DICTIONARY OF MODERN ARAB HISTORY

the practices of Muhammad Ali was the raising of loans; one was needed to finance the railway and others to build fortified palaces in the desert where Abbas lived far from civilisation, surrounded by wild animals and 6,000 Albanian mercenaries. He put IOUs in the Treasury and left debts of some 100 million francs. He took an interest in the Sudan, opening a school there. Abbas was fanatical, cowardly, distrustful, superstitious and reactionary; he was noted for his cruelty, bricking up a servant who had kicked his dog, sewing up the lips of another caught smoking and flogging his women, at least two of whom he drowned. Many of his relatives took refuge abroad. He warned two servants that the following day he proposed to punish them so they murdered him during the night. He was buried in a heatwave, caused, people said, by the gates of hell opening to receive him.

ABD AL-BAQI, Ahmad Hilmi (1882–?)
Palestinian leader. Born in Sidon of Bosnian stock, he served in the Ottoman army before becoming a financial specialist. He rallied to Faysal in Damascus where he was given the Ministry of Finance. After the collapse of the regime he went to Trans-Jordan where the Amir Abd Allah made use of his financial skills. In 1925 he was made Director-General of Charitable Trusts in Palestine and in 1930 was one of the founders of the Arab National Bank. He took an active part in nationalist politics and with Awni Abd al-Hadi revived the *Istiqlal* in 1932. When the Arab Higher Committee was formed in 1936 he was elected its Treasurer. However he approved the White Paper of 1939 and later, with the Mufti Haj Amin al-Hussaini in exile and Raghib al-Nashashibi inactive, he tried with British support to rally the Arabs behind his own leadership. His control of the Arab National Front gave him much influence. During the Palestine War Abd Allah made him Military Governor of Jerusalem with the rank of General. Abd al-Baqi broke with him in September and supported the Egyptians, becoming Prime Minister of the Gaza Government. With its collpase he passed into obscurity.

ABD AL-HADI, Awni (1889–1970)
Arab nationalist leader. He came from an aristocratic family of Nablus and studied law and administration in Istanbul. He continued his law studies at the Sorbonne and being in Paris when the First Arab Congress took place in 1913 attended it as a delegate. He was then one of the early members of the Fatat, the secret nationalist society. One of his uncles was hanged by the Turks during the war. Abd al-Hadi then became secretary to the Amir Faysal, accompanying him to the Versailles Peace Conference. When Syria was taken over by the French, Abd al-Hadi encouraged the Amir Abd Allah to move on from Ma'an and establish himself in Amman. He then practised and taught law in Jerusalem. In 1932 he was one of the founders with Ahmad Hilmi Abd al-Baqi of the Palestinian branch of the *Istiqlal* Party. He was accused of fomenting anti-Jewish riots in 1933 and accepted a temporary ban on political activity rather than a prison sentence. In 1936 he was one of the founders of the Arab Higher Committee of which he became secretary. Abd al-Hadi was regarded

as one of the leaders of the Arab Rebellion and in 1937 was exiled to Syria where he remained until 1941. During this period he was in contact with the Nazis and visited Berlin. By 1943 the *Istiqlal* had become extremely influential in Palestine, controlling much of the Arab press and financial activities and the British hoped to use him as the leader of the moderate nationalists opposed to the Mufti Haj Amin al-Hussaini. In March 1946 he testified before the Anglo-American Committee on Palestine. Abd al-Hadi was a Minister in the Gaza Government established by the Egyptians in September 1948 but soon left it and made his peace with the Hashemites. He became Ambassador to Cairo and served as Foreign Minister in the brief administration of Ibrahim Hashim in the summer of 1956. He later moved to Cairo, working as Chairman of the Legal Committee of the Arab League.

ABD AL-HADI, Ibrahim Pasha (1896–1981)
Egyptian Prime Minister. By profession a lawyer he was, as a young member of the Wafd in the 1930s increasingly troubled by the scandals surrounding his party leaders so he defected to the Saadists of which he was later President. As Foreign Minister he helped to negotiate the Bevin–Sidqi Agreement of 1946 and then was Chef de Cabinet to King Farouq. After the murder of his friend Nuqrashi in December 1948 he became Prime Minister and showed great ruthlessness in repression of the Muslim Brothers and of the Egyptian Communist Party, packing off large numbers to concentration camps in Sinai. A dour, honest man, he did not hide his disapproval of the private life of the King and when it became known that he was looking into the Palace finances, he was summarily dismissed after seven months in office. The harshness of the police activity that he had shown during his premiership was not forgotten after the July Revolution and he was the only politician condemned to death by the Revolutionary Tribunal. The sentence was however commuted to life imprisonment and he was actually released on grounds of ill health in 1954.

ABD ALLAH (c. 1882–1951)
Amir of Trans-Jordan and King of Jordan. He was the second son of Sharif Hussain who in 1893 was ordered to move from Mecca into residence in Constantinople where he remained until 1908. Abd Allah was thus brought up in contact with young Arab nationalists from the whole of the Ottoman Empire. These links were reinforced when in 1909 he gained a seat in the Turkish Parliament as MP for Mecca. In 1911 he took part in his father's campaign against Muhammad b. Ali al-Idrisi but ran into an ambush and had to flee the field. He became friendly with the Khedive Abbas II Hilmi and took advantage of a visit to Cairo in February 1914 to call on Lord Kitchener to enquire whether, in the event of a Turkish dismissal of his father, he could count on British support. As the two Empires were at peace Kitchener evaded the question but even before war broke out he contacted Abd Allah, beginning the exchanges which culminated in the Arab Revolt. In 1916 the first dispatch of British gold was to Abd Allah and when the fighting started his father kept him at hand as Foreign Minister although he also conducted

a leisurely siege of Ta'if. Lawrence described him at this time as "short and thick built, apparently as strong as a horse, with merry dark-brown eyes, a round smooth face . . . open and very charming, not standing at all on ceremony" and possibly more an astute politician than a far-seeing statesman. He spent some time spasmodically besieging Medina and achieved little military success. When the war had ended he determined to use his trained forces to subdue Ibn Saud but a crushing defeat at Turabah in May 1919 when he had to flee in his night clothes, ended his ambitions in Arabia. In March 1920 when his brother Faysal was proclaimed King of Syria, 29 Iraqis present at the Damascus Congress proclaimed Abd Allah their King. In July Faysal was expelled by the French, and in September Abd Allah, announcing his intention to restore him, left Mecca with 500–1,000 tribesmen. He lingered at Ma'an for several months while Faysal was being installed by the British in Iraq. In March 1921 Abd Allah moved on to Amman at a time when the Cairo Conference was meeting to determine British policy in the area. It was not clear whether the bedouin areas east of the Jordan should be regarded as part of Palestine and the Colonial Secretary Winston Churchill went on to Jerusalem. He sent for Abd Allah who agreed to take charge of Trans-Jordan for six months and keep the area free of anti-Zionist and anti-French nationalists in return for a stipend of £5,000 a month and hints that if he behaved well he might yet become ruler of Syria. Abd Allah, however, formed a government almost entirely staffed by strongly nationalist refugees from Syria whose rule was resented by the local tribes; there were five revolts in eighteen months of which that of the Adwan was the most serious and was only suppressed with British help. There was also a series of raids across the frontier of Najd by the Ikhwan which were checked by the RAF. By 1923 London decided to make the situation permanent and Abd Allah was recognised as Amir of a state with a population of 250,000 entirely dependent upon British subsidies: Abd Allah himself was given £36,000 a year paid monthly. He saw Trans-Jordan as no more than a stepping stone to greater things (in 1922 he met Weizmann and volunteered to help to guarantee the establishment of a Jewish national home if the Zionists would help him to become King of Palestine) and at the beginning made no attempt to rule for the benefit of his people. The British Resident Philby said that he was "tyrannical" and other officials regarded him as obstructionist, prodigal, financially dishonest and "languid": Peake, the Commander of the Arab Legion stated he was "a disease which was rapidly destroying" the country. In June 1924 after Abd Allah had departed for the Pilgrimage serious consideration was given to a forceful prevention of his return: in the end he was met at Aqaba by Cox the new Resident who presented an ultimatum as to his future conduct which he tearfully accepted. He realised his complete dependence upon Britain and was prepared to accept limitations on what he could do in internal matters. The relationship was formalised in the Anglo-Trans-Jordanian Agreement of 1928. He allied with the great landowners and formed a group of "Palace" politicians such as Ibrahim Hashim, Tawfiq Abu al-Huda and Samir al-Rifai, men of considerable ability upon

whom he could rely to keep things quiet at home for, restricted in Trans-Jordan, his ambitions lay elsewhere. For many years he did not give up hope of a return to the Hijaz, constantly intriguing to encourage revolts such as those of Ibn Rifada and Hassan b. Ali al-Idrisi against Ibn Saud; although they were formally reconciled in April 1933, the hostility persisted. In the 1930s he had hopes in Palestine, aiming to be recognised as spokesman for the Arabs. Abd Allah plunged deep into Palestinian politics, in alliance with Raghib al-Nashashibi and in bitter hostility to the Mufti Haj Amin al-Hussaini, although he did offer to make him Prime Minister if he himself became King. He was anxious not to antagonise the Jews, encouraging them to invest in Trans-Jordan and selling them land. He also took money from them for political purposes such as trying to keep his own country quiet during times of tension such as the Wailing Wall Incident and the troubles of 1936-9. He ignored the Arab boycott on discussing partition and was the only ruler to endorse it, receiving money and political concessions from London in return. After the death of his brother Faysal he hoped to be seen as the leader of Arab nationalism but was always on bad terms with most of their politicians, partly through his incautious tongue and actions such as alienating the Syrians by visiting Turkey during the Alexandretta Dispute. In September 1939 Abd Allah declared his support for Britain in the war even before some of the Dominions had done so. He won unpopularity with Arab nationalists by allowing the Arab Legion to play a part in crushing the regime of Rashid Ali al-Gilani. After the British invaded Syria in 1941 he hoped that the British would make him its King but they never seriously considered it. Grateful, however, for his loyalty during the war, the British gave Abd Allah considerably more independence and the title of King in the Anglo-Trans-Jordanian Treaty of March 1946. As Palestine moved towards partition Abd Allah intensified his efforts to ensure that at least the Arab portions fell to him. He held a series of secret meetings with Jewish leaders, Golda Meir found him "a small, very poised man with great charm", stressing their mutual hostility to the Mufti. With Sharrett he offered to take over Palestine giving full rights to Jews or to agree to partition if he were given access to the Mediterranean. In February 1948 he sent Glubb Pasha and his Prime Minister Tawfiq Abu al-Huda to London where they secured the consent of Ernest Bevin to the Arab Legion's occupation of areas assigned to the Arabs provided that they did not move into the Jewish portion. When the fighting started Abd Allah was made titular Commander-in-Chief of the Arab armies but exercised no control over the others. His restraint of the advance of his forces was seen by many as treacherous and he was most unwilling to resume fighting after the first Truce. When fighting started again he ordered the abandonment of Ramla and Lydda and he further harmed his reputation by welcoming the Bernadotte Plan. There was a strong movement to expel him from the Arab League. His main pre-occupation was to prevent any other Arab authority emerging in the rump of Palestine and, alarmed by the formation of the Gaza Government under Egyptian auspices, summoned the Jericho Conference in December 1948 which called for the annexation of the West Bank to Trans-Jordan. Secret meetings with the Israelis were resumed: in January 1949 he tried to obtain from Moshe Dayan a passage to the Mediterranean and at Shunah in March the terms of an armistice were negotiated. Later there were even proposals for a non-aggression pact. Even his staunch friend Kirkbride said that Abd Allah's policy over Palestine was "basically selfish" but in February 1949 he became the only Arab Head of State to concede full citizenship to refugees and in May he brought Palestinians into his Cabinet. In June 1949 he changed his title to King of Jordan. Realising that there was no further hope of expansion immediately to the West, Abd Allah now switched his attention to Syria, proposing union in November 1950. Nazim al-Qudsi said that Egypt also should be consulted but undeterred Abd Allah proposed to Riad al-Sulh that an Islamic Bloc be established in the Fertile Crescent as a bulwark against Communism. At the same time he made advances to Iraq. Abd Allah had long regarded his eldest son, Crown Prince Talal whom he had treated abominably, as unfit to reign and he proposed that he himself should be King of a united Iraq and Jordan and that his young nephew Faysal II should succeed to both thrones. He had not abandoned these hopes when on 20 July 1951 while entering the Aqsa Mosque in Jerusalem he was murdered by four Palestinians, one a cousin of the Mufti. The main instigator took refuge in Egypt which was generally believed to have been behind the plot. The four assassins were executed. In his memoirs, amidst waspish comments upon his brother Arabs, Abd Allah declared that historically they had only achieved greatness through the Hashemites and this conviction governed his policies. He saw himself as the embodiment of Arab nationalism. He was a poet of ability and above all else enjoyed learned and humorous conversation with an abundance of proverbs and games of chess. He travelled widely, in his early years spending the winter camping in the Jordan valley, and was extremely accessible to his people whom he treated in the manner of a kindly patriarch or old-fashioned tribal chief; although he granted a Parliamentary Constitution he took little notice of debates in the Chamber. He was self-reliant and decisive, often impetuous and expected unqualified obedience.

ABD AL-RAZIQ, Ali (1885–?)

Egyptian Islamic controversialist. He was the son of a rich landowner and attended al-Azhar at the age of 10. Subsequently he went to lectures by European orientalists at the Egyptian University and to Oxford. He was working as a religious judge and lecturer when in 1925, after the abolition of the Caliphate, he published a book, *al-Islam wa-usul al-hukm* (Islam and the bases of power), arguing that it should never have existed. He stated that the Prophet Muhammad was merely the Messenger of God and had no political function and that his successors had merely political and no religious functions. The form of government adopted by a state had nothing to do with religion and it would be quite legitimate to have a system based on Western ideals. The book was fiercely attacked by the ulema for whom the traditionally accepted view of early Islamic history had become a matter of doctrine: they objected that

Abd al-Raziq was following Christianity by introducing a distinction between the Kingdom of God and this world. The matter became a political one because King Fuad, anxious to get rid of his Liberal-Constitutional ministers, exploited Abd al-Raziq's connections with that party, causing a Cabinet crisis. Abd al-Raziq was dismissed from his judgeship but later became a Senator. He rejected Pan-Arabism, stating that the Arabs had always been divided into separate nations. His brother Mustafa Abd al-Raziq was also an influential thinker and was Rector of al-Azhar from 1945 until his death in 1947.

ABD AL-RAZZAQ, Arif (1914–)

Iraqi Prime Minister. He was the son of a small landowner in a village near Ramadi. He trained as a pilot in England and attended Staff College before being given command of Habbaniya air base which he took over for the Free Officers during the July Revolution of 1958. He was briefly arrested after the Mosul Uprising but returned to duty and was able to facilitate the use of aircraft in the Ramadan Revolution of 1963 in which Abd al-Krim Qassim, who had shown no enthusiasm for unity with Egypt was overthrown. In May, after supporters of President Nasser were dropped from the Government, Abd al-Razzaq was again briefly imprisoned. After the November Revolution he was appointed Minister of Agriculture and then Commander-in-Chief of the Air Force. As the leading supporter of unity with Egypt President Abd al-Salam Aref on 6 September 1965 appointed him Prime Minister, reputedly feeling that he would be less dangerous in an office than commanding the Air Force. His Cabinet, mainly chosen by the President, contained more civilians than usual including Abd al-Rahman al-Bazzaz as Deputy Premier. On September 15 while Arif was attending the Casablanca Summit Abd al-Razzaq attempted a coup which failed ludicrously as it had been anticipated. He fled to Egypt which was embarrassed but gave him refuge. Bazzaz who succeeded him pointedly denied that any outsiders had encouraged the attempt. Abd al-Razzaq was granted an amnesty in April 1966 but on June 30 he attempted a second coup to enforce socialism and unity with Egypt. His followers seized Mosul airport and attacked Baghdad but loyal forces, in the words of the President "made them scurry like rats". It was announced that Abd al-Razzaq would be put on trial but he and the other conspirators were released at the end of May 1967, probably as a result of Egyptian intervention. In January 1970 he was amongst those named as plotting against the Baath regime.

ABD AL-SHAFI, Haidar (1920–)

Palestinian leader. After qualifying as a doctor he practised in Gaza. He was a founder-member of the Palestine Liberation Organisation and was Deputy Speaker at the first meeting of the Palestinian National Congress in 1964 but after it was outlawed by the Israeli Government he had no further formal contact with it. He became Head of the Red Crescent in Gaza where he became used to seeing the sufferings of people under occupation and act as their spokesman. He was, however, little known to the outside world when he was appointed formal leader of the Palestinian members of the Jordanian/Palestinian negotiating team at the Madrid Peace Talks in October 1991. His obvious integrity commanded respect but his participation brought him violent criticism from opponents of the peace talks such as Hamas. He angered them further by public condemnation of the killing of collaborators. In January 1993 he said that the summary deportation by the Occupation authorities of over 400 alleged members of Hamas to Marj al-Zuhur marked the "death-knell" of the Washington Peace talks and that he would attend no further meetings. He was, however, persuaded by the PLO to continue although he was later replaced by Faysal al-Hussaini as leader of the delegation. Subsequently he criticised the Israel–PLO Agreement as ignoring the problems of settlements, particularly in Jerusalem and announced his retirement from politics.

ABD al-QUDUS, Ihsan (1919–92)

Egyptian journalist. He was the son of a civil engineer who became a stage and screen actor and of Rose al-Yusuf, a leading actress who founded a political and cultural journal named after herself. He trained as a lawyer at Cairo University but abandoned law for journalism. In 1945 after the end of wartime censorship he was imprisoned for attacks on the Government. After his release his mother made him Editor of her magazine which he used to attack the corruption of King Farouq and his ministers, in particular for their failure to equip the army to fight the Palestine War; this led to his imprisonment for the second time. He opened his columns to Neguib who attacked government policies as "The Unknown Soldier" and to Nasser and Sadat who also wrote under pseudonyms. Abd al-Qudus gave strong support to the idea of Arab unity and his radical views attracted the attention of the Free Officers who made some of them their own. After they had seized power in the July Revolution his attacks on military dictatorship brought him his third and worst imprisonment. He continued to investigate scandals but turned more of his attention to writing short stories and novels, which, adapted for the cinema, made him probably the most popular Arab writer. In 1961 he was appointed to the Permanent Committee on National Guidance of the National Union and later he was editor of the semi-official *Akhbar al-Yawm*. In 1966 one of his novels, exposing double standards of morality, caused such an uproar that there were demands for its banning but Nasser insisted that he should have the right to defend himself in front of the National Assembly and stopped the banning. In 1972 his outspoken attacks on Russian policy led to angry rebuttals in *Pravda* and in 1974 his criticisms of Qadafi led to an attempt on his life. Abd al-Qudus was described as hardly waiting to finish one battle before starting on the next.

al-ABDI, Isa b. Umar (1842–1924)

Moroccan tribal leader and Minister. His family, which claimed to be of Hijazi origin, were the chiefs of a small faction of the Abda tribe of the Safi area. Isa, who succeeded his brother as Caid in 1879 so impressed Hassan I that he allowed him to extend his authority over any of the neighbouring dissident tribes that he could himself subdue. Isa proved an exceptional warrior, he was said to have killed 7,000 men during

his career, but also an unusually efficient administrator who kept an iron grip on an increasing area. In 1894, on the death of the Sultan, there was a general uprising against the tyranny of Isa which he managed to defeat after killing rebels to whom he had promised a safe conduct. As Pasha of Safi, working closely with the Grand Wazir Ba Ahmad, he was practically an independent ruler and in the campaign against Bu Hamara he took the field at the head of 1,500 cavalry and 1,500 infantry raised and maintained at his own expense for 19 months. He subsequently rallied to Mulai Hafid who, to his horror, put him in charge of foreign affairs of which he admittedly knew nothing. After a long delay he arrived in Fez accompanied by his 40 sons and large numbers of slaves, horses, hounds and hawks. Shrewd, direct and realistic, he charmed British diplomats who regarded him as an honorary English country gentleman, but upset the French. In July 1910 he was put in charge of the Ministry of Justice until the signature of the Fez Treaty when he thankfully returned home. He refused to collaborate with the Protectorate authorities and was sent into exile. His misfortune was, that unlike the Great Caids, otherwise his equals, his fief was easily accessible and did not adjoin a dissident area.

al-ABID, Izzat Pasha (c. 1857–?)

Adviser to Sultan Abd al-Hamid. He came from a Kurdish family which had settled in Damascus, was inter-married with most of the leading families there and held high office in the Ottoman Empire. Izzat was educated by the Jesuits in Beirut and then went to Constantinople, studied law and was appointed a judge in Macedonia. Izzat then obtained a transfer to the Commercial Court in the capital and was engaged in cases concerning foreigners which brought him to the notice of Abd al-Hamid who was impressed by his intimate knowledge of the vital provinces of Syria and Macedonia. He wielded great power as Second Secretary to the Sultan from 1895 until the Revolution of 1908. With Shaykh Abu al-Huda he urged a pan-Islamic policy and more participation by Arabs in running the Empire. He was a very strong advocate of the building of the Hijaz Railway as a unifying factor, while at the same time making considerable sums by speculating in land along the route. He was also involved in development in Damascus. The British regarded him as "one of our greatest enemies" because of his strong support for moving Turkey into the German orbit – probably his motives for this were venal. He was an extraordinarily astute man, cunning and agile with an unerring insight into the motives of disreputable characters – a most valuable gift in the Constantinople of the time. He foresaw the Revolution and left just before it started, living for a time in London before moving to Nice. He expressed strong pan-Arab sentiments and in May 1917 King Hussain wanted to nominate him as his envoy in Paris but the Allies regarded him as unacceptable.

al-ABID, Muhammad Ali (c. 1870–1939)

President of Syria. The son of Izzat Pasha al-Abid, the Secretary of Sultan Abd al-Hamid, he was born in Istanbul and educated at a leading school there and in Paris. He joined the Ottoman diplomatic service and in 1908 was Minister in Washington. He held the post for six weeks before the Young Turk Revolution forced his father into exile. Muhammad Ali joined him in Paris and during the war lived on the Riviera mixing in the highest French society. He expressed pan-Arab sentiments and moved to Syria in 1919. He was reputed the richest man in Damascus, perhaps in Syria, carefully ensuring that a large part of his wealth was safe abroad. He was regarded as having little political influence until he became Minister of Finance in the Cabinet of Subhi Barakat. In June 1932 when the French introduced a new system of government they procured his election as President as a non-controversial figure after the first round of voting showed no result. He appointed the original French candidate for the Presidency, Haqqi al-Azm as Prime Minister. In May 1934, after he had pardoned a man who had attempted to assassinate the local hero Ibrahim Hananu, bombs were thrown at his hotel while he was visiting Aleppo with the Prime Minister Shaykh Taj al-Din al-Hassani. In December 1936 when the National Bloc won power, he resigned. Subsequently he spent most of his time on the Riviera. A British official described him as "a wily old man".

ABU AL-ABBAS, Mahmud (c. 1947–?)
Palestinian terrorist. Originally a follower of Ahmad Jibril, he broke away from the Popular Front for the Liberation of Palestine – General Command when, at the behest of Syria, it fought against Fatah. Abu al-Abbas founded the breakaway Palestine Liberation Front which specialised in raids into Israel. His most notorious exploit was the *Achille Lauro* hijacking of October 1985 after which he was one of the five men held by the Italians after the Americans had forced down the Egyptian aircraft on which they had been given safe conduct to Tunis. To the fury of the Americans, the Italians let him go free. He went to Yugoslavia which refused to extradite him to America. In July 1986 he was sentenced *in absentia* to life imprisonment. He became a member of the Executive Council of the Palestine Liberation Organisation. In January 1988 the Americans withdrew because of insufficient evidence a warrant that they had issued against him. Although he had formally denounced terrorism against civilians in May 1990 he was implicated in an attack on an Israeli beach. Washington demanded his expulsion from the Executive as the price of continued discussions with the PLO but Yassir Arafat refused. Abu al-Abbas had close relations with Saddam Hussein and in September 1990 threatened to strike at US interests if they attacked Iraq; he also urged the overthrow of regimes which co-operated with them. His men were reported active in Kuwait during the Iraqi occupation. In September 1991 he said that he would not stand for the Executive when it became clear that he would not be re-elected: he had not anyway attended for over a year. In August 1992 a report that he was under arrest in Baghdad was denied.

ABU al-DHAHAB, Muhammad (?–1775)
Ruler of Egypt. A Caucasian Mamluk, he became the right-hand man of Ali Bey who made him immensely rich. When Muhammad himself became a Bey in 1764 he was able to scatter gold coins instead of the cus-

tomary silver to the poor and thus acquired the nickname "Father of Gold". He murdered several Beys who threatened to become dangerous to his master. In 1769 he campaigned in Upper Egypt subduing the bedouin tribes. In 1770 he led a force across Sinai and down to Mecca to install a new Amir. In 1771 Ali put him at the head of an army which invaded Syria in alliance with Zahir al-Umar but after capturing Damascus in June, Abu Dhahab inexplicably withdrew. It has never been established whether he had become involved in the savage intrigues of the al-Umar family or whether he had made an arrangement with the Sultan to become ruler of Egypt if he ousted Ali who had been showing desires for complete independence. He fled from Cairo in January 1772 but was joined by all the malcontents including bedouin tribes and the underpaid army which had been sent against him. In April he defeated Ali at a battle in the Delta and was recognised as *Shaykh al-Bilad*. Ali was lured back into Egypt and murdered. Abu Dhahab abolished many taxes but imposed a heavy new one to celebrate the abolition of tyranny. He made an agreement with the East India Company which enabled it to trade in the Red Sea and he promised to bring water there from the Nile if necessary. Although he chased out one Pasha sent by the Sultan, in general he was more deferential to Constantinople than his predecessor had been. In March 1775 at the request of the Sultan and in alliance with Jazzar Pasha he again invaded Syria, this time to overthrow Zahir al-Umar. He sacked Jaffa with a ferocity that frightened Zahir's capital Acre into surrendering. Shortly afterwards he died unexpectedly, slain some said by the Prophet Elias whose sanctuary on Mt Carmel he had violated. In contrast to Ali Bey who had some aspects of creativity and statesmanship, Abu Dhahab was nothing but a jealous, greedy and treacherous thug.

ABU AL-HUDA, Hassan Khalid (1870–1936)
Chief Minister of Trans-Jordan. The son of Shaykh Abu al-Huda, the adviser of Sultan Abd al-Hamid, he was born in Aleppo but brought up in Constantinople where he became a friend of the future Amir Abd Allah. Speaking excellent French, he was appointed representative of the Sultan to the Khedive Abbas II Hilmi in Cairo. In 1922 he was in Vienna when Abd Allah passed through and took him into his service. He became Chief Minister in September 1923. He brought more native Trans-Jordanians into what had been virtually a government of Syrian exiles. In April 1924 the British Resident Henry Cox, determined to instil more financial discipline and to prevent raiding into Syria, had him removed from office. In June 1926 after the dismissal of Ali Ridha al-Rikabi he returned to power and in February 1928 he signed the Anglo-Trans-Jordanian Agreement which regulated the status of the country until the Anglo-Trans-Jordanian Treaty of 1946. In the same year he was much attacked for assisting Abd Allah's plans to encourage Zionist investment. In February 1931 after difficulties with the Legislative Council over the Budget he resigned and was succeeded by Abd Allah Sarraj. When similar trouble caused the dismissal of Sarraj, Abd Allah proposed to bring back Abu al-Huda but this was vetoed by Cox who said that he could not co-operate with him. Abd Allah referred to

him as "one of the best men in the Arab nation – sincere in friendship and on occasions unable to conceal enmity".

ABU AL-HUDA, Shaykh (al-Sayyadi) (c. 1850–?)

"Abu al-Huda" was the nickname of the son of a village notable born near Aleppo who later added the "al-Sayyadi" after a local saint from whom he claimed descent both spiritually and genealogically. He became a member of the Sufi order of the Rifai. About 1870 he went to Istanbul but although he failed to be appointed guardian of the Sayyadi tomb, he made useful contacts amongst the religious and political establishment. In the winter of 1876/7 he was introduced to the new Sultan Abd al-Hamid to whom he became a close adviser and although he received high rank in the religious establishment, his importance stemmed from his ready access to the Ruler. After some years of competition, he managed to discredit Jamal al-Din al-Afghani, as an alternative source of religio-political advice. He also made trouble for his fellow-Aleppan Abd al-Rahman al-Kawakibi and for Rashid Rida. A British diplomat described him as "probably the most intimate confidant of the Sultan". Since the foundation of the Ottoman Empire no Arab had ever been in the centre of power and many believed that his influence was due to the superstitious Sultan regarding him as an astrologer or soothsayer although it was said that he did not have much faith in his own reading of the stars and persuaded secretaries to hold up incoming telegrams until he had read them and predicted their contents. It is more probable, however, that it was due to his mastery of Arab and religious politics in which Abd al-Hamid took such interest. Abu al-Huda spread throughout the Arab provinces of the Ottoman Empire a network of Rifai *zawiyahs* which acted as props for the Hamidian regime at a time when Arab nationalism was starting, particularly in Syria. Many of the early nationalists were Christians and by stressing the universal Caliphate, Abu al-Huda hoped to prevent the Muslims from making common cause with them. As part of the policy of binding Muslim Syrians to the Islamic world, he was a strong advocate of the Hijaz Railway. In 1908 he was believed to be the only person who could convince the reluctant Sultan to accept the new Constitution and having been brought into the Council on a sick-bed, succeeded in doing so. Abu al-Huda was a prolific author with over 200 titles attributed to him in which he called upon Muslims to show loyalty to the Sultan as Caliph and glorified the Rifai order and proclaimed his own descent from the Prophet. He stressed the authoritarian origins of Islam and the duty of people to obey their rulers as the shepherds who led them to God. He was described by a British lawyer who knew him well as of "short stature with a keen, intelligent and not unkindly face, he looked like one who feared no mortal".

ABU AL-HUDA, Tawfiq (1895–1956)

Prime Minister of Jordan. He was born in Acre and served in the Ottoman army. He worked for the Amir Faysal in Damascus and when that government was overthrown he was one of the nationalists who took service under Amir Abd Allah in Trans-Jordan. He had a successful career in the civil service, becoming Director of the Agricultural Bank before in September 1938 he was appointed Prime Minister. In general he was a strong supporter of the British connection and in return could count upon their backing. In 1939 he supported the White Paper on Palestine and took advantage of the London–Palestine Conference to obtain some financial advantages for his master. He attended the Alexandria meeting that led to the formation of the Arab League. In October 1944 he was replaced by Samir al-Rifai and did not resume office until December 1947. In February 1948 he went to London and with Glubb Pasha was received by the Foreign Secretary Ernest Bevin who gave his approval to the advance of the Arab Legion into those parts of Palestine assigned to the Arabs under the Partition Plan. He also negotiated a revision favourable to his country of the Anglo-Trans-Jordanian Treaty. Subsequently he loyally carried out the policies of Abd Allah and he welcomed the Resolution of the Jericho Congress. In May 1949 he took advantage of a reshuffle to bring Palestinians into his Cabinet and worked hard to integrate the two Banks. Suffering from exhaustion Abu al-Huda left office in April 1950 but the following year when Abd Allah was murdered it was generally felt that he, as the shrewdest statesman and best administrator in the country and the leader of the "Palace" politicians close to the Monarchy, should take charge. His efforts probably prevented the newly-created state from splitting into its East and West Bank components. He ensured that the Crown Prince Talal was not pushed aside and proclaimed him as King. He carried out the hesitant moves towards greater democracy desired by the new Monarch and despite misgivings promulgated a more liberal Constitution but in August 1952 had to tell him that he was unfit to rule because of his mental condition. He remained in office during the Regency but as soon as Hussain came of age he dismissed Abu al-Huda in a move to appease the opposition and open the way to more liberal policies. In May 1954 after dangerous riots in which the country appeared to be falling apart in disputes over the continuation of the British connection Abu al-Huda was again felt to be the best man to deal with the crisis. He dissolved Parliament, banned opposition parties and closed hostile newspapers. He held elections which were generally seen as rigged and meant that opposition could only be manifested on the streets, necessitating firm measures of repression. He tried to lessen dependence on Britain by asking for the subsidy for the Arab Legion to be paid to the Government and by paying court to Saudi Arabia. The problem of the Baghdad Pact for which the Prime Minister's lack of enthusiasm upset the King continued to split the country and in May 1955, Abu al-Huda whose health was giving way, resigned. Suffering from cancer he hanged himself the following year. Glubb who worked closely with him for many years described him as the best of Jordanian Prime Ministers; he had a clear, methodical realistic mind and much moral courage but he was all intelligence and no emotion. He was domineering, cold and calculating, inclined to blame subordinates when things went wrong and disliked meeting people. Perhaps, suggested Glubb, with his love of detail and routine, Abu al-Huda should have passed his life as an accountant.

ABU DAOUD (Muhammad Daoud Auda) (1937–)

Palestinian terrorist. He was born in Selwan near Jerusalem. He worked as a teacher in Jordan and Saudi Arabia and was then employed by the Ministry of Justice in Kuwait. He joined Fatah and with Abu Nidal was sent for training in China before acting as Chief of Intelligence for operations inside Israel and Lebanon. After being expelled from Amman in 1970 he was based on Lebanon and Syria. Abu Daoud was believed to have been the main planner of the operations of the Black September Organisation including the Munich Olympics Murders. In February 1973 he was caught entering Jordan with 17 other armed men with the purpose of kidnapping Ministers and carrying out sabotage. He was shown on television making a confession which his friends declared was faked. He was sentenced to death but King Hussain commuted it to life imprisonment after personal requests from King Faysal and the Russian President Podgorny. Eight of his followers then seized the Saudi Embassy in Khartoum to demand his release and killed the American Ambassador before they surrendered. In September another group took over the Saudi Embassy in Paris. Soon afterwards Abu Daoud was included in a general amnesty for Palestinian guerrillas. He was a member of the Fatah Council and was closely associated with Iraq. In January 1977 he went to Paris to attend the funeral of a Palestinian guerrilla and took part in talks with the French Foreign Ministry. On the same day he was arrested at the request of the German Government in connection with the killings in Munich. After four days he was released despite vehement protests from Israel which had demanded his extradition. The way that Yassir Arafat had reacted to the Israeli invasion of South Lebanon in March 1978 and the subsequent cease-fire led to a split in Fatah and in April Abu Daoud and 123 others, who were said to have come from Iraq to cause trouble were arrested by Fatah loyalists led by Abu Jihad. Mediation by Abu Iyad patched up the quarrel but it appeared that Abu Daoud, possibly in alliance with the other Baghdad-based Palestinian dissident Abu Nidal, was trying to create an autonomous left-wing grouping. At the Palestine National Council in January 1979 in Damascus Abu Daoud was dropped from the leadership but was back in favour by early 1983. Abu Daoud was a straightforward thug with no pretensions to political thought.

ABU DHABI – DUBAI WAR (1945–9)

In the mid-1940s Shaykh Shakhbut al-Nihayyan of Abu Dhabi and Shaykh Rashid al-Maktum of Dubai were competing for influence in the interior and skirmishes between their supporters caused gradually worsening relations. In September 1945 Shaykh Rashid started building a fort on territory claimed by Abu Dhabi. The British intervened as his movement of armed men by sea had been in breach of the Maritime Peace in Perpetuity Treaty of 1853 and ordered him to withdraw under threat of sanctions. Fighting continued unchecked by land and spread far into the desert with the Abu Dhabi forces often led by the Shaykh's brother Zaid b. Sultan al-Nihayyan. In 1946 the British again intervened after Dubai had refused to return some looted camels and secured their release by refusing travel facilities and cancelling the call of the mail steamer at Dubai. In November 1947 the Dubai tribes won a significant victory but there was further sporadic fighting until the end of 1948 when the Political Resident established a new frontier. The war led to a personal animosity between Shaykhs Rashid and Zaid that affected the politics of the United Arab Emirates a quarter of a century later.

ABU GHAZALA, Muhammad Abd al-Halim, Field Marshal (1930–)

Egyptian Military Commander and Minister. He was born in al-Bihaira and studied at the American Army War College and in Russia, winning degrees in Economics and Military Science. He specialised as a gunner and was Chief of the Artillery Corps when in 1974 he was appointed Director of Military Intelligence. Two years later he went as Defence Attaché in Washington, where he was involved in planning Egyptian participation in the Rapid Deployment Force and working closely with Husni Mubarak in the acquisition of American weaponry. He returned to become Chief of Staff in 1980 and in 1981 he was appointed Commander-in-Chief, Minister of Defence and Military Production. He was sitting next to Sadat when the President was assassinated and, although wounded, took charge of the evacuation of the casualties and the arrest of the killers. In 1982 Abu Ghazala was promoted Deputy Prime Minister and Field Marshal, seen as the second man in the country, dominating Prime Ministers such as Ali Lutfi. He controlled enormous patronage, running large industrial, housing, shopping and educational projects. He also enjoyed great prestige in the army, raising its morale by his professionalism and his skill in winning for it large sums of money which he used to improve equipment and subsidised services. His support for Mubarak proved essential in critical moments such as after the forcing down by the Americans of the Egyptian aircraft which contained the hijackers of the *Achille Lauro* and during the Gizeh Mutiny. Abu Ghazala was criticised by the left as Washington's man and there were reports that American pressure as well as his own power base frustrated Mubarak's desire to be rid of too independent a subordinate. Abu Ghazala was embarrassed when an Egyptian attempt to smuggle US missile parts to Egypt was uncovered. In April 1989, possibly after demands that his unique position be recognised with the rank of sole Vice-President and for the cancellation of cuts in the military budget, he was removed from office and given the honorific post of Presidential Assistant. In April 1990, as a champion of free enterprise, he was given responsibility for monitoring privatisation of state industries. Fluent in English, French and Russian, Abu Ghazala wrote several books including a *History of the Art of War* in five volumes, studies of Soviet Strategy and *Mathematics and Warfare*. He had great powers of leadership, was eloquent, dashing and ambitious. Unlike the wives of other leading figures, Mme Abu Ghazala wore the traditional Muslim *Hijab*.

ABU IYAD (Salah Khalaf) (1933-)

Palestinian resistance leader. He was born in Jaffa and after 1948 had to go into exile in Gaza. He attended Cairo University where, with his fellow student Yassir Arafat he founded an organisation for Palestinian students which later developed into Fatah. Khalaf fought in the Suez War, returned briefly to Gaza and then taught Arabic in Kuwait to raise funds for the Palestinian resistance. In 1967 he was sent to Damascus as a full-time Fatah worker. He was always anxious to prevent the Palestine Liberation Organisation from falling under the control of any one Arab state and managed to extract arms from Nasser and money from King Faysal. He stood for the elimination of Israel as a Jewish state and its replacement by "a non-sectarian Palestine in which Arabs and Jews live as equals". He was captured by Jordanian forces during the fighting of Black September, was saved from execution by the intervention of Nasser and later took part in trying to negotiate a *modus vivendi* between the Government and the guerrillas. When this broke down and the Palestinians were expelled, Abu Iyad toured Arab states calling for the overthrow of King Hussain and was believed, although he denied it, to have been one of the founders of the Black September Organisation which killed Wasfi al-Tall. He was accused of planning the Munich Olympics Massacre. In 1974 he admitted trying to have the King murdered during the Rabat Summit. In the early 1970s he was in charge of negotiations with the Maronites over the conditions upon which guerrillas could operate from Lebanon and in 1977 he concluded the Shtaura Accord as a *modus vivendi*. After Camp David he urged that the Palestinians should employ a scorched earth policy in the Middle East. He led the PLO delegation to the UN World Conference on Palestine in August 1983 at which he declared that the armed struggle would continue. Abu Iyad played an important part in the process of reconciliation of guerrilla factions which took place at the Palestine National Council meeting of April 1987. Enjoying wide popular support, particularly in the refugee camps he continued to be regarded as the second man in Fatah and the leader of its left wing. His principal work was maintaining good relations with Arab governments but in his *Palestinien sans patrie* he urged that the PLO should stay out of inter-Arab feuds and that groups should make concessions to each other to stay united: all revolutions conceived in Palestine had been betrayed in Arab capitals. Abu Iyad was regarded as intransigent in his ultimate objective of a free Palestine but was flexible and respectful of facts in his methods. He was a calm persuasive man who lived a simple family life.

ABU NUWAR, Ali (1925-)

Jordanian military conspirator. Abu Nuwar, who was born in Salt, was commissioned in the Arab Legion, fought in the Palestine War and received further training in Britain. He first came to political attention in 1952 when he was reported to be seeking an interview with King Talal to propose that Jordan should end the British connection and rely more on other Arab states. Glubb Pasha sent him as Military Attaché in Paris to keep him out of harm's way but there he acted as tourist guide to King Hussain and succeeded in winning the young Monarch's confidence. He also became friendly with the Egyptian Military Attaché, Sarwat Ukasha and made no secret of his admiration for President Nasser; he appeared a typical young radical officer. In November 1955 Hussain had him recalled and made him his personal adjutant and undoubtedly Abu Nuwar used this intimacy to urge the dismissal of Glubb and other British officers. Shortly afterwards, promoted from Major to Major-General, he was appointed Chief of Staff, reorganising the army, placing supporters in key posts and thus antagonising the traditionalist bedouin commanders. After the Suez War there was a very sharp division between pro-Westerners headed by the King and left-wing pan-Arabists headed by the Prime Minister Sulayman al-Nabulsi. Abu Nuwar, who was believed to be receiving large sums from Egypt, concluded that this struggle had to be resolved by the overthrow of the Monarchy. Despite the opposition of the King the Cabinet voted for diplomatic relations with Russia and Abu Nuwar went to Damascus to contact their Embassy in a quest for arms and the promise of support for a coup. On April 8 1957 Abu Nuwar ordered an armoured car regiment to move on Amman apparently with the intention of deposing the King but Hussain questioned him about the manoeuvre and the General, either losing his nerve or unsure of the allegiance of the troops, replied that it was a training exercise and ordered a return to barracks. After the dismissal of Nabulsi, Said al-Mufti was nominated as Prime Minister but immediately resigned in the face of threats from Abu Nuwar. On the evening of April 13, hearing that there was fighting between units, Hussain insisted upon Abu Nuwar's accompanying him and the Zerka Incident showed that the bedouin regiments were overwhelmingly loyal to the King. They wished to kill the General as a traitor but Hussain protected him and allowed him to leave the country although later he was sentenced *in absentia* to 15 years' imprisonment. A search of Abu Nuwar's office showed a sample flag for a Jordanian Republic. The treachery of the man he had believed his closest friend was a deep shock to Hussain. Abu Nuwar went to Damascus where in April 1963 he proclaimed the Jordanian Republic and set up a government in exile with its own radio station. Later he lived in Cairo, returning to Jordan in 1965. In 1970 he was appointed a personal representative of the King and later Ambassador to Paris. Abu Nuwar, a dapper, ingratiating man who could however be truculent and bullying always denied that he had plotted to overthrow the Monarchy.

ABUJA TALKS (1992/3)

Various African states were anxious to end the war that had lasted almost a decade in the Southern Sudan, causing famine and floods of refugees. In April 1992 Ethiopia, on whose border much of the fighting was taking place, invited the main rebel group, the Sudan People's Liberation Movement to a conference in Addis Ababa to discuss humanitarian issues and the following month Nigeria, Chairman of the OAU, called for a full-scale peace conference in its capital Abuja. The SPLM had previously split into two factions, "Torit", mainly Dinka followers of John Garang who was represented by William Nyuon and "*Nasir*", mainly Nuer led by Dr

Lam Akol. The conference looked as if it might never begin as both the Government team led by Muhammad al-Amin al-Khaifah and the rebel factions rejected the other's initial proposals but neither wanted to offend the Nigerians by walking out so talks opened on 28 May under the chairmanship of the Nigerian Interior Minister Tunji Olagunji who had prepared the agenda. The Government accepted the Nasir demand for a discussion of a referendum on self-determination. Akol, arguing that the South was African not Arab, then proposed a confederation of five states and a multi-party democracy – no other solution would be acceptable and the country should break up. This was opposed by Khaifah who ruled out any dissolution of the Sudan and by Nyuon who called for a united secular Sudan with multi-party democracy. The Nassir and Torit factions then found common ground on self-determination. The Nigerians explained systems of federalism and a 15-man committee was set up to study them. On 3 June the talks ended with the Sudanese agreeing to take home and study the Nigerian draft, possibly reassembling after two months. The final communiqué did not mention a referendum, a secular state or de-escalation of fighting but did call for an equitable sharing of wealth between North and South. In July the Government said that it was prepared to resume talks at any time but in November Garang said that resumption was delayed because the Government insisted on inviting splinter groups opposed to the SPLM. In March 1993 a cease-fire was proclaimed to prepare for a new round. Before delegates reconvened both Garang and General Bashir separately visited Abuja. Talks started at the end of April with an agreement that the state's role in religion should not be discussed. The Nigerian Vice-President Augustus Aikhomu took the chair and attempts were made to involve the President of Kenya and Uganda. The Southerners asked for confederation which the Northerners said was tantamount to independence. Garang himself took part in the talks and Khaifah eventually agreed to the establishment of an interim government in the South which should not control a separate army. There were difficulties over foreign policy, exchange control and justice during an interim period: it was agreed that *Shariah* should not be withdrawn but should apply only to Muslims. The Southerners rejected a surprising proposal to move the capital from Khartoum to Juba. Talks were adjourned at the end of May.

ABU JIHAD (Khalil Ibrahim al-Wazir) (1936–88)

Palestinian leader. He was born in Ramleh, the son of a grocer who had to flee to Gaza after expulsion by the Iraelis. He was one of the first Palestinians prepared to use force to take home in the hope of expelling the Israelis and in 1954 he led a raid into Israel. This provoked reprisals and he was arrested by Nasser who was unwilling to be dragged into a war. About 1957 he was one of the founders of Fatah and played a key role in developing its military wing *al-Asifah*. Thereafter he was always the leader who was most in touch with rank-and-file guerrillas who held him in the highest esteem. In 1964 he was one of the first to be an official representative abroad of the Palestine Liberation Organisation being

sent to Algiers with which he later maintained close links. He had good relations with Yassir Arafat, accompanying him on a secret mission to Peking and often acting as his deputy and like him was imprisoned by the Syrians who feared that his activities would provoke reprisals: his wife acted for him as Chief of Operations. In 1968 he was in Damascus building secret cells inside the occupied areas. During Black September he fought in Amman but nevertheless he was regarded by King Hussain as the best of the guerrilla leaders. Politically he was moderate, prepared to recognise Israel within its 1948 boundaries in return for an independent Palestinian state in the occupied territories. His moderation and loyalty to Arafat led to at least two attempts on his life. In April 1978 his influence over the *fidayin* may have saved Arafat during the rebellion of Abu Daoud. When the Syrians turned against Arafat, Abu Jihad was expelled from Damascus and went to Amman which he had to leave when Hussain quarrelled with Arafat in 1986. Abu Jihad went to Tunis from where he was able to have considerable influence on the early course of the *Intifadah* and he was believed to have organised the killing of three workers at the atomic research installation at Dimona. He was widely respected and able to end quarrels such as that between Arafat and Qadafi. He was not given to bombast or empty rhetoric. In April 1988 he was murdered by seven gunmen who were landed near his villa and there was no doubt that the Israeli Mossad was responsible although they tried to shift the blame onto Arafat or the Syrians. There were riots in the occupied territories in which the Israelis killed 14 demonstrators. His wife Umm Jihad (Intissar al-Wazir), who was also his cousin, was already known as a leading guerrilla in her own right and in August 1989 she became the first woman to be elected to the Central Committee of Fatah.

ABU LUTF (Faruq Qaddumi) (1931–)

Palestinian leader. He was the son of a landowner in Nablus who died shortly after his birth and the family moved to Jaffa where he was educated. In 1948 he returned to Nablus where he joined the Baath Party. In 1950 he obtained a post with ARAMCO working at the same time as a clandestine organiser for the Baath. In 1954 Qaddumi was accepted as a student at Cornell University but was refused an American visa as "a dangerous communist". Instead he studied economics at the American University in Cairo coming into contact with Yassir Arafat, Abu Iyad and Abu Jihad. He was thus one of the founders of Fatah. In 1958 he worked briefly for the Libyan Government but was expelled as "a trouble-maker". He had another year in Saudi Arabia working in the oil department of Abd Allah Tariqi and then moved to Kuwait where he spent six years in the Ministry of Health. During all this time he was active in organising Palestinian activists and maintained close links with other Fatah leaders. Expelled from Kuwait in late 1965 he went to Damascus as Secretary-General of the Fatah Central Committee. After the June War he was the principal Fatah representative in Cairo where he established close personal relations with Nasser. In 1969 he was appointed Head of the Popular Organisation, responsible for cadre training, of the Palestine Liberation Organisation of which in 1973 he also became "Foreign Minister". During Black September Qaddumi and Abu Iyad were arrested by Jordanian forces but released on the intervention of Nasser. Qaddumi was one of the first to call for the establishment of a Palestinian entity on the West Bank as a first step towards a secular democratic Palestine and played a major role at the Rabat Summit of 1974 when this was endorsed as official Arab policy. He travelled widely, making frequent visits to Russia whose policies he generally supported. He enjoyed access to many West European Foreign Ministers and was also an active lobbyist at the United Nations. He always saw the Palestinian struggle as part of a worldwide battle against imperialism. A friendly, affable man, he showed considerable qualities of tact, flexibility and open-mindedness.

ABU MUSA DISPUTE

Abu Musa is an island of 25 square kilometres, 42 kilometres off Sharjah and 67 kilometres from the Persian coast. It is chocolate coloured because of deposits of red oxide, an essential ingredient for paint used on the keels of ships. In the nineteenth century it belonged to the Qawasim who, in addition to Sharjah and Ras al-Khaymah, also controlled Lingah and other places on the Persian side of the Gulf. In 1887 the Persians took control of Lingah. When in 1903 the Persians started to introduce a more efficient customs administration, the British advised the Shaykh of Sharjah to hoist his flag on Abu Musa and the Tunb Islands as a sign of his sovereignty. In April 1904 the Persians took down the flags, hoisted their own and established a post but were ordered to withdraw after British diplomatic pressure on Tehran. In 1906 Salim b. Sultan al-Qasimi, the ousted Shaykh of Sharjah who claimed Abu Musa as a personal possession, gave a mining concession to a firm associated with the German concern of Wonckhaus, which had long been regarded by the British with suspicion. The Resident, Percy Cox, persuaded the Ruler, Saqr b. Khalid al-Qasimi to cancel the concession on the ground that it was a breach of the Exclusive Agreement of 1892. When the concessionaires were slow in departing they were expelled by a British warship and armed followers of the Shaykh in an incident in which it was alleged that shots were fired. The German press reacted furiously but the matter was sorted out amicably between diplomats and lawyers. In 1921 when Ras al-Khaymah was recognised as independent of Sharjah, Abu Musa remained with the latter. In 1923 Persia revived its claim but was again warned off by the British. In 1930 Tehran signified its willingness to drop its claim on Abu Musa if it were ceded the Tunbs, but the Shaykh of Ras al-Khaymah refused to bargain. When the British were about to withdraw from the Gulf in 1971, in order to remove Persian objections to the formation of the United Arab Emirates and the independence of Bahrain, they persuaded Shaykh Khalid b. Muhammad of Sharjah to negotiate with the Shah. An agreement was reached by which Sharjah would retain its sovereignty but about a third of the island would be occupied by Iranian troops. If oil were found it would be shared but until Sharjah had its own oil revenues, Iran would pay it $1.5million annually. According to this agree-

ment, on 30 November 1971, two days before the British left, the Iranians landed without resistance on Abu Musa. The deal caused a storm of protest in the Arab world and may have been a contributory cause of the murder of Shaykh Khalid shortly afterwards. The Iranians built a military base for speedboats and helicopters and they controlled the only port. In April 1992 they started to expel expatriate workers, such as the Indians who kept the amenities running, who had refused to apply for Iranian papers. In August 1992 they turned away a ship which was bringing back over 100 passengers including the Egyptian teachers and their families who served the two schools maintained by Sharjah. Stating that they were acting "for security reasons", the Iranians brought pressure upon the 2,000 inhabitants, many of whom left. Diplomats saw the Iranian action as preparation for a naval base and a reminder that they should be consulted in matters involving Gulf security at a time when they were buying submarines. In September the Foreign Ministers of the Gulf Co-operation Council condemned the Iranian action as did the Arab League and Egypt which was anxious to stress its role as the defender of the Gulf States under the Damascus Declaration while the Syrians tried to mediate. At the end of the month a two-day meeting of Iranian and UAE officials in Abu Dhabi produced no result. Both the Americans and the Russians supported the UAE. Early in November the Iranians permitted the return of the Egyptian teachers but did not drop its claim to full sovereignty whereupon the UAE announced that it was referring the dispute to the UN. In February 1993 both Iran and the UAE reaffirmed their claims but neither seemed to bring the matter to a head, agreeing to resume talks after a visit by the Iranian Foreign Minister to Abu Dhabi in May.

ABU NIDAL (Sabri al-Banna) (1937–)

Palestinian terrorist. He was born in Jaffa, the son of the eighth wife of a very rich orange grower whose land was seized by the Israeli Government in 1948 when the family fled to a refugee camp. He spent two years studying engineering at Cairo University but did not graduate. He worked as a teacher in Nablus and then as an assistant electrician in Saudi Arabia where he joined the illegal Baath Party. He was tortured and expelled from the Kingdom. Some time in the 1960s he joined Fatah and was sent to Khartoum in 1969 and then to Baghdad as its representative. Later, with Abu Daoud he was sent for guerrilla training in China where he became strongly influenced by Maoism. Abu Nidal urged that only complete commitment to the armed struggle would result in the "total destruction of the Zionist entity" and regarded all attempts at compromise as treachery; there could be no alliance with reactionary Arab regimes. In September 1973 he organised an attack on the Saudi Embassy in Paris which was occupied for 28 hours and hostages were held for the release of his old comrade Abu Daoud from a Jordanian jail. Based on Baghdad, he established the Fatah Revolutionary Council which acted independently of the main Fatah organisation whose leader Yassir Arafat, Abu Nidal plotted to kill. In October 1974 Fatah condemned him to death for mutiny but he remained in Iraq which found him useful in attacking Syrian targets.

Under the name of Black June his men twice attempted to kill Abd al-Halim Khaddam, in October 1977 killing the UAE Foreign Minister Sayf b. Ghabbash instead. Syrian Embassies in Rome and Islamabad were attacked. In September 1976 Abu Nidal was held responsible for seizing the Semiramis Hotel in Damascus with 90 hostages, about 40 of whom were wounded when troops stormed the building: the surviving gunmen were publicly hanged. In another operation in November three of his men, including a Japanese, were killed trying to take over the Intercontinental Hotel in Amman. In 1978 he started attacking representatives of the Palestine Liberation Organisation including those in London, Paris, Brussels and Kuwait and killing moderates such as Said Hammami and later Isam Sartawi. Abu Nidal was responsible for attacks in Europe on Israeli diplomats and Jewish property, including a school in Antwerp. Abu Nidal formed links with other terrorist groups such as the Armenian Secret Army, co-operating in order to confuse security authorities. He also collaborated with East European intelligence organisations, particularly that of Poland where he ran a business network in order to raise funds. In June 1982 the attempted murder of the Israeli Ambassador in London by Abu Nidal followers, probably at the behest of Saddam Hussain, was seized upon by Begin as an excuse for launching Operation Peace for Galilee, the invasion of Lebanon. In September 1983 a Gulf Air plane was blown up in mid-air with all 122 on board killed. In November the Saudis, whose financial help was essential in the Iran – Iraq War brought pressure on Baghdad to expel Abu Nidal who went to Damascus. In March 1984 he threatened to kill Queen Elizabeth on her State Visit to Jordan. In June 1984 he quarrelled with the Syrians, disbanded the Fatah Revolutionary Council and moved back to Baghdad where he was granted permanent asylum. He was said to be afflicted by heart trouble and in November his death was widely reported. However he was soon back in action and in June 1985 the British Airways office in Madrid was attacked with bombs, grenades and guns. In December 1985 seventeen passengers were killed at the El Al counter of Rome airport (he was sentenced to life imprisonment *in absentia* in February 1988 for this crime) and his men put bombs in Paris department stores. In 1986 12 Jews were killed in a synagogue in Istanbul and in 1988 a Greek tourist boat was attacked with 11 deaths. He stood aloof from the general reconciliation of the guerrilla groups at the Palestine National Council meeting in April 1987. In 1987 he moved to Tripoli where he was given training facilities but in January 1990 Qadafi, seeking better relations with the West and with other Arab countries restricted his activities and in April he returned to Iraq. Abu Nidal was a terrorist organiser of near genius. With never more than a few hundred disciplined and fanatical followers, using a bewildering profusion of names in well-controlled cells, with meticulous planning he defeated the most sophisticated security services in the world and created a stir quite out of proportion to his strength. An estimate was that they had killed or wounded 900 people in at least 20 countries. He was a typical revolutionary plotter, suspicious to the point of paranoia, even of his family and closest

friends, unwilling to speak on the telephone or eat or drink anything that he had not seen prepared. He was utterly ruthless and cruel. In November 1989 a power struggle was reported inside the Abu Nidal group which was temporarily settled by the leader's inviting twenty of his colleagues for a discussion and having them murdered: an estimated 300 perished in all. Many of his followers in South Lebanon were also liquidated. Dissidents within his group accused him of trafficking in arms and drugs.

ABU SHARIF, Bassam (c. 1947–)

Palestinian nationalist leader. He was educated at the American University of Beirut and claimed to have had no interest in politics until he graduated on the day that the June War began. He thereupon joined the Popular Front for the Liberation of Palestine and worked in the Beirut office of its newspaper *al-Hadaf*. In September 1970 he was summoned from Beirut to act as spokesman for the hijackers who had diverted civilian aircraft to Dawson's Field and became regarded as an associate of terrorists. In July 1972 he was wounded by an Israeli letter bomb sent to him at the *al-Hadaf* office, losing one eye and five fingers and was made largely deaf: his chief editor Ghasan Khanafani was murdered by the Israelis. While in hospital he was sent a box of poisoned sweets. Abu Sharif was one of the first to advocate a single, democratic, secular state for Palestine, later switching to a two-state solution: this involving recognition of Israel rather than its destruction led to his divergence from the PFLP. During the Beirut Siege of 1982 he became close to Yassir Arafat, serving as one of his principal advisers. His breach with the PFLP was completed when it continued to accept Syrian patronage after President Assad had used the Shaih militia Amal to attack Palestinians loyal to Arafat in Burj al-Barajinah. Abu Sharif served as the main link between the Palestine Liberation Organisation and London where he made several visits, proving an articulate and persuasive debater as an advocate of a negotiated peace settlement. In September 1990 he tried to distance the PLO from Arafat's support for Saddam Hussain and the threats of George Habash to attack Western interests if Iraq were invaded. In March 1991 he resigned after saying that he would agree to a non-PLO delegation negotiating with Israel, that he would accept less than the whole of the West Bank and Gaza Strip and that Arafat would not necessarily be President of any Palestinian state that might be established. Later in the year he played a key part in persuading the PLO not to oppose the Madrid Peace Talks.

ABU TAYI, Auda (c. 1870–1924)

Arabian tribal chief. He was the leader of a section of the Huwaytat, a bedouin tribe which dominated an area from Tayma in the Hijaz to Karak and from the Gulf of Aqaba to Wadi Sirhan. About 1900 he was put in charge of the tribe by the Turks but ignored authority to become the most famous raider of the time. He attacked Ibn Hadhal of the Amarat on the Euphrates and raided almost as far north as Aleppo. In a skirmish he killed two Turkish soldiers who had come to collect taxes. In 1914 he robbed Captain Shakespear who was crossing Arabia of nearly all his money and his decorated camel girths. He was said to have torn out the heart of a vanquished foe to drink his blood. In 1915 he was reported killed in action. He was at feud with most other tribal leaders, including many of those serving in the army of the Amir Faysal in the Arab Revolt so it took considerable diplomacy on the part of the Amir in settling numerous blood-feuds before Auda could join him. This he did early in April 1917, according to Lawrence, dramatically smashing the false teeth which had been a gift from the Turks and having to go meatless until an Allied set could be procured. His adherence opened up the way to Aqaba which he entered after a sweeping detour at the beginning of July, thus enabling the Arab army to move on from the Hijaz into Trans-Jordan. In addition to fighting the Turks he was busy intriguing for recognition as paramount chief of the Huwaytat. He continued with the army into Damascus, where he is said to have saved Lawrence from a murderous attack by Abd al-Qadr al-Jazairi. When the Amir Abd Allah left the Hijaz in 1920 to try to win a kingdom, he was so penniless that he had to borrow from Auda at Ma'an but later Auda transferred his allegiance to Ibn Saud. He was imprisoned in Salt, and escaped, but was then reconciled with Abd Allah. Lawrence described him as "inimitable" and portrays him as almost a figure from a novelette "his hospitality is sweeping: his generosity has reduced him to poverty and devoured the profits of a hundred successful raids. He has married twenty-eight times, has been wounded thirteen times, and in his battles has seen all his tribesmen hurt, and most of his relations killed. He has only reported his 'kill' since 1900, and they now stand at seventy-five Arabs; Turks are not counted by Arabs when they are dead ... He sees life as a saga and all events in it are significant and all personages heroic". Lawrence said that he had made his section the finest fighting force in Western Arabia. He died in hospital after an operation. Lawrence had said "when he dies, the Middle Ages of the desert will have ended".

ABU ZAABAL

Abu Zaabal was a concentration camp in the Egyptian desert, known as Maqbarat al-ahya ("the cemetery of the living"), used to detain opponents of the Nasser regime. Conditions were horrifying and members of the Egyptian Communist Party were particularly ill-treated when complaints about their detention were made abroad. They were later joined by members of the Muslim Brothers and it was said that many of the best brains in the country were amongst the political prisoners. During much of the 1960s, according to Mustafa Amin, himself a prisoner "if you were guilty you went to prison: if innocent to a concentration camp". Releases became frequent under Sadat and in October 1971 it was announced that Abu Zaabal and all the other concentration camps had been closed.

ACHILLE LAURO HIJACKING (1985)

Four Palestinian guerrillas boarded at Genoa the cruise ship *Achille Lauro* bound for Egypt and Israel where they planned to disembark and take hostages in order to demand the release of Palestinian prisoners. Between Alexandria and Port Said, on 7 October 1985, the crew

discovered them cleaning weapons so they abandoned their original intention and took over the ship with 180 passengers and 331 crew (600 passengers had disembarked at Alexandria). They sailed for Syria which refused to let them land, then to Cyprus which also refused and finally back to Port Said. On the voyage they murdered a crippled American Jew, throwing his body overboard. On 9 October the Egyptian Government, assisted by Abu al-Abbas who was believed to have masterminded the plot, persuaded them to surrender in return for a safe passage to Tunis. The main Palestine Liberation Organisation disavowed the hijacking and promised to put the terrorists on trial: Reagan briefly agreed, implicitly recognising the PLO. The Americans, who had no legal standing in the hijacking of an Italian ship in Egyptian waters, intercepted the Egyptian aircraft bound for Tunis and forced it to land in Sicily. There the aircraft was surrounded by Italian troops ordered to take the men into custody but the Italians were in turn surrounded by American troops who demanded the surrender of the prisoners but were eventually ordered to withdraw as the Italian Government insisted that they be tried in Italy. President Mubarak denounced the action against the Egyptian aircraft as "piracy" but his inability to do more damaged his prestige at home. The Italian Government allowed Abu al-Abbas who had been on the aircraft to go free, leading to vehement American protests and the resignation of the Italian Defence Minister, who claimed that he had not been consulted. Prime Minister Bettino Craxi thereupon resigned but was asked by President Cossiga to continue in office. Yugoslavia, where Abu al-Abbas had gone, also refused to extradite him to the US and was roundly abused. Eventually the four hijackers were sentenced in Genoa to between 4 and 9 years' imprisonment. The whole incident was a gift to Arabs and Israelis opposed to the peace process.

ACHOUR, Habib (1913–)

Tunisian trade unionist and politician. Born in Sfax, the son of a fishery guard, he attended a technical school and became a rebel after being beaten for stepping on the hem of a French boy's coat. Working as a municipal labourer, he became famous as an amateur boxer. In 1940 he led a strike of tanners. In the mid-1940s with his cousin Farhat Hashid he started organising dockers and drivers into a trade union which worked extremely closely with the Neo-Destour. He was strongly anti-communist. In 1945 he helped Bourguiba in his famous escape to Libya. In August 1947 Achour led a general strike which stopped all transport in Sfax: French troops opened fire killing about 30 workers and wounding over 150 including Achour. He was sentenced to five years in jail followed by twenty in forced residence. After his release he led a small breakaway union, the Union des Travailleurs Tunisiens in competition with the larger Union Générale Tunisienne du Travail led by Ahmad Ben Salah. In November 1955, at the Neo-Destour Sfax Congress, Achour's saying that "the workers are Bourguiba's troops", played an important part in the defeat of Salih Ben Yusuf. In 1957 the split between the unions was healed and Ahmad Tlili headed the combined UGTT until March 1963 when he was dismissed by Bourguiba for opposing the policies of Ben Salah: Achour was appointed his successor. In 1964 Achour became a Deputy and a member of the Politburo of the Parti Socialiste Destourien. He became, however, involved in a struggle with the Party Manager, Muhammad Sayah who aimed to make the unions completely subordinate to the Party bureaucracy and with Ben Salah whose economic plans necessitated devaluation and keeping down the pay of the workers. Achour cultivated links with foreign trade unions for support in his domestic battles. In June 1965 a UGTT-owned ferry-boat sank, drowning seven tourists and Achour was accused of forging an insurance document and contempt of court. He was expelled from the Party, his parliamentary immunity removed, and in March 1966 he was sentenced to six months' imprisonment. The World Federation of Trade Unions interceded with Bourguiba and Achour was included in an amnesty in June. In July 1967 he was back in the Assembly and the Politburo. During the 1970s the UGTT was the only national organisation apart from the PSD and became a haven for many diverse opponents of the regime, including young intellectuals who had no other organisation where they could voice criticisms. It also appeared the only possible force for change as the PSD ossified under Hedi Nouira. Twice during 1977 during a time of strained relations between Tunisia and Libya over the continental shelf, Achour visited Tripoli for discussions with Colonel Qadafi and the dissident leader Muhammad Masmoudi. During that year he strongly criticised police terror at the University and led 41 strikes in six months. There were also mysterious reports of an attempt on his life. Early in January 1978, after a meeting of the UGTT National Council, Achour and his deputy resigned from the Party, declaring the Government "orientated towards the consolidation by all means of a capitalist class to the detriment of the national interest" because of its links with foreign exploiters. They called for a general strike and ten days later Tunis erupted in violence on Black Thursday; immediately afterwards Achour and 10 out of 13 members of the UGTT Executive were arrested. Achour was sentenced to ten years' hard labour but after eleven months this was reduced to house arrest. The new leadership of the UGTT condemned Achour's arbitrary decisions and the organisation was paralysed by internal feuds. After the retirement of Nouira the new Prime Minister Muhammad Mzali was concerned to conciliate the opposition and Achour was released. The UGTT Congress in April 1981 appointed a new Secretary-General but Achour remained President. In August 1982 he had a formal reconciliation with Bourguiba and in April 1984 he signed an accord with Mzali by which in return for an agreement not to strike until dialogue had been exhausted, the unions would be consulted over economic policies. During 1984 there were several reports that Achour was proposing to found a Labour Party on the British model and despite his age he was believed to have Presidential ambitions. In December he was reappointed Secretary-General of the UGTT and in April 1985 relations between the unions and the Government started to deteriorate over wage claims. For the first time the UGTT refused to support PSD candidates in elections. In July the union news-

paper was banned. In August Achour started a new campaign of strikes at the very time when Qadafi started to expel Tunisian workers, thus exacerbating the problem of unemployment: Achour was accused of collaborating with him. In October in an attempt at conciliation, Mzali appointed the son of Farhat Hashid as Minister of Labour but he also sent pro-PSD unionists to take over from UGTT officers loyal to Achour. In November Achour was put under house arrest and in December he was sentenced to eight months' imprisonment. Nevertheless he was in January 1986 re-elected Secretary-General but in April he was sentenced to a further three years. He was released after the fall of Bourguiba in November 1967, going straight into a Paris hospital. Achour, the father of eleven children, was an impulsive, rugged, outspoken man who was intimidated by no one.

ACROPOLE HOTEL (KHARTOUM) MURDERS (1988)

In April 1988 Israeli agents murdered the Palestinian leader Abu Jihad. The following month five Britons, a woman teacher, an aid worker, his wife and their children aged three and one, and two Sudanese were murdered by Palestinian terrorists in attacks on the Acropole Hotel, Khartoum and on a club in the city. It was widely accepted, although the killers denied it, that the attack was a reprisal ordered by Abu Nidal. The murderers were sentenced to death in October but, under the *Shariah* imposed by the Nimeiri regime in the September Laws they would escape execution if the relatives of the victims accepted blood money (*diyah*). The relatives of the Sudanese were paid large sums and agreed to the release of the murderers which took place in January 1992 despite British protests.

ADDI OU BIHI, Brahim Zedki (?–1961)

Moroccan tribal leader. In 1948, having been Caid of Kerrando in the Central Atlas he was dismissed by the French for abuses of power but he retained great influence in the area. He refused to join other tribal leaders in the plot hatched by the French and Thami al-Glawi to force out Sultan Muhammad V in 1953. In 1956, when independence had been achieved, he was appointed Caid of the Tafilalet. Addi ou Bihi apparently assumed that the old pre-Protectorate *Bilad al-Siba* would be resumed. He strongly opposed the attempts to modernise tribal administration of which the most obvious sign was the abolition of the old Berber Customary Law Tribunals and the appointment of Arab judges and other officials by the *Istiqlal* Party and refused summonses to Rabat. He received a consignment of rifles from sympathetic French officers and encouragement from the former Interior Minister, his fellow-Berber Lahsen Lyoussi. In January 1957, when the King left the country for a cruise ou Bihi believed that he was escaping from the machinations of the *Istiqlal*. Declaring fanatical loyalty to the Monarch, whom he wished to save from "the evils of the Fassis", he expelled all government officials from his province. The future King, Hassan II, sent two regular army battalions against him and he surrendered. He was then held in a palace for two years while the *Istiqlal* demanded that he be brought to trial. He was condemned to death but reprieved after a few days and died in jail.

ADDIS ABABA AGREEMENT (1972)

For many years Southern resistance to the rule of Khartoum had been fragmented amongst competing groups but eventually it was practically united as the Southern Sudan Liberation Movement under the leadership of Joseph Lagu who was able to negotiate on behalf of them all. Haile Selassie, anxious to end the war on his frontier with its repercussions on his own Eritrean rebels, played an important part in bringing North and South together, giving a personal guarantee that the insurgents would be fairly treated. Actual negotiations were conducted in Addis Ababa by the Sudanese Vice-President, Abel Alier, the Foreign Minister Mansur Khalid and the former Minister Izbone Mandiri and resulted in an agreement signed in February 1972. Although the word "Federation" was not used, a series of compromises created in effect a Federation of two Regions. There was to be the gradual establishment of local autonomy in which the three Southern Provinces, Equatoria, Upper Nile and Bahr al-Ghazal, were to be united into a Region. A Regional Assembly would be elected by universal suffrage within 18 months and there was provision for a Regional President who would at the same time be a national Vice-President, and a Regional Executive Council which would control Southern affairs apart from defence, foreign affairs, currency and social planning which would remain under the Khartoum Government on which the South would be fairly represented. The Regional framework could not be changed without a three-quarters majority of the People's National Assembly and a two-thirds majority in a referendum held in the three Southern Provinces. The Regional Executive could impose taxes although in practice it required subsidies from the North. About 6,000 Anya Nya guerrillas were incorporated into the Sudanese army and would serve in the South with an equal number of Northern troops under the command of an equal number of Northern and Southern officers. Arabic was to be the official language while English would be recognised as a "common language" and taught in the schools. There was no longer a possibility that Sudan might adhere fully to the Federation of Arab Republics with Egypt and Libya. For many years the Agreement worked well and appeared to be one of the greatest achievements of the Nimeiri regime but in 1983 he broke several of its provisions, setting off a second Southern uprising, Anya Nya II.

ADIB, Auguste (1859–1936)

Lebanese Prime Minister. He was a Maronite, born in Constantinople and his mother came from a Florentine family long established there. In 1884 he entered the Egyptian Ministry of Finance, rising to become its Director-General. He was also the President of the Cairo Committee which called for Lebanese independence. He returned after the French had installed themselves in Beirut and was appointed Secretary-General of the Government. In May 1926 when under a new Constitution Lebanon became a Republic, the President Charles Dabbas appointed Adib as its first Prime Minister. He published a Utopian programme but the Constitution proved unworkable with constant French interference and bad relations between the Ministry, the Senate and the Chamber, all divided into interest groups. So little was achieved that people referred to "The Sleeping Cabinet". There were simultaneous demands for reduced taxation and increased government expenditure and after just under a year in office Adib resigned in despair after losing a vote of confidence. Bishara al-Khouri who had reputedly launched a successful intrigue against the Prime Minister who was absent in Paris negotiating over the Ottoman Debt followed him in office. During his brief period Adib had been a strong defender of the separation of Lebanon from Syria. In March 1930 the stern measures adopted by Emile Edde to deal with a financial crisis led to a vote of no-confidence in his government and Adib took office with a Cabinet of only four colleagues. It was considered unlikely that Adib would long survive but in fact his Cabinet lasted over two years, a record for longevity that lasted over 30 years. He carried on the economic cuts of his predecessor but in a less abrasive fashion. He never overcame the inherent difficulties of the system and had further problems with rioting students, industrial unrest, boycotts, episcopal feuding and bloody quarrels between Armenian factions. In May 1932, faced with the additional problem of a Presidential election likely to be fiercely contested, the High Commissioner Henri Ponsot abolished the Constitution and empowered the President, presiding over a Council of Directors, to legislate by Decree. Adib played no further part in public affairs. He wrote a book in French and Arabic on the finances of Lebanon.

al-ADL wa-l-IHSAN (Morocco)

The decreasing number of French school teachers and their replacement by Arabs led to a growth of Islamic fundamentalism amongst young Moroccans. At the same time, as in other North African countries, Islam was seen as the only cure for economic misery. In 1982 the followers of Shaykh Abd al-Salam Yassin were refused permission to register as a party under the name of al-Adl wa- al-Ihsan (Justice and Benevolence) but continued to exist undisturbed, being particularly strong in the Universities. Other clandestine groups were not tolerated and in September 1985 14 members of Jeunesse Islamique led by Abd al-Krim Mottei, who had thrice been sentenced to death and later lived in exile in Libya, were charged with plotting the overthrow of the Monarchy, having received arms, money and training from Algeria. Death sentences were imposed on 14 and imprisonment of up to life on 26. The following month 28 of a second group calling itself Mujahidin were sentenced. In December 1989 17 of al-Adl were convicted of belonging to an unauthorised organisation and possessing documents threatening state security and Yassin himself placed under house arrest. In January 1990 the Government banned al-Adl, arresting five of its presumed leaders and they received sentences of up to two years. In May the trial of some Islamic militants who had demonstrated outside Shaykh Yassin's house set off a major riot in which an estimated 2,000 were arrested, beaten and then released. In February 1991 al-Adl leaders claimed that 25,000 of its members had taken part in a march against Western intervention in the Gulf War. In May Adl members and others demonstrated in Casablanca, demanding popular sovereignty with the King no longer governing and opposing a referendum in the Western Sahara which should be simply annexed by Morocco. During the summer there were further arrests, followed by quick releases and in September the Government offered Yassin and his colleagues official recognition in return for acceptance of the Monarchy and a petition for pardon. They insisted upon being released before there could be any discussions. In April 1992 Adl supporters occupied a University building near Casablanca after one of them had been killed in a clash with police and in the autumn there were violent clashes at Universities between Islamic and left-wing students: after the worst at Oudjda in November 60 fundamentalists were arrested after three leftists had been hacked to death.

ADWAN REBELLION (1923)
The Adwan were the most numerous settled tribe in the new, largely bedouin state of Trans-Jordan and were therefore the easiest to tax. When they found that their hereditary enemies the Bani Sakhr had been exempted from tax their Shaykh Sultan Adwan led a party of 200 armed men to discuss their grievances with the Amir Abd Allah who promised that their complaints would be dealt with. Nothing happened and the tribe lost patience. In September 1923, supported by some town politicians they demanded a representative assembly and more participation by native Trans-Jordanians in the largely Syrian Government. About 500 men marched on Amman where there was panic. Arab Legion cavalry supported by two armoured cars of the RAF attacked them and some 86 people including 13 women were killed. Sultan Adwan took refuge with the Syrian Druzes but was later allowed to return. The British Representative, Philby, considered that their protests had had general support against the "reckless tyranny" of Abd Allah. The Adwan Rebellion was the most serious of a number of tribal uprisings between 1921 and 1923.

AFRO-ASIAN PEOPLES' SOLIDARITY CONGRESS, CAIRO (1957/8)
In April 1955 the leaders of 23 independent states in Asia and six from Africa, nine of them Arab, met in Bandung at the initiative of President Sukarno and Prime Ministers Nehru and U Nu. The Conference made worthy declarations of principle and was strongly anti-imperialist, calling also for bringing Aden under Yemeni rule and the rights of the Palestinians. It was attended by Nasser who said that it "was a landmark in his political understanding". He realised the political benefits and the increased bargaining power that could accrue from leadership of a large number of members of the UN and also from making Cairo the capital of Africa. He gave encouragement to African nationalist movements, allowing them to use Cairo Radio for propaganda. Asian Solidarity Committees were set up in various countries with the active but often clandestine backing of the Russians. In October 1957 a steering committee of Egypt, Syria, the Soviet Union and Communist China was set up to convene a Con-

gress in Cairo which met from 26 December 1957 until 1 January 1958 which was attended by 500 official and unofficial delegates from 46 countries, including exiled nationalist movements. Unlike Bandung, the Russians were invited but some of the more conservative states such as Morocco, Malaysia and Pakistan which had attended the first Conference refused to attend as communist domination was so obvious. The Egyptian representatives argued that there was no question of neutrality in the struggle against imperialism, which was condemned in all its forms and manifestations. It denounced the Baghdad Pact and the Eisenhower Doctrine and supported the particular interests of its members by demanding that the Portuguese should abandon Goa and the reunification of Korea and Vietnam. Israel was "the base of imperialism". There should be an unconditional ban on nuclear tests. Nasser felt that it would be dangerous if the enthusiasm of some members got out of hand and managed to get control of the Secretariat that was established, appointing Yusuf Sibai as Secretary-General. This Congress showed the benefits to both of Russo-Egyptian co-operation. It was followed by an Economic Conference of representatives of Chambers of Commerce which convened in Cairo in December 1958 which also set up a secretariat but was weakened by protests at the non-invitation of anti-communist states. A second Congress was held in Conakry in January 1960, chaired by Sadat, was mainly preoccupied with African issues but did discuss the formation of an international brigade to fight for Algerian independence. Further Congresses were held, the most recent being the sixth held in Algiers in May 1984. The organisation which now has 75 members aims to ensure the economic, social and cultural developments of its members but is of minor political importance.

AHARDAN, Mahjoubi (1921)
Moroccan political leader. He came from a family of tribal notables of the At Sgougou in the Middle Atlas and was educated at Azrou. He then graduated from the Military Academy in Meknes and reached the rank of Captain in the French army during the war, fighting in Tunisia, Italy and Germany. He resigned his commission rather than fight the nationalists in Indo-China but in 1949 he was appointed Caid of Oulmes. He married a French wife. Ahardan was dismissed in 1953 with other local leaders who had refused to endorse the deposition of Muhammad V and with Dr Abd al-Krim Khatib began a clandestine campaign for independence. When the Armée de Libération Nationale emerged in 1955 he was one of its principal leaders. After independence he worked closely with the future Hassan II to integrate the former guerrillas into the newly created Moroccan army. Ahardan was then appointed Pasha of Rabat. In November 1957 he and Khatib announced the formation of the Mouvement Populaire designed to put forward the interests of the rural Berbers, many of them his old followers of the ALN. The Istiqlal Government, incensed at the challenge to their efforts to establish a one-party state, had Ahardan dismissed from his post and later briefly imprisoned in October 1958. His arrest led to disturbances in Berber areas. In February 1961, the death of

Muhammad V was totally unexpected and was kept secret while the new King used Ahardan to alert the police and the army where he had great influence as the majority of senior officers were Berbers. In June Hassan handed over the Ministry of Defence to Ahardan who completed the integration of the ALN and also concluded an arms deal with the Soviet Union. In 1963 he took his MP into the coalition of royalist parties, the Front pour la Défense des Institutions Constitutionelles but he never found it easy to work with smooth urban politicians. In July 1964 he was transferred to the Ministry of Agriculture to carry through reforms desired by the peasants but in February 1966 he returned to the Defence Ministry. The suspension of Parliament in June 1966 led to a split between Ahardan and Khatib who resigned from the Government and subsequently formed his own party. Ahardan resigned in February 1967 and was out of office for ten years until March 1967 when he and the other major party leaders became Ministers of State in order to give credibility to the forthcoming elections. When Ahmad Uthman subsequently reformed his Cabinet Ahardan remained as the first Minister of Posts. In November 1983 Ahardan was again Minister of State in a pre-election government.

In October 1986 internal disputes in the MP led to the replacement of Ahardan as leader by an 8-man collective. In 1990 he created his own Mouvement National Populaire with more stress on religion, taking with him a dozen Deputies. In May 1990 he was nominated to the King's Consultative Council on Human Rights. During the 1993 campaign for the parliamentary elections, Ahardan proved a very effective television performer and was credited with winning several seats for his party. Ahardan, a slight, tense, impulsive man was a gifted poet and painter. He embodied the Berber tradition that combined opposition to corrupt government with deep loyalty to the Sultan.

AHD

In 1909 Aziz Ali al-Misri founded the Qahtaniyyah to forward his ideal of turning the Ottoman Empire into a Dual Monarchy on Austro-Hungarian lines with its Arab provinces enjoying internal independence but united in a kingdom of which the Turkish Sultan should be sovereign. The Qahtaniyyah was believed to have been infiltrated by a government spy and allowed to lapse. Misri then in 1914 formed the Ahd (Covenant) with membership limited to army officers. It has been estimated that out of a total of 490 Arab officers in the Ottoman army, 315 (mostly Iraqi) joined the Ahd. Nuri al-Said, an early member, said that they had no thought of secession from the Empire but wanted a local administration run by Arabs, recognition of Arabic as an official language and that they were in touch with Turkish officers, including the future Ataturk, who favoured a federation of two autonomous states. Misri was sentenced to death on a trumped-up charge but reprieved. When the war started the Arab officers were deliberately scattered throughout the Empire but some in Syria managed in 1915 to work out with the civilian Fatat the Damascus Protocol which, agreed by the Hashemites of Mecca, was the basis of the terms on which the Arabs would assist the British by rising

against the Turks. These terms were brought to Cairo by Muhammad Sharif al-Faruqi, an Iraqi member of the Ahd who had deserted at Gallipoli. Once the Arab Revolt had started, many members who had been captured or deserted, helped to train the Arab army. After the war former members played major roles in Arab history, five of them becoming Prime Ministers of Iraq and one, Ali Ridha al-Rikabi, serving as the first Prime Minister of both Syria and Trans-Jordan. Later Nur al-Said used the name Ahd for a short-lived, loosely-organised group of his supporters in the 1930s.

al-AHDAB, Khayr al-Din (c. 1895–?)

Lebanese Prime Minister. He was a Muslim originally from Tripoli, one of the few Muslims who studied law in Paris before the First World War. After the war he worked with the French administration but opposed the concept of a Greater Lebanon, feeling that it favoured the Maronites. With Riad al-Sulh he founded a newspaper *al-Ahd al-Jadid* which took an Arab nationalist line. In 1934 he was elected a Deputy for Beirut and came to abandon his pan-Arabism in favour of Lebanese separatism. He had a Christian wife and established friendly links with Maronite politicians, especially Emile Edde. When the Constitution was restored in January 1937 President Edde appointed Ahdab Prime Minister, setting the tradition of Maronite President and Sunni Premier. Ahdab found himself in an impossible position as he commanded only 13 votes in the Chamber whereas Bishara al-Khouri who refused to co-operate had 12 and Deputies changed sides two or three times a day. In March he had to reconstruct his Cabinet, bringing in Michel Zakkour, a supporter of Khouri as Minister of the Interior; Zakkour, however, died in June and the Khouri faction left the Government which had to be reconstructed for the third time. There was occasional street violence with clashes between the Communists and what emerged as the Parti Populaire Syrien. In October there were elections with keen bargaining over the nominated Deputies. In November Ahdab had to reform his Cabinet to take account of the new Chamber. He had to cope also with the frequent interventions of the Maronite Patriarch but introduced some useful measures including the dissolution of paramilitary organisations which led to clashes with the Kataib and loss of life. In January 1938 Ahdab changed his government for the final time before resigning in March. His prestige had grown in office and the President became jealous, intrigued against the Prime Minister and made no effort to rally support when it was needed in the Chamber. A British consular report described Ahdab as "intelligent and tactful".

AHMAD, Abd al-Rahim (1944–91)

Palestinian guerrilla leader. He was born near Lydda but his family moved to Jordan after 1948. He attended school in Jordan and then took a degree in Agriculture from Damascus University. As a teenager he was a member of guerrilla groups and of the Baath. When in 1970 the Iraqi Government decided to form its Palestinian adherents into the Arab Liberation Front, Ahmad was one of the earliest members. In 1970 he was elected to the Executive Committee of the Palestine Liberation

Organisation. After the assassination of Abd al-Wahhab Kayyal, Ahmad became leader of the ALF. He fought against the Israelis in Lebanon and after the Beirut Siege was evacuated by sea. He was generally regarded as a moderate, supporting the policies of Yassir Arafat. In 1989 he was found to have malignant brain tumours from which he died in June 1991.

al-AHRAM

Literally "The Pyramids", *al-Ahram* has been an influential Egyptian newspaper since its foundation in Alexandria by two Lebanese immigrants, Salim and Bishara Taqla in 1876. Since 1898 it has been published in Cairo. In its early days it was moderately pro-French and before the First World War supported Mustafa Kamil. Under the Monarchy it was not affiliated to any political party but tended to support the government of the day. After the July Revolution it lost much of its importance until in 1957 Muhammad Hassanain Haykal was appointed its Editor. In 1960, with the rest of the press, it was put under the ownership of the National Union. Owing to Haykal's close relationship with Nasser, the paper became regarded as the mouthpiece of the Egyptian Government and was often given information denied to its rivals – for example in April 1961 it was given the text of a shouting match between Khruschev and Anwar Sadat. Haykal's weekly column "Frankly Speaking", the only uncensored article in any publication, was studied throughout the world as an indicator of possible future policies and was permitted some criticisms of the regime. Sometimes it seemed less anti-American than some official policies. It also published articles by intellectuals not well-regarded by the regime such as Lewis Awadh or Magdi Wahbah. Under Haykal *al-Ahram* became a large-scale publishing house with, for example, an economic weekly founded by Butros Butros-Ghali. Its circulation, perhaps half a million, rising to 750,000 on the day of Haykal's article, was by far the largest in the the Arab world. In 1974 Haykal was dismissed, being replaced by Ali Amin, an exile under Nasser. Later leftists were purged by Yusuf Sibai.

AIN AL-RUMMANAH MASSACRE (1975)

Lebanese Christians became increasingly disturbed at the activities of Palestinian refugees on their territory and it appeared as if they were being exploited by Kamal Jumblatt in his schemes to end Maronite predominance. In February 1975 Palestinian guerrillas had joined forces with left-wing Muslims in a clash in Sidon in which 5 soldiers and 11 civilians had been killed. Tension rose and then subsided until Sunday 13 April when gunmen in a car drove up to a church where the Kataib leader Pierre Gemayel was attending a service and killed four people including his bodyguard and two officials of his Party. In revenge Kataib gunmen ambushed a bus at Ain al-Rummanah, a suburb of Beirut near the main refugee camps, and killed 27 of its Palestinian occupants and wounded 19 more. The Kataib claimed that the Palestinians had been armed and killed three of their men. This massacre was followed by a week of prolonged fighting in which the official figure of 150 killed was a gross underestimate. In retrospect the Ain al-Rummanah massacre can be seen as the start of the civil war and the disintegration of the Lebanese state.

AISHA (1930–)

Moroccan Princess and pioneer of female emancipation. Lalla Aisha was the eldest daughter of Muhammad V and was educated in the Palace school in Rabat. She had already made public appearances unveiled before in 1947, on the occasion of her father's Tangier Speech, she herself made a speech, partly in English, in which she stated that Morocco, although an Arab and Islamic nation, was part of the Western world and that women had a role in fighting for its independence. Later she campaigned actively for women's rights and was a popular broadcaster. From 1953 to 1955 she shared her father's exile in Madagascar and after independence acted as his official hostess as her mother never appeared in public. In 1956 she accompanied her brother the future Hassan II to Washington to appeal for aid but her main activity was as President of Entre'aide Nationale set up to help the poor. She did much to organise relief for Agadir after its destruction in the earthquake of 1960. In 1965, at a time when no Moroccan woman held high public office, her brother appointed Lalla Aisha Ambassador to London where she remained for four years before being posted to Rome. She became Honorary President of the National Union of Moroccan Women upon its foundation. She married an industrialist and had two daughters. Lalla Aisha was extremely informal, always ready to defy protocol to get action in a matter that she regarded as important.

AIX-LES-BAINS CONFERENCE (1955)

Two years after the exiling by the French of Muhammad V it was clear that their position in Morocco was becoming untenable. It was attracting increasing condemnation at the UN. About 6,000 acts of violence in which 700 people including 100 Europeans had been killed had taken place, culminating in the massacre of 49 French citizens at Oued Zem, the puppet Sultan Muhammad ben Arafa had lost all credibility unable to form any body of supporters but refused to step aside while the Resident General, Gilbert Grandval, was the target of the venomous hatred of the colons. The Prime Minister Edgar Fauré summoned a meeting of representatives of all shades of Moroccan opinion at Aix-les-Bains from 22 to 27 August 1955. He attended in person accompanied by Robert Schuman the Minister of Finance, Antoine Pinay Minister of Foreign Affairs, Pierre July Minister for Morocco and Tunisia and the Defence Minister General Koenig. On the first day the conservatives, the Pasha of Marrakesh, Haj Thami al-Glawi and Sharif Abd al-Hayy al-Kattani argued against the recall of Muhammad V while the centenarian Grand Wazir Muhammad al-Mokri was more concerned about the position of the traditional ruling classes. On the second day the Parti Démocratique de l'Indépendance represented by Abd al-Hadi Boutaleb and on the fourth day the Istiqlal Party represented by Mehdi Ben Barka and Abd al-Rahim Bouabid declared that nothing could be done until Muhammad V had returned. This was the first time that the French Government had spoken directly to the nationalists. On the third day tribal notables gave varying opinions. It was then, despite the objections of French conservatives, decided that the first step should be the removal of Muhammad ben Arafa and his replacement by a Council of the Throne to prevent a vacuum. Muhammad V would be moved from Madagascar to a more dignified residence in France. Next a widely-based Moroccan coalition government should be formed to negotiate a new statute of relations with France. Finally that the approval of Muhammad V was an essential prerequisite to these moves and the liberal General Catroux should go to Antsirabe to obtain it. Grandval would also be replaced. The delay in recalling Muhammad V led to the denunciation of the agreement by Allal al-Fassi.

AKKARI, Nazim (1902-)
Lebanese Prime Minister. A Sunni Muslim he was born in Beirut and educated in the Ottoman school there. Entering the administration he was appointed *Kaymakam* of the Shuf and then Governor of Zahle under the French Mandate. When an independent government was established in 1943 he became Secretary-General of the Cabinet. In the late summer of 1952 the Presidency of Bishara al-Khouri was evidently collapsing with all the major politicians leagued against him and even under attack in the Chamber by his own Prime Minister Sami al-Sulh. On 9 September the President appointed Akkari as Prime Minister, Minister of Foreign Affairs and of the Interior with two other non-politicians as colleagues. Five days later Khouri was able to find in Saeb Salam a Sunni prepared to serve as Prime Minister and Akkari returned to his previous post as Secretary-General of the Cabinet which he held until his retirement in 1971.

AKKAWI, Mustafa Abd Allah (1956-92)
A pharmacist, he was one of about 70 Palestinians detained in January 1992 after a series of attacks on Jewish settlers on the West Bank. The police admitted that he had not personally been involved but alleged that he had been a member of the Popular Front for the Liberation of Palestine. He was not allowed to speak to a lawyer. His death in Hebron jail a fortnight later was described by American pathologists as "bordering on homicide . . . triggered by the treatment he received". The previous day a judge had ordered a medical check upon him after seeing him severely bruised. Although suffering from a heart condition, he had been beaten, kept standing with a hood over his head in a freezing corridor and deprived of sleep. Later he had been put in the "refrigerator", a cell two-feet wide. He had been handcuffed with his hands behind his back and his legs were shackled. He had eight broken ribs. The Israeli Police Minister, Ronni Milo, denied that his men had acted improperly.

al-ALAMI, Musa (1897-1984)
Palestinian leader. He was born in Jerusalem and his father, Mayor and MP for the city in the Ottoman Parliament, sent him to study Law at Cambridge. He joined the Legal Service of the Palestine Government and rose to become Government Advocate. Alami married a niece of the future Syrian Prime Minister

Saad Allah al-Jabiri. At the time of the Arab Rebellion he held aloof from all the political factions, although critical of the extremism of his distant relative the Mufti Haj Amin al-Hussaini and his brother-in-law Jamal al-Hussaini. Although he had maintained personal contacts with Zionist leaders, he was dismissed from his post as a result of Jewish pressure and went to live in Beirut for some years. He attended the London Palestine Conference in 1939 and then spent some time in Baghdad before being allowed to return home in 1941. As the Arab Higher Committee had been banned, there was no formal body to represent Arab opinion and in 1944 he was selected to speak for the Palestinians at the meeting which produced the Alexandria Protocol and led to the formation of the Arab League. He persuaded the League to agree to the opening of Bureaux to put the Arab case in the major capitals of the world and chose young intellectuals to staff them. He also started the Arab Development Society with the objective of helping Palestinian farmers in bad times so that they would not need to sell their land and in good times would be able to borrow to modernise. The intrigues of the Mufti led to the closure of his Bureaux and the events of 1948 made his agricultural plans impractical. His reactions were two-fold. Firstly, like Constantine Zurayq he published an analysis – *Ibrat Filastin* – The Lesson of Palestine – in which he discussed both the specific mistakes, the lack of unity, commitment and preparation and also more general problems such as the lack of political consciousness on the part of the people and the lack of contact between them and their governments. As a first move unity between Jordan, Syria and Iraq should be sought. Secondly, he was one of the first to recognise that the exile of the refugees would almost certainly be permanent and, using his own money he determined to do what he could for their children. In 1950 he obtained a 2,000 acre concession of barren land in the Jordan valley near Jericho and, finding water there, turned it into a prosperous farm with a home for orphans who were taught trades. Partly he saw this as a political gesture to show that Arabs, like the Jews, could make the desert bloom and the success of his farming inspired neighbouring land-owners and brought a new prosperity to the area. In 1955 during a period of political crisis the settlement, denounced as "a nest of traitors and imperialists" was attacked and almost destroyed by a mob. With the aid of loans, Alami started again only to lose it all again in 1967. After that he lived for some time in London before returning to Jerusalem and Amman where he took no further part in public life. Alami stood out from many other leaders as a thoroughly good, conciliatory, moderate and honourable man and a genuine philanthropist. Despite his sufferings at the hands of the British he bore no malice. A former Ambassador in Amman, Sir Geoffrey Furlonge published in 1969 a biography of Alami based on long conversations with his subject.

al-ALAWI, (Muhammad) Larbi (1880-1964)
Moroccan religious and political leader. His family were descended from the Prophet and related to the ruling dynasty. Studying at the Qarawiyin, he came under the influence of Shaykh Abu Shuaib al-Dukkali. He was

imprisoned for marrying, without permission, a girl from a non-Sharifian family but was released by Sultan Hafid, to whose children he later acted as tutor. In 1915 the French appointed him a Qadi in Fez and he also taught in the Qarawiyin. Although paid by the Government, standing out from the rest of the ulema, he supported resistance by the areas that had not been subjugated and was one of the leading critics of the Berber Dahir. Arguing that there was no distinction between religion and politics, he influenced his students to see a connection between a purified Islam and an independent Moroccan nation and was a leading figure in the Salafiyyah Movement, attracting young Muslim nationalists such as Allal al-Fassi who referred to him as his "illustrious teacher". Mulai Larbi was appointed Minister of Justice, using his access to the Sultan Muhammad V to put the views of the young nationalists. When in 1944 the Sultan was coerced into denouncing the call for independence of the newly-formed Istiqlal Party, Mulai Larbi refused to do so and was dismissed and exiled to the Tafilet. He was allowed to return two years later but resumed his teaching and in 1951 was exiled to the Middle Atlas. So many people visited him that he was brought back to Fez where he was kept under surveillance. In 1953 Mulai Larbi called for *jihad* to expel the colonialists and when in August Muhammad V was exiled by the French he refused to sign allegiance to the French-imposed Muhammad Ben Arafa, saying that they could cut off his arm. He was banished to Tiznit. Upon independence he was appointed a special adviser to the King with the rank of Minister but in December 1959 he resigned in order the join the new leftist party, the Union Nationale des Forces Populaires. He earned his living by selling the milk from his three cows and the eggs from his own hens. He criticised the Constitution of 1962 as giving too much power and a spurious Islamic legitimacy to Hassan II. Mulai Larbi had a rare reputation as a man of courage and wisdom, a true Muslim and a true patriot.

ALEXANDRETTA DISPUTE

The *Sanjaq* of Alexandretta was an area of less than 2,000 square miles with a population of about 220,000; 85,000 Turks were the largest homogeneous group while the more numerous Arabs were divided into Alawites, Sunnis and Christians and there were also Armenians, Kurds and Circassians. Lord Kitchener regarded it as the most important strategic point in the Middle East, dividing the Turkish and Arabic parts of the Ottoman Empire and had wished to land there in 1914–15 instead of at Gallipoli. The Sykes–Picot Agreement assigned it to France and this was confirmed in the Sèvres Treaty but the Franklin–Bouillon Treaty gave Turkish nationals rights identical to those of the local inhabitants. When the French created the State of Aleppo in September 1920 Alexandretta was made part of it but enjoyed full internal autonomy; this situation continued when Syria was reunited in 1924. The Franco-Syrian Treaty of 1936 which envisaged Syrian independence led to demands by Ankara that Alexandretta should not be included in an Arab-ruled state. In October the Turkish press announced that their army was ready to cross the frontier and violent clashes and inter-

communal boycotts were provoked by their agents. In December the matter was referred to the League of Nations which had laid down that no part of Mandated Syria might be surrendered. Long public sessions were held while French and Turkish delegates negotiated privately: Paris, threatened by the loudly-expressed territorial ambitions of Mussolini was anxious to appease Ankara but did not wish to alienate the Arabs. In January 1937 a compromise was reached by which Alexandretta would become a demilitarised autonomous *sanjaq* with its own constitution, a 40-member elected Assembly and Turkish an official language leaving France responsible for foreign affairs, customs and currency which would be linked to Syria. A committee of specialists was appointed to draft a constitution. This came into effect in November 1937. Tension continued between the communities and there were vehemently anti-French demonstrations in Damascus where the issue raised much emotion. In June 1938 martial law was imposed. As the aggressive intentions of Hitler increasingly worried the French, the Turks escalated their demands. In July 1938 there was an agreement for joint defence of the *sanjaq* and Turkish troops arrived as a garrison. The Turks insisted upon an electoral law that gave them 22 out of 40 seats and the House of Representatives declared the independence of the Republic of Hatay (the land of the Hittites) with a Turkish President, an entirely Turkish Government which would operate on Kamalist principles with Turkish currency and laws. In June 1939, with war approaching, the French abandoned any claim to the area and recognised Turkish sovereignty over it in return for a Declaration of Mutual Assistance. Most of the Armenians and large numbers of Arabs left their homes. In July 1939 Alexandretta, now renamed Iskanderun, was declared the 63rd Vilayet of the Turkish Republic. Syrian resentment at French rule was increased by the cynical sacrifice of the territory, a resentment felt by many other Arabs. It led also to Arab hostility to Turkey that continued for decades.

ALEXANDRIA PROTOCOL (1944)

In May 1941 Anthony Eden's Mansion House Speech stated that the British Government would welcome moves towards Arab unity and although he said later that the initiative would have to come from the Arabs themselves, considerable diplomatic efforts were put into urging friendly leaders to come together. In March 1943 Mustafa al-Nahhas committed the Egyptian Government to a series of bilateral meetings with other leaders to work out a programme for an "Arab Union". In September 1944 a Preparatory Committee under his presidency met in Alexandria. Syria, Lebanon, Iraq and Trans-Jordan were represented by their Prime Ministers, Saad Allah al-Jabiri, Riad al-Sulh, Tawfiq Abu al-Huda and Hamdi al-Pachachi. Saudi Arabia sent Yusuf Yassin and Yemen Hussain al-Kibsi. Other prominent figures attending were Nuri al-Said, Jamil Mardam and Ahmad al-Hilali, a lawyer who actually drafted the Protocol. It was taken for granted that the Arabs would present a common face towards the outside world but the main issues were the extent to which each state was prepared to surrender sovereignty and the form of procedures for settlements of disputes. Syria alone was prepared to surrender sovereignty for full-fledged unity while Yemen and Lebanon advocated loose co-operation and consultations. An Egyptian compromise whereby the sovereignty of each state would be retained in principle by making resolutions subject to unanimity with certain qualifications in defence, foreign policy and settlement of disputes where there would be majority decisions was accepted. Egypt and Saudi Arabia wished to make arbitration of disputes compulsory while Iraq insisted that it should be voluntary but suggested the creation of an Arab Court of Justice. Consensus was finally reached on a loose federation without binding procedures for settling disputes which could be brought before the Council on a voluntary basis. The establishment of a Court of Justice was postponed. The Protocol, signed on 7 October 1944, created the Arab League with a Council of equal states. It was envisaged that sovereignty would be gradually surrendered. Decisions would be binding on those that accepted them. No force would be permitted between members nor a foreign policy prejudicial to the League. Alliances with outside states and within the League were permissible. The Council would intervene to prevent war between members. There should be co-operation in economic, financial, cultural, social and health policies and over communications. A Special Resolution concerning Lebanon affirmed its right to independence. Another declaring Palestine part of and the responsibility of the Arab world, demanded the cessation of Jewish immigration although it deplored the wrongs done to them by Europeans. A Sub-Committee should meet in Cairo in February 1945 to draft the Arab League Pact.

ALEXANDRIA SUMMIT (1964)

The Cairo Summit of January 1964, the first general meeting of Arab Heads of State was widely considered a success and it was decided to hold a second Summit in Alexandria from 5 to 11 September 1964. Those attending were Kings Idris and Hussain, Crown Prince Faysal, Amir Abd Allah al-Salim al-Sabah, Presidents Nasser, Abboud, Ben Bella, Abd al-Salam Arif, Amin al-Hafiz, Helou and Sallal. Tunisia was represented by Bahi Ladgham and Morocco by a Prince. The Palestinian leader Ahmad Shuqayri was also invited. The Summit identified the national objective as the liberation of Palestine and stated that it had "adopted adequate resolutions for the implementation of the Arab plans" – especially with regard to the Jordan Waters Dispute. It welcomed the establishment of the Palestine Liberation Organisation, to which Hussain had withdrawn his objections, and its plans for a Liberation Army although Hussain would not accept it in Jordan. The Summit proclaimed its will to resist "hostile forces, foremost amongst which is Britain" and its determination "to enter into a struggle against British imperialism" in Oman and South Yemen and to help the "princelings" of the Gulf states. It studied means of consolidating unified action in the military, political and economic spheres. There was agreement that each state should keep part of its forces permanently ready for an emergency. They emphasised that an attack on any Arab state would be resisted by all as a result of a Joint Defence Pact. It decided to set up an

Arab Council for Atomic Research and an Arab Court of Justice. There would also be a Follow-up Committee to meet monthly and an Executive Committee of Prime Ministers to convene every four months, while the Summit would meet annually in September. Anxious about Israeli activities in Africa it declared "Arab-African co-operation forms a base of Arab policy by reason of history, geographical position, interests and common objectives" and expressed support for liberation movements and ended with a denunciation of imperialism. During the Summit Faysal and Nasser discussed the Yemen War but were unable to reach any agreement.

ALGIERS, Battle of (1957)

During the summer of 1956 the Algerian War of Independence reached a particularly vicious stage in the capital itself. Guerrillas of the Front de Libération Nationale shot down civilians at random, 49 in three days, while women such as Jamila Bouhired, organised by Yasif Saadi, placed bombs in public places. The colons hit back with attacks on innocent Muslims. On 28 December 1956 a prominent Mayor was murdered. On 7 January 1957 the Governor-General Robert Lacoste decided that the 1,500 police could not control the situation and called in the 4,500 parachutists of General Jacques Massu whom he made responsible for the maintenance of order. Under a system dubbed *quadrillage*, Algiers was divided into squares which were cordoned off with checkpoints for house-to-house searches which with the help of informers reputed to number 1,500 led to mass arrests without warrants and brutal interrogations. Three weeks later Massu smashed a general strike, timed to coincide with the discussion of Algeria at the UN, after eight days by forcing shops to open and rounding up truants from schools. Women continued to place bombs undeterred by ruthless searches until bomb factories were found in intensified searches of the Qasbah. On 25 February the FLN commander Larbi Ben M'hidi was captured and later met his death in custody. Other leaders such as Ben Yusuf Ben Khedda and Ramdan Abane fled abroad. The French made increasing use of torture in interrogations which led to protests not only in France but amongst those ordered to apply it. During March no bombs were thrown but spasmodic incidents, including a bomb at the Casino in June which killed 9 young dancers and blew the legs off many others, continued until the capture of Saadi in September. Many nationalist leaders regarded the Battle of Algiers with the loss of many of their best men, as a severe defeat.

ALGIERS, Bombardment of (1816)

After the overthrow of Napoleon the European Powers determined to repress the Barbary pirates who had exploited the wars of the previous 20 years. Acting as their representative, a Royal Navy squadron under Lord Exmouth, who had won fame as Sir Edward Pellew, forced Yusuf Karamanli of Tripoli and Mahmud Bey of Tunis to renounce the taking of Christian slaves. The Dey of Algiers, Umar b. Muhammad refused, insulted the Admiral, mishandled some of his officers and imprisoned the British Consul General. Having gone home for instructions Exmouth returned to Algiers

ABANE, Ramdane (1920–57)

Algerian Revolutionary Leader. He came from a poor Kabyle family but educated himself to get his baccalaureat and gain a post as a municipal clerk in a *commune mixte*. He was a supporter of Messali Haj and was involved in the Setif Uprising. In 1950 he was sentenced to five years imprisonment during which time he studied the writings of revolutionary leaders, emerging with the belief that Algeria could only be freed by violence. He also undertook the longest hunger strike in a French jail, giving himself ulcers which permanently soured his temper. In the spring of 1955 he assumed charge of the nationalist network in Algiers and succeeded in winning the allegiance of many intellectuals and of members of competing nationalist groups although quite prepared to kill those who dissented. He provided an ideology for the Front de Libération Nationale which while neither fundamentalist Muslim nor Marxist-Leninist, could attract adherents of both. He out-manoeuvred the communist leadership whose members and military arsenal were absorbed by the FLN. Abane was the first to advocate urban terrorism as he saw that the killing of innocent civilians attracted more attention and inspired more fear than attacks on the military. He was the dominant figure at the Soummam Valley Conference which asserted the primacy of those fighting in the interior over exiled leaders such as Ben Bella and of the political over the military, setting up the supreme Comité de Coordination et d'Exécution of which he was a leading member to provide collective rather than one-man leadership. He took part in the Algiers Battle of early 1957 but when he realised that it would be lost, he escaped to join the exiles in Cairo where he found himself in a minority as the Soummam decisions were reversed by a new CCE upon which the military predominated. His quarrels with Colonels Abd al-Hafid Boussouf and Belkasim Krim were especially savage. In December 1957 they lured Abane to Morocco on the pretext of a meeting with King Muhammad V and strangled him, although it was announced that he had fallen in battle against the French. After independence one of the main streets of Algiers was renamed in his honour. Abane was described as the Robespierre of the Revolution, the best brain in the FLN, a skilled organiser and propagandist, decisive, fanatical, violent, brutal, radical, uninterested in the trappings of power. In person he was short with a round cheerful face.

ABBAS, Farhat (1899–1986)

Algerian nationalist leader. He came from a family of notables of Kabyle origin and was born near Constantine where he attended secondary school before doing three years conscription in the French army from which he was demobilised as a sergeant. He then studied pharmacy at Algiers University where he was President of the Association of Muslim Students. Abbas then opened a pharmacy at Setif, married a French-woman and entered politics as a member of the Municipal Council and the Délégations Financières. He joined the Fédération des Elus Indigènes agreeing with Dr Ben Jalloul in the demand for the absorption of the local élite into French society and the end of the Indigénat Code. In 1932 he founded a newspaper *L'Entente* in which he published a famous statement that there had never been and could never be a separate Algerian state – "one cannot build on wind". He called for political and cultural equality within one France from Dunkirk to Tammanrasset, stressing that the French Revolution had been the champion of the rights of man and was the heritage of all mankind. He was active in the Algiers Muslim Congress of 1936 but his secular views led to a split with the Association des Oulemas Algériens. Having come to believe in a separate Algerian personality he quarrelled also with Ben Jalloul who continued to stand for complete integration with France while Abbas called instead for autonomy and equality in a political federation. With the slogan "Algeria is a French country and its inhabitants must evolve within the cadre of the French nation" he founded the Union Populaire Algérienne but although he toured widely trying to attract support, he was never very successful being too honest to make demagogic promises and being opposed by all the other active political forces, the ulema, Ben Jalloul, the communists and the Parti du Peuple Algérien of Messali Haj. At the start of the war he enlisted in the French army sanitary service. After demobilisation he addressed an appeal to the Vichy Government setting out a programme of agrarian reform and political restructuring based on communes; there was a curt rejection. In February 1943 he was the principal creator of the Manifesto of the Algerian People which demanded a Constitution guaranteeing independence for all the inhabitants of Algeria which he presented to the French authorities and the Anglo-American leaders. This, after consultation with Messali, was followed by an *Additif* which for the first time called for full political autonomy for Algeria. This was vetoed by General de Gaulle and Abbas was briefly sent into forced residence in the

Sahara for "provocation to disobedience in wartime". He then founded the Amis du Manifeste et de la Liberté which opposed "annexation and assimilation" and was suppressed after the Setif Uprising. Abbas himself was imprisoned until March 1946. Upon his release he founded the Union Démocratique du Manifeste Algérien and was elected to the French Parliament for Setif, although ballot-rigging soon ensured that he lost his seat. He hoped for progress through the sympathy of French liberals and had no wish to be a revolutionary so various attempts to work with the Mouvement pour le Triomphe de la Liberté et de la Démocratie never lasted long as its leader Messali believed that only force would work. After the War of Algerian Independence began in November 1954 Abbas was at first convinced that it would fail and worked for reconciliation although the guerrillas deliberately murdered his nephew in the Philippeville Massacre. By early 1956 he saw the hardening of attitudes on both sides and despaired of achieving his aims by peaceful means; he therefore joined the Front de Libération Nationale proclaiming that "insurrection is the most sacred of duties". He settled in Switzerland in charge of FLN propaganda but also travelled widely in the Arab world although he never managed to speak literary Arabic. At the Soummam Valley Conference of August 1956 he was elected to the Conseil National de la Révolution Algérienne and was later co-opted on to its "War Cabinet", the Conseil de Coordination et d'Exécution. Always enthusiastic for Maghrib unity, he represented the FLN at the Tangier Conference of April 1958. In September 1958 when the FLN formed the Gouvernement Provisoire de la République Algérienne he was elected its President, perhaps to provide a moderate and internationally known front. He visited China where he was seated on Mao's right hand on Revolution Day and Moscow where he obtained some form of recognition from Khruschev. In August 1961 to facilitate negotiations with de Gaulle, with whom it was said that the 1943 Manifesto and the attempt to involve the "Anglo-Saxons" still rankled, the GPRA replaced Abbas with Ben Khedda. In the struggle for power after the conclusion of the Evian Agreement Abbas at first supported the GPRA but then adhered to the side of Ben Bella and Boumédienne. He was appointed President of the Chamber but in August 1963 he resigned in protest at the drafting of the Constitution by the Party instead of by the Assembly and was expelled from the FLN. He accused Ben Bella of trying to turn "democratic and humanistic socialism" into "Marxist-Leninist socialism" and his relations with the President became so bad that in the summer of 1964 he was sent into forced residence in the Sahara. He was released before Boumédienne took power and refused to serve him as a figurehead, preferring to live in retirement. He refused to comment on public events until in March 1976 in conjunction with Ben Khedda he broke his silence and issued a Manifesto accusing Boumédienne of totalitarianism and personality cult, doctrinaire socialism and sabotaging North African unity by his needless quarrel with Morocco. He was put under house arrest and government history books were rewritten to excise his part in the national struggle. He was rehabilitated by Chadli and decorated as a hero of the war of which

he published an account. In 1984 he published his last book, *L'Indépendance Confisquee* attacking the regimes of Ben Bella and Boumédienne, denouncing one-party rule, calling for democracy, Maghreb unity and a return to Islam. Abbas was never a charismatic leader, always the respectable bourgeois, but he was honest, brave, generous and without hatred, preferring honourable compromise to violence.

ABBAS HALIM (1897–1960)
Egyptian Prince and Trade Union leader. A great-grandson of Muhammad Ali, he was brought up in Germany at the Court of the Kaiser and served with the Turkish army in the First World War. Returning to Egypt he organised golf and boxing clubs, presided over the Royal Automobile Club and went big game shooting. In 1930 he published a manifesto stating that the dismissal of Nahhas Pasha who had recently won 90% of the popular vote in an unusually free election might lead to civil war. King Fuad was affronted and struck the Prince's name from the list of the Royal Family. Abbas Halim then worked to encourage the individual Trade Unions, persecuted by the police, to get new strength by collaboration and brought them together into a Federation with the support of the Wafd. In 1934 he was imprisoned for three weeks after an affray. He then quarrelled with the Wafd and formed another Trade Union Federation. In 1937 he went to England to study how to create a Labour Party but did not pursue the idea. British officials described him as very popular but obstinate and stupid.

ABBAS I HILMI (1813–54)
Ruler of Egypt 1849–54. He was the son of Tussin, second son of Muhammad Ali but as the oldest member of the family he became heir on the death of his uncle Ibrahim. He had fought in the Syrian campaign and spent some time in Arabia. From the beginning he set out to reverse the policies of his grandfather, persecuting his old ministers, expelling his foreign advisers and closing down factories as innovations – he even wished to destroy the Nile Barrage. He ended state monopolies such as that on the sale of corn. He sold Muhammad Ali's fleet and shut the translation school which he regarded as promoting foreign influences. He felt that if Egypt had to have foreign friends, the Turks as fellow-Muslims were preferable to Europeans and he tried to ingratiate himself with the Sultan by sending considerable sums of money and later 15,000 troops to take part in the Crimean war. The Ottomans insisted that the Tanzimat reforms, including the tariff of 1838 and the provision that only the Sultan could approve death sentences should apply to Egypt but Abbas secured the dropping of these demands through British mediation, rewarding the British with a concession to build a railway from Alexandria to Cairo which Muhammad Ali had refused. Thus he reversed his grandfather's foreign policy by a preference for England and Turkey rather than for France; when the Russians tried to persuade Britain not to intervene in the Crimean war by suggesting it should instead annex Egypt, a French diplomat remarked that this was unnecessary as British influence there was anyway all-powerful. The French tried intrigues to replace Abbas. Another break with

work and research over the years and the interpretation of the material are Bidwell's also.

Bidwell himself clearly had an individualistic and rather complicated presentation in mind for his *Dictionary*. He appears to have had in mind the idea of grouping entries with a comprehensive cross-referencing system rather than presenting them all together in alphabetical order. He may well have determined on indices also. The decision has had to be taken to simplify this process which could not be fully understood from what notes he left behind. The reader will now find all entries together in a single alphabetical order and in a book already bursting at the seams it has also been decided to exclude indices.

By far the most difficult editorial problem has been the spelling of certain words and phrases – mostly Arabic – contained in the *Dictionary*. They are for the most part names of people and places, but there are the names of parties, groups and institutions also. Bearing in mind that Bidwell dealt with sources for the most part in European languages and that, in any case, he writes for the general as much as for the academic reader, spellings of proper names have in most cases been left as he produced them. The only changes are minor and are made simply to bring about consistency throughout the work. Spellings of Arabic technical terms or Arabic phrases have been adjusted to represent the original as closely as possible without any attempt at some formal system of transliteration.

For fourteen years, then, Bidwell laboured on the *Dictionary*, almost to the exclusion of all other academic activity. He ransacked the spate of scholarly – and not so scholarly – books and articles which poured forth over the years; he devoured any organ of the press which proved of relevance, whether published in Europe, North America or in the Middle East; he met and sometimes formally interviewed some of the players on the Middle Eastern scene. All this material he digested and interpreted as only he could to present this *Dictionary* to the interested public. The work will for many years to come stand as a worthy monument to Bidwell's scholarly achievement in modern Middle Eastern history. It will be also a constant reminder of his profound love for, and understanding of, the Middle East and above all of his great affection for its people with whom he spent so many happy times.

G. REX SMITH
April 1996

PREFACE

The publication of the late Robin Bidwell's *Dictionary of Modern Arab History* comes as good news. The publishers are to be commended for having, with the aid and support of Professor Rex Smith, persevered in bringing this book into the public domain in spite of the tragic death of its compiler only a short time after the manuscript had been submitted.

Knowing Bidwell's meticulous care over such details as dates, locations and various contacts of political and diplomatic significance, for which he had an exceptionally sharp eye, clearly his *Dictionary* will provide a work of reference as useful as it is needed by all those concerned the better to understand modern Arab history. Henceforth they, and, in the field of diplomacy, commerce, strategic studies, and cultural exchanges, they are many, will have at hand the work of a man who, as Professor Smith reminds us in his Introduction, had visited and known every Arab land.

The fact that, as Rex Smith also mentions, the ground work of the *Dictionary* was entirely Bidwell's, so that the work is that of, not a committee, but one individual, endows it with a special kind of liveliness. As a human document, its achievement owed to one man's dedication, it is idiosyncratic and, since Robin Bidwell was always firm in his opinions and extremely honest in expressing them, this means that there will probably be entries by which some of those who refer to the book will be riled.

Never mind, for not only is this book idiosyncratic, it also happens to be the accomplishment of a man almost unique – I can only think of one or two others – in his knowledge of Arabian personalities. Such knowledge as this is of peculiar importance for students of the regions with which the *Dictionary* is concerned. For in areas where, in a modern and secular sense, politics have not become by any means entirely institutionalised, the role, character and individual attitudes of prominent personalities remain very important.

Hence, one of the main reasons why this work is so welcome rests on Bidwell's unusual degree of familiarity with leading political figures in the modern history of a world which was rudely awakened from the dream of Islamic invulnerability when Napoleon invaded Egypt in 1798, the opening date of Dr. Bidwell's encyclopaedic compilation.

Cambridge, March 1998   Peter Avery

INTRODUCTION

When Robin Bidwell died suddenly at his desk in Coney Weston in Suffolk in June 1994, he had already spent fourteen years at work on his *Dictionary*.

Bidwell was educated at Downside and Pembroke College, Cambridge, where he gained a first in History. His first taste of the Middle East came when he was posted to the Suez Canal Zone in Egypt as a sergeant in the Intelligence Corps. In 1955 he became a political officer in the Western Aden Protectorate, serving in such places as Subaihi country, Ahwar and Lodar. His real Middle Eastern travels began after 1959 when he left Aden for a post as Oxford University Press travelling editor and it was his proud boast when he returned to Cambridge in 1965 that he had visited every single Middle Eastern country without exception. Back in Cambridge, he worked for his Ph.D. degree under the supervision of the late Professor Bob Serjeant. He took the degree in 1968, his thesis being on the subject of the French administration in Morocco. From 1968 until his retirement in 1990, Bidwell held the dual office of Secretary and Librarian of the Middle East Centre in Cambridge. His achievements there were many: he created the Centre library; he taught an undergraduate course in modern Arab history; he successfully supervised a steady stream of Ph.D. students; he instituted a thriving seminar programme; he was a founding editor with Serjeant of *Arabian Studies* in 1974 and of *New Arabian Studies* in 1993.

Wholly committed and enthusiastic as he was for the task in hand, Bidwell never made any secret of the problems of organisation and presentation which the *Dictionary* constantly threw in his path. Other major decisions too had to be taken: who to put in – and thus who to leave out? When should the line be drawn chronologically, bearing in mind that many subjects are still alive and still in the process of making history? How much space should be spent on so-and-so or such-and-such and is the balance right? Whether Bidwell got the answers to these questions right or not is left to the decision of the reader. The organisational and presentational problems he bequeathed to the editorial team which has dealt with the work since his death. It is indeed difficult to state precisely how ready the text was for publication. We can safely say that all the entries were there, although some were incomplete in the sense that they existed wholly or partially in note form. All these latter have now been completed relying solely on Bidwell's notes. It is clear too that some entries are more polished than others and it is highly probable that he was intending to come back to the less well polished before submission to the publishers. No attempt has been made to 'improve' them since his death. With the exception of the completed notes, the texts of the entries are entirely those which Bidwell himself produced, just as all the hard

To Leila, with love

DICTIONARY OF MODERN ARAB HISTORY

AN A TO Z OF OVER 2,000 ENTRIES FROM 1798 TO THE PRESENT DAY

ROBIN BIDWELL

WITH AN INTRODUCTION BY G. REX SMITH

KEGAN PAUL INTERNATIONAL

LONDON AND NEW YORK

First published in 1998 by
Kegan Paul International
UK: P.O. Box 256, London WC1B 3SW, England
Tel: (0171) 580 5511   Fax: (0171) 436 0899
E-mail: books@keganpau.demon.co.uk
Internet: http://www.demon.co.uk/keganpaul/
USA: 562 West 113th Street, New York, NY 10025, USA
Tel: (212) 666 1000   Fax: (212) 316 3100

Distributed by

John Wiley & Sons Ltd
Southern Cross Trading Estate
1 Oldlands Way, Bognor Regis
West Sussex, PO22 9SA, England
Tel: (01243) 779 777   Fax: (01243) 820 250

Columbia University Press
562 West 113th Street
New York, NY 10025, USA
tel: (212) 666 1000   Fax: (212) 316 3100

Set in Plantin by Intype London Ltd
Printed in Great Britain by
Bookcraft (Bath) Ltd

ISBN 0–7103–0505–2

British Library Cataloguing in Publication Data
Bidewell, R. L. (Robin Leonard), 1927–1994
Dictionary of modern Arab history: an A to Z of over 2000
entries from 1798 to the present day
1. Arab countries – History – 1798–   2. Middle East – History
– 1517–
I. Title
956

ISBN 0710305052

Library of Congress Cataloging-in-Publication Data
Bidewell, Robin Leonard.
Dictionary of modern Arab history: an A to Z of over 2000 entries
from 1798 to the present day / Robin Bidewell; with an introduction
by G. Rex Smith.
ISBN 0–7103–0505–2 (alk. paper)
1. Arab countries—History—1798—Dictionaries.   I. Title.
DS38.9.353   1996
909'.0974927—DC20   96–24299
CIP

and, joined at its own request by a Dutch flotilla, demanded satisfaction. When it was denied the ships bombarded Algiers for six hours, firing 118 tons of powder and 500 tons of shot, destroying half the city and sinking all the corsair ships. Algerian batteries responded with heavy fire killing 118 British and 13 Dutch sailors and wounding 690 and 52. The Dey surrendered, released 1,642 slaves, mostly Italian although there were 18 English, promised that future captives would be treated as prisoners of war and not as slaves, returned some tribute extorted from Italian states and apologised publicly to the British Consul General. In his dispatch Exmouth recorded his thanks for being "a humble instrument, in the hands of Divine Providence, for bringing to reason a ferocious Government and destroying for ever the insufferable and horrid system of Christian slavery".

ALGIERS, Charter of (1964)

Before Algeria achieved its independence programmes for its future were laid down in the Soummam Valley Conference of August 1956 and in the Tripoli Programme of June 1962. These were elaborated in the First Congress of the Front de Libération Nationale which assembled in Algiers in April 1964. A Preparatory Commission, dominated by Trotskyist followers of Ben Bella was formed in November to draft an ideological platform. It declared Algeria an "Arabo-Islamic country" whose struggle for the consolidation of independence was indissolubly linked with socialism which was both Islamic and Marxist. Some parts had been developed more than others and this unevenness had to be remedied. Self-management, nationalisation and agricultural reform were necessary. The economy and the infrastructure was too dependent upon the former colonial power. The Government had to support the masses against the privileged classes by planning and controlling welfare. There was to be a new conception of culture with stress on Algerian values which required emphasis on the use of Arabic in order to oppose cosmopolitanism. Art had to be socially responsible. The FLN needed to renew itself perpetually to ensure that it remained an avant-garde, neither a mass nor an elitist party, eschewing bureaucratic formalism. Labour Unions should not confine themselves to demanding benefits for their own workers but should press for socialism. A Peasant Federation would be created. There should be one unified Youth Organisation which would conform with the Party line. Women should be liberated and involved in national reconstruction. The Party should not be merged into the State and should have separate structures. The people should exercise sovereignty through a National Assembly for which candidates were to be selected by the Party. The Army should be "a school for the citizen and the militant", the defender of revolutionary gains. The Charter was presented as looking to the future rather than the past and concentrating upon policies rather than on personalities. It was, however, open to criticism in seeing Algerian politics as dominated by the class struggle instead of by more personal quarrels.

ALGIERS DECLARATION (1978)

The Tripoli Declaration of December 1977 marked the establishment of the Steadfastness Front, whose leaders, Presidents Boumédienne and Hafiz al-Assad, Colonel Qadafi, Abd al-Fattah Ismail and Yassir Arafat reassembled in Algiers in February 1978. Other Palestinians present included George Habash, Nayif Hawatmah and Ahmad Jibril while Zuhair Muhsin of Amal also attended. Early statements denounced Anwar Sadat for his presumption in speaking for the Palestinians and for attempting "to place the Arab homeland under imperialist influence" by excluding the Soviet Union from the peace process. Other countries such as Jordan should be careful not to be drawn in. Libya promised financial aid to the Syrian and Palestinian forces. The 11-point Declaration denounced Sadat, reaffirmed that only the Palestine Liberation Organisation could speak for the Palestinians and reasserted the need for co-operation with Russia and the non-aligned states. It stressed the need for the Syrians and Palestinians to work together and expressed solidarity with the "nationalist and progressive Egyptians" opposed to Sadat and isolation from the Arab nation. To gratify Algeria and South Yemen "extreme anxiety" was expressed about the French military intervention in the Western Sahara and the foreign military presence in Oman where nationalist strugglers should be supported. African nationalist and liberation movements should be helped and so should the left-wing Ethiopian regime then under attack by the Western-supported Somalis. The Algerian Foreign Minister Abd al-Aziz Bouteflika regretted that Iraq, which shared all these principles, would not join the Front because of its hostility to Syria.

ALGIERS PACT (1975)

During OPEC talks in Algiers at the beginning of March 1975 President Houari Boumédienne arranged two long meetings between the Shah and Saddam Hussain who dramatically embraced in the Conference Hall. Iraq surrendered its claim to exclusive control of the Shatt al-Arab and agreed that the border should be the middle of the deepest shipping channel (*thalweg*) and drew a mutually acceptable boundary through a disputed oilfield. In return the Shah promised "strict and effective control" of the northern frontiers in order to "end all subversive infiltration". This in practice meant the end of help for the Kurdish Revolt II which immediately collapsed. Another clause allowed 10,000 Iranian pilgrims access to the shrine of Ali Abi Talib at Najaf: as the exiled Ayatollah Khomeini was then living there this facilitated his spreading of his message in Iran. The Pact formed the basis of a Treaty which was signed by the Foreign Ministers in Baghdad in June. When in 1980 Iran seemed hopelessly weakened by the Ayatollah's Revolution, Saddam seized the opportunity to denounce the Algiers Pact and launch the Iran–Iraq War. In October 1982 with defeat apparently at hand, Saddam offered to renew the Pact in return for peace. The Iranians refused but in August 1990, after his invasion of Kuwait, he repeated the offer which this time was accepted.

ALGIERS SUMMIT (1973)

The October War of 1973 was followed by a period of intense inter-Arab diplomacy resulting in an announcement that a Summit, the sixth, preceded by a Foreign Ministers meeting, would be held in Algiers from 26 to 28 November. Absentees were Presidents Bakr and Qadafi and King Hussain, represented by Bahjat al-Talhuni, was believed to have stayed away because of the attendance of Yassir Arafat leading a delegation of the Palestine Liberation Organisation. The President of Mauritania and President Mobutu of Zaire, invited to show Arab gratitude for African support, were also present. In his opening speech President Boumédienne declared that the Arabs had emerged victorious from the war, showing unity and recovering their self-respect. He thanked the African and socialist states for their support and called for a total boycott of Portugal, Rhodesia and South Africa. The Summit recognised the PLO as the sole representative of the Palestinian people despite Jordanian protests. The Summit declared that the present cease-fire was not a peace which could only come after Israeli withdrawal from occupied territories, beginning with Jerusalem, and the restoration of the rights of the Palestinians. It stressed the importance of the oil weapon and declared that restrictions might be lifted upon any state supporting the Arab cause. It decided to give full military support to the Egyptian and Syrian fronts. Support would also be given to African liberation movements, an Arab bank for industrial and agricultural development in Africa with an initial capital of $12.5 million would be created and diplomatic, cultural and economic relations should be broken off with Portugal, Rhodesia and South Africa. Envoys should be sent to express appreciation to those states which had supported the Arabs. Future Summits should take place annually in April. Finally it was agreed that President Sadat should have a free hand at the forthcoming Geneva Peace Conference. The suggestion that a Palestinian Government in Exile be created was dropped.

ALGIERS SUMMIT (1988)

The Amman Summit of 1987 had been mainly concerned with the Iran–Iraq War and had paid little attention to the problem of the Palestinians. The *Intifadah* brought it again into the forefront and it was the main topic of the Summit which assembled in Algiers in June 1988. The only absent Heads of State were those of Iraq, Oman and Somalia while Egypt was still excluded. The Summit promised "all possible means of support" for the *Intifadah* and reasserted that the question of Palestinian rights was, for the Arabs, the most important of all and that the Palestine Liberation Organisation was their sole legitimate spokesman. This was fully endorsed by King Hussain. The participants agreed to provide financial support, an additional £23million a month, for the PLO which represented a rebuff for the USA which had been trying to persuade its friends to refrain from doing so. Washington was also criticised for having no policy except for unlimited support for Israel. The Summit was a triumph for the diplomacy of Chadli and for Yassir Arafat who re-emerged as a key figure. It was also remarkable for the eccentric behaviour of Colonel Qadafi who wore extraordinary robes and white gloves to avoid touching "impure hands".

ALI, Bey (?–1773)

Ruler of Egypt. He was born in the Caucasus, sold as a slave and brought to Egypt where he entered the household of the leading Mamluk Ibrahim Bey. He distinguished himself as a military leader, defending the Pilgrimage caravan from marauding bedouins and himself became a Bey in 1747. After the death of Ibrahim in 1754 there was a period of quarrels within the leadership which ended in 1760 with Ali supreme, officially recognised as Shaykh al-Bilad. He eliminated opposition by murder and confiscation and packed the ruling *diwan* with his own men including Ahmad Jazzar and Abu al-Dhahab. Ali was determined to rule more absolutely than any of his predecessors and also to establish complete independence from the Ottoman Sultan, chasing out Pashas sent by Constantinople. He struck coins in his own name, a sign of sovereignty as was the mention of his name in the *khutbah*, although he pretended to disapprove of this. So great was his success that Voltaire thought that he was King of Egypt. Ali administered justice and collected taxes strictly but fairly, encouraged trade and agriculture, repressed the bedouins who made life insecure even as close to Cairo as the Pyramids and hoped to win popular support for his regime. Ali took a great interest in trade with India, contemplating the cutting of a Canal across the Suez Isthmus and a great entrepôt at Jiddah. In 1767, caught trying to poison a colleague, he was briefly overturned and fled to Syria where he made friends with Zahir al-Umar who was also trying to establish his own independent principality and who gave him help to return. Abu Dhahab, his closest associate, had meanwhile murdered two other potential rivals. In 1770 at the request of the Sultan he intervened in the Hijaz but did not bring it under Constantinople but under Cairo for the first time since Saladin. In the same year he invaded Syria in support of Zahir al-Umar and in alliance with the Russians to whom they promised ports in the Levant. The allies occupied Damascus but were robbed of success by the treachery of Abu Dhahab. Ali's position was increasingly weakened by the intrigues of the other Beys and early in 1772 Ali exiled Abu Dhahab. Abu Dhahab returned in March with a force that caused Ali to flee in his turn, taking refuge once more with Zahir, whom he helped to capture Jaffa. The following year Ali was lured back to Egypt by letters written under duress by his astrologer, and his small force was defeated by Murad Bey. Soon afterwards Ali died, either of wounds or of poison. His career foreshadowed in many ways that of Muhammad Ali Pasha who learned from his predecessor's mistakes. Ali never tried to make a fresh start by massacring his fellow Mamluks, he did not make use of native Egyptians or call in foreigners for technical advice. He made no effort to build a modern army, antagonising what there already was by deliberately underpaying it, hoping that the troops would desert so that he could replace them with Algerian mercenaries. He was too extravagant, both in his private life and weakening the country by expensive foreign adventures. He also had to rely upon treacherous fellow-Mamluks who betrayed him when it was in their own interests to do so unlike Muhammad Ali who was able to put complete trust in sons like Ibrahim Pasha and Ismail Kamil. Nevertheless Ali Bey was regretted by the people of Egypt who knew him as "the *Jinni*" or "*Bulut Kapan* – The Cloud Catcher".

ALIER, Abel (1933–)
Sudanese politician. An Anglican Dinka from Borr, he was one of the first Southerners to earn a Law Degree from Khartoum University before doing advanced legal studies in London. After some years as a barrister he was appointed a District Judge. He was active in the Southern Front from its foundation in 1964 and was one of its representatives at the Round Table Conference of 1965. He was Member of Parliament for Borr South in 1968/9. He supported the new regime of Nimeiri after extracting a guarantee that there would be regional autonomy, joining the Cabinet as Minister of Housing, later being transferred to Supply and to Public Works. He was sent to Europe in the spring of 1971 to justify Nimeiri's Southern policy, addressing the World Council of Churches which sent a delegation to make contact with the guerrillas to encourage a settlement. After the Minister of Southern Affairs, Joseph Garang was hanged following the communist plot of July 1971, Alier's appointment to succeed him and later as a Vice-President reassured the South. He led the government team which negotiated the Addis Ababa Agreement which brought peace after eight years of Anya Nya guerrilla warfare. He was then appointed President of the High Executive Council established for the Southern Region. He presided over the resettlement of the Anya Nya guerrillas, improved the infrastructure and founded a University at Juba. He worked extremely hard to promote economic development although there were protests that an unfair proportion of the benefits, particularly the Jonglei Scheme, went to Dinka areas and he accepted Nimeiri's decision that the refinery for Southern oil should be at Kosti in the North. In February 1978 when it became clear that his supporters, regarded as too deferential to the North, would be defeated in a general election he withdrew and was replaced by Joseph Lagu as Regional President. The following election of March 1980 restored him to office. In February 1981 Nimeiri proposed to divide up the Southern Region into three autonomous units: Alier opposed the plan and in October he was dismissed and the Regional Assembly dissolved; he retained the office of Vice-President until July 1982 when he was replaced by Lagu. He protested against the September Laws as contravening the Addis Agreement but joined Nimeiri's last government as Minister of Construction. After the fall of Nimeiri Alier became a member of the Permanent Court of International Arbitration at The Hague. Moderate, pragmatic and very highly respected, Alier was able to combine Sudanese patriotism with loyalty to his Southern origins. He wrote a useful book *Southern Sudan* subtitled *Too many Agreements Dishonoured*.

ALI, Kamal Hassan (1921–93)
Egyptian Military Commander and Prime Minister. He came from a middle-class Cairo family and graduated from the Military Academy in 1942, fighting in the Western Desert and the Palestine War of 1948. He specialised in armoured warfare and attended courses in Britain and in the Soviet Union. As Chief of Operations in the Yemen War his lack of veracity surprised a foreign correspondent. He distinguished himself and was wounded during the June War. Ali was Director of Armour before being appointed Assistant Minister of War and Chief of Intelligence in 1975. In 1978, as a Lieutenant-General, he was made Minister of Defence and Commander-in-Chief. He was head of the military section of the Egyptian negotiators at Camp David and later negotiated in Washington with Moshe Dayan. He also negotiated a large package of American aid for Egypt. From 1980 until 1984 Ali was Minister of Foreign Affairs and Deputy Prime Minister. He showed himself extremely flexible in pursuit of Egyptian interests while paying little attention to the Palestinian side of the settlement: he was the first senior Egyptian to go to Jerusalem after the assassination of Sadat but he also began the process of ending Egypt's isolation in the Arab world and also ended the breach with the Palestine Liberation Organisation. In July 1984 Ali was appointed Prime Minister, showing social concern by creating new Ministries of Housing and National Education. Despite his military background he was a mild-mannered man, disinclined to give strong leadership and he believed in giving Ministers a free hand and so bore responsibility for their errors. He was often fiercely attacked with opposition newspapers seeking material to discredit him and his family but he was well regarded in business circles. Ali was crippled by arthritis and his Cabinet gave an impression of drift. There were difficult relations with Israel which tried to renege on its obligation to return all of Sinai by retaining Taba. It was also a period of economic difficulty with IMF demanding socially divisive measures in return for credit. President Mubarak felt that he needed a technocrat as Prime Minister and replaced Ali with the Harvard-trained economist Ali Lutfi in August 1985. Ali became Chairman of the Egyptian Gulf Bank. He was a plump, cheerful man, widely respected. Ali wrote a book, *The Negotiating Warriors* about his dealings with the Israelis.

ALI, Salim Rubai (c. 1938–78)
President of South Yemen. He came from a tribal family in Abyan and attended the local secondary school. After brief service in the Tribal Guards he became a village schoolmaster. About 1960 Ali joined the Arab Nationalist Movement, organising a cell in Hadhramawt. In 1963 he became a member of the Command Council of the National Liberation Front and was a leading guerrilla commander, winning a considerable reputation under the name of "Salimin". In 1966 he was one of the "second-level" leadership which rejected the Egyptian sponsored merger of the NLF with the Front for the Liberation of Occupied South Yemen. He was not a member of the first government after independence and worked with Abd al-Fattah Ismail to organise leftist opposition to it within the Party. In June 1969 they joined forces with Muhammad Ali Haytham to depose President Qahtan al-Shaabi who was replaced by a five-man Presidential Council with Ali as Chairman and the other two as members. The first act

of the new government was to recognise East Germany and in internal affairs to institute a reign of terror in which real or imaginary plots provided justification for mass arrests, purges and torture, suppression of freedom of speech and intense politicisation of the army and police. Ali was particularly active in spreading the revolution to the countryside, especially after a visit to China where he was influenced by Maoist ideas, created a Poor Peasants Union and encouraged the takeover of land by force. He promoted local development schemes which were often administered by officials whose loyalty to himself compensated for their lack of competence or integrity. In 1970 he also signed decrees nationalising businesses and concentrating most economic activities in the hands of the state. The following year Haytham tried to encourage local businessmen to invest in new industries and Ali joined with the dogmatic Marxist Ismail to dismiss him. With Ismail immersed in Party matters, Ali appeared to dominate the Government. At home the strict repression continued and there was a drive to bring ideology into the lives of women and peasants. In foreign affairs he tried to keep a balance between Russia and China as sources of aid and inspiration. Communist aid, however, was not enough in Aden's desperate financial situation and Ali, seeing that it was pointless to quarrel for purely ideological reasons, moved to end the hostility to the rich oil states which had persisted since independence. In August 1977 he visited Riyadh. Relations with Great Britain improved and Aden acquired the BP Refinery by agreement. After all their predecessors had been feted, aircraft hijackers were turned away. In October 1977 at the UN Ali made preliminary overtures to the USA. In 1972 the presence of armed South Yemeni refugees on the territory of the North, as well as ideological disputes, had been a cause of friction which in September became open war. This was ended by Arab League mediation and the signature in November of the Tripoli Agreement that the two states would unite. Despite the willingness of President al-Iryani to implement this, little progress was made until after the accession to power of Colonel Ibrahim al-Hamdi in 1974. He and Ali, both facing mounting internal opposition, had their own reasons for collaboration and in two meetings seem to have established a genuine personal friendship. In March 1977 Ali attended the Taizz Conference which Saudi Arabia and Egypt hoped would lead to an anti-Russian alliance of Red Sea states but he was unable to commit Aden to this. However Ali's *rapprochement* with the conservative states and with the West and his friendship with China alarmed Ismail and other supporters of exclusive alliance with Russia. There were also increasing political difficulties with Ismail insisting on the need to concentrate all power in the hands of a "Vanguard Party" which the masses had only to follow while Ali opposed bureaucracy and wished, Maoist fashion, to rely upon the revolutionary spirit of the people and on the countryside against the urban proletariat which followed Ismail. In October 1975 Ali suffered a setback with the creation of the United Political Organisation – National Front which was controlled by Ismail although Ali was Assistant Secretary-General. The struggle continued with each man trying to get supporters into key posts and Ismail was able to have Ali Antar made Minister of Defence. Ali endeavoured to woo the Saudis but Ismail established close relations with the new communist regime in Ethiopia and isolated Aden from most Arab states by sending troops to support it. Having lost Hamdi, the President may well have tried to establish the same links with his successor Ghashmi, sending a special messenger to Sanaa in June 1978 at the very moment that he himself was expecting the arrival of an American envoy; a bomb exploded in the Adeni's briefcase killing both him and Ghashmi. Immediately afterwards fighting broke out in Aden, either because Ali tried to arrest his opponents or because Ismail ordered an attack, in which it is said that Russian and Cuban elements took part, on the Presidential Palace. After heavy fighting Ali was captured and with two companions found guilty by a "special court" and shot two minutes after sentence. He was subsequently accused of "loathsome mistakes" and "the most terrible crimes". Although a convinced and ruthless revolutionary, he had shown some responsiveness to the feelings and welfare of the people which he was prepared to put above dogma. He was also, having fought to end the domination of Great Britain, unwilling to accept that of Russia.

ALL-AFRICAN PEOPLES' CONFERENCE, CAIRO (1961)

The Third Conference of the All-African People's Organisation was held in Cairo in March 1961 was attended by 200/300 delegates from about 30 countries and 60 organisations. Mehdi Ben Barka represented the Moroccan opposition. In his opening address President Nasser denounced imperialism in Africa, particularly in the Congo, French nuclear testing in the Sahara and Israel as the tool of Western imperialism in Africa. Committees were set up to deal with the liberation of non-independent states, neo-colonialism and the UN, democratic development and African solidarity. Proceedings were marred by an angry clash between Ethiopia and Somalia. Delegates were taken to see refugee camps in the Gaza Strip. A series of routine anti-imperialist resolutions was passed and in closing Nasser declared that moral forces were more effective than atomic weapons, national unity was essential and that the UAR would support the struggles of the African peoples. The Conference was followed by an intensification of Nasser's efforts to present himself as an African leader, providing bases for liberation movements, University places for students etc.

ALL-AFRICAN PEOPLE'S CONFERENCE, TUNIS (1960)

The All-African People's Conference, an unofficial body representing nationalist movements, political parties and Trade Unions rather than states, was constituted in Accra in December 1958. Its objectives were formulated as the liberation of the Continent from colonialism and imperialism and the promotion of unity leading to a United States of Africa. Abdoullaye Diallo of Guinea was appointed to head a permanent secretariat and Tom Mboya chaired a steering committee. The second Conference was held in January 1960 in Tunis. The main issue was the War of Algerian Independence and Mahjoub Ben Sadiq called for the establishment of a symbolic African volunteer army to assist it. President Bourguiba, however, said that it would not be allowed to operate from Tunisian territory. Full support was pledged for a boycott of South African goods and the mixed-race South African Liberal Party was given membership of the Conference – the first whites admitted. The Conference recommended the creation of an All-African Trade Union Federation.

ALL SAINTS' DAY UPRISING (1954) (Algeria)

The Comité Revolutionnaire d'Unité et d'Action during the summer of 1954 made plans for a nationwide uprising against the French. The country was divided into six *wilayas* and their commanders were ordered to strike at 0300 hours on 1 November – All Saints' Day a holiday for Catholics. Many of the attacks were designed to seize arms and explosives: Ben Bella said that the insurgents had only 350–400 guns amongst possibly 2,000 men. In the Aures the first French officer was killed a few moments after 0300 hours and a liberal schoolteacher and a loyal Caid were murdered. In Algiers none of five attacks was successful as homemade bombs proved ineffective. In the Oranie weapons expected from Morocco had not arrived and the insurgents in attacks on isolated farms succeeded only in killing an unarmed civilian. In all seven people were killed and four wounded. In Kabyle some damage was done to communications. The Front de Liberation Nationale broadcast on Cairo Radio a call for a recognition of Algerian nationhood but it was some time before the Algerian War of Independence was taken very seriously by the French.

AMAL (Lebanon)

In the mid-1970s the leader of the Lebanese Shiah, the Imam Musa Sadr formed an organisation to support the poor of the South against feudal landlords, win a fairer share of political power for them as they were now the largest single community in the country, and to defend the villages against the Israeli attacks which followed raids by Palestinian guerrillas. This was named *Afwaj al-Muqawama al-Lubnaniyya* (The Lebanese Resistance Battalions" and was shortened to Amal which also meant "Hope" in Arabic. Amal gave a new cohesion to what were previously localised groups. In the early months of the civil war which started in April 1975 it took no part beyond defending its own villages. After the Israeli invasion of March 1978 the area was further troubled by the exactions and rapine of its surrogate South Lebanon Army and more and more Shi'ites moved to Beirut, spreading the influence of Amal. In August 1978 the Imam vanished in Libya and leadership eventually passed into the hands of Nabih Berri. Amal was primarily a political party agitating for a secular Lebanon and not over-concerned with external affairs such as the Palestine problem and like all other political parties formed its own militia. By 1980 it had over 10,000 fighting men, a figure which later grew to about 30,000 whereas the strongest Christian group, the Lebanese Forces had about 5,000 full-time militiamen. Three of its members became Ministers in the Cabinet of Shafiq al-Wazzan in October 1980: pressure was brought on them to resign

but they continued in office. During the winter of 1981/2 there were frequent clashes with the Palestinians, 30 being killed in a single fight in January 1982. When the Israelis in the course of Operation Peace for Galilee invaded the Lebanon in June 1982, the Amal members in the South generally welcomed them as liberators from the Palestinian guerrillas whereas those in Beirut fought with the Palestinians against them. The more religious-minded members started to leave to form Islamic Amal and, more importantly Hizbullah which called for all-out war against Israel and an Islamic Republic on the lines of the one set up in Iran by Ayatollah Khomeini: Amal, on the other hand, wanted a Lebanese state which, as the largest sect, they could aspire to rule. Berri insisted that Amal was a purely Lebanese movement with no links with any outside power but generally he worked closely with Walid Jumblatt, following his leftist and pro-Syrian line. Amal and Hizbullah combined to harass the withdrawing Israelis in the summer of 1983 and later their suicide attacks led to the policy of the "Iron Fist". They continued active in the South often skirmishing with the South Lebanon Army and occasionally with UNIFIL. In August 1983, after a clash with the army in which the Multi-National Force became involved, the Shiah established themselves as the major force in South Beirut. In April 1985, assisted by the army Sixth Brigade which was mainly Shiah, they wrested control of Muslim West Beirut from the Sunnis. Later that year, having been given nearly 50 tanks by the Syrians, they undertook the task that the Syrians were unwilling to do themselves by attacking the Palestinian refugee camps which had come under control of elements loyal to Yassir Arafat and the ruthlessness with which they besieged Burj al-Barajinah caused disgust in the Arab world. In February 1987 during the siege Amal was attacked in West Beirut by a combination of the Sunnis, the Druze and the Communists and was only saved by Syrian intervention. Amal's attacks on the Palestinians increased the hostility of Hizbullah and fighting broke out between the two Shiah factions and in the spring of 1988 there was heavy fighting between them in West Beirut and in South Lebanon, gravely embarrassing Syria and Iran, which although allies found themselves backing different sides. Amal improved its position in the South but lost ground in Beirut. In June 1988 Berri declared that Amal would disband its militiamen who should join the regular army but nothing seems to have happened. In January 1989 renewed fighting brought mediation by very senior figures fom Syria and Iran: it was agreed that Amal should be responsible for security in the South although Hizbullah should have a presence there while Syria should control security in Beirut.

AMAMOU, Muhammad (1935-)

Born Kairouan – as a student he was a militant and Secretary-General of UGET. He was a diplomat in charge in Amman during Black September. Ambassadorin Beirut at the start of the civil war later Ambassador to Zaire, Morocco and Syria. He was nominated adviser to Tunisia's president Ben Ali before his three-year appointment as Secretary-General of AMU on 22 October 1991.

AMER, Abd al-Hakim, Field Marshal (1919–67)
Egyptian Vice-President. He was the son of the village
headman of Istal in Minya Province and was commissioned in 1939. He fought in the Palestine War and
was given exceptional promotion for valour in the field.
He also assisted the irregular forces of the Muslim
Brothers. He was then an Instructor at the Army School
of Administration and on the staff of General Neguib
whom he brought into the Free Officers, of which he
was a member of the original Executive. Only he and
Nasser knew all the cells. Amer did much of the detailed
planning for the July Revolution during which he took
over the army HQ. He was a member of the Revolutionary Command Council and in June 1953
succeeded Neguib as Commander-in-Chief. In November 1954 it was Amer who arrested Neguib. In
September 1954 he was made Minister of War and on
paper he was at various times in command of Syrian,
Saudi and Jordanian forces. He set out to win a special
place for the army in the state and for himself within
it, winning great privileges for its officers and he found
posts for them in Embassies and in business and
allowed them to traffic in land and drugs. He was more
than tolerant of corruption and a smuggling ring operated from his office. In October 1956 he strongly
advised Nasser to accept the Allied ultimatum but later
was so confident that he could defeat the Israelis that
he resisted orders to bring back troops to defend the
Canal. His poor showing and that of the Egyptian army
in the Suez War had no effect on his career. In 1957 he
was a member of the committee that vetted election
candidates of the newly established National Union but
he was less authoritarian than Nasser and less keen
on transforming society by some form of socialism. In
March 1958 he was promoted Field Marshal. In
October 1959 Nasser sent him as Governor of the
Syrian Province of the United Arab Republic with full
powers and a brief to organise the National Union
there. His relations with Abd al-Hamid al-Sarraj who
controlled security in Syria were never good. He was
personally not unpopular but there were many complaints about the arrogance and corruption of his
entourage. He was taken completely by surprise at the
break-up of the Union in September 1961, was arrested
in his pyjamas and expelled. Nasser blamed him for the
fiasco and also became worried at the extent of his
control over the army and the independence that he
showed. He tried to kick Amer upstairs but was unable
to weaken his grip. Amer would have liked military
aid from the West and resisted Russian influence. He
claimed to have developed the Arab World's first submarines and rockets. He used his power over the
military to thwart Nasser's intention to give the new,
pliant Imam Badr a chance to make Yemen a loyal
ally of Egypt and set off the Revolution in Sanaa. He
frustrated several attempts at peace during the Yemen
War because it gave his officers opportunities for promotion and corruption. When he took control of
operations, he was unsuccessful. Meanwhile he had left
the War Ministry and become Nasser's official deputy
in March 1964 and chaired the Commission for Liquidation of Feudalism and the Higher Committee of the
Public Sector which gave further opportunities to those
such as Shams Badran who manipulated him to feather

their own nests and Amer himself was believed to have
acquired a large land holding. Before Nasser demanded
the withdrawal of UNEF from Sinai Amer had assured
him that he was able to defeat the Israelis: Mahmud
Riad said that he was frantic and irrational and looking
forward to the conquest of Beersheba. But the Egyptian
army had been fatally weakened by the incompetence
and corruption which he had allowed to prevail. At
the start of the June War Amer insisted on personally
directing operations, ordering a precipitate withdrawal
from Sinai, overruling Nasser and the Chief of Staff,
General Muhammad Fawzi. On 9 June he was dismissed and started to fortify his house in Giza, stockpile
weapons there and with the help of Badran to plan a
coup. He felt that the dismissal of some 50 senior
officers had been unfair. On 25 August Nasser invited
him for a discussion and had him arrested. On 14 September he committed suicide with cyanide that he had
concealed under a plaster. It was believed that Nasser
never recovered from the treachery of his best friend,
who he said, had been "closer to him than a brother"
and he said that Amer's suicide had been a crueller
blow than the actual defeat. Amer was described as a
pleasant but slow-witted man, extremely generous with
an almost obsessive loyalty and indulgence towards his
subordinates of whom he was a particularly poor
chooser. He relaxed with women, hashish, the writings
of Agatha Christie and chess with Nasser.

AMERICAN UNIVERSITY OF BEIRUT
In 1920 the Syrian Protestant College was renamed the
American University of Beirut and in 1923 President
Bayard Dodge stressed that although a Protestant institution, its students had full freedom of worship. The
following year it admitted its first female student, a
veiled Egyptian lady who was accompanied by her
husband. In the early 1930s Antun Saadeh who formed
the Parti Populaire Syrien was amongst its students. By
1941 it had more than 2,000 students and was regarded
as having the highest academic standards in the Middle
East. At the foundation meeting of the UN in San
Francisco there were more AUB graduates (15)
amongst the delegates than those of any other University. After 1948 two medical students, George Habash
and Wadia Haddad took over its student society,
turning it into the seed-bed for the Arab Nationalist
Movement. It continued to attract students from all
over the Arab world, some of whom appeared to regard
it merely as a pretext for living in Beirut and one of its
graduates, the hijacker Leila Khalid described it as "a
finishing school for the rich children of the Middle
East"; few came from poor homes. In 1974 there were
4,283 students – 83% of them Arabs (56% Lebanese),
32% women and 56% Christians – occupying 81 buildings on a 75-acre site. Many of the staff of 570 (72%
from the Middle East and 19% from North America)
had close links with the CIA and its large bureaucracy
was mainly financed from the US. In March 1974 the
students went on strike against a 10% rise in tuition
fees, demanding also more participation in the government of the University. Buildings were occupied and
the home of the President, Dr Samuel Kirkwood was
besieged. Classes were suspended for six weeks until
the police stormed the campus and charged more than

60 students with subversion. After the start of Civil War its hospital won the highest praise for its treatment of the wounded of all sides. Violence spread to the campus and in 1976 a militia officer placed his artillery on the football field and two Deans were killed by a student who blamed them for his expulsion. In the same year an annexe was opened in East Beirut for 30 Christian students who felt it unsafe to go to the campus in Muslim West Beirut: eventually 1,300 students attended the annexe. In July 1982 after the Israeli invasion Operation Peace for Galilee, the Acting President David Dodge was kidnapped and taken to Iran where he was held for a year. In January 1984 the President, Malcolm Kerr an eminent historian, was murdered outside his office: Islamic Jihad claimed responsibility but many of his colleagues believed that he was killed for alerting the American Government to some of the plans of President Amin Gemayel. The following month 17 rockets hit the students' sleeping quarters. In 1985 and 1986 there was a series of kidnappings and killings of Faculty members – some of whom were held for years as hostages in Lebanon and the President Frederic Herter was reduced to administering the Univerity from New York. During this time the proportion of foreign students naturally decreased and standards were lowered as threats and force were used to procure the entry of unqualified students and to influence their grades. When the Syrian army began policing West Beirut in 1987, large quantities of weapons were found in the dormitories. Despite all the violence, apart from a strike in May 1986 after the kidnapping of a Lebanese staff member, the West Beirut campus remained open until March 1989 when General Michel Aoun began his campaign to oust the Syrians. During that period at least 88 shells hit the University and three students were killed. The hospital remained open treating most of the casualties of shelling of West Beirut. In October the University reopened with over 5,000 students. In 1990 the annexe in East Beirut was closed and its members were integrated into the main campus. In May 1991 President Herter spoke of the possibility of his early return to Beirut.

AMGALLA CLASH (1976)
The Madrid Tripartite Agreement of 14 November 1975 had provided for a Spanish withdrawal from the Western Sahara and within a few days Moroccan troops crossed the frontier to take possession of the country. They were resisted by local guerrillas of the Polisario which had the support of Algeria which also sent troops into the area. On 27 January 1976 Algerian soldiers escorting supplies clashed with Moroccan soldiers at Amgalla, some 180 miles within the Western Sahara and 250 miles from the nearest Algerian base at Tindouf. The Moroccans were superior in number and achieved tactical surprise. Their commander, Colonel Ahmad Dlimi showed reporters captured missiles, mines and artillery and claimed to have killed 200, and taken 100 prisoner: he put Moroccan casualties at 2 dead and 12 wounded. The Algerians stated that they had killed 400 Moroccans. The Algerians, using Russian tanks and aircraft, mounted a major operation and recaptured Amgalla but denied their troops had taken part, stating that the men involved had been

Polisario guerrillas. Rabat admitted the loss of 300 soldiers in the battle, many of them to attacks from aircraft which Polisario did not possess. Two days later the Moroccans regained the oasis as the Algerians withdrew because of difficulties of communications. There was a possibility that the incident might escalate into a war which might eventually involve the Super-Powers but Arab leaders, in particular Crown Prince Fahd intervened and there was no further fighting. Morocco broke off diplomatic relations with Algeria which had recognised Polisario's self-transformation, in February 1976, into the Saharan Arab Democratic Republic which it continued to assist. There were frequent reports that the Moroccan army was urging King Hassan II to authorise "hot pursuit" of guerrillas into Algerian territory and politicians such as Abd al-Rahim Bouabid and Muhammad Boucetta called for attacks on their bases there but there was no further fighting between regular troops of the two armies until August 1978 when Moroccan soldiers were killed by Algerians 45 miles inside their own country. There was fighting involving tanks the following month and again possibilities of war but the illness and subsequent death of President Boumédienne, whose personal jealousy of the Moroccan King had been a main force of Algerian policy defused the situation although in January 1979 the Moroccans alleged that Algerian regulars had participated in a raid on Tan-Tan. Later that year the Moroccans attempted to buy off the Algerians with the offer of a corridor to the Atlantic but the Algerians' influence over Polisario was frequently challenged by Colonel Qadafi, who lobbied intensively for the inclusion of the SADR in the OAU. Hostility persisted between the neighbours until the King met Chadli in February 1983.

AMIN, Ahmad (1886–1954)
Egyptian educationalist. He was the son of a peasant who, having taught himself to read, became a proofreader at Bulaq Press. Ahmad studied law at al-Azhar, became a judge and a Professor of Law. He was a friend of Taha Hussain and like him, had a rather idealised view of liberal Western thought which he tried to reconcile with traditional Islamic beliefs. His book *al-Sharq wa-al-Gharb* (East and West) called for a union of the scientific spirit and rational economic system of the West with the spirituality of the East: this he saw as leading to a renewal of Islam which would be separated from the state. He edited numerous journals in which he tried to introduce modern critical methods into Arab historical writing and encouraged the young to test new ideas. In 1945 he was appointed the first Director of the Cultural Section of the Arab League. He wrote an autobiography and a book on ethics for schools in which he argued for a system based on reason and intuition rather than solely upon tradition based upon religious texts.

AMIN, Mustafa (1914–)
Egyptian journalist. After the Universities of Cairo and Georgetown, where he took a degree in Political Science, he started his journalistic career in 1927, becoming Editor of a weekly in 1938. In 1944, joined by his twin brother Ali who had studied engineering at Sheffield and then worked for various Ministries, he

founded *Akhbar al-Yawm*. They attacked the corruption prevailing under King Farouq and Mustafa was jailed 26 times. Even before the July Revolution they were close to Nasser whom they supported against Neguib. They were used for unofficial diplomacy, Ali with Britain and Mustafa with the US, passing information that Nasser did not wish to go through official channels. In July 1965 when Nasser became convinced that the Americans were trying to starve Egypt into obedience, he had the brothers accused of espionage. Ali escaped to London but Mustafa in August 1966 was sentenced to life imprisonment with hard labour, deprived of essential medicines and tortured by the Intelligence Chief Salah Nasir. He wrote a book in which he described being hung upside down on a wheel for long periods and being attacked by dogs trained to tear trousers without tearing flesh. Nasser's treatment of an old friend whom he knew to be a loyal Egyptian was one of his most shameful actions. In January 1974 the brothers were pardoned by Sadat and later in the year Ali replaced their former employee Hassanain Haykal as Chairman of *al-Ahram* and then went back to *al-Akhbar* where Mustafa was already Editor. They acted as the principal mouthpieces for Sadat. Ali died in April 1976 but Mustafa was still active as a journalist in his late seventies.

AMMAN ACCORD (1985)

During 1984 Yassir Arafat, who the previous year had been expelled from Tripoli by the Syrians, re-established his authority in the Palestine Liberation Organisation by working with Jordan and Egypt for a political settlement involving some degree of confederation between the East and West Banks to prevent total Israeli absorption of pre-1948 Palestine. In November the Palestine National Council met in Amman and, boycotted by pro-Syrian factions, endorsed Arafat as leader and agreed to his policy of working with Jordan to recover the West Bank. King Hussain addressed the PNC, calling for peace on the basis of Resolution 242 and an international conference. On 11 February 1985 a formal agreement between the King and Arafat was announced. There would be a confederal relationship between Jordan and an autonomous Palestinian entity. The PLO would remain the sole legitimate representative of the Palestinian people and would take part in a joint delegation with Jordan to negotiate, at an international conference, what would in effect be a "territory for peace" settlement with Israel. The Accord, denounced by Syria as "an attempt to liquidate the Palestinian cause", led to a split in the PLO and the formation of the Palestine National Salvation Front but was endorsed by the majority attending the Casablanca Summit in August 1985. As it neither explicitly recognised Israel nor renounced violence it failed to persuade the US to admit the PLO to the peace process. In the winter of 1985/6 there was a *rapprochement* between the Syrians and the Jordanians who in February 1986 declared that Arafat was incapable of keeping his word and denounced the Accord. It was subsequently disavowed by the Palestine National Council meeting in Algiers in April 1987.

AMMAN SUMMIT (1980)

Since the Tunis Summit of November 1979 there had been increased Israeli repression on the West Bank, the change in the Jerusalem Status, the recognition of the Palestine Liberation Organisation by India and Japan, the Venice Declaration which showed the European Community to be more sympathetic to the Arabs than was the US, the Soviet intervention in Afghanistan and the outbreak of the Iran–Iraq War. These last two events had increased the divisions in the Arab World. The Syrians, angered by Jordanian support for Iraq, demanded the postponement of the Summit due to be held in Amman from 25 to 27 November 1980 and when they failed to secure their way, boycotted it and persuaded Lebanon and their partners in the Steadfastness Front, Libya, Algeria, South Yemen and the PLO to follow suit. Following Camp David, Egypt was still excluded. The Syrians moved troops to the frontier of Jordan which also deployed troops there: a menacing situation was only defused by Saudi mediation after the Summit. In these circumstances the truncated Summit was unable to produce any major new initiatives and the proposal of a previous Ministerial meeting to subscribe $15 billion to fund "the decade of Arab development" was reduced by two-thirds. The Summit expressed full support for Iraq and praised its offer of a negotiated settlement. Routine condemnations of Zionism, America and Egypt, rejection of Resolution 242 and support for the Palestinians were somewhat muted. This, the eleventh Summit, represented a particularly low point in inter-Arab relations.

AMMAN SUMMIT (1987)

King Hussain wanted to organise a united Arab response to the Resolution 598 which called for a cease-fire in the Iran-Iraq War which had been accepted by Iraq but upon which Iran had not committed itself. Syria had supported Iran throughout the fighting but in April 1987 the King succeeded in bringing together Hafiz al-Assad and Saddam Hussein on Jordanian soil. In November a Summit was held in Amman which both had agreed to attend after Assad had won his point that issues other than the Gulf War should be discussed. The principal absentees were King Fahd, who was ill and also irritated by recent Syrian attacks but was represented by the Crown Prince, and Colonel Qadafi who refused to attend unless he could discuss fighting the Americans, creating a federal state and building atomic weapons. The Summit expressed "solidarity with Iraq", despite objections from Syria and called upon Iran to withdraw from territory that it had occupied but Syrian opposition defeated calls for a complete Arab break with Tehran. Syrian opposition also prevented the readmission of Egypt, ostracised after Camp David to the Arab League, but it was agreed that any state which wished to resume individual relations with it might do so. The Summit agreed also to support any steps that Saudi Arabia might feel necessary to avoid repetition of the Mecca Massacre. It called for an international peace conference at which the Palestine Liberation Organisation would be represented as "the sole legitimate representative of the Palestinian people" on "an equal footing" with other participants.

This thirteenth Summit was generally regarded as a success for the diplomacy of King Hussain.

AMMASH, Salih Mahdi, General (1924–)

Iraqi politician. He was born in Baghdad, the son of a peasant-entrepreneur and graduated from the Military Academy. He joined the Baath in about 1952 and became head of its military wing; later he joined the Free Officers. He was one of the founders of the Baathist National Guard and in October 1959 he was involved in the Baathist attempt to assassinate Abd al-Krim Qassim. Ammash was retired from the army before the Ramadan Revolution of February 1963 but he had already been involved in its preparation and after its success was promoted from Lieutenant-Colonel to Lieutenant-General and made Minister of Defence. In October when it was agreed that Iraq and Syria would unite their armies, Ammash was nominated as the Commander-in-Chief. As the Baath split into extremists, represented by the National Guard and a more moderate group, Ammash and the Prime Minister Ahmad Hassan al-Bakr tried to keep the party together. They failed and Amash tried to mitigate military action to crush the Guard in the November Revolution. President Abd al-Salam Arif, now secure, dropped his Baathist supporters including Ammash who spent much of the next five years abroad. He returned in time to take part in the coup which ousted President Abd al-Rahman Arif after which he was appointed Minister of the Interior. He was therefore strongly placed to overthrow the new Prime Minister Abd al-Razzaq al-Nayif a fortnight later. Ammash kept his Ministry and was also appointed Deputy Premier. He visited several East European countries including Moscow where he concluded an oil agreement and most Arab countries. There were persistent reports of splits within the Party and the armed forces between factions supporting Ammash and the more militant followers of Air Marshal Hardan al-Takriti. In April 1970 both were appointed Vice-President but stripped of their Ministries. In September 1971 Ammash, regarded by many as the likely successor to the President was squeezed out as Saddam Hussain consolidated his grip, being removed from the political scene with the post of Ambassador to Moscow from where in February 1974 he was transferred to Paris and later to Finland. He wrote several books on military and political matters as well as poetry.

al-AMRI, Hassan b. Hussain (1916–)

Prime Minister of Yemen. A tribesman from the (Hashid and) Bakil confederation he had limited education before being selected for officer training at the Baghdad Military Academy. He specialised in signals and was able to play an important part in the coup in which the Imam Yahya was murdered and Saiyyid Abd Allah al-Wazir seized power in February 1948. Subsequently he was imprisoned for seven years before being pardoned at the request of the Crown Prince Badr whom he accompanied on some of his missions abroad. In September 1962 he was a colonel and after the overthrow of the Imamate he became a Minister and a member of the Revolutionary Command Council. He was clearly one of the strongest peronalities in the country and became a Vice-President the following year, often deputising for Marshal Sallal. In February 1964 he was made Chairman of the Executive Council but a new Constitution in April created the post of Prime Minister which went to General Hamud al-Jaifi. After the attempt at the Erkowit Conference of November 1964 failed through the intransigence of Sallal and the Egyptians, the moderate Republicans resigned and Jaifi's Cabinet melted away. Amri who was regarded as strongly pro-Nasser became Prime Minister in January 1965. In April the regime was shaken by the murder of Muhammad Mahmud al-Zubayri and was forced to replace Amri by Ahmad Muhammad Nu'man who was committed to a policy of peace through negotiations with the tribes. When the military recovered their self-confidence and obstructed Nu'man he resigned and Amri resumed office. With Sallal away he ran the country for the next year, during which, although he was still determined to crush the Royalists, he became impatient of Egyptian control. He particularly resented the Egyptian policy of preventing him from approaching the Russians directly for arms and he was refused access to Kosygin then visiting Cairo. In September 1966 he tried to prevent the return of Sallal by occupying the airfield but superior Egyptian forces compelled him to withdraw. Sallal then became Prime Minister in defiance of his own Constitution and Amri led a delegation to Cairo to ask for his removal. He was detained by Nasser who refused to return him to face charges of treason, preferring to keep him for future use. When Sallal was overthrown in November 1967 Amri returned as Commander-in-Chief and soon became a member of the three-man Presidency Council. When the following month there was a serious possibility that Sanaa might fall to the Royalists, he took over as Prime Minister. During the 70 days of the siege his leadership proved decisive. He armed the citizens, inspired their fighting spirit and shot dissidents. He also obtained crucial military support from the Russians. Determined to establish the state on a firm basis he then ruthlessly crushed attempts by the left-wing National Liberation Front, which was supported by Aden to seize a cargo of arms in Hodeidah in March 1968 and an uprising in Sanaa in August. In these events he had to rely upon tribal support thus bringing the shaykhs back into the mainstream of politics. He also reconquered much of the country, often commanding in person and he purged left-wing officers. He conducted an extremely active diplomacy, visiting Moscow, Morocco and Libya amongst other countries. In January 1969 he crushed another attempted coup by the leftwing, causing strained relations with Aden. In March he reformed his government, promising administrative reform and development, especially in agriculture but in July he resigned on grounds of ill-health, going to Cairo for a rest. In November he was reappointed C.-in-C. In August 1971 after a ten-week government in which he came to despair of settling the country's economic and administrative problems, Nu'man resigned as Prime Minister and Amri, regarded as the nation's "strong man" formed his seventh government. He promised an "administrative revolution", helped by international experts and formed a Supreme Committee attached to his own office to supervise all economic matters. A week later, obtaining a wrong number on the telephone, he was insulted by a drunken photographer who thought a friend was playing a prank: Amri sent his guards for the man and personally shot him. Later it was suggested that he had intended to ring a senior officer about a military takeover. He was dismissed by President Abd al-Rahman al-Iryani who refused to have him executed and he went into exile in Beirut. He returned in January 1975 and played no further part in politics. Known as "The Sword of the Republic", Amri was harsh, arrogant, intolerant and hot-headed and not particularly intelligent but he possessed the qualities of leadership and proved himself extemely skilful both on the battlefield and in politics. In an army not noted for smartness, his immaculate uniforms and military bearing made him an outstanding figure.

ANFAL CAMPAIGN (1988)
In February 1988, as the Iran–Iraq War was drawing to a close, Saddam Hussain ordered a massive operation to punish those Kurds who had in many cases collaborated with the enemy. Under the command of Ali Hassan Majid troops and loyal Kurds surrounded villages and removed their population. Estimates of the number affected vary from 100,000 to 250,000 and some 4,500 villages were destroyed. Houses were flattened, wells filled with concrete and trees cut down. The men were separated from the women and taken South and most were not seen again. The women and children were driven out into the desert and abandoned: many made their ways to towns where they lived in appalling conditions. Where villages resisted, they were bombarded from the ground or attacked from the air – the most notorious example being Halabja which was destroyed in March. The operation seems to have finished before the onset of winter.

ANGLO-AMERICAN COMMITTEE OF INQUIRY ON PALESTINE (1946)
Even before the war it was becoming obvious that the British Government could not solve the Palestine question and its last effort, the MacDonald White Paper of 1939, had been rejected by the Arabs, the Zionists and the Mandates Commission of the League of Nations. The revelation of the atrocities committed by the Nazis, Jewish terrorism in Palestine, illegal immigration and virulently anti-British propaganda spread by Zionists in America made the problem even worse. The Cabinet decided in November 1945 not to try again on its own, or even as in the London Palestine Conference to involve the friendly independent Arabs but to invoke the assistance of the United States. A joint Committee of Inquiry was set up with instructions "to examine political, economic and social conditions in Palestine as they bear upon the problem of Jewish immigration and settlement therein (and) to examine the position of the Jews in those countries in Europe where they have been the victims of Nazi and Fascist persecution". The British delegation of six, headed by a High Court judge included three politicians, most notably the newly-elected Marxist intellectual R. H. S. Crossman. None had previously spoken on Palestine. The Americans also headed by a judge, included two, Bartley Crum and James McDonald who were firmly committed to Zionism. The initial meetings held in Washington where most witnesses, including Albert Einstein, supported the Zionists and attacked the British. At the end of January there was a session in London lasting a week where again most testimony was pro-Zionist, touching particularly on the fate of the European Jews. The Committee spent most of February travelling in Europe visiting Dachau and refugee camps before reassembling in Cairo. Witnesses there included Abd al-Rahman Azzam, Hassan al-Banna, Fadhl Jamali and Habib Bourguiba. They moved to Palestine where they met Weizmann, Ben Gurion who was evasive to the point of untruthfulness, Jamal al-Hussaini and Awni Abd al-Hadi. The Committee then spent most of a month in Lausanne writing its Report which stated that Palestine alone could not meet the emigration needs of the victims of persecution but that 100,000 should be admitted. Many should remain in Europe. A Declaration was needed that Palestine should be neither an Arab nor a Jewish state. The Mandate should continue temporarily and work for an improvement in Arab living standards. Jews should not have an automatic right to enter Palestine. The restrictions on land transfers should be lifted. Discussions should be held with the Jewish Agency and neighbouring Arab states about development projects. The Committee was "profoundly impressed" by the achievements of the Jewish Agency but urged it to co-operate with the authorities against terrorism and illegal immigration. It concluded that "Palestine is an armed camp", especially on the Jewish side and "if British forces were withdrawn there would be immediate and prolonged bloodshed the end of which it is impossible to predict". The main outcome of the Report was a dispute between the British and American Governments with President Truman, principally for electoral reasons, insisting upon immediate implementation of the recommendation that 100,000 Jewish immigrants be admitted while Bevin said that this could "only be enforced by British bayonets" and that the US should refrain from carping and take a more responsible attitude. The Report was condemned by the Arabs as reneging on the promises of 1939 and by the Zionists for its rejection of a Jewish state. Crossman and Crum wrote books about their experiences on the Committee.

ANGLO-EGYPTIAN TREATY (1954)
In October 1951 Nahhas Pasha unilaterally denounced the Anglo-Egyptian Treaty of 1936 which he had himself negotiated. There were two causes of friction between the two states, the future of the Sudan and the presence of British troops in the Suez Canal Zone. After the July Revolution of 1952 General Neguib was able to reach an understanding with political leaders in Khartoum that led to the Anglo-Egyptian Agreement on the Sudan which was signed in February 1953. Discussions on the Canal Zone in April and May were indefinitely adjourned and Neguib spoke of a "great battle ahead". During the summer firstly Pandit Nehru and then the Pakistani Ambassador, added to considerable American pressure, managed to bring the two sides together but constant violence in the Zone led to the rupture of negotiations in October. A strong group of Conservative MPs, with which the Prime Minister

Winston Churchill had some sympathy, opposed any concessions to Egypt but early in July 1954 talks were resumed. On July 27 an agreement was initiated by Nasser and the War Minister Anthony Head which formally ended the privileges accorded by the 1936 Treaty. It provided for a phased withdrawal of British troops before 19 June 1956. The base would then come under Egyptian command but for the next seven years it would be maintained by a maximum of 1,200 British civilian technicians, of whom not more than 800 should be expatriates. In the event of an attack upon an Arab country or on Turkey, the British would again have the use of the base but would have to withdraw immediately afterwards. If there were only a threat, the two states would consult. The British were given over-flying rights. The Treaty reaffirmed that the Canal was an integral part of Egypt and the validity of the Constantinople International Convention of 1888. The Agreement was a triumph for Egypt but was accepted by the House of Commons on 29 July and formally signed on 19 October 1954. It was quickly followed by a resumption of British arms sales to Egypt which had been halted in 1951. It was a triumph for Nasser to obtain the withdrawal of British troops after 72 years but some of the Muslim Brothers blamed him for abandoning the Sudan and linking Egypt in a defence arrangement with the West; a week later one attempted to assassinate him. On 1 January 1957 after the Suez War Nasser abrogated the Treaty.

ANGLO-OTTOMAN AGREEMENT (1913)

After the Turks occupied the Hasa Province in 1871 there occurred a series of disputes with the British over Bahrain, Qatar and finally Kuwait. Attempts to avoid them were delayed firstly by the divisions between the Foreign Office and the Government of India over the British negotiating position and then by Turkish preoccupation with wars firstly in Libya and then in the Balkans. An Agreement was finally reached between Sir Edward Grey and Hakki Pasha on 29 July 1913. The Turks renounced all claims on Bahrain in return for a British undertaking not to annex the Islands formally. The Turks also gave up claims on Qatar which would be autonomous under Jasim b. Muhammad al-Thani while the British pledged themselves to prevent any Bahraini interference there. Kuwait was to remain part of the Ottoman Empire but would enjoy autonomy and the Turks recognised the validity of the Agreements signed by Shaykh Mubarak b. Sabah al-Sabah with the British Government. The islands of Bubiyan and Warbah which had nearly led to armed clashes were assigned to Kuwait. A blue line drawn from a middle point of the Gulf of Bahrain to the 20th Parallel and a violet line drawn diagonally from that point to the Aden Hinterland divided the two Empires. It was significant that the Agreement contained no reference to Ibn Saud. It was envisaged that there would be further Treaties involving the Baghdad Railway and thus removing other possible causes of international tension. The Anglo–Ottoman Agreement had not been ratified by October 1914 when Britain and Turkey went to war, as a result of which it became out of date.

ANGLO-TRANS-JORDANIAN AGREEMENT (1928)

The British, having acquired a Mandate to rule Palestine were uncertain what to do with the bedouin areas East of the Jordan. As a temporary measure in the spring of 1921 they agreed that their wartime ally Sharif Abd Allah might act as ruler in Amman while they decided whether the territory should be administered as part of Palestine. In February 1923 they announced that they would recognize an independent government there provided that it was constitutional and in alliance with Britain. An Agreement was not actually signed until February 1928. This provided that the Amir should exercise legislative and administrative powers on behalf of Britain with the advice of a Resident. He could not legislate against Britain's commitments under the Mandate. Abd Allah agreed to be guided by British advice in foreign affairs, the budget, financial administration, exploitation of minerals and jurisdiction over foreigners etc. Officials from outside the country could not be appointed without British approval. He could not raise military forces without British consent or object to the stationing of British troops and London would subsidise the Government and its armed services. Some relaxations of British control were later granted and the agreement was finally replaced by the Anglo-Trans-Jordanian Treaty of 1946.

ANGLO-TRANS-JORDANIAN TREATY (1946)

The Anglo-Trans-Jordanian Agreement of 1928, placed almost total restrictions upon the freedom of action of the Amir Abd Allah. As a result of the loyalty shown by him during the Palestine troubles and in the war British control was relaxed by an agreement of July 1941 but Trans-Jordan, still subject to the Mandate, continued to appear a client state when its neighbours Syria and Lebanon became independent in 1945. It was refused admission to the UN. Abd Allah and his Prime Minister Ibrahim Hashim negotiated a new Treaty which was signed in March 1946. This ended the Mandate and proclaimed the full independence of Trans-Jordan. This was in fact restricted by the country's continued dependence upon British subsidies and while British troops remained stationed in the country. In May 1946 Abd Allah was proclaimed King. A new Treaty signed by the British Ambassador Sir Alec Kirkbride and the Prime Minister Tawfiq Abu al-Huda in March 1948 restricted the British presence to RAF units at Amman and Mafraq. Their presence however provided the Russians with a pretext to withhold UN membership until 1955. After the annexation of the West Bank that area was regarded by Britain as part of Jordan and so covered by the Treaty. In March 1957 the Nabulsi Government abrogated the Treaty.

ANGLO-YEMENI *MODUS VIVENDI* (1951)

The Sanaa Treaty of 1934 put an end to 15 years of sporadic conflict between the Imam Yahya who regarded the whole of South Arabia as part of the legacy of his Himyaritic and Zaidi ancestors and the British who were determined to maintain a paramount influence over those tribes which had been accepted by the Ottomans as being within the Aden Protectorate. The Treaty had provided that there should be no change in the frontier (*hudud*) but whereas the British interpreted this to mean the actual border line, the Yemenis maintained that it referred to the area behind the frontier. When therefore in March 1949 Sharif Hussain al-Habili of Bayhan, with British agreement, built a customs post at Najd Marqad, three miles within his own state, the Yemenis strongly protested and started to build a fort on the Bayhan side of the border. At the beginning of September the half-completed fort was destroyed by British aircraft. At the same time the British took a renewed interest in Shabwa, still further exasperating the Imam Ahmad. The situation was rendered more difficult by the fact that Ahmad had not reversed his father's veto on the presence in Sanaa of foreign Ambassadors so there were no diplomatic relations between the two states. The British invited the Yemenis to London and a *modus vivendi* was agreed in October 1950, approved in January 1951 and published in March. It provided for the exchange of resident envoys. The British would help the Yemen Government in the spheres of economic development, education, hygiene and other matters as requested. A Joint Commission, consisting of an equal number of representatives of each country with the power to co-opt an impartial Commissioner would be set up to demarcate the disputed areas and determine what had been the *status quo* in 1934 and what it was in 1950. There should be no troops or administrators in Shabwa and the customs house at Najd Marqad and the nearby Yemeni fort should be evacuated. There should be an end to hostile propaganda and arrangements were made for dealing with fugitive offenders. The *hudud* were still not defined and the Yemenis did not give up their claim to the whole of the Protectorates. Shortly after the Agreement was reached, a new Governor of Aden, Sir Tom Hickinbotham, launched a vigorous forward policy in the sensitive areas of Awdhali and Awlaqi to which the Imam responded by handing out money and arms to Protectorate dissidents.

al-ANSAR Organisation (Palestine)

The Ansar Organisation was formed in March 1970 by the Jordanian Communist Party at the behest of the Russians so as to obtain a footing within the Palestine Liberation Organisation. It was joined by communists from neighbouring countries. In accordance with Russian policy it did not demand the destruction of Israel and it echoed Russian disapproval of the acceptance by Nasser of the Rogers' Plan (II). It appears to have played little part in the fighting of Black September beyond putting up posters. The organisation attracted little popular support and was never accepted by the PLO although its leader Fayik Warrad was a member of the Palestine National Council in a private capacity. After the expulsion of the guerrillas from Jordan its 400-odd members settled in South Lebanon where after the PLO improved relations with Russia, it collaborated with Fatah and al-Saiqa and with local communists. Early in 1972 the communist party decided to dissolve the Ansar telling its members to join Fatah.

ANSAR (Sudan)

As Muhammad Ahmad al-Mahdi had struggled to recreate the theocratic organisation of the Prophet, his religious and political followers assumed the name of Ansar as those of Muhammad had done. The Ansar stood religiously for a renaissance of Islam and total faith in God and the Mahdi. Politically, they had an abiding hatred of Egyptians and Turks. After the overthrow of the Khalifah Abd Allahi the British encouraged orthodox religious leaders and the heads of rival *tariqahs* such as the Mirghani/Khatmiyyah to denounce the Ansar as heretics, but, particularly during the First World War Saiyyid Abd al-Rahman al-Mahdi began to co-operate with the British who came to regard the Ansar with benevolence, using them as a sort of rural militia. Their great strength lay on the White Nile and in the West. In 1945 Saiyyid Abd al-Rahman turned his followers, then estimated to number about three million, into an ordinary political party, the Umma, which pursued his aim of an independent Sudan achieved through alliance with the British. Many of the Ansar even wished to see him recognised as King of the Sudan. When the Umma party was suppressed by the military regimes of Abboud and Nimeiri its members presented their activities as purely religious and continued active as Ansar. In 1961 al-Hadi al-Mahdi became Imam of the Ansar; he was deeply conservative and many of the younger members put more trust in his nephew Sadiq al-Mahdi and the organisation was split. In March 1970 the supporters of the Imam revolted but were crushed at Aba Island and al-Hadi was killed. Sadiq who was regarded as acting Imam presided over the rebuilding of the movement in refugee camps mostly in Libya and the Ansar provided the backbone of an almost successful attempt to overthrow Nimeiri in July 1976. It was not, however, fully united as the older members tended to support Sadiq's uncle Ahmad al-Mahdi. The Ansar joined in the National Reconciliation of the following year but opposed the imposition of the *Shariah* on non-Muslims in the September Laws. They boycotted the elections of 1980. They were, however, numerous in the army, with one of their members, General Khalil, serving as Minister of Defence and Commander-in-Chief. After the fall of Nimeiri the Umma party was able to re-emerge and it played a major role in government until parties were suppressed again by General Bashir. Then, once again, the Ansar provided a cover for its political activities.

ANTSIRABE ACCORD (1955)

At the Aix-les-Bains Conference in August 1955 decisions were made which would put Franco-Moroccan relations on a new footing. They were dependent upon the consent of Sultan Muhammad V who had spent nearly two years in exile in Antsirabe in Madagascar. General Catroux, a known liberal and a long-time personal friend of the Sultan was sent to see if he would accept a regency under a Council of the Throne, a continuing link with France with Morocco enjoying internal autonomy and endorse these proposals in a message to his people which would also reaffirm that he would abstain from political activity. In return the Sultan would be given residence in France. The future King Hassan II played an important part in the discussions which ended with an exchange of letters on 8/9 September. Catroux, addressing his to "His

Majesty" whom he called "Sire" noted that they had agreed to "make Morocco into a free, modern and sovereign state, bound to France by permanent ties of freely accepted interdependence with the reservation that in view of the indissoluble nature of the ties that bound the two countries, France's major rights and interests in strategic, political, diplomatic, economic and cultural matters should be guaranteed" and French nationals should be accorded a special status. The Sultan's reply rejected the ties as a condition of independence but spoke of "freely accepted interdependence in areas strategic, diplomatic, political, economic and cultural". He agreed to accept the Council of the Throne and promised to take no part in political activities while resident in France. Although Catroux had clearly exceeded his instructions and French conservatives were outraged, the government of Edgar Fauré reached the conclusion that there was no alternative to the return of Muhammad particularly as this was now supported by Haj Thami al-Glawi. The Sultan arrived in Nice on 31 October and the following week at La Celle St Cloud his meeting with Foreign Minister Antoine Pinay led to his return to Rabat and rapid independence for Morocco.

ANYA NYA II

The first Anya Nya Insurrection ended with the Addis Ababa Agreement of 1972 which kept peace in the Southern Sudan for a decade despite several attempts in the North to overthrow President Nimeiri. It was agreed that of the 12,000 troops stationed in the South, 6,000 should be former guerrillas integrated into the regular army. A regional government was established but in the early 1980s was near collapse through corruption and tribal tensions. The South had other grievances: only one-fifth of development funds went to the region and the main project, the Jonglei Canal, appeared to do ecological damage to the South while mainly benefiting the North. Nimeiri arranged that the oil found in the South should be refined in the North and that much of its exploitation should be entrusted not to local people but to his business associates such as the Saudi entrepreneur Adnan Khashoggi. Southerners also deplored the Integration Charter signed with Egypt in 1982 as making them an even smaller minority. Early in 1983 Nimeiri broke the Agreement by redividing the semi-autonomous Southern Region into its original three Provinces which would be administered directly from Khartoum and also by ordering that the former guerrillas should be posted to the North and replaced by Northerners: there were rumours that these men might be sent to fight in the Iran–Iraq War. In January 1983 dissidents attacked the town of Aweil in Bahr al-Ghazal, killing twelve Northern Sudanese merchants. In February a battalion of 1,000 officers and men fled into the bush with their weapons. Nimeiri tried to conciliate the area by bringing the Dinka leader Abel Alier back into government but in May mutinous soldiers seized the Dinka centre of Borr and further mutinies spread in the Bahr al-Ghazal and Upper Nile Provinces. The insurrection attracted support from Libya and Ethiopia, the enemies of Nimeiri. In July 1983 five foreign aid workers were seized by the guerrillas. In August most of the dissident factions were co-ordinated in the Sudan People's Liberation Movement and its fighting men banded together as the Sudanese People's Liberation Army. These, however, saw themselves as a National Liberation movement and not as fighting for a separatist South. Some groups, mostly from the Nuer tribes, continued guerrilla activities as Anya Nya although they attracted much less attention than the SPLA. Their leader, William Abd Allah Ochwal Deng made an agreement with Nimeiri in October 1984 after which they collaborated against the mainly Dinka SPLA. The policy of encouraging inter-tribal warfare was continued by the government of General Siwar al-Dhahab and in the summer of 1985 there was fierce fighting between the Anya Nya and the SPLA in Bahr al-Ghazal and Upper Nile in the course of which Deng was killed and succeeded by Gordon Kong Ochwal. In the autumn of 1986 the Anya Nya split with some factions wanting to negotiate with the SPLA.

AOZOU STRIP

Aozou is an area of approximately 43,000 square miles, believed to contain uranium and other minerals, which has been for many years a matter of dispute betweeen Libya and Chad. An agreement of 1935 between the French, then ruling Equatorial Africa, ceded it to Libya, then an Italian colony, but the agreement was never ratified nor the Strip transferred. When Libya became independent it recognised its existing border with Equatorial Africa. In 1973 while Chad was in turmoil Libya moved troops into the area and consolidated its position without the government of either country publicly mentioning the fact. The Chad Intervention of Colonel Qadafi meant that relations between Tripoli and Ndjamena constantly fluctuated according to who was in power there but generally the party of Hissein Habre demanded the withdrawal of the Libyans while his opponents, needing Qadafi's help, apparently acquiesced in his annexation of Aozou. In September 1975 Tripoli officially denied newspaper reports of the annexation of 6,000 square miles while Ndjamena said they were true and the land should be returned. In 1977 Chad protested to the OAU which established a mediation committee which made no headway owing to Libya's failure to co-operate. The problem might have been solved if the full union between the two countries proposed by Qadafi in 1981 had come to fruition. In July 1984 he stated that Aozou was "an integral part of Libyan territory" and in September, having signed an accord with Libya which involved the withdrawal from Chad of the troops of both nations, the French Defence Minister stated that this did not apply to Aozou which was a question for the UN. In July 1987 President Habre, visiting Paris, said that Chad was determined to "liberate the Aozou Strip by one means or another" and in August 1987 his army which had chased the Libyans from its territory moved on into Aozou. The French, however, whose air cover had played an essential part in earlier victories, refused to extend it over the disputed area and the Libyan air force was thus able to bomb the Chadians without reprisal until they withdrew after three weeks. A cease-fire was arranged and in July 1989 Qadafi met Habre at an OAU Summit in Mali and subsequently King

Hassan II and President Chadli and others acted as mediators. It was agreed that the Strip be demilitarised and the question of sovereignty referred to the International Court at The Hague.

ARAB BOYCOTT OF ISRAEL

In December 1945 the Council of the Arab League decided that the products of Jewish industry in Palestine should not be admitted into Arab countries and at its Bludan Session in June 1946 recommended that an office be established in each state to supervise the boycott of Zionist goods and services. In August 1950, after the creation of Israel, it was decided to set up a Central Boycott Office in Damascus with a Commissioner, appointed by the Secretary-General, assisted by a Liaison Officer from each state to co-ordinate and implement decisions. A Unified Law, adopted by individual member states, prohibited persons or businesses entering into transactions with persons or firms in Israel, of Israeli nationality or acting in the interests of Israel. Ships and aircraft were to be blacklisted if they called at an Arab and an Israeli port on the same voyage or carried war material to Israel. Banks or other institutions establishing branches in Israel would be boycotted after being given an opportunity to explain or disengage. An estimate in 1963 was that 606 firms, including 167 in America were on the blacklist. Attempts to apply boycott policies often caused great indignation in industrialised countries and were skilfully exploited by Zionists to discredit the Arabs. A famous example was the removal of the pro-Zionist Lord Mancroft from the chairmanship of the Norwich Union Insurance as a result of Arab pressure in 1963. In 1966 after Ford Motors could not be dissuaded from building an assembly plant in Israel, it was banned from selling to the Arab world. A similar threat in April 1966 caused Coca-Cola to refuse a franchise to an Israeli bottling firm but intense domestic pressure forced the company to reverse the decision; it was therefore barred from Arab markets. The Arabs at times brought ridicule upon themselves by banning certain foreign films and records. It is not possible to quantify how much harm was done to Israel by the boycott. In 1992 the President of the Israeli Chamber of Commerce said that over 40 years it had cost the country 10% of both exports and imports worth $80,000 million, but certainly it damaged the country's trade, particularly with Africa and Japan, and inhibited investment. After the June War its application became more difficult as trade with the occupied West Bank was not prohibited. In May 1976 the Jewish lobby in the US secured the passage of the Ribicoff Amendment to the Internal Revenue Act which ordered businesses to report any requests for information from the Boycott Office and removed tax concessions from those that complied. There were other measures taken by Export Administration Acts in 1977 and 1979. The opening of the frontier with Egypt after peace was signed and the strong Israeli presence in Lebanon after 1978 effectively rendered futile further attempts to enforce the boycott. In August 1991 there was a suggestion that the boycott could be ended if Israel stopped building settlements in the Occupied Territories but Tel Aviv argued that this was putting the two activities on an equal legal footing. The American Government, particularly after the election of Clinton, put pressure on friendly Arab states to end the boycott, having some success in the case of Kuwait, but in June 1993 an Arab League official stated that it was still official policy.

ARAB BUREAU

By the middle of 1915 Britain had troops in action in Egypt, the Sudan, Cyrenaica, Aden, Mesopotamia, East Africa and Gallipoli and feared the establishment of submarine bases on the Red Sea and subversion amongst the Muslims of India resulting from Ottoman attempts to proclaim *jihad*. The Foreign Office was concerned with Egypt and Western Arabia, the War Office with the fighting fronts except for Mesopotamia which with Eastern Arabia came under the India Office. There was no mechanism for co-ordinating policy or sharing intelligence. In January 1916 a committee rejected a proposal for an Islamic Bureau but recommended that an Arab one be established in Cairo. Its first function was to harmonise political activity in the Middle East and inform government departments about it and upon Turco-German policy. Members of staff were sent on most secret missions to Arab rulers and advised the highest British authorities. The Bureau published the highly secret *Arab Bulletin* for this purpose and also a series of area handbooks and maps. It provided carrier pigeons to bring intelligence obtained from sympathisers between the Turkish lines and intercepted the wireless signals of the garrison in Medina and also of its ally King Hussain. It spread propaganda, subsidising and where necessary creating newspapers such as *al-Qiblah* in Mecca. It certainly played some part in persuading Hussain to start the Arab Revolt and initially handled all its military requirements, shipping large quantities of arms, mules, barbed wire etc. It acted also as its paymaster, almost flooding the Hijaz in gold sovereigns and as the area historically could not feed itself it sent monthly stores such as 70,000 bags of rice and 2,000 bags of sugar. When Hussain permitted, it assisted the new Hijaz Government by providing liaison with Egyptian Government Departments, arranging the travel of its officials, keeping its accounts, designing postage stamps and passports etc. After the war the Bureau continued to assist the Hijaz Government and had additional responsibilities for the repatriation of refugees and Turkish prisoners who had fought for the Arabs. There were disputes between various Ministries with the War Office wishing it to become a large-scale intelligence organisation but this was opposed by the Foreign Office. However the Bureau was abolished, mainly for reasons of economy, in 1920.

ARAB COLLECTIVE SECURITY TREATY
(1950)

Arab armies emerged from the Palestine War with little credit and had shown neither the willingness nor the ability to act together. Soon afterwards the intensification of the "Cold War" led to the formation of NATO and it was clear that the Western Powers would have liked to draw the Arab states into their anti-Soviet grouping. The Arab League decided that its seven members should "co-operate for the realisation of mutual defence and the maintenance of security and peace". A Treaty was signed on 13 April 1950, based on Article 51 of the UN Charter, laying down that aggression against one of the members was to be regarded as against them all. A Joint Defence Council, consisting of Ministers of Foreign Affairs and Defence, would operate under the supervision of the League Council. Decisions could be taken by a two-thirds majority. A Permanent Military Commission composed of representatives of the general staffs was charged with drawing up plans for joint defence and ways to implement them. A Supplementary Protocol established a Consultative Military Council of Chiefs of Staff. A Military Annex to the Treaty provided for the appointment of a Commander-in-Chief in the event of war but not in peace time although this was changed by the Cairo Summit of 1964 which set up the Unified Arab Command. The Yemen objected to some of the provisions and delayed its ratification for three years.

ARAB CO-OPERATION COUNCIL
After a meeting of their Prime Ministers in Amman, the Heads of State of four Arab countries ineligible to join any other regional organisation such as the Gulf Co-operation Council or the Arab Maghrib Union met on 16 February 1989 in Baghdad. Egypt, North Yemen and Jordan had all been strong supporters of Iraq in the Iran–Iraq War. They agreed to form the Arab Co-operation Council as an Arab organisation adhering to the Charter of the Arab League. Its objective was to "achieve the highest level of co-operation and solidarity . . . and gradually upgrade relations", working for gradual economic and monetary integration in a common market of 80 million people through practical measures allowing free movement of labour and capital within the bloc; they hoped to double trade between its members in a few years. There would be joint projects in transport, communications, finance, industry, culture, technology, tourism, social affairs, health and agriculture. It would encourage investment and joint ventures between public and private sectors within the group which others would be invited to join. They established a Supreme Council of Heads of State with Saddam Hussain as its first Chairman to meet annually and a Ministerial Council to meet every six months. The General Secretariat would be in Amman. They called for the withdrawal of Syrian troops from Lebanon. There were reports that a secret defence pact was also signed, causing some alarm in the Gulf States. At the second Summit, held in Alexandria in June an Egyptian Hilmi Mahmud Najjar, Chairman of the Egyptian Budget Committee, was appointed Secretary-General. Some travel restrictions were removed and it was agreed that citizens of member states should be given priority in recruitment for jobs. The third Summit, meeting in Sanaa in September saw the signing of 16 economic and trade agreements, a motion of support for the Palestine Liberation Organisation after receiving Yassir Arafat and a call for clearing the debris of war from the Shatt al-Arab. There were projects for a joint pharmaceutical industry, a joint airline and a railway linking Egypt, Jordan and Iraq. At the fourth Summit in Amman in February 1990 both Russia and America were condemned for the influx of Russian Jews into Israel and Iran for delaying a peace

settlement. There were agreements for co-operation in industry, oil and gas, health, air transport and tourism. South Yemen automatically joined with unification in May. There were numerous bilateral agreements, Iraq sent oil experts and Jordan teachers to Yemen which, gaining access to more advanced technology, profited most from the Organisation. In August 1990 Saddam Hussain invaded Kuwait and President Mubarak took the lead in calling the Cairo Summit which demanded his immediate withdrawal. This was the effective end of the ACC although both Jordan and Yemen opposed the deployment of Western troops in Arabia. In May 1992 Ali Abd Allah Salih tried to revive it in the hope that close links with Egypt would bring Yemen and Jordan back into favour with the victorious allies. He suggested that Egypt should host a Summit of the three of them: Iraq would not be invited but would attend subsequent meetings in Amman and Cairo. Mubarak, although willing to improve relations with Yemen and Jordan refused to countenance a revival of the ACC.

ARAB FUND FOR ECONOMIC AND SOCIAL DEVELOPMENT
AFESD was established in 1968 by the Economic Committee of the Arab League and began operations in 1973. Its original capital, which was later increased, was 400 million Kuwaiti Dinars, largely subscribed by Kuwait itself, Saudi Arabia, Libya and Algeria. It granted loans to the poorer Arab countries on easy terms and provided technical expertise. A considerable proportion went to the occupied West Bank but by 1991 it had made over 250 loans for such projects as roads in Yemen and Bahrain, irrigation in Morocco and Syria, iron ore production in Mauritania and a thermal power station in Jordan. Its report for 1992 stated that in that year it had agreed to lend $585.6 million towards 11 projects in 8 Arab states bringing its total since 1974 to $5,560 million.

ARAB HIGHER COMMITTEE
al-Lajnah al-Arabiyyah al-Ulya. In April 1936, at the beginning of the unrest which culminated in the Arab Rebellion, the Mufti of Jerusalem, Haj Amin al-Hussaini proposed that the six Arab groups in Palestine should form a united front as a spokesman for them all, Muslims and Christians. He became its President and its objectives were to end Jewish immigration, ban the transfer of Arab-owned land to Jews, end the Mandate and establish an autonomous government. Almost immediately it called for civil disobedience and organised strikes, boycotts and anti-Zionist propaganda. The Committee established relations with the independent Arab rulers such as Ibn Saud and the Amir Abd Allah. In October 1936, at their request, it called off the general strike of Arab workers that was paralysing the country. Contrary to their advice, however, it boycotted the Peel Commission until the very last moment. In July 1937 the more moderate members, led by Raghib al-Nashashibi and his National Defence Party left in a dispute over the attitude of the Committee towards the Peel Report and the increasing violence of the Arab Rebellion. In September 1937 it was officially banned on the grounds that it had instigated terrorism, including the murder of British

officials. The Mufti fled into exile and five of the other leaders were arrested and deported to the Seychelles where they remained until January 1939. The Committee functioned as best it could from abroad, rejecting the MacDonald White Paper. It was reconstituted with 12 members in Palestine after the war, claiming the right to represent the Arab population but stressing that it was not a continuation of the Committee that had been banned. The Arabs, however, continued, split between followers and opponents of the Mufti and members of the Istiqlal Party who established their own Arab Higher Front. In 1946 the Arab League, tired of the wrangling between the two Palestinian organisations, resolved to dissolve them both and reconstitute them as a new grouping. The Chairmanship was assigned to the Mufti but as he was unable to enter Palestine its effective leader was the Vice-Chairman, his kinsman Jamal al-Hussaini. He attended the Conference in London at which the Bevin Scheme was formulated and held discussions at the UN. He also gave evidence to the Anglo-American Committee. In December 1947 its Jaffa office was blown up by Jewish terrorists. Spurred on by the Mufti it revived its intransigence at the end, refusing a cease-fire in Jerusalem, but by that time it had become an irrelevance. It lingered on in Beirut, occasionally publishing propaganda material.

ARAB–ISLAMIC REPUBLIC (JERBAH DECLARATION) (1974)

From the time he seized power Colonel Qadafi made a series of determined efforts to merge Libya with another Arab state. By the end of 1973 the Federation of Arab Republics had clearly failed but already in December 1972 on a visit to Tunisia Qadafi had publicly called for its union with Libya. President Bourguiba had mocked him for youthful *naïveté* but in January 1974 agreed to meet him in Jerbah. On 12 January they agreed to merge as the Arab Islamic Republic with "a single constitution, flag, president, army, legislative, judicial and executive authorities". Bourguiba said that there would be a referendum to approve it on 18 January, although this might be postponed. He declared that the union would "change the course of history" and enable the Arabs to crush their enemies, particularly Israel. He hoped that Algeria and Mauritania and possibly Morocco might join. On 13 January the Tunisian Prime Minister Hedi Nouira hurried back from a visit to Iran and persuaded Bourguiba to dismiss the Foreign Minister Muhammad Masmoudi who was regarded as the architect of the merger and having tricked Bourguiba into signing it. It became clear that there were also divisions in the Libyan Revolution Command Council over its advisability. Later Nouira, declaring that he was not willing "to leap into the unknown" stated that it would take months to prepare for a detailed referendum. Bourguiba went to Switzerland for medical treatment and although Qadafi followed him there to press for implementation of the agreement, the Arab–Islamic Republic was clearly dead within 48 hours of its birth. Qadafi blamed the failure on President Boumédienne of Algeria who feared having a powerful neighbour.

ARAB LEAGUE

For two decades after the First World War there was little interest in Arab unity as the new states created by colonial rule pursued their individual struggles for independence. The Arab Rebellion in Palestine, however, attracted wider interest as was shown in the first meeting of leaders from Eastern Arab states in the Bludan Conference in 1937 and subsequently at the London Palestine Conference of 1939. During the war Anthony Eden's Mansion House Speech of 1941 provided a new impetus which led on to the Alexandria Protocol with its decision to establish a League of Arab States. The Arab League Pact of March 1945 set up a grouping of independent states with no powers to coerce its members. Independent Arab states had a right to join; unanimous decisions were binding upon all but majority ones only on those that voted for them. The supreme organ was the League Council, consisting of one representative of each state and scheduled to meet twice a year although a special meeting could be held at the request of two members. Permanent committees to deal with Cultural, Economic, Social, Legal, Communications, Information, Petroleum, Health, and Financial and Administrative matters were set up and in 1946 was added a Political Committee at Foreign Minister level. A permanent secretariat was formed in Cairo under Abd al-Rahman Azzam who had been the leading advocate of Arab unity and offices were opened in most major capitals. The original members were Egypt, Saudi Arabia, Trans-Jordan, Iraq, Lebanon and Yemen. Syria joined in February 1946, Libya in March 1953, Sudan in January 1956, Morocco and Tunisia in November 1958, Kuwait in July 1961, Algeria in August 1962, South Yemen in December 1967, Bahrain, Qatar and Oman in September 1971, the UAE in December 1971, Mauritania in November 1973, Somalia in February 1974 and Djibouti in September 1977. Palestine was represented at first by a nominated official until the Palestine Liberation Organisation was given observer status in 1964 and full membership in 1976. A number of specialised agencies dealing with matters varying from music to standardisation and tariffs have been created and also organisations such as the offices for the Arab Boycott of Israel, an Arab Development Bank and OAPEC. Despite the Arab Collective Security Treaty of 1950 the League has never established an effective body for military co-ordination owing to a lack of unanimity amongst its members. The main task of the League has been to endeavour to present a common Arab front to the world, particularly in the United Nations and in its first attempt to do this successfully urged independence for Lebanon and Syria. Its second major involvement was in the crisis that followed the murder of the Imam Yahya in February 1948: the League confined itself to sending a fact-finding mission which proved an irrelevance as his son Ahmad triumphed by force of arms. At the end of April 1948 the Military Committee discussed sending Arab armies to Palestine and on 12 May the League declared that it would set up a civil administration there. On 26 May it rejected a UN appeal for a cease-fire which it accepted on 1 June. The aftermath of the Palestine War brought the first internal dispute as King Abd Allah announced that the West

Bank had been incorporated into Jordan. His action was unanimously condemned but calls for his expulsion ended in June 1950 in a compromise formula. Soon after he came to power Nasser removed Azzam whom he considered too independently minded and replaced him by Abd al-Khaliq Hassouna, an administrator rather than politician, under whose regime the League became little more than an instrument of Egyptian policy. Countries at odds with Egypt such as Jordan or Saudi Arabia could expect little comfort from the League as Lebanon found after its complaints about Egyptian incursions in 1958 and, later in the same year, Tunisia after alleging that Nasser had encouraged the conspiracy of Salah Ben Yusuf to assassinate Bourguiba. Tunisia boycotted the League for three years – the first prolonged boycott. Its example was followed for two years by Abd al-Krim Qassim during the Kuwait–Iraq Dispute after the League had dispatched an Arab Security Force to the area. The League did, however, fulfil its role in keeping the Palestine question and the demands of the North African countries and Aden for independence before the UN. African rather than Arab leaders mediated between Morocco and Algeria in the Tindouf Dispute. In 1968 Tunisia again walked out, criticising Egyptian misuse of the League for its own purposes. The practice of regular meetings of Heads of State, starting with the Cairo Summit of 1964 somewhat reduced the importance of the League Council: the Yemen War was settled directly between Nasser and King Faysal. Most major decisions, such as that to launch the October War were taken bilaterally between states concerned. Others such as that to send the Arab Deterrent Security Force to Lebanon were taken at Summits: they were not debated within the format of the League. In June 1972 Mahmud Riad was nominated by the Egyptian Government to replace Hassouna. The general ineffectiveness of the League was shown by its failure despite efforts over many years to settle the Oman–South Yemen Dispute. The Arab states were deeply split by the policies of Anwar Sadat after whose visit to Jerusalem, Syria, Libya, South Yemen, Algeria and the PLO set up the Steadfastness Front which refused to attend Council meetings in Cairo. In July 1978 the League censured South Yemen for its part in the murder of Ahmad Ghashmi and for the presence of Soviet, Cuban and East German military personnel: in the absence of the Steadfastness Front it was not possible to achieve the unanimity necessary for its expulsion but its membership was suspended – the strongest punitive measure yet taken against any state but one which soon lapsed under the pressure of more important events. After the Camp David Agreement all the members except for Egypt, which had not been invited, met at the Baghdad Summit of November 1978 and, after giving Sadat an opportunity to repent, decided to move the Head Quarters of the League fom Cairo to Tunis and subsequently to expel Egypt. The League then elected a Tunisian, Chadli Klibi to replace Riad but he had the greatest difficulty in reorganising the League as Egypt simply refused to release the files or the funds which were held in a Cairo bank, maintaining that only the rump in Cairo had legitimacy. In the absence of Egypt, the most important Arab state, the League lost much of its credi-

bility and much of its routine work lapsed. The further divisions caused by the Iran–Iraq War made it still more difficult for the League to operate as a unity. The Casablanca Summit of May 1989, at which Egypt was readmitted, gave a new life to the League which had its first major success for many years when its Assistant Secretary-General, Lakhdar al-Ibrahimi, was the principal mediator in bringing about the Taif Parliament which provided a framework within which to settle the Lebanese civil war. It was determined to return the HQ to Cairo but there was considerable controversy over the timing of the move after the strong opposition of Husni Mubarak to the invasion of Kuwait by Saddam Hussain. The Cairo Summit of August 1990 was one of the least united in history. Before the transfer of the HQ took place, in September 1990 Klibi unexpectedly resigned, complaining that some Arab governments accorded him insufficient respect. Assad al-Assad, who had been appointed interim Secretary-General, announced at the end of October that the transfer had been completed.

ARAB LEGION

Following the establishment of the Amir Abd Allah in Amman and the creation of the state of Trans-Jordan there was a period of tribal unrest of which the Adwan Rebellion of 1923 was the most dangerous. There was the additional threat of invasion by the Ikhwan and many of the officers who commanded Abd Allah's followers were supporters of the Istiqlal, more interested in pan-Arabism than in the security of Trans-Jordan. A British officer, F. G. Peake who had taken part in camel warfare against Ali Dinar and in the Arab Revolt was sent to organise a security force which would be controlled and paid for by London. He established the Arab Legion which dealt with tribal unrest, collected taxes and established a skeleton of administration outside the towns. In 1925–26 the budget for the Legion was £140,000. By 1926 the force had grown to over 1,500. In 1926 a new force, the Trans-Jordan Frontier Force, directly controlled by the High Commissioner in Jerusalem, with all senior posts held by British officers, was created and took over the artillery, machine-guns, etc. of the Legion which was reduced to an almost static gendarmerie of less than 1,000 men. The TJFF proved ineffective, tribal raids into his Kingdom angered Ibn Saud, and in 1930 the Desert Patrol under the command of J. B. Glubb was set up as part of the Legion. This recruited bedouins who were trained into a most effective fighting force. In 1939 Glubb succeeded Peake and imposed his philosophy of mechanisation and mobility. He established a great personal dominance through intimate knowledge of his men and of their tribal background. There was a rapid expansion of the Legion which showed its efficiency in the operations against Rashid Ali al-Gilani and later in Syria; some were even sent to Sinai in case Rommel crossed the Suez Canal. By the end of the war the Legion had about 8,000 men, officered almost entirely by Arabs. There was a mechanised brigade and three regiments. It was regarded as an élite force and recruits could gain admission only after approval by three officers, two of whom had to be Arabs. Its costs were covered by a British subsidy of £9 million. In the Palestine War the Legion showed itself the most effective of the Arab armies, inflicting heavy casualties on the Israelis at Latrun and in Jerusalem. It was hampered, however, by the refusal of the British to supply enough ammunition or to allow, as a result of American pressure, its officers to play their full part and by the equivocal war-aims of the King. After the Rhodes Armistice the Legion fulfilled garrison duties on the West Bank where some saw it as "the Anglo-Hashemite Army of occupation". There were complaints that it did not take enough action against Israeli attacks and its failure to intervene when Qibya was destroyed caused much criticism. It was greatly expanded and by 1953 numbered about 20,000 men, fully equipped with tanks and artillery, while King Hussain took a keen interest in the creation of an air force. Some of its officers, however, particularly Major Ali Abu Nuwar, started to become involved in politics and there was strong feeling that Glubb was not giving them the same opportunities of those in other Arab armies. In March 1956 the King determined to dismiss him, holding to his decision despite urgent pleas from London and Glubb had to leave the next day. About half the British officers, those who had played a part in putting down the riots against the Baghdad Pact were also sent home. The title of the Force was changed to the Jordan Arab Army. It had played an important part in forming the state and had shown that very close comradeship was possible between Arabs and British officers, loyal both to their duty and to their own country. About 25–30 British officers remained after Glubb as trainers and advisers. They were dismissed during the Suez War entry.

ARAB LIBERATION FRONT

In 1968 the Syrian Baath Party founded al-Saiqa in order to have a Palestinian guerrilla group under its own control. In April 1969, for similar reasons, the rival Iraqi Baath Party founded the Arab Liberation Front. The name echoed Baathist ideals in stressing that the struggle against Israel concerned all the Arabs and not merely the Palestinians who were in a minority amongst its membership. The ALF was soon claiming victories in the West Bank but from the beginning it was opposed by Syria which refused to allow it to operate on its territory. Three hundred commandos were expelled to Jordan. The ALF lost credibility when the 12,000 Iraqi troops then stationed in Jordan did not intervene to help it during Black September but some 500 survivors set up camps in South Lebanon. It was represented on the Executive Council of the Palestine Liberation Organisation and joined the Rejection Front on its formation in 1974. It carried out some operations in the Occupied Territories and had several clashes with UNIFIL. After the outbreak of the Iran–Iraq War the ALF came into conflict with Shiah militias such as Amal and Hizbullah. Its leader Abd al-Wahhab Kayyal was murdered in Beirut in December 1980 and succeeded by Abd al-Rahim Ahmad. Its Lebanese bases were frequently attacked by the Israelis until August 1982 when its members were evacuated from Beirut, going mostly to Iraq and Tunis. Subsequently it did not join the radicals against Yassir Arafat and was generally regarded as a moderate force, working for reconciliation.

ARAB MAGHREB UNION

After the signing of the Arab Maghreb Unity Treaty in Marrakesh in February 1989 Hassan II hoped that the next six months would see rapid progress in dismantling customs and immigration controls. The first activity of the AMU was, however, to send a delegation to Nouakchott to mediate in a dispute between Mauritania and Senegal. In June a follow-up committee met in Rabat and the inaugural session of the Consultative Assembly held in Algiers called for intensification of contacts between professional and political groups. Service Ministers such as those of Transport and Post conferred. In October the Foreign Ministers agreed to establish four ministerial committees to integrate economic and financial policies and consider food, security, infrastructure and human resources. In October the Consultative Assembly met in Rabat and the Foreign Ministers prepared for the *First Summit* which was held in Tunis in January 1990. There had been some doubts as to whether Qadafi would attend and the meeting had twice to be postponed. It was agreed to extend defence co-operation, to double the Consultative Assembly to twenty representatives of each state and to establish a permanent headquarters instead of a secretariat attached to the Chairman but a Tunisian proposal to extend his term to a year was rejected. Differences over the Western Sahara War were ignored but the Summit called for a Middle East Peace Conference and better treatment for over two million North Africans in Europe. Also in January it was agreed to unite Employers' Organisations. In February the Tunisians proposed a single energy market. In March a unified identity card was approved. In April the Tunisians called for a special fund to create local jobs to reduce emigration. In May it was agreed to co-ordinate national airlines as a step towards a joint airline and to improve rail links: a competition for a flag and an anthem was announced. The *Second Summit* met in Algiers in July 1990 with the rise of Islamic militancy in the front of leaders' minds. It was agreed to establish a unified tariff by 1991 and a "genuine customs union" by 1995 although only 6% of foreign trade was with each other. Agreements on double taxation and safeguarding investments were made. It still proved impossible to agree on a headquarters. After the occupation of Kuwait in August the AMU Foreign Ministers met several times but could not agree on a common policy although they rejected the use of force in inter-Arab disputes: the crisis proved that although the AMU could not act as a body it did not disintegrate. In January 1991 a joint AMU initiative to prevent a Gulf War was rejected by the Western Allies. Qadafi twice held meetings in Libya with Egyptian, Sudanese and Syrian leaders to which his AMU partners were not invited and there were inevitable speculations that North Africa took second place in his plans. In October 1990 AMU Foreign Ministers had agreed with the Western Mediterranean members of the EC to promote multilateral co-operation and in November they went as a group to Brussels to discuss financial aid and trade concessions. A Charter for the Environment was promulgated. The *Third Summit* was postponed and when it assembled on 10 March 1991 at Ras Lanuf, 600 km east of Tripoli, King Hassan was absent as he had requested a further postponement to study the consequences of the Gulf War. It was decided to establish a foreign trade bank with $100 million subscribed by each member to fund joint ventures and work towards an integrated economy. A Court with two judges from each state was created. There were plans for a further Summit in Benghazi in June but it was cancelled following a political crisis in Algeria. In July Mauritania, because of ethnic tensions and political unrest, gave up its turn to host a meeting so the *Fourth Summit* was held in Casablanca in September 1991 amidst feelings that there had recently been no visible progress. Major Jalloud represented Qadafi. Organisational decisions were finally taken and it was agreed that unanimity would no longer be needed. The permanent secretariat would be based in Morocco with a Tunisian chief, the Consultative Assembly would be in Algiers, the Supreme Court in Mauritania, the Investment Bank in Tunis and the Academy of Science in Libya. The Summit called for an end to sanctions against Iraq and Libya and for a Charter of Rights for North Africans in Europe. It condemned Israeli intransigence and agreed to be represented at the Madrid Peace Conference. In October the Tunisian Muhammad Amamou was appointed Secretary-General. Also in October the AMU began in Algiers what was to be a series of meetings with the Western Mediterranean members of the EC with Malta present as an observer – the "Five plus Five" but the sanctions imposed on Libya after its refusal to surrender the Lockerbie suspects prevented concrete developments. In December Foreign, Economic and Agricultural Ministers discussed closer co-operation and plans for a Maghreb Autoroute were agreed although there were no signs of action two years later. The *Fifth Summit* was twice postponed because the Libyans, resenting the lack of support over sanctions, made difficulties over attending with Qadafi threatening to leave the Union. When it assembled in Nouakchott in November 1992 he was absent and King Hassan was represented by Prime Minister Lamrani. The communiqué condemned all extremism opposed to "civilisation and secular traditions". Amamou was given a proper budget of $1,700 million for a staff of 40. A year's tenure for the Chairman was finally agreed. Progress had been slow for Morocco was preoccupied with Europe, Libya with Egypt, Mauritania with West Africa and Algeria with Islamic militants and only Ben Ali had attended every Summit and Tunisia was the only country to have ratified all 15 conventions. Morocco and Algeria were not on good terms after the assassination of Boudiaf. The Committee of Defence Ministers had never met and the Consultative Council was paralysed by the absence of an Algerian Parliament. In January 1993 Ben Ali, again Chairman, called for a more determined effort to co-ordinate strategy towards Islamic militancy and towards the EC and for a revival of the Five plus Five. In March a joint driving licence was agreed. In April the first Population Conference forecast that the population of the five states would exceed 60 million by AD 2005, causing further problems. In September Qadafi upset Tunisia by saying that

there was no reason for its existence and that it should be absorbed in Libya.

ARAB MAGHREB UNITY TREATY (1989)

Upon achieving independence Morocco, Tunisia and Algeria all included in their Constitutions aspirations towards Maghreb Unity and this was echoed in the communiqué of the Tangier Conference of 1958. Their economies fitted well with Morocco, the only one without oil having a surplus of agricultural and consumer goods which the others lacked. In practice there turned out to be numerous problems over frontiers, most notably the Tindouf Dispute between Morocco and Algeria. In January 1970 a Treaty of good neighbourliness, brotherhood and co-operation was signed between Algeria and Tunisia which was followed by agreements for economic co-operation. The incessant desire of Colonel Qadafi to find a partner led to the aborted Arab–Islamic Republic in January 1974 and an agreement with Algeria in December 1975 that he interpreted as a prelude to union. The possibility of a united North Africa was then set back by the Western Sahara War with Algeria and Libya supporting Polisario against Morocco and Mauritania. In the late 1970s there was a series of disputes between Tunisia and Libya over the continental shelf and emigrant workers. The adherence of Mediterranean states to the EEC gave the North African states a new need to negotiate with it as a bloc rather than as isolated individuals and in March 1983 Algerian and Tunisia signed a Treaty of Fraternity and Concord to which in December Mauritania adhered. In August 1984 the Oudjda Declaration brought about an astonishing union of Morocco and Libya which lasted on paper for two years. The Tunisian Government tried repeatedly to organise a Summit of all five Maghreb states but was always frustrated by the insistance of Algeria that Polisario should participate which would inevitably have meant that the proceedings would be boycotted by Morocco. In April 1986 delegates from the ruling parties of Algeria and Tunisia and the two main parties in Morocco met in Tangier and agreed to establish a Consultative Committee and in June a call for a Maghreb Constitutional Assembly was made by King Hassan II. In February 1987 the Tunisian Premier Rashid Sfar visited Algiers and Rabat to press for unity and in June the Central Committee of the Algerian Front de Libération Nationale stated that a Maghreb Union was "imperative and answered the logic of history". In July Hassan felt so isolated in North Africa that he publicly applied for membership of the EEC, although he was later to say that he did not regard this as conflicting with membership of a possible Maghreb Union. Throughout 1987 Qadafi urgently wooed Algeria, predicting union by the end of the year and telling its National Assembly in October that he would sign whatever terms it drafted: in December four bilateral treaties dealing with manpower, culture, social insurance and tourism were signed between the two states. Relations between Libya and Tunisia were no longer hostile after the fall of Bourguiba in November 1987. President Chadli would have liked a Union which excluded Morocco but Tunisia was unwilling to be compelled to take sides between Algeria and Morocco. In December 1987 the

Foreign Ministers of Algeria, Tunisia and Mauritania discussed extending their Treaty to include all five states. Chadli, visiting Tunis and Tripoli in January 1988, wished to preside over a Summit but this would have lacked conviction without Hassan and diplomatic relations, severed in 1975, were resumed in May. Immediately afterwards Qadafi and Ben Ali called for a Maghreb without frontiers, agreed on a common identity card, linkage of national grids and other utilities and settled the problem of the continental shelf. After the main Algiers Summit in early June the North African Heads of State met at Chadli's Zeralda Palace in the presence of King Fahd who had done much to reconcile Morocco and Algeria. A committee of Foreign Ministers and five sub-committees, each chaired by one of the states, were established to draft proposals for common economic, social, financial, information and cultural policies. The following month Hassan said that the Maghreb, with its common religion, language and history of struggle against colonialism could unite more quickly than Europe which was scheduled to be transformed by the end of 1992. Also in July Algeria and Libya agreed to hold a referendum on a merger. In October the Foreign Ministers meeting in Fez agreed that Morocco should draw up a document on a coherent structure to co-ordinate political as well as economic policies. In December further technical agreements were made between Libya and Tunisia. There were differences between Qadafi, with some support from Tunisia, who wanted an immediate united state which would include Chad, Mali, Niger and the Sudan and Chadli who wanted gradual progress towards an Arab union. Compromises were reached and the Maghreb Unity Treaty was signed in Marrakesh on 17 February 1989 by Hassan II, Chadli, Ben Ali and Maaouya ould Sid Ahmad of Mauritania and Qadafi which declared that "the peoples of the Maghreb have close links based on common history, religion and language" and wished for a union to advance towards more complete integration. It would enable them to play a bigger part in the world and was seen as a step towards complete Arab unity and a greater union of Arab and African countries. The Union would consolidate fraternal links, ensure progress and the defence of people's rights, keep peace based on justice, work out common policies in various fields and lead to the free circulation of people, trade and capital. There would be exchanges of teachers and students, co-ordination of diplomacy, defence, cultural and economic policies. There would be a Presidential Council of Heads of State which would meet every six months with a rotating chairman, beginning with the King, and it would be the sole decision-making body and had to be unanimous. The Prime Ministers would meet as necessary. A Minister for the Union would be appointed by each country and there would be a General Secretariat under the Moroccan nominee Muhammad Seqat. A Consultative Assembly of ten (later expanded to twenty) from each country would meet once a year and if summoned by the Presidential Council and a Court of Justice of two from each country would be set up. Each state would have freedom to make treaties with outside countries. Aggression against one would be against all – a provision that delighted Qadafi who saw himself

pursued by the spite of the USA. Members would not support each other's dissidents – a provision which led to a diminution of Algerian support for Polisario. By June 1989 the Treaty had been ratified by all the partners.

ARAB MILITARY INDUSTRIES ORGANISATION

The Rabat Summit of 1974 discussed the creation of an Arab-controlled weapons industry to lessen dependence upon external powers. In May 1975 an Establishment based in Cairo was created with an initial capital of $1,040 million subscribed equally by Egypt, Saudi Arabia, the UAE and Qatar, not subject to the laws and tax regulations of the member states. It aimed to build a modern military industrial complex to manufacture sophisticated weapons under licence from Western firms, at reasonable prices with the ultimate aim of Arab self-sufficiency. Work started on jeeps, an adaptation of a British anti-tank missile and jet aircraft. In October 1978 its Director-General, Ashraf Marwan, who had marriage connections with the family of Nasser was dismissed for corruption. In May 1979, after the decision of the Baghdad Summit to end economic relations with Egypt the three Gulf States declared their intention of liquidating the AMIO. The Egyptians declared the decision illegal and said that it would deprive them of expected investments of $1,500 million and endanger 15,000 jobs. Sadat retained the name of AMIO and appointed himself Chairman of a purely Egyptian organisation. In the 1980s it produced about $100 million worth of arms annually, mostly for the Egyptian forces, assembling under licence French aircraft with local components.

ARAB MONETARY FUND

The AMF was established in 1976 by the Economic Committee of the Arab League as a step towards Arab economic integration. Previously the Central Bank officials of the OAPEC countries had recommended the creation of a unit of account for joint economic projects. This, called the Arab Accounts Dinar, was to be based on a basket of Arab currencies, weighted according to foreign trade, gross national income and financial reserves. This Dinar was equivalent to 3 IMF Special Drawing Rights. Each country paid its share in convertible currencies. The AMF worked to promote stability of exchange rates between Arab countries, assist members in balance of payments difficulties, co-ordinated the policies of members towards monetary problems and provided technical assistance to banking institutions. It had the ultimate aim of a unified Arab currency. It made loans to members in balance of payment difficulties at favourable rates of interest, repayable within three years. In 1987 the first Managing Director of the Fund was convicted of financial malpractices by a court in Abu Dhabi where the AMF is based. In May 1990 the AMF participated in the creation of the Arab Trade Financing Programme to increase inter-Arab trade in goods and services but excluding petroleum.

ARAB NATIONALIST MOVEMENT

Harakat al-Qawmiyyin al-Arab. After the Palestine War young Arabs, particularly students at the American University of Beirut, were profoundly impressed by the thesis of Dr Constantine Zurayq that Zionism could only be defeated by a total, radical transformation of Arab society. Almost equally important were the writings of Sati al-Husri on Arabism. Led by the medical students, George Habash and Wadia Haddad from Palestine and Ahmad al-Khatib from Kuwait and a Syrian political scientist Hani al-Hindi, they converted the supposedly non-political society *al-Urwah al-Wuthqa* into a group dedicated to "Unity, Liberation and Vengeance". Arab unity was the only path to the liberation of which they were the vanguard. They were equally hostile to Zionism and to the corrupt, reactionary regimes that had failed to protect Palestinian rights and called for a united, revolutionary Arab state. Although opposed to communism as an ideology they recommended that the Arabs should accept Russian help. Cells spread rapidly in schools and universities in Lebanon and as the founders graduated, in the places where they worked. The rise of Nasser gave them a charismatic figure to follow even at the expense of their ideological and organisational independence. After demonstrations against the Baghdad Pact the *al-Urwah* was banned and students who were expelled were welcomed in Egypt. Early in 1956 the first National Conference transformed a network of autonomous groups into a hierarchical system. The attempt of Habash to establish the Movement in Jordan was crushed after the imposition of martial law but Khatib was more successful in Kuwait; eventually he and three of his colleagues became Members of Parliament. There was no actual ANM structure in Egypt but student members there managed to convert exiles such as Qahtan al-Shaabi. Relations with the Baath Party which was notionally socialist, were usually strained as the ANM was purely nationalist and supported Nasser. The ANM welcomed any move towards Arab unity, even the Arab Federation and was enthusiastic about the establishment of the United Arab Republic. The breakup of the UAR was a profound shock to Arab Nationalists and caused urgent reappraisals within the Movement. Led by the Lebanese Muhsin Ibrahim, editor of the official journal *al-Hurriyah*, there was a strong call for a shift to the left and later for absorption in the wider Nasserist movement. This was resisted by Habash and Khatib as inapplicable in Jordan and Kuwait and the ANM practically ceased to exist there. The seizure of power by the Baath in both Syria and Iraq early in 1963 crushed the ANM in those countries despite efforts at a come-back in alliance with Nasserite officers. After the June War and the consequent disillusionment with Nasser, the ANM effectively disintegrated as a pan-Arab organisation. Its leftward drift alienated the bourgeoisie without winning the workers and peasants and all that remained was a few Marxist intellectuals. Habash and Nayif Hawatma formed a Palestine Regional Command that was later to become the Popular Front for the Liberation of Palestine. Only in South Yemen where al-Shaabi was President until the Glorious Corrective Move of June 1969 did the ANM hold power: he maintained contact with other former members. The Dhofar Liberation Front, an offshoot of the ANM, remained active under various names until the 1980s but was largely isolated. A dozen ANM members were imprisoned in Libya for subversion in February 1968. The Lebanese section was amongst the leftist groups legalised in August 1970 by Kamal Jumblatt with whose Progressive Socialist Party it had long collaborated but its membership was later swallowed up in other groups. The failure of the ANM showed that the time had not come for Arab unity as the states, although artificially created after the First World War, had taken on a life of their own with strong interest groups committed to their preservation and entanglements with outside powers that limited their freedom of action. Perhaps its main achievement was to keep alive interest in Palestine between the débâcle of 1948 and the creation of the Palestine Liberation Organisation in 1964.

ARAB NATIONAL UNION

Political parties were banned in Jordan upon the declaration of martial law in 1957 but in September 1971 King Hussain announced the creation of a Jordanian National Union which would be the only authorised political organisation and represent both East and West Banks. A committee of 300 was set up to draft a charter which stated that Jordan was a constitutional monarchy and an integral part of the Arab nation. Attempts to divide East and West Banks were "treasonable". It promised freedom of expression, work for a better economic, cultural and social future and the solution of problems "through democratic methods based on scientific and realistic analysis" rather than through force. Members of the "childish Left and senile Right" and other "imported ideologies" would be barred. After the announcement of the United Arab Kingdom plan in March 1972 the JNU was renamed the Arab National Union. In April 1974 the ANU was reorganised as the King dismissed its Secretary-General and greatly reduced the numbers of its Executive and Council. In April 1976 the ANU was dissolved. At its peak it had perhaps 100,000 members but little political importance.

ARAB PEOPLE'S CONFERENCE (1983)

Held in Tripoli, 1–5 February 1983, the Arab People's Conference was attended by Ali Nasir Muhammad, "revolutionary leaders" and members of legal oppositions from Morocco, Jordan, the Sudan, Kuwait, Tunisia and the Lebanon. Three hundred and fifty deputies representing 235 organisations were reported to have attended. Many issues were aired: that the Gulf nations impose an oil embargo on the US; that Libya arm Palestinian and the Lebanese forces; an agreement not to fight the regime in Iran. Delegates highlighted the impotence shown in Lebanon, and spoke of the need for a pan-Arab force to support people's struggles and to oppose racist, fascist Zionist organisations which threatened Arab unity. Pan-Arab support was demanded for national forces in Iraq, Jordan, Sudan, Somalia and Polisrio, and revolutionary forces were urged to unite with Syria and Libya against Zionism and with South Yemen against imperialist and reactionary plots.

ARAB REBELLION

After Zionist pressure had secured the nullification of the Passfield White Paper the Arabs of Palestine came to feel that they had no political means of making their voices heard and that their interests were disregarded in London. The vast increase in Jewish immigration (60,000 in one year) following the coming of power of Hitler added to their worries. In November 1935, at a time when Iraq had gained its independence and Syria and Lebanon appeared on the point of doing so, Arab leaders in Palestine put forward demands for a democratic government, a ban on transfers of land from Arabs to Jews and the immediate stopping of immigration. Some concessions were made but the discussion of the establishment of a Legislative Council was cut short by Zionist objections to it. During this time a Syrian refugee Izz al-Din al-Qassam led a guerrilla band in the hills until he was killed by the police near Janin; many saw him as an inspiration. In April 1936 there was considerable inter-communal strife, enflamed by rumours, with killings, attacks on vehicles, etc. on both sides. The Arab leaders proclaimed a general strike, scheduled to last six months, and this proved extremely effective and was accompanied by spontaneous assaults on Jews and destruction of their crops. Simultaneously armed groups of Arabs took to the hills and raided government installations. The adventurer Fawzi al-Qawukji attempted to impose himself as Commander-in-Chief and achieved some successes so that the British garrison had to be doubled to 20,000 men. The recently formed Arab Higher Committee attempted to direct the activities of their followers until in October at the request of Ibn Saud and other independent Arab rulers they called off the strike. There were indications that some at least of their demands would be met. The guerrilla bands dispersed and their leaders including Qawukji fled abroad. During this period 37 members of the security forces, 82 Jews and an unknown number of Arabs were killed. In July 1937 the British Government published the Peel Report which recommended partition which would have left large numbers of Arabs either living under Jewish rule or being resettled. There were sporadic terrorist incidents, security deteriorated and a senior British official was murdered by Arabs. In the autumn the Rebellion flared up again and in October the Arab Higher Committee was banned and the Mufti of Jerusalem Haj Amin al-Hussaini escaped into exile. There were at times about 1,500 armed Arabs, operating mostly in Galilee and Samaria, attacking the British and the Jews in a series of skirmishes that had some of the features of a peasant uprising and some of a people's revolutionary war. There was no sophisticated organisation and little liaison between groups, indeed there was often violent fighting between them. Many were poorly armed with pre-war weapons but the Arab police, anticipating that there might be an independent government, could not afford to be too zealous. It was estimated that the total killed in 1937 was less than 100. The worst year was 1938 in which there were over 5,000 incidents and those killed included about 70 Britons, 100 Palestinian members of the security forces, 200 Jews, 450 Arab civilians and over 1,000 armed Arab rebels. About 100 Arabs were hanged after conviction by military courts. For a time a large part of the country including Jaffa and Hebron was effectively outside government control. During that year, after much wrangling between the British political authorities, reluctant to use force, and the military, reinforcements were brought in and effective security measures with curfews and passes, stopping just short of martial law, were introduced. In a series of clashes gang after gang was wiped out and the killing of the last leader in March 1939 meant the effective end of the rebellion and in July detainees were released and restrictions relaxed. During the first six months of 1939 219 Arabs were killed by the security forces, 260 Arabs by other Arabs and 87 Jews by Arabs. Like the Spanish Civil War, with which it almost exactly coincided, the Arab Rebellion marked a changing point in history. In the decade before 1914 there had been hopes of an Arab nation but after these were disappointed in the Peace Settlement, there had been little thought of unity as Syria, Iraq, Egypt and other countries became preoccupied with their own local struggles for independence. The question of Palestine gave them a new common interest as was shown by pan-Arab gatherings such as the Bludan Conference and the Arab Parliamentary Congress. At the same time the Jews, most of whom had hoped to live as peaceful agriculturalists, were made to realise the necessity of their own armed forces and, inspired by Captain Orde Wingate, formed anti-terrorist squads that provided the nucleus for the Israeli Army.

ARAB REVOLT

During the reign of Sultan Abd al-Hamid the Arabs could hope for an increasing share in the government of the Ottoman Empire and considerable regional autonomy but the centralisation and Turcification of the Committee of Union and Progress showed that they were condemned to a minor role. Their disappointment took different forms. In Istanbul there were secret societies such as the Qahtaniyyah out of which came a grouping of army officers, the Ahd. In Damascus the Fatat consisted of young nationalists, many of them former students in Paris or Istanbul. Meanwhile the Imam Yahya, Muhammad b. Ali al-Idrisi of Asir and Shaykh Mubarak b. Sabah al-Sabah of Kuwait had gained practical autonomy and in December 1913 the British Ambassador reported a rumour that Sharif Hussain of Mecca, Ibn Saud, Thalib al-Naqib and the Regent of Saud b. Abd al-Aziz al-Rashid were planning a meeting in Kuwait to co-ordinate a revolt in which they hoped for British support. Sharif Hussain established links with the Ahd and Fatat groups through his sons Abd Allah and Faysal and in April 1914 sent Abd Allah to Cairo to see Lord Kitchener to ask if British aid would be forthcoming in the event of an Arab Revolt. As London and Istanbul were at peace, no promise could be made but in September with Britain at war with Germany and hostilities with Turkey looming, Kitchener sent a message to Abd Allah asking what would be the attitude of the Sharif if the Turks tried to force him into war against Britain; he received the reply that the Arabs would rise if guaranteed support. Kitchener replied that Britain would "provide every assistance against external aggression" and dangling the hope of the Caliphate. However when war was declared in October the majority of the Arabs supported the Turks, none deserted during the fighting on the Suez Canal, and it was not until the hanging of nationalists in Damascus and Beirut by Jamal Pasha in May 1915 that their attitude changed. In London the India Office argued that Ibn Saud should be supported as the Arab leader while the Foreign Office, pressed by Sir Reginald Wingate in Khartoum, urged that it was rather the Sharif with his links with the Syrian nationalists and whose religious status could lend dangerous credibility to a Turkish declaration of *jihad* who should receive the British backing. The Imam Yahya continued loyal to the Turks throughout the war while Ibn Saud was heavily involved in his own battles against the Al Rashid and the Ajman but in May 1915 the Idrisi became the first Arab leader to agree to attack the Turks in return for a subsidy. In July 1915 a letter in which the Sharif claimed to speak for all the Arabs initiated the Hussain–McMahon Correspondence which went on slowly until October when an Iraqi officer of the Turkish army, Sharif Muhammad Faruqi deserted at Gallipoli and was hurried to Cairo with a speed that gives the impression that he had been expected. He convinced the British that unless they accepted the demands of the Sharif, the full backing of the Arab nationalists would be given to the Germans. An agreement was reached and in January 1916 McMahon wrote that he would leave the timing of the rising to the Sharif. In March the Sharif offered the Turks to mobilise the tribes for *jihad* in return for amnesty for nationalists and hereditary amirates for his sons. There was then alarm about the appearance of a German mission in the Hijaz and the loss of some documents caused the Sharif to fear that his dealings with the British would be discovered and in May 1916 3,000 picked Turkish troops arrived in Medina to march through the Hijaz to reinforce those besieging Aden. These events and the difficulty and expense of holding his men together forced the Sharif into action and on 10 June he initiated the Revolt by firing a rifle shot from his palace in Mecca. His subsequent proclamation was couched in religious and not in nationalist terms. Mecca was quickly liberated and so was Jiddah with the help of the Royal Navy. Ta'if resisted for some time against Abd Allah while the Arabs failed completely at Medina where Fakhri Pasha held out until after the Armistice. In November 1916 there occurred the Rabigh Crisis when for a time it appeared that the Turks might be able to recapture Mecca and end the Revolt. The capture of Wijh in January 1917 removed the danger to Mecca and provided a base for Faysal, commanding a mixed force of regulars, mostly deserters from the Turkish army, and tribesmen whose blood-feuds he had to settle as he advanced; large sums in gold were provided by the British for the task. Operations were hampered by the obstruction of the French who had been promised control of Syria under the Sykes–Picot Agreement and by the intrigues of Hussain who became jealous of the successes and increasing independence shown by his sons. Helped by the advice of his Liaison Officer T. E. Lawrence, Faysal adopted the strategy of isolating Medina where the garrison of 23,000 was too strong to overrun by cutting the Hijaz

Railway, the first attack on which occurred in March 1917. In July the capture of Aqaba enabled operations to start outside the Hijaz. The war became less irregular and more orthodox and operations were co-ordinated with the British army which had for a long time been held up in Sinai. In November Jerusalem was liberated and in January 1918 there was a major battle at Tafilah in which the Turks suffered a defeat at the hands of the Arabs. Subsequently the Arabs operated as the right-wing of the British army east of the Jordan, helping Field Marshal Allenby by giving the misleading impression that he intended his main advance should be there. In May the Sharif, alarmed by the publication of Sykes–Picot and the Balfour Declaration made a last attempt to treat with the Turks but in June the Declaration to the Seven promised "complete and sovereign independence" for all the territories liberated by the Arabs themselves. Spurred by this Faysal's troops were the first to enter Damascus on 1 October. It was estimated that about 120,000 Arabs at different times took part in the fighting but Lawrence said that the number of regulars never exceeded 9,000. The British provided about £11 million as well as all the arms and ammunition, and naval and air support. The Revolt left the Hashemites the main spokesmen for Arab nationalism and made the reputations of many such as Jafar al-Askari and Nuri al-Said who showed military gifts. It also secured the Arabs a place at the Peace Conference which was denied to Egypt. The Arabs were greatly disappointed that Syria, Palestine and Iraq were not awarded to them and found it difficult to realise that, important although the Revolt had been to them, it was in global terms, as Lawrence said, "the side-show of a side-show": the war had been won in France where the number of Britons killed in a day on the Somme was greater than that of all the Arabs who fought against the Turks.

ARABSAT

The first Arab satellite earth station, linked to world networks, was opened in Bahrain in 1969 and in 1976 the Arab League set up an Agency to improve telephone, telex, data transmission and radio and television between member states. It was based on Riyadh and in February 1985 its first satellite built by the French Aerospatiale was launched from French Guiana. The first 598-kilogram satellite failed to work but a second, taken up in June by the American space shuttle *Discovery* proved successful. Amongst the crew of the shuttle was the first Arab astronaut, a grandson of Ibn Saud, Prince Sultan b. Salman. It provided a broadcasting channel and 10,000 telephone circuits. A second satellite designed as a reserve was leased to India. In 1990 the organisation was netting $30 million a year but did not expect to be really profitable until 1995.

ARAB SOCIALIST CONGRESS (1967)

The first Arab Socialist Congress opened in Algiers on 21 May 1967 with 100 delegates representing most Arab countries apart from Iraq, Tunisia and Yemen. There was a delegation from the Front for the Liberation of Occupied South Yemen. In a message President Nasser welcomed "a valuable opportunity for an exchanges between all progressive forces". After a week of routine denunciations of colonialism, imperialism and reaction, castigation of the USA for supporting Israel and reactionary regimes and praise for the Communist Bloc it was decided to plan for permanent institutions based on Algiers, to consider publishing a socialist review and to hold a second conference in Damascus. The outbreak of the June War the following week provided Arab governments with more important things to do and nothing further seems to have been heard of the Socialist Congress.

ARAB SOCIALIST UNION (Egypt)

Despite the failure of the Liberation Rally and the National Union, Nasser never understood that a successful political movement cannot be imposed by a government but can only grow from a few committed members. After the break up of the United Arab Republic he made his third attempt to form an organisation that would give him vigorous support and galvanise the masses behind him without expecting to receive any share in power. The Arab Socialist Union for "the working masses . . . peasants, workers, intellectuals, soldiers and national capitalists in a stage of socialist transformation" started with four million members. At the same time it was to form an élite vanguard, isolate reactionaries, melt class differences and attract progressives in other Arab countries away from the Nasser's *bête noire*, the Baath Party. It would also serve as a guide to national feeling, spy on potential dissidents and provide political indoctrination. From 7,000 village and urban districts representatives were sent to regional committees whose delegates formed district committees which elected the national leadership. Membership was not compulsory but no one who was not an ASU member could exercise a profession such as journalist and the ASU owned all newspapers and periodicals. Its Executive nominated the candidates for election to the National Assembly. In the 1963 Cairo Unity Talks Nasser was able to fend off Iraqi and Syrian requests for unity by insisting that their Baathists be eventually absorbed in the ASU. In April 1965 the Egyptian Communist Party dissolved itself and its members joined the ASU where, as activists, they acquired some influence. Nasser himself was its first Secretary-General but in September 1965 he handed over the office to Ali Sabri. Sabri, generally regarded as one of the most left wing of Nasser's entourage had no independent power base so he concentrated, with the help of the communists, in building the power and influence of the ASU so that it should become, in his words, "the spine of every activity in society". In April 1966 the truculence of one of its officials engaged in land reform led to his murder which was followed by the establishment of the Committee for the Liquidation of Feudalism which challenged traditional authority in the countryside and conducted a wholesale persecution of those disliked by Party members. The ASU started to claim the right to intervene in matters affecting the army, the trade unions and the bureaucracy and it acquired youth organisations and study centres. In about 1966 Nasser, fearing that the ASU might become a power centre that could challenge him and at the same time feeling that he might need it to counterbalance the army from whose affairs Field Marshal Amer was trying

to exclude him, established a secret organisation under Sharawi Jumaa of utterly dependable loyalists within it. When, during the June War, Nasser resigned, it was the task of the ASU to get the crowds on to the street to demand he stay in power. Shortly afterwards he resumed the Secretary-Generalship, perhaps as a counterbalance to the sullen and resentful armed forces, but this did not prevent Hassanain Haykal stating in August 1967 that the ASU was trying to take over the Government. In January 1968 Nasser reappointed Sabri but two months later in the March 30 Programme he demanded reforms in the Party with elections for Committees even to the previously appointed Supreme Executive. In May he replaced all four senior executives and in October 1968 the President defined the duties of its central Committee as implementing decisions of its Congress, laying down broad lines of internal and foreign policy, debating the national economic plan and that it would be in continuous session until "the elimination of the consequences of the Israeli aggression". In July 1969 Nasser chose the ASU Congress of 1,700 members to make a major speech on the state of the nation and to propose further measures of land reform. In September Sabri, who had been caught smuggling, was dismissed and replaced by Sharawi Jumaa, who being with Nasser the only man to hold office in Party and State, was clearly one of the most important men in the country. After the death of Nasser it was the endorsement of the Central Committee that made Sadat his successor. He appointed himself as Chairman and Abd al-Muhsin Abu al-Nur, a former General and Deputy Prime Minister, as Secretary-General. The ASU was then the scene of fierce infighting as supporters of Sabri tried to press left-wing policies on Sadat and for a time it seemed that they might prevail. The announcement in mid-April 1971 that Egypt was to join Libya and Syria in a Federation of Arab Republics brought matters to a head. In May leaders of the ASU laid on a mass demonstration at Helwan to frighten the President. Sabri, Jumaa and Abu al-Nur were arrested after a police officer gave Sadat taped evidence that they were plotting his overthrow and all received long prison sentences; 67 others were also jailed. Sadat declared that the ASU elections of 1968 had been rigged and new ones were held in July followed by constitutional reforms that abolished the post of Secretary-General. These were followed by further changes in February 1972 and Sadat's close ally Saiyyid Marai was put in charge with orders to weaken its potential for opposition. In August 1974 Sadat issued a 7,000 word paper in which he criticised the ASU for being only nominally voluntary as it was impossible to obtain important jobs without membership, for permitting power centres to impose their own notions and for being too intimately linked to the Government to furnish constructive criticism and he later said that he had no objection to rightists, centrists and leftists forming their own "platforms" or "pulpits" (*manabir*) to express their viewpoints within the ASU. A Socialist Democratic (led by the President's brother-in-law Mahmud Abu Wafia) and a Free Democratic (led by Mustafa Kamil Murad, a former member of the Wafd) Platforms were set up in October 1975: the former called for adherence to socialism and justice in the distribution of the national wealth and the latter for restricting the public sector to infrastructure and strategic industries and the introduction of private capital elsewhere, freedom of judiciary and the press. Sadat stated that he had no objection to these developing into separate parties. Three Platforms were licensed in February 1976, the Centre (the Arab Socialist Organisation) under the Prime Minister Mamduh Salim, the Right (Socialist Liberals) under Murad and the Left (National Progressive Union) under the former Free Officer Khalid Mohieddin. In elections in October they won respectively 280, 12 and 2 seats while 48 Independents were successful. This was followed in November by their formal recognition as separate political parties. Although losing its monopoly the mainstream ASU, now the Egyptian Arab Socialist Party was by far the largest. In the Bread Riots of January 1977 ASU offices were a primary target of the mobs. In August 1978 Sadat formed his own National Democratic Party and the ASU merged into it, formally dissolving itself in May 1980.

ARAB SOCIALIST UNION (Libya)

Political parties were banned in Libya under the Monarchy. In June 1971 Colonel Qadafi as Chairman of the Revolution Command Council announced the formation of the Arab Socialist Union, replacing the tribal system as an organ of mass mobilisation to link the people and the Government. Closely modelled on the Arab Socialist Union of Egypt, Qadafi declared that it would bring about true democracy with all participating from local to national level, eliminate class distinctions and formulate a new socialist ideology, based on Islam, rejecting Marxism. There would be a group in every neighbourhood and institution which would elect a Basic Committee of up to ten of its members who would elect two or more representatives to a Governorate Congress which would choose ten or twenty to participate in the National General Congress. At least half the members of each Committee had to be workers or farmers. Despite this democratic structure the ASU was in practice closely controlled from the top with the RCC empowered to annul any resolution or dissolve any branch: Qadafi was its first President. Trade Unions were incorporated into the ASU as it was ideologically unsound to suggest that the workers needed a separate organisation. The first Congress started at the end of March 1972 with the representatives of 371 basic units with a reputed membership of 322,000 out of the million eligible. Qadafi made a five-hour speech and he and other RCC members debated with the delegates over freedom of the press and the right to strike. In April 1973 in his Zuwarah Speech, Qadafi proclaimed the Libyan Cultural Revolution and the people were instructed to form in every village and work-place committees that were to be the primary instrument of the Revolution. At the second National Congress in November 1974 the administrative system of governorates and directorates was abolished so that there should be direct contact between the Government and the people and the committees were placed under the supervision of the ASU. It became clear that the ASU was failing to arouse revolutionary enthusiasm amongst the masses or to reflect their interests while simultaneously pushing government policies, monitoring political activities and stifling dissent. There was a lack of cadres and as Nasser had found, it was impossible to impose a political party from above. In April 1975 Qadafi decreed a General People's Congress should "turn the whole people into an instrument of rule", replacing the ASU Congress: this 618-strong body met in November. It met again in January 1976 to approve the budget, demand that all opposition be crushed and pledge allegiance to Qadafi. Membership of the ASU was opened to all Arabs although few non-Libyans seem to have joined. The Sabhah Congress in 1977 abolished all institutions of government, apparently including the ASU.

ARAFAT, Yassir (1929–)

Palestinian leader. He was born Rahman Abd al-Rauf Arafat al-Qudwa al-Hussaini in Jerusalem, or possibly in Gaza, into a lower middle-class family with distant connections with that of the Mufti, Haj Amin al-Hussaini. He took part in the Palestine War after which he went to Gaza where he was much moved by the sufferings of his fellow refugees. Arafat studied engineering at Cairo University and also underwent military training. From 1952 to 1957 he was President of the Palestinian Students Union, associating with the more militant to form a clandestine nationalist group. He served in a demolition squad in the Egyptian army in the Suez War and after graduating in 1957 worked as an engineer in Kuwait where he earned enough, with the help of rich Palestinian exiles, to become the full-time organiser from about 1964 of a group which expanded into Fatah. Arafat was known amongst them as Abu Ammar. He founded a periodical *Filastin-na* (Our Palestine) which started appearing in 1959. Realising that the Palestinians could not rely upon other Arabs to liberate their country, with Abu Jihad, Arafat acquired arms to form a commando unit which, under the name of *al-Asifa* carried out its first attack on an Israeli target on 1 January 1965. Arab governments feared that such actions might escalate into a war with Israel for which they were not ready and Arafat was imprisoned for 51 days in Damascus. After the June War he showed great conspiratorial skills, slipping in and out of the Occupied Territories, forming a network of cells. After the battle of Karamah Fatah emerged into the open with Arafat its acknowledged leader, quickly becoming an internationally recognisable figure with his Palestinian *kufiyah* headdress, inevitable pistol, bulging eyes and carefully cultivated stubble. In February 1969 he was elected to replace Ahmad Shuqayri as Chairman of the Palestine Liberation Organisation. With the support of Nasser he worked to transform it from a ponderous bureaucracy into an umbrella organisation which could accommodate *fidayin* groups of widely differing political ideologies. Desperately anxious to keep the PLO together he always tried to play down differences until Palestine should be free and not to antagonise minorities to the extent that he was frequently unable to impose discipline upon the unruly such as George Habash, Nayif Hawatma or Abu Nidal. This meant that he lost credibility through being unable to commit the PLO to any consistent policy. However he did succeed in ensuring that the problem of Palestine was not dropped from world's agenda and that its people maintained a distinct identity in their own eyes and in those of the international community. He alternated very long office hours, mostly at night, with incessant travelling. He was an excellent chairman, patient and adept at finding a compromise. He was also an efficient administrator, exercising personal control over the large funds at the disposal of the PLO, using them to finance social benefits for widows and families of guerrillas, medical and educational development amongst Palestinians and the establishment of large and profitable business enterprises at the same time attracting a grateful clientele. Although a conservative nationalist, with long-term links with the Muslim Brothers, he proved sufficiently flexible to work with Nasser or the Syrian Baath Party and he established a good working relationship with the Soviet Union. Arafat was able to keep on friendly terms with mutually hostile Arab states and was often able to perform useful services as a mediator between them: when this was impossible he cleverly played off one against another. He managed to emerge personally unscathed when Abu Nidal attacked Saudi targets. Arafat was also able to become reconciled with Arab leaders after the most bitter of quarrels with them. In 1970 Arafat had to flee from Jordan during Black September but in 1974 at the Rabat Summit King Hussain accepted that the PLO led by him was the sole legitimate representative of the Palestine people: in February 1985 they were the closest of allies before quarrelling again. In the early 1970s Arafat, though still Commander-in-Chief of the Palestine Liberation Army seems to have left operations against Israel largely in the hands of Abu Jihad and to have concentrated upon diplomacy and it often seemed as if he personally would have been prepared to settle for less than the total elimination of Israel in exchange for a smaller territory where the Palestinians could establish their own state but was unable to carry others with him: Habash, Ahmad Jibril and others formed the Rejection Front to oppose his policies. Arafat frequently expressed disapproval of terrorist activities and aircraft hijackings. Arafat achieved a diplomatic triumph by being invited to address the UN General Assembly in November 1974, was welcomed as a Head of State, and received a standing ovation after greatly impressing delegates in a speech in which he declared that he was bearing "an olive branch and a freedom fighter's gun". He played a large part in the virtual takeover by the Palestinians of Southern Lebanon to the extent that the area became known as "Fatahland". He tried to keep them out of the fighting between the Maronites and the adherents of Kamal Jumblatt but again was unable to control Habash and other hardliners. The military success of the Palestinians brought the intervention of the Syrians to save the Lebanese Government and Arafat was forced into hostility to Hafiz al-Assad. An uneasy truce was made between them but when the Israelis invaded Lebanon in Operation Peace for Galilee in June 1982 the Syrians rapidly sought a cease-fire leaving the Palestinians in the lurch. After heavy fighting in the Beirut siege Arafat with 8,000 *fidayin* and 2,600 PLA men were evacuated by sea. Arafat was greatly weakened by loss of the "governmental

machinery" that he had established in South Lebanon which he could not recreate in his new base in Tunis. He returned several months later to Lebanon but recent failures had shaken his authority which he attempted to bolster by placing in key commands men loyal to himself but who were regarded as cowardly, corrupt and incompetent. With Syrian backing a section of Fatah rebelled against him and Arafat was besieged by them in Tripoli, Lebanon, for the second time having to be saved by evacuation by sea. He was expelled from Damascus in June 1983 but compensated for the hostility of Syria by a *rapprochement* with Egypt (which caused a breach with Libya) and with Jordan with whose help he "packed" the seventeenth Congress of the Palestine National Council in Amman so that it rejected his rather theatrical offer of resignation. He concluded the Amman Accord with Hussain which envisaged an arrangement by which the Palestinians would have received territory which they would federate with Jordan in return for peace with Israel. Again Arafat was unable to convince the radicals who regarded him as too confident that his personal diplomacy could achieve results and after a year the King accused Arafat of failing to keep his word and denounced the agreement. This prepared the way for a reconciliation between Arafat and most of the rejectionists including Habash at the eighteenth PNC in Algiers in April 1987. At the Palestine National Council Algiers Meeting of November 1988 he won support for his policy of accepting Resolution 242, implicitly recognising Israel and negotiating with the Americans for a peace settlement. The Israelis, however, still regarded him as a terrorist and ensured that the Americans refused him a visa to enter the US to address the General Assembly. The UN session therefore moved to Geneva for Arafat's speech after which he formally renounced terrorism and explicitly accepted the right of Israel to exist. Dialogue was opened between American and PLO representatives and continued for a year until June 1990 when the Palestine Liberation Front carried out a raid on a beach near Tel Aviv. Arafat deplored the action was unable to bring himself formally to condemn his colleague Abu al-Abbas. The Americans therefore ended the dialogue. He appeared to be gaining acceptance after being received by the Pope and President Mitterand and being modelled by Mme Tussauds in London, but lost much credibility by giving support to Saddam Hussain, and his foolish behaviour at the 1990 Cairo Summit antagonised Mubarak. The Tunis raid was a deliberate attempt by the Israelis to eliminate him. In July 1991 his leadership was seriously under question over his insistence on a peace conference and by the failure in South Lebanon. In April 1992 he was thought lost in the Libyan desert after an aircraft crash and questions were raised as to who might succeed him. With Abu Jihad and Abu Iyad dead, it became clear that he had no real successor and despite his subsequent brain surgery, his leadership was never really in question. Moreover, it was revealed that he was the only one who knew where the PLO's money was. It has been estimated that there have been over 50 attempts on his life, some by Israelis and others by dissident Palestinians and he has been forced to keep constantly on the move, rarely sleeping two successive nights in the same place and often changing his travel plans at the last moment. He does not smoke or drink alcohol or coffee, preferring large quantities of herb tea sweetened with honey. He sneers at the kiss and hug style of other world leaders. He married in 1992. He admitted that the PLO lost a great deal by supporting Saddam Hussain – in purely financial terms an estimated $12bn. He had predicted that the US would not fight and that the war would last six years. His support for Hussain was contrary to his general policy of taking care not to put all his political eggs in one basket. However, this did not appear to harm his position with the Palestinians and he gained credit for persuading Hussain to release hostages. He realised that the US was the only Super-power and that the Arab countries had to go along with the Madrid agreement, persuading the majority not to split the movement. In January 1993 he told Israeli TV in an interview that he felt that Hamas was the main obstacle to peace. Later in 1993 there were reports that he was prepared to resign as head of Fatah following accusations of political and financial mismanagement and criticism over his handling of peace talks, including his endorsement of the PL-J Confederation. He was a tremendous success in the US, being visited by the Presidents Carter and Bush, prompting the resignation of five members of the PLO executive. He began being received as potential head of state and the equal of Rabin. He always said that he would accept one square metre of Palestine as a start. He was taken by surprise at the start of the Intifadah but worked hard to show he was rightful leader. His role in the uneasy peace of the last two years may be seen as the summit of his achievement for the people he has led for so long, with the handshake on the lawn of the White House representing victory rather than compromise. He maintains a crucial role in the protracted negotiations and it is still difficult to see who his successor might be.

ARAMCO

In 1923 Major Frank Holmes of the Eastern and General Syndicate received from Ibn Saud a concession for about 30,000 square miles in al-Hasa province but in 1928 he let it lapse after his geologists had concluded that drilling would be a pointless gamble. The rights were taken by Gulf Corporation which had to relinquish them under the Red Line Agreement. The value of the concession was transformed by the discovery of oil in Bahrain in 1932. In May 1933 after hard bargaining with Abd Allah Sulayman, in which the explorer Philby was involved, Standard Oil of California obtained a concession for sixty years for 360,000 square miles in the al-Hasa province in return for an immediate loan of $30,000 with a further loan of $20,000 in eighteen months and a first annual rental of $5,000 – all in gold. The Iraq Petroleum Company also bid but failed because it could only offer rupees. Drilling began in 1935 but the first six wells sunk proved dry and Socal which had set up the Californian-Arabian Standard Oil Company to exploit the concession invited Texaco to take half share in what became Caltex. Oil was found on 4 March 1938 and a 43-mile 10-inch pipe was built to enable the first export on 1 May 1939. A Supplementary Agreement in 1939 gave an additional 85,000 square

miles on payment of $140,000 and rent increase to $25,000. Exports amounted to 510,000 tons in 1939. Wartime difficulties prevented much increase in production but the company, renamed ARAMCO in 1944, took on a significant role in the development of the country. It provided the Government with communications, educational and health services throughout the Eastern Province where it also started agricultural and industrial projects. It also acted as banker for the King. It fought to exclude British interests from the area and consistently championed Ibn Saud, securing his inclusion in the Lease-Lend arrangements although technically they were only for belligerents. In 1944 the parent companies fought off an attempt by the US Government to acquire a shareholding to build a pipeline to the Mediterranean. A pipeline, built in 1945, enabled Saudi oil to be refined in Bahrain. In 1947 the need for capital for expansion led to Standard Oil of New Jersey and Socony-Vacuum taking respectively 30% and 10% shares in ARAMCO and in Tapline, the pipeline to Sidon. During this time American oil interests tried hard but without success to alter the pro-Zionist stance of President Truman in the process of the creation of Israel. More wells were drilled and production rose from 2.5 million tons in 1945 to 41 million in 1952 when the company had about 20,000 employees. In 1950, after a serious crisis, a new financial agreement was negotiated by which payments through royalties and income tax, the Saudi Government would receive half of ARAMCO's operating profits after agreed deductions. In 1952 two Saudis were appointed to the Board of Directors and the company's HQ was moved from New York to Dhahran. The country's budget for 1952/3 included about $59 million from direct oil revenues while the only other significant sum was about $8 million from customs, much of it related to the oil industry. In addition ARAMCO constructed fuel storage tanks throughout the country and built a 355-mile railway from Riyadh to Dammam which could never be economic but pleased Ibn Saud. Dissatisfaction at the differing conditions in which American and Arab staff were paid and housed led to the first strike in October 1953 when 5,000 soldiers had to be drafted into the area to guard the installations and keep order. Pressure for further territory where oil might be found led to Saudi intervention in Buraymi and Jabal Akhdar in which ARAMCO staff acted as propagandists, rewriters of history and smugglers of war materials on behalf of the Government. An ARAMCO party attempting illegally to work in the Eastern Aden Protectorate was chased out. The company dragged in its wake the American Government which by now regarded it as the most important and valuable foreign economic asset ever developed by US citizens. The ARAMCO labour force, mainly composed of potentially disaffected Shiah, was the only organised, literate group in the country and a strike in the spring of 1956 was believed to have had political rather than industrial causes; it was savagely suppressed and further strikes prohibited. The first Saudi oil minister, Abd Allah al-Tariki who had served in ARAMCO became convinced that the company was too secretive, autocratic and self-interested and was not contributing as it should have to the development of the country and he became the driving force behind the creation of OPEC. This enabled the host states to assert themselves more effectively against the oil companies and in 1968 Tariki's successor, Shaykh Yamani stated publicly that the Kingdom aspired to a 50% stake in ARAMCO. The claim was brushed aside but the Tehran Oil Agreement of 1971 showed that OPEC members could ultimately impose their wills on the companies. In March 1972 ARAMCO conceded the principle of a 20% stake. In October a General Agreement on Participation gave Saudi Arabia, Kuwait, Abu Dhabi and Qatar an immediate 25% shareholding in their local companies which would rise progressively until 1981 when it would reach 51%. In June 1974 the Saudi stake was raised to 60% and the takeover was completed in March 1980 after which the company became purely a provider of services. In 1988 Saudi ARAMCO became a legal entity. In the sixty years after its inception the company had discovered more than 60 viable oilfields, seven of them offshore and was capable of pumping 9 million barrels a day, half of which it hoped to refine locally. It was also expanding its interests within North America with a sales deal in June 1988 with Texaco. In November 1991 its President, Ali Naimi announced plans for expansion into related fields, new fields were discovered in the central regions and in June 1993 it took over SAMAREC, the marketing and refining company. It employed about 45,000 staff of 50 nationalities with Saudis holding 76% of the supervisory posts. ARAMCO played the major part in switching Saudi Arabia from the British to the American sphere of influence and the protection of its oilfields shaped American foreign policy, affecting such decisions as the creation of the Rapid Deployment Force in 1977. In addition few, if any, privately-owned companies can have done so much to transform the primitive economy of a backward state into opulence and sophistication in so short a time.

ARIF, al-Rahman Muhammad (1916–)

Iraqi President. He was born in Baghdad, the son of a draper and the elder brother of Abd al-Salam Arif whom he preceded to the Military Academy. He also joined the Free Officers and led his armoured regiment into Baghdad in the July Revolution. Abd al-Rahman was apparently regarded as so harmless that he was not molested while Abd al-Salam was imprisoned under sentence of death on charges of plotting and attempting to murder Abd al-Krim Qassim. He was retired in 1962 but returned to command a division after the Ramadan Revolution when his brother became President. He was then promoted Acting Chief of Staff the post he was holding when Abd al-Salam was killed in a helicopter crash. The joint military and civilian National Defence Council elected him as a non-controversial President after Abd al-Rahman al-Bazzaz who had obtained more votes on the first ballot stood down. A simple, amiable, unambitious man, he lacked the energy, cunning, decisiveness, aggression and political cunning of his predecessor and seemed always to have doubted his own fitness for the post – a doubt which communicated itself to others. Abd al-Salam had placed trusted people from his own tribal area in key posts and they remained under his brother but Abd al-Rahman was unable to

control the feuding military cliques and was prepared to leave decisions to others. Officers procured the dismissal of Bazzaz, the Prime Minister most likely to solve the country's problems, especially that of the Kurds and his succession by General Naji Talib. In June 1966 key officers remained loyal to him at the time of the attempted coup of Arif Abd al-Razzaq and he tried to strengthen his standing among them by making military agreements with President Nasser and with Syria and obtaining sophisticated equipment from France. No progress was made towards Arab unity, constitutional reform, the dispute with the Iraq Petroleum Company or peace with the Kurds. He maintained friendly relations with Iran and Turkey, paying state visits to their capitals. In May 1967, unable to find anyone more suitable, Arif himself took the Premiership, forming a Cabinet in which nine out of twenty members were officers. In the June War Iraq sent troops into Jordan but Israeli air action prevented them from achieving anything. The subsequent need for intensive inter-Arab diplomacy made it impossible for Arif to hold both Presidency and Premiership so on July 9 he handed over the latter office to the efficient but corrupt General Tahir Yahya. On July 17 1968 two of his closest associates, Colonels Abd al-Razzaq al-Nayif of Military Intelligence and Ibrahim al-Daud of the Republican Guard who had allied with the Baath politely informed him that he should go into exile. Pausing only to be assured that his pension would be paid, Arif went to London and then, after a period in Istanbul, settled in Cairo.

ARIF, Abd al-Salam Muhammad (1921–66)

Iraqi President. He was the son of a draper from a tribal area of the Middle Euphrates who had migrated to Baghdad. He passed out of the Military Academy in 1941, fought in the Palestine War and in 1957 was commanding a battalion in Jordan. There he was recruited by his Brigadier, Abd al-Krim Qassim who had known him since 1942, into the Free Officers. In the July Revolution of 1958 Arif played the major part in the Revolution, taking over command of an armoured brigade which he led into Baghdad to storm the Royal Palace. Arif was appointed Qassim's deputy as Prime Minister and Commander-in-Chief and Minister of the Interior. Within a week he was sent to see President Nasser to seek help in case of foreign intervention but ignoring his instructions, stated that Iraq would join the United Arab Republic and that Qassim would be pushed aside like General Neguib. Arif made a series of speeches praising Nasser and disparaging Qassim and set afoot intrigues amongst nationalist officers, who resented Qassim's failure to establish a Revolutionary Command Council. In September, therefore, Qassim relieved him of his posts and appointed him Ambassador to Bonn. Arif protested violently and, alone with Qassim, drew his revolver either for murder or suicide. He then agreed to go to Bonn but returned secretly and was arrested. Charged with plotting treason and attempting to kill Qassim, he was given a secret trial in the Mahdawi Court and condemned to death. Qassim did not endorse the sentence and kept Arif in prison until October 1961. He was then closely watched but managed to conspire with pan-Arab officers and with the Baath who felt that they could use him as a figurehead to take the place of Qassim. On February 8 1963, the Ramadan Revolution, Arif with Colonel Ahmad Hassan al-Bakr led tanks into Baghdad and, after a final interview with Qassim, had him shot. The National Council of the Revolution appointed Arif President and Bakr formed a Cabinet which contained Baathists and Nasserists but in May dropped the latter in a reshuffle. Arif was apparently reduced to a puppet as the Baathists and their Syrian colleagues engaged in violent polemics with Nasser after the failure of the Unity Talks and their National Guard insulted, arrested and even tortured and murdered opponents including army officers. With the help of his brother Colonel Abd al-Rahman Arif and moderate Baathist officers such as the Chief-of-Staff Tahir Yahya, Arif carried out his third coup, the November Revolution of 1963 smashing the National Guard and turned himself from a dummy into a strongman. He had earlier been regarded as vain, emotional to the point of instability, noisy and impetuous but he now proved an astute, moderate, religious and mature statesman. Unlike his predecessor who never left Baghdad he spent much time travelling around the country making attractive speeches and listening to grievances and became generally popular. Arif appointed himself the first Field Marshal in Iraqi history, Commander-in-Chief and President of the Council with full powers which he used to get rid of the moderate Baathists and to model his regime closely upon that of Nasser. A group of officers from his own tribal area provided his essential power base as he placed them in key posts. Arif announced a new provisional constitution on Egyptian lines, stressing Islam, socialism and democracy, introduced nationalisation measures and created a sole party also called the Arab Socialist Union. In May 1964 he and Nasser agreed to set up the Unified Political Command to bring about union within two years but this was clearly impossible while all Iraqi Cabinets suffered from acute internal dissensions and the country itself was so divided. In the interests of Arab unity he intensified efforts to bring the Kurds to heel and very heavy fighting ensued. Arif concluded an arms deal with Russia, meeting Khruschev whom he advised to become a Muslim, receiving missiles and bombers but at the same time he kept on good terms with the West. In July 1965 he attempted to improve relations with the Iraq Petroleum Company which had become very difficult since Qassim's takeover of much of their concession. Arif's enthusiasm for union with Egypt appeared to cool as experience taught him the possible difficulties and the unpopularity of socialism and military rule but, perhaps to neutralise him, chose in September 1965 the ardent Nasserist Arif Abd al-Razzaq as Prime Minister. Then, having taken precautions against a possible coup by his Prime Minister, he went off to attend the Casablanca Summit. Abd al-Razzaq duly attempted to seize power and was humiliatingly unsuccessful. Arif then appointed Abd al-Rahman al-Bazzaz a distinguished lawyer to be the first civilian Premier since the Revolution with a brief to reduce socialism and the intervention in government of conflicting military cliques and take cautious steps towards a more demo-cratic form of government. A greater openness and efficiency became apparent, the air of tension diminished and the economy improved with more scope for private enterprise, but before really decisive changes could be made, Arif was killed when his helicopter crashed in a sandstorm while he was on a speech-making tour. He was genuinely mourned and unusually for the Arab world there was no suggestion that the sudden death of a leader had been caused by foul play. His memoirs were published in an Egyptian periodical.

al-ARISH KILLINGS (1985)

On 5 October 1985 a 24-year-old Egyptian conscript, serving as a security guard, opened fire on a party of Israeli tourists, killing seven of them. He then turned his weapon against his comrades, killing his commanding officer. He came from a village near Alexandria where 46 children had died in April 1970 in an Israeli air raid which hit a primary school. He was praised as a hero by fundamentalists but at his trial it was not clear whether he had known that his victims were Israelis. On 29 December he was found sane and guilty but on 7 January 1986 he was discovered hanged in a prison hospital where he was undergoing treatment for bilharzia.

ARMÉE DE LIBÉRATION NATIONALE (Algeria)

The morning of the All Saints' Day Uprising, the Front de Libération Nationale called for volunteers between the ages of 18 and 40 to join its Army. Hampered by lack of organisation and arms, the guerrillas in the six *wilayas* could launch little more than hit-and-run raids and try to attract or terrorise the population into supporting them. Some of the most bitter fighting was against the rival Mouvement National Algérienne. French intelligence sources in April 1956 estimated the number of ALN fighters (*mujahidin*) at 8,500 with over 21,000 auxiliaries (*musabilin*) providing food, shelter and information. There were also *fidayin* who acted as saboteurs and killed traitors. The Soummam Valley Conference of August 1956 introduced a formal system of ranks and a pay scale ranging from 1,000 francs (then about $20) per month for a private to 5,000 francs for a colonel: there were no generals. French successes drove large numbers of the ALN over the frontiers into Tunisia and Morocco where they were able to receive better training and weapons. By the end of 1956 there were probably 10,000 of them in Tunisia and to prevent their returning the French built the Morice Line along the frontier: a lesser deterrent was built along the Moroccan frontier. Daily there were local clashes, usually on quite a small scale but when the French concentrated on a single objective as they did in the Algiers Battle of 1957, there was little that the ALN could do. French reprisals caused a constant increase in the number of recruits and at the beginning of 1958 the French put the number of ALN regulars at 30,000, of whom about half were operating in the interior at any one time with an additional 30,000 irregulars. Despite French claims that over 25,000 were killed or captured in the first eight months of that year, the Information Minister Muhammad Yazid claimed 100,000 had been enrolled at the end of it, although not all had weapons.

Relations were often extremely bad between the political authorities, as represented by the Gouvernement Provisoire de la République Algérienne, and the field commanders, five of whom convicted of plotting to overthrow it, were court-martialled and shot in November 1958. During 1959 General Challé won a series of victories which were stated to have disposed of over 26,000 in the interior and captured another 11,000 leaving only 8,000 in scattered and demoralised groups: meanwhile the exterior forces, now numbering about 40,000, remained on the sidelines. During 1960 it was estimated that 3,000 fighters in the interior were killed or wounded each month. In February 1960 a General Staff was created under Colonel Houari Boumédienne, assisted by Major Ahmad Kaid, which established complete control over the external forces and showed minimal deference towards the GPRA, administering its own budget and establishing its own ancillary services. The General Staff was supposed to have jurisdiction in the interior but it took little interest in the fighting there as each *wilaya* commander regarded himself as supreme in his own fief. In September 1961 President Ben Khedda of the GPRA, attempted to assert control by abolishing the General Staff and creating separate ones for the interior and the exterior, both subordinated to himself but Boumédienne ignored him. After the conclusion of the Evian Agreement in the struggle between the GPRA and the Politburo formed by Ben Bella to rule the state when independence came the ALN at first appeared to stand aloof. On 30 June 1962, however, Ben Khedda sought to dismiss Boumédienne who thereupon rallied to Ben Bella and ordered his troops to march on Algiers. At first it appeared that the troops coming from outside might be resisted by some of the *wilaya* commanders who rallied to Ben Khedda but the mood of the Algerian people was that seven years' bloodshed had been enough. Ben Khedda resigned, Boumédienne became Minister of Defence and integrated the internal and external forces as the Armée Nationale Populaire.

ARMÉE DE LIBÉRATION NATIONALE
(Morocco)
The exiling by the French of Sultan Muhammad V in August 1953 was followed by some spontaneous acts of violence but for two years there was no sign that these were organised. Then Abd al-Krim Khatib and Mahjoub Ahardan started to approach Moroccans serving as officers in the French army and also to recruit ex-servicemen. Most of these were Berbers, many of whom had fought in Europe or Indo-China or taken part in guerrilla activities in the Algerian War of Independence which had just started and which made it difficult for Riffis to migrate there for seasonal work. On 19 August 1955, the day before the anniversary of the deposition of the Sultan, Zayyan tribesmen brandishing portraits of Muhammad V attacked government buildings in Khenifra and in clashes with the Foreign Legion 40 people were killed. The following day Smaala tribesmen captured Oued Zem, savagely massacring 49 French residents including women and children and on the same day other Berbers smashed up the mines at Khourigba killing more Frenchmen. This defection of the Berbers was a devastating blow to the French who

since the Berber Dhahir of 1930 had been relying upon their support against Arab nationalism. These attacks were followed by a series of raids on military and police posts throughout the Riff and Middle Atlas in which arms were seized and in October Allal al-Fassi announced the existence of an Armée de Libération Nationale, pledged to expel the French from the whole of North Africa. It was linked to the Istiqlal Party through one of its leaders, his cousin Abd al-Kabir al-Fassi. In a fortnight in October the French claimed that 100 ALN members were killed and 2,000 wounded in the Riff and a further 40 killed and 100 wounded in the Middle Atlas and admitted its own losses in the following two months as 101 killed, 17 in a single ambush. The Sultan returned in November but guerrilla activities, including attacks on posts loyal to him continued and during the winter of 1955/6 much of the mountainous areas came under the control of the ALN which by now numbered about 10,000 men. They received covert help from the Spanish whose town of Nador served as their headquarters. Regarding independence as incomplete they were particularly active along the Algerian frontier, tying up French troops needed in Algeria and further groups were formed in the extreme South. There were as yet no Moroccan regular forces but the future King Hassan II negotiated with the ALN group by group to integrate them into the army that he was forming. At the end of March 1956 30 ALN leaders paid homage to the King but this led to factional fighting in which the ALN Chief of Staff Abbas Masadi was murdered. The Istiqlal, particularly Mehdi Ben Barka, were competing for their allegiance but by July some 6,000 had been incorporated in the new regular army and 3,000 in the police. Khatib declared that their work was not complete and about 3,000 continued to attack French forces in the South and in Mauritania. In November 1957 their attack on the Spanish precipitated the Ifni Crisis. It was not until 1959 that the Government could exercise control over outlying areas of the South and the ALN faded away. Many of the former guerrillas later formed the nucleus of the Berber Mouvement Populaire created by Khatib and Ahardan.

ARSLAN
The Arslan family, who claim descent from pre-Islamic kings, have been leaders amongst the Lebanese Druzes for generations, ranking second only to the Shihab; their stronghold was in the Gharb east of Beirut. From the beginning of the eighteenth century, heading a group of clans known as the Yazbaki, they had to struggle for influence against the more active house of Jumblatt until the heads of that family were sent into exile in 1825. When the Dual Kaymakamate was established in 1842 the Amir Ahmad Arslan was appointed as the head of the Druze area. He was in prison at the time of his appointment and had to return to jail to consult his colleagues as to whether he should accept. He demanded the revival of all feudal rights, was again imprisoned and restored to power before in 1845 he was replaced by Amin Arslan. The British established friendly links with the Arslans although these were not as close as those with the Jumblatts. When the Turks tightened their grip on the Lebanon after 1860, the Amir Mustafa Arslan was chosen as *Kaymakam* of the

Shuf. He had powerful connections in Istanbul, shunned close relations with foreign powers and dominated the area into the twentieth century. In August 1902, fearing the reforming zeal of the new Mutasarrif, Muzaffar Pasha, he attempted to resign in favour of his nephew Shakib Arslan but found himself replaced by Nasib Jumblatt. Amir Mustafa took this with ill grace and headed a series of intrigues and in 1908 regained his old office, on friendly terms with the Young Turks and converting to Islam. During the French Mandate the Arslans, unlike the Jumblatts, were considered nationalists and Amir Amin tried to arrange terms for those involved in the Druze Revolt and was later an ally of Riad al-Solh. After the war Amir Fuad was one of the most outspoken critics of collaborationist politicians but Rafiq was Director of Agriculture after the Constitution was suspended in July 1939. Shakib and his brother Adil (1882–1954) were amongst the leading opponents of colonialism. Adil remained loyal to the Turks during the war and later was one of the founders of the Istiqlal Party. He was in exile during most of the 1920s and 1930s and again after the Allies occupied the Levant in 1941. He entered Syrian politics and was Foreign Minister during the military rule of Husni al-Zaim. Majid Arslan held a Cabinet post once before independence and at least sixteen times after it. Members of the family have the honorary title of *Amir*.

ASHIQQA

The Ashiqqa (literally Brothers from the same womb) was the first genuine political party formed in the Sudan. It grew out of the Graduates General Congress under the leadership of Ismail al-Azhari and its membership consisted of the educated young, government clerks and townspeople. Its main demand was for union with Egypt with equal rights for the two peoples and a joint army. It therefore opposed the policy of advance towards independence under British tutelage favoured by Saiyyid Abd al-Rahman al-Mahdi and his Umma Party and enjoyed the patronage of the rival Saiyyid Ali al-Mirghani. It refused to co-operate with the British and boycotted the conference that led to the creation of the Legislative Assembly. In 1949 some of its members, dissenting from Azhari's extreme pro-unionist views, split away to form the National Front and in 1952 it merged with other unionist groups to form the National Unionist Party.

ASHRAW, Hanan (1946–)

Born Ramallah her father was a descendant of the family that founded Ramallah and participated in the first meeting of PNC. Her mother was Lebanese. She took a first degree in textual criticism from AUB and a Ph.D. in medieval comparative literature from Virginia. She was head of Bir Zeit English department for eight years and was later appointed Dean of the Faculty of Arts. She came into prominence during the Gulf War when spoke of the suffering of the Palestinians. Her view was that the Palestinians had no choice but to opt for peace and that armed struggle was suicidal. She is married with two children. Her husband is a film-maker and musician.

ASWAN DAM

In 1894 after building a dam across the Tigris, the famous engineer Sir William Willcocks was commissioned by Colin Scott Moncrieff, in charge of irrigation in Egypt under Lord Cromer, to build a dam across the Nile. The objective was not to impede the flood but to store water for use in the summer. There was considerable debate because the proposals would lead to the flooding of the temple at Philae and the country could not afford at the same time both to build a dam and to reconquer the Sudan: the Caisse de la Dette was unlikely to allow expenditure on a new project without drastic cuts elsewhere. However the contractors agreed to accept payments by instalments; work started in 1898 and was finished in 1902 at a cost of £E3,500,000. Its value was immediately apparent and there was a demand for its heightening which was done between 1907 and 1910. It was then the largest in the world, a mile and a quarter long with sluices closed by iron gates weighing up to 30 tons each. Eventually it consisted of 1 million cubic metres of masonry compared with the 2 million in the Great Pyramid. By 1912 the cotton crop had been trebled and the sugar crop doubled. In 1934 it was raised again, increasing the reservoirs to five times their original capacity. In the late 1950s industrial developments such as an electricity generating station and a fertiliser factory utilised the power it produced. In 1960 work started on the Aswan High Dam five miles south of the original Dam.

ASWAN HIGH DAM

In about 1947 an Egyptian engineer of Greek extraction suggested building a new dam on the Nile above the existing Aswan Dam. It envisaged a rock-filled dam, the largest in the world with a core of clay which would create a lake with an area of 4,000 km. It was estimated that as well as providing electricity, it would enable the cultivation of an additional million *feddans* with a further 700,000 converted to perennial irrigation. The proposal was ignored until after the July Revolution when the Revolutionary Command Council grasped it as a prestige symbol that would fire popular imagination; Nasser called it "our new pyramid". The estimated cost, over £E400 million, ($11 billion) was beyond Egypt's resources. In November 1955 the Finance Minister Abd al-Munim al-Qaissuni arranged an unconditional loan of $56 million from the US Government and an additional $14 million from the UK. As the Czecho-Slovak Arms Deal had just taken place Prime Minister Eden considered that "in our dealings with Egypt it could be trump card". In January 1956 the President of the World Bank signed an agreement to lend a further $200 million but on terms which implied some form of supervision over Egyptian finances. At this point the Egyptian Government infuriated Secretary Dulles by recognising Communist China and American cotton farmers lobbied against help for the Dam. The Russians offered to lend £100 million. On 19 July the Americans abruptly withdrew their offer in terms that Nasser considered deliberately insulting and which Eden criticised as unwise. A week later Nasser, without warning, nationalised the Suez Canal to use its revenues to build the High Dam. After the Suez War the Russians advanced credits of about $320 million and provided technicians and equipment. Work started in January 1960 and the first stage, the diversion of the river, was completed in the presence of Khrushchev in May 1964. There were problems as the Sudanese population up-river had to be evacuated as Lake Nasser rose and an elaborate rescue was needed for the temple of Abu Simbel. There were criticisms that the population would rise faster than the benefits could accrue despite government encouragement of birth control. There were technical fears that as the Nile no longer carried silt there would be erosion along the riverside and on the coastline, that bilharzia would spread and fish stocks decline. There were fears that the Dam might be bombed by the Israelis. Much of the progress was due to the energy of the Minister in charge of the High Dam, Sidqi Sulayman. The reservoir, the largest in the world, started to fill in 1967, power generation started 1968 and in 1971 it was formally inaugurated by Presidents Sadat and Podgorny. By 1980 it had allowed farmers to double their crop yield and the Dams supplied almost half the power used in the country. In 1988 there were fears that the prolonged drought in Ethiopia would make the level of Lake Nasser too low to operate the turbines.

al-ATASI, Hashim (1875–1960)

Syrian Prime Minister and President. He came from a leading landowning family of Homs of which his father was the Mufti and a Deputy in the Ottoman Parliament. Atasi trained at the Administrative College in Istanbul, served in the bureaucracy for twenty years, became Governor of Acre and remained loyal to the Turks throughout the war. In 1919 he represented Homs in the Syrian General Congress of which he was elected Chairman. In May 1920 when the Congress was pushing Faysal into confrontation with the French, he appointed Atasi Prime Minister. He formed a Cabinet which included radical nationalists such as Dr Shahbandar. He opposed the Mandate from the outset and in February 1926 was arrested for leading a boycott of elections and imprisoned on Arwad Island off Tartus. In October 1927 he presided over the conference that led to the formation of the National Bloc and in June 1928 he was elected President of the Constituent Assembly. He was one of the first to call for a Treaty to lead to the independence of Syria in alliance with France. In June 1932 he was a candidate for Head of State but withdrew in favour of Muhammad Ali al-Abid to keep out Subhi Barakat. He was widely respected as a calm, serious and honest politician and this was shown by his nomination as one of the group that tried to mediate between Ibn Saud and the Imam Yahya at the time of the Saudi–Yemeni War. In February 1936 at a time of great unrest he proclaimed that only a nationalist solution would be acceptable and the following month he led to Paris the delegation that negotiated the Franco-Syrian Treaty which was so favourable to Syria that it was unacceptable to the French Parliament. When the National Bloc won the election of December 1936 the Assembly was nearly unanimous in electing Atasi as President of the Republic. It proved a difficult time as to disputes over the ratification of the Treaty were added those over Alexandretta and the status of the Druzes and Alawites.

The National Bloc Government fragmented, there were angry quarrels with Dr Shahbandar and his followers and a neutral government under Nasuhi al-Bukhari resigned over the French attitude to the minorities. The High Commissioner suspended the Constitution, dissolved Parliament and put power in the hands of a Directorate of civil servants. Atasi immediately resigned. In March 1943 General Catroux, the representative of De Gaulle proposed to reconstitute the position as it had been in 1939 with Atasi as President committed to signing a Treaty favourable to the French. Atasi would have liked to accept but under pressure from Shukri al-Quwatli finally refused. In December 1948 after the government of Jamil Mardam had collapsed under the unrest caused by its inefficient and corrupt conduct of the Palestine War Quwatli, now President, asked Atasi to form a government but he was unable to do so. He "unconditionally extended full support to the coup" of Husni al-Zaim in March 1949 but in August when Colonel Hinnawi overthrew Zaim, Atasi agreed to become Prime Minister. Although the army had officially withdrawn from politics, it is clear that they had strong influence over Atasi's Cabinet which contained representatives of the People's Party and the Baath. After elections a Constituent Assembly in December 1949 elected Atasi as provisional President of the Republic, an office he retained after the coup of Colonel Shishakli the following week. The People's Party leader Nizam al-Qudsi attempted to form a government but the army objected, Atasi offered to resign if the army interfered but Qudsi withdrew. In September 1950 the Constituent Assembly approved the new Constitution and Atasi formally took the oath as President encountering great difficulties in trying to keep political life going despite constant interference from the army and the divisions over the country's future stance in the Arab World. At the beginning of December 1951 Shishakli formally took power and Atasi resigned the Presidency. Although by now in his mid-seventies he opposed military rule so strongly that he was put under house arrest in Homs. When Shishakli published a new Constitution Atasi denounced the unprecedented powers given to the President. After a Druze uprising in January 1954 Atasi was again arrested. The following month Shishakli fled and Atasi once again became President. Despite a stroke, he struggled to get political leaders to work together to govern without army interference and although his sympathies lay with the People's Party he gave others a chance. He made no attempt to win another term of office, retiring in September 1955. A moderate, sensible, soothing man, he was one of the more principled of Syrian politicians.

ATIF, Sidqi

Saudi Prime Minister, appointed November 1986. In December 1986 he reduced exchange rates, increased interest charges, energy and agricultural prices, and provided incentives for investment.

al-ATRASH

Leading Druze family, said to have originated in Mount Lebanon. Ibrahim was the first prominent member of the family being killed fighting against the occupation of Hawran by Ibrahim Pasha in the late 1830s. His son Ismail led a contingent from Syria to Lebanon to participate in the Dayr al-Qamr Massacre of 1860. He died in 1869 and his son Ibrahim established the family as the lords of Jabal Druze with their "capital" at Suwaydah. In 1878 the Druzes sacked a village and the Governor of Damascus, Midhat Pasha sent an expedition against them which, after some successes, suffered a heavy defeat. Ibrahim's younger brother Shibli won popular support by distributing some of the family lands, which had been a quarter of the entire area, to the peasants. In 1888 there was another clash with the Turks, followed by the arrest of Shibli and more trouble in 1890. Shibli succeeded his brother as head of the family in 1892 and was soon stirring up unrest. In 1896 after four Turkish battalions had been massacred Marshal Tahir Pasha mobilised 30,000 men against the Druzes, 300 of whose leaders were exiled to Anatolia while captured tribesmen were sent to serve in garrisons in Tripoli. In 1900 the Turks released the leaders and Shibli was received by Sultan Abd al-Hamid. He died in 1904 and was succeeded by another brother Yahya whose early years were marked by a blood feud against another leading Druze family, the Miqdad. After a series of raids and skirmishes the Young Turks determined to bring Jabal Druze under control. In August 1910 they sent a military force of some 18,000 men under General Sami Pasha to put down what had become a revolt. Leading members of the Atrash, including Yahya who was arrested by treachery, were carried off in chains and sentenced to death. Yahya later submitted and was restored as Governor of the Jabal. He died in 1914 and was succeeded by yet another brother Salim. Salim remained loyal to the Turks during the war, doing much to alleviate the famine that raged throughout Syria but another important member of the family, Sultan al-Atrash helped the forces of Amir Faysal, harrying the Turks in the Biqaa. After the war Salim corresponded with the French authorities in Beirut and kept his post as Governor of the Jabal when they established control over Syria; he was given a French Adviser and allowed considerable autonomy. When Sultan revolted in the summer of 1922 Salim continued to support the French. He died in September 1923 and the family was too divided to agree upon a successor. A *Majlis* was held and requested the appointment of a French officer, Captain Carbillet as Governor. His reforms alienated the Atrash leaders and in July 1925 three of them who went to complain to the French High Commissioner General Sarrail were arrested. Sultan thereupon set off the Druze Revolt after the collapse of which he had to remain in exile until 1937. Hassan, the son of Yahya (born 1908) also went into exile but was able to return in 1928 and established himself as the leading man on the Jabal. The family was divided between those who wanted integration in the Syrian state and those led by Abd al-Ghaffar who demanded for the Druzes an independent status, linked with France. Amir Hassan was appointed Governor of the Jabal early in 1938 but resigned after a year following a demonstration against the High Commissioner. He was succeeded by a French officer. In the Cabinet of Husni al-Barazi Amir Hassan was War Minister. Hassan and Sultan tried to block the

elections of 1947 which would have led to the choice of an opponent of feudal rule but President Shukri al-Quwatli instigated a peasant rising against them and enlisted Saudi help by alleging that they were intriguing with King Abd Allah. Hassan then helped Husni al-Zaim to overthrow Quwatli. Early in 1954 he was arrested for planning an uprising against the dictatorship of Adib al-Shishakli but the following year he was Minister of Agriculture in the government of Sabri al-Asali and was later in the Cabinet of Said al-Ghazzi. Late in 1956 he was charged with collusion with the British in plotting a rising in favour of union with Iraq and smuggling arms and sentenced *in absentia* to death. In 1968–69 he was tried for involvement in another abortive coup but escaped to Jordan. He was kidnapped and brought back. He was condemned in 1970 to two years imprisonment but owing to his age did not serve the sentence. Two other members of the family achieved fame in a different sphere. Farid al-Atrash (1916–74) was perhaps the best-known singer and composer of popular songs of his period and his sister, known as Asmahan, was also a singer and a film star who died in mysterious circumstances in Cairo in 1944 at the age of 26.

al-ATRASH, Sultan b. Hamud (c. 1882–1982)

Druze leader. He was one of the heads of the al-Atrash family which dominated Jabal Druze after about 1870. Sultan had to struggle against his relatives and during Ottoman times he generally managed to keep out of trouble so as not to antagonise the Pasha of Damascus. He corresponded with Faysal during the Arab Revolt, during the last stages of which he harried the Turks in the Biqa. He does not appear to have been very active during Faysal's reign but in July 1922, enraged by the arrest by the French of a criminal who had sought asylum in his village, he raised the countryside in a revolt. His house was bombed and he fled to Trans-Jordan where he received no welcome from the Amir Abd Allah. He was forced to make his peace and pay a heavy fine. Sultan was on bad terms with the Governor of the Jabal, Salim al-Atrash who died in September 1923 and, as the family were unable to agree on a successor, was replaced by a French colonial officer who set out to introduce drastic changes including land reform. In February 1925 a Druze delegation invited to put their complaints to the French High Commissioner was imprisoned. Sultan who had suspected treachery and remained behind gathered a force and attacked the French garrison at Suwaydah. During the consequent Druze Revolt he proved himself an effective guerrilla leader. He formed an alliance with the Damascus nationalist Dr Shahbandar and with Fawzi al-Qawukji of Hama thus turning a local into a national uprising. It has been stated that Shahbandar hailed Sultan as King of Syria; he was certainly recognised as Commander-in-Chief. When the Revolt was crushed early in 1927 Atrash escaped into Trans-Jordan from which he was expelled by British armoured cars. He was, however, welcomed by Ibn Saud. He was sentenced to death by a French military tribunal. In April 1937 he was amnestied and returned but had to struggle for dominance of the Jabal with his cousin Hassan. A British report at this time described him as uneducated, of low intelligence, crafty and treacherous. Sultan was on bad terms with the National Bloc which opposed Druze autonomy in its demand for a unitary state. He called for boycott of the 1947 election which would have led to the election of a candidate from a rival clan and President Quwatli instigated a peasant rising against him which proved unsuccessful. In 1954 for the third time he had to flee to Jordan after the army under Brigadier Shishakli had arrested one of his nephews, setting off the chain of events that led to the end of army rule. He then returned home. In *Who's Who* he claimed to have had one wife and 24 children.

AWACS DEAL

The AWACS was a Boeing aircraft adapted to carry special electronic equipment which enabled it to monitor air and ground movements with a range of up to 400 miles and also to co-ordinate military operations. In October 1980 after the start of the Iran–Iraq War President Reagan sent 4 AWACS to Saudi Arabia to operate under US command. This move was denounced by the Russians. In April 1981 there was discussion of the use of AWACS in an integrated command of the Rapid Deployment Force and the forces of the Gulf Co-operation Council to prevent Russian encroachments upon the Gulf and the oilfields but the Saudis wished to have an independent fleet as a guarantee against a possible American withdrawal. President Reagan agreed to sell five of the aircaft to the Saudis for $8.5 bn and to enhance the potential of their 52 F-15 fighters. This would be the largest single arms deal in American history and the aircraft were to be delivered by the end of 1987. The proposal was strongly attacked by Israel and by the Zionist lobby in the US but in opposition a big business lobby, led by Mobil, pointed out that trade links with Saudi Arabia were worth $35,000 million and affected 700 companies in 42 States. In September Begin and Sharon visiting Washington said that the sale would upset the security balance in the Middle East and were rebuked by Reagan for attempting to change his foreign policy by lobbying: they were later compensated by the signature of a Strategic Co-operation Agreement. Congress had not been consulted and it was possible that the proposal might be voted down but in the event although defeated in the House of Representatives it was approved by a majority of four votes in the Senate in October after intensive lobbying by the President in person. The difficulties in getting Congressional approval led the Saudis to look elsewhere for modern weapons, contributing to the signing of the Yamamah Deal with Britain. Later the AWACS provided an essential part of the Peninsula Shield Force.

AWADHALLAH, Babikr (1917–)

Sudanese Prime Minister. He started his career as a clerk in the Legal Department before studying law in Khartoum. He then qualified in London as a barrister and served as a District Judge in Kordofan. In 1954 he was elected to the first Sudanese Parliament as a member of the National Unionist Party and appointed Speaker. Awadhallah resigned in 1957 and returned to the Bench. In 1964 he played an important part in the popular movement that led to the overthrow of General Abboud, leading a strike against the rough handling of protesting students. He was then appointed Chief Justice. After the death of Siddiq al-Mahdi in 1961, Awadhallah, with the support of the Mirghani/Khatmiyyah and the Sudanese Communist Party was seen as the principal leader of the opposition. He was never a member of the SCP but he held strongly Marxist views. In May 1967 he resigned in protest against the interference of the Supreme Council in matters concerning the judiciary, specifically its decision to support the government of Muhammad Ahmad Mahjoub in disregarding a High Court ruling that a ban on the SCP was contrary to the Constitution. He was mentioned as the probable candidate of the left if the Presidential elections proposed for 1970 took place. When Mahjoub was overthrown in a military coup led by General Nimeiri in May 1969 Awadhallah who had foreknowledge of the event was the only civilian appointed to the Council of the Revolution and was also Prime Minister and Minister of Foreign Affairs. He was anxious to dispel impressions of a military dictatorship and his Cabinet included only three officers with Nimeiri himself at Defence and others at Internal Security and Communications. It did, however, include nine alleged communists. His first action was to recognise East Germany and to announce that Sudan would not resume relations with West Germany and the USA while they supported Israel. He criticised the Americans in UN General Assembly and received a Soviet economic mission. He was a strong supporter of the Palestinians and Sudan was one of the first Arab states to break off relations with Romania which had resumed them with Israel. He visited East Berlin where he said that communists provided the indispensable vanguard of the Sudanese regime. This apparently upset Nimeiri who in October decided to assume the Premiership himself with Awadhallah as his Deputy and Minister of Justice. Unlike the SCP, the pro-Egyptian Awadhallah strongly supported the adherence of the Sudan to the Federation of Arab Republics. In June 1971 the communists attempted to overthrow Nimeiri and Awadhallah broke with them. In a reshuffle in October he lost his offices but was appointed First Vice-President. He appeared, however, to have lost his influence and in May 1972 he resigned on grounds of ill health and later settled in Cairo.

al-AYNI, Muhsin b. Ahmad (1932–)

Yemeni Prime Minister. He was a member of a family of tribal notables of the (Hashid and) Bakil and was one of the "Famous Forty" – young Yemenis sent abroad for education by the Imam Ahmad. After study at Cairo University and the Sorbonne he became a teacher in Aden. He was soon prominent in left-wing nationalist politics and became Secretary-General of the newly-formed Socialist People's Party. When British relations with the Imam improved in January 1961 he was expelled to Cairo where he represented the Aden Trade Union Congress. On the overthrow of the Imamate he was appointed the first Foreign Minister of the Republic but was soon sent off to the UN where he ably presented his country's case after frontier incidents with the British and the Saudis. When Ahmad Muhammad Nu'man became Prime Minister in April

1965 with the policy of ending the Yemen War through negotiations with the tribes, al-Ayni was recalled as Foreign Minister but as his sympathies were generally believed to be with the Baath rather than with Nasser, his appointment weakened the Government by giving offence to the Egyptians. When Nu'man resigned, al-Ayni returned to the UN. On the overthrow of Sallal became Prime Minister but immediately the Royalists began a dangerous siege of Sanaa. He called for Russian support which helped to save the Republic but, after a month in office, was replaced by a war cabinet under General Hassan al-Amri. He returned to the UN and also served as the diplomatic representative of President Abd al-Rahman al-Iryani. The following year he became Ambassador to Moscow. In July 1969, at a time of acute financial difficulty, he was recalled as Prime Minister but failed to form a government and returned to Moscow. In February 1970 he once again became Prime Minister and his diplomacy played an important part in creating the National Reconciliation which ended the civil war. He took advantage of an Islamic Foreign Ministers' Conference to reassure King Faysal that the Republic presented no threat and gained his official recognition. Many Royalists returned and joined his Cabinet. A new Constitution was proclaimed in December 1970 but it proved impossible to devise an electoral system which would reconcile the interests of the tribal shaykhs, the Shafais and the city-dwellers. This and the financial crisis caused his resignation in February 1971 and he went off as Ambassador to Paris. After the short-lived governments of Nu'man and Amri, he again became Prime Minister in September. He attempted some reforms, announced plans for a University and unsuccessfully tried to end the chewing of qat. He also visited nearly every Arab capital, Russia, China and India to end his country's isolation. The following year relations with South Yemen deteriorated rapidly owing to the presence in the North of considerable numbers of refugees, armed and financed by Saudi Arabia which provoked frontier incidents. Al-Ayni refused to "police" them and at the end of September 1972 actual war broke out. After a fortnight the Arab League succeeded in arranging a cease-fire and at the end of October al-Ayni and the South Yemeni Prime Minister Ali Nasir Muhammad met in Cairo and signed what was to become the Tripoli Agreement to unite the two countries. In December, however, seeing the opposition amongst conservative groups to implementing the Agreement, al-Ayni resigned, becoming Ambassador to London. In June 1974 after Colonel Ibrahim al-Hamdi had ousted President Iryani, he appointed al-Ayni as Prime Minister. He seemed the ideal choice, the only man with links both with the tribal leaders as he was related by marriage to the powerful Abu Lahum family, and with the left-wing in Aden. Ambitious plans for the reform of the judiciary, the administration, education and health were announced and steps taken to reduce corruption. There were also proposals for greater public participation in government. Al-Ayni was anxious for development without excessive dependence upon Saudi Arabia and his progressive ideas upset Riyadh and the conservatives. It was also felt that a more professional financier was needed to solve the unending problems of the economy.

In January 1975 he was replaced by the technocrat Abd al-Aziz Abd al-Ghani and went off as Ambassador to Paris and subsequently to Bonn. Al-Ayni was a very sociable, tolerant, agreeable man, of great administrative and diplomatic ability but perhaps lacked the ambition and the ruthlessness to stay at the top.

al-AYYUBI, Ata (c. 1877–?)
Syrian Head of State and Prime Minister. He came from a rich Damascus family which claimed descent from Saladin and was trained at the Administrative College in Istanbul. Before 1914 he was Mutasarrif of Lattakia and during the war British reports described him as pro-Turkish. However he became a close confidant of King Faysal and undertook missions for him in Beirut. He was in the government of Ala al-Din al-Durubi and later Director of the Ministry of the Interior. He was Minister of Justice under Subhi Barakat and was one of the group that tried to mediate in the Druze Rebellion and the nationalists regarded him as pro-French. He was again Minister of Justice in the government of Taj al-Din al-Hassani until in February 1936 during a period of strikes and civil unrest the French considered that he would make a more respectable Prime Minister than his chief. Ayyubi included some moderate nationalists in his Cabinet, released some detainees and the strikes were settled. He held office while the Franco-Syrian Treaty was negotiated and then made way in December 1936 for a purely nationalist government under Jamil Mardam. A British report at this time described him as one of the cleverest men in Syria, an experienced administrator and a very pleasant person. After Nasuhi al-Bukhari resigned in May 1939 Ayyubi was asked to form a government but he refused. In March 1943 after Hashim al-Atasi and Shukri al-Quwatli both refused to take office Ayyubi was appointed Head of State to conduct elections. He appointed a skeleton government of only three Ministers. He stepped down in August after the elections.

al-AZHOURY, Najib (c. 1870–1916)
Arab nationalist leader. He was a Greek Catholic, born in South Lebanon, who studied in Constantinople and at the Sciences Politiques in Paris. From 1898 until 1904 he was assistant to the Governor of Jerusalem but after quarrelling with him went to Paris where he founded the Ligue de la Nation Arabe. It never attracted more than a handful of members. He set forth his ideas in Le Réveil de la Nation Arabe and in a short-lived periodical L'Indépendance Arabe. He called for the independence of the Arab provinces of the Ottoman Empire although this would not include Egypt, "a nation of African Berbers" who were unfit to govern themselves but were fortunate to have good British rule. The Arabs of Asia he saw as a single nation with their divisions artificially created by outsiders. He called for a liberal Sultanate, held possibly by the Egyptian Khedive, and a purely religious Caliphate based on Mecca. He held that the Turks had ruined the Arabs, the Kurds and the Armenians and that they should all be freed from Ottoman rule with the help of Western liberal powers, particularly France in whose pay he was believed to be. He was allowed to use French postal

services in the Levant to distribute his propaganda and although he claimed to have secessionist followers in every large Arab city, he was taken more seriously in Europe than in the Middle East. He was one of the first to warn of the dangers of Zionism and he also had a great distrust of Russia.

al-AZM

The Azm have been one of the leading families in Damascus since at least 1725 when Ismail Pasha al-Azm was appointed Governor of the city. Although he held power only for four years he made great sums by monopolies and did much building. Other Azms governed Sidon and Tripoli. After four years they lost their patron in Istanbul and the new Sultan Mahmud ordered the imprisonment of all Azms and confiscation of their wealth. In 1734, however, Sulayman al-Azm became Pasha and apart from a break while he was Pasha of Egypt, held office until 1742 when he died campaigning against Zahir al-Umar in Galilee. He was succeeded by his nephew Assad and by 1755 Azms again governed Damascus, Tripoli and Sidon. In 1757 Assad was posted to Aleppo and then ordered to go to Egypt but there occurred a notorious massacre of the *Hajj* caravan by the Bani Sakhr in which 20,000 were said to have died. The Pasha of Damascus was traditionally responsible for its safety and the Azms, as Arabs, had always been able to maintain good relations with the bedouins; there were suggestions that the crime had been instigated by Assad Pasha to show his indispensability and he was executed. In 1771 Muhammad, of the third generation of Azms became Pasha and was ruling when the Egyptians under Abu al-Dhahab briefly occupied Damascus. He declined to compete with Jazzar Pasha for hegemony in Syria and concentrated on building and encouraging poets and sufis. On his death in 1783 his son Abd Allah succeeded but he was the last Azm Governor, dying in 1803. In their period of power the Azms, although they maintained a private army to keep order, were content to work within the Ottoman Empire and never aimed at independence. They developed alliances with the main trading families and showed their wealth by building palaces, mosques, baths and schools. They continued to be the most influential family in Damascus, also holding high administrative posts in Istanbul and sitting on every Council and Court in Syria. At the beginning of the twentieth century Muhammad Fawzi al-Azm was President of the Municipality and a Minister in Istanbul and was later Director of Works for the Hijaz Railway. He strongly opposed the Arab Revolt seeing it as treachery against the Caliph and he sent a telegram to Enver Pasha assuring him of Syrian loyalty. A British report described him as "cool, calculating, intelligent, always on the strongest side". He was Chairman of the General Syrian Congress and patched up differences with Faysal before his death in November 1919. On the other hand, Rafiq al-Azm was one of the founders of the Ottoman Decentralisation Party and one of the nationalists to whom the Declaration to the Seven was made. Another founder of the party was Haqqi al-Azm who was later Prime Minister. Muhammad Fawzi's son Khalid al-Azm was also Prime Minister.

al-AZM, Haqqi (c. 1870–?)

Syrian Prime Minister. He was a member of the very distinguished Azm family of Damascus and educated at a missionary school there and at the Military College in Istanbul. He entered the Ottoman bureaucracy and became Inspector-General to the Ministry of *Awqaf* until it came under the control of the Young Turks. In 1912 he stood against them on a liberal platform but was heavily defeated. He moved to Cairo where he was one of the founders of the Ottoman Decentralisation Party and became a close associate of Rashid Rida. He married a very wealthy divorcee through whom he came to own much land in Egypt. He entered into contact with the British and with Sharif Hussain but decided to throw in his lot with the French. He returned to Damascus after its liberation but quarrelled with Faysal and attempted without success to form an anti-monarchist party. When the French ended the brief period of Syrian independence, they divided the country into nominally separate states. Azm accepted office as Governor of the State of Damascus. He used his position for the financial advantage of himself and his numerous family and made himself ridiculous by excessive pomp while merely rubber-stamping all French decisions. In December 1922 he resigned but became a Minister in the collaborationist Cabinet of Subhi Barakat. In 1929 he founded the short-lived Syrian Reform Party. In January 1932 the French supported his election to the Assembly as a check upon the nationalists and in June at first appeared to be backing him as their candidate for the Presidency. However they switched their support to Muhammad Ali al-Abid and perhaps as a consolation Azm was appointed Prime Minister. He included two nationalists Jamil Mardam and Mazhar Raslan in his Cabinet. He found, however, the problems of the Franco-Syrian Treaty too much for him and he was dismissed, together with numerous officials, in February 1934 when the French thought a fresh approach was necessary and that Shaykh Taj al-Din al-Hassani would be even more pliable. A British report two years later described him as "a wise old man but spineless".

AZZAM, Abd al-Rahman *Pasha* (1893–1976)

Egyptian diplomat and first Secretary-General of the Arab League. The Azzams were a family of bedouin origins and preserved many of the traditions of the desert. Abd al-Rahman was the son of the Deputy for Giza and studied medicine at London University. During the summer vacation of 1913 he put his skill at the disposal of the Turkish forces fighting in Albania, returning to continue his studies. After leaving without qualifying in 1915 he provided medical services to Ahmad al-Sharif al-Sanusi in his invasion of Egypt and after that failed, was taken to Germany by submarine for military training. Azzam returned to Libya as one of the leaders of the resistance to the Italians and, working closely with Ramadan Shutawyi, was one of the founders of the Tripolitanian Republic in 1918. He was condemned to death by the Italians. He returned to Egypt after the defeat of the Republic in 1923, joined the Wafd and the following year became the youngest Member of Parliament. Although he had been close to Saad Zaghloul, he later turned against the Wafd with its narrow Egyptian perspective and started to work for

Arab unity. In 1932 he published *Les Arabes, peuple de l'Avenir*, comparing their situation with that of Italy and Germany a century earlier. The High Commissioner Sir Percy Loraine described him as "an attractive young fanatic with the bedouin qualities of courage (moral no less than physical), acute sense of honour – together with a sense of humour and a large measure of sportsmanship and idealism . . . in the best sense of the word an adventurer and his personality stands out in a land of *fellahin*". In 1936 he was appointed Ambassador to Saudi Arabia and Iraq, using the position to urge their Rulers towards Arab unity. He was accredited also to Tehran where the British Minister commented upon his friendliness, abilities and support for the Anglo-Egyptian Treaty of 1936. Upon his appointment as an Ambassador, the Italian Government annulled his death sentence. In 1939 he worked hard for Arab unity at the London Palestine Conference. Later that year he joined the anti-British government of Ali Mahir as Minister of *Awqaf* and later of Social Affairs. He was also Commandant of Territorial Forces and later Minister for Arab Affairs, using his position to push Egyptian leaders towards Arab unity. When the Arab League was established in May 1945, Azzam became its first Secretary-General and directed its first action which was to demand French withdrawal from Lebanon and Syria. Although accused by some such as Nuri al-Said of "hijacking" the League for Egypt, it was undeniable that despite a certain lack of administrative ability, his forcefulness, strong sense of history and of Arab destiny and ability to see the Arab world as a whole played a vital part in making it a reality. Indeed by 1947 the British thought that he had created a "Frankenstein" but rejected plotting to replace him as too risky. Azzam, however, was not really anti-British, stressing the need of London to gain Arab confidence. Azzam hoped to see the Jews of Palestine represented in the Arab League which, he said, had "no spirit of racial exclusiveness or sterile chauvinism". He acted as Arab spokesman over Palestine, confusing Count Bernadotte by speaking simultaneously of his love of peace and readiness to fight to the death. He also tried to unify Arab strategy in the Palestine War. After Nasser took power he wanted an administrator rather than a policy-maker, particularly one associated with King Farouq, at the Arab League and he had Azzam replaced by Abd al-Khaliq Hassouna in September 1952. Azzam went abroad, became an adviser to King Faysal whose daughter he married and did not return to Egypt until 1972. He wrote memoirs serialised in Egyptian and Lebanese journals in 1950 and 1972. Volatile, he was a brilliant talker with great charm. He was an expert horseman who won many amateur races. In appearance he was tall and thin with a sparse moustache.

BAATH Party (Iraq)

The Baath Party (Syria) was founded in 1944 by Michel Aflaq and Salah al-Din al-Bitar and students trained in Beirut and Damascus started to spread its ideals throughout the Eastern Arab world. In Iraq its members were first mentioned as participating in riots in 1952 and its first publications appeared late the following year. It did not have the resources to contest the elections of May 1954 but in June 1955, after riots against the foundation of the Baghdad Pact, 22 leaders including the Regional Secretary Fuad al-Rikabi, a Shiah from Nasiriyyah, were arrested. As it then had fewer than 300 members this briefly paralysed its activities but it had already recruited some officers such as Brigadier Ahmad Hassan al-Bakr and Major Salih Mahdi Ammash who, as Free Officers were involved in the July Revolution of 1958. Rikabi became a member of the first Cabinet formed by Abd al-Krim Qassim but he was dismissed with other pan-Arabists at the end of September. Baathists were angered by Qassim's lack of interest in Arab unity and by his alliance with their enemies the communists and in February 1959 a committee of the Regional Command planned his murder. The attempt in October failed and Rikabi fled to Syria leaving the remnants of the organisation in the hands of Ali Salih al-Saadi, a man with ideal gifts, courage, ruthlessness and organising ability, for the underground struggle. He rebuilt the Command, created a militia – the National Guard – and formed alliances with other pan-Arab groups, discontented officers and even the Kurds against Qassim. Baathist officers including Bakr and the pilot Major Mundhir al-Wandawi played an essential part in the Ramadan Revolution of 1963. The new government amongst other Baathists had Bakr as Prime Minister, Saadi as Deputy Premier and Interior Minister, Ammash at Defence and Brigadier Hardan al-Takriti as commander of the Air Force. The Party still had less than 1,000 members with about 15,000 associates but it determined to dominate the country and to assist in this Saadi built up the National Guard, commanded by Wandawi, until by the late summer it had over 35,000 armed members. In March the Syrian Baath seized power in Damascus and during the spring both parties held the Unity Talks with President Nasser who after their failure declared that he could never again work with the Baath. In Baghdad Saadi announced his conversion to Marxism, demanding such radical measures that they were disavowed by Aflaq although they were accepted at the Party's Sixth National Congress. This and the refusal of "the left" to relinquish control of the National Guard alienated the moderate Baathists and particularly the military such as Bakr, Ammash, Takriti and the Chief of Staff General Tahir Yahya and in the November Revolution they allied with President Abd al-Salam Arif to smash the radicals and the National Guard. This group remained in office until Arif felt secure enough to drop them. Saadi was replaced as Secretary-General by Bakr but the real power in the Party was held by the Assistant Secretary-General, his relative Saddam Hussain who gathered all the levers into his own hands. The Shiah who had backed Saadi lost influence to the Sunnis, mainly those from Takrit who were strongly represented amongst army officers. In Syria the Baath remained in power but fell under the leadership of a group led by Colonel Salah al-Jadid which ignored pan-Arabism in favour of carrying out a radical revolution within its own country. They expelled Aflaq but the Iraqis still recognised him as Secretary-General and the two Regional Commands exchanged bitter insults. On July 17 1968 Colonel Abd al-Razzaq al-Nayif, a disgruntled officer ousted President Abd al-Rahman Arif in alliance with the Baath and became Prime Minister with Bakr as President. The experiences of 1963–64 determined the Baath never again to share power and a fortnight later Bakr arrested Nayif and appointed himself Prime Minister of a Baathist Cabinet. The Party consolidated its rule with months of terror. In-fighting amongst the Party leadership led to a victory for the civilians as Takriti and Ammash were relegated to Embassies abroad: this was largely due to Bakr who used his prestige in the army to give victory to the civilians. The Party was determined never again to lose power and felt that it had to control every aspect of life and penetrate every level of society. Baathists were given preference in employment over abler non-party members who were frequently moved around to prevent them from acquiring power bases. The Baath expanded enormously until it had about 25,000 members organised in a pyramidical structure based on local cells. In addition there were 1.5 million organised supporters, many of them constituted as an armed militia, and structures to dominate the affairs of women, youth and other groups and a network of informers. Opponents were tortured and killed as a matter of routine. In 1972 the Baath decided to allow other groups some participation in government and two members of the Iraq Communist Party joined the Cabinet and the following year the ICP became a junior partner in a National Patriotic Front which also included some Kurdish representatives. The Baath might have had many of its leaders murdered in the Kazzar Plot but the subsequent purges and the election of a new Regional Command still further strengthened the position of Hussain and the identity of Party and State. The ten-fold increase in the country's oil revenue in the five years after the October War enabled the Party to buy friends abroad and at home but the disproportionate spending in Sunni areas led to Shiah resentment. In October 1977 the Iraqi Baath restaked its claim to be the pan-Arab National Command of which Aflaq was re-elected Secretary-General with Bakr as his Deputy and Hussain as an Assistant while the Regional Command was absorbed into the Revolutionary Command Council. In March 1979 the Patriotic Front broke up and persecution of communists began. In July 1979 after Bakr had retired in favour of Hussain the discovery of a plot was announced after which 22 senior members of the Party were shot. The Party which Aflaq had founded with the object of bringing the reign of love had become an obsessively secretive instrument of repression to keep a brutal clique in power and no other discernible policy or ideals. In 1990 an American Human Rights group stigmatised it as one of the most brutal and repressive regimes in the world.

BADEA

Following the October War, the Algiers Summit of 1973 was particularly concerned with winning support in Africa for the Arab cause. The Banque Arabe pour le Développement Économique en Afrique was established with an initial capital of $524.75 million, mostly subscribed by Saudi Arabia, Iraq, Kuwait, the UAE and Algeria. The subscription was later doubled. Based on Khartoum, BADEA provided technical assistance and small loans at low interest and by 1991 had contributed to about 150 projects ranging from a sewerage network in Burundi to abattoirs in Zimbabwe. More than half its money went on infrastructional development.

al-BADR (Muhammad) (1927–)

King of the Yemen and Zaidi Imam. He was the son of Ahmad who gave him a traditional and religious upbringing although amongst his tutors were the liberals Muhammad Mahmud al-Zubayri and Ahmad Muhammad Nu'man. In April 1955 when a coup to oust Ahmad appeared to be succeeding, Badr rallied the Hashid and Bakil and hurried to his aid; he arrived too late for his help to be needed but he was rewarded with the appointment of Crown Prince, to the chagrin of his uncle Hassan who, according to Zaidi law, had an equal right to claim the Imamate. Ahmad used his son as a special Ambassador and he obtained arms, trade and development help from both Moscow and Peking, declaring "we are Russia's friends". In London he failed to settle the frontier disputes with the Aden Protectorates. He also went to Cairo where he fell under the spell of Nasser and became a supporter of radical Arabism. In April 1969 Ahmad went to Rome for treatment of his morphine addiction and Badr was left in charge. Still fearing that his uncle Hassan might dispute the succession, Badr determined to seize the opportunity to win support. Having himself hailed on the radio as the "Treasure and Hope of the Nation", he promised liberal reforms, rapid development and a pay-

rise of 25% for the army. He brought in numerous Egyptians, officers, teachers and doctors. However the money for the reforms did not exist and the Egyptian presence was resented; there was considerable unrest to quieten which he had to resort to traditional methods and call in the Hashid and Bakil. In August his father returned, rapidly restored order and, according to rumour, put Badr briefly under arrest. However Ahmad reverted to morphine after an attempt on his life in March 1961 and power gradually passed into the hands of Badr. He succeeded to the throne without opposition on 19 September 1962, assumed the regnal name of al-Mansur Billah and immediately announced plans for sweeping reforms to raise political, economic and social standards. He proclaimed a general amnesty, ended the hostage system, remitted taxation for the rest of the year and decreed the establishment of an Advisory Council which would be half elected and also of elective municipal councils. He appointed himself Prime Minister to ensure that these measures were carried through and raised the pay of the army. He received a message of support from Nasser but on the night of 26 September, with Egyptian help, military units attacked his palace. The Imam was reported killed and a Republic proclaimed under Colonel Abd Allah Sallal, whose career and probably life were due to the patronage of Badr. His uncle Hassan was proclaimed Imam. However Badr had made a dramatic escape and after being sheltered by a woman who gave him an ordinary soldier's uniform, hurried north, attracting tribal following as he went. On 10 November he gave a conference to international journalists, resumed the Imamate and made Hassan Prime Minister. He established his HQ in caves near Jabal Qara, 40 miles south west of Sada where he assumed overall leadership but, contrary to Imamic tradition, neither personally led his followers in battle nor provided them with spiritual guidance. In August 1964 an Egyptian offensive forced him to withdraw to caves near Jabal Dhada close to the Saudi frontier. By the time of the first moves to end the Yemen War – the Erkowit Conference of November 1964 – took place, his supporters and even his family were prepared to agree to his exile in return for that of Sallal. Badr had previously been known for self-indulgence and his health deteriorated. He spent some months of 1966 in Saudi Arabia for medical treatment and after his return in November he virtually handed over power to his cousin Muhammad b. Hussain who had gained the reputation of being the best of the fighting princes. In 1968 he opposed but could not prevent the major offensive by which Prince Hussain hoped to capture Sanaa after the Egyptian withdrawal and in June Badr was reported deposed by his cousin. He spent much time in Saudi Arabia but in March 1968 managed to reassert control. When the Royalist cause crumbled, Badr took refuge in England, living quietly near Bromley. He is a gentle, intelligent, well-meaning man but an exceptionally poor judge of character – most of the people in whom he put his trust betrayed him. The history of his ancestors showed that only an exceptional man could successfully rule the Yemen and Badr was all too ordinary.

BADR, Zaki Mustafa (1934–)
Egyptian Minister. A professional policeman, he won a
reputation for toughness as Governor of Asyut Province, the hotbed of the Islamic militant *Jihad* group. In
February 1986, after the regime had been shaken by
the Gizeh Mutiny he was called to Cairo as Minister
of the Interior. It was calculated that during the next
five years he presided over the arrest of 20,000 people,
mostly Muslim fundamentalists but also including communists and the nationalist left-wingers of Egypt's
Revolution. He ordered the police to ignore normal
rules of procedure, disciplined those who refused to
do so, sanctioned collective punishment and torture,
declaring that violence could only be met with violence.
After any breach of security there were wholesale arrests
and prolonged detention of suspects. He appeared to
consider all Muslim activists dangerous, unable to distinguish between impoverished peasants of the south
and sleek members of the Cairo establishment. Badr
later openly admitted that he had tampered with the
results of the election of April 1988. In August 1989 he
ordered the harsh crushing of a peaceful strike at
Helwan. In December 1989 the first truck bomb used
in Egypt was an attempt on his life; he foiled another
aimed at the American Embassy. The brutality of his
behaviour was matched by the brashness of his language: fundamentalists were "mad dogs", human rights
activists "perverts and homosexuals" and journalists
were a particular target. He was widely unpopular even
within his own Ministry and his reputation for harshness was seen to reflect on the Government as a whole.
In January 1991 after a series of his obscene comments
on politicians came to light he was replaced by a less
provocative figure. Badr was a very large man with a
very red face.

BADRAN, Mudar Muhammad (1934–)
Jordanian Prime Minister. He was born in Jerash and
took a degree in Law from Damascus University. He
immediately entered the military security service and
was Director of Intelligence in 1970 when King Hussain
made him Secretary-General to the Royal Court and
later Security Adviser and Head of the Executive Office
for the affairs of the Occupied Territories. He held the
rank of Major-General. In May 1973 Badran became
Minister of Education in the government formed by
Zaid al-Rifai, holding the office until November 1974
when he was brought into the inner circle of advisers
as Chief of the Royal Court. In July 1976 when Rifai
resigned after three years as Prime Minister and Minister of Defence and Foreign Affairs Badran was named
to succeed him. His loyalty was beyond doubt but he
was little known abroad although it was said that he was
politically moderate. Badran was believed to opposed
excessive demands from the Palestinians; he had fewer
of them in his Cabinet and their militants were harassed
by the police. In July 1976 he set up a Bureau of Occupied Homeland Affairs which was attacked by militants
as an attempt to influence affairs on the West Bank. He
continued his predecessor's close links with Syria and
was criticised by other Arab states for supporting its
presence in Lebanon. The main emphasis was on development and technocrats were encouraged. Amman
profited from the troubles of Beirut and greatly

increased as a financial centre. After Camp David he
refused to be cajoled into bilateral negotiations with
Israel. Badran was the first Prime Minister of the
decade to visit Libya from which he returned with a
loan. Relations improved with the Palestinians and
Yassir Arafat returned to Amman for the first time since
Black September. A nominated National Consultative
Council was created to take the place of the Parliament
dissolved in 1974. When Badran resigned in December
1979 it was generally agreed that his government had
presided over a period of unusual tranquillity and prosperity. In August 1980 after the unexpected death of
Abd al-Hamid Sharaf Badran again became Prime
Minister and soon found the country at odds with Syria
over its support for Baghdad in the Iran–Iraq War.
Relations became extremely bad as Syria accused
Jordan of encouraging Muslim fundamentalists and still
claiming to speak for the Palestinians. In 1981 five
Syrian army officers who had entered the country to
kill Badran were shown on Jordanian TV. Badran welcomed the Reagan Initiative and after a meeting with
Arafat advocated in December 1982 "special and dis-
tinctive relations between Jordan and a liberated
Palestine". He soon realised that the peace process
could only really start once the Americans had recognised the Palestine Liberation Organisation which the
Israelis would never allow them to do. The economy,
although still heavily dependent upon aid and remittances, expanded considerably although Badran
claimed no special expertise. A new Five-Year Plan for
1981–5 was introduced. Less was heard about democratic reforms although women had the vote for the
first time in the local elections of 1981. In January 1984
the King decided on one of his characteristic "fresh
starts" and recalled the survivors of the 1974 Parliament: at the same time he appointed Ahmad Ubaydat,
another former Intelligence officer, to replace Badran.
In April 1989 riots in traditionally loyal South Jordan
brought down the Cabinet of Rifai and led to a freely
conducted general election, after which, on 6 December
Badran again became Prime Minister. He appointed a
mainly technocratic Cabinet but although on good
terms with the Muslim Brothers, the largest single
group in Parliament, could not persuade them to join
as he was unwilling to meet their demand for the Ministry of Education. However he won their general
support by introducing reforms that brought the legal
system closer to the *Shariah*, setting up a *Shariah*
Faculty at the University and restricting sales of alcohol.
Badran tried to grant greater democracy without relin-
quishing control. He made concessions at an
unexpected rate: martial law after it had been in existence since the June War of 1967 and he curbed the
Intelligence Service. He gave up controls on newspapers introduced by Rifai. Top civil servants had to
declare the sources of their wealth. In January 1990 after
a critical debate Parliament approved his programme by
65 votes to 9 with 6 abstentions. King Hussain and
Badran started to run into trouble after the Iraqi
invasion of Kuwait when Jordan was one of the few
Arab states to support Saddam Hussain and to assist
in the breaking of UN sanctions. In January 1991 he
reformed his Cabinet bringing in five Muslim Brothers.
Work on the National Charter was completed and it was

published in June. A few days later the King, anxious to win back the favour of the West, sacrificed Badran, replacing him with Tahir al-Masri. A stocky, balding man, he was calm and moderate, able to face demands for change.

BADRAN, Shams al-Din (1929–)

Egyptian officer and politician. He graduated from the Officers' School in 1948 and after the July Revolution worked in the bureau of the Commander-in-Chief Field Marshal Amer, over whom he seems to have acquired great influence. He used this to control military intelligence and the careers of brother officers, for many of whom he found well-paid sinecures. His power within the armed forces became practically unlimited. In 1965 he directed the repression of the Muslim Brothers after they were alleged to have plotted against the life of Nasser. He was also one of the leading members of the Committee for the Liquidation of Feudalism which harassed the richer farmers and looted their property. In September 1966 he was appointed Minister of War and presumably bore some responsibility for the atrocities committed by the Egyptian army in the Yemen War and by Egyptian trained terrorists in Aden. Confident of easy victory in a conflict with Israel, he placed incompetent friends where he thought that they would get credit for the inevitable success. In May 1967 he went to Moscow and gave the impression on his return that Russia would support Egypt. Although himself partially responsible for the defeats suffered in the June War, he blamed Nasser for not attacking first and urged him to resign. When Nasser announced on TV that he would do so, Badran used troops to try to prevent demonstrations in the President's favour. Failing, he and Amer resigned, collected arms and supporters and prepared to carry out a coup while Nasser was at the Khartoum Summit; Badran was to be Prime Minister. The plot was discovered and Badran was arrested. In January 1968 he and 54 others accused of treason were placed on trial and in August he was sentenced to hard labour for life. In October 1974 he was released in a general amnesty proclaimed by President Sadat and went abroad, settling in England on a farm. In June 1977 he was sentenced *in absentia* to 30 years' hard labour for torturing Muslim Brothers and other political prisoners.

al-BADRI, Abd al-Qadir (1916–)

Libyan Prime Minister. A landowner, he was Minister of Housing and Government Property in the Cabinet of Hussain Maziq before succeeding him as Prime Minister in July 1967. He showed solidarity with the Arab cause after the defeat of the June War by continuing until September the oil boycott of the West and by demanding the closure of British and American bases. At the Khartoum Summit Libya won considerable prestige through its undertaking to subsidise Egypt although it was itself suffering more than most countries through its refusal to sell oil to the West. Tougher than most other politicians, Badri put on trial the oil workers whose strike had brought down the previous government but he became extremely unpopular. In October 1967 he resigned on the plea of ill health. After the

Revolution he was sentenced to four years' imprisonment for corruption.

BAGHDAD SUMMIT (1978)

In September 1978 Egypt and Israel reached the Camp David Agreement which was regarded by many Arab states as a betrayal of past commitments and of Arab unity. Iraq was the first to call for a Summit to discuss an Arab fund of $5 billion annually to help to "meet Egypt's heavy financial burden, in the event that its government would renounce the Camp David agreements" – at the same time another $4 billion would go to the other confrontation states. Syria laid aside its quarrel with Iraq and Hafiz al-Assad went to Baghdad for a reconciliation with Ahmad al-Bakr. This ninth Arab Summit, to which Egypt was not invited, met on 2 November 1978 and was attended by eleven Heads of State and Yassir Arafat: Algeria, Jibouti, Libya, Morocco, Oman, Somalia, Sudan, Tunisia and North Yemen sent representatives. It agreed that the cause of the Palestinians could never be abandoned and that, as this was a collective national responsibility, it was inadmissible for any one state to attempt to solve the problem in its own: only a full Summit could do this as had been decided at previous meetings and peace could only come after total Israeli evacuation of the territories occupied in the June War. Hard-line calls for sanctions and boycotts were rejected and Egypt was invited to abrogate its agreement with Israel and return to the Arab fold. It was further decided to hold a Summit annually in November and to launch a propaganda drive to put the Arab case. In a further secret agreement a fund of $3,500 million was established to aid the confrontation states and the Palestinians. A four-man delegation led by the Lebanese Prime Minister Salim al-Hoss was sent to Cairo on 4 November with a message from the Summit but President Sadat refused to receive it. It was then decided that the headquarters of the Arab League should be moved from Cairo to Tunis. The Summit also agreed to study reconstruction aid for Lebanon and to end the sanctions imposed on South Yemen for its suspected involvement in the murder of President Ghashmi. After the signature of the Sinai Agreement in March 1979 a conference was held in Baghdad of Arab Foreign and Economic Ministers except for those of Sudan, Oman and Jibouti. This decided to break off diplomatic relations with Egypt, to expel it from the Arab League and seek its expulsion from the Non-Aligned Movement, the Organisation of African Unity etc., to operate a financial and economic boycott, to remove all pan-Arab organisations from Cairo and to ban the import of Egyptian publications. Egypt was to remain in official, although decreasing isolation until the Casablanca Summit of May 1989.

BAGHDAD SUMMIT (1990)

Saddam Hussain, at the request of the Palestinians, called a Summit in Baghdad from 28–30 May 1990 to discuss the "threat to Pan-Arab security" posed by the Russian decision to allow an increased flow of Soviet Jews into Israel. King Hassan II, Sultan Qabus and Presidents Chadli and Assad declined to attend. Yassir Arafat called for sanctions against all who facilitated the Jewish immigration. Saddam attempted to project himself as the leader of the Arabs by threatening Israel with mass destruction if it used nuclear weapons and said that the USA was intimately associated with Israeli aggression but President Mubarak urged against escalating tension saying that "any message to the outside world should be humane, logical, realistic and consistent with the values and concepts of the age". King Hussain said that Israel had selected Jordan as the "point through which to penetrate the Arab nation" and the struggle to prevent this had "exhausted all the material capabilities" of his country which desperately needed economic and military aid. Qadafi in a jocular speech described how he had challenged President Reagan to a duel in Switzerland and urged the Arabs to multiply until they numbered one billion. The Summit expressed its support for Iraq in its frontier claims against Iran, although Saddam hinted that relations might improve. Despite the efforts of Mubarak and King Fahd the final communique was a victory for the confrontationalists although it did not endorse Arafat's call for sanctions. The US was criticised as the protector of Israel. The greatest challenge to the Arabs was said to be in the scientific and cultural fields and there was a demand that the advanced states increase the transfer of technology. Yemeni unity was welcomed. Following the excitement generated by the apparent discovery of an Iraqi Super-Gun the Summit declared that the country had "the right to take all measures to defend its security". The Summit expressed total support for Jordan and said that aid should be negotiated bilaterally. Ominously, in the light of future events, Saddam accused the Gulf States of waging economic war against Iraq by refusing to cut their production of oil, thus keeping the price low and depriving Baghdad of the revenue essential for rebuilding the damage done in the Iran–Iraq War.

As part of his policy of liberalisation President Gorbachev facilitated the departure of Russian Jews, many of whom proceeded to Israel. In the spring of 1990 the Palestine Liberation Organisation and Jordan called for an emergency summit to discuss this "threat to pan-Arab security" and Jordan was also desperate for money as only Iraq had been giving the aid promised. Despite intense pressure Hafiz al-Assad refused to attend a meeting in Baghdad and Algeria, Morocco, Lebanon and Oman sent only representatives. Otherwise all the Heads of State assembled in Baghdad on 28 May 1990. There was an emotional appeal from King Hussain who argued that the Israelis intended to penetrate the Arab world through Jordan which lacked the financial backing to confront them alone: the security of Jordan was the security of all the Arabs. Saddam Hussain threatened Israel with mass destruction in the event of an attack. Yassir Arafat denounced the Americans as bearing "basic responsibility as the state which provides Israel with the means to defy the international community" but Hosni Mubarak and King Fahd prevented any call for sanctions and made the final communiqué less confrontational. The Summit called on the UN to set up an international supervisory mechanism to ensure that Russian Jews were not settled in the Occupied Territories. Measures should be taken against states that recognised Jerusalem as the capital of Israel.

It extended the mandate of the tripartite committee set up at the Casablanca Summit of 1989. It condemned recent "aggressive threats" against Iraq which had the right to get whatever weapons it needed. Financial support for Jordan should be arranged bilaterally. It was agreed that a regular Summit should be held in Cairo in November 1990. Qadafi rejoiced that the Baghdad Summit, generally seen as a success for Iraq and the PLO, had "wiped out the shame of Casablanca".

al-BAGHDADI, Abd al-Latif Mahmud (1917–)
Egyptian Vice-President. He was born in Dakhaliya Province and was a member of the new class that was able to aspire to officer status in the expansion of the Egyptian forces that followed the Anglo–Egyptian Treaty of 1936. He graduated from both the Infantry and Air Force Academies but attempted to resign his commission as he was one of the officers who resented the humiliation of King Farouq in the Abdin Incident of January 1942. Thereafter he did his best to hamper the British war effort, organising sabotage and flying over their lines to take photographs that were smuggled to Rommel. After the war he was attached to Air Misr, gaining commercial experience and contacts in industry. During the Palestine War he went to Damascus in the hope of persuading Syrian air force officers to fly support missions for the Palestine Liberation Army. Baghdadi was an early member of the Free Officers, was on the executive formed in 1949 and acted as a link with the Muslim Brothers. Before the July Revolution, as a Wing Commander, he was commander of Almaza air base which he took over. He was a member of the Revolutionary Command Council. In June 1953 he was appointed War Minister and later that year presided over the Revolutionary tribunal of which Anwar Sadat and Hassan Ibrahim were the other members. They sentenced former political leaders, condemning four to death by hanging and imprisoning others. He took part in the negotiations for the Anglo–Egyptian Treaty of 1954 and in the same year was moved to Ministry of Municipal and Rural Affairs to which Planning was later added. He was thus involved in a major rebuilding of Cairo, proving himself a tough-minded administrator. He was particularly close to Nasser who kept him at his side during the Suez War, during which he poured scorn on those who thought of surrender. When a form of parliamentary life was introduced in July 1957 Baghdadi was in charge of screening the candidates for the sole party, the National Union. On the formation of the United Arab Republic he was one of the two Egyptian Vice-Presidents and he continued to hold the title after the break up while he was in charge of the Treasury. Baghdadi criticised the waste of Egyptian resources in the Yemen War and the President's increasing reliance upon the Russians and upon left-wingers. He deplored, also, the concentration of all power in Nasser's hands and he came to be on bad terms with Field Marshal Amcr, to whose defects the President seemed perversely blind. In March 1964 he resigned. Before the outbreak of the June War he warned Nasser not to give Israel any excuse for an attack. When Nasser's health was failing he wished for the succession of Baghdadi whom he invited

to become First Vice-President and Prime Minister; it was only upon his refusal that Sadat was chosen. After Nasser's death Baghdadi was the leader of a group which urged Sadat to return to collective leadership, to allow some opposition and press freedom and restrict the secret police. In April 1972 he was the best known signatory of a memorandum to Sadat saying that it was time to end excessive dependence upon Russia and to balance between the Super-Powers. He criticised the Camp David Agreement as sacrificing the Palestinian cause and cutting Egypt off from the rest of the Arabs. He was regarded as one of the most likeable of the Egyptian leaders and the one most ready to mix with ordinary people.

BAHNINI, Ahmad (1909–71)

Moroccan Prime Minister. After studying at Mulai Idris College in Fez, he qualified as a lawyer and practised in Fez. He was one of the signatories of the Manifesto of the Istiqlal Party in January 1944. After independence he was appointed Director of Political Affairs at the Ministry of the Interior before becoming Minister of Justice in 1963. Bahnini was a leading member of the Front pour la Défense des Institutions Constitutionelles which was formed by Reda Guedira to band together supporters of King Hassan II. In May 1963 Guedira as Minister of the Interior rigged parliamentary elections to provide a majority for them and their allies, the Mouvement Populaire. In November when Bahnini formed a government mostly from these two parties, he was generally seen as a front-man for the Palace *camarilla* and after three months there was a general impression that the Government was out of its depth in an economic and political crisis. The opposition Istiqlal and the Union Nationale des Forces Populaires brought about a parliamentary stalemate and, after narrowly surviving a vote of confidence, Banhini had to suspend Parliament to prevent debate on his failure to bring forward measures that were widely demanded. The trial of alleged UNFP conspirators was seen internationally as a farce. In February 1964 there were riots against police brutality in Khenifra. In foreign affairs the Government had a better record, diplomatic relations broken off over the Tindouf Dispute were restored with Algeria, Tunisia and Egypt but the Americans suspended aid as Morocco refused to break with Cuba. The FDIC fell apart and in May 1964 Bahnini became President of a new Parti Socialist Démocratique, also founded by Guedira, which aimed to establish wide support for the King through a "liberal" socialism which would combine with private enterprise. In September key Ministers including Guedira resigned and Bahnini had to reform his Cabinet bringing in Ahmad Tayba Ben Hima Benhima at Foreign Affairs and General Oufkir at the Interior. Despite harsh enforcement of Ramadan in January 1965, the Government was still attacked by Allal al-Fassi for "lack of Islamic spirit". In March 1965 student demonstrations against an educational reform which they saw as damaging their prospects of government employment set off the Casablanaca Riots in which there were some estimates that 400 people were killed. Observers thought that the regime might collapse until the King proclaimed a state of emergency with suspension of

Parliament and revision of the Constitition. He himself replaced Banhini as Prime Minister. Bahnini was later appointed President of the Supreme Court. In July 1971 he was one of those killed in the Skhirat attempt on the life of the King.

BAKER PROPOSALS (1989)

The harshness of the Israeli attempts to repress the *Intifadah* made the new American administration of George Bush less susceptible to Zionist influence than had been that of Reagan and it put considerable pressure upon them to make concessions in the interests of peace. Elections in the Occupied Territories were reluctantly offered in the Shamir Plan but under conditions that the Palestinians could not accept and an attempt to make them more palatable in the Mubarak Peace Initiative was rejected by Shamir. In October 1989 Secretary of State Baker formally abandoned the traditional American policy that Israel should negotiate with the Palestinians through Jordan, last set out in the Shultz Initiative and rejected at the Algiers Summit of 1988, and urged that Israel should negotiate directly with the Palestinians. He understood that Egypt could not negotiate on their behalf but he called for a meeting in Washington with its Foreign Minister and that of Israel within two weeks to discuss such matters as a list of the Palestinians with whom the Israelis would talk. He understood that Israel would talk with them on the basis of the Shamir Plan but other matters could be discussed. The Palestine Liberation Organisation rejected the proposals as it did not acknowledge their title as the sole representatives of the Palestinian people. The Israelis did not accept the invitation and their intransigence was formally deplored by the US Government which subsequently considered them insincere in the search for peace.

BAKHIET, Jafar Muhammad Ali (1926–76)

Sudanese Minister. He was born in El Obeid and studied at the Universities of Exeter and Cambridge where he was awarded a doctorate. After working as a local government official in Darfur and the South, he taught political science at Khartoum. His support gave intellectual respectability to the regime of Jafar Nimeiri whose government he joined in February 1971 as Minister of Local Popular Government. He argued that administration, instead of being a natural product of social relations had become state-sponsored backing of local autocrats and advocated the establishment of a local government system by removing the concept of two-tier method in favour of a pyramid linking local communities directly to the top. He put forward a Local Government Act setting out regional autonomy for the South which formed the basis for the Addis Ababa Agreement of 1972 which he played a major part in negotiating. Bakhiet was also one of the architects of the Sudan Socialist Union which he saw as a mass movement of political participation. With his colleague Mansur Khalid he did most of the drafting of the Constitution of 1973 which provided for a strong executive presidency which a People's Assembly and the SSU would prevent from becoming dictatorial. He saw his Ministry as a transforming organ of government and stood up to anyone including Nimeiri, opposed preventive detention, fought against centrists blocking local initiatives and denounced the "hypocritical sloganism" of pressing Islam on Christians. In January 1975 Bakhiet was demoted to leader of government business in the Assembly and Assistant Secretary-General of the SSU. He was Chairman of the University and Editor of the official newspaper and died of overwork while writing his daily article. He had just been asked to mediate in the Eritrean problem. Mansur Khalid called him "a cerebral giant".

BAKKUSH, Abd al-Hamid (1935–)

Libyan Prime Minister. He was born in Tripoli and unlike his predecessors had no tribal affiliations. He took a Law Degree in Cairo, became Legal Adviser to an Oil Company, and was a protégé of the Muntasir family before being appointed Minister of Justice in March 1964. In October 1967 he became Prime Minister, reputedly the youngest in the world, heading a Cabinet of youthful technocrats. He symbolised the post-war generation, the educated bourgeoisie, and he gave a new impetus to affairs. Bakkush tried to gain a new level of public participation by explaining his policies on the radio, visiting the Universities and Libyanising posts. He appointed dynamic young planning officials and inaugurated a new oil policy setting up a company to undertake joint ventures. He was anxious to bring his country more into the mainstream of Arab affairs and visited most Arab countries, although in February 1968 94 people accused of belonging to the Arab Nationalist Movement were jailed. He was anxious that Libya should be able to defend itself, thus reducing its dependence upon the West, expanded the army and made an enormous (£100 million) arms deal with Britain which included the purchase of missiles. His activity and his progressive policies upset the conservative circle around King Idris, with whom he disagreed over appointments, and he was also accused of favouritism and corruption. In September 1968 he unexpectedly resigned and was appointed Ambassador to Paris. He later stated that during his period there he had warned the Americans there of an impending army coup but they had been confident that they could control Qadafi and his group of young officers. Although the independent, self-confident and vigorous policies of Bakkush had foreshadowed those of the Revolution, he was imprisoned immediately after it. In 1970 he was accused, along with another former Prime Minister Maziq, of plotting to overthrow the regime and in September 1971 he was sentenced to four years' imprisonment. Upon his release he sought political asylum in Cairo where he was made welcome by Sadat. He became a focus of organised opposition to Qadafi. This so enraged the Colonel that in 1984 he paid a gang of mercenaries to murder Bakkush. The plot failed but Bakkush collaborated with the Egyptian police to fake his own death, thus bringing ridicule on the Libyan Government which had announced his "execution by an heroic suicide squad". A second attempt the following year also failed. In April 1986 Bakkush gave whole-hearted support to the American effort to topple Qadafi by the Tripoli Bombing.

BAKKUSH, Hedi (1930–)

Tunisian Prime Minister. He was born in Hammam-Sousse in the Sahil and became an active nationalist while still at school. In 1950 he was imprisoned but later went on to study in France where he became President of Neo-Destour students. In 1962 Bakkush was appointed joint Director of the Party bureaucracy with Muhamad Sayah, initiating a period of rivalry between them which lasted a quarter of a century. He spent some years as Governor of Bizerta and then of Sfax and early in 1970 was appointed Director of the National Social Security Fund. Bakkush had been an enthusiastic supporter of the socialist policies of Ahmad Ben Salah and shared his disgrace. In May 1970 he was convicted of using illegal methods to force collectivisation and received a five-year suspended sentence. He managed, however, to win the favour of the economic liberal Prime Minister Hedi Nouira who sent him as Ambassador to Algeria. In June 1978 Nouira recalled him to the task of rejuvenating the Parti Socialiste Destourien and his struggle with Sayah was renewed. Bourguiba apparently preferred Sayah and Bakkush returned to the Embassy in Algiers. In March 1984 the Prime Minister Muhammad Mzali made him Director of the Party as a Minister attached to his own office. In September 1986 he became Minister of Social Affairs and Labour and just over a year later, on seizing power, President Ben Ali made him Prime Minister. Seen as a wily politician, Bakkush was dubbed "the thinking head of Ben Ali". On taking office he promised "to make pluralism a reality" in a genuine multi-party democracy, greater press freedom and to hold early elections although these were not due until 1991. He did not rule out relations with the militant Mouvement de la Tendance Islamique, saying that Islam, devoid of fanaticism, had an important role although later he was to say that mixing religion and politics was "the work of the Devil". In July 1988 he reshuffled his Cabinet, dropping Bourguiba appointees, and bringing in two generals and two first ever non-party civilians, including the leader of a Human Rights organisation who had been prosecuted under the old regime. In February 1989 Bakkush tried unsuccessfully to get an all-party coalition to contest the elections after which he again reshuffled the Cabinet leaving out 32 Ministers only 4 who had served Bourguiba. At the time Ben Ali paid tribute to him as "indispensable . . . he makes the Government work and co-ordinates its activities". Shortly afterwards in September, unexpectedly, Ben Ali dismissed him. Tunisia was in a bad economic situation and Bakkush was seen as too negative a figure to deflect blame from the President. In July Ben Ali had called for sacrifice, warning that there was "no future for a people who consume more than they produce" and in August there were large price rises with aid for needy families. Bakkush, faced with a national debt that demanded $1,000 million a year for servicing, felt that the measures urged by the country's creditors were too risky politically. In September he told an extraordinary session of Parliament that the private sector had failed to fill the gap caused when the state cut investment on World Bank insistance in 1986 and he opposed further privatisation. Bakkush had not played

a major role in foreign affairs although he went to Libya
to co-ordiate joint ventures.

al-BAKR, Ahmad Hassan, Field Marshal (1914–82)

Iraqi President and Prime Minister. The son of a small
landowner from Takrit he taught in a village school
before joining the army. As a young officer he supported
Rashid Ali al-Gilani, was dismissed but subsequently
reinstated. It is possible that he joined the Baath in the
early 1950s and in 1955, as a Colonel, Bakr was
recruited into the Free Officers. He took part in the
July Revolution of 1958 but was soon retired from
the army when he made known his dissatisfaction
with the unwillingness of Abd al-Krim Qassim to negotiate for union with Egypt. He kept up contacts within
the army and, with Abd al-Salam Arif led a force of
tanks to attack the Defence Ministry in the Ramadan
Revolution of 1963. Bakr was appointed Prime Minister
and although Arif became President, it appeared as if
he were the weaker of the two. However an extreme
group of Baathists led by Ali Salih al-Saadi opposed
the more moderate policies of Bakr and their National
Guard became increasingly irresponsible. Bakr therefore supported their crushing in the November
Revolution but immediately afterwards the Premiership
passed to General Tahir Yahya while Bakr was "promoted" to the meaningless post of Vice-President. In
January 1964 he lost even that, receiving a sinecure in
the Foreign Ministry and later again was retired from
the army. About 1967 he began working actively
against the Prime Minister General Yahya, regarded by
the Baath as a renegade, and in April 1968 petitioned
President Abd al-Rahman Arif to dismiss him.
Receiving no response Bakr played a part in organising
a conspiracy of independent officers and Baathists to
remove the two. On July 17 1968 they succeeded and
Bakr became President. A fortnight later he dismissed
the independents and installed an administration totally
dominated by the Baath with himself as Prime Minister,
Commander-in-Chief and Chairman of the Revolutionary Command Council. He promoted himself
Field Marshal the following year. His first moves were
to cut taxes, call for a settlement of the Kurdish Revolt
(I) and declare relations with other countries would
depend on their attitude towards Israel. Bakr surrounded himself with people from Takrit and worked
with the National Command of the Baath, including
its founder Michel Aflaq and moderates like General
Salih Ammash and his relative Saddam Hussain against
the left-wing which was supported by Damascus while
posing as above factionalism. In December 1969 he
brought a communist into the Cabinet and later
announced a new Constitution making the Revolutionary Command Council the supreme body in the
state. There was a series of mass arrests, political trials
and executions and Bakr was described by Hassanain
Haykal as "an excellent organiser of public square hangings but no good on the battlefield". In 1970 he issued
the March Manifesto which brought a temporary end
to the Kurdish War. He rejected the Rogers' Plan and
any proposals for a foreign force to police the Gulf
and denounced many Arab states for moderate foreign
policies although he refused to intervene in Jordan

during Black September. Bakr declared union with
Egypt and Syria "a sublime aim" but in inter-Arab
affairs his deeds usually failed to match his words. In
November 1971 he proclaimed a National Charter for a
broad coalition including the communists and Kurdish
parties to work for a permanent constitution and to
take over the oil industry. In June 1972 he in fact
nationalised the Iraq Petroleum Company and created
a new Iraqi Company for Oil Operations. Two months
earlier he had signed the Russo-Iraqi Treaty which
brought Soviet influence to the Gulf and the boundaries
of the Peninsula. In July 1973 the late arrival of his
aircraft frustrated the Kazzar Plot for his assassination
after which 36 conspirators were hanged. In the
October War he criticised other Arab countries for not
making full use of the oil weapon. The Kurdish Revolt
(II) started in March 1974 as the Government had
failed to honour its pledges but by this time there were
increasing reports that Bakr's health was failing and it
was not clear to what extent he was in charge of affairs.
On July 16 1979 he formally resigned all his offices on
grounds of ill health, giving full support to his successor
Saddam Hussain. He was granted the titles of "Father
and Comrade". In the autumn of 1982 while the
Iran–Iraq War was going badly for Baghdad there were
calls for his return to power but he died on October 4:
some Syrians alleged that he had been murdered by his
successor. Bakr was a strict Muslim who neither
smoked nor drank and with his image of paternal
respectability and long record of nationalism rather
than socialism enjoyed great prestige in the army and
with the middle class.

BALAFREJ, Ahmad (1908–90)

Moroccan Prime Minister. His family were rich aristo-
crats of Andalusian origin and he was born in Rabat
where he attended a French school before receiving
higher education in literature and law in Cairo and
Paris. In 1927 he founded an association for North
African students in Paris. In 1930 he was associated
with Allal al-Fassi in protests against the Berber Dhahir
and, after inheriting a legacy, founded a school in
Rabat. He worked with Shakib Arslan and in quest of
support for Moroccan nationalism visited the Spanish
zone, Paris, Geneva and Berlin where he remained for
some time, making several broadcasts. He returned in
1943 and the following year was one of the founders of
the Istiqlal Party which demanded complete independence and of which he was Secretary-General. He was
arrested, accused of collaboration with the Germans,
and exiled to Corsica until June 1946. After his release
he worked closely with Muhammad V, putting the Moroccan case before the UN in 1952 and travelling widely
to seek support for the Sultan who had been exiled
in August 1953. When Muhammad returned in 1955
Balafrej played an important part in negotiating the
details of independence and became Foreign Minister
in the first independent government. In May 1958 he
succeeded Mubarak Bekkai as Prime Minister at the
head of a predominantly Istiqlal Cabinet although some
of the Party criticised him for including three Ministers
whose primary allegiance was to the King. He continued to hold the Foreign Ministry, conducting
prolonged negotiations with the Americans over the

bases that they had been granted by the French. He announced a programme designed to encourage investment, protect local industry and overhaul the educational system. He was unwilling to take tough action against striking Trade Unionists or against rebellious tribesmen in the Riff, both of which groups opposed the extension of control by Istiqlal. Balafrej was also criticised for not taking a strong line against the West at a time when American and British troops went into Lebanon and Jordan. He was out of touch with the younger more progressive members of the Party and in October 1958 his Deputy Prime Minister Abd al-Rahim Bouabid in protest against the indecisiveness of his leadership. The left wing of the Party broke away under the leadership of Mehdi Ben Barka and in December Balafrej resigned the Premiership although he continued Secretary-General of Istiqlal. He refused office in May 1960 when Muhammad formed his own government but in November 1960 he visited several countries to put Morocco's claim to sovereignty over Mauritania. He agreed to resume the Foreign Ministry when Hassan II formed a Cabinet in June 1961. He continued in office until November 1963 when he was appointed a Personal Representative of the King, for example putting the Moroccan view of the June War to General de Gaulle and the UN. He was a member of the Cabinet and also stood in for the King on ceremonial occasions such as the funeral of Nasser and OAU Summits. In June 1972 he retired and the following year his son Anis was sentenced to 15 years' imprisonment for involvement in the revolutionary plot of Abraham Serfaty. Balafrej was highly intellectual, with a great respect for French culture but was accused of haughtiness and lack of understanding of the ordinary people that he appeared to despise.

BALFOUR DECLARATION (1917)
In 1896 Dr Herzl, a Viennese journalist published *Der Judenstadt* in which he advocated the in-gathering of the Diaspora Jews in their own sovereign state and then organised the First Zionist Congress in Basle in 1897. The proposal for the establishment of a state in Palestine became, after some consideration of alternatives such as Argentina, Uganda, Libya and the Hasa Province, the official policy of the World Zionist Organisation. A headquarters was established in Berlin with branches in other capitals, the one in London headed after 1904 by Dr Chaim Weizmann. He proved extremely successful and before the outbreak of war had won over the Conservative leader A. J. Balfour who felt it "not a dream but a great cause" and leading Liberals such as David Lloyd George and Winston Churchill. The idea also coincided with British strategic interests. During the war-time discussions over the future of the Ottoman Empire the British, seeking a buffer between Syria, which would be controlled by the French, and Egypt urged that Palestine should become part of their share but in the Sykes–Picot Agreement had to concede that it would be under international rule. This, anyway, conflicted with the promises made to the Arabs in the Hussain–McMahon Correspondence. Early in 1917, at a particularly critical period in the war with Russia apparently collapsing and America still neutral it was felt that the backing for the Allies of

World Jewry might be of great value. There were fears that the Germans might win American approval by persuading their Turkish allies to endorse a Jewish home in Palestine or even that France or Italy might do so. After Sykes had sounded out the Zionists in what Omsby-Gore, an Assistant Secretary of the War Cabinet called "a deliberate act of the Cabinet, as part of their general foreign policy and their war aims", instructed Balfour, now Foreign Secretary to make a statement calculated to enlist Jewish support. With the assistance of Lord Rothschild and Weizmann a letter was drafted addressed to the former stating that "HMG view with favour the establishment in Palestine of a national home for the Jewish people and will use their best endeavours to facilitate the achievement of this object, it being clearly understood that nothing shall be done which may prejudice the civil and religious rights of the existing non-Jewish communities in Palestine". The Cabinet accepted this despite opposition from Lord Curzon, the only member with a practical knowledge of the Middle East and from Edwin Montagu, the only Jewish member who feared that it would differentiate Jews from other Englishmen. Churchill never claimed that there had been humanitarian motives for the "measure taken . . . in due need of war with the object of promoting the general victory of the Allies, for which we expected and received valuable and important assistance". President Wilson expressed approval and it was issued on 2 November 1917. Balfour later admitted "literal fulfillment of all our declarations is impossible, partly because they are incompatible with each other and partly because they are incompatible with facts". Hogarth, Head of the Arab Bureau stated that the Government had not realised that Palestine was already "settled land in occupation" by Arabs "who had not been so greatly oppressed by the Turks as to welcome a liberation at the price of a new subjection": clearly the Jews would not be content to remain a minority. The Arabs never accepted the legality of the Declaration but Balfour said that Zionism was "of far profounder import than the desires and prejudices of the 700,000 Arabs who now inhabit that ancient land".

BARAKAT, Subhi (c. 1886–)
Syrian Head of State. He was born into a Turkish family in Antioch and was educated in the local secondary school. After an undistinguished career in the Ottoman Army he deserted when Allied troops got near. Barakat then led a band of guerrillas in the Alawite area fighting the French until June 1920 when in return for a substantial bribe he submitted. In September 1920 the French set up separate states in Syria including one in Aleppo in which Barakat became very influential. In November 1922 the French reorganised the separate states into a Confederation and appointed Barakat its President. At the inaugural banquet his speech had to be read for him as he was fluent neither in Arabic nor French. In November 1923 he became President of the Aleppo Representative Assembly and the following month when delegates from the Assemblies met to elect a Head of State, Barakat was chosen with the support of the French who wished to check the nationalists of Damascus. Barakat's Cabinet was appointed by the French. He hated and was hated by the Damascenes,

worked to foment trouble between the French and the nationalists to safeguard his own position, tried to move the capital to Aleppo and was the centre of a network of nepotism and corruption. In 1925 he was President of the Syrian Union Party which the French hoped to use against the People's Party of Dr Shahbander. During the Druze Revolt he remained indifferent as the Damascus Bombardment shattered the capital. By 23 December 1925 the French came to regard him as a liability and his resignation was announced. The British Consul regarded it as "inevitable and unduly delayed" as he was unfitted for the post. Dropped by the French, he turned into a vocal nationalist. When in 1932 a new Constitution provided for an Assembly, Barakat's house was attacked and subsequently a student attempted to murder him. He hoped to become President but although at first it seemed as if the French would support him, in the event they preferred Muhammad Ali al-Abid and Barakat became Speaker of the Assembly. Later he was active during the Alexandretta Dispute. A British report of 1939 described him as "a 'whole-hogger' nationalist, truculent but not above truckling on his own behalf . . . A man who has played, always unsuccessfully, many parts".

BAR-LEV LINE

The June War ended with the Israelis on the east bank of the Suez Canal but from the cease-fire Nasser proclaimed his intention of reconquering Sinai. Egyptian commandos carried out occasional raids across the Canal and in October 1968 the Israeli Chief of Staff, General Haim Bar-Lev ordered the construction of defences. This was a new concept in Israeli military thinking which had always preferred fighting in the open but was dictated by the political consideration that it was necessary, in the words of Defence Minister Dayan, "to buzz in the ears of Nasser". Along the entire length of the Canal, itself lined with concrete banks, the Israelis built a sand dune 60 feet high and as thick at the base. On the eastern side of the rampart, at a lower level out of sight of the enemy across the Canal, there was a road for tanks with firing positions every hundred metres. Inside the sand wall were reservoirs filled with inflammable liquid that could be squirted at would-be crossers. Behind the rampart was a series of 35 self-contained multi-storey forts protected by minefields and barbed wire, equipped to hold out for a week. They were usually about three miles apart but near likely crossing points were clustered only 1,000 yards apart. They could be defended by an infantry brigade and were protected by a further three armoured brigades totalling 360 tanks. Behind them, between 8 and 11 kilometres from the Canal were a further 11 bunkers. They were invulnerable to anything but a direct hit from a 1,000-pound bomb although the Israelis often suffered casualties during the War of Attrition. According to Hassanain Haykal the Egyptians anticipated that to breach the Line would cost some 26,000 casualties. In fact the attack that began the October War, mounted by 8,000 soldiers in 1,000 rubber boats, supported by 4,000 guns and aircraft achieved complete surprise and the sand wall was washed away by high-pressure hoses. The first fortress was captured within half an hour of landing and the crossing of the Canal

was one of the greatest triumphs achieved by the Egyptian army. Specially designed bridges were then put in place and in 18 hours they put across 90,000 men with 850 tanks and 11,000 other vehicles.

al-BARAZI, Husni (c. 1893–)

Syrian Prime Minister. He came from a very rich landowning family of Kurdish origin in the Hama area and was educated at Istanbul Law Institute. Barazi served in the Ministry of Justice during the rule of King Faysal. In 1926 he was Minister of the Interior in the Cabinet of the *Damad* Ahmad Nami but was arrested and exiled for protesting at the Damascus Bombardment. In 1928 he was amnestied and allowed to stand in elections, becoming Deputy for Hama. He was one of the founders of the National Bloc but by 1931 left it to form his own party of large landowners. In March 1934 he made his break with the nationalists clear by taking the Ministry of Education in the Cabinet of Taj al-Din al-Hassani, resigning with him in February 1936. He was then appointed *Muhafiz* of Alexandretta at the time when the French were negotiating over its future with the Turks and helped the nationalists against both of them. A British report of this time described him as "an agreeable intriguer" whose wife was a noted feminist. In April 1942 he became Prime Minister but had an extremely difficult time owing to the distress caused by food shortages and soaring cost of living. Measures to procure grain upset both the landowners and the hungry and Barazi was accused of corruption. He received no help from the French authorities and quarrelled with the President Shaykh Taj al-Din and resigned in January 1943. In 1949 he was appointed Administrator of Northern Syria by the military regime of Husni al-Zaim. He then became a leading advocate of the concept of a Fertile Crescent uniting under Hashemite rule all the countries threatened by Israel. As the owner of about 20 villages (and incidentally a leading grower of hashish) he became a particular target of Akram al-Hawrani who had acquired great influence during the period that the army under Adib Shishakli allowed a façade of parliamentary rule to continue under the nominal Premiership of Nazim al-Qudsi. Barazi claimed that "Parliament is a toy in the hands of the army" and that "the law of the jungle is at present prevailing" and was attacked by Qudsi as a "traitor and foreign agent". In November 1951 when Shishakli carried out a second coup, Barazi was imprisoned. After his release he went to live in Turkey and Lebanon. Sir Edward Spears said that "his face was puffy and sagged in unexpected places – he looked like a pudding a cook had given up in despair".

BARI RADIO

Mussolini was determined to increase Italian influence in the Arab world and in March 1934 Radio Bari started to transmit eastern music by high-class performers to attract an audience for its news in Arabic. Through short-wave rebroadcast from Rome it could reach most of the area from Morocco to the Red Sea and in order to increase its audience the Italian Government provided cheap radios for Arab customers. After the start of the invasion of Ethiopia the hallmark of Bari Radio was violent attacks on the British in an attempt to whip up

Arab nationalist agitation. At a time when the British authorities in Palestine reckoned that 60% of the licence holders listened to Bari, the radio declared that the Jews were being allowed to import arms to slaughter Arabs. The British made diplomatic protests without avail, considered jamming Bari, and eventually, after a long battle on the part of the Foreign Office to persuade the BBC, started their own Arabic Service in January 1938. Shortly afterwards the Anglo-Italian Agreement caused the Radio to end its anti-British propaganda and switch its attention to the French. After a year attacks on Britain were resumed and continued during the war and provided a platform for exiles such as the Mufti Haj Amin al-Hussaini and Rashid Ali al-Gilani. The obvious untruthfulness of much of its material meant that Bari had little credit but was the first attempt to spread propaganda by wireless in the Arab world and as such set the path for later transmissions such as those of Sawt al-Arab.

BARUDI, Jamil (1905–)

Saudi diplomat. He was born in Suq al-Gharb, Lebanon and educated at the American University of Beirut. He spent much time in London and New York where he worked for the 1940 World Fair and the Arabic edition of *Reader's Digest* and lectured at Princeton. In 1945 he was adviser to Prince Faysal who led the Saudi delegation to the founding conference of the UN at San Francisco in 1945. He spent many years at the UN in the Saudi delegation, firstly as assistant to Ahmad al-Shuqayri and then as Permanent Delegate. His habit of speaking on every issue with verbosity, exaggeration and pedantry over points of detail infuriated some of his colleagues while it amused and delighted others and he became one of the best known characters at the UN.

al-BARUDI, Mahmud Sami Pasha (1839–1940)

Egyptian Prime Minister. He was half Turk and half Egyptian and both his grandfathers were killed by Muhammad Ali in the Mamluks Massacre. He served the Khedive Ismail, who gave him a wife from his own harem, as representative in Constantinople, guard commander, private secretary and secret agent as well as fighting in Crete between 1865 and 1867. He was Minister of War at the time dissatisfaction started to develop amongst the Egyptian-born officers and, sympathising with them, he was dismissed by Riaz Pasha. He was then regarded as the brains or "evil genius" (Milner) and possibly the financier of the Arabi movement. On the insistence of the army he became Minister of War again in the Cabinet of Sharif Pasha and published the Nationalist Manifesto in January 1882. When Sharif was dismissed in February, Barudi succeeded him as Prime Minister with Arabi as Minister of War. One of his first actions was to issue a new Constitution. Cromer wrote that there was little doubt that there was a military conspiracy to depose the Khedive and make Barudi Governor-General and there was talk also of an independent republic to which Syria and the Hijaz might later adhere. Barudi knew no foreign language, had no understanding of the Western mentality and was quite incapable of dealing with foreign diplomats as the crisis deepened with the arrival of British warships in Alexandria. He resigned in May. He played a

muddled and possibly equivocal role in the campaign of Tel el-Kebir and after it was exiled with Arabi to Ceylon where he devoted his energies to poetry. He made several anthologies and his own original verses were regarded as influencing the subsequent development of Arabic poetry. Wilfrid Scawen Blunt saw Barudi as a patriot and reformer of great culture whereas for a *Times* journalist he was "a thorough scamp of considerable ability for low eastern intrigue".

BARZANI, Ahmad (?–1969)

Kurdish leader. The Barzanis were originally religious leaders but who, after settling in the Kurdish village of Barzan in the nineteenth century, became tribal chieftains and exercised a powerful influence over a wide area. Ahmad became head of the family after his grandfather and brother had been hanged by the Turks and his father killed in a tribal skirmish. He established friendly relations with the British who did not attempt to establish administrative control in his area. In 1920 he was involved in the murder of two officers, declared an outlaw and Barzan was destroyed by troops but not occupied. In 1922 he welcomed Turkish agents and practised banditry until the Turks withdrew whereupon he submitted to the authorities. For the next few years he ruled his villages until in 1931 he began a private war with a neighbouring shaykh whom he drove into Persia, burning his villages behind him. Iraqi troops intervened to restore order but had to be rescued by the RAF and the Barzani leaders fled to Turkey where they were interned. His brothers escaped and resumed fighting but they surrendered in July 1933 and were pardoned. The Turks then handed over Ahmad on condition that his life be spared. He was detained in Mosul but that was too close to home and he was soon involved in fresh intrigues so he was moved to Baghdad. He was allowed home in 1944 but got into further trouble and was detained once more until the July Revolution. He opposed Kurdish Revolt (I) and remained in Baghdad hoping to mediate. By that time his religious eccentricities seem to have turned into insanity and effective power over his people was exercised by his brother Mulla Mustafa Barzani.

BARZANI, Masud (1946–)

Iraqi Kurdish leader. The son of the famous tribal leader Mulla Mustafa Barzani he was born in Mahabad where his father was one of the leaders of a briefly independent republic and his early years were spent in Russia where his father had taken refuge. After Mulla Mustafa's return to Iraq in 1958 Masud assisted him during the period of virtual autonomy that preceded the Kurdish Revolt (I), running the Kurdistan Democratic Party which involved much fighting against the followers of Jalal Talabani and the brief Kurdish Revolt (II) after which he fled to Iran. On the death of Mulla Mustafa in 1979 Masud and his brother Idris took over leadership of the KDP which, despite several splits, they attempted to modernise and make less tribal. In the Iran–Iraq War the Barzanis supported Iran and in 1983 8,000 of the tribe were arrested and never seen again while others were gassed at Halabja. After the death of Idris in Tehran in 1987 Masud became the sole chief of the tribe and the KDP. In May 1988 he was reconciled with Talabani forming the Iraqi Kurdistan Front under their joint leadership. In July 1989 he visited London where he succeeded in persuading the Government not to sell £300 million worth of aircraft to Iraq, warning that they might be used against Kuwait. Before Operation Desert Storm the Americans urged the Kurds to rise against Saddam Hussain but when they actually did so in March 1991 they provided no support and the Kurdish Uprising was ruthlessly crushed. In May Barzani entered into negotiations with Saddam convinced that both sides had learned that nothing could be achieved by war, that the Kurds could not rely upon support from outside and that they had suffered enough. Barzani believed that he had secured agreement for a democratic multi-party Iraq and this led to a split with Talabani who felt that Saddam could not be trusted and Barzani's willingness to abandon the Kurdish claim to Kirkuk was too high a price to pay. In November 1991, though Iraqi armies were attacking Irbil and Sulaymaniyyah and 200,000 Kurds were in flight before them, Barzani again went to Baghdad in the hope that it would honour earlier commitments. Barzani was always careful not to antagonise Turkey by appearing to favour the dissident Kurds of the Marxist PKK and he had meetings with President Ozel and Prime Minister Demirel. As the independent Kurdish area had no proper authorities Barzani proposed that elections should be held in May 1992. His KDP won slightly more votes than Talabani's Patriotic Union of Kurdistan but they agreed on an equal division of ministerial portfolios. The two party leaders felt that they would be freer to deal with the outside world if they were not Ministers in an unrecognised government and they made several tours together, meeting, for example President Mitterand. Barzani became a leading figure in the opposition Iraqi National Congress and was one of a delegation received in Washington in July 1992 by Secretary of State Baker. In November the INC meeting in Salahuddin elected a three-man Presidency of which Barzani was one. Barzani, who spoke fluent Arabic, Farsi and English, was respected for his integrity and subtlety but was regarded as brooding and self-sufficient. There were at least two attempts on his life.

BARZANI, Mulla Mustafa (c. 1900–79)
Kurdish leader. "Mulla" was his personal name and not a religious title. He was descended from a family of *Sufi* shaykhs who had become tribal leaders and were frequently in conflict with the authorities or with neighbouring tribes or with both. It is said that Mulla Mustafa had his first experience of prison at the age of one when the whole family was locked up by the Turks. His brother Shaykh Ahmad Barzani continued the tradition of turbulence and Mulla Mustafa was involved in some savage fighting in 1931 when they burned the villages of a neighbour whom they pursued into Persia. Iraqi troops were sent to restore order but were defeated by the Barzanis who were then forced by the RAF to seek refuge in Turkey where they were interned. Mulla Mustafa escaped and resumed fighting but in July 1933 he was pardoned. He was detained for a decade in Sulaymaniyah then escaped and raised a gang of outlaws to attack government posts. He was himself always in the forefront of any fighting. He appealed to

the British Ambassador for Kurdish rights and, unlike other tribal chiefs combined raiding with politics, forming the Freedom Party in February 1945. In September 1945 he led his followers, estimated at between 10,000 and 35,000 to Mahabad to form the army of the independent Kurdish Republic established there under Russian auspices. The force wore uniforms provided by the Russians and Barzani assumed the rank of Marshal. When the Republic was overrun by the Iranians at the end of 1946 Barzani fought on until the spring when he led his men on "the Long March" to Russia where he remained until 1958. He was received by Stalin and studied at the Academy of Languages but was never a communist and would much have preferred help from the West to secure Kurdish independence. After the July Revolution he was invited to return by Abd al-Krim Qassim whom he supported against the pan-Arabists. He was regarded as a hero, given an official house and car, and assumed the leadership of the now legal Kurdistan Democratic Party. Mulla Mustafa spent much of the winter of 1960–1 in Russia and returned saying that he wanted legitimate Kurdish aspirations without harming the integrity of Iraq. He went back to Barzan where his tribesmen complained of settlements of Arabs on Kurdish land and economic injustices. In July 1961 the Barzanis defeated neighbouring tribes which they thought that the Government was preparing to use against them and at the end of August Mulla Mustafa sent an ultimatum to Baghdad demanding the end of Qassim's exclusive rule, recognition of Kurdish autonomy and the restoration of democratic liberties. In mid-September the army moved against him, winning initial successes but having to withdraw at the onset of winter. The Kurdish Revolt (I) had started. The Government tried to undermine his position by subsidising old tribal enemies against him and stirring up rivals in the KDP such as Jalal Talabani but no one doubted that Barzani was the leader of the revolt and his *Pesh Mergas* bore the brunt of the fighting. He became an international figure, obtaining help from Iranian and Turkish Kurds and training and arms from Israel while Syrians assisted Baghdad. He rarely made excursions outside his own area, preferring to let his enemies come to him. There were several attempts at peace which were renewed after Barzani had given help to the Baath to overthrow Qassim in the Ramadan Revolution. In February 1964 a cease-fire was announced and in June Barzani held talks with the Prime Minister General Tahir Yahya but in the meanwhile relations with Talabani had deteriorated to the extent that there was fighting between their factions: Barzani relied on tribalism and was determined that left-wing politicians should not take over the leadership. In July 1964 he reasserted control over the KDP and in October he accused the Government of settling Arabs in Kurdish areas and of making no effort to implement its promises of development. Clashes and talks alternated until April 1965 when the Government launched a major offensive and fighting continued until the civilian Prime Minister Abd al-Rahman al-Bazzaz in 1966 issued the Declaration of the Twenty-ninth of June which conceded many of the Kurdish demands. A cease-fire followed and in October Mulla Mustafa met President Abd al-Rahman Arif who was touring the North. Peace continued until October 1968 when the Government sent forces to help Talabani and fighting became so severe that Mulla Mustafa appealed to the United Nations to prevent genocide. In April 1969 he survived an attempt on his life when he was ambushed by Talabani supporters and on another occasion the Government tried to blow him up with the gift of a tape-recorder made into a bomb. A year of secret negotiations and heavy fighting preceded the March Manifesto of 1970 which appeared to have ended the war. The Government did not carry out its undertakings and in March 1974 Barzani resumed fighting, spurred by the promise of CIA funding through the Shah but his dependence on Iran damaged his prestige. The Kurdish Revolt (II) lasted a year for on March 5 1975 the Shah and Saddam Hussain signed the Algiers Pact that closed the Iranian border to the Kurds, depriving them of military aid. The revolt collapsed and thousands of Kurds, including Mulla Mustafa and his sons fled to Iran. He later went to the USA where he died of lung cancer, a broken man claiming that he had been betrayed by the Americans and the Iranians. Barzani was no opponent of Arab nationalism provided that it allowed autonomy to Kurds and at the time of the Suez War urged the Russians to help Egypt and later he hoped that President Nasser would mediate between him and Baghdad. He prevented the Kurds from distracting the Iraqi Government during the June War and the October War. Barzani was a boisterous, charismatic figure with piercing black eyes and an air of reckless authority. He had seven children by two wives and two of his sons, Idris (died January 1987) and Masud, were politically active after his death, running the KDP and then fighting on the Iranian side in the Iran–Iraq War.

BASH HAMBA, Ali (c. 1875–1918)

Tunisian nationalist leader. He came from an aristocratic family of Turkish mamluk origin. He was educated at the Zeituna Islamic University and at the Sadiqi and also studied for a French law degree. In 1907 with Bashir Sfar he started the weekly *Le Tunisien* calling on the people to struggle for their rights. Inspired by his ideas a group known as the Young Tunisians grew around him. He demanded reforms rather than immediate independence, universal elementary education and modernisation of the Qur'anic schools, asserting that science could not be taught in Arabic. The Italian invasion of Tripoli made him stress the importance of Islamic unity in association with the Ottoman Empire. In 1912 when he was exiled as part of the repression of the Young Tunisians, he went to Istanbul where, despite French objections, he was made an Inspector in the Ministry of Justice. He became closely associated with Shakib Arslan and during the war was in charge of a bureau spreading propaganda for the unity of North Africa against the Allies. In 1916 it was decided that he should be smuggled into Tunisia to organise resistance as Sulayman al-Baruni was doing in Tripolitania. He fell ill, however, before he could go. His brother Muhammad was also an active nationalist, establishing himself at Geneva during the war and publishing a journal *La Revue du Maghreb*.

BASHIR, Umar Hassan (1938–)

Sudanese President and Prime Minister. Born in Shendi, his family were members of the Mirghani/Khatmiyyah *tariqah*. He trained as a paratrooper in Egypt and the USA and fought in the June War. Later he fought in the South, commanding a town which was later overrun by the Sudan People's Liberation Army. In February 1989, a Brigadier, he was one of the officers who issued an ultimatum to the Prime Minister Sadiq al-Mahdi demanding immediate negotiations for peace. He was not then known to have played any part in politics although he was believed to have assisted General Siwar al-Dhahab in the overthrow of President Nimeiri. On 18 June there was an attempted coup which led to the arrest of 18 officers and 28 civilians, leaving Bashir the most senior officer opposed to the Government. On 30 June 1989 he overthrew it without any bloodshed, proclaimed a state of emergency and declared himself Head of State, Chairman of the 15-man Revolutionary Command Council for National Salvation, Prime Minister, Minister of Defence, a Lieutenant-General and Commander-in-Chief. He immediately abolished the Constitution, dissolved the National Assembly and all political parties and trade unions, and arrested senior politicians such as Saiyyid Sadiq, Hassan Turabi and Muhammad Uthman al-Mirghani and some 1,500 others. Forty civilian newspapers were closed. Egypt was the first country to recognise his regime which was welcomed by Iraq, Saudi Arabia and Libya: Bashir and Qadafi drove a bulldozer to knock down Kobar Prison setting free 1,300 inmates. He included three Southerners in the RCC, declared a unilateral cease-fire with the SPLA and offered an amnesty. Stating that the "revolution will amputate any who stand in its way", he decreed the death sentence for any found with foreign currency and set up special courts to deal with hoarding and profiteering. His position was not secure and in his first year there were four attempted military coups for which 40 officers were shot. He quickly released Turabi whose National Islamic Front, although technically illegal, came to be regarded as the main prop of his regime – almost as its dominating force. Bashir promised a Sudanese model of an Islamic state after "an incessant revolution for progress and achievement". Opponents of the NIF, doctors, academics and 57 judges were either forcibly retired or imprisoned, held as hostages against possible uprisings and tortured in "ghost houses" which were condemned by Amnesty International. Local Committees, copied from those in Libya, terrorised their neighbourhoods and the British Foreign Secretary denounced the regime's "complete contempt for human rights". After a Cabinet reshuffle in April 1991 which increased the influence of the NIF, 31 officers were shot after a coup attempt. In November 1991 measures to compel that mass media conform with Islamic values were introduced. During 1990, after food had been exported to buy arms, famine spread throughout the country but Bashir, declaring "we eat what we grow, we wear what we make", refused to admit its existence or ask the international community for help. Inflation ran at 150% and the IMF in 1990 declared the Sudan in default for failing to meet its obligations. The country's problems were increased by the vagaries of Bashir's foreign policy. In March 1990 he signed a "declaration of integration" with Libya and later in the year at the Cairo Summit he refused to condemn the Iraqi occupation of Kuwait. Later he denounced King Fahd for "defiling the Holy Places" by admitting Western troops and the Egyptians warned him against an attack on the Aswan Dam: the loss of Western and Gulf aid probably cost Sudan $300 million. In December 1991 the Iranian President Rafsanjani visited Khartoum promising oil and military aid. Some of this was used to set up training camps for the Islamic militants of Egypt and Tunisia which broke off relations in August 1992. All Sudan's problems were compounded by the continuation of the war in the South. Bashir had originally hoped that it could be settled "soldier to soldier" and was even prepared to accept secession but his attitude hardened under the influence of the NIF. Talks held in Addis Ababa and Nairobi broke down when Bashir refused to withdraw the *Shariah*. In February 1991 he called a Constitutional Conference and divided up the country into 9 or 66 provinces with 281 local government areas given some autonomy. Later in the year he set up a Transitional National Assembly of 300 members in which the police and army were heavily repesented but which did contain some former politicians. In February 1992, in order to conciliate the IMF, subsidies on essential commodities were removed, leading to some riots, some measures of privatisation were introduced and the Sudanese pound was devalued by 70% and floated, promptly losing another 8% of its value. There were further reports of the execution of officers and the University of Khartoum was closed. During 1992 the European Community and the General Assembly both criticised abuses of human rights and so on a visit to Khartoum did the Pope in February 1993. In August 1993 the US placed the Sudan on the list of countries sponsoring terrorism as Egypt, Ethiopia and Eritrea complained of guerrillas being sent across their borders. There was a further quarrel with Egypt over Halaib. In October 1993 the RCC dissolved itself after appointing Bashir President and in a Cabinet reshuffle he handed over the Defence Ministry. At the same time the curfew which had been in force since his takeover was lifted: Bashir claimed that Khartoum was one of the safest cities in the world but there were persistent reports of kidnappings of Southern children who were forcibly brought up as Muslims and sent to fight their kin. In November 1993 Bashir announced a new Constitution which retained the *Shariah* and promised presidential and legislature elections for 1995. The nine provinces were given further autonomy and in February 1994 the number of states was increased to 26. Bashir appointed 140 Ministers for them, including the first woman Governor and a Christian as Governor of a Northern state. In January 1994 Archbishop Carey decided not to visit Khartoum following the expulsion of ambassadors. In the same month agreement was reached with Libya on the freedom of movement and work. The UN condemned human rights abuses and estimated that 3.7 million in the South were starving and talked about famine. In March 1994 Sudan's only independent newspaper was closed amid attacks on imperialists and accusations that Israel was supplying the South with arms. The IMF, which in 1986 had declared Sudan bankrupt and in 1990 refused to co-operate with the country when it failed repeatedly to settle arrears, running at about $1.2 bn, threatened to expel the country. In April Sudan offered a token payment to the IMF and exporters asked for the devaluation of the currency which on the black market was changing hands at 500 to the dollar. A devout Muslim, Bashir has ruled with extraordinary incompetence, improvising continually with a series of incoherent policies.

BAT GALIM AFFAIR (1954)
Despite the Rhodes Armistice the Egyptian Government prevented the passage of ships flying the Israeli flag, or ships of any flag proceeding to or from Israel, through the Suez Canal. This blockade was condemned by the Security Council in September 1951 and January 1954 but a Russian veto prevented any action. On 28 September 1954, with the obvious intention of provoking a reaction at a time when, under the Anglo–Egyptian Treaty British troops were being withdrawn from the Suez Canal Zone, the Israeli cargo-ship *Bat Galim* sailed into the Suez roadstead where it was halted by the Egyptian authorities who stated that it had fired on fishing boats killing two seamen. The Israelis denied this. The ship was then detained. The Israelis appealed to the UN but in a Security Council debate on 7 December, the Egyptian Representative declared that his government would continue to refuse passage to Israeli ships but that it did not prevent cargoes bound for Israel in other ships unless they were considered war contraband. The debate was adjourned until mid-January 1955 by which time the Egyptians had freed the ship and its crew. They continued to deny passage to Israeli ships until 1979.

BAT YAM INCIDENTS (1992)
Even during the *Intifadah* over 40,000 Arab workers daily left the Gaza Strip to work in Israel, many of them going to work on large construction sites in Bat Yam, a suburb of Tel Aviv. On 24 May 1992 one of them stabbed to death a 15-year-old Israeli girl. An angry crowd of Jews then attacked passing Arabs, stabbing two until they were dispersed by the police. The following night a large crowd shouting "Death to the Arabs" attacked any that they could find and more than 150 were arrested. A bulldozer was used to attack a primary school where Arab children were sheltering before police intervened. Gaza was temporarily sealed off. In July the murderer was sentenced to life imprisonment. The Bat Yam Incidents provide an example of how quickly violence could escalate in the climate engendered by the *Intifadah*.

BAYT SAHOUR, Siege of (1989)
In September 1989 the 12,000 mostly Christian inhabitants of the West Bank town of Bayt Sahour stopped paying taxes to the Israeli occupation authorities, although they had done so without protest before the outbreak of the *Intifadah*. They declared that they received practically no municipal services in return for their money which merely benefited their oppressors. The Israelis then sealed off the town from the outside world, cutting telephone contact and barring journalists

while they launched a wholesale campaign of confiscation of everything from household goods such as umbrellas and baby clothes to the machinery of family workshops on which the town depended; over $1.5 million worth was seized. There was world-wide sympathy for the inhabitants of a small town resisting, without violence, foreign occupiers, delegations expressed support and the matter was raised at the UN. After 42 days the embarrassed Israelis raised the siege. Many of the inhabitants continued to refuse to pay, were faced with exorbitant demands and deprived of essential documents. There was also random violence by Israeli soldiers and in one incident of random shooting soon after the Rishon Le Zion killings of May 1990 at least fifteen people were injured. The South African leader Archbishop Tutu made a point of visiting the town which was itself nominated for the Nobel Peace Prize.

BAZOFT EXECUTION (1990)

Farhad Bazoft (born 1958) was an Iranian-born journalist who reported for the London *Observer* and whose coverage of the Iran–Iraq War had not offended the authorities in Baghdad. They therefore invited him in September 1989 to observe elections being held in Kurdistan. The day that he arrived there were reports of a massive explosion which had occurred in a vast military complex near Hillah: rumours spoke of sabotage and of up to 700 killed. Bazoft and other journalists wished to investigate the matter but only he, with the help of a British nurse Mrs Daphne Parish who worked in Baghdad, managed to get to the site. They were arrested, accused of espionage. After six weeks in prison Bazoft was shown, in a deplorable state, confessing on Iraqi TV that he had spied for Israel. Saddam Hussain promised a "full and fair trial" but the British press were excluded from the court and on 10 March 1990 he was sentenced to death and Mrs Parish to 15 years' imprisonment. British Government appeals for clemency were dismissed as "flagrant interference" in the internal affairs of Iraq and the Foreign Secretary was told not to visit the country. King Hussain, Yassir Arafat and the UN Secretary-General also appealed for mercy but Bazoft was executed on 15 March. The incident revealed to many who were not normally in touch with Middle Eastern events the savage brutality of the Iraqi regime.

al-BAZZAZ, Abd al-Rahman (1913–73)

Iraqi Prime Minister. He came from a family of ulema of Baghdad and after studying law there, took a Doctorate in London. He was strongly nationalist, seeing it in religious terms and was briefly imprisoned for supporting Rashid Ali al-Gilani in 1941. In 1955 he became Dean of the Law School but was dismissed by Nuri al-Said whose policy over the Suez War Bazzaz opposed. After the Revolution he was appointed a judge but, like other pan-Arabs, quarrelled with Abd al-Krim Qassim and was imprisoned. He then went to Cairo where he was Director of the Institute of Arabic Studies and published a book calling for a federal Arab union. Abd al-Salam Arif who succeeded Qassim was an old friend of Bazzaz and selected him to put the Iraqi case in the Cairo Unity Talks of March 1963 in which Bazzaz

did much to draft the Tripartite Agreement to form a union after two years' preparation. He was then appointed Ambassador to London, where he was very popular and successful, and then Secretary-General of OPEC. Arif wanted Arab unity without subjugation to either Nasser or the Baath and he also sought a return towards civilian rule after 17 years of feuding officers. He therefore appointed Bazzaz Deputy Prime Minister in the Cabinet of the air force commander Arif Abd al-Razzaq in September 1965. A fortnight later Abd al-Razzaq failed in an absurd attempt at a coup, fled to Egypt and Bazzaz succeeded him as Prime Minister. He was the first civilian to hold the office since the Revolution and formed the first largely civilian Cabinet. Demanding a return to "the rule of law" and the end of military interference in government, he put forward a programme of non-Marxist "prudent socialism", administrative efficiency, eventual federal union with Egypt and, above all, settlement of the Kurdish problem. One of the few politicians trusted by them, Bazzaz realised the difficulties of combining the aspirations of the Kurds with Arab unity and in 1966 he put forward the Declaration of the Twenty-ninth of June which won the approval of their leader Mulla Mustafa Barzani. His expertise in oil matters was helpful in solving disputes between his own and other Arab governments and the international companies. In February 1966 he signed an agreement reaffirming the Unified Political Command with Egypt. His foreign policy was generally pro-Western but he went to Moscow to win help in building dams. He also improved relations with Turkey and Iran. Having the backing of no military faction his position was, however, very much dependent upon his personal relationship with the President who, unfortunately for Bazzaz, was killed in an air accident in April 1966. He was briefly Acting President and stood for election but realised that the army would not accept him. The military resented their exclusion from power and disapproved of his Kurdish policy and promises of elections and they prevailed upon President Abd al-Rahman Arif in August to replace Bazzaz with an officer. He went to London but was also involved in an attempt to mediate between Egypt and Saudi Arabia in the Yemen War. After the Baath took power in July 1968, against the advice of his friends, he returned home and was sentenced to 15 years' imprisonment for spying for America and Israel. In jail he was tortured and released after a year paralysed and almost blind. His wife brought him to London for treatment but nothing could be done and he returned home to die. Bazzaz, the only genuinely popular Iraqi leader after the Revolution, was an honourable, sincerely religious man, moderate, friendly, humorous, frank to the point of occasional indiscretion with a lively intelligence and great energy.

BEIRUT AIRPORT ATTACK (1968)

On 26 December 1968 two members of the recently formed Popular Front for the Liberation of Palestine attacked an El Al Boeing 707 on the ground at Athens airport, killing a passenger and wounding a stewardess. The Israelis had been awaiting a chance to attack a weak Arab state as a warning not to harbour guerrillas so on 28 December it launched a 45-minute raid on

Beirut airport. Several dozen commandos carried by eight helicopters destroyed 13 aircraft, eight belonging to Middle East Airlines, estimated to be worth £11 million. A storage tank was destroyed and runways damaged. Lebanon appealed to the Security Council which unanimously condemned the Israeli action with even the Americans saying that it was unjustified although they refused to agree to any sanctions against Tel Aviv. Resolution 262 condemned "premeditated acts of violence", warned against a repetition and considered that Israel should pay compensation. Israel rejected the Resolution as showing "the bankruptcy" of the UN. General de Gaulle embargoed arms shipments to Israel. The ineffectiveness of the response of the Lebanese army led to the fall of the government of Abd Allah al-Yafi.

BEIRUT, Siege of (1982)

The Israeli invasion of Lebanon, Operation Peace for Galilee which began on 6 June 1982 was an immediate military success and within a week they had encircled the capital and its population of 600,000. For seventy days they pounded Muslim West Beirut by land, sea, and air, often killing over a hundred people a day, 90% of them civilians. There was no pretence of aiming at military targets and nearly all the 25 hospitals in West Beirut suffered damage as did innumerable schools and 134 embassies or diplomatic residences. Electricity and water supplies were cut off while the Israelis prevented the delivery of food, fuel and medical supplies. The commander of an Israeli armoured brigade resigned his commission rather than go on killing civilians. The resistance came from about 12,000 Palestinian guerrillas and some of the local Muslims and left-wingers while most of the Christians remained aloof in East Beirut. Mild American protests were disregarded by the Israeli Government which knew that words would not be followed by action against them. The Israelis stated that they would continue until the Palestinians left which on 30 July they stated that they would do but negotiations about where they would go were prolonged. On 1 August in a 14-hour bombardment the Israelis killed about 165 people. On 12 August after the Israelis had bombed the city for eleven hours without stopping they announced a cease-fire which the UN Security Council called for UN officers to monitor. An American envoy, Philip Habib then negotiated a settlement by which a Multi-National Force would go to Beirut to supervise the withdrawal of the guerrillas and provide security in West Beirut which would then be left defenceless. On 21 August the evacuation of the guerrillas started and it was completed on 1 September. On 10 September the MNF started to withdraw. On 14 September the newly elected President of Lebanon Bashir Gemayel was assassinated and the following day in contravention of previous understandings, Israeli troops occupied West Beirut. This was immediately followed by the Sabra-Chatila Massacre in which many of the women and children of the guerrillas were slaughtered.

BEKKAI, Mubarak b. Mustafa (1897–1961)

Moroccan Prime Minister. He was a Berber from a family of notables of the Beni Snassen near the Algerian frontier and had a distinguished career in the French army, reaching the rank of Colonel and losing a leg in battle in May 1940. He was appointed Pasha of Sefrou but in 1953 he was dismissed for refusing to sign the petition demanding the deposition of Muhammad V which had been organised by the Pasha of Marrakesh, Haj Thami al-Glawi. Bekkai thereupon went into exile. He played an important part in convincing the French that only the return of Muhammad from exile in Madagascar could prevent a descent into anarchy and was a member of the Throne Council which operated in the interregnum. He was one of the few Moroccans regarded by the King as a personal friend and upon independence, determined to have as representative a government as possible, Muhammad chose Bekkai who had great prestige but no party allegiance, as his first Prime Minister in December 1955. The Cabinet consisted of four other Independents, nine from the Istiqlal Party, five from the Parti Démocratique de l'Indépendance and a representative of the Jewish community. In March 1956 Bekkai signed the Agreement by which France formally recognised Moroccan independence. He tried not to antagonise the French and was slow to accord any overt support for the Algerians who were just beginning their War of Independence. Other Agreements were signed by which Spain surrendered its protectorate over the North and the international status of Tangier ended. Law and order was re-established, a start was made with the integration of the turbulent Armée de Libération Nationale into the regular armed forces and with the creation of a new civil service. Bekkai was anxious to govern in the interests of the King and of the country and he soon fell foul of the Istiqlal leaders who considered that their part in the national struggle entitled them to a monopoly of power. In October 1956 they provoked a crisis over the preparations for elections to replace the nominated National Consultative Assembly and Bekkai was forced to reshuffle his Cabinet eliminating the PDI. Relations with France became strained after Ben Bella, Boudiaf and others were hijacked on a Moroccan aircraft flying out of Rabat and French citizens were killed in a subsequent riot in Meknes. At the same time there was fighting between elements of the ALN and the Spanish army in the enclave of Ifni. There were several local Berber uprisings, most notably that of Addi ou Bihi against what appeared an Arab-dominated government, leading to the formation of the Berber Mouvement Populaire by Mahjoubi Ahardan. Early in 1958 the dispute over the preparations for elections again came to a head and the Istiqlal members of the Cabinet resigned as Bekkai struggled to obtain more rights for minority parties. Bekkai found it impossible to continue and resigned at the end of April. He went into retirement but in May 1960 he was recalled as Minister of the Interior. He made attempts to purge provincial governors and caids who had been appointed for purely party reasons but died in office less than a year later. Bekkai, tall, thin, very upright with a remarkable hooked nose and a wide mouth with exceptionally large teeth which gave him a resemblance to a horse, always maintained the bearing and speech of a senior officer with dignity, integrity and loyalty to his King.

BELGRAVE DIARIES

Feb 24 "The Arabs there (Budeya) are a bad lot and not on good terms with the Shaikh, being Dowasir, and the sons of the headman are notorious".

Apr 18 "Commander of the seaplanes on their first visit offered to take the Shaikh to Doha. After much conversation he accepted. Really he didn't seem very keen about it as he said it was Friday, they were not expecting him and the Arabs of Doha had never seen an aeroplane before. Much discussion as to what he should wear, he was very anxious to take his sword".

1930 Feb 19 "Abdel Latif's sons came in, one of them had been summoned and didn't come so I sent him to the Fort for a night to teach them to respect the Government. They are a saucy crowd, all the Dawasir crowd are. They are the people with whom we had so much trouble when Daly was here and most of them retired from Bahrain to the mainland in a huff".

Feb 23 "Various people came to see me . . . the sons of Abdel Latif the Doseri Shaykh who said their father was in his dotage and they wanted the Govt. to take over his estates, all quite untrue . . ."

Apr 2 "Joint Court. Some business about one of the Dawasir Shaikhs who the Shaikh insisted on giving some money to encourage him to settle in their town of Bedya. He was very obstinate about it in spite of my telling him that we are now 50,000 rupees down in our Budget".

Apr 15 Major Holmes came. "Very glad to see him again. I like him though like all these oil people he is very dodgy and one can't believe much he says when about his oil business". "Prior showed me a lot of confidential papers from London about the oil business. It is quite amazing the way the Colonial Office have behaved, in about six months they have completely reversed their policy, instead of standing out against an American Company they now allow it. All the arrangements have been done without consulting the Shaikh. It makes me very angry. I suppose it is this Labour Government. The whole business is really disgraceful and there looks as if some of the C.O. people were too intimate with these wealthy oil people. Holmes himself admits that we have been badly treated. There is more of what I consider dishonest business about oil than any other thing in this part of the world. As far as I can gather, and I have seen all the letters about it from Passfield and the India Office, they divided up all the oil bearing land in this part of the Near East between England, France and America without even telling the rulers of the various countries to whom it belonged. When they had done this they told Irak and Bahrain that it had been arranged. Of course we shall get a handsome royalty on it but even so the Shaikh ought to have been consulted. Holmes' Company is now really American though it was definitely laid down that it should be English and at first the Colonial Office was very insistent on this, now they have entirely given way. Of course actually it doesn't matter to us where the money for the development comes from but they ought not to change about so much".

Apr 16 The Shaikh meets Holmes who "was very full of all the advantages that we are going to get from the oil and talked as if it were already a sure thing".

Apr 17 The Shaikh and Belgrave go to the Agency "when it came to the oil business Prior said that he was asked by the Brit Govt to obtain the Shaikh's agreement to the transfer of the concession from one company to another. The Shaikh asked if it was an English Company and was told it was registered in Canada and London. Abdulla asked whose money was in it and Prior said that it was partly American and partly Canadian but the Brit Govt advised the Shaikh to agree to the transfer. He, of course, said that he did. Afterwards they came over to our house again and we found Shaikh Rashid and Sulman also calling on Holmes. They all crawled about the drawing room making plans of where the oil wells were to be".

May 13 The Shaikh came "it was about some Arabs from Dohar who came to Bahrain, actually they are Bahrain subjects. The Shaikh of Dohar, Kattar, is very angry at our not sending them back and has sent several messengers about it. We went over to the Agency and drafted a reply to the Shaikh of Dohar, then came back and had a long talk with the messenger. The Shaikh was really quite clever as he talked unceasingly about his love for his "brother" the Shaikh of Kattar, so that the messenger hardly got a word in, whenever there was a pause he drew me into the conversation and I carried on in the same way, eventually we sent him off with a vague reply that we would consider the matter after the diving season, typically Arab to put a thing off". . . . "The down mail came in with two American men belonging to the "Bahrain Petroleum Company Ltd". This is the name of Holmes' show nowadays".

May 19 Shaikh Abdulla "thinks there is a danger of trouble in Muharrak as there are so many foreigners there, wild bedus from the south of Arabia and a lot of Dawasir and some Somalis who would welcome a bit of a riot as a chance of doing some bazaar looting".

Jun 12 "The Shaikh came in to the Agency and signed the document of the transfer of the oil concession".

Jul 10 "Dined with Major Holmes, quietly, nobody else there. He is very fed up with Prior who because he personally dislikes the idea of oil here seems to be violently opposed to the whole show. I am all in favour of it and don't pretend not to be".

Nov 1 Shaykh Muhammad "talked about the return of the Dawasir, they want to come back with no questions asked about the accounts of their divers who are known to have been abominably swindled over their accounts. I see no point in giving in to them as they have always been a nuisance and we get on better without them. The Shaikh doesn't like to see their town falling into ruins".

Nov 4 Visited Shaykh Isa "I asked him what he thought about the oil and said they intended to bore a mile into the ground, he seemed moderately interested and said only Allah knew what was under the earth".

Nov 28 "Had to go down to see the Shaikh with Major Holmes to get a paper signed about the oil business. Holmes is a very popular person with the Shaikh, in fact with all the Khalifah, as he never worried them but "keeps their hearts good" by frequent handsome presents to get what he wants from them. He is now after an extension of the area of the concession but the Political people, Govt of India are I know against".

Jan 20 "Holmes stayed to dinner and talked about oil

politics, he thinks that the Resident is going into Hassa to try to persuade the King not to give Holmes' Company a concession over there".

Jan 23 "Went out to see the Shaikh and stayed a long time, Sulman and Abdulla were there, he talked about Holmes' application for a further extension of the oil concession and also about the royalty.

Jan 26 "Tea with Holmes. He is trying to get this oil concession in Arabia from the King, Ibn Saud and showed me the Concession which interested me very much. It is not agreed yet and his difficulty is to state the terms of the payment which have to be corresponding to gold, but as in these days the value of the £ is moving up and down so fast it is a very hard thing to arrange".

Feb 29 "Holmes showed us a bottle of oil which they got from the well, there was no doubt about its being oil, it burned splendidly and smelt like petrol. They got it at 1,640 feet down".

Mar 15 "Holmes talked oil very interestingly . . . he is putting in for a large piece of country on which to build refineries, stores etc.".

Apr 13 Holmes "wants a clause in the Concession altering. My object is to get some return for the oil as soon as possible".

Apr 20 "Talked to the Shaikh about the area applied for by Holmes for the oil business, he did not seem very interested but agreed that Om al Hassan, Essex Point was Government ground. He seemed relieved at the idea of the Refinery being so far from Sakhrir, any inconvenience to Manama which is after all the capital, does not interest him in the least".

Apr 23 Saw Prior "Holmes has put in for an extension of the Prospecting Licence for two years from the time that it expires, that is in about seven months. I suppose he meant to all the time though he did not say so before. Two years is the maximum time he can get as an extension, and he has to show reason for needing it. The Shaikh came in later . . . we explained it all to him, but I doubt if he understood much of it at all, it is bad enough in English to understand. He was very decided on one point and that was that two years was too long and he was inclined to allow one year only, but as he did not really grasp the whole thing his decision is rather absurd, however as he decided that himself we will take it as his opinion".

Apr 27 "Went to see the Shaykh to show him the letter that I had written for him about the oil business, he gave his opinion but asked for advice from the Colonial Office".

May 5 Very gloomy at the oil camp. "They are going to start again and dig down to 2,500 feet. There is apparently not enough gas to push the oil up though there is some oil there but they don't know how much".

May 6 "Heard that the oil well is practically a wash out, very disappointing. Prior said that though everyone else seemed to be sad about it he was very pleased".

May 30 "Out to dinner at the Oil Camp where I heard the good news that yesterday they got a flow of oil of 600 barrels a day, or it may be tins, I forget".

Jun 8 "Skinner seemed quite cheerful but he says that the amount of oil they have got now is still not enough to start on commercially but if they get several wells about the same amount it will be a real proposition".

Jun 20 "Holmes is leaving on the up boat for Kuwait I fancy in order to meet Faisal at Kuwait and try to get his oil concession fixed up. Holmes was in a great rage still about one of the oil men who said he intended going across to the mainland to examine the land over in Kattar, apparently they had a real row and both lost their tempers".

Jun 24 "Skinner had a long talk with Luard (of APOC) about the rumour that APOC were buying up the Bahrain Oil Coy. Luard seemed very worried at such an idea having got round and said that there was not a word of truth in it but he put it down to Yusuf Kanoo. Skinner said he thought it was Haji Williamson, who is here now". Later the Shaikh said to Luard that "he hoped soon they would be running the Bahrain oil, which was perhaps hardly tactful".

Sep 15 "Holmes stayed a long time and discussed oil matters, he is very annoyed at some important questions being held up but I cannot do anything about them until Prior comes back".

Sep 21 "Shaykh Abdulla (came) to discuss some business about a share which he has in the oil company which was given to him really as a bribe by Holmes when he was trying(?) to get the original concession from the old Shaikh. Now the Company offer to buy it back".

Dec 4 "Heard news that the Persians have cancelled the Agreement of the APOC. This is very exciting and if true is very serious . . . If anything happens to Abadan the oil in Bahrain will become of great value and importance".

Dec 13 Went to the Shaikh "took a document about the oil concession, granting them another year on the present lease, for signature".

BEN ALI, Zain al-Abdin (1936–)

Tunisian President. He was born in Hammam Sousse near Monastir and as a youth, served a brief prison sentence for nationalist activities. After independence he was one of the first officers selected for overseas training, qualifying in France in electronics and artillery and in the USA in security and intelligence. From 1958 to 1974 he was Head of Military Security before being sent to Rabat as Military Attaché. At a time of increasing tension between the Government and the powerful trade union organisation, he was recalled as Director-General of National Security, civil and military, in which capacity he put down the riots of Black Thursday. In 1980 Ben Ali was sent as Ambassador to Warsaw, perhaps as some form of exile, but was brought back as Secretary of State for National Security after the Bread Riots of 1984. The first Tunisian army officer to hold political office, Ben Ali won the confidence of Bourguiba who made him in April 1986 Minister of the Interior and in June one of three Assistant Secretaries General of the Parti Socialiste Destourien. He dealt sternly with student unrest, conscripting some into the army, putting police posts on the campus and threatening to close the University Arts Faculty for a year. In May 1987 his rank was raised to Minister of State and on 2 October Bourguiba appointed him Prime Minister in place of the colourless Rashid Sfar. Ben Ali had to deal with a capricious and obstinate President who endorsed his Cabinet, changed his mind and then appeared to approve the Cabinet but not his Prime Minister. Bourguiba was also outraged that the trial of 90 members of the Mouvement de la Tendance Islamique had led to only seven death sentences and ordered Ben Ali to reopen the process to secure more hangings. The Prime Minister summoned a Cabinet from which Bourguiba's closest adherents were excluded and it was agreed to depose the President on grounds of senility: seven doctors provided certificates to justify the action. On 7 November, starting his speech with a Qur'anic quotation, Ben Ali announced that he had taken over in the cause of national reconciliation. His assumption of power was widely welcomed, the opposition leader Ahmad Mestiri saying that it had saved the country. He appointed Hedi Bakkush as Prime Minister and some of Bourguiba's closest associates were briefly imprisoned. At the end of the month, however, the Government announced the arrest of 76 people, some of them security officials and the discovery of an arms cache: it was believed that there had been a plot to prevent the succession of Ben Ali. Ben Ali at once raised the basic wage and declared a fiscal amnesty. Some press restrictions were lifted and although he refused a general amnesty, over 4,000 prisoners deemed to have received excessive sentences were released. Exiled politicians were allowed to return and there was talk of political plurality from which the MTI was not necessarily excluded. Setting out to impose democracy from above, he promised to disentangle the State from the Party which would be reformed to provide new leadership and was renamed the Rassemblement Constitutionnel Démocratique. A Constitutional Council and a National Security Council were created. The post of President for Life and the automatic succession of the Prime Minister were abolished. The Party Politburo was reduced from 20 to 13 members, leaving few Bourguiba men. The State Security Court was abolished and new safeguards provided for people arrested. In January 1988 Ben Ali reshuffled his government, assuming the Defence Ministry and dropping more Bourguibists. His predecessor had been seen as trying to turn Tunisia into a secular European state but Ben Ali set out to reverse this, setting up a Supreme Islamic Council, establishing an Islamic University, permitting the *Azzan* on television and reaffirming its Islamic and Arab identity in a new Constitution promulgated in April 1988. He attempted to conciliate the MTI, now renamed al-Nahdah but still illegal, releasing its leader Rashid Ghannouchi in May and a further 3,000 political prisoners by July but he insisted that no political party could claim a monopoly of Islam. Realising the intransigence of the fundamentalists, he set out to woo the secular opposition: his consistent objective was, for both internal and external appearances, to have as wide a participation as possible without destroying the leading role of the RCD. In July he appointed for the first time since independence a Minister who was not a member of the ruling party and in the same month he increased the freedom of the press by making it subject to the courts rather than to the executive. He declared his intention of liberalising the economy by 1991 and

started a programme of privatisation. Ben Ali favourably impressed the poor by going to the suq to see their difficulties. He received all the opposition leaders and representatives of unions, women's and youth groups etc. and on the first anniversary of his takeover, called for a National Pact to create guidelines for a pluralist democracy including proportional representation and he brought forward to April 1989 the parliamentary elections not due until 1991. He failed to create a national coalition and was embarrassed by the overwhelming victory of the RCD which won all the seats: as the sole candidate for the Presidency he himself won 99%. He then reshuffled his Cabinet leaving only 4 of its 32 members who had held office under Bourguiba. In foreign affairs he had during his first year ended the old quarrel with Libya which he tried to reconcile with the USA and he also set up an executive committee to work towards unification of the two countries. Ben Ali was deeply concerned with co-operation with his neighbours, seeing unity as a necessity to confront the shared problems of Islamic militancy and relations with the EC, particularly the status of North African workers in Europe. He persuaded Algeria to end its hostility to Morocco and played an important part in drafting the Arab Maghreb Unity Treaty and later was the only Head of State to attend all its Summits. He addressed the UN on Third World debts. Ben Ali maintained traditional good relations with European and Gulf States and was one of the first Arab leaders to re-establish links with Egypt. He went to Washington in May 1990 where he put the case for the Palestinians: the presence of the HQ of the Palestine Liberation Organisation made it easy for him to act as a go-between. In the meanwhile at home Ben Ali had, in September 1989 replaced Bakkush, who was regarded as too much under the thumb of Party apparatchiks with Hamid Karoui and in January 1990 introduced reforms which would guarantee the opposition one third of seats in the forthcoming municipal elections but he was unable to satisfy them that his reforms were genuine because in a really fair poll Nahdah would triumph: Muhammad Muada, the leader of the Mouvement des Démocrates Socialistes accused Ben Ali of trying to hand pick his opposition. In June all the opposition parties boycotted the local elections leaving the RCD with another meaningless victory. On his third anniversary, concerned by increasing criticism of torture of political prisoners, he set up a Human Rights Commission as Muada complained that there had been little substantial change and that the country was slipping towards despair as Islamic militants represented a real threat. Although Ben Ali refused definitely to disentangle the State and the Party, in April 1991 he ordered that the six legal opposition parties should receive state funds for administrative purposes, that their local branches should not be harried by the police and that government officials should have time off to work for them. He had by then won considerable popular support by his attitude during the crisis that followed the Iraqi invasion of Kuwait. He had little love for the Gulf States which were financing Nahdah and after failing to get the Cairo Summit postponed while he went to see Saddam Hussain, boycotted the meeting while attempting his own mediation by receiving

Kuwaiti and Iraqi Ministers. Later he denounced the bombing of Baghdad as inhuman and was punished by the cutting off of American aid. Nevertheless he quickly regained the friendship of the Allied nations, making a special effort to show off his democratic credentials. He offered to give the opposition the nine vacant seats in the Assembly without contest but still could not persuade them to co-operate. Showing ostentatious piety in Ramadan, he tried to present himself as the defender of modern Islam against reactionary militants, 279 of whom were put on trial in July 1992 accused of plotting to shoot down his aircraft. He made great efforts to rally the support of women, frightened of fundamentalist rule, promising them "new horizons". He set out to attract foreign investment, giving Tunisia an almost East Asian free market as the World Bank praised it as a model for developing countries although the prosperity was not universal. It was announced in December 1992 that the dinar would be made convertible. He permitted Greenpeace to open its first office in an Arab capital. On his fifth anniversary he created an Ombudsman to investigate complaints of government malpractice and in January 1993 he announced electoral reforms to ensure that the opposition was represented in Parliament. Under Ben Ali Tunisia was seen as a useful member of the world community, sending troops to Somalia and Bosnia and helping with the negotiations that led to the Israeli-PLO Agreement. He agreed that Tunisia should be the first Arab state to host one of the Multi-Lateral Peace Talks. He was the leading advocate of Trans-Mediterranean links. In March 1994 Ben Ali, seen as a force for peace, stability and economic progress, was re-elected unopposed with 99% of the votes. Ben Ali once said that he was "unaffected by all forms of pressure" and alone would decide the pace and scope of reform and that he mananged the country from a computer in his office. He rarely toured and, taciturn and uncharismatic, always spoke from a prepared script. He had no vision on great matters, how, for example to reconcile Islam and modernisation, but was prepared to deal with each problem as it arose.

BEN BARKA, Medhi (1920–65)
Moroccan political leader. He was born in Rabat, one of seven children of a poorly-paid mosque reader and brought up by an uncle who was a road mender. He was educated at a Franco-Muslim school where he showed such brilliance at mathematics that but for the war he would have gone to Paris to take a doctorate. Instead he went to Algiers University where in 1941 he was elected leader of the North African students. Upon graduating he taught at a French school in Morocco and was selected as one of the tutors of the future Hassan II. When the Istiqlal Party, demanding the end of French rule, was created in 1944, Ben Barka was an early member, appointed assistant to the leader Ahmad Balafrej, editing its newspaper and playing an important part in transforming what had started as groups of Fez Islamic traditionalists and Westernised intellectuals into a mass-movement. In 1948 he went to New York to lobby the UN for Moroccan independence. The French regarded him as a particularly dangerous enemy, Marshal Juin called him "the apprentice Lenin", and he was several times imprisoned, kept in solitary con-

finement, or sent into forced residence in the Sahara. After the exiling of Muhammad V he was active in organising demands for his return and was again imprisoned. He was released to take part in the negotiations at Aix-les-Bains. After independence he was ruthless in trying to subjugate all other resistance groups, the civil service and the armed forces to the Istiqlal and was even accused of involvement in the murder of an opponent. Restless, imaginative, exuding exceptional energy and vitality, he was seen as the "dynamo" of a new Morocco although his open agnosticism caused many to suspect him. In 1956 he formed the National Union of Moroccan Students (UNEM). When the King created a Consultative Assembly, Ben Barka was appointed its President. Ben Barka started to feel that the Istiqlal leadership was too conservative and not doing enough for the poor and he moved increasingly to the left. He spoke of "socialist democracy" and only later stated that this did not exclude constitutional monarchy. Having originally declared himself a supporter of the West he began to see merits in "popular democracy" as practised in Russia and China. In August 1958 he resigned the political directorship of the Istiqlal newspaper and in September 1959, with the support of Abd al-Rahim Bouabid and Mahjoub Ben Sadiq, he founded the Union Nationale des Forces Populaires which spoke in Marxist terms of a class struggle, co-ordinating the organised workers, the peasantry and the old resistance. In February 1960 11 UNFP members were accused of plotting to murder the Crown Prince and although the Government took no action against Ben Barka, he went into exile in Paris. There, through close contacts with left-wing journalists, he carried on a press campaign against the Moroccan Government. He also visited Peking and Hanoi and was a leading figure in the anti-colonialist movement on such occasions as the All-African Peoples' Conference in Cairo and a Conference on Solidarity of Afro-Asian Peoples in Lagos. He was also active in Arab politics, trying to mediate between Nasser and the Baath Party. Ben Barka published a book in which he set out a development strategy for Morocco and North Africa as a whole as he was an early advocate of a unified Maghreb. In May 1962 he returned to Morocco but in November he received injuries when a police car tried to force his vehicle off the road into a steep ravine. In the parliamentary elections of May 1963 he was elected by an overwhelming majority in a poor district of Rabat. In July before the communal elections 130 of the UNFP were charged with plotting the overthrow of the Monarchy and the Government believed that Ben Barka, then in Cairo, had been instrumental in supplying Egyptian funds for the purpose. In October after fighting broke out between Morocco and Algeria in the Tindouf Dispute, Ben Barka declared his own country the aggressor and urged the army not to fight. He was condemned to death *in absentia* in November 1963 and again in March 1964 for his part in the UNFP plot. He settled in Geneva. In March 1965 after violent riots in Casablanca the King issued an amnesty in an attempt to restore national unity and he hinted that this might apply even to Ben Barka. It was said that Ben Barka agreed to return after he had attended an anti-Western Tricontinental Conference in Havana. In

October he went to Paris to discuss the making of an anti-colonial film and, on the Boulevard St Germain, he was hustled into a car and never seen again. The full story of his kidnapping will probably never be known but it was generally believed that he was tortured to death by the Moroccan Interior Minister General Muhammad Oufkir in a cellar near Orly Airport. Oufkir, who would not have welcomed a reconciliation between the King and Ben Barka had apparently conspired with some corrupt French security officials and their gangster associates. The repercussions of the affair included a French warrant for the arrest of Oufkir, the withdrawal of Ambassadors between Morocco and France and some Arab countries which had condemned the kidnapping, several suicides or murders and even calls for the resignation of General de Gaulle. In June 1967 a French counter-espionage agent and the former head of the Paris narcotics squad and several gangsters were sentenced to imprisonment but Colonel Ahmad Dlimi, who had surrendered to the court in order to take the heat off the King and Oufkir, was acquitted. In person Ben Barka was short, plump, voluble with very bright eyes, a brilliant speaker with a most effective humour. His enemies saw him as unscrupulous, opportunistic and overweeningly ambitious.

BEN BELLA, Ahmad (1916–)
Algerian President. He was born in Marnia near the Moroccan frontier, the son of a trader of Moroccan origin and had a secondary education in Tlemcen, winning a reputation as an unusually good footballer. During the war he served with the French army in Italy, ending as a warrant officer and receiving two high decorations for valour, the second from General de Gaulle in person. After demobilisation he entered local politics, being elected to Marnia Council as a member of the Mouvement pour le Triomphe de la Liberté et de la Démocratie. After being one of the MTLD candidates defeated by fraud in the elections of 1948, Ben Bella came to realise that Algerian Muslims would never escape from foreign rule by politics alone and was one of the founders of the Organisation Spéciale, dedicated to the achievement of independence through force; he became its Chief when it was felt preferable to have an Arab to the Berber At Ahmad. The OS was chronically short of money and to obtain some in April 1949 Ben Bella robbed the main post office in Oran escaping with over 3,000,000 francs. In May 1950 he was captured and sentenced to eight years' imprisonment but in March 1952 he escaped, seeking refuge in Cairo, where he attempted to win support for Algerian independence but encountered difficulties owing to his poor knowledge of Arabic. In 1954 he was one of the former OS leaders contacted by Muhammad Boudiaf to split away from the MTLD and establish the Comité Révolutionnaire d'Unité et d'Action to plan a Revolutionary war. After the All Saints Day Uprising, Ben Bella, a flamboyant man of great charm and energy, able to present a more attractive public image than Boudiaf, was used as the main spokesman for the newly created Front de Libération Nationale and came to be regarded as its leader. One of his tasks was to negotiate in Libya for the transhipment of arms to the guerrillas in the *wilayas*. During 1956 French Intelligence tried to

assassinate him, once in Cairo and once in Tripoli. A struggle developed over the direction of the Algerian War of Independence between the "externals" such as Ben Bella, Ait Ahmad and Boudiaf and the "internals" led by Belkasim Krim and Ramdan Abane and a Conference was called in the Soummam Valley in August 1956 to resolve matters. The "externals" were invited but Abane managed to make it impossible for them to attend and the "internals" established a parliament, the Conseil National de la Révolution Algérienne and a small executive. Despite his disavowal of the proceedings, Ben Bella was made an Honorary Member of the CNRA and Vice-President of the Gouvernement Provisoire de la République Algérienne when it was set up in September 1958. Before that, however, in October 1956 the aircraft on which he, Boudiaf, Ait Ahmad and Muhammad Khidr were returning to Tunis after a meeting with Muhammad V about possible peace moves was hijacked to Algiers and they were all arrested. After de Gaulle came to power their conditions were relatively comfortable and Ben Bella claimed to have read 700 books while in prison and he improved his literary Arabic. In captivity Ben Bella became more firmly established as the symbol of the Independence Movement and after being consulted about the Evian Agreement, he emerged from captivity in March 1962 as its obvious leader. In a speech in Tunis in April he set forth a programme of socialism, neutralism, development of a national culture, war on illiteracy and the leadership of the FLN as the only legitimate party. At the CNRA meeting in June his supporters put forward these concepts as the Tripoli Charter and argued for the replacement of the GPRA and of the Provisional Franco-Algerian Executive headed by Abd al-Rahman Faris with a Politburo consisting mainly of the five leaders who had been imprisoned together but the five split amongst themselves. Ben Bella allied with Colonel Boumédienne against the GPRA, headed by Ben Khedda who went to Tizi-Ouzou and then to Algiers still declaring itself the legitimate government. Ben Bella announced the appointment of a seven-man Politburo to undertake "the direction of the country and the construction of the State" and went to Tlemcen where he was joined by the respected moderate Farhat Abbas and by Boumédienne and some 35,000 well trained and well equipped regulars of the Armée de Libération Nationale and another 10,000 guerrillas from three of the six *wilayas*. Public opinion stopped the commanders of the other *wilayas* from resisting Ben Bella's advance on Algiers where on 7 August Ben Khedda handed over power to him. In September a general election with a single list of candidates approved by the Politburo, although some opponents were permitted to stand, produced a National Assembly which appointed Ben Bella Prime Minister. He formed a government which included Boumédienne as Defence Minister and later Vice-President and members of the Oudjda Group, the adherents of Boumédienne, and he made Khidr responsible for organising the FLN as one of the principal props of the regime. Saying that "there is no place for an opposition", one of his first moves was to outlaw the Communist Party and to bring the Trade Unions under control. Influenced by Trotskyist advisers and by the example of Yugoslavia he issued the March Decrees which handed over lands and businesses left by the French to the peasants and workers who were to manage them themselves under a system of *Autogestion*. This Ben Bella regarded as a triumph for "Algerian Socialism" but in fact it produced economic chaos. Even barbers were nationalised. He was now the hero of the peasantry but, ignoring the realities of power, he began the process of getting rid of those who had helped him to office. He ousted Khidr after disputes over the role of the Party and At Ahmad went dissident after accusing him of aiming at dictatorship. In August 1963 Ben Bella introduced a new Constitution which led to the resignation of Farhat Abbas and his own accession to the Presidency with an official 96.8% vote in a referendum. Each government reshuffle meant the dropping of another of the Oudjda Group and the assumption of more offices by Ben Bella who was at the end of 1964 President, Prime Minister, Minister of the Interior, Finance and Information and Secretary-General of the FLN. He wished to do everything himself but he was a poor although an over-confident and over-optimistic administrator, incapable of taking long views, driven by emotion rather than logic, susceptible to flattery and liable to attach as much importance to gossip as to official reports. He had a sincere compassion for the down-trodden and was given to flamboyant gestures, sending food from the Presidential Palace to the war-wounded, leading 2,000 children to a fruit market during Ramadan and telling them to help themselves, mobilising volunteers to plant trees and forcing the shoe-shine boys to give up work and go to school which left them penniless. He did much for women, improving their chances of education and participation in political life. Despite opponents' charges of a reign of terror only six people were executed, and that for armed rebellion, in nearly three years and about 2,500 imprisoned for offences with political implications. Ben Bella's conduct of foreign policy also showed impulsiveness rather than calculation. A month after becoming Prime Minister he visited Washington, gaining promises of aid from President Kennedy but went straight on to Cuba where he praised Castro so enthusiastically that American aid was indefinitely postponed. The victory of the FLN had been possible owing to the bases provided by Tunisia and Morocco but within months Tunisia had broken off relations when Ben Bella gave asylum to men who had attempted to assassinate Bourguiba and Morocco had gone to war with Algeria over Tindouf. Addressing the General Assembly Ben Bella committed himself to "the liquidation of colonialism in both its classic and disguised form" but he never included France, upon which Algeria depended for aid, personnel (especially teachers) and markets for its produce, amongst the imperialists. Declaring "no Algerian can consider himself free while his African brothers remain in colonial serfdom", he supported Liberation Movements, providing bases and training for guerrillas. Ben Bella established cordial relations with Russia, which awarded him the Lenin Peace Prize, visiting Moscow, but although he took aid from China, he refused to go to Peking. His relations with Nasser were so close that there were rumours that he was applying for union with Egypt but he refused to support

him in his quarrel with the Baath. Ben Bella gave enthusiastic support to the newly-created Palestine Liberation Organisation and broke off relations with West Germany which had recognised Israel although it meant sacrificing aid. He aspired to recognition as a leader of the Third World, sporting a Mao tunic and in 1964 he spent 75 days abroad in communist and developing countries and as much time welcoming leaders ranging from Haile Selassie to Chou En Lai in Algiers. The first Congress of the FLN in April 1964 revealed the worsening of relations with Boumédienne who criticised the President for relying upon Marxists rather than upon those who had fought the war and for trying to dilute the power of the army by forming a national militia. Ben Bella made overtures to former enemies such as At Ahmad and Boudiaf in the hope of forming an alliance against his Vice-President. He spent the early months of 1965 preparing for an Afro-Asian Summit to be held in Algiers in July which he hoped would give him sufficient backing and prestige for the dismissal of Boumédienne. To ensure personal control over the proceedings he demanded the resignation of his Foreign Minister Abd al-Aziz Boutaflika, the last of the Oudjda Group. To prevent this in the early hours of 19 June 1965 the army took over the country, arresting Ben Bella in his bed. A proclamation gave the reasons for his overthrow as his cult of personality, ideological confusion which had led to the imposition of foreign socialism inconsistent with Islam, discrediting the heroes of the Resistance, improvidence with national resources and "diabolical dictatorship in imposing policies and men according to his mood, whim, and caprice": the book of his treasons promised by Boumédienne never appeared. There was complete surprise and no demonstrations in his favour although Russia deplored his fall. He spent the next six years in solitary confinement, sometimes in an underground cell, but in 1971 his mother arranged a marriage for him with a left-wing journalist. His name was expunged from official history. In July 1979 President Chadli released him to house arrest in M'sila near Constantine and then in 1980 set him free. Ben Bella went to Paris where he launched a journal which described Islam as the basis for a democratic new order throughout Muslim world. Although he had always been an observant Muslim, never smoking or drinking, he attacked fundamentalists for violating human rights. He further admitted that one-party rule had been a mistake, producing corruption on the scale of that practised by the Shah, but he still defended *Autogestion*. In 1983 the French authorities raided his house and encouraged him to move to Switzerland and the following year he set up the Mouvement pour la Démocratie en Algérie. Some of his associates were arrested in Algiers for smuggling arms. In 1985 he joined At Ahmad in a call for a unified opposition to work for "a return to the founding ideals of the Algerian Revolution", ideological freedom and political pluralism. In the summer of 1990 he went back to Algiers expecting a return like that of General de Gaulle but found that he had been generally forgotten, less than 50,000 and no officials coming to greet him. He called the Government "a gang of bandits" which should resign and fight for Saddam Hussain and he went immediately to Baghdad. It appeared that although he was still as rhetorical and irrational as he had been in 1962, his charisma had disappeared. Although he declared that "Islam is the core of our identity", he had no success in attracting moderates away from the Front Islamique du Salut and in June 1991 his announcement that he would stand in the forthcoming presidential election was largely ignored. During the elections of December 1991 he proclaimed his readiness to rejoin the FLN if it would nominate him for the presidency. After the overthrow of Chadli he showed contempt for the ruling Haut Comité d'État and readiness to talk to the FIS. After the murder of Boudiaf Ben Bella complained that the French and the Americans had prevented him from succeeding him as a punishment for his attitude to Iraq. During 1993 he and At Ahmad refused several times to hold political discussions with the HCE although he was several times suggested as a potential mediator with the Islamic militants.

BEN BOULAID, Mustafa b. Ahmad (c. 1917–56)

Algerian Revolutionary leader. He came from the Aures Mountains and won several decorations as a warrant officer in the French army in Italy. After the war he became a miller and then operated a bus service. He had seven children. Ben Boulaid was defrauded of a seat in the elections of 1948 and, losing faith in democratic methods of gaining advancement for the Muslim population, joined the Organisation Spéciale, dedicated to expelling the French by force. Ben Boulaid was one of the Neuf Historiques who planned the All Saints' Day Uprising. His men in the Aures were the first to go into action and the first to kill a French officer. He kept his band of about 350 together in extremely difficult circumstances in the Aures until he was captured in February 1955 near the Libyan frontier on his way to meet Ben Bella in Tripoli. He was sentenced to death in June, given the benefit of a mistrial and again sentenced to death in October. In November he escaped with ten others from Constantine jail and rejoined the guerrillas in the Aures who had become demoralised in his absence. He restored morale by putting some of them to death. In March 1956 the French arranged for Ben Boulaid to find a military radio set: it was booby-trapped and blew him to pieces as he examined it. His death was kept secret and he was nominated for the Conseil National de la Révolution Algérienne many months after it had occurred.

BEN HALIM, Mustafa (1921–)

Libyan Prime Minister. He was born in Alexandria where his Cyrenaican father had sought refuge from the Italian occupation and he trained at the University there as an engineer. His abilities greatly impressed a fellow exile, Ibrahim al-Shalhi, the intimate adviser of the future King Idris. After independence he was called back to Cyrenaica to serve as Minister of Public Works responsible for rebuilding its war-damaged cities. He was then Minister of Communications before becoming Prime Minister on the fall of the Saqisli Government in April 1954. He was the only technocrat in a Cabinet of traditionalists. His three-year period of office was marked by personal and regional struggles within the

Cabinet which had to be reshuffled five times. It was, however, a period of great activity particularly in foreign affairs which, in the days before oil had become plentiful, he exploited as a means of obtaining aid through careful balancing. The keynote of his policy was alliance with the West although he changed this from exclusive dependence upon Britain by allowing the Americans, after a visit to Washington, to establish an airbase at Wheelus, near Tripoli, in return for aid. He also signed a Treaty with the French by which they withdrew from the Fezzan and provided some aid despite the fact that he was allowing arms to pass through Libya to the insurgents in Algeria. He received further aid for endorsing the Eisenhower Doctrine and from Italy after settling problems caused by the past relationship. On the other hand he established diplomatic relations with the Soviet Union which lifted its veto on Libya's entry into the UN although Ben Halim made it clear that he would not tolerate communist activities within the country. He was careful also not to offend Arab sentiment; in March 1956 he declared that Libya would help any Arab state against Israeli aggression. He supported the nationalisation of the Suez Canal and ensured that the British bases in Libya were not used in operations against Egypt but at the same time he prevented Egyptian diplomats from distributing arms for attacks upon them with the result that Nasser later accused him of being hostile. He refused to join the Baghdad Pact and facilitated the passage of arms through Libya to the nationalists fighting the French in Algeria. He was anxious to avoid too much dependence upon Egypt by cultivating good relations with Turkey and with Tunisia, then hostile to Nasser with which he signed a twenty-year Treaty of Friendship. Despite his weakness in Cabinet he tried to solve the problem of the relationship between the central government and the provinces by proposing a decentralised unitary system and he tried to avoid the succession issue by suggesting that the King should become President for life. One of his most important contributions was to ensure that, unlike Iraq or Saudi Arabia, no one country had a monopoly of Libyan oil, dividing the country into numerous small concessions which were offered to as many companies as possible. Ben Halim gave much attention to improving the educational system. He resigned in May 1957 after a decision of which he was known to disapprove was passed by a decree of the Royal Diwan during his absence abroad. After leaving office he spent two years as Ambassador in Paris and then started a business as an engineering contractor in Tripoli. After the Revolution he was sentenced *in absentia* to 15 years' imprisonment. Ben Halim, friendly, informal, enormously fat and incurably optimistic was clearly one of the ablest of Libyan Prime Ministers.

BEN HIMA, Muhammad Taiyba (1924–80)

Moroccan Prime Minister. He was born in Safi and received a French education before going to Nancy University where he qualified as a doctor. After a few years in practice he went into health administration before in 1960 he was appointed Governor of Agadir with the task of rebuilding the town after its devastating earthquake. Ben Hima entered the Cabinet in 1962 as Minister of Public Works and then of Industry. He was moved in 1965 to Education where he was criticised for restraining Arabisation in favour of Western languages: he agreed to the establishment of an American University at Tangier and also established the first Military School for Girls. In May 1967 he reverted to Public Works but in July, after holding the Premiership himself for two years Hassan II passed the office to Ben Hima with the brief of improving the economic situation. Parliament had been suspended but a Council for National Development and Planning was created as a form of replacement. He represented the King at the Khartoum Summit. In April 1969 he went to Algiers to sign a series of technical agreements and to prepare for a state visit by the King as part of the process of improving relations after the Tindouf Dispute and he also worked to improve relations with France, still suffering in the aftermath of the Ben Barka affair. There were frequent Ministerial reshuffles, six in one year as the Government tried to grapple with the problem of speeding up development to keep pace with the birth rate. In August 1969 he was given additional responsibility for planning but in October he was replaced as Prime Minister by Ahmad Laraki. Ben Hima was put in charge of Agriculture and Agricultural Reform and it was officially stressed that the post was so important that it should not be considered demotion. However in August 1970 he was dismissed amidst allegations of corruption when a land dispute led to the death of six peasants. In April 1972 Ben Hima was brought back as Minister of the Interior in the government that Karim Lamrani formed to prepare for elections, which were postponed shortly afterwards. In August he presented the official government line about the mysterious circumstances surrounding the death of General Oufkir and he was responsible for a crack-down on the Union Nationale des Forces Populaires after the March Plot of 1973. In May 1973 he resigned on grounds of ill health but later in the month was appointed Minister for Co-operation and Training to organise two years' civil national service for all graduates in order to end the shortage of trained managers. In 1977 as Minister of the Interior he organised elections that were generally reckoned as amongst the fairest ever conducted in Africa. In March 1979 he retired on grounds of ill health. He was described as a bluff, plain-speaking man, energetic and pragmatic. His brother Ahmad Taiyba Ben Hima (born 1927) had a distinguished diplomatic career, being appointed Permanent Representative at the UN in 1961. He was Minister of Foreign Affairs from 1964 until January 1966 when he was given the key post of Head of the Royal Cabinet. After a year he returned to the UN. In May 1972 he was again Foreign Minister and was much involved in gathering support for a Moroccan takeover of the Spanish Sahara and in the diplomacy that followed the October War. He was transferred to Information in April 1974 organising a propaganda campaign in the Sahara. He died in 1980.

BEN KHEDDA, Ben Yusuf (1920–)
Algerian political leader. Born near Blida, the son of a magistrate, he attended a French school and qualified at Algiers University as a pharmacist. While still a student he joined the Parti du Peuple Algérien and in 1943 was detained for eight months. On its formation he became a member of the Mouvement pour le Triomphe de la Liberté et de la Démocratie of which he rose to become Secretary-General. The elections of 1948 in which MTLD candidates were either arrested or fraudulently declared defeated confirmed his existing belief that only violence could compel the French to treat the Algerians with justice and he was concerned in the running of the Organisation Spéciale. In May 1952 the MTLD split with Ben Khedda heading the opposition of the Central Committee to the pretensions of Messali Haj. After the All Saints' Day Uprising he was imprisoned for protesting against the mass arrests that followed it. Released after five months, he immediately joined the Front de Libération Nationale. He represented Algiers at the Soummam Valley Conference of August 1956 and was co-opted on to the 5-man Comité de Coordination et d'Exécution which attempted to run the War of Algerian Independence. Ben Khedda was one of the leaders of the Algiers battle, trying to turn the Qasbah into a fortress but was hunted intensely by the French army. After a perilous journey he escaped to Tunis. When in September 1958 the Gouvernement Provisoire de la République Algérienne was set up, Ben Khedda became Minister of Culture and Social Affairs and in November he headed the first FLN mission to China which was of great psychological importance as underlining recognition and securing arms. He also toured Latin America. When the GPRA was reformed in January 1960 he was omitted but continued to go on diplomatic missions and to write theoretical articles in FLN publications. In August 1961 when the GPRA was again reformed, Ben Khedda who was not regarded as belonging to any of the competing factions, was chosen as President. He committed the revolution to socialism and neutralism. During the winter of 1961/2 his public moderation, for example in a speech to the Non-Aligned Nations Conference in Belgrade, contributed towards peace negotiations and he was the first to announce the conclusion of the Evian Agreement as "a great victory for the Algerian people". In June 1962 the Conseil National de la Révolution Algérienne met in Tripoli to formulate an ideology and set up a government Ben Khedda was challenged by Ben Bella who declared that this should be done not by the GPRA but by a Political Bureau headed by himself. Ben Khedda walked out and then attempted to assert his authority by ordering the dissolution of the General Staff and the arrest of its leader Boumédienne. He lost the struggle and, accompanied by a few loyal Ministers, went to Tizi Ouzou and then to Algiers, declaring himself still Head of the legitimate government. Some of the *wilaya* commanders rallied to him but ultimately were not prepared to fight the well-equipped and more numerous troops of Boumédienne. On 7 August Ben Khedda formally resigned and the following month he was excluded from the National Assembly. He dropped out of politics and resumed his old business, running a pharmacy in Algiers. In July 1964 at the time when the opponents of Ben Bella combined to criticise him Ben Khedda was amongst those imprisoned. He did not engage in politics again until March 1976 when with Farhat Abbas he issued a manifesto condemning Boumédienne's "totalitarian

rule and personality cult". When in 1989 the formation of political parties was permitted, Ben Khedda formed the Umma Party but had little success in the parliamentary elections. In March 1992 Ben Khedda denounced the enforced dissolution of Front Islamique du Salut. He was an old, reserved, quiet-spoken, rather austere man with doctrinaire Marxist leanings. He always wore dark glasses and suffered chronic ill health.

BEN M'HIDI, Larbi (1923–57)

Algerian Revolutionary Leader. The son of a prosperous farmer, he was born at M'lila near Constantine and was arrested at the time of the Setif Uprising. He became an actor and played minor parts on Algiers Radio. A member of the Organisation Spéciale, he was one of the Neuf Historiques who planned the All Saints' Day Uprising. Ben M'hidi was put in charge of raising the Oran region but encountered exceptional difficulties as the area had recently been hit by an earthquake and arms promised from Morocco had not arrived. He then spent some months with the "external" leadership in Cairo. In August 1956 he handed over Oran to Abd al-Hafid Boussouf and assumed command in the capital. He played an important part at the Soummam Valley Congress, arguing for the primacy of the "internals" doing the fighting over the "externals". With Ramdan Abane and Belkasim Krim he was elected to the Comité de Coordination et d'Exécution in charge of running the Algerian War of Independence. He was mainly responsible for launching the Algiers Battle in January 1957 but at the end of February he was captured and tortured by French parachutists. A few days later French officials stated that he had committed suicide by hanging himself with strips torn from his shirt but his comrades thought it unlikely that such a devout Muslim would have taken his own life. After independence one of the smartest streets in Algiers was renamed in his honour.

HUBEN SADIQ, Mahjoub (c. 1921–)

Moroccan nationalist and trade union leader. He came from a poor family in Meknes and started working on the railways. He was soon active in the trade union movement, then under the domination of French communists, and in 1944 he was one of the first members of the Istiqlal Party. In December 1952, with his colleague Taiyib Bouazza, Ben Sadiq was one of the leaders of a demonstration against the murder of the Tunisian trade unionist Farhat Hashid which led to bloodshed in Casablanca. The French used this as a pretext for a general round-up of nationalists and Ben Sadiq was jailed until September 1954. In 1955 he was again accused of involvement with a terrorist group, arrested and tortured, his head thrust into a bucket of urine, but not prosecuted. In March 1955 with help of Istiqlal, he played a major part in creating the Union Marocain du Travail of which he became Secretary-General. The UMT was a definitely nationalist organisation for it refused to admit non-Moroccans and it deliberately dispelled French allegations of Istiqlal links with Moscow by refusing to join the communist-dominated WFTU, a stance brought it financial aid from Washington. After independence he was Vice-President of the Consultative Assembly set up by Muhammad V.

The UMT now claimed 600,000 members and was, with the army, the best organised body in the Kingdom. Ben Sadiq played an important part in securing laws favouring the workers in such matters as health insurance, occupational safety and minimum wages. In September 1959 with Mehdi Ben Barka and Abd al-Rahim Bouabid Ben Sadiq broke away from Istiqlal in order to form the more left-wing Union Nationale des Forces Populaires. The Istiqlal retaliated by creating its own trade union movement, the Union Générale des Travailleurs Marocains and later the Union Socialiste des Forces Populaires also had its own union, the Confédération Démocratique du Travail: these unions cooperated or competed according to the policies of their parties. In January 1963 Ben Sadiq broke his formal links with the UNFP but in general followed much the same policies. He was actively concerned with the establishment of links with other African trade unions and was President of the All-Africa Trade Union in 1964. He had close relations with Hassan II, to the extent that he was sometimes reviled as a stooge of the Palace but in July 1967 he was sentenced to 18 months' imprisonment for insulting remarks about the Government's collusion with Zionism. There were internal and foreign protests against the sentence and he was included in an amnesty in December 1968. Ben Sadiq continued to run the UMT which he kept out of the strikes that set off the Casablanca Riots of 1981 and the Fez Riots of 1990. He was re-elected for another term in 1989. In the 1990s it was estimated that the UMT had 700,000 members, the UGTM 650,000 and the CDT 300,000. Ben Sadiq was a small, slender man with a feline walk.

BEN SALAH, Ahmad (1926–)

Tunisian politician. Born in Moknine, he was educated at Sadiqi College and the Sorbonne where he became General Secretary of the students' branch of the Neo-Destour. With a degree in Arabic literature he began teaching at Sousse where he joined the civil service trade union and was head of the local Party branch. In 1954, after the murder by French right-wingers of Farhat Hashid, he became Secretary-General of the main Trade Union Organisation (UGTT), frequently representing it abroad. He proved an inspiring leader, making clear his socialist views by declaring "we shall nationalise all companies whatever their importance". In 1955 his ability to deliver the support of the UGTT played an important part in the victory of Bourguiba over Salih Ben Yusuf. In April 1956 he was elected Vice-President of the Constituent Assembly. Later in the year, however, having claimed for the UGTT an equality with the Party in economic policy-making, he quarrelled with Bourguiba and was dismissed. Ben Salah was quickly forgiven for the following year he was appointed Secretary of State for Health and Social Affairs. In 1961 he was transferred to the Ministry for the National Economy and in 1968 he was given additional responsibility for Education. He published an ambitious 10-year plan, aiming for self-sufficiency and high living standards for the poor and received aid from the Americans as a "pilot country". In March 1964 his third 4-year plan was welcomed by foreign investors and in September he devalued the dinar, increased prices and froze wages. He also announced major reforms for Tunis University. In 1964 Bourguiba made him Assistant Secretary-General of the Party. Apart from the President he now appeared the most powerful man in the country and when in March 1969 Bourguiba had a heart attack, Ben Salah was widely regarded as his obvious successor. He had, however, in aiming to restructure the country, made powerful enemies. His plans for farming collectives – his saying "it is folklore that ten people should own a single olive tree" – typified his arrogance, authoritarianism and misunderstanding of the mentality of the majority of peasants whom he made little effort to convince. At the same time his plans for state-run factories and retail outlets angered the middle class led by the Governor of the Central Bank, Hedi Nouira. He pushed for "economic decolonisation", the reduction of the influence of foreign businesses, and nationalised foreign-owned land. He made no secret of his intention to change the life of every citizen. In January 1968 the Defence Minister Ahmad Mestiri resigned from the Government in protest at Ben Salah's "wild collectivisation". In January 1969 Ben Salah accelerated his collectivisation policy by creating a National Union of Co-operatives under his immediate control and quadrupling the area of collectivised land by taking over private holdings including olive groves: landowners would retain their titles but decisions over production and marketing would be made by co-operative managers under government supervision. These measures, often enforced by his officials before they had become law, were greeted by violent demonstrations: peasants were imprisoned for refusing to join the co-operatives and slaughtered their animals or smuggled them into Algeria rather than turn them over to the state. In some areas, for the first time since independence, troops had to be called upon to support the police. In September 1969 power over the economy was taken from Ben Salah and given to Bahi Ladgham and in November he was dismissed also from Education, expelled from the Party and put under house arrest with Bourguiba criticising his "juggling empty slogans of shadowy socialism" which had been leading towards "an abyss". There were allegations of corruption amongst his entourage and his edifice of collectivisation was demolished with rapidity. In March 1970 he was put on trial for treason for violating the Constitution, abuse of power and deceiving the Head of State: he was accused of "a real breach of trust . . . a veritable plot against state security" in authorising expenditure on the co-operatives without Cabinet approval and providing false statistics. He pleaded that he had always acted in good faith and was unaware of details of any injustices. In May he was sentenced to ten years' imprisonment. Bourguiba admitted that he himself had been mistaken but said that no one else could have saved the country from Ben Salah. In February 1973, with the aid of a warder, he escaped to Algeria from where he fled to France. He was sentenced to an extra five years for escaping with an additional six months for illegally crossing the frontier; his brother received three years and the warder, *in absentia* 11 years. In August Bourguiba made an offer to all fugitives of an amnesty if they returned before 31 December 1973 and guaranteed

to abstain from politics: Ben Salah who would have had to stand trial again ignored it, later claiming that he was pursued by a pack of killers. In exile in Paris he published a Manifesto *Vers une nouvelle Tunisie* and announced the formation of the Mouvement de l'Unité Populaire to fight for his political ideals. In August 1977, after some MUP members had been arrested for sedition, Ben Salah was sentenced *in absentia* to a further eight years' jail for creating an illegal organisation. After the overthrow of Bourguiba, he was cleared of all charges against him and returned to Tunisia in June 1988. Although hardly active politically, he was soon in conflict with the new regime and went into exile in Switzerland. In May 1991, with his fellow exiles Muhammad Mzali and Rashid Ghannouchi he issued a Manifesto condemning Ben Ali for repression and terror.

BEN SULAYMAN, Sulayman (c. 1906–86)

Tunisian nationalist leader. After studying medicine in Paris he was an early member of the Neo-Destour, becoming a member of its Politburo in 1937. His arrest in April 1938 set off riots which led to the arrest of Bourguiba, Mongi Slim and others: they were all freed when the Germans overran Vichy France in 1942. While in jail he became a close friend of Bourguiba on whose behalf he managed the Party while the leader remained in exile. They quarrelled, however, because while Bourguiba aimed at independence through working with the West, Ben Sulayman considered that it could only be won through alliance with the Russians. In 1949 Ben Sulayman was expelled from the Party. In 1960 he was allowed to start an intellectual left-wing journal but in 1962 it was closed and he was purged from his hospital post for his embarrassing support of Vietnam. In 1976 he was reconciled with Bourguiba. Just before his death his son was arrested for political agitation.

BEN TOBAL, Lakhdar (1923–)

Algerian Revolutionary leader. The son of a peasant from Mila near Constantine, he was a schoolmate of Ahmad Boussouf. He was active in the Mouvement pour le Triomphe de la Liberté et de la Démocratie and joined its armed wing, the Organisation Spéciale. In 1950 he came under suspicion and went underground. He was one of the Twenty Two who met in July 1954 to plan the All Saints' Day Uprising. He then showed himself one of the most courageous, skilful and ruthless of the guerrilla leaders, and in August 1955 planned the Philippeville Massacre in which women and children were slaughtered in scenes of revolting savagery. The reprisals of the outraged colons brought further recruits to the Front de Libération Nationale. Ben Tobal was one of the delegates at the Soummam Valley Conference and from July 1957 a member of the nine-man Committee that controlled the Algerian War of Independence. His command of the North Constantine area, on the Tunisian frontier, was strategically one of the most important. When in September 1958 the Gouvernement Provisoire de la République Algérienne was established, Ben Tobal was nominated as Minister of the Interior. He was with Boussouf and Belkasim Krim in day-to-day charge of running the war and was one of the negotiators at Evian. After independence he supported the GPRA against Ben Bella and refused to be a candidate for National Constituent Assembly. He went into business and played no further public role. Ben Tobal was a small slight man of Malay appearance.

BEN UTHMAN, Muhammad (1920–)

Libyan Prime Minister. He was the son of a Qadi in the Fezzan who gave him a religious education and later employed him as an assistant. When the French drove out the Italians in 1943, Ben Uthman was appointed a teacher but he resigned after a year, having become an active nationalist and a supporter of a united Libya under Idris in opposition to the French who had aspired to annex the Fezzan. He led the Fezzanese delegation to the first Parliament and was involved in the drawing up of the Constitution. He was appointed Minister of Health in the first federal government. When the Qubar government fell through a corruption scandal in October 1960 the King felt it time that a Fezzanese should become Prime Minister. Ben Uthman was widely respected for his integrity and restored confidence in the Government. He cultivated good relations with the Palace clique but this was complicated by the King's decision to establish himself at al-Beidha, making him difficult of access. Ben Uthman also tried to involve the people more in government by travelling around the country and by propaganda, greatly increasing the educational material published by the state. He appointed the first Minister for Oil and oil exports began during his period of office; he worked hard to persuade the people that Libya could not develop this source alone and that the Western companies were helping and not plundering the country. He took Libya into OPEC in September 1961. He settled the disputed boundary between Tripoli and Fezzan. In August 1961 he locked up 61 members of the Baath Party which had been campaigning against corruption and against the British bases and declared the Party illegal. He also imprisoned some trade unionists. Ben Uthman established friendly relations with Nasser, cultivated other African states and concluded a Treaty with Morocco and allowed the Gouvernement Provisoire de la République Algérienne to establish itself in Tripoli. In March 1963 he unexpectedly resigned, officially on grounds of health: it was suggested that the real reason was his despair at his inability to resolve disputes between the Palace and the politicians, to avoid which he was considering a return to a federal rather than a unitary state.

BEN YAHYA, Muhammad Sadiq (1932–82)

Algerian Minister. Born at Djidelliin Kabyle, he trained as a lawyer at Algiers University where he was a leading student organiser. After qualification he was prominent in defending militants accused of subversive activities. He escaped to Cairo before he could be arrested, represented the Front de Libération Nationale in Jakarta and worked closely with Farhat Abbas as President of the Gouvernement Provisoire de la République Algérienne. He represented the GPRA at the Melun Talks and was one of the negotiators of the Evian Agreement. Although he was on the staff of Ben Khedda as Secretary-General of the GPRA, he deserted him for Ben Bella and was a member of the committee that drafted the Tripoli Charter. He was elected to the National Assembly but soon afterwards was sent as Ambassador to Moscow where he had the important responsibility of assuring the Kremlin that the overthrow of Ben Bella meant no change in Algeria's anti-imperialist stance. Transferred to London, Ben Yahya's stay was brief as Algeria broke off relations over Rhodesia. When Boumédienne started replacing politicians with technocrats in his government, Ben Yahya was in October 1966 appointed Minister of Information and switched in July 1970 to Higher Education where he had to confront a major student strike. Later he was again Ambassador in London. In March 1979 when Chadli was beginning to divest himself of those most closely connected with his predecessor, he appointed Ben Yahya to replace Abd al-Aziz Boutaflika who had dominated Algerian foreign policy for over a decade. Ben Yahya played a decisive part in securing the release of the 50 Americans held hostage in their Embassy in Tehran and won great respect internationally. In March 1980 he negotiated an important agreement by which India supplied technical personnel and teachers in return for oil. In May 1981 he had a miraculous escape when an aircraft taking him to an OAU meeting crashed near Bamako. Later in 1981 he met Hassan II, moving towards the restoration of relations broken off five years earlier over the Western Sahara War. Having established good relations with Iran over the hostages, he was asked to mediate in the Iran–Iraq War and was on his way to Tehran when his aircraft crashed in mysterious circumstances, possibly shot down by the Iraqis. The Ayatollah Khomeini ordered three days' of national mourning in Ben Yahya's honour. Ben Yahya was very much a lawyer, cool, secretive, calculating and precise.

BEN YUSUF, Salih (1908–61)

Tunisian nationalist leader. He was born in Jerbah and qualified as a lawyer. He was an early member of the Neo-Destour and was one of the closest associates of Bourguiba, who brought him on to the Politburo in 1937. In 1938 he was arrested with the other leaders and freed when the Germans overran Vichy France. In March 1945 it was at his urging that Bourguiba escaped to Cairo and during the following years Ben Yusuf as Secretary-General ran the Party although there were already suggestions of rivalry between them. He devoted much effort to organising workers into trade unions and gaining their support for the nationalists. In August 1950 when Muhammad Chenik formed a "Government of Negotiations" to seek firstly autonomy and then independence in agreement with France, Ben Yusuf, with the consent of the Party, became its first Minister, accepting the Ministry of Justice. He accompanied the Prime Minister to Paris for talks and in January 1952 he put the case for Tunisia's independence to a Security Council meeting. Later in the month when the French arrested Chenik and other Ministers he escaped to Cairo where he became an admirer of Nasser. In June 1955 after the signature of the Franco-Tunisian Autonomy Agreement which gave less than complete independence Ben Yusuf remained in Cairo, vehemently attacking it as binding Tunisia too closely to France to the detriment of links with the

Arab and Islamic world and as betraying Morocco and Algeria which were still resisting French rule: he accused Bourguiba of concentrating on narrowly Tunisian interests. Bourguiba persuaded him to return which he did in mid-September to be greeted with a great show of reconciliation and party unity. Shortly afterwards Ben Yusuf in front of a large crowd denounced the convention as a sell-out to colonialism, demanded complete independence and a meeting of the National Congress of the Party which he expected to dominate. The Bourguibist Politburo dismissed him as Secretary-General and expelled him from the Party. Ben Yusuf tried to rally support in public meetings but these were broken up by Bourguibists and he had to make himself ridiculous by appealing to the Government for protection. The Congress was summoned in mid-November for Sfax where, as a Jerban, Ben Yusuf could expect little popular support. He declared the Congress illegal as only he, as Secretary-General, was empowered to convoke it, then called for a boycott and refused to appear in person. Bourguiba outmanoeuvred him by gaining the support of both those who aspired to full independence, by asserting that he was the most likely man to win it, and of Ahmad Ben Salah and the trade unions. Ben Yusuf then made a forlorn attempt to organise a rival party and when that failed called for an armed rebellion, killing some of Bourguiba's supporters and receiving some help from the Algerians who were just beginning their War of Independence. In January 1956, after Ben Yusuf had fled into Libya, a search of his house revealed large stocks of arms, money and treasonable literature. He took refuge in Cairo but armed unrest, particularly in his native South, continued until June when it was crushed with the help of French troops. Some of his guerrillas were hanged. In Cairo he attempted to raise a Tunisian Liberation Army and on 24 January 1957 he and six of his followers, *in absentia*, were sentenced to death for treason. In October 1958 Tunisia broke off relations with Cairo which it blamed for connivance in a "Yusufist" plot against Bourguiba. In May 1961 Ben Yusuf acceded to Bourguiba's request for a meeting in Switzerland but there was no reconciliation. In August Ben Yusuf was murdered in a hotel in Frankfurt. The assassins were never caught but they were publicly praised by Bourguiba for "ridding Tunisia of a viper". Despite his murder his vision of a Tunisia linked with the radical Arabs rather than with the West continued and his followers were implicated in another attempt on the life of Bourguiba in December 1962. In March 1989 President Ben Ali awarded Ben Yusuf the country's highest honour. Ben Yusuf was described as "primarily a political animal, intelligent and passionate . . . He possessed the art – by his lucidity, sincerity, tricks, calculations – of electrifying a crowd", energetic, buoyant, impulsive and outspoken and there was only room for one man of that kind in Tunisia. In person he had a square jaw and bulging eyes behind thick spectacles.

BERRI, Nabih (1937–)
Born in Freetown, Sierra Leone, he lived in South Lebanon before studying law at AUB, where he was a Baathist, and then at the Sorbonne. He joined his father in Sierra Leone then lived in the US where he married an American. He returned to Lebanon in 1975 and joined Amal, becoming Secretary-General in 1978 and taking over the leadership in 1981 when it was no longer being kept vacant for Musa Sadr. He brought Shiah into mainstream political life. He opposed the May Agreement although he did not formally join the National Salvation Front. In August 1983 Kataib made an attempt on his life. Generally pro-Syrian he allied himself with Jumblatt, sometimes trying to restrain his wilder policies. He attended the Geneva Reconciliation talks. He was brought into the Karami Cabinet of April 1984 as Minister of Justice but refused to take his seat until he was given the additional post of Minister for South Lebanon. He tried to work with Karami and even Gemayel but boycotted many meetings later calling for Gemayel's resignation. He spent a great deal of time in Damascus. The more extreme Shiah split away to form the Hizbullah and Islamic Amal, calling for an Islamic Republic. Berri wanted to preserve the existing state with a larger share for Shiah. In September he suggested a Presidency rotating between the leaders of the six sects. He opposed the separatism of the Maronites and Jumblatt and in December 1985 signed the Three-Militia Agreement with Jumblatt and Hobeika. In 1984–5, in alliance with Jumblatt, he got control of West Beirut, then attacked Palestinian camps on Syria's behalf. His importance was shown in June 1985 when he secured the release of an American aircraft hijacked by Shiah on Syria's behalf.

BIDUN
After the discovery of oil, Kuwaiti citizenship became so valuable that steps were taken to restrict it. Under the Nationality Law of 1959 only those resident in Kuwait before 1920 and their direct descendants in the male line became entitled to it. Naturalisation could be granted to Arabs after residence of ten years but only 50 individuals could be granted citizenship in one year. By 1990 there were about 230,000 Arabs, 10% of the population, mostly of bedouin origins, who had no claims to nationality either of Kuwait or of any other country: they were known as *bidun* – "without" (citizenship). Many of them served in the army or the police and most were loyal during the Iraqi occupation. After the liberation, however, the Kuwaiti Government refused to allow back those who had been deported or had escaped without a rigorous investigation of each case. At one time 2,000 were detained in a single camp.

BILQASIM, Sharif (1933–)
Algerian politician. He came from a bourgeois family of Beni Mellal, Morocco and studied law at Rabat University. He strongly supported the Algerian War of Independence and headed its student organisation in Morocco. In 1956, under the name of Si Jamal, he joined the guerrillas in *wilaya* V on the Moroccan frontier, rising to become its Chief of Staff and a close associate of Boumédienne. After independence he was elected Deputy for Tlemcen. In September 1963 he was appointed Minister of National Orientation which grouped education, youth and sports. In April 1964 he became a member of the Central Committee of the Front de Libération Nationale but after outspoken criti-

cism of Ben Bella he was demoted. After he had helped his patron Boumédienne to seize power in June 1965 Bilqasim was put in charge of the education and reorganisation of the Party. In March 1968 he was appointed Minister of Finance but in 1970, after disputes with the Industry Minister, Belaid Abd al-Salam he was transferred to Minister of State, in which capacity he carried out numerous missions on behalf of the President to Arab, African and East European countries. He also often acted official spokesman. At this time he was regarded as one of the most important men in the country. In July 1975 he was summarily dismissed without any reason being given publicly. Little was heard of him until before the parliamentary elections of 1991 when he was reported to be trying to rally former Boumédienne loyalists to form a party and in 1993 when he said that he had no intention of returning to politics although there was a need to end the corruption of the Chadli years and also the terrorism of the Islamic militants.

BILTMORE PROGRAMME (1942)

In May 1942 an Extraordinary Zionist Congress was held in the Biltmore Hotel in New York attended by some 600 American Jews and several from abroad including Chaim Weizmann and David Ben Gurion. It denounced the British White Paper of 1939 with its restrictions on immigration and land settlement and demanded that "the gates of Palestine should be opened" and that the Jewish Agency should be "vested with control of immigration and with the necessary authority for building up the country, including the development of its unoccupied and uncultivated lands". Palestine should "be established as a Jewish Commonwealth integrated in the structure of the new democratic world" which it was hoped would emerge after the war. It advocated the formation and recognition of a Jewish military force under its own flag. It adopted the policy of Ben Gurion that the Jews could not rely upon British good will and, with the background of Nazi persecution of European Jews, should trust to the conscience of mankind. If Jews could not legally enter Palestine they should be smuggled in. This was the first claim for the establishment of a Jewish state and was opposed by many Zionists on the grounds that it was bound to lead to the partition of Palestine and conflict with the Arabs.

BIR AM and IKRIT

Bir Am and Ikrit were Christian villages in the north of Palestine near the Lebanese frontier and prior to 1948 were on cordial terms with the Jewish settlers in the local Kibbutz. In November 1948 although the Palestine War was effectively over, the 1,050 inhabitants, who had been given Israeli citizenship, were told to leave their homes for a fortnight for security reasons and dispersed to the surrounding villages. At the end of the fortnight Moshe Carmel commanding the region told them that they could not return because of a curfew on the frontier but it became apparent that the real reason was that their land was coveted by the Kibbutz. The villagers appealed to the High Court but on Christmas Day 1950, ten days before the verdict was due, the army blew up all the buildings in Ikrit apart from the church: the decision that the expulsion had been unjust had no effect. Similarly in September 1953 when the Bir Am appeal was pending, the entire village was destroyed by the Israeli air force. The plight of the villagers attracted the sympathy of liberal Israelis who in August 1972 approached Prime Minister Golda Meir who replied that to help them would recognise the right to return of other Arabs who had been expelled. In February 1977 Shmuel Toledano who had been adviser to the Labour Party on Arab affairs took up their case, also without success. The injustice done to the Arab villagers foreshadowed many similar cases after the occupation of the West Bank.

BIR ZEIT UNIVERSITY

In 1924 a wealthy Palestinian woman founded a village school at Bir Zeit, 15 miles north of Jerusalem. By 1935 it had become a high school and in the 1950s it started running two-year degree courses in arts and sciences. After the occupation of the West Bank it adopted four-year courses and was accepted as a fully fledged University in 1975. Its students helped the surrounding villages with literacy campaigns, agricultural development, tree planting etc. It had already become regarded as a centre of Palestinian nationalism, denounced by an Israeli official as "a terrorist cell disguised as a school". With 2,500 students it was the most prestigious of the six Arab Universities in the Occupied Territories. The Occupation authorities regularly interfered with its teachers, finance and curriculum, removed books from its shelves, put heavy taxes on new equipment and hampered access with frequent road blocks: at times there appeared a deliberate campaign to starve young Arabs of higher education and to prevent its work in preserving the historical and cultural Palestinian people. Closure was a form of collective punishment banned under the Fourth Geneva Convention, an international law flouted in numerous ways by the military authorities. In November 1974, after widespread demonstrations celebrating the recognition of the Palestine Liberation Organisation by the UN, the University President, Dr Hanna Nasser was deported to Lebanon, blindfolded and in handcuffs. The University was closed for some time. In March 1976, to stop a demonstration, Israeli troops attacked the dormitories, arresting 5 students and severely injuring 13. The student council was dominated by representatives of nationalist groups, sometimes co-operating and at others in dispute. In March 1979 the University was again closed: during the next eight years it was closed on 13 occasions for periods varying from a week to three months. In November 1980 the closure was the result of Israeli objections to its syllabus: 16 students were wounded demonstrating against the decision. These restrictions upon a University angered some Israeli intellectuals who set up a Committee of Solidarity with Bir Zeit University and were dispersed with tear gas. There were also support groups in other countries. In December 1986 two students were killed by Israeli soldiers. Bir Zeit University was again closed after the outbreak of the Intifadah in December 1987 although there were no accusations of terrorism against its students. The teaching staff operated a "University in Exile", holding classes wherever they could. In January 1992 the Professor of Archaeology, was murdered. In April 1992, long after other Universities had been permitted to reopen, Bir Zeit was allowed to resume after 51 months. It had lost 60% of its funding since the Gulf War and 63 of its students were in prison without trial. Its role in Palestinian nationalism was shown by the fact that of the negotiators at the Washington Peace Talks six had either studied or taught there including the official spokeswoman Dr Hannan Ashrawi. In November elections for the student council showed that two thirds of them supported the PLO and the peace process and that one third, backing Hamas, opposed it.

BISHARA, Abd Allah b. Yakub (1936–)
Kuwaiti diplomat. He was the son of a famous seaman who left him a strong sense of identification with the Gulf. After higher education at Cairo University and Oxford, he was briefly a teacher before joining the Kuwaiti diplomatic service, representing his country at the UN from 1974 to 1981. He returned home as diplomatic adviser to the Government but in 1982 he was chosen as the first Secretary-General of the Gulf Co-operation Council. Bishara had won a reputation for bluntness and independence. His arrangement of an interview between the US Ambassador and a PLO official led to the enforced resignation of the American and bitterness against the Arabs amongst the blacks.

BITAT, Rabah (1927)
Algerian political leader. Born in Constantine, he volunteered for the French army seeing it as a force for freedom but was disillusioned after the harsh repression of the Setif Uprising. He joined the Mouvement pour le Triomphe de la Liberté et de la Démocratie and was a member of the Organisation Spéciale. He was then one of the Neuf Historiques who planned the All Saints' Day Uprising in which his task was to attack a police post in Blida. He was unsuccessful in capturing any weapons and lost three men killed. He was then put in command of the resistance in Algiers but in March 1955 he was captured and his organisation broken up. He remained in captivity, latterly in France, until after the signature of the Evian Agreement in March 1962. During his imprisonment he was regarded as an Honorary Minister of State in the Gouvernement Provisoire de la République Algérienne and he attempted to mediate between it and the supporters of Ben Bella. He later married a resistance heroine who had spent five years in prison. After independence Bitat was appointed Deputy Prime Minister and with Muhammad Khidr put in charge of transforming the Front de Libération Nationale from a fighting force into a political party. In September 1963 he quarrelled with Ben Bella, resigned and went abroad. After Boumédienne took power he appointed Bitat Minister of State and sent him on missions to African countries. After October 1966 he headed a newly created Ministry of Transport for a decade before becoming Speaker of the National Assembly. In that capacity he acted as Head of State after the death of Boumédienne and also presided over the first session of the Consultative Assembly of the Arab Maghreb Union. In October 1990 he resigned the Speakership in protest at what he considered the excessive speed of reform of the Hamrouche government.

BIZERTA CONGRESS (1964)
The seventh Congress of the Neo-Destour Party was held in Bizerta from 19 to 22 October 1964 and was officially called "The Congress of Destiny". It met while Ahmad Ben Salah, as Minister of Planning and Economic Affairs was imposing collectivisation on the farmers. President Bourguiba stressed that a developing country needed a state-controlled economy. The structure of the Party was reorganised, according to the President to bring in younger men, with the creation of a new Central Committee of 40–50 which would consist of the old Politburo with other ministers and regional governors and from it the President would choose a new Politburo of 10–15 members. In the event of the President's death the Central Committee would elect a successor within 48 hours. Bourguiba declared that it was the duty of trade unions to ensure that their members accepted government policies. The Congress was seen as marking a shift away from the sometimes illiterate veterans of the struggle for independence towards younger educated men. The Congress had been attended by about 1,300 delegates, one chosen by each cell, and it was decided that there should be fewer, chosen regionally, for future Congresses. Each region would have a Governor and a Party Secretary working together with a committee of co-ordination. The commitment to socialism was marked by the change of name from Neo-Destour to Parti Socialiste Destourien which was to act as the motor of the state. After the Congress Muhammad Sayah was appointed Director of the Party, charged with ensuring the discipline of its members and made the post one of the most important in the country.

BIZERTA INCIDENT (1961)
At the beginning of July 1961 President de Gaulle unexpectedly received what he termed a "threatening letter" from President Bourguiba demanding the immediate French evacuation of the leased naval base at Bizerta and a rectification of the frontier with Algeria to give Tunisia some territory believed to contain oil. These points had previously been raised by the Tunisians who had not shown any urgency although the French were now seeking more land to extend the Bizerta airfield for new fighters. Bourguiba's motive was probably to regain prestige after a period of economic difficulties and attacks by Nasser that he put Western interests above those of the Arabs. When no reply had been received after a fortnight, a "spontaneous" collection of about 10,000 Tunisian troops, police, civilians, women and children blockaded the French forces. In order to clear the perimeter the French counter-attacked with naval gunfire, bombing from the air and they also dropped in 7,000 parachutists. Fighting continued for three days, spreading throughout much of the town. Official Tunisian figures put their dead at 1,365 while other sources put it at over 800: French losses were 24 killed and 100 wounded. France was censured at the UN on 26 August by 66–0 with even the NATO countries Norway, Denmark and Turkey voting against her. The condemnation of France

increased de Gaulle's determination to leave Algeria but deprived him of the possible services of Bourguiba as a mediator with the Gouvernement Provisoire de la République Algérienne. The Bizerta Incident also moved Tunisia into closer relations with the more radical Arab and African states. Diplomatic relations between France and Tunisia were restored in July 1962 and the Bizerta base was evacuated in October 1964 with the French abandoning installations worth £35 million.

BLACK JUNE

"Black June", the month of 1976 when Syrian troops entered Lebanon to assist the Maronites against the Palestinians, was a title assumed for terrorist activities by followers of Abu Nidal. The name was first used in September when four of its members seized the Semiramis Hotel in Damascus holding 90 hostages. In a shoot-out one terrorist and four hostages were killed and the three surviving terrorists publicly hanged. Fatah denied any association with the group which was believed to be financed from Iraq. In October there were attacks on the Syrian Embassies in Islamabad and Rome and in November three out of four raiders, including one Japanese, were killed in an attack on the Intercontinental Hotel in Amman. A fortnight later Black June claimed responsibility for the first of several attempts to murder the Syrian Foreign Minister Abd al-Halim Khaddam. In October 1977 in Abu Dhabi one of its members tried again, missed him and instead killed the UAE Minister of State for Foreign Affairs. It later claimed to have carried out attacks on Israeli supporters in Europe and upon moderate Palestinians for which it was blamed by Abu Iyad. Subsequently the followers of Abu Nidal seem to have used other titles.

BLACK SEPTEMBER (1970)

After the June War large numbers of Palestinians in Jordan became increasingly militant and their relations with the Government were often extremely tense. They formed a state within the state, interfering in Jordanian politics while their men openly carried arms and operated road blocks. On 10 February 1970 King Hussain banned the storage or firing of arms in populated places and this was followed by clashes in which 30 people were killed. Other Arab states warned the King not to act against the *fedayin* but early in June there was nearly a week of heavy fighting in which it was estimated that up to 500 people were killed before a cease-fire was agreed between Hussain and Yassir Arafat. The Tripoli Summit in June established a committee of representatives of Egypt, Libya, Sudan and Algeria to mediate between the Jordanian Government and the guerrillas. Early in July a compromise was reached and an agreement signed between the Prime Minister Abd al-Munim al-Rifai and Arafat but later in the month the situation deteriorated when Hussain accepted the Rogers' Plan (II) for a cease-fire with Israel. He was under great pressure from the army, some of whose officers had been deprived of their commands at Palestinian insistence, and other hardliners to bring the guerrillas to heel and there was a real fear that the exasperated soldiers might mutiny. At the beginning of September there was an attempt on the King's life and the hijacking by the Popular Front for the Liberation of Palestine of three airliners to Dawson's Field. This showed that the more extreme elements were beyond Arafat's control. Heavy fighting in Amman and northern Jordan followed and on 16 September Field Marshal Habis al-Majali was appointed Military Governor with absolute powers. The newly-appointed Prime Minister Brigadier Muhammad Daoud defected. Syrian troops invaded the country to support the guerrillas but were expelled with the reported loss of 90 tanks after the Defence Minister Hafiz al-Assad refused to commit the air force to their support. There were also 25,000 Iraqi troops stationed in Jordan and for a while, until they were restrained by their Defence Minister Hardan al-Takriti, it appeared that they might intervene on the side of the Palestinians. Meanwhile Kuwait cut off financial aid, Libya threatened unspecified action and the Israelis let it be known that they would bomb the guerrillas if they moved near the frontier. On 25 September President Nimeiri, at risk of his life negotiated a cease-fire. President Nasser invited other Heads of State, Hussain and Arafat to Cairo and an agreement was signed on 27 September under which the guerrillas withdrew from Amman to bases in the north. An observer mission and a Supreme Follow-up Committee were appointed to supervise it. A "comprehensive agreement" was signed in October. Later in the month, however, the King appointed as Prime Minister the tough Wasfi al-Tall who later drove the commandos from the country. It is not known how many people were killed in the fighting; the best estimate is 1,500 to 2,000. The Black September Organisation was formed by men determined to avenge the events of September 1970 by terrorist methods.

BLACK SEPTEMBER ORGANISATION

After the fighting between the Jordanian army and the Palestinian guerrillas in Black September 1970 about sixty mainly well-educated young people formed a group to take revenge. It was sometimes called the Ali Abu Iyad group after a guerrilla killed by the Jordanians in the Jerash–Ajloun Fighting in July 1971. "Black September" was regarded by some as the terrorist arm of Fatah which strongly, although not always convincingly, denied this: it was said to take orders from Abu Iyad. Its main target was probably always King Hussain himself but it first came to prominence with the murder of his Prime Minister Wasfi al-Tall in Cairo in November 1971 which was quickly followed by an attempt on his Ambassador in London, Zaid al-Rifai. It then extended its activities to other targets, blowing up a factory in Hamburg which produced generators for Israeli aircraft and in August 1972 blowing up oil storage tanks in Trieste. Before that four terrorists hijacked a Belgian aircraft to Lydda and threatened to blow it up with its 100 passengers unless Palestinians in Israeli jails were released: the aircraft was stormed and the two male hijackers were killed and the two females captured. Their most spectacular action was the Munich Olympics Murders which was condemned even by Albania and disavowed on behalf of the Palestine Liberation Organisation by its London representative Said Hammami. In December 1972 they seized the Israeli Embassy in Bangkok taking six hostages but the incident ended peacefully after mediation by the Cambodian Crown Prince. They also killed Israeli agents and suspected Arab collaborators in Europe. It was believed that many of these acts were planned by Abu Daoud after whose arrest in February 1973 eight Black September members seized the Saudi Embassy in Khartoum, demanding his release together with that of the killer of Robert Kennedy and members of the German Baader-Meinhoff terrorist gang. When their demands were refused they murdered the American Ambassador and the Belgian Chargé before surrendering. In August 1973 two men, claiming membership of Black September, attacked passengers in a crowded transit lounge at Athens airport killing 3 and wounding 55 before surrendering. They were condemned to death but reprieved after Pakistani terrorists had seized a Greek ship in Karachi. On 5 September 1973 five Septembrists (all Arabs but none Palestinian) were arrested in Rome in possession of missiles which they had intended to use to attack Israeli aircraft. On the same day another five took over the Saudi Embassy in Paris holding the staff hostages before taking them to Kuwait in a commandeered aircraft. They released the hostages and surrendered and although the Kuwaiti Government said they would be put on trial, they were eventually released to take part in the October War. Subsequently no further major actions were claimed by Black September and it is probable that many of its members were absorbed into other groups such as that of Abu Nidal and Black June. Although it obviously had links with foreign terrorist organisations, Black September was of all the Palestinian groups the most successful in maintaining secrecy and it was believed that this was probably due to its having no real "permanent staff" but assembling *ad hoc* groups for individual operations. Many Palestinians felt that Black September espoused violence for its own sake and that its activities were harmful to their cause.

BLACK THURSDAY (Tunisia) (1978)
During 1977 economic, political and social discontent mounted in Tunisia and most of it, whether Islamic or Marxist, coalesced under the banner of the Trade Union Movement (UGTT) led by the veteran Habib Achour. The hardline Prime Minister Hedi Nouira in December 1977 rid the Cabinet of his more conciliatory Ministers and in January the UGTT leaders adopted a resolution critical of government measures with Achour resigning from the Politburo of the Parti Socialiste Destourien. The Government used the police and the Party militia to beat up strikers and UGTT officials whereupon the UGTT called for a general strike for 26 January 1978. On the day violence got out of hand as unemployed youth looted, burned and clashed with the security forces on a scale unprecedented since independence and also for the first time army units with tanks were needed to support the police. According to official figures 51 people were killed (unofficial estimates were 200), 346 wounded of whom 181 were from the security forces and 1,187, including Achour and 10 out of the 13-member UGTT executive, arrested. Nouira denounced a "premeditated attempt at rebellion" and declared a state of emergency and a curfew which lasted a month. The Government claimed that arms were found in UGTT offices and that there had been Libyan involvement. A new, tame UGTT leadership was installed and a new Service Civile was created into which the unemployed were conscripted and kept in camps. Most of those arrested were released without charge but in September Achour and 29 others were put on trial. Despite prosecution calls for death sentences none was condemned to more than ten years or actually served more than one. "Liberals" such as Ahmad Mestiri said that Nouira had created "an unbridgeable chasm" between government and people and Nouira made no attempt to conciliate the moderate opposition which came to see its salvation in Islam rather than unionism.

BLUDAN CONFERENCE (1937)
The Peel Report of July 1937 recommended the partition of Palestine, a solution profoundly distasteful to local Arab leaders such as the Mufti of Jerusalem, Haj Amin al-Hussaini. An unoffficial pan-Arab Congress met at Bludan, a summer resort in the Syrian Anti-Lebanon, for three days in September 1937. Over 400 delegates assembled, 160 from Syria, 128 from Palestine, 65 Lebanese, 30 Trans-Jordanians, 12 Iraqis, 6 Egyptians and a solitary Saudi. The best known of them were Shakib Arslan, Lutfi al-Haffar, Riad al-Sulh, and Naji al-Suwaydi who was elected President. The Conference passed resolutions calling for the end of the British Mandate in Palestine which should be replaced by an arrangement similar to the Anglo-Iraqi Treaty of 1930 and the revocation of the Balfour Declaration. Palestine was declared "an inseparable part of the Arab homeland" and Jewish immigration and proposals for partition should be abandoned. In economic matters no Arab should sell land to Jews and there should be a general boycott of Jewish goods. British goods could suffer the same fate for London had to choose either Arab or Jewish friendship. Inter-Arab trade should be encouraged. Propaganda offices to put the Arab case should be established. The Bludan Conference marked the first attempt of the Eastern Arab world to act as a unit and showed how widespread was the interest in Palestine. The British, who believed that many of the delegates had been subsidised by the Italians, were quite relieved that the general tone was not more anti-British.

BLUDAN SESSION (1946)
Shortly after the meeting of Arab rulers that led to the Inshass Declaration a special session of the Political Committee of the Arab League met at Bludan on 9 June 1946 to discuss Palestine. It was clear from the beginning that there were profound conflicts of interests. Both King Abd Allah, represented by Ibrahim Hashim and the Syrians, led by Faris al-Khouri, aimed to occupy as much of Palestine as they could grab. Abd Allah was then prepared to negotiate with the Zionists while the Syrians were not. The Mufti Haj Amin al-Hussaini wanted the expulsion of the Jews and the country placed under his own rule. Iraq (Fadhl Jamali), Yemen and Lebanon all advocated armed intervention but were unable or unwilling to do much about it. Egypt (Makram Ubayd) and Saudi Arabia (Yusuf Yassin) had no wish to become involved in hostilities with the Jews

backed by the USA. Brigadier Clayton of the British Embassy in Cairo was also present. No positive conclusions could be agreed upon so the decisions reached represented face-saving compromises. The official communiqué stated that it had been decided to send memoranda to Britain and the USA about the Report of the Anglo-American Committee of Inquiry on Palestine, to form a Palestine Committee of Arab states based in Cairo and another, under the Mufti, to represent the Palestinian Arabs, (this entailed sorting out the rivalry between the Arab Higher Committee and the Arab Higher Front), to punish absentee landowners who sold property to Zionists and to boycott Jewish goods. Further secret resolutions were adopted: to urge the Arab nation to assist the Palestinians by all ways, funds, arms and soldiers. If the recommendations of the Committee of Inquiry were implemented they would withhold any new concessions from British or American interests, consider cancelling existing concessions, refuse to support them at international gatherings, boycott them morally, and appeal to the UN. Jamali attacked the ineffectiveness of these Resolutions so vehemently that his speech was expunged from the record. This was the first Arab League conference at which specific proposals were made on Palestine and also provided the British Government with ammunition to use to restrain the vehement American support for the Zionists.

BLUE LINE

The Anglo–Ottoman Agreement of 1913 laid down a boundary between the British and Turkish spheres in the Arabian Peninsula and the Gulf. This was designated the Blue Line, running due south from a middle point on the Gulf of Bahrain to the 20th Parallel from which point the Violet Line ran diagonally to a point in the Aden Hinterland in the vicinity of Bayhan. After Ibn Saud had established his Kingdom, the British considered that as the successor state to the Ottomans, even though it had never been ratified, he was bound by this Agreement but he refused to accept it. He regarded it as particularly unsatisfactory in that it left the whole of Qatar as well as most of the Empty Quarter on the British side of the line. There were prolonged negotiations, during which in April 1935 Ibn Saud proposed a Red Line which would have given him much of Southern Qatar, including Udayd, cutting it off from the Trucial States and also a large area in the Empty Quarter. The British, hampered by the fact that their negotiator, the Minister in Jiddah, Sir Andrew Ryan, was colour-blind, replied with a Green Line, followed by Yellow and Brown Lines. After negotiations in London, Ryan became the first British Ambassador to visit Riyadh where he offered the Riyadh Line which conceded most of Ibn Saud's demands in the Empty Quarter but not Udayd. This was rejected and after further discussions in 1938 the question of the eastern boundaries of Saudi Arabia lapsed until 1949 when Ibn Saud revived it with demands for Udayd and Buraymi. It was said that one of the simpler Gulf Shaykhs, told that his frontier was the Blue Line, sent men on camels to search the desert for it.

BLUM–VIOLETTE PROPOSALS (1936)

Very few Algerian Muslims took advantage of their entitlement to apply for French citizenship under the Senatus Consulte of 1865 or the Jonnart Laws of 1918–19 because doing so entailed their subjection in personal matters to French civil law rather than to the Muslim *Shariah*. Maurice Violette who had been Governor-General from 1925 to 1927 was firmly in favour of their assimilation believing that "the Algerians have no country, let them enter the French nation or they will create one of their own". He became a Minister in the Popular Front government formed in June 1936 by Leon Blum and persuaded him to extend full citizenship to certain categories without their having to renounce their Muslim personal status. These included former officers and NCOs and decorated soldiers, holders of certain diplomas, Muslims elected to various representative bodies, government officials and holders of medals. There would be a single electoral body in which the number of Muslims with the suffrage would increase from about 8,000 to about 30,000 compared with the 250,000 colons with the vote. The project was violently opposed by the local Europeans, the mayors voting 300–2 against, and by right-wing politicians in Paris who were able to prevent the matter from even being debated in Parliament. In Algeria it was opposed by Ben Badis as creating a gap between the educated élite and their fellow Muslims and by Messali Haj as merely enfranchising a few bourgeois. Its eventual abandonment by the French Government was a grave blow to the trust in French liberalism of such assimilationists as Farhat Abbas. The categories listed and some others were eventually enfranchised by the Algeria Decree of 1944.

BMARIAM AND KFAR MATTA MASSACRES (1983)

Following the May Agreement of 1983 the Israelis withdrew from the northern parts of Lebanon that they had occupied and there was a fierce struggle for territory between the Christians and the Druze. In August the Druze attacked the Christian village of Bmariam in the Metn area and 24 of the inhabitants, mostly women, were knifed to death. In October the Kataib captured the Druze village of Kfar Matta and shot 110 people, including 65 from a single family. Amongst those murdered was a Canadian television man.

BOUABID, Abd al-Rahim (1920–92)

Moroccan political leader. Born in Sale, his father was a mosque carpenter who later ran a shop and his mother a sewing woman. He did so well at the École des Fils de Notables that he went on to higher education, qualifying as a teacher and studying law in his spare time. During this period he became friendly with Mehdi Ben Barka. Having suffered from social snobbery during his education he made contacts with communist party members but found them too dependent upon the French Party and opposed to independence for Morocco. He also had contacts with anti-Vichy French officers. In 1944 he was one of the early members of the Istiqlal Party and a signatory of its Manifesto. Later he edited its newspaper *al-Alam*. He spent most of two years in prison and upon his release he was excluded from teaching, although he was considered by Muhammad V as tutor to the future Hassan II: the post went instead to Ben Barka. He went to Paris where he organised support amongst Moroccans for the Istiqlal, finished his law studies and married a Frenchwoman. After his return he was active with Mahjoub Ben Sadiq in trying to get Moroccans into the French-dominated Trade Unions and they were both imprisoned after the Casablanca riots of December 1952. After his release he went to Paris where he already had good contacts with left-wing politicians and also made friends amongst the right. He was credited with influencing the Prime Minister Edgar Fauré to call the Aix-les-Bains Conference and later to bring back Muhammad V from exile. In the first government formed by Mubarak Bekkai in December 1955 Bouabid was Minister of State charged with negotiating with France the details of Moroccan Independence which was formalised in March 1956. When Bekkai reshuffled his Cabinet in October 1956 a special Ministry of the Economy grouping Finance, Industry, Commerce and Mines was created for Bouabid who was assisted by three junior Ministers. There was little enthusiasm amongst other politicians for this post as there were few Moroccans qualified to reconstitute an economy which had been run for the benefit of the colons. He had to reform the customs administration which had also been run for their benefit. Bouabid was extremely active, establishing a National Bank, drawing up the first Five-Year Plan, creating an Irrigation Authority and playing a large part in promoting Operation Plough which, it was hoped, would transform the countryside. His good relations with the Trade Unions helped to restrain excessive pay demands. He was sometimes criticised for excessive reliance upon left-wing French advisers but was retained and even promoted Deputy Prime Minister with Agriculture added to his responsibilities when Ahmad Balafrej formed a government mainly from the right-wing of the Istiqlal in May 1958. Bouabid grew increasingly unhappy at the Prime Minister's hesitancy in disavowing tribal disorders in the Riff and in October he resigned although the fact was kept secret for two months. In December 1958 when Abd Allah Ibrahim formed a government from the left-wing of the Istiqlal, Bouabid was again Deputy Premier and Economy Minister until the dismissal of the Government in May 1960. He had encouraged Ben Barka and others to split away from the Istiqlal and form the Union Nationale des Forces Populaires although he did not immediately join the new party. Bouabid was therefore not involved when 130 leading members of the UNFP were arrested in July 1963 accused of attempting to overthrow the monarchy but he took over the leadership of the Party as Ben Barka remained in exile. He supported the Government during the Tindouf Dispute although other left-wingers did not. He was the chief defence lawyer when in June 1971 193 left-wingers were accused of plotting against the security of the state. Bouabid, always rigorously legal, saw a democratic monarchy as a barrier against extremism although he said that the Skhirat attack would not have taken place if Hassan II had been prepared for dialogue with the opposition: he later had frequent meetings with the King. During the

early 1970s there were doctrinal differences within the UNFP and in April 1973, after the March Plot, the Rabat branch led by Bouabid was officially suppressed and a thousand of its members arrested. These did not include Bouabid but he was not permitted to act as their defence counsel. In September 1974 he was permitted to reconstitute the Rabat branch of the UNFP as the Union Socialiste des Forces Populaires with himself as Secretary-General. After the death of Allal al-Fassi in 1974 Bouabid was the most respected politician in the country. He gave complete support for Morocco's claim on the Western Sahara and in March 1977 was one of opposition leaders who joined the Government to ensure fair conduct of parliamentary elections. He himself, having unwisely challenged a local Berber doctor who campaigned in Berber in the Berber area of Agadir, failed to be elected, to the embarrassment of the Government. In September 1981 after Bouabid and two other members of the Politburo of the USFP had criticised the King for agreeing to a referendum on the Western Sahara they were sentenced to a year's imprisonment but were pardoned in February 1982 at the intercession of President Mitterand as Bouabid was always greatly respected by French socialists. During his period in jail Bouabid wrote his memoirs. In January 1983 the King persuaded him to promise that the USFP would not boycott forthcoming elections. There were rumours that Hassan offered to make him Prime Minister of a transitional government, probably with the intention of having a scapegoat if things went wrong with the economy and with the Saharan referendum. Bouabid submitted a list of reforms that he would wish to see implemented which the King found unacceptable. He did, however, take office again in November in the Cabinet that Karim Lamrani formed to prepare for the poll but increasing ill health prevented him from playing much part in it. He was mourned by the King as "an intimate friend and companion of the road" and the Crown Prince presided over the renaming of a boulevard in his honour. In his early days Bouabid was described as a Byronic figure, pale, silent, chain-smoking, while intellectuals saw him as Hamlet.

BOUABID, Maati (1927–)

Moroccan Prime Minister. Born in Casablanca, he was educated at the local Lycée before taking a degree in law from Bordeaux University. He then practised in Casablanca often defending nationalists. After independence he was appointed King's Prosecutor in Tangier. Bouabid married a cousin of Hassan II. He was an early member of the Union Nationale des Forces Populaires and served as Minister of Labour and Social Affairs in the government of Abd Allah Ibrahim, forming lasting links with the trade unions. After leaving office in May 1960 he returned to Casablanca where he became a leading member of the Bar and head of the town council. In the elections of May 1963 he was returned as a Deputy for Casablanca. Bouabid defended UNFP members accused of treason, caught a magistrate and police officers tampering with evidence, and ostentatiously withdrew from a case which had already shown up Moroccan justice as a farce. He was expelled from the UNFP when he was appointed

Minister of Justice in October 1977. During the winter of 1978/9, despite the national unity brought about by the Western Sahara War, there had been a series of strikes for economic reasons, closing phosphate mines, banks, transport, health services, schools etc. And in January Polisario guerrillas had shocked the country by raiding Tan-Tan, well within its borders. In March 1979 the King decided to appoint Bouabid, known to be a skilled negotiator, as Prime Minister to deal with the labour unrest and to move Ahmad Uthman to a newly created National Defence Council to handle the war. Bouabid made only minor changes in the coalition Cabinet and quickly announced a 30% wage increase, to be followed by a 10% increase to take effect in the new year. In July in an emergency budget he imposed a national solidarity tax which mainly affected the rich. In 1981 after a disastrous drought the country was hit by another economic crisis. The deficit absorbed half its reserves and the Government, under pressure from the IMF, raised prices of some essential commodities by up to 90%, claiming that rationing was the only alternative. This set off in June 1981 the Casablanca Riots in which it was officially admitted that 67 people were killed. The Government was forced hastily to reduce prices. In the long term Bouabid attempted to solve the chronic financial crisis, Morocco's debt of $24,000 million was the highest, *per capita* in the world, by working for self-sufficiency and at the same time by encouraging foreign investment. Foreigners were permitted to take a 100% ownership in a Moroccan company, appoint a majority of foreign directors and repatriate profits. In January 1983 he announced the formation of a new party, the Union Constitionelle specifically aimed at the educated young. In June Bouabid's fledgling UC emerged as the single largest party and he won the nickname of "the Pressure Cooker" for the extraordinary speed of his achievement. In November, in order to prepare for parliamentary elections, the King, as usual required a non-party Prime Minister and Bouabid stood aside for Karim Lamrani and was himself appointed a Minister of State. When the postponed parliamentary elections were held in September 1984 the UC was again the major winner. He continued as party leader but did not take ministerial office although his followers were regarded as part of the Government coalition. Bouabid was a populist, a strong supporter of social justice but without any particular ideology.

BOUCETTA, Muhammad (1925–)
Moroccan political leader. Born in Marrakesh, he received a French education before taking a law degree in Paris. While there he was an active member of the Istiqlal Party which he represented at international student gatherings. In 1951 he established himself as a lawyer in Casablanca where he became noted for defending militants and lobbying for support amongst French liberals. He ran the party newspaper and after the exile of Muhammad V, was for a time the leading nationalist at large in Morocco. Upon independence Boucetta became assistant to Balafrej, the first Foreign Minister, and was active in negotiations over the American bases and at the UN. He was not in the government of Abd Allah Ibrahim but joined that

formed by the King in 1961 as Minister for the Civil Service and he was later Minister of Justice in the Cabinet of Hassan II. In December 1962 the Government split after the sentencing to death of three Bahai's for proselytisation and the King's reshuffle which would have weakened Istiqlal representation. Boucetta and others withdrew into opposition. In 1974 he succeeded Allal al-Fassi as Secretary-General of the Party. In 1977 when the King offered general reconciliation, Boucetta returned to government as Minister of Foreign Affairs. He stood in for the King at the Baghdad Summit of 1978 and at Summits of the OAU. He continued the traditional irredentism of his Party, being an ardent supporter of the annexation of the Western Sahara and would have liked to have seen the Presidios brought under the Moroccan Crown. Boucetta travelled very widely in Africa seeking to exclude Polisario from the OAU and in the Arab world, after the assassination of Sadat, arguing for a new understanding with Egypt. In 1983 his diplomacy and enlistment of mediators ended the seven-year dispute with Algeria. In 1985 he was replaced as Foreign Minister but remained active politically as leader of Istiqlal. The Party, nominally in opposition, supported the Government on major issues and the advice of Boucetta was often sought. During the Presidios Troubles he denounced Spain as "racist and colonialist like South Africa and Israel". He opposed the holding of a referendum in the Western Sahara as unnecessary. In the various electoral campaigns Boucetta proved one of the most effective campaigners on television. In October 1993 the King offered him and other party leaders government office but it proved impossible to agree on conditions. In February 1994 he stressed that for Morocco Istiqlal provided a barrier against the Islamic militancy that was troubling its neighbours and announced his impending retirement.

BOUDIAF, Muhammad (1919–92)
Algerian Head of State. He was the son of a farmer in M'sila in the Constantinois, and was conscripted into the French army in which he became a senior NCO. Influenced by Messali Haj, he organised a nationalist group within the army and after demobilisation set up a branch of the Organisation Spéciale while working as a tax official. In 1950 Boudiaf was sentenced *in absentia*, firstly to eight years and then to ten years as a threat to the security of the state. Between June 1953 and February 1954 he was the leader of the Mouvement pour le Triomphe de la Liberté at de la Démocratie in France when it split between supporters of Messali and those of Ben Khedda and the Central Committee and he took the initiative in creating a new force to launch a revolutionary war. He arranged a series of clandestine meetings with veterans of the disbanded OS and organised them into the Comite Révolutionaire de l'Unité et de l'Action going himself secretly to Algiers in July to plan the All Saints' Day Uprising. Boudiaf was at this time effectively the leader of the Front de Libération Nationale, the most influential of the Neuf Historiques, although the more personable and flamboyant Ben Bella was allowed to appear so. He went to Cairo where he took charge of organising arms shipments and he was also the main link between the

guerrillas in the mountains and the external leadership. In October 1956 he was returning to Tunis from a meeting with King Muhammad V when his aircraft was diverted to Algiers and he was arrested. Boudiaf remained in prison in reasonable comfort, incessantly quarrelling with Ben Bella and beating the others at ping-pong until March 1962. He was made an Honorary Member of the Conseil National de la Révolution Algérienne and the Gouvernement Provisoire de la République Algérienne of which he became a Vice-President after his release. In the power struggle of the summer of 1962, he was briefly abducted by troops of the Armée de Libération Nationale but released on the intervention of Ben Bella. Despite this and an offer of the Foreign Ministry, Boudiaf refused to join the Politburo with which Ben Bella was trying to replace the GPRA and refused also to be a candidate for the National Assembly. Instead he set up the clandestine Parti de la Révolution Socialiste, Marxist but not collaborating with the communists. In *O va l'Algérie?* he criticised Ben Bella for his lack of commitment to socialism and failure to purge the party and the civil service of anti-socialists concerned only with keeping their privileges at the expense of the masses. He called for immediate nationalisation of key sectors of the economy, state control of foreign commerce, the organisation of a truly revolutionary party and the creation of a powerful autonomous trade union body. Always a strong supporter of Maghreb unity, he blamed Ben Bella for a pointless quarrel with Morocco over Tindouf. In June 1963 on the charge of conspiring against the Government he was exiled to a Saharan oasis but after a hunger strike in which he lost 40 lbs he was released without trial in November. In April 1965, *in absentia*, he with Ait Ahmad and Muhammad Khidr was sentenced to death. He continued to criticise the regime after Boumédienne had seized power, calling for the end of one-party rule which was bound to be authoritarian and corrupt. He settled in Kenitra in Morocco where he ran a brick works and often gave interviews, including one in 1976 when he condemned Boumédienne's denials of fundamental liberties. In 1986 he refused to join Ben Bella, whom he continued to regard as the author of the country's troubles in opposition to Chadli. After the generals took over in January 1992 Boudiaf, seen as a popular hero of the resistance, untainted by recent scandals and known to be a practising but not fundamentalist Muslim, was invited back to become Chairman of the Haut Comité d'État to act as Head of State until the expiration of Chadli's term in December 1993. Three quarters of the population had been born during the 27 years that he had been in exile. The legitimacy of the HCE was challenged by all the political parties including the FLN and it was seen as a self-constituted body serving as a front for the military, particularly for General Nezzar. Boudiaf confirmed this impression by calling for order, security, submission to the state and the end of the use of mosques for propaganda and declaring that he would not allow the exploitation of Islam as a means to take over the country. He offered the fundamentalist Front Islamique du Salut freedom to operate within the law but its leaders demanded elections. On 9 February as it appeared that an Islamic Insurrection was beginning

Boudiaf declared a state of emergency which was followed by the arrest of some 6,000 FIS members. Boudiaf promised houses and jobs and the Prime Minister Sid Ahmad Ghozali began a desperate search for foreign aid. At the end of February Boudiaf attempted to conciliate the FIS by bringing three Ministers with Islamic backgrounds into the Cabinet and starting the release of detainees. Boudiaf, despite obstruction by bureaucrats and the military who had censored his speech calling for an attack on corruption, set in train investigations which resulted in arrests of several important figures including a senior general. In April the HCE announced the names of a 60-member Consultative Council to replace the dissolved Assembly but it was rejected by most political parties and early in June Boudiaf decided to appeal to the people over the heads of the military and the politicians by calling for the formation of a Rassemblement Patriotique National "to impose the radical changes we need" with committees in every village and workplace to lay the foundation for a genuine multi-party democracy with a free market economy. On 29 June, while opening a cultural centre in Annaba, Boudiaf was assassinated. Although the event was being televised it was uncertain whether this was the act of a lone killer and the presentation of an investigating committee, several times postponed and finally presented with 76 out of 111 pages missing, was uninformative: attempts to throw the blame on militant Muslims were unconvincing and many, including his widow, blamed corrupt officials. There were emotional scenes at his funeral and he was genuinely mourned, particularly by women who saw him as their defender against religious bigotry. In foreign affairs Boudiaf had greatly improved relations with Morocco which he regarded as his second home, co-ordinating action against fundamentalists as he did with Tunis. He also had good relations with other Arab states and with the West, glad that the threat of an Islamic takeover had been averted. Boudiaf, cautious, secretive, hardworking was generally respected as an honest man with a genuine interest in the welfare of the people.

BOUHIRED, Jamila (c. 1935–)

Algerian Revolutionary heroine. After her father had been killed by French soldiers, she became extremely active in the Algiers Battle. She had a close relationship with Saadi Yacef who was the principal organiser of a bombing campaign which was carried out mainly by young women such as Bouhired and Jamila Boupacha who would conceal home-made bombs under flowing Muslim dress. Bouhired was arrested in January 1957 and accused of implication in two bomb attacks. After a sensational trial in which she stated that she had been tortured, she was sentenced to death. Her trial attracted great attention in France and throughout the world. She was reprieved in March 1958 and later released. After independence she married her defending lawyer but then divorced him. Apart from one mission to China she had no political role and became bitter at the non-recognition, particularly in the Boumédienne years of the part played by women in the Algerian War of Independence. She prospered, however, in business, running the Algerian branch of an international cosmetics firm.

BOUMAZA, Bashir (1927–)

Algerian politician. The son of a small merchant in a little town near Setif, he went to France where he worked as a carpenter. He joined the Mouvement pour le Triomphe de la Liberté et de la Démocratie and acted as secretary to its leader Messali Haj. Soon after the All Saints' Day Uprising he joined the Front de Libération Nationale and was put in charge of many of its activities in France. In December 1958 he was arrested and remained in Fresnes jail where he organised the Algerian prisoners until he escaped in October 1961. He was one of the co-authors of the famous book *La Gangrene*, an account of the tortures to which the French subjected Algerian prisoners and its effect upon the torturers. After the Evian Agreement he supported Ben Bella against the GPRA and was appointed Minister of Labour and Social Affairs. Boumaza was recognised as one of the Trotskyists in the immediate entourage of the President and showed his political stripe in his next post of Minister of Industry by nationalising a series of businesses. A few days before the coup in which Boumédienne seized power, Ben Bella publicly blamed Boumaza and another of his closest associates, Ahmad Mahsas, the pioneer of Autogestion for the country's economic ills. Boumaza kept his post on the Politburo of the FLN but was demoted to Minister of Information. In this capacity he established a state monopoly of publishing and importing books, newspapers and magazines but justified the arrest of communists. In October 1966 he announced that he had defected to join the opposition Organisation Clandestine de la Révolution Algérienne. In November the President ordered that Boumaza and Mahsas who had also fled the country would be tried in their absence for "grave crimes against the state".

BOUMÉDIENNE, Houari (c. 1927–78)

Algerian President. He was born Muhammad Boukharouba, one of seven children of a poor farmer at Guelma near Bone. His mother is said to have come from Tindouf which might have affected his attitude towards Morocco. He received an Islamic education in Constantine and then, to avoid conscription, went on to the Zaytuna University in Tunis and al-Azhar where he also attended courses at the Commando School. At this time he met Ben Bella who had taken refuge in Cairo after his escape from jail and other exiled members of the Neuf Historiques. He adopted the *nom de guerre* of Boumédienne after the famous saint of Tlemcen. After returning to Algeria he organised in 1955 the distribution of arms that had been smuggled to the coast near Oran in a yacht owned by the Queen of Jordan. His efficiency was noticed by Boussouf, the commander of *wilaya V* who made him his adjutant and then his successor. During the Algerian War of Independence Boumédienne was the youngest Colonel in the Armée de Libération Nationale and a fine organiser both of guerrillas and of regular soldiers. He was appointed to command the western front consisting of three *wilayas* and, after presiding over the trial and execution of four dissident colonels, was made Chief of Staff of the ALN when the forces in Morocco and Tunisia were put under a single command. He adopted the strategy of abandoning attempts to infiltrate his

soldiers into Algeria to take part in the fighting, holding them back in order to be able to control the largest and best-armed force to exercise a decisive role either before or after independence. At the same time he formed around himself the Oudjda Group of able and ambitious young military politicians to hold key appointments should he come to power. He opposed the Evian Agreement as making too many concessions to the French so Ben Khedda, the President of the Gouvernement Provisoire de la République Algérienne, attempted to dissolve the General Staff and arrest Boumédienne in July 1962. Boumédienne thereupon allied with Ben Bella and his troops marched on Algiers causing the fall of the GPRA. When Ben Bella formed a government, Boumédienne was appointed Minister of Defence and the following year Vice-President. He was always insistent upon the ideological training of the army and of its role as an instrument of social change, independent of the Front de Libération Nationale. Boumédienne's reputation suffered in 1963 when the army proved ineffective in dealing with the revolt of Ait Ahmad in Kabyle and in a brief war with Morocco over Tindouf. Ben Bella attempted to weaken Boumédienne's hold on the army, seizing the opportunity of the absence of the Defence Minister in Moscow in a quest for military equipment to take away his appointment of Chief of Staff which, without consultation, he gave to Colonel Taha Zbiri. Boumédienne came increasingly to see the President as a Marxist rather than a Muslim and more concerned with words and flamboyant gestures than with practical measures to benefit the country. Boumédienne had insisted that members of the Oudjda Group be appointed to senior posts in the Government in order to support his interests but in Cabinet reshuffles Ben Bella contrived to divest himself of them one by one and in June 1965 he dismissed the last of them, Abd al-Aziz Boutaflika. Ben Bella was also apparently planning a popular militia to counterbalance the army and was due to preside over an Afro-Asian Summit which would increase his prestige both at home and abroad, giving him sufficient support to dismiss his Vice-President. In the early morning of 19 June Boumédienne seized power in a swift and bloodless coup which was greeted by the people with a mixture of fear and indifference. The Constitution and the National Assembly were immediately suspended and after some delay a 26-man Revolutionary Council, consisting almost entirely of army officers and former *wilaya* commanders was announced. Boumédienne was President of this Council and after a number of politicians including the veteran Farhat Abbas had refused to serve as a front for the army, he was also Prime Minister. At first, aware that he lacked the charisma of his predecessor he stressed collective leadership and refused to appear on television, his voice rasping from a blacked-out screen but later although he often went on tour, taking the whole Cabinet with him to deal with local issues, he never had a popular touch or mingled with the crowds. Announcing that "verbal socialism is dead", he prepared to introduce "very specifically Algerian socialism, not imported" with the objectives of building the state, achieving complete independence through control of all wealth and laying the basis for the economic transformation of a backward agricultural country into a modern socialist industrial state. Boumédienne pressed for centralisation, firstly ending warlordism in the *wilayas* and then building a huge, tangled bureaucracy whose powers were increased in almost every issue of the *Journal Officiel*. Autogestion was ended as demagogic and wasteful. Organisations such as trade unions and even the Government party, the FLN, had their wings clipped. Ben Bella's old Trotskyist advisers were expelled, being replaced by technocrats and men whose main qualification was subservience to the Leader. People who had played major roles in the struggle for independence were imprisoned, exiled or ignored: none were given a second chance: only 8 of the Revolutionary Council still held office at Boumédienne's death. Potentially dangerous opponents were either murdered like Muhammad Khidr or jailed, like Ben Bella, in harsh conditions. Men of independence, like Zbiri, found this intolerable but his revolt was suppressed in December 1967 and Boumédienne also survived the machine-gunning of his car in April 1968, escaping with a cut lip. A Three-year Plan introduced in 1967 was described as making an "inventory of potential wealth" and led to nationalisation of the oil industry in March 1971. In November 1971 and January 1972 decrees were promulgated nationalising the land of absentees and large estates so that no one could own more than he could cultivate single-handed. Peasants and nomads were forced, by the army if necessary, into "Socialist Villages" but the country remained unable to feed itself. Foreign trade and much of the domestic means of distribution were brought under control. The 1970 Plan put the highest proportion of the GNP into development of any country in the world and the whole resources of the state were devoted to an almost Stalinist concentration on heavy industry which Boumédienne saw as a locomotive pulling behind it light industry and agriculture. The heads of great state enterprises like SONATRACH became international figures. Whole factories were bought and Algeria went heavily into debt. The provision of free schools and medicine was hampered by the problem that half the population was under 19 years of age and 75% of those over 10 years of age were illiterate: despite a chronic shortage of skilled manpower hundreds of thousands sought work in France, the number of emigrants rising from 425,000 in 1962 to 780,000 in 1973. Boumédienne appeared little concerned that his regime had no claim to democratic legitimacy although candidates approved by the FLN contested municipal elections in February 1967 and *wilaya* elections in May 1969. In June 1975 on the tenth anniversary of his seizure of power Boumédienne announced that a National Charter would be submitted for debate and, in a referendum, a new Constitution and that there would be parliamentary and presidential elections. He himself was the only presidential candidate in December 1976, receiving 99.38% of the votes. He refused to nominate a Vice-President and continued as Prime Minister, Defence Minister and Chief of Staff, later assuming charge of civil service and religious affairs. He took a particular interest in the latter, declaring that "Islam is not only a spiritual path but a social and political programme". He often stressed the part that it had played in preserving the Algerian personality under colonial rule. In April 1975 a new civil code conformed with Islam by forbidding gambling except on state-run football pools although its also set up a tribunal of army officers to try offences against state security. The veteran nationalists Abbas and Ben Khedda who in March 1976 ventured to criticise Boumédienne's "totalitarian rule" were put under house arrest. The use of Arabic was declared an integral part of the Revolution although it should not be used to obstruct progress. The ousting of Ben Bella was not welcomed by the Egyptians or by the communists while the West hoped that there would be less anti-colonial rhetoric. Indeed Boumédienne hesitated for a long time before following many Third World countries in breaking off relations with Britain over Rhodesia and his visit to Moscow in December 1965 was distinctly low-key although he returned with promises of military and industrial aid including a steel mill for Annaba. After that for nearly two years Boumédienne left details of foreign policy to Boutaflika until the June War when he sent troops and aircraft to the front, visited Cairo to urge Nasser not to stop fighting and went on to Moscow to demand support. He stopped oil supplies to London and Washington, put American companies under state control and refused to attend the Khartoum Summit. Relations continued reasonably good with France until 1971 when he nationalised their oil interests: friendship was later restored by a visit of President Giscard in April 1975 and French money was borrowed to finance development. In the October War Boumédienne again sent troops to Suez, stopped oil to the US and Holland, visited Arab capitals and Moscow to call for intervention and replacement of Arab arms; he also warned the Americans against attacking Saudi Arabia. His importance in Arab councils was shown by his chairmanship of the Algiers Summit which followed the war. Later he strongly opposed the peace policies of Anwar Sadat and was one of the most intransigent members of the Steadfastness Front. He supported liberation movements, even the American Black Panthers and one for independence for the Canary Islands. On most of his visits to the Middle East Henry Kissinger visited Boumédienne. Although Algeria was economically linked with the West, diplomatically it was closer to Russia which supplied 2,000 teachers and the same number of military advisers but Ait Ahmad's jibe that Algeria had become a "Soviet fief" was exaggerated. In the 1970s Boumédienne was one of the first to grasp the need for a new relationship between the industrialised countries and the underdeveloped Third World which, he forecast could, by the year 2000 lead to an unstoppable surge of hungry humanity towards the North. African countries should be enabled to take control of their own resources without incurring impossible debts and profits should be invested in the country of origin or in other Third World states rather than accruing to Western business. This shift of balance would necessitate reform in the United Nations including the abolition of the Security Council. Boumédienne worked to co-ordinate policy with African states, although he tended to keep aloof from the more extreme. In September 1973 he presided over the fourth conference of the Non-Aligned Movement which was attended by 105 delegations which elected him Chairman for three years and in January 1974 on their behalf he called for a special emergency meeting of the UN to "establish a new system of co-operation in international economic relations". At the session in April he called for restructuring the world economic system to ensure a fair distribution of benefits. He chaired a further conference of 104 developing nations in Algiers in February 1975, repeating his call for them to take economic charge of their own destinies. Boumédienne saw a major role for OPEC in developing the Third World and at the summit that he chaired in March 1975 he achieved a diplomatic triumph by reconciling the Shah with Saddam Hussein. In the late 1970s Boumédienne was particularly involved in the problem of the Western Sahara in which most Arab states supported Morocco. In September 1970 he apparently agreed with King Hassan II and President ould Daddah of Mauritania that their two countries should take over the Spanish colony while Morocco abandoned its claim to Tindouf. Later he came to resent the aggrandisement of his neighbours and gave support to Polisario in its resistance to them. He sent Algerian troops into the Sahara and after a clash at Amgalla there was a possibility of a second war with Morocco which was perhaps only prevented by the onset of his fatal illness. He spent October 1978 in a Moscow hospital, returning to Algiers where he was attended by 62 international specialists. In his last years it was clear that his economic policies were not working, his agricultural reforms had failed, there was a feeling that sacrifices were not fairly distributed, there was widespread unemployment, there were strikes which even he admitted were justified and there was no enthusiasm for his undeclared war with Morocco. In person Boumédienne was lean, ascetic and gaunt, with high cheek bones, intense green eyes and red hair. He was taciturn, humourless and ruthless. A chain-smoker, he was believed a confirmed bachelor until it emerged that he had married a barrister in 1973/4. He was indifferent to the feelings of ordinary people, putting ideology above their daily welfare, apparently unable to understand that many of them were not happy at having to wait for a glorious future in fifty years time. Unemployed peasants flocked to Algiers, trebling its population, and the capital was rat-infested and dilapidated. The first steps of his successor Benjadid Chadli were to promise continuation of his policies but gradually to humanise them.

BOUMENDJEL, Ahmad (1908–)

Algerian Revolutionary leader. The son of a teacher, he was born in Michelet in Kabyle. He qualified as a lawyer in Paris and in 1939 he defended the nationalist leader Messali Haj. In 1946 he joined the more liberal nationalist group, the Union Démocratique du Manifeste Algérienne of Ferhat Abbas and was elected to the French Assembly. When the Algerian War of Independence began he stood aside although he later defended Ben Bella. In March 1957 his brother died in mysterious circumstances while in a French prison whereupon Boumendjel went to Tunis and joined the Front de Libération Nationale. He was put in charge of its weekly newspaper and also of rallying support amongst independent African states. In April 1958 he was one of the Algerian delegates at the Tangier Conference. When

the possibility arose of a negotiated settlement to the war in June 1960 Boumendjel was chosen to lead the Algerian team at the Melun Talks which came to nothing. Later his preliminary talks with Georges Pompidou in Lucerne in February 1961 led to the beginning of the negotiation of the Evian Agreement in which Boumendjel again represented the FLN. In the struggles that followed the Agreement on Independence Boumendjel supported Ben Bella and Boumédienne against Ben Khedda and the Gouvernement Provisoire de la République Algérienne. He was Minister of Reconstruction in Ben Bella's first Cabinet but he was dropped in December 1964 and played no further part in politics. Boumendjel was a plump and jovial man of much charm.

BOUPACHA, Jamila (1937–)

Algerian Revolutionary heroine. Her working-class family lived in Algiers. In February 1960 she was arrested on the charge of having placed a bomb in the University Restaurant in Algiers in September 1959. She admitted having done this but claimed that she confessed after being subjected to revolting tortures including deflowerment with the neck of a bottle after which she had been unconscious for two days. She was also tortured with electrodes and members of her family, arrested at the same time, were beaten up. The case caused outrage in France and was taken up by prominent left-wing intellectuals including Picasso, François Mauriac and Simone de Beauvoir. She was taken to France and moved from prison to prison while the case was investigated despite the shameless lying of the French military authorities who were never brought to justice. She was released in April 1962 after the signature of the Evian Agreement. On her return to Algiers she addressed large crowds calling for a greater role for Algerian women, but like the other heroine, Jamila Bouhired she was to be disappointed.

BOURGUIBA, Habib (c. 1903)

Tunisian President. He was born in Monastir, the son of an army officer. The whole family invested in his schooling at Sadiqi College but he had to leave through ill health. He went to Paris in 1924, to study law and politics, there he married a French lady. In 1927 he returned home and started to build a considerable reputation as a lawyer. He later said that it was the triumphalism of holding a Catholic Eucharistic Congress in Tunis in 1931 that awoke his nationalist feelings and he joined the Destour Party, writing for its newspaper. He soon came to consider it too remote from ordinary people and too cautious and upper class and in 1934 he started campaigning around the villages, speaking in colloquial Arabic, unlike most politicians who strained after classical oratory. Although religion sat lightly upon him he realised its importance to the peasantry to whom he also stressed the colon threat to their land. In March 1934 at Kassar Hallal he launched the Neo-Destour of which he was Secretary-General. The movement appeared an immediate success, especially amongst the workers whom he was the first to court. The French were alarmed and in September Bourguiba and other leaders were sent into restricted residence in the South. In 1936 the Popular Front government of Leon Blum freed Bourguiba who reorganised the Party and used tough tactics to destroy the old Destour. He also campaigned in France for the end of the Protectorate. In April 1938, after there had been a riot he and others, who had shown themselves ready to employ violence, were imprisoned without trial. After the outbreak of war the nationalist leaders were transferred to a fortress near Marseilles from which they were freed when the Germans occupied Vichy France. Bourguiba went to Rome but refused to collaborate with the Axis, having already written in August 1942 to Dr Thameur, who was organising the underground in Tunis, that the Allies were bound to win and ordering him to collaborate with local Gaullists. In April 1943 he returned home and made contacts with the Allies who entered the city a month later. The French made no concessions towards Tunisian independence and Bourguiba determined to bring his struggle to the attention of the world, in particular to that of the newly-formed Arab League, and in May 1945 he fled in disguise to Cairo, covering on foot part of the route across the Libyan Desert. Though disappointed at the lack of interest shown by the Eastern Arabs, he campaigned with a mixture of ideology and opportunism winning an international reputation both in the Arab states and in the wider world. He published his speeches and articles in *La Tunisie et la France*. In December 1951 the French, who had appeared likely to make some concessions, started a new hard line and Bourguiba returned home to step up the struggle, declaring "it is necessary that blood flows". A month later he was again arrested, imprisoned firstly in the Sahara and then on an isolated rock off Bizerta until May 1954 when he was transferred to another island off Brittany. Meanwhile in Tunisia there was increasing bloodshed, with atrocities committed both by the nationalist *Fellagha* and colon extremists until in July 1954 a new French Prime Minister, Pierre Mendes-France accepted the principle of internal autonomy for Tunisia in his Carthage Declaration. The negotiating team included Neo-Destour Ministers who kept Bourguiba fully informed and in May 1955, just before the signature of the Franco-Tunisian Autonomy Agreement, he returned home to a rapturous welcome. Bourguiba, unlike many other Arab nationalists, had the statemanship to realise that he could not win his full objective with one bite and was prepared to accept this less than ideal agreement, consolidate his gains and then win more. Only Bourguiba could have persuaded the Neo-Destour to accept such a compromise and it was bitterly opposed by his old colleague and rival Salih Ben Yusuf who tried to organise the Party against it but was worsted in the Sfax National Congress. Ben Yusuf then set off an armed insurrection but with the help of the French Bourguiba prevailed.

He then exploited the situation to gain complete independence in the Franco-Tunisian Protocol on Tunisian Independence which was signed on 20 March 1956. Elections were organised for a Constituent Assembly in which every seat was won by Bourguiba's National Unity List. When the Assembly met Bourguiba became Prime Minister and created the Ministries of Foreign Affairs and Defence, both of which initially he held himself. In July 1957 Tunisia became a Republic

with Bourguiba as its President, abolishing the post of Prime Minister and divesting himself of his other Ministries.

He established an overwhelming position through the force of his personality with minimal repressive power for the army and police were proportionally far smaller than in other Arab states.

He dispensed with the services of French officials, took over some colon land, modernised the judiciary and introduced new rights for women including the prohibition of Islamic divorce and polygamy which Tunisia was the first Muslim country after Turkey to enforce. In June 1959 a Constitution was promulgated which vested great powers in the President who was later to say "Ministers are not independent, they will carry out my policies" and "if a people have a Bourguiba why should they contradict him?"

The Constitution provided for an electoral system that made one-party rule inevitable and Bourguiba regarded the Party as "the motor of the State". Although the Constitution had paid deference to Islam, almost immediately afterwards Bourguiba took over Habus land and later he was to denounce the veil and publicly to break Ramadan to stress that production should take priority.

Saying that "the people must be taught to be shocked at what they had taken for granted", he saw himself as a schoolmaster, instructing his people in political science, economics, hygiene, history and good manners, for example banning the mini-skirt although generally he prefered persuasion to coercion. Genuinely paternalistic, Bourguiba was convinced that he alone could provide the education and prosperity to give his people a better life. He was rarely vindictive, usually prepared to give opponents a second chance, although he did order the murder of Ben Yusuf: leading figures from the Protectorate regime were not harassed although two former Prime Ministers were briefly imprisoned. In the first years after independence relations with France were difficult for Bourguiba allowed Tunisia to be used as a base for guerrillas fighting the Algerian War of Independence. This led to the Sakiet Sidi Yusuf Bombing in 1958 but early in 1961 Bourguiba had separate meetings with General de Gaulle, Hassan II and Farhat Abbas in an attempt to mediate a settlement. However the Bizerta Incident in July led to a breach with France which cancelled promised aid that Tunisia tried to replace through Britain and America. Relations with Egypt, acccused of supporting Ben Yusuf in an attempt to assassinate Bourguiba, were very bad and their two leaders bandied charges: Bourguiba publicly regretted that the Suez War had not led to the overthrow of Nasser. There was also a quarrel with Morocco as Tunisia recognised the independence of Mauritania and in December 1962 with Algeria, also accused of implication in a plot to kill Bourguiba. In the meanwhile a drastic change had taken place in domestic affairs. Priority had first been given to private enterprise but in 1961 Bourguiba was apparently converted to socialism by Ahmad Ben Salah for he declared "the idea of absolute ownership has had its day". The 1961 Plan set out a restructuring of economic and social life and at the Bizerta Congress of 1964 Bourguiba spoke of "continuous revolution" and changed the name of the Neo-Destour to the Parti Socialiste Destourien. In 1962 Bourguiba, having divorced his French wife, married Wassila Ben Ammar, a member of a wealthy family that stood to lose heavily if all the plans of Ben Salah reached fruition. In 1964 Bourguiba was re-elected President for five years with 96% of the poll. In 1965 his tour of the Middle East resulted in a series of speeches attacking Arab leaders and in the Bourguiba Proposals which advocated recognition of Israel in return for a settlement of the Palestinian refugees. There was a barrage of criticism and Bourguiba became the first leader to boycott an Arab Summit – Casablanca in September. Thereafter for some years, dissociating himself from the Arab League which he termed, "a wasps' nest", he concentrated on relations with the Maghreb and Africa, taking little interest in Arab affairs, breaking off relations with the Palestine Liberation Organisation and withdrawing recognition from the Yemeni Republic: the Syrian Prime Minister Yusuf Zuayyin called him "an imperialist tool". He supported Egypt in the June War but then offered to mediate with Israel, leading to further quarrels and a second breach with the League. Bourguiba had two heart attacks in the first months of 1967 and thereafter he frequently went abroad for extended periods for medical treatment, conveniently enabling him to distance himself from unpopular acts of his government. Ben Salah appeared to dominate the country, imposing collectivisation that encountered growing resistance with the Defence Minister Ahmad Mestiri resigning with the complaint that the Government, entirely dependent upon Bourguiba's personal prestige, had seized up. In the autumn of 1969 Bourguiba asserted himself, and Ben Salah was dismissed as "a criminal who took advantage of the President's ill health". In 1968 he had said that he would nominate his own successor, although, as he admitted, having created the state around his own personality, he would not be easy to replace and, in November 1969, having been re-elected President for another five years with 99.76% of the votes, he reorganised the Government to reduce his own work load, apparently preparing to retire. For the first time he appointed a Prime Minister, Bahi Ladgham, and then retired to France for six months for treatment for hepatitis. Ladgham, however, had ideas of liberalising the system and had, through his work in the Black September crisis, become an international celebrity in his own right and in November 1970 Bourguiba replaced him with the colourless, conservative Hedi Nouira whom in March 1972 he nominated as his successor. At home there was a period of prosperity and in June 1972 Bourguiba paid a state visit to Paris, an invitation which he regarded as "the crown of my career". In 1973 he made another controversial pronouncement on Arab politics suggesting dialogue with Israel and that Jordan should disappear to make way for a Palestinian state: King Hussain broke off relations. In December 1972 he had ridiculed the call of Colonel Qadafi for unity between their two states, rebuking him in public but in January 1974, apparently under the influence of his Foreign Minister Muhammad Masmoudi, Bourguiba signed the Jerbah Declaration forming the Arab–Islamic Republic of Tunisia and Libya. Nouira who had not beeen consulted prevailed

upon Bourguiba to disavow the document and dismiss Masmoudi for misleading him: many have seen in this incident the first signs of Bourguiba's decline into senility. Bourguiba had always taken an interest in Maghreb unity but after the outbreak of the Western Sahara War, in which he supported Morocco against Algeria, this became unlikely. During this time there was increasing dissatisfaction at autocracy and unwillingness to share power but the Monastir Congress of September 1974 showed that Bourguiba was in total control both of the State and the Party which, he said, merged in his person. In November 1974 he was elected for a fourth five-year term with 99.98% of the votes and in March 1975 the National Assembly proclaimed "The Supreme Combatant" President for Life. He was regarded as the embodiment of the nation, a monarch surrounded by courtiers bickering over the succession rather than advisers, and the cult of his personality was carried to extraordinary lengths to hold the country together. He himself appeared on television to tell his astonished subjects that he disciplined Ministers by spitting in their faces and that he personally had only one testicle. Mme Bourguiba, often compared with Mme Mao, intrigued against the rigid conservatism of Nouira and the Party boss, Muhammad Sayah while Bourguiba played them off against liberals such as Mestiri and the trade unions led by his old comrade Habib Achour. Economic hardships led to strikes which culminated in January 1978 in the bloodshed of Black Thursday when for the first time since independence troops fired on a crowd. Following the rejection of his unity hopes Qadafi made difficulties for Tunisia and in January 1980 dissidents that he controlled carried out a raid on Gafsa which led to a breach in relations with Tripoli and showed that France, which sent warships, was still prepared to defend Tunisia. After Nouira had a heart attack, Bourguiba apppointed, in April 1980, as Prime Minister the comparatively youthful, liberal and Arab-inclined Muhammad Mzali who attempted to bring in a new breath of fresh air. Opposition groups were permitted to organise themselves and publish journals. Early in 1984 price increases decreed by Mzali set off Bread Riots which nearly brought down the Government. Bourguiba appeared on television to reverse the rises but confirmed Mzali as his successor. Tunisia gave the PLO a headquarters after its expulsion from Beirut and Bourguiba welcomed Yassir Arafat, continuing to support him after his expulsion from Damascus. The Israelis attempted to kill Arafat in the Tunis Bombing of October 1985 and Bourguiba was shocked by American support for this aggression. Close links were established with Algiers and Bourguiba, visiting there in June 1983, had the warmest welcome of any visitor since Nasser as he spoke of the two countries forming the spinal column of a Greater Maghreb. By early 1984 he appeared to be preoccupied with building his mausoleum in Monastir and to have withdrawn from day-to-day government. He intervened occasionally to reshuffle Ministers to prevent any from becoming too entrenched and to encourage the young and others who might have become embittered. Knowing from his early career the strength of Muslim feeling in the country, he became increasingly worried about the rise of fundamentalism, which he saw as a threat to all that he had stood for, and prevented Mzali from legalising the Mouvement de la Tendance Islamique. It was, however, anger at corruption that gave him a new lease of life early in 1986 when he sharply ended the intrigues around him by dismissing his son from a government post and then divorced his wife, offically for contradicting him. She was sent into exile and subsequently Bourguiba was frequently photographed swimming with his niece, Saida Sassi. In June, apparently so feeble that he had to be supported and prompted during his speech at the Party Congress he again endorsed Mzali as his successor but twelve days later dismissed him from office, appointing the colourless Rashid Sfar to deal with an economic crisis caused by unemployment and stagnation and with student troubles. Early in 1987 the Government appeared to be oscillating chaotically between repression and clemency with people being arrested, freed and rearrested against a background of apparently meaningless Cabinet changes, accusations of corruption, student and trade union strikes. In September 90 members of the MTI were put on trial and only 7 were sentenced to death. Bourguiba was dissatisfied and ordered General Ben Ali whom he had just appointed Prime Minister to stage a retrial, apparently threatening to replace him with Sayah if he demurred. Ben Ali summoned a Cabinet meeting from which leading supporters of Bourguiba were excluded, secured agreement to depose him and on 7 November he announced that a panel of seven doctors had found the President "totally incapable of fulfilling his duties" and that he had been taken to an official residence. There was no opposition but widespread regret that a man who had done so much for his country should have been unable to realise that he could have rendered one last service by stepping down gracefully.

BOURGUIBA PROPOSALS (1965)
In February and March 1965 during a tour of the Middle East in which he had been struck with horror by the state of the Palestinian refugees Habib Bourguiba made a series of speeches in which he analysed the state of the Arab world. He accused leaders of "drugging the masses with provocative slogans and unanswered promises" and criticised calls to break off relations with West Germany which had recently established an Embassy in Tel Aviv. Bourguiba recalled that Tunisia had gained independence through accepting compromises and then asking for more, not expecting to get all it wanted the first time. Arab unity was inevitable but could not happen until social structures were more similar. He proposed a negotiated settlement of the Arab–Israel conflict on the basis of Resolution 242, saying that the refugees had been kept going by "chimerical hopes and sterile hatreds" because the Arabs could never win a war while many of their weapons were "scrap iron". Israel should hand back those parts of the territory not assigned to it in Resolution 181 but which it had subsequently overrun to form a Palestinian state with which it could live in harmony if both sides rejected extremists. Refugees should be allowed to return to their homes. A spokesman for the Syrian Baath Party declared that such views were treason while the Iraqis withdrew his invitation. The officially-controlled Cairo press said that Bourguiba was "raving mad" and a mob set fire to the residence of the Tunisian Ambassador: Bourguiba accused Nasser of aiming at "exclusive leadership" of the Arabs and boycotted the Casablanca Summit in the autumn. Of the Arab states only Morocco, Libya and Saudi Arabia did not criticise the proposals while the Israeli Deputy Prime Minister Abba Eban said that it was now impossible to return to the situation of 1947. Bourguiba was generally praised in the West for his frankness and realism.

BOUSSOUF, Abd al-Hafid (1926–)
Algerian Revolutionary leader. Of a notable but impoverished family, he was born at Mila near Constantine and was a schoolmate of Lakhdar Ben Tobal. He qualified as a teacher and held a diploma in psychology. Boussouf joined the militant nationalist Organisation Spéciale but his activities came to the notice of the police so he fled to Oran where organised an underground network. He was co-opted on to the Comité Révolutionnaire d'Unité et d'Action and was involved in the actual planning of the All Saints' Day Uprising.' He assumed command of wilaya V covering the Oranie. where with the help of his deputy, Houari Boumédienne he proved perhaps the most efficient of all the Colonels, training and arming some 3,000 men. He directed operations from Oudjdah in Morocco. He believed most firmly that the Algerian War of Independence should be controlled by the military commanders and was involved in the murder of Ramdan Abane who stood for the primacy of the political leadership. In April 1958 Boussouf represented the Algerian military at the Tangier Conference. He was then with Ben Tobal and Belkasim Krim in charge of running the war. When the Gouvernement Provisoire de la Republique Algérienne was set up in August 1958 Boussouf was nominated Minister of Liaison and Communications which put him in charge of Intelligence. In February 1960 he changed to Minister of Armaments and in May visited Moscow and Peking, returning with promises of increased help. In the struggles for power before independence he supported GPRA, of which he was regarded as the most powerful member, against the General Staff but was later reconciled with Boumédienne. He retired from politics, going into business, but was mentioned as a possible Prime Minister after the coup of June 1965. There was apparently too much opposition to his appointment but he sometimes carried out special missions abroad for the Government. In March 1976 it was reported that Boussouf had been arrested after criticising the President: he had been one of the last of the old guard to retain favour. Bousouf was a tough but jovial man with a large round face, cropped black hair and with his eyes concealed behind dark glasses.

BOUTAFLIKA, Abd al-Aziz (1937–)
Algerian Minister. He was born in Oudjda, the son of the Algerian owner of a Turkish bath and was educated locally and at the University of Algiers. On the outbreak of the War of Algerian Independence he abandoned his studies to join the Armée de Libération Nationale. As Commandant Abd al-Qadr he was a political commissar at wilaya V on the Moroccan frontier, serving on the staff of Colonel Boumédienne: he was thus a

member of the Oudjda Group. In 1961 he was deputed
to attempt to open a new front in the Sahara which
necessitated diplomatic visits to neighbouring West
African countries. In February 1962 he acted as the
contact between Ben Bella, still in detention, and Boumédienne. When Ben Bella formed his first government
in September 1962, he appointed Boutaflika Minister
for Youth and Sports, promoting him in September
1963 to take charge of Foreign Affairs. In practice Ben
Bella attempted to control diplomacy himself through
his own office and there were constant disputes between
them: Boutaflika was later to describe Ben Bella's
foreign policy as "vulgar catchwords and impulsive
frenzy". Ben Bella was also concerned to eliminate
adherents of Boumédienne from the Government. In
May, as Ben Bella recalled all Ambassadors to discuss
the forthcoming Afro-Asian Conference, the quarrel
between the two men came to a head and he tried to
dismiss Boutaflika. This precipitated the coup in which
Boumédienne overthrew Ben Bella, after which Boutaflika, denounced by Ben Bella's friend Fidel Castro as
"an enemy of revolution", resumed his post. For some
years Boumédienne was preoccupied with establishing
his position and with domestic matters, leaving Boutaflika a free hand. In October 1965 he secured the
approval of General de Gaulle for the new regime and
in December he broke off relations with Britain over
Rhodesia, threatening to prepare troops for its liberation. One of the world's most active Foreign Ministers,
Boutaflika led Algerian delegations to numerous international gatherings as well as conducting much bilateral
diplomacy. He was an effective instrument of Boumédienne's policy of encouraging the "Poor South" to resist
economic domination by the "Rich North" by
assuming control of its own resources, making Algeria
the leader of the developing countries. After a visit to
Havana he was reconciled with Castro and still further
angered the Americans by receiving Mme Binh, the
Viet-Cong Foreign Minister, in February 1973, hailing
her country as "a shield to and a sword for the Third
World". He caused more offence when, as President of
the General Assembly of the United Nations in
December 1974 he allowed Yassir Arafat to address the
world body, according him the treatment of a Head of
State. He always took a strongly pro-Palestinian line,
supporting Egypt in its wars with Israel and denouncing
its quest for peace. In the late 1970s he had to carry
out Boumédienne's policy of hostility to Morocco over
the Western Sahara: in March 1976 he denounced Moroccan "genocide" and later in the year attempted to
persuade the French to mediate and the Americans
to stop supplying Hassan II with arms. He devoted
some attention to Party matters, declaring "we will
mercilessly wipe out any tentative introduction of
foreign ideology, whether Communist, Baathist or
Nasserist . . . Algeria will not allow others to think for
it". He was clearly the second man in the state and
there was frequent speculation that he would be
appointed Vice-President or Prime Minister: he was
in charge of the Government during Boumédienne's
terminal illness. There was much support, amongst
technocrats and government officials for Boutaflika to
succeed as President but the Party officials and army
officers considered him out of touch with ordinary

people and criticised his extravagant lifestyle. The
Presidency therefore went to Colonel Chadli who
almost at once removed Boutaflika from the Foreign
Ministry, giving him the title of Councillor. This
marked the beginning of the end of his political career
for in January 1980 he was dropped from the Cabinet
and during 1981 from the Party Politburo and then
from Central Committee. Boutaflika was a pleasantly
unpompous man with a friendly smile.

BOUYALI, Mustafa (1940–87)
Algerian religious guerrilla leader. He was born in
Achour near Algiers and took part in the Algerian War
of Independence, being imprisoned from 1958 to 1960.
He had already become noted for his strong religious
views and saw a democratic political system as the
natural corollary of Islam. He opposed the expulsion
of Ben Khedda by Ben Bella and later took part in
the revolt of Ait Ahmad. Bouyali formed a group of
supporters which was harried by the police after it had
condemned the execution of Saiyyid Qutb. In October
1981 plain clothes policemen tried to abduct him but
he was rescued by neighbours. His associates now
included the future leaders of the Front Islamique du
Salut, Abbas Madani and Ali Belhadj and Shaykh
Nahnah, later the leader of Hamas. In April 1982 as
the police came to arrest him, he escaped over a wall.
He later started to organise armed groups which took
the name of the Armed Algerian Islamic Movement. In
December he escaped at a checkpoint by wounding a
policeman and took on the aura of a Robin Hood,
raiding banks, jewellers and petrol stations for cash and
hospitals for medicine and terrorising corrupt officials.
In January 1983 47 of his supporters were arrested and
another 100 were captured by May: he was condemned
in his absence to life imprisonment. He denounced the
Government as "a band of atheists". In August 1985
his men attacked a police college, killed a guard and
captured weapons. In October, Bouyali and 23 others,
ambushed by police with helicopters, shot their way
out, killing 5 gendarmes but losing 2 killed and 17
prisoners in the biggest gunfight since the end of the
war. There were further skirmishes in November and
at intervals until, betrayed by a driver, he was killed by
the police in January 1987. In June 200 Islamic militants, 20 of whom were alleged to be members of
Bouyali's gang went on trial for murder, sabotage and
theft. Four were condemned to death and 184 others
received sentences of up to life imprisonment.

BRAHIMI, Abd al-Hamid (1936–)
Algerian Prime Minister. He took a Doctorate in Economics from Harvard and soon after independence was
appointed Governor of Annaba. He was then Director
of Franco-Algerian Industrial Co-operation, a Lecturer
at Algiers University and Representative of SONA-
TRACH in the USA before in 1979 being appointed
Minister of Regional Planning and Development. He
was criticised for excessive zeal in breaking up public
corporations but was little known when in January 1984
President Chadli selected him as Prime Minister. He
was believed to have little commitment to the socialism
of the Boumédienne era and most of his Cabinet were
non-political. As an executive of the President's poli-

cies, particularly in the economic sphere, rather than an initiator of his own, Brahimi stressed hard work and austerity and travelled widely trying to promote efficiency rather than rhetoric. In December 1987 he passed six new laws which weakened top-heavy bureaucracy, giving more powers to local managers of state industries. He also created new *wilayahs* in the South to give more local initiative. He cut government expenditure as the value of oil exports fell and the dinar declined 30% against the dollar. Brahimi was determined not to reschedule the national debt which rose from $15,000 million to $22,000 million under his administration, preferring to restrict imports even of essential foods. The economic distress, particularly unemployment and poor educational opportunities amongst the young, set off the October Riots of 1988 which nearly brought down the regime. In November he was replaced by Kasdi Merbah. During his period of office there had been great progress towards Maghreb Unity and relations were restored with Morocco. He resumed his career as a Professor of Economics but in April 1990 created a sensation by alleging that in the previous decade the state had been swindled out of $26,000 million, more than the total national debt, by corrupt practices such as the pocketing by officials of 20% commission on contracts. The picture was hardly improved by the statement of Prime Minister Mouloud Hamrouche that only $2,000 million had been stolen. In October 1990 he resigned from the Central Committee of the Front de Libération Nationale, complaining of lack of democracy within the Party. Later he worked for reconciliation between the FLN and the Front Islamique du Salut, saying that a synthesis was possible between Islam and nationalism. He headed committees to help FIS members held as political prisoners.

BREAD RIOTS (Tunisia) (1983–84)

At the end of 1983 Tunisia was in economic difficulties with a rapidly rising trade deficit and increasing bankruptcies amongst small businesses as prices were held down to prevent demands for higher wages. In October 1983, under pressure from the IMF, Prime Minister Mzali announced that subsidies would have to be reduced in the New Year. In December it became clear that this would involve doubling of the price of bread, to take effect from the New Year. Riots started amongst the unemployed of the South, who burned anything belonging to the Government, and rapidly spread throughout the country. At least 15 people were killed as tanks fired upon the crowds and on 3 January the Government declared a state of emergency. The brutality of its reaction set off further riots in which, officially, 89 people were killed (unofficial reports said 140), 938 (including 348 of the security forces) wounded and 2,000 arrested. Parts of Tunis were on fire when on 6 January President Bourguiba personally announced the cancellation of price rises. Mzali admitted that he had "overestimated the spirit of sacrifice of the people" and, unlike Black Thursday or the Gafsa Raid, no attempt was made to blame outside intrigue: indeed, embarrassingly, Qadafi offered help. The emergency was not lifted until 2 February. This was the first time since independence that the Govern-

ment had been forced to change its policies as a result of street pressure and its security forces which had looked near to collapse had to be completely overhauled. The Minister of the Interior was sentenced, *in absentia*, to ten years' imprisonment and about 300 others were brought to trial; the vindictiveness of the sentences showed how frightened the Government had been. Eight adolescents were sentenced to death but reprieved after international outcry while others received up to 30 years. The banned Mouvement de la Tendence Islamique, with the slogan "There is no god but Allah and Bourguiba is His enemy", claimed leadership of the riots. Mzali himself took over the Interior Ministry and brought in General Ben Ali as Secretary of State for National Security.

BREZHNEV GULF PROPOSALS (1980)

In January 1980 the Carter Doctrine declared that the US would use force to prevent any outside power from dominating the Gulf. On 10 December President Leonid Brezhnev, addressing the Indian Parliament, in effect offered Soviet restraint in the area in return for Western recognition of its position in Afghanistan. He said that the Americans were unjustified in building up forces against a "Soviet threat" as, despite a natural interest in a neighbouring area, there was no "intention of encroaching either on the Middle East oil or its supply routes". He called upon the US and other Western Powers, Japan, China and others to agree to five mutual obligations. The first was not to establish foreign military bases in the Gulf or in adjacent islands and not to deploy nuclear or other weapons of mass destruction there. The second was not to use or threaten to use force against states of the area and not to interfere in their internal affairs. The third was to respect their non-alignment and not to attempt to draw them into alliances. The fourth was to respect their sovereign right to their natural resources. Lastly not to raise any obstacles or threats to normal trade or sea lanes. The first proposal would have meant that the Americans would have to give up their facilities in Bahrain and Oman and their base in Diego Garcia while the Russian facilities in Aden and Ethiopia would not be affected. The second would not involve the Russian position in Afghanistan where they claimed to have been invited by the legitimate government. The third would prevent the Americans from making bilateral agreements with states which would never have considered making them with Russia. The fourth would prevent any Western attempt to counter the Oil Weapon which could never anyway be used against the Soviet Union. Only the final one could be accepted by the West with mutual benefit so the Brezhnev Proposals were basically a call for the West to surrender advantages without any return. They were generally regarded as a piece of propaganda and not taken seriously by any of the Arab states involved although Kuwait did see some "positive points in them".

BREZHNEV PEACE PLAN (1982)

The Israeli aggression in Lebanon, Operation Peace for Galilee, of June 1982 was followed by the peace proposals of the Reagan Plan on 1 September, followed a week later by those of the Fez Summit. On 15 September Brezhnev put forward his six proposals, beginning with that of the inadmissibility of the seizure of land through aggression: Israel should return all its conquests from the June War after which the borders between it and its Arab neighbours would be inviolable. The Palestinians had a right to their own state to which refugees should be permitted to return or receive compensation. Eastern Jerusalem should be returned to the Arabs with free access to the shrines for all. Fourthly all states had a right to independent existence. Fifthly the state of war between the Arabs and Israel should be ended and further disputes settled peacefully. Sixthly the settlement should be guaranteed by the the permanent members of the Security Council or the Council as a whole. The Palestine Liberation Organisation was the sole legitimate representative of the Palestinian people. There should be an international conference on the Middle East. His Peace Plan was presumably put forward in the hope of winning some friends amongst the Arabs as, given Reagan's obsession with keeping "the Evil Empire" out of the Middle East and Begin's refusal to consider surrendering an inch of land, Brezhnev could hardly have expected any favourable response to it.

BUBIYAN–WARBAH DISPUTE
Bubiyan and Warbah are two small islands to the west of the main channel of the Shatt al-Arab. Warbah, the northern one, is the smaller, about six miles long and three wide while Bubiyan is 27 by 15 miles. Both are mudflats, usually uninhabited but used by nomadic fishermen. Before 1899 they were regarded like Kuwait as part of the Ottoman Province of Basra but in that year Mubarak b. Sabah al-Sabah signed a secret agreement with the British which was the first step towards the independence of Kuwait. He claimed that the islands belonged to the Al Sabah. In 1902 a Turkish force of about 20 men landed on Bubiyan, possibly in connection with the search for a terminus for the Baghdad Railway. The Viceroy, Lord Curzon, feared that if they fortified the islands it would be possible to build an impregnable naval base on the deep water Khawr al-Zubayr and that the Turks would no longer be dependent upon Basra which could only take shallow-draft vessels. He wished to expel them by force if necessary but was overruled by London which contented itself with a protest. In the Anglo-Ottoman Agreement of 1913 they were recognised as belonging to Kuwait but as the Agreement was not ratified, remained under Turkish control until after the outbreak of war. In 1923 Iraq, then under British domination, recognised them as Kuwaiti and this was reiterated after independence by Nuri al-Said in 1932. During the Second World War the Iraqis, with British help, built a port at Umm Qasr on the Khawr al-Zubayr which later developed into a naval base and an oil terminal. In 1961 after the British granted Kuwait independence, Abd al-Krim Qassim demanded the whole state including the islands for Iraq; no Arab state supported his claim. His fall ended the larger claim but Iraq thereafter exploited the claim to the islands and indeed the whole frontier as a means of putting pressure on Kuwait. In March 1973 there was a clash in which soldiers on both sides were killed. This was followed by a formal claim to

Bubiyan and Warbah with the Iraqi Foreign Minister saying "without them we could not become a Gulf State". In August a visit to Baghdad by Jabir b. Ahmad al-Sabah failed to resolve the matter but nothing further happened. In May 1975 Iraq offered to accept Warbah and a lease on the northern part of Bubiyan in return for a formal recognition of other frontiers. In 1978 a joint Committee was established to delimit the frontier but nothing was achieved. In 1981 Saddam Hussain revived the claim and asked for a 99-year lease of half of Bubiyan but was placated by a large "loan".

al-BUKHARI, Nasuhi (c. 1881–)
Syrian Prime Minister. He came from a religious family of Damascus and was educated the Military College in Istanbul. During the war he commanded a Brigade on the Caucasus front until he was captured by the Russians. He escaped from a prisoner-of-war camp in Siberia and made his way back to Turkey through China and America. He then commanded a division in Palestine but deserted to join the army of the Amir Faysal. He was Minister of Education and then of Agriculture in the 1920s. Early in 1939 there was a period of crisis in Syria as the nationalists agitated against the rejection of the Franco-Syrian Treaty, the cession of Alexandretta and the special status that the French wished to accord to the Druzes and Alawites in order to maintain their own position if Syria became impossible to rule. Jamil Mardam resigned the Prime Ministership on 18 February, Lutfi al-Haffar was able to hold office for only three weeks and two other leaders declined to try to form a government. Bukhari, widely respected and regarded as a man of principle, agreed to do so on 6 April. His neutral Cabinet lasted until 15 May when he resigned over the question of the minorities but he was persuaded to stay on while two other politicians attempted to form governments. On 10 July the Resident General Puaux suspended the Constitution and replaced the Government by Directors.

BURJ AL-BARAJINAH, Siege of (1986–87)
After the Beirut Siege in the summer of 1982 Palestinian guerrillas were evacuated from Lebanon leaving their families behind in refugee camps. Within a few years perhaps 1,000 fighting men returned and the fact that they were mostly loyal to Yassir Arafat caused them to be viewed with hostility by Syria and its Lebanese ally the Shiah militia Amal. In May 1985, having defeated the Sunnis for control of West Beirut, Amal launched "the war of the camps" with attacks on the survivors of Sabra-Shatila and the nearby camp of Burj al-Barajinah. They overran the first two but although they cut off water, food and medical supplies Burj al-Barajinah held out for a month after which the indignation of Arab Governments forced the Syrians to bring about a cease-fire. UNWRA calculated that in this first round 500 Palestinians were killed and 15,000 out of the 40,000 forced to flee. Spasmodic attacks followed until in May 1986 Amal, now joined by the Shiah Sixth Brigade of the Lebanese Regular Army with tanks and heavy artillery attacked again. The Palestinians, with some help from Hizbullah, Amal's rival for the allegiance of the Shiah, held out for 36 days and even increased their territory before there was another cease-fire. In Sep-

tember 1986 there was another attack which was successfully repulsed. In November while Amal was trying to extend its sphere in Southern Lebanon, Palestinians occupied the strategically-sited village of Maghdushah, cutting them off from Beirut. In reprisal Amal once again attacked Burj al-Barajinah. All supplies were cut off and women and children leaving to forage were deliberately shot in the legs. On 6 February 1987 the inhabitants, declaring that they had eaten all the cats, dogs and mules in the camp, asked for a *fatwa* from religious leaders as to whether it would be legal to eat human flesh. The following day volunteers manned a relief lorry full of food but Amal blew it up in sight of the camp. There was widespread revulsion and on February 18 a small convoy was permitted to enter and some of the wounded were allowed to leave after the Palestinians had agreed to evacuate Maghdushah. The siege was not finally lifted until April 6 when Syrian troops moved in. It was estimated that about 250 people had been killed. Amongst those who emerged alive was a British surgeon Dr Pauline Cutting who had tended the wounded without medical supplies, water, electricity or food. A modified siege continued and it was not until November that the inhabitants were allowed to bring in materials to rebuild their homes. There was not complete freedom of movement until January 1988. In July 1988 there was further fighting when the camp was taken over by supporters of Abu Musa and 120 Arafat loyalists were driven out.

AL BU SAID, Qabus b. Said (1940–)
Sultan of Oman from 1970. The son of Said b. Taymur Al Bu Said by a Dhofari tribeswoman, he was born in Salala where he received his early education. As a teenager he was sent to England for private tuition and after graduating from Sandhurst, served with a Scottish regiment in Germany and with a local government office. After a world tour he returned home in 1966 to find that his father, far from regarding him as a collaborator, kept him a virtual prisoner. Before his accession he had never visited Muscat and knew very few Omanis. In July 1970 with the help of British officers Qabus staged a palace coup and was installed in his father's place. With British advisers he proceeded to reverse most of the policies of Said. Qabus was faced with two problems, the preservation of the country by crushing the Dhofar Rebellion and the development of one of the most backward countries in the world. His first speech demonstrated that a new age had begun as he changed the national flag and title and apparently delegated authority with the appointment of a Prime Minister and a Cabinet. Although they had not met for at least a decade he invited back his exiled uncle Tariq b. Taymur Al Bu Said who had a reputation as a liberal. Innumerable petty restrictions, including those on education, travel and the importation of foreign goods were removed. Despite difficulties in persuading Arabs and others that not under the thumb of the British, Qabus ended Oman's isolation by joining the Arab League and the UN. He ended the country's traditional hostility to Saudi Arabia after visiting King Faysal in 1971. He was a strong advocate of Gulf unity and recognised the importance of this for the defence of the Middle East. He strengthened Oman's ties with Britain and forged

links with other Western states. He refused to break with Egypt over the Camp David agreement. Qabus was close to the Shah of Iran, whose pompous uniforms and ritual he copied and whose troops helped crush the Dhofar Rebellion. In 1980 he provided defence facilities to the US and played and important part in keeping the Gulf sea lanes open during the Iran–Iraq War, refusing to bow to pressure. During the dispute with the Yemen he neither sought nor avoided confrontation.

Qabus' rule balanced fairness with determination. He ended the Dhofar Rebellion with a mixture of force and generous amnesties. He increased the power of the walis at the expense of the sheikhs. In 1981 he set up the State Consultative Council with 45 nominated members. He appointed his uncle Prime Minister but kept the ministries of defence and finance in his own hands or put them in the hands of expatriates. He took a personal interest in building up the armed forces. In the early days of his reign the pace of reform was often frantic which resulted in chaos and spiralling prices, although things improved following the first five-year plan of 1976. He initiated grandiose building plans including a new palace and an international airport at Muscat. He encouraged urban expansion and under him Atrah became the nation's principal city. He took frequent tours outside of Oman, liked Western classical music. Shy, stiff and formal, he has a tremendous sense of his position as Head of State. Married to the daughter of Tariq he seemed unaware of the importance of providing a successor.

AL BU SAID, Tariq B. Taymur (1922–c. 86)
Omani Prime Minister. He was a son of Taymur b. Faysal Al Bu Said by a Circassian lady and was educated in Turkey and Germany before serving with the Indian Army on the North West Frontier. His brother Said b. Taymur Al Bu Said employed him as Administrator of Muscat Municipality and then in negotiations with the Imam Ghalib b. Ali al-Hinai. He then commanded troops in the Jabal Akhdar Campaign, winning much praise from British officers. In 1958 he quarrelled with his brother, who, he said, had no spark of human feeling and went abroad, living partly in Germany and partly in the Middle East as representative of a German construction firm. During this time he was often seen gambling in Beirut nightclubs. To some extent he became regarded as the embodiment of liberalism and reform. In July 1970 when Said was overthrown, Tariq was invited back to Muscat by his nephew Qabus b. Said Al Bu Said and appointed Prime Minister. The appointment was a disaster as there was little mutual trust between them and the Prime Minister's duties were ill-defined as the new Sultan kept matters of defence, security, finance and concessions in his own hands or in those of the expatriates who surrounded him and they ensured that the Prime Minister was excluded from major decisions. Tariq had no staff, for some time not even a secretary, and was unable to follow up his ideas, although he launched a vague Five-Year Plan and was the first to suggest use of natural gas. He created a ministerial system, adding new departments to the skeleton administration that his brother had maintained. He also spoke of constitutional monarchy and possibly even of a republic. Tariq played

an important part in getting the country accepted as a member of the Arab League. It had never been clear who was responsible for foreign affairs and the reported appointment of an American former Treasury Secretary, a Lebanese and a Libyan to conduct them seemed to be the cause of Tariq's departure for Germany in December 1971, leaving behind a letter of resignation. The official reason was ill-health but Tariq was too strong a personality and too intelligent a man for the post that he had been given. The Sultan himself took the Premiership. In March 1972 Tariq returned as an Adviser to his nephew who, in March 1976, married his daughter Kamilla. He was also Chairman of the Central Bank. Tariq was a very large dynamic man, fluent in four languages with a considerable sense of humour.

BUSH ASSASSINATION PLOT (1993)

In April 1993 ex-President Bush visited Kuwait to receive an honorary degree and ten days later the Kuwaiti Government announced that it had arrested 14 out of 17 members of a terrorist gang which had come from Iraq to assassinate him with a car bomb and commit acts of sabotage. Iraq immediately denied any involvement and when in June the prisoners were put on trial their evident ineptitude made it improbable that they had been on a mission organised by an intelligence service, although some experts said that the explosives were of a type used by the Iraqis. Two Iraqis, however, pleaded guilty amidst doubts of the fairness of the trial. Before the process had been concluded, President Clinton, whose muddled policies in Somalia and the Balkans had aroused much criticism, determined to show himself a strong leader by ordering a missile attack on Baghdad without consulting the Security Council. On 27 June, 23 missiles were aimed from warships in the Gulf and Red Sea at the Iraqi intelligence HQ; some missed, killing at least six innocent civilians including a well-known artist. The President's rating rose in American opinion polls. Even pro-American Arab Governments, apart from Kuwait, condemned the attack but it was obsequiously praised by the British Government of John Major. The Iraqi Government complained to the Security Council which took no action. The trial resumed in Kuwait but was adjourned until 4 September.

BUSH PROPOSALS (1991)

Speaking at the Air Force Academy Graduation ceremony in Colorado on 29 May 1991 President Bush outlined a programme to eliminate weapons of mass destruction from the Middle East, calling for a "freeze on the acquisition, production and testing" of surface to surface missiles, leading to their "ultimate elimination" and an end to the production or import of plutonium or weapon-grade uranium needed for nuclear weapons. All Middle Eastern countries should adhere to the Geneva Biological Weapons Convention. The states of the region should only be allowed to buy such conventional weapons as "they legitimately need to deter and defend against military aggression" and arms suppliers should work out rules to avoid "destabilising" deals and should notify each other ahead of concluding "certain sales". Shortly afterwards the

US made enormous sales to the Gulf States and nothing more was heard of the Bush Proposals.

BUTROS-GHALI, Butros (1922–)

He was born in Cairo into a wealthy Coptic family with large estate in southern Egypt. His grandfather was the assassinated Prime Minister Butros-Ghali and an uncle was Foreign Minister in the 1920s. He studied at Cairo University, took a Doctorate at the Sorbonne and was a Fulbright Scholar at Columbia. Butros-Ghali then taught international law and headed the politics department at Cairo University, frequently going abroad to lecture and attend conferences, making valuable contacts throughout Africa and Asia. In 1960 he was asked by UNESCO to make a feasibility study for an Institute of Diplomatic Studies for East Africa and inaugurated a Latin-African Dialogue. He was also a member of the political bureau of the Arab Socialist Union and President of the Centre for Political and Strategic Studies at *al-Ahram* where he had earlier helped to found and edit a weekly economic magazine. He considered that journalism prevented him from becoming too academic but he wrote 12 books on international affairs in Arabic, French and English. In 1972 Butros-Ghali helped in the negotiation of the Addis Ababa Agreement which ended the war in the Southern Sudan. In October 1977 he was appointed Minister of State for Foreign Affairs and acted as Foreign Minister when Ismail Fahmy and Muhd Ibrahim Kamel resigned in protest at the policies of President Sadat, whom he accompanied to Jerusalem and also to Camp David. Married to a Jewess, he saw the Palestinian problem as the most important of all international disputes and had assembled groups to consider details even before his appointment. He led the Egyptian team in negotiations with Israel in Washington. He then played an important part in getting Egypt readmitted to the Third World organisations from which it had been expelled. In 1987 he was candidate for the headship of UNESCO but decided not to oppose a fellow African. In 1985 he set up a trilateral co-operation between Egypt, Japan and Black Africa and in 1989 he mediated a settlement between Mauritania and Senegal. Later he had a key role in securing the release of Nelson Mandela. He was appointed Deputy Prime Minister for Foreign Affairs and Minister of State for Emigration and Expatriate Egyptians. In the summer of 1991 he campaigned vigorously for election as Secretary-General of the UN, holding discussions with Bush and Shamir. He also lobbied in Peking, urging that, with the end of the Cold War, a new type of UN was needed to democratise international relations. There were doubts, however, because he had always been less a creator of policies than the implementor of those of others. There was considerable anger when it appeared that the Developed World was considering putting forward a Western candidate but the feeling that it was "Africa's turn" prevailed. The British regarded him as too Francophile but abstained in the voting as did the Yemen and two other states and he was elected unanimously in November. He started in January 1992 in a UN short of money (85 members, notably the US were behind with contributions) but facing increasing demands for peace-keeping operations in Cambodia, Yugoslavia and

West Sahara. He had various suggestions for strength-ening the role of the Security Council and was anxious to streamline UN bureaucracy and to give more say to smaller nations. He tried to avert sanctions against Libya over their refusal to hand over Lockerbie sus-pects. In July 1992 he complained that the UN was more interested in the "War of the Rich" in Yugoslavia than in sufferings of Somalia. He annoyed ambassadors by going over their heads to Foreign Ministers and snubbed the Security Council by not turning up. In August 1992 Douglas Hurd denied that the British had initiated a whispering campaign which Butros-Ghali said was "maybe because I am a wog". He had differ-ences with Lord Carrington as EC mediator over Yugoslavia and there were suggestions that he had com-plained to the media instead of to officials. In September he warned that the world could splinter into 400 economically crippled mini-states. In October there was criticism when the Special Envoy to Somalia was forced to resign after speaking out against UN manage-ment. He is seen as too autocratic and unwilling to delegate. In his early life he was keen on fencing, shooting and flying. He is frquently ill-tempered and abrasive but under his leadership the UN has been assuming new responsibilities. In January 1993 the US deplored what it terms the "Third Worldism" of the UN, what it saw as the failure of the UN to reform and its tolerance of corruption, favouritism and slipshod administration. Butros-Ghali annoyed the US in calling for the return of the Marj al-Zuhur deportees despite a promising start when he abolished four Under-Sec-retary posts, although he later replaced two of these. Things improved, however, after his meeting with Clinton. In February 1993 he visited Japan and Germany and persuaded them to help in Mozambique and Somalia. He saw the UN role as second-generation peace-keeping – the rehabilitation of devastated areas such as Cambodia. In March he was trying to get talks restarted in Cyprus.

CAIRO CONFERENCE (1921)

In January 1921 Winston Churchill was appointed Colonial Secretary "entrusted with the task of reordering British policy towards the Arab world" and in particular Palestine and Iraq for which Mandates had been received at the the San Remo Conference. Although Churchill did not consider Iraq, unlike Egypt, to be vital to imperial strategy, the costly repression of the Iraq Revolt showed the necessity of establishing a government in Baghdad that enjoyed local support. Churchill summoned forty leading officials and experts from the area between Persia and Somaliland to meet at the Semiramis Hotel in Cairo on 12 March. The best known Arab invited was Jafar al-Askari. A Political Committee and a Military and Financial Committee held over forty sessions in secret. Frequent cables to and from London meant that the Cabinet participated in decisions. The first decision was to establish a monarchy in Iraq and after the rejection as possible rulers of Ibn Saud, Shaykh Khazal of Muhammarah, Sayyid Thalib al-Naqib, the Agha Khan and a Turkish prince it was decided that Faysal for whose plight after his expulsion by the French from Syria the British felt some responsibility, offered "hope of the best and cheapest solution". The method of installing him with a show of popular support was then discussed. It was decided that the Kurdish areas should be part of Iraq and not constitute an independent state. It was further decided that the British garrison in Iraq should be substantially reduced and that security would be the primary responsibility of the RAF, assisted by local Levies. This is the first time in any empire that such an experiment was made and it was at once extended to Aden which it was decided should be amalgamated with British Somaliland. The policy of subsidies to Arab rulers was discussed; Ibn Saud received an increase from £60,000 a year to £100,000 while that of King Hussain would be continued conditionally upon his good behaviour. Iraqi business concluded, the Conference was joined by Sir Herbert Samuel, High Commissioner for Palestine, to discuss how the Balfour Declaration could be implemented without antagonising the Arabs and also the position of Trans-Jordan. Churchill and other members of the Conference then moved to Jerusalem where he received a deputation from the Haifa Convention led by Musa Kazim al-Hussaini which demanded repudiation of the Declaration, the end of Jewish immigration, an Arab government and some form of union with other Arab states: Churchill bluntly refused. A subsequent Jewish delegation was warned to conciliate the Arabs. He then decided to install the Amir Abd

Allah as governor of Trans-Jordan for six months with a salary of £5,000 a month and orders to keep the area free from anti-Zionist and anti-French nationalists. It is ironical that this final short-term decision should be the only one surviving after 70 years but the Conference had been over-optimistic in believing that desert princes could introduce democracy in more developed areas. T. E. Lawrence, who had been one of Churchill's advisers in Cairo, concluded that it had "made straight all the tangle, finding solutions fulfilling (I think) our promises in letter and spirit (where humanly possible) without sacrificing any interest of the peoples concerned".

CAIRO SUMMIT (1964)

At the end of 1963 the Arab world was in disarray. King Hussain had broken off diplomatic relations with Egypt in 1961 and after the outbreak of the Yemen War King Saud had done the same while Morocco and Algeria had been at war over Tindouf. Syria was at odds both with Egypt and Iraq. There then occurred the Jordan Waters Dispute and President Nasser feared that as the aspiring leader of the Arabs he might be forced into a war with Israel. He determined that other Heads of State should share the responsibility for whatever happened so he invited them all to meet together for the first Summit meeting to be held in Cairo from 13–16 January 1964. This represented a reversal of his previous stand that he could collaborate only with those Arab states which were ideologically compatible. All those invited, Kings Saud, Hussain and Hassan, Shaykh Abd Allah b. Salim al-Sabah and Presidents Ben Bella, Abd al-Salam Arif, Bourguiba, Sallal, Amin al-Hafiz and Abboud attended while King Idris was represented by his Crown Prince and President Shihab by the Prime Minister Rashid Karami. The final communiqué stated that Israel was planning a "serious aggression" by diverting the Jordan waters "with the object of realising Zionist expansionist ambitions". Unspecified practical technical resolutions had been taken to thwart this plan – later this was shown to be the diversion of the Litani and Hasbani Rivers. As there was a danger of war it was agreed to set up a Unified Arab Command under the Egyptian General Ali Ali Amer. Support was expressed for the Front for the Liberation of Occupied South Yemen, for the Dhofar Liberation Front and for nationalists in Angola and elsewhere. The Summit called upon independent African nations to support the Arab cause. A recent Russian call for a partial ban on nuclear tests was welcomed. There was discussion of the creation of some organisation to represent the Palestinians under the leadership of Ahmad Shukayri. Various bilateral matters were settled, Hussain and Nasser met for the first time in seven years, and the leaders, at least formally reconciled, agreed not to attack one another in public. It was generally felt that the Summit had been a success and that in future the Heads of State should meet at least once a year.

CAIRO SUMMIT (1970)

During Black September of 1970 there was heavy fighting in Jordan as the army tried to control the Palestinian guerrillas. On 17 September the Secretary-General of the Arab League, Abd al-Khalik Hassouna appealed to all Arab states to help to end the bloodshed and two days later Bourguiba suggested a special Summit. All Heads of State with the exception of King Hussain arrived: he was at first represented by his Prime Minister Brigadier Muhammad Daoud who promptly defected before the King himself arrived. A Mediation Committee under Nimeiri made a one-day visit to Amman and subsequently reported that there had been "a pre-arranged plot to crush the Palestinian people". On 27 September Kings Faysal and Hussain, Presidents Nasser, Nimeiri, Franjiyah and Qadafi, Amir Sabah al-Salim al-Sabah and representatives of Tunisia and North Yemen and Yassir Arafat signed an agreement "designed to put an end to Arab bloodshed". It called for an immediate ceasefire, cessation of military movements, release of prisoners and the establishment of a supreme follow-up committee under the chairmanship of the Tunisian Prime Minister Bahi Ladgham to supervise the working of the agreement and to work for better relations between the Jordanian Government and the Palestinians. All the signatories would unite against the side which violated the cease-fire. The Summit represented a success for Hussain as there was no challenge to his rights to rule the West Bank. It was most probably the stress of these meetings that caused Nasser to have a fatal heart attack on 28 September.

CAIRO SUMMIT (1976)

In June 1976 Syrian troops entered Lebanon to support the Government against the Palestinian guerrillas with whom there had been heavy fighting. On 15 October King Khalid invited Presidents Assad, Sadat and Sarkis, Shaykh Jabir al-Ahmad al-Sabah and Yassir Arafat to discuss the situation. This led to the Riyadh Resolutions which legitimised the Syrian presence as the Arab Deterrent Security Force and provided for the resumption of normal Lebanese Government. These decisions were put to a full Summit, the eighth, which assembled in Cairo on 25 October. There were 14 Heads of State and Morocco, Algeria, Iraq, Oman and Tunisia sent representatives. Qadafi who had originally announced his intention of boycotting the meeting because he had been criticised by Sadat, also sent a representative. The decisions taken at Riyadh were confirmed despite divisions over the composition of the ADSF and its financing. It was agreed that each Arab country should contribute "each according to its ability" to the reconstruction of Lebanon. Egypt refused to send any troops. A fund of $90 million was set up to finance the Force for six months.

CAIRO SUMMIT (1990)

A few days after Saddam Hussain had invaded Kuwait, President Mubarak called for a Summit to attempt to find an Arab solution to the developing crisis: otherwise, he warned, there would be massive Western involvement. It was attended by 15 Heads of State and representatives of five others but boycotted by Tunisia. Shaykh Jabir al-Sabah attended but left before the Iraqis spoke. After a day's delay to allow for informal talks the Summit opened on 10 August. Mubarak pleaded with the Iraqi Foreign Minister to withdraw from Kuwait but Tariq Aziz defended the annexation on historical grounds, declaring it "eternal and irreversible" and denied that Saddam had assured the Egyptians that there would be no invasion. Mubarak declined to fly to Baghdad for fear of being held there as a hostage. The Summit called for immediate Iraqi withdrawal and the restoration of the legitimate government, confirming the sovereignty and territorial integrity of Kuwait. It endorsed the Saudi call for US help and Kuwait Annexation, Security Council Resolutions 660, 661 and 662 which imposed an economic blockade on Iraq. Fifteen states with Jordan, Sudan and Mauritania expressing some reservations agreed that an Arab force should be sent to protect Saudi Arabia: Iraq, Libya and the Palestine Liberation Organisation voted against the resolution while Algeria and Yemen abstained. The inability to find an Arab solution was welcomed by the USA. Mubarak admitted that the Summit had been a failure and refused later requests to call another one. Saddam called it "a cover for US aggression".

CAPUCCI, Hilarion, Archbishop (1922–)

Capucci, who was born in Aleppo, was educated locally and studied for the priesthood in Jerusalem. He was in charge of a seminary in Damascus before being appointed Greek Catholic Archbishop of Jerusalem in 1965. On 18 August 1974 he was arrested by Israeli authorities and accused of being a courier for Fatah and of smuggling arms and explosives. It was widely believed that he had been framed by Israeli intelligence, embarrassed by his outspoken attacks on ill-treatment of Palestinians. In December he was sentenced to 12 years' imprisonment. The sentence was deplored by the Vatican and attacked in Arab states. Always declaring his innocence, he went on hunger strike several times while in jail. Guerrillas in several operations demanded his release. In November 1977, his health having seriously deteriorated, he was released at the request of Pope Paul VI and flown to Rome on condition that he should not return to the Middle East. He later went to South America and was made an honorary member of the Palestine National Council.

CARTER DOCTRINE (1980)

In the winter of 1978/9 the US suffered several setbacks in the Middle East. In November its Embassy in Tehran was seized by students and its staff held hostage and the following month Russian troops entered Afghanistan. The Russians had a foothold in Baghdad through the Russo-Iraqi Treaty whereas the US did not even have a diplomatic representative there. There seemed a distinct possibility that the Russians might strike towards the Gulf, disrupting the oil supplies of the

Western world, so in his State of the Union message on 23 January 1980 President Carter declared "Let our position be absolutely clear: an attempt by any outside force to gain control of the Persian Gulf region will be regarded as an assault on the vital interests of the USA and such an assault will be repelled by any means necessary, including military force". The statement gave some assurance to the Arab states although its reference to "outside force" did not necessarily apply to attempts to export the Iranian Revolution. The speech was followed by the build-up of the Rapid Deployment Force and the quest for bases in the Indian Ocean region.

CASABLANCA BLOC
In December 1960 at the height of the Congo crisis 12 pro-Western Francophone countries established the Brazzaville Bloc which was presented as the first step towards African unity. As a response Muhammad V invited the Heads of State of the countries which had contingents in the Congo but India, Indonesia, Ceylon, Ethiopia and some others refused and only the leaders of radical states, Ghana, Guinea, Egypt (President Nasser making his first visit to the Arab West) and Ferhat Abbas representing the Gouvernement Provisoire de la République Algérienne accepted. Libya and Ceylon sent observers. Habib Bourguiba who had opposed Morocco's claims upon Mauritania was not invited. The Conference opened on 4 January 1961 in Casablanca. Nasser proposed direct military intervention in support of the Lumumbists but was dissuaded by Nkrumah who wanted to work through the UN. The Conference condemned Israel as an "imperialist base" and supported Morocco's claim to Mauritania and Algeria's to independence. It opposed Western military bases in Africa and French nuclear tests in the Sahara. It was decided to establish an African Consultative Council with political, economic and cultural committees and an African High Command to co-ordinate action against foreign intervention. All were invited to subscribe to an African Charter of non-alignment and liberation from colonialism and neo-colonialism. Nasser described the Conference as "an historic event incarnating African unity and the common anti-imperialist struggle", making nonsense of attempts to divide Arab and Black Africa while Nkrumah said that it had "laid the foundations for political unity of the African continent". The proceedings were disapproved of by the West and applauded by the communist states. Various committee meetings took place during 1961 but interest in the Bloc waned and after Morocco and Algeria had fought over Tindouf nothing more was heard of it.

CASABLANCA RIOTS (1965 and 1981)
On 22 March 1965, angered by a decree from the Ministry of Education that students over the age of 17 should be barred from enrolling in the second stage of high school education instead being relegated to technical schools, students demonstrated in Casablanca against a measure which effectively barred them from careers in government service. This, at a time of economic distress, with a parliamentary opposition linked to the trade unions, obstructive but powerless, set off a

wave of sympathy strikes, escalating into violent riots and burning of public buildings which spread to Rabat, Fez and Marrakesh. All transport and most industries were paralysed. The Government panicked, imposed a curfew, cut telegraphic communications with the outside world and sent in the troops. For 48 hours observers thought that the regime would collapse but the ruthless methods of General Oufkir restored order. The official estimate put the toll at 7 dead, 43 wounded and 168 arrested, the opposition said 300–400 killed and credible witnesses suggested 109 including 6 policemen. Moroccan students abroad staged sit-ins at their Embassies. Hassan II ordered the release of 120 students but later some 700 rioters received prison sentences of up to six months. Subsequently the King tried to form a government of national unity, failed, imposed a state of emergency and dissolved parliament. In 1981, under pressure from the IMF, the Government led by Maati Bouabid, cut subsidies on essential foodstuffs, leading to price increases of up to 90% while wages rose by only 20%. The Confederation Démocratique du Travail, associated with the opposition Union Socialiste des Forces Populaires, called for strikes which led on 21 June to scenes of utmost violence in which it was reported that soldiers were stoned to death and police dogs set on fire. Heavy tanks confronted tens of thousands of rioters. Official figures were 66 dead and 110 seriously injured but the USFP put the number of dead at 637 with thousands wounded. The number of arrests was put by a French civil rights lawyer at 6,000 – 8,000, *some children of eight*. Their trial was clearly unfair, foreign observers were barred and some received sentences of up to 20 years' imprisonment. The King put most of the blame on the USFP whose leaders were amongst those jailed. Prices were hastily reduced and he promised a complete review of domestic problems and a major programme to create almost a million new jobs in the next five years.

CASABLANCA SUMMIT (1965)
The third Summit was held in Casablanca from 13–17 September 1965. It was attended by Kings Hassan, Faysal and Hussain, the Libyan Crown Prince, Amir Abd Allah al-Salim al-Sabah, Presidents Nasser, Helou, Boumédienne, Abd al-Salam Arif, Azhari, Amin al-Hafiz and Sallal. Tunisia, smarting under the vehemence with which some of them had attacked the Bourguiba Proposals earlier in the year, refused to attend – the first Summit boycott. After a welcoming speech in which King Hassan warned against disunity, Nasser was elected Chairman. The participants agreed to end radio campaigns and not to support subversive movements against each other. Ahmad Shuqayri complained that there was insufficient support for the Palestinians but it was agreed to form a Palestinian army. General Ali Ali Amer, the Egyptian General of the Unified Arab Command reported that the Arab armies would not be ready for war for at least three years. It would be necessary to station troops on each other's territory – Jordan and Lebanon were hesitant about this. Jordan warned that in the Jordan Waters Dispute the Israelis were already drawing off water from Lake Tiberias and this could not now be stopped: the Arabs should therefore press ahead with the diversion

of the Hasbani and the Banyas Rivers for the East Ghor Canal. The Summit expressed support for African Liberation Movements, mentioning those in Angola, Mozambique, South Africa and Rhodesia and also for those in Dhofar and South Arabia. It hoped that the Indo–Pakistani dispute over Kashmir could be settled peacefully. Aid should be given to those states of the Gulf which had not found oil. The leaders demanded the "liquidation of foreign bases which threaten the security of the Arab world and international peace". Opportunities were taken to end or at least defuse the quarrels between Faysal and Nasser over the Yemen War and between Hafiz and Nasser over the treatment of the latter's supporters in Syria.

CASABLANCA SUMMIT (1985)

King Hassan called for a Summit to discuss the attacks by the Syrian-sponsored Amal militia on Palestinian camps in Lebanon that had followed the Amman Accord by which King Hussain and Yassir Arafat had agreed to set up a joint Jordanian-Palestinian team to negotiate a peace settlement with Israel on the basis of "territory for peace". The Summit, assembling on 4 August 1985 was poorly attended, boycotted by the Steadfastness Front of Syria, Algeria, South Yemen and Libya and by Lebanon while King Fahd and Shaykh Jabir al-Sabah sent representatives. The Summit endorsed the Amman Accord, declaring that it did not conflict with the principles laid down in the Fez Summit of 1981–2. Hassan was asked to go to Washington to present the Arab viewpoint to Reagan who was about to meet Gorbachev. The Summit was seen as a qualified success for Hassan but a breach in the concept that Arab policy was reached through consensus rather than by a majority.

CASABLANCA SUMMIT (1989)

The fourteenth Arab Summit met in Casablanca in May 1989 to discuss the *Intifadah* and the situation in Lebanon which had no representative present as it was impossible to agree upon one. Eighteen out of 22 Heads of State attended in person. Before the Summit met President Mubarak arrived and insisted upon attending the first session without a formal invitation to rejoin the Arab League. He was effusively welcomed by Colonel Qadafi, his most vitriolic critic for over a decade and less enthusiastically by Hafiz al-Assad who would need his support to avoid condemnation of Syrian activities in Lebanon. The absence of such a condemnation led to the angry withdrawal of Saddam Hussain. The Summit officially endorsed the decisions of the Palestine National Council Algiers Meeting, its proclamation of a Palestinian state and its endorsement of Resolution 242 and Resolution 338 – thus accepting the legal existence of Israel. There was much praise for the courage of the militants in the West Bank and Gaza. The Summit accepted the Syrian refusal to withdraw its troops from Lebanon, despite the demands of General Aoun but decided to set up a committee of Kings Hassan and Fahd and President Chadli to "undertake contacts, and take all measures that seem necessary" to create a climate in which a new President could be elected with a reformed Parliament to create a government of National Unity. This led to the meeting of the Ta'if Parliament and the election as President of Rene Muawad.

CHAD, Libyan Intervention in (1970–87)

In 1960 the French gave independence to Chad but retained there 2,000 troops and considerable influence, giving support to the Christian south in its competition with the Muslim north where King Idris of Libya took an inherited interest. He gave some discreet support to the Muslim insurgents Frolinat who had in 1966 taken up arms against President François (later Ngarta) Tombalbaye and his government in Ndjamena. After Colonel Qadafi had seized power he made no attempt to disguise his support for the rebels and his interest in obtaining the Aozou Strip which was believed to be rich in uranium and other minerals. In August 1971 Tombalbaye broke off diplomatic relations, accusing Libya of backing an attempted coup which had aimed at making Chad "an Arab domain", embarrassing his French allies who had no wish to quarrel with Tripoli. Qadafi riposted by recognising Frolinat as the sole legitimate representative of the Chadian people. As a result of the mediation of Niger, diplomatic relations were resumed in April 1972 and later a deal was done by which Libya would cease supporting the insurgents and give money to the government in Ndjamena in return for its breaking off diplomatic relations with Israel and concessions over Aozou. In December 1972 Tombalbaye paid a state visit to Tripoli, receiving a loan and a promise to expel Frolinat members. Qadafi returned the visit in March 1974. In the meanwhile the Libyans had started to occupy Aozou. Guerrilla warfare continued in northern Chad with some successes for the rebels led by Hissein Habre and Goukouni Oueddai. In 1974 a French lady archaeologist was kidnapped by Frolinat who the following summer seized her husband who had gone to rescue her. After General Felix Malloum ousted Tombalbaye in April 1975 Libya was the first state to recognise the new regime. In June 1976 Libyan troops probing southwards from Aozou clashed with those of Habre who had by now broken with Oueddai who therefore became the ally of Qadafi who had previously imprisoned him. Chad denounced Libya at the UN and closed the frontier despite the avowals by Qadafi that he was its disinterested friend. In 1977 Qadafi secured the release of the French couple while pro-Libyan rebels increased their hold in northern Chad. In February 1978 with Libyan backing FROLINAT captured the important centre of Faya Largeau, destroying almost half the Chadian army (FAT) which had to be rescued by the French air force and the Foreign Legion in a major battle at Ati in Central Chad. At the end of March at a meeting in Sabha in the Fezzan Malloum agreed to a truce which appeared to regularise the Libyan gains in the north. In August 1978 Habre, now supported by the anti-Libyan governments of Egypt and Sudan, became Prime Minister in Ndjamena in uneasy alliance with Malloum. The following month he angrily accused Qadafi of planning to divide the country at the 14th parallel. After a series of upheavals in the early months of 1979, Malloum was chased out and a provisional government (GUNT) was established with Oueddai as President and Habre as Defence Minister. The new regime, predominantly

Muslim, was under threat from the Christian south and from rebels from FAT with whom Qadafi formed a brief alliance and attacked in the north but was repulsed. In April 1980 the French withdrew their forces from Chad and shortly afterwards GUNT came apart with a violent civil war; Oueddai called for Libyan assistance and signed a mutual defence agreement in June. In December 1980 4,000 Libyan troops with air support chased Habre's troops (FAN) into Cameroon. This led to a deterioration of relations with France which expressed "grave concern" and with most of the countries of West Africa, where anyway Qadafi had been meddling incorrigibly; they either expelled Libyan diplomats or broke relations altogether. An emergency summit of the OAU called for the withdrawal of all foreign troops from Chad. In January 1981 Qadafi declared that Libya and Chad were indissolubly united "by history and blood" and announced "full unity" under the rule of General People's Congresses and that Oueddai had requested the help of Libyan troops. Oueddai who was visiting Tripoli was reportedly threatened with execution if he demurred. Twelve countries bordering the Sahara met at Lome and denounced the merger which France saw as "a threat to the security of Africa" and suspended an oil agreement. Some of FAN rallied in the Sudan whereupon Qadafi attempted to overthrow the government of President Nimeiri and bombed villages across the frontier. FAN, with the overt assistance of the Egyptians, scored military successes whereupon Oueddai canvassed for support amongst Qadafi's African enemies: Qadafi thereupon gave his backing to Oueddai's rival within GUNT, Acyl Ahmat. French diplomacy arranged for the establishment of an OAU force in Chad whereupon Qadafi announced that his proposal had entained a "unity of peoples" not "a political unity as constitutionally understood" and withdrew his forces. In June 1982 Habre supported by Qadafi's foes, which meant much of the international community, overthrew GUNT and became President: Oueddai took refuge in Tripoli. Qadafi had long cherished the ambition of presiding over an OAU Summit but his insistence that Oueddai should represent Chad led to a boycott and in June 1983 at an OAU Summit in Addis Ababa he was isolated and virtually humiliated. Upon his return he sent a force of 1,500 Libyan troops and 3,000 mercenaries of his "Islamic Legion" to reinstall GUNT. There was heavy fighting, Faya Largeau changed hands three times and Libyan aircraft indiscriminately bombed Chadian villages. Zaire sent troops to help Habre, Egypt and Sudan gave other assistance, France and the US sent weapons and later the French sent troops and fighter aircraft while the Americans sent AWACS surveillance planes to the Sudan. Despite overwhelming evidence Qadafi consistently denied having any troops in Chad which was effectively partitioned at the "red line" and in a state of drought and famine. In January 1984 the Libyans shot down a French aircraft and in September Qadafi promised them "a worse lesson than Dien Bien Phu". It was therefore a surprise when a few days later he announced an agreement with them that both sides would withdraw all their forces from Chad. Even after a meeting between the Colonel and President Mitterand in Crete it was not clear that the Libyans had

kept their word. In March 1985 Habre accused the Libyans of building a military airfield in Wadi Doum but otherwise it was a year of uneasy stalemate with further splits developing in GUNT. In December Qadafi toured West Africa to propose a new African force for Chad without the French: he was received without enthusiasm. He also offered to negotiate with Habre but in February 1986 supported a GUNT offensive across the "red line". They were driven back and the French bombed the Libyans at Wadi Doum whereupon a Libyan aircraft raided the airfield at Ndjamena. GUNT split again and Qadafi backed Acheikh Ibn Omar against Oueddai whom he imprisoned and whose followers he attacked with napalm in Tibesti. Taking advantage of the confusion, Habre who had consolidated his hold in the south, launched an offensive across the "red line" which resulted in a total defeat of the Libyans at Fada where they were estimated to have lost 2,000 men. Attempts at mediation failed and a second offensive by the Chadians in March 1987 resulted in the Libyans flying in confusion, many perishing of thirst in the desert, and abandoning aircraft, tanks and great quantities of arms. In August the victorious Chadians overran Aozou but the French refused to extend the aircover which had played a considerable part in their earlier success and they were bombed out by the Libyans after just over a fortnight. Thereafter, apart from a Chadian raid on a military base 180 miles inside Libya, there was no further serious fighting and on 11 September OAU mediation brought a cease-fire. In June 1988 Qadafi recognised the government of Habre with which he established diplomatic relations in October. In December 1990 he hastened to congratulate Idris Deby who had overthrown Habre. At this time there were still 2,000 Libyan soldiers held in Chad as prisoners of war of whom some 600 were enlisted by the Americans as the nucleus of an anti-Qadafi army. Qadafi had conceived a plan for expanding Libya into a Saharan Islamic Empire under his rule and in pursuit of this chimera he had quarrelled with a score of countries, devastated a neighbour, incurred vast expense, been exposed as a compulsive but incompetent intriguer and been humiliated. In September 1988 Qadafi admitted that his involvement in Chad had been a mistake but a complaint to the World Court by President Deby in June 1993 that Libya was trying to destabilise his country showed that perhaps the dream persisted.

CHADLI, Benjadid (officially 1929 but almost certainly earlier)

Algerian President. The son of a small farmer of Tunisian origin, he was born in a village near Constantine and received little education. He became a stone mason and served in the French army. He was active in the Mouvement pour le Triomphe de la Liberté et de la Démocratie and volunteered for service upon the outbreak of the War of Algerian Independence which he ended on the staff of Colonel Boumédienne. Chadli was particularly trusted by him and was sent to take over command of the Eastern Front but the guerrillas in the field refused to accept him: they arrested him but he escaped. In 1964 Chadli was given command of the Military District of Oran, a post he retained until

1979. When Boumédienne seized power in 1965 he had made Chadli a member of the 26-man Revolutionary Council but he was generally unknown to the public until during the President's terminal illness he was put in charge of the army. In January 1979 Chadli became Secretary-General of the Front de Libération Nationale and so sole candidate for the Presidency. The other contenders, Boutaflika and Yahyawi, both of whom had lost touch with public opinion, might have engendered a split between the Government and the Party, and the army, seeing its prime duty as the maintenance of national unity, put forward Chadli, the oldest and most senior member of the Revolutionary Council. His nomination was confirmed by 94% vote in an election in which 94% voted. Chadli like Sadat, was seen as an innocuous stopgap, and he, like Sadat, while vowing to continue the policies of his predecessor, started to modify them, showing surprising self-confidence. Socialist jargon was abandoned, anti-Western rhetoric toned down and the vision of Algeria as the leader of the Third World quietly dropped. Political prisoners, including Ben Bella, were released and Boumédienne's closest associates lost much of their power: Merbah was moved from Intelligence, Boutaflika from the Foreign Ministry and military commanders and Ambassadors from their fiefs although, unlike Boumédienne, Chadli was never vindictive. In March he appointed Muhammad Abd al-Ghani Prime Minister, for the first time splitting the office from the Presidency although he retained the Defence Ministry. He enlarged the Politburo of the FLN so that more strands of opinion might be represented and he relaxed Boumédienne's rigid centralisation such as the monopoly of overseas trade, letting in more consumer goods and lifting travel restrictions. He tried to end the drabness which had characterised the Boumédienne regime and his own pragmatism and open enjoyment of luxury contrasted with the dogmatism, harshness and austerity of his predecessor. The Five-Year Plan gave priority to agriculture, irrigation, housing and education and the breakneck pace of industrialisation was slowed down. He was later to refer to much of the heavy industry as "scrap-iron" which operated at a third of its capacity. Chadli's changes were resented by FLN ideologues and apparatchiks, some of whom were pursued for corruption but his grip on the Party was strengthened at an Extraordinary Congress in June 1980 which empowered him to select the members of the Politburo. In February 1981, for the first time, he made a speech which did not mention his predecessor and later in the year most of his possible rivals were dropped from Party office. In January 1982 he called for a national debate on the role of women and for the first time one was appointed to the Cabinet. There had also been changes in foreign policy as Algeria gradually distanced itself from the Steadfastness Front, giving cautious approval to the Fahd Plan and he ended Boumédienne's jealous hostility to Morocco, holding a dramatic meeting with Hassan II in February 1983 although he did not cease giving aid to the Polisario guerrillas. In the name of "positive good neighbourliness" he settled old frontier disputes, arranged annual summits and signed a Treaty of Fraternity and Concord with Tunisia. He declared "construction of a Greater Arab Maghreb amongst our

foremost preoccupations". Chadli had already condemned Russian actions in Afghanistan and played a helpful part in securing the release of the American hostages held in their Tehran Embassy and he went on to buy military equipment from the West, welcome Vice-President Bush and in November 1983 pay the first state visit by an Algerian President to France; he was photographed walking hand-in-hand with Mitterand who said that they were "brothers". In Middle Eastern matters Chadli always worked for conciliation, trying to end the Iran–Iraq War and disputes such as those between Assad and Arafat and between the various factions in the Lebanese Civil War. In January 1984 Chadli, again the sole candidate, was re-elected for another five years with 95% of the votes. Now clearly leader in his own right, Chadli started to undo the "irreversible commitment to socialism" that he had inherited in the National Charter and he appointed as Prime Minister Abd al-Hamid Brahimi who was seen as a technocrat rather than a politician. Women were given greater rights, the number of provinces increased to give more local responsibility and military reforms made the army less of a political force with the revival of a General Staff and a new emphasis reducing its role in internal security. The great state corporations were decentralised and the banking system reformed to help agricultural development. During 1985 Chadli, to allow more scope to private enterprise, concentrated on reform of the Charter itself, although to reassure the old guard that socialism would not be destroyed, he had to term it "enrichment". A revised Charter was pushed through a special Congress of the FLN and approved by over 98% in a referendum in January 1986. By this time only 6 of the 48 Ministers had held office under Boumédienne. Liberalisation of the economy brought new problems at a time when the price of oil had fallen and one-third of export earnings, derived exclusively from hydro-carbons, was required to service the foreign debt, which the Government, for reasons of prestige and unwillingness to admit IMF intervention, refused to reschedule. The population had grown faster than the food supply, 70% of which had to come from abroad, but imports had to be restricted while the new élite was demanding luxuries from overseas. The restriction of imports led to a shortage of spare parts and factories closed contributing to unemployment of over 17%. The Berbers claimed more support for their culture and opposed a new drive for Arabisation while liberals demanded more human rights but most of the discontented turned towards Islamic militancy. In October and November 1986 there were riots in Algiers and Constantine in which portraits of Chadli were defaced: the Government made no attempt at conciliation, crushing them by force. During 1987 the effort to create a viable private sector continued, though hampered by a corrupt bureaucracy and the lack of an educated workforce. Farmers were given greater freedom and the great state corporations broken up into autonomous units. There was an unparalleled wave of strikes. In September 1988, in a sombre broadcast, Chadli spoke of "a deep and permanent crisis" in which interested groups prevented his reforms from being implemented while management refused to take responsibility for shoddy goods. A spontaneous explosion of anger set off the October Riots which so threatened the regime that Chadli, on 6 October, imposed a state of siege while the army, regardless of the cost in human lives, restored order. The President made no public statement for four days, leading to rumours that he was dead or deposed but then promised reforms to be approved by a referendum. The Prime Minister should be accountable to Parliament and not solely to the President. Chadli, distancing himself from the Party, dismissed his hated Party Deputy Muhammad Sharif Messaadia and conceded that independents should be allowed to contest elections, but still refused to allow the formation of other parties, probably fearing that one based on Islam would be uncontrollable. These reforms were approved by 92% in a referendum on 3 November. The tough and respected Merbah replaced Brahimi as Prime Minister. On 22 December Chadli was re-elected for a third term by 81%. In February 1989 Chadli introduced a new Constitution in which stress was laid on the rights of individuals and collectives rather than upon those of the Nation. The word "socialist" was dropped from the title of the state and the army relieved from its duty of building socialism. A powerful Constitutional Council was created and the right to strike guaranteed. The press was given more freedom and soon 128 newspapers were competing. A multi-party system was at last permitted and within a year 50 parties represented a wider range of opinion than in any Arab country except the Lebanon. Despite the other preoccupations of 1988 Chadli was active in foreign affairs, presiding over the successful Algiers Summit in June which united the Arabs in support of the Intifadah. Immediately afterwards he chaired a meeting of the North African Heads of State which laid the groundwork for the Arab Maghreb Unity Treaty of February 1989. After the Casablanca Summit in May Chadli was elected with Kings Hassan and Fahd to a committee to bring peace to the Lebanon – a sign of the respect in which he was held by Arab rulers. In September 1989 Chadli replaced Merbah, whom he regarded as insufficiently interested in reform by Mouloud Hamrouche who formed a government of liberal politicians to press forward to multi-party democracy while further dismantling socialism and encouraging foreign investment. Muslim militants formed the Front Islamique du Salut which in the local elections of June 1990 won an absolute majority of the votes. It was possible that the President had encouraged their success in order that they should have an opportunity to discredit themselves by dogmatism and inefficiency and their leader Abbas Madani, while calling for parliamentary elections to be brought forward from 1992, expressed willingness to serve as Chadli's Prime Minister. Chadli's tolerance of an Islamic party worried his partners in the Arab Maghreb Union and they differed further in their reactions to the invasion of Kuwait by Saddam Hussain: Chadli abstained in a vote over sending Arab troops to Saudi Arabia. The most active of Arab leaders in seeking a peaceful solution, in December 1990 he made an extensive tour of the Middle East in an effort to find a peaceful settlement, going also to Paris and Rome. At home rising prices and unemployment were blamed on the policies of Hamrouche and there was in March

1991 the first general strike since independence. At the beginning of April Chadli announced that parliamentary elections would be held on 27 June and a new electoral law, designed to hamper the FIS was introduced. On 23 May Madani called for an indefinite general strike and the resignation of the President. After days of bloodshed on 5 June Chadli proclaimed a state of siege, postponed the elections indefinitely and apparently reached an agreement with Madani who called off the general strike in return for the replacement of Hamrouche by Sid Ahmad Ghozali who formed a politically neutral government. Chadli announced his resignation from the FLN and refused to proscribe the FIS despite pressure from the army which, since handing over the Defence Ministry in July 1990 to General Nezzar he no longer directly controlled. For the next six months he appeared to take a back seat while his Prime Minister prepared for elections of which the first round was held on 26 December. They brought an enormous success for FIS which was bound to win an outright majority on the second round due on 16 January 1992. Chadli refused to cancel the election and expressed readiness to cohabit with a government formed by FIS but they demanded an immediate presidential election. Chadli failed to persuade either the unemployed to desert FIS and trust him to improve their lot or the army to accept the inevitable result of the poll. Under intense military pressure he resigned on 11 January "to safeguard the interests of the country" and retired from public life. Generally popular and respected during his period of office, although there were few public expressions of regret at his fall, he was later the target of much criticism centring upon his alleged tolerance: Brahimi said that $26,000 million ($2,000 million more than the entire national debt) was misappropriated by officials during what became known as the "Black Decade". In February 1993 one of his closest associates, General Mustafa Beloucif was sentenced to 15 years' imprisonment for the theft of $12 million. Chadli's wife, Halima Bourekba a former teacher, was believed to have interfered in politics in her own financial interests. When financial scandals were uncovered in Italy Chadli's name was mentioned. In retrospect he was seen as another Brezhnev, mediocre, living off the past and allowing problems to mount up but King Hassan referred to him as "a man without any wickedness". He was a practising Muslim, making several visits to Mecca and he enjoyed swimming, sailing, cards and cigars.

CHAMOUN, Dany (1934–90)

Lebanese politician. The son of President Camille Chamoun, he was educated at Loughborough Secondary School where he became a keen rugby player. After qualifying as an engineer at the American University of Beirut he went into business on the West Bank and, after it was overrun by the Israelis, in Beirut as an urban planner. He was a keen sportsman with a reputation as a playboy but after the start of the civil war was one of the leaders of his father's militia, "The Tigers". He attempted to save some of the women and children at Tall al-Zatar but took a full part in fighting the Syrians in East Beirut. "The Tigers" were effectively destroyed by their fellow Christians, the Lebanese

Forces led by Bashir Gemayel in June 1980 and Chamoun looked to the Israelis to defend Maronite interests, holding numerous meetings with political and military leaders. Dany succeeded his father in 1987 as leader of the National Liberal Party and in 1988, after repeated denials, put himself forward for the Presidency, urging reform of the National Pact to give Muslims equality with Christians. He rejected partition and called for the removal of all armed foreigners including Palestinian guerrillas. When no election could be held, common hostility to Lebanese Forces led him to support General Aoun although he always maintained a close personal friendship with Walid Jumblatt. After the overthrow of Aoun he rejected advice to leave East Beirut and a week later he and his wife and his sons aged 7 and 5 were murdered in cold blood by three hooded gunmen who broke into their flat: his ten-month-old daughter and the family dog were spared. Jumblatt and others ascribed the crime to Samir Geagea who vehemently denied it while others thought that Syria was responsible. The motive was probably to remove a rallying point for Aoun loyalists. Chamoun was a very handsome man, charming, sophisticated, witty and athletic.

CHATTI, Habib (1916–91)

Tunisian politician and diplomat. He was born in M'saken, a village in the Sahil and educated at Sadiqi College. He became a journalist, acting as a leading propagandist for the Neo-Destour and in 1952 and 1953 was imprisoned by the French. In 1954 when Tahar Ben Ammar formed a government to negotiate autonomy with Paris, Chatti was put in charge of persuading the French public of the justice of the Tunisian case. After independence he was Director of Information, wielding influence far above his nominal rank. In 1956 he was elected to the Constituent Assembly of which he became Deputy Chairman. He then began an Ambassadorial career which took him to Damascus, Beirut, Baghdad, Ankara, Tehran, London, Morocco and Algeria as well as to the UN. It fell to Chatti to make public denunciations of the interference of Nasser in the affairs of other Arab states. In 1971 he became a member of the Central Committee of the Parti Socialiste Destourien. In August 1972 he was put in charge of the Presidential Secretariat, a post of great power. In January 1974 when the Foreign Minister Muhammad Masmoudi was dismissed for persuading Bourguiba to sign the Jerbah Declaration, setting up a union with Libya under the name of the Arab–Islamic Republic, Chatti was appointed to succeed him to deal with the consequent diplomatic problems. Qadafi had been infuriated by the set-back and there was a series of problems including a major dispute over an oil platform which Chatti managed to defuse. He re-stablished good relations with Tunisia's traditional partners and wooed the Gulf States, securing aid from all of them. His diplomacy also brought assistance from France, West Germany, Russia, China and Hungary. He remained Foreign Minister until December 1977 when he resigned with several other Ministers after Hedi Nouira had insisted upon no compromise with the Trade Unions. In October 1979 he was unanimously elected Secretary-General of the Organisation of the Islamic Conference and was immediately confronted by the Russian take-over of Afghanistan to which he tried to organise an Islamic response working closely with Pakistan. The following summer Saddam Hussain invaded Iran and Chatti tried on numerous occasions with other Muslim leaders to put a stop to the Iran–Iraq War: with Sekou Toure of Guinea he visited both capitals in October 1982 in an unsuccessful mediation attempt. He also tried to secure the rights of minority Muslim groups such as those of the Philippines who had fallen foul of President Marcos. Chatti played an important part in the OIC meeting in Casablanca in January 1984 which marked the beginning of the end of the ostracism of Egypt which had followed Camp David. Chatti retired in April 1985 and was succeeded by the Pakistani Attorney-General, Sharifuddin Pirzada.

CHEQUERS MEETING (1956)

Even before the nationalisation of the Suez Canal in July 1956 the British and French Governments of Eden and Mollet were determined to overthrow Nasser. They used the time of the London Maritime Conference to move troops to Cyprus and prepare Operation Musketeer which involved a two-day air offensive to neutralise the Egyptian air force, followed by a landing by parachute and amphibious troops at Alexandria. After about seven days it was anticipated that there would be a break-out and an advance on Cairo. This represented the hardline view of the War Office, supported by the Chancellor Macmillan that it would be necessary to conquer Egypt but was dropped early in September in favour of a more limited operation to seize the Canal by landing at Port Said. There was the difficulty that Nasser had not behaved provocatively enough to justify an invasion and attempts to stir him into an action that could be presented as hostile had failed. The French had recently delivered 75 modern fighters to Israel, in breach of the Tripartite Declaration of 1950 and certainly envisaged collusion with Israel against Egypt. On 3 October the British Cabinet agreed to collusion with Israel although they were worried that this might destroy the Baghdad Pact and that the Israelis might attack Jordan which they were committed by the Anglo-Jordanian Treaty to defend. However they insisted that the Egyptian ban on the use of the Canal by Israeli ships be lifted – either to provide a *casus belli* or as a return for anticipated help. On 14 October the acting French Foreign Minister Albert Gazier and the Deputy Chief of Staff General Maurice Challé went with great secrecy to Chequers to propose that Israel be invited to overrun Sinai and that the British and French should order "both sides" to withdraw forces from the Canal in order to enable allied troops to occupy it under pretext of "extinguishing a dangerous fire" and saving it from damage. According to Anthony Nutting, Eden was surprised by the idea but this is difficult to believe. Two days later he and the Foreign Secretary Selwyn Lloyd went to Paris to agree to planning with the Israelis. French determination to act was reinforced by the interception, the same day, of an Egyptian ship running arms to the Algerian rebels. The Franco-Israeli-British plot was formalised in the Sèvres Accord of 22 October.

CHURCHILL WHITE PAPER (1922)

Before the League of Nations ratified the assignment by the San Remo Conference of the Mandate for Palestine to Great Britain the Colonial Secretary, Winston Churchill issued in June 1922 a White Paper setting out the intentions of the Government. Reaffirming the Balfour Declaration it stated that the Jewish people would "be in Palestine as of right and not on sufferance but HMG have no such aim as that Palestine should become as Jewish as England is English". The Arab population, language and culture would not disappear or be subordinated and the whole population would be regarded as Palestinian. There was no statement as to whether it would attain self-government as a dual-national state but a Legislative Council was promised. Jewish immigration would be limited by the capacity of the country to absorb new arrivals. The Zionist Executive was not entitled to share in the Government. Any community feeling aggrieved might appeal to the League of Nations. At the same time Trans-Jordan became a separate Amirate under Sharif Abd Allah. The Zionists accepted the White Paper, the Arab leaders rejected it, fearing that they would be swamped in a Legislative Council and the lack of precision in the restriction of immigration.

CLEOPATRA BOYCOTT (1960)

On 13 April 1960 the 8,193 ton Egyptian cargo vessel *Cleopatra* was prevented from unloading its cargo in New York by picketing from the Seafarers' International Union which complained of the threat to American sailors' jobs posed by the Arab boycott of Israel and of alleged mistreatment of its members in Arab ports. This embarrassed the American Government and the State Department stated that while it did not condone the boycott it deplored attempts by a private group to coerce a foreign government into changing its policies. American courts upheld the seamen's right to picket and a retaliatory boycott began of American shipping by harbour workers in Egypt, Syria, Libya and Lebanon. Nasser stated that the US was dominated by "Zionist–Jewish–Israeli imperialism" and was "slack" in dealing with the incident. On 6 May, after negotiations at the State Department, Union representatives agreed to call off the picketing in return for a Government declaration of support for freedom of the seas and transit of the Suez Canal for all nations, investigation of the seamen's grievances and to seek a solution of the Arab–Israeli dispute on "every suitable occasion". Unloading of the *Cleopatra* began on 9 May and the boycott of American ships was lifted on the same day.

COALITION OF ARAB DEMOCRATIC POPULAR FORCES

After the condemnation by the majority of Arab states of the Iraqi invasion of Kuwait at the Cairo Summit of August 1990 a meeting was held in Amman in September to support Saddam Hussain. Organised by the "Jordanian Arab National Democratic Alliance", it was attended by about 120 people including George Habash and Nayif Hawatma who were making their first visit to the country since Black September of 1970. There were also anti-Western religious figures such as Hassan Turabi. The conference was opened by the Jordanian

Speaker on behalf of King Hussain who personally endorsed its proceedings. It denounced the West for meddling in Arab affairs, condemned the "US-led military campaign against Iraq as an act of aggression against the Arab nation" and supported the struggle of the Palestinians.

COMITÉ RÉVOLUTIONNAIRE D'UNITÉ ET D'ACTION (Algeria)

By the beginning of 1954 the nationalist party, the Mouvement pour le Triomphe et de la Liberte et de la Démocratie, was badly split and appeared incapable of providing positive leadership in a struggle for Algerian independence. Muhammad Boudiaf appears to have been the man who called together in Switzerland meetings of known militants from the various factions to form a unified organisation to start a revolutionary war. These, now known as the Neuf Historiques, constituted themselves the Comité Révolutionnaire d'Unité et d'Action but as three of them, Ahmad Ben Bella, Hocine Ait Ahmad and Muhammad Khidr were in exile they could not take part in the detailed planning. This was done in Algiers by a Committee of Twenty-Two which divided the country into six *wilayas* and assigned to their commanders their tasks for the All Saints' Day Uprising. The exiles had, however, an important role in obtaining money and arms from independent Arab countries, and, owing to their access to foreign media, were able to present themselves as the real leaders of the War of Algerian Independence. This was resented by those doing the actual fighting inside the country who, under the leadership of Ramdan Abane who at the Soummam Valley Conference in August 1956 decided to replace the CRUA by an elected Assembly, the Conseil National de la Révolution Algérienne and a three-man executive committee.

COMMITTEE FOR THE LIQUIDATION OF FEUDALISM (Egypt)

In May 1966 an official of the Arab Socialist Union who was engaged in implementing land reform at Kamshish in Upper Egypt was murdered. The authorities blamed a local landowning family that they described as "feudalists" and seized upon the crime to distract public attention from other problems such as an economic crisis, the recent plot by the Muslim Brothers, and the nostalgia shown for the days of the Wafd at the funeral of Nahhas Pasha. A Committee was set up under the second man in Egypt, Field Marshal Abd al-Hakim Amer which included the former Prime Minister Ali Sabri, the Head of Intelligence Salah Nasr, the War Minister Shams Badran, and the Interior Minister Sharawi Jumaa. Its procedures were completely arbitrary and Sadat later accused it of "practising the worst types of terror, repression and humiliation. Its members played havoc with life in Egypt". It was used largely to settle old scores. Several hundred alleged feudalists lost their land or their employment or were arrested and nearly 60,000 *feddans* were seized. Some of the decisions caused such outrage that they had immediately to be rescinded and the whole episode showed the worst type of police state. The Committee did not survive the fall of Amer and many of its decisions were reversed when Egypt's greatest agricultural expert Sayyid Marai returned to the Government after the June War.

CONSEIL NATIONAL DE LA RÉVOLUTION ALGÉRIENNE

The Conseil National de la Révolution Algérienne was set up at the Soummam Valley Conference in August 1956 as the sovereign body of a future independent nation. At the same time a 5-man Comité de Coordination et de'Exécution was chosen exclusively from leaders within the country. The 34 members of the CNRA, on the other hand, included the eight surviving members of the Neuf Historiques although most were in exile. It also included men such as Farhat Abbas who were generally regarded as moderates. Later the CNRA was expanded to over 70 members not all of whom can be identified with certainty. The second session of the CNRA was held in Cairo in August and September '57 after it had become clear that the Algiers Battle had been lost. A new CCE, larger but dominated by the military was elected and the primacy of the "internals" over the "externals", established at Soummam was reversed. The CNRA lost its theoretical supremacy with the creation, in September 1958, of the Gouvernement Provisoire de la République Algérienne. Another competitor for power emerged during 1959 – the external army, the Armée de Libération Nationale, effectively controlled by its Chief of Staff Colonel Boumédienne. The third session of the CNRA took place in Tripoli, lasting 33 days, in December 1959 and January 1960. It reformed the GPRA which relinquished its military powers to the General Staff of the ALN. It also endorsed the Boumédienne strategy of ending costly assaults on the Morice Line in favour of building up the ALN on the friendly territories of Tunisia and Morocco. In a provisional constitution the CNRA declared the FLN the sole party, pursuing independence by revolution. The fourth session of the CNRA took place in Tripoli in August 1961 and, following the failure of the Melun Talks, discussed the renewal of peace negotiations. It replaced Farhat Abbas as President of the GPRA with Ben Khedda who, it was felt, would be more able to reach agreement with General de Gaulle. The fifth CNRA meeting was held, also in Tripoli, in February 1962. The first stages of a peace agreement had already been worked out and the Council gave its approval for its conclusion in talks at Evian. The final meeting of the CNRA was held in Tripoli in June 1962 before the referendum which was to ratify independence. It had to face two tasks, to provide an ideology for the new state and to decide upon its future leadership. The Tripoli Charter, providing a mixture of Islam and socialism dealt with the first problem but the second was only resolved by military force. After independence an elected National Assembly replaced the CNRA.

CONSTANTINE PLAN (1958)

On 28 September 1958 an overwhelming majority, both in Metropolitan France and Algeria amongst Muslim voters, endorsed the new Constitution put forward by General de Gaulle who had been brought to power in May. On 5 October in Constantine he offered a "profound transformation" to Algeria "so vital and so courageous, but so difficult and so suffering". An ambitious Five-Year Plan would turn the country into a modern industrialised nation. Nearly 500,000 new jobs would be created at wages comparable to those in France. Over 600,000 acres of new land would go to Muslim farmers who would be given help in modernisation. Housing for a million people would be provided. Administrative posts would be made available to Muslims at a ratio of one to ten with those of the Mother Country. There would be a great improvement in educational opportunities for Muslim children. Financial experts calculated that these measures would need the investment of $4,500 million. In the forthcoming elections, Algeria would vote under the same conditions as France but at least two-thirds of her representatives would have to be Muslims. He concluded his speech with a direct appeal to the Front de Libération Nationale to allow "a new blossoming of hope all over the land". A fortnight later de Gaulle again offered a *paix des braves*. His left-wing opponents saw the Plan as neo-colonialism and the FLN demanded not a cease-fire but political negotiations: the colons saw it as conceding too much to rebellious natives.

CORAL SEA INCIDENT (1971)

On 11 June 1971 the tanker *Coral Sea* carrying a cargo of Iranian oil bound for Israel came under rocket fire as it passed through the Straits of Bab al-Mandab. There were no casualties and the ship suffered only minor damage. According to the crew the attack had been carried out by men in a speedboat lowered from a fishing craft. Later the Popular Front for the Liberation of Palestine claimed credit and said that four of its guerrillas were being held in North Yemen. They stated that they had operated from Aqaba but it is more likely that they came from Perim. The Israelis for whom keeping the Red Sea open was vital for their economy threatened severe measures if there were a repetition and the Egyptians and Saudis were also alarmed as there had been a tacit understanding that tankers on both sides should be free from attack. Presumably Arab pressure was put on the guerrillas and there was no repetition of the incident.

CURIEL, Henri (1915–1978)

Egyptian communist. His father was a very rich Jewish banker and he first showed signs of social concern by distributing medicines to workers on the family estates. He then concluded that palliatives were not enough and that revolutionary change was necessary. Curiel started a left-wing bookshop in Cairo which attracted the young and, after his first arrest in 1941, was in contact with the forerunners of the KGB. In about 1943 he started organising the Egyptian Movement for National Liberation, running Party schools on his estate and also going around factories, showing a great gift for convincing the workers that he really cared about their problems. Curiel took a special interest in Sudan, recruiting the future Communist leader Abd al-Khaliq Mahjoub and financing a newspaper in Omdurman. He was twice arrested in 1946 and in 1948–49 he was interned for opposition to the Palestine War. In 1951 he was expelled by King Farouq and went to France where he spent most of the rest of his life, never, to his sorrow, seeing Egypt again. After the July Revolution, he was full of enthusiasm for it but was disillusioned after the Kafr al-Dawar Riot. He claimed to be an orthodox Marxist-Leninist but was too independent-minded always to follow the Russian line. He saw that Egypt was more concerned with national liberation than with pure socialism so he often supported Nasser whereas the Egyptian Communist Party under Sabri Abd Allah attacked him. It is possible that, through French communist contacts, he obtained some of the plans for the Suez War, which he forwarded to Nasser. Unlike most Parisian intellectuals he saw that the Algerian struggle was nationalist rather than communist but he helped it by smuggling money out to Switzerland. He was imprisoned for these activities from October 1960 until June 1962, being released after the signature of the Evian Accord. Later he was financed by Ben Bella as a sort of "salesman of world revolution". Curiel was the leader of *Aide et Solidarité* which provided finance for clandestine movements, even non-communist ones, in many countries. He had strong connections with Cuba and Angola. He organised secret meetings of moderate Israelis and Palestinians. He was accused in the French press of being an agent of the Kremlin and a supporter of terrorists such as the Japanese Red Army. He was shot dead outside his house in the Latin Quarter by two men who were never found but were probably members of the Organisation de l'Armée Secrète. Even his opponents spoke of his generosity and sincerity and it was said that if he had been an Arabic-speaking Muslim the history of the Middle East might have taken a different form.

CZECHOSLOVAK ARMS DEAL (1955)

The Gaza Raid of February 1955 showed the military inferiority of the Egyptian armed forces to those of Israel and Nasser approached Egypt's traditional weapon suppliers in the West for up-to-date equipment. He was refused, the British saying that he would have to stop opposing the Baghdad Pact and therefore turned to the Eastern Bloc. On 27 September 1955 he stated that "feeling insecure" since the Gaza Raid he had made "repeated requests" to the West but had only been offered some "on conditions incompatible with the aims of the Egyptian Revolution". Israeli sources later claimed that he received from the Communist states 100 Stalin heavy tanks, 200 Czech T-34 tanks, 100 artillery pieces, 150 out of a promised 200 MiG-15 fighters, 45 out of 60 promised Ilyushin-28 jet bombers, 2 destroyers and 19 Motor Torpedo Boats. American officials estimated the value of the arms, some of them outdated, at between $90 million and $200 million to be paid with cotton and rice over a long period. This military aid was followed by help in building civilian industries. Arab nationalists were greatly heartened to find that there was an alternative to dependence on the West and the Czech Arms Deal was the start of Nasser's rise to heroic status, Salah Salam comparing him to Christ. Nasser denied that he was opening the door to Communism but in fact he gave the Russians their first real opportunity since the creation of Israel to get a foothold in the Arab World. He did not, however, bring the Cold War into the area as it was already there with Western attempts to recruit Arab states but he did convince Western leaders, in particular Eden, that he was a menace both to peace and to British interests.

DABBAS, Charles (1885–1935)

Lebanese President. Although a Greek Orthodox, he studied Law at the Jesuit University of Beirut where he was an active member of the nationalist Beirut Reform Society. He welcomed the Young Turk Revolution and felt that Lebanon should sacrifice some of its special privileges in the interests of reforming the Empire. Dabbas continued his law studies at Montpellier and the Sorbonne and married a Frenchwoman. Opposing the Turkification policy of the CUP, he was one of the organisers of the First Arab Congress in Paris in June 1913, serving as its Secretary so he remained in France during the war being condemned to death *in absentia* by the Turks. Returning to Lebanon he was active as a lawyer, newspaper editor and adviser to the French authorities. When the French proclaimed the country a Republic in May 1926 they appointed Dabbas as President, confident of his loyalty and anxious to show that it was not their intention that the state should be totally dominated by their Maronite allies. One of his first actions was to declare that not an inch of Lebanese territory would be surrendered, a statement that caused the Syrian Prime Minister, the *Damad* Ahmad Nami to offer his resignation and to a demonstration against Dabbas in the Grand Mosque in Beirut. In general, however, he had excellent relations with the Sunnis, particularly with the Assembly Speaker Muhammad al-Jisr as he was determined to show that the President should be above sectarian squabbles. He worked very closely with the High Commissioner Henri Ponsot and in October 1927 they introduced a new Constitution which abolished the Upper Chamber. Dabbas proved an able and popular President and was re-elected in March 1929. In May 1932, fearing violence in the forthcoming Presidential elections Ponsot suspended the Constitution and appointed Dabbas Head of State with full executive and legislative powers – subject to complete French control. There was some feeling that Dabbas should have resigned rather than accept the scrapping of the Constitution that he had sworn to defend but he acted resolutely to deal with economic difficulties, even reducing his own salary by a third, and introduced a number of administrative reforms. Despite the practical achievements of the non-constitutional regime there was increasing opposition to it and the new High Commissioner, Count Damien de Martel decided to make a fresh start. Dabbas resigned in January 1934 but became President of the new Chamber. He resigned before the end of the year and retired to France where he died some months later.

DAFALLAH, Jazuli (1935–)

Sudanese Prime Minister. He was born in a village near Wad Madani and qualified as a gastroenterologist in London. He became Chairman of the Doctors' Union and, like many of the professional classes, opposed the regime of President Nimeiri by whom he was imprisoned. When the National Alliance for National Salvation, consisting of the opponents of Nimeiri came into existence, he was elected its chairman. In April 1985 after the overthrow of Nimeiri Dafallah was invited by General Siwar al-Dhahab, the Chairman of the Transitional Military Council, to become Prime Minister. He formed a government of technocrats which included two senior officers, three Southerners, one as Deputy PM, and two Muslim Brothers. The formal task of the Government was to prepare for multi-party elections to take place in April 1986. Overtures were made to the Southern leader John Garang, whom Dafallah praised as the first to oppose Nimeiri, and the Government declared a unilateral cease-fire but Dafallah and Siwar al-Dhahab, both devout Muslims were unwilling to withdraw the September Laws in which Nimeiri had imposed the *Shariah* although the floggings and mutilations were stopped. There were constant rumours of plots, a minor mutiny in September was mishandled and it was unclear whether the Cabinet or the TMC which seemed to look upon it merely as administrators was actually running the country. The Cabinet itself appeared unable to take any positive measures and by September seemed near collapse. The economic situation inherited from the previous regime was disastrous and while financial ministers and experts favoured accepting the advice of the IMF, Dafallah and other ministers disagreed. In February 1986 the IMF refused further credits. Such was the economic chaos that there was a strike of Sudanese diplomats. In October an interim constitution appeared mainly designed to postpone difficult choices until after the elections. In foreign affairs there was a reconciliation with Libya which Dafallah visited in March 1986 leading to the cooling of previously intimate relations with Egypt and the joint organisations set up under the Integration Charter were formally abolished. Relations deteriorated with the USA which withdrew its Ambassador but improved with Iran. Meaningful negotiations with the Sudan People's Liberation Movement kept being postponed although in March 1986 there was a meeting at the Koka Dam in Ethiopia. The following month elections took place and Dafallah handed over office to the leader of the single largest party, Sadiq al-Mahdi.

DAMASCUS Bombardment of (1945)

In May 1945 when it appeared that the French were not taking active steps to implement the granting of independence to Syria promised in June 1941 and confirmed in the De Gaulle–Lyttelton Agreement there were riots in several cities that got completely out-of-hand. Many French officials had no doubt that these had been stirred up by the British. There was street fighting in Hama and Homs and both cities were shelled by the French. On the evening of 29 May the French commander in Damascus lost his head and ordered heavy shelling and bombing which lasted until noon the next day. British Staff officers tried to arrange a cease-fire but sporadic shelling, looting and mob violence continued until on the morning of 1 June the senior British officer gave the French commander a written order to withdraw all his troops and confine them to barracks: it was made clear that British troops would intervene in the event of non-compliance. British military control was established until the Syrian Government could resume administration. According to Winston Churchill 400 civilians and 80 gendarmes were killed. Much of the modern quarter including the Parliament building was destroyed.

DAMASCUS, Bombardments of (1925, 1926)

On 18 October 1925 at a time when the Druze Revolt was spreading, some of the insurgents penetrated into Damascus and killed some Circassian and Moroccan troops of the French army who had been responsible for atrocities. As they advanced many of the citizens, including policemen welcomed them and erected barricades to hamper the deployment of French tanks. At sunset, without warning the European residents, the French withdrew their troops and started an indiscriminate bombardment of the city which, also employing aircraft, they resumed the following morning. The notables persuaded General Gemelin to desist which he did, imposing a fine of 100,000 Turkish pounds in gold and 3,000 rifles and making them responsible for preventing the entry of further rebel bands. The bombardment, presumably caused by panic, was admitted by the French to have caused 150 civilian casualties although Municipality calculated that 1,416 people had been killed including 336 women and children. The Amir Said al-Jazairi, following the example of his grandfather Abd al-Qadr in the Damascus Massacre took vigorous action to save Christians from angry crowds. The British Consul protested angrily at the bombardment which also caused great indignation throughout the Muslim world and led to the recall of the High Commissioner, General Sarrail. On 7 May 1926, alleging that the people of the Maydan Quarter were sheltering rebels, the French carried out a second heavy bombardment. Estimates of the number killed varied from 200 to 1,000, mostly women and children, with about 1,600 houses destroyed, some by the shelling and some by deliberate incendiarism; the fire brigade was forbidden to enter the area for three days and there was widespread looting by French and African troops. Later the orchards that distinguish the *Ghutah* were systematically destroyed on the pretext that they afforded shelter to rebels.

DAMASCUS DECLARATION (1991)

After the defeat of Iraq in Operation Desert Storm the Foreign Ministers of the Arab states, Egypt, Syria and the six members of the Gulf Co-operation Council, that had formed part of the coalition met in Damascus. Morocco where the war had been extremely unpopular at home did not attend. On 6 March they published a 7-point Declaration that called for for co-operation in a new Arab order, non-interference, equality of sovereignty, commitment to solving disputes by peaceful means etc. and declared the non-permissibility of seizing land by force, denouncing Iraq for destroying hopes of united Arab action. They would seek to make the Middle East a nuclear-free area, encourage development through private enterprise, conduct joint scientific research, cultural exchanges etc. These activities would be carried on through regular ministerial meetings. Any Arab state had the right to invite Egypt and Syria to station troops on its territory. This last point was understood to have been given practical form in secret clauses in which Egypt would commit 100,000 men and Syria 50,000 to provide security in the Gulf and in return would receive aid amounting to $15,000 million. Western navies should be invited to sit over the horizon. By May it was clear that this was not going to work. The Kuwaitis showed that they preferred to have American rather than Egyptian soldiers on their territory and played down the part played by Egypt and Syria during the war. They appeared unwilling to pay for Egyptian troops to remain and did not give Egypt its fair share of rebuilding contracts. The Egyptians became dubious about an agreement which seemed to regard their men as cannon-fodder and in May President Mubarak announced that he was recalling his 36,000 troops but that this was not the end of the Damascus Declaration as they could return if a subsequent agreement were reached. In July a meeting of Foreign Ministers in Kuwait brought no results as the Gulf States were unwilling to pay for a large permanent force but wanted a commitment to send troops if needed. The Egyptians were disturbed by proposals to include Iran. The last Egyptian troops left in September. Before that a 10-year agreement was signed between Kuwait and Washington for the stationing of American forces although the British refused to set up a permanent base. In September 1991 Kuwait agreed to stockpile American arms and later established defence links with Russia and China. At the GCC Summit in Kuwait in December 1991 it became clear that the the Gulf leaders preferred to build up their own deterrent force, strengthening Peninsula Shield to 100,000 and doubling air forces without relying on other Arabs. An expected meeting of the signatories in Qatar in March 1992 did not take place. In April President Assad made one of his rare excursions from Damascus, visiting the Gulf trying to get an arrangement that did not leave its defence dependent on the Americans but Mubarak was more inclined to abandon the project. Suggestions of a Summit and Ministerial meetings did not materialise although in September 1992, with the revived Iranian threat to Abu Musa, the Foreign Ministers met in Doha and there was a meeting of Finance Ministers to discuss proposals for economic co-operation. In April 1993 Egypt and Saudi Arabia signed a defence agreement.

DAMASCUS MASSACRE (1860)

The Muslim citizens of Damascus felt their position threatened by what they saw as the increasing arrogance of the previously humble Christians who had benefited from the Tanzimat. There was also a new factor of interference from the European Consuls who had been permitted to reside in the city. In July 1860 a scuffle flared up into a general massacre of Christians and 5,500 were killed in a day; many more were saved by the intervention of the Amir Abd al-Qadr who took personal risks to protect them. The Jews were not harmed. The Ottoman Government, anxious to settle the matter before the European powers could intervene, sent the Foreign Minister Fuad Pasha to mete out punishment. The Pasha was hanged without trial and 100 soldiers and 50 civilians were also executed and the city was fined £200,000. Nevertheless, Napoleon III, anxious for prestige, used the Massacre as a pretext for sending troops to the Levant.

DAMASCUS PROTOCOL (1915)

The outbreak of the First World War gave Arab nationalists the possibility of escaping from the rule of the Young Turks in Istanbul. They realised that they could only do this with the help of the British but they had no wish to exchange Turkish for British domination. Members of the two secret societies, the Ahd and the Fatat met in Damascus in the spring of 1915 and drew up the terms on which they would rise in support of the British. These were firstly that the British would recognise the independence of the Arab countries bounded to the North by a line Mersin–Adana–Urfa–Amadia to the Persian frontier, to the East from the Persian frontier down to the Gulf, to the South by the Indian Ocean with the exclusion of Aden (whose status would be maintained) and to the West by the Red Sea and the Mediterranean back to Mersin. Secondly all exceptional privileges granted to foreigners under Capitulations should be abolished. Thirdly the conclusion of a defensive alliance between Great Britain and the future independent Arab state. Fourthly the grant of economic preference to Great Britain. These terms were given to the Amir Faysal who had been in touch with the groups and he agreed to put them to his father, Sharif Hussain of Mecca, whereupon the leading members of the groups swore to recognise the Sharif as the spokesman of the Arabs. These terms later formed the basis of his demands put in the Hussain–McMahon Correspondence and were confirmed when a member of the Ahd, Muhammad Sharif al-Faruqi, deserted to the British at Gallipoli.

al-DAMLUJI, Abd Allah (c. 1890–)

Saudi and Iraqi Minister. He was born in Mosul and claimed to have studied medicine in Constantinople and Paris. He was with the Turkish army in the Hasa Province when it was overrun by Ibn Saud into whose service he passed. With his experience of the outside world, which his master lacked, he became the leading expert on foreign affairs. In 1921 he undertook a mission to Baghdad for Ibn Saud and in 1922 signed the Uqayr Protocol as his representative. He accompanied the Amir Faysal to London in 1926 and began the negotiations which brought about the Jiddah Treaty. In Arabia his European outlook and his addiction to drink, cards and reputedly other vices, made him unpopular and he lost influence to Fuad Hamza and Yusuf Yassin and in 1928 he went to Haifa to attend a conference on the Hijaz Railway and did not return. He then became Iraqi Consul-General in Cairo and in 1930 Foreign Minister. He held that office again in 1934 and at other times was Director-General of Health and Court Chamberlain, exercising, British officials believed, a sinister influence over King Ghazi. He had, however, made an enemy of Nuri al-Said who in December 1939 moved him to an obscure post in the Ministry of Health. Both in Arabia and Iraq his financial integrity was more than suspect.

DAOUD, Muhammad (c. 1917–72)

Jordanian Prime Minister. A Palestinian, he served in the Palestine Police until the end of the Mandate when he joined the Arab Legion. He was appointed to the Jordanian side of the Mixed Armistice Commission with Israel of which he became Head with the rank of Brigadier. At the height of the Black September Crisis of 1970 King Hussain asked him to form a military government. On September 16 Daoud announced a Cabinet of twelve officers with himself also holding the Foreign and Justice Ministries. Practical power, however, was in the hands of the Commander-in-Chief General Habis al-Majali. Heavy fighting continued and there was the possibility of a Syrian invasion. The Arab League arranged a special summit for which Daoud went to Cairo. Upon his arrival on 24 September he resigned, leaving a letter for the King saying that only a civilian government could negotiate a settlement with the Palestinians. Daoud was subsequently reported to be living in Libya as Egypt refused him political asylum. He had proved himself a competent police officer during his service with the Commission but the post of Prime Minister in a crisis was too much for him.

al-DAOUQ, Ahmad (1892–)

Lebanese Prime Minister. A member of one of the leading Sunni families of Beirut, he was educated at the Christian Brothers College there then trained as an engineer in France. During the war he worked in the Egyptian sugar refining industry and after that was for a time a technical adviser to King Hussain of the Hijaz. Daouq returned to Beirut after the French had taken control and combined engineering with finance and insurance. He was a Municipal Councillor after 1927. In April 1941 when a non-political government was established under Alfred Naqqash Daouq was made Minister of Public Works and Posts. Later in the year when the formal independence of the Lebanon was proclaimed, Naqqash on French advice made Daouq Prime Minister. He resigned after six months, despairing of solving a food crisis, and started a new career as a diplomat holding posts such as Ambassador to France and Spain and Representative at the United Nations. In May 1960 he was appointed Prime Minister to supervise elections, holding office until the beginning of August. He returned to diplomacy which he combined with business, founding a bank, a shipping company, a textile company, and administering real estate and a radio station. He was described as a moderate nationalist, courteous, diplomatic and highly cultured but not a forceful character.

al-DAWAH (Iraq)

Literally "the Islamic Call" was a Shiah group formed in the Holy City of Najaf in the late 1960s. It was inspired by the teachings of Sayyid Muhammad Baqir al-Sadr (born 1930), a member of one of the leading families of *ulema* who wrote works on philosophy and economics stressing that all power and all property belong to God and that this forbids political or economic domination over anyone. The presence in Najaf of the exiled Ayatollah Khomeini after 1964 also inspired some of the underprivileged Shiah to look for an Islamic solution for their problems. The Iraq Communist Party was also competing for their allegiance but a leading Iraqi Ayatollah Muhsin al-Hakim (died 1970) issued a *Fatwa* forbidding them to join it. The Dawah was a secret organisation with a clandestine newspaper but the suspicions of the Government had clearly been aroused for in December 1974 five *ulema* were executed, the first, it was said of several hundred. In February 1977 the depth of Shiah feeling was shown in the Karbala Riots during the Shiah commemoration of *Ashura* in which they claimed hundreds had been killed after which the Baath made conciliatory gestures. The Revolution in Iran in February 1979 gave the Shiah new confidence and led to open attacks on the Government. Sadr who had in June 1979 declared Baathist membership incompatible with Islam, was arrested and hanged with his sister in April 1980 after a Shiah had tried to assassinate the Deputy Prime Minister, Tariq Aziz. Early in 1980, preparing to launch the Iran–Iraq War, Saddam Hussain expelled a number of Shiah estimated at between 15,000 and 40,000 of Persian origin although many had been resident in Iraq for generations. In April 1980 Saddam decreed that any Dawah member who did not surrender within a month could be executed. The Dawah had always had to compete with another Shiah movement, the Mujahidin which recruited Western-educated but religious-minded intellectuals and received support from the Shah, also started to split after 1980 into a moderate reformist and a radical wing. Five Shiah were taken into the Cabinet in June 1982 but in August the terrorist wing exploded a car bomb in Baghdad killing 30 people while Ayatollah al-Hakim's sons Muhammad Bashir and Mahdi organised exiles in Tehran and Europe: the Government rounded up about 80 of the family, executing six. The Grand Ayatollah Abu al-Qassim Khoei, opposed to any involvement in politics, refused to denounce the Government but the Dawah formed alliances with the communists and with Kurdish groups opposed to the Baath. Despite other car bombs terrorists found it difficult to operate in Iraq, where they stated that 500 cadre and sympathisers had been killed between 1974 and 1980, so they turned their attention to Kuwait, bombing the French and American Embassies there in December 1983 after which 25 members were arrested and six condemned to death. To secure the release of 16 of them (believed to be 2 Lebanese, 6 Iraqis and 8 Kuwaitis of Iranian origins) their colleagues hijacked an aircraft to Tehran in December 1984 and attempted to assassinate the Amir Shaykh Jabir al-Ahmad al-Sabah

in May 1985. Dawah gunmen also operated in Lebanon, closely linked with Hizbullah and were believed to be holding Western hostages there. They claimed to have 50,000 armed men. In December 1986 they were believed to have been involved in the hijacking of an Iraqi aircraft over Saudi Arabia in which 62 people were killed: several senior army and intelligence officers suspected of complicity were executed. In January 1988 Mahdi al-Hakim was murdered in Khartoum, presumably by Iraqi government agents. During 1989 and 1990 Dawah members claimed to have attempted to kill Saddam in Fao and also King Hussain and President Mubarak. During the confusion that followed the Iraqi invasion of Kuwait in August 1990 the prisoners there appear to have escaped. During Operation Desert Shield Dawah leaders put out pamphlets condemning Western intervention. In March 1991 they claimed responsibility for the Shiah Uprising but fear of their extremism was one of the factors which discouraged Western help. Later they appealed for world help to topple Saddam and criticised the Kurds for negotiating with him. Dawah members linked with other Shiah groups in Tehran to form the Supreme Council of the Islamic Revolution in Iraq which participated in the meeting of the Iraqi National Congress in Salahuddin in September 1992.

DAWSON'S FIELD

At the end of July 1970 Egypt and Jordan both announced their acceptance of the Rogers' Plan (II) which involved a cease-fire with Israel. The Palestinian guerrillas felt abandoned by their friends and resolved to show their determination to continue to fight. Within a few hours on 6 September the Popular Front for the Liberation of Palestine hijacked three aircraft and failed to hijack a fourth – an El Al Boeing 707 en route from Amsterdam to New York. In the latter case one hijacker was killed and the other Leila Khalid detained at Heathrow. A Pan Am 747 with 170 passengers and crew flying from Amsterdam to New York was taken to Beirut and then on to Cairo where it was blown up the next day. A TWA Boeing 707 from Tel Aviv to New York with 145 on board and a Swissair DC-8 from Zurich to New York with 155 were flown to Dawson's Field, a disused RAF airstrip in Northern Jordan. On 9 September these were joined by a BOAC VC-10 from Bahrain to Beirut with 115 passengers and crew. Meanwhile on 7 September the PFLP issued an ultimatum that unless Khalid, three guerrillas imprisoned in Switzerland for an attack on an El Al airlines and three others held in West Germany for an attack on El Al passengers were released, they would blow up the planes with their passengers. The threat prevented the Jordanian army from intervening. The PFLP prevented a convoy of food, organised by al-Fatah from reaching the hostages. The Swiss and Germans agreed to release the guerrillas and on 11 September the hostages were moved to hotels in Amman, 360 of them including all the children and most of the women were released the next day. The hijackings were condemned by King Hussain as "shame for the Arab world", by Egypt and by the Security Council. The main Palestine Liberation Organisation suspended the membership of the PFLP. There were fears that the Americans might try to rescue the hostages by force and on 13 September the three aircraft were destroyed. Some of the remaining hostages were freed by the Jordanian army in the fighting of Black September and all were released by the end of the month.

DAYFALLAH, Abd al-Latif (1929–)
"Prime Minister" of Yemen. He entered the army and was trained at the Egyptian Military Academy where he acquired Nasserist sympathies. He was later an instructor of Yemeni officers, selecting some for the group planning to overthrow the Imamate and at the time of the coup of September 1962 he held the key position of Director of Signals. He was appointed a member of the High Command and Minister of the Interior. In April 1963 Marshal Sallal in one of his many attempts to create a form of government which would appear democratic yet enable himself to keep power, drew up a new Constitution which provided for a Presidential Council which would be the supreme body collectively responsible for political, economic, social and administrative matters and an Executive Council which would draw up laws, budgets etc. Dayfallah became Chairman of the Executive Council, in effect Prime Minister. In October he was replaced by the abler Abd al-Rahman al-Iryani but subsequently held other important positions such as Deputy Prime Minister for Health and Agriculture 1964, Chief of Staff 1966 and Deputy Prime Minister for Internal Affairs 1976.

DAYR AL-ZUR DISPUTE (1919–20)
Under the Ottoman Empire Dayr al-Zur was a special *Sanjak*, like Jerusalem and not subject to the Governors of Syria, as the population was largely bedouin but also contained many Kurds. In November 1918 with the collapse of Turkish rule, the inhabitants asked the British to send a Political Officer to keep order. When he arrived he found that an Arab *Mutasarrif* had been appointed by the Sharifian Governor of Aleppo and was recruiting gendarmes; particularly galling was the fact that they were being paid at excessive rates from subsidies provided by the British to the Hashemites. The Syrian representative was withdrawn after three weeks of disputes but propaganda agitation about the precise location of the frontier continued. In December 1919 tribesmen occupied the town, declared loyalty to a Sharifian Governor and held prisoner the British Political Officer whose life was only saved by the timely appearance of aircraft from Mosul. The British decided to abandon the area which became a centre for raids and propaganda against them until the fall of the regime of King Faysal in July 1920. The King disavowed these actions but they were carried on by one of his most faithful adherents Maulud Mukhlis. The French were unable to occupy Dayr al-Zur until they had formed a special camel corps early in 1921. They came under constant attack and it took large-scale military operations lasting until the end of the year to bring the area under control.

DEATH OF A PRINCESS (1980)
In July 1977, on the instructions of her grandfather Prince Muhammad b. Abd al-Aziz, the elder brother of King Khalid, Princess Mishail and her lover were publicly executed in a Jiddah car park for adultery. The appearance of the story in a British newspaper in January 1978, followed by a Foreign Office spokesman's description of it as "a tragedy", caused great indignation in Saudi Arabia and the Foreign Secretary, Dr David Owen sent a private letter of apology. Subsequently an independent journalist made a "dramatised documentary" of the story with actors playing the parts. *Death of a Princess* was shown on Independent Television on 9 April 1980. The Saudi Royal Family regarded the film, particularly a scene in which princesses were shown driving around ogling men, as an intolerable intrusion into their private affairs and were embarrassed that it revealed that they, the Guardians of the Holy Places, had punished the offenders not according to the *Shariah* but under tribal custom which orthodox jurists regarded as unIslamic. The British Ambassador was expelled, there were suggestions that the entire British expatriate community of 30,000 would suffer the same fate, the King's proposed State Visit to London was cancelled and there were threats of economic reprisals. The Foreign Secretary, Lord Carrington publicly expressed personal but not official regret for the "understandable offence" that had been caused and the film was strongly criticised by businessmen with interests in the Kingdom. The Saudi Government made strenuous efforts to prevent the film from being shown in other countries with limited success. In America there was intense lobbying and it was blacked out in several states but permitted in others. The rift between London and Riyadh did not last long and the British Ambassador returned in mid-August.

DECLARATION OF THE TWENTY-NINTH OF JUNE (1966)
Abd al-Krim Qassim failed to understand the strength of Kurdish demands for autonomy and determined to crush them by force. The conspirators, such as General Tahir Yahya who were aiming to overthrow him promised autonomy in return for support to Mulla Mustafa Barzani who agreed and ordered a cease-fire after the success of the Ramadan Revolution. Prolonged negotiations over the exact terms failed and fighting resumed with President Abd al-Salam Arif considering Kurdish demands harmful to Iraqi unity. The Defence Minister General Abd al-Aziz al-Uqayli was convinced that the Kurds could be crushed by force and launched an offensive that achieved nothing. In April 1966 Arif died, Uqayli was replaced in a Cabinet reshuffle and the civilian Prime Minister Abd al-Rahman al-Bazzaz was able to make a peace initiative. After negotiations he made on 29 June a Declaration of his peace proposals. Kurds and Arabs would enjoy equal rights, the Kurdish language and education in it would become official, parliamentary elections would be held with the Kurds obtaining representation, political, administrative, judicial, military and diplomatic posts in proper proportion to their population. Officials in the area would be Kurds, dismissed employees and soldiers who had deserted should regain their old jobs under a general amnesty. The University would pay special attention to Kurdish and open branches in the area. The Kurdish

Democratic Party would be legalised. It is possible that a secret clause arranged for the *Pesh Mergas* to remain in being, paid as a militia. Before the programme could be put into effect military pressure led to the dismissal of Bazzaz but a *de facto* cease-fire lasted for over a year.

DE GAULLE–LYTTELTON AGREEMENT (1941)

After the Germans overran France in June 1940 Lebanon and Syria under General Dentz declared loyalty to the government established in Vichy and the Levant states were used as a base for anti-British activities. This provided a dangerous threat at the time that Rashid Ali al-Gilani in Baghdad was seeking support from the Axis and in June 1941 British troops with a small Free French contingent marched into Syria. At the same time General Catroux on behalf of General de Gaulle and Sir Miles Lampson, British Ambassador in Cairo, issued declarations recognising the independence of Syria and Lebanon. Dentz surrendered to the British on terms which appeared to ignore the Free French and de Gaulle feared that the British aimed to establish permanent political control in the region. He also complained to Oliver Lyttelton, Cabinet Minister in the Middle East, about the activities of various officials such as Sir Edward Spears, the Liaison Officer which also appeared aimed at the Free French. After Lyttelton had endured what Spears called "the insane assaults of de Gaulle's ugly temper" agreement was reached and set down in an exchange of letters. The British declared both sides were pledged to the independence of Syria and Lebanon but when this had been achieved they would recognise the historic position of France upon which they had no intention of encroaching; they had no interests beyond winning the war. The French recognised British military preponderance in the area and accepted British command. De Gaulle made no reference to Lyttelton's stipulation that independence should precede the re-establishment of French influence. Most of the agreement dealt with military matters such as the Free French being permitted to recruit Vichy troops, the disposal of war material and chains of command. The Agreement was later confirmed by Winston Churchill.

(Popular) DEMOCRATIC FRONT FOR THE LIBERATION OF PALESTINE

The Popular Front for the Liberation of Palestine grew out of the Arab Nationalist Movement which had contained many right-wing nationalists. In 1968 the leftists led by Nayif Hawatma split off to form the PDFLP which was recognised by the Palestine Liberation Organisation as a separate group the following February. The break was acrimonious and Fatah leaders had to intervene to protect members of the new faction which was unique in that its fighters were unpaid. Calling for a general Arab revolution as a prelude to the liberation of Palestine, it did not limit its activities to operations against Israel but called for campaigns against the more conservative states, Jordan, Saudi Arabia, Oman, Egypt and even against Fatah. Seeing the Palestinian struggle as part of a world revolution, it cultivated relations with Western Trotskyist groups but allowed them to lapse when they proved unproductive, switching instead to Eastern Europe. It also had close links with the radical wing of the Syrian Baath Party before the assumption of power by Hafiz al-Assad. The PDFLP tried, also, to co-operate with left-wing Israeli groups in the interests of a Marxist-Leninist binational Palestine: in the meanwhile it was ready to accept a temporary socialist state in the West Bank and Gaza. It disagreed with the PDFLP policy of spectacular hijackings abroad and tried to build grass-roots support for left-wing policies in Jordan and the Occupied Territories. The PDFLP was seriously weakened after the expulsion of the guerrillas in Black September but attempted to rebuild its influence through an active role in the Palestine National Front. In April 1973 its HQ in Beirut was attacked by Israeli commandos and some of its leaders killed: the feeble response of the Lebanese army led to the resignation of the Prime Minister Saeb Salam. It officially dropped the "Popular" from its title in 1974. In May 1974 it claimed to have carried out the Maalot Killings in order to sabotage the peace process. It refused, however, to join the Rejection Front, established by George Habash later in the year and was seen as one of the "mainstream" supporters of Yassir Arafat. It was active in the refugee camps where it established social services. At the thirteenth session of the Palestine National Council its advocacy of a "mini-state" led to this becoming official policy. Arafat's attempts to maintain good relations with Egypt after peace moves towards Israel by Sadat and his links with Saudi Arabia caused the DFLP to move towards the Rejection Front and Hawatma joined Habash in May 1978 in calling for a restructuring of the PLO to provide a more collective leadership. It opposed also Arafat's *rapprochement* with King Hussain. In January 1979 it lost three guerrillas in a second attack on Maalot from a base in South Lebanon. The DFLP at this time was receiving money from Libya and its estimated fighting strength of about 1,000 made it the largest guerrilla force after Fatah and Saiqa. In May 1981 its second national congress was held in Damascus, demonstrating its links with Syria, which were intensified after the closure of its Baghdad offices on the suspicion that it had contacts with the Iraq Communist Party. It published a clandestine newspaper in Jordan and continued to criticise the Saudi regime. The DFLP rejected the Fahd Plan which implied recognition of Israel. During 1980 and 1981 its bases in Lebanon were frequently attacked by the Israelis. After the expulsion of Palestinian guerrillas from Beirut in August 1982 most of DFLP men were evacuated to North and South Yemen. The DFLP immediately rejected the Reagan Plan as failing to recognise the right of the Palestinians to an independent state but by the mid-1980s it was regarded as one of the more moderate factions, joining the Democratic Alliance, and taking part in the general reconciliation at the PNC meeting of April 1987. On several occasions the DFLP was on the same side as the PFLP and there was talk of reunion. It carried out occasional attacks on Israel – in April 1988 three of its members were killed after crossing from Lebanon. In November 1988 the DFLP refused to go along with the decision of the Palestine National Council Algiers Meeting implicitly to recognise Israel by accepting Resolution 242. In May 1991 the DFLP offered to swap the body of an Israeli soldier for detained comrades. September saw the formation of a split non-Maxist wing led by Yair Abd Rabbu who was close to Arafat and just before the Third Palestine National Congress three guerrillas were shot dead in an attempted raid on Golan. In October 1991 supporters in Ain Halwah mutinied over the PLO decision to go to Madrid. In April 1992 the DFLP said it was prepared to accept confederation with Jordan after independence. In December 1992 after the Hamas deportations the DFLP said it should withdraw from peace talks. In May 1993 it called for a Palestine referendum on talks but was still split. By September 1993 part of the rejection movement were reckoned to have 350 armed men in South Lebanon.

DEMOCRATIC UNIONIST PARTY (Sudan)
In December 1967 the National Unionist Party and the People's Democratic Party which had split in 1956 reunited to form the Democratic Unionist Party. Ismail al-Azhari was President of the Party which had the blessing of Saiyyid Ali al-Mirghani. In the elections of May 1968, when the Umma Party was split, it won 101 out of 218 seats, taking three-quarters of the vote in the North and Kassala areas, the traditional stronghold of the Mirghani and over 40% nationwide. It formed an alliance with the conservative wing of the Umma opposed to Sadiq al-Mahdi and provided the majority of the Ministers in the last Cabinet of Muhammad Ahmad Mahjoub. It played a full part in the quarrels and intrigues which brought it down. Like other parties the DUP was banned after the coup of Nimeiri but continued a shadowy existence. The National Reconciliation of 1977/8 split the party with the Mirghani faction participating in government while that of Yusuf al-Hindi remained hostile and in exile. In the elections of February 1978 it was estimated that about 20 of those successful, nominally members of the Sudan Socialist Union, were DUP supporters. Its former Secretary-General, Ahmad al-Saiyyid Hamad was a member of the SSU Central Committee and a Minister. When the DUP was formally revived after the fall of Nimeiri its leading figures were Muhammad Uthman al-Mirghani and Zayn al-Abdin al-Hindi but after the death of Sharif Yusuf the Hindi faction lost ground while the Mirghani group benefited from its good relations with Egypt. In March 1986 the DUP refused to endorse the Koka Dam Declaration which set out proposals for a secularised Sudan. In the elections of the following month the DUP was badly organised, sometimes putting up more than one candidate for a seat. Nevertheless it remained strong in the North and East and, although it did badly in urban areas, gained 29.5% of the votes and 63 seats. The DUP was not apparently clear whether it supported repeal or amendment of the September Laws which had imposed *Shariah* but its leaders were certain that they wanted ministerial posts so they joined the Umma in a coalition under Sadiq al-Mahdi, Ahmad al-Mirghani becoming Head of State and Zayn al-Abdin al-Hindi Foreign Minister. The party was never fully united and in April 1987 the Secretary-General resigned because of differences over leadership. In November 1988, with Egyptian encouragement, the DUP negotiated an agreement with the Sudan People's Liberation Movement which was rejected by its coalition partners

so it withdrew from the Government. It was brought back again just before the overthrow of parliamentary government by General Bashir in June 1989 when parties were again banned. DUP leaders were imprisoned and it was not until December 1990 that Muhammad Uthman al-Mirghani was released to house arrest while the Secretary-General Sid Ahmad al-Hussain was freed. In January 1991 in a statement issued in London the DUP denounced the anti-Saudi policies of the Bashir government and its reliance upon the fundamentalists of the National Islamic Front.

DHAHRAN AIR BASE
During the Second World War the Americans wanted an airbase that would facilitate the movement of forces between Europe and the Far East and it was decided to site it in Saudi Arabia, the only place in the area not subject to British influence. In March 1945 an agreement was signed with Ibn Saud which permitted the construction of a base in Dhahran in return for training for local personnel. Building by the US Corps of Engineers was finished in March 1946. Training courses started the following year. In 1951 the US negotiated a five-year renewal of the lease in return for a commitment to supply arms and to train the Saudi forces, replacing the British military mission which had been in the country since 1947. The facilities were expanded. The lease was renewed in 1957 in return for military aid. As at Wheelus in Libya, the existence of an American base on Arab soil was attacked by nationalists and early in 1960 King Saud stated that the lease would not be renewed. In December 1962 after attacks by the Egyptian air force on Saudi territory after the start of the Yemen War the Americans were again allowed to use the airfield which was run by an American firm associated with the businessman Adnan Khashoggi. In 1990 and 1991 Dhahran was the principal base in the build-up of the Allied forces sent to expel the Iraqis from Kuwait.

DHOFAR LIBERATION FRONT
Jabhat al-Tahrir al-Zafari. At frequent intervals after its annexation in 1829 by Said b. Sultan Al Bu Said the non-Arab population of Dhofar rebelled; a rising in 1895 was so serious that British naval help was needed. In the 1950s Said b. Taymur Al Bu Said regarded the area as a private fief and adamantly refused to permit change. At the same time Dhofaris started to go for work to the oil states where some of them absorbed Arab nationalist and even Marxist ideas, contrasting progress there with the total lack of development at home. About 1962 some of them formed the Dhofar Charitable Association with the ostensible purpose of building mosques and helping the poor. The members had mixed political views but were generally anti-Sultan and anti-British. A Shaykh of the Bayt Kathir, Musalam b. Nufl, a mechanic on the Sultan's staff, turned them into the Dhofar Liberation Front. Their first attacks were on oil company vehicles in April 1963. Bin Nufl fled to Saudi Arabia where he was welcomed by Imam Ghalib b. Ali al-Hinai, in exile since the Jabal Akhdar Campaign and by the Saudi authorities. He went later to Iraq where he was trained in guerrilla tactics and enrolled others. Relations were established with the

South Yemeni National Liberation Front and with radical Palestinian groups and financial and other backing was obtained from President Nasser but many members were still conservative and wished to maintain Islam and the traditional tribal structure. At the beginning of June 1965 they held their first Congress and elected an 18-man executive and called for all Dhofaris to unite against the Sultan. The Front regarded 9 June 1965, the date of a successful ambush, as the start of the Dhofar Rebellion. In April 1966 DLF members in the army attempted to assassinate the Sultan. At first arms came from Saudi Arabia and later from China where selected members were sent for training and indoctrination. This and the assistance of the revolutionary government in South Yemen gave a strong Marxist-Leninist slant to the Front and many of the original tribal dissidents left. The changed character of the movement was reflected at the second Congress held in Hamrin in Central Dhofar in September 1968 when it decided to rename itself the Popular Front for the Liberation of the Occupied Arab Gulf.

DHOFAR REBELLION

In about 1962 dissatisfaction at the total refusal of Sultan Said b. Taymur Al Bu Said to sanction any progress or development led Jabali tribesmen, in particular those who had, while working in the newly-rich oil states, been exposed to Arab nationalist or even Marxist ideas, to form the Dhofar Liberation Front. There had been local unrest for some time but according to the DLF the rebellion started on 9 June 1965 with an attack on lorries belonging to an oil company. After that date the Sultan's Armed Forces were permanently deployed in the province. They were hampered by poor equipment, maps and intelligence and could do little beyond send out patrols in the hope of finding the dissidents and maintain security on the mountain road which was the only land connection between Salala and the rest of Oman. Fighting had to stop during the monsoon season from July to September. British officers under contract to the Sultan played a leading role and the first one was killed in March 1966. In April 1966 DLF members in his bodyguard attempted to kill the Sultan who subsequently rarely appeared in public. By early 1967 there was a military stalemate with the DLF inactive, as the Saudis were no longer supplying arms or money. British officials pressed the Sultan to make political concessions, convinced that that could end the war but he refused. Although revenues from oil were now starting to flow he refused also to permit any development or buy essential weapons such as helicopters. The situation was transformed by the British withdrawal from Aden and the coming to power there of the revolutionary National Liberation Front which gave the DLF a secure base with a port enabling arms to brought from China, Russia and other allies. The rebels evolved from a tribal to a Marxist-Leninist force and this was signalled by their adoption of the title of the Popular Front for the Liberation of the Occupied Arab Gulf. By this time there were about 2,000 hardcore fighters with about 4,000 militiamen but they were supported by most of population of the Jabal where the Sultan's Forces were seen as a foreign army of occupation. By the end of 1969

the rebels controlled practically the whole of Dhofar apart from a heavily fortified enclave around Salala. In June 1970 another rebel group calling itself the National Democratic Front attempted to extend the war to the Nizwa area but was defeated and almost completely wiped out. On 23 July 1970 the Sultan was deposed and his son Qabus ascended the throne. He announced a series of radical reforms including the building of schools, hospitals etc. in Dhofar, released prisoners and offered an amnesty and financial help for any rebel who surrendered. British aid was increased, a medical team was sent and so was a contingent, which eventually numbered 120, of the élite Special Air Service and more air support was made available. In September 1970 the original leader of the revolt Musalam b. Nufl surrendered and his example was subsquently followed by an average of 20 men a month. These were formed into well-armed and well-paid *firqahs* each of about 100 men from a single tribe, trained by the SAS and which operated against their former comrades. Eventually they numbered about 3,000 and played an essential part in the war. In October 1971 a joint SAS and *firqah* group re-established itself on the Jabal, dug a well, set up a clinic, a veterinary officer, a school, a store and an information centre surrounded by a perimeter guarded by the *firqah* and connected to the coast by a motorable track. This was the start of a pattern of similar settlements designed to win over the population. This was followed by moving troops by helicopter to build the Leopard Line across the Jabal isolating dissidents in the extreme eastern area. There were frequent skirmishes – the PFLOAG reported 290 in three months – culminating in July 1972 with a major attack by over 200 dissidents on the coastal village of Mirbat which was only saved by an unexpected break in the clouds enabling the garrison to call for air support. The rebels were reported to have lost 70 killed and never again attacked positions off the Jabal. In the summer the Sultan for the first time received help from an Arab state, Jordanian intelligence officers and engineers arrived, and were later joined by 3,000 men of the Iranian Special Forces with numerous helicopters. In December 1972 members of PFLOAG attempted a rising in Muttrah but 77 of them were brought to trial and 10 shot. In 1973 the Hornbeam Line was built 80 km east of the border with the PDRY. Made of at least 15,000 coils of barbed wire and using 4,000 anti-personnel mines, it was 50 km long and about 150 rebels were trapped behind it. Omani oil revenues were now about £300 million a year with half going on the armed forces which numbered about 15,000 men and much of the remainder spent on developing the newly pacified areas. In March 1974 the Foreign Ministers of the Arab League sent a delegation in the hope of ending the fighting but PFLOAG were intransigent. In October 1974 a final attempt at a rising in the north near Rustaq was defeated. In January 1975 the Iranians carried out a successful offensive and established the Demavend Line between Hornbeam and the frontier. A final offensive in October pushed the remaining rebels back into the PDRY and on 11 December Sultan Qabus stated that the rebellion had finally been crushed. In fact a few further skirmishes took place and there were intermittent clashes between Omani and

South Yemeni troops. A series of amnesties brought home all but a handful of former rebels. After the Iranian Revolution in 1979 the Ayatollah Khomeini recalled the Iranian units which were replaced by Egyptians. The South Yemenis maintained a pointless and largely verbal hostility and the Oman–South Yemen Dispute continued until relations were normalised in November 1982. The war would never have been won without political reforms and a determined effort to win the confidence of the tribal population.

DIDOUCHE, Murad (1927–55)

Algerian Revolutionary leader. He was originally a supporter of Messali Haj but then joined the more militant Organisation Spéciale. In the early 1950s worked underground in Paris with Muhammad Boudiaf setting up nationalist cells amongst expatriate workers. In March 1954 they returned together to Algeria to organise activity there. He was a member of the Comité Révolutionnaire d'Unité et d'Action and is recognised as one of Neuf Historiques, the youngest of the group. Didouche was put in charge of the Second *wilaya* covering North Constantine but was killed in action two months after the start of the War of Algerian Independence.

DIOURI AFFAIR (1991)

Abd al-Mumin Diouri, who was born in Kenitra in 1938 was the son of an early nationalist leader who, in 1953, was murdered by French settlers. The following year his mother and other members of his family died in suspicious circumstances in a car accident. The accounts that Diouri gave of himself frequently varied and he cultivated an air of mystery but it seems that he inherited a prosperous farm and went to France to study in 1959. In Paris he established links with Algerian nationalists, particularly Abd al-Hafid Boussouf and Moroccan exiles such as Ben Barka. Returning home in 1962 he joined the Union Nationale des Forces Populaires and may have been involved in buying arms from American servicemen. In June 1963 he was arrested and, under torture from General Oufkir, appears to have given away the names of his associates. In March 1964 he was sentenced to death but was released from prison after thirteen months. From 1965 until 1971 he lived on his farm in Kenitra and Diouri has said little about this period although respectful letters that he wrote to Hassan II have been published. In 1970 he was involved in a swindle when a parliamentary candidate claimed to have paid a large sum in the expectation that it would secure his election. Diouri, distrusted by the legitimate opposition, stated that he had formed an armed republican movement and went to Paris where in 1972 he published *Requisitoire contre un Despote: pour une République au Maroc*. He travelled widely on business in which he was extremely successful. In 1982 he published *Réalités Marocaines*, another attack on the Monarchy. In June 1991 Diouri announced that he was about to publish *A qui appartient le Maroc?*, an exposure of dubious business dealings and exploitation of state monopolies that had made Hassan one of the world's richest men. Franco-Moroccan relations had been strained the previous year by the publication of another attack on the King, *Notre Ami le Roi* by Gilles Perault

and Paris, extremely worried by the rise of Islamic militancy in Algeria and Tunisia felt its whole position in North Africa under threat. The French Government, therefore, stating that Diouri was a security risk because of alleged contacts with Libya and Iraq determined to expel him: the decision caused a public outcry. Switzerland, saying that it could not guarantee his safety, refused to accept him but eventually Gabon agreed to do so. Upon his arrival there he was imprisoned but his expulsion was declared illegal by a French court and he returned to Paris. In October his publisher announced that he was postponing bringing out the book as he had received death threats.

DLIMI, Ahmad (1931–83)

Moroccan General. Born at Sidi-Qasim, he was trained at the Moroccan Military Academy and in France and fought in the Tindouf Dispute. In 1964 he was attached to the staff of General Oufkir as Assistant Director-General of Security. After the disappearance of Mehdi Ben Barka in October 1965, Oufkir and Dlimi were amongst those charged with his murder. The trial opened in Paris in their absence and appeared to be leading towards a verdict which would cast guilt upon Oufkir and possibly even upon Hassan II when Dlimi unexpectedly surrendered to the French police in order to shield his superiors and prevent serious damage to Franco-Moroccan relations. After nine months in prison he was acquitted in a second trial which ended in June 1967. On his return he was promoted, posted to the King's Military Cabinet and later was made Director-General of Security. He was one of the King's closest associates, in charge of both internal and external intelligence. It may have been Dlimi who killed Oufkir after the failure of the Royal Boeing Plot: he had himself been one of the passengers on the aircraft. In 1975, now the only General, he was put in charge of the campaign in the Western Sahara, in the early days of which he defeated a regular Algerian force at Amgalla. Later he drove the Polisario guerrillas from the settled parts and was the architect of the wall that confined them to the desert; later he started offensive probes beyond the wall. In January 1983, after a meeting with the King at Marrakesh he was killed when his car exploded and his chauffeur burned alive. Later his adjutant who had been imprisoned escaped to France and stated that Dlimi, who was of Saharan origin, had wanted to make peace with Polisario, considering total victory impossible, but had found the King adamant in refusal. Dlimi had plotted to make Hassan abdicate and go into exile but had been discovered. He was then killed and his body, which his family were never allowed to see, put in a vehicle filled with explosives. His death was followed by the arrest of dozens of senior officers, giving credence to the theory of a military plot.

DRUZE REVOLT (1925–27)

The leading family of Jabal Druze, the al-Atrash was divided between those who collaborated with and those who opposed the French Mandate: Salim was Governor with a French Adviser whereas Sultan al-Atrash had been bombed and fined. When Salim died in September 1923 no successor was generally acceptable and the *majlis* agreed to the appointment of a French officer,

Captain Carbillet. Carbillet started an active programme of reforms, based on his experience in West Africa, including those of land tenure which greatly upset the notables and public works by forced labour which alienated the peasantry. In February 1925 a group of the Atrash who had gone to complain to the High Commissioner General Sarrail was treated with contempt and on 11 July a second mission which had been invited was detained. Sultan who had remained behind prepared to revolt. On 20 July with about 600 followers he advanced on the principal town of Suwaydah and shortly afterwards ambushed a French detachment of about 175 men. A column 3,000 strong advancing to the relief of Suwaydah was destroyed by Sultan and his horsemen in a night attack. The Druzes raided to within four miles of Damascus. The Damascus nationalist leaders, Dr Shahbandar and Hassan al-Hakim met Sultan late in August and agreed that they would fight together to end the Mandate. A Provisional Government was proclaimed and Sultan assumed the title of Commander of the Revolutionary Armies and issued a proclamation about the principles of the French Revolution. As the French brought in reinforcements insurrection and plain brigandage spread. In September the French abandoned Suwaydah. In October Fawzi al-Qawukji, an officer in the French army, attacked government buildings in Hama and although defeated started a guerrilla war in the area. In the same month insurgency in the district led to the Damascus bombardment by French forces. The following month Sultan's brother Zaid led a force into Southern Lebanon, captured Marjayun and hoped to link up with the Druze of Mount Lebanon. After very heavy fighting he failed to take the fort of Rashayya and had to withdraw; this marked the turning of the tide. Sarrail whose mishandling had led to the crisis was replaced by a civilian Henry de Jouvenel who was prepared to adopt more conciliatory policies. In December he received a delegation of leading nationalists led by Faris al-Khouri but insisted that laying down of arms should precede amnesty and constitutional advance. De Jouvenel announced elections for a Constituent Assembly but they were either boycotted or unconvincing. From the beginning of 1926 the military situation turned in favour of the French. The defeat of Abd al-Krim in the Riff meant that troops could be brought from Morocco while in Syria the insurgents were weakened by heavy casualties and defections of the more opportunistic. In April the French reoccupied Jabal Druze although Sultan and Shahbandar remained in the field and fighting continued in other areas, particularly in the *Ghutah* around Damascus. In May Damascus was bombarded for the second time. In July major operations expelled the rebels from that area and after that fighting became more and more sporadic and confined to remote areas. Qawukji continued raiding until April 1927 but then escaped abroad, at the same time as Sultan al-Atrash and Shahbandar. In March 1928 the French proclaimed a general amnesty except for a blacklist of 64 of the leaders. The Revolt was estimated to have cost the lives of 600 of the rebels and left 100,000 homeless. The Revolt had been profoundly anti-imperialist and had attracted the support of all classes, landowners, peasants, tribesmen and the

bourgeois intelligentsia, both Western and Muslim educated; the revolutionary Shahbandar had worked well with the conservative Sultan al-Atrash. The French had clearly not been interested in Syrian welfare and had merely exploited the country. It had sharpened religious differences and while doing little for social services had spent heavily on security and the creation of artificial states. The Druze Revolt was the last and greatest of a series which had included that of Subhi Barakat in Alawi country and Ibrahim Hananu in Aleppo. Its failure caused the nationalists to look to political means to achieve independence which they did by creating the National Bloc.

DUAL KAYMAKAMATE

In May 1840 Ibrahim Pasha ordered the imposition of conscription for Mount Lebanon and the whole population rose in revolt. The strong old Amir, Bashir II Shihab fled and under his weak successor Bashir III Shihab civil war flared between Maronites and Druzes. Bashir III was deposed and the Shihab Amirate declared abolished. The Ottomans tried to establish direct rule but the political incompetence of Umar Pasha al-Namsawi only made the situation worse. The French were backing the Maronites and the British the Druzes and in the interests of European harmony at the end of 1842 the Austrian Chancellor Prince Metternich negotiated a settlement by which the Mountain was divided at the Damascus road – the northern Christian part under a Maronite Kaymakam and the southern under a Druze. A complicated system of local administration was set up but quickly broke down in further sectarian strife. In 1845 the Ottoman Foreign Minister Shakib Effendi published a new organic law. Each Kaymakam was to have a council (*majlis*) comprising his deputy and a judge and adviser for each of the Sunni, Maronite, Druze, Greek Orthodox and Greek Catholic sects and an adviser for the Shiah. Shakib Effendi appointed these officials, regarded as whole-time and paid a salary for life but subsequent vacancies were to be filled at the choice of the head of the appropriate sect. The *majlis* decided upon the assessment and distribution of taxes, heard judicial cases and supervised local administration. This solution was not regarded as satisfactory because the Maronites felt that their superior numbers had not been taken into account and that the Mountain had lost its traditional autonomy as the Kaymakams were appointed by the Ottoman Pasha of Sidon whose approval was also necessary for new council members. The European Consuls continued to intrigue on behalf of their clients while the old feudal families resented the admission of peasants to the *majlis*; they therefore obstructed its working whenever they could. It was a formalisation of civil war – a recognition that the Maronite and Christian communities found it hard to live peacefully together. By 1858 the country was again in turmoil and, after the massacres of 1860, the Dual Kaymakamate was replaced by the Règlement Organique.

DUBAI AGREEMENT (1968)

Early in 1968 the British Government under Harold Wilson announced its intention of withdrawing from the Gulf. Realising that their states were too weak to stand alone Shaykhs Zaid b. Sultan al-Nihayyan and Rashid b. Said al-Maktum signed the Simayh Agreement of 18 February 1968 to federate Abu Dhabi and Dubai and at the same time invited the Shaykhs of Bahrain and Qatar and the other five Trucial States to become parties to the agreement. They met in Dubai on 25 February 1968 for what most probably assumed to be a preliminary meeting on the possibilities of union but found themselves confronted with a draft already prepared by Qatar. This, amongst other things envisaged that the five small Shaykhdoms, Sharjah, Ajman, Umm al-Qaiwain, Fujayrah and Ras al-Khaymah, should form a single unit, the United Arab Coastal Emirates. This was indignantly rejected by their Rulers. Other precise details in the draft were omitted in favour of a vaguer document but the Dubai Agreement, signed on 27 February provided for the establishment of a Federation of Arab Emirates which would come into being on 30 March. There was to be a Supreme Council of the Rulers which would draw up a permanent Charter and formulate higher policy on international, political, economic, cultural and other affairs. The Chairmanship would rotate annually. The Budget would be fixed by the Supreme Council with the share of each member regulated by law. Executive functions would be exercised by a Federal Council. The Emirates would strengthen their armed forces and co-operate against outside aggression. There would be a Supreme Federal Court. Each Emirate would exercise those powers not reserved for the central government. It was entirely an agreement of Rulers and no provision at all was made for the participation of ordinary citizens. No British officials were present during the discussions but London welcomed the agreement as did most other states apart from Iran which had claims on Bahrain and South Yemen, Algeria and Syria which saw it as an imperialist plot. There were no decisions upon such practical matters as the site of a capital or how the various states would be represented and after three years of fruitless discussions, the attempt to set up a Federation of the Nine had to be abandoned.

al-DUKKALI, Abu Shuaib (1878–1937)

Moroccan religious reformer. Born near Casablanca, his family belonged to the *tariqah* founded by Larbi b. Ahmad al-Darqawi. In 1896 he enrolled as a student at al-Azhar where he was much influenced by the ideas of Muhammad Abduh that true understanding of the meaning of Islam was a force for modernisation not for reaction. In 1904 the Sharif of Mecca Awn al-Rafiq who had adopted some of the Wahhabi tenets such as smashing the tombs of saints and curbing *tariqahs* asked the Rector of al-Azhar to send a preacher and teacher. Dukkali was selected and remained in Mecca for three years. In 1908 he was invited back to Morocco by the new Sultan Mulai Hafid whose hostility to *tariqahs* was shown by his flogging to death Sharif Muhammad al-Kattani. Dukkali taught in the Qarawiyin, reforming its syllabus to weaken the hold of tradition and was largely responsible for the spreading of Salafiyyah doctrines amongst intellectuals. In 1911 Dukkali was appointed Qadi of Marrakesh and in 1912 Minister of Justice. After the establishment of the Protectorate he led the attack on the *tariqahs* which were seen as supporters of French rule. Regarded as "the Moroccan Abduh", he influenced through his student Mulai Larbi al-Alawi the generation of Allal al-Fassi and the subsequent nationalist movement.

DURDAH, Abu Zaid Umar

Libyan "Prime Minister". He was Governor of Misurata Province when in July 1972 he was appointed Minister for Information. In a reshuffle in November 1974 he was made Acting Minister for Foreign Affairs. Later he held other "Secretariats", Municipalities, Economic Affairs, and Land Reclamation and Reform until October 1990 when he replaced Umar al-Muntasir as Secretary-General of the General People's Committee, effectively Prime Minister. The "Cabinet" was restructured with new posts created for Integration with the Maghreb, Egypt and the Sudan while those dealing with Mobilisation and Revolutionary Guidance were abolished. In June 1991 Durdah officially denied Libyan responsibility for the explosion which destroyed and American aircraft over Lockerbie but the problems posed by the subsequent sanctions dominated his Premiership. He visited Arab countries to put Libya's case and had to deal with the financial problems: in January 1994 he declared that it was necessary to cut the budget by several thousand million dinars. Although in November 1992 he had reshuffled his Cabinet to bring back the Western-inclined Muntasir as Foreign Minister, Durdah was believed to oppose the handing over of the suspects. In January 1994 he was moved to be Deputy Speaker of the General People's Congress: this was probably not demotion as the GPC was coming to be regarded as more important than the Cabinet.

al-DURUBI, Ala al-Din (?–1920)

Syrian Prime Minister. He was came from a noble family of Homs and entered the Ottoman service, rising to become a Provincial Governor. A British report of 1917 remarked that he was rich and influential but was selfish, unreliable and anti-Arab. Nevertheless he was appointed Minister of the Interior in the first Syrian Cabinet formed by Ali Ridha al-Rikabi and was known to be in favour of conciliating the French despite their demands upon King Faysal. On 25 July after the defeat at Maysalun the King, about to flee the capital, appointed Durubi Prime Minister, hoping that he could negotiate some arrangement to save the throne. His government contained several politicians known to be anti-nationalist. After leaving Damascus Faysal remained for some time on Syrian territory at Dera'a; on the instructions of the French Durubi sent him several telegrams asking him to leave. The district of Hawran refused to accept French rule and on 21 August, Durubi and a colleague went to persuade them not to resist. At the station of Khirbet al-Ghazaleh near Dera'a they were dragged from their railway carriage by Hawranis and murdered.

EAST GHOR CANAL

In the early 1950s the Jordanian Government, with the encouragement of UNWRA, started planning for a development project which would take water from the River Yarmuk through a canal running parallel with the Jordan for about 45 miles to irrigate about 30,000 acres in the Zerka area. At one time it appeared that this scheme might form part of a larger project to share the waters of the Jordan under the Johnston Plan but this was eventually rejected by the Arabs as it implied recognition of Israel. The original project, started in 1958, was completed in 1964 at a cost of about $85 million but in 1962 the Seven-Year Plan drawn up by the government of Wasfi al-Tall aimed to extend it a further 20 miles to the south to bring another 36,000 acres under cultivation. In 1966 work began on a large storage dam at Mukheiba but the following year after the June War the Israelis occupied the northern bank of the Yarmuk up to a point close to Mukheiba. In 1968 a plan to extend the Canal another five miles was announced. In June 1969 after some guerrilla activity in the area a conduit was blown up by the Israeli forces which subsequently fired upon attempts to repair it and in August further damaged it by bombing. The Jordanians complained to the United Nations at this attempt to "destroy the backbone of the economy" and the Americans brought pressure upon Israel to permit repairs. Water started flowing again in May 1970. In 1971 a new plan which would irrigate a further area sufficient to support a population of 150,000 was announced. In 1973 the Jordan Valley Commission was created to co-ordinate a whole series of development schemes including one to extend the canal for another 11 miles and build a sprinkler irrigation system.

EDDE, Emile (1886–1949)

Lebanese Prime Minister and President. A Maronite, originating from Byblos, he was educated by the Jesuits in Beirut before taking a law degree in Paris. He returned to Beirut and went into practice with the French consulate amongst his clients. He spent the war in Egypt working for the French and was brought back to Lebanon in a French warship and appointed Adviser to the High Commission. In 1919 he was one of a delegation sent to the Peace Conference at Versailles by the Patriarch to demand that Lebanon should not be incorporated in Faysal's Kingdom of Syria but be administered by France. In 1925 when he had already been Chairman of the Beirut Bar and President of the Assembly, he hoped to be elected Governor of the Lebanon but this was vetoed by the anti-clerical High Commissioner General Sarrail because of Edde's links with the Maronite clergy. He was always anxious to ensure a Christian majority in the country and in 1926 supported an attempt by the new High Commissioner to restore the largely Muslim districts of Tripoli and the Biqaa to Syria. His fears of an eventual Muslim majority, reinforced by the census of 1932, convinced him that French rule constituted the main prop for Christian predominance. This, and personal ambitions, differentiated him from his rival for the political leadership of the Maronites, Bishara al-Khouri. Edde called his faction the National Bloc but it was hardly a political party. In May 1929 after Habib al-Saad, failing to cope with factional strife in the Chamber and a financial crisis, resigned, Edde refused to become Prime Minister. Bishara al-Khouri took office but gave up after five months and Edde formed a five-man Cabinet vowed to drastic economies. Assisted by the French he obtained permission to legislate by decree and reduced expenditure on administration by abolishing large numbers of posts; both the poorer Muslim community and Christian vested interests were damaged. Nearly all government hospitals and orphanages were shut down. He also closed over 100 schools which strengthened the influence of missionaries and offended Arab nationalists who were already upset by Edde's support for the claim that the Lebanese were Phoenicians. The resultant outcry brought down the Government at the end of March 1930. In January 1936 the Chamber was given the power to elect a President for a period of three years and Edde prevailed over Bishara al-Khouri. He immediately dismissed the Sunni State Secretary who held full executive powers subject to a French Adviser and replaced him with the Protestant Ayyub Thabit but a year later when the post of Prime Minister was reconstituted he appointed his close Sunni associate Khayr al-Din al-Ahdab. During the next three years Khouri was the main leader of the opposition while Edde appointed two more Sunni Premiers, *Amir* Khalid Shihab and Abd Allah al-Yafi. The President himself, stretching the prerogatives of his office, ensured some efficiency and continuity while the French also played a large part in the administration. He negotiated a Franco-Lebanese Treaty which was approved by the Chamber in November 1936 but which led to rioting between the Muslim and Christian communities. In October 1937 Edde's term of office was extended to six years. In September 1939 to ensure control during wartime, the High Commissioner abolished the Constitution but while retaining Edde as President reverted to the system of concentrating executive power in the hands of a State Secretary with a French Adviser; Edde sulked at the limitations of his authority. In March 1941 there were riots against food shortages, corruption and inequality of political opportunity and Edde resigned in April being replaced by Alfred Naqqash as Head of State. When the Constitution was restored in September 1943 Edde hoped to resume the Presidency but the Assembly instead preferred Khouri. Edde was still a wholehearted supporter of the French and to counter this Khouri allied himself with the British whose troops were the main occupation force in the Lebanon. Khouri initiated measures to bring the country nearer to independence and in the early morning of 11 November he and most of his Ministers were arrested by the French. Jean Helleu, the High Commissioner issued a Decree appointing Edde as President but no Lebanese politician would consent to serve with him. After ten days intense British pressure compelled the French to back down and Khouri was restored to power. The Assembly declared Edde guilty of high treason and expelled him but he was not otherwise harmed. However his own political career was effectively ended but his faction was carried on by his sons Pierre and more particularly Raymond Edde. Alarmed by Khouri's National Pact and his taking Lebanon into the Arab League Emile Edde feared that the Christian identity of Lebanon would be submerged in a tide of Arabism and tried to win allies by intriguing with the Zionists whom he saw as another minority struggling to establish a place in an area dominated by Muslims. He moved in a small French-speaking clique of rich Christian and Muslim merchants and had few contacts amongst Arabic speakers. He was generally regarded as very clever and dynamic but too restless, impulsive, arrogant, short-tempered and unwilling to listen to other viewpoints. Spears alleged that he made a very large fortune by filching the lands of villagers in the Biqaa by very questionable legal means.

EDDE, Raymond (1913–)

Lebanese politician. He was born in 1913 in Alexandria where his father, the future President Emile Edde had gone to be out of reach of the Ottoman authorities. He trained as a lawyer in the Jesuit University in Beirut. In 1949 he succeeded his father as leader of the National Bloc and four years later entered the National Assembly where his brother Pierre had preceded him. The Eddes allied with Camille Chamoun to bring down President Bishara al-Khouri and Pierre became Minister of Finance. The two brothers were enthusiastic champions of private enterprise and Raymond was largely responsible for the drafting of a law on banking secrecy which enabled Lebanon to profit from the oil money starting to flood into Arabia. Despite Raymond Edde's support for Chamoun's resistance to pan-Arabism he opposed the President's aspirations to extend his term in office and called for his resignation. Although it was clear that the country wanted General Fuad Shihab as President, Edde insisted on standing against him to show that there was a choice: he received 7 out of 55 votes. Shihab then persuaded Edde to serve in the four-man Salvation Cabinet formed by Rashid Karami: he held the portfolios of the Interior and Labour, proving an effective

and liberal Minister particularly helpful to small farmers. After a year he became disillusioned with "Shihabism" which he condemned as military rule in disguise and leading to socialism. In 1961 Shihab revoked Edde's passport and he remained in opposition after Charles Helou became President. In 1967 Edde formed with Chamoun and Pierre Gemayel a Triple Alliance, the Hilf, to oppose growing Palestinian influence in Lebanon. In October 1968 when Prime Minister Abd Allah al-Yafi reformed his troubled Cabinet he brought in Edde in charge of several departments as one of the three other Ministers. As Palestinian guerrillas raided from Lebanon into Israel, attracting reprisals, Edde called for the stationing of a UN force on the frontier and subsequently he opposed the Cairo Agreement. In 1970 despite his scorn for the lack of sophistication of Sulayman Franjiyah, the "anti-Shihabist" candidate, he agreed not to stand against him for the Presidency in return for a promise of representation for his Party in the Government. As the country plunged into civil war Edde criticised the violence and involvement with Israel of Gemayel's Kataib militia and that of Chamoun and also the pro-Syrian policies of Franjiyah and thus found himself isolated from the other Maronite leaders and on better terms with the traditional Sunni politicians Saeb Salam and Rashid Karami and even Kamal Jumblatt. He established the National Unity Front but it had little influence. In 1976 he attempted to stand for the Presidency but the Syrians were determined to impose Elias Sarkis. Edde had no armed backing and many of his followers deserted him in favour of more militant chieftains. He spent much time working for the release of victims of kidnapping. Distancing himself from the bloodshed and bitterness he withdrew to Paris hoping that if peace were restored he could be the public figure with the fewest enemies and at last realise his ambition to lead his country. In 1982 he attempted to contest the election of Amin Gemayel but he attracted only the support of Walid Jumblatt and not a single vote. He probably hoped to be a candidate in 1989 but could not stand in the face of Syrian opposition. A life-long bachelor Edde was a colourful witty politician, not a man of deep thought or much organising ability and inclined to be petulant and excitable.

EDEN'S MANSION HOUSE SPEECH (1941)

At the end of May 1941 the British had just been driven from Greece and most Arab states were under unfriendly governments – Egypt under King Farouq, Lebanon and Syria under Vichy and Iraq under Rashid Ali al-Gilani while Italian troops were on the Egyptian frontier: it appeared essential to regain Arab friendship which had been damaged by pre-war events in Palestine and by the propaganda efforts of Bari Radio. The Foreign Secretary, Anthony Eden declared in a speech at the Mansion House that "many Arab thinkers desire for the Arab peoples a greater degree of unity than they now enjoy. In reaching out towards this unity they hope for support. No such appeal should go unanswered . . . HMG will give their full support to any scheme that commands general approval". He followed this in the House of Commons on 24 February 1943 by stating that "the British Government would view with sympathy any movement amongst the Arabs to promote economic, cultural or political unity, but clearly the initiative in any such scheme would have to come from the Arabs themselves". The Arab states were now under friendly governments and a period of intense diplomatic activity with and between them followed. The first proposal, put forward by Nuri al-Said early in 1943, was for a union of the Fertile Crescent but this was generally rejected as a plan for the aggrandisement of the Hashemites. Shortly afterwards, in March 1943 Mustafa al-Nahhas announced that the Egyptian Government would start a series of bilateral talks in Cairo with other Arab states to ascertain their views on "Arab Union". The favourable response that he obtained enabled the meeting of a Conference in September 1944 which led to the Alexandria Protocol and the creation of the Arab League.

EGYPTIAN COMMUNIST PARTY

There were some active Trade Unions in Egypt before the First World War and many more after it. The first Communist Party in Egypt was started by the amalgamation of three small groups in 1919–20. Its main figures were a lawyer, Antun Marun, a jeweller Joseph Rosenthal and the leader of the Alexandrian Workers' Party, Husni al-Arabi, who was one of the very few Muslims in a group almost entirely composed of Jews, Copts, Greeks, Armenians and Italians. Although in 1923 it affiliated to the Communist International its membership never exceeded a few hundred. After some of its members were believed to have fermented a series of strikes it was savagely repressed in 1924, Marun died in prison, the Party was formally banned and there was no further communist activity until after the outbreak of war in 1939. This was followed by a series of "study-groups", one led by Marcel Israel who was friendly with the leader of the Lebanese Communist Party, Nikola Shawi, who secured him a meeting with Midoyan, the Comintern agent for the Middle East. This, the establishment of a Soviet Embassy in Cairo in 1942, and the prestige won by the Red Army at Stalingrad gave a new impetus. Georges Pontet, a Swiss Professor at the Cairo Police School, instilled the need for action rather than theory. Henri Curiel founded the Egyptian Movement for National Liberation to which he recruited some native Egyptians although the membership was still mostly foreign. Other groups led by Marcel Israel and Hillel Schwartz (Haditu in Arabic) joined Curiel in the Democratic Movement for National Liberation which organised strikes and created cells in the University, the army, the police and even al-Azhar. There were constant splits and in 1946 there was a severe crack-down by the police. The factions reunited in 1947 but split again over the Palestine War the following year and there was another series of arrests. There was a continual emergence of new groups, one under a professor of Political Economy, Ismail Sabri Abd Allah, calling itself the Egyptian Communist Party. A further split followed the July Revolution which was welcomed by Curiel and the DMNL but opposed by the others particularly after the killing of workers in the Kafr al-Dawar Riot. Some of the Free Officers, especially Yusuf Sadiq and Khalid Mohieddin were inclined towards Marxism but they

lost influence and in April and May 1954 there were wholesale arrests and several hundred were interned in camps, chained day and night in intense heat. Many, including Abd Allah who was put on trial but acquitted, were tortured. Nasser declared that they were "the best allies of Zionism . . . indistinguishable as to ideology". Their treatment depended upon the relationship that was growing between Nasser and Khruschev, who expressed unease when they were persecuted but was ultimately unwilling to push the matter far while Nasser was pursuing an anti-Western line. Members of most of the groups were released during 1956 and they came together again as the ECP in January 1958. They issued a statement praising Arab nationalism as anti-imperialist and welcomed the formation of the United Arab Republic. Later they expressed support for Abd al-Krim Qassim who was then collaborating with the Iraqi Communist Party against the Nasserists and this led to another severe repression with Sadat in September 1958 threatening to "torture them out of existence". Many were arrested in 1959 and 1960 but most were released in 1963 and 1964 and many were given official posts: the apparent influence of the communists at this time led to the resignation of conservative leaders such as Abd al-Latif al-Baghdadi. It is estimated that at this time the ECP, now entirely Egyptian in membership, numbered about 600 with perhaps 2,000 sympathisers. In January 1965, on Russian advice, the Party dissolved itself and its supporters joined the Arab Socialist Union in which, under the patronage of Ali Sabri they achieved considerable influence and were able to use as cover for publications and propaganda. Some were later purged by Sadat but in 1971 he took Abd Allah and another former leading communist, Fuad Mursi, into his Cabinet. In August 1975 the ECP reconstituted itself in Beirut, issuing a manifesto that echoed Russian criticisms of Sadat. Within Egypt, however, after three political parties were authorised in 1976 most left-wingers joined the National Progressive Unionist Rally of Khalid Mohieddin. Despite their small numbers, communists, including the Communist Labour Party provided a convenient scapegoat for the Bread Riots of January 1977. The Government announced that 22 cells were uncovered and 230 supporters arrested. The ECP was officially dissolved in 1978 but in 1980 held their first Congress in Egypt which focused on liberation from Zionism. Faride Mujahid was appointed General Secretary and membership was estimated at 500. In November 1984 six suspected leaders were arrested. In 1985 there was a second Congress. In November 1987 10 members of NPUR were arrested accused of forming a communist ring.

EGYPTIAN-LIBYAN BORDER CLASHES (1977)

Egypt and Libya were theoretically united in the Federation of Arab Republics when in August 1972 Sadat and Qadafi agreed to a complete union of their two countries by 1 September 1973. So little progress was made that in July 1973 Qadafi organised a march of 30,000 Libyans who crossed the Egyptian frontier to demand immediate unity. Although Sadat was prepared to use force to stop them, a further merger agreement was signed. Again nothing happened and Sadat began and ended the October War without informing his theoretical partner. Relations deteriorated rapidly and in the spring of 1975 Egyptians working in Libya were harassed and the media exchanged personal insults about the two Presidents. Qadafi was the most vehement critic of the Sinai Disengagement Agreement and Sadat declared that the Libyans, who had concluded a large arms deal with the Russians, were collaborating with them against him. In July 1976 Libya was implicated in a plot to overthrow President Nimeiri of the Sudan who then joined Egypt in a defence agreement. Libya was accused of causing bomb explosions in Cairo and Alexandria and of fomenting the Bread Riots of January 1977. The Libyans hanged an Egyptian accused of spying and expelled others. Qadafi said that it would take 50 years to normalise relations after the "high-treason of the hangman Sadat" while Cairo declared that Qadafi was planning to annex the Western Desert with the aid of 7,000 Cubans and was financing an "Egyptian Liberation Front"; each side complained to the Arab League. Moscow warned Sadat against any adventure. Owing to the total divergence of the accounts given by Egyptian and Libyan authorities and the absence of impartial witnesses, precise details of what happened are unclear. The Egyptians claimed to have captured a 4-man "sabotage team" and that the Libyans had fired on a frontier post. On 21 July Sadat ordered an invasion "to teach the crazy red agent a lesson he will never forget". Airfields and radar installations, allegedly used by the Russians to monitor American naval movements, were bombed and the Egyptians claimed to have destroyed 40 tanks and 30 other military vehicles in fighting near the Mediterranean. The Libyans said that the USA and Sudan were helping their enemies. On 22 July Sadat said that all Egyptian forces were back on their own side of the fontier but the Libyans said that fighting was continuing. On 24 July after mediation by Boumédienne and Yassir Arafat Sadat ordered a cease-fire. A month later about 100 prisoners were exchanged. Sadat had probably hoped that the Libyan people would rise to overthrow the regime and certainly for a few days Qadafi appeared uncertain whether he should trust his forces. The incident showed how few supporters Qadafi had amongst the Arabs. Although there were no further frontier incidents, relations between Egypt and Libya continued bad until Qadafi formally severed them in December after Sadat's Knesset Speech.

EGYPT'S REVOLUTION

Thawrat Misr. In 1984 an Israeli official in Egypt was wounded and two others were murdered in 1985 and 1986 while two American Embassy security men were wounded in 1987 and these crimes were blamed on an organisation calling itself Egypt's Revolution. A group with the same name claimed responsibility for the Malta Hijacking of November 1985 although others "credited" this to Abu Nidal. Egypt's Revolution was receiving money and arms from Libya. In 1987 the brother of its leader Mahmud Nur al-Din quarrelled with him and fled to the American Embassy where he gave details of the gang. Before they could be apprehended, Khalid, the son of President Nasser took refuge

in Yugoslavia. The Egyptian Government was particularly embarrassed because Nur al-Din had been a senior army officer who had worked in Nasser's security office before being posted to the London Embassy to spy on Israeli diplomats. Others had also been in the Intelligence service and one was believed to be a senior officer although this was not mentioned in public. The trial began in November 1988 with 120 lawyers rallying to the defence and in June 1989 Khalid Abd al-Nasser unexpectedly returned to join the others in the dock. The defendants claimed that they were heroes fighting the national enemy while the prosecution accused them of damaging the country's relations with America and Israel for financial gain. The presence of Abd al-Nasser and the previous official careers of the others caused great embarrassment to the Government. In April 1991 Abd al-Nasser was acquitted but Nur al-Din was condemned to 25 years' imprisonment, five received between three and 15 years, six received suspended sentences of up to a year and four others were acquitted. By this time leftist secularists were far less significant as opponents of the regime than Islamic fundamentalists.

EILAT, Sinking of (1967)

On 21 October 1967, four months after the end of the June War, the 2,300-ton Israeli destroyer *Eilat*, the former Royal Navy warship *HMS Zealous*, was sunk by missiles fired from two Egyptian patrol boats with the loss of 47 sailors. The rest of the crew, 155 men, were rescued but 91 had been wounded. The Egyptians stated that the warship had been within the 12-mile territorial limit off Port Said but the Israelis claimed that it had been in international waters. As a reprisal Israeli artillery opened fire across the Suez Canal setting ablaze two oil refineries at Port Suez. About 80% of Egypt's refining capacity was destroyed and Nasser ordered the evacuation of 350,000 civilians from Suez and Ismailiyyah. The fear that the situation might escalate into a renewal of the war gave an impetus to Security Council discussions and Resolution 242 was issued the following month. There were no further major incidents for another year when the War of Attrition started in earnest.

ENTEBBE HIJACKING (1976)

On 27 June 1976 an Air France A-300 airbus with 245 passengers and 12 crew on a flight from Tel Aviv to Paris shortly after taking off from Athens was hijacked by three men and a woman, led by a German. It landed briefly at Benghazi and after being refused permission to land in Khartoum, came down in Entebbe with little fuel remaining. Six more terrorists joined the original hijackers. President Amin of Uganda, revelling in the spotlight, took personal charge of negotiations with the hijackers who demanded the release of 40 prisoners in Israel, including Archbishop Capucci and the Japanese survivor of the Lydda Airport Attack, and others in West Germany, France, Switzerland and Kenya. These international links indicated that the action had been planned by Wadei Haddad. On 30 June 47 women, children and invalids were released and Amin advised governments concerned to meet the hijackers' demands. On 1 July Israel expressed readiness to negotiate and 100 hostages were freed. On the night of 3–4 July 150 Israeli commandos in three C-130 Hercules transport aircraft landed at Entebbe achieving complete surprise. They had flown undetected down the Red Sea between Saudi and Egyptian airspace and then at great height over Ethiopia and Kenya. There was resistance from Ugandan soldiers guarding the airfield and 20 of them were killed as was the Israeli commander. Seven out of the ten kidnappers were killed and the others escaped. George Habash of the Popular Front for the Liberation of Palestine categorically denied that his group had been involved. Amin executed three Ugandan air traffic controllers for negligence. In Israel the release of the hostages was hailed as a classic of enterprise and daring (three films were made about it within a year) while Western governments welcomed the release of the hostages and ignored the violation of Ugandan territory.

EQUALITY DAY (1987)
The Arab population living within the pre-1967 borders of Israel had Israeli citizenship but their civil rights and social services were not equal to those enjoyed by Jewish citizens. On 24 June 1987 they organised a protest against discrimination, the "apartheid policy", in the provision of municipal services, job opportunities and education. The main issue was the unequal distribution of budgets for local councils and municipalities for expenditure *per capita* in Arab areas was approximately 25–33% of that in equivalent Jewish. Strikes were widely observed in Arab cities such as Acre and Nazareth.

ERKOWIT CONFERENCE (1964)
At the Alexandria Summit in September 1964 Crown Prince Faysal and President Nasser met for the first time since their countries had been fighting the Yemen War by proxy and agreed to bring it to an end. It was decided that Royalist and Republican leaders should assemble at Erkowit, a hill resort in the Sudan on 30 October. The Royalists were led by Ahmad Muhammad al-Shami and the Republicans by the moderate Muhammad Mahmud al-Zubayri who were old friends from the days of the Ahrar. They agreed that there should be a cease-fire to take effect on 6 November and that a National Congress of 63 *ulema*, 63 tribal chiefs and 18 members of a preparatory commission should meet in Yemen on 23 November. It was understood in private conversations that the Egyptian army should be withdrawn and both the Imam Badr and President Sallal would be required to step down. The cease-fire came into effect but it was violated almost at once by the Egyptians and fighting resumed. The Republicans claimed that they should nominate 2–3 of the delegates and the Royalists refused to accept this. It also proved impossible to agree on a meeting place so the Congress never took place.

ERZERUM, Treaty of (1847)
Turkey and Persia ended wars in 1639, 1746 and 1823 with peace treaties which left the boundaries between them ill-defined. There were constant disputes over the allegiance of the Kurdish tribes and in 1842 Britain feared another war between two Muslims states which it wished to see strong as a barrier between India and

Russia. It therefore invited the Russians to participate in a commission with the two contestants. In 1847 a Treaty was signed in Erzerum in which Persia surrendered claims to lands to the west of the province of Zohab in return for recognition of its sovereignty over Muhammarah, the island of Abadan and the lands of the eastern bank of the Shatt al-Arab. British and Russian surveyors laboured until 1865 (with a break for the Crimean War) to produce maps which it took another four years to agree. Persian ships were to be permitted to navigate freely on the Shatt and the question of whether the international boundary was the east bank or, as was more usual, the middle of the river was not deemed of any importance until after the exploitation of oil. Then it became a cause of bitter dispute, being in 1980 one of the factors leading to the Iran–Iraq War exploitation of oil.

EURO-ARAB DIALOGUE
The doubling of oil prices in 1973 left the Arabs with huge amounts of petro-dollars and there were proposals that these should be mixed with European expertise in the interests of development. The Euro-Arab dialogue was seen as "the product of a joint political will towards establishing a special relationship". A General Committee was set up with about thirty working groups to prepare specific projects such as the creation of a Euro-Arab Centre for the Transfer of Technology. There were also arrangements for academic and cultural exchanges. The Arabs generally provided up to 80% of the necessary finance. The Camp David agreement and the expulsion of Egypt from the Arab League caused the suspension of all activities. The Venice Declaration of June 1980 which stated the necessity of associating the Palestinians with any peace settlement led to a resumption of the Dialogue at all levels and there were plans for a first meeting of European Community and Arab Foreign Ministers the following summer. This did not take place but working parties were resumed. In December 1989 a large-scale meeting was held in Paris chaired by President Mitterand and King Hassan. The Dialogue resumed after the Kuwait war but was restricted to technical matters, the EC saying that with the peace process there were other channels for political discussion. The EC was unwilling to work with Libya or Iraq, preventing a possible ministerial meeting but there was a meeting of experts in Lisbon in April 1992. The Algerian Summit decided to send four Ministers to the EC Summit in Copenhagen in December 1973. In 1974 the Rabat Summit accepted the idea of the Dialogue. In 1975 there was an export meeting in Cairo. In 1976 the first meeting of the General Commission of the EC in Luxembourg was followed by an agreement on co-operation with individual states. In October 1992 Ismat A Majid in Brussels decided on common projects such as studying land desalination and a European-Arab University at Granada. Europe wanted small technical groups not representatives of all Arab countries. Trouble then arose over the PLO which the EC did not want represented but there was eventually a decision that the Dialogue should be between groups able to choose their own representatives and not countries. In 1989 there was a resumption of the Dialogue after Egypt rejoined, with France keen to assert a

mediating role. Little was achieved – not wholesale economic dialogue but a bilateral agreement. Arabs had not hoped for an understanding of Arab culture but had nevertheless seen a change in the European attitude towards Palestine, which was now seen as a national rather than a refugee problem. The EC seemed more concerned in dealing with the Gulf Co-operation Council and Arab Maghreb Union.

EVIAN AGREEMENTS (1962)

The first attempt at ending the Algerian War of Independence at the Melun Talks in June 1960 failed because General de Gaulle had been unwilling to appear to recognise the legitimacy of the Gouvernement Provisoire de la République Algérienne and also because he hoped that it might be possible to find a different negotiating partner. A year later, disgusted by the intransigence of the colons, after several delays, he authorised the reopening of talks which began in Evian on 20 May 1961. The French team was led by Louis Joxe, Minister of State for Algeria, and the Algerians by the GPRA Foreign Minister Bilqasim Krim. The French wanted guarantees for their citizens opting to remain in an independent Algeria but Krim argued that this would still mean colonialism. Secondly the French wished to retain the Sahara where oil had been discovered at Hassi Messaoud and where they could test nuclear weapons. The Algerians categorically refused. By 13 June talks had reached an impasse and were adjourned for a month. After a second brief session at the end of July they were suspended indefinitely. During the summer the hard-line officers and colons in the Organisation de l'Armée Secréte stepped up terrorism in France, including an attempt to murder de Gaulle, and against Muslims in Algeria: violence on both sides escalated until there were sometimes 40 a day killed in Algiers alone. In January 1962 after a meeting in Morocco the GPRA decided to renew negotiations provided that the assent of Ben Bella and his imprisoned colleagues was obtained. In February Joxe and Krim met secretly at a ski lodge at Les Rousses near Geneva and after a telephone intervention by de Gaulle reached a preliminary agreement. A formal conference opened in Evian on 7 March and concluded with the signature of a 93-page document on 18 March. Arrangements were made for a cease-fire and the release of prisoners. The full sovereignty of Algeria was recognised. The colons were to have special rights during a transition period of three years at the end of which they had to choose either French or Algerian citizenship. France had a year in which to reduce its troops in Algeria to 80,000 and a further two years in which to withdraw them completely. The great naval base at Mers-el-Kebir near Oran would be leased to France for 15 years in the first instance and other essential bases would be retained for an unspecified period. France would continue the aid promised in the Constantine Plan for at least three years. Algeria would remain part of the franc zone and Algerian workers would be free to remain in France. France would retain existing oil concessions in the Sahara and would have preferential treatment for new development for the next six years. It would retain nuclear testing facilities in the desert. A Provisional Executive of equal numbers of Algerians and French would rule during a transition period and would organise a referendum in not less than six months. Most Algerians considered the Agreement a triumph although some such as Ben Bella felt that too much had been conceded. Most of Metropolitan France was glad that the war was over while the colons felt betrayed and about 1,500,000 of them left Algeria.

FAHD (1921–)

King of Saudi Arabia. He was the eleventh son of Ibn Saud, the eldest of his seven sons by Hassa al-Sudairi and he received a more modern education than his elder brothers before pursuing religious studies in Medina. In 1945 he was one of the Saudi delegation to the founding conference of the UN and represented the Kingdom at the Coronation of Queen Elizabeth. In 1953 his brother Saud appointed him the Kingdom's first Minister of Education at a time when there was a single secondary school in Mecca and a total of 35,000 receiving education. He concentrated on building up from the bottom but was also instrumental in founding Riyadh University and a programme for the education of girls. He also led Saudi delegations to sessions of the Arab League. In the power struggle of the early 1960s he sided with Faysal, to whom he was always close, and who in 1962 made him Minister of the Interior and Second Deputy Prime Minister. In Saudi terms he proved himself a liberal but attracted much criticism by his behaviour during his long periods outside the country, particularly gambling on the Riviera. He presided over the drafting of the first Five-Year Plan. There was speculation that Fahd might become the next King as Crown Prince Khalid was believed to be in poor health and reluctant to accept the throne but on the murder of Faysal Khalid did succeed, appointing Fahd Crown Prince and First Deputy Prime Minister and delegating to him much of the day-to-day responsibility for administration. Fahd was helped by the oil boom and channelled much of the revenue into major development projects such as those at Yanbu and Jubayl. He took a particular interest in desalination and irrigation, aiming, apparently regardless of cost, to make the Kingdom self-sufficient in agriculture. In foreign affairs he maintained a very close alliance with the Americans, providing money for covert operations in Nicaragua and Afghanistan which Congress would not allow the US Government to carry out. He was critical, however, of American support for Israel, refused an invitation after Camp David for fear of coming under pressure to endorse it and in 1981 launched his own initiative, the Fahd Plan which was attacked with equal vehemence by the Steadfastness Front and the Israeli Government. In June 1982 he ascended the throne and there was some expectation that, freed from the innate conservatism of Khalid, he would introduce some major reforms. In fact, frightened by the fate of the Shah, he was more concerned with preserving the consensus and not alarming the ulema. Anxious to keep their goodwill he did not cut the religious budget at a time when all others were slashed and in 1986 he dropped the title of King in favour of "Custodian of the Two Holy Places". In 1984 he spoke of creating a "Parliament like any other country" but no immediate steps were taken to increase political participation and his unwillingness to admit that the Government could ever be wrong led to criticism of his attitude after the Mecca Tunnel Disaster. His dislike of seeing members of the Royal Family overshadowed by a commoner was probably a major reason for his abrupt dismissal of Shaykh Yamani in 1986 who was advocating a more realistic oil pricing policy than that demanded by the King. A large, heavy man, Fahd is charming, courteous, kind and generous but not especially charismatic. He is a heavy smoker and said to be indolent, although in bursts is a hard worker, and in particular late at night. He has a remarkable grasp of detail and tends towards the lenient, hating never to say no. Stories of his extravagance must be balanced against the immense wealth of the Kingdom. Fahd lavished money on his teenage son Abd Allah and in 1985 ordered a Jumbo jet which he equipped as a flying palace complete with a three-storey lift for a reputed $150 m. He heavily subsidised farming, paying five times the world price for wheat. He encourages the making of money almost as much as he encourages the making of sons. :He channels vast sums establishing religious universities and to fund the Holy Places. In July 1990 he established political relations with Peking and later with Muslim states. The new generation in the Kingdom is not really interested in tribal Najd and prefers intellectuals of Hijaz and businessmen. In March 1992 he set up a Consultative Council and established basic law establishing constitutional rights and freedom from arbitrary arrest. His reforms were, he said, based on Islamic principles of decency and popular consultation and he denied that he was moving away from his religious roots. He established elected regional assemblies and an Electoral College of about 500 princes eligible to be named king who will have to endorse his successor. He attacked the US Middle East Watch as codifying royal absolutism.

FAHD PLAN (1981)

In August 1981 Crown Prince Fahd gave an interview in which he criticised the American Government for failing to realise that Camp David did not provide a satisfactory basis for peace in the Middle East and making no further effort. He then put forward his own eight-point plan. The Israelis should withdraw from all territory occupied in 1967 including East Jerusalem; settlements should be dismantled. There should be freedom for all religions in the Holy Places. Palestinians driven from their homes should have the right of return and compensation. There should be a transitional period of several months under UN auspices in the West Bank and Gaza. An independent Palestinian state should be set up with Jerusalem as its capital. All states in the region should be allowed to live in peace. The UN should guarantee to implement these proposals which were General Assembly decisions, not his own invention. They needed "an end to unlimited American support for Israel", "an end to Israeli arrogance" and "recognition that the Palestinian factor is the basic factor in the Middle East equation". It appeared to recognise the right of Israel to exist by its reference to "all" states but Begin said that it was designed "to liquidate Israel by stages". It was dismissed by Sadat and the Americans as containing nothing new although Reagan regarded it as "potentially important" but welcomed by the Europeans. The Fahd Plan was a rare example of the Kingdom's launching a diplomatic initiative and perhaps even aspiring to Arab leadership. It failed in its main object of reuniting the Arab world, split between the moderates and the Steadfastness Front, Libya saying that anyone who supported it was "a traitor", and the Fez Summit, meeting in November to discuss it, broke up after a single session.

FAO, Battle of (1986–88)

Fao stands on a mud-spit near the mouth of the Shatt al-Arab about 75 miles from Basra. During the Iran–Iraq War, on the night of 9 February 1986 the Iranians made a surprise crossing of the river and occupied the Peninsula. It was reported that 140 mullahs inspiring the troops were killed in the operation. Subsequently about 85,000 soldiers and fanatical volunteers (*Basij*) tried to push on to Basra but they were held in fighting so bloody that the entire Baghdad taxi fleet and a whole train were commandeered to bring back Iraqi corpses. In the fighting that followed it was estimated that 10 million shells were fired as the Iraqis constructed impenetrably fortified lines. The firing was often heard in Kuwait. Maintenance of such a large force on the other side of the Shatt proved such a burden on the Iranian supply system that it weakened their efforts elsewhere. In mid-April 1988 the Iraqis launched a meticulously-planned operation which, with the help of poison gas, overran the Iranian defences in two days. The area was totally devastated.

FARIDA (1921–88)

Queen of Egypt. She was born Safinaz Zulfikar, daughter of a wealthy judge in Alexandria and a lady-in-waiting to Queen Nazli, wife of King Fuad. At the age of 17 she married the 18-year-old King Farouq, changing her name to conform with the new tradition that all members of the Royal Family should have names starting with "F". The couple were extremely handsome and charming and became very popular. She had three daughters and not the son that the King desired and during and after the war his life became increasingly scandalous. In 1948 he divorced her, greatly increasing his own unpopularity. After the Revolution, the private wealth of the Royal Family was expropriated and Farida was allotted a pension of $52

a month. She therefore went abroad and earned her living as a painter. Her works were exhibited in Europe and America. She returned to Egypt in the 1970s, living very quietly in a small apartment in Maadi and continued to work until she became ill. She was unable to afford hospital treatment and eventually this was provided at the expense of the state on the orders of President Mubarak.

FARIS, Abd al-Rahman (1911–)

Algerian political leader. He was born in Algiers and qualified as a lawyer in the University there. He entered politics as a moderate nationalist, in favour of integration with France and was President of the Algerian Assembly. In September 1955, nearly a year after the All Saints' Day Uprising he was one of 61 prominent Muslims who passed a majority resolution that total integration was still the best solution. A year later, however, he declared that the Front de Libération Nationale was the only valid spokesman for the Algerian people and in December he formed a committee to help students striking in obedience to its orders. He continued to hold a legal position under the French Government and in October 1958, after the announcement of the Constantine Plan, Faris was used by President de Gaulle in attempts to negotiate a *paix des braves* with the FLN. In 1961 he was arrested by the French but in March 1962 after the signature of the Evian Agreement he was released to head a Provisional Executive, a mixed French-Algerian caretaker government, until an Algerian Government could be formed. On 3 July as Acting Head of State he formally acknowledged the letter of General de Gaulle recognising Algerian independence. He was, however, as a middle-class moderate, distrusted by the former guerrillas and his Executive was elbowed aside, being dissolved on 24 September. In July 1964 Faris was arrested as a counter-revolutionary for opposing Ben Bella and spent a year in jail before being released after Boumédienne had seized power.

al-FASSI, (Muhammad) Allal (1906–74)

Moroccan nationalist leader. He was born in Fez into a very distinguished family of Andalusian origin which claimed descent from Uqba b. Nafi, the original Arab conqueror of North Africa. His father was a Professor and the Librarian of the Qarawiyin University where Allal received a purely Arab education and came under the influence of the Salafiyyah Movement. In 1930 he was twice imprisoned for attacking the Berber Dahir and he went to see the young Sultan Muhammad V who promised him not to surrender any of the rights of the nation. Although he had passed his examinations with great distinction the authorities refused him a licence to teach but he was able to give evening lectures on the life of the Prophet which he used to make contemporary political points. He carried forward the philosophical and political thought of Muhammad Abduh and also wrote nationalist poetry which had a wide appeal. In August 1933, expecting arrest he fled to Paris but he returned the following year to play the leading part in the foundation of the National Action Bloc and the drafting of the Plan de Réformes Marocaines. In November 1936 he was arrested after demonstrations in Fez and held for two months and in October 1937 he was banished to Gabon where he was held in isolation but he used the opportunity to learn French and to write a book in which he set out his creed of theocracy. He refused to support General de Gaulle who would give no assurances about future independence. In June 1946 he was allowed to return home where he found himself accepted as the leader of the Istiqlal Party which had been formed during his absence. In May 1947 Si Allal moved to Cairo where he was appointed Secretary-General of the newly formed Maghreb Bureau which had been set up by the Arab League to work for the independence of the whole of North Africa. He had great prestige and travelled widely, lobbying in the free Arab countries, Europe, Africa, Latin America and at the UN. After the exile of Muhammad V he made many broadcasts from Cairo calling for the continuation of the armed struggle which he went secretly to Spain to organise. He was not involved in the negotiations for independence which he criticised for not applying to the whole Maghreb and he refused any settlement which did not immediately bring the return of the Sultan. In October 1955 he called for a joint Algerian–Moroccan war against France, the only Istiqlal leader to do so. He was at this time on the margins of the Party, although still its titular leader. He returned to Morocco in March 1956 but although his party formed the majority of the Government, he refused to take a Ministry or to participate in day-to-day party politics. He was active in purging supporters of the former regime and in trying to prevent Berber separatism. He criticised the Government for not pressing a claim to the whole of Mauritania and in 1957 founded Le Sahara Marocain to do so. He encouraged the guerrilla activities that led to the Ifni Crisis and even claimed the Canary Islands. During 1958 the Istiqlal started to split with the younger leaders such as Mehdi Ben Barka and Abd al-Rahim Bouabid regarding the Balafrej government as reactionary and bourgeois. The King asked Si Allal who had not endorsed either group to form a government of reconciliation but he was unable to do so. In January 1960 as President of Istiq he used his position to encourage the young, trying to dissociate himself from the old impression of the Fez bourgeois by appealing to workers and peasants to push Islamic socialism. In June 1961 he was minister for International Affairs. In November 1969 he was elected President of Conseil Constitutionnel and in 1970 allied with the UNFP against Khatib. He was always loyal to the monarchy but also to Parliament. In July 1971 he was present at Skhirat. He was a heavily built man with a red beard, very blue eyes and a deep voice. He was frugal, eloquent to the point of grandiloquence, even in private conversation, and utterly incorruptible. He died in Bucharest.

FATAH

"FATAH" is a reversed acronym of *Harakat al-Tahrir al-Falastini* – Movement for the Liberation of Palestine and also means "Victory". Its origins are obscure but about 1959 young Palestinians in Cairo and the Gaza Strip including Yassir Arafat, Abu Jihad, Abu Iyad and Abu Lutf started publishing a journal *Our Palestine*. Their ideas were nationalist and close to those of the

Muslim Brothers rather than socialist but they wished to avoid ideological discussion until victory had been won and they were anxious not to be tied to any Arab government although they received some help from Saudi Arabia. Many of them went to the oil states so as to earn money for the organisation. They created a military wing *al-Asifa* with Arafat as Commander-in-Chief and Abu Jihad as Chief of Staff and established training camps in various countries to escape the exclusive control of Nasser. Asifa carried out its first operation on 1 January 1965 blowing up an Israeli pumping station at the time of the Jordan Waters Dispute. The first Israeli reprisal took place in May but according to Israeli sources Fatah staged over 30 raids in that year. Its military doctrine was influenced by the Algerian War of Independence and the lessons of Vietnam and "Che" Guevara. The Unified Arab Command which, fearing to provoke Israeli reprisals before the Arab armies were ready for war, had vetoed guerrilla activity, ordered the arrest of Fatah members – Arafat was imprisoned in Damascus. The June War which showed that the Arab regular armies could not defeat Israel gave a new impetus to the *fidayin* and Fatah was reborn in a general Congress which reaffirmed the need for a long-term people's war. Its reputation was enhanced by its part in repelling an Israeli attack on Karamah in March 1968. Fatah ceased to be clandestine and in April Arafat was publicly named as its leader. The fourth Congress of the Palestine National Council recognised that Fatah was the strongest of the guerrilla groups and its predominance was further recognised by the election of Arafat as Chairman of the Palestine Liberation Organisation at the fifth Congress in February 1969. The practical identification of Fatah with the PLO, which it attempted to aggrandise so as to claim equality with independent Arab states, was much resented by radical groups such as the Popular Front for the Liberation of Palestine which demanded equality of representation. Fatah was, however, by far the richest, most organised and most numerous faction with 20,000 fighting men whereas no other had more than 1,000 although Syria and Iraq both formed their own commando groups to compete with it. In January 1969 Nasser gave it a radio station in Cairo. Fatah established bases in Lebanon and Jordan for raids into Israel and the Occupied Territories where it enjoyed overwhelming popular support. The Israeli reprisals that these provoked led to some restrictions upon its activities in Lebanon by the Cairo Agreement and the arrogance that it showed in Jordan led to its expulsion after heavy fighting in Black September. These setbacks led to a series of disputes within Fatah, some advocating a return to secrecy and violence while others wanted to achieve political respectability at the same time as a right wing called for closer ties with conservative Arab regimes and leftists wanted relations with the Soviet Union and revolutionary movements in the Arab world and elsewhere. The leftists, led by Abu Iyad triumphed, Arafat went to Moscow and there was a mending of fences with the PFLP and other leftist factions. Fatah started training international revolutionary groups such as the Popular Front for the Liberation of the Occupied Arab Gulf and dissidents from other countries such as Turkey and

Iran and at the same time sent some of its own men for training in Eastern Europe. A Fatah member, Abu Daoud was believed to have planned the terrorist activities of the Black September Organisation including the Munich Olympics Murders although he subsequently stated that he had acted on the orders of Abu Iyad, who was generally regarded as the most important man in Fatah after Arafat. In Southern Lebanon it established such a presence that the area was often called "Fatahland" and was used for raids into Israel including one by sea in March 1975 when eight Fatah guerrillas seized a hotel in Tel Aviv. While conducting these activities Fatah opposed terrorist action outside the Middle East and sentenced to death Abu Nidal, its former representative in Baghdad who formed the Fatah Revolutionary Council which attacked Syrian targets in addition to Israeli interests in Europe. Fatah was regarded as one of the more moderate groups in the PLO and the belief that it was prepared to negotiate for a peace settlement on terms less than the total elimination of Israel, possibly a "two-state " solution, led to the creation of the Rejection Front led by George Habash, calling for force not diplomacy. Despite Arafat's attempts to keep out of the civil war in Lebanon Fatah became heavily involved after the Palestinian refugee camps such as Tall al-Zatar were attacked by the Maronites and this brought it into conflict with Damascus after Syrian troops entered the country to support the Government. This led to attempts by Sadat to win Fatah's acquiescence in his efforts to reach a negotiated settlement with Israel but instead it moved closer to Syria, thus alienating Iraq. Fatah men suffered heavy casualties during the Israeli invasion of Lebanon in March 1978 but fought sufficiently well to prevent the capture of Tyre despite its indiscriminate bombardment with shells and cluster bombs. The subsequent cease-fire which mutineers against Arafat's leadership headed by Abu Daoud wished to defy led to 123 of them, mostly from Iraq, being arrested by loyalists such as Abu Jihad. Casualties and the various splits, demonstrated in the fourth Congress in Damascus in May 1980, had by then reduced Fatah, according to Israeli estimates, to about 8,000 fighting men. The Israeli invasion of South Lebanon, Operation Peace for Galilee, deprived Fatah of its main base and later its fighting men were left in the lurch by Syrian acceptance of a cease-fire. The survivors were evacuated in August 1982 after the Beirut Siege but many returned to Lebanon. Arafat re-established relations with Egypt and King Hussain and appeared willing to consider the Reagan Plan while at the same time appointing as military commanders men loyal to himself who had not distinguished themselves in the recent fighting. This led to a major mutiny led by Colonel Abu Musa in May 1983 who, it soon became clear, had Syrian backing. Arafat and about 4,000 loyalists were besieged in Tripoli from September until they were evacuated under the UN flag in December: about 400 Palestinians had been killed in the fighting. Abu Musa was expelled from Fatah and later most of his followers rejoined the mainstream. The PNC meeting of November 1984 showed that Fatah was still the dominant force in the PLO and was prepared to follow Arafat in peace moves co-ordinated with King Hussain. When these broke down

Hussain tried to sponsor a puppet Fatah of those based in Jordan but it never won significant support. Fatah was formally reconciled with most of the other groups at the Algiers PNC meeting in April 1987. The old Fatah policy of negotiating to obtain even a mini-state on Palestinian soil was accepted by practically the whole of the PLO at the Palestine National Council Algiers Meeting in November 1988. Earlier that year three Fatah members were murdered by Israeli intelligence officers to frustrate a possible propaganda coup with the Ship of Return. The outbreak of the *Intifadah* showed the support that Fatah still enjoyed in the Occupied Territories but later the fear that Arafat might concede too much to obtain peace led to a coalition against it of the PFLP and local organisation such as Hamas. Fatah had largely re-established its position, with about 5,000 men in South Lebanon where in September 1990 it fought off a challenge from the followers of Abu Nidal in clashes in which over 70 were killed and in which it had the support of Amal and Huzbullah. In April 1991, there was more fighting against Abu Nidal in South Lebanon. In March 1992, after a debate in the Ruling Council, terms were agreed for a confederation with Jordan. In April 1992 there was more fighting in South Lebanon against Abu Nidal and 25 were killed. In June Hamas denied any agreement to collaborate. The affiliated organisation of Black Panthers carried out killings and collaborated on the West Bank. They were hunted by undercover units and 38 were killed in the three years to December 1992. In August an Israeli unit commander and two Black Panthers were killed in Janin. A similar group of Fatah hawks was formed in Gaza. In early September, despite the old willingness to accept "one square metre" of Palestine there was dissent in central Committee from veterans like Khalid al-Hassan. On 23 September Fatah loyalists were killed in Gaza by opponents of peace, but it is not clear if these were from within Fatah.

FATAH REVOLUTIONARY COUNCIL

In 1973 Abu Nidal broke away from the main Fatah organisation to form his own group which hoped to liberate Palestine through terrorism against anyone dealing with Israel. He received the backing of Iraq and his followers, using the name Black June, were active in 1976 and 1977 in attacking Syrian Embassies. Later the FRC killed moderate Palestinians such as Isam Sartawi and representatives of the Palestine Liberation Organisation in Arab and European capitals. Attempts were made on the lives of Yassir Arafat and Abu Iyad. Attacks were also made on Arab diplomats and after Camp David upon Israelis in Egypt. Aircraft were hijacked in November 1973 and November 1974. In the interests of Iraq the FRC attempted to murder the Israeli Ambassador in London in June 1982 as Saddam Hussain hoped that subsequent Israeli reprisals in Lebanon would embarrass Syria. In November 1983 when Saddam was desperate for Saudi aid during the Iran–Iraq War he was pressed to expel Abu Nidal who with his followers became clients of Syria. In the spring of 1983 there was growing dissatisfaction within Fatah at the leadership of Arafat after the evacuation of the guerrillas from Beirut and Arafat's *rapprochement* with King Hussain to discuss the Reagan Plan. He was regarded, also as preferring political to military action and over-tolerant of corruption. In May 1983, with Syrian encouragement, Colonel Said Musa, a Sandhurst-trained former Jordanian officer who had switched to Fatah after Black September revolted after Arafat had attempted to replace him with another officer judged to have shown cowardice during recent fighting. They took over Fatah offices and bases in Damascus and the Biqa and besieged Arafat and 4,000 of his supporters in Tripoli where they held out for a month before being evacuated. This group also assumed the name of Fatah Revolutionary Council when it constituted itself in Damascus in June, although it was more generally known as the Fatah rebels. It collaborated with the followers of Abu Nidal. The Fatah rebels opposed Arafat's conclusion of the Amman Accord with the King but the Syrian use of Amal to attack Palestinian refugee camps in Lebanon in 1985–86 caused most of its members to rejoin the mainstream of Fatah. The Abu Nidal faction, moved back to Baghdad in June 1984 and resumed its terrorist activities especially against Jordanian targets. There were several incidents involving grenades and bombs in Athens. In 1985 the faction was responsible for attacks with grenades and guns on British Airways offices in Madrid and Rome and that winter the FRC was blamed for the Malta Hijacking and the Rome and Vienna Airport Attacks. It put bombs in Paris department stores and in 1986 12 Jews were killed in a synagogue in Istanbul. It refused to be reconciled with other groups and did not attend the session of the Palestine National Council in Algiers in April 1987. It stood for the total elimination of Israel and refused the idea of a Palestinian state on only part of the territory. During 1987 Abu Nidal moved to Tripoli but most of his men remained in Lebanon. There they became involved in vicious infighting and in 1988 an estimated 150 of them were liquidated on the orders of Abu Nidal. They became involved, also, in a struggle with Fatah for dominance over the camps of South Lebanon and after murders on both sides, Arafat loyalists inflicted severe losses upon them in June 1990. In September 1990 there was further fighting with 80 killed in one day. In 1987 they claimed to have seized a yacht with six Belgians, French women and two children, who were later released. April 1988 saw the Acropole murders. The FRC strongly supported the invasion of Kuwait and some members were arrested for their involvement in the killing of a passenger on an Israeli bus. In July 1992 two FRC leaders were killed after Fatah commanders were murdered in the Lebanon.

al-FATAT

Fatat, also known as the Young Arab Society, was a secret group dedicated to the achievement of Arab independence from the Ottoman Empire founded by seven students in Paris in 1911. It represented a significant advance from the positions of the Ottoman Decentralisation Party and the Qahtaniyyah which aimed at improving the status of Arabs while remaining within the Empire. Its members, eventually numbering about 200, were bound by oaths and carefully screened; nearly all were Muslims. In April 1913 its members, together with those of the Decentralisation Party organised the

First Arab Congress in Paris but later that year after the leaders had returned home, it was centred firstly on Beirut and then on Damascus. The future King Faysal may have become a member. Fatat, together with the Ahd was responsible drawing up the Damascus Protocol, the terms on which the Arabs would assist the British by revolting against the Turks and in pressing the Hashemites to take the lead. Of its founders, three were hanged by the Turks, Jamil Mardam, Shukri al-Quwatli and Awni Abd al-Hadi headed governments and Rustum Haidar became the closest adviser to Faysal. After the war its members kept in touch as the pan-Arab *Istiqlal* Party.

FAWZI, Mahmud (1900–81)

Egyptian Prime Minister. He studied law at Cairo University before joining the diplomatic service in which he was posted to Rome where he took a Doctorate in Criminal Law. He spent several years in Kobe where he learned Japanese and also served in the USA and in Greece. From 1937 to 1940 he was Consul-General in Liverpool, finding time to take further courses at the University there. After a brief period in the Foreign Ministry in Cairo he was Consul-General in Jerusalem before becoming the first Egyptian Representative at the UN, deeply engaged in the Palestine question. Fawzi had just been appointed Ambassador in London when he was recalled to become Foreign Minister after the July Revolution. He held this post throughout the Nasser period. When Eden became Prime Minister Fawzi chaired a committee to study his possible policies and later played an important part in negotiating the Anglo-Egyptian Treaty of 1954 and in the diplomatic activities of the Suez War. In 1958 he accompanied his chief to Moscow to negotiate arms deals. He was Deputy Prime Minister and then Presidential Assistant for Foreign Affairs. After the June War Fawzi toured Western countries to restore damaged relations. He worked with the Russians at the UN and was mentioned as a possible Secretary-General for the Arab League. After Nasser had announced that there would be free elections within the ASU, he put Fawzi in charge of organising them in May 1968 and then of preparing the agenda for the Congress. Fawzi did much to persuade Nasser to accept the Rogers' Plan (II). On 21 October 1970 he was the first civilian since the Revolution to become Prime Minister, probably because he was neutral in the struggle between Nasser's heirs and it was thought that his diplomatic skills would be useful in building new bridges to the West without alienating Russia. After three weeks he reformed his Cabinet with a group of Deputy Prime Ministers concentrating on general policy and inter-departmental co-ordination, grouping together several Ministers and declared that increased democracy and scientific research were the highest national priorities. He was involved in the negotiations for the creation of the Federation of Arab Republics which formally came into being in May 1971. Opposition to it led to a plot against Sadat in which several Cabinet Ministers had been involved and Fawzi had to reform his government. He reformed it again in September, abolishing several Ministries. Fawzi, although a skilled diplomat, was not a successful Prime Minister, he was too old, had had no experience of domestic politics nor of the formulation of policy, having spent his life carrying out instructions from superiors, and in January 1972 Sadat replaced him with an able technocrat, Aziz Sidqi whom he considered would do a better job of preparing the country for war. Fawzi was given the honorary position of Vice-President which he held until he retired in 1974. He was a natural linguist, even learning Amharic.

FAWZI, Muhammad, General (1915–)

Egyptian soldier and conspirator. He commanded a division in the Palestine War. In 1957 he was Commandant of the Military Academy and in 1961 he was nominated as Chief of Staff of the African High Command that was theoretically established by the Casablanca Bloc. After commanding a corps in the Yemen War, Fawzi was Chief of Staff when in November 1966 it was agreed that in the event of war he should command Egyptian and Syrian forces. In May 1967 he wrote the letter demanding the withdrawal of UNEF observers from Sinai that gave Israel the pretext for launching the June War. As Egyptian resistance was collapsing, Fawzi, on the orders of Nasser, arrested Field Marshal Amer whom he succeeded as Commander-in-Chief. In January 1968 he was appointed Minister of War and by now was one of the President's "inner circle". He attended the Khartoum Summit and the Rabat Summit making specific requests for assistance with troops and weapons. During the War of Attrition he was in constant contact with the Russians seeking weapons and training. He also worked closely with service chiefs of the Arab countries. In May 1971 it was announced that he had resigned and in July that he was to be court-martialled for treason. It was stated that he, Ali Sabri and Sharawi Jumaa had immediately after the death of Nasser started a conspiracy to overthrow Sadat; Fawzi was to have provided the troops and to become the new head of State. He was believed to have opposed better relations with America and the formation of the Federation of Arab Republics. He was said, with Jumaa, to have paid a spiritualist medium to put him in touch with Nasser to receive orders. In court he appeared weak and emaciated, answering all questions with "I don't know" and complaining that his memory had been affected by prison food. The Prosecutor demanded the death penalty but Fawzi was sentenced to 15 years' imprisonment and released in April 1974. According to Haykal, Nasser called Fawzi the "cruel disciplinarian", a harsh, unimaginative man but who had the qualities to pull the army together after the favouritism and incompetence of the Amer years.

FAYSAL (c. 1905–75)

King of Saudi Arabia. He was the third son of Ibn Saud, the only one by a descendant of Muhammad Ibn Abd al-Wahhab, but his mother died soon after his birth. He received a traditional Islamic education but in 1919 became the first of his family, at the invitation of the British Government, to visit Western Europe. In addition to being received by George V he attended numerous functions in Wales, Ireland and France. Soon after his return he was put in nominal command of operations against Ali b. Muhammad al-Idrisi in Asir.

Faysal had a major role in the war against King Hussain and after its conclusion was appointed Viceroy of the Hijaz. As foreign representatives were confined to Jiddah, Faysal was responsible for dealing with them and became in effect Foreign Minister although much of the routine work was done by Fuad Hamza. Diplomatic reports at this time show him as a rather dissolute young man but he was used by his father in responsible posts such as President of the Consultative Council and in 1926 he was sent to London again for frontier negotiations. In 1932 Faysal visited Britain, France, Turkey and the Soviet Union whence he returned overland via the oilfields. Faysal's corps was responsible for the conquest of the Tihamah in the Saudi–Yemeni War of 1934 while that of his elder brother Saud remained largely immobile in the mountains. Faysal led the Saudi delegation to the London Palestine Conference of 1939 and to the San Francisco Conference of 1945 which founded the United Nations. King Abd al-Aziz was determined that after his death his two oldest sons should rule in tandem so when he created the Council of Ministers he appointed Saud Chairman with Faysal as his Deputy and decreed that after Saud became King, the succession would go to Faysal and not to a son of Saud. At first after Saud had inherited the throne in November 1953 this arrangement appeared to work smoothly but it became apparent that the efficient Faysal was becoming exasperated by the incompetence of the new King with his tolerance of waste and corruption. Faysal spent much of 1957 in Europe and America where he underwent two operations. By March 1958, despite enormous oil revenues the country was practically bankrupt and in foreign affairs Saud had demeaned it by a clumsy attempt to procure the murder of Nasser. A Council of the Royal Family decided that Faysal should be given full powers to restore the situation. Faysal banned foreigners from the Cabinet and set in train rigid economies, stablised the currency, producing the country's first Budget; soon half-finished palaces were to be seen all over Riyadh. Some reforms were introduced but apart from one initiating education for girls, they were in no way revolutionary and there was no suggestion of inviting public participation in decision-making. The King started a clever campaign to rebuild his support – he persuaded the younger liberal Princes such as Talal b. Abd al-Aziz al-Saud that he was in favour of representative government, the ulema of his traditionalism and the tribes of his past and future lavishness. In December 1960, refusing to sign the Budget that Faysal presented, he took his brother's protests as a resignation which he instantly accepted. Faysal declined to revert to Deputy Prime Minister, withdrawing from public life for over a year. Saud's health declined and in March 1962 he invited his brother to return as Deputy Premier and Foreign Minister and started to spend increasing periods abroad. In August the Kingdom was shaken by the defection of Talal and from September by the presence of Egyptian troops such as Talal b. Abd al-Aziz al-Saud, engaged in the Yemen War, on its frontiers. Faysal, in Washington at the time, warned Kennedy that the Imamate had been overthrown by an Egyptian plot, not by a popular revolution. In November Faysal became Prime Minister, forming a Cabinet which brought in some of the young, modern-minded princes such as Fahd. Allowances to the Royal Family were sharply cut. A major programme of reforms began with the freeing of slaves with compensation for their owners, a Judicial Council of twenty leading ulema and a special drive to find water and build desalination plants in the hope of achieving agricultural self-sufficiency. The situation became critical with the Yemeni leader Marshal Sallal and the Egyptian radio calling for the overthrow of the Saudi monarchy while after Egyptian aircraft had bombed villages in the South West, diplomatic relations were broken. They were restored, however, with Britain after the breach over Buraymi and the Suez War while the Americans gave an air demonstration of their readiness to support the Kingdom. In March 1964 Saud demanded the restoration of all his powers but was forced instead to accept their curtailment: he continued to intrigue and in November was deposed and Faysal became King. As sovereign he initiated great programmes of development while insisting that all was done within the framework of Islam. Hundreds of schools were built, one every three days at one stage, a free health service and road networks created and television programmes started and after the great oil-price rises of 1971 and 1973 huge sums were available. Faysal aimed at diversification beyond oil to achieve ultimate self-sufficiency rather than mere profitability. Able young technocrats like Ahmad Zaki Yamani and Hisham Nazir enjoyed royal patronage and were given great responsibilities. All his seven sons received their higher education in the West. Although provinces were given some local government, Faysal adamantly rejected any form of political assembly or even the existence of trade unions. In 1969 there were reports of attempted coups and in October it was admitted that 250 people, including some young officers, had been arrested. Rumours in 1972 and 1974 linked the sons of Saud with further conspiracies. Punishments were administered according to Islamic law. "The Holy Qur'an", he declared provided "the oldest and the best of Constitutions", making the country "one big Family" in which "anyone oppressed has only to come and see me". He spent endless hours in his *majlis* dealing with petitions from all classes but was obsessed with fear and hatred of communism. While Faysal dominated his country he was also a major figure in international affairs, exercising more influence than any Arab leader for centuries. Apart from the Communist states, he visited and received nearly all world leaders, using state visits as an instrument of policy. His foreign policy had three overriding principles: no other power could be permitted to dominate the Arabian Peninsula, Islamic solidarity had to be maintained and Zionism, "the mother of Communism", had to be resisted. He was determined that Yemen should not come under Egyptian control and provided bases, arms and money for the Royalists while at the same time trying to reach a settlement with Nasser over their heads as in the Jiddah Agreement of August 1965. Faysal came, however, to regard the Egyptian leader as totally untrustworthy and used the Yemen as a battleground to resist his pretensions to leadership of the Arab world. He distrusted Nasser's socialism as preparing the ground for communism and, hoping to use Muslim solidarity against Arab

nationalism, toured the Islamic world from Iran and Pakistan to Mali and Guinea warning against "alien and atheistic influences". He collaborated with Nasser's Arab foes such as King Hussain whom he subsidised. During 1966 Nasser's propaganda machine hurled frantic insults at Faysal who rarely replied in kind although he took the precaution of concluding large arms deals with the USA and the UK. During a state visit to London in May 1967 he made strenuous efforts to persuade the Wilson government to reverse its decision to withdraw from Aden which he feared would come under Nasser's control but he resisted British suggestions that he should himself intervene there. The situation was radically altered by the June War from which Faysal emerged as the real victor with Nasser humiliated and reduced to becoming his pensioner. After the withdrawal of Egyptian troops from the Yemen and the overthrow of Sallal, the government of Abd al-Rahman al-Iryani also depended upon Saudi money and provided bases for refugees, subsidised and armed by Faysal, from the new left-wing government in Aden which the King refused to recognise and made several attempts to overthrow; frontier clashes took place, most notably at al-Wadiah. He provided help to Sultan Qabus to defeat the communist-supported Dhofar Rebellion and encouraged other Gulf rulers to reject demands from their subjects for political participation, although for three years, maintaining the old claim to Buraymi, he refused to recognise the UAE. He accepted the Nixon Doctrine under which he and the Shah, both heavily armed, were responsible for Gulf security. In November 1968 they agreed to a delimitation of their offshore areas. Another result of the June War, the annexation of Jerusalem by Israel, obsessed the King for the rest of his days. He saw its recovery as a task for Islam as a whole and after the Al-Aqsa Mosque burning issued several calls for *Jihad*. Intense diplomatic activity, much of it conducted personally, led to the first meeting of Islamic Foreign Ministers in Jiddah in March 1970 and the subsequent creation of the Islamic Conference Organisation, the Islamic News Agency, the Islamic Development Bank etc. Faysal tried to mediate between King Hussain and Fatah which he subsidised so as to prevent the Palestine Liberation Organisation from becoming controlled by the more revolutionary groups. He tried to win support from moderate African states by subsidies and by joining the boycott of Rhodesia. In order to acquire an independent source of weapons Faysal did much of the funding of the Arab Military Industries Organisation. In the meanwhile he was dependent upon the West for arms which he could not bring himself to seek from Russia. He made major purchases from France in 1972 and Britain in 1973. Relations with these countries, and also America, were often difficult as he saw them as being in thrall to Zionist trickery but nevertheless he hoped to win them over to the Arab cause by the use, at the appropriate time, of the Oil Weapon. In the meanwhile his moderation won him the hostility of radicals such as Qadafi, the Syrians who supported a "Saudi Liberation Front" and the Iraqis who saw him as the servant of colonialism. The King maintained close links with Anwar Sadat, who came three times in one year and he was one of the very few privy to the plan for the October

War during which he sent troops to the front. He was so incensed by the extent of American support for Israel that he cut off all oil supplies to them but relations were soon cordial again and in June 1968 Nixon visited Riyadh and spoke of co-operation in desert agriculture and in harnessing solar energy. The war made Syria and Jordan as well as Egypt financially dependent upon the Saudis as the subsequent quadrupling of the oil price made the Kingdom incomparably rich. There were more large arms deals but also the establishment, in September 1974 of a fund to help the developing states and $4,500 million were given in two years. In the same month a $1,000 million loan was made to Japan. On 25 March 1975, while holding his *majlis* the King was shot three times by his nephew Faysal b. Musaid whom he was in the act of embracing. The assassin who as a student in America had a history of drugs and drink was publicly executed. The *Washington Post* stated that the King had done more harm to the West than anyone since Hitler. Faysal's immense experience, tenacity, self-control and patience made him realistic to the verge of cynicism. In person he was of medium height, slim, with thin, acquiline, austere features which rarely relaxed although he could be humorous and charming. He remained married to a single wife, Iffat, for forty years. His rule was based as his father's had been on alliances with the ulema, the tribes and the leading families and he completed the work of his father who had built a Kingdom but not found a place for it in the modern world. Faysal did so without abandoning its traditional values, accepting modern technology while resisting the shoddier aspects of Western culture.

FAYSAL-CLEMENCEAU AGREEMENT (1919)
The Arab Revolt had concluded with the Amir Faysal setting up a government in Damascus but at the end of November 1918 his father King Hussain ordered him to Europe to represent the Arabs at the forthcoming Peace Conference. In London he was told by Lloyd George that under the Sykes–Picot Agreement the British had no option but to support French claims to supremacy in Syria and advised him to make the best deal with them that he could. In April 1919 Faysal met Prime Minister Clemenceau who assured him that France had no wish to conquer the country but asked that as a minimum French troops should replace the British still there. Faysal, hoping that the King–Crane Commission would report in favour of Syrian independence and that this would be accepted by the Great Powers, was non-committal. The situation in the area was later complicated by the defeat suffered by the French at the hands of resurgent Turkish nationalism in Cilicia and fears that Faysal might ally himself with it, spurred on by the unrealistic demands of nationalists in Damascus. In October Faysal reached a provisional agreement with the French Prime Minister which was so favourable to the Arabs that Clemenceau, fearing that it would jeopardise his bid for the Presidency, insisted that it should be kept secret. France would rule a Greater Lebanon and exercise the loosest type of Mandate over Syria which, with French advisers would be practically independent and over which he would recognise Faysal as King provided that he maintained order. France would guarantee Syria against external

aggression and handle its foreign relations and provide assistance in organising a treasury, an army and a police force. It is possible that he even promised to try to get Faysal's Kingdom to include Palestine. In November the last British troops were withdrawn from Syria. Then Clemenceau was defeated for the Presidency and retired from politics and the General Syrian Congress proclaimed Faysal King and refused any connection with the French. The San Remo Conference in April 1920 formally assigned the Mandate for Syria to France and the stage was then set for the battle of Maysalun and the French takeover of Syria.

FAYSAL–WEIZMANN AGREEMENT (1919)
The British Government sent Chaim Weizmann, the Zionist leader, out to the Middle East and Allenby, the Commander-in-Chief arranged for him to meet the Amir Faysal near Aqaba in June 1918. Weizmann stated that the Jews did not propose to set up any government of their own in Palestine but to develop and colonise the country. Faysal did not object to Jewish immigration provided that Arab farmers were also helped. They agreed on the necessity for future co-operation and Faysal accepted Weizmann's offer to represent both of them in the USA although he said that political decisions could only be taken by his father King Hussain. This first meeting was merely making of acquaintance with no practical outcome but in January 1919, Faysal wanting allies at the Versailles Peace Conference, signed an Agreement with Weizmann. It provided for "the closest collaboration" between "the Arab State and Palestine", the boundaries of which would be determined by a joint commission. They endorsed the Balfour Declaration and agreed to encourage "large-scale" Jewish immigration while the rights of Arab farmers should be protected. Faysal added a handwritten note making the carrying out of the Agreement conditional upon the Arabs receiving their independence as he had demanded in a Memorandum around the same time. Many Arabs later claimed that Faysal had been misled by T. E. Lawrence into signing a document for which he had no proper authority and of which he had probably not fully understood the translation.

FEDERATION OF ARAB EMIRATES
The Dubai Agreement of February 1968 established a Federation of Nine Gulf states, Bahrain, Qatar and the seven Trucial Shaykhdoms, due to come into being on 30 March, but it did not address the practical problems that were bound to arise. Nothing happened on 30 March as it became clear that no agreement could be reached on the election of a President, the siting of a capital or the voting power allotted to each member. Treating as equals Bahrain with 250,000 inhabitants and Ajman with 5,000 was clearly absurd and the inequalities of wealth and consequent contribution to the Federal Budget were just as wide. There were also problems about a defence force and a central bank. A meeting of advisers to the Rulers in Abu Dhabi in May showed wide divergence of views on every topic with Qatar pressing for immediate progress while Bahrain and Abu Dhabi advocated caution. A two-day meeting of the Rulers themselves on 25 and 26 May produced

only a vague commitment to strengthen the union. Meanwhile the British Conservative Party was declaring that should it come to power it would reverse the withdrawal decision and Iran issued threats of reprisals should the Union take effect. In July in Abu Dhabi the Rulers agreed to appoint a Legal Adviser to draft a Constitution and to establish a Provisional Federal Council under the chairmanship of Khalifah b. Hamad al-Thani of Qatar who was the most active promoter of unity. This Council met in September and decided to set up a number of committees. A meeting of the Rulers in Doha in October set up further committees and agreed to form federal armed forces. There followed a period in which bilateral agreements were made and many of the Rulers went separately to Iran. A meeting of the Rulers in May 1969 in Doha failed to solve any of the problems and although it agreed to establish a Cabinet, could not agree who would hold the posts or be Federal President. In October 1969 the nine Rulers met in Abu Dhabi and agreed that Shaykh Zaid b. Sultan al-Nihayyan should be President, Shaykh Rashid al-Maktum Vice-President and the Deputy Ruler of Qatar Prime Minister with a 13-man Cabinet. Abu Dhabi was to be the temporary capital until a permanent one could be constructed on its border with Dubai. As there were differing drafts for a Constitution these were referred to a committee. The communiqué had not been signed when a message arrived from the British Political Resident who deplored their lack of progress. Some members walked out in protest against this interference and it was decided to reconvene the meeting in Abu Dhabi in November. This was postponed indefinitely while Qatar suggested a series of bilateral meetings. In December Shaykh Isa b. Salman al-Khalifah announced a reorganisation of the Bahraini Government which would institutionalise popular participation which did not exist in the other states. In March 1970 Qatar promulgated a provisional constitution and it was difficult to see how such arrangements could exist in what was envisaged as an integrated union. After two postponements the Deputy Rulers met in Abu Dhabi in October 1970 but talks broke down after Bahrain demanded representation on the basis of population which would give it nearly half the total voting power and it further suggested that the Federal Assembly should be elected by popular suffrage. Saudi Arabia and Kuwait attempted to bring about agreement and so, less publicly, did the British. The report of the Bahrain UN Commission led to the dropping by the Shah of his claim on the Shaykhdom, removing the main obstacle to its becoming independent on its own. This it did in August 1971, followed by Qatar in September. This ended the possibility of a Federation of the Nine, clearing the way for the transformation of the Trucial Shaykhdoms into the United Arab Emirates.

FEDERATION OF SOUTH ARABIA

For most of a century after their capture of Aden in 1839, British policy was to interfere in the affairs of the Hinterland as little as possible, taking action only when outside powers encroached or trade routes were threatened. The Western Aden Protectorate in the 1950s covered an area of approximately 14,000 square miles with a population of less than 500,000 divided between some 20 Sultanates and Shaykhdoms in addition to minor units, none capable of existence as an independent modern state. This fragmentation made the establishment of efficient administration impossible and hampered development; commercial vehicles, for example, had to pass through customs posts every few miles. In January 1954 the Governor of Aden, Sir Tom Hickinbottam, invited Rulers to hear plans for a form of federation which had largely been drawn up in London: he himself would be Head of State with responsibility for defence and foreign affairs while the Federation would deal with education, public health, communications etc. There was no mention of future independence. Fiercely independent and mutually jealous chieftains would have had to surrender their sovereignty and South Arabia would become very similar to a conventional Colony. The Rulers agreed in principle but killed the project by calculated inertia. The mere proposal, however, appeared to the Imam Ahmad a breach of the *status quo* provided for by the Sanaa Treaty of 1934 and if successful might have proved a magnet for his own Shafai subjects; he therefore greatly increased interference in the Protectorate leading to widespread insecurity which reached a peak in 1957/8. At the same time other Rulers were alarmed at the activities of Ali b. Abd al-Krim al-Abdali, Sultan of Lahej the most advanced state, who, using the South Arabian League, apparently aimed at uniting the area under his own rule. With discreet British prodding, the three most dependable Rulers, Sharif Hussain al-Habili of Bayhan, Sultan Salih al-Awdhali and Naib Ahmad b. Abd Allah al-Fadhli called for a Federation of Arab Emirates of the South which would eventually achieve independence. After a Treaty with the British extending to the new entity the Protectorate Treaties previously concluded with individual states, this grouping of the three plus the Amiri of Dhala, the Afifi of Lower Yafai and the Upper Awlaqi Shaykhdom came into existence in February 1959. At the signing ceremony the Colonial Secretary pledged help to prepare for independence. A new capital, al-Ittihad, was built and other states joined until there were 17 members. From the first the new state was completely dependent upon British money and British officials as the Sultans, in their capacity as Cabinet Ministers, were mostly without experience of administration. The Federation therefore appeared a British puppet and was weakened by the determined hostility of the Yemen and many of the other Arab governments. Nevertheless much economic progress was made and in November 1961 it acquired its own armed forces when the Aden Protectorate Levies were handed over and its officers gradually Arabised. In 1961 Whitehall felt that the security of the base at Aden, seen as strategically vital, was threatened by the turbulence engendered by the Trade Union activities led by Abd Allah al-Asnaj and determined to swamp them by uniting the Colony with the Federation. Many Adeni politicians were strongly opposed to this but enough were coerced or bribed or, like Hassan Ali Bayoomi genuinely believed in it, to force the agreement to merge through the Legislative Council in September 1962. This took effect from January 1963 and the title changed to the Federation of South Arabia. Adenis joined the Supreme Council and the renamed state appointed its first Foreign Minister in Shaykh Muhammad Farid al-Awlaqi. It never had either a President or a Prime Minister, the Chairmanship rotating monthly amongst the members of the Supreme Council. The grievance of many Adenis attracted hostility towards the Federation amongst members of the British Labour Party (to become the Government in November 1964) and in the UN, as did the Radfan Campaigns. The Federation was greatly hampered by the refusal of the important states of the Eastern Aden Protectorate to join and although the *Federalis* (Rulers and officials) said in February 1964 that it was vital, the British refused to become involved. It had difficulties, too, through its ambivalent position within Aden Colony. Constitutional discussions, arranged for December 1963 had to be postponed when a grenade was thrown amongst the Rulers assembled at Aden airport and did not take place until June 1964. For a month the Federalis were relentlessly bullied by the Colonial Secretary Duncan Sandys and it was announced that independence would come in 1968 and that there would be a President and a Prime Minister, an elected Assembly and complete Arabisation of the civil service. The pressure from Sandys was so intense that one of the founding members, Sultan Ahmad al-Fadhli defected and joined the nationalist opposition in Cairo. A few months later Sharif Hussain decided to withdraw to Bayhan after his old friend the High Commissioner, Sir Kennedy Trevaskis, was removed by the incoming British Labour Government and although remaining Minister of the Interior, played no further part in Federal affairs. There were two potential leaders, the Awdhali Sultan and Muhammad Farid, neither willing to play second fiddle so no Constitutional progress was ever made. The Hone–Bell Commission was created to devise a workable form of government. Terrorism increased in Aden and spread from Radfan to other parts of the Federation despite much material progress there. Financial difficulties and the need to appease internal party critics led the Wilson government to decide that there was no longer a need for the Aden base, the security of which had been one of the paramount reasons for creating the Federation, and that there would be no further military presence there after South Arabia achieved independence in 1968. This was announced in a White Paper in February 1966 and the *Federalis*, realising that they had isolated themselves from much of the Arab world by supporting Britain, felt that they had been betrayed. There was a frantic race against time to prepare South Arabia to stand alone and British subsidies were used to increase the security forces. The High Commissioner, Sir Richard Turnbull, however, disliked the *Federalis* and did little to help them and self-confidence and prestige ebbed away leaving them an anxious and leaderless group. London tried various expedients, including the UN, a promise of short-term security cover and trying to arrange a power-sharing agreement between the *Federalis* and the National Liberation Front but finally concentrated on withdrawing British personnel with the minimum of casualties. A short-lived military mutiny on 20 June 1967 showed the weakness of the *Federalis* and there was a desperate attempt to organise a new government under an Adeni Prime Min-

ister which failed owing to the jealousies of the others. Much of the Hinterland fell to the NLF and on 28 August 1967 the Chairman of the Supreme Council admitted that it had lost control and invited the army to take over. On 5 September the High Commissioner, Sir Humphrey Trevelyan, said that the Federation had ceased to exist. The British decided that they preferred the independent but left wing NLF to the Egyptian controlled Front for the Liberation of Occupied South Yemen and assisted it to take power. This was formalised by a meeting at Geneva on 21 November and the formal declaration of independence on 30 November 1967. The brief period of the existence of the Federation was an essential bridge between the local particularism of the past and the strongly centralised state of the future. The lesson of the need for a party to enforce the Government's will in every corner of the land was not wasted on its successors.

FELLAGHA (Tunisia)

Fellagha was a local word for bandits which was later adopted as a title of honour. In 1952 hopes that Tunisia would obtain autonomy by negotiation with France were dashed by the arrest of Prime Minister Chenik and some of his Ministers. At the same time French extremists, the Red Hand, carried out terrorist attacks on nationalists, killing amongst others the labour leader Farhat Hashid. In March 1954 groups of Tunisian militants started attacks on police stations, post offices, French-owned farms and factories, coaches and even trains. They also distributed propaganda on behalf of the Neo-Destour Party with whom there were close links at local levels and although it was never clear if their activities were centrally co-ordinated the Assistant General-Secretary of the Party, Hedi Nouira resigned in protest at its association with violence. Many of the *fellagha* were illiterate and only a few had any military training, probably in Libya. They numbered about 2,500, hunted by some 15,000 French troops. According to French figures between March and July 74 European civilians were killed and 67 wounded and of the security forces 21 were killed, 52 wounded and 5 missing. In July 1954 the Carthage Declaration by the French Prime Minister Pierre Mendes-France that France would concede complete internal autonomy to Tunisia brought a lull in the activities of the *fellagha* but they started up again in September with attacks on colon farms and pro-French Tunisians. In a little over a month 50 Tunisians and 16 French were killed. At the beginning of November a cease-fire came into effect as each group was contacted by a mixed team of French and Tunisian officials and responded to a Neo-Destour order to "lay down your arms for Bourguiba" in return for pension, government posts etc. According to official French figures, between 1 May and 1 November 147 *fellagha* were killed and 51 taken prisoner. Some former *fellagha* late in 1955 briefly took up arms in support of the demand of Ben Yusuf for complete independence but, unlike the Moroccan Armée de Libération Nationale, they never constituted a threat to the newly independent government.

FEZ RIOTS (1990)

During 1989 and 1990 there was increasing discontent amongst Moroccan workers and students at economic and employment prospects. Youth unemployment was reckoned at 30%. Fez was particularly affected with a Minister admitting that its population had doubled although no new houses had been built and suggesting that 100,000 should leave. There had also been riots at the University for which 28 students had been jailed for up to five years. In April 1990 two trade unions, the Confederation Démocratique du Travail, led by Muhammad Nubir Amawi which was affiliated to the Union Socialiste des Forces Populaires and the Union Générale des Travailleurs Marocains associated with Istiqlal called a general strike. The Government promised negotiations so the strike was called off. The Unions demanded a doubling of the minimum wage to $250 a month and Prime Minister Izz al-Din Laraki made such vague promises that Amawi felt that he could not be trusted. A second strike call was therefore issued for 14 December on which the workers should stay at home. There was little response in Rabat or Casablanca but in Fez some 20,000 demonstrators, most aged between 15 and 25, started a two-day riot in which the Merinid Hotel, owned personally by Hassan II, was burned down amidst looting of other conspicuous signs of wealth. Troops were said to have fired on crowds in narrow alleys. Official figures were that five demonstrators were killed but other estimates put the number at up to 170 including 20 of the security forces. There were over a thousand arrests. Demonstrators were also killed in Tangier and there were simultaneous riots in Meknes and Kenitra. The opposition demanded an independent inquiry and dismissed the commission set up by Laraki as an attempted whitewash. The King absolved the unions from blame which he placed on criminals and foreign (apparently French) intrigues. On 18 December the Government promised pay rises. By the end of January 1991 about 350 had been jailed in Fez for up to 15 years but, as usual, many were soon included in amnesties.

FEZ SUMMIT (1981/2)

The Fahd Plan announced in August 1981 appeared to recognise the right of Israel to exist in peace and was therefore attacked by the leaders of the Steadfastness Front while it was formally endorsed by those of the Gulf Co-operation Council. After intensive diplomatic activity the twelfth Summit assembled on 25 November at Fez in an attempt to re-establish Arab unity. The previous week Colonel Qadafi announced his intention of boycotting the meeting and at the last moment Hafiz al-Assad also refused. Only 8 out of 20 Heads of State attended in person but Iraq, Sudan, Oman, Mauritania, Algeria, Libya and Syria were represented. Yassir Arafat was present and Egypt was not invited. The host, King Hassan deplored the "irresponsibility" of those who had not attended in person, merely sending delegations without authority and this nearly caused a walk-out by the Syrian Foreign Minister Abd al-Halim Khaddam. Fahd offered to withdraw his Plan from the agenda but was persuaded not to. The Summit then passed a Resolution condemning Israeli actions in Lebanon and asking the Americans to bring pressure on Israel to make it obey UN decisions. After four hours the Summit adjourned with Hassan saying "more information was needed, not because we had divergences". In June 1982 Israel invaded Lebanon in Operation Peace for Galilee and Libya was the first to call for a Summit to co-ordinate a united response while Bourguiba offered to host it in Tunis. It was decided instead to reconvene the adjourned twelfth Summit which therefore reassembled on 6–9 September, boycotted only by Qadafi. Kings Fahd, Hassan and Hussain attended while Assad and Saddam Hussain met for the first time in three years. Peninsula rulers except for Qabus were present while Algeria, Tunisia (Bourguiba was ill) and Lebanon (in the process of electing a President) sent representatives. Nimeiri failed to secure an invitation for Egypt. Divisive issues such as the Western Sahara and the Oman-PDRY dispute were kept off the agenda and enabled general agreement. After discussion of the recently revealed Reagan Plan, the Fahd Plan was modified by replacing the Arab recognition of Israel by a Security Council guarantee of peace for all states including an independent Palestine. Reference to the Security Council admitted a Russian role in the area. The Fez Plan also specifically mentioned the Palestine Liberation Organisation which the Fahd Plan had not. The Summit expressed strong condemnation of the Israeli aggression against Lebanon and called for implementation of Security Council Resolutions. It rejected Lebanon's request for the ending of the mandate of the Syrian-controlled Arab Deterrent Security Force saying that this should be discussed between the two governments. On the Iran–Iraq War it praised Iraq's "withdrawal" of its forces from Iranian territory, declared its commitment to the defence of Arab territory, saying that aggression against any Arab country was aggression against all, and called for a cease-fire. The Summit supported Somalia in its dispute with Ethiopia and called for a peaceful solution of the Ogaden question. Finally a Committee was established to contact the permanent members of the Security Council about the Fez Plan. The second Fez meeting after the boycotts of the first, which followed those of the Amman Summit restored Arab morale by showing that its leaders could meet and agree on decisions which on the whole were a success for the moderates without alienating the radicals.

al-FIKINI, Muhi al-Din (1924–)

Libyan Prime Minister. He trained as a lawyer, taking a Doctorate at the Sorbonne and served as Ambassador to Cairo, Washington and the United Nations before becoming Minister of Justice in the Ben Halim government. In March 1963 he was appointed Prime Minister in succession to Muhammad Ben Uthman. He was anxious to lead a liberal and reformist administration and to replace the federal system with a unitary one. The country was divided into ten administrative districts instead of three provinces which had enjoyed a large measure of autonomy: the Provincial Assemblies were dissolved and governors were made responsible to the Legislative Assembly instead of directly to King Idris. Women were given the vote. Fikini established a Development Board and a Five-Year Plan which paid special attention to agriculture and raising living standards and public services in rural areas. Fikini visited the three other Maghreb countries, calling for unity and signing agreements with them. He would have liked to have been rid of foreign bases but although he managed to get the French out of Sabha, the King insisted that the Americans should stay at Wheelus. In September 1963 he denounced apartheid at the UN. In January 1964 President Nasser convoked the first meeting of Arab Heads of State to discuss the Jordan Waters Dispute but Idris refused to attend the Cairo Summit. There was a student riot in Benghazi with demands for a more positively Arab foreign policy and for the removal of British and American bases. The Cyrenaican Defence Force reacted with what was seen as excessive harshness, killing two students. Fikini demanded the dismissal of their commander who was the brother-in-law of the King's adviser, Busayri al-Shalhi but Idris, even threatening abdication, refused. Fikini thereupon resigned and returned to his law practice.

FIRST ARAB CONGRESS (1913)
The Congress was organised by the secret Fatat society and the Ottoman Decentralisation Party and 24 delegates met in Paris in June 1913. They were almost exactly divided between Christians and Muslims, and were mostly Syrians although two came from Iraq and three represented the Arab communities of the USA. Amongst the participants who later became famous were two future Presidents of the Lebanon, Charles Dabbas and Ayyub Thabit, the future Syrian and Iraqi Prime Ministers Jamil Mardam and Tawfiq al-Suwaydi and the Palestinian leader Awni Abd al-Hadi. Although Sharif Hussain of Mecca sent a telegram to Istanbul denouncing its proceedings as treasonable, there was no talk of secession from the Ottoman Empire and speakers stressed their need of its protection against foreign encroachments, provided that the Arabs were regarded as a unity and as partners in a decentralised form of government. The Turkish Government, having failed to persuade the French to ban it, made conciliatory gestures towards the Congress whose members swore that they would accept no office until their demands had been met. In fact the Turks made no changes in their policies and those offered a government post took it. In retrospect it assumed some importance as the first small step towards Arab unity. On the last day the doors were thrown open to the public and the proceedings were in French; altogether about 200 people attended.

FIRST ARAB PETROLEUM CONGRESS (1959)
Abd Allah al-Tariki, the first Saudi Arabian official with an understanding of the international oil market was also the first to work for co-operation between the countries where it was produced. In 1957 he concluded an agreement with Iran to exchange information and he maintained contact with the Venezuelan Oil Minister Dr Perez Alfonso. Tariki was the driving spirit behind the first meeting of Arab oil exporting states to discuss the technical, economic, legal and political aspects of the industry which was held in Cairo in April 1959. Iraq and Bahrain declined to attend. Western oil men, representing 35 companies, feared that it would provide a platform for Arab extremists but in fact the

tone was moderate as there were still strong memories of the problems encountered by Iran after it nationalised Anglo-Iranian in 1951. There was no demand for nationalisation although a member of Tariqi's staff presented a paper arguing that sovereign states had no right to alter contracts unilaterally. Tariki proposed an Arab pipe-line linking Saudi, Kuwaiti and Iraqi oilfields with the Mediterranean as the Suez Canal would be unable to cope if production reached 11 million barrels a day. Tariki was responsible for two other proposals; the first was that all petroleum agreements should be periodically renegotiated as conditions changed and the second was for voluntary curbs on production when prices fell as they had just done. The Lebanese businessman Emile Bustani called for each country to set aside 5% of profits for development. The final communiqué proposed that national companies should operate alongside private companies. Despite its moderation this Congress constituted the first step in the complete reversal of the balance of power between the producing countries and the international companies which followed the establishment of OPEC.

FRANCO-LEBANESE TREATY (1936)
The Anglo-Iraqi Treaty of 1930 which ended direct British rule and provided for League of Nations membership for Iraq led to similar demands from Syrian nationalists. It was not until June 1936 that a Franco-Syrian Treaty was signed and then negotiations began in Beirut leading after less than a month of talks to the signature of a Treaty on 13 November in almost identical terms. France would recognise Lebanese independence and sovereignty and the country should join the League of Nations before the end of 1939. The Treaty should last for 25 years and be renewable and provided for perpetual friendship and alignment of foreign policies. France should have the use of all Lebanese facilities in the event of war. There was also a military convention by which Lebanon would engage only French instructors and use only French equipment while providing bases for all three services. An exchange of letters guaranteed equality of civil and political rights between all nationals and equal representation of all sections in the public service. Muslim objections, however, to the Treaty which had been negotiated mainly by the Maronite President Emile Edde and the Protestant Secretary of State Ayyub Thabit led to riots in Tripoli and Beirut. The Treaty was unanimously approved by the Lebanese Parliament four days later but it suffered the same fate as the Syrian Treaty. The left-wing government of Leon Blum which had negotiated it fell from power and its right-wing successor made no effort to put the Treaty to the French Assembly for ratification. It never therefore came into force.

FRANCO-SYRIAN TREATY (1933)
The Anglo-Iraqi Treaty of 1930 which provided for independence and League of Nations membership for Iraq in the near future stimulated demands by Syrian nationalists for the end of the French Mandate leading to considerable agitation. In 1932 the French established a Syrian Government under the Presidency of Muhammad Ali al-Abid with which it could negotiate.

In November 1933 a Treaty of Friendship and Alliance was signed by the French High Commissioner Comte Damien de Martel and the Prime Minister Haqqi Bey al-Azm to regulate relations after the end of the Mandate. It was very similar in many of its terms to the Iraqi Treaty. There would be perpetual friendship and the two countries would consult over relations with other powers and France would represent Syrian interests abroad where there was no direct Syrian presence. They would consult if any threat of war arose. Although the new Syrian state would be responsible for defence and security French forces would remain in the country with extra-territorial rights. The French would provide training and officers, magistrates, civil servants and technical councillors. The Syrian state would guarantee the protection of minority rights. The special status of the Alawites and Druzes and their administration by France would continue. France would exercise certain financial powers. The Treaty would be valid for 25 years. Over the next four years the French would progressively associate Syrians with their conduct of foreign affairs. The French would be consulted on the identity, posts and powers of European officials to be retained. France would recommend Syrian entry into the League at the end of the "preparatory period". The main nationalist objection was to the continued dismemberment of the country by the separation of the Alawis and Druzes and it was clear that the Treaty would be rejected by the Assembly which was then suspended by the French. The French authorities learned their lessons and the Franco-Syrian Treaty of 1936 met many of the objections of the nationalists.

FRANCO-SYRIAN TREATY (1936)

An attempt to conclude a Franco-Syrian Treaty in 1933 was defeated by the opposition of nationalist politicians to such provisions as the continuation of special regimes for the Alawis and Druzes, French military and economic control and the dilatory progress towards independence. A second attempt was made when a Syrian delegation led by Hashim al-Atasi and including Jamil Mardam, Saad Allah al-Jabiri and Faris al-Khouri negotiated with the new left-wing government of Leon Blum. The French gave way on the more objectionable proposals of 1933. The Alawi and Druze areas were to be annexed to the Syrian state although some French troops would remain there for five years. The French military presence elsewhere would be unobtrusive. France would be allowed facilities including communications in wartime. A national army would be formed with the help of a French military mission and advisers and technicians would be sought only from France. Parity of currency would be maintained. Foreign policies would be aligned and rights and obligations assumed by France during the Mandate would devolve upon the new Syrian state. Nothing was said about Lebanon. The Treaty of "friendship and alliance" would last for 25 years from the admission of Syria to the League of Nations which was assumed to occur in the next three years. News of the Treaty was received with great joy in Syria and the negotiators treated as heroes. Mardam signed the Treaty of 22 December and it was unanimously ratified by the Syrian Parliament within a week. However the Blum Cabinet fell and the right-wing government that succeeded it made no attempt to push the Treaty through the Assembly and it was therefore never ratified by France.

FRANJIYAH, Sulayman (1910–)

Lebanese President. A Maronite, he was born in the mountainous area of Zghurtah near Tripoli; his father was a wealthy businessman with a seat in Parliament in which he was succeeded by his eldest son Hamid. Hamid was a leading nationalist politician and was several times Foreign Minister. He resigned that post in 1955, opposed to the pro-Western policies of Camille Chamoun who was also intriguing with the rival Maronite clan in Zghurtah. Hamid was expected to be a strong candidate for the Presidency in 1958 but in October 1957 he was left paralysed by a stroke. Sulayman was then a successful farmer and contractor and had also managed "constituency affairs" showing himself tough and ruthless. In 1957 he took part in a shoot-out with the pro-Chamoun faction in a village church in which 23 people were killed. He fled to Syria where he formed a close and lasting friendship with Hafiz al-Assad then a junior air force officer. After President Nasser who had admired Hamid interceded on his behalf, President Fuad Shihab allowed Franjiyah to return and he succeeded to his brother's parliamentary seat. He quickly became Minister of Posts under Saeb Salam but lost office when Rashid Karami who was from the same area and supported a rival Maronite clan-leader became Prime Minister. Franjiyah was considered a possible candidate for the Presidency in 1964 but did not hold office again until 1968 when he was Minister of the Interior in the Cabinet of Abd Allah al-Yafi. He was by then closely allied with Salam, the leading opponent of the Shihabists, and on friendly terms with other disgruntled Maronites such as Pierre Gemayel, Raymond Edde and even Chamoun. Franjiyah won a reputation for toughness in conducting the elections of 1968 and this was contrasted with the weakness of President Charles Helou in defending Lebanese interests. In August 1970 he was elected President by 50 votes against the 49 of the Shihabist candidate Elias Sarkis as some of his supporters flourished firearms in the Chamber. It was widely said that the fact that he did not appear to have any political ideas of his own helped his cause and enabled the anti-Shihabists to agree upon him. He appointed Salam Prime Minister and together they re-established political control over the bureaucracy and the Military Intelligence which had been so powerful under the previous two Presidents. Contrary to expectations, however, in other fields Franjiyah did not prove a strong President. Although before election he had promised social reforms, he made no effort to introduce any. He said that Palestine was a Holy Land for the Arabs but the Palestinian guerrillas became increasingly powerful and Maronite resentment grew causing their leaders, including Franjiyah, to arm their own followers. In March 1971 he became the first Lebanese President to visit Damascus where his friend Assad now ruled. In April 1973 Israeli commandos landed in Beirut and killed three Palestinian leaders. Salam demanded the dismissal of the officer responsible but the President refused as the man came from Zghurtah; the Prime Minister resigned. Franjiyah then had difficulty in finding Sunnis of stature to fill the office, appointed minor figures such as Amin al-Hafiz and even experimented briefly with a military government before reluctantly turning to Karami. In November 1974 he addressed the United Nations on behalf of the Palestinians. Meanwhile Kamal Jumblatt, who had provided the crucial votes to secure Franjiyah's election, was forming a coalition dedicated to a complete transformation of the political system and the country became increasingly polarised. After the Ayn al-Rummanah Massacre of April 1975, Lebanon was in a state of civil war. By January 1976 the President, in common with other Maronite leaders, saw the conflict as being between Lebanese and Palestinians who had not honoured their pledge of non-intervention in the affairs of their host country. Without reference to Karami, who was both Prime Minister and Minister of Defence, he ordered the air force to intervene on the side of the Christians at Damour and the armed forces started to disintegrate. Henceforth he was seen as the boss of a faction rather than as the neutral Head of State. In the summer Franjiyah retired to Zghurtah, paralysing the political system as Karami refused to assemble the Cabinet there. His only hope appeared to be that the Syrians could solve all the problems. In September Edde and Saeb Salam demanded his resignation. In February 1976 Franjiyah went to Damascus where with the help of Assad he drafted a new "Constitutional Document" which would amend the National Pact to give equal representation to Muslims and Christians and make the Prime Minister, still necessarily a Sunni, practically equal to the still Maronite President. There would be more social justice and deconfessionalising the civil service except for the top posts which would be equally divided between Christians and Muslims, more independence for the judiciary and reforms in the army, the economy and the educational system. The document was still being discussed when the Sunni officer commanding in Beirut seized the radio station and demanded the resignation of Franjiyah. The call was endorsed by two-thirds of the Members of Parliament but the President ignored it: his palace was bombarded and he had to flee to Jouniah. Syrian troops moved into Lebanon and a few days later Parliamentarians amended the Constitution to bring forward presidential elections by six months. Sarkis was chosen but Franjiyah was allowed to serve out his term until September. During this time he openly supported the Maronite Lebanese Front, working very closely with Chamoun. Franjiyah retired to Zghurtah where he built up his own militia, the Marada, under his son Tony. When Chamoun and Gemayel opposed the Syrian presence in the early summer of 1978 Franjiyah continued to support it and in June the Kataib militia under Bashir Gemayel attacked the ex-President's home, perpetrating the Ihden Massacre in which Tony Franjiyah, his wife and small daughter were killed. Franjiyah renounced the Maronite grouping and entered into alliance with his old foes Rashid Karami and Walid Jumblatt and assisted the Syrians to occupy the historic Maronite heartland. Early in 1982 he was hoping to regain the Presidency with Syrian support but the Israeli invasion in June

destroyed his chances. He never forgave the Gemayels, applauded the murder of Bashir and in June 1983 with Karami and Jumblatt formed the National Salvation Front to oppose President Amin Gemayel and intensify opposition to Israel. He stood with his allies against the Maronite majority in the Geneva Reconciliation Talks. Later he rebuilt contacts with the Maronites including Chamoun. In 1988 the Syrians supported him for a second term as President but the Lebanese Forces prevented Deputies from reaching the Assembly and there was no quorum. Franjiyah wrote a book *My Country Is Always Right* but he always saw things as the feudal lord of Zghurtah rather than from a national perspective. Clannish, of limited intellect, vindictive, arrogant, stubborn, narrow-minded, tolerant of corruption particularly that of his own family (his insistence that his son Tony should hold a lucrative Ministry complicated Cabinet-making), incapable of understanding idealism, he played a role on a stage too big for him.

FRANKLIN-BOUILLON TREATY (1921)
After the end of the First World War the French occupied Cilicia as well as Syria but were faced by the growing strength of the Turkish nationalist movement under the leadership of Mustafa Kamal (Ataturk). Having secured his regime Mustafa Kamal started attacking French troops in the Turkish-speaking areas. After being driven from several towns, the French decided to evacuate Cilicia altogether. A Treaty negotiated in October 1921 by Franklin–Bouillon and the Turkish Foreign Minister Yusuf Kamal Bey achieved this objective. It represented a breach of faith with the British as the Allies had agreed not to deal separately with the Turkish nationalists. From the Arab point of view it meant the loss of territory which had always been part of the Vilayet of Aleppo and infuriated the Syrian nationalists who saw part of their country ceded in the wider interests of French diplomacy. Their anger was intensified when they lost more of the area in the Alexandretta Dispute.

FREE OFFICERS (Egypt)
Dubbat al-Ahrar. The Anglo-Egyptian Treaty of 1936 led to a large increase in the size of the Egyptian army and to the acceptance for officer training of youths from lower social classes than before. Many of those that entered for a one year's crash course instead of the normal three years in the spring of 1937 were the sons of minor officials and landowners. After commissioning several of them including Gemal Abdul Nasser, Anwar Sadat and Zakariah Mohieddin were posted to Manqabad in Upper Egypt and became aware of each other's dissatisfaction with the British occupation, the corruption of politicians and the inequalities of the social system. They were also inspired by the veteran nationalist General Abd al-Aziz al-Misri. The humiliation of King Farouq in the Abdin Incident added to anti-British sentiment and some took positive action to assist the German army on the Egyptian frontier while others did not. From about 1942 Nasser was their undisputed leader and he has recorded that there were regular meetings of dissident officers after 1944. They sought a strong independent Egypt but otherwise had no single ideology. Some such as Sadat, Kamal al-Din

Hussain, Hussain al-Shafai and Abd al-Munim Abd al-Rauf were close to the Muslim Brothers while others such as Hassan Ibrahim were members of Young Egypt and others such as Khalid Mohieddin and Yusuf Saddiq had strong left-wing connections. Yet others, such as Sarwat Okasha, had links with the Wafd. Some of the members were involved in political assassinations, including an attempt on the Prime Minister Nahhas Pasha. After 1946 they occasionally produced leaflets, some published anonymously and others put in the mail-boxes of potential supporters. The corruption and incompetence displayed by the Government during the Palestine War made them into revolutionaries and in November 1949 they set up an Excutive Committee consisting of Nasser, who was elected Chairman, Sadat, Abd al-Latif al-Baghdadi, Abd al-Hakim Amer, the brothers Gemal Salim and Salih Salim, Khalid Mohieddin, Hussain and Ibrahim. Their average age was 33. Later four others, Shafai, Saddiq, Zakaria Mohieddin, and Abd al-Munim Amin were added and finally General Neguib who may not have become a member until after the July Revolution. Nasser, aided by his position as an Instructor in Staff College and Amer were mainly responsible for organising a network of cells of five to ten officers each in key units, completely unknown to British Intelligence and Egyptian security officials. The number of Free Officers is uncertain, Nasser has said about 90, Neguib "several hundred" while Sadat put it improbably high at 1,000. At the elections for the Committee of the Officers' Club in December 1951 the Free Officers were able to secure for their slate 276 out of the 334 votes cast. The result, particularly the choice of Neguib as President, infuriated the King and set in train the events that ended with the July Revolution, after which the Executive transformed itself into the Revolutionary Command Council. They then proceeded to purge some 400 senior officers, many of the Colonels and most of the higher ranks. They knew what they wanted to destroy but not what to build and a radical programme was only formulated later. Some of them entered the Cabinet in June 1953. Sadat says that 60 Free Officers were elected to Parliament in 1957. The lack of a definite ideology meant that many of the Free Officers fell away and by the death of Nasser only Sadat and Shafai of the Executive were politically active. The title and cell organisation were later used in other countries such as Yemen.

FRONT DE LIBÉRATION NATIONALE
(Algeria)

The Mouvement pour le Triomphe de la Liberté et de la Démocratie split in mid-1954 with the more militant setting up the Comité Révolutionnaire d' Unité et d'Action which planned the All Saint's Day Uprising of November 1954. It broadcast a proclamation from Cairo Radio and scattered leaflets throughout Algeria announcing that "a group of responsible young people and dedicated militants" had set up the Front de Libération Nationale which it invited all patriots to join. Its stated aims were the restoration of a democratic Algerian state within the principles of Islam. It called for the rooting out of corruption and for North African unity "in its national Arabo-Islamic context" and prom-

ised that in return for a recognition of independence French economic and cultural interests would be respected and that French citizens wishing to remain would have the option of Algerian citizenship or retaining French nationality with status of foreigners. It forecast a prolonged struggle to achieve these aims. The FLN established a network of cells in Algeria and amongst immigrant workers in France which initially often obtained members or supporters by coercion of rival groups such as the Mouvement National Algérienne and terrorising the non-committed but by January 1956 it had been joined by nearly all those opposed to French rule and even by former assimilationists including Farhat Abbas. Some of its fighting men, the Armé de Libération Nationale, were in action in the *wilayas* while others received training in neighbouring states. The leadership was also divided between "externals" with internationally known figures in Cairo having little contact with the "internals" doing the fighting and there were also disputes between the political leaders and the Colonels commanding the *wilayas*. The first attempt at sorting out these differences at the Soummam Valley Conference in August 1956 led to the establishment of the Comité National de la Révolution Algérienne as a Parliament with a small "internal" Comité de Co-ordination et d'Action to control the war. The FLN received a heavy blow in October 1956 when the most prominent of the "external" leaders were kidnapped by the French. Despite this the Soummam decisions were reversed in a CNRA session in Cairo which set up a larger, military-dominated Comité de Co-odination et d'Exécution. The FLN received some international recognition at the Bandung Conference and at the Tangier Conference of April 1958 in which it participated as an equal with the leading Parties of Morocco and Tunisia, the Istiqlal and the Neo-Destour. Following advice received there in September 1958 the FLN set up the Gouvernement Provisoire de la République Algérienne in Tunis with the moderate Abbas as President. Its negotiating stance at Melun and Evian showed that it had not changed its original war aims but after the cease-fire it became clear that it had given little thought to its role in an independent Algeria. The Tripoli Charter of June 1962 marked its transformation from a resistance movement into a political party, led by a Politburo dominated by Ben Bella. It declared itself a socialist party permeated by Islam. Muhammad Khidr was appointed Secretary-General and set up a nationwide organisation. He aimed at a mass party which would control the Government and the army and this brought him into conflict with Ben Bella who wanted an élite vanguard party which would have "the exclusive right of working out the thought of the nation": it was to be for the people rather than of the people. Ben Bella prevailed and assumed the office of Secretary-General. After a sharp struggle the Trade Union movement (UGTA) was brought under Party control which was extended to organisations for students (UNEA), youth (JFLN) and women (UNFA). After two years of independence the FLN claimed 153,000 full members and 619,000 aspirants. The Algiers Charter of April 1964, laid down at the first full Party Conference, elaborated its ideology. After his seizure of power Boumédienne put an Executive Secretariat over the FLN; it was headed by Sharif Bilqasim who was also in charge of education and reorganisation. Other shadowy parties ceased to exist and the FLN acquired a monopoly, nominating all the candidates whenever elections were held. The rigid centralisation practised by Boumediénne effectively deprived the Party of a role and many of its members fell away while others engaged in what he considered idle debate. In December 1967 he dismissed the Executive Secretariat and ordered one of his closest associates Ahmad Kaid to build a well-organised and dynamic political body to control all national organisations and divert initiatives into the desirable channels of socialism, pan-Arabism and non-alignment. Boumédienne declared "every person who believes in the Revolution must be a member of the Party or, from this day forward, he will not be given a place at any level of the political leadership". Kaid failed to shake the FLN out of increasing lethargy and corruption and resigned in December 1972 after which Boumédienne himself ran the Party with the aid of Muhammad Yahyawi as ideologue and Executive Secretary. The 1976 Constitution referred to its "vanguard leadership, organising the people towards the aim of building socialism". After the death of Boumédienne the FLN held a five-day Congress at the end of January 1979 during which Colonel Chadli was named as its new Secretary-General and thus automatically sole candidate for the Presidency: he was empowered to appoint the Party's executive, the Political Committee, subject to the approval of the supreme body, the Central Committee of between 120 and 160 full and 30–40 alternate members. The Cabinet appointed by Chadli in March appeared a mainly administrative body with policy-making in the hands of the Political Committee which he enlarged from 8 to 31 to represent a wider spectrum of opinion. In June 1980, firmer in the saddle, Chadli abolished Yahyawi's post, showing the downgrading of the importance of ideology, and reduced the Politbuiro which became less involved in the daily running of the country, taking on a more advisory role as greater initiative was given to regional authorities. Later the revival of a General Staff weakened the grip of the Party over the Army and Chadli, ignoring the Party, increasingly relied upon the army and upon technocrats. During 1981 the closest associates of Boumédienne, Boutaflika, Yahyawi, Ghozali and Abd al-Salam, were dropped from the Central Committee. In parliamentary elections in March 1982 the Party gave the voters a choice between three of its members for each of the 281 constituencies: in the event only 68 former Deputies were re-elected with many idealogues being replaced by technocrats and teachers. In December 1983 the FLN held its Fifth Congress which marked a further move from the policies of Boumédienne by encouraging private sector growth without formally disavowing socialism and giving priority to agriculture over industry and to the provision of schools and hospitals. In 1984 Chadli publicly worried about "parasitic elements", engaging in corruption and sabotage within the FLN but it became popularly regarded as a Mafia with all perquisites reserved for war veterans. In June 1985 the FLN jealously defended its monopoly by declaring illegal a newly-formed Human Rights organ-

isation of the type permitted in Morocco and Tunisia and imprisoning its leaders. In December 1985 a Special Congress, its members mainly chosen by the President, gave approval to his new version of the National Charter which, by down-playing socialism, largely deprived the Party of any recognisable ideology. This upset the hardline apparatchiks who opposed any moves towards liberalisation. In the parliamentary elections of February 1987 again three FLN candidates contested each seat but four-fifths of those elected were new Deputies under 45 years of age. In September 1988 Chadli publicly rebuked Party officials who "exploited the Revolution" and the luxury which they and their families enjoyed in the midst of poverty were the primary cause of the October Riots in which Party offices were a main target. Later in October Chadli, though ruling out competing parties, said that Independents might stand in future elections, removed professional organisations from Party control and he replaced the reactionary Director of the FLN Secretariat, Muhammad Sharif Messaadia, the most hated politician in the country, with the more conciliatory Abd al-Hamid Mahri. At the Sixth Party Congress at the end of November, originally summoned to endorse Chadli as the Party candidate in the forthcoming presidential election, he distanced himself from it by handing over as Secretary-General to Mahri. Although opponents of reform such as Messaadia remained on the Central Committee the Congress perforce accepted its disentanglement from the State and agreed to admit differing opinions. In February 1989 a new Constitution deprived the FLN of its monopoly, permitting the registration of other parties which did not "threaten national unity, territorial integrity, independence or the sovereignty of the people" and decreed that its Secretary-General would no longer be the sole candidate for the presidency: Chadli hoped that the need to compete would revive the FLN. In March 1989 the official representatives of the army withdrew from the Central Committee stating that the forces could no longer be identified with one party. Despite these setbacks the FLN claimed 400,000 new recruits and took over the two leading newspapers. In November an Extraordinary Congress showed a growing number putting Islam above socialism but was seen as a victory for the old guard with Boutaflika, Abd al-Salam, Kasdi Merbah and others restored to the Central Committee. The FLN, with its financial resources, organisation and the backing of local officials was generally expected to win easily in the first multi-party elections for communes and provinces of June 1990. In the event, however, it was not even able to find a candidate for every seat and was trounced with 31% of the votes compared with 55% for the Front Islamique du Salut: it took 14 provincial and 487 municipal councils compared with 32 and 853 for the FIS. It failed to take a single commune in the main cities of Algiers, Oran and Constantine. In the same month, after scenes of violence to which police had to be called, the trade union organisation UGTA voted out all the old-guard leadership and severed formal links with the Party. In July the Prime Minister Mouloud Hamrouche and the Foreign Minister Sid Ahmad Ghozali resigned from the Politburo saying that the Party had to renew itself and get rid of obstructive bureaucrats. In October more than 30 of the Central Committee, including former Ministers, denounced the programme of Hamrouche as undermining the public sector. In the spring of 1991, in preparation for parliamentary elections called for June, the Party did not renominate more than 80% of its sitting Deputies and redrew the constituency boundaries, increasing the number from 295 to 542: most of the new seats were in areas it expected to win. This gerrymandering set off a general strike, bloodshed, a state of siege and postponement of the elections. Chadli resigned the Chairmanship, completing the breach between government and party: in September 1989 Mahri had said that 13,000 FLN officials were paid by the state. In the autumn Ghozali, now Prime Minister forced through a constituency revision with 430 seats. After the December poll, with 206 results declared, the FLN had won 16 with 1.25 million votes compared with the 3.25 million votes and 167 seats for FIS: it did not even come second as the Front des Forcés Socialistes had won 25 seats. This was the first time in Arab history that a once sole ruling party had been defeated at the polls. In the shock divisions appeared with Mahri ready to negotiate with the FIS, Yahyawi seeking an alliance with moderate groups against FIS while Hamrouche wanted a coalition of all secular parties against political Muslims. In these circumstances some leaders welcomed the military takeover in January 1992 while others, notably Mahri, condemned it. Relations with the new ruling Haur Comité d'État were not easy and in May 1994 Abd al-Salam as Prime Minister took back 3,000 buildings belonging to the state which the party had been allowed to use. The HCE made several attempts to enter into dialogue with the old parties but early in 1993 Mahri was the only leader willing to talk. In January 1994, however, when a National Dialogue Commission invited debate on a new political system, not even he was willing to participate.

FRONT DES FORCES SOCIALISTES (Algeria)
In September 1963 At Ahmad, complaining that the socialism of Ben Bella was vague and wordy rather than practical, announced in Tizi-Ouzou that he was forming an opposition Front des Forces Socialistes. Its first publication called for a boycott of the forthcoming referendum on the new Constitution. From the beginning it attracted strong support in Kabyle where the Berbers felt that they were being neglected by the Government in its work of post-war reconstruction. At Ahmad was joined by Colonel Mohand Ou al-Haj with over 3,000 fighting men and the country appeared on the verge of civil war. Ben Bella claimed that the FFS was supported by King Hassan II, the CIA and West Germany and was able to exploit the patriotic sentiment evoked by the war with Morocco over Tindouf to detach ou al-Haj and, without military support, the revolt collapsed. At Ahmad went into hiding but sent representatives to join the group of the exiled Boudiaf in the Comité National pour la Défense de la Révolution. In October 1964 At Ahmad was captured and several hundred members of the FFS subsequently received prison sentences varying from a few months up to twenty years. In June 1965 preparing for a showdown with Boumédienne Ben Bella sought the support

of FFS members still in the *Maquis* and they announced a cease-fire. In April 1966 At Ahmad escaped abroad and kept the FFS in nominal existence until 1989 when the monopoly of the Front de Libération Nationale was ended. In November the FFS was granted legal recognition and in December At Ahmad returned to a mass welcome. The Party opposed the politicisation of Islam and called for greater rights for women and Berbers. It had, however, to compete in Berber areas with the strongly secularist Rassemblement pour la Culture et le Démocratie. In June 1990, unlike the RCD, the FFS called for abstention in the municipal elections and the fact that only 20% voted in some Berber areas attested to the strength of its support. In March 1991 a Congress of 2,300 delegates unanimously elected At Ahmad as Secretary-General and applauded his call for the party to provide a locomotive of democracy, neither wildly liberal nor authoritarian socialist, to confront the Front Islamique du Salut. The FFS claimed that 100,000 demonstrated against new laws imposing use of Arabic but of its National Council only 261 out of 630 were Berbers. In the parliamentary elections of December 1991 the Party put forward 322 candidates for 430 seats, winning in the first round 25 which made it the largest party after the FIS. In the bargaining that preceded the second round, the FFS refused to join the FLN against FIS and was one of those accused by Prime Minister Ghozali of behaving like ostriches. After the military take-over of January 1992 the FFS consistently refused to talk to leaders of the new regime. At Ahmad spent much time abroad and the day-to-day leadership was in the hands of Hamdani.

FUDA, Faraj (1945–92)
Egyptian political writer. Born near Damiettat he attracted attention while a student by publishing vernacular poetry and leading a demonstration against the dictatorship of Nasser. He then taught economics at Ayn Shams University and became known for his liberal ideas which he spread in typed or hand-written posters throughout all the Universities of Egypt, contributing to a new intellectual climate amongst the young. He argued for tolerance and for multi-party democracy. Fuda was a pious Muslim but he refused to accept religion as a political programme. In *The Trick* he pointed out Islamic Banking had caused large numbers of peasants to lose their savings. In *The Absent Truth* he argued against the main doctrines of the Jihad group, denying the possibility of an Islamic Republic. His final book, *Terrorism*, was seen as a direct challenge to the Islamic Group and, six months after its publication, he was murdered. In January 1993 his complete works were banned by al-Azhar as contrary to Islam. In the same month 13 people were charged with his murder. In April the trial was adjourned for a month.

FUNDAMENTAL LAW (Morocco) (1961)
On 8 May 1958 Muhammad V proclaimed a Royal Charter which restated his often expressed views that the best form of government for an independent state was democratic and that a true democracy, in which the people would participate increasingly in the affairs of government, could be evolved within the frame-

work of a constitutional monarchy. He promised the eventual election by universal suffrage of a National Assembly. Before that the old tribal organisation would be replaced by local communes (it was estimated that 3,000 communes would be formed from some 600 tribes) which would elect councils which would elect delegates to a Deliberative Assembly which would share legislative power with the King. There would be written clarification of the responsibilities of Ministers which implied some delegation of the King's executive powers and there would be a Bill of Rights allowing freedom of association, speech, the press, etc. These promises were made more specific in a Charter of Public Liberties issued in November. It also required new political parties to register and restricted the rights of foreigners to take part in Moroccan politics. His son Hassan II, in June 1961, soon after his accession to the throne, issued the Fundamental Law of the Kingdom. Morocco was stated to be "an Arab and Muslim Kingdom . . . on its way to becoming a constitutional monarchy". The State had to oppose anything likely to cause division within the national community. It promised equality for all, protection of basic rights, independence of the judiciary, Moroccanisation of national resources and Arab–Islamic education. Foreign policy would be based on "non-dependence", anti-colonialism and faithfulness to the UN, the Arab League and the Casablanca Bloc. The King set up a small group of advisers to draft a Constitution which was issued in November 1962 and approved by referendum in December. It contained 100 articles, one of which explicity prohibited the establishment of a one-party state. The 1962 Constitution was replaced by another in 1970 which extended the powers of the King.

GAFSA RAID (1980)

Since the intervention of Prime Minister Nouira had aborted his hopes of a union of Libya and Tunisia as the Arab–Islamic Republic, Colonel Qadafi had nurtured resentment against him. Between 1,200 and 2,000 Tunisian dissidents received shelter and military training in his camps and in May 1979 the Algerian authorities intercepted a Libyan convoy smuggling arms into Tunisia. On 27 January 1980 a group estimated at 50 seized hostages and the police and army barracks in Gafsa, calling for a nationwide uprising against the Government while Libyan radio mounted a barrage of propaganda. The day chosen was the eve of a national strike to commemorate Black Thursday and Gafsa, a stronghold of the miners' union, was suffering from a decline in the phosphate industry upon which it depended: the Government ignored the economic discontent in the South. A few locals joined the rebels and the armed forces were slow in responding. It took an entire day before authority was re-established at a cost, according to official figures, of 22 security personnel, 15 civilians with 4 insurgents killed and 42 arrested. Unofficial estimates put both the raiding party and the casualties at 300. Sporadic fighting on the hills outside continued for another two days. In March 67 citizens, including 29 Libyans, were put on trial: 13 were hanged, 20 acquitted and the rest received prison sentences. While the issue was in doubt the French sent warships and aircraft to the Tunisian coast to prevent armed Libyan intervention: the Arab League merely condemned the French and a Tripoli mob burned down the French Embassy. It was learned that the incursion had been mounted from Algerian territory but the Algerian Government, blaming local officials, denied involvement. The Gafsa raid showed the irresponsible meddling of Qadafi in the affairs of other states and was condemned even by his Tunisian friends such as Muhammad Masmoudi. Relations with Libya continued bad until they were broken off in September 1985. The Gafsa Raid and the continuing Libyan threat showed the dependence of Tunisia upon the West for its security through the weakness of its own armed forces: the Government embarked upon massive arms purchases, adding to its financial problems. The stress of the incident was blamed for the heart attack which compelled Nouira to retire.

GARANG (DE MABIOR), John (1945–)

Southern Sudanese leader. A Dinka from Borr, he was educated in a small village school in Tanzania. As a youth he fought against the Sudanese Government with the Anya Nya guerrillas until peace was made in the Addis Ababa Agreement. He then joined the Sudanese army becoming a protégé of the Southern general and politician Joseph Lagu who arranged for him to go to the USA where he spent nine years, graduating from the School of Infantry and then winning a doctorate in the economics of development from Iowa State University. Garang returned to become Deputy Director of the Military Research Branch at army HQ. In 1983 as a Colonel he was sent to quell a mutiny of Southern soldiers in Borr but instead he assumed command of them. Garang became leader of the Sudan People's Liberation Movement and Commander-in-Chief of the Sudan People's Liberation Army. He demanded for the South a bigger share of political power and of the national wealth and later the repeal of the September Laws in which President Nimeiri imposed *Shariah* upon the country. He strongly denied that he was a secessionist, anti-Arab or anti-Muslim, insisting that he wanted to overthrow Nimeiri and establish a democratic secular Sudan. Garang advocated "Sudanism" – a national unity based on cultural diversity. The Saudi entrepreneur Adnan Khashoggi and other business associates of the President who were anxious to exploit the oilfields in the South unsuccessfully pressed him to negotiate with Nimeiri who in 1984 offered to make him Vice-President in charge of the development of the South but in March 1985 he did agree to attend a constitutional conference. He denied any links with Israel but admitted to receiving arms from Ethiopia. Militarily he was ruthless, besieging towns in which he bombarded the civilian population and threatening to shoot down Red Cross aircraft bringing food to the starving. Garang was also accused of kidnapping children who were conscripted into his forces and sent for training in Cuba. He refused to negotiate with the government of Dr Jazuli Dafallah which was unable to commit itself to repeal of the September Laws, refused to participate in the elections of April 1986 and then declared the result unrepresentative but he had several meetings with the next Prime Minister, Sadiq al-Mahdi. Garang was extremely active in attempting to secure international recognition, visiting Europe and America appealing for investment in the area under his control and OAU Summits calling for it or the UN to intervene. His position was weakened by the fall in May 1991 of his ally, the Ethiopian leader Mengistu and in August there was a split in the SPLM with a group which became known as the Nasir faction saying that he was autocratic, contemptuous of human rights and oppressive of other tribes: they also called for the secession of the South. Garang claimed to have retained the support of 10 out of 13 members of the SPLA High Command. In the spring of 1992 the government of General Bashir launched a major offensive in which they regained much territory, even driving Garang from his base at Torit. In November his proposal for two confederated states, each with a separate constitution but joint defence against external aggression was rejected by the Government. In September 1992 he accused the UN of hostility and aid workers in the Sudan were attacked. In January 1993 there was a split within the Garang faction and calls were made for his resignation. In February Museveni in Khartoum said that Garang was ready to play a personal part in the peace talks. In April he went to Abuja before the talks to meet Babangida. In August 1993 a government offensive started to push back against Uganda. At the end of October 1993 it was reported that he was reconciled in Washington with Maher both to help famine relief and to fight the Government. Garang is tall, strongly built and bearded.

GARANG, Joseph (?–1971)

Sudanese Communist leader. A lawyer, he was the only Southerner prominent in the Sudanese Communist Party of which he was a member of the Central Committee. He had no real support in the South and was heavily defeated in all the elections that he contested there. During the military regime of General Abboud he attracted attention by challenging in the courts the right of the Government to ban the SCP after one of its student members had blasphemed against the Prophet. He welcomed the seizure of power by Nimeiri who appointed him Minister of Supply in May 1969. Garang held this post for less than a month before he was put in charge of the affairs of the South where the Anya Nya guerrillas had been fighting for nearly a decade. He made strenuous efforts to crush the revolt which he saw as conducted by stooges of Imperialism and Zionism who had taken advantage of economic inequality; nevertheless he held meetings with their leaders in an attempt to persuade them to return. Many believed that his ultimate objective was to build a socialist state in the South which might eventually become independent of Khartoum. In July 1971 extreme left-wing officers carried out a coup to replace Nimeiri with Colonel Babikr al-Nur after the failure of which Garang and other communist leaders were hanged despite protests from the Soviet Union. Garang was a broad-minded man, who did not reject alliance with capitalist powers. He edited the communist newspaper *Advance* and wrote *The Dilemma of a Southern Intellectual.*

GAZA GOVERNMENT

After the second cease-fire between the newly-proclaimed State of Israel and the Arabs in July 1948 the Egyptians were left in occupation of Gaza while other areas were held by the Arab Legion, the Arab Liberation Army and Iraqi forces. In September the Egyptians encouraged the establishment of a "Government of All Palestine" which claimed sovereignty over all the territory of the Mandate. The Prime Minister was Ahmad Hilmi Abd al-Baqi and it had the support of the Mufti of Jerusalem whose cousin Jamal al-Hussaini was Foreign Minister. Awni Abd al-Hadi was Minister of Social Affairs and it contained many respected Palestinian leaders. A rudimentary form of administration and taxation were created and this caused intense annoyance to the Amir Abd Allah of Trans-Jordan who was determined to annex the areas not assigned to Israel. He called a conference of Palestinians in Amman which made little impression but in the resumed fighting in October most of the territory claimed by the Gaza Government, except for the Strip, was overrun by the Israelis. After that an Egyptian Military Governor administered the area and the Gaza Government, although not formally abolished until 1952, existed merely on paper; its headquarters was a villa in Cairo. It was never recognised by a major Power.

GAZA RAID (1955)

After September 1954 *Fida'i* started making raids into Israel from the Egyptian-occupied Gaza Strip – according to the Israelis there were 27 attacks in the following six months for which there were no reprisals. At the same time, as a result of the *Bat Galim* Affair and the Lavon Affair Israeli morale was at a low point. Ben Gurion who had come out of retirement to be Minister of Defence determined to restore it with a spectacular success. On 28 February 1955 two platoons of Israeli troops crossed two miles into the Strip and demolished a military post and a pumping station in an action in which 38 Egyptian and 8 Israeli soldiers were killed. Both sides appealed to the UN and UNTSO which put the blame on Israel and condemned its "brutal attack . . . ordered by Israeli authorities". On 29 March Israel was unanimously condemned by the Security Council which also called for closer co-operation with UNTSO. The incident was to have great importance because before it Nasser, preoccupied with domestic matters, had paid little attention to the Palestine question. The demonstration of Egyptian military inferiority was to lead to the Czechoslovak Arms Deal which set in motion the events that were to lead to the Suez War.

GAZA STRIP

The Gaza Strip came into an existence separate from the rest of Palestine after the Palestine War when it was occupied by the Egyptians. It is an area of about 135 square miles, 25 miles long and up to 9 wide. Its pre-war population was estimated at 30,000 but after 1948 an influx of refugees, many of them born there, took it to over 500,000 by the 1980s. The Egyptians set up a puppet Gaza Government but practical administrative power was in the hands of a Military Governor. At the Lausanne Talks of 1949 the American representative suggested that the Strip be given to Israel in return for acceptance of refugees: some Egyptian Ministers favoured the idea but King Farouq and the Israelis did not. Many of the earliest Fatah activists came from Gaza. In the early 1950s it was a base for *fidayyin* who raided into Israel: the Israeli reprisal Gaza Raid of February 1955 led to Nasser turning to the Eastern Bloc for arms. In the Suez War it was overrun and savagely treated by the Israelis who perpetrated the Khan Yunis Killings in a refugee camp. They were compelled to withdraw whereupon Gaza once again became a major military base where units of the Palestine Liberation Army were stationed. UNEF maintained a substantial presence. In the June War the Strip was again conquered by Israel. A Military Governor, later replaced by a Civil Administrator, was appointed. The area was ignored by the Palestine Liberation Organisation which preferred to concentrate on the more politicised West Bank but seethed with unrest aggravated by economic exploitation. The economy was systematically linked with that of Israel, practically unable to trade directly with anyone else and so forced to pay or accept whatever prices Tel Aviv dictated. A densely populated mass of sprawling refugee camps it was noted for poverty, hatred, violence, drugs, crime and poor sanitation. A large proportion of the people were dependent on rations distributed by the UN. In the summer of 1971 Ariel Sharon bulldozed houses and forcibly deported refugees suspected of trouble-making. A businessman Rashad al-Shawwa was then appointed Mayor but his pro-Jordanian attitude caused criticism both from Israelis and the nationalists who attempted to murder him in September 1972. He was dismissed in October 1972 but reinstated three years later. He conducted an active diplomacy with frequent consultations with the Egyptians, Jordanians and the PLO and after the Camp David agreement he worked for Palestinian participation in any autonomy talks. Shawwa made fund-raising trips to the Gulf States to seek funds for development. The Iranian Revolution brought a significant increase in Islamic fundamentalism. There was insufficient work available locally and the men had to cross into Israel where they were poorly paid. The educated youth had no prospects and were forced to emigrate. The press was heavily censored. The presence of the security forces was all-pervasive. Suspects were tortured. About 5,000 Jewish settlers lived apart in fortified villages built on confiscated Arab land. In the circumstances it was hardly surprising that the Intifadah started in Gaza and that the violence there was greatest. There were constant strikes and curfews, the one imposed during the Gulf War lasted over a year, and the schools were frequently closed – in one year 40% of school days were lost. After five years nearly all the young men in refugee camps had been in jail. The economy was ruined as the workers who went daily to Israel, 44,000 out of a total workforce of 99,000 were frequently banned from leaving the Strip, depriving it of $2,000,000 a day. Poverty was increased when the Gulf States ceased subsidising the PLO, which had distributed funds locally, as a punishment for its support of Saddam Hussain. A doctor estimated that 97% of Gazan children had had their homes raided, 60% had been beaten by the occupation forces and 19% had at least one family member in detention. Children were often arrested and had to be ransomed by their parents. Hamas appeared the most active group, elbowing aside Fatah although in elections for the Chamber of Commerce in November 1991, supporters of the PLO won 13 out of 16 seats, showing that there was local support for participation in the Madrid Peace Conference. In July 1992 Yassir Arafat appealed for co-operation between the PLO and Hamas in the Strip. In October over 100 Arabs were wounded in a single demonstration and Israeli army figures showed that during the year 121 Palestinians had been killed, mostly in Gaza. When in December over 400 alleged Hamas members were deported to Marj al-Zuhur, the majority came from Gaza, several of them teachers at the University. This led to a great increase in violence and in the first three months 18 Israelis were murdered and the security forces killed 34 Palestinians, 12 of them children under the age of 13. In March the Israeli commander ordered his men to "shoot without hesitation" and two Palestinians were killed and 100 wounded in two days. The Israeli left wing Meretz Party called on Prime Minister Rabin to pull out of Gaza and the belief grew that the Government would be glad to do so if this could be done without abandoning it to Hamas : the Egyptians declined to resume responsibility for it. At the end of March the Israelis sealed off Gaza from the rest of the world, turning the area into one large prison, declaring the closure of the frontier indefinite. In April there was a general strike in protest against further Palestinian participation in the Washington Peace Talks. There were further attacks on Israelis in May and 55 Palestinians were wounded in a single day. In May Amnesty International stated that 70 Arabs had been killed since the deportations and criticised the destruction of Palestinian houses without notice, usually followed by wanton destruction of property. In June the restrictions on movement were lifted and in September, the signature of the Israel–PLO Agreement provided for an Israeli withdrawal from Gaza and the establishment there of a Palestinain administration. Apart from some HAMAS zealots, the news was greeted with wild enthusiasm although it was realised that vast amounts of foreign aid would be required to make the statelet economically viable.

GAZODUC MAGHREB-EUROPE

As Algeria developed its market for the sale of liquified natural gas it signed in October 1977 a contract for a 2,500 km pipeline to carry it across Tunisia under the Mediterranean to Italy. It was obviously desirable to have a second pipeline across Morocco and the Straits of Gibraltar to Spain and Portugal but Morocco and Algeria were at loggerheads over the Western Sahara War and it was not until September 1988 that relations were restored after a 12-year breach. This was quickly followed by the signature in February 1989 of the Arab Maghreb Union Treaty for economic co-operation. Plans were then drawn up for a 1,225 km pipeline from Hassi R'mel to Seville – 527 km would be in Algeria and 545 in Morocco and the pipe would start by taking 7,200 million cubic metres a year, doubling its capacity by AD 2000, probably also extending to France and Germany. A meeting of Energy Ministers in Casablanca in November 1990 agreed that Morocco would receive 2,000–2,500 million cubic metres a year as transit fees, thus reducing its energy imports and helping industrialisation. The Gazoduc would have important political implications in making very costly a quarrel between the neighbours and furthering Morocco's hopes of close association with the EC. In March 1993 their Energy Ministers agreed to set up a joint Moroccan-Spanish company to build the Moroccan section. Algeria had some difficulty in obtaining credit but received a loan from the EC and in August 1993 signed a contract by which Bechtel would construct its section with 48 inch pipes for $305 million. The work would take two years and it was hoped that the first stage would be operational by the end of 1995.

GEMAYEL, Amin (1942–)

Lebanese President. The son of Shaykh Pierre Gemayel, the founder of the Kataib, he was born in the family home at Bikfaya, educated at a Jesuit school and trained as a lawyer at the Jesuit University. For some years he practised, representing amongst other clients Eastern Bloc airlines and he also administered the Party's very large business interests, including a radio station. In 1970 he entered Parliament where he showed himself politically moderate with good relations with other communities and, unlike his vehement younger brother Bashir Gemayel, was not prominent in the extreme Maronite Lebanese Forces. He was not involved in collaboration with Israel. In August 1982 with Beirut under Israeli occupation, Bashir was elected President but was assassinated ten days later before taking office. Amin, supported by Muslims who would never have endorsed Bashir, was chosen to succeed him by 78 out of 80 votes cast. His only opponent was Raymond Edde as former President Camille Chamoun withdrew before the poll. The new President pledged to continue the policies of his brother but in practice rejected his Maronite separatism. Gemayel kept on as Prime Minister Shafiq al-Wazzan who was trusted by the Muslims of West Beirut and he was able to bring about the reunion of the capital for the first time for years. He saw Lebanon as essentially part of the Arab world, in need of a government strong enough to free itself of Israel, Syria and the Palestinians but unable to solve its problems on its own and in particular he wanted to keep the Multi-National Force. He stressed this in a speech at the UN in October when he also said that the Palestinians had a right to their own state. In December 1982 he asked for a new "Marshall Plan" to reconstruct the damage caused in the Israeli invasion which he estimated at $2,500 million. He was unable to persuade the Lebanese Forces to disband and they went their own way under Samir Geagea. Gemayel secured Israeli agreement to withdraw from the country in the May Agreement in 1983 but the very heavy price that he had to pay the invaders to go made the terms negotiated unacceptable to the Syrians and their allies who formed the National Salvation Front to reject it. Gemayel kept therefore delaying his signature of the Agreement and in September the Israelis started unilaterally to withdraw. The resulting scramble for the territory that they evacuated caused some of the heaviest fighting ever and resulted in a defeat for the Lebanese Forces at the hands of the Druzes who penetrated to within 4 km of the presidential palace at Ba'abda while the Shiah Amal took over much of Sunni West Beirut in August 1983. The President ordered the army into action against their illegal encroachment whereas he had refused to allow it to operate against the equally illegal control that Maronite militias were exercising in East Beirut. In the sectarian fighting the Lebanese army, which the President was working hard to rebuild, disintegrated and Gemayel was never again

credible as a national figure above sectarian groupings. However Gemayel struggled for compromise and managed to persuade all the leading figures to assemble for the Geneva Reconciliation Talks at the end of October 1983 but nothing was achieved. In February 1984 Gemayel went to Damascus where he was persuaded by President Hafiz al-Assad to abrogate the May Agreement and to announce a package of reforms which he did at the Lausanne Reconciliation Talks which also ended without agreement. Meanwhile Wazzan had resigned, disapproving of the President's lack of impartiality. Gemayel then called upon the veteran conciliator Rashid Karami to form a "Last Chance Government" bringing in leaders of all political groups including the President's own father, Chamoun, Walid Jumblatt and Nabih Berri. The diversity of interests was too great and it simply did not work and the President and the Prime Minister could not collaborate, not meeting for months. The entire Cabinet assembled only on one occasion in 1986 and usually the Christian Ministers conferred only with the President while the Muslims dealt with the Prime Minister. Jumblatt, often in the most abusive terms, and Berri called for Gemayel's resignation. The beleaguered President, who could travel only by helicopter or with decoy cars, was confined to the Maronite enclave and was unable to visit the East and South and only rarely the North. He showed considerable courage in continuing work with his Palace being shelled but sought respite in frequent foreign tours in which he enjoyed great pomp. By mid 1985 the President had lost any control of the Lebanese Forces and was no longer the principal figure even on the Christian side. Thus important negotiations took place with militia leaders such as Elie Hobeika rather than the President speaking for the Maronites and the result was the Three-Militia Agreement which he refused to endorse. Gemayel was unwilling to commit himself to such radical reforms and opposed total subservience to the Syrians although he realised that it was impossible to get them out. After the murder of Karami, he appointed Salim al-Hoss but found it difficult to work with him. When his period of office expired it was clearly impossible to hold Presidential elections so Gemayel merely appointed General Michel Aoun as Prime Minister and left the country. Gemayel, handsome with a soft round face, dark eyes and thick black hair was devoted to gadgets and spent much time on computer technology. In 1975 he had established *Dar al-Mustaqbal*, a research and scientific institute for development and academic documentation and contacts with appropriate bodies abroad. His other recreation was tennis.

GENERAL PEOPLE'S CONGRESS (Libya)

In April 1975 Colonel Qadafi decreed a reform of the Arab Socialist Union to bring about more participation at grass-roots level. He ordered the creation of Basic People's Congresses in all villages, offices and workplaces. All Libyan citizens were automatically members of the BPC under whose jurisdiction they lived and no one could join a union or a professional association without membership of a BPC. In a city the Municipal Popular Congress consisted of the leadership of several BPCs. Although split into geographic areas they were not limited to discussion of local issues but had a right to formulate policy on any matter including international affairs. Responsibility for implementing their decisions rested with a secretariat selected by and accountable to each Congress. Each was assisted by a series of People's Committees which dealt with matters such as housing and health but had no decision-making powers of their own. Policy for the country as a whole, arising out of the debates in the BPCs, was co-ordinated by the General People's Congress which met annually in January or February attended by officials of each BPC which gave it a membership of about 1,000. The GPC acted as an executive and legislative body and often held suprisingly free-ranging debates on development policies and foreign affairs. In February 1985 the GPC overruled Qadafi's proposed conscription of women but in 1987 they were not allowed to debate the involvement in Chad. Ministers had been abolished by the Sabhah Congress of 1977 and a People's Committee for each aspect of public affairs from foreign affairs to agriculture carried out the policies of the GPC which they had no power to change or dispute. The Secretaries in charge of these Committees formed the General Popular Committee whose Secretary-General was in effect Prime Minister; the post was held by Qadafi himself from 1977 to 1979. By 1987 there were over 2,000 BPCs. The GPC also elected a General Secretariat which originally consisted of the surviving members of the Revolution Command Council to prepare its agenda. In addition there were Revolutionary Committees, which appeared to have the power to intervene in any matter they chose and act as watchdogs over the BPCs, the police and the armed forces. Some RCs were established amongst Libyans abroad where they murdered exiled dissidents – the "stray dogs" – and occupied Embassies, rechristened People's Bureaux. They were chosen for their zealous devotion to Qadafi and at times of crisis seemed to constitute his principal support.

GENERAL SYRIAN CONGRESS (1919–20)
Soon after the end of the war Amir Faysal suggested to Allenby the Allied Commander-in-Chief that a Constitutional Congress be summoned in Damascus. Owing to the delay in settling the future of the country nothing was done until after the appointment of the King–Crane Commission to enquire into the wishes of the population. In May 1919 groups of notables decided to form a Congress to give more status to representations to the Commission and to draft a Constitution. Deputies in the former Ottoman Assembly became members, others were elected in differing ways and 35 tribal and religious leaders joined *ex officio* the elected 85. Apart from the Alawites and Maronites, all the communities of Syria, Lebanon and Palestine were represented. Meeting in June under the presidency of Rashid Rida, the Congress elected Hashim al-Atassi as Chairman and declared itself the legal representative of all Syria. Delegates were chosen to give evidence to the Commission. It called for the repudiation of the Sykes–Picot Agreement and the Balfour Declaration. It was prepared to accept an American or less willingly a British Mandate but not a French one and in November 1919 discussed a declaration of war on France. Faysal, trying

to negotiate with Paris, was embarrassed and suspended the Congress on 4 December. In February 1920, with the French now firmly established in Lebanon and making demands upon Syria, Faysal, needing nationalist support, recalled the Congress. It declared independence for a united Syria and Palestine and denounced Zionism. It declared its willingness to co-operate with the Allies and their economic interests and safeguard the rights of minorities. On 8 March the Congress invited Faysal to be constitutional King of Syria. At the same time the Iraqi members meeting separately offered a throne in Baghdad to his brother Abd Allah. The Members started drafting a Constitution and acted briefly as a legislature. It showed no sympathies with Faysal's attempts to appease the French. After a French ultimatum was received, the Congress declared illegal any government that accepted it and demanded the right to approve of any agreement made. On 20 July, just before the battle of Maysalun Faysal suspended the Congress. The vehement Syrian nationalism showed by the Congress was a strong contrast to the pan-Arabism of the earlier movements like al-Fatat and indeed of Faysal's father King Hussain who regarded the acceptance of thrones by his sons as acts of disloyalty.

GENEVA OIL AGREEMENTS (1972 and 1973)
The Tehran Oil Agreement showed that if the OPEC countries maintained a united front they were more powerful than the companies. The point was further proved in December when after the Shah's seizure of Abu Musa, Qadafi nationalised BP's interests in Libya without suffering any reprisals. During 1971 the value of the dollar, in which prices were calculated, had declined and the OPEC countries, claiming that their purchasing power had decreased, demanded a price rise. At Geneva in January 1972 they compelled the companies to accept an 8% increase and a formula linking further rises to the fall of the dollar. They also called for an immediate 20% participation agreement leading to eventual 51% ownership of the companies' assets. This would mean the complete subjugation of the companies, reducing their role to extracting oil as instructed and paying a price dictated by the host state. By May 1972 most of the major companies had conceded the principle of 20% and in June Baghdad got away with nationalizing the Iraq Petroleum Company. Early in 1973 the dollar had declined by 11% which, according to the formula, should have triggered a rise of 6%. Instead in the second Geneva Agreement of June 1973 OPEC demanded 12%, settling for 11.9%. This signalled the capitulation of the oil companies and later in the year, with less success, the Arabs tried to coerce Western governments by using the Oil Weapon.

GENEVA PEACE CONFERENCE (1973)
Shortly after the end of the October War of 1973 the US Secretary of State Henry Kissinger and his Assistant Joseph Sisco visited the Middle East and several European countries and on 21 November Kissinger said that "sufficient progress" had been made for peace talks which would be held at Geneva the following month. This was partly a sop to the Russians whose prestige had been dented by the American initiatives in stopping

the fighting. Egypt, Israel and Syria, having accepted the principle, then proceeded to impose conditions and Kissinger made another brief visit to the area. After a postponement the Secretary-General of the UN Kurt Waldheim presided over the opening session on 21 December: Egypt, Jordan and Israel sent Ismail Fahmi, Zaid al-Rifai and Abba Eban. The US and the USSR were represented by Kissinger and Gromyko who later shared the chairmanship. Syria refused to attend and, on the insistence of Israel, no Palestinian delegation was invited. No progress was made and the talks lasted only a few days. A Jordanian proposal that all forces should be withdrawn from a zone five miles each side of the River Jordan was rejected by Israel. At the same time military disengagement talks were held between Egyptian and Israeli officers in Geneva and although there was no progress in these either, a settlement was reached through the mediation of Kissinger at Kilometre 101 in January 1974. This encouraged the US to decide to attempt a peace settlement on its own without further involving the Russians.

GHANNOUCHI, Rashid b. Mahmud (1941–)

Tunisian political and religious leader. He was born near Gabes and educated locally and at the Khalduniyyah religious university. He then taught in Gabes for two years before going to Damascus University where after four years he took a degree in Philosophy. Returning home in 1969 he again worked as a teacher. Influenced by the thought of Ghazali (died 1111) and Saiyyid Qutb, with Abd al-Fattah Mourou, he set up an Islamic group and published two journals. He advocated the use of *Ijtihad* to present Islamic answers to all contemporary problems, supported the equality of the sexes and opposed the veil, and was a member of the government-sponsored Association for the Preservation of the Qur'an which was encouraged to compete with Marxists for recruits in Universities. He argued that Islam, which rests on *Ijma* (consensus) is not anti-democratic and that imported ideologies in development models caused materialism and moral corruption, making Muslims strangers in their own country. Ghannouchi opposed violence, and was shocked by the brutal repression of the workers that followed the Black Thursday Riots of January 1978. His concern with current realities brought him increasing popularity with students, workers and the middle classes and led to harassment by local Parti Socialiste Destourien officials. Islamic dissent was inspired by the success of the Iranian Revolution and in 1979 Ghannouchi received *bay'a* as Amir from a number of groups. In 1981 when the government of Muhammad Mzali appeared ready to tolerate political pluralism Ghannouchi applied for registration of his followers as a party under the name of the Mouvement de la Tendance Islamique. It was refused and he was sentenced to eleven years' imprisonment for terrorism in collaboration with a foreign power, presumably Iran. He was tortured in jail but pardoned in 1984 at the request of Gulf Shaykhs. He resumed leadership of the MTI which he made further efforts to have legalised. In 1986, having already attacked the Americans for supporting undemocratic governments such as that of Bourguiba, he led a demonstration against the Tripoli Bombing.

Later that year he was resident in Saudi Arabia. In March 1987 Ghannouchi was arrested for preaching in a mosque, contrary to the terms of his release in 1984. Although he was thus in jail when Islamic militants bombed tourist hotels in August, he was brought to trial with them in September. The Prosecutor demanded a death sentence but he was sentenced merely to life imprisonment. Bourguiba's insistence upon a retrial as sentences on the militants had been too light, was a major cause of his overthrow. The new President Ben Ali released Ghannouchi in May 1988 and received him several times. As his civil rights had not been restored Ghannouchi was unable to play much part in the parliamentary elections of April 1989 and shortly afterwards he went abroad. In Algeria he attempted to mediate between President Chadli and the Muslim fundamentalists. After the invasion of Kuwait by Iraq, Ghannouchi opposed Saddam Hussain as a secularist but declared that the Gulf States had excluded themselves from the Muslim world by accepting foreign troops and he called for *Jihad* and a boycott of Western goods: this stance caused a breach between him and Mourou. He led delegations of ulema around several capitals trying to mediate. He went into exile and linked up with other opponents of the regime, Mzali and Ahmad Ben Salah to accuse it of terror and repression. In October 1991 the Tunisian Government recalled its Ambassador from the Sudan after Khartoum had given Ghannouchi a diplomatic passport. It tried to present him, Hassan Turabi and Umar Abd al-Rahman as leaders of a worldwide Muslim conspiracy. In August 1992 he was sentenced, *in absentia* to life imprisonment for masterminding a plot to seize power after causing a power vacuum by the assassination of Ben Ali. He moved to London and was, in August 1993, despite the opposition of some MPs, given political asylum. He gave frequent interviews declaring that democracy was not incompatible with Islam which saw it as a means to win power without violence.

al-GHASHMI, Ahmad b. Hussain (1940–78)

President of Yemen. He came from a family of tribal notables and entered the army after a very limited education. When Colonel Ibrahim al-Hamdi ousted President Abd al-Rahman al-Iryani in June 1974, Ghashmi was a Lt Colonel and generally regarded as unambitious and unintelligent. In October he was made a member of the Military Command Council and shortly afterwards Chief of Staff. He made several trips abroad seeking new sources that would weaken the army's exclusive dependence on Russian arms and advisers. In October 1977 Hamdi and his brother were murdered. There were some reports that the crime took place in the house of Ghashmi and the bodies later moved. Ghashmi was appointed to succeed him and, amidst scenes of widespread mourning, almost immediately survived the first of several attempts on his life. The supporters of Hamdi, in particular Shafai officers led by Major Abd al-Alim attempted an uprising in Taizz but Ghashmi rallied enough support from Zaidi tribal units to put it down. Although he declared his intention of following the policies of his predecessor, he tacitly abandoned the hope of pursuing an independent line by loosening the close relations with South

Yemen and strengthening the weakened ties with Saudi Arabia. He was too preoccupied with problems of day-to-day survival to take much initiative in development although the International Development Conference planned by Hamdi took place with considerable success. He expressed the wish to see democracy flourish but moved extremely cautiously towards it, nominating a 99-man Constitutional Assembly which dissolved the MCC and declared Ghashmi President. On 24 June 1978 he was receiving a personal envoy from Salim Rubai Ali when the Adeni's briefcase exploded, killing both men. It is still unclear who committed the murder and why. It is unlikely that it was planned in Sanaa for there it caused total surprise and no group was poised to exploit it. It is more likely to have been a by-product of the power struggle in Aden between Ali and the extreme left wing. Ghashmi had neither the time in office nor the ability to make a significant mark on the history of the Yemen.

GHOZALI, Sid Ahmad (1937–)

Algerian Prime Minister. Born in Marnia on the Moroccan frontier, he was educated at the University of Damascus where he took a degree in Philosophy and at the Cole des Ponts et Chausses in Paris where he took a degree in civil engineering. He worked briefly for a French oil company and as a teacher before attracting the attention of Ben Bella who also came from Marnia. The incarnation of a technocrat, speaking perfect French, always wearing a bow tie, he was in 1964 made Under-Secretary for Public Works with charge of the oil industry. In 1966 he was put in charge of SONATRACH which he built into an enormous industrial empire with some 80,000 employees. He did much to pioneer new technology and developed the export of liquid gas. In May 1977 Ghozali was put in charge of the newly created Ministry of Energy and Petrochemicals when Boumédienne broke up the much resented concentration of industrial power that Belaid Abd al-Salam had enjoyed. When Chadli formed a government in March 1979 he moved Ghozali to the Ministry of Irrigation to attend to a sphere that had been neglected in Boumédienne's drive for industrialisation. In December 1981 he was one of the old associates of Boumédienne dropped from the Politburo of the Front de Libération Nationale and in June 1984 he was sent to Brussels as Ambassador to the EC. After the October Riots of 1988, which had been largely caused by economic distress, Chadli appointed him Minister of Finance. The following year he was transferred to the Foreign Ministry where he proved a great success at raising money, quickly securing a large loan from France. He worked extremely hard in an attempt to end the Western Sahara War. Later he was associated with Chadli in trying to prevent the crisis that followed the invasion of Kuwait by Saddam Hussain from escalating into war. In August 1990 he called for a Summit to settle it as a dispute amongst Arabs and later he denounced sanctions against Iraq and the seizure of its assets as "the hold-up of the century". In May 1991 the Front Islamique du Salut began a series of violent demonstrations against a new electoral law patently framed to prevent them from winning the forthcoming parliamentary elections. Co-operation with FIS was

obviously necessary but as Mouloud Hamrouche, the Prime Minister, was unwilling to do this, on 5 June, Chadli offered the post to Ghozali who was known to be a practising Muslim and was seen as capable of maintaining the confidence of Algeria's foreign creditors. A 4-month state of emergency was imposed. Ghozali had been little involved in domestic politics but he aimed to form a non-partisan coalition to conduct the elections, reportedly consulting 200 people before accepting. It took him a fortnight to name a Cabinet which included 23 technocrats, two women, to the annoyance of FIS, the first Minister of Human Rights in the Arab world, and a Minister for Small Businesses. He retained General Nezzar at Defence and was inevitably regarded as a front for army rule: Ghozali indeed saw the army as the ultimate guarantor of independence, national dignity and social justice. He promised war on poverty, help for the unemployed, measures to help business with the establishment of a free market over three years and a continuation of the democratic process. Parliament approved his programme by 259 votes to 5. His first Cabinet meeting accepted an IMF package, involving a loan of $550 million which showed that economic liberalism would continue. He invited all party leaders to discuss electoral procedure but although 48 accepted, FIS and three others did not and no consensus was reached. Ghozali expressed readiness to sell state assets including the oilfields of Hassi Massaoud to reduce the national debt: this was much resented by FLN diehards and by bureaucrats and Ghozali dismissed Ministers and bureaucrats considered too close to the Party or hostile to the army. The Prime Minister had trouble with the FLN-controlled Parliament which refused, with an election looming, to cut subsidies as demanded by the IMF or to pass a fairer electoral law. Ghozali himself joined a demonstration of women protesting against the casting of their votes by their husbands. In September the dinar was devalued by 22%. In October he reshuffled his Cabinet, himself taking the Finance Ministry and bringing in General Belkheir to supervise the elections. The participation of FIS remained in doubt and Ghozali feared for the democratic process, admitting in November that "we have lied too much to the people". He pressed on, with some success, with efforts to secure foreign investment. In December the elections took place with 5,712 candidates from 49 parties contesting 430 seats with so little disorder that Chadli congratulated Ghozali upon their conduct. The result, however, a triumph for FIS which had belatedly decided to participate, "sealed", said Ghozali, "the collapse of the democratic parties" which "had behaved like ostriches" in failing to work together. He said that he would resign after the second round due in January. It did not take place for the army ousted Chadli whom it replaced with a Haut Comité d'État. Although not a member of the HCE, Ghozali expressed entire solidarity with the new regime, staying on as Prime Minister as a sign of continuity and promising elections within two years. There were mass arrests, many as Ghozali admitted, of innocent people. He reshuffled his Cabinet, abolishing the Ministry of Human Rights but bringing in one of the founders of FIS as Minister of Employment. A survey showed that only 29 out of 189 state enterprises were financially healthy and he admitted that the economy was "100% in shambles". He put forward plans for combatting the growing Islamic Insurrection by rapid development for which he needed massive imports which he hoped to pay for by raising $8,000 million through foreign participation in the oil industry. In April he promulgated a decree dissolving FIS-run Councils and there were continual clashes. In June the Government abolished food subsidies. Ghozali's economic liberalism was not entirely to the taste of the new Head of State, Muhammad Boudiaf who had been advocated some state control. On 7 July, after the assassination of Boudiaf, Ghozali resigned to enable the new Head of State Ali Kafi to make a fresh start: he was appointed Ambassador to France. Ghozali was widely regarded as an honest man, genuinely concerned with the man in the street.

GLORIOUS CORRECTIVE MOVE (1969)
At the Zinjibar Congress of March 1968 the split between the right and left wings of the ruling National Liberation Front in South Yemen came out into the open. The left had prevailed but their victory was nullified by the President Qahtan al-Shaabi, who, in alliance with the army arrested or dismissed his opponents. They managed to regroup but the President was so contemptuous of them that he even promoted some to his Cabinet in April 1969. In June Qahtan quarrelled with his Minister of Defence Muhammad Ali Haytham over the posting of an officer and dismissed him. Haytham who had considerable influence with the army and the tribes thereupon joined forces with the leftists. In a bloodless coup the President and his Prime Minister and cousin Faysal Abd al-Latif al-Shaabi were deposed for "individualistic actions" and "blatantly violating" the Party's Charter by failing to consult the General Command. The office of President was replaced by a five-man Council headed by Salim Rubai Ali and including Haytham as Prime Minister and Abd al-Fattah Ismail. The move to the left was immediately shown by a call for the export of the Revolution to neighbouring countries, closer relations with Russia and recognition of East Germany which had all been strongly opposed by Qahtan.

GOUVERNEMENT PROVISOIRE DE LA RÉPUBLIQUE ALGÉRIENNE
The accession to power of General de Gaulle in May 1958 and the possibility that he might bring about a peace settlement with the Muslims within Algeria alarmed the leaders of the Front de Libération Nationale in exile in Cairo. On 19 September Farhat Abbas, speaking in French, announced the formation of a Government in Exile headed by himself. It included the five leaders imprisoned in France, Ben Bella as Vice-President and the others as Ministers of State. The total of 16 Ministers included Bilqasim Krim as Vice-President and Minister of the Armed Forces and the wilaya commanders Boussouf and Ben Tobal. Its capital was to be in Tunis where various offices gave young Algerians useful experience of administration. The Arab and radical African countries and most of the communist states although not initially the USSR, recognised it as the legitimate government of Algeria.

The Arab League provided financial support. The GPRA never exercised full control over the individual wilayas or over the Armé de Libération Nationale and attempts to assert authority were greatly resented. In January 1960 the GPRA was reduced in size with Krim becoming Foreign Minister to travel widely in quest of support. At first it rejected any suggestion of negotiations with France but in June after an appeal by de Gaulle the GPRA authorised Ahmad Boumendjel to meet his emissaries for the Melun Talks but these came to nothing. An overwhelming majority in a vote in the UN General Assembly in December 1960 showed support for the GPRA but de Gaulle still refused officially to recognise it. At the fourth session in Tripoli in August 1961 members of the "Parliament", the Conseil National de la Révolution Algérienne decided that Abbas was not the man to conduct the final search for a peace agreement and, considering that Krim would be too divisive, selected Ben Yusuf Ben Khedda to replace him. Peace negotiations ended with the signature by Krim on behalf of the GPRA of the Evian Agreement in March 1962 which amongst other measures set up a French–Algerian Provisional Executive headed by Abd al-Rahman Faris which the GPRA worked to sabotage. Ben Bella, who with the other imprisoned members of the GPRA had been released, immediately repudiated the Agreement as a sell-out to France and demanded that a programme for the independent state should be drafted by a Politburo of the FLN dominated by himself and his nominees. He was supported by Colonel Boumédienne on behalf of the ALN. At the final Tripoli meeting of the CNRA no agreement could be reached and Boumédienne attempted to arrest Ben Khedda who with his loyalists fled firstly to Tunis and then established their headquarters on Algerian soil at Tizi-Ouzou. Ben Khedda as President ordered the arrest of Boumédienne whereupon Ben Bella, as Vice-President, asserted that this action terminated the legitimacy of the GPRA. For a moment the country appeared on the brink of civil war but there was a general feeling that seven years of bloodshed had been enough. Support ebbed away from Ben Khedda and on 7 August he formally handed over power to the Politburo. The GPRA ceased to exist after elections for a National Assembly in September.

GREAT MAN-MADE RIVER PROJECT (Libya)
In the 1960s prospectors for oil in the Fezzan and Kufra areas found enormous reserves of fossil water several thousand years old in an underground ocean covering 8,000 square km. Although agriculture accounted for only 5% of Libya's GDP and according to FAO figures only 2% of the country was cultivable and 5% suitable for livestock, from the time he seized power Colonel Qadafi took a particular interest in its reform, confiscating all lands not in use and taking over Italian-owned properties. The state directed organisation of land use but development plans merely resulted in production decreasing, partly through misuse of water. As his ideology developed Qadafi came to believe that no nation that imported its food could be truly independent and that self-sufficiency had to be achieved even if home-grown corn cost five times as much as imports. Desalination plants would have been cheap but depen-

dent upon the West for spare parts. He therefore devised a plan for the "eighth wonder of the world", a $25,000 million scheme which in five phases would for fifty years move 6,000 million cubic metres of water a day from 960 wells with a depth up to half a kilometre, through 3,380 km of concrete pipes, 4 metres in diameter and each weighing 75 tons to bring an extra 100,000 hectares into cultivation. It would require the moving of ten times as much earth as the Aswan Dam. The Great Man-Made River Authority was set up in October 1983. Two factories had to be built to make the pipes. For the first phase, a 1,860 km twin pipeline, taking 2 million cubic metres a day from 108 wells near Tazerbo to an immense reservoir at Ajadabiyyah for distribution to Benghazi and Sirte on the coast at a cost of $3,290 million. The South Korean company Ah Dong was chosen for its low cost and highly disciplined labour force of which 8,000 were sent to Libya and the contract was signed in November 1983 and work started in August 1984 and was completed in August 1991. The inauguration ceremony, illuminated by lighting obtained second-hand from Blackpool, was attended by North African Heads of State. A $5,300 million contract for the second phase, 1,100 km pipeline from the Fezzan to Tripoli was signed with Ah Dong in August 1989 despite some difficulties over payment. The third stage envisaged was to bring water from Kufra into the Tazerbo-Ajadabiyyah pipeline, the fourth from Ajadabiyyah to Tobruk and the fifth from Tripoli to Sirte. These extensions would make possible the cultivatation of an extra 450,000 acres in winter and 250,000 in summer although, given Libyan unwillingness to work on the land, large-scale imports of Egyptian labour would be necessary: the figure of one million was suggested. The entire project was due for completion by 1997 and was financed by a 10% special levy on petrol, cigarettes and some services. Although Qadafi said that it showed the Libyan desire for peace, there were fears that it might be bombed by the Americans; there were also worries that it might damage the acquifer system of the whole of North Africa. In January 1994, the former Prime Minister Jadullah al-Talhi was made Minister in charge of the Project.

GREEN BOOK (Libya)

In April 1973 Colonel Qadafi in a speech at Zuwarah launched the Libyan Cultural Revolution, sweeping aside the past, and later that year he outlined the Third Universal Theory which was to replace capitalism and communism. Having handed over all his duties to Abd al-Salam Jalloud in order to concentrate on ideology, he set out to provide "the comprehensive solution of the problems of human society so that the individual may be materially and spiritually liberated to attain his happiness". In 1976 he published the first Volume, about 6,000 words, of his *Green Book, The Solution of the Problem of Democracy. The Authority of the People* which stated that "representation is a falsification of democracy", the representative usurps the authority of the people, that majority rule is unfair to the minority and that "the supervision of the people by the people" can only be achieved by popular congresses. All contemporary systems are merely the result of past struggles for power between instruments of governing

and political parties, representing a class or an interest group only give rise to "negative and destructive struggles". Like Rousseau he considered that the general will would be sovereign and infallible. Volume II *The Solution of the Economic Problem – Socialism*, also about 6,000 words, appeared in 1977. In it he declared that Socialism had been invented by the Arabs, that the producer must become the consumer as profit participation would "abolish wages, free man from slavery to them and return to the natural laws that prevailed before the appearance of classes, man-made governments and artificial laws". The individual would be freed by having his needs taken care of and no one should have power over another or collect rent by owning more than one dwelling. Money, the concept of profit and the private retail trade would eventually disappear. In Volume III *The Social Bases of the Third Universal Theory* which appeared in 1979 Qadafi differentiated between the State which would disappear and the Nation, which ideally should have a single religion to prevent conflict. He set out controversial views on women (they cannot be equal although "equal as human beings"), education ("all existing methods should be destroyed" as a curriculum is coercion against human freedom and everyone should learn what they wish), minorities, melody, arts, sport (all should take part and none should watch). The whole was presented as a new Gospel. *The Green Book* was attacked by the ulema as it undermined the whole of traditional Islamic jurisprudence by saying that only the Qur'an had validity and dismissing the *Hadith* and the *Sunna* of the Prophet whom Qadafi appeared to be attempting to replace with what was described as "anarchic syndicalism".

GREEN MARCH (Morocco) (1975)

In May 1975 the Madrid Government announced its intention of giving independence to the Western Sahara as soon as possible and shortly afterwards started withdrawing its troops. The UN had called for a referendum on whether the territory should become a sovereign state or be partitioned between Morocco and Mauritania. Hassan II maintained that the historical claims of Morocco to the territory were irrefutable and that he would not recognise a vote for independence. As a judgement from the International Court of Justice on the validity of the claims was awaited the King declared on 16 October 1975 that he would personally lead a peaceful march of 350,000 unarmed civilians (the number chosen was that of the annual births in the Kingdom) to recover the Sahara. Volunteers could register at special offices throughout the country and would be taken by special trains to Marrakesh from where they would set out in 8,000 lorries, accompanied by 470 doctors and 220 ambulances with 17,000 tons of food and 36,000 tons of water. His call was greeted with overwhelming enthusiasm from the entire population, even those politically opposed to his regime, and nearly 650,000 volunteered within four days: all Moroccans donated a week's pay towards the expenses of the March. The first group of 20,000, led by the Prime Minister Ahmad Uthman set out for the frontier from Ksar al-Suq on 21 October. On 1 November the Spanish Government told the Security Council that it would use force to stop the march and asked Secretary-General Waldheim to intensify efforts for a peaceful solution. On 6 November, however, the first group of 44,000, 10% of them women, crossed the frontier led by the Prime Minister, the King having decided to stay at a command post. They were to brandish the Qur'an and the Moroccan flag and not to reply if fired upon – the army would protect them. On the same day the Security Council deplored their action. They had not gone far when they had to halt at a "dissuasion line" manned by the Spanish Foreign Legion and protected by minefields. On 9 November the King unexpectedly called off the March, saying that it had achieved its object. On 14 November the Madrid Tripartite Agreement provided for a complete Spanish withdrawal by 28 February 1976. The Green March provided a tremendous boost for the position of the King as the national leader and its spirit of national unity was invoked by him on numerous occasions when he found himself in political difficulties.

GUEDIRA, (Ahmad) Rida (1922–)

Moroccan political leader. He was born in Rabat and took a law degree in Paris where he was active as a student nationalist. Establishing himself in practice in Morocco, he often defended people accused of terrorist offences. Guedira was the founder of the Liberal Independent Party, a small group of intellectuals which did not like the traditionalism of the Istiqlal Party or the republicanism of some of the Parti Démocratique de l'Indépendance. He was extremely close both to Muhammad V and the future Hassan II. After independence he was appointed the first Minister of Defence, charged with the preliminary steps towards forming a national army. When Bekkai reshuffled his Cabinet in October 1956 Guedira was moved to the Ministry of Information which worked directly with the Palace. He was out of office during the Premiership of Abd Allah Ibrahim and, with the encouragement of the Crown Prince, he ran a journal criticising the administration. He was strongly pro-American and supported the retention of their bases as an element of stability. In 1961 he was appointed Minister of the Interior and of Education and also Director-General of the Royal Cabinet, making him effectively the King's deputy. After a careful study of other nations' constitutions he was the principal architect of Morocco's Fundamental Law and was largely responsible for the clauses ruling out a one-party state. In the autumn of 1961 he set out the Promotion Nationale, an ambitious plan for development in rural areas which he hoped would also bring him some personal support in the *bled*. In May 1963, declaring political parties anachronistic and totalitarian, he put together the Front pour la Défense des Institutions Constitutionelles, a coalition of monarchist groups to fight the elections: the success it obtained in just failing to win an outright majority was regarded as mainly due to his manipulation. In November 1963 at the time of the Tindouf Dispute with Algeria, Guedira was moved to the Foreign Ministry to win support for Morocco's case. He became involved in a dispute with the US which forced Morocco to stop buying sugar from Cuba. In May 1964, with the FDIC falling to pieces, he founded the Parti Socialiste Démocratique

which advocated a "liberal" socialism with "state guidance" of private capitalism. His relations were cooling with the King and in August 1964 after his advice on courts dealing with corruption had been rejected, he resigned. He was in private practice until 1968 when he was appointed Director of Planning and Development for which he was made Minister of State in February 1969. In August after student riots he was made Minister of Education and later that year he toured the Arab world to persuade leaders to attend the Rabat Summit. In February 1970 he was made a scapegoat for more student riots and dismissed. In 1977 the King recalled him as a Councillor of the Royal Cabinet and used him on a series of highly delicate missions. In June 1981 he negotiated a deal which ended years of Libyan hostility to Morocco: Qadafi ceased to support Polisario in return for a withdrawal of Moroccan help for the factions opposing him in Chad. In June 1983 Polisario claimed that they had been talking secretly with Guedira. The following year he was closely involved in the drafting of the Oudjda Declaration and subsequently he visited Algeria and Tunisia to reassure them that it was not directed against them. In November 1984 after a Polisario delegation had gone to the UN, Guedira led a mission mainly composed of Sahrawis to put the Moroccan case. In 1985 he was several times in Algeria seeking reconciliation and eventually succeeded in bringing about a resumption of relations. Guedira was involved in all the most secret activities of Moroccan diplomacy from persuading reluctant leaders to attend Summits to handling negotiations with Israel. The King found him equally useful in domestic politics, making him the main channel for communication with the opposition parties and in October 1992 appointing him to head a Commission to see that the preparation and conduct of the forthcoming parliamentary elections were regarded as fair by all participants. Guedira was an immensely hard-working man, frank, realistic and highly efficient.

GULF CO-OPERATION COUNCIL

The outbreak of the Iran–Iraq War caused the Arab oil states to think seriously about their future and gave them the opportunity to form a group without including either of the larger Gulf powers. They realised that they were dependent upon a single, finite, resource and they needed to co-operate to diversify their economies by creating a manufacturing infrastructure and also to reduce their total dependence on the West. There was also the problem of defence although there was no unanimity on how this should be achieved with Oman wanting formal alliance with the West, Kuwait hoping to exclude both Super-Powers while the remainder wished Western assistance to be available at a reasonable distance. There was also a feeling of a shared destiny and that a united Gulf would have a larger voice in international affairs. Following a series of meetings by Foreign Ministers, six Heads of State signed in Abu Dhabi on 25 May 1981 a Charter setting out the objectives of "co-ordination, integration and interconnection" in economic and financial matters, commerce, customs and communications, education and culture, social and health affairs, information and tourism, and legislation and administrative affairs: there was no mention of defence. It established a Supreme Council of Rulers with the Chairmanship rotating annually, a Ministerial Council of Foreign Ministers meeting quarterly, and a Secretariat of some 300 officials headed by the Kuwaiti diplomat Abd Allah Bishara with its headquarters in Riyadh which also housed the Commission for the Settlement of Disputes. The following month the Finance Ministers signed an equally fundamental document, the Unified Economic Agreement which arranged for co-ordinated import/export policies, building up strategic food stocks, freedom of movement and capital, joint ventures, harmonisation of banking procedures, transfer of technology with the aim of a Common Market by the end of the 1980s. Annual Gulf Co-operation Council Summits, at which decisions needed unanimity, were held. Joint institutions such as a Gulf Investment Corporation and a Gulf Standards Organisation were set up. The role of the GCC in Arab politics was defined as one of conciliation, it brought about the end of the Oman–South Yemen Dispute and tried to mediate in the Iran–Iraq War and in the Hawar Dispute. It always expressed strong support for the Palestinians. The first phase came into effect in March 1983 when tariff barriers between the members were abolished. Professional people such as doctors or industrialists could practise or set up business in any member-state. GCC members co-ordinated their pricing policies and operated as a group within OPEC. Militarily the key-note was "self-reliance" and, as it appeared possible that Tehran might win the war and move on into Arabia, it was agreed at the Kuwait Summit of 1984 to establish a defence force, the Peninsula Shield. Agreements were made on other spheres, Ministers of Agriculture harmonised regulations on technical matters, Ministers of Industries endorsed a common strategy, there were discussions of new road and rail links and a Causeway joining Bahrain to the mainland was built, studies were commissioned for a regional power grid, increasing water supplies etc. There were also frequent meetings of officials and during its first decade, the GCC made real progress towards economic unification working towards unity of tariffs, standardisation of banking laws, co-ordination of regional and international aid programmes, development loan policies, investment to acquire technology, standards of imported food, etc. which were necessary for negotiating with the EC as a single unit. Member states were committed to settling disputes peacefully, respecting borders and non-interference in each other's affairs. GCC members supported each other in international affairs such as the Iraqui invasion of Kuwait, the Iranian threat to Abu Musa or Western threats to impose a tax on crude oil imports. They negotiated as a bloc with Egypt and Syria in the Damascus Declaration. There were also numerous unofficial events such as meetings of Chambers of Commerce and sports tournaments between universities of GCC states. In December 1992 Fahm b. Sultan al-Qasimi was appointed to succeed Bishara as Secretary-General.

GULF CO-OPERATION COUNCIL SUMMITS

The *First Summit* of the leaders of six Arab Gulf States was held in Abu Dhabi in May 1981 and took the formal decision to set up the Gulf Co-operation Council. It appointed a Secretary-General, Abdallah Bishara, a secretariat and five specialist committees to formulate a unified oil policy and to co-ordinate economic and social planning, industrial, commercial and cultural policies. It failed to agree on a joint defence force but was unanimous in opposition to foreign interference in the region, the peace of which depended upon settlement of the Palestinian problem.

The *Second Summit* in Riyadh in November 1981 ratified the unified economic agreement. It declared opposition to foreign military bases.

The *Third Summit* was held in Bahrain in November 1982 approved agreements by Finance Ministers which exempted GCC products from customs duties, permitted, subject to certain provisos, citizens to work in any member state, eased movement of vehicles and established the Gulf Investment Corporation. It also agreed to accept Saudi specifications and standards. There was still no agreement over defence.

The *Fourth Summit*, held in Doha in November 1983 was almost disrupted by an attempted coup, which led to a complete ban on the entry of all foreigners. Bishara's report suggested extending joint economic activity to include tourism, pharmacy and the unification of charges for utilities, the possibility of a railway link and network of gas pipes and the location of food reserves. Measures were approved which increased free movement of labour between states and eased restrictions on economic activities. The leaders expressed satisfaction at the degree of co-operation so far achieved in economic matters and made some advance in military matters. They hoped for peace in Lebanon and between warring Palestinian factions. They called for adherence to Security Council Resolutions condemning attacks on shipping in the Gulf.

The *Fifth Summit*, held in Kuwait in November 1984, agreed to set up, as a temporary measure, a joint strike force of 10,000 men from all six member states – Peninsula Shield. It approved proposals to give priority to local products and a document on development policies and discussed land ownership regulations.

The *Sixth Summit*, meeting in Muscat in November 1985 approved measures of integration in the common agricultural policy and industrial development to protect the environment. It agreed that educational and professional qualifications would be valid in all member states. It put Sultan Qabus in charge of an attempt to find a peace settlement to end the Iran–Iraq War and sent an Omani Minister to Baghdad with proposals.

The *Seventh Summit* took place in Abu Dhabi in November 1986. It approved an agreement by which investors could obtain loans within any state of the GCC with the right to engage in trade on the same terms as the locals. In foreign affairs it reiterated support for the PLO and called for an immediate ceasefire in the Iran–Iraq War with withdrawal to previous frontiers and the independence of Lebanon. It regretted the breach between Britain and Syria which had resulted from the Hindawi affair. It praised the development of the Peninsula Shield forces and set out a media charter to protect the heritage of the area.

The *Eighth Summit* took place in Riyadh in December 1987. It called for an end of oil price discounting and for sticking to quotas and ratified an oil-loaning system.

It urged a common defence strategy including standardisation of equipment. It also stressed the need to maintain contacts with Iran in pursuit of a peace settlement although it deplored recent missile attacks and expressed support for the *Intifadah* which had just begun. More restrictions on business activities between states were eased.

The *Ninth Summit* in *Bahrain* in December 1988 approved further economic integration. Citizens could buy shares in any state and there should be co-ordination of industrial projects. It approved a regional emergency plan for petrol and equal access to all medical services. It agreed on a single business tax. It ratified an agreement with the European Community and called for more co-operation between OPEC and non-OPEC states. It welcomed the cease-fire in the Iran–Iraq War and Yassir Arafat's proclamation of an independent State of Palestine.

The *Tenth Summit* in Muscat in December 1989 welcomed moves towards a unified tariff.

The *Eleventh Summit* in Doha in December 1990 called for Iraqi withdrawal from Kuwait and payment of reparations. It issued a 8-point Doha Declaration supporting the Palestinians. It welcomed the resumption of trade with Iran and called for further contacts. Sultan Qabus was put in charge of the Higher Security Committee for the Region.

The *Twelfth Summit* in December 1991 took place in Kuwait after its liberation, while expressing sympathy for the Iraqi people for their sufferings, rejected any dealings with its Government until it had complied with all its obligations under the cease-fire and called for the international community to maintain pressure upon it. It approved the Damascus Declaration. It expressed its determination to continue the "joint action march" and

urged Ministerial committees to continue to work for unification. It approved the Madrid Peace Conference and looked forward to bilateral negotiations with Israel but it deplored its expansionism. It welcomed the new independence of Muslim states of the former Soviet Union. It was agreed to establish a fund of $10,000 million for Arab economic development. It hoped for a completed common market by the end of century but warned that the fostering of local industries had to be done without upsetting other trading blocs as had happened over petrochemicals with the European Community.

The *Thirteenth Summit* assembled in Abu Dhabi on 21 December 1992. As a result of the Khofous Incident there had been doubts about the attendance of Qatar but its dispute with Saudi Arabia was settled just in time. Iran had recently annexed Abu Musa and relations with Tehran dominated discussion of defence and security matters. The proposals for a standing army of 100,000 men were postponed but it was agreed that the Peninsula Shield should be strengthened and the importance of the Damascus Declaration, "the nucleus for a new Arab order", was reaffirmed. Fahm b. Sultan al-Qasimi of the UAE was appointed to succeed Bishara as Secretary-General. The Summit expressed the need to press ahead with tariff unification in order to negotiate with the EC, due to be changed on 1 January 1993 and there was minor progress towards economic integration with agreements on patents and retailing. The Rulers condemned Iraq for failing to comply with UN Resolutions and the UN for failing to help the Muslims in Bosnia and for imposing an arms embargo upon them. It also called for pressure on Israel to compel it to take back the Hamas members expelled to Marj al-Zahour.

HABASH, George (1926–)

Palestinian political and guerrilla leader. A Greek Orthodox, he was the son of a successful corn merchant in Lydda and was educated in Jerusalem before entering the American University of Beirut as a medical student in 1944. His family suffered in the Lydda Expulsions and he fought with the Syrians in the Palestine War. Returning to AUB he became President of the students' society *al-Urwah al-Wuthqa* which he politicised, turning it into the basis of the Arab Nationalist Movement calling for pan-Arabism and the elimination of Israel by violent means. In a book *Joint Defence* Habash demanded revenge on the West and on the Arab leaders who had let down Palestine. He qualified in 1951 and went to Amman where, with Dr Wadia Haddad he founded a "people's clinic" where they gave free treatment to refugees, formed a school and started a newspaper which attacked Jordan's ties with Britain. It was suppressed and Habash, after a brief period in hiding, was imprisoned. He emerged to stand unsuccessfully in the elections of October 1956 but went underground again when martial law was proclaimed in April 1957. After an unsuccessful attempt at a bombing campaign, with Nayif Hawatma he fled to Damascus after the proclamation of the United Arab Republic. By now his hero was Nasser who provided money but at times seemed insufficiently extreme. Habash went into hiding after the breakup of the UAR but was caught and imprisoned from July 1962 until the Baath Party seized power in March 1963. He came to see the issue of Palestine as part of an inevitable world revolution which he hoped would be led by China rather than Russia. Disillusioned with Nasser after the June War, he concluded that the Palestinians could rely only upon themselves to liberate their country so in December 1967 he founded the Popular Front for the Liberation of Palestine. In March 1968, having criticised the Syrians for refusing to permit guerrilla activities from their territory and seizing arms destined for guerrillas, he was imprisoned in Damascus. He was liberated by his friends in November while being transferred from one jail to another but in the meanwhile dissatisfaction both from the right and the left had arisen within the PFLP. Ahmad Jibril broke away to found the Popular Front for the Liberation of Palestine – General Command while his old colleague Hawatma formed the (Popular) Democratic Front for the Liberation of Palestine. In August 1968 the PFLP carried out the first of a series of aircraft hijackings for which it became notorious. Habash justified this by saying "When we hijack a plane it has more effect than if we had killed a hundred Israelis in battle . . . For decades world opinion has . . . simply ignored us. At least the world is talking about us now". Habash was the first guerrilla leader to realise that modern communications made possible worldwide publicity for anything spectacular and spoke of the struggle continuing for twenty years and his willingness to risk a world war to destroy Zionism and reactionary Arab regimes. He also declared that the future Palestinian state would be based on Marxist-Leninist principles. He refused to join the Palestine Armed Struggle Command because of jealousy of the predominance of Fatah. The PFLP hijackings to Dawson's Field and the bellicose attitude of Habash towards the Jordanian Government were principal causes of the expulsion of the guerrillas from Amman after the fighting of Black September 1970. In March 1972 after Russian and Chinese pressure, Habash formally renounced hijackings as an instrument of policy. In May he had a heart attack for which he received treatment in Moscow. In August 1973 the Israelis abducted a Lebanese airliner in the belief that Habash was one of its passengers. Golda Meir justified the action by saying that of all the terrorists "Habash is the worst of the lot". Habash continued to criticise Fatah and stood aloof from the Palestine Liberation Organisation when denied equal representation with it. In August 1974, fearing that Yassir Arafat might accept Resolution 242 with its implied recognition of Israel as the price for participating in the Geneva Peace Conference, Habash formed the Rejection Front demanding "no negotiation, no peace with Israel and no recognition of Israel". His intransigence was one of the causes of the full involvement of the Palestinians in the fighting in Lebanon after 1975 and his subsequent hostility towards Syria led to his reliance upon Iraqi support. He gradually moved towards the more moderate stance of Arafat and did not join the Syrian-backed National Alliance against him. In April 1987 Habash was reconciled with the majority of the commando groups and the following year at the Palestine National Council Algiers Meeting he went along with the decision to accept Resolution 242 and the renunciation of terrorism. By early 1990 he was questioning whether these concessions had been worth while and was allying himself with HAMAS to intensify the *Intifadah*. After Saddam Hussein had annexed Kuwait, Habash threatened terror attacks on American interests if they intervened. He revisited Jordan for the first time since 1970 to attend the Conference of the Coalition of Democratic Popular Forces and was received by King Hussain. At the twentieth meeting of the Palestine

National Council it was clear that he had failed to grasp that the end of Super-Power rivalry had radically altered the Middle East situation and he later withdrew from the Executive, prepared to split the PLO rather than endorse the Madrid Peace Conference. In January 1992, amidst conflicting reports that he had had another stroke or that he was merely seeking a check-up, he arrived in Paris for medical treatment. The subsequent furore shook the French Government, two of the most senior civil servants in the Foreign Ministry were dismissed and there were rumours that Cabinet Ministers would follow, Israel appeared likely to apply for extradition whereupon the PFLP warned that French interests would be at risk. Habash was then put under guard at the hospital and expelled after three days. In October 1992 he met Arafat to urge that the PLO dissociate itself from further participation in Peace Talks. Habash, with his evident sincerity, was capable of attracting whole-hearted loyalty from his followers. Outside politics he was described as a modest, warm and friendly man.

HADDAD, Wadia (1928–78)

Palestinian guerrilla leader. A Greek Orthodox, the son of a merchant, he was born in Safad and studied medicine at the American University of Beirut where he became a close friend of a fellow medical student George Habash. Together in the 1950s they founded the Arab Nationalist Movement which, as the principal group outside Egypt which followed the leadership of Nasser, attracted membership in most Arab states. They also opened together a "people's clinic" in Amman where they gave free treatment to the inhabitants of refugee camps and ran a school which served as a recruitment centre. Haddad was suspected of involvement in some bombing incidents in 1957 and after a brief imprisonment, joined Habash in Damascus. Habash and Haddad became more left wing in the mid 1960s and in 1968 the ANM split into independent groups. Habash and Haddad had by then founded the Popular Front for the Liberation of Palestine which soon became known for its terrorist activities, in particular, hijackings of Israeli aircraft. In July 1970 rockets were fired into Haddad's Beirut flat but he and his wife and eight-year-old son escaped with minor injuries. Haddad did much of the organisation which led to the hijacking of three aircraft to Dawson's Field. After 1972 the PFLP officially ceased hijacking aircraft, considering it injurious to the Palestinian cause, Haddad continued his terrorist activities, forming links with the German Baader-Meinhoff Gang, the Japanese Red Army and the notorious "Carlos". Haddad received financial support from Qadafi, South Yemen and Iraq. The Western press dubbed him "the god-father of international terrorism" and he was involved in incidents which stretched across frontiers such as the OPEC Ministers Kidnapping of December 1975, the Entebbe Hijacking of July 1976 and the Mogadishu Hijacking of October 1977. The PFLP formally dissociated itself from these actions and Habash announced that his old friend had been expelled from the group. Mogadishu was probably Haddad's last action because in March 1978 he died of cancer and was buried in Baghdad with a eulogy pronounced by Habash.

al-HAFFAR, Lutfi (1891–)

Syrian Prime Minister. He came from a wealthy family of Damascus textile merchants and received a traditional education locally. In their teens he and his comrades founded one of the first secret nationalist groups. In 1925 he was one of the earliest members of the People's Party. He served in the pro-French government of the *Damad* Ahmad Nami but in June 1926 during the Druze Revolt he was arrested on the charge of contacts with the rebels and exiled to the desert. He was amnestied in March 1928 and immediately joined the new National Bloc of which he was regarded as one of the leaders. An able businessman, who had been President of the Chamber of Commerce, he won considerable prestige by bringing a major new supply of water to Damascus. Haffar was Minister of Finance in the Cabinet of Jamil Mardam whom he succeeded in February 1939 at a time when the National Bloc was divided over what action take following the failure of the French to ratify the Franco-Syrian Treaty of 1936. He was not on good terms with the President Hashim al-Atasi, was unable to control the Alawite area where the "Mahdi" Sulayman al-Murshid enjoyed practical independence with French support and he could not persuade the French to withdraw a decree which enabled Muslims to change their religion and Muslim women to marry outside the faith. There were parades and street demonstrations and Haffar's Cabinet lasted less than a month. In July 1940 after the murder of his opponent Dr Shahbandar he fled to Iraq but was exculpated and able to return the following year. During the war he was Minister of the Interior in the government of Saad Allah al-Jabiri and was also in the Mardam Cabinet, resigning in November 1948 at the time of discontent over the mishandling of the Palestine War. He was pro-Western and supported the adhesion of Syria to the Baghdad Pact and resigned from the National Party owing to their opposition to it and their increasing links with the Baath; this in February 1945 brought down the government of Faris al-Khouri. In June 1956 President Quwatli asked Haffar to form a Cabinet but the Baath refused to serve with him and he was forced to withdraw. Haffar was a moderate, practical politician with an unusual grasp of economics. He wrote two volumes of *Memoirs*.

al-HAFIZ, Amin Ismail (1926–)

Lebanese Prime Minister. A Sunni Muslim, he was born in Tripoli the son of a magistrate. He was educated at the Christian Brothers College there, Cairo University and the American University of Beirut before taking a Law Doctorate in Lausanne. He also attended The Hague Higher Academy of International Law but worked as an economist and was Director of the Industrial Research Institute. He also lectured on economics at the Lebanese University. He was elected MP for Tripoli in 1960, 1968 and 1972. On 10 April 1973 Israeli commandos killed three Palestinian leaders in the centre of Beirut and the Prime Minister, Saeb Salam resigned after the President Sulayman Franjiyah refused to dismiss the Maronite army commander who had offered no resistance. Franjiyah appointed Hafiz who was known to be sympathetic to the Palestinians and who as a minor political figure had no strong independent base and he became Prime Minister and Minister of Health and Information on 25 April 1973. He brought new faces into the Cabinet and tried to combine all political forces even a leftist. The appointment of Hafiz was resented by the traditional Sunni *zu'ama* such as Rashid Karami and Saeb Salam and by Kamal Jumblatt who had his own candidate for the post. He was unable to prevent further clashes between the army and the Palestinians, 12 soldiers were killed in a single clash and over 100 Palestinians in a few days, Syria closed its frontier stating that the Lebanese were trying to wipe out the Palestinians and on 8 May Hafiz attempted to resign. He was persuaded to remain but the Sunni Mufti, Shaykh Hassan Khalid declared that Hafiz lacked the authority to speak for the community and that it was under-represented in the Government. On 13 June two of his Sunni Ministers refused to support Hafiz in a vote of confidence and he resigned the next day. Hafiz published a treatise on the economic and political structures of Lebanon and Syria. His relaxation was swimming.

HAIFA CONVENTION (1920)
The overthrow of the rule of the Amir Faysal in Damascus by the French in the summer of 1920 signalled the end of hopes of a Greater Syria including Lebanon, Palestine and Trans-Jordan under his leadership. Palestinian leaders had to consider a policy of their own and called a Congress at Haifa in December 1920. The 37 delegates, claiming to speak for all the population, declared that "Palestine, the Holy Land, belongs to the Christian and Muslim worlds and the administration of its affairs should not be entrusted to non-Muslims and non-Christians". A National Government responsible to a Council elected by all Arab-speaking people resident there at the outbreak of war should be established. The existing government set up by the British had no power to legislate without a representative Council or the approval of the League of Nations. Moreover it unfairly favoured the Zionists, permitting their immigration, appointing them to administrative positions, recognising Hebrew as an official language etc. It established an Executive Committee with Musa Kazim al-Hussaini as Chairman to represent it.

al-HAJRI, Abd Allah (1912–77)
Prime Minister of Yemen. He was a member of the hereditary *Qadi* class and received a traditional religious upbringing before entering government service. During the Yemen War he remained loyal to the Imam Badr, to whom he was a close adviser, and did not return until 1970. He was soon made Ambassador to Kuwait and was later a member of the three-man Republican Council. In November 1972 after a brief war with South Yemen, President Abd al-Rahman al-Iryani signed the Tripoli Agreement committing the two states to unity. This greatly alarmed the conservative tribal leaders – surreptitiously supported by Saudi Arabia which feared that Sanaa might fall under the influence of communist, atheist Aden. The Prime Minister, Muhsin al-Ayni realised the strength of the opposition and resigned. Hajri who was known as a strongly religious conservative was appointed to succeed him. He took office on

1 January 1973, saying that union was an immediate necessity but determined to do nothing to bring it about. He quickly went to Riyadh to reassure the Saudis, receiving financial aid in return for renouncing the Yemeni claim to Asir and Najran which although formally surrendered in the Taif Treaty of 1934, had been revived when the Kingdom had been the leading opponent of the Republic. As Prime Minister Hajri lacked administrative ability and force of character and his Ministers pursued their own policies without reference to him or to each other. Corruption was rife amidst general inefficiency and no progress was made in development or towards the Constitutional government which the President wanted. At the end of May the Shafai member of the Republican Council was murdered and Hajri seized the opportunity to blame this on the Aden Government and to unleash a ferocious repression of supporters of union, executing about 40 people. The President, disapproving, went into voluntary exile in August. Iryani was persuaded to return and spent the winter building up support against his Prime Minister. In February he felt strong enough to replace him with the abler and more progressive-minded Dr Hassan Makki. Hajri subsequently served as deputy chief of the Supreme Court. In April 1977 on a visit to London he and his wife were murdered.

al-HAKIM, Hassan (1886–)
Syrian Prime Minister. He was born into a prominent Damascus family and trained at the Administrative College in Istanbul. Hakim was an Inspector of Finance and later Director of Posts under King Faysal and was said to have been responsible for a delay in sending off a reply to a French ultimatum which gave them the pretext to invade Syria. He fled to Trans-Jordan and worked as a financial adviser to the Amir Abd Allah. He was allowed to return in 1921 but was soon active in nationalist politics, becoming a founder-member of Dr Shahbandar's People's Party. With Shahbandar he escaped arrest during the Druze Revolt by fleeing abroad and went to Baghdad to ask for Iraqi help for the uprising. Hakim then managed a bank in Jaffa before being allowed to return in 1937. He became Director-General of *Awqaf* and later Minister of Education in the Cabinet of Nasuhi al-Bukhari. Although he had a reputation as a nationalist, it was as a neutral that he became Prime Minister in September 1941. He was on bad terms with the President Taj al-Din al-Hassani whose nepotism and other vices he refused to condone and could not overcome the country's economic problems. His Cabinet split and he resigned in April 1942. After the war, with Husni al-Barazi he was one of the strongest supporters of Arab unity under the Hashemites and received money from Abd Allah to build a Monarchist Party. In 1947 he stood for election as one of the leaders of the Liberal Party vaguely pledged to respect the constitution, equality, social justice and an end to "economic colonialism". As a respected independent he was appointed a Minister of State in the government which Nazim al-Qudsi formed as a façade for the rule of Colonel Adib al-Shishakli but soon resigned when he found that promised reforms were not being implemented. After a crisis following the fall of the short-lived Cabinet of Khalid al-Azm in

August 1951 Hakim became Prime Minister with the military leader Colonel Fawzi Silu as Defence Minister. He received a vote of confidence for a programme of economic and administrative reforms but encountered difficulties as the army would tolerate no cut in its budget. He threatened to dismiss striking civil servants and returned to the Treasury the secret funds for propaganda – to the annoyance of journalists. Even more controversial was his outspoken call for alignment with the West; he argued that otherwise the West would be forced to rely on Turkey and Israel to the disadvantage of Syria. His Foreign Minister Faydi al-Atasi, however, declared that Syria would reject any Western invitation to a defence pact. Hakim's Cabinet was pilloried as a tool of the army and then split over control of the militia as well as over foreign policy. On 10 November Hakim resigned. Early in 1953 Hakim was invited by Shishakli to form another Cabinet but said he would only do so if the army pledged to stay out of politics. Always regarded as one of the more honest of Syrian politicians he continued active for a few more years. Hakim wrote two volumes of memoirs.

HAKIM, Ibrahim (1946–)

Western Saharan/Moroccan politician. Ibrahim ould Darwish (Hakim was a *nom de guerre*) was a tribesman of the Reguibat, born on the frontier between the Spanish Sahara and Mauritania where he was educated. After Mauritanian independence he was employed by the Ministry of Health before taking a diploma in International Studies in Geneva. He then served in the Mauritanian Embassies in Tunis and Algiers before resigning to qualify as a lawyer which he did in 1974. He had already been in contact with Sahrawi students in Morocco who wished to see the end of Spanish rule and the incorporation of the territory in Morocco. He was one of the 15 young men who formed Polisario in May 1973. Early in 1975 Hakim was appointed representative of the Front in Algiers. After the Green March he went to New York to put the Sahrawi case to the UN. He then became Foreign Minister of the SADR, travelling widely to obtain recognition in Africa. After this was achieved he became Minister of Information. In 1988 Hakim signed a letter calling for peace and was arrested by the Sahrawi President Muhammad Abd al-Aziz. He was quickly released in case his tribal faction made trouble and was appointed Ambassador to Algeria. In August 1992 Hakim defected to Morocco and was extremely active in convincing people to vote in Moroccan elections. His former colleagues alleged that he had been involved in financial swindles. Hakim was hardly a typical desert nomad, a genial *bon viveur*, usually seen with a large cigar.

HALABJA, Destruction of (1988)

Halabja was a town with an estimated population of up to 40,000 in Iraqi Kurdistan near the border with Iran. During the Iran–Iraq War many of the local people, members of the Kurdistan Democratic Party, had collaborated with the Iranians who captured the town on 15 March 1988 in an operation in which they claimed to have killed 3,000 Iraqi soldiers and captured 300 Russian tanks. Three days after its loss it was heavily attacked by Iraqi bombers using chemical weapons.

The Iranians reported that 5,000 civilian Kurds were killed and another 10,000 badly gassed. The rest of the population fled. Foreign journalists reported seeing heaps of bodies unmarked by any wounds. It was regarded as part of the policy of Saddam Hussain to terrorise Kurds into resettlement in Southern Iraq.

HALAIB DISPUTE

In 1899 after the Anglo-Egyptian conquest it was agreed between the two governments responsible for the Condominium that "the Soudan" should be regarded as the area south of latitude 22 with a salient at Wadi Halfa. In 1902 the Egyptian Ministry of the Interior decreed that an area south of the line which was used as a grazing ground by the Egyptian Ababda bedouins should be administered from Cairo and an area north of it near Halaib, used by the Sudanese Bisharin, from Khartoum. These were administrative rather than international boundaries but this altered with Sudanese independence. The people of Halaib voted in the Sudanese parliamentary elections of 1953 but not in the Egyptian presidential election of 1956. The Egyptians determined that they should participate in the referendum on the formation of the United Arab Republic and not in the almost simultaneous general election in the Sudan so in February 1958 they suddenly occupied the area north of the 22nd parallel. The Sudanese also sent troops but they were turned back by an Egyptian steamer. The Egyptians offered to exchange the areas north and south of the parallel but the Sudanese appealed to the Security Council which took no action beyond hoping for a peaceful solution. The traditionally anti-Egyptian Umma Party exploited the issue which helped it in the election. The Egyptians withdrew their troops and nothing more was heard from the area until in December 1991 the Sudanese Government awarded a concession there to the International Petroleum Company of Canada. The General Petroleum Corporation of Egypt declared that this was illegal. The dispute came when Egyptian–Sudanese relations were bad as Cairo had accused Khartoum, with the help of Iran, of providing training and assistance for the Islamic terrorists operating in the Dayrut area. No senior figure from either country had visited the other for 18 months but in February 1992 the second most important man in the Sudanese military junta, General Zubayr Muhammad Salih went to Cairo and it was agreed that a committee should meet in Khartoum where it might discuss joint control of the area. At the same time there were reports that Egypt was trying to settle 4,000 of its citizens in Halaib. Early in April President Mubarak declared that his country would not abandon "a single grain of sand". Two days later two Sudanese policemen were killed and four wounded in a skirmish but the Egyptian Government apologised and offered compensation. The talks in Khartoum in May in which the Egyptian side was led by Usama al-Baz produced no result and a meeting planned for Cairo was several times postponed. In December 1992 the Sudanese complained to the UN that the Egyptians had sent a further 600 troops to the area, doubling their border posts to 20, and took over some Egyptian-run schools and later the branch in Khartoum of Cairo University. In Januay 1993 Sudan complained that the Egyptians were prospecting in Halaib for manganese which it had agreed to export, paving more roads, building mosques and schools, sending Defence Ministry officials and issuing identity documents. The Sudanese press threatens "violence" and General Bashir said that the area was 100% Sudanese. However in February, after intervention by Yassir Arafat, the committee of officials held its third meeting but this produced no result nor did a meeting of the Foreign Ministers in April. In May there were reports that the Sudanese were mobilising and had given an ultimatum but Mubarak ruled out any possible use of force. In June the Sudanese closed two Egyptian consulates, leading to warnings that this was escalating the situation. Early in July, however, relations improved while Bashir was in Cairo for an OAU Summit. He denied that he was helping the terrorist campaign of Islamic Jihad. The Foreign Ministers met later in the month amidst speculation that there would be an agreement to share.

(Abd al-) HALIM, Muhammad Pasha (1831–94)
He was the fifth son of Muhammad Ali Pasha and received a military training at St Cyr. He was on the first train from Alexandria to Cairo in 1855 which crashed into the Nile when a bridge collapsed but, being a strong swimmer was one of the few survivors. According to the *Firman* granted by the Ottoman Sultan to Muhammad Ali in 1841, Halim was the destined successor to his nephew Ismail but the Khedive, in 1866, in return for a large sum of money, won a new decree restricting the throne to his own direct descendants. Abd al-Halim plotted against Ismail, possibly trying to kill him with a poisoned dart and had to flee to Constantinople. He was engaged in a series of conspiracies, trying to get the army to depose the Khedive. He also intrigued with the Freemasons. In 1878 he attempted to win the support of Ismail's numerous creditors by ensuring that the press obtained a letter by him urging reforms. After declaring Ismail deposed, the Sultan tried to impose Halim as Khedive but the Powers put such pressure on him that he had to consent to the accession of Tawfiq. Halim increased his efforts to stir up the army but even the success of Arabi, whom the British suspected of being his tool, did not bring him to the throne, despite another effort by the Sultan. Apart from these activities he was an enthusiastic musician, teaching his eleven children to play different instruments to form a family orchestra. He was also said to be the first to write down Turkish music in European notation. His son, Muhammad Said Halim Pasha (1865–1921) was Grand Wazir of the Ottoman Empire at the start of the First World War but was unable to influence events as all power was held by the Young Turks who did not even inform him of their plan to attack Russia.

HAMADAH, Sabri (c. 1902–76)
Lebanese politician. His family were Shiah feudal lords in the Baalbek area and dominated parts of the Maronite Mountain until the middle of the seventeenth century. Sabri was elected to Parliament for his fiefdom in 1925 and held the seat for the rest of his life. He was one of the founders of the Constitutional Bloc which under the leadership of Bishara al-Khouri worked firstly for a Franco-Lebanese Treaty and then for independence and he continued a member of the party for many years. In 1938 he was Minister of Public Works in the Cabinet of Abd Allah al-Yafi but most of his career was spent as Speaker of the Assembly, a post to which he was elected 24 times, 1943–50, 1946–51, 1959–63, 1965–67 and 1968–70. He was a key figure in the manoeuvring of *zu'ama* (local bosses) that constituted Lebanese politics. He worked closely with Presidents Khouri, Shihab and Helou and was regarded as an expert in manipulating procedure in the interests of the Government. He also filled the Speaker's office with his own retainers and those of his father-in-law, Ahmad al-Assad, who had an equally feudal grip on the Shiah of the South and also held the Speakership, an office reserved for Shiah, several times. Hamadah was not, however, on good terms with Camille Chamoun who ousted him from the Speakership. In 1957 he joined with Sunni leaders to oppose the foreign policy of the President and in May 1958 he was reported to be distributing Syrian arms to his adherents. In August 1970 he was in the Chair during the Presidential election when he ruled that the 50 votes for Sulayman Franjiyah did not constitute a significant majority as 49 had been cast for his own preferred candidate Elias Sarkis. Franjiyah and some of his supporters produced firearms in the Chamber and prevailed upon Hamadah to declare that a majority of one was sufficient. He was Minister of Public Works under Saeb Salam in May 1972 and of Agriculture in the Cabinet of Taqi al-Din al-Sulh in July 1973 and stood for the Speakership a last time in 1974 but was defeated by one of the Assads. By this time, he had come to realise that the Shiah would no longer blindly follow their feudal lords but had become politicised under the influence of the Imam Musa Sadr and his revolutionary movement, AMAL. Nevertheless his son succeeded to his Parliamentary seat.

HAMAS
Harakah al-Muqawamah al-Islamiyah (Islamic Resistance Movement), an acronym of which means "zeal" in Arabic. It was founded by a blind preacher Shaikh Ahmad Yassin in the Gaza Strip, growing out of the Muslim Brothers and it issued its first leaflet on 14 December 1987 a week after the traffic accident which set off the *Intifadah*. It received financial backing from Kuwait and soon was well organised with five districts in Gaza and three commands to deal with military, political and propaganda affairs. In the area it controlled it punished alcohol drinkers, sex criminals and collaborators. Hamas regarded the secular leaders of the PLO as "eaters of pork and drinkers of wine", remote from what was happening on the ground and too ready to seek a political solution. It recruited from the same constituency as Fatah which it accused of violence against it and this led the Israelis, briefly, to hope it might be used. However, it became clear that *Hamas* refused to recognise Israel, totally opposed any political settlement or two-state solution regarding the whole of Palestine as "the Waqf of God", no part of which could be surrendered. It was anxious to escalate violence, many of its members showing a real desire for martyrdom, and prepared to work with Marxists such

as the PFLP. Yassir Arafat failed to persude Hamas to be represented at the Palestine National Council Algiers Meeting of November 1988 at which the decision was taken to recognise Israel. Its ultimate aim was an Islamic State firstly in Palestine and then throughout the Muslim World. In 1989 Shaykh Yassin was sentenced to life imprisonment while the co-founder Dr Abd al-Aziz al-Rantissi (born 1947), a resident of Khan Yunis refugee camp received 30 months. Nevertheless Hamas continued to grow, attracting many who had been educated abroad, and during 1990 the Israeli military believed that 50% of the residents of Gaza and 25% of the West Bank supported it. In May 1990 it was criticised by Abu Iyad for aspiring to replace the PLO and for refusing representation on the PNC unless it received half the seats. In September 1990 its leaders gave strong support for Saddam Hussain and called for *jihad* against the West but they then came under pressure from Saudi Arabia and Kuwait and demanded Iraqi withdrawal before the Allies left. This led to further disagreements with the PLO. In December 1990 four Hamas leaders were deported after three Israelis were murdered in Jaffa and the rest responded by calling for escalation. In February 1991 the occupation authorities claimed to have arrested a further 350 members. In October 1991 Hamas called for a general strike in protest against the Madrid Peace Talks. There were clashes in Gaza and Tulkarm against supporters of Palestinian participation. The popularity of Hamas was shown when in February 1992 it won many seats (on what) including 10 out of 11 on the Ramallah Chamber of Commerce. In June 1992 it again denied reports of any agreement with Fatah. In December 1992, after probably having been responsible for the killing of a number of Israeli soldiers within a few days, Hamas kidnapped an Israeli frontier guard, and after offering to exchange him for Shaykh Yassin, murdered him. In retaliation Prime Minister Rabin ordered the rounding up about 1,600 alleged Hamas members; deporting over 400 to Marj al-Zahour. It was clear that Israel had not broken the organisation for after the killing of one of their secret agents, 22 members of a Hamas "hit-squad" were arrested early in January 1993. The deportations did, however, lead to talks in Khartoum with the PLO as Turabi attempted to reconcile. They broke down in April when the PLO decided to continue to give its backing to the Washington Peace Talks. Muhd Sharatha (b. 1957), commander of the military wing, was sentenced to three consecutive life sentences for killing Israeli soldiers. In October 1992 Iran, which was subsidising Hamas with $30 million a year, provided the organisation with an office in Tehran, recognising it as the sole legitimate representative of Palestine Jihad and started to work with Jibril against the PLO, Israel instituted the strategy of using the PLO againt Hamas. Arafat offered reconciliation talks in Sanaa in September but formed a rejectionist front with Habash. In April 1993 representatives toured the Gulf for money. In June the Israeli army rounded up over 100 alleged Hamas members and in July talks with the PLO in Amman were renewed after a previous round of talks broke down in April. In August Hamas claimed responsibility for an attack on a West Bank village in which two soldiers were killed.

HAMAS (Algeria)

Set up in November 1990 with government encouragement as a rival to the FIS, its aim was to get the support of liberal Muslims and after a rally claimed 15,000 supporters. Its founding leader was Mahfud Nahnah, former associate of Bouyali. Madini claimed he was being stabbed in the back but Nahnah offered an alliance which Madini turned down. A few days earlier another religious group was recognised by the Government – the Islamic Renaissance Movement of Abd Allah Djallabah.

al-HAMDI, Ibrahim b. Muhammad (c. 1943–77)

President of Yemen. He was the son of a respected *Qadi* and received the education for government service traditional in his class. On the outbreak of the Yemen War, however, he switched to the army and made a name as an able and ambitious officer. By 1970 he was commander of the General Reserve Forces and later was Deputy Commander-in Chief. These posts enabled him to form a group of progressive-minded young officers. In September 1971 he was Deputy Prime Minister for Internal Affairs in the government of Muhsin al-Ayni and worked closely with modernising young civilians. He became prominent in schemes for economic and social development and was first President of the Local Development Association which worked at village level. In 1974 under the vacillating President Abd al-Rahman al-Iryani and the incompetent Prime Minister Abd Allah al-Hajri the Government appeared on the verge of collapse with financial crisis and widespread corruption. In what he described as a "corrective move", Hamdi took power as Chairman of the Military Command Council in a bloodless coup. He suspended the Constitution and the Consultative Council and appointed as Prime Minister his former chief Muhsin al-Ayni who had the tribal connections that he himself lacked. Possible military rivals were posted abroad as ambassadors but for some months Hamdi's hold on power appeared extremely tenuous, but gradually he became immensely popular. With his inspiring oratory, evident honesty and sincerity, his youth – he was the first young Ruler that even the oldest Yemeni could remember – he appeared to represent a new generation and a new hope for the future after decades of harsh rule and civil war. For some months he and al-Ayni acted vigorously together to reform the administration, threatening to cut off any hand proved to have taken a bribe but in January 1975 feeling the need of a technocrat with financial skills, Hamdi appointed Abd al-Aziz Abd al-Ghani as Prime Minister. He travelled widely visiting nearly every Arab country in addition to Iran and he paid the first State Visit of a Yemeni Ruler to Europe. From most of these trips he returned with money for new projects. Trade also expanded, helped by the remittances of thousands of Yemeni workers profiting from the prosperity of the oil states after the price rise of 1973. State revenue was increased by reform in tax collection and Hamdi determined that much of this new money should benefit the neglected rural areas; he was active in providing better health, housing and educational facilities, electrification and improved communications. His development plan of 1977 was the most ambitious that the countryside had ever seen. He paid much more attention than was usual to the concerns of the Shafai regions and encouraged small men to become independent by starting their own businesses. Although a pious Muslim he removed out-of-date restrictions that hampered progress particularly for women and the number of girls attending the University rose from a few dozen to several hundred. He reformed the army, aiming to make it a third pillar of the state with the ulema and the shaykhs and tried to lessen its dependence on Russian arms and advisers and on tribal leaders for its officers. Hamdi wanted a strong centralised government with wide political participation but it was impossible to devise any scheme that would not harm the interests of the great Zaidi shaykhs of northern mountains who were practically independent of Sanaa whose armed strength they could match. Some of them went dissident and in the summer of 1977 there was actual fighting as he ordered the air force to bomb their strongholds. Realising the difficulty of either subjugating or coming to terms with them he allowed the emergence of left-wing activists that was to take shape as the National Democratic Front. Hamdi's troubles with the shaykhs led him to seek better relations with South Yemen. The Tripoli Agreement of 1972 pledging unity between the two countries was officially still in force but opposition from the tribal leaders backed by Saudi Arabia had prevented it from being implemented. President Salim Rubai Ali also needed help against internal opposition so the two leaders were natural allies and seem to have liked one another personally. They realised that a total merger could not be created overnight but required steady growth through increasing co-operation in economic, financial, agricultural and educational links, and to press these forward they established a high-powered committee to meet twice annually with themselves in the chair. Hamdi was about to visit Aden when on the night of 11/12 October 1977 he and his brother were murdered. It was never established whether the motives were political, to prevent the journey to Aden, revenge for the bombing of the North or personal – with his admitted chronic suspicion his associates might have feared that he was planning a purge. His death was greatly mourned, particularly by the young and educated who felt that he had pioneered the vision of a modern civilised Yemen that would no longer be dependent upon outside powers.

HAMID AL-DIN, Muhammad b. Yahya (?–1904)

Zaidi Imam. After the Turks returned to the Yemen in 1849 the Zaidi Imams were content to be religious leaders of their community and played little part in politics, apart from bickering with rival candidates. Muhammad was at the time of his election in 1891 regarded merely as a pious, non-political preacher in Sanaa but he took the regnal title of al-Mansur Billah in conscious imitation of his ancestor Qasim who had led the revolt which ended the first Ottoman occupation in the seventeenth century. He found himself the focus of national discontent and fled to Sada from which had been the seat of the first Imam a millennium before. He issued proclamations accusing the Turks of "not giving Allah His due", of wine-drinking and homosexuality, of excessive deference to Jews and Christians

and of "losing every feeling of benevolence and pity towards the Muslims". Soon the whole country was in flames and even the Shafai south accepted his rule. In the highlands only Sanaa where 2,000 Turks resisted a tribal force consisting largely of the Hashid and Bakil held out. Muhammad entered into relations with Sultan Fadhl b. Ali al-Abdali of Lahej and possibly with Awn al-Rafiq, Sharif of Mecca. He ensured that surrendered Turks were well treated. Constantinople sent a notoriously tough and ruthless Pasha, Ahmad Faizi, who burned 300 villages and relieved Sanaa by man-handling his guns over roadless mountains, some of which rose to 8,000 feet. Muhammad retired to the north. There were further uncoordinated risings which the Turks managed to keep under control and occasional negotiations. In 1902 Muhammd rejected a call for an alliance with the Turks against the British. He spent his last days grooming his son Yahya to succeed him and preparing for another major national uprising.

HAMMADI, Saadun (1930–)

Iraqi Prime Minister. A Shiah, born in Karbala, he studied at the American University of Beirut and at Wisconsin University where he took a doctorate in Agricultural Economics. Before the July Revolution he taught Economics in Baghdad and after it he left to become Deputy Head of Economic Research at National Bank of Libya. When the Baath Party shared power in 1963 he was Minister of Agrarian Reform and on their overthrow the following year he went to Syria, still under Baathist rule, as Economic Adviser to the Presidential Council and was also Economic Expert to the United Nations Planning Institute in Damascus. After the Baath seized power in 1968 Hammadi, regarded as one of its few real intellectuals, was appointed Chairman of the Iraq National Oil Company and the following year Minister of Oil. With an ideological dislike of multi-national companies, he pressed hard on the Iraq Petroleum Company before nationalising all its assets in June 1972. He went immediately to Moscow where he secured an agreement on oil cooperation. He also signed, in 1973, an agreement to build an oil pipeline across Turkey that lessened Iraq's dependence upon shipping through the Straits of Hormuz and was extremely active in negotiating deals for oil sales, particularly to Third World countries. After the October War Hammadi refused to follow other Arab countries in reducing output, instead announcing plans to increase it by 50% in two years. In November 1974 he was transferred to the Foreign Ministry. He accompanied Saddam Hussain on several foreign tours. In 1975 he played a major part in negotiating the Algiers Pact in which Iraq abandoned its claim for exclusive control of the Shatt al-Arab in return for the Shah's promise to cease support for the Kurdish Revolt (II) and argued, in front of the Arab League, Iraq's case in the Euphrates Dispute. Hammadi showed continued hostility to Syria and readiness to accept isolation in the Arab world by refusing to endorse the Riyadh Resolutions which authorised Damascus to send troops to Lebanon. In 1978, at the Baghdad Summit, he brought Iraq into line with the Arab majority by denouncing Egypt for signing the Camp David Agreement. In 1981 at the United Nations he denounced Israel for the

Osirak Raid and later articulated Iraqi opposition to the Fahd Plan which appeared to recognise the right of Israel to exist. He was Minister of State 1983–8, member of the Revolutionary Command Council and later Chairman of the National Assembly. He took over as Prime Minister on 23 March 1991 and concentrated on trying to tackle Iraq's economic problems and to get the support of Kurds and Shiahs. Hammadi made an unsuccessful attempt to woo the West promising a free press, to liberalise trade and to work for multi-party democracy but on 14 September 1991, when Saddam felt the crisis was over, Saddam dismissed him, although he later made him an adviser with the Rank of Cabinet Minister. He may have suggested that Saddam temporarily step down. He has written books on revolution and on agriculture.

HAMMAMET DECLARATION (1983)

In April 1983 a group of 35 Arab poets, scholars and political activists met at Hammamet to discuss the lack of human rights and democratic freedoms in the Arab world. They declared that these had vanished in the past thirty years with governments saying that they had to be sacrificed in the interests of socialism, development, unity, defending independence or the struggle against Israel. The Arabs had been deprived of the freedom of thought and expression. "The Arab people are today desperate and without hope, without faith in themselves or in their regimes". All political prisoners should be released or brought to trial, emergency regulations abolished and illegal activities of secret police forces ended. The link between power and responsibility had been lost and regimes were based on intimidation and favouritism. This has led to the absence of critical thought and "cultural and intellectual life have been effectively destroyed". The signatories, the best known of whom was the poet Adonis, called for the creation of human rights groups in each Arab country and summoned a larger conference on the crisis of democracy in the Arab world. As no Arab country would host a second meeting, it was held in Cyprus in December and set up a permanent Organisation for the Protection of Human Rights.

HAMMAMI, Said (1941–78)

Palestinian leader. He was born in Jaffa and brought up in Amman. He studied English literature at Damascus University and became a member of the Baath Party. He later joined Fatah and became close to Yassir Arafat. Hammami was active as a guerrilla in the Golan Heights after 1967 but after Black September he moved to Beirut. He became extremely active in policy discussions, arguing for compromise with Israel that would lead to a Palestinian state on the West Bank and Gaza as part of a secular democratic state for Jews, Muslims and Christians in all Palestine. In 1972 he was sent to London as representative of the Palestine Liberation Organisation. His willingness to engage in genuine dialogue and his sense of humour made him extremely popular. He always expressed his abhorrence of atrocities such as the Munich Olympics Massacre but stressed that such events were the inevitable consequence of the wrongs done to the Palestinians. He strongly opposed any idea that the Palestinians should revert to the rule of King Hussain. Like Isam Sartawi he had public discussions with moderate Israelis. Hammami saw the cycle of terrorism and repression as merely inflicting more suffering upon his people and he was denounced by extremists such as those of the Popular Front for the Liberation of Palestine as a "fifth columnist" because of his moderation. It was, however, a member of the Abu Nidal group who on the afternoon of 4 January 1978 murdered Hammami in his office in Mayfair. The gunman escaped. British politicians were amongst those who paid tribute to his memory.

HAMROUCHE, Mouloud (1943–)

Algerian Prime Minister. The son of a peasant of the Constantinois he participated as a teenager in the Algerian War of Independence in which his father was killed. He took a degree in political science from Baghdad University and while in the army was spotted by Boumédienne who recruited him into his office. He was also active in the Front de Libération Nationale, serving on its Central Committee. He continued at the Presidency under Chadli, first as Director-General of Protocol and then as Secretary-General of the Government. Hamrouche had therefore no ministerial experience when in September 1989 he was appointed Prime Minister in succession to Kasdi Merbah who was regarded as dragging his feet over reforms: gradual changes were not working and acceleration was necessary. Hamrouche gave the impression of being dynamic and effective with very clear ideas of what needed to be done. He selected a young, reform-minded team, 15 out of 23 Ministers were new, designed to ensure control by the President in whose office many of the Ministers, including Ghazi Hidouci who was given wide-ranging powers over the economy, had served. The Ministries of Information and Culture were abolished as not being the concern of the Government which guaranteed press freedom. Hamrouche put to Parliament a 20-page programme in which he promised transformation into a multi-party democracy, a market-based economy with priority given to holding down inflation and job creation, punishment for speculators, free wage bargaining, more control for local managers, and transparency in decision-making: he let it be known that he would dissolve the Assembly if thwarted and it was approved by 281 to 33. Hamrouche declared that he would end the "bicephalisme" of the State and the Party in an effort to hustle the country from one system to another. The economy, hit by an average of 250 strikes a month, was in disarray with problems of youth unemployment, shortage of housing and spare parts, and a heavy external debt. In November 1989 he began a drive for foreign partners, starting with a joint venture with Fiat, liberalisation of exports and imports and encouragement to businessmen to look to the banks rather than to the treasury. In January 1990 he attempted to float the first local bond issue but it was too much of an innovation to be a success. His efforts were not enough to check the rise of the Front Islamique du Salut as the voice of economic distress and in June 1990 it won an overwhelming success in the municipal elections: the defeat of his party showed that they had been fairly conducted. Hamrouche, whose policies had been criticised by hardliners in the FLN resigned with his Ministers from its Politburo and there were suspicions that, regarding the party as incapable of reforming itself, he was aiming to form a "Chadlist" party. He reformed his Cabinet, bringing in seven new Ministers none of whom were closely associated with the FLN and which included General Khalid Nezzar who took over Defence from the President. He rejected calls from the FIS for early elections, urging the need to consolidate his economic reforms. In August he ended the state monopoly of imports except for food and allowed competition from private companies; later the need for licences was removed. In September he promised a market economy by early in 1991, convertibility of the dinar, availability of foreign currency at the official rate and autonomy for state enterprises. His policy of cutting subsidies in favour of direct aid to the needy was criticised by the trade unions. In December he authorised the establishment of a stock exchange, although at first it was to be limited to public corporations. During the crisis that followed the Iraqi invasion of Kuwait Hamrouche largely abstained from comment, preferring to press on with his reforms, although in December he wooed the nationalists by decreeing that all business, even in private companies, should be conducted in Arabic. In Februrary 1991 he permitted eight joint ventures with foreign companies in the hitherto sacrosanct petrochemicals sector. After Chadli in December 1990 had promised multi-party elections in six months, he refused to replace Hamrouche by a politically neutral Prime Minister. In March 1991 resistance to the Government's moves towards a market economy involving price rises and lay-offs led to a 48-hour general strike, the first since independence. Realising that economic misery, the dinar had lost 95% of its value between August 1990 and April 1991, had still further increased support for FIS, he attempted to hamper their election by a new law which reduced the number of constituencies in the cities where they were strong while increasing the number in areas where the FLN could expect support. This led to a fortnight of violent demonstrations by FIS which ended on 5 June when Chadli declared a state of emergency and postponed the elections. Negotiations with FIS were clearly necessary but Hamrouche was unwilling to deal with them and resigned. Seeing that the elections in December could produce another victory for FIS, Hamrouche tried desperately but without success to revive the FLN and ally it with other secular parties. After the military take-over of January 1992 Hamrouche, apart from advocating a government of national unity, appears to have played little part in public life.

HAMZA, Fuad (c. 1900–51)

Saudi Minister. A Druze, he was educated at the American University of Beirut and had a varied early career as an Inspector of Schools in Damascus, a clerk in the Palestine Public Health Department, and a teacher in Acre and Jerusalem. He became involved in nationalist politics and after a brief spell as an English teacher in Cairo, went to Mecca at the end of 1926 to give English lessons to the sons of Indian merchants. His compatriot, Yusuf Yassin, then acting as Foreign Minister in the absence of Abd Allah al-Damluji

recruited him and in 1928 the two of them successfully intrigued to get rid of the Iraqi. The Amir Faysal, Viceroy of the Hijaz was appointed Foreign Minister but British Consular officials regarded Hamza, his Assistant, alert, intelligent, well-informed and industrious, as exercising the effective power. In 1932 he accompanied the Prince to London and took the leading part in the difficult frontier negotiations. He was believed to pay no more than lip-service to Wahhabi principles but to be enthusiastic for development and for Arab nationalism of which he saw Ibn Saud as the embodiment. He attended the London Palestine Conference of 1939 and did his utmost to further the Arab cause. He was suspected by the British of receiving money from the Italians and the Germans while the Germans thought him in British pay. In 1939 he was sent as Ambassador to France and was later Ambassador to Turkey and Minister of State for Development Affairs.

HANANU, Ibrahim (1869–1935)

Syrian nationalist leader. He was the son of a wealthy rural notable from the Aleppo area and after secondary education in that city, went on to study administration and law in Istanbul. After a period as an Ottoman bureaucrat in Aleppo, he left to manage his estates. Hananu fought with the Arab army of Amir Faysal and in 1919 he was a member of the General Syrian Congress. He soon came to the conclusion that words and diplomacy would not deter the French from taking over Syria and he raised a resistance army of some 700 men even before the French entered Aleppo. Then his movement spread all over the area west and southwest of Aleppo, overran French outposts and controlled several towns. Hananu established close links with the Turkish nationalists of Mustafa Kamal who was trying to eject the French from Cilicia and with the Amir Abd Allah who provided help. He also claimed a direct link with Lenin. By the spring of 1921 about 5,000 well-armed guerrillas were confronting over 20,000 French troops. However the French had started the negotiations with the Turks that led to the Franklin–Bouillon Treaty and Hananu received no further help from Ankara. In July his stronghold at Jabal al-Zawiyah was overrun and he sought refuge in Trans-Jordan. In August when he was visiting Jerusalem he was arrested by the British and handed over to the French. In March 1922 he was tried for organising rebel bands, brigandage, murder, etc. and surprisingly acquitted. He continued to oppose the French Mandate and was one of the founders of the National Bloc. He was always immensely popular in Aleppo, respected even by his opponents, and was one of its delegates to the Constituent Assembly of 1928 of which he was elected Chairman of the Committee set up to draft the document. During the elections of January 1932 Hananu was ill and Aleppo was taken over by the moderates. He was always worried at the possibility that Aleppo might be subordinated to Damascus and this caused dissensions in the nationalist ranks. Hananu had hopes of becoming President in June 1932 but the French ensured that this would not happen. There was an attempt on his life. The pardon of his assailant by the President Muhammad Ali al-Abid led to bombs being thrown at al-Abid during a visit to Aleppo. After Hananu's death his residence became known as the House of the Nation and served as a centre for nationalist activities.

HARADH CONFERENCE (1965)
In the Jiddah Agreement of August 1965 King Faysal and President Nasser decreed that the Yemen War should be ended by a meeting at Haradh near the Saudi frontier of the Royalist and Republican leaders. A city of 200 tents was erected, two Saudi and two Egyptian observers were appointed and 6,000 Egyptian troops lurked nearby. The delegations, each 25 strong, were headed by Ahmad al-Shami for the Royalists and Abd al-Rahman al-Iryani for the Republicans. At Jiddah it had been agreed that a transitional government should draft a new constitution and hold a plebiscite but had not stated whether it should be Royalist or Republican. Meetings discussing appointments, representation at the UN and the form of the plebiscite occurred at intervals for a month during which the Egyptians showed no signs of withdrawal although this was due to start on the same day as the Conference. Faysal visited the Shah, an act which Nasser saw as aimed at him. Nasser sent word to Iryani that he would be "buried alive" if he abandoned the Republican form of government. On 24 December the Congress went into recess, proposing to meet again on 20 February 1966 at the end of Ramadan. Before that Nasser had decided to stay in the Yemen indefinitely so the Congress did not reconvene.

HARIRI, Rafiq (1944–)
Lebanese Prime Minister. He came from a poor family in Sidon and left the Arab University before graduating. In 1965 he moved to Jeddah where he taught mathematics before working for a construction firm. In 1970 he started his own business and quickly became extremely rich with wide interests in building and banking. He became a personal friend of King Fahd and was given a Saudi passport. Greatly concerned about the plight of the poor during the Lebanese Civil War, he provided blankets and medicines for Shiah of the South and built a large hospital near Sidon which was subsequently looted by the South Lebanon Army. The Hariri Foundation dispensed $100 million annually, much of it to Lebanese students abroad. He was involved in various peace talks and he defrayed much of the expense of the Ta'if Parliament of 1989. When peace came he provided a residence for President Hrawi and he put forward a grandiose, extremely controversial plan for rebuilding Beirut which involved bulldozing 135 ha which would be replaced by skyscrapers and shopping malls: he was said personally to own 10% of the city with an estimated value of $3,000 million. In October 1992 he flew from Riyyadh via Damascus to Beirut following his appointment as Prime Minister. This appointment was welcomed by Patriach who had led a boycott of the polls but opposed by Hizbullah. Hariri formed a 30-man Cabinet with himself as Finance Minister. Eight members were technocrats but the moral authority of the Cabinet was weakened by the appointment of Hobeika. His appointment was greeted with unrealistic hopes – the value of the currency increased 10% in 12 hours and the US agreed to send

symbolic military aid for the first time since 1984. Inflation was running at 100% and he said that his first priorities would be to stabilise the currency, attract back Lebanese money from abroad, obtain foreign aid, stamp out corruption, get essential services working, build up the army and extend the authority of the state. He also vowed to get Israel out of the Security Zone. Tension between various groups reduced as they all supported him. He was given no exceptional powers for reform. He returned quickly to Damascus after his appointment and co-operated closely with Syria in an attempt to implement the Brotherhood Treaty. In December he initiated a crackdown on crime, targeting drug traffickers, and moved troops into the Shiah district of Beirut. With Syrian help he brooked no resistance. In December he refused to co-operate with Israel over Mark al-Zuhur and gained the full backing of the Lebanese people – the first move for years by a Prime Minister supported by the whole country. In March he refused to grant nationalisation to Palestinians or to disarm Shiah while Israel was still in occupied territory. In February 1993 he declared Israels occupation "a poisoned bullet in Lebanon's body".' He went on the first of several tours of the Gulf briefing on rebuilding plans estimated to cost $13 billion. In May marijuana and opium fields were flattened. During Operation Acountability he refused to act against Shiah saying they have the right of resistance and that he will do so after Israel leaves the Security Zone. He resisted US pressure to deal unilaterally with Israel and in August toured the Gulf seeking financial support to rebuild the army. He hoped to raise $500 million. He is not on good terms with Hrawi who through his son-in-law, Foreign Minister Faris Bouez, tries to keep him out of foreign policy. Thin-skinned, kindly and generous, his favourite son was killed in a car accident in the US.

HASHIM, Ibrahim (1884–1958)
Prime Minister of Jordan. He was born in Nablus, studied law in Istanbul and held legal posts under the Ottomans. He then served Faysal in Damascus as Attorney-General and after the overthrow of that regime entered the service of the Amir Abd Allah in Amman as Minister of Justice. He held that post until in November 1933 he became Chief Minister as the British Representative Sir Henry Cox refused to accept Hassan Khalid Abu al-Huda. Hashim was regarded as the leading jurist and a staunch supporter of the dynasty and able to conciliate the Legislative Council which had refused to co-operate with his predecessor Abd Allah Sarraj. He remained in office until September 1938 when he resigned, desperate, according to Abd Allah, at the restrictions that Cox put upon his actions. In May 1945 he was again Chief Minister, proclaiming a policy of working for Arab unity with British help and later accompanied Abd Allah to London where he negotiated the Anglo-Trans-Jordanian Treaty. In 1946 he chaired the Bludan Session of the Arab League in Bludan where it was decided secretly to take measures against Britain and the USA if they enforced the partition of Palestine. In February 1947 he resigned because he disapproved of Abd Allah's friendship with Turkey which had annexed the Syrian area of Alexand-

retta. In 1948 Hashem was appointed Military Governor of the newly-occupied West Bank where he confirmed regulations previously imposed by the British. Then he became President of the Senate, a member of the Throne Council during the minority of Hussain and, greatly respected and believed above political quarrels, was appointed Prime Minister on 20 December 1955 to preside over elections after some 40 people had been killed in street rioting over the determination of Hazza al-Majali to join the Baghdad Pact. However the dissolution of Parliament was held to be constitutionally illegal and he resigned after 17 days in office. In July 1956 when elections were to be held he once again took office and ensured the carrying out of the fairest elections in the country's history, retiring on the formation of the government of Sulayman al-Nabulsi in October. After the chaos caused by the dismissal of Nabulsi in April 1957 he again became Prime Minister and assisted King Hussain in restoring order and purging pro-Nasser officials. He negotiated with Nuri al-Said the formation of Arab Federation of which he became Deputy Prime Minister. He was therefore in Baghdad on the day of the July Revolution of 1958 when Hashemite rule was overthrown and he was murdered in the course of the coup.

al-HASSAN, Khalid (1928–)
Born in Haifa and associated with Muslim Brothers, he was Secretary of the Development Directorate in Kuwait when he joined Arafat in founding Fatah. His responsibility was for relations with Arab States. A moderate, in 1990 with his brother Hanio he opposed Arafat's support for Saddam. In 1991 he called for a government in exile. In March 1992 he favoured a confederation with Jordan. In August 1993 he appealed for collective leadership and in September opposed the signing of the Israeli–PLO agreement.

HASSAN (1947–)
Jordanian Crown Prince. The third and youngest son of Talal, he was educated at Harrow and christ Church, Oxford. In April 1965 he was appointed Crown Prince as the son of his brother King Hussain had an English mother. He was extremely close to the King either accompanying him on his tours or acting as Regent during his frequent absences abroad. He also carried out confidential missions to other Arab rulers. In 1966 he was made an honarary General and in 1967 was given the job of meeting anyone who wanted to see King Hussain. He involves himself particularly with economic matters snd general development plans. On his frequent trips abroad he is received by Heads of State. In 1971 he chaired the recently formed Council of Tribal Sheikhs, dealing with tribal affairs. In 1982 he attacked Syria for dividing Arab states by supporting Iran. In 1968 he married the daughter of a former Pakistani Ambassador to London and has four children. Unlike the King he has an interest in intellectual matters and he founded the Royal Scientific Society of Jordan. He has written several books including a study of the West Bank and another on Jerusalem.

HASSAN II (1929–)
King of Morocco. The eldest son of Muhammad V he received both an Islamic and a modern education in a school that his father established within the Palace and which was attended by children of various social backgrounds. He was present at the Anfa Meeting between his father and President Roosevelt in 1943 and on the occasion of the Tangier Speech in 1947. Hassan was a keen footballer and a show-jumper of international quality. In 1948 he began legal studies which led to a degree from Bordeaux University. He also had a period of training on a French warship. In the early 1950s he worked closely with his father to mobilise Moroccan opinion against the continuation of French rule travelling widely particularly in the *Bled*. On 20 August 1953 they were both deported to Corsica and later to Madagascar, returning home in November 1955. He assisted in the negotiations that led to independence. In April 1956 Hassan was appointed Chief of Staff of the Armed Forces with the task of creating a new army that would pose no danger to the monarchy and he also used it for social purposes such as building rural schools and roads. He took overall command of operations in the Atlas against Addi ou Bihi, in the Riff and in the South during the Ifni Crisis. In July 1957 in a breach of Moroccan tradition, his father invested Hassan as Crown Prince. In February 1960 members of the newly-formed left-wing Union Nationale des Forces Populaires were charged with plotting against his life. He made numerous foreign visits and was also involved in all major matters at home. When Muhammad V himself took over as Prime Minister in May 1960 he appointed Hassan his deputy and effective Head of Government. Hassan kept Muhammad's unexpected death on 26 February 1961 secret until he had completed preparations for a smooth succession which he personally announced on the radio. He continued as Prime Minister but, lacking his father's almost magical prestige, he had to organise right-wing support against the UNFP and the Istiqlal, although, reforming his government in June, he was able for a time to bring the latter uneasily into his Cabinet. Hassan always ensured that it, and other opposition groups that later came into his governments should not have access to independent sources of power and only his most trusted servants were given the Ministries which controlled the army or the police. He was helped by being able to announce, in March 1961, that the last French troops would leave in October, two years before schedule. In March 1962 he set out the Promotion Nationale, civil mobilisation for public works, nationalisation of the infrastructure and Moroccanisation of the administration: throughout his reign he frequently tried to disarm the opposition by adopting their policies. In foreign affairs he was less non-aligned than Muhammad, although he received Brezhnev and Chou En-Lai, moving towards the West. He gave strong support to the Algerians in their War of Independence, played a part in negotiating the release of Ben Bella and was the first Head of State to visit after independence. Morrocco was a founder member of the OAU in 1963. At home he determined to keep to his father's timetable of granting a Constitution in December 1962 and elections in May 1963 before which, with the help of his

close associate Rida Guedira, he put together a royalist party, the Front pour la Défense des Institutions Constitutionelles, which just failed to win an absolute majority. In July 1963 a second UNFP plot against the Monarchy was discovered and severe sentences were handed down. As Hassan was to do with other matters affecting national pride, he exploited the Tindouf Dispute with Algeria to rally the country behind him and in November he handed over the Premiership to Ahmad Bahnini who was clearly little more than his puppet. There was increasing opposition to the Government's economic policies and the National Assembly became extremely factious leading the King to declare that there was a fundamental incompatibility between parliamentary democracy and real democracy. In March 1965 there were in Casablanca riots so violent that it appeared that the Monarchy might fall. Ruthless action by General Oufkir restored order and the King granted an amnesty. Having failed to woo the UNFP and the Istiqlal into a government of national unity, on 8 June he proclaimed a state of emergency, suspended Parliament, announced projected revisions of the Constitution and formed a new government with himself as Prime Minister, heavily reliant upon Oufkir as Minister of the Interior. Almost immediately their partnership attracted international reprobation with the murder in Paris of the opposition leader Mehdi Ben Barka which nearly led to a complete breach of diplomatic relations with France. Hassan continued to speak of a return to parliamentary life but in March 1967 Mahjoubi Ahardan, the last party leader in the Government, resigned and there were eight reshuffles in two years with the King warning his Ministers that if he wished he could replace them with his chauffeur. Always concerned to be able to dissociate himself from direct blame if things went wrong, in July he handed over the Premiership to Muhammad Taiyba Ben Hima whom he hoped could improve the economic situation. The King was prepared to send Moroccan troops to the June War but it was over before they could arrive, and, as tradition demanded, he took the local Jewish community under his personal protection. He broadcast that the Arabs had been defeated because they were "disunited and sinful", and he called for a Summit in Rabat in December to discuss Resolution 242: Syria refused to participate and he was forced to abandon the idea. Hassan realised that the Palestinian cause both won support at home and celebrity abroad and after the burning of al-Aqsa Mosque in August 1969 he chaired the Rabat Islamic Summit which issued a declaration that there could be no settlement in the Middle East without the return of Jerusalem to Arab rule and he also chaired the Rabat Summit in December which ended in failure with King Faysal and Nasser both threatening to walk out. Continuing his efforts to find a solution to the Palestinian problem, in June 1970 Hassan had a "cordial" meeting with Nahum Goldman, President of the World Jewish Congress, initiating a series of contacts, both overt and clandestine with Jewish leaders: for this he was fiercely attacked by Syria. In September he met Boumédienne and President ould Daddah of Mauritania and they agreed that Morocco would drop its claim to Tindouf in return for Algerian support in the Spanish Sahara. Meanwhile, at home,

attempts to use these external events to unite the nation failed and economic distress continued to cause political unrest until the King seemed to be relying mainly upon the army for support. The replacement of Ben Hima by Ahmad Laraki in October 1969 was followed by a referendum which appeared to give unanimous assent to a new Constitution which, though ending the state of emergency, considerably increased his powers at the expense of Parliament. This was followed by elections boycotted by the opposition. In July 1971 the King was celebrating his birthday at Skhirat palace when about 1,400 young cadets burst in spraying the guests with machine-gun fire, killing about a hundred: the King managed to hide in a bathroom and later emerged to receive the homage of the attackers and lead them in prayer. What the attackers intended to do with the King is unknown for the leaders, generally regarded as conservative and honourable officers, were shot out of hand. There was a widespread feeling that people in high places, possibly even the Monarch, were involved in corruption with foreign business interests and that there was a need for reform in the distribution of wealth and the spheres of education, administration and justice and in August Hassan appointed a new Prime Minister, Karim Lamrani, with exceptional powers and orders to put things right in 18 months. The opposition still refused to collaborate and most of the Ministers were technocrats although Oufkir was moved to Defence to purge the armed forces. In February 1972 the King promulgated yet another Constitution which diminished his powers by making him an arbiter with executive authority vested in the Government which would be responsible to Parliament. Despite a boycott called by the opposition, 93% of the electorate was said to have voted, giving 98.75% approval. Hassan tried once more to form a national unity government to supervise elections but still the opposition refused to participate and the elections were postponed. In June the King presided over a Summit of the OAU in Rabat at which all African countries except Malawi were represented. In August it was probably Hassan's quick thinking that foiled an attempt by Moroccan fighter aircraft to shoot down the Royal Boeing in which he was returning from a private visit to France: the implication of Oufkir whose death in mysterious circumstances occurred the same night led him to say that he would never trust anyone again and himself to take over the Defence Ministry. Again the King unsuccessfully tried to persuade the opposition to share responsibility and in November he made his non-political brother-in-law Ahmad Uthman Prime Minister. Colonel Qadafi had openly expressed his regret that the two attempts to kill the King had failed and in 1973 his hand was seen behind the March Plot for an insurrection in the mountains and civil unrest, fomented by the UNFP in the cities: subsequently there were 15 executions. Hassan again adopted the policies of the opposition, taking over more foreign-owned land and industries and by extending Moroccan territorial waters from 12 to 70 miles, leading to a confrontation with Spain over fishing rights. During the October War he won over disgruntled students and urban politicians by sending 1,800 troops to the Golan Heights. Hassan's constant search for an issue on which he could call for national unity was rewarded by the Spanish commitment to end colonial rule in the Sahara. The whole country responded when in November 1975 he declared that he personally would lead a Green March of 350,000 unarmed civilians across the frontier. In the event he remained at a command post and called off the March a few miles inside Spanish territory. For the moment it appeared that his prestige might have been irreparably damaged but it reached a new peak when it was learned that he had already concluded the Madrid Tripartite Agreement by which the Spanish would withdraw within three months. Polisario resisted the Moroccan take-over and the Western Saharan War began with the Algerian involvement making a war between the neighbours a distinct possibility: Hassan claimed the right of hot pursuit across the frontier. With the country united, it was possible to hold communal elections in November 1976 and parliamentary elections in June 1977 which produced a large majority of independent royal supporters despite being acknowledged as amongst the freest and fairest ever held in Africa; their extension to the Sahara reinforced Moroccan claims. Subsequently debate in the Assembly was remarkably open and the King could claim to be presiding over a genuine democracy and that he was succeeding in his task of bringing on a new young élite. At times, however, he appeared uncertain as to whether to play the role of the leader of the progressive forces or that of the arbiter who stood above politics. Despite always keeping on personally cordial terms with opposition politicians, he could, by using referenda, play the demagogue and appeal to the people over their heads. He was always quick to exploit his thirty-ninth generation descent from the Prophet, the *barakah* which had apparently saved his life in assassination attempts, and his title of Commander of the Faithful and the traditional trappings of the Monarchy and its function as the main source of patronage. He was never seen to make concessions such as his frequent amnesties under pressure, able always to present them as his unilateral gift. Hassan was skilled in arguing that opposition was to policies of the Government, not to his person or to the regime. The revelation during a trial in Casablanca in January 1977 that there had been a plot to establish a republic under a Jewish mining engineer Abraham Serfaty evoked more amusement than alarm and during the year rumours that Hassan had cancer showed that even the communists regarded him as preferable to the only conceivable alternatives – anarchy or a military take-over. In the autumn of 1979, however, a leaked CIA report forecast his downfall within a year. In the meanwhile Hassan had shown his importance in the Arab world by presiding over the successful Rabat Summit of October 1974 and by sending troops to join the Arab Deterrent Security Force in Lebanon in 1976. He was also head of the al-Quds Committee which kept Muslim views on Jerusalem before world leaders including the Pope. The death of Oufkir ended the period of strained relations with France and during a visit by President Giscard in May 1975 Hassan started a campaign for close association with the EEC including the construction of a bridge across the Straits of Gibraltar. He conducted also an active diplomacy in Africa, lobbying against recognition of Polisario and

in 1978 sent troops to Zaire to help President Mobutu to suppress a rebellion. In 1978 he made what he described as "the contract of the century", a major trade deal with Russia which had never tried to exploit his problems. Despite its lack of full support for his Saharan policies, he kept on good terms with Washington and gave his backing to Camp David. In May 1981 a rumour that he had met the Israeli Labour leader Shimon Peres was officially denied and in November he presided over the unsuccessful Fez Summit which was unable to a agree on a plan for negotiations for a peace settlement. In May 1982 the King, hailed by Reagan as a "firm friend" visited Washington where he exploited a recent defeat in the Sahara to get military and development aid in return for making some airfields available. In September 1982, after the Israeli invasion of Lebanon, Hassan seized exactly the right moment to reconvene the Fez Summit which delegated him as the principal spokesman of the Arabs to put peace proposals to the Permanent Members of the Security Council. The Saharan War dragged on and much of Hassan's foreign policy revolved around it. The war had caused a breach of relations with Algeria but these improved after the King met Chadli in February 1983. Libya had been one of the main supporters of Polisario but in August 1984, the King and Qadafi astonishingly agreed in the Oudjda Declaration to unite their two countries: this had no practical effect other than to end fifteen years of hostility. In November 1984 Morocco walked out of the OAU after the majority of the states agreed to seat Polisario. At home, despite economic hardships which culminated in 1981 in the Casablanca Riots there was little political dissent: the King was so dominant that the opposition was marginalised with its leaders joining a National Defence Committee and some serving in the Government. Later the King felt compelled to subsidise the opposition parties to keep them in existence, declaring that he would "subvert by democracy my people's national instinct towards anarchy". The municipal elections of June 1983 produced a large majority for the centre-right supporters of the King and they were also successful in the parliamentary elections of September 1984, winning 206 out of 306 seats: Lamrani continued as Prime Minister until September 1986 when he was replaced by Izz al-Din Laraki who under pressure from the IMF started a programme of privatisation and other measures to attract foreign investment. The King spoke of a system of "Moroccan socialism" which helped the poor without harming the rich and expressed the ambition of making Morocco "the workshop of the North serving the South, of the East serving the West"; he made a formal application to join the European Community. There was criticism abroad of abuse of human rights in Morocco while there was also a rise of Islamic militancy under the leadership of Shaykh Abd al-Salam Yassin. A rather unsuccessful Casablanca Summit in August 1985 ended with Hassan being deputed to put the Arab case in Washington and other capitals but he outraged the radical states by publicly holding the Ifrane Meeting with Peres, now Prime Minister, in July 1986. He regained his authority amongst the Arabs with a successful Casablanca Summit in May 1989, achieving a major objective of his foreign policy by ending the isolation of Egypt. He was also asked to chair a committee to try to end the Lebanese Civil War. Earlier in the year he had chaired the congress in Marrakesh at the Arab Maghreb Unity Treaty was signed. His international prestige was further shown by a request for his mediation in a dispute between Belgium and Zaire. In February 1990 he said that the mass emigration of Russian Jews to Israel was a catastrophe which necessitated a full international peace conference. Attention was, however, diverted by the Iraqi invasion of Kuwait and in September Hassan met King Hussain and Chadli to try to find a solution. He sent 1,300 troops to Saudi Arabia despite considerable opposition which he branded an illegitimate questioning of royal prerogative. He propitiated public opinion by declaring that "our hearts are with Saddam Hussain although our heads are against him", denouncing the bombing of Baghdad and refusing to adhere to the Damascus Declaration. He emerged from the crisis with credit for moderation, the Gulf States under obligations to him and the pro-Iraqis not alienated and made successful visits to Washington and to the Gulf from which he returned with $900 million in aid. He tried to push forward peace negotiations, expressing readiness to meet Prime Minister Shamir and offering Morocco as a venue for an international conference; within a few days he received Secretary of State Baker and Yasser Arafat. He claimed "a consultative role" in the process which led to the signature of the Israel-PLO Agreement after which Prime Minister Rabin stopped at Rabat on his way home from Washington. Fighting in the Western Sahara officially ended with a cease-fire in September 1991 with the future of the area to be decided in a referendum which Moroccan immigration and money spent on development making its integration with the Kingdom practically certain: Hassan refused to countenance any other outcome. He refused also to negotiate with the Polisario leaders, calling them "errant sons" whom he would treat graciously after they had submitted. His handling of the issue over twenty years showed great skill, subtlety, strong will and quickness to seize every advantage. In October 1992, partly to impress Europe, he declared war on drug abuse, saying that if parents did not teach their children the dangers, he would do so himself. One of the features of the reign of Hassan II was the adroit way in which he mixed traditional Islamic monarchy with modern political leadership and this was demonstrated by his assertion that as Commander of the Faithful he had the duty to chair a meeting of government and opposition figures to discuss a new electoral law. In August 1992 he promulgated the fourth Constitution of his reign, describing it as a "passport to make our entry into the modern world". It gave more power to the Prime Minister without really diminishing the supremacy of the King and the majority which approved it in a referendum was so overwhelming as to excite ridicule. The parliamentary elections, several times postponed, considerably increased the opposition parties and the King spoke of taking a Prime Minister from their ranks but although he offered them Cabinet posts, he was unable to tempt them into a national coalition. In 1993 he published his Memoirs in which he said that he was thinking of retiring: he had already

had the succession of his eldest son, whom he had carefully trained, confirmed by a referendum in May 1980 and built the most lavish mosque in the world as his mausoleum. Hassan saw himself as Arab, Western and African all at once and his long-term strategy was to mould Morocco in this fashion into a dynamic power in all three areas by dealing with each problem tactically as it arose: his Memoirs cheerfully admitted that 60% of his decisions had been wrong but he had survived, usually by managing to claim credit for success while contriving to put blame for failure upon others. He had also, sometimes by dubious means, acquired great wealth, owning seven palaces and chateaux in France: all had golf courses on which he appeared in flamboyant costumes. He also enjoyed the spectacular in state craft, both diplomatic and domestic. His dealings both with foreign potentates and his own subjects, he toured widely to keep in touch with the countryside, were often marred by an unpunctuality that appeared unworthy arrogance. He was a skilled orator with a deep sense of loyalty to his dynasty and his nation. His wife, from a leading Berber family, never appeared in public, but his two sons and three daughters received modern educations

al-HASSANI, Taj al-Din (1885–1943)

Syrian Head of State and Prime Minister. He was the son of a very respected religious leader of Algerian origin on the strength of whose reputation he was appointed *Qadi* of Damascus. The French dismissed him as a supporter of Faysal and the British but in January 1926 at the time of the Druze Revolt they invited him to form a government. In order not to alienate the nationalists Shaykh Taj laid down conditions such as a Franco-Syrian Treaty, eventual admission to the League of Nations and the return of the Biqa to Syria. Negotiations failed and the French appointed the *Damad* Ahmad Nami. In February 1928 the French wished to make a fresh start so they dismissed the *Damad* and appointed Shaykh Taj to form a provisional government to oversee elections although they regarded him as "a conceited puppet". The British Consul remarked that the French wanted someone subservient and had overlooked the fact that Taj had neither the experience, the talent nor even the education for the post. He had, however, considerable political wiliness and a very shrewd idea of how to fill his own pockets and those of his friends whom he appointed to posts in the Government and bureaucracy. Although he spent large sums from the secret funds he was unable to rig the elections to his complete satisfaction. He made a tactical alliance with the leaders of the National Bloc but double-crossed them by sending supporters with police protection to stuff the ballot-boxes. Even so the Constituent Assembly would not produce the required results and had to be suspended. The Prime Minister was the most unpopular politician in Syria, booed when he appeared in public and denounced from the pulpit when he went to a mosque. The British Consul reported that he was "apt to be oriental towards women when drunk, and caused embarrassment at official functions". In November 1931 the French were anxious that there should be a respectable government with which they could negotiate a Treaty so Shaykh Taj was curtly dismissed but given a large gratuity. He had already been active in the elections but was again unsuccessful. He dropped out of political life but in the summer of 1933 went to Paris to canvass support. In March 1934 with the future of the country extremely unsettled the High Commissioner reappointed the pliable Shaykh Taj who had frankly said that he was prepared to take office on any terms with the support of any party. His Cabinet again included the most distrusted politician in the country, his relative Jamil al-Ulshi. His first official visit to Aleppo was greeted with bombs. His Ministers took no initiatives except in enriching themselves and their corrupt administration set off a general strike in February 1936. The French decided that a more respectable Prime Minister might settle things down and dismissed Shaykh Taj. He knew himself to be so unpopular that he fled to Paris where he stayed until the fall of the National Bloc Cabinet early in 1939. In September 1941 after the arrival of the Free French, De Gaulle's representative General Catroux appointed Shaykh Taj, whom he described as enjoying the favour of the moderates and much loved by the lower classes "a man of courage, decision, political sense, skill in manoeuvre and energy" and completely loyal as Head of State. His interference and nepotism caused his two Prime Ministers to resign in despair but he did stand up to the French over the retention of Syrian grain. In January 1943 he died in office. Sir Edward Spears at this time described him as "the shape of a child's balloon stuffed into grey pinstripe trousers cut on the model of a lavatory basin".

HASSI MASSAOUD (Algeria)
In 1945 French oil companies started prospecting in the Sahara and shortly after the All Saints Day Uprising of 1954 a major strike was made at Edjele near the Libyan frontier. A more important field, however, was found further north on the Tunisian frontier at Hassi Massaoud and the first oil flowed there on 7 January 1958. It was estimated that production in the first year would be 5,000,000 tons, rising to 14,000,000 in 1962 and sufficient to satisfy all France's requirements by 1980. This enormously raised the stakes in the War of Algerian Independence: France could hope to end its dependence upon Middle Eastern oil and the Suez Canal but anticipated "Anglo-Saxon" plots to take control of it. Despite the fighting large-scale investment took place with an oil pipeline from Hassi Massaoud to Bougie was opened in November 1959 and there were plans for a gas pipe line from Hassi R'mel to Arzew. At the first Evian meeting in 1961 the French maintained that the oil belonged exclusively to France to be exploited for the benefit of all the former French colonies surrounding the Sahara to which Algeria had no historic claim as it had only been administered from Algiers since its conquest by the French. The insistence of Bilqasim Krim that the desert was an integral part of Algeria which could not even be discussed was a major factor in the breakdown of the negotiations. At the second Evian meeting in March 1962 it was agreed that French oil companies should keep their concessions and receive preferential treatment for new exploration and development contracts over the next six years. After

independence Ben Bella regarded these arrangements, and particularly the fact that the Algerian Government received far lower royalties than did the Middle Eastern countries as unsatisfactory: apart from a 40% share in one oil company the country did not participate in the exploitation of its major asset. After twenty months of difficult negotiations an agreement was signed in July 1965 which created a French and an Algerian state oil company (SONATRACH) to co-operate as equal partners in the exploitation of designated oilfields. This was the first oil agreement involving private companies that was negotiated exclusively between governments. The companies retained their concessions but were subjected to a new system of taxation. In February 1971 President Boumédienne announced that Algeria proposed to take a 51% interest in the two French companies operating in there and to nationalise outright the gas resources and the oil and gas pipelines. The French denounced this breach of the 1965 agreement, calling for an internationl boycott of Algerian oil, but in September an arrangement was made by which the French companies continued as minority partners in return for guaranteed supplies.

HASSI MASSAOUD MEETING (1975)
During 1975 Colonel Qadafi narrowly survived an attempted coup and faced the unremitting hostility of Egypt. Algeria was uncertain as to whether its opposition to the Moroccan take-over of the Western Sahara might lead to war. Early in December Colonel Boumédienne visited Tripoli and at the end of the month he and Qadafi met again at Hassi Massaoud. In a joint statement the two countries promised to help each other if either were threatened and also that they would "institutionalise" their relations. "Organic or vital links" would be created and they would have regular summits. Qadafi presented the agreement as a first step towards unification, claiming priority when Algeria established close links with Tunisia in the Treaty of Fraternity and Concord of 1983. In the immediate aftermath of the agreement Libya was reported to have put 100 Mirage fighters at the disposal of Algeria.

HASSOUNA, (Muhammad) Abd al-Khaliq (1898–1992)
Egyptian Minister and Secretary-General of the Arab League. He was born in Cairo, the son of a leading Muslim scholar and studied law at Cairo and Cambridge Universities. Hassouna joined the diplomatic service and served in Brussels and Rome before in 1942 being appointed Governor of Alexandria. While holding that office he arranged with the Prime Minister Nahhas Pasha that he should go secretly by night to meet the advancing forces of Rommel and arrange that the city should be surrendered and not defended inch-by-inch as Montgomery had proposed; the British victory at El Alamein made this unnecessary. He entered the government of Sirri Pasha in 1949, served under Ali Mahir, and in 1952 was Minister of Foreign Affairs. In September 1952 when the Revolutionary Command Council decided that they wanted an administrator rather than a policy-maker at the head of the Arab League they appointed Hassouna to replace Abd al-Rahman Azzam. Hassouna regarded himself very much

as the servant of the Egyptian Government rather than of that of the League as a whole. He worked hard to prevent the deterioration of relations between Nasser and the British although later he worked to undermine the British position in South Arabia. In 1961 during the Kuwait–Iraq dispute he played an important part in obtaining the admission of Kuwait into the League and the replacement of British troops by a force drawn from Arab states. During the Yemen War he showed support for FLOSY rather than the NLF. In May 1967 Nasser was critical of his visit to Bonn which had been approved at council. In 1969 he tried to mediate between the Kingdom of Arabia and the People's Democratic Republic of Yemen. His term was several times extended as there was no agreement on his successor. The appointment of a third Secretary-General in March 1970 left Hassouna in charge only of finance and protocol. In April 1972 he welcomed the members of the Palestine National Congress who had assembled to denounce the proposal of King Hussain for a united Arab Kingdom, and in the same month announced his retirement. He was succeeded by Mahmud Riad.

HAWAR DISPUTE
Hawar is a group of islands, containing two villages, a mile and a half from the west coast of Qatar. While the Al Khalifah family ruled both Bahrain and Zubarah there was no dispute over their ownership but later they were claimed by Qatar after the delimitation of maritime frontiers became important in connection with the granting of oil concessions. In 1936 Hamad b. Isa al-Khalifah established a Bahraini military post there at which Abd Allah b. Jasim al-Thani of Qatar complained to the British Political Resident. The more sophisticated Bahrainis obtained professional legal assistance in presenting their case which the Qataris were unable to contest in similar form. In 1939 the Political Resident awarded the islands to Bahrain, a decision which his successor felt was unfair but was unwilling to cause trouble by reopening. During the 1940s Hawar was used as a place of punishment for members of the Ruling Family whose private lives provoked scandal. In 1965 the islands were included in an oil concession granted by Bahrain. In 1967 the Qataris revived their claim and did so on other occasions. In 1978 after Bahraini manoeuvres in the area, the Qataris detained some Bahraini fishermen. In March 1982 there was further trouble when the Bahrainis named a warship *Hawar* and the Qataris vehemently protested. Linked with the Hawar dispute was a further incident in April 1986 when the Bahrainis were reclaiming land for a new coastguard station on Fasht al-Dibal reef. The Qataris launched a helicopter attack and carried off British, Dutch and Filipino workmen. There was much anger on both sides until Saudi Arabia headed a mediation committee. It was decided to blow up the reclaimed land.

HAWATMA, Nayif (1934–)
Palestinian nationalist and guerrilla leader. He was born in Salt to a Christian family of bedouin origins. Thanks to an uncle, a chicken farmer, he received a secondary education in Amman where he came into contact with George Habash and joined the Arab Nationalist Move-

ment. Hawatma took part in the nationalist conspiracy of Ali Abu Nuwar and after its repression was sentenced to death. He escaped to Damascus and was sent to Iraq to organise a branch of the ANM. There he was involved in the pro-Nasser events of the Mosul Uprising and was imprisoned from the end of 1961 until February 1963 seizure of power by the Baath Party which released but soon deported him. Hawatma became a committed Marxist and managed to swing the ANM away from the Nasserism of Habash into support of "scientific socialism". He paid several visits to Aden where he helped to draft the Marxist programme of the National Liberation Front and wrote a book on *The Crisis of the South Yemen Revolution*. He disagreed with the Fatah policy of keeping out of inter-Arab disputes, feeling that there should be active participation on the side of "progressive" states and saw the liberation of Palestine as part of a wider struggle which also involved overthrowing the bourgeois regimes of Egypt and Jordan. He returned to Beirut in 1966 as a philosophy student at the Arab University and joined Habash in founding the Popular Front for the Liberation of Palestine but soon came to see it as insufficiently revolutionary. He broke away, therefore, to form the (Popular) Democratic Front for the Liberation of Palestine which cultivated relations with international anarchist groups. Hawatma established links with left-wing Israeli groups and called for a de-Zionised binational state of Palestine, rejecting a smaller entity on liberated territory. He opposed terrorism outside the area but in July 1972 refused to be bound by a Palestine Liberation Organisation decision to freeze operations from Lebanon. In May 1974 he deliberately sabotaged moves towards peace by ordering the Maalot Killings. Hawatma, however, refused to join the Rejection Front and for many years was regarded as a supporter of Yassir Arafat. In May 1975 he collaborated with Abu Iyad in an attempt to work out a *modus vivendi* with the Lebanese Government. Hawatma played a major role in the general reconciliation of the guerrilla groups in 1987/8. In 1988 he refused to accept the Palestine National Council Algiers Meeting acceptance of Resolution 242. In 1990 he urged that dialogue with the US should be kept going.

HAYCRAFT REPORT (1921)
After the Jaffa Riots of May 1921, the first serious clash between Arabs and Jews since the British had taken responsibility for Palestine, the Government in Jerusalem set up a Commission of Inquiry under the Chief Justice Sir Thomas Haycraft. He reported that the disturbances had been initiated by the Arabs but had been unpremeditated, and implied that they had been provoked by the feeling that the authorities were favouring the Jews with a disproportionate share of government jobs. There was also the fear that the Arabs would be swamped by Jewish immigrants and capital. Many Arabs distrusted what they understood to be Zionist policies, and were particularly affronted by the fact that many of the immigrants appeared to hold extreme socialist views.

HAYKAL, Muhammad Hassanain (1923–)

Egyptian journalist and politician. After a degree from Cairo University in economics, law and journalism, he became a war correspondent, covering the Greek civil war, the Palestine War, where he first met Nasser, and Korea. In 1949 he was the youngest editor in Egypt but his period of real importance started when he was appointed Editor of *al-Ahram* in 1957. He was one of the very few people, perhaps the only civilian, fully trusted by Nasser, whose book *The Philosophy of the Revolution* he was generally believed to have written. Haykal may have invented the phrase "positive neutralism" and he enunciated the concept that while Egypt as a state had relations with reactionary powers, Egypt as a revolution was entitled to plot against their regimes. He always accompanied Nasser on foreign trips and visiting journalists could obtain access to the President only through him. Haykal was used to slander foreign opponents of the regime, to launch new campaigns and to test public opinion: his weekly column 'Frankly Speaking' (*Bi-Saraha*) was the only uncensored writing to be found in the country; he did, however, expose corruption. In a famous series of articles "I Accuse" (*Inni Attahim*) in 1963 he blackguarded the Baath as clownish saboteurs of Arab unity. *Al-Ahram*, quintupling its circulation, became one of the most-quoted newspapers in the world. He was generally seen as right-wing, criticising government hostility to the US, arguing that only with American neutrality would it be possible for the Arabs to defeat Israel and advocating a relaxation of the harsher aspects of police control. He was a member of the Central Committee of the Arab Socialist Union. Haykal several times refused office but in April 1970 agreed to become Minister of National Guidance. At times he acted as Foreign Minister and was sent on delicate missions such as to discover the sentiments of Colonel Qadafi who had just seized power. He was present at Nasser's death and resigned as a Minister shortly afterwards. In February 1974 Sadat dismissed him from *al-Ahram* amidst accusations that he was trying to make his newspaper an alternative source of power; he had also criticised the policies and motives of Kissinger. In 1976 he founded a Nasserite party but was not allowed to contest the general election. In 1978 he was banned from leaving the country. In September 1981 during a crackdown on all forms of opposition, Sadat had Haykal arrested on the charge of defaming Egypt abroad; he was, however, released in November by the new President Mubarak. He wrote several books on the inner workings of the Egyptian Government under Nasser and Sadat which are entertaining although every detail cannot be taken literally.

HAYTHAM, Muhammad Ali (1940–93)

Prime Minister of South Yemen. He was born in Dathinah of a tribal family and trained as a teacher, subsequently working at the school in his home village. He became a secret member of the Arab Nationalist Movement and later of the National Liberation Front. In June 1966 at its Jiblah Congress he was one of the "second-level" leaders elected to the Executive but he was generally unknown when appointed Minister of the Interior by Qahtan al-Shaabi in the first government after independence in November 1967. He was responsible for organising the beginnings of a police state with ruthless repression of opponents, purges and control of the press etc. In June 1969 he quarrelled with the President over the posting of an official and was dismissed. He thereupon joined forces with the extreme left wing of Salim Rubai Ali and Abd al-Fattah Ismail, assisting them with his influence with the army and the tribes to depose the President in the Glorious Corrective Move. He became Prime Minister and a member of the five-man Presidency Council. His period of office was a time of terror, with constant speeches about conspiracies, mass arrests with special courts untrammelled by ordinary law to "review anti-state activities". Purges and indoctrination produced an army and police force subordinated to the party. Large numbers of citizens escaped abroad and early in 1970 it was estimated that a quarter of the population had fled. Even so there was widespread unemployment in a financial situation that Haytham called "chronic". Many businesses were nationalised. Relations with Great Britain were icy and there were none with the USA as Aden advised other Arab states to confiscate all American assets. Haytham called for Revolution in the "Occupied Gulf", refused to recognise the independence of Bahrain, Qatar and the UAE and provided a base for the rebels of the Dhufar Liberation Front. Continuous radio warfare with Saudi Arabia was punctuated with occasional frontier clashes such as one at al-Wadiah in November 1969. He received Leila Khalid after her release. However attempts were made to improve relations with the YAR and in November 1970 he became the first South Yemeni Prime Minister to visit Taizz where he urged unification. Haytham's quarrel with al-Shaabi had been personal rather than doctrinal but although he did fully share the ideology of his partners, he generally acquiesced in their policies. He was not an all-out revolutionary and came to realise that as the foreign policy of the regime attracted no investment from abroad he would have to encourage local businessmen to start small industries. His more doctrinaire colleagues Ali and Ismail united against him and in August 1971 he was dismissed. He went into exile where he became a vociferous opponent of the regime that he had helped to create, forming the Yemen United Front in Cairo. In May 1975 he appeared in Muscat, making a speech supporting the Sultan against the rebels in Dhufar. In October 1975 in Cairo there was an attempt on his life after which two diplomats from the PDRY were arrested. There was another attempt to murder him in 1976. In 1980 he joined forces with his old foe Abd al-Qawi Makkawi to set up the National Grouping of Patriotic Forces under the auspices of the Iraqi Government. It was clear, however, that his belated conversion to multi-party democracy carried no conviction and that he attracted little support or respect.

HEBRON ISLAMIC COLLEGE ATTACK (1983)

Hebron, where the Jewish quarter had been destroyed during the Wailing Wall Riots of 1929 was perhaps the place where there was most unrest after the Israeli occupation of the West Bank particularly after settlers arrived in the area and talked of rebuilding. On 26 July 1983 four masked members of the so-called "Jewish Underground" carried out an attack with machine-guns and army-issue grenades on the Islamic College there. Two teachers and a student were killed and more than 30 Arabs wounded. Prime Minister Begin denounced the action as "a despicable crime". In 1985 25 Jewish terrorists were put on trial including two who admitted participation in the Islamic College attack. They were amongst those condemned to life imprisonment but the sentences were reduced three times by President Chaim Herzog and they were finally released in December 1990.

HEBRON MASSACRE (1944)

There is a long history of histility in Hebron. In 1929 67 Jews were killed at the Wailing Wall, and although 30 Jewish families returned in 1931 they were forced to leave following riots in 1936. On 25 February 1994 at Friday prayers 48 Muslims killed and 70 wounded, mainly shot in the back, while praying. President Clinton said that negotiations should switch to Washington to show US involvement. The massacre showed the threat of extremists to the negotiations. Palestinians called on Israel to disarm immediately all 130,000 settlers. Baruch Goldstein, aged 42, a doctor and reserve captain who had settled 10 years before from Brooklyn, led the massacre. He was dressed in army uniform and left a suicide note at council offices. Many of the victims were shot by soldiers who fired in panic. Following eruptions outside the mosque a further six people were killed. Rabin described the massacre as "the bloodiest single incident since the Israeli occupation – a loathsome criminal act".

HELOU, Charles (1912–)

Lebanese President. A Maronite, he was born in Beirut where he received a French education, graduating in Law from St Joseph University. He married one of the first Lebanese women to become a lawyer, the niece of President Petro Trad in whose office he practised. He was a founder-member of the Kataib but later became a follower of Bishara al-Khouri editing a journal that supported him. Khouri, as president, appointed Helou to represent Lebanon at the Vatican and at UNESCO. In 1949 he was Minister of Justice in the Cabinet of Riad al-Sulh, a post he later held under President Camille Chamoun. Later he came to oppose Chamoun and was one of the Maronite leaders who condemned the President's attempt to alter the Constitution in order to secure re-election. He was briefly a Minister under President Fuad Shihab but in 1960 he announced his retirement from politics, becoming Chairman of the Office of Social Development and later founder of the National Tourist Board. In September 1964 when it became clear that the President would refuse to be re-elected those around him wished to continue "Shihabism", the principle of the primacy of administration over politics, and there was a general unwillingness to put power into the hands of a single Maronite boss, Chamoun, Khouri or Raymond Edde. A neutral candidate was needed and the choice fell upon Helou who had no particular enemies and no significant following of his own. In general therefore he had to rely upon the elements that really owed their allegiance to his predecessor, the Intelligence Service and young army officers and technocrats and his Presidency was

regarded as a prolongation of "Shihabism". He continued reforms of the bureaucracy and although he was not always able to enforce his will, a drastic purge was carried through in 1965. He was, however, less enthusiastic in planning development on a national basis. Helou was unable to maintain the alliance with Kamal Jumblatt which had been so helpful to his predecessor. During his period of office Lebanon found itself drawn deeper into inter-Arab affairs. In October 1964 he attended the Cairo Summit which dealt with the Jordan Waters Dispute, agreeing to proposals which could have involved the country in reprisals by Israel and he had to accept also the presence of armed Palestinians on Lebanese soil. This was to lead to what appeared to Maronites such as Pierre Gemayel a distortion of the National Pact, which, owing to the weakness of the President, had to be countered by the formation of armed militias. In the June War of 1967 Lebanon loudly proclaimed its solidarity with the Arabs but took no military action although it briefly expelled the British and American Ambassadors. The Arab defeat increased the number of militant Palestinians, Israeli incursions, the apprehensions of the Maronites and the virulent Arabism and socialism of Jumblatt. The country started to split while Helou was unable to do anything as his control over government machinery weakened. In December 1968 Lebanon was humiliated by an Israeli raid on Beirut airport which had met with practically no resistance. During 1969 as armed clashes between Palestinians and the Lebanese army flared, politicians became more intransigent. The Cairo Agreement of November 1969 brought a temporary respite and Helou was able to finish his term of office in September 1970. In his farewell address he claimed that agricultural and industrial output had trebled under his administration and social services greatly improved. Later he opposed the Syrian presence in Lebanon and was regarded as close to the Lebanese Forces. In July 1979 he was appointed Minister of State in the Cabinet of Salim al-Hoss with the task of trying to pave the way for national dialogue but in less than three weeks he realised that he could not bring about reconciliation even within the Maronites and resigned. Helou was a highly intelligent, thoughtful man of unquestioned integrity. He was subtle, as his nickname "The Jesuit" implied but not forceful.

HELWAN

After the July Revolution the Egyptian Government determined to prove wrong experts who said that steel could not be economically produced in the country by building a plant at Helwan, about 16 miles south of Cairo using iron ore mined near Aswan and transported by barge. In February 1954 the Egyptian Iron and Steel Company was set up with a government grant of £E2 million. It was to be built and equipped by West Germans who undertook to produce 300,000 tons of ingots annually at well below the price at which they could have been imported. It was seen as very much a prestige project, almost as much as the Aswan High Dam, to show that Egypt could become an industrialised country. For many years it ran at a loss, the Germans were accused of selling substandard furnaces and installing them badly, some of the technology was obsolete by the time the works were completed, the ore was of poor quality and the price of imported coke much higher than anticipated. There was a shortage of skilled local labour. In 1963 it was only producing 144,000 tons and Aziz Sidqi, the Minister of Industry, decided to increase the scale of operations awarding, in May 1968, a £430 million contract to the Russians to modernise the technology to produce 1.75 million tons of cast iron and 1.5 million tons of steel, using electricity from Aswan, and creating 12,000 new jobs by 1976. The project was hailed as a model for co-operation between an industrial power and a Third World State. The complex of factories also produced military equipment. These were, in February 1968, the scene of the first anti-government riot in Egypt since Kafr al-Dawar in 1952. At least 2,000 workers demonstrated against the leniency of the sentences imposed upon four officers judged responsible for the incompetence shown by the air force in the June War. The police fired on the crowd; officially 23 were said to have been wounded while other estimates were that 17 had been killed. There were protests in Cairo and Alexandria where the Universities were closed. There were allegations that the incident was instigated by the Minister of the Interior, Sharawy Jumaa to embarrass Nasser who went in person to address the workers, saying that the police had mishandled it and promising the liberation of every inch of Arab territory.

HIJACKED BUS INCIDENT (1978)

The peace moves of Anwar Sadat in the winter of 1977/8 alarmed the Palestinian Liberation Organisation which would have been excluded from any settlement. Their leaders therefore determined to disrupt the process by a major raid on Israel. On 11 March 1978 eleven guerrillas landed from two dinghies on a beach about 20 miles south of Haifa and hijacked a bus into which they forced 100 hostages. They drove towards Tel Aviv but were stopped at a road block. In the course of heavy fighting, during which the bus which had been wired with explosives, blew up, 9 guerrillas and 28 civilians were killed and 82 wounded. Two guerrillas were captured and stated that they had intended to seize a tourist hotel in Tel Aviv and trade hostages for Palestinians and the Japanese survivor of the Lydda Airport Attack. There was considerable criticism within Israel of the failure of the security forces to prevent this attack from the sea. The Israelis had for some time been intending to attack guerrilla bases on South Lebanon and seized upon the raid as a pretext. On the night of 14/15 March 25,000 soldiers invaded the country and within 15 hours occupied a strip along the 80 km frontier varying in depth from 5 to 20 km. Refugee camps were bombed and accounted for most of the 600 people killed or critically wounded. On 19 March the Israelis launched a second stage of the invasion occupying the area up to the Litani River and besieging Tyre which they had attacked with cluster bombs. The Lebanese Government appealed to the Security Council which on 19 March passed Resolution 425 calling for an Israeli withdrawal and establishing UNIFIL to supervise it. When a cease-fire came into force on 20 March it was estimated that 1,168 Lebanese and Palestinians had been killed in the invasion.

al-HIJAZI, Abd al-Aziz Muhammad (1924–)

Egyptian Prime Minister. He trained as an economist in the Universities of Cairo and Birmingham, where he was awarded a doctorate for a dissertation of the philosophy of controlling accounts. Hijazi was Dean of the Faculty of Commerce at Ayn Shams University when he was appointed Minister for the Treasury in March 1968. One of his first tasks was to plan the financial aspects of the March Programme put forward by Nasser which included nationalisation of some industries. He also had to find the money to replace the military equipment lost in the June War. In March 1973 when Sadat became Prime Minister, Hijazi was appointed First Deputy Prime Minister in charge of the Economy, Finance and Foreign Trade. He urged the increase of inter-Arab trade to lessen dependence upon the Super-Powers and negotiated Arab finance for the SUMED project after it had proved impossible to make an agreement with European bankers. He played a leading role in the Intifadah, transforming state socialism to private enterprise, working for a wedding of Arab capital and Western technology on Egyptian soil. In July 1973 he lifted all restrictions on foreign trade and established a "parallel market" in currency exempt from official rates. Free zones were created where foreign capital could be invested and American banks given permission to open branches. In September 1974 Sadat handed over the Premiership to Hijazi with instructions to prepare a transitional 18-month development plan. He took over Sadat's Cabinet almost in its entirety, making only 4 changes in 37 Ministries. The President retained full control over foreign affairs but the Prime Minister arranged aid from the oil countries, stressing that the armed forces necessary for confrontation with Israel swallowed a third of the national income. Hijazi ended the state monopoly of transport to demonstrate that the age of Nasserite socialism would not return and he claimed that 500 proposed development schemes showed the success of the "Open Door". In January 1975, however, there were demonstrations against the rising cost of living and low wages; troops had to be used to restore order and Hijazi offered his resignation. In April Sadat accepted it, appointing the tough policeman Mamduh Salim to restore order. Almost immediately afterwards there were allegations that Hijazi had been involved in some dubious import deals; he was cleared by the National Assembly but played no further part in politics, working as a managerial consultant. Hijazi was described as cautious and taciturn.

al-HINDI

A family of Sudanese religious and political leaders, claiming descent from the Prophet. I about 1840 Muhammad al-Amin moved from the Hijaz to Sudan where he founded his own *tariqah* which, a century later, was estimated to have about 50,000 members. His son Yusuf Muhammad al-Amin (c. 1865–1942) originally fought for Muhammad Abd Allah al-Mahdi but rallied to the British. He married a daughter of the slave-trader Zubayr Pasha and was one of the leaders who went to London in 1919 to congratulate George V on the victory of the Allies. He received considerable financial help from the Government and enjoyed great influence particularly in the Gezirah but later was over-shadowed by Saiyyid Abd al-Rahman al-Mahdi and Saiyyid Ali al-Mirghani. His tomb at Burri near Khartoum became a place of pilgrimage. His son Abd al-Rahman (died 1964) exercised mainly local influence although he founded his own Nationalist Party which merged with the National Unionist Party. Another son, (Hussain) Yusuf (1925–82) was one of the leaders of the Democratic Unionist Party and a Minister, usually of Finance, in various governments. He took a leading role in opposing Nimeiri and was involved in the Ansar rebellion of 1970 after which he went into exile. He had close relations with the Saudis and in 1972 King Faysal arranged for a meeting between him and Nimeiri but no agreement was reached. Hussain was one of the founders, with Sadiq al-Mahdi of the National Front which in July 1976 organised a major plot involving 2,000 heavily armed civilians trained in Libya infiltrating Khartoum to overthrow the regime. He was then sentenced to death. When in 1977 Saiyyid Sadiq returned to the Sudan and took part in the National Reconciliation, Sharif Yusuf remained aloof. In April 1978 Nimeiri made a further attempt at a reconciliation but Hindi insisted that he should give up his support for Sadat and the Camp David Agreement. He also demanded more democracy within the sole party, the Sudan Socialist Union, greater rights for citizens and trade unions, and a solution to the problem of the South offering in return to disband the 6,000 armed exiles who still supported him. He put out propaganda from Iraq and Ethiopia and in March 1979 was suspected of organising an attempt on Nimeiri's life with Iraqi support. While in exile he showed himself an extremely successful businessman. He died in Athens but was buried at Burri. Zain al-Abdin al-Hindi (born 1938), graduated from al-Azhar and was a member of the Assembly before the take-over by Nimeiri. He withdrew from politics to concentrate on farming and then went abroad. When political life resumed, he became Secretary-General of the DUP, although the party was split between his faction and that of Muhammad Uthman al-Mirghani. In May 1986 he joined the government of Sadiq al-Mahdi as Foreign Minister and Deputy Prime Minister.

HIZBULLAH (Lebanon)

"The Party of God" came into existence soon after the Israeli invasion of Lebanon, Operation Peace for Galilee in the summer of 1982. Members of the Shiah party Amal had not distinguished themselves by showing any of the sect's traditional readiness to seek martyrdom and the more militant broke away under the guidance of Ali Akbar Mohtashami, then Iranian Ambassador in Damascus who was one of the strongest supporters of the Islamic Revolution of the Ayatollah Khomeini. Mohtashami commanded the Revolutionary Guards and arranged for some of them to train Hizbullah fighters at Baalbek. The new group rejected any compromise with anyone and called for the total destruction of Israel. It did not have a formal Chairman but was headed by a Council of 12 religious leaders with Shaykh Muhammad Fadhlallah as its spiritual guide. Soon it had about 6,000 fighting men, paid and armed by Iran. It maintained close links with the other

Iranian-backed organisation al-Dawaa and had a general Pan-Islamic tendency which was opposed to Amal's exclusive preoccupation with Lebanon. Hizbullah joined with Amal in harassing the retreating Israelis in the summer of 1983 and later its suicide attacks upon their forces led to the policy of the "Iron Fist" and it established a strong presence in the South. Hizbullah was suspected of being behind much of the kidnapping and hi-jacking of the middle and late 1980s with its adherents using different names such as "The Organisation of the Oppressed on Earth" and "The Revolutionary Justice Organisation". During 1985 it became increasingly important in the Shiah districts of South Beirut at the expense of Amal. It refused to endose the new political system negotiated by the Amal leader Nabih Berri in the Three-Militia Agreement at the end of 1985. Hizbullah also opposed the attempt of Amal, at the behest of Syria, to root out supporters of Yassir Arafat in the refugee camps and tried to mediate in the siege of Burj al-Barajinah. In the South it attacked UNIFIL, the South Lebanon Army and the Israelis. In February 1987 it resisted attempts by the Syrians to impose order on West Beirut and lost some ground there although the Syrians did not dare to go into South Beirut; during the fighting some Hizbullah men were murdered in cold blood leading to a protest from Iran. A year later there was conflict with Amal and Hizbullah, with the backing of Iran, regained parts of Beirut but was weakened in the South. In November 1988 it showed its total intransigence by denouncing Arafat for his willingness to recognise Israel. In January 1989 the warfare with Amal was so ferocious that Syria and Iran were emabarrassed at the behaviour of their clients and intervened at high level to mediate a peace by which Amal was to control security in the South although Hizbullah was guaranteed a presence there while Syria itself would be responsible for security in Beirut. Leading members were the Hamadi family, Hussain Musawi and Imad Mughnieh, who had a cousin imprisoned in Kuwait.

HONE–BELL CONSTITUTIONAL PROPOSALS (1966)

The Federation of South Arabia started in February 1959 as a grouping of six small tribal Emirates and by 1965 comprised 17 members including the Colony of Aden with its large commercial and labouring population. Although committed to eventual independence it lacked the institutions of modern state, having neither a President nor a Prime Minister and the Chairmanship of the Supreme Council rotated monthly. A Minister held office regardless of his abilities because his shaykhdom was entitled to a seat in the Cabinet. Local administration remained in the hands of the old ruling families who applied such Federal legislation as they thought convenient. There was no Parliament and apart from Aden itself only two states had held even a pretence of elections. Many Adenis complained that they had been forced against their will under the rule of backward feudal Sultans and urban resistance was growing. In order to prepare for independence the British Government pressed the Supreme Council to commission a study for a possible Constitution. The matter was put in the hands of Sir Ralph Hone, Legal Adviser to the

Commonwealth Relations Office and a former Governor of North Borneo and Sir Gawain Bell, former Governor of Northern Nigeria. Their proposals, published in February 1966 recommended the establishment of a United Republic of South Arabia with two elected legislative bodies. The Council of States with limited delaying powers would have two representatives from each of the shaykhdoms and four from the capital territory which would be Aden. The National Assembly would be directly elected by manhood suffrage; Rulers would be debarred from being candidates. The two bodies would elect a President with limited personal powers to hold office for five years. The President would appoint a Prime Minister who could select his Cabinet from either House. The Cabinet would be responsible to the National Assembly. There were also proposals for an independent judiciary and other basic human rights. This gave the nationalists everything they said that they wanted but the Constitution was still-born for the following week the British Government announced that it planned to leave South Arabia in 1968.

HOPE SIMPSON REPORT (1930)
The Shaw Report following the Wailing Wall Incident recommended an investigation into whether Palestine could support a larger agricultural population. This was carried out by Sir John Hope Simpson, a former Indian Civil Servant and a member of the League of Nations Commission for the resettlement of Greek refugees. He reported that there was little space left for further Jewish immigration and it was not true that the Government could make large areas available for further settlement. Some of the methods by which the Jewish National Fund acquired land were "objectionable". Some 14% of the cultivable land had been bought by Jews and the original Arabs dispossessed. Many of them were living on the edge of destitution and the situation was deteriorating. The existing population was increasing but perhaps 20,000 more families might be admitted but not all of these should be Jewish. He criticised the refusal of Jewish settlements and of the labour organisation Histadrut to employ Arab labour and it was wrong that Jewish workers should be imported while there were Arabs unemployed. He considered that agriculture could be further modernised but that there was little chance of industrial development, for example a large-scale textile industry as proposed by the Jewish Agency.

al-HUNI, Abd al-Munim Tahir (1941–)
Libyan politician. He came from a middle-class family of Tripoli and joined the army. As a Captain in September 1969 he played an important part in taking over Tripoli and he was one of the first to be named as a member of the Revolution Command Council. He was placed in charge of Intelligence, sometimes holding office as Minister of the Interior, failing to organise during 1970 the kidnapping of Umar al-Shalhi but successfully frustrating attempted coups by Shalhi and by a member of the former ruling family in the Fezzan. In November 1972 he ceased to be a Minister but accompanied Qadafi on numerous visits abroad, including a prolonged stay in Cairo in a quest for unification and to Malta where agreements were signed for

technical co-operation and shipbuilding. In November 1974 he received the formal title of Minister of Foreign Affairs. At this time he was seen as a possible replacement for Qadafi but differing from him in giving more importance to Libyan national interests than to Pan-Arab idealism. In August 1975 another RCC member, Major Umar al-Muhayshi suddenly fled the country after having failed to mount a military coup. In the autumn, while the quarrel between Qadafi and Sadat was at its height, Huni was sent on a mission to Cairo and decided to remain. In November he announced that he would work for the Revolution in Cairo and was founding an opposition Libyan National Alliance. Qadafi tried to woo him back but when this failed, to kill him. In March 1976 a Libyan hit-squad seeking Huni and Muhayshi was arrested in Cairo and Huni failed to board an aircraft from Cairo to Rome which it had been intended to divert to Tripoli. In April 1982 he was named with the former Prime Minister Bakkush and Muhayshi as one of the leaders of a new Front for the Liberation of Libya. In January 1987 he was mentioned as the co-ordinator of eight opposition groups in Cairo. He later had a meeting with Qadafi in Algiers in July 1987 which caused a split in the opposition with some supporting his policy of negotiating with Qadafi while others led by Mansur Kikhia refused. After 1989, when Qadafi was reconciled with Mubarak, Huni's importance in Cairo waned. In December 1993 a Basic People's Congress sentenced him to death.

HUSSAIN IBN NASIR, Sharif (1906–)
Jordanian Prime Minister. He was born and brought up in the Hijaz but in 1925 he became an official at the Court of King Faysal I of Iraq. Subsequently his nephew King Ghazi used his house as a place of revelry. Sharif Hussain was unable to remonstrate but in 1935 managed to escape to a diplomatic post in Ankara. After Ghazi's death he returned as Deputy-Director of Protocol until 1946 when he went to Jerusalem as Iraqi Consul-General and also acted as Chargé in Amman. King Abd Allah invited him to stay and gave him his daughter in marriage. He spent most of the 1950s as Ambassador to Paris and Madrid before in November 1961 being appointed by King Hussain as Director of the Royal Cabinet. In March 1963 he was made Minister of the Royal Court. The following month during a crisis that followed a parliamentary vote of no confidence in Samir al-Rifai the King wanted a Prime Minister in whom he could have absolute trust, so he appointed Sharif Hussain who also took the Ministry of Defence and subsequently that of Foreign Affairs. He held office until July 1964 when the King wanted a more political figure and replaced him with Bahjat al-Talhuni. In March 1967 he was again appointed Prime Minister to preside over elections. When they had been completed he stepped down in favour of Saad Jumaa but continued as Minister of the Royal Court. Sharif Hussain was a man of no great ability but of undoubted loyalty to the King and the dynasty. His pastimes were bridge, stamp-collecting and tennis.

HUSSAIN, Kamal al-Din (1921–)
Egyptian Vice-President. He came from a land-owning family of Banha and graduated from the Military

Academy as a gunner in 1939. He was close to the Muslim Brothers and in 1947 resigned his commission to train their guerrillas with whom he saw action in the Palestine War. His report of the dying words of his commanding officer "Remember that the real struggle is in Egypt" had a profound affect on Nasser and on other Free Officers, of whose founding executive he was a member. He was a Major at Staff College at the time of the July Revolution, much of the detailed planning of which was done at his house. Although younger than the others, he was an influential member of the Revolutionary Command Council and in 1953 preached in numerous mosques that their policies were not incompatible with Islam. In January 1954 he was appointed Minister of Social Affairs with the task of bringing the Trade Unions to heel. As Commander of the National Guard he was responsible for bringing in crowds from the provinces to demonstrate for Nasser against Neguib. As Minister of Education he purged the Universities, dismissing over 40 Professors and numerous students for left-wing sympathies and was described as having the mentality of a sergeant-major. Hussain resisted the demand of the National Assembly that all who had completed secondary education should be allowed to proceed to higher education, was defeated and resigned but Nasser reinstated him and dissolved the Assembly. He forced through the modernisation of al-Azhar. In August 1956 he was put in charge of raising a National Liberation Army which included Women's and Youth groups for guerrilla activity in the event of a British and French invasion and during and after the Suez War harassed their troops. As early as 1959 he criticised Russian interference in Egyptian affairs. Later that year he oversaw the creation of the National Union as the sole political party. In July 1960 he was appointed Governor-General of the Southern Region of the United Arab Republic. In August 1961 he was appointed Vice-President and moved from Education to Local Government, setting up loyal district councils. In March 1964, with Abd al-Latif al-Baghdadi he resigned, criticising the growing dictatorship of Nasser, increasing socialism, involvement in the Yemen War and repression of the Muslim Brothers. In October 1965 he was imprisoned for attempting subversion in the army. After the June War Nasser invited Hussain back to organise guerrillas in the Canal area but would not accept his condition that detained Muslim Brothers should be freed and he continued under house arrest until 1971. On the accession of Sadat, Hussain was one of the surviving Free Officers who asked him to relax the more repressive features of the Nasser regime and later to restrain Russian influence. In October 1976 he was elected to the National Assembly but was expelled for attacking the repressive legislation that followed the Bread Riots of January 1977 as "legitimising injustice". Later he criticised the Camp David Agreement as cutting Egypt off from the rest of the Arabs. Hussain was a devout, hard-working man who always remained in touch with the people of his own district.

HUSSAIN, Taha (1889–1973)

Egyptian scholar and political thinker. He was born in a village in Upper Egypt and lost his sight at the age of three. At the age of 13 he went to al-Azhar where he remained for ten years. His account of his early life, *al-Ayyam* has been translated into twenty languages. He then took a doctorate at the Sorbonne and married a French lady. On his return in 1920 he was appointed Professor of History and Arabic at Cairo University. For the next thirty years he was probably the leading intellectual in the country. He applied the criteria of Western scholarship firstly to the ancient poetry of Arabia and then to the Qur'an itself, claiming that some texts could not be authentic. This provoked outrage and the book that he published on this in 1926 was denounced by Rashid Rida as "apostasy" and had to be withdrawn. He was also politically active in the "Jaridah Group" and in the Wafd and was dismissed from the Deanship of the University in 1932 by the government of Ismail Sidqi. In works in the 1930s he argued that Egypt was part of Mediterranean civilisation, having little in common with Arabs or Africans. He idealised ancient Greece and nineteenth century liberal Europe, which provided the example for Egypt to follow. Pan-Arabism he condemned as leading to religious fundamentalism and oriental despotism. During the war he spoke on the BBC Arabic Service and became the first Rector of Alexandria University. From 1945 to 1950 he wrote a series of books denouncing social injustice, exploitation and political corruption. In 1950 Nahhas Pasha made him Minister of Education and he tried to enforce old laws ensuring free and compulsory primary education and to make secondary and technical education freely available. After the Revolution he took no further part in politics.

al-HUSSAINI, Faysal (1940–)

Palestinian leader. He was born in Baghdad where his father Abd al-Qadr, a leading nationalist, and his cousin the Mufti, Haj Amin al-Hussaini had sought refuge after being expelled from Jerusalem by the British. His father was killed in the Palestine War and he was brought up in Cairo before receiving military training in Egypt and Syria. Hussaini returned to Jerusalem in 1964 as head of one of its most patrician families with a large clientele. After the Israeli occupation he became one of the most prominent nationalist leaders, organised a guerrilla camp in Lebanon and was arrested for storing weapons in 1968. Hussaini was always loyal to Yassir Arafat whom he had known since 1949. In 1980 he founded the Arab Study Centre in Jerusalem where he was regarded as the champion of any Arab in trouble. Although he was in prison, without trial, when in December 1987 the *Intifadah* started, the security authorities nonetheless regarded him as one of its leaders. He was briefly released in mid-1988 and drafted a declaration of independence which influenced that of the Palestine National Congress Algiers Meeting some months later. He dropped his early demands for driving the Jews out of Palestine and advocated a two-state solution through dialogue which, he believed, could be brought about by civil disobedience and the mobilisation of international support. He ended six months' detention in June 1988 but was again imprisoned from July until January 1989. By now he was regarded as the leading Palestinian "moderate" and held numerous meetings with members of the Knesset and others interested in peace. In October 1989 the Israeli army closed off parts of Jerusalem to prevent foreign correspondents reaching his press conference. He was again imprisoned in January 1990 for three days on the charge of giving $450 to activists to buy uniforms. In April 1990 Hussaini went to Moscow to object to mass exodus of Russian Jews and Zionist zealots said that he should not be allowed to return home. In June 1990 he toured the US with the daughter of Moshe Dayan, calling for American action to solve the Palestine problem. He was then banned from going abroad. In August 1990 he deplored the invasion of Kuwait by Saddam Hussain as distracting attention from Palestine and said that the Iraqis should withdraw. In October 1990 Hussaini was accused of planning the demonstration that led to the Temple Mount Massacre and was imprisoned for 16 days. When Secretary of State Baker undertook the series of visits to the area that was to lead to the Madrid Peace Conference of October 1991, he always saw Hussaini who was obviously the most important nationalist leader in the Occupied Territories and who was believed to have played a major role in persuading the Palestine Liberation Organisation to agree to the negotiations. He was unable to take part officially in the Washington Peace Talks owing to the refusal of Shamir to allow residents of East Jerusalem to participate but he was present as an "adviser" and was regarded as the real leader of the Palestinian delegation. In July 1992 he was allowed to reopen his Institute which had been closed for four years and in August he published in a Jewish newspaper an article calling for a confederation of Jordan, Israel and an independent Palestine. His moderation enraged the extremists and his life was threatened by Hamas. After Rabin replaced Shamir as Prime Minister Hussaini was in frequent contact with his Ministers and was allowed to lead the Palestinian delegation in Washington. In August 1993 he and two other leading members of the delegation to the Talks went to Tunis to resign in protest at the readiness of the PLO to bypass the delegation and shelve the question of Jerusalem in the quest for peace but he was assured of the confidence of the Organisation and persuaded to continue, recognised as one of its officials. He called for the formation of a "government of national salvation" of which it was generally assumed he would be leader. Hussaini is described as non charismatic, quiet, reasonable, unemotional, without bombast, a very likeable man unaffected, modest and humorous.

al-HUSSAINI, Haj (Muhammad) Amin
(c. 1895–1974)

Palestinian leader. He came from one of the three most distinguished families of Jerusalem, of which his father and grandfather had been Muftis. He himself studied at al-Azhar although he was not there long enough to qualify as a Mufti; he made the Pilgrimage at this time. During the First World War he was an officer in the Ottoman army and then, having been invalided home to Jerusalem, supported the Amir Faysal, working for the unification of Syria and Palestine and recruiting troops for the Arab army. He then served in the HQ of the British Military Governor of Jerusalem but in April 1920 he was sentenced to ten years' imprisonment for demonstrating against the pro-Zionist commitments of the Mandate. Hussaini fled to Trans-Jordan but four

months later was pardoned at the request of the notables. In May 1921, now regarded as pro-British, he was appointed after much lobbying to succeed his brother as Mufti of Jerusalem, partly because Raghib al-Nashashibi, head of a rival family had been made Mayor and the authorities did not wish to appear to favour one group. The following year he was appointed Chairman of the Supreme Muslim Council which gave him control of considerable funds and a patronage network throughout the country. A man of great energy and organising ability he exploited this to become both spiritual and political leader of the Palestinian Arabs, gradually undermining more moderate leaders such as his relative Musa Kazim al-Hussaini. Though taking care not to antagonise the local Christians he imparted a religious dimension to the struggle against Zionism, striving with building projects and propaganda to enhance the importance of the *Haram al-Sharif* to the Islamic world as a whole and he used the Wailing Wall Incident to emphasise that they were in danger. The Shaw Report exonerated him from any blame for the rioting but from then onwards Zionist supporters saw in him their main enemy and he was vilified in the press and Parliament. He organised the Jerusalem Islamic Congress of 1931 to discuss the threat and the possible foundation of an Islamic University in Jerusalem. He was elected Chairman of its permanent organisation and used the international standing that this conferred upon him in an attempt to mediate in the Saudi–Yemeni War of 1934. The Mufti worked hard to make the rulers of the independent Arab countries feel that they had to become involved in support of the Palestinians and also he had some relations with the Mussolini government in the early 1930s. As Jewish immigration increased after Hitler came to power, the Mufti formed the Arab Higher Committee to bring together all the political groupings in a united front. This did not, however, last long as the political and family hostility between him and the Nashashibis was too deep. He widened his Axis contacts to include the Germans in July 1936. He was unwilling to co-operate with the British, refusing to meet the Peel Commission until strong pressure was brought upon him by the rulers of the independent Arab states. As violence spread in the Arab Rebellion the Mandate authorities blamed the AHC and arrested the members that they could catch but did not touch the Mufti. Shortly afterwards he fled in a fishing boat and took refuge in Beirut. The British refused to permit him to return or to hold discussions with him although they did allow his kinsman and right-hand man Jamal al-Hussaini to speak for him at the London Palestine Conference of 1939. After the outbreak of war he went to Baghdad where he was soon mixing with anti-British elements such as Rashid Ali al-Gilani and the officers of the Golden Square. When the British overthrew Gilani, he and the Mufti and Fawzi al-Qawukji escaped to Iran where the British again failed to catch them. The Mufti hid in the Japanese Embassy then, helped by the Italians, fled across Turkey in disguise. He was received by Mussolini and later by Hitler who was convinced by Hussainis red beard and blue eyes that he had Aryan ancestry and promised to regard him as the principal Arab leader. The Mufti was then employed on propaganda and in trying to raise Arab and Muslim troops from the Balkans to fight on the Russian front. A plan to send him to North Africa was frustrated by Allied victories there. As the Third Reich collapsed he fled to Switzerland but was refused permission to stay. He crossed into France where he was kept in a villa near Paris but, learning that he might be tried as a war criminal, he escaped to Cairo on an American military aircraft and was welcomed as a guest by King Farouq. Although the British refused to allow him home he was once again recognised as the leader of the Palestinians, calling out for strikes, boycotts and violence. He intransigently refused all compromise or discussion of partition, insisting that the only possibility was a Palestinian Arab state under his own leadership. When the Gaza Government was established the Mufti was elected President of the Supreme Council. It is probable that he organised the assassination of his old enemy King Abd Allah, a deed that was carried out by one of his family. He often represented Palestine at gatherings such as the Bandung Conference. In later years Nasser determined to control the Palestinians himself and had little use for the ageing Mufti who ceased to have more than minor importance. He died in Beirut. He had an impressive bearing, great charm, an agile and extremely devious mind and an ability to impress most of the people that he met. However his controversial personality and policies and unwillingness to settle for anything other than complete victory did immeasurable harm to the Palestinian cause of which he felt that he alone was the embodiment.

al-HUSSAINI, Jamal (c. 1893–1982)

Palestinian politician. He was a member of a leading Jerusalem family and a relative of the Mufti Haj Amin al-Hussaini. He studied medicine at the American University of Beirut and although he did not graduate owing to the war, he was later employed in the Health Department of the Government of Palestine. He then worked as secretary for his uncle Musa Kazim al-Hussaini who until shortly before his death was generally regarded as the leader of the Palestinian Arabs, accompanying him on delegations abroad. He was also closely associated with the Mufti, serving as Secretary of the Supreme Muslim Council and playing an important part in the organisation of the Palestine Arab Party of which he became President. He was a member of the Arab Higher Committee and when it was banned by the British in September 1937 on the grounds that it had been organising terrorism in the Arab Rebellion, Hussaini avoided arrest by escaping to Arabia where he was taken into the service of Ibn Saud. Despite the warrant against him he was allowed to go to England

early in 1939 to lead the Arab delegation in the London Palestine Conference. Hussaini then went to Iraq where he was an active ally of Rashid Ali al-Gilani upon the collapse of whose regime he escaped to Iran. He was caught there by the British and exiled to Rhodesia where he remained until 1945. Hussaini was allowed back into Palestine in January 1946 and succeeded in reviving the AHC. Opponents of the Hussaini faction formed a rival body but in 1946 both were suppressed by the Arab League which formed a new Arab Higher Executive with Hussaini as Vice-Chairman. As the Chairman, the Mufti was not permitted into Palestine or to visit London, Hussaini acted as the leader of the Palestinian Arabs. He gave evidence at the Anglo-American Committee, and headed delegations to London and the UN. He tried also to organise the Palestinians for military action. Hussaini then became Foreign Minister in the short-lived Gaza Government but unlike many of his colleagues, never made his peace with the Hashemites. He subsequently settled in Saudi Arabia where he became an Adviser to the King. He took no further part in Palestinian affairs although he wrote political articles and novels.

al-HUSSAINI, Musa Kazim (c 1847–1934)

Palestinian leader. He was a member of one of the most prominent families of Jerusalem and the son of a mayor of the city. He was trained as an Ottoman official and held various posts such as *Mutasarrif* of Hauran and Governor of Jaffa. He was appointed Mayor of Jerusalem by the British in succession to his brother in 1918 but he was dismissed in April 1920 for leading an anti-Zionist demonstration in protest at the recognition of Hebrew as an official language: as Mayor it was his duty to represent all citizens impartially. In December 1920 he was elected President of the Palestine Arab Congress at the Haifa Convention which set up the Arab Executive with Hussaini as Chairman. The following year he headed a delegation to discuss the future of the country with the visiting Colonial Secretary Winston Churchill and another to London. He led other missions to London and on all these occasions, with the greatest charm and suavity, refused to make the slightest concession. He agreed, however, in 1929 to the proposal to form a Legislative Council. In 1931 he was prominent at the Jerusalem Islamic Congress. He was by this time a distinguished rather than an effective figure and the leadership of the Palestinian Arabs was passing into the more violent hands of his relative the Mufti, Haj Amin al-Hussaini or into those of his family rival Raghib al-Nashashibi. In October 1933 he was injured in a riot and he died the following March.

IBN BAZ Abd al-Aziz b. Abd Allah (1912–)

Saudi religious leader. Born in Riyadh becoming blind at the age of 16, he studied there with the leading ulema. From 1938 until 1953 he worked as a Qadi. He was then appointed Lecturer in *Shariah* at King Saud University and later Rector of the Islamic University in Medina. In 1966 he caused a sensation by issuing a *Fatwa* that it was blasphemous to state that the earth was not flat and that it revolved around the sun. This embarrassed King Faysal and Ibn Baz partially retracted. Generally he stressed that the ulema were the allies of the Government and were not Ayatollahs seeking an Islamic Republic. However, some of his former students were involved in the Mecca Mosque Seizure although he himself condemned the action. He advocated the education of girls so that they could teach the Qur'an to their children and perform medical services as mixed staffs in hospitals were improper. He declared that marriage was a duty and established a fund to enable poor Saudis to meet the bride price. In 1993 he warned against foreign travel as corrupting morals. As president of the Supreme Religious Council he had frequent and direct access to successive Kings and he was also a Minister and Grand Mufti. Ibn Baz was a leading member of many International bodies, preached regularly at the principal mosques in Mecca, Medina and Riyadh and wrote numerous books on religious topics.

IBRAHIM, Abd Allah (1918–)

Moroccan Prime Minister. A descendant of the Prophet, he was born in Marrakesh where he studied poetry and Arabic literature at the Ben Yusuf University. He was active in nationalist activities, was imprisoned and was an early member of the Istiqlal Party. He later went to the Sorbonne where he took a particular interest in Trade Union organisation. In 1949 he returned to run the Istiqlal newspaper and also acted as an adviser to the illegal Trade Union movement. He was again imprisoned between 1952 and 1954. On independence he joined the Bekkai government as Minister of Information and then of Labour where he strengthened the Union Marocaine des Travail by ordering that all union officials be Moroccans. As the Istiqlal started to split he sided with the younger left-wingers such as Ben Barka, refusing a post in the Balafrej government whose reactionary leadership he spent much of 1958 attacking throughout the country. In May he broke with the official Istiqlal and was later briefly detained. In December 1958 after Allal al-Fassi had refused to become Prime Minister Muhammad V

invited Ibrahim "in a personal capacity" and not as a leader of Istiqlal breakaways to form a government to prepare for the first communal elections. Ibrahim took the Foreign Ministry and gave other portfolios to left-wingers and technocrats but the King insisted upon keeping control over the army and the police. Ibrahim stressed the importance of removing the Moroccan economy from French domination and land was taken from the colons and developed as communes. He tried also to improve agriculture by better use of water resources and worked for industrial development, helped by his excellent relations with the unions. His government introduced social security with old age pensions and other measures and tried to increase the teaching in Arabic of scientific subjects. In foreign policy he wanted increased co-operation with Arab states and went to Washington to try to expedite the withdrawal of French troops and of American forces stationed in Nouaceur under NATO agreements. His opponents accused him of communist sympathies and it was not always clear to what extent he was his own man or whether he was acting as a front for radicals like Ben Barka and Ben Sadiq. He was expelled from the Istiqlal but did not join the Union Nationale des Forces Populaires upon its foundation in September 1959. Early in 1960 some rebels in the Riff declared that they were acting in his support and after an attempt on the life of the future King Hassan II in February, for which 11 UNFP members were arrested, the King thought that his Prime Minister was showing insufficient zeal in pursuing the plotters. He was also understood to have opposed a ban on the Moroccan Communist Party. Ibrahim then made a determined effort to win control of the police and the removal of French security officials. In May, just before the communal elections in which the King feared that the UNFP might gain embarrassing success, he dismissed Ibrahim, thanking him for accomplishing the task assigned to him, and himself assumed the Prime Ministership. Ibrahim later joined the UNFP and edited its newspaper. Ibrahim declared that the battle for democracy would be harder than that for independence and in May 1963 he denounced "absolute monarchy of the feudal type and egoistic bourgeois". From 1963 onwards he always called for boycotts of elections and referenda. After the disappearance of Ben Barka in 1965 Ibrahim was recognised as leader of the UNFP. In July 1970 he was a member of a National Front formed to oppose a referendum on a new constitution. In 1975 he was the only party leader to refuse to endorse the Moroccan claim to the Western Sahara, causing a split with his old ally Abd al-Rahim Bouabid which weakened the UNFP.

Small man with a slight stoop, preoccupied expression but ready smile, almost timid in manner, keen sense of humour, secretive.

IBRAHIM, Fatima Ahmad (1935–)

Sudanese communist and feminist leader. At the age of 17 she was one of the founders of the *Ittihad al-Nisa'i*, the Women's Union which was a front organisation for the Sudanese Communist Party and which in the early 1960s had a membership of 15,000. She edited its journal and became its President in 1956. She campaigned strongly against female circumcision and for equal rights for women, publishing books on the subject. She had to go underground during the military regime of General Abboud but was able to play a part in the demonstrations which brought him down. In 1965 Ibrahim became the first Sudanese woman to be elected to Parliament. She was prominent in the politics of SCP as she was an independent thinker and did not automatically follow the Moscow line. After the failure of the attempted coup of Babikr al-Nur in July 1971 President Nimeiri turned on the communists. Ibrahim's husband Shafai Ahmad al-Shaykh, a prominent member of the communist dominated World Federation of Trade Unions, was hanged and she herself was put under house arrest for two years. Despite official harassment she continued her activities until she was again imprisoned in 1976. In 1990 she was allowed to go abroad. She then became the first woman from the Third World to be elected President of the World Federation of Democratic Women.

IBRAHIM, Hassan (1917–90)

Egyptian Vice-President. He graduated from the Air Force Academy and was soon in touch with other discontented young officers such as Anwar Sadat. He was closely connected with Young Egypt. In 1942 he was disciplined after lending another pilot his aircraft to take photographs of British positions and a draft for Egyptian independence to Rommel. With Abd al-Latif al-Baghdadi he went to Damascus during the Palestine War in an attempt to persuade Syrians to provide air support for Palestine guerrillas. In 1949 Ibrahim was one of the Executive Committee of the Free Officers. He was a Wing Commander at the time of the July Revolution in which he helped to seize a major airbase. Ibrahim was a member of the Revolutionary Command Council and of the Tribunal which investigated corrupt politicians of the old regime. In 1954 he was one of the officers who arrested General Neguib and he was then made Minister for Presidential Affairs. In 1956 he was put in charge of the Economic Agency, dealing with development planning and of raising finance for the Aswan High Dam but he had little sympathy with socialism and proved ineffective. Ibrahim was then found sinecures in business before being brought back into government as a member of the Presidency Council and from February 1964 as one of seven Vice-Presidents. He. eloped with the wife of an Alexandrian doctor and was told by the puritanical Nasser that he had to renounce either the lady or his office; he chose to keep the former and resigned in January 1966,

returning to business. In May 1967 he warned Nasser that demanding the removal of UNEF would lead to war. Later he was a strong supporter of Sadat.

IBRAHIMI, Ahmad Talib (1932–)

Algerian Minister. Born in Setif he had a largely Muslim education before going to Paris where he qualified as a haematologist. He joined the nationalist student movement in France, published a journal and was imprisoned from 1957 until just before independence in 1962. Returning home he was again imprisoned, this time for opposition to Ben Bella. He was released after the take-over by Boumédienne and immediately made Minister of Education. His main task was to replace the Frenchmen who still predominated in Algerian schools and although in 1969 he spent a fortnight in the Soviet Union recruiting teachers, most of those that he brought in were from the Arab world. Subsequently some blamed the rise of Islamic militancy upon the changes that Ibrahimi brought about. In 1970 he headed a delegation to the States of the Peninsula to urge a united front against colonialism and Zionism. In July 1970 he was transferred to the Ministry of Information and Culture which he held for seven years, during part of which time he was also a member of the Executive Council of UNESCO. He argued for the retention of the French language and declared that "Algerian blood is Arab–Berber with Berber dominant". He had frequently accompanied Boumédienne on trips abroad, for example to the Far East in 1974, and in 1977 he was appointed Minister-Councillor to the President, a post he continued to hold under Chadli until 1982 when he became Foreign Minister. Ibrahimi was particularly concerned to build good relations with the West as a source of financial aid and a customer for hydrocarbons. He was active in mediating disputes, helping Qadafi to disengage from Chad and trying to end quarrels between factions in the Palestine Liberation Organisation and between the PLO and Hizbullah. He played a major part in persuading Chadli to reject as too risky Qadafi's proposal for a union of the two countries in 1987 and instead to work for a larger Arab Maghreb Union. The election of Algeria to the Security Council in October 1987 showed the respect in which its diplomacy was held. Ibrahimi left the Foreign Ministry in September 1989. Subsequently he was involved in trying to find an accommodation between the modern state and Islam which, he said, was a permanent revolution against exploitation. In September 1991 he called for the release of the imprisoned leaders of the Front Islamique du Salut and was seen as a possible President, able to bring reconciliation. His name was put forward after the assassination of Boudiaf and again in January 1994 but on both occasions, however, he preferred to remain in Paris. Ibrahimi, an elegant, courteous man, was a member of many learned societies, particularly those connected with Islam and the Arabic language.

IBRAHIMI, Lakhdar (1934–)

Algerian diplomat. He studied at the Institut des Sciences Politiques in Paris where he was active in student politics and he was an early member of the Front de Libération Nationale. During the Algerian

War of Independence he represented the FLN in South East Asia. After independence he was briefly General Secretary of the Ministry of External Affairs before being sent as Ambassador to Egypt where he became a close friend of Nasser. From 1971 until 1979 Ibrahimi was an extremely successful Ambassador in London, travelling widely to address academic and business groups. He was then a member of the Central Committee of the FLN until 1984 when he was appointed Assistant Secretary-General of the Arab League. He was particularly involved in trying to bring peace in the Lebanese Civil War, being one of the authors of the Ta'if Agreement and going to Beirut during the defiance of General Aoun. After the resignation of Chadli Klibi in September 1990 it was widely expected that Ibrahimi would succeed him as Secretary-General but the Egyptian Ismat Abd al-Majid was chosen. In June 1991 he was called home as Foreign Minister. One of his first tasks was to reassure the Americans that Algeria was not proposing to develop nuclear weapons. After the military take-over of January 1992 he went to the Gulf to explain the background and to seek financial aid. In February 1993 he was unexpectedly dismissed amidst reports that the Prime Minister Belaid Abd al-Salam wished to take more control of foreign affairs. Shortly afterwards Dr Butros-Ghali appointed him Special UN Representative in Zaire.

IDHEN MASSACRE (1978)

Ihden, a village in the mountains of Zghurtah, was the base of the Lebanese President Sulayman Franjiyah and there his son Tony raised and trained a militia. By the spring of 1978 the Maronites were deeply divided between those like Franjiyah who were allied with Syria and those like Pierre Gemayel and Camille Chamoun who were prepared to accept the support of Israel. In the early morning of 13 June Bashir Gemayel sent a force of 100 men led by Samir Geagea to attack Ihden where they killed Tony Franjiyah, his wife and baby daughter and 29 other people. In Lebanese politics, where alliances changed so frequently, it was unheard of to murder important leaders. The result of the massacre was that the Maronite side was irretrievably split as Sulayman Franjiyah co-operated with the Sunni Rashid Karami and the Druze Walid Jumblatt and the Syrians secured a firm foothold in the northern Maronite heartland.

IFNI CRISIS (1957–58)

In 1476 fishermen from the Canary Islands established a settlement on the Atlantic coast of Morocco which they named Santa Cruz de la Mar Pequena. After about fifty years it was overrun by the Moroccans and disappeared. After their defeat in the Tetuan Battle of 1859 the Moroccans signed the Gualdras Convention in which, amongst other provisions, it was stipulated that Santa Cruz de la Mar Pequena should revert to Spanish rule. There was, however, no agreement as to its location and for fifty years there were intermittent attempts to identify it. After the French secured their Protectorate in the Fez Treaty of 1912, they agreed with the Spanish that the site was Ifni where there was little except for the tomb of a *marabout*. Its borders were vaguely defined but finally it was agreed that it was an enclave approximately 40 miles long and 15 miles deep. The population was about 30,000, mostly Berbers of the Ait Ba Amran although there was also a small semi-nomadic tribe of Arabs, the Abuya. It was not until the French had completed the conquest of Southern Morocco by their victory at Jabal Sagho in 1934 that the Spanish could take possession of Ifni and eventually there was a European population of about 4,000. There was little economic activity and most of the native population sought employment in the French zone. After Morocco regained its independence in 1955 nationalist leaders such as Allal al-Fassi claimed that it should include Ifni, the Western Sahara and Mauritania and the Ba Amran declared their loyalty to Muhammad V. In November 1957 about 1,200 guerrillas of the Armée de Libération Nationale attacked Ifni and many of the locals rose to assist them. The Moroccan Government disclaimed responsibility and the Spanish increased their garrison of 2,000 to over 10,000 with air and naval support. Arab countries backed Morocco. Fighting lasted for some months with the frontier post of Tiliounine under siege for over a fortnight. The Spanish admitted 61 killed and claimed to have inflicted hundreds of Moroccan casualties, 60 in one day. Local resistance groups spread the fighting into the Western Sahara including an attack on the capital Al-Ayun. The French who still controlled Mauritania sent 5,000 troops to join the Spanish and there were allegations that poison gas was used. In April 1958 the Moroccan regular army moved South after a Spanish threat of a reprisal attack on Agadir. Fighting died down and the Spanish agreed to evacuate the Cape Juby area. In December 1965 the UN called for negotiations over the future of Ifni and the following year called for its transfer to Morocco. In January 1969 an agreement was signed by which the Spanish evacuated Ifni in August.

IFRANE MEETING (1986)

Hassan II, particularly after becoming Chairman of the Arab League, considered that he had a special responsibility for finding a solution to the Palestinian problem. He had already had several secret meetings with Israeli leaders, with Defence Minister Moshe Dayan in 1975, with Prime Minister Yitzhak Rabin in 1976, with Opposition leader Shimon Peres in 1979 and 1981 and in France in 1984. In May 1984 a session of the regular Congress of the Moroccan Jewish community was attended by the Crown Prince and some Ministers while a delegation of eight Members of the Knesset who had been invited was welcomed by the Interior Minister. The King personally received the President of the World Jewish Congress Edgar Bronfman. In October 1985 when Peres was Prime Minister, leading an uneasy coalition with the hard-line Likud Party, Hassan ruled out "all direct contact" with him but in December said that he would invite him "with great pleasure" if he brought specific proposals to discuss. On 22 and 23 July 1986 the two men met at the King's holiday retreat of Ifrane in the cedar forests on the slopes of the Middle Atlas. The communiqué said that the frank talks, which had lasted only three hours, centring on the Plan produced at the Fez Summit of 1982, had been "purely exploratory" and there had been no negotiations. The King urged a full-scale peace conference including the Palestine Liberation Organisation and the Russians but Peres was only prepared to talk to residents of the Occupied Territories who had renounced violence. Hassan claimed that he had been expecting realistic proposals, breaking off talks when none were forthcoming, and that the meeting had shown that while the attitude of the Arabs towards peace had been positive, that of the Israelis had been negative. Reactions to the first overt meeting, since those of Sadat, of an Arab Head of State and an Israeli Prime Minister, were mixed. President Mubarak was delighted and the Gulf rulers abstained from comment but Syria denounced "black treason" while Qadafi, still hoping to salvage something from the Union established by the Oudjda Declaration, called the King brother and traitor in the same breath. Hassan seized the opportunity to renounce the Declaration, thus improving relations with Washington and he also resigned as Chairman of the Arab League. Moscow condemned the meeting as "US-inspired".

INSHASS DECLARATION (1946)
In May 1946 following the publication of the Report of the Anglo-American Committee of Inquiry on Palestine a meeting was held at Inshass, a country palace belonging to King Farouq. Others attending were Amir Abd Allah, Crown Prince Saud, Regent Abd al-Illah of Iraq, Crown Prince Ahmad of Yemen and Presidents Shukri al-Quwatli and Bishara al-Khoury. Originally it had been intended that they should discuss co-ordinating activities against Communism but Palestine became the principal topic. They issued a Declaration that Palestine was a problem that concerned not merely the Palestinian Arabs but all Arabs. Palestine being an Arab country it was the duty of all Arab countries to see that this position was maintained. They opposed Jewish immigration as a violation of the MacDonald White Paper of 1939. They hoped that their friendly relations with the Western Allies would not be damaged by actions harmful to the Palestinians.

INTEGRATION CHARTER (Egypt–Sudan) (1982)
Al-Mithaq al-Takamul. In November 1970 Egypt, Sudan and Libya agreed to form the Federation of Arab Republics which was later joined by Syria. Bad relations, however, between Colonels Qadafi and Nimeiri meant that Sudan's participation never became effective. By 1974 the relations between Sadat and Qadafi were even worse so in February he and Nimeiri agreed in Cairo on moves towards political and economic integration "away from emotionalism and impulsive actions". A Higher Ministerial Committee was to meet twice a year to discuss specific joint projects and a Higher Political Committee, meeting every three months, would co-ordinate actions between the Arab Socialist Union and the Sudan Socialist Union. A Joint Technical Committee would plan specific agricultural projects, form joint companies for navigation and fisheries on the Nile and eliminate difficulties to free trade and movement. The Presidents would meet at least once a year. In July 1976, after an insurrection in Khartoum organised by Libya and the National Front had failed, they signed a defence agreement establishing a

Joint Defence Council and a Joint Staff; later there were combined manoeuvres and guarantees of mutual support against aggression. In the following years there was considerable co-operation, Sudan opposed the ostracism of Egypt after Camp David and there were joint parliamentary sessions in Cairo in 1977 and Khartoum in 1979. The hostility to both countries shown by Qadafi ensured that the relationship survived the murder of Sadat and in July 1982 an Office for Integration Affairs was established under the direct supervision of Nimeiri who said that the process could only be stopped "when the Nile ceased to flow". In October Mubarak signed in Khartoum the Integration Charter of 41 articles which provided for the integration of the two countries' policies in the political, economic, military, social and cultural fields within ten years. A Supreme Council headed by the two Presidents was to supervise the process; the Secretary-General would be Sudanese. An independent Integration Fund, headed by an Egyptian, with a capital of $500 million was to finance joint development projects. There was also to be a Nile Valley Parliament of 60 members from each country which would meet twice a year to make recommendations to the Supreme Council. The Charter would strengthen popular ties, assure equal treatment for citizens of both countries and integrate the legal framework. The integration would be based on Islamic, Arab and African values but from the beginning it was opposed by the non-Muslim Southern Sudanese and by political leaders such as Sadiq al-Mahdi and Yusuf al-Hindi who saw it as extending American influence. The Parliament was inaugurated in Khartoum in May 1983 but never reassembled. After the overthrow of Nimeiri in April 1985 the new leader General Siwar al-Dhahab pledged continuation of the process of integration but in March 1986 his government formally abolished the organisations set up under the Charter. Later Sadiq al-Mahdi as Prime Minister moved closer towards Libya but in February 1987 he and the Egyptian Prime Minister Atif Sidqi signed a Brotherhood Charter which appeared to replace the concept of integration by one of mutual co-operation. After General Umar Hassan al-Bashir took power, relations between Sudan and Egypt were extremely bad and there was no question of integration.

INTIFADAH
The Gaza Strip, as a result of economic exploitation and repressive rule, was seething with discontent when on 8 December 1987 a Jewish-driven truck crashed into two vans carrying Arab workers, killing four of them and wounding six. A rumour spread that this was no accident but deliberate murder and a demonstration began outside a refugee camp upon which the army fired, killing three. This set off spontaneous rioting which grew into an uprising which spread to the West Bank. Both Arab and Jewish leaders were taken by surprise and there was never any suggestion that the *Intifadah* had been planned but it was fuelled by the brutality of the Israeli reaction. There were almost daily incidents with unarmed demonstrators being repressed by the security forces who killed an average of at least one Palestinian a day: before the end of December 21 had been killed, 179 wounded and over 1,000 arrested.

194

On 22 December the Security Council passed a Resolution "strongly deploring" Israeli actions and early in 1988 another condemned the Israeli policy of deporting suspects without any judicial process: these were the first for six years critical of Israel that had not been vetoed by the Americans. After six months UN officials calculated that 202 Palestinians had been killed and 10,000 injured. Many stone-throwers, who could receive up to a year's imprisonment or have their houses demolished, were children, of whom 160 under the age of 16 were killed and thousands injured by gassing or beating in the first two years of the uprising. Over 300 Palestinian houses were blown up in three years and their owners deported. In January 1988 the first leaflet bearing the name of the Unified National Command of the Uprising appeared, calling for a general strike which was widely observed: during the following two years some 50 further "Calls" were issued demanding such actions as refusing to pay taxes or the resignation of those employed by the authorities. The Israeli Defence Minister Itzhak Rabin ordered a policy of harsh beatings of suspects, "force, power and blows", saying that this would be more "humane" than shooting. There were, however, cases of Arabs being buried alive or having their bones deliberately broken by the dropping of heavy weights. The fact that many of the atrocities were televised caused disquiet in Israel. The Israeli army, reduced from defending its country against foreign enemies to distasteful police duties, was particularly unhappy and in the first six months 25 soldiers were sentenced for refusing to serve in the Occupied Territories. In the first fifteen months 700 cases of "excessive force" were reported but very few soldiers were punished and one who beat a man to death was sentenced only to 18 months' imprisonment. Vigilante squads of Zionist fanatics often acted unchecked. For the first time since 1948 Israeli Arabs showed concern over what was happening in the Occupied Territories and an unprecedented general strike on 21 December 1987 was completely observed. Until his murder by the Israelis in April 1988 the Palestine Liberation Organisation leader Abu Jihad seemed to exercise some control over the *Intifadah* but after that the UNCU appeared to organise events with a minimum of outside intervention. This was the first time that "insiders" rather than exiles had called the tune in Palestinian affairs. The legitimacy of the UNCU was shown by the fact that its orders were obeyed and the fundamentalist groups Hamas and Islamic Jihad competed with the PLO for its leadership. King Hussain in his Separation Statement of July formally severed administrative and legal links with the Occupied Territories and stopped paying salaries of officials there. In February 1989 Rabin put the number of Palestinian dead at 360 but other estimates suggested 500. In May 1989 the Hamas chief Shaykh Ahmad Yassin, suspected by some Israelis of being not merely the spiritual but the organisational leader of the Intifadah was arrested. Also in May 1989 400 Israeli Professors petitioned that the Arab schools and universities which had been closed for 18 months be reopened and this started gradually from July. During 1989 the repression became harsher, 20 were killed in Gaza in May, and the number of children under 5 years of age being beaten increased

by 100% while there was an increase of 1,400% in children under 10 with bullet wounds. The average age of children shot dead was 12. Torture, although officially denied, was routine. At any one time perhaps 5,000 Arabs were being held in detention. Youths were killed after being forced to climb electric pylons to remove Palestinian flags. When an Israeli soldier was killed, houses within a hundred metre radius might be destroyed and the Israeli Human Rights organisation Bet Selem said that at least 430 had been demolished by January 1990. An incident in July 1989 when an Arab from Gaza seized the steering wheel of a bus travelling from Tel Aviv to Jerusalem, causing it to crash into a ravine killing 16, caused particular horror. In February 1990 Ariel Sharon resigned from the Israeli Cabinet which he felt was too lenient with the Palestinians but in the same month the hundredth Israeli soldier, a major, was sentenced for refusing to take part in the repression. In June 1990 an Israeli soldier threw a tear-gas grenade into a UN maternity centre, injuring 60 children. The feeling grew that despite the claims of Prime Minister Shamir the *Intifadah* could not be repressed by force alone as savagery merely strengthened nationalist fervour and worldwide sympathy for the Palestinians. The Syrians were compelled to prevent their surrogate Amal militia from attacking refugee camps in Lebanon and Yassir Arafat was treated with a new respect by Arab leaders. It became clear that mere physical integration of Gaza and the West Bank into the Israeli infrastructure would not create an irreversible fact. In May 1990 the Americans blocked an otherwise unanimous Security Council decision to send a delegation to investigate alleged Israeli atrocities. In June 1990 the new Israeli Defence Minister Moshe Arens changed strategy by withdrawing troops from villages, using instead undercover agents. This led to a great decrease in violence with only one Palestinian killed in August after an average of twenty a month. The constant strikes seemed to do little harm to the Israelis but bankrupted Arab shopkeepers. Some felt that the *Intifadah* was over but the situation was changed by the invasion of Kuwait by Saddam Hussain which was received with enthusiasm in the Occupied Territories. The West, and in particular the Americans, lost interest in Israeli violations of Human Rights and its support for Iraq cost the PLO the financial backing of the Gulf States which went instead to Hamas which was able to subsidise the families of its "martyrs". In October, after the Temple Mount Massacre, some external leaders such as George Habash urged that the insurgents should adopt firearms but it was generally felt that more was to be gained by maintaining the image of stone-throwing children confronting soldiers bristling with weapons. In December the Israelis who had deported 60 Palestinians in the first months of the uprising before, under American pressure, desisting in April 1990 resumed the practice, extending it later to women and children despite a promise to the Supreme Court not to do so without permission. In January 1991 as Operation Desert Storm began a curfew was imposed on the Occupied Territories. From the beginning there had been lynchings of suspected collaborators and this increased until the *Intifadah* appeared to be degenerating into gang warfare between Arabs. In May 1991 8

Palestinians were killed by the Israeli army but 28 were killed by other Palestinians. An Amnesty International report of July 1991 stated that more than 30,000 people, some charged only with non-violent expressions of political opinions, had been tried since December 1987 and convicts were kept in harsh conditions in Ktziot detention camp in the Negev; many were convicted after torture or on the testimony of informants planted in the jails. In December 1991, on the fourth anniversary of the *Intifadah* official Israeli army figures stated that 723 Arabs had been killed by the security forces and 506 by other Arabs while Bet Selem estimated that of the Arabs killed by the army, 168 had been children under 16; it added that a further 41 Arabs had been killed by settlers and put Israeli deaths at 12 soldiers and 14 civilians. The Israeli Chief Military Prosecutor reported that 75,000 Palestinians had been arrested since 1987, 45,000 prosecuted and 4,000 were in detention. In January 1992 a Security Council Resolution, number 726, unanimously condemned Israeli deportations in the middle of the Washington Peace Talks. The breakdown in the Talks in March 1992 gave a new impetus, led by Hamas and the Democratic Front for the Liberation of Palestine, to the Uprising and statistics published in December showed that an additional 250 Arabs had been killed by the security forces and vigilantes, over 150 Arabs by other Arabs while the Israeli total had risen to 109 including 21 soldiers. The number in prison had risen over 6,300. The deportation of over 400 alleged members of Hamas to Marj al-Zuhur further intensified the violence and the repression: in six weeks up to the end of January 1993 182 children were treated in UN and other hospitals for gunshot wounds. This showed that children as young as eight had become politicised and, often ignoring the instructions of their parents to keep out of trouble, preferred to follow street leaders. Soldiers had orders not to fire at children unless their own lives were at risk but Bet Selem investigated 38 cases in which these were ignored, including that of an 18-month-old boy. Allegations of torture became more frequent, complaints from the Red Cross and a UN investigative committee were brushed aside, but in June the Israeli Medical Association instructed its members not to sign certificates that prisoners were fit for torture and the left-wing Meretz Party introduced a bill to outlaw the practice. Upon signature of the Israel–PLO Agreement in September 1993 Arafat ordered the "Hawks", an offshoot of Fatah, to cease-fire: the Israelis stated that the "Hawks" had been responsible for half the attacks carried out on their forces. Hamas continued some sporadic violence, including assassinations of Fatah members. The euphoria of 1988 that the world would help an unarmed struggle for justice had changed into despair in 1990– as the Israelis refused to negotiate, the nationalist movement split and poverty broke spirits but, as Hannan Ashrawi said, the *Intifadah* had given the Palestinians a new faith in themselves and had contributed to peace as had the disgust of many Israelis at the role that they had had to play; nearly 200 soldiers had been sentenced for refusing service in the Occupied Territories. The final estimates were that 1,120 Palestinians, 232 of them under 16, and 143 Israelis had been killed in 5 years.

IRAN–IRAQ WAR

Saddam Hussain was worried that the Revolution of the Ayatollah Khomeini might affect the Shiah majority of the Arabs of Iraq but thought that the Iranian Government and armed forces were on the verge of collapse: President Bani-Sadr was having difficulty in holding off Muslim extremists and after arrests and purges the army had declined from 200,000 to 110,000 while the American embargo on military spare parts meant that only 30% of the aircraft and tanks were serviceable. Iraq had a larger and much better equipped army and, exporting 3 million barrels of oil a day, could well afford a brief war. It seemed an ideal opportunity to assert himself as the leader of the Arabs against the historic enemy Persia and to reverse the Algiers Pact of 1975 in which he had ceded Iraqi claims in the Shatt al-Arab in return for the Shah's ending support for the Kurdish Revolt (II). A propaganda war started in April 1980 and diplomatic relations were broken off on 26 June. About 200,000 Shiah were expelled from Iraq, usually for no stated reason. Some real or fabricated frontier incidents provided a pretext and on 22 September 1980 the Iraqis bombed Iranian airfields, hoping to catch their planes on the ground, and also launched a three-pronged invasion of Khuzistan. It was immediately successful in overrunning some 10,000 km capturing the port of Khorramshahr and surrounding the oil refinery at Abadan. There the *Blitzkrieg* was halted, partly due to the inefficiency of the Iraqi General Staff which had dispersed its efforts and managed to get only 3 out of its 12 divisions in action at any one time. Its navy and air force fought their own separate unco-ordinated wars. On September 24 Hussain offered peace if Iran agreed to evacuate Abu Musa and the Tumbs, and give autonomy to its Kurdish, Arab and Baluch minorities but from the first Khomeini was adamant that the war would continue until the overthrow of the Iraqi regime and the public trial of Hussain. Despite the Russo-Iraqi Treaty Moscow deplored what *Pravda* called "a destructive military adventure" as it had no wish to see a fragmented Iran on its frontier or the Americans exploiting an opportunity to intervene: it therefore assured Tehran that it would not make trouble in the North so that Iranian troops could be concentrated in Khuzistan and it stopped all military supplies to Iraq. The Russians sent advisers to Iran and provided rail facilities for its exports and imports. On 28 September the first of the Iran–Iraq War, Security Council Resolutions Number 479 called upon the participants to "refrain from any further use of force" but it did not demand the withdrawal of Iraqi troops from occupied territory thus alienating Tehran which thenceforward never saw the UN as impartial. The UN Secretary-General Kurt Waldheim chose the former Swedish Prime Minister Olof Palme as a mediator and he made five trips to the area. On 5 October Hussain declared a cease-fire which gave the Iranians time to regroup. The war split the Arabs with Syria, which in April 1982 broke off diplomatic relations with Iraq and ended the transmission of Iraqi oil through the pipeline, and Libya supporting Iran while Jordan, which sent a Brigade, and the Gulf States which, provided vast sums of money after it could no longer export its own oil, supported Iraq.

Later 15,000 Egyptian and some North Yemeni volunteers fought on the Iraqi side. The Gulf States, however, seized the opportunity presented by Baghdad's preoccupation with the war to establish the Gulf Co-Operation Council without it in May 1981. In October 1981 Iranian bombing of oil installations in Kuwait added to the alarm in the Gulf. The Iraqi army was neither trained nor equipped for a prolonged occupation of hostile territory, for, contrary to some expectations, the Arabic-speaking population of Khuzistan had not welcomed them just as the majority of the Iraqi Shiah had remained loyal to their own government rather than rallied to their co-religionists. At the end of September 1981 the Iranians relieved Abadan and thenceforward they held the military initiative and when fighting resumed after the winter they launched a series of offensives. In May 1982 Khorramshahr was recaptured with 12,000 Iraqi prisoners and in June, stating that his forces were being regrouped to confront Israel which had just invaded Lebanon, Hussain withdrew them all from Iranian territory. In the same month he lost much prestige by announcing that since it had been bombed, Baghdad could no longer act as host for the Non-Aligned Summit. Iraq made frequent offers of cease-fires for religious occasions and of peace, offering to accept the Algiers Pact and practically anything else demanded except the removal of the Baath from power but the Iranians rejected them all, demanding $150 billion in reparations and when this sum was offered by the Fez Summit, refused, saying Iraq alone must pay. They declared that they would liberate Jerusalem after passing through Baghdad. Casualties on both sides were enormous, an estimated 175,000 after the first three years, but Iran with three times the population was bound to win a war of attrition. The Iranians advanced in "Human Waves" consisting mainly of *Baseej*, partially trained and part-time volunteers, and *Pasdaran*, the Revolutionary Guards controlled by the Mullahs while the improving regular army fought a more conventional war. The Ayatollah "as a special favour" permitted 12-year-old boys eligibility for martyrdom by sending them to the front after a week's training and 5,000 Iranian teenagers were killed clearing a minefield ahead of the advance after animals originally tried for the task had stampeded. Basra was under threat but protected by the creation of an artificial lake. The war was then costing each side about $1 billion a month. In the winter of 1982–83 Russia, angered by Iranian support for Afghan *mujahidin* and by a purge of local communists, resumed arms supplies to Iraq. Iran, exporting more oil than it had done under the Shah, had no difficulty in buying weapons, particularly from South Africa, Israel, Libya and North Korea. During 1983 as the Iraqi air force grew stronger, the Iranian became weaker so the Iraqis, knowing they could not win on land, initiated the War of the Tankers to prevent the export of Iranian oil: Iranian reprisals brought Western warships into the Gulf. Iraq had to earn American support by moderating its line on Palestine. Fighting spread to the Kurdish areas with each side arming the other's dissidents. In March 1984 Iran announced the "final offensive" by 500,000 men but after capturing the Majnun oilfields was halted by the use of poison gas and there was little movement for a

year amidst scenes reminiscent of the First World War. The similarity was intensified by the Iraqi use of poison gas which was condemned by the United Nations.

In March 1985 Iran advanced through the Marshes and cut the Baghdad–Basra road but could not hold the positions as their mass formations were ideal targets for helicopter gunships and they reportedly lost 20,000 killed. The Iranian strategy of concentrating so much of its effort in the southern sector was ill-advised. Again there was stalemate on land but action at sea and the intensification of pro-Iranian terrorism in Lebanon by groups such as Hizbullah which took Western hostages. In February 1986 the Iranians won a major success in the capture of the 160 square miles of the Fao Peninsula which enabled them to threaten Basra from the south and caused great alarm in Kuwait where the gunfire could be heard. The Iraqis replied by stepping up the War of the Cities hoping that indiscriminate attacks on civilian targets would cause revolt amongst the Iranian people who continued loyal to Khomeini's dictum "compromise is eternal ruin". In May 1986 the Iraqis carried out their first offensive since the beginning of the war, recapturing Mehran from which they were expelled three months later. During 1986 the fall in oil prices cut Iran's ability to buy weapons and to a loss of morale. A major offensive directed by the Assembly Speaker Rafsanjani, who appeared to be in supreme command of the Iranian forces, was heavily defeated with severe losses in December and further offensives failed in March and April 1987. By this time it was calculated that 250,000 Iranians and 105,000 Iraqis had been killed. In July 1987 the Super-Powers certain that Iraq could never hope to win, threatened after Security Council Resolution 598, to apply sanctions against the combatant which refused a cease-fire. The obstinacy of the Ayatollah, however, kept the war going long after it became clear that the bloodshed was achieving nothing and that Iran could not win by numbers and ardour alone. In a final battle at Majnun in June 1988 the Iraqis deployed 2,000 tanks against 60. Rafsanjani and the Ayatollah's son Ahmad convinced the old man to "drink poison" and agree to a cease-fire on 17 July. The Iranian National Liberation Army, based in Baghdad made a brief and futile attempt to establish itself on Iranian territory before the arrival of the UN force UNIIMOG on 10 August. The Ayatollah had called the invasion "God's Mercy" and it certainly enabled Iran to postpone tackling numerous political and development problems that had arisen as a result of its Revolution: emotion was concentrated on the "Martyrs' Cemetery" where the fountains ran red. Saddam Hussain by skilful propaganda and good care of the families of the killed was able to present himself as the embodiment of Iraq, repeatedly evoking Qadissiyah, the battle in 633 in which the Arabs had overthrown the Persians and at the end the Iraqis saw themselves as victors, ready to assume leadership of the Arab world. The war gave legitimacy to both regimes, uniting both nations: the Shiah were much more integrated into Iraq than ever before. Nothing came of the Iranian hope of establishing a shadow Iraqi Government of dissident officers on occupied territory although some particularly successful Iraqi generals met their deaths in suspicious circumstances. It was astonishing that a war in such a sensitive area did not spread, apart from attack on Kuwait and "accidental" Iraqi attacks on the Abu Dhabi oil installation. Although Iran and Iraq had exported one-sixth of the OPEC oil total in 1979 prices did not rise and Western interests suffered little damage. The strategic importance of the Straits of Hormuz declined because of the construction of pipelines across Saudi Arabia. The War brought Egypt back into the Arab fold after the ostracism that had followed Camp David. Human casualties were put at 500,000 and the longest conventional war in the twentieth century was immensely expensive. It was estimated that in the first three years Iraq spent $17.6 billion on arms whereas Iran spent $5.4 billion. Iraq ended the war about $80 billion in debt while Iran was believed to have lost $600 billion in revenue and its reconstruction costs were put at between $700 billion and $1,500 billion.

IRAN-IRAQ WAR, Security Council Resolutions
Iraq, confident of the success of its *Blitzkrieg* managed to hold up a meeting of the Security Council after its attack on Iran but Resolution 479 of 28 September 1980 was issued less than a week after the start of the fighting. Sponsored by Mexico it called upon both parties to "refrain from any further use of force", avoiding the term cease-fire. Other states were asked "to refrain from any act which may lead to a widening of the conflict" and the Secretary-General to attempt to resolve the dispute. Although Iraqi troops were on Iranian soil it did not demand their withdrawal, thus convincing the Iranians that the UN was prejudiced against them. After Iraqi troops had been driven from Iran and the Iranians had entered Iraq, Jordan sponsored Resolution 514 of 12 July 1982. This Resolution did call for the withdrawal to the recognised frontiers and for the dispatch of UN observers. Iran took no part in the proceedings. By the autumn of 1982 Iraq was desperate for peace at any price except for the stepping down of Saddam Hussain and the Baath regime. In October Resolution 522 repeated the call for a cease-fire and expressed gratification that one combatant was prepared to accept it although it contained implicit censure of Iraq's actions in the War of the Cities. Resolution 540 of 31 October 1983 showed a move towards the Iranian demand that Iraq should be condemned for aggression by calling for an "objective examination of the causes of the war". Resolution 552 of 1 June 1984 was sponsored by the Gulf States and issued at a time of increasing civilian casualties due to the War of the Tankers as well as the War of the Cities. It condemned these attacks and called for free navigation to and from states that were not party to the hostilities, specifying Kuwait and Saudi Arabia. As these countries were making large financial contributions towards the Iraqi war effort, Iran saw the Resolution as one sided.

Resolution 582 of 24 February 1986 made a gesture towards the Ayatollah by deploring "the initial aggression". It also deplored recent escalation, the bombing of civilians, attacks on neutral shipping and the use of chemical weapons. On 21 March 1986 Iraq was censured by the Security Council for use of poison gas. The Iranians achieved successes in the first part of 1986, winning the battles of Fao and Mehran. Resolution 588 of 8 October 1986 called for an immediate cease-fire and withdrawal of all troops to the internationally recognised frontier. It urged the Secretary-General Perez de Cuellar to intensify his efforts at mediation and to send a representative to the area. Iran rejected the Resolution as not condemning Iraqi aggression. In the summer of 1987 the five Permanent Members of the Security Council agreed to impose an arms embargo on the state which refused a cease-fire. Resolution 598 of 20 July 1987 demanded an immediate cease-fire and the dispatch of observers to monitor it. This Resolution was at once accepted by Iraq and implicitly by Iran a year later thus bringing an end to the war. It was clear throughout the war that neither side saw the United Nations as doing more than provide a platform for attacks on its opponent and for enlisting support.

IRAQ COMMUNIST PARTY
The first communist group in Iraq was probably founded in Basra in 1927 by a Comintern agent with others slightly later in Nasiriyyah and Baghdad. Several of the members, including their eventual leader "Fahd" were Christians and the majority had at least secondary education at a time when there were few industrial workers. The various groups united in 1935 and put out an illegal newspaper which incensed the authorities and numerous arrests crippled the Party. Some activities continued and although General Bakr Sidqi threatened to crush them they replied by leading a series of strikes. The Party was led by a journalist Zaki Khairi until he was imprisoned in November 1937. Soon afterwards "Fahd" returned after instruction in Moscow and Comintern activities in Western Europe and took charge of building an effective network of well-trained cells. The Party backed Rashid Ali al-Gilani but after the German invasion of Russia supported the Allies. There were splits in the leadership but in May 1943 many dissidents were arrested although "Fahd" managed to escape and consolidate his grip and drew up the National Charter of the Party in March 1944 which called for justice for the poor rather than revolution. The Party probably never exceeded a few hundreds and was often plagued by factionalism and actual treachery amongst its leaders. In January 1947 the leaders were rounded up by Nuri al-Said and charged with receiving money from foreign states and organisations, subversion and propaganda in the armed forces and they received long prison sentences. A considerable proportion were Jews. "Fahd" continued to direct Party policy from inside jail until he was hanged in February 1949. The Party began to revive under the leadership of a Kurdish student Baha al-Din Nuri, managed to capitalise on the grievances of students and workers, establish a front organisation, the Partisans of Peace, and even spark off such a large-scale demonstration in November 1952 that martial law was declared. A new Charter in December caused a large number of defections of "right devationists" who set up a rival faction. In April 1953 Nuri was caught by the police and the leadership passed to a Kurdish schoolmaster Abd al-Krim Ahmad al-Daud who was ineffective both as a theorist and an organiser and

was replaced when Hamid Uthman, a Kurdish petition-writer who had been imprisoned since 1949, escaped and took charge in June 1954. Uthman was a hot-headed Maoist and hoped to prevent the creation of the Baghdad Pact by street violence: he failed and after exactly a year was replaced by Hussain Ahmad al-Radi, a Shiah schoolmaster from Najaf. He managed to unify the various factions and formed a partnership with Amr Abd Allah, a Sunni lawyer of *sayyid* descent, and Jamal al-Haidari, a Kurdish professional revolutionary who were still leading the IPC at the time of the July Revolution of 1958 in which the IPC claimed, with little justification, to have played a significant part. When Abd al-Krim Qassim formed his first Cabinet no member of the Party was included although Dr Ibrahim Kubbah, a former Professor who became Minister of Economic Affairs, was believed to be a close associate. All Party members were quickly released from prison and soon the IPC was obviously the most effective political organisation in the country with supporters in key posts in the Government, army, University, Trade Unions, the press etc. and controlling strong front organisations. Qassim came under intense pressure from pan-Arabist officers to declare for immediate union with Egypt – a policy opposed by the IPC because President Nasser was persecuting Egyptian communists and their Shiah and Kurdish members had no wish to see the submersion of Iraq, in which they had hopes of power, in a larger Arab unity: their powerful militia engaged in frequent street clashes with nationalists. They approved, also, of Qassim's agrarian and social reforms and provided his principal support during the Mosul Uprising of March 1959. The following month the communists demanded Cabinet seats and Qassim, feeling that they were over-reaching themselves, refused but promoted some of their sympathisers. In July 1959 the Kirkuk Killings discredited the Party and although there was no indication that its national leaders had been involved it never fully recovered. Despite all these activities the Party, like all others had remained technically illegal but in January 1960 Qassim's Law of Associations permitted their registration. The Central Committee headed by Zaki Khairi and Hussain al-Radi applied and so did a small group headed by Daud al-Sayigh, a Christian lawyer from Baghdad: the latter was licensed and the main group, having refused to change its title, was not. The Sayigh party soon disappeared but the old IPC had been greatly weakened, its membership declined from an estimated 20 to 25,000 maximum in 1959 to about 10,000 by 1963, and it lost its grip on the Unions and became isolated without either a voice in the Government or in the clandestine opposition that was gathering around the Baath and other nationalists. After the Ramadan Revolution the Baathists took a ferocious revenge on the communists, al-Radi was hanged and hundreds were slaughtered while others fled abroad. After the November Revolution although officially still banned its situation improved and it cautiously resumed operations. In 1967 there was a major split and a militant pro-Chinese group, the Central Command led by Aziz al-Hajj, started guerrilla activities and held out for two years until captured in the spring of 1969. After the Baath take-over of July 1968 communists were released from prison and even offered Cabinet posts which they refused unless the Party were legalised and full civil rights restored. The government of Ahmad Hassan al-Bakr combined persecution of communists with blandishments to them to enter a National Front and the Party endorsed the National Charter of November 1971. In May 1972 Amr Abd Allah and another Central Committee member entered the Cabinet and the following year the ICP joined the Baath in Progressive Patriotic and Nationalist Front. It was a junior partner in the Government for five years although relations began to deteriorate in 1976. In May 1978, shortly after a communist coup in Afghanistan and some criticism in a communist newspaper that the Government was wooing the West, the Baath accused the ICP of "subservience to Moscow", of attempting to set up a secret organisation within the armed forces and of plotting with the Shiah and the Kurds. Within a few days 20 communists, some of whom had been in prison for years, were hanged and over 1,000 arrested. Some attempts were made to end the dispute but without success and in October Aziz Muhammad who had succeeded al-Radi as Secretary-General escaped to Moscow while other Central Committee members were arrested and the Party accused the Government of mass arrests. In the spring of 1979 the ICP was expelled from the PPNF, its Ministers dropped from the Government and exiled members including students at foreign universities harried. In July 1979 a leading Baathist declared "There is no need for a Communist Party . . . if they want to become martyrs we will oblige them". Some communists fled north and after the start of the Iran–Iraq War allied with the Kurdistan Democratic Party and armed several hundred *Pesh Mergas* who were soon in battle with the KDP's enemies the Patriotic Union of Kurdistan. The Party had always been strong in Kirkuk and Sulaymaniya but Kudistan was marginal to their main interests in Iraq. The ICP even allied with the Shiah al-Dawah to bring down Saddam Hussain. Aziz Muhammad, who had addressed the Congress of the Soviet Party had several meetings with Hafiz al-Assad and received some support from Syria.

IRAQ DEVELOPMENT BOARD

In 1950 Iraq produced over 6.5 million tons of oil and it was clear that this would increase rapidly and bring enormous revenues. To the great credit of Tawfiq al-Suwaydi a Law was promulgated that these revenues should be used for capital development and paid not to the Government but directly to a newly-created Development Board in order to prevent political decisions upon expenditure. Revenue rose so sharply that in 1952 the Board's share was reduced to 70% but that still left more than could easily be spent. The Board consisted of the Prime Minister and Finance Minister and six salaried officials, experts in various fields, appointed for five years with a British Secretary-General in charge of finance and an American irrigation engineer. Later a Ministry of Development was created. Modelled on the Tennessee Valley Authority it concentrated on flood control, dams, irrigation canals etc. in the hope of making Iraq once again a great grain producer. There was also much expenditure on communications and electricity and later on hospitals and schools, summer resorts and a museum. It did extremely valuable work but inevitably there were tales of blunders such as building railway stations far from the tracks or houses without doors. It also caused resentment as much of the benefit was inevitably long-term while people wanted immediate results. Furthermore much of the development took place in the neglected countryside, for example the import of pedigree bulls or a million dinars for forestry and not in politically conscious Baghdad where it was seen as too powerful and serving only landowners. It was abolished immediately after the July Revolution.

IRAQ PETROLEUM COMPANY

In 1925, under strong British pressure, King Faysal granted a concession that covered the whole of Iraq to the Turkish Petroleum Company, a consortium in which eventually nearly half the shares were held by Shell and Anglo-Persian, nearly a quarter each by French and American groups and 5% by the Armenian financier Calouste Gulbenkian. The TPC changed its name to the Iraq Petroleum Company in 1929 and subsequently transferred some of its areas to associated companies for Basra and Mosul. Oil was found in abundance near Kirkuk in October 1927. In 1931 the IPC concession was extended to 75 years. In 1935 King Ghazi officially opened two pipelines, carrying about 4 million tons a year to the Mediterranean which started from Kirkuk, split at Haditha on the Euphrates, and ended at Banyas and Haifa – the northern 522 miles long and the southern 620. In the 1930s and 1940s the Company, helped by official British Government pressure, acquired concessions in the Gulf States and sought them in the Hijaz. Production varied little between 1935 and 1949 after which it inceased ten-fold in ten years. Enormous revenues became available and were paid not to the Government but to the Iraq Development Board for capital investment. The IPC was also the main provider of industrial training. Apart from occasional arguments over royalties relations with the Government were good and in 1952 a 50:50 profit sharing agreement was signed. The losses incurred by Iran after Musaddiq took over the assets of Anglo-Iranian served as a warning and after the July Revolution of 1958 Abd al-Krim Qassim declared that existing agreements would be honoured and he urged an increase in production. In 1959 and 1960 the international companies reduced their posted prices which cut Government revenues in all the oil states and led in September 1960 to the formation of OPEC. The government greatly increased port dues in Basra but lost money as IPC reduced output. Negotiations between Qassim, in a bitter and truculent mood, and IPC began in the spring of 1959 and eventually broke down in October 1961 because the Company, aware of the world surplus of oil, was unwilling to make major concessions. In December 1961 Iraq enacted Public Law 80 which expropriated 99.5% of IPC's area without compensation. They were left with some 800 square miles being actually exploited with a reserve of a further 80 square miles. IPC, fearful of setting a precedent which might affect other countries, particularly Saudi Arabia, refused to accept the Law and called for arbitration, further negotiations and compensation. The

Iraqis, unable to sell oil themselves and with no alternative source of revenue to replace the 80% derived from oil, did not wish to push matters too far and negotiations continued for a decade. Qassim had proposed to set up a National Oil Company to exploit the other areas but was killed before this could be done and eventually the Iraq National Oil Company was created up by Public Law 11 in February 1964. A draft agreement between INOC and IPC for co-operation in exploiting the important North Rumaila field belonging to IPC where oil had already been discovered was initialled in June 1965 but not ratified by the Government. In September 1966 the Syrian Government demanded an increase in the transit and loading fees for the pipelines and its doctrinaire leftist Prime Minister Dr Yusuf al-Zuayyin made the issue a matter of national sovereignty and called for pan-Arab support for an Iraqi take-over of the IPC. Despite the consequent loss of revenue as the flow of oil ceased, the Iraqi Prime Minister General Naji Talib felt it politically impossible to persuade Syria to compromise and the dispute dragged on for over six months. During the June War of 1967 Iraq banned oil exports to the West. Public Law 97 of August 1967 gave INOC exclusive rights to develop expropriated areas and North Rumaila. Later in the year INOC assigned some of its areas to French and Russian interests. In April 1968 INOC ignored IPC's continuing claim to Rumaila, believed capable of producing 20 million tons a year, and announced that it would itself exploit it. The Baath, now in power, had an ideological distaste for international companies, controlled from outside the Arab world. In March 1972 after INOC invited bids for three unexploited areas seized under Law 80, IPC declared that it would take legal action against companies that took them up. In May the Oil Minister Dr Sadun Hamadi claimed that IPC was reducing output in order to embarrass the Government and deprive it of revenue and presented an ultimatum demanding an increase in production, a share in assets and a retrospective increase in royalties. On the expiry of the ultimatum on 1 June President Ahmad Hassan al-Bakr announced the nationalisation of IPC and the transfer of its assests estimated at £136 million to a new Iraqi Company for Oil Operations. At the same time Syria took over the pipeline. The Basra and Mosul Companies were not affected. The nationalisation was widely applauded in the Arab world and IPC failed to persuade other companies, particularly French ones, not to buy Iraqi oil. At the end of February 1973 Bakr announced that an agreement had been made that IPC would agree to the loss of its assets in the north in return for 15 million tons of crude oil worth about £128 million delivered to the pipeline terminals and IPC would settle back royalties for £141 million.

IRAQ REVOLT (1920)

Iraqi resentment against British administration grew during 1919. Many of the educated classes expected complete independence, the religious leaders in Najaf and Kerbela considered the acceptance of rule by non-Muslims as sinful and the tribes resented a newly efficient system of taxation. Under the Ottomans 70% of the administrative posts had been held by local men but now all the senior posts were held by Britons and many of the clerical jobs by Indians. The Acting Civil Commissioner, Colonel Arnold Wilson, was autocratic, totally convinced that only firm British rule of the colonial type could keep the country from anarchy, and had little contact with General Sir Aylmer Haldane, the recently arrived commander of a rapidly diminishing garrison which had only 4,200 British and 30,000 Indian soldiers available for active service out of 130,000. Wilson dismissed a delegation of notables seeking independence with contempt while many of the Political Officers were young and brash, showing little respect for tribal leaders or customs, often making rapid changes without consultation or explanation. There was a general belief that nationalism was flourishing with Syria having apparently gained independence under Faysal and the Turkish revival under Mustafa Kamal. Iraqis in Damascus at the General Syrian Congress offered the crown to Amir Abd Allah but the San Remo Conference in April 1920 formally invested Britain with a Mandate for Iraq but the status of the country remained undefined. There was disorder in the Dayr al-Zur area and in June a raiding party from there reached Tel Afar, 40 miles from Mosul, killing two British officers and two sergeants but was chased back into the desert. A second clash in July after the arrest of a Shaykh led to the cutting of the Baghdad–Basra railway at Rumaytha and set off an uprising that affected about a third of the country and in particular the middle Euphrates area. The main trouble was in the Diwaniyyah and Hillah divisions where religious leaders called for *jihad* and were able to distribute money received from abroad. The rebels had no overall leader although tribal chiefs and former officers, returning after the fall of Damascus to the French, had local influence and their efforts were totally unco-ordinated. There was, however, an unprecedented co-operation between Sunnis and Shiah. The Kurds and the main cities remained quiet. Several political officers including the famous Colonel Leachman were murdered as were the crew of a riverboat, left to roast in intense heat and altogether the British lost 450 men killed, 1,228 wounded and 615 missing and prisoners and the repression cost £40 million. Arab losses were estimated at 8,450 killed and wounded. By mid-October security was restored and the more pragmatic Sir Percy Cox, instructed to introduce a more representative system of government, took over from Wilson. Although some British officials saw the Iraqi revolt as part of a worldwide conspiracy directed from Moscow or Berlin, it was a spontaneous uprising against a harsh foreign government and led to the creation of the Iraqi monarchy under Faysal after the Cairo Conference.

IRAQI NATIONAL CONGRESS

By 1990 there were a large number of exile groups, some little more than phantoms, which called for the overthrow of Saddam Hussain. There were several Shiah groups, of which the most important was al-Dawah, which were based in Tehran and formed the Supreme Council of the Islamic Revolution in Iraq under the leadership of Muhammad Bakr al-Hakim. They did not participate in a meeting of 17 organisations which included Kurds, liberals, communists,

dissidents from the Baath Party, Arab nationalists, etc. in Damascus in December 1990 which agreed to resolve old disputes amongst themselves and called for a provisional government in Iraq to organise free elections and the evacuation of Kuwait: the Kurdish problem should be settled on the basis of the March Manifesto of 1970. In December 1991 the Kurdish leader Jalal Talabani said that a united opposition could overthrow Saddam in a week. In January 1992, after Hakim had visited President Assad, SCIRI took part in a Joint Committee meeting in Damascus and in the same month it claimed that its supporters had killed some senior officers in an attack on the air force HQ in Baghdad: later 80 officers including two Brigadiers, said to be members of SCIRI were executed. After al-Hakim had seen King Fahd, another group meeting was held in Saudi Arabia although it was missed by the Kurds who had not received invitations in time. In June 1992 200 delegates assembled in Vienna constituted themselves the Iraqi National Congress, set up a National Assembly of 87, including 4 women, and an executive of 17. There were resolutions on human rights, economic recovery and a call to the UN for the release of frozen Iraqi assets for humanitarian purposes and a reduction in the indemnities for the Iran–Iraq War. It was proposed to set up a base in Northern Iraq from which Saddam could be attacked. Much of the organisation was done by Ahmad Chalabi from London and the chief spokesman, also from London was Laith Qubba, a Shiah intellectual. Forty groups were represented but the meeting was boycotted by factions based in Syria which was worried about a possible break-up of the Iraqi state, Saudi Arabia which was supporting former Baathists, and Iran. Although President Bush had increased secret funds for overthrowing Saddam from $15 million to $40 million, the INC denied receiving financial backing from Washington but in July Secretary of State Baker received a delegation which consisted of Talabani and the other Kurdish leader Masud Barzani, Qubba, a Shiah leader Muhammad Bakr al-Allum, a secular Sunni Dr Salah al-Shaikhly and the former Prime Minister Arif Abd al-Razzaq and promised not to abandon them. There was general agreement on what to do once the INC had overthrown Saddam but a shortage of ideas on how this was to be done. Another delegation was received by President Ozel and Egypt also expressed support. During the summer of 1992 there were several reports of plots in Iraq, after one of which 100 officers were said to have been executed. In January 1993 Bush's National Security Adviser admitted that these had been backed by the US and come "pretty close" to success. During the summer there were also various meetings of leaders and groups which led, at the invitation of Barzani, of a conference of over 70 delegates from 30 groups, including for the first time SCIRI, in Irbil in September. Anxious to allay the fears of neighbouring states that Iraq might break up, it called for a federal system such as that of Germany with local government for Kurds. The conference agreed on a 3-man Presidency, a 21 to 25-man executive committee and an Assembly of 174. It backed the recent imposition of a no-fly zone in the South. In late October 300 delegates, although those from six groups in Damascus were prevented from attending, met in the mountain resort of Salahuddin. There was a steering committee consisting of Talabani, Allum and Muhammad Haidari who represented SCIRI but another prominent figure was Masham al-Jaburi who had worked in Saddam's office until his flight in 1988 since when he had organised three attempted coups. The meeting endorsed the principle of a federated of Iraq which was to be approved by referendum after the fall of Saddam and stressed the need for amnesty to win over minor figures of the regime. The Troika Head of State was to comprise Generak Hassan Naqib, Barzani and Allum. There was a call for a safe haven to be set up in the South. Delegates were sent to Turkey, Iran and Syria requesting corridors into Iraq but the Foreign Ministers of these states, meeting in Ankara, declared the Salahuddin decisions invalid and reaffirmed that Iraq should not be divided. The unity established at Salhuddin was short lived for many Shiah felt that the others were indifferent to what was happening in the Marshes and all except Allum withdrew from the executive council. Many disapproved of Chalabi, who had once been convicted in Jordan of absconding with the funds of a bank, while others agreed with Kubba that the Troika emphasised ethnic differences rather than Iraqi unity. Naqib's Independent Iraqi Alliance started recruiting army officers in the South. In March Talabani, Allum and Bakri were received by the British Prime Minister John Major and then went to Washington. In March there were policy differences, with the Kurds seeing the INC as Shiah. They were unwilling to integrate into a single army or let in Hakim's Badr Brigade as controlled by Iran. Some wanted to keep Saddam Hussain as a guarantee of Western support. In April Abd al-Razzaq, claimed wide contacts in the army called for a new opposition grouping – the Iraqi Central Committee for Dialogue and Follow up. Reports surfaced of a plot. In June Hakim was in Damascus and Kuwait asking for support from the world's Muslims. In June there was a bomb in Baghdad and in August SCIRI asked the UN to send aid to the Marshes. Responsibility was claimed by the committee for Defence of Democracy for a further bomb outrage in Baghdad in August and some officers were shot in the South by al-Majid. Another attempted coup was followed by 20 arrests and allegations against Saad Jabr of the Free Iraq Council. Two former ambassadors Hisham al-Shawi and Hamidal-Jubari defected.

IRAQI "SUPER-GUN"

In April 1990 when Anglo-Iraqi relations were at a particularly low ebb owing to the execution of Farhad Bazoft and the seizure at Heathrow of Kryton triggers for nuclear weapons destined for Baghdad, there was intense excitement when Customs officials at Middlesbrough detained pipes which they suspected to be part of the barrel of what would have been the largest gun ever designed. Eight tubes were impounded and it was revealed that 44 had already reached Baghdad. Their manufacturers, a specialist foundry in Sheffield, believed that they were for use in a petrochemical plant as the Iraqi authorities claimed. Ballistic experts, however, considerd that these pipes could have formed the barrel of a gun 155 metres long, with a calibre of one metre, capable of firing shells that could deliver up to two tons of nerve gas on Jerusalem or Tehran with a possible range of 1,150 miles. It was later discovered that a Brussels-based Canadian scientist Dr Gerald Bull who had been in Baghdad several times and invented specialist gun-carriages used in the Iran–Iraq War had built a very long gun which had fired a shell 118 miles into space and it was possible that the Iraqis intended to launch a space vehicle. A Swiss company was making breech blocks while propellant was made in Belgium. Bull had been murdered the previous month and it was suspected that Mossad had been responsible. The British Trade Minister, Nicholas Ridley stated that he was "entirely satisfied" that the pipes were part of a "Super-Gun" and other components were seized in Italy, Germany and Turkey while in Greece a British lorry driver with a suspect load was detained. There was political controversy in London over whether the Government had known full particulars when the pipes had been ordered. Eleven people were charged with illegally exporting arms but in November the Government unexpectedly decided not to proceed with the case. A Committee of the House of Commons was set up to investigate but was hampered by Government obstruction and could not produce a proper report before it was dissolved by a General Election. Nevertheless it was believed that, as in a subsequent case of laser equipment for making fuses for Iraq, British Intelligence had reported what was happening and that Whitehall was guilty either of collusion or incompetence. It seemed also as if the discredited Bank of Commerce and Credit International was involved and the affair was linked to the murder of a former Belgian Deputy Prime Minister in July 1991. In July 1991 when the Iraqis were compelled to disclose their weaponry after their defeat in Operation Desert Storm a prototype, "Baby Babylon" with a 52.5 metre long barrel and a calibre of 350 mm was found at Jabal Hamryan, 150 km north of Baghdad: it was destroyed. Parts of the "Super-Gun" ended up in the London Imperial War Museum and the expert view was that it had been an interesting curiosity, by no mans worth what it had cost.

al-IRYANI, Abd al-Rahman (c. 1912–)

President of Yemen. He came from a *Qadi* family in the Ibb area and received a traditional Islamic education. He had progressive views and became an adviser of Crown Prince Ahmad who was then encouraging young progressives. Iryani was closely associated with the Ahrar led by his friends Ahmad Muhammad Nu'man and Muhammad Mahmud al-Zubayri and like them was involved in the coup of February 1948 in which the Imam Yahya was murdered. He spent six years in Hajjah jail where he wrote and edited poetic works. After his release he briefly acted as an adviser to Ahmad once more but then took refuge in Cairo. After the overthrow of the Imamate he returned home to become Minister of Justice. In October 1963 he was appointed a Vice-President and Chairman of the Executive Council and often acted as Head of State in the absence of Marshal Sallal. A year later, tired of seeing their country used as a battlefield between Egypt and Saudi Arabia, a group of moderate Republicans led by Zubayri, Nu'man and Iryani attempted to end the Yemen War by negotiating with the moderate Royalists at Erkowit. When their effort was frustrated by the intransigence of Sallal and the Egyptians the three resigned in December 1964. Zubayri attempted to found a Third Force of moderate Republicans but was murdered in April 1965 and the revulsion caused by this crime brought to power Nu'man who was pledged to ending the war by negotiations with the tribes. A Conference of 4,000 tribal leaders assembled at Khamir under the chairmanship of Iryani and worked out peace proposals and a new Constitution but their efforts were again blocked by Sallal. Iryani continued to work for peace, although he was always determined that the Imamate should not be restored, and in December 1966 when it was clear that Sallal was still set on crushing the Royalists by force, Iryani went to Cairo to protest. He was detained there by Nasser and could not return home until Sallal had been ousted in November 1967. Iryani headed the three-man Council which exercised Presidential functions and immediately called for peace although he was still adamant that the Republic should survive. His religious background and the general respect in which he was held, both by Zaidis and Shafais, played an important part in enabling it to do so in the absence of 60,000 Egyptian troops previously considered indispensable. He gave full backing to his Prime Minister General Hassan al-Amri in crushing left-wing radicals and this, coupled with King Faysal's alarm at the actions of the new regime in Aden caused the ending of Saudi financial support for the Royalists whose leaders, many old friends of Iryani, returned in 1970. Later that year a Constitution, in the drafting of which Iryani had a major role and which reflected both his Islamic background and his gift for compromise was promulgated. Under his aegis the first General Election held in the Yemen took place in March 1971. In 1973 he attempted to found a political party, the National Yemeni Union but it never had time to take root. In internal affairs he had to take account of conservative shaykhs, grown more powerful as a result of the weakening of centralised government, ulema and of young modernisers anxious for reform. In dealing with them he had to contend with an endemic financial crisis, rising prices, large-scale corruption and an incompetent administration although a start was made towards improving it. He was often regarded as indecisive as he tried to keep a balance. In foreign affairs he succeeded in creating good relations with all the Arab states and with the West while not losing the friendship of Russia. However the financial position made Sanaa dangerously dependent upon Riyadh which, determined to overthrow the regime in Aden, maintained its armed opponents on North Yemeni soil. The resulting border clashes led to a war in September 1972 which ended in the Tripoli Agreement in which Iryani and Salim Rubai Ali undertook to unite their states. Iryani sincerely wanted this merger but was unable to impose it upon the tribal chiefs and the ulema backed by Saudi Arabia. He was thwarted at every turn by the tribally-dominated Consultative Council and there were times when the country appeared upon the verge of anarchy. In August 1973 he went into voluntary exile in Syria, as a means of emphasising his own indispensability – a

variant on his usual technique of resigning two or three times a year. He was persuaded to return but the situation did not improve. In June 1974 a plot backed by Iraq was discovered and Iryani opposed any strong reaction. When the tribal leaders and the army insisted he resigned and this time it was accepted. He went into exile in Syria where he remained until he returned to Yemen in October 1981. Appearing to rule almost as a Regent for an absent Imam, his character and record legitimised the Republic and prepared the way for a new generation. Combining Islamic tradition and a desire for progress he presided over the reintegration of the Royalists and the start of modernisation, however halting.

ISLAMIC CHARTER FRONT (Sudan)
al-Jabhat al-Mithaq al-Islami. During the Second World War the Muslim Brotherhood began to spread in the Sudan, being particularly strong in the University of Khartoum. Its original leader was Rashid al-Tahir (Bakr) but after Hassan Turabi had returned from higher education abroad he became its dominant figure. The movement opposed the military regime of General Abboud and took part in the transitional government of Sirr al-Khatim al-Khalifah. About this time the Brotherhood organised itself as a political party under the name of the Islamic Charter Front. It participated in the Round Table Conference on the affairs of the South. Tahir who represented in the Cabinet was detained for arms smuggling; although he maintained that the weapons were for the Muslim Eritreans resisting the Christian regime of Haile Selassie, it was generally believed that they intended them for a coup. The ICF remained in the Government after the left was purged in February 1965 and in the elections of April won five seats, two of them in the Graduate Constituencies. After 1965 it was generally in opposition, campaigning for a permanent Constitution based on Islam. Helped by the general spread of Islamic fundamentalism after the June War it won three seats in the elections of 1968. Like all other parties it was banned by Nimeiri but continued to exist in shadowy form. In 1973 it joined the National Front opposition to the regime but took part in the National Reconciliation of 1977/8 after which it became extremely influential working within the Government with Turabi one of the President's closest advisers. In the elections of February 1978 about 20 of its members were returned under the label of the sole party, the Sudan Socialist Union. It played an important part in the formulation of the September Laws which imposed *Shariah* on the country and in resisting all attempts at making peace with the Sudan People's Liberation Movement at the price of repealing them. When political parties were again legalised under the government of General Siwar al-Dhahab it reconstituted itself as the National Islamic Front.

ISLAMIC INSURGENCY (Algeria)
In the late 1980s FIS training camps were established in Algeria. Isolated acts by fundamentalists followed. In December 1990 hotels in Algeria holding New Year's Eve parties were attacked and prostitutes targeted. An attack on an RCD meeting left 48 injured. At the end of November 1991 a gang of 34 Muslim extremists led

by Tayib the Afghan attacked a frontier post killing three police officers and capturing weapons. The perpetrators were hunted down and a large number killed. Twenty-seven died in ensuing skirmishes. Extremists also fired on security forces and attacked government offices. After the military take-over Hashni said there would be no violence despite mass arrests. Violence continued, however, and Hashani was arrested for calling for a rebellion in the army. The FIS claimed that 500 were arrested in clashes at mosques. In January 1992 one soldier and two police officers were injured in a machine-gun and bomb attack at a roadblock near the Algerian border. On 26 January Kabir said that the Government was trying to provoke civil war. The 31 January saw the first bomb attack on the US Embassy since independence. On 5 February the Government said that 15 were killed at Batna where dynamite was found in a mosque. Clashes extended over three days. FIS said that 20 were killed with the army firing on the crowds from helicopters. On 9 February a state of emergency was declared for up to one year after a week of rioting. It was claimed that the Government was trying to provoke insurrection. On 10 February Afghans killed eight police and in the ensuing shoot-out a further six were killed. There was fighting outside mosques as the Government tried to install subservient Imams in the universities. On 4 March FIS was outlawed. There were 5,000 arrests in the first three weeks of February, according to Haroun Hurimim. Camps were opened in the Sahara and at least 50 were reported killed. Incidents occurred all over the country. Tayib Afgh was captured and on 4 May the courts passed 13 death sentences. This number quickly doubled. The first death sentences were carried out on the three Hizbullah for murder in the course of stealing explosives. Belkeir reported that there were 103 dead (including 31 security forces), 414 wounded (144 from the security forces) and more than 9,000 arrested. In retaliation there were attacks on the security forces in an attempt to seize arms. On 9 May anti-FIS newspapers were bombed. By mid-June 70 police were dead in what Nazzar described as "an implacable war". The weekend after the murder of Boudiaf five police were shot, taking the total to about 80. In July there were attacks on electricity and telecommunication lines. In August clandestine radio said that the killings of police were internecine. Clashes occurred almost daily. A ten-man gang was wiped out, one of whom had killed 22 police, in the three-hour gun battle. In August an airport bomb killed nine. British and American citizens were told not to travel to Algeria and American citizens were ordered home. In August a state prosecutor was killed – the first attack on a magistrate – followed by attacks on replacements for FIS mayors. The Government said they had a list of 274 wanted men. On 4 October a new anti-terrorist law was passed which gave suspects two months to surrender or face trial by special streamlined courts with secret judges and prosecutors with powers to sentence for anything from five years' imprisonment to the death penalty. Five years was the punishment for being an "apologist" for terrorism. There was an increase in arrests and killings on both sides. One hundred and forty members of the security forces had been killed since February. On 16 November

relations with Iran were downgraded following reports that Iran had arranged for terrorists to travel in the Sudan. On 29 November the Prime Minister declared total war stating that the State must go on the attack. Over 300 municipal government officials were dismissed. On 4 December a curfew from 22.30 to 5.00 was imposed in Algeria and in five surrounding *départements* where an estimated 60% of the population lived. Army units with helicopters were stationed in mountains. In the fortnight after the imposition of the curfew 337 militants and 17 security men died. In four months 211 officials were killed and 3,800 arrested. In January 1993 the first two executions were performed – soldiers involved in attacking a naval base. About 30, mostly officers, appeared before a military court in quargla. In February the emergency was indefinitely extended after 250 security forces were killed. By February 1993 48 had been sentenced to death. In March a Minister was killed – the Head of the Institute for Planning Social Strategy and in June his successor was killed; his throat was cut in front of his daughter. There were also attacks on members of the Consultative Council. In March there was a major offensive on a military barracks – terrorists were let in by accomplices and 18 other soldiers were killed. Twenty-three were lost in a week-long hunt. In March relations broke down with Tehran and Ambassadors from the Sudan were recalled. By May 76 death sentences had been carried out. In June 1993 there were more murders of officials – a Professor of Psychiatry, Prosecutor-General and Chief of Security, Laghoust. In May 1993 the curfew was renewed and extended.

ISLAMIC LIBERATION PARTY

The *Hizb al-Tahrir al-Islami* was founded in about 1950 in Jordan by Shaykh Taqi al-Din al-Nabhani. He was a former official of the Muslim Brothers but created the ILF in opposition to it. It was a right-wing Muslim group which rejected all foreign ideologies and advocated Arab unification and the restoration of the Caliphate. The circumstances of Jordan in the 1950s made it extremely anti-British and it tended to see any act deleterious to the Muslims as being ultimately inspired by London. It attempted to form a political party in Jordan but was banned in 1952 but continued underground. It never won more than 7,000 votes but secured a seat in the Parliament of 1956. The ILP supported King Hussain in the crises of 1957 but in November 1969 16 members, including Nabhani, *in absentia* were put on trial for plotting to overthrow the Monarchy. Fourteen were condemned to death but in March 1970 the sentences were commuted to 20 years' imprisonment. Nabhani died in the 1970s; no successor was named and underground activity continued. It established a network of clandestine cells in most Arab countries, particularly in Tunisia, and was active in Turkey and amongst Muslim communities in Europe. The ILP was believed to have the ultimate aim of a totally Islamic world, achieved by revolution and in the meanwhile it rejected territorial divisions between Muslim states. In the 1980s it offered the Caliphate to Ayatollah Khomeini. It recruited particularly in schools and universities and amongst the armed forces.

ISMAIL, Abd al-Fattah (1939–86)

President of South Yemen. He was born of a low-class family in North Yemen and received little formal education. In 1957 he went to Aden and worked as an unskilled labourer in the BP Refinery. From at least 1959 he was a convinced supporter of the Arab Nationalist Movement, forming a cell at his workplace. After the overthrow of the Imamate he went North, coming into contact with other cell leaders who eventually amalgamated to form the National Liberation Front. He returned to Aden where he became one of the main organisers of terrorism, reputedly killing British and Arab opponents with his own hands. In the first government after independence he was appointed Minister of Culture, Guidance and Yemeni Unity Affairs. He was by now an all-out revolutionary, prepared to destroy all existing institutions and rebuild them according to socialist principles and to spread revolutionary ideas throughout the Arabian Peninsula. This brought him into conflict with the President, Qahtan al-Shaabi who wanted to rebuild the state using existing institutions and, by conciliating neighbouring monarchies, obtain financial aid from them. At the Zinjibar Congress of March 1968 the left demanded that Ismail should be appointed Prime Minister but immediately afterwards Qahtan, with the help of the army, re-established control and Ismail was dismissed from office. He spent the next year secretly gathering support against the President and in June 1969, in the Glorious Corrective Move with Salim Rubai Ali and Muhammad Ali Haytham succeeded in overthrowing him. Ismail became a member of the five-man Presidential Council and obtained the key post of Secretary-General of the Party. While taking a full share in the purges, indocrination and nationalisation that followed and in a foreign policy firmly aligned with Moscow, Ismail devoted much energy to gaining control of the Party and establishing relations, on a Party basis, with Russia, the East European satellites and Cuba. Under the pressure of economic reality, to which Ismail was always indifferent, Haytham tried to encourage local businessmen to set up small industries, whereupon Ismail joined forces with Ali to dismiss him. Ali concentrated on the government while Ismail was preoccupied with building support within the Party for unlike Ali he had no popular following except amongst some of the urban proletariat and unlike Ali Nasir Muhammad and Ali Antar, he had no tribal backing. In 1970 he became Chairman of the Permanent Committee which dominated the People's Supreme Council and when a Politburo was established in 1972, he was its Secretary-General. From these positions he controlled the indoctrination of the armed forces and organised a Militia which came directly under himself as Party chief and served as propagandists and informers. He demanded ever more sacrifices from the people for the sake of building a socialist future and was glad when the middle class and even skilled workers escaped abroad, thus removing internal opposition. He called for friendship with the communist countries and hostility towards the rest of the world even if it meant isolation and bankruptcy. His relations with Ali deteriorated as the President, struggling to provide a better life for the people, relaxed some of the harsher repression and tried

to win financial aid from the rich Arab states and the West by a less revolutionary foreign policy. Ismail worked to counter this by building an all-powerful Vanguard Party consisting entirely of his own supporters and achieved a first step towards this by the creation of the United Political Organisation – National Front in October 1975. He had a major success when his associate Ali Antar became Minister of Defence. In June 1978 Ali was preparing to receive an American envoy at a time when Aden had become even more strategically important to Russia as a base from which it was possible to help the struggling new communist regime in Ethiopia and Ismail sent Ali Antar to Moscow to get approval for the overthrow of the President. Seizing, perhaps manufacturing, the opportunity of the murder of the North Yemeni President Ahmad al-Ghashmi which Ismail blamed upon Ali, Ismail's supporters, reportedly backed by Russian and Cuban forces, stormed the Presidential Palace. Ali was shot after a drumhead trial. Ismail went quickly ahead with the formation of the Yemeni Socialist Party and in December 1978 became formal Head of State. He refused totally to compromise and it is said that even Brezhnev warned him against extremism. In February 1979 a second war with the North ended in an agreement of the two states to unite but Ismail worked to overthrow the Sanaa Government by providing full backing of the National Democratic Front. It was a general surprise when he resigned on 20 April 1981 on grounds of ill health. Although he was known to have tuberculosis and a chronic stomach ulcer and may well have been exhausted after two decades of relentless revolutionary activity, there were reports that he had been dismissed for making concessions to Russia in a Friendship Treaty beyond those approved by his colleagues or for administrative incompetence and impracticality and lack of personal appeal. He was given the honorary title of President of the Party and went into exile in Russia where he had previously spent long periods. In February 1985 he returned to Aden and later in the year was back on the Politburo. He was soon working against President Ali Nasir Muhammad as he had done against others who had put practical above rigid doctrinal considerations and was in alliance again with Ali Antar. In January 1986 Ali Nasir determined to arrest or kill his opponents at a Politburo meeting. In the general bloodshed Ismail simply disappeared and his body was never found. After being at first denounced by the Russians as a "counter-revolutionary", he was later officially pronounced a "martyr".

ISMAIL (ALI), Ahmad, Field Marshal (1918–74)

Egyptian Military Commander and Minister. He graduated from the same class in the Military Academy as Anwar Sadat and fought in the El-Alamein campaign. Ismail was an early member of the Free Officers. He commanded a battalion in the Palestine War and a brigade in the Suez War and a division in the June War after which he built a defence line west of the Suez Canal. He had had prolonged training in Russia. In 1968 he was appointed Chief of Military Operations and in March 1969 Chief of the General Staff. He kept this post only until September 1969 being dismissed by Nasser after the Egyptian forces were humiliated by Israeli commando raids during the War of Attrition. After involvement of senior officers in the plot of Ali Sabri to overthrow Sadat in May 1971, Ismail was brought back as Chief of Military Intelligence. In October 1972 the War Minister, the strongly anti-Russian General Sadiq was dismissed amidst rumours of an attempted military plot at a time when Sadat was working for a reconciliation with Moscow and Ismail was chosen to replace him. According to his rival, General Saad al-Din Shazli, Ismail was dying of cancer and the President knew that he could control him. Ismail had a major part in the planning of the crossing of the Canal and in joint planning with the Syrians. Shazli criticised his conduct of the October War, saying that he was a "weak man, alternating between submissiveness and bullying" and that he was deeply unpopular with the troops. However in February 1974 he was promoted Field Marshal and in April Deputy Prime Minister. Ismail died of lung cancer in London in December. Haykal described him as a large, honest, professional soldier, strict, rigid and above politics.

ISMAIL Bey (?–1791)

Ruler of Egypt. He was a Mamluk of Ali Bey and remained faithful to him after his expulsion by Abu al-Dhahab. After the death of the latter he rallied the former adherents of Ali Bey against the new rulers Ibrahim Bey and Murad Bey the leaders of the Abu Dhahab faction. In 1776 he managed to expel them and they took refuge in Upper Egypt until the following year when they drove him out and he in turn fled to Upper Egypt. In 1786 a Turkish expedition restored Ismail to power but Ibrahim and Murad continued to make trouble in the South. In 1789 Ismail asked the French Consul if officers could be sent to modernise his army but the outbreak of the Revolution prevented this. In 1791 the Turkish troops had to be withdrawn because of war with Russia. Ismail's regime was on the verge of collapse, with open rebellion in Cairo when he died of the plague.

ISMAILIYYAH BUS ATTACK (1990)

On 4 February 1990 an Israeli tourist bus near Ismailiyyah was attacked with grenades and machine-gun fire. Six Israelis and two Egyptians were killed outright, three more died later and more than twenty were wounded. The Egyptian Government announced that the attack had been plotted abroad and carried out by non-Egyptians. A gang calling itself "the Organisation for the defence of the oppressed in Egypt's prisons" claimed responsibility. This was thought to have been either a front for the Islamic Jihad or for Ahmad Jibril.

ISTIQLAL PARTY (Iraq)

The Istiqlal was the most right-wing of the five parties that were formed in Iraq in April 1946 upon the ending of martial law. Its leader was Muhammad Mahdi Kubba. It called for strong Arab nationalism and moderate social reform and the British regarded it as "the spiritual – and probably the actual descendant of the pro-Nazi movement led by Rashid Ali al-Gilani". It distrusted Nuri al-Said for his willingness to work with the British and called for neutrality between East and West and its paper stated that Communism was preferable to Zionism. When the other four parties were either suppressed or ceased voluntarily to operate in 1948, it alone survived. In 1951 when Mussadiq nationalised British oil interests in Iran, the Party demanded similar measures in Iraq. In November 1952, in common with the other parties, it was dissolved by General Nur al-Din Mahmud but later resumed action. In June 1954, in alliance with the National Democratic Party it contested the elections winning two seats. In September 1954 Nuri dissolved all political parties and the Istiqlal was never formally revived. Its leaders, however, tried in 1957 to form a National Unity Front with members of the NDP, the Baath and the Communists but did not receive government authorisation to do so.

ISTIQLAL PARTY (Morocco)

In the late 1930s there were two strands of opposition to the continuation of the French Protectorate in Morocco. There were in the Salafiyyah those such as Allal al-Fassi who had received a religious education and saw resistance primarily in Islamic terms while others, such as Ahmad Balafrej who had received a modern schooling, saw it in terms of Western nationalism. These two groups had come together to form the National Action Bloc but that was dissolved by the French authorities in 1937. At the end of 1943 they came together again to form the Istiqlal (Independence) Party which issued its Manifesto with 58 signatures on 11 January 1944. Unlike previous demands which had been for reform of the Protectorate, the Charter explicitly demanded independence with a constitutional monarchy and the participation of a sovereign reunited Morocco in the post-war world organisation. It called for social legislation to help the poor and nationalisation of public utilities. It requested Muhammad V to take the movement under his patronage and declared that it would refrain from violence. Its membership consisted of the grand bourgeoisie of Fez, intellectuals, the *Vieux Turbans* and under the leadership of Mahjoub Ben Sadiq, workers, and it soon claimed 100,000 members with local cells, sports clubs, schools etc. The French arrested some of the leaders, setting off riots and demonstrations. Muhammad Lyazidi, effectively the leader until al-Fassi and Balafrej returned from exile in 1946 petitioned the UN for membership. Istiqlal then launched a vigorous campaign to win foreign support for Moroccan independence which it refused to discuss with the French until the principle was conceded. Its newspaper *al-Alam* attracted a wide readership. The French tried without success to weaken Istiqlal by encouraging the growth of "tame" nationalist movements. In December 1950 Lyazidi and other Istiqlal members on the Government Council defied the Resident General, Juin, walked out and were immediately received by the Sultan. After riots in Casablanca in December 1952 the French arrested those leaders that they could catch but others continued to organise resistance from Tangier and Cairo. The refusal of the Sultan to denounce the Party led to his deposition by the French in August 1953 and at the same time the Party was banned. For the next two years violence escalated with terror gangs in the cities and guerrilla warfare in the mountains but, apart from al-Fassi this was not approved by the leadership. An important part in the struggle was played by Union Marocaine du Travail which the Party helped to form under Ben Sadiq. When independence was conceded by the French late in 1955 the Istiqlal considered that its achievements entitled it to be the leading if not the sole party but the King insisted upon the formation of a national government with nine of its members and six from its rival Parti Démocratique de l'Indépendence under the Premiership of the non-party Mubarak Bekkai. The Istiqlal absorbed the Party of National Reform which had been active in the Spanish Zone and set to work to gain control of the local administration and of the armed forces by placing sympathetic officials in key posts: the appointment of urban Arabs to Berber areas touched off unrest and led to the revolt of Addi ou Bihi. It also used violence against supporters of the PDI which it managed to eliminate from the Government in October 1956. Its insistence upon "homogeneous government" led to the creation of a purely Istiqlal administration under Balafrej in May 1958. Its first Party Congress, held in December 1955, had shown personal and political differences emerging between the traditionalists and a younger, more left-wing group and at the second Congress in August 1956 there had been difficulty in agreeing a party programme acceptable to all. During 1958 the gap became unbridgeable and the dissidents led by Mehdi Ben Barka and Abd al-Rahim Bouabid formed their own Union National des Forces Populaires. The Balafrej government collapsed and was succeeded by a largely UNFP Cabinet led by Abd Allah Ibrahim. In January 1960 al-Fassi was elected Secretary-General of the Party which could still claim over 1.5 million members. As Ben Sadiq had joined the UNFP the Istiqlal set up its own Trade Union movement, the Union Générale des Travailleurs Marocains and it was strong in other unions such as that of the students. The municipal elections of May 1960 gave it 44% of the seats, practically twice that of the UNFP, its nearest rival. Muhammad Boucetta represented the Party in the Cabinet formed by Muhammad V in May 1960 and continued to serve in that of Hassan II in which he was joined by al-Fassi and others. In July 1962 its Congress urged that Morocco should regain its "natural frontiers" and work for a unified Maghreb. The Istiqlal campaigned vigorously in favour of the Constitution which was endorsed by referendum in December 1962 but its Ministers resigned from the Government in January 1963, resenting the concentration of power in the hands of their opponent Reda Guedira, and went into opposition. In a new Manifesto it demanded the expropriation of all foreign-owned land, agrarian reform, nationalisation of key sectors of the economy, stress on Arabic in education and sovereignty over Mauritania and all Spanish North Africa. In the general election of May 1963 it emerged as the strongest single party with 41 seats out of 144 but it contested the results as rigged and in alliance with the UNFP boycotted the subsequent local elections. After the imposition of the state of emergency in June 1965 the Party called for the restoration of Parliament although it stressed its loyalty to the Monarch. In 1969 it denounced the apparent willingness of the Government to recognise the independence of Mauritania. In July 1970 Istiqlal was the largest component of a National Front formed with the UNFP and the communists of Ali Yata to boycott the parliamentary elections: despite this 9 out of the 240 successful candidates were regarded as being its supporters. In 1974, on the death of al-Fassi, Boucetta succeeded him as Secretary-General. In the municipal elections of 1976 the Istiqlal, awarded 16% of the votes although it claimed to have won 36%, came second after the Independents with 2,184 seats in 13,500 contested. After the outbreak of the Western Sahara War in 1975, the Istiqlal put victory above domestic political concerns. In March 1977 when Ahmad Uthman reformed his Cabinet to conduct parliamentary elections, Boucetta was one of the party leaders who joined as Minister without Portfolio. Campaigning on a platform of social and economic equality, ending corruption, pan-Arabism and pan-Islam Istiqlal emerged the second strongest party with 49 seats in the 176-man Assembly. When in the autumn the King reshuffled the Cabinet to form a government of National Unity, Boucetta took the Ministry of Foreign Affairs and four other important Ministries and three Secretaryships went to members of Istiqlal. In April 1978 the tenth Party Congress gave priority to the need for an Arab, Muslim Maghreb. In March 1979 when the 10-member National Defence Council was established, Istiqlal was given two seats. In the local elections of June 1983 Istiqlal was declared to have taken 18% of the vote with 2,605 seats but Boucetta scorned the figures as the most fraudulent ever. In the parliamentary elections of September 1984 Istiqlal, although it fielded more candidates than any other party, lost half its seats to finish with 23 and 15.5% amongst widespread feelings that it was rigid and out of date. Its associated UGTM won two indirect seats. In April 1985 Karim Lamrani reformed his Cabinet which the Istiqlal, disliking his economic proposals, with its ally the Union Socialiste des Forces Populaires, refused to join: it was thus out of government for the first time since 1977. In 1990, sensing the rise of Islamic fundamentalism throughout North Africa, it demanded that Friday be the rest day and that sales of alcohol and tobacco be banned. The UGTM in April 1990 proposed to call a general strike unless wages were increased and although it was cancelled, a second call in December set off the bloody Fez Riots. In October 1991, with the USFP, Istiqlal set out a Declaration of Democracy, complaining that the Gulf War had been used as an excuse for denying reforms: unlike the USFP it laid stress on the *Shariah*. In May 1992 the Istiqlal, the USFP and the Parti du Progèrs et du Socialisme formed a Democratic Bloc, demanding separation of powers, fairer elections, a stronger Parliament, a lower voter age and an attack on corruption. In September Istiqlal and the USFP boycotted the referendum on a new Constitution which it described as "mere tinkering". In October Istiqlal did well in the municipal elections, ending as the largest opposition party with 12.5%, regaining a majority in Fez and holding up well in other areas. In February 1993 the Bloc temporarily withdrew from the electoral commission in protest against its procedures. In the parliamentary elections on June 1993 the USFP agreed not to oppose each other's candidates – Istiqlal in 118 seats and the USFP in 104 – fighting on a programme sufficiently vague to offend no one and promises of further details after victory. The opposition won 45% of the votes in the direct elections in which Istiqlal nearly doubled its seats to 43. In the indirect elections it gained only a further nine. Subsequently, despite the King's offer of 19 portfolios, the Bloc refused to join a coalition.

ISTIQLAL PARTY (Palestine)

Many Arab nationalists who had served the Government of the Amir Faysal in Damascus continued to see him as the personification of pan-Arabism, particularly after Iraq achieved its independence. A group of his former adherents led by Awni Abd al-Hadi and Ahmad Hilmi Abd al-Baqi formed in August 1932 the Istiqlal Party in Palestine as a branch of the Pan-Arab Movement. Their Manifesto declared "Palestine is an Arab country, a natural part of Syria". They argued that the individual Arab states would first have to be liberated from foreign domination and then they would be able to federate. Their hostility was therefore directed mainly against the British and only secondarily against the Jews whom they saw as mere tools of imperialism. The membership was mainly young Muslim intellectuals, tired of the feuding between followers of the Mufti Haj Amin al-Hussaini and Raghib al-Nashashibi and was strong in Haifa. Although some members were pro-Hashemite (others were pro-Saudi) they opposed the willingness of the Amir Abd Allah to sell land to Zionists and in the autumn of 1933 organised demonstrations against illegal Jewish immigration which led to over 20 deaths. Their anti-British sentiments caused them to flirt with the Italians and the Germans. In January 1936 they alone of the Arab groups expressed outright opposition to the idea of a Legislative Council. In the same year they contributed two members of the Arab Higher Executive. After the White Paper of 1939 they dropped their opposition to the British and were alarmed by the ambitions of the Mufti; they became a dominant force amongst the Arab population, controlling the press and the Arab banks. The British attempted to use them as representatives of moderate Arab nationalism but as the conflict with the Jews increased after the war, the Istiqlalists lost ground to the extremists. Later they participated in the Gaza Government but then, as an organised force, ceased to exist.

ISTIQLAL PARTY, (Trans-Jordan)

The Istiqlal Party grew out of the secret Arab nationalist groupings, the *Ahd* and the *Fatat* that had existed in the pre-war Ottoman Empire. It aimed at the unification of Syria, Iraq and Palestine as an independent Arab state. They put their hopes in King Faysal in Syria and on the overthrow of his regime many of them went into exile in Trans-Jordan where the newly-established Amir Abd Allah, nursing hopes of a throne in Damascus, made them welcome. They were given a predominant role in government and the first two Chief Ministers, Rashid Tali and Mazhar Raslan were members of the party. However they did not accept the validity of the British Mandate and Abd Allah's willingness to collaborate with it to maintain his own position led them into opposition. The withdrawal of his patronage caused many of them to leave and their main base moved to Palestine where Awni Abd al-Hadi established a branch. Their strength in Trans-Jordan probably never exceeded 150 supporters. They did not apply for registration when this was granted to political parties in 1947.

ISLAMIC JIHAD (Palestine)

Islamic Jihad was founded in the early 1980s in Gaza by Dr Fathi Shkaki as an uncompromising underground guerrilla network. It demanded the destruction of Israel and the creation of an Islamic polity throughout the Middle East East. Shkaki wrote a pamphlet on Khomeini. It has a small membership but much popular support. It claimed responsibility for a bombing in a Jerusalem suq and also for bus suicide killings. It says there is no distinction between civil and military support. In July 1989 a member of Islamic Jihad grabbed the steering wheel of an Israeli bus killing 17. In November 1990 it claimed the killing of four Israeli civilians by a man crossing from Egypt. In April 1991 *The Independent* had a reference to the *Palestine Islamic Jihad* said to have been set up in opposition to the secular and political approach of Abu Jihad, feeling that Islam's main weapon – fundamentalism fanaticism – should be exploited. Its organisers were Main Tahir and Munir Shafiq. Islamic Jihad has also been linked with Islamic Jihad for the Liberation of Palestinian – hostage holders in the Lebanon. An operation in Cyprus failed when a bomb exploded prematurely killing two members. In April 1991 a cell was found in Cyprus planning an attack on the British Consulate in Patras – a bomb killed the carrier and six Greek passers-by. An arms' cache was found in Thessalonika and links unearthed with the official PLO mission in Athens, six members of which were expelled together with 20 other Palestinians. In May 1992 Islamic Jihad was blamed for an attack on Eilat Beach in which an Israeli civilian and two guerrillas were killed. In December 1992 they fought a nine-hour gun battle in Jenin killing an Israeli officer.

JABAL AKHDAR CAMPAIGN

In 1913 the conservative religious and tribal leaders of Inner Oman revived the Imamate as a protest against the ending of traditional ways and the laxity and British domination to be seen in Muscat. The Sib Treaty of 1920 made the Imam Muhammad b. Abd Allah al-Khalili a practically independent ruler and two separate regions co-existed taking little notice of each other. Khalili, who as a strict Ibadhi refused to have dealings with the Saudis whom he stigmatised as Wahhabis, was prepared to co-operate with Sultan Said b. Taymur Al Bu Said to expel them from Buraimi but the operation was vetoed by the British. Khalili died in May 1954 and was succeeded by Ghalib b. Ali al-Hinai who was sponsored by the tribal leader Sulayman b. Himyar al-Nabhani; both men were believed by the British to be in contact with the Saudis and with American oil interests. The imprecision of the Sib Treaty made it possible to argue that the oil concession granted to the British by the Sultan in 1937 did not apply to areas under the influence of the Imam. The British were prospecting at Fahud near the disputed frontier with Saudi Arabia and to secure this area and to cut the Imam from direct links with Buraimi, the Sultan's forces occupied Ibri which had been ruled by the Imams since 1925. The Imam then declared Oman an independent state and in November 1954 applied for membership of the Arab League. In the autumn of 1955 without resistance except in Rustaq where the Imam's more determined brother Talib put up a fight, the Sultan's forces took over the whole area. Ghalib who formally abdicated and Ibn Himyar submitted to the Sultan but Talib fled to Saudi Arabia and Cairo to rally support. In Dammam he received money and arms supplied by the Saudis and ARAMCO which provided facilities for his guerrillas and from Cairo vituperative radio support. In January 1957 he returned and started a resistance movement which was for some weeks successful, winning control of most of inland Oman and Jabal Akhdar. British infantry and the RAF supported the Sultan's troops and by the end of August much of the lowland was regained at the cost of one man killed, four wounded and £270,000. The rebels, however, held out on Jabal Akhdar which was generally regarded as impregnable. It has a circumference of about 700 miles and only 12 guarded tracks led to a plateau 6,000 feet high above which cliffs and peaks arose another 4,000 feet. Occasional military supplies, particularly of American-made land-mines continued to reach them. It proved impossible to dislodge them by air action so in January 1959 the Mountain was stormed by members of the Special Air Service. The leaders fled to Dammam where they set up a government in exile which for some years lobbied international meetings with complaints about the British and the Sultan. There were occasional acts of terrorism but after a visit in August 1963 a UN envoy Herbert de Ribbing declared that the rebellion was over.

JABAL ALI

In August 1976 Shaykh Rashid b. Said al-Maktum ordered the building of a new deep-sea port at Jabal Ali, 30 km west of Dubai, and by 1982 there were 15 km of quays, making it the largest man-made port in the world. In order to promote industrial development in May 1980 he decreed that it should be a free trade zone and this came into force in 1985. Within it a foreign company could own 100% of a firm, compared with 49% in the rest of the state. There were no exchange controls and the few tax restrictions that applied in the rest of Dubai were not applicable. There was a 15-year guarantee of no tax on any operation that was constantly renewed. One of the first plants was to produce phosphoric acid and 25 textile factories were set up. By 1990 some 240 licences had been issued to foreign companies, some world-famous, that wished to operate in Jabal Ali.

JABAL SAGHO, Battle of (1933)

Although the French had established their Protectorate over Morocco by the Fez Treaty of 1912 parts of the mountains had still not been subdued twenty years later. In 1931 the Middle Atlas was finally subjugated and about 1,500 Berber tribesmen unwilling to submit had congregated on part of the High Atlas and on Jabal Sagho, a wild range of mountains in the South, separated from the Atlas by the fertile valley of Wadi Dades. After Adolf Hitler had taken power the French Government became concerned not to have troops tied up in Morocco and ordered a major operation led by Generals Giraud and Catroux which started in mid-February 1933. The core of the resistance was provided by the Ait Atta tribe, led by Hasso ou Baslam. The French used tanks in the plains but the assault on the mountain was launched by the Foreign Legion, 9 goums and 8,000 partisans, members of tribes that had already submitted. In a fortnight's very fierce fighting little progress was made despite heavy losses, one goum lost six out of its seven French officers and half its Moroccan personnel, and General Hure who had taken overall command had to resort to a blockade. This lasted over three weeks with continual bombardments.

There were then generous terms of surrender – the tribesmen had to make a formal submission to the Makhzen, there would be a general amnesty, no taxes would be levied for a year, and there would be a census of firearms which they were allowed to retain. Later Hasso ou Baslam was appointed a Caid. The battle for Jabal Sagho was regarded as the culmination of the pacification although there was some further fighting in the High Atlas, particularly for Jabal Baddou and it was not until the following year that final pockets of resistance in the Anti-Atlas and Wadi Draa were mopped up.

al-JABIRI, Saad Allah (1893–1947)

Syrian Prime Minister. He came from a leading family of *Ashraf* in Aleppo and was educated at the Ottoman Administration College in Istanbul. While there he became an ardent Arab nationalist. Jabiri was conscripted into the Turkish army and fought in the Caucasus before returning home in 1919. He was elected to the General Syrian Congress and fled to Egypt when Faysal was expelled by the French. He returned in 1921 to take part in the revolt of his fellow-Aleppan Ibrahim Hananu and was imprisoned for six months. He was again arrested during the Druze Revolt but managed to harangue a crowd through the window of his cell. He was amnestied in March 1928 and in the same year was one of the founders of the National Bloc of which he was elected Vice-President. In May 1933 he was jailed for demonstrating against the first official visit to Aleppo of the pro-French Shaykh Taj al-Din al-Hassani and in February 1936 he was again arrested in connection with a general strike. The following month he was one of the delegation that went to Paris to negotiate the Franco-Syrian Treaty and when in December Jamil Mardam formed a National Bloc Government, Jabiri became Syria's first Foreign Minister. The British Consul found him "a pleasant personality combined with a certain ability". In July 1940 after the murder of his old political opponent Dr Shahabandar he fled to Iraq but was officially exculpated and returned the following year. In August 1943 when Shukri al-Quwatli became President he appointed Jabiri, whose list had won decisively in Aleppo, as Prime Minister. The Cabinet contained most of the veteran nationalist leaders but they had little sympathy with the special areas such as the Druzes and Alawites and no ideas for social or economic reform. In September 1944 he was at the meeting that produced the Alexandria Protocol, leading to the formation of the Arab League. In October 1944 his Cabinet fell to pieces and he resigned, becoming Speaker of the Assembly. Exactly a year later he again became Prime Minister and encountered difficulties over foreign policy. At a time when many Syrians wanted close relations with Iraq, Jabiri was unwilling to upset the Egyptians and the Saudis and he had a life-long hatred of the Turks, who had cordial relations with Baghdad. In December 1946 he resigned. Six months later he died, greatly regretted as a brave and straight politician. His brother Ihsan al-Jabiri was also active in nationalist politics as a close associate of Shakib Arslan and was banished from Syria from 1924 to 1937.

JAFFA RIOTS (1921)

On May Day 1921 a demonstration of the Jewish Labour movement in Jaffa became involved in a clash with members of the illegal communist group MOPSI in which no one was hurt. No Arabs were involved but some of them seem to have seen the disorder as a threat to them and attacked the immigration centre in Jaffa killing 13 Jews. Then the Jewish agricultural settlement at Petah Tikvah was attacked by about 2,000 Arabs, some of them with firearms but managed to hold out until rescued by British troops. As in all subsequent clashes there are no exact figures of casualties but it was estimated that 48 Arabs and 47 Jews were killed and 73 Arabs and 146 Jews wounded. The Government of Palestine temporarily halted Jewish immigration and set up a Commission of Inquiry under the Chief Justice Sir Thomas Haycraft.

al-JAIFI, Hamud (c. 1917–)

Prime Minister of Yemen. He was one of the batch of officers sent by the Imam Yahya for training in Baghdad and like his companions Abd Allah Sallal and Hassan al-Amri returned critical of the lack of modernisation in his homeland. After the murder of Yahya in 1948 he was imprisoned with many others in Hajjah jail but was released in 1955 through the action of Crown Prince Badr. In 1962 he was Commandant of the War College and it is said that when in September the young officers overthrew the Imamate, General Jaifi was their first choice to be the senior figure needed as Head of State. He refused, but briefly became Minister of Defence under Sallal before going to Cairo as Ambassador. In April 1964 after Nasser's visit to Sanaa where he was horrified at the administrative chaos, Sallal was stripped of most of his executive powers which were given to Jaifi. In June he made the first external telephone call from Sanaa. After the first attempt at peace at the Erkowit Conference in November 1964 Jaifi was prepared to accept the return of the royalists except for the Imam but would not agree to the withdrawal of Egyptian forces. In December the lack of progress towards peace and democracy, together with excessive Egyptian influence caused Muhammad Mahmud al-Zubayri, Muhammad Ahmad Nu'man and Abd al-Rahman al-Iryani to leave his Cabinet which disintegrated. In January 1965 Sallal returned from Cairo and replaced Jaifi who continued to hold Ministerial and military posts. In February 1966 as Commander-in-Chief he personally led a major offensive. In September 1966 he accompanied Amri to Cairo to petition for the permanent exile of Sallal and was briefly imprisoned there. He was later again Commander-in-Chief and played a part in the defence of Sanaa. After peace came, he retired. Jaifi was generally seen as a moderate, decent man and widely respected.

JALLOUD, Abd al-Salam Ahmad (1944–)

Libyan Prime Minister. He came from a poor family of the powerful Megarah tribe and was born in an oasis in Fezzan. He attended Sabhah Preparatory School where he, Muammar Qadafi and other boys held clandestine meetings to study the actions of Nasser. Most of them continued to Misurata Secondary after which Jalloud, who had been planning to go to medical school, at the urging of Qadafi, instead joined the army. He attended a signals course in Texas and was a Major at the time of the coup of 1 September 1969 in which he led armoured cars to disarm the police and the British-officered Tripolitanian Defence Force. His importance was shown by his leading the first delegation to Nasser, the Mentor of the Revolutionaries, negotiating with the British about the evacuation of their bases and by an incognito visit to Peking in an attempt to buy an atomic bomb for dollars. In January 1970 when Qadafi took over as Prime Minister, Jalloud was nominated as his Deputy and Minister of the Interior and of Local Administration. In this capacity he disbanded the Sanusi *tariqah* and tried to weaken tribal links by promoting a sense of national identity. He was involved in the formation of the Arab Socialist Union and he started the process of transferring power over oil production to the state and away from the oil companies. This was demonstrated by the bullying methods, including placing a revolver on the table, by which he secured in the Tripoli Oil Agreement of March 1971 terms more favourable than those enjoyed by any other government and increased the national revenue by 50%. In March 1972 Jalloud finally overcame Qadafi's aversion to any dealings with communist states and led the first ever high-level Libyan delegation to Moscow where he signed economic agreements which also benefited Egypt with which he was working hard to make the union prescribed in the Federation of Arab Republics a reality. In July 1972 he took over from Qadafi as Prime Minister with the brief of running domestic affairs and supervising technocrat Ministers in charge of the first Development Plan. His determination ensured that Libya got at least its fair share of the great increase in oil revenues that followed the October War of 1973. At the beginning of April 1974 it was announced that, in order that the Leader of the Revolution should be free to concentrate on ideological matters, Jalloud was taking over Qadafi's ceremonial duties, including such matters as meeting Heads of State and administrative tasks such as that of Executive Secretary of the General People's Congress. He was seen as a technical, managerial figure, an advocate of industrialisation and encouraging Western investment. In May 1974 he arranged in Moscow a major arms deal, estimates of which varied between $1,000 million and $12,000 million. He was also much engaged in trying to end the overt antipathy between Qadafi and President Sadat. In the summer of 1975 Jalloud's quarrel with the Planning Minister Umar Muhayshi over the allocation of national resources caused the latter to weave a military conspiracy and, after its failure, lead a dissident movement from Cairo. During 1976, as the Lebanese Civil War developed, Jalloud attempted to organise help for the Palestinians. In April 1976 after students at Benghazi University had denounced government interference in their affairs, Jalloud addressed them, firing shots in the air as a call for "popular revolution" and the expulsion of reactionaries. There had been regular reports that, trying to run the country efficiently, he was angered by the often bizarre notions of Qadafi in giving power to the people, and might elbow the "Supreme Thinker" aside but in February 1977 he praised the decision of the Sabhah Congress to abolish the state and served as

his deputy as Secretary-General of the GPC. Although seen as the only other person given broad authority and as a possible scapegoat if things went wrong, he was replaced in 1979 by a civilian as Deputy Secretary-General. In July 1978, having failed to get help from France, he tried to persuade India to collaborate on an atomic bomb and in August he went to Peking, establishing diplomatic relations. In April 1979 he led a large mission to Tehran to congratulate the Ayatollah Khomeini but failed to persuade him to resume the diplomatic relations broken off in the days of the Shah because of suspicion of Libyan involvement in the disappearance of Musa Sadr. In June 1980 he justified the killing of "stray dogs", the exiled opponents of the regime but in the autumn he accused the Revolutionary Committees of abusing their powers: they responded by summoning him to justify himself and arresting his brother-in-law. There were increasing reports that Jalloud was frequently erratic and incapacitated by alcohol and drugs and there were occasions when he appeared to lose touch with truth or reality; for example he accused the British Government of murdering a policewoman outside the Libyan Embassy so as to gratify the Americans. In March 1986 when it was apparent that the Americans were looking for a pretext to attack Libya he was put in charge of security and after the Tripoli Bombing he, rather than Qadafi, steadied the country. He then went to Moscow but failed to get new credits although he was given some help in upgrading air defences. In November Jalloud went to Damascus, apparently in an attempt to mediate between the Palestine Liberation Organisation and the Syrians but the siege of Burj al-Barajinah continued. In January 1987 Qadafi recalled and humiliated him in public: Jalloud returned to Syria taking his family amidst reports that he was defecting, having disagreed with Qadafi over Chad. In April, however, he represented Libya at the Amman Summit that was such a humiliation for his diplomacy that he accused most Arab governments of being paid by the Americans and made his exit spitting. In June he negotiated economic agreements with Algeria and pushed for unification of the two countries; he was later the the main Libyan negotiator for the Arab Maghreb Unity Treaty. In January 1991 he went to Baghdad, Amman, Tehran and Ankara in the hope of averting war after the Iraqi occupation of Kuwait. In 1993 while Qadafi was trying to improve relations with the West Jalloud was sometimes seen as the defender of the revolutionary past but unassailable as Qadafi needed the support of the Megarah: Jalloud's Megarah connections made him oppose the handing over of the Lockerbie suspects, one of whom came from his tribe. In October he was reported under arrest after an army mutiny had been repressed. Jalloud in later years was described as impetuous, erratic, foul-mouthed and an insatiable womaniser.

AL-JAMA'A AL-ISLAMIYYAH

Egyptian militant group. Trouble started in May '92. Umar had denounced tourists even though one in five of the population made their living from tourists who brought in $3 billion a year. On 14 May 1992 there were a number of killings at Manshiet Nasser, near

Dayrut. In June al-Jama'a al-Islamiyyah used Dayrut as the base for 1,000–3,000 men. Following an attack in Dayrut in which four were killed (two merchants and two police) 450 extremists were arrested. The extremist leader Gamal Faragallah Haridie, an army reserve officer, was blamed for the Dayrut killings and arrested. A militant group of zealots guarded by armed police surfaced in Sanabau led by a butcher who called himself Amir. He was killed on 19 June. In June Farag Fouda, a secularist Muslim, was killed and 22 imprisoned for one year in Damitta for attacks using swords on cafés and shops showing TV. On 28 June a curfew was imposed in Dayrut, two were killed and three wounded. There were also allegations that the police were using torture. On 22 July Mubarak denounced the violence and introduced a new anti-terrorism law. On 10 August a police station and video shops were burned in Dayrut. On 23 August the curfew in Dayrut was extended after police killed seven people in a raid on a flat in Manwqabad where arms were found. On 17 September Bdr Makhluf, a lawyer said to be a leader in Qna, and six others were arrested in a shoot-out and accused of organising attacks on tourists. A communiqué from Gam al-Isl warned foreigners to stay away – rocks were thrown at buses and incendiary bombs were discovered at tourist sights. The catalogue of killings continued: on 29 September a policeman was killed in an ambush; on 6 October three police were killed when a bomb was thrown from a train in Dayrut; on 16 October four were killed in attacks on Copts; an English woman tourist was killed when a bus was shot at in Dayrut (a 17-year-old student was later arrested); on 23 October a Nile steamer was fired on near Nag Hammadi. al-Jamaat declared that it would attack tourists (the second target after the government leaders) unless the regime freed all detainees, abandoned torture and "Allowed the call to God to resume". Two lawyers were arrested. On 29 October the trial of 18 Islamic fundamentalists (and four in their absence), said to be Takfir, started in Alexandria. Twenty-six members of the Jihad group, including the brother of Islambuli and Hani Shazli, were accused of involvement in the murder of Mahjoub. On 1 November gunmen fired on a bus carrying 55 Copts. On 7 November the Interior Minister Muhd Ahalim Musa said he was determined to crush the militants. Jamaat claimed responsibility for attacks on a British woman and three attacks on Nile steamers and there were calls for an armed campaign to topple the Government and to install a religious state. On 9 November Nile cruises were suspended, blamed on low water. A bomb was thrown into a police compound at Dayrut and the army started using helicopters to look for militants. On 11 November a proposal was mooted to bring all private mosques under the Ministry of Waqf and extra preachers were appointed. Jamaat took over the Bar Association. On 12 November six German tourists and two Egyptians were wounded when snipers fired at a bus. A number of fundamentalists condemned this the eleventh attack on foreign tourists since June. Four suspects of the 12 November attack were arrested in Alexandria. On 10 November a bomb was thrown into a police camp at Dayrut which sparked off renewed fighting. A curfew was introduced in Assyut and 150 were arrested in a dawn raid. They were accused of plotting to seize "vital targets". One of the officers was said to belong to the extremist wing of Jama'a al-Islamiyyah. By this stage 76 had been killed, 120 wounded and 1,000 were in prison under the emergency laws. Luxor reported the tourism, its main currency earner, was down by nearly 50%. On 23 November 48 people were arrested and accused of attacking video shops. On 25 November two police were shot in Alexandria. On 4 December eight Islamic Jihad militants were sentenced to death by an Alexandrian military court. The General-Judge banned reporters and the Supreme Court later ruled that they should not have been tried by the military. On 6 December a bomb was thrown in Dayrut which wounded passers-by. On 10 December 600 were rounded up in Cairo by 14,000 troops which enforced Islamic law in the Imbab district. A government spokesman said that "the phenomenon is being finished". Shaykh Jabir, who had been captured, was said to have confessed to ordering bombs in 22 Cairo cinemas. Islamists claimed that they had been more efficient than government at earthquake relief in Upper Egypt. In December 24 Copts were hatcheted to death in front of their families and 33 houses and churches burned. Many of those arrested were despairing unemployed labourers. Shaykh Hamid Abu al-Nasir's *Supreme Guide of MB* was denounced as unIslamic and harming Egypt. In mid-December Mubarak-said that 90% of Jama'a al-Islamiyyah had been netted. He toured sites in the South. Six hundred and fifty were arrested in Imbaba, Mubarak confirmed the first death sentences. On 31 December four were arrested after a shoot-out at an Alexandrian bomb factory. Violence increased in 1993. On 5 January 1993 two buses carrying holidaymakers were attacked in the South and 80 were arrested in Dayrut after three attacks on churches. On 5 January Arab Interior Ministers met in Tunisia to co-ordinate action. Sudan and Iran offered help. Twenty Japanese were shot at near Dayrut. On 8 January attacks in Cairo started. Warnings were circulated to travel agents: "tourism teaches our youth decadence but we have no wish to kill individuals". Tourism was down by over 50%. In January there was an attack on a tourist bus near Pyranida. Jama'a al-Islamiyyah warned foreigners to keep away so as not to be caught up in the struggle against the Government. A leaflet threatened to turn Cairo into an "arena of holy war". On 11 January, eight sentences of life imprisonment were given for the killing of suspected extremists. On 20 January Mubarak called on Ulama to repudiate the violence. Rumours circulated of car bomb attacks planned on foreign embassies. On 24 January two police were killed in Cairo. On 30 January police were accused of trying to cover up attacks on the tourists. By early February four militants had been killed. On 9 February a German tourist bus was bombed near Dayrut. On 17 February four, mostly German, buses were attacked at Manfaloyut on their way South. On 26 February a bomb in Tahrir Square killed four, including two tourists. Eighteen others were wounded and 100 suspects arrested. On March 6 49 were charged in military courts with trying to change the Government by force and of attacking foreigners between Cairo and Aswan. All complained of torture. On 9 March Jama'a al-Islamiyyah denied connection with the bombing of New York Trade Center. It claimed it never attacked innocent people. On 11 March 14 militants and police were killed in a shoot-out at the Aswan mosque. Eighty were arrested. At least 21 were killed in 24 hours in four incidents in Imbaba. On 12 March Tutankhamun was reopened. On 13 March, 52 were hurt after an attempt to burn a Protestant church in Delta Qalyub. On 16 March a bomb exploded near the Egyptian Museum. The Government was blamed for relying on force and arrested Shaykh Yahia had links with Umar and was found with militant leaflets. On 17 March 12 were killed in Asyut in a police attack. Over 100 were rounded up. Jama'a al-Islamiyyah threatened businesses in an intensification of security. On 20 March five soldiers and three militants were killed near the Libyan frontier. On 21 March a militant was shot and five arrested in Asyut. On 27 March police were killed in a fire station. On 28 March in a bomb attack on a civil defence HQ one policeman was killed in a shoot-out in a metro station. Fifty were arrested when bombs were found. On 29 March there was a bomb in the Chephren pyramid. On 30 March there was a bomb in a police building and a British citizen was stabbed near the Opera. On the same day Interior Minister Ahalim Musa demanded that Ulama condemn militant attacks. On 3 April Mubarak travelled in the West. On 9 April a Nile cruise ship was fired on. On 11 April bombs were placed on a German tourist bus in Cairo. A brigadier and two staff were killed near Asyut. Seventy-five were arrested. By the end of April there had been 15 attacks on Western tourists: three were killed and more than 20 wounded. One hundred and forty had been killed already in that year. In a single day there were bombs in Cairo, Delta and Upper Egypt. On 18 April Interior Minister Ahalim Mousa was blamed for letting militants flourish and for reacting too late. He also accepted Ulama's attempt to mediate without consulting Mubarak. He was replaced by General Hassan Muhd al-Alfi, Governor of Asyut. Alfi had said there was a need to tackle economic difficulties. On 20 April following an attemped assassination of information Minister Safwat Sharif more than 500 were arrested. Ulama attempted to mediate but on May Day Mubarak said there could be no truce. The Education Minister said that 200,000 video tapes were seized in a single week. On 10 May two police were killed in the Asyut area.

On 18 May the Government cut direct telephone links with Pakistan, Afghanistan, Iraq, the Sudan and Iran. On the same day Mubarak ratified seven death sentences. On 19 May 800 members of the Vanguard of the New Holy Struggle running secret cells in universities and schools were arrested. On the same day the mayor of Xtn was killed near Asyut. On 21 May a bomb outside a Cairo police station killed seven. On 24 May three soldiers were killed for their weapons in an attack on a camp. Four tourists were injured at Simbel by police after a bus did not stop. On 27 May six death sentences were passed by Safwat making 23 since the first in December. On 3 June the Interior Minister said that a plot financed from abroad for attacking during Eid had been foiled. On 5 June 400 were arrested after Imbaba December went on trial. On 8 June five Britons were wounded in a bus near the Pyramids. One hundred and fifty were arrested. On 12 June the first militant since Sandat was hanged. Fourteen more died in the next month. The next day six bombs were defused. Mubarak pledged $1 billion for social improvements to defuse the situation. On 18 June seven were killed by a nail bomb in a Cairo slum thus targeting ordinary Egyptians. Jihad were accused and Cairo residents denounced the escalation of violence. All mosques came under state control and 2 million video tapes were confiscated. It was estimated that 44 groups were operating in Egypt – allies and rivals. Jihad specialised in infiltrating forces and attacking senior officials; Shawkiun specialised in raiding jeweller's shops and killing Copts; Afghans specialised in Islamic fatah Vanguard. Early July saw the first arrests in the Red Sea area. On 8 July seven militants were hanged and five more on 17 July. The 18 July saw attempts to kill General al-Alfi in Cairo and on 8 August the police Chief of Qena was killed. On 21 August four more militants were sentenced to hang in Cairo.

JARRING MISSION (1967–73)

Resolution 242 by which the Security Council hoped to restore peace after the June War requested the Secretary-General U Thant to send a special envoy to the area "to promote agreement and assist efforts to achieve a peaceful settlement". He selected Dr Gunnar Jarring (born 1907) a Professor of Turkic Languages and previous President of the Security Council, currently Swedish Ambassador in Moscow. The Khartoum Summit ruled out direct negotiations with Israel but seemed to leave an opening for indirect talks. After an initial visit to the area, seeing all those concerned separately, except Syria which refused to receive him, Jarring reported at the end of March 1968 that he had failed because Israel insisted upon direct talks which the Arabs refused. He continued throughout the year, showing infinite patience in flying from one capital to another, frustrated each time by a new incident. In March 1969 he undertook another series of visits after which he practically gave up. The Rogers' Plan (I) of June 1969 envisaged a further role for Jarring but when that failed to win acceptance he returned in October to his post in Moscow. In February 1970 he met U Thant in Geneva and they agreed there was insufficient basis to reactivate the Mission but the acceptance of Rogers' Plan II of June 1970 led to its resumption. In February 1971 he specifically asked Israel if it were prepared to withdraw its forces from all occupied territories and seek a genuine solution to the refugee question: at the same time he asked Egypt if it were prepared to end the state of belligerency, guarantee freedom of navigation, recognise the rights of all states to live in peace and prevent its territory from being used as a base for guerrillas. Israel refused point-blank while Egypt would only agree to negotiate after the Israelis had withdrawn. This effectively ended the Jarring Mission although he continued to pay visits to the Middle East and to negotiate with Arab and Israeli leaders in New York or Geneva. After the October War Jarring retired as Ambassador to Moscow and played no further part in Middle Eastern affairs.

al-JAZAIRI, (Muhammad) Said (c. 1872–?)

Syrian politician. As grandsons of the Algerian leader Abd al-Qadr, he and his brother Abd al-Qadr inherited great wealth and influence. They flirted with Arab nationalism before the war and one of the family was hanged by Jamal Pasha in 1915 and the rest temporarily exiled. Abd al-Qadr was released at the urging of the ex-Khedive Abbas Il Hilmi and went to Mecca to join Sharif Hussain. Despite warnings from the French that he was in the pay of the Turks, Amir Faysal told Lawrence "I know he is mad. I think he is honest" and he was allowed to accompany the Arab army. Lawrence said that he was "half-insane with religious enthusiasm and a most violent belief in himself". Abd al-Qadr was joined by his brother Said whom Lawrence described as "a low-browed degenerate with a bad mouth and as devious as his brother but less brave". In November 1917 they deserted the Arab army, collaborated with the Turks, and tried to establish themselves as rulers of Jabal Druze. On 29 September 1918 when the Arab army was about to enter Damascus, Abd al-Qadir persuaded the Turks to leave peaceably and they then forced a gathering of notables at the Town Hall to nominate Said as Head of State. Two days later Lawrence dismissed the brothers, whereupon Abd al-Qadr tried to knife him but was prevented by Auda Abu Tayi. Immediately afterwards they launched a sudden and fanatical revolt in the course of which Abd al-Qadr was killed resisting arrest. The French protested that he had been murdered in the interests of the Hashemites and some believed that he had been working in their interests. Said was briefly exiled to Haifa. A Foreign Office report of 1921 said that he was "rash and ignorant and had committed three acts of homicide through carelessness"; he was also believed to be intriguing with Amir Abd Allah. In 1925, echoing his grandfather, he saved some of the Christians of Damascus during the Druze Revolt and later tried to arrange a general peace settlement. In 1928 when the French were reported to be choosing a King for Syria, Said hoped to be selected. In 1931 he founded the Party of the national Pact and later he played some part in boycotts. He was frequently in debt, selling some of his property in Palestine to Zionist settlers and in 1934 his son tried to murder him because of his supposed stinginess. A British official report of 1937 remarked "Not very clever, nor entirely sane. Rather a joke with everyone". In November 1956 he offered to raise a force of Algerians to fight Imperialism and Zionism.

JERASH–AJLOUN FIGHTING BATTLES (1971)

During 1970 relations between the Jordanian Government and the Palestine Liberation Organisation deteriorated until they reached open warfare during Black September. After intervention by other Arab states King Hussain and Yassir Arafat signed an agreement by which the guerrillas withdrew from Amman and were concentrated in the Jerash-Ajloun area. The King still suspected that the Palestinians planned to seize power and appointed as Prime Minister the strongest advocate of keeping them in check – Wasfi al-Tall. Clashes continued and in January 1971 the Jordanian army launched a major attack near Jerash which was followed by another agreement as the Arab states called for a cease-fire. In April Hafiz al-Assad tried to mediate and his failure was followed in June by representatives of King Faysal and Anwar Sadat. In July Hussain announced unilateral abrogation of agreements with the Palestinians and Jordanian land and air forces started a major assault on the estimated 3,000 commandos in the Jerash–Ajloun area. After four days of heavy fighting about 2,300 guerrillas were taken prisoner and expelled from the country, going mostly to South Lebanon. Nearly 100 crossed into Israel and surrendered. Tall said that government casualties had been 31 dead and 90 wounded but no accurate figures were available for Palestinian losses amongst whom was Ali Abu Iyad, almost the only leader who had not fled when the fighting started. The Black September Organisation often invoked his name. Several Arab states broke off relations with Jordan and the Saudis called a conference in Jiddah which failed to work out a new relationship between the King and the PLO which continued bad for several years.

JERICHO CONFERENCE (1948)

After the creation of the State of Israel, King Abd Allah was determined to annex the remaining part of Palestine. Alarmed by the creation of the Gaza Government under the auspices of Egypt in September 1948 in the same month he invited a group of pro-Hashemite Palestinian leaders to Amman. They obligingly repudiated the Gaza Government and called for the unification of Palestine with Trans-Jordan but the number and known sympathies of those involved carried no conviction. In October the Israelis overran much of the territory "administered" by the Gaza Government and the northern areas which had been occupied by the Arab Liberation Army. There was therefore little possibility of an independent Arab state and in December Abd Allah called a second conference in Jericho. This was attended by 2,000 delegates and, thanks to capable stage-management, was able to create an image of popular support for annexation of the West Bank although it called also for the unity of Palestine which it saw as a preliminary to greater Arab unity, presumably also under Abd Allah. The decision led to a series of attacks upon Abd Allah by other Arab states but met with the approval of the British who extended their security guarantee to the enlarged state and of the Americans and Israelis.

JERICHO–GAZA

Due to be taken over on 13 January 1994, the withdrawal was completed in April. In June all elements of the military administration were due to be destroyed and elections were scheduled for July. On 13 September the World Bank proposed $3 billion aid for development over ten years. There was an urgent need for water, sewerage, power, transport and education. The PLO wanted $11.6 billion. Usuf Sayugh said that the priority was to provide employment. It was also hoped that a desalination plant and refinery would be built. In October two Israeli hikers were murdered near Jericho. On 22 October Assad Saftawi, leading moderate in Gaza and head of the UN school, was murdered. On 24 October fighting broke out within Fatah in Gaza. Starting 13 October, Israel was due to hand over control of education, tax, culture, health and social affairs and to set up police in Gaza.

JERUSALEM, Annexation of (Security Council Resolutions)

During the June War of 1967 Israeli forces captured East Jerusalem which it declared that it would never give up. On 4 July General Assembly Resolution 2253 declared Israeli measures to change the status of Jerusalem invalid and that they should be rescinded. Despite the similar Resolution 2254 the following week, the Israeli Government in August declared the City the country's capital. A unanimous Security Council call on Israel on 27 April 1968 "to refrain from holding" a military parade there was defied. On 21 May Security Council Resolution 252 sponsored by Pakistan and Senegal calling on Israel to rescind measures taken to change the international status of the City was passed unanimously although the USA and Canada abstained. On 3 July 1969 Resolution 267, passed unanimously apart from American abstention, "deplored the failure" of Israel to heed previous Resolutions, censured all measures to change its status and demanded their cancellation. Israel contemptuously rejected the Resolution. On 15 September, after the burning of the Al-Aqsa Mosque Resolution 271 deplored the sacrilege, recognised that the destruction of Holy Places could endanger peace, called on Israel not to interfere with the plans of the Supreme Muslim Council for its rebuilding and again declared that the acquisition of territory by force was inadmissible. Resolution 298 of 25 September 1971 declared "expropriation of land, transfer of populations and legislation aimed at the incorporation of the occupied section totaly invalid". In July 1993 the Deputy Mayor Avraham Kahila stated that whereas in 1967 there had been no Jews in Eastern Jerusalem their present number, 160,000, had surpassed that of the 155,000 Muslim and Christian Arabs.

JERUSALEM ISLAMIC CONGRESS (1931)

During the Mecca Conference Haj Amin al-Hussaini, the Mufti of Jerusalem established friendly links with Shawkat Ali and other Indians influential in the Khilafat Movement. Both were anti-British, in search of allies, and disappointed at the lack of suppport forthcoming from Ibn Saud who was doing nothing about organising a standing committee or a second Congress. The Mufti wished to gather Muslim support for the Palestine Arabs and called for a Conference to discuss the threat to the Holy Places and the need for an Islamic University in Jerusalem. Other matters for the agenda were the threat to the Hijaz Railway posed by French actions in Damascus, propaganda and general Muslim co-operation. Although the Indians supported his call there was considerable opposition: Ibn Saud, King Fuad, and the Turks all feared a demand for the revival of the Caliphate, perhaps in the person of the Ottoman Pretender or King Faysal of Iraq. The Italians, who had recently executed Umar al-Mukhtar, expected to be attacked and asked the British to forbid a Conference as did the Zionists. The Palestinian politicians Raghib al-Nashashibi and Hussain Fakhri al-Khalidi, fearing the aggrandisement of the Mufti, were also hostile. However it attracted a far wider participation than its predecessor with delegates from Bosnia, Morocco, Nigeria, Indonesia and the Tatar region of the USSR. A leading Shiah *alim* also attended when the Conference opened in December 1931. The best known delegates were Sir Muhammad Iqbal, Rashid Rida, Abd al-Aziz al-Thaalibi, Riad al-Sulh, Shukri al-Quwatli, Abd al-Rahman al-Azzam, Awni Abd al-Hadi, Shakib Arslan, Abd al-Khaliq Torres and Muhammad al-Makki al-Nasiri. The Mufti, controlling the invitations, contrived to keep out his opponents. In fact little was achieved although many felt that it had been the most successful piece of inter-Muslim co-operation for centuries. The debates were often acrimonious with some delegates arguing that a British presence was a safeguard for the Holy Places and Azzam was expelled from the country for a virulent attack on the Italians. There were disputes over the curriculum for the proposed University, the very idea of which was vehemently condemned by representatives of al-Azhar. An Executive Committee of 25 with the Mufti as Chairman and Ziyad al-Din Tabatabai, a former Prime Minister of Persia, as General Secretary was created with a seven-man permanent secretariat. Christian missionary activities amongst Muslims were condemned as were Imperialism and Zionism. The restoration of the Hijaz Railway to Muslim control was demanded. It was proposed that there should be another Congress in two years time but funds were not available either for this or the University so nothing further happened. The main result was to enhance the prestige of the Mufti who gained further *kudos* by exploiting his position as Chairman in an attempt to mediate in the Saudi–Yemeni War of 1934.

JIBRIL, Ahmad (1938–)

Palestinian terrorist. He was born near Jaffa with a Palestinian father and a Syrian mother. After the Palestine War he fled to Syria where he joined the army, reaching the rank of captain. He had close links with the Baath Party and was dismissed upon the formation of the United Arab Republic. In 1959 he founded the Palestine Liberation Front which, organised into small cells, was designed more as a fighting than a political force. After its first operations he joined Fatah but left when it fell foul of the Syrian Government. Jibril established links with the Russians, East Germans and Bulgarians. In October 1967 he merged his group into the Popular Front for the Liberation of Palestine but a year later he quarrelled with its leader George Habash whom Jibril considered too involved in left-wing politics and ideological disputes to set up his own Popular Front for the Liberation of Palestine – General Command which was to be more concerned with terrorist operations. It specialised in suicide actions within Israel and its first known operation was the killing of eight Israeli schoolchildren when it fired rockets at a bus in May 1970 and its most notorious the Qiryat Shemona Killings of 1974. That was a deliberate attempt to disrupt possible peace talks because Jibril refused to accept any compromise, insisting upon the complete liberation of all Palestine and considering Yassir Arafat too anxious to reach an agreement with the Americans. He was believed to have close personal links with Hafiz al-Assad and refused to join other Palestinian groups in resisting the Syrian troop movements into Lebanon in June 1976. This led to a split in the PFLP-GC with Abu al-Abbas forming the Palestine Liberation Front. In May 1977 Jibril was expelled from the Rejection Front. In August 1978 Jibril was suspected of being behind the bomb that blew up the HQ of Abu al-Abbas in Beirut with the loss of 200 lives. Jibril was on friendly terms with Qadafi and some of the leaders of the Iranian Revolution. In July 1981 he attempted to sabotage a cease-fire agreement in southern Lebanon but was frustrated by Arafat. During the *Intifadah* he claimed close links with Hamas and the Islamic Jihad. Jibril's support for Hizbullah against the Syrian-backed Amal brought the possibility of further splits in the PFLP-GC. He was strongly suspected of having organised the planting of the bomb that blew up an American airliner over Lockerbie in December 1988 and President Assad promised to hand him over if a case against him were proved. Foreign journalists found him a chatty, smiling, avuncular, stocky little man with a clipped military moustache.

JIDDAH AGREEMENT (1965)
After the failure of the Erkowit Conference in November 1964 fighting was resumed in the Yemen War between the Royalists backed by Saudi Arabia and the Republicans supported by Egypt. By the following summer President Nasser was anxious to end the commitment to what he regarded as "my Vietnam" as it was proving expensive and unpopular with his troops. He saw too that his difficulties were being exploited by the Russians as a means of putting pressure upon him. Increasing dissatisfaction with Egyptian domination was also showing amongst the Yemeni Republicans. He therefore went to Jiddah in August 1965 and according to Saudi sources, begged King Faysal to "save the prestige of the Egyptian Army". On 24 August an agreement was signed providing for an immediate cease-fire which should be supervised by a joint Saudi-Egyptian Commission which would also watch ports and frontiers to see that no reinforcements arrived. The Saudis would cease to supply the Royalists. Egyptian troops would withdraw in ten months from 23 November. On the same day a Yemeni National Congress would assemble at Haradh to decide upon a Transitional Government which would work out the terms of a plebiscite to outline the future form of government which should be put to the people not later than 23 November 1966. As far as is known, no Yemenis were present at the meetings of the leaders.

JIDDAH MEETING OF THE ORGANISATION OF THE ISLAMIC CONFERENCE (1992)
After the break-up of Yugoslavia, Serbs seized large areas of the predominantly Muslim state of Bosnia–Herzegovina, committing appalling atrocities including the mass rape of young girls. This was discussed by the Foreign Ministers of the Organisation of the Islamic Conference at an emergency meeting in Istanbul in June 1992. They called upon the Security Council to co-ordinate action to restore peace and also condemned Israeli actions in South Lebanon and the Occupied Territories. As the situation did not improve, King Fahd called a second emergency meeting in Jiddah in December. It was attended by the Bosnian President Izetbegovic and the UN mediator Lord Owen. The

King opened the meeting by saying that Saudi Arabia was already supplying food and cash for Bosnia and called for the end of the international ban on sending weapons. He also expressed support for the *Intifadah*. Foreign Minister Saud al-Faysal al-Saud called on the UN to use force to defend the Bosnian frontiers as 51 Security Council resolutions had been ignored: a war crimes tribunal should also be created. He said that some Arab volunteers were already fighting in Bosnia. The final communiqué called for the implementation of Security Council resolutions by 15 January 1993, after which force should be used. The meeting showed Saudi Arabia, strongly supported by Iran, taking the lead in a matter of concern to all Muslims. Fahd also took advantage of the presence of the Qatari Foreign Minister to take the first steps towards ending the Khofous Dispute.

JIDDAH, Treaty of (1955)
On 20 October 1955 Egypt and Syria signed a Mutual Defence Pact and the following week Saudi Arabia signed a similar Treaty with Egypt. They agreed to co-operate if either of them were attacked and to establish a Supreme Council consisting of their Foreign and Defence Ministers and a War Council of their Chiefs of Staff. The War Council would prepare plans for military industries, statistics, plans, etc. There would also be a Joint Command. The Treaty would be for a term of five years and automatically renewable. In April 1956 the Imam Ahmad signed the adherence of the Yemen to the Treaty of Jiddah. The main effects of this were that the Saudis gave some money to the Yemen for the purchase of arms while Egypt decreased its support for the Ahrar and other political exiles in Cairo.

JOHNSTON PLAN
In 1953 President Eisenhower in an attempt to bring peace to the Middle East by getting Israel and its Arab neighbours to co-operate for their joint economic benefit, commissioned Eric Johnston (1896–1963), President of the American Motion Picture Corporation, to draw up a plan for "an effective and efficient use" of the water of the River Jordan "disregarding political boundaries". This problem had arisen because Jordan was planning to build the East Ghor Canal to utilise the waters of the Yarmuk River, the main eastern tributary of the Jordan. As the Arab states (assisted by Egyptian experts) refused to negotiate directly with Israel Johnston had to deal with them separately but he managed to secure substantial agreement. Jordan would receive 829 million cubic metres (46.7%), enough to irrigate 120,000 acres, Israel 427 million (38.5%) for 104,000, Syria 50 million (11.7%) for 7,000 acres and Lebanon 3.1%. The distribution would be supervised by neutral experts. Lake Tiberias would be the main reservoir both for Jordan and Israel with canals leading off each side and there should be a low storage dam at Maqarin on the Yarmuk instead of the high one planned by Jordan. In 1956 Johnston produced a revised version of his plan which divided the water 60% for the Arabs and 40% for Israel. The main reservoir would now be at Makarin, which was a gain for Jordan as Israel dominated Tiberias but some of the waters could be used for the Negev which represented a gain for Israel.

In the end the Israelis thought that they would get more water by acting independently while the Arab states, at Syrian insistence, decided not to sign an agreement which implicitly recognised the existence of Israel and brought it economic gain even if they lost by it themselves. In practice the Johnston division was tacitly accepted and both sides continued their own development until the Jordan Waters Crisis of 1964.

JONGLEI CANAL SCHEME
As the White Nile flows north from Juba it enters an enormous swamp known as the Sudd and when it has emerged some 300 km further on it has lost nearly half its volume. As early as 1904 there were discussions on the possibility of dredging a canal through the Sudd which would have shortened the river journey from Khartoum to Juba by some 250 km. In 1974 a scheme was drawn up to dig a canal 360 km long, 40 metres wide and 4 metres deep from the confluence of the Nile and the Subat near Malakal past the village of Jonglei to Borr which would take 25% of the water which would normally flow into the Sudd and divert it to rejoin the main stream north of the marsh. There would be a series of dams. Under the Nile Waters Agreement of 1959 half the increased flow of 4,000 million cubic metres which would otherwise have evaporated would go to Egypt but it was still estimated that it would be possible to irrigate an additional 3.5 million acres in the Sudan. There would be considerable ecological consequences upon the tribes that had pastured their flocks in the area and rumours that two million Egyptians might be brought in to work the new lands caused riots in Juba in October 1974. There was a general feeling in the South that the Canal would benefit the North at their expense. Finance came from French and Arab sources and Egypt agreed to meet half the costs estimated at £Sudanese 90 million. Work started in 1978 with giant bucket-wheel excavators. Later it was found that a longer and more expensive route would be necessary. In 1980 the Compagnie des Constructions Internationales renegotiated a $148 million contract. In December 1983, after some 260 km had been completed the Anya Nya II guerrillas attacked the French construction workers and work stopped. After that the area was never secure but work resumed on a limited basis in 1988.

JORDAN COMMUNIST PARTY
There were probably no communists at all in Trans-Jordan but members of the former Palestine Communist Party became Jordanian citizens after 1948. They could not operate openly but formed front organisations such as the League for National Liberation (*Usbah al-Taharrur al-Watani*), the Popular Front (*al-Jabhah al-Shaabiyah*) and the Partisans for Peace (*Ansar al-Salam*). These groups aimed to influence Trade Unions and issued a series of publications. Three members of the Popular Front were elected on the West Bank in the elections of 1951. The Party itself was formally constituted in 1951 with Fuad Nassar as Secretary-General and about 700 members. Supported by intellectuals and students it stood for national liberation, social justice, republicanism, abolition of links with Britain and rights for women and the press. In the

elections of 1951 two members were successful and one in prison in Nablus received 25% of the votes. In 1952 Nassar was imprisoned and on 8 December 1953 the Party was formally banned with penalties of 15 years' hard labour. It continued to exist, however, winning three seats in the free elections of 1956 and a place in the Cabinet of Sulayman al-Nabulsi. The Party played a prominent part in the crises of 1957 and King Hussain declared that the formation of the Arab Federation with Iraq was "a natural result of its growth". In April 1966 three of its officials were sentenced to five years' imprisonment. It formed close links with the Palestine Liberation Organisation and members of West Bank origin participated in the Palestine National Front of 1973. In 1977 the JCP was reported to have held its first Congress for seven years although the place and date were not specified. Early in 1978 it joined with other opponents of the Government to form the Alignment of Popular Forces, based on Damascus, and in the wake of riots in March most of its leaders were arrested, receiving up to ten years' imprisonment from a three-man military tribunal. It was estimated that the majority of 100–200 political prisoners in the country were communists. After the death of Nassar, Faiq Warrad held office as Secretary-General for a time before he was succeeded by Yakub Zayadin. In the early 1980s, estimated to have about 200 members, the JCP moderated its attitude towards the Monarchy, declaring that to struggle for its overthrow detracted from the main battle against imperialism and Israeli occupation and it was compared to a radish "red on the outside, white within". It maintained links with the Israeli CP. In May 1986 three students were killed and 30 wounded in a riot at Yarmuk University and the King spoke of "an unholy alliance" of the communists, Fatah and Islamic fundamentalists. After the riots of April 1989 about a hundred alleged sympathisers were arrested but in the fair elections of November one avowed Party member and two supporters were elected. In January 1990 the law of 1953 was repealed, Zayadin looked forward to more public activity and in April he was received by the King.

JORDAN WATERS DISPUTE
After the failure of the Arab states and Israel to agree on the division of the Jordan waters laid down in the Johnston Plan, the riparian states went ahead on their own schemes. In practice, however, they observed the Johnston division of 45% for Jordan, 40% for Israel and 15% for Syria and Lebanon. The Arabs were particularly concerned that the river should not be used for large-scale irrigation in the Negev, opening the desert to Jewish settlers from abroad and were thus alarmed at Israeli preparations to divert water from Lake Tiberias which were due to come into operation in 1964. They were, however, at the time even more than usually divided with Egypt engaged in bitter disputes with Syria and Jordan and clashing with Saudi Arabia in the Yemen War. President Nasser believed that these three states were trying to push him into war with Israel and determined that all Arab leaders should share responsibility for whatever might happen. He therefore called on all Heads of State to meet for the first time at the Cairo Summit in January 1964. At that meeting the

Arab leaders decided against military action to stop the Israeli diversion of the water but instead to divert the Hasbani River from the Jordan partly westward into the Litani and partly eastward into the Banyas in Syria from which the waters would flow into the Yarmuk to be stored at a dam at Mukheiba for use in the Jordanian East Ghor Canal. The project would be financed by the oil states, in particular Kuwait. Realising that this might lead to war, they established the Unified Arab Command. The Israeli Prime Minister Eshkol confirmed that in 1964 his country would draw water from Tiberias up to the limit set by Jonhston and warned that Arab attempts to sabotage this would be met by force. In the event the Israeli "National Water Carrier Scheme" went ahead in 1964 without interference and work on the Arab scheme started in 1965 but the diversion works were hampered by Israeli raids, inter-Arab disputes and Lebanese lack of enthusiasm. After the June War the Arab scheme was clearly impractical.

JUFAIR AGREEMENT
Jufair, on the Bahraini island of Manama, was used for many years as a base by the Royal Navy. When the British withdrew from the Gulf in 1971 the Bahraini Government offered naval and air facilities to the Americans in return for military training and a payment of $4 million a year. A flagship and two others enjoyed "home-port" rights and the American establishment there was about 300 personnel including families. After the October War the Bahrainis cancelled the docking facilities as a protest against American support for Israel but this apparently made little difference for in October 1975 it was stated that the facilities would be available only until June 1977. The "home-port" privileges were then withdrawn but the ships were still allowed to call to take on supplies and about 60 personnel remained for logistical purposes. The importance of Jufair to the Americans was shown during the War of the Tankers and in the operations after the Iraqi occupation of Kuwait.

JULY LAWS Egypt (1961)
In June 1961 President Nasser began what he called The Second Revolution or The Social Revolution. "From now on", he declared, "there will no longer be one class sucking the blood of the other". It started with the nationalisation of the cotton trade and all export-import firms were put under government control. On 23 July, the anniversary of the First or Political Revolution he announced the nationalisation of a large part of Egyptian industry and commerce. All banks, insurance companies, heavy and basic industries, including motor transport, shipping and electricity, were taken over. In 83 companies (plus 12 in Syria) the state took over half the share capital, replacing them with 15-year bonds bearing 4%. In a further 147 medium-sized companies (plus 11 in Syria) individual holdings were restricted to £10,000 – the rest going to the state. Estates which had been limited to 200 *feddans* in 1952 were now restricted to 100 with a maximum of 50 *feddans* for rented land. The transfer of the ownership of nearly 500,000 acres was involved. Farmers would no longer have to pay interest on

government loans. No income in any organization was to exceed £5,000 and there was to be a new progressive tax of up to 90% on incomes above £10,000. All officials were to declare the source of their revenue for the previous ten years. Employees were to have elected representatives, in the proportion of one to seven on boards of management. They were to share 25% of the profits of the organisation in which they worked. The working week was cut to 42 hours without loss of pay in 370 named businesses. Government departments and companies with public participation were not to give contracts worth more than £E30,000 to companies without public participation: no contractor should receive more than £E30,000 in a single year. Nasser claimed that there had been no confiscation and saw the participation of workers as a move towards social justice not towards a Marxist State. The measures were decreed without consultation with the National Union or with representatives of Syria, to which, as a part of the United Arab Republic, they also applied. There they played a large part in causing the dissatisfaction that led to the breakup of the Union two months later.

JULY REVOLUTION (1952) (Egypt)
After the Palestine War the leaders of the Free Officers concluded that Egypt could only be reformed after a Revolution which they did not think that they could prepare before 1954–5. The election of General Neguib to the presidency of the Officers' Club in December 1951 alerted King Farouq to the dissatisfaction amongst middle-ranking officers and on 18 July 1952 he ordered the dissolution of the Club committee. In the meanwhile, following the burning of Cairo on Black Saturday there had been no stable government and the King, inviting Hussain Sirri Pasha to form a government on 2 July wished to impose upon him General Sirri Amer, a known opponent of reform as War Minister while the Prime Minister wanted Neguib. As they could not agree, on 22 July the King nominated Ahmad Hilali Pasha as Prime Minister and his own brother-in-law, Ismail Shirin as War Minister, promoting him colonel although he had no military experience. This was seen as an insult to the army and a danger as a Free Officer, Sarwat Okasha, was warned by his journalist brother-in-law that the King knew of their plans. They therefore determined to forestall probable arrest. As none of them was widely known, according to some accounts, they invited the famous nationalist General Aziz Ali al-Misri to become their nominal leader but according to himself, Neguib was already their Chairman. Their organiser, Colonel Nasser, alerted the leaders of the cells that he had created in key units to act at once. The plan was to take over firstly the army, then the Government and then deal with the King. Ali Sabri, who had contacts with the American Embassy, assured them the coup would not be anti-Western and asked it to inform the British. The King, himself at Alexandria, suspecting trouble, had ordered the most senior officers to assemble at GHQ in Cairo to take measures to prevent it but the building was surrounded by the tanks of Khalid Mohieddin and then entered by Abd al-Hakim Amer who arrested 20 senior officers: two guards were killed. Simultaneously the tanks of Hussain al-Shafai occupied the radio and railway stations, air-

ports and the telephone exchange. The brothers Gemal Salim and Salah Salim had been sent to take over the important garrison at al-Arish. Early the following morning, 23 July, Anwar Sadat read a proclamation on the radio in the name of Neguib saying that the army, shaken by instability acting in the name of the people, who had been debased by corruption, had taken power to purify its ranks. The King agreed to accept Ali Mahir as Prime Minister with Neguib at War. It was generally thought that the King might be allowed to remain but there were reports that he had asked for help from the British in the Suez Canal Zone and there was debate amongst the Officers as to whether he should be put on trial for his life. Nasser swayed the vote in favour of deposing him and the troops of Zakaria Mohieddin surrounded Ras al-Tin Palace on the morning of 26 July; six guards were wounded in an exchange of fire, the King abdicated in favour of his infant son Ahmad Fuad and sailed into exile the same evening to a 21-gun salute. A Council of Regency was established, the Executive of the Free Officers became the Revolutionary Command Council. The July Revolution was unusual in that it was conducted with apparent moderation, spreading over several days.

JULY REVOLUTION (Iraq) (1958)

Iraqi officers in the mid-1950s turned against the Monarchy because of its adherence to the Baghdad Pact which was seen as a new form of subjection to Western imperialism, the favouritism and arrogance of the Regent Abd al-Illah in army matters, the attacks of President Nasser, the hero of Arab nationalism on the ageing and pro-British Nuri al-Said, and a sense of social injustice felt by the majority of them who came from poor or lower-class backgrounds: the Government was out of touch. During 1953 the Free Officers Movement, consisting mainly of colonels, came into being in small, private meetings. In the summer of 1954 they recruited a senior officer, brigadier Abd al-Krim Qassim and he became their undisputed leader. Qassim seized the opportunity to carry out a coup provided by the passing of an armoured brigade through Baghdad on its way to reinforce the Jordanians. The General commanding the Brigade was not a member of the Free Officers but was persuaded by one of his battalion commanders, Colonel Abd al-Salam Arif to go on ahead to select a bivouac. As soon as he had left Arif seized command, arrested those officers who refused to collaborate, and led the brigade to take over key installations. One battalion surrounded the Royal Palace, shelled it and machine-gunned King Faysal, two elderly Princesses and the Regent when they emerged. Qassim arrived later and assumed command. General Nuri briefly escaped but was recognised although dressed as a woman and torn to pieces by a mob. There were further atrocities but no real resistance and the whole Revolution was accomplished in the single morning of 14 July. Air force personnel under Colonel Arif Abd al-Razzaq took over the British-administered base at Habbaniya without a shot. Originally it was suspected that Nasser, with Russian backing, had been involved but it soon became apparent that it was a purely Iraqi operation.

JUMAA, Saad Muhammad (1916–)

Jordanian Prime Minister. He was born in Amman and took a Degree in Law from Damascus University. After some years as a barrister he entered government service as head of publicity and was Secretary-General to the Prime Minister's Office and to the Ministry of the Interior before in 1957 being appointed Governor of Amman. He then held posts in the Foreign Ministry and was Ambassador in Tehran, Damascus and Washington before becoming Minister of the Royal Court in 1965. He also represented Jordan at the Arab League. Jumaa was generally regarded as pro-Western and anti-Nasser but in April 1967 he was appointed Prime Minister, instructed by King Hussain to work for an Arab summit to end the quarrels with Cairo and Damascus that had so marked the Premiership of Wasfi al-Tall. He promised decentralisation, an attack on corruption, private enterprise and investment and settlement of the bedouins but warned that austerity was inevitable. In May he supported Nasser's declaration of a blockade of Israel and accompanied Hussain to Cairo where they signed a military agreement. After the June War in which Jordan lost the West Bank, Jumaa offered his resignation to allow the King to form a new government to cope with the changed situation but he was asked to continue in office. He blamed disunity for the defeat and declared that Jordan would not recognise the Israeli annexations but could not act alone. On October 7 Hussain replaced him with Bahjat al-Talhuni but he remained a close adviser and was appointed the House of Notables and of the Royal Consultative Council. In 1969 he was sent to London as Ambassador where he spent a year, after which he was still often used on diplomatic missions and also was appointed a Senator.

JUMAA, Sharawy Muhammad (1920–)

Egyptian politician. Born in Upper Egypt, he made a career in the police force and in security intelligence. He was Governor of Suez before being appointed Minister of the Interior in September 1966. He became deeply interested in ideology or perhaps thought that the profession of socialism was a way to ingratiate himself with Nasser. He was a member of the Commission for the Liquidation of Feudalism which terrorised the middle classes and farmers. He was extremely active in the Arab Socialist Union, firstly heading the Secretariat for Organisation through which he established a semi-secret Vanguard Organisation which trained leadership cadres and attended to the political indoctrination of the army, and, after September 1969, as Secretary-General. He was thus the only man, apart from the President, to hold office in both the Government and the Party and was seen as very much the rising man. Jumaa was in charge of security, harshly repressing the riots of early 1968 which followed the derisory sentences on some officers found guilty of incompetence during the June War and which some said that he had himself instigated to bring pressure on Nasser and show his own indispensability; he also closed universities and high schools after more demonstrations in November 1968. He was also in charge of civil defence during the War of Attrition with Israel; after the humiliation at Nag Hammadi there were calls for his dismissal. In November 1970 Sadat appointed him Deputy Prime Minister. In February 1971 he was said to have visited Russia without informing the President and in May he was dismissed with Ali Sabri, accused of being a Soviet agent and plotting a coup to overthrow the Government: it is probable that he had hoped to become Prime Minister. Sadat further accused him of bugging the President's office and ordered the wholesale destruction of tapes and the closure of detention centres as a sign that the days of repression were over. Jumaa was also accused of trying to obstruct the formation of the Federation of Arab Republics and in December he was sentenced to life imprisonment. It was subsequently stated that he had employed a medium to hold seances in which he hoped to receive instructions from Nasser but the children of the late President accused him of treating the family very badly after their father's death. He was released on health grounds in 1976. Jumaa had a very round face and a pronounced lisp; he was probably not financially corrupt but was over-ambitious.

JUMBLATT

A family of Kurdish origin whose name originally meant "soul of steel" and claiming kinship with Saladin, they have been powerful in the Lebanon since the early eighteenth century. Before that they had exercised some authority in Aleppo. The Jumblatts became Druzes and successfully competed for leadership of the sect with the more aristocratic Arslan family, attracting followers by useful marriages and generosity. After assisting the Shihab *Hakims* to establish their power, Ali Jumblatt was rewarded with the lordship of the Shuf, establishing his headquarters at Mukhtara. Bashir Jumblatt formed an alliance with Bashir II Shihab and was practically his equal in power until he came to resent the *Hakim*'s exalting Maronites above Druzes. He revolted against Bashir II, was defeated with the help of Ahmad Jazzar Pasha and submitted. He rose again in 1825 and was again defeated. Bashir Jumblatt was strangled in jail and his sons lived in exile until the overthrow of Bashir II in 1840. During this period they established cordial relations with the British who arranged for the education of Ismail in England; he returned with "a disordered mind" and leadership of the family passed to the "energetic and ferocious" Said Jumblatt. With British help he managed to re-establish the influence of the family, and became notorious as "a wayward, overbearing and unscrupulous marauder" with a reputation for land-grabbing. The Ottomans preferred the Arslans, appointing one of them as the Druze representative in the Dual Kaymakamate. In 1845, however, they helped Said against attacking Maronites at a time of general disorder. After the Dayr al-Qamr Massacre of 1860 led to all-out war Said Jumblatt was the most savage of the Druze leaders and called in the help of the Hauran Druzes under Ismail al-Atrash. His sister Naaify also led attacks on Christians and presided over massacres of women and children at Hasbayyah while Salim Jumblatt simultaneously attacked Janin. During the atrocities Said, claiming to be unable to control his followers, continued to express loyalty to Britain, who after peace was restored, arranged for his comforts in prison where he died in 1861. Said's son Nasib maintained the family policy of friendship with the English and hostility to the Arslans. He served as a *Kaymakam* until 1904, frequently embarrassed by the cupidity of his family. One of his sons, Rashid, was convicted of having swindled a French banker in Paris; another, Fuad, was an inspector in the militia. During the French Mandate the family collaborated with the French who appointed Fuad *Kaymakam* of the Shuf. He was killed in 1921 chasing bandits and for many years the leader of the family was his formidable widow, Nazira who served as the model for the heroine of Pierre Benoit's novel *La Chatelaine du Liban*. She succeeded in maintaining the family inheritance until her son Kamal Jumblatt came of age. In the meanwhile Hikmat Jumblatt held various Ministries in the late 1930s.

JUMBLATT, Kamal (1917–77)

Lebanese political leader. Born in Mukhtara, the seat of the aristocratic Jumblatt family, he inherited the leadership of his community at the age of four. He was educated by the Lazarist Fathers in Beirut and at the Sorbonne where he studied sociology and philosophy. He received a further degree in Law from the Jesuit University of Beirut and as soon as he had completed his education, took his family seat in the Assembly in 1943. Initially a supporter of Emile Edde, he turned against him regarding his devotion to the French as treason. Jumblatt from the first disliked the National Pact which meant that he, as a Druze, could never aspire to the highest posts but in December 1946 accepted office under Riad al-Sulh as Minister of Agriculture and Social Affairs. He resigned after a few months and bitterly attacked the corruption of the regime of Bishara al-Khouri. Jumblatt was a great admirer of Gandhi and throughout his career paid frequent visits to India, living in *ashrams* and discussing Hindu mysticism with his guru. He also regularly practised yogi and spent much time pondering philosophical questions such as the morality of the existence of the State. He had married the daughter of Shakib Arslan and the Palestine War completed his formation as an ardent Arab nationalist. He was genuinely convinced that the majority of politicians ignored socio-economic problems and were indifferent to the underprivileged. In 1949 he founded the Progressive Socialist Party, called for sweeping reforms and distributed some of the family estates while still insisting upon his status as feudal leader of the Druzes. In 1952 he and Camille Chamoun worked closely together to frustrate Khouri's attempt to alter the Constitution in order to secure a second term in office. The alliance, however, did not last because Jumblatt was temperamentally and ideologically incapable of collaborating with anyone for long and he quarrelled with the President's pro-Western foreign policy. They both came from the Shuf and Chamoun worked with Majid Arslan, the rival for Druze leadership to weaken Jumblatt's influence. In 1957 Jumblatt lost his parliamentary seat. After the creation of the United Arab Republic Jumblatt went to Damascus where he arranged for some 600 of his followers to receive arms and guerrilla training. Despite his Gandhian principles, Jumblatt was never averse to the use of violence to achieve political aims and he played a leading part in plunging Lebanon into civil war to bring down the President. He supported the new regime of General Fuad Shihab under whom he held office from 1961–4 as Minister of Education, then of Public Works and later of the Interior. He worked hard to bring benefits to the poorer areas although at times he made himself ridiculous by such measures as attempting to regulate the *déshabillé* of nightclub performers. Jumblatt moved further and further to the left and after a visit to Peking in 1964 returned an outspoken supporter of Chinese Communism and other Third World causes. At the same time he used left-wing ideology to weaken the hold of the traditional Sunni leaders upon their younger followers and he exploited Nasserism for the same purpose. Jumblatt continued his alliance with the Shihabists by supporting the election of Charles Helou but later quarrelled with him on both personal and political grounds. In March 1965 he announced the formation of the National Struggle Front, aimed at ending Maronite domination of the political system. In the June War he showed fervent support for the Palestinians and then encouraged them to start a war of liberation on the model of those in Vietnam and Angola, forging alliances with leaders such as George Habash, Naif Hawatmeh and Ahmad Jibril. He aimed also to use the large numbers of Palestinian refugees now in Lebanon as his allies to overthrow the existing order. He worked also with the Communists, both factions of the Baath and the Syrian Socialist Nationalist Party. Pierre Gemayel accused him of aiming at a socialist state such as Algeria or Syria. He demanded conscription to fight Israel. Though he had previously criticised Rashid Karami for repression, he accepted the Ministry of the Interior under him in November 1969 and tried to implement the Cairo Agreement. He used his position to attack Army and Intelligence interference in politics and to legalise the previously outlawed parties such as the Communists with which he was allied. In June 1970 Jumblatt proposed Jamil Lahoud for President but when he saw this would be unsuccessful he gave Sulayman Franjiyah the four votes of the National Struggle Front which enabled him to win by a majority of one. In the next two years he supported and organised a series of strikes and demonstrations in favour of the Palestinians and received the Lenin Prize in Moscow. He venomously attacked Chamoun and the Prime Minister Saeb Salam for corruption and sympathy with Zionism and Gemayel for arming his followers, regardless of the enormous arsenal that he was himself acquiring in Mukhtara. He continued, however, to enjoy good relations with the President and attempted to woo the Shiah. After the Ayn al-Rummanah Massacre in April 1975 which is generally seen as the start of the Lebanese civil war,

Jumblatt often became so vehement that many thought that he was actually insane. He worked to keep Rashid al-Sulh in power but refused co-operation with any government that had representation of Gemayel's Kataib and joined forces with his old enemy Saeb Salam to wreck the military cabinet of Nur al-Din al-Rifai. Jumblatt then put forward his Five Demands for the abolition of the confessional system, a new constitution regulating the executive, change in the electoral law, reorganisation of the army and extension of citizenship to many immigrants who were mostly his own supporters. Jumblatt became extremely critical of the growing involvement of Syria in Lebanese affairs. In December 1975 he broke from Franjiyah who was refusing to use all the forces of the state against Gemayel and for inviting Syrian intervention. His followers, the so-called Army of Fakhreddin, launched a series of attacks on Christian villages and in March 1976 they moved against the Presidential Palace. In the same month after declining two invitations he saw the Syrian President Hafiz al-Assad and peremptorily set out his plan for a total transformation of Lebanon under socialist and Palestinian domination. He failed to convince Assad who feared that this would bring about Israeli intervention and the following month Syrian troops entered the country to support the Government. Jumblatt did his utmost to obstruct the policies of Assad and pushed Yassir Arafat further than he wished to go along the same road. In the presidential election of 1976 he supported Raymond Edde and boycotted it when it appeared that Elias Sarkis, the Syrian candidate would prevail. With little internal and no external support there appeared no political future for him and in January 1977 he announced his retirement and his intention of withdrawing to India. A few days later he put forward a proposal for an Arab Confederation on the Swiss model. When he was murdered, the furious Druzes massacred 140 Christian villagers but few doubted that his killing was on Syrian orders. Jumblatt was an enigmatic and constantly changing mixture of idealist and gangster-politician. Borrowing from Teilhard de Chardin he held that when human beings were completely formed they would seek togetherness resulting in harmony and world fellowship with society providing the perfect niche for each individual, none being inferior to any other: in the meanwhile he was often extremely practical in ensuring that he got his share of the political spoils. He wrote numerous books and pamphlets on a variety of subjects including poetry, the medicinal use of herbs, translations of Hindu mysticism and his memoirs which were published after his death. In person he was lanky, donnish and untidy with piercing eyes. His son Walid Jumblatt took over his mantles of communal and political leadership.

KAFI, Ali Hussain (1928–)

Algerian Head of State. He was born in Constantine, the son of a Mufti and trained as a teacher in Constantine and Tunis. He was one of the members of the Mouvement pour le Triomphe de la Liberté et de la Démocratie who moved across to the Front de Libération Nationale. During the War of Algerian Independence he rose to the rank of colonel, commanding *wilayah II* and twice making the dangerous crossing of the Morice Line. After independence he was Ambassador to a series of Arab states. In 1979 Kafi was nominated to the Central Committee of the FLN and he was also Secretary-General of the Mujahidin, the organisation of war veterans that was widely seen as part of the corrupt establishment. When the army ousted Chadli in January 1992 Kafi was appointed to the Haut Comité d'État, the group that was to exercise presidential functions until there was a new election. On 2 July, after the murder of Boudiaf, Kafi succeeded him as Chairman of the HCE. At Ahmad said that he lacked the calibre of Boudiaf and credibility as a symbol of democracy; and was also less likely than his predecessor to have ideas of his own and was prepared to serve as a front for the military under General Nezzar. Although uninspiring, he was believed honest. In his first speech after pledging to continue fighting extremism, he offered to talk to all other politicians. He set up a commission to investigate the murder of Boudiaf but made no apparent effort to ensure that it produced a factual report. To emphasise a break with the economic liberalisation of the Chadli era, he appointed as Prime Minister Belaid Abd al-Salam, the embodiment of the state control of the time of Boumédienne. To deal with the Islamic Insurgency special courts were set up in October and a curfew imposed on the capital and its neighbourhood in December. Having dropped Boudiaf's plan of forming a Patriotic Front to appeal to the people over the heads of the politicians, in January 1993 in an attempt to gain some legitimacy for the HCE and provide an excuse for its failure to hold elections he announced a referendum and invited party leaders for discussions upon political reform. Although he simultaneously issued an amnesty for some 6,000 detainees belonging to the Front Islamique du Salut, apart from the FLN no politicians were ready to talk to him and in February the state of emergency was extended indefinitely. In March he promised that the referendum would be held by the end of the year and to expand the nominated Consultative Council which had replaced Parliament. In June he proffered a blueprint for democratic reforms to begin

in December when the HCE had promised to retire and take two or three years. In October Kafi set up a National Dialogue Commission to find a successor to the HCE. It included three senior officers and failed to persuade the politicians to collaborate. In December therefore the HCE renewed its own mandate. Kafi played little part in foreign affairs: his first visit after becoming Head of State was to Nouakchott in November 1992 for the Summit of the Arab Maghreb Union and his second to Tunis three months later.

KAFR AL-DAWAR RIOT (1952)

The July Revolution was seen by many Egyptians as the start of a new age and three weeks later, on 12 August, a group of union workers at the Kafr al-Dawar textile mill, about 12 miles from Alexandria, assembled in front of the factory office and demanded "in the name of Muhammad Neguib and the Revolution" an increase in wages and the dismissal of two company officials. It was believed that the organisers were members of the illegal Egyptian Communist Party. Security guards tried to disperse them but the workers occupied the buildings. The police then opened fire on them and the workers burned down two of the buildings, shouting "Long live the Revolution of the Army and the People". The next morning troops arrived and stormed the factory, killing 8 and wounding more than 20. The next day two workers regarded as ringleaders were sentenced to death by court martial and twelve others to long terms of imprisonment. After much debate, the Revolutionary Command Council, despite the opposition of Nasser, Amer and Khalid Mohieddin, upheld the sentence with Neguib declaring that disturbance of public order was treason. The two men were hanged and the harshness of the repression of workers, following the clemency shown to King Farouq, caused many on the left to lose confidence in the new regime.

KAFR KASSIM KILLINGS (1956)

Kafr Kassim is an Arab village within Israel about 8 miles north-east of Tel Aviv. During the Suez War the Israeli authorities feared that there might be incursions from Jordan which the villagers might help and so a curfew as imposed from 5 p.m. to 6 a.m. Border police arrived to enforce the curfew at 4.30 p.m. on October 29 but were told by the *Mukhtar* that it would be impossible to inform all the people, particularly those who worked outside the village. Regardless, the police killed those returning after 5 p.m. including a twelve-year-old boy who had been pasturing his goats. In all 47 Arabs were killed and a number wounded. Prime

Minister Ben-Gurion expressed detestation of the crime and eventually eleven policemen were put on trial. On 12 October 1958 eight including a major who was sentenced to 17 years' imprisonment were found guilty and three acquitted. Subsequently, on 24 December 1958 the Lieutenant-Colonel commanding the police brigade was put on trial for murder. Undoubtedly similar orders were received by other platoons which had allowed obviously innocent villagers to go to their homes.

KAHAN REPORT (1983)

After the Sabra–Chatila Massacres there was a widespread belief in Israel and amongst Jews abroad that the Israeli army could and should have done more to prevent the slaughter. Prime Minister Begin refused to establish an official inquiry but international pressure and a demonstration of 400,000 people in Tel Aviv forced him to change his mind. Itzhak Kahan, President of the Supreme Court, was appointed to bring to light "all the facts and factors connected with the atrocity carried out by a unit of the Lebanese Forces". His Report, published in February 1983, distinguished between the "direct responsibility" of the Lebanese Forces and the "indirect responsibility" of the Israeli military and political authorities. He rebutted any suggestion that Israeli soldiers had participated in the killings as "baseless libel" and that those who had enabled the Lebanese Forces to enter the camps were accomplices in the crime. The Defence Minister Sharon and some senior officers had been guilty of sending in the Lebanese Forces without considering the danger that they would carry out a pogrom and of not taking "energetic and immediate action" to restrain them once it had become clear what they were doing. Disregarding the statements of many survivors, the Report said that there was no evidence that the Israeli-controlled South Lebanon Army had taken part in the massacre. Sharon was forced to resign and the officers involved censured. Many saw the Kahan Report as a whitewash while others regarded it as admirably impartial.

KAID, Ahmad (1924–78)

Algerian military and political leader. He came from a bourgeois family of Tiaret where he attended a French school before going to the French military school. He was a supporter of Messali Haj but rallied to the Armée de Libération Nationale after the All Saints' Day Uprising. As Commandant Slimane, he commanded a district in the Southern Oranie until on the creation of a General Staff in February 1960 he was appointed Deputy to Colonel Boumédienne. He was therefore one of the original Oudjdah Group. In March 1962 he represented the General Staff in the Evian negotiations. In the subsequent power struggle Kaid was dismissed by the Gouvernement Provisoire de la République Algérienne and briefly imprisoned. In September 1963 Ben Bella appointed him Minister of Tourism but in December 1964 he resigned after the President had accused him of embezzlement and slapped him in public. Kaid naturally supported Boumédienne's coup of June 1965 after which he was appointed Minister of Finance. He also acted as the principal spokesman of the new Revolutionary Council. In December 1967

at a time when the Government appeared to be under threat from dissident officers and from its own left wing, Kaid was appointed to take charge of the ruling party, the Front de Libération Nationale and to reorganise it to provide effective support for the Government. He was now seen as the second most powerful man in the country and there were at least two attempts on his life. Kaid became disillusioned, finding it impossible to galvanise the FLN out of its lethargy and corruption and he was also critical of Boumédienne's agrarian policy. As a supporter of a unified Maghreb he also opposed the President's personal hostility towards Morocco. In December 1972 he suddenly resigned on grounds of ill health and went into exile. Kaid became exceedingly bitter, in June 1975 declaring that Algeria was "sick and in chains" and "in a state of anarchy" with all power in Boumédienne's hands and in 1976 he was ordered out of France for harming relations between the two countries. He settled in Rabat where he died. He was described as voluble and given to noisy explosions of rage.

KARAMAH, Battle of (1968)

Unable to operate in Palestine the al-Fatah guerrillas resorted to shelling Israeli border posts and settlements with Russian Katyusha rockets from within Jordanian and Lebanese territory. On 21 March 1968 the Israelis launched a major attack with two brigades, about 15,000 men, against the guerrilla camp at Karamah, three miles east of the river and six miles north of the Jericho–Salt road with the probable objective of pushing on to Amman itself. Before dawn helicoptered paratroops attacked the camp which was defended by 300 guerrillas who were overwhelmed and Karamah was systematically destroyed. There followed a major battle between the Israelis, closely supported by their air force, and two Jordanian brigades which lasted for fifteen hours and ended with the Israelis being forced to retreat. According to Jordanian figures the Israelis lost 250 killed and wounded, more than 40 tanks destroyed and four fighter-bombers severely damaged; the Jordanians lost 207 killed and wounded and 25 tanks: the commandos lost 80 killed or wounded and 40 prisoners. It was a great psychological victory for the Jordanians and the Palestinians who could claim a success over the Israelis greater than any hitherto achieved by any other Arab troops: the Palestinians overestimated their contribution to the success, leading to the arrogance which caused Black September.

KARAMI, Rashid (1921–87)

Lebanese Prime Minister. A Sunni Muslim born in Tripoli, he was the son of the Prime Minister Abd al-Hamid Karami who, as a former *Qadi*, gave him a strict religious upbringing that influenced him throughout his life. Unlike most of his Lebanese contemporaries who preferred to study in Beirut or in Europe he took his law degree in Cairo and then practised for some years. On the death of his father, Karami, in 1951, inherited his Tripoli constituency and almost immediately became Minister of Justice in the Cabinet of Abd Allah al-Yafi. Having witnessed the misrule of King Farouq, Karami welcomed the Egyptian Revolution and formed his own Arab Liberation Party which, however, attracted little following. He opposed the attempts of Bishara al-Khouri to prolong his presidential term and then became Minister of the Economy under Sami al-Sulh. When that government collapsed in September 1955 President Camille Chamoun appointed Karami to be the youngest Prime Minister in the country's history. He had established a personal friendship with Nasser, whom he is said to have dubbed "a Super-man", and in March 1956 resigned in protest at Chamoun's pro-Western foreign policy. Karami vehemently opposed the President's acceptance of the Eisenhower Doctrine and when civil war erupted in the summer of 1958 he led the anti-Chamoun forces in the North. Immediately General Fuad Shihab took over as President in September 1958 he appointed Karami Prime Minister in a bid to reassure both Nasser and the Lebanese Muslims that there would be no continuation of his predecessor's policies. Karami, holding also the portfolios of the Interior and Defence, formed a Cabinet that appeared so strongly to support radical Arab causes that the Kataib launched a general strike and renewed violence to bring it down. After three weeks Karami resigned and reformed his government as one of "National Salvation" including two Maronite chiefs in its four members. Essentially a pliable, reasonable man, Karami worked very well with Shihab in attempting to give the Muslim population a fairer share of the national wealth and affronting neither the pan-Arabs nor the West. Substantial reforms were made to improve administrative efficiency and honesty. In May 1960 he was replaced by Ahmad al-Daouq who formed a neutral government to conduct elections. When they had been concluded the President decided to appoint Saeb Salam, a stronger man than Karami, as Prime Minister with instructions to reform the administration. After a year Salam proved to have too much of a will of his own to suit Shihab who in October 1961 brought back Karami who formed the Democratic Parliamentary Front of 30 Deputies to group the "Shihabists". This government which included both Pierre Gemayel and Kamal Jumblatt presided over a period of prosperity, social advancement and success in not getting involved in other people's quarrels. Karami attended the first Arab Heads of State meeting, the Cairo Summit of January 1964. The following month he left office to allow Hussain al-Uwayni to form a neutral Cabinet to preside over elections. This government actually lasted over a year and it was not until July 1965 that Karami formed his fifth Cabinet, remarkable for the fact that he was the only Deputy in its ranks. Some major ministrative reforms were carried through and corrupt bureaucrats sacked but the Government was unpopular with professional politicians and at the end of March 1966 Karami resigned. The Yafi government that followed had little success and at the beginning of December Karami formed another Cabinet of civil servants and technicians. With the help of the future President Elias Sarkis the Government managed to restore confidence after the Intra Bank Scandal. During the June War the Prime Minister would have liked to take positive steps to assist the Arab armies but leading Christians prevailed upon the Maronite Commander-in-Chief General Emile Bustani to say that it was militarily impossible and Karami had to content himself with

expelling the British and American Ambassadors and banning Coca-Cola. The war had, however, an important effect on Lebanon by greatly increasing the number of Palestinian refugees and leading to greater radicalism amongst the Sunnis who had been docile followers of their traditional zu'ama. In February 1968 Karami stepped down to allow a neutral Cabinet under Yafi to conduct elections. During 1968 there were clashes between Palestinian guerrillas and Israeli forces culminating in an Israeli attack on Beirut airport at the end of December. Criticism of the inefficiency with which the army dealt with the humiliation brought down the Yafi government and after an eight-day crisis, Karami who was known for his support for the Palestinians formed a 16-man government representing all parties except the Chamounists. He declared that the Palestinians had a right to fight for their homeland and that his government backed their cause "with all its might". He planned to introduce conscription, reinforce border villages and co-ordinate policies with other Arab states. These measures led to the resignation of the Christian leaders Gemayel and Raymond Edde and Karami had to reshuffle his Cabinet. Strong pressure from the Muslims to do more for the Palestinians conflicted with his unwillingness to upset the existing balance too drastically. Clashes between guerrillas and security forces intensified and in April 1969 Karami declared that his government, and indeed the entire country, was divided in its attitude to the Palestinians and resigned. President Charles Helou persuaded him to stay on as a caretaker. Political deadlock continued as fighting became bloodier and there were threats of Syrian and Israeli intervention. By the end of October the Lebanese army was almost daily in battle against the guerrillas and Karami repeated his resignation saying that he could not take responsibility for actions of which he disapproved. On 25 November, after the Cairo Agreement had laid down rules for Palestinian activities in Lebanon, he put together a Cabinet of 16 members representing all political parties. The Government lasted nearly a year – a period in which Cabinet Minister Gemayel and Jumblatt armed their militias, the Kataib fought the Palestinians, the Shiah grew militant under Imam Musa Sadr and the young became increasingly disillusioned with establishment figures such as the Prime Minister. Optimistic almost to the point of absurdity, he remained confident that parliamentary discussion and compromise would solve all problems and was one of the few leaders who did not form his own militia. As custom dictated Karami resigned at the end of September to allow the newly elected President Sulayman Franjiyah his choice of Prime Minister. After a difficult period with Saeb Salam, Franjiyah tried to govern through second-rank Sunnis such as Amin al-Hafiz and Rashid al-Sulh and then set up a military government under Brigadier Nur al-Din al-Rifai. This caused such an outcry that Karami, although regarded as one of the leading opponents of the President in alliance with Salam and Raymond Edde was appointed Prime Minister in May 1975, mainly through Syrian pressure. It took him more than a month to form a government of National Salvation in which he showed his skill in persuading bitter enemies to sit together and which included his old adversary Chamoun as Minister of the Interior. For months on end the President and Prime Minister did not meet and no formal business could be done. Karami tried desperately to re-establish peace but the country was now in a full-scale civil war with incidents such as the Black Saturday Massacre and, the destruction of Damour in which the President and Chamoun ordered the air force to intervene without reference to the Prime Minister who was also Minister of Defence. Karami resigned but was persuaded to remain in office while Tall al-Zatar was besieged and Syrian troops crossed the frontier. In September 1976 Karami submitted his resignation to the new President Elias Sarkis but agreed to stay on until early December when Salim al-Hoss was able to form a non-political Cabinet. Out of office, he spent much of his time trying to keep the peace in Tripoli. After the Israeli invasion of 1982 he opposed all compromise with the aggressors and joined with Franjiyah and Walid Jumblatt in the National Salvation Front to reject the May Agreement. In April 1984 President Amin Gemayel called upon Karami to form his tenth "Last Hope" Cabinet which included Chamoun, Pierre Gemayel and Walid Jumblatt. Karami announced his objectives as ending the Israeli occupation of the South, restoration of law and order and revision of the National Pact in favour of the Muslims. He had established such good relations with the Syrian President Hafiz al-Assad that the Maronites attacked him as a quisling. The Government never functioned as a unit as the warlords pursued their own policies and Jumblatt, in particular, appeared as an opponent rather than as one of its members. Karami found it impossible to work with the President and virtually went on strike, refusing to convene his Cabinet. In April 1985 he resigned but stayed on at the urging of Assad but in June he suggested that both he and the President should resign. In January 1986 he refused to meet Gemayel to discuss the Three-Militia Agreement. During 1986 the Cabinet only once met as a body as normally Christian Ministers conferred with the President in East Beirut while Muslims met the Prime Minister in West Beirut. In April 1987 the Cabinet met but proved so divided that Karami announced his resignation but Gemayel procrastinated in accepting it. At the beginning of June the helicopter in which Karami was travelling was blown up by a bomb. It was not clear who had placed it and every faction found reason to blame its opponents; one suggestion that it was his Tripoli opponents the Tawahid. His death, however, caused surprisingly little stir. A kindly, usually courteous man, Karami was ridiculed for his slow ponderous speech in classical Arabic. He never married. His pastime was shooting but he kept a small private zoo with the animals named after his political colleagues.

KARBALA RIOTS (1977)

Karbala is a holy city for the Shiah containing the tomb of the Prophet's martyred grandson Hussain. After the Baath took power educated Shiah resented the domination of Sunnis from Takrit while the poor felt that they were not receiving their fair share of increasing prosperity. This led, in about 1968 to the foundation of an underground Shiah party, al-Dawah. In December 1975 it was reported that five Shiah leaders had been hanged. In February, at the height of the annual mourning for Hussain the Government stated that a religious procession had attacked a police station and fired on officials. There were scuffles in which perhaps a dozen, although Shiah sources said hundreds, were killed before the army arrived and made numerous arrests. Then it was announced that "an agent of the Syrian regime", quarrelling bitterly with Iraq at the time, had been apprehended carrying a bag containing ten kilograms of explosives into the Shrine. The frontiers with Kuwait and Syria were closed. The bomber, a Syrian sergeant, confessed on television that he had been ordered by his intelligence service to blow up the Shrine while the Syrians claimed that he was a deserter working for the Iraqi Government. A Special Tribunal, presided over by two senior Baath Party members, sentenced eight, including the sergeant, to death and fifteen to life imprisonment. The two judges were subsequently removed from the Council of Ministers for "lack of faith in the principles of the revolution". The riots took the Government by surprise and reminded it that it could not rely upon the loyalty of the Shiah.

KAROUI, Hamid (1927–)

Tunisian Prime Minister. Born in Sousse, he qualified as a doctor in Paris, where, a nationalist from the age of 15, he was a leader of the Neo-Destour students. He returned on independence but did not seek political office, practising as a chest specialist even though he was known as a socialist and the brother-in-law of Ahmad Ben Salah. In 1983 he became a member of the Party Politburo and Vice-President of the National Assembly. In 1986 he was appointed Minister of Youth and Sport and in 1987 Minister of Justice where showed himself hard upon corruption. In September 1989 President Ben Ali, considering that Hedi Bakkush was too much under the influence of Party officials, replaced him as Prime Minister by Karoui. There were no other changes in the Cabinet. Karoui followed Ben Ali in trying to persuade the opposition parties to co-operate in a National Pact to stand against the threat of Islamic militancy as represented by al-Nahdah. In January 1990 he invited them to discuss possible amendments of the electoral system which was so heavily weighted in favour of the Rassemblement Constitutionnel Démocratique that it held all the seats both in the Assembly and on local councils in the hope that they would be encouraged to contest some forthcoming by-elections and municipal elections: only three minor parties agreed to meet him and Nahdah had not been invited. He made some unilateral changes but even so the opposition boycotted the municipal elections in June. Karoui continued his attempts to unite the country against extremism and in December 1990 criticised the opposition for not publicly condemning a plot to overthrow the state by force. In the same month his budget set out an ambitious programme of economic liberalisation with the eventual aim of achieving the convertibility of the dinar: there would be privatisation of state businesses, removal of price and import controls and cutbacks in free education and health. He saw that the task was also to reduce unemployment and the social costs of the change to greater private enterprise and he outlined plans for offshore facilities. In the meanwhile Saddam Hussain had invaded Kuwait. Karoui did not condemn the action although he declared that international frontiers had to be respected. In September 1990 he went to Baghdad with a five-point plan which included the replacement of Western troops by Arabs and the release of hostages. Later he said that concern for international legitimacy should extend to the problems of the Palestinans. Tunisia observed the sanctions against Iraq and Karoui restrained the press from attacks on the Allies. With the crisis over, in April 1991 Karoui set up a High Council of the plan to involve the opposition in proposals for privatising all non-strategic industries, cutting subsidies and aiming for a 6% annual growth. Many pointed out the contrast between economic liberalisation and political repression as human rights organisations angered the Government by pointing to the treatment of political prisoners. In the summer of 1992, Karoui twice reshuffled his Cabinet, creating a Ministry for Foreign Investment and also setting up a Department of Women's Affairs to defend their rights against Islamic militants. He signed an economic agreement in Ankara and in August went to Algiers to urge a renewal of interest in the Arab Maghreb Union. In January 1993 he eased foreign exchange controls and there was a feeling that Tunisia was doing well economically: there was 8.6% growth in 1992, inflation was the lowest for 15 years and the World Bank held up Tunisia as a model for other developing countries. Karoui, whose honesty was never in doubt, is an elegant, courteous, rather aloof man with a quick temper; he was also a football enthusiast.

KATAIB (Lebanon)

The Kataib or *Phalanges Libanaises* was founded by five young Lebanese Christians disillusioned with professional politicians in November 1936. Their leader, Pierre Gemayel had been influenced by the harnessing of the dedication and idealism of the young by the Hitler Youth which he had seen in Berlin and by Antun Saadeh in his Parti Populaire Syrien which called for the absorption of Lebanon into a Greater Syria. The Kataib stood for an independent, Western-orientated, Christian-controlled Lebanon and consisted mainly of the French-educated middle and professional classes, with a few Muslims. Any male Lebanese between the ages of 18 and 35 with the required "moral and physical attitudes" was eligible for membership. Striving for a patriotic mind in a healthy body it was more like the Boy Scouts than a Fascist movement as it was in no way racist or anti-intellectual and eschewed strident propaganda and divisive ideology. It soon had 8,000 members, organised in a strict hierarchy based on "patrols" of six members, culminating in the Phalanges of 600 men. The Kataib engaged in street brawls with the PPS and in November 1937 the French authorities banned it and other paramilitary groups. The Kataib resisted, there was loss of life and it turned into an undercover independence movement. It showed no sympathy with the Axis Powers during the war. By 1943 it had a membership of 39,000 which it was able to mobilise quickly upon the streets and was therefore the most effective force in demonstrating against the French arrest of President Bishara al-Khouri and his

Cabinet after their declaration of independence. In December 1943 it was recognised as a legal organisation and, although still officially a youth movement, unsuccessfully contested a by-election in 1945. In July 1949 after street violence it and all other youth groups were dissolved. It officially, but briefly, changed its name to the Lebanese Federation Party and in 1951 won three seats in the Assembly. As a mass national party the Kataib differed from the others which were merely the followers of a particular boss by having an ideology which could be described as "Lebanonism", the building of a strong independent pro-Western state, above sectarianism, not socialist but concerned with social security for the poor, friendly with but not part of the Arab nation. It published its own daily newspaper *al-Amal*. At the same time it maintained a militia with about 3,000 men under training at any one moment and an efficient intelligence service based on adherents in key posts. In 1958 the Kataib were amongst the most active fighters for President Camille Chamoun in his resistance to attempts to force Lebanon into the United Arab Republic, showing their power and also that nearly 10% of their strength was Muslim, mainly Shiah. Considering that the Cabinet subsequently formed gave too much to their former opponents, they brought it down by a general strike and a threat of renewed civil war and Gemayel became a Minister for the first time. In 1960 he also became a Deputy for the first time, one of six for the Kataib. For much of the 1960s the Kataib supported Presidents Fuad Shihab and Charles Helou and its numbers continued to grow from a claimed 54,000 in 1964 to an estimated 80–90,000 in 1970 – including some 5,000 overseas. After the June War of 1967 the Kataib became increasingly anxious that the Lebanon was being dragged by the presence on its soil of 400,000 Palestinian refugees into both internal and external situations which could threaten its existence. It therefore joined with other Maronite groups in the Hilf Triple Alliance and increased its military preparations at very considerable expense. It also established discreet links with Israel and received covert help from the Americans. In March 1970 for the first time it clashed with Palestinian guerrillas. By the early 1970s the Kataib militia was under the command of the energetic and ruthless Bashir Gemayel and when the civil war started it became noted for its savagery in such incidents as the Ayn al-Rummana Massacre and those of Black Saturday and Tall-al Zatar. From 1975 the Kataib operated its own two radio stations and rather than a political party with a militia, it was now a revolutionary army. In the summer of 1976 the Kataib was briefly allied with Syria but seeing that the Syrians did not intend to withdraw, it resumed and intensified its contacts with Israel. Bashir Gemayel turned on the other Christian militias, killing President Franjiyah's son in the Ihden Massacre and then destroying the Tigers of Camille Chamoun: the remnants of these groups were absorbed into the Lebanese Forces in which the Kataib had a dominating part and which controlled East Beirut. When the Israelis invaded Lebanon in June 1982 the Kataib openly collaborated with them. After the murder of Bashir Gemayel the Kataib, with the backing of the Israeli military perpetrated the Sabra-Shatila Massacres. After the Israelis left the Shuf, the Kataib attempted to take it over but they were defeated and also lost ground south of Beirut to the Shiah Amal militia. President Amin Gemayel never effectively controlled the Kataib which opposed his attempts to negotiate with the Lebanese opposition and with the Syrians and it even deprecated its founders joining the pro-Syrian government of Rashid Karami. When Shaykh Pierre died in August 1984 he was succeeded by Elie Karami who was later replaced by Georges Saadeh in June 1986. In October 1985 the Lebanese Forces took over the Kataib radio station and in October 1988 they absorbed the remnants, about 1,000 men, of the Kataib militia. Saadeh continued active in politics, there was an attempt on his life in January 1989, but politics were less important than guns in the Lebanon of the late 1980s.

KARAMI, Abd al-Hamid (1893–1950)

Lebanese Prime Minister. The son and grandson of Muftis of Tripoli, Karami had a traditional religious education, became a Qadi and was all his life a strict and conservative Sunni Muslim. Although he had supported the Turks throughout the war he later welcomed emissaries from Faysal. He opposed the French Mandate and was dismissed. In 1926 the French arrested him for active encouragement of the Druze Revolt. His family were in competition in Tripoli with the Mukaddam family and in the early part of his political career he was more concerned with building his home base than with national matters. He worked well with the local Christian leaders, the family of Sulayman Franjiyah. In 1936 he took part in the Conference of the Coast which supported the integration of most of Greater Lebanon with Syria, leaving independence for the Mountain alone and was arrested for demonstrating against the Franco-Lebanese Treaty. Later Karami came to accept the permanence of the state and his alliance with Riad al-Sulh brought together the two principal Sunni areas. During the war both collaborated with the British to obtain their support for Lebanese independence. After the promulgation of the new independent Constitution, Karami was one of the leaders arrested by the French in November 1943. In January 1945 he became Prime Minister and Minister of Defence. In April there was an attempt on his life at a time of general disorder. His government only lasted until late August when he was succeeded by Sami al-Sulh. He was followed by his son Rashid Karami as leader of the Sunnis of Tripoli and later as Prime Minister.

KAZZAR PLOT (Iraq) (1973)

Colonel Nadhim Kazzar, sometimes called "the Beria of Baghdad", was put in charge of security by Saddam Hussain after the Baath took power in July 1968 and he presided over a period of terror. In January 1969 14 people accused of spying for Israel were publicly hanged and in May there was another group of ten convicted. Leading politicians like the former Prime Minister Abd al-Rahman al-Bazzaz were tortured in prison and Kazzar was believed to be responsible for organising the murder of exiled opponents of the regime. In January 1970 44 accused of plotting on behalf of the CIA, oil companies, Zionism and British imperialism

were executed and the Iranian Ambassador asked to leave. Kazzar was especially hostile to Kurds, even though they were not at the time in revolt, and attempted to blow up their leader Mulla Mustafa Barzani and to communists, personally torturing them. In June 1973 as the Iraq Communist Party was moving towards an alliance with the Baath, Kazzar started to fear for his position and realised that the power he had amassed was alarming President Ahmad Hassan al-Bakr whom he therefore determined to kill. On 30 June Bakr was due to arrive on an aircraft from Bulgaria and be welcomed back by leading officials. Kazzar invited the Ministers of the Interior and Defence to inspect some new spying equipment, seized them as hostages and sent assassins to the airport. His men panicked, either because of extra security precautions or because the plane was late and made no attempt to carry out their mission. Kazzar, watching the President's arrival on television realised that his plot had failed and fled towards Iran with the two Ministers demanding as the price of their release that Iraqi troops should be sent against Israel, that war against the Kurds should be resumed and that named officials should be dismissed. Troops were sent to pursue him but before he was caught he killed one Minister and seriously wounded the other. After a trial before a special tribunal Kazzar, seven security and thirteen army officers were executed on 7 July, followed by thirteen civilians the next day. The plot enabled the Government to blame Kazzar for previous excesses, dubbed "embarrassing mistakes", amend the Constitution to enhance the powers of the President and place security in the charge of a brother of Saddam Hussain whose position was further strengthened by the purging of a senior Party member who had been implicated, probably against his will, in the affair.

KHALID (1912–82)

King of Saudi Arabia. He was the son of Ibn Saud by one of his favourite wives, Jauhara of the family of his close comrade Ibn Jiluwi and he received a traditional religious education in Mecca. He was also brought up amongst the tribes, performing his first public duty in 1928 when during the Ikhwan Rebellion he was sent to watch the Trans-Jordan frontier. Although born the seventh, Khalid was by now the fourth surviving son of the King. In 1934 he was deputed to sign the Ta'if Treaty which ended the Saudi–Yemeni War. In 1938 he visited Europe and was entertained by Hitler. In 1943 he accompanied his brother Faysal to Washington and London. During the next few years he showed little interest in administrative work but spent much time amongst the bedouins, enjoying falconry and other sports. When the divergence between King Saud and Faysal became unbridgeable Khalid supported the reforming policies of the latter. In October 1962 Faysal appointed him Deputy Prime Minister. The Amir Muhammad b. Abd al-Aziz, Khalid's elder and only full brother, was judged unsuitable for kingship because of violent temper and alcoholic excesses and Khalid was now the next senior Prince, an avuncular figure in the eyes of the younger family members. He was also probably the most popular, sympathetic, humorous, aloof from factional disputes and above suspicion of financial irregularities. His generosity and traditional ways gave him a large following amongst the tribesmen. He was appointed Crown Prince and despite doubts about his health after heart surgery in 1972 and about his willingness to accept the throne, succeeded as King on the murder of Faysal in March 1975. Khalid saw his main duty as holding the family and the country together while delegating much of the day-to-day authority and detail to his younger brother Fahd whom he permitted to introduce administrative rather than political reforms while he himself still appeared to continue the conservatism of Faysal. Khalid, by no means a figurehead, showed greater social concern by creating new Ministries such as Housing, Rural Affairs and Higher Education. He spent at least a month each year touring amongst the tribes. He kept in close touch with the Gulf States to see that political reforms there did not get out of hand. Although less active on the world stage than his predecessor he nevertheless embodied moderation and conciliation in Saudi foreign policy, for which he was constantly and stridently attacked by Qadafi. Kissinger called him "perhaps the most important stabilising factor in the Middle East". In May 1975, in a clear reversal of Faysal's policies, he stated that Saudi Arabia would accept the right of Israel to exist within pre-1967 boundaries if it accepted a Palestinian state on the West Bank. He also ended Faysal's refusal to deal with the Aden Government, giving aid to it as a move to buy out Russian influence which he fought to restrict in Somalia and Iraq. He was always ready to mediate in inter-Arab quarrels, sending Fahd in an attempt to mediate in the Western Sahara. Khalid played an important part in the Riyadh Resolutions of 1976 which put the Arab Deterrent Security Force, largely paid for by the Saudis, into Lebanon. Around the same time, with the backing of the King, Shaykh Yamani led the moderate faction in OPEC, trying to restrain excessive price rises in the interests of long-term stability. In February 1977, amidst rumours that he would soon abdicate, Khalid underwent hip surgery in London. After the Camp David Agreement the King reiterated the Saudi commitment to the liberation of Jerusalem and rather reluctantly went along with punitive measures against Egypt. In October 1978, accompanied by a retinue of 200, he went to Cleveland, Ohio for a second heart operation. In 1979 he welcomed Queen Elizabeth, returning the State Visit in 1981. Between the two visits there had been a brief crisis in relations between Riyadh and London for in 1977 Khalid had reluctantly acquiesced in the condemnation to death by his brother Muhammad of a granddaughter who had attempted to elope with a lover. Comments in London and the film Death of a Princess led to the expulsion of the British Ambassador. The King continued Faysal's efforts for Muslim unity but he broke one of the strictest of Islamic traditions by calling upon French commandos to end the Mecca Mosque Seizure. In 1981 he presided over the Ta'if Islamic Summit. Later that year he calmed down the excitement which arose from the belief that the Israelis had flown over Saudi territory to destroy the Iraqi nuclear reactor in the Osirak Raid. Khalid frequently expressed the hope that money spent on armaments could be channelled into Third World development.

He was regretted as an honourable man and a pleasant one.

KHALID, Leila (1946–)

Palestinian hijacker. She was born in Haifa from where her family fled to Lebanon. After education at the American University of Beirut she worked as a schoolteacher in Kuwait. She then trained as a guerrilla in Lebanon as a member of the Popular Front for the Liberation of Palestine and first came to notice when she and a companion forced a TWA Boeing 707 with 113 people on board on a flight from Rome to Lod to land at Damascus. The plane was destroyed and she was briefly imprisoned before going to Amman. The PFLP stated that it was a reprisal for the American sale of 50 Phantom jets to Israel. On 6 September 1970 three aicraft were hijacked by PFLP guerrillas and taken to Dawson's Field but Leila Khalid failed to take over an El Al Boeing 707 with 155 passengers flying from Amsterdam to New York. Her accomplice was shot dead and she was overpowered and the aircraft landed at Heathrow where she was arrested. The Israelis demanded her extradition but the PFLP threatened reprisals on the passengers and crews held at Dawson's Field and on 30 September she was deported to Cairo with six other guerrillas who had been held in Germany and Switzerland. The passengers of the hijacked aircraft admired her beauty, intelligence and courtesy and she received worldwide publicity. Later she undertook propaganda activities for the PFLP and survived Israeli attempts on her life. In 1980 she was Secretary of the General Union of Palestinian Women and attended a conference in Copenhagen. In 1988 she was reported to be living near Damascus with her two children, still advocating the armed struggle.

KHALID, Mansur (1933–)

Sudanese politician. He trained as a lawyer in Khartoum University and then did post-graduate studies at Pennsylvania and the Sorbonne. He was Attorney-General from 1957 until 1959. Khalid then joined the UN Legal Secretariat, serving in Algiers and at UNESCO in Paris with a period as Visiting Professor at Colorado. He was one of the intellectuals who rallied to the military regime of Jafar Nimeiri who appointed him Minister of Youth and Social Affairs. He represented Sudan at the General Assembly of the UN before becoming Foreign Minister in August 1971. During his period of office Sudan moved decisively from a pro-Russian to a pro-Western stance. A strong believer in a polyethnic Sudan he worked vigorously for reconciliation with the Anya Nya guerrillas and did the diplomatic work which led to the signature of the Addis Ababa Agreement in 1972. In the same year he was President of the Security Council. He played a major role in drafting the Constitution of 1973 with its strong Presidency held in check by a sole party, the Sudan Socialist Union. In 1975 he was transferred to the Ministry of Education which he held until August 1976 when he was appointed Presidential Adviser on Foreign Affairs with Prime Ministerial rank and in February 1977 again Foreign Minister. He was less pro-Egyptian than his predecessors at a time when alliance with Cairo was the keystone of Nimeiri's policies and in September he was dismissed with the President stating that he wished for "a foreign policy of development not of attending cocktail parties". He was, however, appointed Assistant Secretary-General of the SSU for Ideology and also Chairman of its publishing house but in July 1978 he was again dismissed with Nimeiri saying that "his outlook was not close to the people". This marked his final breach with the regime which he attacked in a witty but bitter book *Nimeiri and the Revolution of Dismay*. He became a consultant on international affairs, based mainly in Switzerland. He established close relations with the Sudan People's Liberation Movement, editing a volume of the speeches of John Garang and, to the indignation of Northern politicians, representing him at the Koka Dam meeting in 1986.

al-KHALIDI, Hussain Fakhri (1894–1962)

Palestinian politician. He was a member of one of the great families of Jerusalem which claimed descent from Khalid b. al-Walid who had conquered the city in 638. He qualified as a doctor at the American Univerity of Beirut and practised medicine until in 1934, in alliance with the Mufti Haj Amin al-Hussaini but also attracting Jewish voters, he defeated Raghib al-Nashashibi for the Mayoralty of Jerusalem. The following year he organised his supporters into the Reform Party. In April 1936 he was one of the founder members of the Arab Higher Committee. When the British in September 1937 dissolved the AHC, accusing it of organising terrorism, Khalidi was one of the members arrested and exiled to the Seychelles. He was released in 1938, allowed to attend the London Palestine Conference in 1939 and settled in Beirut before returning to Palestine in 1943. In 1945 he was a member of the revived AHC but left it to join the more moderate Arab Higher Front formed by the Istiqlal Party. He was then appointed by the Arab League a member of the reconstituted AHC. In 1948 he was briefly a member of the Gaza Government but soon made his peace with the Hashemites. He held various Ministerial posts in Jordan until April 1957 in the crisis that followed the dismissal of Sulayman al-Nabulsi by King Hussain, Khalidi was appointed Prime Minister. He remained in office only nine days before giving way to the firmer Ibrahim Hashim. He then retired from politics. He was described as a man of great sincerity and integrity with charming old fashioned manners but stubborn, with a narrow outlook.

al-KHALIFAH, Hamad b. Isa (c. 1870–1942)

Ruler of Bahrain 1923–42. He had been appointed Crown Prince by his father Isa b. Ali al-Khalifah in 1898 and succeeded him in power if not in formal title in 1923 when the British compelled the old Shaykh to abdicate. In 1925 Hamad went to England and returned with an interest in modernisation, exemplified by one of the first motor cars seen in Bahrain. He was persuaded by the British to engage a Personal Adviser, Charles Belgrave, who was to remain for 30 years. Hamad put great trust in Belgrave and fully supported him in creating a modern system of government in a state which previously only had Departments of Police and Customs. Education, health and justice were given priority but communications and public works were also undertaken on a considerable scale, making Bahrain the most advanced state in the area. In the early days, as the pearl trade declined, there was little money but oil was discovered in 1932 and a refinery started operating in 1935. Hamad had problems caused by scheming and corrupt relatives and by the perpetual discontent of the Shiah majority. Later the increase in education produced young men who resented the paternalism of Hamad and Belgrave and started to demand political participation, preference for Bahrainis in jobs, codification of the law etc. Hamad's relations with the British were not always good as he felt most strongly that the Al Khalifah had been robbed of Zubarah, their ancestral home, through their lack of support but on the outbreak of war he announced that he had had a dream in which he saw himself sending a telegram congratulating King George VI on the Allied victory. He also contributed generously to wartime charities. He was described as a kindly, good-natured man, perhaps inclined to be over influenced by handsome young men, and his death was sincerely mourned.

al-KHALIFAH, Isa b. Ali (c. 1859–1932)

Ruler of Bahrain 1869–1923. He was acting as Governor of Qatar when his father Ali b. Khalifah al-Khalifah was murdered during the invasion of Bahrain by his uncle Muhammad b. Khalifah al-Khalifah. The British restored order and appointed Isa as Ruler. In his early years there were nervous moments as the Turks took control of the Hasa Province while after 1880 he was threatened as the descendants of Abd Allah b. Ahmad al-Khalifah who had been deposed in 1843 prepared to reassert the claims of their branch by force with the acquiescence of the Turks and the active assistance of Jasim b. Muhammad al-Thani who had established himself as independent Shaykh of Qatar. In 1880 Isa signed an Exclusive Agreement with the British binding himself not to negotiate with other governments nor to allow them to establish diplomatic or consular representation or coaling stations without the consent of the Political Resident. This was supplemented by a further Exclusive Agreement in 1892 in which he agreed not to sell or mortgage any territory to other Powers. Isa was deeply interested in Zubarah but in 1875 and 1878 he was warned by the British not to interfere on the mainland. Later in 1895 the Al Bin Ali, a dissident tribe of Bahrainis, established themselves there with the help of Jasim but as it was believed that they were planning an invasion, the British destroyed their warships. Isa incurred the displeasure of the Indian Government on several occasions and the offences alleged against him ranged from murder and complicity with pirates and gun-runners to maltreatment of British subjects and financial irregularities. In general, though, Isa although always jealous of his independence, was sufficiently intelligent to know how far he could safely go. British officials considered him shifty, irresolute in dealing with his troublesome relatives, stubbornly obstructive in matters such as reforming his administration and tyrannical in his treatment of his Shiah subjects. In 1900 a British Political Agent was posted to Bahrain despite Isa's opposition and the largest house on the island was built as his Residence – a sure sign of permanency.

Troubles continued and in 1904 the servants of one of Isa's unruly nephews beat a German merchant and were later involved in a brawl with Persian traders; to avoid giving these governments a pretext for intervention the British, overriding Isa's objections, publicly flogged the culprits. They then demanded the expulsion of his nephew Ali and when Isa demurred, sent gunboats which threatened to bombard his palace. Ali escaped, probably with the connivance of the Shaykh but later surrendered and was taken off as a prisoner to India. The Resident, Percy Cox, told Isa that in future rejection of British advice on important matters would not be tolerated. In 1909 the British assumed jurisdiction over foreigners in Bahrain, in effect making the state a protectorate, and the following year Isa undertook not to assign oil concessions without British approval. The threat from the Turks which had risen periodically throughout his reign was ended by the Anglo-Ottoman Agreement of 1913 and then by the collapse of their position in Arabia. When British troops arrived in October 1914 on the way to Iraq, Isa proved most helpful and was later given a Knighthood. After 1917 there was general misgovernment, involving oppression of the Shiah majority who were treated as serfs and who paid far more than their fair share of taxes; communal troubles culminated in Sunni attacks on Shiah villages in 1923. The British prevailed upon Isa to hand over power to his son Hamad b. Isa al-Khalifah. Ibn Saud told a British officer that the deposition of Shaykh Isa had done more harm to their reputation than any other action in the Gulf for a century – "we, the Arabs, particularly my own house, looked up to him as the father of the whole of Arabia and would have died for him had he asked for help". Isa apparently bore no grudge and received numerous British visitors whom he impressed as a slight, very regal man of great dignity and courtesy.

al-KHALIFAH, Isa b. Salman (1933–)

Shaykh of Bahrain from 1961. The son of Salman b. Hamad al-Khalifah, who became Shaykh in 1942, he was educated locally but also travelled extensively, with frequent visits to India and in 1955 a prolonged tour with his brother of Europe and America. In 1956, at time of agitation in the Higher Executive Committee and discord between the Sunni élite and Shiah poor, he was appointed President of the Municipal Council. Al-Khalifah is reported to have dispersed an anti-British demonstration single-handedly and in 1958, when Bahrain was for the first time able to hold elections, he became Heir Apparent. In November 1961 he became Shaykh. As Shaykh, al-Khalifah ran development schemes, showed an interest in housing and parks, and built mosques and wells. In Shiah villages he increased the number of schools and concerned himself with improving the daily life of his people. He welcomed new technology such as Concorde, kept open Majlis exploiting traditional paternalism and introduced Western administrative methods and social services – using oil for the good of the people. He prepared Bahrain for independence, making sweeping changes: in 1966 he introduced the country's own coinage; in 1986 he set up the National Guard under his son Shaykh Hamad; in January 1969 he created the Depart-

ment of Foreign Affairs; and in December 1969 announced proposals to reorganise government giving his people a part to play. In 1970 he transformed the Administrative Council into a Cabinet, appointing his brother Khalifah Prime Minister with complete authority over internal and external affairs while he retained sovereignty. In December 1970 he declared himself in favour of the Gulf Federation, which he described as a necessity. He also promised a Constitution and hinted at elections. He visited the Shah and took part in negotiations for the Gulf Federation. In August 1971 he declared independence and signed a Treaty with Great Britain, applying for membership of Arlea. In 1972, despite family opposition, he announced elections for one half of a Constitutional Assembly. In June 1973 he approved a Constitution and announced further elections for a National Assembly the following December. In August 1975 members of Assembly were critical of a public-security ordinance and of proposed ties with the US, so he dissolved the Assembly and gave full legislative powers to the Cabinet. In November 1992 he said he would appoint a new 30-member council as the principles of *Shariah* had existed for generations.

Al-Khalifah has sufficient popular backing to have survived coups and periods of unrest. He is generous and highly sociable and likes to invite visitors to his private beach. His horses are his only real luxury.

al-KHALIFAH, Khalifah b. Salman (1936–)

Bahraini Prime Minister. He was educated locally and in London. He held various posts in education, finance, administration and technical assistance before becoming President of the State Council in January 1970. In 1973 he became Prime Minister. In August 1975 he said that the left washindering the Government's work and that the Assembly was a "vehicle for anarchy". He tried to make Bahrain a centre for banking and light industry. In October 1975 he signed the Jufair Agreement with the US, which allowed the US "home-port" rights until June 1977.

al-KHALIFAH, Sirr al-Khatim (1917–)

Sudanese Prime Minister. He joined the Ministry of Education in 1938 and later was in charge of education in the South and Principal of Khartoum Technical Institute. In October 1964 after a series of demonstrations had brought down the military regime of General Abboud, al-Khalifah was invited to head a transitional government which included one representative of each of the traditional parties. The Sudanese Communist Party, for the first time, and the Islamic Charter Front were also included and the Professional Front assumed particular importance giving his government a left-wing weighting. It supported national liberation movements in Aden, the Congo and Eritrea. A special court was established to look into corruption, women were to receive the vote, a commission was appointed to advise on agricultural reform and a new economic strategy to help local business was inaugurated. Above all Sirr al-Khatim gave priority to settling the problems of the South, releasing prisoners, curbing excesses by the military, and appointing the Southerner Clement Mboro as Minister of the Interior. He made a goodwill tour of the area and summoned a Round

Table Conference which assembled in March 1965. From the beginning the Government was never united and the right-wing suspected that the illegal enrichment court would be used to purge its supporters and the Professional Front felt that the new Assembly would give too much weight to workers and peasants. In February 1965 the Prime Minister resigned and then reformed his Cabinet omitting the radicals. After the elections of April the Umma Party and the National Unionist Party united against him to bring Muhammad Ahmad Mahjoub to power in June. Al-Khalifah was sent as Ambassador to Rome and then London where he was notably popular and convivial. In April 1972 he was recalled to become Minister of Higher Education which he remained until President Nimeiri reshuffled the Government in January 1975. He later spent much time abroad but in March 1985, just before his overthrow, Nimeiri appointed him chairman of a committee set up to make peace with the Sudan People's Liberation Movement. Sirr al-Khatim was a man of great integrity and much charm.

KHAMIR CONFERENCE (1965)

Before his murder Muhammad Mahmud al-Zubayri was trying to create a Third Force to end the Yemen War without victory either for a despotic Imam, dependent upon Saudi Arabia or a military dictatorship backed by the Egyptian army. The revulsion caused by the crime brought his old friend Muhammad Ahmad Nu'man to power in April 1965 and immediately he called for a conference of tribal leaders to meet at Khamir, about 30 miles North of Sanaa to discuss the future of the country. As it was within Republican-held territory the chiefs of the Royalist tribes refused to attend but about 5,000 tribal notables met under the chairmanship of the Acting President Abd al-Rahman al-Iryani. During the discussions they drafted the first Constitution produced by Yemenis for themselves, declaring the state an Islamic Republic, with an Assembly able to dismiss the President. They approved proposals for an 11,000 strong People's Army to replace the Egyptian forces and for trying to involve other Arab countries, ending the exclusive dependence upon Egypt. It was agreed to establish a permanent committee of five tribal leaders and four *ulema* to draw up peace terms that the Royalists could accept. Shortly afterwards Nu'man resigned and although some of the permanent committee went to Saudi Arabia for discussions, the hope of an independent Yemeni initiative to end the war was lost.

KHAN YUNIS KILLINGS (1956)

On 3 November 1956 during the Suez War advancing Israeli troops occupied the town of Khan Yunis in the Gaza Strip. The Director of UNWRA subsequently stated that 275 civilians were killed. The Israelis claimed that this had occurred during the fighting but Palestinian refugees said that the resistance had stopped and that Israeli troops had gone through the town and shot unarmed men while searching for weapons.

KHANKA CLASH (Egypt) (1972)

Khanka, about 12 miles north-east of Cairo, was the scene of the most notable of a series of clashes between Muslims and Copts at a time when Islamic fundamentalism was beginning in Egypt. These occurred during a period of national frustration for the "Year of Decision" in the regaining of Sinai announced by President Sadat for 1971 had passed with no result. In July 1972 the Grand Shaykh of al-Azhar and the Coptic Pope Shanuda III issued a call for unity after there were reports of sick Muslims being cured and converted in Alexandria by a miracle-working priest. Shanuda, young and newly-elected, was also urging more representation for Copts in the Government. In September a Bishop was stoned and a new church set ablaze at Damanhour. On 6 November, the first day of Id al-Fitr which ended Ramadan, the church at Khanka was set on fire. The following week Shanuda ordered 50 priests to march to Khanka to celebrate a Mass of protest although the authorities warned against it. Six Christian houses and two shops were attacked. Sadat, backed by the press, intervened to defuse the situation but clashes continued being particularly severe during Ramadan of 1977 in Asyut and Faiyyum. A law proposed by Sadat himself that any Muslim accepting Christianity should be put to death caused particular offence and Shanuda and the 44 Bishops began a protest fast which was called off after the Prime Minister Mamduh Salim promised that it would be dropped. There were further sporadic incidents particularly after the creation of the *Takfir wa al-Hijrah* and *Jihad* groups. In March 1980 Shanuda cancelled the Easter celebrations which included an exchange of greetings with the President and banned pilgrimages to Jerusalem. The Copts also claimed that official figures distorted their proportion of the population. There were allegations that Colonel Qadafi had encouraged the inter-religious tension as a means of embarrassing Sadat who always insisted on his credentials as a pious Muslim. In two days of rioting in the Cairo suburb of Zawiyyah al-Hamra in June 1981 at least 17 people were killed and in August three more when a grenade was thrown into a church during a wedding. In September, as part of the purge of his opponents Sadat ordered that Shanuda should be confined to a monastery and his functions exercised by a committee. He was released by Mubarak and there were no further official confrontations although there were many incidents, particularly in the Asyut area. These multiplied after the rise of *al-Jama'a al-Islamiyyah* in the spring of 1991.

KHARTOUM SUMMIT (1967)

As a result of the June War the majority of the radical states were prepared to end their quarrels with the conservative monarchies in the interests of Arab unity. The fourth Summit assembled in Khartoum on 29 August with the Heads of eight of the eastern states present, the four Maghreb countries represented by delegates and Syria boycotting the meeting. Before the main agenda was reached King Faysal and President Nasser were reconciled and agreed to end their support for the contestants in the Yemen War. On 1 September the leaders declared they would "unite their political efforts at the international and diplomatic level to eliminate the effects of the aggression" within the framework of the "main principles by which the Arab states abide, namely no peace with Israel, no recognition of Israel, no negotiations with it, and insistence on the rights of the Palestinian people in their own country". It was agreed that the oil states should resume the supplies to the West that they had cut off during the war and that Saudi Arabia, Kuwait and Libya would subsidise Egypt and Jordan to compensate for their losses in the war. They agreed to expedite rearmament and to press forward with the elimination of foreign bases from Arab soil. They agreed to a Kuwaiti proposal to set up an Arab Fund for Economic and Social Development. The Summit did not rule out indirect negotiations with Israel but showed there was no intention of abandoning the Palestinians.

KHASHOGGI, Adnan (1935–)

Saudi Arabian businessman. He was born in Mecca, the son of the King's physician and was educated at Victoria College, Alexandria, Chicago State University and Stanford which he left after one term. He founded the Triad Corporation and acted as middle-man in a series of enormous deals, particularly involving weapons and aircraft. He had a close relationship with the Saudi Air and Defence Minister Prince Sultan b. Abd al-Aziz in whose Department his uncle was a senior official. He associated with American Presidents and international celebrities, statesmen and film stars. In 1975 he was named in the Lockheed bribes scandal as a conduit through which money reached Saudi officials: he himself was said to have made $184 million on a single deal for F-5 fighter aircraft. He was also involved in various deals with the Sultan of Brunei and in the earlier stages of the American covert arms deal with Iran. He said that "money showered down like peanuts" and it was estimated that at his peak he was getting $100 million a year. Khashoggi invested in oil, industrial and agricultural ventures in the developing countries. He was said to be one of the richest men in the world with a fortune estimated at $4 billion, and the most flamboyant spender with an enormous yacht, 12 fully-staffed houses and private jets. His pastimes were given as skiing and water-skiing but his private life, with gambling and call-girls, attracted much attention in the tabloid press. He was already reported to be in some difficulties when, in April 1989, he was charged in New York with assisting the disgraced President and Mrs Marcos steal $400 million of Philippine Government funds. He was extradited from Switzerland but released on bail of $10 million on condition that he wore an electronic ankle tag. After a three-month trial he and Mrs Marcos were acquitted but in June 1991 he was charged on the Riviera with violating customs laws in connection with 38 paintings by masters including El Greco, Cézanne, Gauguin and Picasso which he had bought on behalf of Marcos.

HUKHATIB, Abd al-Krim (c. 1920–)

Moroccan nationalist and political leader. He was born in Mazagan with an Algerian father and a Moroccan mother and qualified as a doctor at the Universities of Algiers and Paris where he came into contact with other nationalist students. He then worked as a surgeon in Casablanca where he became known for free and secret treatment of militants injured in clashes with the French authorities. After the exiling of Muhammad V in

August 1953 Khatib concluded that independence could not be gained by political action alone and started to organise guerrilla resistance in the Riff and Middle Atlas. By the end of 1955 this had grown into some 10,000 fighting men, the Armée de Libération Nationale. He had been largely responsible for raising the necessary funds for its operations. Khatib was deeply loyal to the King and played an important part in bringing former resistance fighters into the framework of the new state. He was not, however, prepared to accept the demands of the Istiqlal Party that it should have a political monopoly and with his old colleague of the ALN, Mahjoubi Ahardan, he founded the Mouvement Populaire in November 1957. This led the following year to his being briefly imprisoned for sedition by the Istiqlal Government. In May 1960 when Muhammad formed his own Cabinet he brought in Khatib as Minister of Labour. In the subsequent Cabinet of Hassan II he was Minister of State for African Affairs and later for Health. In January 1964 he was elected Speaker of the National Assembly. During that year his relations cooled with Ahardan whose Berberism he regarded as excessive. After riots in Casablanca in March 1965, the King invited Khatib to become Prime Minister but it proved impossible to agree upon conditions for the appointment. In June the King dissolved the Assembly and proclaimed a state of emergency. This led to a definite split in the MP and both Ahardan and Khatib declared the other expelled. In February 1967 Khatib announced the formation of the Mouvement Démocratique Populaire, later the Mouvement Populaire Constitutionel et Démocratique under his own leadership. It never flourished, and its best effort was 2% of the votes in 1977. Khatib handed over the leadership to Ashur Bekkai and left politics. He was a large, jovial, bearlike man of great vitality and good humour which was shown by frequent and enormous guffaws.

al-KHATIB, Bahij (c. 1893–)

Syrian Head of Government. He was born in Lebanon and educated at the Syrian Protestant College. He worked in a minor capacity in the government of King Faysal in Damascus and when it collapsed he went to Palestine. In 1923 he returned and joined the Ministry of the Interior working his way up through the bureaucracy. He continued to serve during the Druze Revolt and during the administrations of Taj al-Din al-Hassani and Haqqi al-Azm, whose private secretary he was, and the nationalists regarded him as pro-French. He became Chief of Police in Aleppo and was accused of manipulating election results. Khatib was then sent as *Mutassarif* to Dayr al-Zur but when Shaykh Taj al-Din became Prime Minister he was brought back as Director-General of Police, in which capacity he repressed the riots of 1936 and charged the nationalist leader Jamil Mardam with corruption. When the National Bloc won power they removed him but he was then sent to Jabal Druze where he won praise for keeping order during an election campaign. A British report of this time said that he was very much the bureaucrat, moderate and experienced and he had "earned the unusual reputation of being a painstaking and incorruptible public servant". In July 1939 at a time of crisis the French Resident Puaux suspended the Constitution, removed the Ministers and replaced them by a Council of Directors-General of Departments. Khatib was put in charge of the Interior and chaired the Council. By the end of 1940 his position had become extremely difficult, the defeat of June had destroyed French prestige, the Germans and Italians were interfering in Syria, there were disorders provoked by food shortages and the measures to combat them; also Khatib's government was unrepresentative and opposed by the nationalists. He resigned in March 1941. Later that year he was Minister of the Interior in the government of Hassan al-Hakim.

KHIDR, Muhammad b. Yusuf (1912–67)

Algerian Revolutionary leader. The son of a poor farmer, he was born in Biskra and worked as a bus driver. A nationalist from an early age, as a follower of Messali Haj, he was elected to the French Parliament in 1946. In 1950 after his car had been used in the robbery by Ben Bella of the Oran Post Office, his immunity was lifted and he fled to Cairo. He was extremely active amongst European immigrants in building a network and raising funds for an armed uprising against the French and was regarded as one of the Neuf Historiques. With his brother-in-law Ait Ahmad he put the case for Algeria at the Bandung Conference and he undertook other diplomatic tasks including the first secret negotiations with the French in April 1956. In October 1956, leaving Rabat with Ben Bella and others after talks with Muhammad V, their aircraft was diverted to Algiers where they were arrested. The five men were kept in reasonable comfort in France until March 1962 and were all appointed Honorary Ministers in the Gouvernement Provisoire de la République Algérienne. After his release he resigned from the GPRA and supported Ben Bella. After independence he was put in charge of the Front de Libération Nationale, organising its transformation from a resistance movement into a political party. He differed, however, from Ben Bella upon its role: the President wanted an élite party as a vanguard while Khidr wanted a mass party which would control the Government and the army. His party was to be based on the possessing classes, traditional forces and the religious leaders, to conciliate whom he advocated a witchhunt of those who failed to keep Ramadan. He opposed the March Decrees with their introduction of *Autogestion*. In April 1963 Khidr attempted to by-pass Ben Bella by calling an immediate Congress of the FLN but Ben Bella dismissed him and himself took over the post of Secretary-General: the wartime funds of the FLN, some £6,000,000, still remained, however, at Khidr's disposal in anonymous accounts in Swiss banks. In the autumn, however, Khidr attempted to mediate in the growing dispute between the President and Ait Ahmad but he refused to attend the FLN Congress and went into exile. In January 1964 there were reports of foreign plots to restore Khidr and the ousted Congolese leader Tshombe and in June there were rumours of an attempted military coup and the establishment of a government in exile of the opponents of Ben Bella financed by the money to which Khidr had access. The Algerian Government demanded the return of the money but the Swiss would do no more than freeze some of it whereupon the Algerians sentenced Khidr to hard labour for life. In September the Swiss expelled Khidr for illegal political activities. In April 1965 Khidr, Ait Ahmad and a third Historique, Muhammad Boudiaf were sentenced to death by a revolutionary criminal court in a parody of justice for crimes against the security of the state. On 3 January 1967 Khidr was murdered in a street in Madrid in front of his wife. Ait Ahmad formally accused President Boumédienne of responsibility but the crime may have been committed by one of his agents without explicit instructions. The money apparently remains still frozen in Switzerland.

KHOEI, Ayatollah Abu al-Qassim (1899–1992)

Shiah religious leader. His family were provincial clerics in the Azerbaijani town of Khoi where he had a traditional education in Arabic religious texts and Persian poetry before at the age of 13 going to study theology at Najaf. He was regarded as exceptionally learned, recognised as an Ayatollah while in his early thirties and generations of his pupils were to be found in all major Shiah centres. He wrote more than 90 books on law and exegesis and was a prolific editor of texts. He also wrote poetry in Arabic, Persian and Turkish. In the 1960s he formed his own theological college and charitable foundation for the educational and social welfare of Shiah with offices in London, Bombay, Karachi and New York. He also paid for the installation of water supplies in remote villages. A strict traditionalist, he refused take sides on political issues, declaring that a religious leader should not become involved in affairs in which he would have to compromise. Although he was regarded as the Grand Ayatollah, the supreme authority for 150 million Shiah, his views were challenged by the activist Ruhollah Khomeini who was in exile in Najaf from 1965 to 1978 and the two men rarely met. In November 1978 Empress Farah came specially to Najaf to request Khoei to make a statement supporting the Shah but he refused to break his rule of non-intervention in politics; he did, however, organise relief for Shiah sufferers in Lebanon and Afghanistan. During the Iran–Iraq War his unwillingness to endorse either side was seen as opposition by Saddam Hussain. In March 1991 as the Iraqi army collapsed as a result of Operation Desert Storm, the Shiah Uprising broke out. Khoei nominated a committee of *mujtahids* to "protect the public interest" while Najaf was free. He appealed to the world to help the Shiah and issued a *fatwa* condemning Saddam as anti-Islamic – his first real intervention in politics. After a fortnight the Iraqi army returned and over a hundred of Khoei's family and staff were arrested and he himself taken to Baghdad where he was shown on TV praising Saddam. He was then placed under house arrest in Kufa where he died 18 months later. Both Iran and Iraq proclaimed three days of national mourning but his family declared that he was buried hurriedly without ceremony to prevent demonstrations.

KHOFOUS INCIDENT (1992)

At the end of September 1992 the Qatari Government stated that Saudi forces had overrun their frontier post at Khofous killing two soldiers. It denounced and called

for the renegotiation of a frontier agreement of 4
December 1965. The precise location of the boundary
seemed unclear, having possibly been altered by the
settlement of the Udayd Dispute in 1974. The Saudis
denied that their forces had been involved but admitted
that there had been "firing between bedouins" inside
Saudi territory which the Qataris had begun and in
which one Saudi had been killed and another wounded.
King Fahd refused renegotiation but pointed out that
the third article of the agreement provided for joint
selection of an international committee to demarcate
the frontier but this had not been done. Relations were
straind as Qatar was angry at the lack of Saudi support
in the Hawar Dispute while Riyadh was angry that
Doha had resumed relations with Tehran. Saad b. Abd
Allah al-Sabah offered to mediate but Qatar recalled its
troops from Peninsular Shield, boycotted the Gulf Co-
operation Council Defence Ministers' meeting and
threatend to boycott the forthcoming Summit. President Mubarak went twice to Riyadh and twice to Doha
and succeeded in broking an agreement that was signed
in his presence in Medina by the two Heads of State.
A joint commission was appointed to complete a final
demarcation of the boundary within a year. Khofous
showed how a matter which could have been sorted out
by two police officers could escalate into an international incident when Arabian frontiers were involved.

al-KHOURI, Bishara (1882–1964)

Lebanese Prime Minister and President. He came from
a distinguished Maronite family, his father and his uncle
Habib Pasha al-Saad being senior officials in the
Ottoman administration. He was educated at the Jesuit
school in Beirut and then studied law in Paris. In 1912
Khouri returned and entered the law office of Emile
Edde. He had been in contact with the French, secretly
urging them to take over the Lebanon when he heard
that the Turks had seized the Consul's papers so he
fled to Egypt where he practised at the Mixed Courts.
He returned with the French, was appointed Secretary
of Mount Lebanon and in 1925 President of the civil
section of the Court of Appeal. He married the sister
of Michel Chiha an influential banker who played a
large part in drafting the first Lebanese Constitution.
In May 1926 when Auguste Adib formed the first Lebanese Cabinet, Khouri was Minister of the Interior.
A year later Adib resigned having failed to make the
Constitution, which encouraged proliferation of factions, work to produce an effective and economical
administration. Khouri succeeded him and pressed
through changes which led to a more powerful executive, abolished the Senate and made the Chamber more
responsible. In January 1928 in the interests of economy
he restricted his Cabinet to three men and started abolishing all unnecessary posts in the administration. This
led to incessant agitation by groups deprived of their
sinecures and in August Khouri resigned. His uncle
Habib al-Saad tried to govern the country but gave up
the effort in May 1929 and, after Edde refused to
become Prime Minister, Khouri formed his second
three-man Cabinet. Again he promised economies but
found it impossible to reconcile demands for less taxation with those for more expenditure and resigned in
August; no one wanted to take over and he had to

remain in office until October when Edde formed a
new government. By now the two men had become
bitter rivals, and their hostility was personal as well as
ideological; Edde was the idealist of a Christian
Lebanon as a Mediterranean state linked with France
and lived in a French-speaking circle while Khouri,
whose family came from the Druze region, was the
more practical politician, lived more with Muslims and
Druzes and saw them as partners in a Middle Eastern
state. Each had his own faction masquerading as a
political party. Khouri's Destour Party was the more
nationalistic so the French cancelled the presidential
election of 1932 which it was evident that Khouri would
win and helped Edde to win that of 1936. Khouri
became in effect the leader of the opposition and sought
allies amongst the Sunni Muslims, forming a close partnership with Riad al-Sulh. They formulated the
Nationa! Pact by which Lebanon should become an
independent state but part of the Arab nation. When
the British occupied Beirut in the summer of 1941
Khouri, realising that the French would always maintain Edde, wooed the British to the cause of ending
the Mandate. When constitutional life was restored in
September 1943 Khouri was unanimously elected President and immediately appointed Sulh as Prime
Minister. They drafted a new Constitution which would
implement the independence that the French had
formally declared but Jean Helleu, the High Commissioner, refused to endorse it. It was nonetheless
passed by the Chamber and signed by Khouri. In the
early morning of 11 November the French arrested
the President and the Prime Minister and confined
them in the fortress of Rashayya. There were widespread riots and a British ultimatum compelled the
French to release the prisoners who had by now become
national heroes. Independence became a fact and
Khouri led the country into the Arab League and the
UN. Once he had secured the removal of all French
troops he made friendship with France a firm principle
of his foreign policy. Lebanon with minimal armed
forces and little motivation did not play a distinguished
part in the Palestine War but benefited enormously
from the fact that Haifa and Jaffa came under Israeli
rule so that trade for Damascus and beyond passed
through Beirut. This brought unprecedented prosperity, encouraged by Khouri's *laissez-faire* policies: he
himself had close links with leading bankers. Corruption became widespread and financial scandals touched
the President's own family. Under Khouri's presidency the country was deeply split into sectarian and
other factional groups, many of them with paramilitary
organisations. The great coalition which had swept him
to power did not last and Parliament was similarly
divided, with the President trying to play off the various
interest groups. He had nine Prime Ministers and Riad
al-Sulh formed six Cabinets. In 1947 a blatantly
crooked election produced a Chamber which amended
the Constitution to give Khouri a second term in office.
His relations with Riad al-Sulh cooled but his death in
1951 weakened Khouri's links with the Muslims while
Camille Chamoun, Pierre Gemayel and Raymond Edde
organised opposition to him within the Maronites.
Kamal Jumblatt formed the Progressive Socialist Party
to denounce corruption and demand reform while the

Parti Populaire Syrien wanted revenge for the execution of their founder Antun Saadeh. These divergent forces combined with the sole purpose of bringing down the President although they pretended to have a common ideology as the National and Socalist Front. In August 1952 Khouri made a final effort to save himself by announcing distribution of state land to the peasantry, reform of the judiciary, dismissal of unnecessary officials and an end to corruption but few took him seriously. In September 1952 the Prime Minister Sami al-Sulh speaking in the Chamber publicly attacked the President for his tolerance of maladministration, miscarriage of justice and financial wrong-doing, even hinting that he had had a hand in the murder of Riad al-Sulh. In an atmosphere of impending revolution with a threatened general strike, Khouri dismissed the Prime Minister and after some difficulty in finding a Sunni Muslim prepared to hold the post appointed Saeb Salam. A number of leading Deputies demanded the resignation of the President and Salam advised him that although he still had the backing of the parliamentary majority he no longer had the support of the people. The Chief of Staff, General Fuad Shihab made it clear that the army would not intervene in a dispute between politicians. A guarantee was given that neither Khouri nor any of his family or entourage would be prosecuted and he therefore resigned on 19 September appointing Shihab to supervise the transition to Chamoun. Khouri retired to private life although in the subsequent crisis of 1958 he was one of the few Maronites not to support Shihab, perhaps still hoping that he might be recalled to the Presidency. Khouri was a brave, shrewd, humorous man with a kindly nature that could be exploited by those around him. His four volumes of memoirs are an important source for the history of Lebanon. His brother Salim and then his son Khalil succeeded him as leaders of his Destour Party.

al-KHOURI, Faris (1873–1962)

Syrian Prime Minister. He was the son of a Protestant carpenter who owned some land in the Biqa and was educated at the Syrian Protestant College. He taught in various schools including the leading Turkish establishment in Damascus until 1908 when he became *Dragoman* of the British Consulate. In his spare time he taught himself law and learned French and Turkish. In 1910 he became Legal Adviser to the Damascus Municipality, a post he held for many years. He had welcomed the Young Turk revolution and in 1914 was elected to the Ottoman Parliament, attending law lectures, his only formal legal training, while in Istanbul. During the war he was suspected of sympathising with the Arab Revolt and was detained and later expelled from Syria. He returned just before Faysal entered Damascus and served in his Cabinet as Minister of Finance, according to British reports, taking the opportunity to line his own pockets. During this time he was also a founder-member of the Arab Academy and the first President of the Damascus Bar Association. In 1922 he was defence council for Dr Shahbandar who was accused of provoking riots against the French occupation which Khouri criticised in court. In 1924 when Shahbandar formed the People's Party, Khouri became its Vice-President. Then, as later, the fact that he was

a Christian gave an impression of national unity. He was one of the delegation that tried to arrange for a peaceful settlement of the Druze Revolt and became Minister of Education in the government of the *Damad* Ahmad Nami. Some months later he was suspected of assisting the insurgents and was exiled. After his amnesty he was one of the founders of the National Bloc. Early in 1936 he was dismissed from his Professorship in Damascus University for nationalist activities but shortly afterwards was one of the delegation that went to Paris to negotiate the Franco-Syrian Treaty. After the victory of the National Bloc in the elections of November 1936 Khouri became Chairman of the Chamber of Deputies, a post for which he was admirably suited. He took a great interest in the Palestinian problem and led the Syrian delegation to the Bludan Conference. In the autumn of 1938 he resigned from the National Bloc as a protest against the concessions that the Prime Minister Jamil Mardam was making to secure French ratification of the Treaty. A British Consular report of this time referred to him as "a prudent, skilful and unscrupulous politician. Entirely venal". When in August 1943 constitutional life was resumed, Khouri was again Chairman of the Assembly and in October 1944 when the government of Saad Allah al-Jabiri fell to pieces, Khouri succeeded him as Prime Minister, the only Christian to hold the office. His government was regarded as feeble and ineffectual but lasted a year, mainly preoccupied with struggling for the independence that Syria had been promised. In February 1946 he led the Syrian delegation to the UN to call for the withdrawal of French troops; he often represented his country there and he presided over the General Assembly. When the National Bloc split up in the spring of 1947 Khouri with other Damascus-based politicians formed the new National Party. After the elections of July 1947 Khouri was again elected Speaker. His reaction to the coup of Husni al-Zaim was ambivalent, privately he said that it was the greatest disaster since the terror of Jamal Pasha and refused to form a government but yet he tried to legalise it by securing the resignation of President Shukri al-Quwatli and supported Zaim's pro-Iraqi and pro-Western policies. After the end of military rule and the elections of October 1954 had produced an Assembly almost half Independents with the remainder split amongst seven parties, neither left nor right could form a government, Khouri managed to form a precarious coalition. He was soon confronted by the formation of the Baghdad Pact and the need to define Syria's attitude towards it. Khouri was anxious not to condemn Iraq and this aroused the ire of the Egyptians. Almost immediately afterwards internal disputes over patronage and the budget caused the Khouri government to split into warring factions. After three months in office he resigned at the beginning of February 1955. Later, though he disliked it, he did not oppose the ending of Syrian independence through union with Egypt, regarding it as the only way to check Communism. In his later years he was widely respected but, a man of words and arguments, was not the strong leader that the times required. He was then described as stocky, white-haired, cheerful and easily accessible. His brother Faiz was also active in nationalist politics and his son became a Minister. His grand-daughter became a leading novelist.

KHURSHID PASHA

Governor of Lebanon. In September 1857 Khurshid Pasha, then Governor of Sidon was in addition put in charge of Lebanese affairs. His main policy was to win the support of the Druzes. It was a time of worsening inter-communal relations and the intrigues of the Consuls of the Great Powers further complicated the situation. He complained that the Government in Istanbul ignored his warnings and that his demands for reinforcements went unanswered. Khurshid was unable to do anything to prevent civil war from spreading in the summer of 1860: some Christians thought that his inactivity was deliberate. He seems to have made little if any attempt to prevent the Dayr al-Qamar Massacre in June. In July he called leaders of all communities to Beirut and produced peace proposals based on forgetting the past with neither side claiming compensation. These terms, in which unofficially he had British encouragement, recognised the victory of the Druzes but the Christians appeared content. Khurshid tried to treat the matter as an internal one in which the Great Powers were not involved but the French suspected that he had exacerbated the situation by encouraging the Druzes to make trouble in order to establish his own direct government in place of the Dual Kaymakamate which had so disastrously broken down. The Turkish Foreign Minister Fuad Pasha who had been sent to restore the situation after the Damascus Massacre subsequently went to Beirut where a senior British naval officer demanded the punishment of Khurshid. He was condemned to perpetual imprisonment and sent to Constantinople where it is probable that he was quietly released.

KIKHIA, Mansur Rashid (1931–)

Libyan diplomat and opposition leader. He came from a distinguished Benghazi family and graduated in Law from the Universities of Cairo and Paris. He joined the diplomatic service and was Consul General in Geneva when in 1967 he was appointed to the Permanent Mission at the UN. In 1969 he was recalled to serve as Under-Secretary in the Foreign Ministry before returning to the UN as Permanent Representative in January 1972. Seven months later he became Foreign Minister. In September he threatened economic war against the West if it continued to support Israel but tried to promote co-operation in the Western Mediterranean. In April 1973 he resigned, possibly having quarrelled with Qadafi over the Libyan Cultural Revolution. Kikhia, who some believed to be a supporter of the Baath Party, practised privately as a lawyer until August 1975 when he returned to his former post at the UN. During 1976/7 he chaired the Security Council and also acted as Vice-President of the General Assembly as well as being active on numerous Special Committees. In September 1980 he defected, living partly in Paris and partly in Missouri where he had a business. He was active in the opposition to the regime, forming his own group the National Libyan Alliance which became part of the National Front for the Salvation of Libya. In December 1993 while in Cairo for a meeting of the Arab Human Rights Organisation he mysteriously vanished. Kikhia had said that he was going to meet a representative of the Libyan Government, which however, said that it knew nothing of the matter. The Egyptian Government stated that it had no evidence of Libyan involvement in his disappearance.

KILOMETRE 101 AGREEMENTS (1973 and 1974)

Kilometre 101 on the road from Cairo to Suez was the furthest point reached by the Israeli forces in the October War which ended with 45,000 Egyptian soldiers encircled on the east side of the Canal. Resolution 338 had called for a cease-fire but after accepting it the Israelis violated it to increase their grip on the beleaguered troops and the town of Suez. Following a visit to Cairo by Secretary of State Kissinger, a Six Point Agreement was signed at Kilometre 101 on 11 November which dealt with strengthening the cease-fire and the passage of non-military supplies to the Third Army and Port Suez. Israeli checkpoints on the Suez–Cairo roads would be taken over by UNEF (II) after which there would be an exchange of PoWs. Talks about further disengagement continued but were broken off on 29 November. An attempt at the Geneva Peace Conference in December to settle the area through the co-operation of the Super-Powers came to nothing but military disengagement talks continued into January 1974. Secretary of State Kissinger between 11 and 14 January made repeated visits to Egypt and Israel and an agreement was reached by which the Israelis withdrew their troops from west of the Canal while the Egyptians reduced their forces on the east bank. The area between the two armies, a 10-kilometre buffer zone would be policed by UNEF and east and west of the zone Israeli and Egyptian forces were to be thinned out and limitations were imposed upon their equipment. The Agreement had been implemented by the end of March. It was stressed that this was not an official peace settlement.

KING–CRANE COMMISSION (1919)

Under strong American pressure the "Big Four" at the Versailles Peace Conference decided in March 1919 to send a commission to discover the wishes of the people of Syria with regard to their future. Britain and France which had already agreed in the Sykes–Picot Agreement to partition the area between themselves determined to sabotage the Commission and did this by refusing to nominate any representatives to it. Therefore only the Americans, Henry C. King, a University Professor who had written on the Bible and Charles R. Crane a manufacturer of sanitary fittings who had financed Woodrow Wilson's election campaign, with three expert advisers, arrived in June in Palestine where they spent a fortnight. They found that the overwhelming number of petitions received (1,364 out of 1,863) called for a unified and independent Syria. There were a few calls (49) for an independent Lebanon, none for an independent Palestine. If there were to be a Mandate at all, 60% wished for it to be exercised by the USA or failing them the British. Only 14% (all from Lebanon) wanted a French Mandate. The greatest unanimity was on the question of Jewish immigration – 85% were opposed.

Their Report recommended a united democratic Kingdom under Faysal of whom they wrote that he was "a unique outstanding figure capable of rendering the greatest service for world peace. He is the heart of the Moslem world . . . a confirmed believer in the Anglo-Saxon race". Admitting that they had been predisposed in favour of Zionism, they recommended that Jewish immigration be restricted and the project for making Palestine a Jewish commonwealth be abandoned. If there were to be a single Mandate the Americans would be more acceptable both to the Arabs, to Britain and France, each of whom would oppose one exercised exclusively by the other. The Greeks had asked for Constantinople but the Report recommended that it should be administered "like the District of Columbia" by the USA. Not merely was the Report never acted upon, it was not even published until 1922: King and Crane attributed this to its disavowal of Zionism. Gertrude Bell described the Commission as "a criminal deception" of the Arabs by arousing hopes that their views would be taken into consideration when Britain and France had already decided their fate. The Report is, however, of historical interest as the only independent survey of local opinion.

KING DAVID HOTEL OUTRAGE (1946)

At the end of June 1946 the British authorities in Palestine succeeded in rounding up a considerable number of Jewish activists who were believed to have been involved in terrorism. The Irgun Zvai Leumi, led by Menahem Begin decided as an act of revenge to attack the King David Hotel in Jerusalem of which the upper floors were used as military and government offices while the lower floors were a normal hotel. At midday on 22 July Jewish terrorists disguised as Arabs smuggled milk-churns filled with explosives into the unguarded kitchen entrance. When they exploded 91 people, British, Arabs and Jews were killed. The head of one victim was blown 50 yards and found spiked on a railing. The Jewish Agency issued a perfunctory disavowal. General Sir Evelyn Barker commanding the troops forbade social contact with the Jewish community to show contempt and cause them financial loss.

KIRKUK KILLINGS (1959)

A massive demonstration by the militia of the Iraq Communist Party had sparked off the Mosul Uprising by pan-Arabs in March 1959 which, aided by Kurdish tribesmen, they had then helped to suppress. Their savagery had terrified their opponents and they determined as a further means of intimidation to hold another rally in Kirkuk where left-wing Kurds were numerous, to celebrate the first anniversary of the July Revolution. Events got out of hand and riots continued for three days in which it was estimated that up to a hundred people were killed: 40 were said to have been buried alive. Kurdish workers with communist sympathies attacked the middle-class Turcomans, their hereditary foes, with barbarous cruelty, mutilating women and children before armoured troops arrived to restore order. Although there was no evidence to prove it, many Iraqis believed that the violence had been deliberately planned by the Communist leadership in Baghdad to frighten their enemies into submission but the revulsion that it caused proved a severe setback to their hopes of sharing power.

KLIBI, Chadli (1925–)

Tunisian Minister and Secretary-General of the Arab League. He was born in Tunis, the son of a senior civil servant and educated at Sadiqi College and then at the Sorbonne where he took a Doctorate in Arabic Literature. Returning home he combined teaching at the University with journalism. In 1958 Klibi was appointed Director of the State Radio and Television Service before creating a Ministry of Information and Cultural Affairs, a post that he himself held for over a decade. He was also Mayor of Carthage and a member of the Politburo of the Parti Socialiste Destourien. From 1974 to 1976 he headed a department in the office of President Bourguiba before returning firstly to Cultural Affairs and then to Information. He inaugurated and was first editor of two vast projects – the Official History of the Nationalist Movement and the Collective Speeches of Bourguiba. After the Baghdad Summit had decided to expel Egypt from the Arab League, moving its headquarters to Tunis, Klibi was elected its Secretary-General in June 1979. As the Egyptian Government refused to hand over either the files or the funds of the League or to allow its citizens, who provided the bulk of the staff, to move to Tunis and Sadat even created an alternative "League of Arab and Muslim Peoples" which, however, quickly withered. Klibi had effectively to rebuild the organisation from scratch while dealing with a host of current problems. He had to try to bring about some common action on the Lebanese Civil War which was resulting in Arab states supporting different factions and was confronted, also, with the problem of the Iran–Iraq War, again with Arab states supporting opposite sides. In 1982 he tried to reunite all Arabs following the Israeli aggression against Lebanon in Operation Peace for Galilee and in support of peace proposals based on the Fahd Plan. He tried to mediate between Britain and Libya after the killing in London of a woman police constable by a Libyan diplomat. In 1986 Klibi condemned the USA for its Tripoli Bombing and later that year he managed to hold the League together after the resignation of its Chairmanship by King Hassan II after the criticism that followed the Ifrane Meeting. In April 1987 he played a part in the "Reconciliation Congress" in Algiers of the Palestine National Council which at least temporarily gave a semblance of unity. Klibi worked hard to bring new life to the Euro-Arab Dialogue and frequently negotiated with the EEC. In 1989 he attempted to minimise the dangers to inter-Arab relations posed by the intransigence of General Aoun. His period of office was marked by the creation of groups within the League, the Steadfastness Front, the Gulf Co-operation Council, the Arab Co-operation Council and the Arab Maghreb Union which weakened its role as the central forum and at times it seemed irrelevant with its Tunis HQ far from the scenes of action. For several years Klibi had worked for the readmission of Egypt and after this took place at the Casablanca Summit of May 1989 it was proposed to return the League offices to Cairo. Before this could be done Saddam Hussain invaded Kuwait and Klibi found himself criticised, particularly by Syria and Saudi Arabia, for not being active enough in organising action against Iraq. On 4 September, although his mandate had been renewed until 1994, Klibi unexpectedly resigned. He complained that he had been accorded insufficient respect on many occasions by Arab officials but his critics said that his demands for a luxury villa overlooking the Nile and a private jet were meeting opposition. Klibi was an unimposing man, lacking the public qualities of leadership although he was an effective worker behind the scenes. He published several works on literary and political matters, notably on Palestine and on cultural policy.

KOKA DAM DECLARATION (Sudan) (1986)
After the overthrow of President Nimeiri the successor regime of General Siwar al-Dhahab met representatives of the Sudan People's Liberation Movement in March 1986 at the Koka Dam in Ethiopia in an attempt to end guerrilla warfare in the South. All the major political parties except the Democratic Unionist Party were represented. An 8-point Declaration, partly drafted by Mansur Khalid who had been a leading Minister under Nimeiri but now supported the SPLM, subtitled "A Proposed Programme for National Action", was issued. It called for "a new Sudan that would be free from racism, tribalism, sectarianism and all causes of discrimination and disparity". Immediate steps were required, the most important of which were lifting of the state of emergency, a cease-fire, repeal of the September Laws of 1983 which imposed the *Shariah* and the "abrogation of military pacts signed by previous regime". A new Constitutional Conference should be held, arranged provisionally for Khartoum in June 1986 with an agenda which included the Nationalities Question and the Religious Question. The SPLM, but not the others, said that "the essential prerequisite" for the conference should be an Interim Government of National Unity, representing all the political forces including the SPLM and the Armed Forces and that development funds should be fairly distributed throughout the country as a whole. The Declaration was endorsed by the political parties except the National Islamic Front which would not agree to the abandonment of *Shariah* and the DUP. Some Southerners argued that all the political parties were to some extent "sectarian" and therefore illegitimate. The following month elections were held which resulted in Sadiq al-Mahdi forming an Umma-DUP coalition. In July he met the SPLM leader John Garang in Addis Ababa but could not commit himself to the repeal of the *Shariah* and the war continued.

KRIM, Belkasim (1921–70)
Algerian Revolutionary leader. Born in Kabyle, he served as a corporal in the French army during the war. On demobilisation he became secretary of a Municipal Council. In 1947 he joined the Mouvement pour le Triomphe de la Liberté et de la Démocratie and was sentenced to death for killing a policeman. Until 1954 he lived in Algeria as an outlaw, receiving another four death sentences. He was one of the Neuf Historiques and a dominant figure on the Comité Révolutionnaire

d'Unité et d'Action. At the time of the All Saints' Day Uprising he had already 200 armed followers who cut communications and attacked police posts. In his Kabyle *wilaya* he would not accept a recruit until he had proved his metal by killing either a Frenchman or a Muslim regarded as a traitor such as a member of the Mouvement National Algérien. He played a leading part in the Soummam Valley Conference of August 1956 at which he was elected one of the five members of Comité de Co-ordination et d'Exécution which ran the War of Algerian Independence. Early in 1957 he was one of the commanders in the Algiers Battle after which he was forced to flee to Tunis fighting his way in a series of skirmishes. Krim was by then the only one of the nine who was still at liberty. When in September 1958 the Gouvernement Provisoire de la République Algérienne was set up in Tunis he was its Vice-President and Minister of the Armed Forces, directing the military side of the War with Ben Tobal and Boussouf. He came under considerable criticism for his inability to get arms to the guerrillas across the Morice Line and in January 1960 was transferred to the Ministry of Foreign Affairs. In this capacity he visited China and Russia and secured promises of arms, artfully leaking this to the West to induce pressure upon France to make peace lest the GPRA fell under communist influences. In December 1960 he attended the UN General Assembly and after meeting Khruschev secured his belated recognition of the GPRA. In May 1961 Krim headed the Algerian negotiators at the first round of the Evian talks, firmly resisting any concessions that would give the colons a privileged position in an independent Algeria or the French Government any control over the Sahara. At the subsequent meeting of the Algerian "Parliament", the Conseil National de la Révolution Algérienne in August it was decided to cast aside the veteran President Farhat Abbas to facilitate negotiations and there was nearly unanimous support for Krim as his successor. It became clear, however, that his choice would be unacceptable to Boumédienne and the General Staff of the Armée de Libération Nationale and he was persuaded to continue as Vice-President; he also changed from the Foreign to the Interior Ministry. He continued, however, in charge of the peace negotiations and in January obtained permission from President de Gaulle to visit Ben Bella and the other imprisoned leaders to ascertain their views. Despite criticism from Boumédienne, he then resumed the peace talks and signed an Agreement on 18 March 1962. He then supported the GPRA against Ben Bella but accepted membership of the National Assembly. Later he clashed with Ben Bella whom he denounced as authoritarian and set up a liaison committee for the Defence of the Revolution. In September 1963 he resigned from the Assembly, declaring "open political war" on Ben Bella for practising "false socialism". Krim gave up politics and sold jewellery. He did not rally to his old opponent Boumédienne when he found that democracy was not being restored but went into exile, living mainly in Morocco. In October 1967 he announced in Paris the formation of a non-socialist Mouvement Démocratique du Renouveau Algérien, declaring that the country was suffering a "social catastrophe" with injustice, incompetence and corruption and was pursuing a whimsical foreign policy quarrelling unnecessarily with its neighbours. He alleged that seven years of independence had been worse than seven years of war. In April 1969 he was tried *in absentia* for conspiracy against the life of the Party leader Ahmad Kaid and sentenced to death. Based on Morocco, he travelled widely contacting opposition groups and on 20 October 1970, he was found strangled in the International Hotel in Frankfurt. Algerian agents were presumed responsible. The Moroccans refused to accept his body so he was buried in Frankfurt. Krim was described as flabby with a strong resemblance to the Corsican bandit of fiction.

KURD ALI, Muhammad (1876–1953)

Syrian politician and journalist. His father, from a family of Kurds long resident in Damascus was an illiterate tailor who prospered and bought a small farm. Kurd Ali had a mixed education, attending a French Catholic school but spending much of his time learning from the *ulema*. He became a journalist, founding in 1906 in Cairo the influential *al-Muqtabas* which attacked Ottoman rule as incapable of reform and opposed to reason and civilisation. After the fall of Abd al-Hamid he moved the journal to Damascus but continued to attack the Turks and twice had to take refuge in Egypt. He never contested the cultural superiority of the West, although he regretted it and felt that the Muslim world had much to learn although Europe should not try to impose its own cultural values. However he came to feel that Ottoman sovereignty was the only protection for the Arabs against foreign occupation and urged its rulers to drop the policy of Turcification which unnecessarily antagonised their Arab subjects. In his Memoirs he stated that he became a member of the Committee of Union and Progress. During the war he wrote ferociously anti-British articles. In 1919 he founded the Arab Academy of Damascus of which he later became President. Kurd Ali was in the government of King Faysal and was later Minister of Education in the pro-French administration of Shaykh Taj al-Din al-Hassani. He always took a particular interest in developing a specifically Syrian form of schooling. He recognised the material benefits of the Mandate regime although he wished to see it ended. After the war he welcomed the coup of Husni al-Zaim as saving the country from disorder. A British report once derided him as "a pompous turncoat" but he did have clear political ideas, if not principles.

KURDISH FEDERATED STATE (Iraq)

The Allied intervention which followed the Kurdish Uprising of 1991/2 meant that an area of about 190,000 square miles with a population of 3.5 million had escaped control from Baghdad which was restrained by some 80 Western aircraft based on Turkey patrolling a no-fly zone north of 36 degrees. After elections in May 1992 a government was set up under Fuad Masum of the Patriotic Union of Kurdistan consisting of seven Ministers each from the two parties which had practically monopolised the votes, the PUK and the Kurdistan Democratic Party, one Christian and a Communist – the Islamic group refused to participate. The area was affected both by the sanctions imposed on

Iraq by the Kuwait Invasion Security Council Resolution 661 and by a blockade ordered by Saddam Hussain and had to depend upon what could be smuggled in. The new Ministers, based on Irbil, had neither telephones nor offices for the Government had no revenue except for some customs dues, most of which went to the political parties to pay their militias (*Pesh Mergas*) but nevertheless within a year it had an army of 100,000, and judicial and educational systems which included a new University at Dohuk and the reopening of the old one at Sulaymaniyyah. The KFS was under constant threat, in June 1992 Saddam Hussain massed 170,000 men near the frontier and the Turks, fearing another exodus agreed to continue to allow the use of the Incirlik base for another six months and there were continual incidents as Iraqi agents placed mines and bombs in Kurdistan to show the weakness of the Government. There were attacks on the UN guards who escorted relief convoys which practically ceased after the United Nations High Commission for Refugees wound up its activities in July. In October the Parliament declared a federated Kudish state within a democratic Iraq but Iran, Turkey and Syria were alarmed at the possibility that it might become the nucleus of a state which their own Kurdish minorities might aspire to join. Their Foreign Ministers met on several occasions to condemn any possible break-up of Iraq, a sentiment echoed in Washington which saw Baghdad as a bulwark against the Islamic fundamentalism of Tehran. The Iranians were alarmed at the links of the KFS with the West and also several times crossed the frontier on the grounds that the KFS was sheltering its dissidents of the Kurdistan Democratic Party of Iran. Relations with Ankara were further complicated when terrorists, said by Turkey to number 7,000, of the extreme left-wing group of Turkish Kurds, the PKK which had been conducting an armed struggle since 1984 in the course of which over 5,000 people had been killed, took refuge on the territory of the KFS. The army of the KFS co-operated with the Turks against their brother Kurds. About 15,000 Turkish troops were allowed to establish a bridgehead "security zone" on KFS territory and soon claimed to have killed 1,800 of the PKK while another 1,500 had surrendered to the Iraqi Kurds. During the struggle the PKK targeted lorry drivers coming from Turkey thus increasing the famine in Kurdistan until mid-November when UN-sponsored aid managed to get through. However the trucks had to use 50 miles of road controlled by the Iraqi Government and during their passage so many had bombs attached to them at Iraqi checkpoints that the UN had to suspend relief until an agreement was negotiated with Baghdad. In January 1993 there were reports that Saddam, possibly hoping to profit by an interregnum in Washington had massed nine divisions along the frontier, probably aimed at capturing Irbil but after four incidents in which American aircraft had fired on Iraqi radar installations in the no-fly zone, he announced their withdrawal as a gesture to the new President. In April Masum gave way as Prime Minister to Abd Allah Rasul Ali, also of the PUK, who was regarded as a more forceful character after the two most important political leaders, Talabani of the PUK and Barzani of the KDP felt that their diplomatic activities would be restrained by formal office. In the same month the economic situation was thrown into worse confusion by the order of Saddam invalidating the Iraqi banknotes that were the principal tender in Kurdistan and it became practically impossible to pay salaries or buy goods smuggled across frontiers. The UN stated that it needed $490 million for relief work in Iraq but that only $2 million had been pledged and also that it was unable to maintain its 236 armed guards who would be withdrawn by the middle of June. The Kurds feared that the world was losing interest in them. In July Save the Children warned that 200,000 Kurds were still without shelter and that a humanitarian disaster might be expected in the winter. There were still threats of Iraqi attacks which brought a warning from the Allies and Turkish approval of the use of their airbase for another six months.

KURDISH REVOLT (II) (1974–75)

On 11 March 1974 Mulla Mustafa Barzani and the Kurdistan Democratic Party issued a statement that the provisions of the March Manifesto, and in particular those relating to the status of the oil province of Kirkuk which had ended the Kurdish Revolt (I), had not been implemented by the Government. The Kurds rejected a new autonomy offer, fighting resumed and five Kurdish Ministers left the Government. It was reported that Barzani had been promised by the CIA without the knowledge of the State Department money and arms which would reach him through the Shah. Barzani with about 40,000 *Pesh Merga* within days controlled much of the frontier with Turkey and major battles took place during the summer with the Iraqi air force using napalm. In July the KDP claimed to have killed 1,600 Iraqi soldiers and shot down 44 military aircraft. The army performed better than it had before but could not crush the rebels while they received help from outside. The situation was complicated by frontier incidents with Iran and reports that Russian pilots were involved on the Government side. On 5 March 1975 the Shah and Saddam Hussain signed the Algiers Pact which cut off aid to the Kurdish guerrillas and the Revolt collapsed. On 13 March there was a cease-fire and an amnesty for those who surrendered within a month. Mulla Mustafa and a reported 250,000 other Kurds sought refuge in Iran.

KURDISH UPRISING (1991/2)

The Anfal Campaign of 1988 in which some 4,000 Kurdish villages were destroyed and between 100,000 and 250,000 people killed or forcibly deported left Iraqi Kurdistan crushed and sullen. Soon after Saddam Hussain had invaded Kuwait in August 1990 the Patriotic Union of Kurdistan leader Jalal Talabani went to Washington to seek American help. In February 1991 when it appeared that Operation Desert Storm might prove costly and difficult President Bush encouraged the Iraqi people to overthrow "the dictator" and promises of help were forthcoming in broadcasts from a radio station in Jiddah controlled by the CIA. Confident of American support the Kurds rose in March and, joined by Kurdish deserters from the Iraqi army, freed much of the area including Kirkuk. There was a difference in objective between the Kurdistan Democratic Party of

Masud Barzani who wanted the autonomy promised in the March Manifesto of 1970 and the PUK, more concerned with liberating all of Iraq from the rule of the Baath Party. The Kurds claimed to have 100,000 men with tanks in the field. The collapse of the Iraqi army in the South meant that their help was no longer necessary and the Americans considered it essential not to upset Egypt, Syria and Saudi Arabia by allowing the disintegration of Iraq while Turkey and Iran would not have tolerated an independent Kurdistan. The Allies therefore stood aside when at the end of March the Iraqis launched an offensive in which it was estimated that 50,000 were killed while they recaptured the major towns including Kirkuk and Sulaymaniyyah. Fearing genocide over a million, perhaps as many as two million Kurds fled towards Turkey and Iran. The French wanted intervention to assist them but the Russians, Chinese and Indians refused to allow the precedent of interfering in the internal affairs of a UN member. Early in April an estimated 200,000 Kurds were trapped without food on snowy mountains on the Turkish frontier while 20,000 vehicles an hour were reported to be fleeing into Iran. The sight on TV of their suffering caused Western public opinion to demand action, relief supplies were sent, and on 5 April the Security Council passed Resolution 688 which condemned Iraqi repression and demanded that Baghdad permit humanitarian access to the refugees. Saddam offered an amnesty which came into effect in mid-April. On the initiative of the British Prime Minister the legal scruples of the UN Secretary-General were brushed aside and British, French and American troops sent to establish "safe havens" for Kurds, building six refugee camps each able to hold about 60,000 returning refugees. The Iraqis were warned that they should take no military action north of latitude 36 degrees leaving an area of 170,000 square miles and over 3,000,000 people under Kurdish control. Barzani and Talabani went to Baghdad and Saddam, anxious for a breathing space, appeared to agree to Kurdish autonomy although he would not accept an international guarantee or cede Kirkuk. There was an uneasy peace with shared control in the towns. At the end of June Saddam made new demands for the handing over of heavy weapons, the closing of radio stations and the ending of links with the Allies. In July there was further fighting which showed that apart from the Republican Guard, the Iraqi army did not have its heart in the battle – some 5,000 surrendered and the Kurds captured Sulaymaniyyah. At about the same time, having resettled 400,000 refugees, the Allied troops withdrew from Iraqi territory but a Rapid Deployment Force of 2,500 British, American, French, Turkish, Belgian and Dutch soldiers remained just across the Turkish frontier with air support available from the Turkish base of Incirlik and carriers in the Mediterranean. The situation was further complicated by clashes between the Turkish Government and its own Kurdish separatists, the PKK to check whom it established a 3-mile buffer zone within Iraq. In October the Iraqis launched an offensive south-east of Kirkuk forcing the flight of another 70,000 Kurds to join the 160,000 still in Iran and the 600,000 homeless in the mountains. The Kurds claimed 4,000 soldiers surrendered: sixty of them were massacred in cold blood in Sulaymaniyyah. Saddam then instituted a blockade with a 350-mile fortified line from Zakho on the Turkish frontier to Qasr-e-Shirin on the Iranian border. No one was allowed to take food or petrol across this line and there were acute shortages, even of cash so that it was impossible to pay salaries. Officially the Kurds were unable to receive much from outside because as Iraqis they were subject to the sanctions imposed in Kuwait Invasion Security Council Resolution 661 although later Iran made supplies available. Saddam ordered the withdrawal of all government officials from the blockaded area where some sort of administration was established by the Kurdistan Front, a coalition of eight parties, including a police force of 2,300 *Pesh Mergas* from the KDP and the PUK. There was deadlock as the Kurds thought that if they held out Saddam would be overthrown whereas he thought that the Allies would lose interest and end the survey flights which prevented him from any activity north of 36 degrees. The Kurdistan Front was paralysed by the right of any party to veto any decision and it was determined to hold elections for a Head of State and an Assembly of 100 members. Saddam declared that he would not tolerate the holding of elections; there were threats of a renewed invasion and some air incursions despite Allied over-flying. The elections were hampered by the lack of an electoral roll and any rules for their conduct. It soon became clear that six minor parties such as the Kurdistan Socialist Party of Mahmud Uthman and the Kurdistan Popular Democratic Party of Sami Abd al-Rahman had little chance and it would be a straight fight between Barzani's conservative, tribal KDP drawing its support from the Kermani speakers in the West and the more urban, left-wing PUK of Talabani which relied on the Surani speakers of the East. Barzani was prepared to accept autonomy within Iraq while Talabani stood out for either a federal state or even independence and the overthrow of Saddam. The elections were four times postponed, the final occasion because it was found that the indelible ink which would mark voters and prevent them from voting twice was easily removable, but took place on 17 May 1992. None of the minor parties won the 7% necessary to qualify for a seat and it appeared that the KDP won slightly more votes than the PUK. The two major parties decided to take 50 seats each and create another 5 for the Christian minority. Parliament met on 4 June in Irbil and elected Jawhar Namiq Salih of the KDP as Speaker and Fuad Masum of the PUK as Head of the Executive and decided to postpone the election of a Head of State. A government of 7 KDP, 7 PUK and one Christian was set up for what later became known as the Kurdish Federated State.

KURDISTAN DEMOCRATIC PARTY
The first political party in Iraqi Kurdistan was probably *Heva* (Hope) which was founded in Kirkuk late in 1942 and spread to other major towns. Its membership was mainly intellectuals, officials and army officers and distinctly left-wing. Although advocating Kurdish autonomy it made no efforts to attract the tribal shaykhs who really controlled the people and so never had much following. Three years later Mulla Mustafa Barzani formed the Freedom Party consisting mainly of tribal

leaders but later in 1945 he went to Mahabad and subsequently to Russia. In his absence, in August 1946 the Kurdistan Democratic Party was formed out of the remnants of the two existing groups, renaming itself in 1954 the United Democratic Party of Kurdistan. The Secretary was a communist lawyer from Sulaymaniyyah, Ibrahim Ahmad and it had an inner Politburo of five which included Jalal Talabani. After the July Revolution of 1958 one of its members joined the Cabinet but Abd al-Krim Qassim refused a request for a degree of Kurdish autonomy or for publication of a newspaper. In October Mulla Mustafa returned and assumed the Presidency of the now legalised UDPK which allied with the communists against the pan-Arabists in support of Qassim. In January 1960 at the insistence of Qassim who wanted emphasis on its regional rather than international character, the UDPK resumed its old name of Kurdistan Democratic Party and dropped demands for autonomy. The tribes became restless at the taxation and agrarian policies of Qassim but the leadership of the KDP condemned breaches of the peace feeling it was not strong enough to tackle the Government and could not hope for outside support; Talabani and a minority, however, were for resistance. In September 1961 Qassim formally dissolved the Party. Relations between Barzani and the Politburo deteriorated as he made clear his contempt for talking rather than fighting men and many of the Party followed him into the mountains. Once the Kurdish Revolt (I) had started, the Party tried to present itself as a movement to establish democracy throughout Iraq. It established control of an area of Southern Kurdistan where it introduced socialist measures such as Peasant Councils and agricultural reform and this alienated the tribal leaders who were the backbone of Mulla Mustafa's forces and he would not allow the KDP into the North. Talabani proved successful in the organisation of guerrillas, the *Pesh Merga* and although he could field only about 650 men they were more effective than the 15,000 that followed Barzani, distinguishing themselves in a major battle at the Ruwandiz Gorge in the summer of 1963. In 1964 Barzani arranged a cease-fire with the Government without consulting the Politburo which censured him. He thereupon expelled Talabani and Ahmad from the KDP and chased them into Iran. His dominance, confirmed by a Party Congress held at Raniya in July 1964, survived an attempt by the dissidents to overthrow him in February 1966, fighting with Talabani who then had the support of the Baath Government in 1968, and continued until the collapse of the Kurdish Revolt (II) in March 1975. Mulla Mustafa went into exile and the KDP disintegrated as its members were scattered. One group reformed in Damascus as the Patriotic Union of Kurdistan while Barzani's two sons Masud and Idris set up a new KDP with the help of their father's old friend Mahmud Osman. Within a year, however, Osman broke away to form a more left-wing Sorani-speaking group which, joining PUK dissidents, became known as the Socialist Party of Kurdistan–Iraq. In the Spring of 1978 the KDP won a major victory over the PUK but lost many of its members to Muhammad Abd al-Rahman (known as "Sami") who formed the less tribal and more progressive Democratic People's

Party of Kurdistan and, like Talabani, accused the Barzanis of accepting aid from the the CIA and Iran. Masud Barzani claimed to have 5,000 *Pesh Mergas* in the field and his successes so alarmed the governments of Baghdad and Ankara that they agreed on joint measures against the Kurds. After the start of the Iran–Iraq War the KDP, stressing that its fight was against the Baath and not against Arab Iraqis, joined an anti-government coalition with the SPK-I, the Iraq Communist Party and the Shiah party al-Dawah and declared itself part of the world liberation movement. The KDP, equipped with missiles from Syria and Libya, fought actively for what it called the "Glorious Iranian Revolution", operating an administration and even a radio station in the mountains, kidnapping Europeans and claiming substantial successes including the destruction of forts and aircraft. It fought also against the PUK and the Democratic Party of Iranian Kurdistan which opposed the Government in Tehran. In February 1987 Idris Barzani died in Tehran and in March 1988 many of its supporters were gassed in Halabja. The end of the war in the summer of 1988 meant that Baghdad was able to concentrate its forces against the Kurds many of whom were transported to Southern Iraq. Reports of sporadic unrest continued.

al-KURSHUMI, Abd Allah b. Hussain (1932–)
Yemeni Prime Minister. He was one of the "Famous Forty" – young Yemenis sent to foreign universities by the Imam Ahmad. After taking a degree in engineering at Ain Shams University, Kurshumi practised as an architect until in September 1962 he was appointed Minister of Public Works in the first Republican Cabinet. For the next seven years he held Ministerial posts while completely avoiding factional politics. He was Minister of Transport in July 1969 when acute financial difficulties brought about the resignation of the Prime Minister General Hassan al-Amri and the failure of Muhsin al-Ayni to form a government. Kurshumi took office in September after a prolonged crisis and stressed that only severe remedies could end the financial chaos. He set up committees to examine means of controlling expenditure and antagonised the army, the tribal leaders and the National Council. He took the first steps towards creating a National Bank and banned luxury imports. After only five months he resigned in February 1970 finding it impossible to obtain agreement to any Budget which made financial sense. He subsequently held numerous technical and Ministerial appointments. He was too abrasive to play the game of politics according to Yemeni rules.

KUT AL-AMARA, Siege of (1915/16)
In July 1915 General Sir John Nixon commanding the Indian Expeditionary Force in Iraq thought that Turkish opposition would crumble in the face of a determined push on Baghdad. His gamble nearly succeeded but unknown to him two fresh Turkish divisions under General Khalil Pasha had arrived from Gallipoli. Major-General C. V. Townshend with the 6th Indian Division and the 6th Cavalry Brigade was checked at Ctesiphon in November and Townshend fell back to Kut al-Amara where he fortified a U-shaped position based on the Tigris. His force of about 3,000 British and 7,000 Indian soldiers was besieged by a slightly smaller number of Turks but was exhausted and had to share diminishing supplies with about 6,000 Iraqi civilians trapped in the town. Two British relief columns failed with considerable loss. At the beginning of April 1916 Captains T. E. Lawrence and Aubrey Herbert of the Arab Bureau were sent with £1 million in gold to attempt to bribe Khalil Pasha to raise the siege but the offer was rejected with disdain; they were still there when on April 29 Townshend surrendered. His troops were harshly treated by the Turks and over half died in captivity. Reprisals were also taken against the Arab population which had welcomed the British. The behaviour of the Turks inspired such fear that when the British entered Baghdad in March 1917 in order to win co-operation their first action was to issue the Maude Proclamation – a firm statement that the Turks would never return.

KUTAYHA, Convention of (1833)
After the Egyptian victory at Konia in December 1832 Ibrahim Pasha continued his advance on Constantinople, hoping to reach the capital before any European Power could intervene. However, a Russian envoy quickly arrived at Alexandria and warned Muhammad Ali Pasha that the Czar would defend the Sultan and prevailed upon him to order his son to halt. Ibrahim was then at Kutayha, about 150 miles from the Bosphorus. The prospect that Russia would establish a paramount position in the Ottoman Empire as its sole defender alarmed Britain and France. The former brought pressure on the Sultan and the latter on the Pasha and an agreement was reached on 8 April 1833 by which Muhammad Ali would be appointed Pasha of Crete and Syria on payment of tribute. This could not be a permanent settlement for it left both the Turks and the Egyptians discontented and it lasted only until 1839 when the Sultan felt strong enough to attempt to drive Ibrahim out of Syria.

KUWAIT FUND FOR ARAB ECONOMIC DEVELOPMENT
The Kuwait–Iraq Dispute, following immediately after the attainment of independence in 1961 showed the Government the need to attract friends amongst the poorer Arab nations. On the initiative of the Finance Minister Shaykh Jabir al-Ahmad al-Sabah the KFAED was set up at the end of 1961 with a capital of 50 million Kuwaiti Dinars (£58 million), which was doubled in 1963 and 1966. It was the first agency of a national government, as opposed to an international agency, created for regional development and was the first case of a non-industrial nation providing economic aid. Loans were made to the poorest countries such as Mauritania with interest as low as 0.5% while more prosperous ones such as Morocco paid 7%; maturity could be up to 40 years. The Fund was not subjected to the vagaries of politics but was able to make loans as it saw fit, continuing, for example, to work with Jordan after Black September had led the Kuwaiti Government to stop aid to Amman. It was less governed by purely economic considerations than organisations such as the World Bank and for social reasons it made loans that conventional financiers

would have thought too risky. It was able to support both public and private enterprise. Unlike other donors it did not insist upon acceptance of its own manufactures as part of the aid. From its earliest days it provided technical assistance in the form of feasibility studies and it served as a training ground for officials in subsequent organisations such as the Arab Fund for Economic and Social Development. In 1974 after the quadrupling of oil prices had led to an enormous increase in its revenues, Kuwait increased the capital of the Fund to KD1,000 million and extended loans to non-Arab states. In March 1981 its capital was doubled. Abd al-Latif al-Hamad who was Director-General from 1963 until 1981 when he became Chairman played the major role in formulating the policies of KFAED. It was always particularly interested in increasing food production, for example in the Sudan, and in providing training facilities such as those for merchant naval officers in Alexandria. It made many loans for long-term projects in housing, health and education and for the development of industries such as a textile factory in Tanzania. For many years Kuwait gave 3% or more of its GNP in aid whereas most countries failed to meet the UN target 0.7%.

KUWAIT INVASION, SECURITY COUNCIL RESOLUTIONS

Resolution 660 of 2 August. This condemned the Iraqi invasion and demanded an immediate and unconditional withdrawal of its forces to the positions which they had occupied on 1 August. It also called upon Iraq and Kuwait to open immediate negotiations to resolve their differences. Yemen, the only Arab member of the Council abstained and the Resolution was carried 14–0.

In Resolution 661 of 6 August the Security Council declared that Iraq had failed to comply with Resolution 660 and decreed that sanctions should be imposed upon it. No state should import goods originating in Iraq or Kuwait nor export to it any products except for medical supplies or "in humanitarian circumstances", foodstuffs. No funds should be made available to Iraq or Kuwait. A committee was appointed to oversee the implementation of this Resolution which was carried 13–0 with Yemen and Cuba abstaining.

Resolution 662 of 9 August, carried unanimously, declared that the annexation of Kuwait announced by Saddam Hussain had no legal validity and should be rescinded.

Resolution 664 of 18 August, again unanimous, demanded that the foreigners held as hostages should be allowed to leave at once and that nothing should be done to harm them. It also demanded the cancellation of the Iraqi decree closing all diplomatic missions in Kuwait.

Resolution 665 of 25 August authorised the use of naval force to halt all shipping proceeding to or from Iraqi harbours to inspect their cargoes and verify their destination. Yemen and Cuba abstained.

Resolution 666 of 13 September decided that the situation regarding foodstuffs in Iraq and Kuwait should be kept under constant review, requested the Secretary-General to seek information about the availability of food and that particular attention be paid to persons who might suffer specially. The Council would decide when humanitarian circumstances arose. Yemen and Cuba voted against this Resolution which was carried 13–2.

Resolution 667 of 16 September, passed unanimously, condemned the aggressive acts committed by Iraq against diplomatic premises in Kuwait and the abduction of foreign nationals whose immediate release was demanded. There should be no interference with foreign diplomats.

Resolution 669 of 24 September, carried unanimously, asked the committee established by Resolution 661 to look into the problems of states prevented by sanctions from trading with Iraq and to make recommendations for assisting them.

Resolution 670 of 25 September extended the naval blockade to air traffic: no cargo except for medical supplies or food for humanitarian purposes should be flown into Iraq. All states should prevent aircraft destined for Iraq from overflying or landing in their territory. Measures should be taken against any state breaching sanctions regulations. Cuba voted against this Resolution which was carried 14–1.

Resolution 674 of 29 October condemned the holding of hostages and demanded that food, water and basic services should be made available in Kuwait. It reminded Iraq that it was liable for losses and injuries resulting from its illegal actions and invited all states to collect information about eventual claims for damages. It trusted the Secretary-General to use his good offices to bring about a peaceful solution. Cuba and Yemen abstained.

Resolution 677 of 28 November, carried unanimously, condemned Iraqi attempts to alter the population balance in Kuwait by expelling natives and replacing them with Iraqis. The Secretary-General was asked to safeguard a smuggled copy of the register of citizens.

Resolution 678 of 29 November noting that Iraq had refused to comply with previous Resolutions, reaffirmed them and gave it until 15 January 1991 to do so. After that date force could be used to ensure compliance. Yemen and Cuba voted against this Resolution and China abstained.

KUWAITI AIRWAYS HIJACKING (1988)

As a result of terrorist activities in Kuwait including an attempt to assassinate the Amir and attacks on the French and American Embassies, at least 17 members of the extremist al-Dawah were imprisoned there. On 5 April 1988 a Kuwaiti Airways Boeing 747 with 97 passengers, including three members of the Ruling Family, and 15 crew flying homewards from Bangkok was hijacked over the Indian Ocean and forced to fly to Mashhad. The hijackers demanded the release of the 17 and the Iranian authorities invited the Kuwaiti Government to send an envoy to negotiate. Twenty-four women and 32 non-Arab men were released. After some shooting the aircraft was refuelled and took off on 8 April amidst mutual recriminations between the Kuwaiti and Iranian Governments. The Syrians refused to allow the pilot to land in Beirut, blocking the runway with tanks, but as he was just about to crash for lack of fuel, the Cypriot Government agreed to accept the plane but refused to refuel it. A Kuwaiti hostage was murdered and his body thrown on the tarmac amidst threats that the hijackers, who had assumed martyrs' shrouds, would kill the rest if denied fuel. Their allies, Hizbullah threatened to kill all the hostages in Lebanon if the aircraft were stormed. Leaders of the Palestine Liberation Organisation mediated and on 13 April the hijackers released 12 hostages and flew to Algiers. The Kuwaiti Government still refused to negotiate and acute tension persisted for another week. On 20 April the hijackers disappeared and the hostages were freed. The success of the Algerian Government in ending the incident without further bloodshed was praised by Arab leaders and by the French but much criticised in London and Washington. It was never exactly clear who the hijackers were and there were suspicions that they were acting on behalf of hardliners within the Iranian Government to embarrass the efforts of Speaker Rafsanjani to end the Iran–Iraq War.

LA CELLE ST CLOUD, Declaration of (1955)

After a meeting with leading Moroccan nationalists at Aix-les-Bains in August 1955 the French Government became convinced that only the deposition of the puppet Sultan Muhammad ben Arafa and the restoration of the exiled Muhammad V could bring an end to the increasing violence in cities and in the Berber areas of the Riff and Middle Atlas where the Armée de Libération Nationale was fighting large-scale actions against the Foreign Legion. There was considerable opposition within the French Cabinet and among the colons and it was not until the end of October, after a dramatic change of sides by Thami al-Glawi, that Ben Arafa abdicated. The French hurriedly brought Muhammad V from Madagascar and on 6 November he met the Foreign Minister Antoine Pinay near Paris. The Sultan then issued a declaration that he would establish representative government entrusted both with negotiations with France and with reforms creating a democratic state with a constitutional monarchy in Morocco. Morocco would build a common future with France, achieving independence within interdependence, without the intervention of any third party. Each affirmed the sovereignty of the other, mutually guaranteed each other's rights and those of their citizens and respected the Treaty rights of foreign powers. The French right-wing saw this abandonment of the Protectorate as a "a diplomatic Dien Bien Phu". Ten days later Muhammad V returned home in triumph.

LADGHAM, (Muhammad) Bahi (1913–)

Tunisian Prime Minister. Although he came from a poor family he was educated at Sadiqi College where he took part in his first demonstration at the age of 17 and was for a time expelled. He also founded a student organisation which was later absorbed into the Neo-Destour Party. Ladgham then worked as a civil servant, becoming in 1939 *Chef de Cabinet* of the Director of Finance. At the same time he was engaging in clandestine nationalist activities. After the arrest of Bourguiba and others in April 1938, Ladgham was responsible for the underground organisation that kept the Neo-Destour alive. In November 1939 he was caught and sentenced to 15 years' hard labour. After five years in Algeria he benefited from an amnesty proclaimed by General de Gaulle. He was briefly imprisoned in 1946. He was Director of the Tunisian Chamber of Commerce when in 1951 he was appointed a political adviser to the government of Muhammad Chenik which hoped to negotiate autonomy for Tunisia. After the talks broke down in 1952 he went to New York where he

opened a Bureau for Tunisian Liberation and lobbied at the United Nations. He returned in 1955 after the signature of the Franco–Tunisian Autonomy Agreement and at the Sfax National Congress which saw the victory of Bourguiba over Ben Yusuf, Ladgham was elected Secretary-General of the Neo-Destour. In July 1957 he was appointed Secretary of State to the Presidency and later Vice-President so for the next 15 years he often served as Bourguiba's personal representative, particularly when the President was ill: many saw him as the next President and Bourguiba said that Ladgham's only defect was excessive modesty. He was also twice Minister of Defence. His interview with General de Gaulle in July 1962 marked the de-escalation of the Bizerta Incident. In November 1969, after the crisis that had led to the fall of Ahmad Ben Salah, Bourguiba, for the first time, determined to appoint a Prime Minister and his choice fell on Ladgham. He stated that his priorities would be an overhaul of government machinery and of the economy and reconsideration of Ben Salah's discredited Plan. Bourguiba thereupon retired to France for six months' treatment for hepatitis, leaving the new Prime Minister to cope without knowing whether his actions would be approved his master's return. It was generally agreed that, without Bourguiba's flamboyance, he did very well. He had, however, paid more attention to Arab and Islamic issues than Bourguiba had ever done, ending quarrels with Nasser and Qadafi. In June 1970 Ladgham reformed his government, trying to bring in representatives of differing political tendencies although he was always determined that the Neo-Destour, of which he was still Secretary-General, should remain the sole party. In September 1970 he was asked to head the Arab Supreme Follow-up Commission which supervised the disengagement of the Jordanian and Palestinian forces after Black September. He spent a considerable time in the country and in negotiation with Heads of State and also represented Tunisia at the funeral of Nasser. In his absence Hedi Nouira was appointed interim Prime Minister. Ladgham apparently expressed anger, delaying his return and Nouira's appointment was made definite on 2 November. So favourable an impression had Ladgham made that he was widely regarded as the logical choice for next Secretary-General of the Arab League and he returned to Jordan when fighting with the Palestinians broke out again in January 1971, also seeing King Hussain in London and Yassir Arafat in Tunis. In April he resigned from the Commission, strongly criticising the King. At the Monastir Party Congress in October Ladgham was clearly the most popular figure but Bourguiba dismissed him from the Politburo and nominated Nouira as his own successor. Ladgham's relations with Bourguiba deteriorated beyond repair and in March 1973 he resigned from the Party and in May the President had him expelled from the National Assembly. Ladgham played no further part in politics.

LAGU, Joseph (1931–)

Southern Sudanese military and political leader. A Protestant from the Madi tribe of Equatoria, he was educated at Rumbeck School and graduated as an officer in 1960. In 1963, while on leave, he deserted and joined the Anya Nya guerrilla movement. In the Equatoria region he proved himself a highly skilled strategist and tactician and eventually united the numerous factions under his command as the Southern Sudan Liberation Front. He had little time for competing politicians and became the most important figure in the South. He was thus able in February 1972 to negotiate the Addis Ababa Agreement with the Government, ending over a decade of bloodshed. Under its terms his warriors were integrated into the army and Lagu became a General. He was appointed Inspector-General and then in October 1974 Commander of the Southern Region. He worked well with Nimeiri. After elections were held in the South for the People's National Assembly its members in February 1978 unanimously elected Lagu as President of the Higher Executive Council. Lagu was too direct and intolerant to be a successful politician and the Council was plagued by divisions, allegations of corruption and a strong opposition which led to a crisis, the resignation of Lagu and dissolution of the Regional Assembly in February 1980. The elections were won by the supporters of the Dinka, Abel Alier who took office as President of the HEC. Lagu started to campaign for greater decentralisation, splitting the South into three separate regions each with its own government. The proposal was taken up by Nimeiri but opposed by Alier and the veteran Clement Mboro. In July 1982 Nimeiri dismissed Alier as Vice-President of the Republic, replacing him by Lagu who held the office until the overthrow of the regime. He was an outstanding personality with considerable charisma, deeply religious, strongly anti-communist but although a supporter of Western democracy, was too direct to be politician. He was intelligent, pleasant, and soft-spoken. He led a simple life and said that he would have preferred to have been a teacher. In 1972 he wrote a book on the Anya Nya.

LAKE HULA DISPUTE (1951)

Hula is a shallow lake, roughly four miles long and up to three miles wide on the River Jordan, ten miles north of the Sea of Galilee, covered in papyrus and surrounded by malarial swamps. The area lay inside Mandated Palestine but in the Rhodes Armistice it was designated a demilitarised zone. In March 1951 the Israelis, planning to settle thousands of immigrants, started drainage works, evicted Arab residents and kidnapped some Syrian citizens; the Syrians protested at a "flagrant violation" of agreements. Skirmishes broke out and as the Syrian army considered inadequate the

response of the ruling People's Party it vetoed an attempt on 23 March by Nizam al-Qudsi to form a new Cabinet. On 4 April, 7 Israeli policemen were killed by Syrian troops whereupon the Israelis bombed Syrian territory. Both sides appealed to the Security Council but two days of fighting south of the Sea of Galilee started on 2 May. On 14 May the new government of Khalid al-Azm called for a meeting of the Arab League at which Iraqi willingness to offer help contrasted with Egyptian reticence. On 18 May the Security Council condemned Israeli actions and ordered a suspension of the drainage work but later the Mixed Armistice Commission decided that it gave Israel no military advantage and it was resumed. Incidents on the border continued but the MAC was unable to meet because all sessions were boycotted by one side or the other. By December 1975 it was calculated that Syria had 568 complaints and Israel 401 that it had been impossible to discuss.

LAMRANI, (Muhammad) Karim (1919–)

Moroccan Prime Minister. He came from a Sharifian family of Fez with a tradition of commerce and government service. He trained as an economist and was appointed to the Ministry of the National Economy soon after independence. He was then put in charge of the Sharifian Phosphates Office, the main earner of hard currency. He returned to the private sector, becoming a prominent businessman in Casablanca and President of its Chamber of Commerce. As Director of the Crédit du Maroc he was unusual in encouraging small companies and showing some sympathy for the left-wing Union Nationale des Forces Populaires. In May 1967 he was reappointed Director-General of the SPO and was also one of a small group of economic experts chosen by Hassan II as advisers. He was able to announce that in 1970 at a time of a world slump in phosphates, Morocco's exports had risen. In April 1971 he was given the additional post of Minister of Finance at a time when corruption was rife. Lamrani's main duty, however, was to put Morocco's relations with the European Economic Community on a good footing. In August 1971, a month after the Skhirat Attempt he was appointed to head a government of technocrats which the main parties refused to join; 10 of its 16 members had served in the previous Cabinet. The King said that it would last for up to 18 months, introducing reforms in education, distribution of wealth, education and justice and he gave it exceptional powers. One of Lamrani's first acts was to go to Washington to seek support from the World Bank and he also met other Finance Ministers and signed a co-operation agreement with the visiting Soviet Prime Minister Kosygin. He hoped to stimulate economic growth by new incentives to investment and simplified regulations, exerted control over the foreign-owned press and distributed land to poor peasants. In April 1972 the King instructed Lamrani to reconstitute the Government to organise elections in the summer but as once again the political parties refused to participate it meant little change except for the creation of some new technical Ministries. Lamrani announced a series of reforms in education, in response to student strikes and that a Four-Year Plan in preparation would transform the development programme. He was Prime Minister at the time of the attempt on the Royal Boeing which showed the disloyalty of the Defence Minister General Oufkir, causing worry as to its prevalence throughout the Armed Forces. The King continued his attempts to form a government of national unity but came eventually to the conclusion that this could not be done under Lamrani whom in November 1972 he replaced with Ahmad Uthman. Lamrani resumed his old post at the SPO. In November 1983 when there was again a need for a national government to organise elections, Lamrani, greatly respected at home and abroad and known to be politically neutral, was called upon to lead it. The leaders of the four major parties sat in the Cabinet as Ministers of State and there were minimal complaints about unfairness in the poll. Lamrani did not neglect the economy, regaining international confidence in the Dirham after rescheduling debts. In April 1985, after the elections, he reformed his Cabinet, omitting representatives of the Istiqlal and Union Socialiste des Forces Populaires but as Prime Minister he never really controlled Foreign Affairs which were the province of the King or internal matters of which Driss Basri was in charge. He did, however, run economic matters and embarked upon a controversial programme of privatisation, "returning to private enterprise everything that naturally belongs to it", which, while increasing efficiency and gratifying the IMF, was bound to lead to greater disparities of wealth within the Kingdom. He proposed to take over 250,000 hectares of French-owned land. The tax system was to be simplified and a Value Added Tax introduced for the first time in a Third World country. He cut back bureaucracy and, close to American business interests, he encouraged foreign investment. In September 1985, after a reduction in food subsidies, he obtained a standby loan of $315 million from the IMF and rescheduling of debts which caused a de facto devaluation. He also introduced some educational reforms laying stress on technical training. In September 1986 he resigned on grounds of ill health but returned to the Phosphate Office from which he retired in July 1991 after a disastrous fall in exports following the loss of a major contract for sales to India. In August 1992 Lamrani became Prime Minister for the third time to preside over the first elections for eight years. Once again he appointed a non-political Cabinet, only one Minister was a member of a party, and was ordered to give priority to dialogue on economic and social matters, particularly trying to find work for the educated young and encourage local investment. He attempted to anchor the economy of Morocco to that of the EC, which he saw as a "separate partner", and announced that the dirham would be made convertible from January 1993. He undertook a major programme of privatisation, for example of eleven sugar companies in January 1993. In July he persuaded the Islamic Development Bank to open its first branch outside Saudi Arabia, providing it with a base for operations in North and West Africa. There were no serious complaints about the conduct of the elections in which the opposition Istiqlal and USFP both did well. The King failed to persuade them to join a coalition, despite the offer of 19 portfolios, and in November reappointed

Lamrani. The reshuffled Cabinet included ten new Ministers, none of whom had been candidates during the elections, a Minister for Human Rights and the first Jew to serve in a Cabinet since 1957. Lamrani's five-point programme included further privatisation, an overhaul of the Stock Exchange, reforms to banking and tax law and a determined effort to end human rights violations. Despite opposition criticism that his programme lacked real content, it was approved by the new Parliament by 202 votes to 118. Lamrani went to Spain, returning with a large credit. In January 1994 his government's budget cut taxes to stimulate growth.

LAND DAY RIOTS (1976)
In March 1976 the Israeli Government announced plans to expropriate 2,000 acres of Arab land, 1,750 acres of Jewish land and 2,250 acres of state land which the Arabs believed had been intended for extending Arab settlements in Galilee. Apart from 250 acres to be used for Arab housing, the rest was to be used for Jewish settlements. A further 375,000 acres in the Negev owned by bedouins were also to form part of the new Lebensraum. As a protest a general strike was called for 30 March 1976 – "The Day of the Land". On the previous evening Arab villagers held up a Jewish military vehicle at Sakhnin and riots escalated with at least six Arabs killed, 260 arrested and 70 including 38 Israeli soldiers and policemen wounded. The anniversary was normally marked by demonstrations.

LARAKI, Ahmad (1931–)
Moroccan Prime Minister. He came from a very distinguished Fassi family and obtained a degree in Law from the Sorbonne. He was one of the first to join the Dipomatic Service after independence and was appointed Permanent Representative to the UN in 1957. He had held the Embassies in Spain, Switzerland and the USA when in March 1967 he was appointed Foreign Minister in the Cabinet of Hassan II. Two of his first tasks were to negotiate the cession by Spain of Ifni which had been a cause of strained relations and to sit on the Tripartite Committee which negotiated the withdrawal of Egyptian troops from the Yemen War. He was also successful in obtaining food aid from the USA. In December 1967 he was severely injured in a car accident while in Jiddah where he had gone in an unsuccessful attempt to persuade King Faysal to agree to a Summit in Rabat. In May 1968 Laraki went to Tehran to encourage co-operation between Iran and Saudi Arabia in anticipation of British withdrawal from the Gulf. Laraki also tried to improve relations with Algeria and signed trade agreements in Eastern Europe. After the burning of the al-Aqsa Mosque it fell to Laraki to make the diplomatic preparations that led to the Rabat Islamic Summit. In October 1969 he was appointed Prime Minister and in February 1970, at a time of student unrest, he took over the Education Ministry. His government presided over a referendum which gave remarkably unanimous approval to a new Constitution and over elections that were boycotted by the opposition. The Cabinet was reshuffled three times in two months and Laraki set out a new programme of financial austerity, encouragement of local investment "to avoid the hazards of foreign aid", ambitious agricul-

tural development including several new dams, gradual Moroccanisation of banking, insurance, etc. and greater encouragement for the teaching and use of Arabic, better rights for workers and an attack on corruption which he said had become "a serious social disease". In foreign affairs he promised to work for North African co-operation and co-operation with the EEC and support for the Palestinians. During 1970 he and the King met both the President of the World Jewish Congress and Yassir Arafat. He also went to Washington to seek Nixon's help to end the War of Attrition. In July 1971 Laraki was one of those who hid with the King in a bathroom during the Skhirat Attempt and then witnessed the execution of the senior officers involved. The following month Hassan decided to make a fresh start and replaced Laraki with Karim Lamrani. In April 1974 Laraki was brought back as Foreign Minister and almost immediately went on a tour of the Gulf in a successful quest for financial support. He was also much involved in the diplomatic manoeuvring that preceded the decolonisation of the Spanish Sahara which Hassan claimed should revert to Moroccan sovereignty, attempting to defuse Algerian hostility. He and the Mauritanian Foreign Minister together toured Black Africa and went to the UN to explain their case and briefed the International Court in The Hague. Subsequently he was one of the signatories to the Madrid Tripartite Agreement which set the timing for the Spanish withdrawal. Laraki also visited China where he signed a long-term trade agreement. In October 1977 when the King was forming a coalition government, he needed an important post for the Istiqlal leader Muhammad Boucetta so he gave him the Foreign Ministry and Laraki left politics.

LARAKI, Izz al-Din (1929)

Moroccan Prime Minister. He came from a very prominent family of Fez and qualified in Paris as a doctor, specialising in pneumology. He then alternated between clinical practice, lecturing and medical administration. As a youth he had joined the Istiqlal and when in October 1977 the Party agreed to join the Cabinet of Ahmad Uthman he was given the Ministry of National Education and Executive Training which he held for the following nine years. Some of his policies were criticised by the Istiqlal and he left the Party when it went into opposition in 1985. He therefore had no Party and no personal following when in September 1986 he was appointed Prime Minister: he was, however, close to Hassan II. He announced a programme that would give priority to the Western Sahara War, and after that to education, self-sufficiency in food production and rationalisation of State industries. He was never, however, in full control of the government for foreign affairs were the preserve of the King and Abd al-Latif Filali while Driss Basri effectively ran internal matters. In March 1987 Laraki secured a rescheduling of the foreign debt and started an austerity campaign and a drive to secure investment. Laraki worked closely with his able Finance Minister, Muhammad Barradi, who in December introduced a budget to stimulate an open, competitive economy. They started relaxing state control over industry, maintaining the strategic sector of essential infrastructure while the rest went for "people's

capitalism". In October 1989 he appointed a Minister of Privatisation and shortly afterwards announced a list of 113 organisations, including four banks and 37 hotels, for privatisation. The Stock Exchange was revived. In November 1989 the King decided to postpone elections for two years so that they would not clash with an expected referendum on the Sahara and Laraki remained in office. In December the Budget increased revenue through reforms rather than tax rises. He had to preside over a period of austerity due to a rise in energy costs and a fall in the exports of phosphates and in February 1990 he appointed the first Minister of Foreign Trade to fight a worsening deficit. He secured rescheduling of the country's debts which amounted to $22,000 million and in May devalued the dinar by 10%. In the same month, for the first time in Moroccan history, a motion of no confidence in the Government was moved in the Assembly by four opposition parties but although Laraki survived by 200 votes to 82 a precedent had been set. During 1990 the King and the Government came under much criticism at home for economic misery and abroad for violations of human rights and in December it was shaken by the Fez Riots: there were also large demonstrations over the Government's active role in supporting Saudi Arabia after the occupation of Kuwait by Saddam Hussain. Laraki quickly raised the minimum wage by 15% and the next Budget promised large increases in health and education. In April 1991 he put forward a 21-point plan to create 100,000 jobs by the end of the year. Laraki pushed for greater cohesion in the Arab Maghreb Union and advocated a bridge across the Straits of Gibraltar and a free trade zone in Tangier. Diplomatically he worked with the Algerian Prime Minister Hamrouche for a common North African policy during the Gulf Crisis and for a common Arab front for the Madrid Peace Conference. In April 1992 Morocco sent troops to assist the UN in Somalia. Laraki's economic policies were praised by the World Bank which in April 1992 gave Morocco a credit of $6,000 million – the highest for any country. He was also extremely successful in attracting foreign investment which in the first half of 1992 was 70% above the figure for the previous year. In April 1992, in an anti-corruption drive, Laraki decreed that all officials should declare their personal wealth. In August 1992, with parliamentary elections pending, his Ministers wished to take part in party politics and Laraki resigned so that a non-political Cabinet might be formed by Karim Lamrani. Laraki was a member of the Royal Moroccan Academy and international learned bodies and published a number of medical papers.

LARNACA AIRFIELD SHOOT-OUT (1978)

On 18 February 1978 Yusuf Sibai, a prominent Egyptian writer and a close friend of President Sadat was murdered by two Palestinian gunmen in the Nicosia Hilton Hotel. The killers seized a dozen hostages including four Egyptians and three representatives of the Palestine Liberation Organisation. At the request of the Cypriot Government, the PLO sent a mission to persuade the murderers to surrender. In the meanwhile, after negotiations with the Cypriot Government, they and their hostages flew out on a Cyprus Airways DC-

8 but were refused permission to land by Libya, Algeria, Kuwait and South Yemen. They were allowed to stop in Djibouti and returned to Larnaca almost 24 hours after they had left it. Almost immediately afterwards an Egyptian Air Force Hercules C-130 landed a 74-man commando unit which came under heavy fire from Cypriot National Guardsmen. Fifteen Egyptians were killed, 16 were wounded and the rest surrendered. The killers of Sibai released their hostages and surrendered to the Cypriot police. Sadat, who had impulsively thought to secure a triumph equal to that of the Israelis at Entebbe personally insulted President Kyprianou and broke off relations with Cyprus. The Egyptians claimed that the Cypriots had agreed to their presence to free the hostages and arrest the murderers and then treacherously attacked them.

LARNACA YACHT KILLINGS (1985)
On 25 September 1985 three Israelis were seized on their yacht in Larnaca harbour by three men, two Arabs and a Briton. After fruitless negotiation conducted by Cypriot, Egyptian and Palestine Liberation Organisation officials, the three Israelis were killed. The terrorists stated that their victims had been Mossad members, responsible for Israeli interference with Palestinian boats. The PLO denied any responsibility for the action but, claiming that it was a reprisal, the Israelis, with American assistance, carried out the Tunis Bombing of the PLO HQ killing 65 people on 1 October. In December the three assassins were sentenced to life imprisonment for premeditated murder.

LATRUN, Battle of (1948)
Latrun, a village about 15 miles west of Jerusalem and 20 miles east of Tel Aviv dominates the main road between the two cities and was the scene of heavy fighting during the Palestine War of 1948. It was occupied by the 4th Regiment of the Arab Legion under the command of the future Field Marshal Habis al-Majali and defied a series of attacks by the Israelis to capture it. In the first stage of the fighting which lasted for about a fortnight until the first truce on 11 June about 700 Israelis, more than the entire casualties in the June War of 1967, were killed. During the cease-fire the Israelis built a temporary road which enabled them to by-pass Latrun but when fighting started again on 9 July it was the object of a major attack by an élite task force of five brigades under the command of Yigal Allon. The first stage, which included the Lydda Expulsions was successful but an attempt to envelop Latrun from the north-west failed. The second truce was due to start in the evening of 18 July but early that morning two crack Palmach Brigades made a final effort to capture the position. A single 6-pounder gun of the Arab Legion destroyed the five tanks that the Israelis used to spear-head their attack and the infantry, although outnumbering the Arabs by eight to one, made no attempt to advance. The two battles of Latrun which cost the Israelis 1,300 killed and wounded, showed that the Legion, although much the smallest of the Arab armies, was by far the most effective.

LAUSANNE, Convention (1923)
The successes of the Turkish nationalists under the Ghazi Mustafa Kamal rendered the humiliating terms of the Sèvres Treaty unenforceable. After eight months of negotiations a revised Treaty was signed in Lausanne on 24 July 1923. It made no difference to the status of the Arab provinces of the former Ottoman Empire except for an agreement to negotiate a frontier with Iraq within nine months. Provisions for Armenian independence, Kurdish autonomy and Greek rule in Smyrna were abandoned. Much of the Treaty dealt with the Greek Islands and the Straits.

LAVON AFFAIR (1954)
During 1954 the Israelis were alarmed at the improvement of Cairo's relations with Britain, shown by the negotiations for the Anglo-Egyptian Treaty, and angered by the Bat Galim Affair. The Minister of Defence, Pinhas Lavon, who was known for his aggressive attitude towards the Arabs, seems to have approved a conspiracy to sabotage Egyptian relations with the West by the placing of bombs in British and American official establishments in Cairo in the expectation that this would be blamed upon the Egyptian Government. The Prime Minister, Moshe Sharrett, had not been informed of the plot. An amateurish spy ring of young Egyptian Jews had been recruited but had already been penetrated by Egyptian intelligence. Some explosions took place, the American Consulate in Alexandria, an American-owned cinema in Cairo and a post office were damaged. The gang was arrested but their detention was kept secret until October when they were put on trial. One of the most important committed suicide in jail. Two were condemned to death, six, including a woman, were given long prison sentences and two were acquitted. The Israeli Government unwisely campaigned noisily for the commutation of the death sentences but they were hanged, despite, it was said, the personal opposition of Nasser who was overruled by his colleagues: some Muslim Brothers had recently been executed and to pardon Israeli spies would have been politically impossible. Lavon denied giving orders for the operation but was contradicted by the Chief of Staff General Dayan and the Chief of Intelligence. Lavon resigned and was replaced by Ben Gurion who came out of retirement. In order to restore shaken Israeli morale, Ben Gurion authorised the Gaza Raid which had immense long-term effects. Ben Gurion's desire to destroy Lavon dominated domestic Israeli politics for a decade.

LAW AGAINST MEETINGS (1986)
During 1986 Israel was governed by an uneasy coalition of the Likud and Labour parties. In August two Bills were presented to the Knesset, one of which was designed to prevent the rise of a racist party such as Meir Kahane's Kach. This was, however, watered down to permit religious quotations in political speeches thus enabling Kahane to continue to incite racism with the backing of the Bible. In order to persuade Likud to vote even for this weakened measure, Labour had to accept a linked law which made it a crime for Israelis to have any contact with representatives of the Palestine Liberation Organisation. Soon afterwards the law was defied by a group of 28, mostly left-wing intellectuals, who flew to Romania to discuss a possible peace settlement with PLO officials: on their return

they received death threats and some were interrogated and charged with breaking the new law. In January 1990 the former Defence Minister, Ezer Weizmann, was dismissed from the Cabinet for contacts with the PLO but, as a Knesset Member, he was not prosecuted. In April 1991 five Israelis met PLO representatives at a Peace Forum in Granada which was also attended by the Secretary-General of the Arab League, Chadli Klibi. The most prominent defier of the law, however, was Abie Nathan whose previous search for peace had included an attempted meeting with Nasser and hiring a boat from which he broadcast *The Voice of Peace* in Arabic. In October 1989 he was sentenced to eighteen months' imprisonment with one year suspended for meeting Yassir Arafat in Tunis. Released in February 1990 he met Arafat again the following month and was again brought to trial. He then went on hunger strike in a tent in a square in Tel Aviv at the end of April 1991 and was taken to court in a wheelchair. The case was adjourned. The Knesset Speaker and Arafat appealed to him to stop but he continued until President Chaim Herzog himself received him. In October 1991 he was sentenced to a further 18 months. In December 1992 Prime Minister Rabin announced that the law would be repealed but this was only achieved by a majority of one.

al-LAWZI, Ahmad Abd al-Krim (1925–)

Jordanian Prime Minister. He was born at Jubayha near Amman and trained as a teacher in Baghdad. After three years in a school in 1953 he joined the Royal Court as assistant to the Chief of Protocol and with a brief interruption as a Deputy, held various posts there before becoming Minister of State for Prime Ministerial Affairs and a Senator in 1965. In 1970 he was Minister of Finance in the government of Wasfi al-Tall upon whose murder he became Prime Minister in November 1971. He took a firm line against Palestinian guerrillas operating within Jordan but said that troops from other Arab countries would be welcomed provided that they were under Jordanian command. He supported the plan of King Hussain for a United Arab Kingdom of East and West Banks, stressing that only Jerusalem could be capital of the West Bank. Lawzi declared that there could be no bilateral settlement with Israel. In May 1973 he was admitted to hospital and resigned shortly afterwards. He was appointed a Senator and in 1978 was first President of the National Consultative Council which replaced the Assembly dissolved in 1974.

LEBANESE COMMUNIST PARTY

During the First World War a group of Lebanese intellectuals published articles attacking capitalism and nationalism and calling for the basic equality of all people. In 1924 some of them were contacted by a Polish Jew on behalf of the Palestine Communist Party who asked them to set up a branch in Lebanon. Instead the Lebanese, led by an author, Yusuf Yazbek, set up their own group, the Communist Party of Syria and Lebanon, and started to organise trade unions. Their leaders were arrested for supporting the Druze Revolt and the Party banned. Yazbek was replaced by a worker and trade unionist, Fuad Shimali under whom the Party expanded, becoming strong in Tripoli and Sidon. A considerable proportion of the membership was Christian, particularly Armenian. In 1936 Khalid Bakhdash who had undergone a long period of training in Moscow took over as Secretary-General at a time when France, under the Popular Front Government, was indulgent towards communism which, although technically illegal, could operate openly and even contest the Lebanese elections of 1937. Bakhdash concentrated on indoctrination and propaganda, translating Marxist works into Arabic, organising demonstrations and building up cadres. It was always dependent upon outside finance, from Palestine, France or Russia. Members had street fights with the Parti Populaire Syrien and the Kataib. There was a crack-down after the Party opposed the war but with the overthrow of the Vichy regime and Russia's entry on the allied side it was again tolerated. Candidates, denying any desire to build a socialist system and stressing the struggle for national independence, stood unsuccessfully in the 1943 elections. Shortly afterwards, after a Congress at which 190 delegates represented 7,000 members, the Party split into its components and the Syrian Communist Party came into existence though a joint Central Committee was maintained for another year. Farajallah al-Hilu led the Lebanese Party until 1946 when he was replaced by Nikola Shawi. The Party split in 1948 as several leaders opposed Russian support for the creation of Israel while others opposed joining the Palestine War seeing it as a British plot to benefit Trans-Jordan. The influx of Palestinians increased its numbers and it put up candidates in the elections of 1947 and 1951 but none of them were able to attract the 10% of the votes needed to save their deposits. In the 1958 crisis it strongly opposed President Camille Chamoun but was not invited to join his other critics in the United National Front. Again its candidates failed in the 1964 and 1968 elections although by now it claimed 10,000 card-carrying members and fellow-travellers in the unions and peace movement: there were, however, divisions between pro-Russian and pro-Chinese factions. In 1969 it joined the National Movement led by Kamal Jumblatt, who as Minister of the Interior legalised the Party in August 1970. It called for strong action to restrain Israeli attacks in the South and Georges Hawi, who was to succeed Shawi in the late 1970s, was jailed for belittling the army. A policy statement in 1974 stressed that it was not fighting for socialism but for a democratic system free from foreign interference, public liberties, and an independent Lebanon co-operating with other Arab States. During the civil war the Party had its own militia, the Partisans, who supported left-wing Palestinians fighting the Kataib which lost it Christian supporters but gained them among the Shiah, particularly in the Biqaa. In 1983 it joined the National Salvation Front opposing the May Agreement of Amin Gemayel with the Israelis. In 1985/6 the communists supported the Druzes and the Syrians in the fighting against the Islamic fundamentalists, the Tawahid, who were trying to control the Party's old stronghold in Tripoli. In 1985/6 they were also fighting Amal which was trying to take over Palestinian camps such as Burj al-Barajinah. It also had some armed men in the South who claimed to make occasional raids into Israel and its Security Zone. In

December 1989 Israeli troops, landing from helicopter gunships, raided its HQs in the Biqa and near Sidon. In October 1990 it agreed to withdraw its militia from Beirut where it still maintained a radio station. In the early 1990s the Party probably had some 3,000 members.

LIBERAL SOCIALIST PARTY (Egypt)

Hizb al-Ahrar al-Ishtirakiyyin. In October 1975 Anwar Sadat permitted the creation of three separate platforms within the only legal party, the Arab Socialist Union. The leader of the right-wing tendency, the Free Democrats, was Mustafa Kamal Murad, former President of the Cotton Exporters Association. They stood for restricting the public sector to infrastructure and strategic industries but otherwise freedom for private capital, the judiciary and the press. In February 1976 they were licensed as the Liberal Socialists and fought the general election in October, winning 12 seats. In November the three platforms were recognised as individual parties, separate from the ASU and Murad was elected Leader of the Opposition. There was little difference between its policies and those of the Government National Democratic Party and the LSP supported *Infitah*, (the "Open Door" policy) and the Egyptian–Israeli Peace Treaty. Murad was the only non-official taken by Sadat to Jerusalem for his Knesset Speech and the Party escaped the purge of September 1981. In the election of June 1979 its representation fell to 3 with Murad losing his seat. It fought the election of May 1984 on a platform of reform of the electoral laws, more freedom, more self-reliance, direct elections for President, non-alignment and less association with the US, more rights for tenants, wage policies geared to inflation, encouragement of foreign investment, an agreement with IMF to make Egyptian currency convertible and criticism of Israel for its refusal to recognise Palestinian rights. Its symbol was a key. The Party only attracted 0.6% of the votes and won no seats. In the April 1987 general election the LSP in alliance with the Socialist Labour Party and, unofficially, the illegal Muslim Brotherhood, shared a million votes and 60 seats, overtaking the New Wafd as the main opposition party. The coalition supported the re-election of President Mubarak. The SLP with the rest of the opposition boycotted the election of November 1990.

LIBERATION RALLY (Egypt)

Haya't al-Tahrir. In January 1953 the ruling Revolutionary Command Council decreed the abolition of all the previously existing political parties and the creation of a single Liberation Rally to replace them. Its Secretary-General, Colonel Nasser said that it was "not a political party (but) a body that would organise the people's forces for the reconstruction of society on a sound new basis". Throughout his career Nasser always wanted a popular organisation that could deliver unconditional support with controlled fanaticism for his policies. The Rally's Chairman General Neguib, on the other hand saw it as a way back towards a multi-party system. It announced an 11-point programme which included complete evacuation of British troops, self-determination for the Sudan, a new constitution, a welfare state, a fair economic system, improved edu-

cation, friendly relations with other Arab States with a regional force to strengthen the Arab League. Its slogans were "Unity, Liberty, Work". In fact the Rally suffered from lack of leadership, experienced cadres, efficient organisation and a real ideology. It was joined by all who wanted government jobs so there were conflicting political, economic and social objectives. It was never given any political power but it was useful to the regime in neutralising the still legal Muslim Brothers, the still popular Wafd and the Egyptian Communist Party and in rooting out their supporters from Trade Unions, student organisations etc. Within a year it had 1,200 centres doing health and welfare work in competition with the Muslim Brothers. It could also produce enthusiastic mobs when required, for example to demonstrate for Nasser in his struggle with Neguib. By the end of 1956 it was clear that the Liberation Rally was too amorphous and inchoate a body to be of further use and it was allowed to lapse. It was replaced by the more disciplined National Union.

LIBERTY, Attack on *USS* (1967)

The *Liberty* was an American naval ship with exceptionally sophisticated equipment for electronic eavesdropping and deciphering and carried intelligence personnel fluent in Arabic and Hebrew. It was armed with two small machine-guns. Anticipating the outbreak of the June War of 1967 it was stationed in international waters off Sinai and after the start of the fighting intercepted Israeli signals which showed that they were trying to mislead Jordan into an attack which would provide an excuse for the annexation of Jerusalem and the West Bank. The Israelis quickly learned what the *Liberty* was doing and decided to neutralise it. On 8 June three Israeli Mirage jets attacked the ship with intense cannon and machine-gun fire, destroying its electronic gear. Three Israeli motor torpedo boats then attempted to sink the *Liberty* but its captain managed to get it safely to Malta. Thirty four Americans were killed and 171 wounded – many of them intelligence personnel. The Israelis quickly apologised for "an innocent mistake" and, to the extreme anger of US naval officers, it suited the American Government, perhaps fearing revelation of its foreknowledge of the Israeli attack on Egypt, to pretend to believe that it had been an accident.

LIBYA–MALTA TREATY (1984)

In 1972 while the British were negotiating with Malta over the future of the military bases that had been on the island for 170 years Colonel Qadafi offered Prime Minister Mintoff financial assistance in return for a guarantee that the bases would not again, as they had been in the June War, be used for flying supplies to Israel. This was followed by a considerable expansion of economic relations. When at the end of March 1979 British forces withdrew Qadafi who had attended the celebrations promised to meet the estimated revenue loss of £35 million. In return he tried to extract the closure of the Egyptian and Israeli Embassies in Valletta and a favourable settlement of a dispute over the maritime boundary. This, however, flared up in August 1980 when a Maltese-chartered oil rig was forced to withdraw by the Libyan navy: Mintoff expelled 50 Libyan technical and military personnel. It was agreed in 1982 to submit the boundary dispute to the International Court. This was reaffirmed and the Treaty of Friendship signed on 19 November between Qadafi and Mintoff for co-operation in economic, social and cultural fields and also for the exchange of security and defence information. Libya was to supply military equipment and training and to have the use of Maltese dockyards. Malta agreed that its territory should not be used for military activities. In June 1985 the International Court gave a judgement that put the maritime boundary 18 nautical miles north of the median line. In April 1986, invoking the Treaty, Mintoff's successor Dr Bonnici warned Qadafi of American aircraft approaching for the Tripoli Bombing. In February 1990 the Treaty was renewed for a further five years but the conservative Prime Minister Eddie Fenech Adami stated that the military clauses which had annoyed the Americans were no longer operative.

LIBYAN BOEING, Destruction of (1973)

In February 1973 a Libyan civilian Boeing 727, with a French pilot, carrying 104 passengers and a crew of nine was shot down by Israeli fighter aircraft when, straying off course in a flight from Tripoli to Cairo, it came over the Sinai Peninsula which was under Israeli occupation as a result of the June War. Amongst the 108 killed was a former Libya Foreign Minister Salah Masud Bawaisir and the Director-General of the Libyan Archaeological Department. The immediate popular reaction was an attack on the American Embassy in Tripoli. There was great resentment at the Egyptian failure to help or join in reprisals and the Egyptian Embassy and other institutions were attacked after the funeral of the victims. The Israeli action was condemned by the UN, whose Secretary-General Kurt Waldheim called it "one of the most shocking incidents in the history of civil aviation". The Israeli Government expressed "deep sorrow" but said that the aircraft had been over a sensitive area, had ignored warning signals, and that they had feared a *kamikaze* attack on Tel Aviv. They agreed to pay $30,000 to the dependants of those that had died and up to $30,000 to those injured. Qadafi was dissuaded by Sadat from bombing Haifa but in May he ordered an Egyptian submarine stationed in Tripoli to sink the British liner *Queen Elizabeth II* which had been chartered to take a party of wealthy Jews to Tel Aviv to celebrate the 25th anniversary of the proclamation of the State of Israel. The submarine commander sought further orders from Sadat who ordered him to sail to Alexandria. Qadafi thereupon decided to resign, distributed copies of resignation in the streets of Tripoli and took his whole family and all his possessions to Egypt where he remained for 18 days. These incidents significantly weakened the Federation of Arab Republics in which Libya and Egypt were linked.

LIBYAN CULTURAL REVOLUTION (ZUWARAH SPEECH, 1973)

In April 1973, on the anniversary of the birthday of the Prophet, at a speech at Zuwarah Colonel Qadafi denounced most Arab states for "slogans of democracy (but) secret oppression" and educated Libyans who refused to work for their country and he proclaimed a Cultural Revolution. It comprised five points. The first was the annulment of all existing laws promulgated by the previous monarchical regime and their replacement by laws based on *Shariah*. Secondly the repression of communism and conservatism by weeding out all political and moral deviates, "sick minds", including atheists and Muslim Brothers. Thirdly the distribution of arms to the people so that they could protect the Revolution. Fourthly administrative reform to end excessive bureaucracy, incompetence, shirking and bribery. Fifthly the promotion of Islamic thought by rejecting any imported ideas inconsistent with it which "have made youth insane and sick". This Cultural Revolution was to be carried through by People's Committees established nationwide in villages and workplaces who would seize power in order to purge and replace management and stimulate the Revolution from below. If these proposals were rejected Qadafi declared that he would recall King Idris and go into retirement himself. It was claimed that 2,000 committees were formed within six months, libraries were sacked and a start made on brainwashing a generation. Qadafi insisted that unlike that of Mao Tse Tung his Cultural Revolution was not innovation but a return to the Islamic and Arab heritage which was carried further by the Third Universal Theory, *The Green Book* and the Sabhah Congress of 1977.

LIBYAN–SYRIAN UNION (1980–1)

In the summer of 1980 there appeared a strong possibility of a further round of Egyptian–Libyan Border Clashes in which Colonel Qadafi felt that he should be supported by the other members of the Steadfastness Front. On 1 September, Revolution Day for which all the asphalt of the main square had been painted green, Qadafi in his broadcast speech invited Syria to form a union "to confront Israel, Sadat, America and the Arab reactionaries". President Assad, apparently forewarned, immediately accepted "deeply moved". The following week he came to Tripoli and a 13-point statement was issued on a "single personality" at the international level with full political, economic and military union as a base for building socialism and confronting Zionism, etc. which others were welcome to join. Nothing was said about a Head of State, the form of government or a capital but it was agreed that the leaders should meet again within a month to arrange details. Qadafi declared that if the Union failed, he would go and fight as a commando in Galilee and he was reported to have paid the Soviet Union $1,000 million to cover past Syrian debts and given Damascus a further $600 million. Assad apparently discouraged a return visit from Qadafi and came back to Tripoli in December when he said that the merger would be "expedited in the shortest time possible". In March 1981 Assad said that they were "searching for a formula that achieves unity with real popular consent" but he declined to dissolve the rigidly centralised Baath Party which could not possibly conform with the Libyan Jamahariyyah system of "people's power". In August Qadafi on a belated visit to Damascus made no progress, blaming bureaucrats and unspecified regional and separatist factions. Though relations, cemented by a common hostility to

Iraq, continued close there seems to have been no further attempt to give reality to what Sadat called "a union of children".

LILLEHAMMER MURDER (1973)

On 21 July a Moroccan waiter Ahmad Bushiki, walking from a cinema with his Norwegian wife, was shot down in cold blood. It became clear that he had been a victim of mistaken identity. After the Munich Olympics Massacre Israeli Intelligence formed squads for revenge killings of people suspected to have been involved with the Black September Organisation. Shortly after the murder the Norwegian police arrested six foreigners at the residence of an Israeli security official who threatened them with a gun. The head of the Legal Department of the Israeli Foreign Minister requested the release of two Israelis. The diplomat was expelled and the six were brought to trial in January 1974. The former First Secretary of the Israeli Embassy in Paris and a half-Jewish South African woman posing as a Canadian were sentenced to 5 years' imprisonment for conspiracy to murder and illegal intelligence work. Three other Israelis of Scandinavian origin received lighter sentences for espionage. The former chauffeur of the Israeli Embassy in Paris was acquitted. The judge remarked that he took it for granted that the Israeli Intelligence had been behind the crime. It later appeared that the victim had been mistaken for Ali Hassan Salama, an active member of Black September, who was blown up by a car bomb in Beirut in January 1979.

"LITTLE" TRIANGLE

The "Little" Triangle, as opposed to the "Large" Triangle which meant most of Samaria, was an area of Galilee around Wadi Arara which in 1948 had a population of about 12,000 Arabs in 15 villages. During the Palestine War its inhabitants, with the help of Iraqi troops, beat off a series of Israeli attacks and it received a further 1,500 refugees. In the Shunah Talks King Abd Allah agreed to cede it to the Israelis as part of the price of their acceptance of his annexation of other parts of the West Bank. The villagers sent a mission to Baghdad in a vain effort to secure the retention of Iraqi troops but on 1 June 1949 the area was handed over to Israel which proceeded to expel all the refugees and many of the original inhabitants.

LOCKERBIE

On 21 December 1988 Pan Am Boeing 747 Flight 103 from Frankfurt to New York with 259 people on board was torn to pieces by an explosion over the Scottish town of Lockerbie and major parts of the wreckage fell on houses, killing another 11 people. The impact at more than 200 mph was with the force of an earthquake 1.6 on the Richter scale and pieces of the aircraft were found over an area of 845 square miles. There were angry recriminations amongst the security authorities of Britain, Germany and the USA as to how the bomb could have been smuggled on board and there were rumours of a CIA operation involving drugs that had gone hideously wrong. Others saw the outrage as revenge for the destruction of an Iranian civil airliner by the *USS Vincennes* and at first the general consensus

was that the operation had been carried out by Ahmad Jibril on behalf of Tehran. The investigation cost over £17 million with 15,000 statements taken in 17 countries, 20,000 names recorded and 35,000 photographs taken. These enquiries suggested that the crime had been planned by the Libyans: the detonator used was identical with some seized from their agents in February 1988 and had been put in a suitcase in Malta. It was also similar to one used to destroy a French aircraft over Chad in 1989 in which 171 people had perished. In June 1991 the Libyan Government officially denied responsibility. In October 1991 it became politically expedient, both for reasons of American politics and to conciliate Syria and Iran, to put the blame firmly on Libya and the American and British Governments demanded the extradition from Tripoli of Abd al-Basit al-Maghrari, a senior Intelligence Officer and Amin Fahimah, who had been Air Libya manager in Malta at the relevant time. It was suggested that they had taken orders from the Chief of Special Operations, Major Abd Allah al-Sanusi whose extradition was demanded in October by the French for the Chad bombing. On 13 November Scottish and American Law Officers issued indictments for murder against Maghrari and Fahimah with hints that if they were not handed over unspecified action would be taken. Colonel Qadafi denied Libyan involvement but arrested the accused and said they could not be legally extradited but would go on trial locally: neither British courts, after a spate of scandals involving alleged Irish terrorists, nor American after the case of General Noriega, could be expected to render impartial justice in cases in which their governments were interested. The prospect of a second Tripoli Bombing alarmed other states, including Italy and Iran, the Arab League officially expressed concern and Qadafi asked friends of the West such as President Mubarak to mediate, offering to hand them over to a neutral court or to assist British or American judges or a UN investigating team in Tripoli. On 20 January 1992 the Security Council passed Resolution 731 urging Libya to make an "effective response" to French, American and British requests. Three weeks later Qadafi, trying to concert his opponents by being conciliatory, said that the French might question their four suspects and the other two could be handed over for trial in a neutral country if the British and Americans re-established normal relations. The Secretary-General Dr Butros-Ghali attempted a settlement. On 31 March Resolution 748, passed by ten votes to none with five abstentions, ordered Libya to hand over the two men by 15 April and show by concrete measures its renunciation of terrorism or face sanctions which would paralyse the Libyan aviation industry, ban arms purchases, and reduce its diplomatic missions: no measures were threatened against oil exports. Libya appealed to the International Court against Western bullying but was told that it had no jurisdiction over the Security Council. After sanctions came into force they were generally applied, even by Libya's partners of the Arab Maghreb Union, thus weakening the organisation: in January 1993 Qadafi briefly closed his frontiers in protest. Sanctions were renewed every 120 days. Qadafi faced the dilemma that handing over the men would anger his intelligence services and Revolutionary Committees and his Deputy, Major Jalloud, a fellow-tribesman of one of them, while intensification of sanctions would antagonise the people with increasing hardships. Libya stockpiled food and shifted some assets to secret accounts abroad. There were complicated legal proceedings in the United States with Pan Am, which went bankrupt, alleging that the Government had been deliberately evasive about what it knew. There were further Libyan hints that the men might be prepared to go before a neutral court, such as one in Switzerland: the Swiss refused but anyway, after such political and diplomatic effort, the West could not risk allowing the suspects to go before any court which might acquit them and rejected a further suggestion of a jury consisting of international judges meeting at The Hague. Mubarak and other Arab leaders still attempted to mediate but in October Resolution 833 freezing Libyan assets abroad, banning the export to Tripoli of oil-related technology, and still further reducing diplomatic missions came into force. The following month Qadafi threatened to set the oilfields ablaze. In February 1994 Qadafi declared that he was closing the Lockerbie file but sanctions were routinely renewed in April.

LONDON AGREEMENT (1987)
The Israeli elections of 1984 meant that no party could form a government and so an agreement had to be made that the Labour leader Shimon Peres should be Prime Minister and the Likud leader Yitzhak Shamir Foreign Minister for two years after which they would exchange posts. This occurred in October 1986. The coalition was deeply divided, particularly on the question of negotiations with the Arabs which implied that some territorial concessions would have to be made in return for peace. Peres hoped that if he could make an agreement with Arab leaders this would break up the coalition and bring about a general election which he would win. In April 1987 Israeli newspapers favourable to him reported that he and the Labour Defence Minister Yitzhak Rabin had held a secret meeting with King Hussain in London at which it was agreed that a Peace Conference would be convened by the Secretary-General of the UN on the basis of Resolution 242 which admitted the right of Israel to exist within secure borders but meant surrender of occupied territory. The Conference would invite the Arabs and Israelis to set up "geographical bilateral committees" to conduct direct negotiations. It was further agreed that the main Conference would not be able to impose or veto any agreements reached in the bilateral talks. The Palestine Liberation Organisation should have no part in the Conference but Israel would negotiate with moderate representatives of the West Bank. The King was said to have stated that Syria would present no obstacle to such a Conference and that Russia, with which Israel had no relations, would have to participate. Peres' supporters further implied that he had secured American backing. The Jordanian Prime Minister, Zaid al-Rifai denied that there had been any agreement and said that the PLO would have to take part in any Conference. In the event Secretary Schultz, having discovered the strength of Likud opposition and unwilling to give

Russia a voice in a Middle East settlement, did not support the idea of a Conference but almost exactly similar arrangements were made for the Madrid Peace Conference of October/November 1991.

LONDON, Convention of (1840)
In 1839 the Ottoman Sultan Mahmud II determined to reconquer Syria which had been lost to Muhammad Ali Pasha at the beginning of the decade but his army was defeated by Ibrahim Pasha at Nizib. The Turkish fleet defected to Egypt and the Ottoman Empire appeared about to collapse. The Foreign Secretary, Lord Palmerston, feared that the situation might develop to the advantage of Russia which could gain either by coming to the aid of Constantinople and securing a dominant position there or by annexing neighbouring areas as they slipped from the Sultan's grip. There was a further problem in that France might gain through its long-standing relationship with Muhammad Ali. Palmerston negotiated a Convention by which Britain, Russia, Austria and Prussia agreed to support the Sultan. Muhammad Ali would be granted the Pashalik of Egypt for himself and his descendants and the Pashalik of Acre for his own lifetime. In return Muhammad Ali would pay tribute to the Sultan, withdraw from his conquests in Arabia, Crete, northern Syria and southern Anatolia and return the Ottoman navy. If he failed to accept within ten days, the offer of Acre would be withdrawn. The Convention was signed on 15 July 1840 and was a triumph for Palmerston as it superseded the Unkiar–Skelessi Treaty to which he had so strongly objected and excluded France from a voice in the settlement. Muhammad Ali did not accept and in September British and Austrian troops landed behind his lines in Beirut and Egyptian troops were subsequently withdrawn from Syria and Arabia. The Sultan later issued a *Firman* setting out the conditions upon which Muhammad Ali was granted the hereditary governorship of Egypt.

LONDON MARITIME CONFERENCES (1956)
After the CzechoSlovak Arms Deal Prime Minister Eden saw Nasser as attempting to unite the Arabs against the West and as a threat to vital oil supplies and determined to overthrow him by intrigue within Egypt or, if necessary, by force. At the same time the French saw him as the "actual leader" of the revolt in Algeria and were equally anxious to oust him. The nationalisation of the Suez Canal on 26 July 1956 appeared to present the ideal opportunity and on 27 July Eden wrote to Eisenhower that it was essential to regain the Canal by force. Eisenhower replied suggesting a conference of the maritime nations most affected. Eden, knowing that the British armed forces were not ready and public opinion not prepared for action, concurred. A meeting of the British, French and American Foreign Ministers in London which ended on 2 August agreed to freeze Egyptian assets and issued a communiqué in deliberately offensive terms condemning "the arbitrary and unilateral seizure by one nation of an international agency". They invited the signatories of the Constantinople Convention and other maritime countries to a conference in London which met from 16 to 23 August. The British wished to exclude Russia and Egypt but

gave way to please the Americans. Twenty-two states were represented, most by their Foreign Ministers: Greece refused to attend because of its dispute with Britain over Cyprus and Egypt declined to participate but sent the President's close collaborator Ali Sabri as an observer. Some of the Third World states were not happy at the assumption that the Egyptians could not operate the Canal and only 18 endorsed the four proposals put forward by Dulles. These were that the Canal should not be controlled by any single country but should be operated by an international board on which Egypt would be represented. There should be fair compensation for the Suez Canal Company, an "equitable return" for Egypt and recognition of Egyptian sovereignty, and the International Court to arbitrate in financial disputes. The Indian representative Krishna Menon urged that the UN should be involved but was opposed by the Western powers. The majority appointed the Australian Prime Minister Menzies to obtain Nasser's acceptance of these terms. The mission failed and on 12 September Dulles put forward a proposal for the creation of a Suez Canal Users Association which would manage the Canal and take the revenues, paying Egypt a fair share. A second London Conference meeting from 19 to 21 September endorsed an altered version of the Dulles plan which he saw as a basis for negotiation but Eden envisaged as an ultimatum. Finally a third Conference of the 15 countries that accepted SCUA met at Ambassadorial level in London on 1 October to start drafting a constitution for it. By this time, however, the British and French Governments had determined that toppling Nasser was of more importance than the operation of the Canal, and were preparing to launch the Suez War.

LONDON PALESTINE CONFERENCE (1939)
With war with Germany likely the British Government was anxious to defuse the Palestine situation which during the Arab Rebellion had tied up considerable numbers of troops. The Peel Report had recommended partition but the Woodhead Report had pronounced this impractical. The Government therefore decided to make one further attempt to find an agreed settlement between Arabs and Jews, failing which it would feel justified in imposing one. Both sides were therefore invited to send delegations to London early in 1939. The Jewish Delegation led by Dr Weizmann contained representatives of various groups from Palestine, Europe, America and South Africa, Zionist and non-Zionist with the exception of the Revisionists. The Arab Delegation contained representatives of the Arab Higher Committee and several of them including the leader Jamal al-Hussaini were released for the purpose. The Mufti, Haj Amin al-Hussaini was, however, banned. The British insisted upon the presence of Raghib al-Nashashibi. Sympathy for the Palestinians had been shown by Arab leaders at the Bludan Conference and the Arab Parliamentary Congress and there was a real danger that they might turn to the Axis for help. Some, such as Ibn Saud and the Amir Abd Allah had proved helpful during the strike that preceded the Rebellion and they, Egypt, Iraq and Yemen were also invited to send representatives. These included Prince Faysal and Fuad Hamza of Saudi Arabia, Nuri al-Said,

Ali Mahir and Tawfiq Abu al-Huda. The first meeting at St James's Palace was addressed by the Prime Minister Neville Chamberlain. The Palestinians refused to sit with the Jews so the two sides had separate meetings with the Colonial Secretary Malcolm MacDonald. The Palestinian Arabs made their familiar case based upon the Hussain–MacMahon Correspondence, as a result of which it was officially published for the first time, and repeated their fear of Jewish domination. They would accept nothing but an independent state and the end of Jewish immigration. The other Arabs had a courteous but fruitless meeting with Weizmann. The Jews also argued on historical lines and refused to accept a permanent position of numerical inferiority. After six weeks the Conference broke up without having achieved any result and six weeks later the British imposed their views in the MacDonald White Paper.

LUTFALLAH, Michel (c. 1880–?)
He was the son of Habib Lutfallah, a Greek Orthodox Syrian who made a fortune in the Sudan and later moved to Cairo as a banker. He was a member of the Ottoman Decentralisation Party and became a strong supporter of Sharif Hussain to whom he lent large sums of money. Michel spent the war raising funds and doing propaganda work for the Arab Revolt which his brother represented in Paris. Michel entered Damascus with Faysal and founded there a Party of Syrian Unity. In 1920 King Hussain conferred upon Habib the title of *Amir* after which Michel claimed to be a Prince. After the overthrow of Faysal's kingdom, Michel became the leader of Syrian exiles in Cairo. In 1921 he financed the Syro-Palestinian Congress to organise opposition to the French Mandate and lobby the League of Nations. The organisation split after a few years with Lutfallah and Dr Shahbandar who were pro-Hashemite and pro-British being opposed by Shakib Arslan and the pan-Arabists. Lutfallah lost credibility when it was learned that he had aspirations in 1928 to becoming King of Syria or of Lebanon and that his relatives the Sursuqs had sold large areas of Palestine to the Zionists.

LUTFI, Ali, (c. 1935–)
Egyptian Prime Minister. He took a Doctorate in Economics at Lausanne and became head of the Economics Department at Ayn Shams University. He was regarded as an expert on taxation and wrote several monographs on financial matters. He was also active in politics and chaired the Economic Committee of the National Democratic Party. Sadat appointed Lutfi Minister of Finance but he resigned in May 1980 when he was not allowed to take measures which would have weighed heavily on the corrupt circle round the President; he also resented the concentration of power in the reformed Ministry of Planning. In August 1985 at a time of financial crisis with which the sick General Kamal Hassan Ali was unable to cope, Lutfi replaced him as Prime Minister. He did not change the main Ministers, one of whom, the Defence Minister General Abu Ghazala administered the expanding military/industrial complex according to his own ideas. He declared that his aim was basic economic reform, cutting subsidies, rationalising exchange rates and reducing foreign debts but in fact Lutfi failed to halt

the decline in the economy and was unable to produce any co-ordinated strategy or stablise prices when the country was under pressure from the IMF. The general dissatisfaction was shown by the Gizeh Mutiny of February 1986. Lawyers held their first strike in 30 years as a protest against the extension of the state of emergency declared after the murder of Sadat and Islamic fundamentalists burned bookshops and bars in Cairo. In March President Mubarak publicly rebuked his government for inaction and in July himself went on a European tour to seek help with debt repayment. In August Lutfi forecast gloom for years ahead. Lutfi was in the middle of negotiations for a credit of $1,000 million and appeared so willing to accept rigid cuts in public expenditure, particularly on food subsidies, that the President thought that his concessions might lead to public disorder. He therefore abruptly dismissed Lutfi in November 1986, appointing another economist Dr Atif Sidqi as Prime Minister.

LYAZIDI, Ahmad (c. 1908–)

Moroccan politician. He was born in Rabat, son of an office messenger and served as a lieutenant in the French army. He then went into business, prospering as a wholesaler of sugar, tea and oil. He was elected President of the Federation of Chambers of Commerce and to the Conseil du Gouvernement where in 1951 he aroused the ire of Marshal Juin by stating that the budget was designed solely to benefit the colons. He was already a member of the Istiqlal Party and in December 1952 he was imprisoned after riots in Casablanca. In 1955 he was Minister of Commerce in the first government after independence but was moved to Defence where he had major tasks in working out the role of the army in a new state with problems over its politicisation, the relationship between the Ministry and the General Staff, then headed by the future Hassan II and the creation of military districts as well as dealing with dissidents in the Riff and the clashes with the Spanish in the South that followed the Ifni Crisis. Later he was President of the National Bank for Development. His elder brother Muhammad Lyazidi was one of the earliest nationalists.

LYAZIDI, Muhammad (c. 1905–)

Moroccan nationalist leader. He was born in Rabat, son of an office messenger, but after education at an élite Franco-Muslim college, he obtained a post as a government interpreter. He was much influenced by the Salafiyyah Movement and was a close associate of Allal al-Fassi. He was dismissed in 1930 for public attacks upon the Berber Dahir. He and Allal were arrested in 1936, charged with preaching sedition in the mosques and Lyazidi was again imprisoned in 1937 and 1938, exiled to the Sahara. He had been one of the signatories to the Plan de Réformes Marocaines, edited a nationalist newspaper and was one of the founders of the Istiqlal Party. In 1944 he was imprisoned for some months charged with collaborating with the Germans. With Allal and Balafrej in exile Muhammad Lyazidi was effectively the leader of Istiqlal and also acted as a link between Muhammad V and the nationalists. In March 1945 he applied to the newly created UN to grant membership to Morocco as an independent state.

With his brother Ahmad, Lyazidi he was imprisoned in December 1952 but was released to participate in the independence negotiations. After independence he refused a Ministry as he was generally in poor health. He was regarded as one of the most traditional conservative members of the Istiqlal but tried to reconcile differences within the Party at the time of the Ben Barka secession. Later, austere, taciturn, greatly respected but always ill he preferred to remain at home, exercising influence through editing a newspaper, rather than through active participation in politics.

LYDDA AIRPORT ATTACK (1972)

The Popular Front for the Liberation of Palestine established links with foreign left-wing terrorist groups including the Japanese Red Army. On 31 May 1972 three Japanese who had undergone training in Lebanon arrived from Rome as tourists at Lydda airport and attacked passengers with Kalashnikov rifles and hand grenades. Twenty-five people, including Puerto Rican pilgrims were killed. Two of the terrorists were killed and the third captured. The attack was condemned by some Arab leaders such as King Hussain. The Israelis blamed the Lebanon for not controlling guerrillas and carried out several raids on what were alleged to be guerrilla bases. The surviving terrorist was in July sentenced to life imprisonment and was one of the prisoners whose release was demanded during the Maalot Killings. He was in fact released in May 1985 as part of a deal arranged by the Popular Front for the Liberation of Palestine–General Command.

LYDDA EXPULSIONS (1948)

As the State of Israel was coming into existence it took violent measures to frighten away the Arab population from the area it intended to control. The most notorious incident before the declaration of independence had been the Dayr Yassin Massacre but during the Palestine War the Prime Minister David Ben-Gurion felt it necessary to expel 50,000–70,000 Palestinians, including 15,000 refugees from areas already seized, from the area of Lydda and Ramla. Israeli aircraft early in July alternately dropped bombs and leaflets over the towns to cause panic. King Abd Allah forbade his army to defend them and they were captured on 12 July. All able-bodied men were rounded up and taken to camps. Shortly afterwards a skirmish erupted and between 250 and 400 Palestinians were killed while the Israelis lost three dead. In an operation organised by the future Israeli Prime Minister Yitzhak Rabin the total population of Lydda was expelled by force and that of Ramla terrified into leaving. The women and children, some of whom died, had to depart on foot and many were robbed of their valuables by Israeli soldiers. The towns were systematically looted, even doors and windows being taken away. In September there were less than 2,000 Arabs remaining in Lydda and Ramla.

LYOUSSI, Lahsen (1903–70)

Moroccan tribal leader. He received little, if any formal education for his tribe, the Ait Youssi Berbers, who lived near Sefrou, resisted the French until 1922 so much of his youth was spent under arms. He was later

Caid but was dismissed in 1953 for refusing to sign the petition organised by Thami al-Glawi calling for the deposition of Muhammad V, of whom he was a personal friend. In the last months of the Protectorate he was involved with the Armée de Libération Nationale, attacking French garrisons in the Middle Atlas, stressing that it was he and the Berbers, not the urban Arab Istiqlal Party who were forcing the French to give way. Upon independence he was appointed the first Minister of the Interior, it was said at the instigation of the Istiqlal who wished to discredit him for, semi-literate, he was obviously incapable of fulfilling such tasks as organising elections. After six months, having mishandled some troubles in Marrakesh he was given the honorary posts of Minister of State and member of the Royal Council. He then toured the Berber areas, calling on the tribesmen to ignore Arab-dominated political parties and rally round the King. He also obtained arms from French officers who hoped for a weakening of the new government by a reversion to anarchy amongst the Berbers. It appears that Lyoussi encouraged the revolt of Addi ou Bihi although later, at the request of the future King Hassan II, he urged him to lay down his arms. When ou Bihi was put on trial, the role of Lyoussi became apparent and he fled firstly to his own tribe, where he stirred up some unrest, and then to Spain. In December 1958 he was sentenced to death but in 1967 he was allowed to return home.

MAALOT KILLINGS (1974)

In the early morning of 15 May 1974 three guerrillas of the Democratic Front for the Liberation of Palestine seized the school at Maalot, an Israeli village about 7 km from the Lebanese frontier in which more than 90 school children were spending the night. Having already killed four other people, they killed the caretaker. Some of the children escaped, two sick girls were released and another child sent out with a list of about 26 prisoners whose release the guerrillas demanded. Amongst them was the Japanese survivor of the Lydda Airport Attack. The guerrillas called for the mediation of the French and Romanian Ambassadors who should escort the released prisoners to Damascus. Half the children would be released when their arrival was reported and the other half would fly with the guerrillas to an Arab country. Probably owing to confusion the guerrillas' deadline passed without anything having happened. The Israeli Government decided to storm the school, a decision which resulted in a shoot-out in which 20 children and the guerrillas were killed. Although the Lebanese Government denied that the guerrillas had operated from their territory, in reprisal Israeli bombers carried out a series of attacks on refugee camps there, killing or wounding more than 300 civilians.

MacDONALD WHITE PAPER (1939)

The Peel Report of 1937 had recommended the partition of Palestine into separate Arab and Jewish states but the Woodhead Report of the following year showed this to be impractical. The London Palestine Conference in the first months of 1939 failed to produce a solution and in April 1939, with war with Germany obviously close at hand, the Prime Minister Neville Chamberlain reached the conclusion "if we must offend one side let us offend the Jews rather than the Arabs". A White Paper issued in May by the Colonial Secretary Malcolm MacDonald declared "unequivocally that it was not part of their policy that Palestine should become a Jewish state". The Government proposed to create an independent Palestinian state in treaty relations with Britain at the end of ten years. The independent state would be one in which "Arabs and Jews share in government in such a way that the essential interests of each community are safeguarded". In the transition period Palestinians would be given an increasing share of power. During the first five years 75,000 Jewish immigrants would be admitted after which further entry would be dependent on Arab consent. The Government was determined to halt illegal immigration. The High Commission would have power to regulate or prohibit the transfer of land. The White Paper was furiously attacked by the Zionists as a breach of the Balfour Declaration and the Mandate and, by condemning them to minority status in perpetuity, a surrender to Arab terrorism. The Arabs rejected it because of the length and indefiniteness of the proposed transitional period and demanded an immediate halt to immigration. In Parliament it was attacked by the Labour Party and by pro-Zionist MPs such as Winston Churchill and Leopold Amery. It was condemned by the Mandates Commission of the League of Nations but the outbreak of war prevented its discussion by the full Council. It therefore remained technically in force throughout the war and was probably partly responsible for the fact that there was no serious anti-British activity amongst the Palestinian Arabs.

MADAGHRI, Ahmad (1934–74)

Algerian political leader. He was born in Oran and qualified as a teacher. During the Algerian War of Independence he served on the General Staff under Colonel Boumédienne, and thus was regarded as a member of the Oudjda Group. In September 1964 he was elected to the National Assembly and appointed Minister of the Interior. In July 1964 Madaghri was forced to resign after quarreling with Ben Bella who took control of the police and demanded that Prefects should report directly to himself and not to the Interior Ministry. Madaghri was then one of the leaders of the coup of June 1965 in which Boumédienne took power and was immediately reinstated as Minister of the Interior. Madaghri was strongly authoritarian and was little interested in the views of the Party hierarchy. He was seen as a possible future President but died the day after attending a Cabinet meeting. He was believed to have been suffering from a painful illness but there were also reports that he had committed suicide after an angry disagreement with the President.

MADRID TRIPARTITE AGREEMENT (1975)

In 1924 the Spanish Government grouped as the Spanish Sahara some coastal settlements such as Rio de Oro and Villa Cisneros which they had acquired in the nineteenth century. They made little attempt to move inland until after 1934 when the French extended their influence in the Western Sahara after their victory at Jabal Sagho. The Spanish Civil War inhibited much activity before 1940 after which geological surveys discovered valuable phosphates at Bu Craa, iron and possibly oil. Upon regaining independence Morocco claimed that historically it had enjoyed sovereignty over the area and after the Ifni Crisis of 1957/8 it took over Cape Juby and later Ifni itself. In 1965 for the first time the UN criticised the Spanish presence which was defended by a Spanish-organised petition in which the local chiefs stated that they wished for no change. In 1967 an elected Yemaa, a tribal assembly representing all Sahrawis, was created but guerrilla activity started in the area in 1971. Soon there were several competing groups with support from Morocco (the FLU) and Algeria but in 1973 what became Polisario, based on Mauritania which also put forward claims to the area emerged as the most important. After 1970 there were annual Resolutions at the UN calling for independence and a referendum in consultation with Morocco and Mauritania: that in 1974 was passed by 108 votes to none with 23 abstentions. As Franco lay dying Spanish determination to hold on to the area weakened and on 21 August 1974 it declared readiness for a plebiscite under UN supervision. This proposal was denounced by Hassan II who said that he would use force if it resulted in a vote for independence. Mauritania also expressed dissent and at the Rabat Summit agreed to partitioning the area with Morocco and joint exploitation of Bu Craa. The King then proposed that the International Court of Justice be asked to rule whether the territory had been without a ruler at the time of its annexation by Spain and if so, what ties it had had with Morocco and Mauritania. During the winter there was increasing violence with clashes between Spanish and Moroccan troops, between Moroccan troops and POLIsario and between Spanish troops and FLU guerrillas. The leader of the Spanish-created Saharan Unity Party defected to Morocco. In May 1975, before the Court had decided, Madrid announced that it would give independence to the Western Sahara as soon as possible and immediately started the evacuation of women and children. As Morocco and Mauritania reasserted their claims there were threats that Algeria would intervene by force to prevent a Moroccan takeover. Violence continued and occurred also to the borders of the *Presidios* of Ceuta and Melilla leading to icy relations between Madrid and Rabat. Early in October a UN mission returned from the area with the recommendation that a UN presence should keep the peace as the Spanish withdrew and stated that most of those that it had seen wanted independence and opposed the territorial claims of Morocco and Mauritania. On 16 October the International Court decided that although there had been legal ties between the area and its neighbours, these were not enough to constitute sovereignty. On the same day, the King, who had been exploiting the gathering crisis to rally all shades of Moroccan opinion, announced that he would lead a peaceful Green March to take over the territory. By the beginning of November the Spanish had withdrawn from two-thirds of the territory, concentrating around the capital Al-Ayoun and the phosphate mines at Bu Craa. After a visit to Madrid by the Moroccan Premier Ahmad Uthman and the Foreign Minister Ahmad Laraki and the Mauritanian Foreign Minister Hamdi Ould Muknass an agreement was signed with the Spanish Prime Minister Carlos Arias on 14 November. Spain affirmed that it would irrevocably end its presence by 28 February 1976. Until then the Spanish Governor would be joined by Assistant Governors representing Morocco and Mauritania with the co-operation of the *Yemaa* whose President had just declared his allegiance to King Hassan. The opinions of the inhabitants, expressed through the *Yemaa* would be respected. It was agreed that the ownership of the Bu Craa mine should be 60% Spanish, 30% Moroccan and 10% Mauritanian. The Green March was called off. Algeria, which had not been invited to participate in the negotiations denounced the agreement with such fury that Hassan said he would not be surprised if there were war between the two countries. Within a fortnight of the signature Moroccan troops had occupied Smara, the second city, and Algeria gave support to Polisario which began a series of military actions against the Moroccans which would continue as the Western Saharan War. The Spanish withdrew two days ahead of schedule on 26 February 1976. The following day the 80 out of 103 members of the *Yemaa* voted to become part of Morocco while Polisario leaders proclaimed themselves the Saharan Arab Democratic Republic. On 14 April Morocco and Mauritania signed a frontier agreement which assigned roughly two thirds of the territory to Morocco and provided for joint exploitation of mineral wealth.

al-MAGHRABI, Mahmud Sulayman (1935–)

Libyan Prime Minister. He was born in Haifa with a Libyan father and a Palestinian mother who in 1948 moved to Damascus where he qualified as a lawyer. He then taught in the Gulf before going to George Washington University where he studied geology and petroleum engineering and to Johns Hopkins where he was awarded a Doctorate in Law. He obtained Libyan nationality and in 1966 was appointed Legal Adviser to Esso in Libya. He was active in forming an illegal trade union amongst oil workers and was believed to have links with the Arab Nationalist Movement or the Baath Party. After the June War of 1967 during which he had led a strike by workers refusing to load Western tankers he was sentenced to four years' imprisonment and deprived of his citizenship. He was released in July 1969 and left the country on an Iraqi passport but was recalled by the Revolution Command Council in September to head the Government after they had overthrown the Monarchy. His Cabinet consisted of four other civilians and two senior officers but the RCC clearly intended to rule through efficient technocrats. There were numerous arrests and restrictions were placed upon the press but the masses looked forward to a better future. No government programme was announced but Maghrabi disavowed any intention of forming a political party or nationalising any industry, saying that he wished to co-operate with the oil companies. He demanded the closure of foreign bases and the £100 million contract with Britain for the supply of missiles was cancelled. The teaching of English in primary schools was stopped and the Government decreed that all signs, including those over shops, street names and menus would be in Arabic only. Foreign banks were brought under control. There was a constant turnover of Ministers with three Ministers of

Guidance in three months. In December the two military members of Maghrabi's Cabinet were arrested for plotting to overthrow Colonel Qadafi who had emerged as the leader of the Revolution. A Provisional Constitution was proclaimed which made the RCC "the highest authority in the Republic". It insisted upon ratifying every decision of the Cabinet and this led to the resignation of Maghrabi in January 1970. In April he was appointed to head a committee to force the oil companies to raise their prices. From January 1971 until 1973 he was Permanent Representative to the UN and he was then transferred as Ambassador to London where he remained until 1976. He wrote several books on modern history.

al-MAHDI, Sadiq (1936–)

Sudanese Prime Minister. He was the son of Siddiq al-Mahdi and was educated at a Catholic school in Khartoum and at Oxford. When his father died Sadiq was considered too young to succeed him as Imam of the Ansar and the office went to his uncle al-Hadi al-Mahdi. The Umma Party, the political wing of the Ansar, was banned under the military rule of General Abboud but Sadiq emerged as a leader of the opposition. When the Party was legalised in 1964 and won the elections of May 1965 Sadiq was still regarded as too young to become Prime Minister so Muhammad Ahmad Mahjoub, an ally of Imam al-Hadi, was appointed. The Party split with a youthful reformist group supporting Sadiq against his uncle and the Prime Minister. In July 1966 he formed an alliance with the National Unionist Party which was able to pass a motion of no-confidence in Mahjoub and Sadiq became Prime Minister. He hoped to settle the problems of the South and also to press through permanent constitutional reforms which, stressing that Sudan was an Islamic nation, would have provided for a strong executive President with a Southern Vice-President. In December 1966 there was a minor revolt after the Government had refused to accept a High Court ruling that the ban on the Sudanese Communist Party was illegal. He advocated reforms in agrarian and social policies which attracted support across traditional party lines but angered others with his gradualist approach. At the same time he alienated the conservative wing of the Umma and the NUP which in May 1967 joined forces to outvote him; Mahjoub resumed the Premiership. The Umma fought the elections of April 1968 as two separate parties with the Sadiq wing winning more votes than the al-Hadi wing although Sadiq himself lost his seat. In November 1968 the breach was formally healed by the marriage of Sadiq to the daughter of his uncle. Soon after he took power in May 1969 Colonel Nimeiri attempted to win the support of Sadiq who refused and was detained in an army camp in the Red Sea Hills. In April 1970 after a rising of the Ansar against the new regime, in which the Imam was killed, had failed, Sadiq was deported to Egypt where he remained until February 1972. When he returned he was rearrested. In May 1973 he was released and subsequently spent much time in Oxford and Riyadh. In exile with Sharif al-Hindi he formed the National Front which was blamed in July 1976 for a plot with Libyan backing to overthrow Nimeiri. Sadiq was sentenced to

death but in July 1977 had a secret meeting in Port Sudan with Nimeiri which led to the National Reconciliation and the dissolution of the Front. Accepting the principle of the one-party state he was appointed to the Central Committee of the Sudan Socialist Union but he remained aloof and resigned soon afterwards because he disapproved of Nimeiri's support for the Egyptian initiative for peace with Israel. He then generally kept a low profile, spending much time abroad, but in February 1982 he called for a transitional government. An advocate of modernising Islam, he opposed Nimeiri's introduction of the September Laws in 1983 as a spurious attempt to win legitimacy by the application of *Shariah* punishments; he also received *Bay'a* as the true leader of the Ansar to the annoyance of his rival, another uncle Ahmad al-Mahdi, who was much closer to Nimeiri. Sadiq was detained without trial in Kobar jail for 15 months, being released in December 1984. In 1985 he published a pamphlet rejecting the idea of a secular state although purely religious duties could not be imposed on Christians: assimilation of the South would end the country's divisions. With the re-emergence of political parties after the overthrow of Nimeiri, Sadiq resumed leadership of the Umma although he never totally controlled it. In the elections of March 1986, contested by 42 parties, the Umma emerged as the largest with 100 out of 270 seats. Sadiq had difficulty in forming a coalition as he himself appeared willing to repeal the September Laws whereas the Democratic Unionist Party with 63 seats favoured their amendment and the National Islamic Front with 51 opposed any change. The DUP leaders, however, agreed to join but his offer of Cabinet places to members of the Sudan People's Liberation Movement was refused despite a meeting with John Garang. In addition to the war in the South he faced economic chaos – Sudan had been declared bankrupt by the IMF. Famine affected an estimated two to three million people, there was rationing for others and currency devaluation caused price rises. The Government was in an almost perpetual state of crisis. In March 1987 the Prime Minister asked the five-man Supreme Council which acted as Head of State to dissolve his Cabinet and in May coalition collapsed after investigations by the Minister of Commerce, a DUP member, into hoarding and economic crimes started to threaten Umma leaders but was reformed with the same composition, 11 Umma, 8 DUP and 5 Southerners. In July the Government declared a state of emergency to end hoarding and inflation and closed all educational establishments indefinitely but it collapsed again in August when the Prime Minister refused to accept the DUP nominee, an old Nimeiri associate, for a place on the Supreme Council. The Government revived after ten days but collapsed again in November when it was agreed that Ministers should continue in office. In October the Sudan had had to accept IMF demands for a 40% devaluation with steep price rises and demonstrations were repressed with tear gas. The Government faced an insoluble problem: the economic situation could not be improved without peace and peace could not be had without repeal of the *Shariah*. Sadiq made repeated promises to do so but the Umma and the DUP were frightened of NIF agitation: the NIF was

prepared to join the Government if the *Shariah* were
replaced by a "more genuine Islamic code" which need
not apply to Southerners but this would not satisfy the
SPLM demand for a secular state. In the meanwhile
the SPLM made considerable advances and many of the
main towns were under siege while the Government
could do little but arm the more Arabised tribes against
them. Foreign affairs presented further difficulties as
friendship with Libya, with which a defence agreement
was signed and which was allowed to operate in Chad
from Sudanese soil, meant cool relations with Egypt
and also the USA which was suspected of helping the
SPLM. In August 1986 the Prime Minister had refused
to go to Cairo, instead visiting Moscow, and the following month Qadafi was in Khartoum and the
Sudanese Embassy in Tehran was reopened. In 1987
Sudan withdrew from joint manoeuvres with the
Americans and declared the Integration Charter with
Egypt abrogated. In 1988 Sadiq visited Tripoli and there
was talk of union with Libya, despite the opposition of
the DUP and the South. Early in 1988 Sadiq dismissed
his Ministers and ruled with civil servants until May
when he formed a new coalition of 10 Umma Ministers,
6 from the DUP, 5 Southerners of dubious credentials
and, for the first time, 5 members of NIF: the appointment of the Prime Minister's brother-in-law Hassan
Turabi clearly ruled out any relaxation of *Shariah*
although Sadiq hinted that it would not be applied to
non-Muslims. At the end of 1987 Sadiq met Garang in
Kampala and then in Djibouti with no progress towards
peace but in November 1988 the DUP made an agreement with the SPLM. The Prime Minister was
equivocal, but it was rejected by the Umma and the
NIF so the DUP left the coalition. This was followed
by massive demonstrations demanding peace and the
calling of indefinite strike by the Trade Unions against
price rises. Trying to buy time the Government put up
wages by 500% not realising it would lead to spiralling
price rises: sugar went up by 600%. In January 1989
Sadiq formed a new coalition with the NIF. There was
a feeling of general drift, there was no sign of peace,
the war costing $1m a day at a time when current
export earnings were only half enough to service the
debt. Judges and journalists went on strike against
government interference. Cliques squabbled while the
country was disintegating and the Prime Minister
dithered. Foreign governments were not prepared to
help. There was persistent rioting and 250,000 died of
famine in a year. The Government was blamed for
inaction after disastrous floods rendered 1.5 million
homeless. In February 1989 Sadiq again reformed his
government, abolishing some departments and making
Turabi Deputy PM. Doctors and University lecturers
went on strike. The Southern capital Juba came under
bombardment. The Commander-in-Chief General
Fathi Ahmad Ali and 156 other army officers presented
an ultimatum giving the Prime Minister one month to
end the civil war, formulate a balanced foreign policy
and economic reforms and bring about national unity.
Sadiq attempted a National Declaration of Peace which
was rejected by the NIF and he formed a new coalition
with the DUP which had 6 Ministers to 8 from the
Umma and 4 from the South. *Shariah* was suspended
and Garang was offered a constitutional conference.

Early in June there were rumours of a plot to bring
back Nimeiri and on 30 June there was a coup led
by General Bashir in which Egyptian involvement was
suspected and which was welcomed by Saudi Arabia,
Iraq and even Libya. Sadiq went on the run but was
caught and imprisoned. Investigations showed no evidence of personal corruption and in November he was
released to house arrest. In June 1990 he was reported
to be confined to a safe house and to be suffering from
an eye complaint and although in June 1992 he was said
to be back in prison, in October he gave a newspaper
interview in which he criticised the nominated Transitional National Assembly and said that since the coup
Sudan had been isolated and worse off. Despite his
sophistication Sadiq never forgot that he was a traditional Muslim leader with considerable charismatic
appeal. Under pressure however he often seemed weak
and irresolute.

MAHJOUB, Abd al-Khaliq (?–1971)
Sudanese Communist leader. While in Egypt in the
early 1940s he was converted to Marxism by Henri
Curiel and was an early member of the Sudanese Movement for National Liberation which became the
Sudanese Communist Party. He became Secretary-
General in 1949 and built it into the largest in the
Arab world. Mahjoub presented the Party as a *tariqah*,
attempting to reconcile Islam with Marxism, opening
his meetings with a prayer. In most matters, however,
he was an orthodox supporter of Moscow, never
tempted by Maoism nor being swayed by purely local
considerations. He was jailed during the Abboud
regime for protesting against the maltreatment of
political prisoners but, having been released after a
hunger strike, played an important part in its overthrow.
He had much influence in the immediately succeeding
government of Sirr al-Khatim al-Khalifah, taking part
in the Round Table Conference on the South, but in
November 1965 was narrowly defeated in a by-election
at Omdurman. In December 1966 Mahjoub was jailed
for plotting against the government of Sadiq al-Mahdi
but released after a few days. In October 1967 after the
discovery of arms in the house of a party member he
was again briefly detained. In the general election of
May 1968 he was returned as an Independent. In
October 1968 he called for self-government for the
South. He welcomed the take-over of power by Nimeiri
in May 1969, hoping to influence the new regime in a
communist direction. He refused to disband the SCP,
leaving its members free to adhere to the single party
desired by Nimeiri and in April 1970 was expelled from
the country. He went to Egypt but returned secretly in
August, was caught and imprisoned. In June 1971 he
escaped and sought refuge in the Bulgarian Embassy.
A fortnight later a pro-communist coup in the name of
Babikr al-Nur briefly succeeded in toppling Nimeiri.
Three days later a counter-coup restored the President
and Mahjoub was brought before a military tribunal,
charged with waging war against the state. The public
was excluded after the first hour of the trial in which
Mahjoub was one of 14 communists sentenced to hang.
The Russian and Bulgarian Governments criticised the
executions and their Ambassadors were expelled. A
man of great intellectual ability he was one of the most

important of Arab communists. His opponents paid tribute to his courage, integrity and affability.

MAHSAS, Ahmad (1923–)

Algerian politician. He was born in Algiers where his family had recently moved from the countryside and joined the Organisation Spéciale which sought to win independence for Algeria by armed struggle. In April 1949 he was associated with Ben Bella in the hold-up of the Post Office in Oran and was imprisoned with him in Blida. In March 1952 they escaped together, Ben Bella saving the life of Mahsas who had injured himself in jumping from the walls. He went underground in France building a militant network amongst immigrant workers. In 1954 he joined Ben Bella in Cairo where he spent most of the War of Algerian Independence organising arms supplies for the guerrillas. He was reputed to have saved Ben Bella from assassination in Tripoli. While Ben Bella was imprisoned after October 1956 he managed to conduct a correspondence with Mahsas who acted as his spokesman, for example denouncing the decisions of the Soummam Valley Conference. After independence he became Ben Bella's Minister of Agriculture in which capacity he strongly insisted upon state control despite the official policy of Autogestion. Mahsas led the effort to diversify production beyond that of vines. Just before his fall in June 1965 Ben Bella castigated Mahsas and his other close associate Bashir Boumaza as responsible for the country's economic ills. After the take-over by Boumédienne he continued in office but in September 1966, like Boumaza, he fled the country and joined the opposition Organisation Clandestine de la Révolution Algérienne. In November Boumédienne stated that Mahsas and Boumaza would be tried in their absence for "grave crimes against the state". He settled in France where he published a book on Autogestion but later returned to live in Algiers.

al-MAJALI, Abd al-Salam (1925–)

Jordanian Prime Minister. A member of a distinguished Karak family, he trained as a doctor at Damascus and Ankara Universities. He was the first Jordanian Medical Officer in the Arab Legion, founding and commanding the first military hospital and rising to the rank of Major-General. In August 1969 he joined the Cabinet of Bahjat al-Talhuni as Minister of Health, retaining the post under Wasfi al-Tall when he was also Minister of State for Premiership Affairs. In August 1971 he was appointed President of Amman University where he was also Professor of Medicine. In November 1976 he returned to the Cabinet as Minister of Education. At the end of 1979 Majali was appointed a Special Adviser to King Hussain and resumed Presidency of the University. In October 1991 he led the Jordanian delegation to the Madrid Peace Conference. In May 1993 Majali was appointed Prime Minister, holding also the Departments of Defence and Foreign Affairs in a transitional, non-party political government. His brief was to prepare for elections, hold Islamic militancy in check, carry forward the peace process and continue distancing Jordan from Iraq while wooing the Gulf States. The signature of the Israel–PLO Agreement brought new problems of how to prevent the new Gaza-

Jericho area from remaining in the Israeli economic orbit. June 1993 he promised to reactivate the economy by encouraging the private sector. He is a jovial man and is married to a Briton.

al-MAJALI, Habis (1914–)

Jordanian Field Marshal. He was born in Karak which had long been dominated by his family and was the first Arab cadet to join the Arab Legion and train at Sandhurst. He originally served in the cavalry but transferred to the police force in 1941. He was the first Arab officer to be entrusted by Glubb Pasha with command of an infantry battalion and greatly distinguished himself in the Palestine War, defeating an Israeli attempt to capture Latrun. In July 1951, as commander of the guard, he was escorting Abd Allah at the al-Aqsa mosque when the King was assassinated. There were reports that Majali intended to use his troops to force the Government to nominate the Amir Naif as King instead of the ailing Talal and he was removed from command. He loyally accepted the situation and soon successfully resumed his career. After the Zerka Incident King Hussain dismissed General Ali Abu Nuwar whose successor General Ali Hiyari almost immediately defected; he thereupon appointed Majali as Chief of the General Staff. Majali built up the army from a four-brigade force of ten infantry and three armoured regiments into an eleven-brigade army of nine infantry and two armoured brigades and greatly increased the artillery. He also made the first systematic attempt to provide the army with a military doctrine and organised structure. Subsequently he was appointed Commander-in-Chief. In August 1960 when his cousin the Prime Minister Hazza al-Majali was murdered he stopped the King from rushing to the scene in case further bombs had been placed. During the June War he was subordinated to the Egyptian General Abd al-Munim Riad whose disregard for Majali's local knowledge and pre-planned strategy led to loss of Jerusalem and the West Bank. In October 1967 he was replaced by General Amer Khammash, becoming Minister of Defence in the Cabinet of Bahjat al-Talhuni. He resigned in April 1968 but continued one of the King's closest advisers on military matters. During the crisis of Black September 1970 when Palestinian guerrillas came near to overthrowing the Monarchy, Majali was again appointed Commander-in-Chief and headed a military government with instructions "to restore Jordanian suzerainty, once and for all". This he succeeded in doing after some heavy fighting. In January 1976 he retired from the army and became Minister of the Royal Court. Majali was a tough, brave, loyal soldier of great professional skill.

al-MAJALI, Hazza (c. 1916–60)

Jordanian Prime Minister. His family was the most important tribal shaykhs of Karak and he trained as a lawyer at Damascus University, where he took part in nationalist demonstrations against French rule. Soon after his return he was appointed Chief of Protocol by King Abd Allah and subsequently was normally one of the closest advisers of the monarchy. He held a series of Ministries and was also Mayor of Amman. He was always strongly pro-Western and while Minister of the

Interior was criticised by the Premier Said al-Mufti for trying to push Jordan into the Middle East Defence Organisation. The widespread opposition to the country's joining the Baghdad Pact led to Mufti's resignation and King Hussain on 15 December 1955 appointed Majali as Prime Minister. Majali refused to adopt the subterfuge of declaring that he would not join the Pact but doing so after the agitation had died down but stated quite openly that he would sign. Egyptian propaganda assisted local leaders such as Sulayman al-Nabulsi to organise such dangerous riots that Majali had to resign five days later; he was the only Jordanian Prime Minister brought down by external pressures. He was then for two years Chairman of the Development Board. In 1958 he was made Minister of the Royal Court and the following year accompanied the King on a world tour. In May 1959 after the Prime Minister Samir al-Rifai had stabilised the situation after the crises of the previous summer, Hussain decided that it was safe to liberalise the political system and, regarding Rifai as too old and conservative to do so, replaced him with Majali. He formed a government which contained moderates of the centre-left as well as ultra-loyalists and on his first day in office he declared that Jordan would stand aloof from all military alignments and conduct a peaceful revolution against communism, corruption, waste and inefficiency. He carried out a limited purge of the administration although in practice this often meant replacing Rifai appointees with his own tribal followers and established a Bureau of Complaints where any citizen could approach him. Local elections took place and preparations were made for parliamentary elections. A major effort was made to improve the job prospects of school-leavers. He tried for reconciliation with Iraq and Egypt but this proved difficult and he forecast his own assassination. A plot to kill him was discovered in March 1960 and another to overthrow the regime failed in July but on 29 August Majalli was killed by a bomb placed in the drawer of his desk. Possibly anticipating that the King would hasten to the scene a second bomb was timed to explode half an hour later: it killed a further ten people. Cairo Radio applauded the removal of "an imperialist agent". There was difficulty in preventing his tribesmen from avenging him but four men convicted of the murder were hanged in December. Majali was impetuous, sometimes overtrusting and naïve, but a genial manipulator and intriguer, able to win over both sophisticated Palestinians and his fellow-bedouins, fond of alcoholic parties, brave, humorous and courteous. He looked a typical bedouin, tall, well-built with a brown face, moustache, arched brows and very bright eyes. He wrote a volume of memoirs.

al-MAHDAWI, Fadhl Abbas, Colonel (1915–63)

President of the Iraqi Special Supreme Military Court. Mahdawi came from a poor family, had an undistinguished military record and although a cousin of General Abd al-Krim Qassim, played no part in the July Revolution. Although he had no legal training he was appointed to head the Court which was set up to try political opponents of the new regime. He turned the Court into a national institution which people flocked into cafés to watch on television. Mahdawi

employed a hectoring manner, was sadistically sarcastic and vulgarly abusive but often extremely funny. He made the Court into a forum for pro-Government demonstrations, permitting poets and singers to join in and allowing dancing in the aisles. The first trials were of Ministers of the Monarchy such as Fadhl al-Jamali and, although many death sentences were imposed, they were generally commuted into imprisonment which was often quickly followed by release. The aim of the authorities seems to have been the humiliation and discrediting of the old politicians rather than their physical punishment. Trials of conspirators against the Government such as Rashid Ali al-Gilani and Colonel Abd al-Salam Arif, military plotters, and the attempted assassins of Qassim were usually held *in camera* and could result in death sentences which were actually carried out. In January 1960 when political parties were permitted, Mahdawi considered forming one but was discouraged by Qassim. In December 1962 Mahdawi's bodyguard beat up students who had teased his son and this set off a series of riots and strikes which culminated in the Ramadan Revolution and the overthrow of the regime. Mahdawi with Qassim and a handful of officers held out in the Ministry of Defence for a day and a half against attacks by tanks and aircraft. After his surrender Mahdawi was put in front of a drumhead court martial and shot.

MAHJOUB, Rifaat (1926–90)

Egyptian politician. He graduated from Cairo University Law School in 1948 and in 1953 obtained a doctorate in economics from the Sorbonne. He held several academic posts, including Dean of the College of Economy and Political Science, before entering politics in 1973 as Minister for Presidential Affairs. Mahjoub was also appointed to the committee to redraft the National Charter and presided over the Supreme Press Council. He was First Secretary of the Arab Socialist Union in charge of ideology and elections when in October 1975 he became Deputy Prime Minister. He was a strong supporter of the peace moves of Anwar Sadat. In 1984 he was appointed Speaker of the People's Assembly, the second man in the country according to protocol as there was no Vice-President. Like a Tudor Speaker, he regarded himself as the servant of the executive rather than of the House and was often brazen in his lack of impartiality. He was frequently attacked by the opposition for attempting to bully them. He ignored a court ruling that 78 seats held by the government party, the National Democrats, rightfully belonged to other parties. On 12 October 1990 he was murdered with three of his bodyguards driving through central Cairo. All sections of Egyptian political opinion condemned the crime which was at first ascribed to radical Palestinian supporters of Saddam Hussain and the annexation of Kuwait which Egypt took the lead in opposing; later it was believed that *Jihad* was responsible. Mahjoub was a tall, lean man, stiff and stern and lacking any popular appeal.

MAKKI, Hassan Muhammad (1933–)

Prime Minister of Yemen. A Shafai, he was one of the "Famous Forty" – the young men who were chosen by the Imam Ahmad to study abroad. Makki returned from Rome and Bologna with a Doctorate in Economics and was appointed an Adviser in the Ministry of the Economy. During the Yemen War at various times he held the Ministries of the Economy, Communications and Foreign Affairs. He was also Chairman of the Bank for Reconstruction and Development. In 1966 he was one of the Yemeni leaders who went to Cairo to protest at the misgovernment and unwillingness to make peace of President Sallal and was detained there until the overthrow of the regime. He returned in November 1967 and was again Foreign Minister but having strong left-wing views, he actively opposed the crushing of the radicals by General Hassan al-Amri and was wounded by government forces. He was sent abroad as Ambassador firstly to Rome and then to Bonn. In 1972 he was brought back as Deputy Prime Minister for Economic and Financial Affairs. The ultra-conservative and financially incompetent Prime Minister Abd Allah al-Hajri was dismissed in March 1974 by President Abd al-Rahman al-Iryani who appointed Makki to succeed him. He revived the project of union with the South which had made no real progress since the signature of the Tripoli Agreement in November 1972 and started strong measures to deal with the financial and administrative chaos that he inherited. He selected the first Yemeni Cabinet in which graduates outnumbered tribalists, drafted a development plan and started to reform the civil service, judiciary and army. His appointment and subsequent actions alarmed the Saudis who made no effort to discourage the overthrow of President Iryani by Colonel Ibrahim al-Hamdi. Makki continued briefly as Prime Minister but was then replaced by Muhsin al-Ayni, a man of similar views who had the advantage of the strong tribal connections that Makki as a Shafai and Hamdi as a member of the *Qadi* class lacked. He later held various important posts such as Ambassador to the UN, President of Sanaa University and Ambassador to Rome before returning to political appointments under President Ali Abd Allah Salih, being in the 1980s Deputy Prime Minister for Foreign Affairs and subsequently for Economic Affairs.

al-MAKTUM, Rashid b. Said (1914–90)

Shaykh of Dubai. His father was Said b. Maktum al-Maktum, a mild man who allowed himself to be dominated by his son from the time that Rashid was still in his early twenties. In March 1939 he used the opportunity provided by his marriage to bring in armed bedouins to expel his cousins who were exploiting the Dubai Majlis to pursue family feuds. Later that year he had the eyes of five of his cousins, who had been intriguing against his financial interests, burned out with hot irons. His attempts to increase influence amongst the tribes of the interior led to the Abu Dhabi––Dubai War of 1945/9 and a life-long rivalry with Zaid b. Sultan al-Nihayyan. Although his father did not die until 1958 Rashid was in complete control of his state and was able to embark upon his policy of economic modernisation. Renowned for his financial acumen, he was said to regard Dubai as a trading company with himself as Managing Director and principal shareholder. He introduced utilities, such as telephone and electricity systems but kept them as monopolies. He

was the first Trucial ruler to grasp the economic potentialities of issuing gaudy stamps to celebrate such unlocal events as space exploration. Rashid built schools, roads and hospitals and set up a police force and an army. He built also numerous apartment blocks which he rented out to expatriates. Rashid was concerned that his people should be self-reliant and not dependent upon state bounty so he took active steps to encourage the creation of jobs and to ensure that the young received proper training. Administration was kept to a minimum although in 1957 he established a Muncipal Council with his son Hamdan as its permanent chairman. In 1954 he issued Creek Bonds enabling him to hire a British engineer to deepen Dubai Creek to give it an advantage over Sharjah, commercial rivalry with whom induced him to build an almost contiguous international airport. Relying upon trade, in which smuggling was certainly not unknown, and the provision of an efficient infrastructure and financial services, Dubai was prosperous years before the great oil boom of the 1970s and able to exploit the wealth flowing into Abu Dhabi and also, to some extent, that of Qatar whose Shaykh, Ahmad b. Ali al-Thani his son-in-law, provided money for a bridge across the Creek and for a water supply and built an enormous palace. Typically Rashid himself had his office in the Customs House from which he could see everything that happened rather than in a palace. To attract expatriate businessmen he made Dubai the most tolerant place in the Gulf, the pleasantest in which to live, saying "we have mosques for those who want them, bars for those who want to drink and jails for those who drink too much". He kept all power in his own hands and had little sympathy with the young who, he felt, should be concerned with making money rather than politics. Rashid was the most open of all the Rulers in expressing his hopes that the British would continue to protect the Gulf but when he realised that they were determined to go, he was the first to see the necessity of unity, agreeing with his old foe Zaid to unite their states in the Dubai Agreement of February 1968. He played a considerable part in the creation of the Federation of Arab Emirates of which he was to have been Vice-President. When this grouping of the Nine collapsed he was a founder member of the United Arab Emirates of which he was Vice-President. He was adamant that Zaid and Abu Dhabi should not dominate the Federation and obstructed all extensions of central authority. He resisted the idea of a united army, fearing that it might interfere in the politics of individual Emirates. His determination to preserve the internal autonomy of Dubai led to the Unification Crisis which lasted from 1976 to 1979 when unity became essential in the face of the Iranian Revolution. In April he agreed to become Federal Prime Minister while remaining Vice-President. He was, however, little interested in politics as such, settled his sons in key positions and got on with making money, particularly through the new industrial complex that he created at Jabal Ali. Late in 1980 he suffered a stroke and, although he retained his positions, was almost completely incapacitated. He welcomed the formation of the Gulf Co-operation Council as providing better business opportunities. Rashid was a tall, wiry man with a thin face and prominent hooked nose. His expression was shrewd and cynical and he enjoyed his legendary reputation for miserliness. He had one wife, a cousin, by whom he had four sons and six daughters.

MALIK, Rida Ahmad (1932–)

Algerian Prime Minister. Born in Batna, the son of a lawyer, he took degrees at the Universities of Algiers and Paris where he was one of the founders of the Union of Maghrebi Students. During the Algerian War of Independence, he ran the mouthpiece of the Front de Libération Nationale, *al-Mujahid*, from Tunis and took part in the negotiation of the Evian Agreements. After independence he served as Ambassador to Belgrade, Paris and Moscow before in 1977 being appointed Minister of Information and Culture: he was also a member of the Central Committee of the Front de Libération Nationale. In 1979 he was Ambassador in Washington where he was involved in securing the release of the Americans held hostage in their Embassy in Tehran and became a friend of Warren Christopher who was subsequently Secretary of State in the Clinton administration. From 1982 to 1985 he was Ambassador in London. When, after the overthrow of President Chadli, the ruling Haut Comité d'État created a Consultative Council in place of the National Assembly which had been dissolved, Malik was appointed its Chairman. After the assassination of Boudiaf at the end of June 1992 he was co-opted to the HCE of which it soon became clear that he was one of the most influential members. He took an important part in trying to woo the less militant Islamists until in February 1993 he was appointed Foreign Minister. One of his first visits was to Rabat to improve relations with Morocco which had become strained as a result of increased Algerian support for the Polisario guerrillas. He also visited Paris where he overcame French distaste for an undemocratic regime. In August he succeeded the unpopular Belaid Abd al-Salam as Prime Minister. Unlike his two predecessors he was not an economist but was faced by a foreign debt that demanded $9,000 million for its servicing out of total export earnings of $11,000 million. He was faced also with an Islamic Insurgency which had reached the scale of a civil war with several killings a day. It took him a fortnight to form a Cabinet. He appointed as Finance Minister Murad Benachenhou who was known to favour rescheduling the debt and also privatisation, two policies strongly opposed by Abd al-Salam. Malik reversed also his predecessor's skirmishing with the press. He tried to win the support of the non-Islamic opposition by creating in October a Commission de Dialogue Nationale to agree on a structure to replace the HCE whose mandate was due to lapse in December. In November Malik urged foreign businessmen not to leave although the fundamentalists had declared them legitimate targets and he tried to encourage investment. In January the parties refused to talk.

On 9 April the dinar was devalued by 40% – an attempt at shock therapy. There was immediate opposition from trade unions. Two days later he was dismissed. It was understood that he opposed Zeroul's readiness to talk to the FIS, which welcomed his dismissal. His was the shortest-lived government since the start of the troubles in 1988 – possibly blamed for the escape of 1,000 fundamentalists.

MALKI, Colonel, Murder of (1955)

Adnan al-Malki, born in 1918, was a prominent and popular officer in the Syrian army, known for his strong support for the Baath Party of which his brother Riad was one of the leaders. In December 1952 he confronted the effective ruler Brigadier Adib al-Shishakli with demands for the dissolution of the only legal party, the Arab Liberation Movement and the removal of the ban on other parties; he and his associates were jailed and the Baathist leaders fled to Beirut. After the fall of the dictator Malki was reinstated and, in alliance with Akram al-Hawrani and Khalid al-Azm led the opposition to negotiations which might have led to Syria's adherence to the Baghdad Pact. Rumours that Malki was about to lead a coup contributed to the resignation of the Prime Minister Faris al-Khouri in February 1955. He then was prominent in negotiations for a military pact with Egypt and it was believed that he was about to be appointed Chief of Staff. On 22 April he was shot dead at a football match by a sergeant of the military police who immediately committed suicide. The assassin, an Alawite, was a member of the Syrian Social Nationalist Party which had been competing with the Baath for influence in the army and despite the denials of its leaders, was believed to be acting on its behalf in a deliberate plot to change government policy. It was alleged that the Americans had inspired the crime. The SSNP was ruthlessly suppressed, 140 members were indicted, 30 of them on capital charges. Malki became a national hero with statues erected and streets renamed in his memory.

MALTA HIJACKING (1985)

On 23 November 1985 an Egyptian Airlines Boeing 737 flying from Athens to Cairo was hijacked by five men styling themselves members of Egypt's Revolution and forced to land at Luqa despite the refusal of the Maltese authorities to accept it. Fighting had broken out during the flight between the hijackers and Egyptian guards leading to the death of a terrorist and the wounding of a guard. Israeli and American passengers were put on the landing steps and shot at: an Israeli woman was killed. The Maltese Prime Minister Dr Carmelo insisted that until all the passengers had been released, the aircraft could not leave. When this produced stalemate he authorised a special 75-man Egyptian commando unit flown in from Cairo to storm the aircraft. Poorly trained, the Egyptians became involved in a prolonged shoot-out in which 60 of the 90 passengers and all the hijackers, except for their leader, a Palestinian, who was hit on the head by an axe wielded by the pilot, were killed. The Palestine Liberation Organisation denied involvement and blamed the maverick Abu Nidal.

al-MANAKH SCANDAL (1982)

The Kuwait Stock Exchange was proudly claimed to be the eighth biggest in the world but it did not trade shares in Gulf-based companies. This was done in an unofficial market, the Suq al-Manakh, where transactions were conducted in post-dated cheques. This system, depending upon the presumption of continuous boom and rising prices, led to wild speculation. Many Kuwaitis had invested in Iraq and in the summer of 1982 it appeared possible that the Iran–Iraq War might end in victory for Tehran; the Manakh market suddenly collapsed. Two thousand speculators had given 29,000 cheques amounting to $96,000 million that they could not meet. One single dishonoured cheque was for $180 million. The debts of the 17 leading dealers accounted for 82% of the total: one debtor entered the *Guinness Book of Records*, owing $20,000 million. To a small, tightly-knit community, the crisis came as a profound shock. The Government had to intervene to restore confidence and to save some 400–500 Kuwaiti citizens from bankruptcy. It spent 756 million dinars to maintain share prices and and gave 500 million in aid to "small investors", those who owed up to $7 million. A clearing company was set up to register the cheques involved. In August 1983 the Assembly passed a law limiting liability in debts. The Minister of Finance resigned because he considered that bailing out investors weakened the credibility of Kuwait as a financial centre. There were some questionable claims – three members of one family claimed 95% of the losses and the Minister of Justice received £2,000,000 in the name of his son. He was forced to resign after questioning in Parliament. By mid-1985 three-quarters of the debts had been settled and in December 1989 small investors (those owing less than $825,000) had most of their debts forgiven. The Government bore the brunt of the losses but it had made the mistake of having provoked the creation of the alternative market through restrictive legislation and then failed to legalise or regulate it. In June 1990 there was talk of reviving the Suq al-Manakh.

MARAI, Saiyyid (1913–)

Egyptian Vice-President. The son of a rich landowner, he took a degree in Agriculture from Cairo University and then worked in pharmaceutical, seed and fertiliser companies, specialising in new techniques and breeding horses. Marai was elected to the Chamber of Deputies in 1944 and astonished his peers by calling for a rent ceiling for tenant farmers. He rallied to the new regime and was appointed to the Higher Committee for Agrarian Reform, a topic on which he wrote several books. He restricted the size of holdings and did much to make credit available for *fellahin*. He was appointed Minister of Agriculture in 1957. During the period of the United Arab Republic he was also in charge of agrarian reform in Syria. In 1962 he was dismissed for telling Nasser that the agricultural policies of Prime Minister Ali Sabri to reclaim 200,000 *feddans* a year were impractical; there were also hints of corruption that were never proved and are unlikely. He became Director of the Bank Misr. In 1964 he was Vice-President of the National Assembly but in June 1967 returned as Minister of Agriculture to repair the damage done to the countryside by the excesses of the Committee for the Liquidation of Feudalism. Marai continued to hold a series of posts such as Deputy Prime Minister for Agriculture, Land Reform and Reclamation until 1972 when he was appointed Secretary of the Arab Socialist Union, with the task of making it more modern and democratic. During the preparations for the October War he headed

a committee set up to prepare the home front before being switched to look after work with Arab states to mobilise the Oil Weapon. In 1974 he was appointed Secretary-General of the World Food Congress. From 1975 until his retirement in 1978 he was Vice-President of the Republic and Speaker of the Assembly. In 1976 Marai chaired a committee which recommended the formation of different tendencies within the ASU. In August 1977 he had a secret meeting with Menachem Begin in Romania to prepare the way for Sadat's Knesset Speech. He was a keen supporter of the ideals of Nasser, with many Marxist friends, but was also close to Sadat whose daughter married his son. Marei was a suave, elegant man with mild Western-style socialist ideas.

MARCH 30 PROGRAMME (Egypt) (1968)

In the wake of the disastrous defeat in the June War the first anti-government demonstrations for 16 years took place in Egypt. At the industrial centre of Helwan and in the Universities there were complaints that officers accused of negligence had been treated too leniently and Nasser himself had had to promise reforms. On 30 March 1968, Muslim New Year's Day, he declared that every inch of territory conquered by Israel would be regained, that the armed forces had been rebuilt, economic stability had been achieved through internal sacrifices and external aid, that "centres of power" had been liquidated and that public trials had given the people the opportunity to look at the mistakes of the past. He went on to promise a new Constitution with as its bedrock a reformed Arab Socialist Union which would be rebuilt with elections at every level: its Central Committee would no longer be nominated. The Constitution would affirm that Egypt was an organic part of the Arab nation. All socialist gains, such as emancipation of women, right to free education and health and the representation given to workers and peasants by the National Charter of 1962 would be protected. There should be freedom of thought and of the press. The spheres of state institutions should be clearly defined. The Constitution would stress the importance of work as the only criterion of the value of man. Property should be guaranteed as should be the right to seek justice from an independent judiciary. There should be a Supreme Constitutional Court. The Constitution should limit the tenure of senior posts. On 2 May these proposals were approved by 99.989% (798 voted against) but Egypt continued to have an autocratic ruler and an all-pervasive secret police.

MARCH DECREES (Algeria)

A year after the signature of the Evian Agreement President Ben Bella, in the midst of a struggle with Muhammad Khidr for control of the Front de Libération Nationale and with the nation angered by a French nuclear experiment in the Sahara, decided upon a gesture to rally popular support. Without consulting the Party or the Parliament, and taking all credit to himself, he issued three decrees that were to put Algeria in the vanguard of socialism. The first on 18 March 1963 ordained that the properties of colons that had been unoccupied for two months and land and businesses no longer operating were effectively nationalised. About 200,000 houses and flats, over 16,000 farms, 450 industrial enterprises and an unknown number of cafés, shops, etc. were taken over. The second decree of 22 March laid down that these *Biens Vacants* should be managed by the workers and set out the system of Autogestion. The third decree of 28 March established the principle that the profits of these enterprises should be shared amongst the workers except for an unspecified percentage which would be taken by the state for its unemployment and development funds. Much of the land in question had in fact already been occupied by the peasants who could not possibly have been expelled but the March Decrees, impractical though they were in application, succeeded in their objective of winning great popularity for the President, enabling him to oust Khidr the following month.

MARCH MANIFESTO (Iraq) (1970)

The Kurdish Revolt (I) which had started in 1961 appeared to have been settled by the Declaration of the Twenty-ninth of June of 1966 but fighting broke out again in 1968. The Baath Government was anxious to be able to concentrate its military strength against Israel and was also subjected to Arab pressure and negotiations were opened early in 1970. These led to an agreement, promulgated on 11 March which amplified the terms of the earlier Declaration. Starting with high-flown prose about "imperialistic-Zionistic-reactionary conspiracies" it set out 15 points. It declared that the Kurds were part of the divided Kurdish people of Kurdistan and their national movement was part of the general Iraqi national movement. The "legitimacy" of Kurdish nationality was recognised, a University teaching Kurdish would be established at Sulaymaniyyah, a Kurdish TV station would be created and more radio programmes would be the responsibility of a Directorate General of Kurdish Culture. Kurdish would be the language of instruction in its own area and widely taught elsewhere. The administration would be decentralised with a new, mainly Kurdish, Governorate of Dohuk and officials should be Kurdish or Kurdish-speaking. The inclusion of Kirkuk, where the oilfields lay, would not be included in the autonomous area until a plebiscite had taken place. There would be a general amnesty and Kurds dismissed would be reinstated. There would be no discrimination in holding public office and Kurds would receive posts in the Legislature and executive in proportion to their numbers. Kurds would have the right to form their own political and professional organisations. Pensions would be paid to dependants of guerrillas "who met with martyrdom in the regrettable hostilities". One Vice-President would be a Kurd. Efforts would be made to raise the living standards and apply agrarian reform in the area. It was believed that a secret clause agreed to the retention of over 10,000 of the guerrillas as a paid militia or border guards. Each side expressed satisfaction that its main objectives had been achieved. A High Committee was set up to supervise the implementation of the agreement after four years but differences over its interpretation and particularly lack of action over Kirkuk led to the Kurdish Revolt (II) in 1974.

MARCH PLOT (1973) (Morocco)

In March 1973 the Moroccan Government stated that two small bands of armed men, trained in Libya, had infiltrated from Algeria and attacked a police post at Khenifra in the Atlas mountains. Bombs were exploded in several cities including Marrakesh, Casablanca (including one under the car of the American Consul General) and Oudjdah. The Government alleged that these terrorists activities were linked with the left-wing Union Nationale des Forces Populaires and there were more than a thousand arrests including student and trade union activists. The plot was said to have been organised by Muhammad Basri, who was in exile in Algeria since 1965 when he had been pardoned after a death sentence the previous year for an earlier conspiracy. Colonel Qadafi who had publicly regretted the failure of attempts in the two previous years to kill Hassan II was believed to have supplied the conspirators with arms and money. In June 157 people including service personnel were charged before the permanent military tribunal at Kenitra and in July a further 81, mostly intellectuals, in Casablanca. Some defendants admitted Libyan and Algerian connections. At the end of August the Kenitra court condemned 16 to death, 70 were acquitted and the rest given prison sentences. The Casablanca court acquitted 14, gave suspended sentences to 11 while the rest received between 18 months and 15 years. Life imprisonment was passed on 25, all *in absentia*: these included the Jewish mining engineer and journalist Abraham Serfaty who was to become Africa's longest serving political prisoner. The Government had clearly been shaken, not all of those acquitted were released and the hunt for suspects continued. Appeals were rejected and on 1 November 15 were executed at Kenitra. The Rabat branch of the UNFP which had been suspended for involvement in the plot was dissolved although its leader Abd al-Rahim Bouabid was not charged: it reformed the following year as the Union Socialiste des Forces Populaires.

MARDAM, Jamil (1888–1960)

Syrian Prime Minister. His family was one of the richest in Damascus, owning land and claiming to have worked in the Ottoman administration since the sixteenth century. As a law student in Paris he was one of the organisers of the First Arab Congress of 1913 and upon returning home was one of the founders of the secret nationalist society al-Fatat. He prudently spent the war years in South America and returned to occupy a post in the Foreign Office in the government of Faysal. He went into exile after the French overran Syria. He was involved in the Druze Revolt, spending three months with the insurgents, and fled to Haifa; he was handed over by the British and imprisoned on Arwad Island. He was then one of the founders of the National Bloc and represented it as Minister of Finance and Agriculture in the Cabinet of Haqqi al-Azm but resigned under pressure from his more intransigent friends. In 1934 he was one of the group that tried to bring peace in the Saudi–Yemeni War while trying at the same time to get the support of Ibn Saud for the Syrian nationalists. In January 1936, calling for a general strike, he was arrested. Mardam was one of the delegation that negotiated the Franco-Syrian Treaty of

1936 and after the election in November he became Prime Minister, forming a government mainly from the Bloc. French Deputies delayed ratification of the Treaty and Mardam went to Paris in November 1937 and August 1938, making further concessions until it was said that he was "a lion in Damascus but a fox in Paris". In a further attempt to appease the French he did not take a strong line in the Alexandretta Dispute. Many nationalists including Shukri al-Quwatli, who resigned from the Cabinet and Dr Shahbandar who saw himself as national leader almost by Divine Right, fiercely attacked Mardam and in June 1938 there was an attempt on his life for which Shahbandar's brother-in-law was accused. There were strong rumours of financial malpractices and the Government disintegrated early in 1939. In July 1940 after the murder of Shahbandar, Mardam was one of the politicians who fled abroad until they were exonerated the following year. After politics were resumed in August 1943 Mardam held the post of Foreign Minister for two years during which he signed the Alexandria Protocol which led to the formation of the Arab League. When the National Bloc fell apart at the end of 1946 he formed his own Republican Party and in December he became Prime Minister. Mardam had spent forty years agitating for independence but now that it had come, he had no idea how to govern. He had no assured majority in the Assembly and tried to keep control by patronage and manoeuvring, with no aim beyond staying in office, managing to hold on after a fraudulent election in July 1947. Politics consisted of bickering and widespread corruption at a time when new strongly-motivated groups like the Muslim Brothers and the Baath were becoming active. The general malaise had also affected the army, Mardam took over Defence when the Minister resigned in May 1948 and it was in this state that Syria stumbled into the Palestine War. The defeat turned parliamentary government into a complete shambles and Mardam determined to close it down. His Cabinet split, there was near anarchy in the streets and at the beginning of December Mardam resigned. He played no further part in politics and went into exile after the military coups of 1949, dying in Cairo. A moderate agreeable man, he was a skilful politician, so opportunistic that he forfeited popular confidence; he had neither the personality nor the vision to be a statesman.

MARJ AL-ZUHUR DEPORTEES (1992/3)

In mid-December 1992, after five Israeli soldiers had been killed in a week, a frontier guard was kidnapped and an offer made to exchange him for the Hamas leader, Shaykh Ahmad Yassin who had been in prison since 1991. When no reply was received, the guard was murdered. On the night of 16/17 December 1992 413 Palestinians, alleged supporters of Hamas or of Islamic Jihad were deported, handcuffed and blindfolded, from the Occupied Territories contrary to Article 49 of the Geneva Convention. They were not charged or given access to lawyers and some had already spent months in detention. They were taken through the Security Zone up to Lebanon but Prime Minister Hariri refused to collaborate with Israel by accepting them. They were therefore dumped on a bleak, snow-covered mountain side where their plight attracted world-wide sympathy. Hariri refused to allow supplies through to them or to permit 10 that the Israelis admitted had been deported in error to return home via Lebanon but food and other necessities were smuggled in by Hizbullah. On 18 December the Security Council passed Resolution 799 "strongly condemning" the deportation and demanding that they should all be permitted to return at once. The USA, however, made it clear that sanctions for ignoring Security Council Resolutions, while rigorously enforced against Iraq and Libya, could not be applied to Israel. On 21 December the deportees attempted to march on the Israeli lines but were dispersed by shell fire and similar attempts in January and February were also thwarted. On 28 January 1993 the Israeli Supreme Court ruled that the deportations were legal. Violence in the Occupied Territories was not diminished by the deportations and subsequently the Israelis admitted that the murderer of the frontier guard had not been connected with Hamas. The Arabs made it clear that the Washington Peace Talks, due to resume on 20 April could not continue until the problem had been settled. In February, influenced by the American Secretary of State Warren Christopher, Prime Minister Rabin offered to take back 101 at once and halve the period for the rest but Dr Abd al-Aziz al-Rantisi, a physician from Gaza, rejected the gesture, stating that this would be to accept the legality of the expulsions and that all should return together as stipulated in Resolution 799. On 25 April sick deportees were flown out by the RAF. Friendly Lebanese smuggled in televisions, telephones and eventually a generator for lighting the tents. The 17 Professors amongst the exiles started running academic courses for the "University of Marj al-Zuhur" but the main worry of the deportees was that they were becoming forgotten particularly after the resumption of the peace talks. In August the Israelis offered to take back 187 in September and the rest at the end of the year. As there were over 100 sick, Rantisi agreed.

MASIRAH

Masirah lies about 10 miles off the south coast of Oman and is a low, barren island about 40 miles long and about 8 miles across at its widest point. It first attracted attention when in 1904 the inhabitants plundered a shipwrecked British crew. It lay on the air route from Basra to Aden so in 1932 the RAF established an emergency landing ground and an oil depot. During the Second World War Sultan Said b. Taymur Al Bu Said agreed to improving its facilities and to its use as a base for anti-submarine operations. He also approved its use by the American Air Force. Many of the local inhabitants, estimated at about 600, departed and were replaced by imported labourers. In 1944 the British Government considered its formal purchase or exchange for the Kuria Muria Islands. Immediately after the war the use of the airfield declined and it was guarded by an RAF officer and a few Arab soldiers. After the loss of Habbaniya in 1958 its importance increased and there were frequent rumours that nuclear weapons were kept there. Although it had some importance during the Dhofar Rebellion, the RAF in 1976 handed it over to the Sultan of Oman's Air Force. The Americans had occasionally used it before the creation, in 1980, of the Rapid Deployment Force which gave it a new importance. The airstrip was increased and improved, and defence radars were installed together with extensive stocks of supplies for air and marine operations.

MASMOUDI, Muhammad (1925–)

Tunisian politician. He was born in Mahdia, the son of a fisherman, and attended Sadiqi College from which he was twice expelled for political activities; he was also arrested. He went on to higher studies in Paris where he was President of the Tunisian students and a leading figure in the Neo-Destour. After graduation he remained in France working as a journalist until May 1953 when, with Hedi Nouira, he was arrested on suspicion of the murder of a moderate. It was not proved and he remained in Paris where, appointed a Minister of State, he was involved in the negotiations for the Franco-Tunisian Autonomy Agreement. He was then Minister of the Economy and at the Sfax National Congress he was elected to the Party Politburo. In 1956 he worked closely with Habib Achour to end the control over the trade unions enjoyed by Ahmad Ben Salah which was threatening the business interests of some of his friends. By now regarded as one of the closest confidants of Bourguiba, he was given the key post of Ambassador in Paris. However his associates intensified a campaign of criticism of the Government and in September 1958 Masmoudi himself was expelled from the Politburo for "grave insubordination". Two months later, apparently satisfied that Masmoudi had learned his lesson, Bourguiba brought him back to the Politburo and made him Minister of Information. In October 1961 Masmoudi published an article attacking the "personal power of Bourguiba", which he regarded as a "menace to the moral health of the nation" and the President's taste for luxury which he contrasted with the austere life-style of Nasser. Bourguiba thereupon dismissed and publicly humiliated Masmoudi. In 1965 Masmoudi was forgiven and sent back as Ambassador to Paris where he remained until June 1970 when he was recalled to be Foreign Minister. He was also made Assistant Secretary-General of the Party. Due to Bourguiba's ill health, he seemed to be master of Tunisia's foreign policy. In May and June 1971 he toured European capitals, arguing for aid and for a new Mediterranean policy, keeping out Super-Power rivalry and taking account of the different state of development of the northern and southern shores. His main effort was, however, devoted to bringing Tunisia more into the Arab world, a task that was easier after the death of Nasser whom Bourguiba had regarded with aversion. He ended a quarrel with Syria and attempted to mediate in several disputes, mostly involving Libya. In January 1974 Bourguiba who had previously scorned Colonel Qadafi unexpectedly signed the Jerbah Agreement uniting the two countries as the Arab – Islamic Republic. The Prime Minister, Hedi Nouira who saw Masmoudi as a rival for the succession for the Presidency convinced Bourguiba that the move would be disastrous. Bourguiba thereupon declared that Masmoudi had misled him and removed him from office. Masmoudi went into exile and was expelled from the Party amidst accusations that he had personally profited

from an aircraft deal with France: in response he attacked Bourguiba's monarchical pretensions. He spent most of the next three years in an expensive Parisian hotel, his bills met by the Libyan Government, but in March 1976 he was briefly arrested in Cairo, accused of involvement in a plot to kidnap two exiled opponents of Qadafi. In 1977 when relations between the Tunisian Government and the trade unions were moving towards a crisis, Masmoudi supported the unions and held meetings in Libya with his old colleague Achour, apparently urging him to challenge the Government. In December 1977, proclaiming himself the "spiritual son of Bourguiba", he returned home, calling upon the unions to resist intimidation and was put under house arrest. In 1980 he was freed after he had condemned the Libyan-backed Gafsa Raid but continued to call for a new Constitution and an end of repression. In 1984 he accepted the post of Libyan Representative at the UN but abandoned it when told that he would forfeit Tunisian nationality. He returned after the deposition of Bourguiba. Masmoudi, a dumpy man, is reserved, occasionally naïve and usually devious.

al-MASRI, Tahir (1942–)

Jordanian Prime Minister. He was born in Nablus and educated there and in Aleppo and in Texas where he took a degree in banking. He worked in the Central Bank of Jordan from 1965 to 1973 when he became a Member of Parliament and Minister of State for the Occupied Territories. In 1975 he went as Ambassador to Madrid, moving on to Paris and eventually, in 1983, to London. He was recalled the following year to be Minister of Foreign Affairs, a post he held until 1989 when he was appointed Deputy Prime Minister for Economic Affairs. In January 1991, at the height of the Kuwait crisis, in which he had shown support for the Iraqi point of view, he was reappointed Foreign Minister, possibly to conciliate the Palestinians. In June 1991 he became Prime Minister, the first Palestinian to hold the office for 20 years. A diplomat was needed to repair relations with the West and with other Arab states who had been alienated by the sympathy of King Hussain for the Iraqis and Masri also had a good reputation as liberal and pro-democratic. There were also Western projects for a peace conference in which Jordan hoped to participate in conjunction with the Palestinians. His position was extremely difficult for the Muslim Brothers, who were adamantly opposed to any negotiations with Israel held 22 seats, the largest single bloc, in the 80-strong Parliament. They had also occupied five seats in the Cabinet of his predecessor Mudar Badran but were dropped by Masri at the King's behest. Nevertheless, after promising that he would implement the National Charter, tackle unemployment which was extremely bad after the return of many Jordanians and Palestinians from the Gulf, reduce state spending and denying that he was pro-American, he received a vote of confidence by 47 to 31. In September he reshuffled his Cabinet to rid himself of more opponents of the peace process including his Foreign Minister. A Parliamentary recess gave him a respite but the economic situation was desperate and there were plans for bread rationing. He needed Parliamentary support for restructuring the economy to appease the IMF and pass an austerity budget but by now more than half the Deputies opposed him on ideological or personal grounds, as a coalition of fundamentalists, leftists and palace loyalists demanded his resignation. In November just as there were reports that he was about to undertake a third reshuffle, he resigned and was replaced by one of the King's toughest and most trustworthy henchmen, Sharif Zaid ibn Shakir. His friends said that he had become exasperated at demands for Cabinet posts in return for votes. He had, anyway, put together a joint Jordanian-Palestinian delegation and policies for the Madrid Peace Conference. He is described as soft-spoken and diplomatic but weak.

MATERI, Mahmud (c. 1896–?)

Tunisian nationalist leader. Although he came from a poor family, he was able to train as a doctor in Paris, sometimes sharing student digs with Habib Bourguiba. He became an active communist but in 1924 was expelled from the party for Trotskyism. Upon his return he joined the Destour Party but in common with other Western-educated intellectuals he came to see it too much a group of traditionally-educated city-dwelling bourgeoisie to agitate effectively for Tunisian rights. In 1932 he joined with Bourguiba to found a newspaper and in 1934 at Kassar Hallal they founded the Neo-Destour Party of which Materi was elected President. In September they were both arrested and spent over 18 months in confinement in the South. In March 1938 most of the Neo-Destour leadership decided upon a campaign of civil disobedience leading probably to violence but Materi dissented and resigned. In August 1942 when Muhammad al-Munsif Bey formed a government to demand concessions from the French, Materi was one of his Ministers. In 1945 he was briefly imprisoned. In 1951 when Muhammad Chenik formed a government to negotiate for autonomy Materi was Minister of the Interior. In March 1952 he wrote a report detailing Foreign Legion atrocities in the Cap Bon area. After independence he was twice elected a member of the National Assembly but he was very critical of Neo-Destour intolerance and was driven from public life. He was rehabilitated after the fall of Bourguiba.

MAUDE PROCLAMATION (1917)

On 11 March 1917 British and Indian troops under General Sir Stanley Maude entered Baghdad and he issued a Proclamation designed to win the collaboration of the citizens and other Arabs. It declared that the British came not as conquerors but as liberators, that Britain and Baghdad had long been intimately connected through commerce and that the Turks and Germans would never return. The people "should not understand that it is the wish of the British Government to impose upon you alien institutions". Other "noble Arabs" had been fighting against "the alien rulers, the Turks, who oppressed them". The Proclamation, which had been drafted by Sir Mark Sykes, continued in his usual verbose and visionary fashion that Britain hoped that the "Arab race may rise once more to greatness and renown" and closed with an invitation to participate in the management of civil affairs "so that you may unite with your kinsmen in North, South, East and West in realising the aspirations of your race". General Maude who wanted strong military administration to maintain security without having to be bothered by civilian collaborators and who realised that the Proclamation did nothing to win the support of the large Jewish population of Baghdad objected to its terms but had to obey orders from London to promulgate it.

MAY CORRECTIVE REVOLUTION (Egypt) (1971)

The "Corrective Revolution" was partly a euphemism for a purge of his opponents carried out by Anwar Sadat in May 1971. He had had little part in the formulation of policy under Nasser and he wished to be rid of the close links with Russia, the "inane socialist slogans" which distorted social justice, the preference given to pan-Arab interests over those of Egypt, the repressive police regime and the Israeli occupation of Sinai that he had inherited. The legacy of Nasser was, however, strongly defended by Ali Sabri and the other left-wingers who were working to make the Arab Socialist Union a "power centre" uncontrolled by the Government. They strongly opposed Sadat's readiness to join the violently anti-communist Qadafi in the Federation of Arab Republics and his suggestion of reopening the Suez Canal in return for an Israeli withdrawal from its banks. Sadat was brought tape recordings which showed that Sabri was plotting with the Interior Minister Sharawy Jumaa, who controlled the police, and the Minister of Defence General Muhammad Fawzi to overthrow him. They were all arrested. Sadat personally set fire to 22,000 tapes of secretly recorded telephone calls and ordered a total overhaul of the ASU. Political prisoners were released and officials dismissed for political reasons reinstated. Saying that there was a need for freedom and democracy and national dialogue about the character of the regime, he asked the National Assembly to draft a new Constitution to replace the provisional one and which should enshrine the "ethics of the Egyptian village" to make the country "one big family with science and faith as its motto". The name of the state was changed back from United Arab Republic to the Arab Republic of Egypt.

MAYSALUN, Battle of (1916–)

In the summer of 1920 it became clear that despite all the efforts of King Faysal to appease them, the French were determined to occupy Damascus. A force of 12,000 men under the command of General Gouraud, mostly Algerian and Senegalese but supported by tanks and aircraft advanced on the Syrian capital. About 4,500 Syrians, a mixture of regulars and irregulars commanded by the War Minister Yusuf al-Adhma tried to halt them at the pass of Maysalun about 15 miles from Damascus. At dawn on 24 July the French attacked and in very heavy fighting in intense heat the Syrians held out for six hours before being overwhelmed. The French claimed that they lost 24 killed and Arab losses were about 150 killed (including al-Adhma) and 1500 wounded. Faysal fled and the French took over Syria.

MAZIQ, Hussain (1920)

Libyan Prime Minister. He came from an important tribal family in Cyrenaica which had long connections with the Sanusis. He received little formal education but was intelligent and hard-working. Maziq worked for the British Military Government and in 1949 he was appointed Minister of Agriculture in the Government of Cyrenaica. In 1953 he succeeded Saqisli as Governor of Cyrenaica. He was Foreign Minister in the second Muntasir Cabinet before becoming Prime Minister in March 1965. Parliamentary elections produced a large majority of loyal supporters but he had to face the usual problem of Cabinets divided by provincial and personal interests and had to reshuffle three times. He attempted to improve agriculture and the road system and introduced reforms in the social services. He brought in conscription and the Libyan navy bought its first corvette. British troops were withdrawn from Tripoli in March 1966. He tried to exercise some measure of control but his period of office was dominated by the feverish expansion of the oil industry. He had good relations, business and otherwise with the Palace and the King persuaded him to give his daughter in marriage to his favourite Umar al-Shalhi. In general his premiership was a peaceful interlude of prosperity which was brought to an end by the June War of 1967. Maziq strongly supported the Egyptians, joined in the boycott of oil exports to the West and formally requested the removal of British and American bases. In July with the war over he wished to resume oil sales as they provided the country's sole source of wealth but this was resisted by the extreme nationalists and there were some strikes and violence. Maziq thereupon resigned on the plea of ill health. In September 1971 he was sentence to ten years' in jail for plotting with Bakkush to overthrow the republican regime.

MBORO, Clement (1917–)

Sudanese political leader. He was a member of the ruling family of the small Ndogo tribe of Bahr al-Ghazal and entered government service in 1940. By the time of independence in 1956 he was the most senior Southern official and was later Deputy Governor of Darfur. After the overthrow of the military regime of General Abboud in October 1964 a group of moderate Southern politicians, anxious to solve, in collaboration with the government led by Sirr al-Khatim al-Khalifah, the problems posed by the guerrilla movement Anya Nya formed the Southern Front of which Mboro was elected President. He was also Minister of the Interior although some of the powers that he would normally have exercised were transferred to Ministries held by Northerners. The successor government of Muhammad Ahmad Mahjoub was less concerned with conciliating the South and Mboro lost office in June 1965. He won a seat in the elections of May 1968 and Mahjoub, reshuffling his government, brought back Mboro as Minister of Industry and Mining. He worked hard to encourage a search for oil and for metals in the Red Sea and to rally the South to the Government. After Nimeiri seized power in May 1969 Mboro was one of the Ministers imprisoned, sentenced to four years' imprisonment for giving a special licence to a Japanese motor company, and remained in jail until October 1971. The Addis Ababa Agreement of February 1972 provided for the establishment of a Relief and Resettlement Commission to co-ordinate the activities of the Government, the regional executive, UN agencies and voluntary bodies and Mboro became its President. After the National Reconciliation he was one of the former opposition appointed to the Central Committee of the Sudan Socialist Union. He was Speaker of the Southern People's Assembly from 1978 until he was forced out by Joseph Lagu in July 1979. In October 1981 Mboro led the protest at Nimeiri's plan to split the South into three regions, founding and presiding over the Council for the Unity of South Sudan. He was charged with forming an illegal party and soliciting funds from Libya and briefly imprisoned. When Anya Nya II started in 1983 Nimeiri tried to get Mboro back from his self-exile in Nairobi to help to re-establish peace but by now the leadership had passed to a new generation.

MECCA DECLARATION (1981)

After very considerable debate the Ta'if Islamic Summit of January 1981 issued a Declaration on *Jihad*. It deplored the loss of moral standards despite material progress and stressed that despite diversities, the Muslims constituted a single nation. There could be no settlement of world problems until the Palestinians obtained their rights. There should be a *Jihad* for the liberation of Jerusalem. It declared full solidarity with Islamic Afghanistan, overrun by the Russians. Security in the Gulf should be maintained by its inhabitants without foreign interference. The Non-Aligned Movement, the Arab League and the OAU should be supported. All peoples had the right to their own natural resources and economic relations should be on a basis of justice. The Islamic principle of *Shura* (Consultation) should be honoured. Islamic thought should be cleansed of what was alien and subversive.

MECCA MOSQUE SEIZURE (1979)

Early in 1979 the success of Islamic Revolution in Iran, coupled with unrest amongst the Shiah of the Eastern Province caused acute tension amongst the leaders of Saudi Arabia. Amongst the uneducated there was excitement because 20 November 1979 marked the beginning of the Islamic year 1400 and there was an old tradition that a *Mahdi* (a Bringer of Righteousness) would appear at the beginning of a new century. On that day a group of armed men, estimated at 200 to 300 although some reports said 700, who had mingled with the worshippers interrupted the dawn prayer at the Grand Mosque at Mecca, the holiest of the Holy Places, with a demand that the Imam proclaim one of their number, Muhammad b. Abd Allah al-Qahtani, as the Awaited One. He refused and the dissidents produced further weapons and supplies of food, killed some 20 of the guards and sealed the 19 gates and 48 doors effectively holding 50,000 worshippers as hostages. The Saudi Government immediately closed its borders, cut off communications with the outside world, put troops around the Mosque and attempted to negotiate. It was unwilling to storm the Mosque but attempted to persuade the rebels to surrender by psychological means and by obtaining a *Fatwa* that they were renegades from Islam. The rebels denounced the Government for "deviation fom the correct path of Islam" and the Royal Family for financial corruption and addiction to alcohol, gambling and sex orgies: they demanded the abolition of television, professional football and the employment of women in public places. In the evening of 24 November, after another *Fatwa* legalising the use of force, tanks broke into the Mosque after heavy fighting and the surviving rebels, perhaps 250 in number, took refuge in the 278 rooms of the basement. King Khalid reportedly wished them to be taken alive and his troops made very slow progress in capturing them until, reversing this policy, he called in French commandos who on 4 December flooded the basement and put high voltage electric cables in the water until the rebels "floated out like kippers". The Interior Minister, Prince Naif announced that in the fighting 127 Saudi soldiers had been killed and 451 wounded, 102 rebels killed and an unknown number wounded and 26 worshippers killed and 109 wounded. The body of the self-proclaimed *Mahdi* was found in the basement. Sixty-three of the captured rebels, 41 Saudis, 10 Egyptians, 6 South Yemenis, 3 Kuwaitis and one each from Sudan, Iraq and North Yemen, were beheaded and the executions were spread around eight cities so as to have the maximum propaganda effect. Many of the rebels were already known to the authorities as religious fanatics but dismissed as harmless cranks. Many were tribesmen, including the military leader Juhayman b. Sayf who was from the Utaybah and had modelled their dress and speech upon the Ikhwan. Although this had been the most severe challenge to Saudi rule since the Ikhwan Rebellion fifty years before, the Royal Family maintained that the motives of the rebels had been religious rather than political and made every effort to prevent the full facts, particularly of rumoured disturbances in other parts of the Kingdom and of the French involvement, from becoming known.

MEHRAN, Battle of (1986)

After its attempt to win the Iran–Iraq War by a *blitzkrieg* in the autumn of 1980 had failed, Iraq won no further successes on land and after June 1982 had been fighting on its own soil. In February 1986 the Iranians won a major victory by seizing the Fao Peninsula and were threatening Basra from two sides. In May 1986, largely for the propaganda reason of showing that they could still attack Iranian territory the Iraqis launched a large-scale attack with 25,000 troops on Mehran, a town in the central sector of the front about 80 miles south-east of Baghdad, although it had been destroyed by shelling and had no strategic value. Its capture was announced as a turning point of the war and there were hopes of exchanging it for Fao. In July, however, the Iranians launched a counter-attack and drove them out, killing at least 500 and capturing 1,100. The battle showed up Iraqi military incompetence as they failed to use their overwhelming superiority in the air in an operation which was anyway ill thought-out.

MELUN TALKS (Algeria)

In May 1960 Si Salah, the guerrilla chief of the Algiers District became so disillusioned with the official leaders of the Algerian War of Independence who were in exile abroad that he made approaches to the French authorities. On 10 June he was received with great secrecy in person by General de Gaulle who had recently offered a *paix des braves*. On 14 June the President broadcast an appeal to the Gouvernement Provisoire de la République Algérienne to negotiate. Si Salah was arrested by his comrades and later died in mysterious circumstances. The GPRA, however, accepted the invitation and sent a delegation headed by Ahmad Boumendjel to meet close associates of de Gaulle in the Prefecture at Melun near Orly Airport. After four days, during which Boumendjel complained that he was being "kept in a golden cage" unable to contact anyone outside, the talks broke down. The French were unwilling to appear to confer legitimacy on the GPRA although the mere fact that it had been invited in some measure did so and also suggested that it was winning. For French diehards the President's action was treachery and contributed to the subsequent revolt by the Generals and colons.

MERBAH, Kasdi (1938–93)

Algerian Prime Minister. Abdullah Khalef, Merbah was a *nom de guerre*, was born in Kabyle and received a limited education. Holding important staff appointments, he attained the rank of Colonel during the Algerian War of Independence after which he was appointed Director of Military Security, the most powerful and feared man in the country after Boumédienne in whose seizure of power he had an important part. He was also in charge of relations with Polisario. Merbah played an influential role in the succession of Chadli who, however, decided to move him from his key position in Intelligence, making him a member of the Politburo of the Front de Libération Nationale and Secretary-General of the Ministry of Defence. In 1982 Merbah became Minister of Heavy Industry but after a few months he was moved to the Ministry of Agriculture which had had a disastrous record. There he proved a success, relaxing bureaucratic controls, breaking up socialist collectives and allowing the peasants to run their farms on 99-year leases. He was then moved to Health where he purged corruption. With a proven record of toughness and efficiency as well as liberalism, he appeared the ideal man to become Prime Minister after the regime had been shaken by the October Riots of 1988. A referendum had made him the first Prime Minister answerable to Parliament and he announced an immediate programme to provide work for the young, particularly in the building industry, and reforms in health and education. For the first time a government programme was debated in the Assembly live on television for four days during which 160 Deputies spoke, and endorsed by 267 to 21. In February 1989 a new Constitution signalled a real breach with the past in ending the monopoly of the FLN and greatly reducing the political role of the army which was no longer to have the duty of building socialism. It also gave public sector workers the right to strike. Long entrenched senior officers were moved or retired and government finances tidied up. Faced with a debt that demanded two-thirds of export earnings for its service, Algeria took for the first time a loan from the IMF which required increased economic liberalism with more prices set by the open market and the legalisation of joint ventures to attract foreign capital. These reforms led diehard followers of Boumédienne to cry treachery while greater efficiency caused further unemployment. Nevertheless Merbah had to admit a stagnating economy, labour unrest, shortage of consumer goods, inefficient industry and struggling agriculture although there was some improvement. He advocated dialogue with the opposition including the increasingly important militants of the Front Islamique du Salut which was allowed to register with other political parties and there was greater freedom for the press. In September 1989 Chadli suddenly announced his replacement by the technocrat Mouloud Hamrouche but Merbah for some days refused to give up his office, declaring in the press that his dismissal was unconstitutional: it certainly appeared unfair after he had borne the main burden of trying to move Algeria towards a Western-style democracy. He resigned from the FLN and started his own party, the Mouvement Algérien pour le Justice et le Développement, which, however, never attracted much popular support. After the invasion of Kuwait by Saddam Hussain he called for support for Iraq as "the last bastion of Arab dignity and hope of renaissance". After the military take-over of January 1992 he refused to accept the legitimacy of the new regime and opposed the banning of FIS which he argued should have been given the opportunity to discredit itself. When the Prime Minister Sid Ahmad Ghozali resigned in July 1992 Merbah was mentioned as a possible successor but he had few friends. In July 1993 he appealed to extremists to lay down their arms and seek a political solution. In August 1993 he was assassinated with his brother and one of his sons, probably by Islamic militants, although his widow put the blame upon Chadli. Ben Bella, calling him "the best-informed man in Algeria", suggested that the motive was his knowledge of corruption amongst army officers while the FIS thought it might have been his opposition to a settlement with Morocco at the expense of Polisario. In October 36 men suspected of involvement were put on trial. Merbah, as befitted an Intelligence officer, was aloof, ascetic and appeared rather menacing.

MESTIRI, Ahmad (1925–)

Tunisian politician. Born in La Marsa, he came from a petit bourgeois family. After secondary education in Tunis Mestiri studied law in Algiers and Paris. He joined the Neo-Destour in 1942 at a time when the French were arresting its members and had an important clandestine role in raising money for terrorists and their families and for propaganda abroad. In 1954 he was *Chef de Cabinet* to Mongi Slim who was charged with the negotiations to secure autonomy for Tunisia. In the first government after independence he was Minister of Justice responsible for creating a native judiciary and also for administering the laws such as the abolition of polygamy that raised the status of women. In 1958 he was transferred to the Ministry of Finance where he supervised the withdrawal of Tunisia from the franc zone. He was also a member of the Central Committee of the Party. In 1960 he was sent as Ambassador to Moscow, then to Cairo and he was in Algiers when in June 1966 he was recalled to

become Minister of Defence. Mestiri was greatly impressed by Israeli military organisation and ordered a study for its possible application to Tunisia. In January 1968 he resigned complaining that "the wheels of the state are not functioning properly" and only worked because of the prestige of President Bourguiba. He also criticised "the wild collectivisation" that the socialist experiment of Ahmad Ben Salah entailed and which was against Party principles. He was then excluded from the Party. He returned to private legal practice but in October 1969 he created a sensation by announcing that he would stand against Bourguiba for the Presidency although he withdrew after a fortnight. His audacity was forgiven and he was readmitted to the Party in April 1970 and appointed Minister of the Interior in June, apparently insisting upon the post as a test of Bourguiba's readiness to introduce reforms. Mestiri proposed that the Government should be responsible to the National Assembly rather than to the President, that the next President be elected rather than nominated by Bourguiba, and that a multi-party system be permitted. In September 1971 Mestiri was dismissed from his Ministry but the Monastir National Congress showed his popularity. Although he received a large vote Bourguiba refused to accept him on the Central Committee. He was expelled from the Party for "disruptive factionalism" and in May 1973 Bourguiba decreed that as he was no longer a Party member he was ineligible for the National Assembly. In March 1976 he was the leader of a group of "liberals" who called for the legalisation of opposition groups and in April 1977 was one of the 160 intellectuals who called for the convocation of a national conference on civil liberties. Six months later he was received by Bourguiba for the first time in six years, asking for a National Pact which would be signed by representatives of all tendencies working inside the Constitution to guarantee freedom of political activity: Mestiri always stressed that he wanted to reform rather than overthrow the system. He also argued for Maghreb unity, starting with an agreement with Libya. As relations between the Nouira Government and the trade unions deteriorated, Mestiri condemned the use of force against strikers. In June 1978 his application for permission to form a Mouvement des Démocrates Socialistes was refused but in 1980 he was allowed to publish a newspaper and readmitted to the Party. In November 1981 he complained of fraud after parliamentary elections in which the total opposition vote was declared to be 5.2%. In March 1982, with other opposition groups, he called for the restoration of political freedoms, the return of exiles, repeal of unconstitutional laws and release of detainees. In November 1983 the comparatively liberal Prime Minister Muhammad Mzali prevailed upon Bourguiba to legalise the MDS and other opposition parties and thereafter Mestiri tried to find a path between submission and revolt. In April 1986, accused of an illegal demonstration against the Tripoli Bombing by the Americans he was sentenced to four months' imprisonment. A sentence of three months or more entailed disqualification from political candidacy but at Mzali's behest it was quashed. After the take-over by Ben Ali, Mestiri met him several times to renew his advocacy of a National Pact but it proved impossible to persuade

Tunisian politicians to work together. elections. In September 1989 Mestiri, tired of controversy within the Party over its attitude to the Government, declined to stand for re-election as Secretary-General and dropped out of politics.

MENZIES MISSION (1956)
The London Maritime Conference, assembling after Nasser had nationalised the Suez Canal in July 1956, decided, mainly on the initiative of the American Secretary of State Dulles, that the waterway was too important to be left under the control of a single state but that it should be administered by an International Authority representing the principal users and Egypt which should receive a fair financial return. A delegation representing the USA, Australia, Sweden, Iran and Ethiopia was selected to go to Cairo, not to negotiate but to secure Nasser's full compliance. Eden, the British Prime Minister, hoped that Dulles would himself head the mission but he declined and so it was led by the Australian Prime Minister Robert Menzies. Eden urged Menzies to put the message in such a way that the Egyptians would be bound to refuse and thus provide a pretext for the use of force. Menzies spent six days in Cairo but failed to make any impression: he was not helped by a statement from Eisenhower that there should be no use of force. Nasser promised freedom of passage, technical improvements and fair tolls, but would not budge on the question of ownership.

MIDDLE EAST SUPPLY CENTRE
After the entry of Italy into the war in 1940 the British Government was faced by a powerful hostile navy in the Mediterranean. After June 1941 there was further pressure on shipping with the need to get aid to Russia through Iran. In order to feed the civilian population of the Middle East it was essential to rationalise imports and increase local production. In July 1941 a member of the War Cabinet was appointed Minister of State in Cairo and a Supply Centre was established. In 1942 the Americans joined, taking for the first time an active role in the area. The MESC introduced many short-term measures, new Western techniques, improvements in agricultural methods, introduction of machinery and fertilisers, and cultivation of food in new areas. It also gave aid to industries and allocated scarce raw materials. Pressure was brought upon Egypt to switch land from cotton to food. Syrian grain was shipped to Alexandria instead of to Marseilles. Local factories were set up to produce military *matériel* and scarce civilian goods. The entire transport system of the Middle East was co-ordinated to reduce congestion at the ports. Essential supplies such as grain, sugar and medicines were purchased in bulk by the MESC and stored in regional depots. A Scientific Advisory Commission was appointed to carry out a survey of problems in the area as a whole and a number of regional conferences were held – for example one on methods of improving statistics. Attempts were made to combat inflation. In 1944 a Middle East Agricultural Development Conference brought together representatives of all the states except Turkey, the first time that Arab leaders had assembled for any purpose other than to discuss Palestine. The

British hoped that the MESC would continue after the war as a unifying and development agency which would consolidate their presence in the Middle East but the Americans were determined thenceforward to conduct their own independent policies in the region and the Arab states, seeking independence, regarded it as dictatorial and a means of reinforcing colonialism. In November 1945 therefore the MESC was dissolved but it had instilled the idea of economic co-operation which was enshrined in Article 2 of the Arab League Pact: it had also reinforced the idea that Cairo was the "capital" of the Middle East. The British hoped that some of the functions of the MESC would be assumed by a new Middle East Office established in Cairo but this never achieved any importance.

MIKI MISSION (1973)
Following the outbreak of the October War in 1973 OAPEC countries resolved to use the Oil Weapon to coerce oil-consuming states into taking a line favourable to the Arabs. States were divided into three categories and those not in the "friendly" or "neutral" lists were to receive no supplies. Japan, totally dependent upon imports of oil for the enormous expansion of its industry, was horrified to find itself excluded from these lists. Measures were immediately taken to reduce consumption. Prime Minister Kakuei Tanaka appealed to the visiting Dr Kissinger to use American influence on oil companies to divert stocks to Japan but received no satisfaction. The Government which hitherto had unquestioningly followed American policy in the Middle East felt bound to dissociate itself from it and on 22 November issued a statement calling for Israeli withdrawal from all the territories occupied in the June War, recognising the rights of the Palestinian people and the inadmissibility of annexing land by force and warning that it might have to reconsider its attitude towards Israel. This declaration led to rebukes from Israel and the USA and threats of boycotts from Jewish Americans but was welcomed by the Arabs who excluded Japan from a subsequent 5% cut. The Deputy Prime Minister Takeo Miki, the most important Japanese official ever to visit the area, was sent to see King Faysal whom he convinced that an oil embargo would ruin the Japanese economy and that of other Eastern nations and lead to the spread of communism. He pointed out that decreased production had caused a fall in supplies of steel and cement to Saudi Arabia. The King therefore agreed to reschedule Japan as "friendly" and so did Anwar Sadat to whom Miki offered a loan of $280 million to assist in widening and deepening the Suez Canal. Miki also visited Syria, Iraq and the Gulf oil states. The shock of the embargo led Japan to seek more of a role of its own in the Middle East and increase diplomatic and cultural ties with Arab states.

MINURSO
In March 1990 the UN Secretary-General Perez de Cuellar visited the main participants in the Western Sahara War and in June he proposed to the Security Council the formation of a force to monitor a cease-fire, a referendum on integration or independence and the withdrawal of troops. It would act as a transitional

government during a period of some five months between the cease-fire and the announcement of the referendum results: the cease-fire would begin 16 weeks after a date had been fixed. Saying that the operation, conducted with the OAU would be "large and complicated", he proposed sending a technical team to work out details and obtain information. The Security Council agreed, a Technical Commission visited the area in July and August, and in April 1991, the same month in which UNIKOM was created, approved by Resolution 690 a 35-page plan calling for the spending of $200 million. There would be 500 military observers, an infantry battalion of 700, with air support, signals, military police, and medics making up a military force of 1,695 men. In addition there would be 300 police and more than 800 civilians. There was also a need for a programme to repatriate Sahrawi refugees costing a further $34 million to be raised by voluntary contributions. Morocco would agree to limit the number of its troops to 65,000 within 11 weeks of the cease-fire and they and Polisario guerrillas would be confined to certain locations which would be monitored. The cease-fire should come into force on 6 September and the referendum take place in January 1992 and if Polisario lost it should disband within four weeks: if the Moroccans lost they should withdraw completely within six. MINURSO would pull out four weeks later. The Special Representative of the UN, a Swiss diplomat Johannes Manz, would be in control. In August Morocco banned the entry of MINURSO complaining of the way in which UN officials were drawing up the electoral roll and Hassan II demanded a postponement of the referendum. He had said that his country had spent $500 million on developing the area and that its rule was "irreversible". There was also the first fighting since November 1989 as both sides sent forces into the "no man's land" outside the Moroccan walls. Nevertheless on 6 September a cease-fire was proclaimed and about 200 UN peacekeepers from 16 countries under a Canadian General Armand Leroy arrived. Tunisia was the only Arab state to contribute and the build-up was extremely slow with less than 450 in place by the end of October. Progress by the Identification Committee on the roll of people entitled to vote in the referendum was even slower. It had been agreed that it would be based on the 73,500 enumerated by the Spanish in 1974 but Rabat claimed that a further 120,000 Sahrawis and their descendants who had taken refuge in Morocco should be added: Polisario declared that the population had been 207,000 of whom 160,000 were under their control. Polisario alleged that MINURSO was helping Morocco, that 170,000 Moroccans had been brought in for the vote and that their supporters were being arrested. In December Manz resigned leaving MINURSO without a political chief. There was deadlock in the UN until 31 December when Resolution 725 laid down the criteria and the incoming UN Secretary-General Dr Butros-Ghali was asked to report within two months. In March Butros-Ghali extended the deadline until 31 May when he gave another three months, threatening to withdraw MINURSO if there were no progress. He also stated that MINURSO had reported that Morocco was responsible for nearly all the cease-fire violations. In

March the Pakistani Yaqub Khan was selected to replace Manz and found himself welcomed by Morocco but not by Polisario. A further problem was that by October 1992 hardly any states had paid their promised contributions. In January 1993 an American committee complained that there were financial irregularities. In July the MINURSO compound in al-Ayun provided a neutral venue for the first face-to-face meeting in the territory between Moroccan and Polisario representatives which ended, however, in failure.

MIXED ARMISTICE COMMISSIONS
The Rhodes Armistice that ended the Palestine War between Israel and its four Arab neighbours provided that on each frontier there should be a Mixed Armistice Commission with the principal tasks of preventing further hostilities, arranging the exchange of prisoners of war, establishing permanent demarcation lines and supervising demilitarised zones and local arrangements such as traffic on specified roads. The MACs consisted of an equal number of officers (usually two) nominated by each side and were chaired by an observer from UNTSO who, as normally one side was complaining about violations by the other, had in practice a casting vote. The Syria–Israel MAC had a particularly difficult time because of the Lake Hula Dispute with most of its sessions boycotted by one side or the other. By October 1966 the number of outstanding complaints of violations in its area was just over 66,000. The Egypt–Israel MAC was unable to hold a formal meeting for ten months prior to August 1952 during which time 314 complaints had accumulated. In 1951 the MAC refused to uphold an Israeli complaint that its shipping was refused passage through the Suez Canal but the Egyptian ban was condemned by the Security Council. During the Suez War Israel repudiated the Armistice and subsequently peace-keeping on that frontier became the responsibility of UNEF. The Israel–Jordan MAC effectively ceased to exist after March 1954, boycotted by the Israelis after it refused to condemn the ambushing of a bus on the Eilat–Beersheba road. Only the Lebanon–Israel MAC had no major problems before 1967. After the June War all the MACs, while not abolished, effectively ceased to operate and when in 1980 UNIFIL suggested the revival of the Lebanon–Israel Commission, the Israeli Government stated that it no longer had any validity.

MOGADISHU HIJACKING (1977)
During 1977 West German terrorists carried out several murders and kidnappings to secure the release of 11 members of the Baader–Meinhoff gang who had been imprisoned since 1972. They sought the aid of Wadei Haddad who had formed links with several international terrorist organisations. On 13 October four of his followers, two men and two women, hijacked a Lufthansa Boeing 737 with 86 passengers and 5 crew flying from Majorca to Frankfurt. The plane was forced to fly to Rome, Cyprus, Dubai and Aden where the pilot was murdered. It was believed that the hijackers expected asylum in Aden but its government, then seeking respectability after criticism for help to terrorists, only allowed them to refuel. They went on to Mogadishu where after nightfall on 17 October the

plane was stormed by German commandos assisted by British experts and equipment. In an extremely well-planned attack three of the terrorists were killed and the fourth seriously wounded: most of the hostages were unharmed. King Khalid, at the request of Western governments had persuaded the Somalis to co-operate. A few hours after the hostages were freed, Baader and two of his associates committed suicide in jail. George Habash of the Popular Front for the Liberation of Palestine formally dissociated his group from the hijacking. The surviving terrorist, a Palestinian girl, was sentenced to 20 years' imprisonment.

MOHIEDDIN, (Ahmad) Fuad (1926–84)

Egyptian Prime Minister. He was the son of a prosperous farmer in the Delta, a cousin of Khalid Mohieddin and Zakariah Mohieddin. He graduated from Cairo University as a radiologist and also took a law degree. He rose through medical administration and party work and in 1957 was elected to the National Assembly. Mohieddin was Secretary-General of the Doctors' Syndicate when in 1965 he was elected a provincial secretary of the Arab Socialist Union. From 1968 to 1973 Mohieddin was Governor firstly of Sharqiyyah, then of Alexandria and finally of Gizeh. He then entered the Cabinet as Minister of Local Government, being transferred to Health in 1974. He was also Chairman of the Assembly's Foreign Affairs Committee. Nevertheless it was a surprise when in May 1978 President Sadat assuming the office of Prime Minister, appointed Mohieddin as his Deputy with full powers to supervise the work of the Cabinet and the Assembly "to expedite work". He also acted as the Government's principal spokesman. Upon the murder of Sadat, Mubarak took over the Premiership but passed it on to Mohieddin in January 1982. Mohieddin was seen as a middle-of-the-road social democrat, a hard worker who supervised details normally left to subordinates, a man with a distaste for personal publicity, honest and not out for personal gain. Mohieddin put forward a Five-Year Plan to alter the balance of the economy away from services by increasing productive investment, reducing the balance of payments deficit by limiting the growth of imports to 4% while increasing exports annually by 8.3%, rationalising consumption, retaining essential subsidies, encouraging the private sector, giving more initiative to the public sector, improving housing and vocational training, restraining expenditure and, above all, cutting the population growth rate. He realised that progress was dependent upon foreign capital which he did his utmost to obtain. In May 1984 he led the National Democratic Party to an overwhelming electoral victory, having supervised the choice of candidates and campaigned vigorously despite a heart attack: the opposition claimed that he was responsible for intimidation and vote rigging. Before Parliament met, however, the Prime Minister died at his desk of a heart attack. All those who had been campaigning against him paid tribute to his decency and integrity.

MOHIEDDIN, Khalid (1922–)

Egyptian political leader. The son of a middle-class farmer, he became an officer in the cavalry. He took a degree in Economics at Cairo University and had strong links with, and may even have been a member of the Egyptian Communist Party. He was an original member of the Executive of the Free Officers, was one of its most active underground pamphleteers and gained much influence over younger officers. During the July Revolution his tanks surrounded the military district of Abbasiyyah. Major Mohieddin was a member of the Revolutionary Command Council but he saw the organisation as too dictatorial and during the dispute between Neguib and Nasser he strongly supported the former and there was a fear that the cavalry might carry out a coup to make him Prime Minister. He was sent on an unspecified but well-paid mission to Europe where he remained for two years. During this time he was in contact with the famous Egyptian communist Henri Curiel. Nasser brought him back in October 1956 and put him in charge of *al-Massa*, a newspaper that he had created to put forward the views of the left-wing. In March 1959 after Iraqi communists had thwarted the attempt of pro-Nasser officers to take power in the Mosul Uprising, Nasser cracked down on the leftists and the newspaper was closed. In 1964 with increasing links with Russia and an impending visit from Khruschev, Mohieddin was made Editor-in-Chief of the leading newspaper *al-Akhbar*. With Ali Sabri Mohieddin worked to make the Arab Socialist Union the dominant force in the state and he also headed the Egyptian Peace Council, receiving a Lenin Prize in 1970. He led peace delegations to many countries and tried to work with Israeli leftists. He opposed the economic liberalisation and pro-American policies of Sadat and when three "platforms" were permitted in the ASU he headed the leftist wing which later became the National Progressive Unionist Party. He also started its newspaper. In 1976 he was one of the only two leftists elected to Parliament but he failed to secure re-election in 1979, 1984 and 1987. In 1979 he was charged with anti-state activities in fomenting the Bread Riots but was not put on trial. Unlike his dour cousin, Zakariah Mohieddin, Khalid was a remarkably good companion, cheerful, frank and generous and Nasser, who was always personally fond of him, permitted him to take liberties in his presence that no one else would have dared.

MOHIEDDIN, Zakariah Abd al-Majid (1918–)

Egyptian Prime Minister and Vice-President. The son of a landowner from Dakhaliyyah Province, he graduated from the Military Academy in the same class as Nasser and Sadat with whom he was subsequently posted to Manqabad in Upper Egypt. Their shared dissatisfaction with the corruption of the political system led to the formation of the Free Officers. Mohieddin fought in the Palestine War and became a Lieutenant-Colonel on the General Staff. During the July Revolution he arrested several senior officers and subsequently led the troops that surrounded the palace of King Farouq whose execution he advocated. He was then a member of the Revolutionary Command Council and Director of Military Intelligence. In June 1953 he was made Minister of the Interior and, bringing army officers into civil security, set up the repressive services that were one of the most hated features of the

Nasser regime. After the disgrace of Salah Salim, he was also in charge of dealings with the Sudan. A man of strong personality, a remarkable organiser and a man of clear judgement he was seen at the time by diplomats as the ablest man in the Government and the best fitted to succeed Nasser but perhaps feared by him as a potential rival – the two were never personal friends. During the Suez War he was in charge of organising guerrilla forces. In 1957 with Abd al-Hakim Amer and Abd al-Latif al-Baghdadi he was in charge of screening parliamentary candidates on behalf of the National Union. He saw the formation of the United Arab Republic as unrealistic but served as its Vice-President, continuing to hold the title after the breakup when he was moved from the Interior to Nationalised Industries. After the muddled socialism of Ali Sabri led to economic chaos while the drift towards Russia had alienated potential Western donors, Mohieddin was appointed Prime Minister in September 1965. He called for sacrifices and rejuvenation of the economy; he purged the bureaucracy, raised taxes and prices, cut subsidies, encouraged private investment and stopped the move towards socialism. He negotiated with the oil companies and the formerly despised Gulf Rulers, obtained a preliminary deal with the US by which Egypt secured cheap grain and advocated devaluation at the behest of the IMF. He rejected numerous pleas to commute the death sentence on the Muslim Brother leader Saiyyid Qutb and introduced the death penalty for drug trafficking. Putting Egyptian interests above Arab nationalism, Mohieddin realised that the Yemen War was the cause of both economic trouble and Western and conservative Arab hostility; even before coming to office he had persuaded Nasser to sign the Jiddah Agreement with King Faysal. His efforts to end the Yemen War infuriated Field Marshal Amer who joined Moheiddin's left-wing enemies and in September 1966 he was dismissed from the Premiership although he remained Vice-President. In June 1967, as a known pro-Westerner, he was deputed to go to Washington to announce a graceful climb-down on Nasser's demand for withdrawal of the UNEF but his mission was forestalled by the Israeli attack. When the magnitude of the Egyptian defeat in the June War had become apparent on 9 June Nasser resigned, appointing Mohieddin as his successor. Mohieddin refused to accept the Presidency but agreed to serve as Deputy Prime Minister under Nasser. He held the office only until March 1968, however, when he was dismissed because of his opposition to increasing dependence upon Russia. He withdrew from politics, settling down as a farmer. He was mentioned as a possible successor on Nasser's death but there was opposition to his intelligence and his right-wing views and possibly a Russian veto. Although Sadat was to introduce economic reforms advocated by Mohieddin he regarded him as a possible rival and kept him under surveillance. Mohieddin opposed Sadat's peace initiative. In sharp contrast to his popular, out-going cousin, Khalid Mohieddin, Zakariah was a dour, reticent organisation man.

MONASTIR CONGRESSES (1971 and 1974)

The eighth Congress of the Parti Socialiste Destourien, the first for seven years and the first since the failure of Ahmad Ben Salah to impose collectivisation upon the country, met at Monastir from 11 to 15 October 1971. It was clear that there would be demands that the Party be reformed so that ordinary members should have more say and some "liberals" led by Ahmad Mestiri had recently resigned from it. President Bourguiba warned against hasty measures, asserting that the people were not mature enough to rule themselves. The Party Director Muhammad Sayah said that the country needed discipline while Mestiri and Bahi Laghham argued for more democracy. Discussions became tense and at one stage Bourguiba threatened to dissolve the Party. He had to give way to demands that future Presidents be elected by universal suffrage and turned down an offer that he himself hold the office for life, but agreed to continue for another four years, after which he recommended that Hedi Nouira succeed him. Proposals that the ruling Politburo be elected by the Congress ended in a compromise that they should elect a Central Council from which Bourguiba would choose the Politburo. There was a debate on the powers of the National Assembly but it was accepted that it should have no powers over the Government. The strength of the "liberals" was shown by Ladgham and Mestiri heading the poll for the Central Council: their weakness by the fact that Bourguiba refused to have either on the Politburo. The ninth Congress was also held in Monastir, sitting from 12 to 15 September 1974. It was attended by 682 delegates representing 411,000 members in 1,400 cells. Before it met Mestiri, Baji al-Sibsi and five other leading members were expelled for a memorandum condemning the exclusion of the Central Committee from its preparation. Proceedings showed that Bourguiba was in complete control over both Party and State, which, he said, were different structures with their own functions but merging in his person. He was acclaimed as President for life of both. This required constitutional amendment and it was stipulated that his successor should not be elected but would be his Prime Minister, Nouira, who would also be Secretary-General of the PSD. Nouira denounced "collectivist socialism" as against freedom and prosperity and there was simultaneous denunciation of "liberalism". Bourguiba appointed a new Politburo of twenty of whom fourteen held Ministerial office, thus demonstrating the identification of Party and State.

MOSUL UPRISING (1959)

Abd al-Krim Qassim was brought to power by a group of nationalist army officers many of whom had expected him to declare for unity with Egypt as a prelude to general Arab unity. Qassim in fact encouraged radical and even communist elements as support against the pan-Arabism of his deputy Abd al-Salam Arif whom he imprisoned at the end of 1958. At the same time landowners and tribal shaykhs began to fear for their estates and the civilian population and officers of Mosul, and in particular their commander Colonel Abd al-Wahhab Shawwaf, felt themselves neglected. It is also known that the Syrian Intelligence chief, Colonel Abd al-Hamid al-Sarraj had agents in the city on behalf of

President Nasser and was having weapons smuggled across the frontier. On 1 March the Baghdad Government announced that it had authorised the pro-communist Peace Partisans to hold a demonstation in Mosul and despite the protests of Shawwaf, official transport brought into the city about 250,000 Partisans, many of them armed. Shawwaf unsuccessfully tried to get the support of officers in Baghdad and Kirkuk to join him in a revolt but on the night of 7/8 March issued a Manifesto stating that "the Glorious Revolution" had been corrupted by a "mad tyrant" and "an anarchistic group" and promising democracy and reform. A nationalist militia was formed and joined by Shammar tribesmen, the Partisans were fired upon and the Nasserist flag raised. However the soldiers of Mosul garrison were mostly Kurds with no interest in Arab nationalism and did not follow their commanders. Qassim sent aircraft to bomb army HQ in Mosul and Shawwaf was slightly wounded and then murdered by a Kurdish medical orderly. No help arrived from Nasser, the nationalist militia and the Shammar vanished, and Kurds and the poor looted the city. Summary trials were held and hundreds hanged or dragged through the streets behind vehicles. The Uprising was badly timed, not co-ordinated with sympathisers elsewhere, poorly planned without any air cover and too narrowly based for success.

MOUROU, Abd al-Fattah (c. 1945–)

Tunisian religious and political leader. He trained as a lawyer and later specialised in cases which involved religious matters. In the early 1980s he was associated with Rashid Ghannouchi in the formation of the religious groups which coalesced into the Mouvement de la Tendance Islamique, which he stressed, was a political party based on the ideas of Hassan al-Banna and Saiyyid Qutb rather than a religious movement. He saw Japan, which had modernised while keeping its own culture, as a model for developing nations and advocated the use of modern technology as coming from God rather than the West. There should be a gradual movement towards an Islamic state through education as it was impossible to impose it or the *Shariah* by force. There should be a simultaneous move towards Muslim unity ending in a confederation like the EC as small states were not viable on their own: there was no possibility of reviving the Caliphate. When Bourguiba was cracking down on Islamic militants Mourou went into exile in Saudi Arabia which, after he had been sentenced to ten years' imprisonment in September 1987, refused to extradite him. After Ben Ali had taken power Mourou was invited back, sentenced to five years' jail and immediately released. The Government had refused on several occasions to register the MTI as a political party so, in order to contest the parliamentary elections of April 1989 it renamed itself al-Nahdah and, with Mourou as Secretary General, applied for official recognition. It was again refused and Mourou complained of the slow pace of reform and the Government's inability to distinguish between violent and non-violent Muslims. In October 1989 he was briefly arrested for demanding the dismissal of the Education Minister as "hostile to Islam". In January 1991 he split with Ghannouchi who had

denounced the Gulf Rulers for inviting Western troops after the invasion of Kuwait by Saddam Hussain and Mourou claimed that he had dismissed him from the Party. He wished Nahdah to operate as a legal party and published a list of its leaders to emphasise that it was not a clandestine organisation. He was, however, unable to control youthful hotheads and after three youths, claiming membership of Nahdah, had attacked an office of the ruling Rassemblement Constitutionnel Démocratique, killing its custodian, he dissociated himself from the Party. He announced his intention of forming a party which, devoting itself to economic and agricultural matters would be acceptable as not based upon religion, but he was unsuccessful. Mourou is an energetic, charismatic man with bulging eyes and a bushy beard who thoroughly enjoyed the limelight.

MOUVEMENT DE LA TENDANCE ISLAMIQUE (Tunisia)

Harakat al-Ittijah al-Islami. After Tunisia achieved its independence in 1956 its ruling élite represented a culture that was Western and secular rather than Arab and Islamic. Bourguiba had banned polygamy and the veil and scorned the keeping of Ramadan. Many complained of the loss of traditional values at the same time as there was economic hardship. All political opposition was banned so, as in Iran, the mosque, where there was comparative freedom of speech, became for the depressed classes the focus of discontent. An intellectual yearning for an Islamic state was to be found in the Universities where a journal edited by Rashid Ghannouchi circulated. Both strands received enormous encouragement from the triumph of the Ayatollah Khomeini in 1979 and coalesced around Ghannouchi as the Mouvement de la Tendance Islamique. During 1981 the comparatively young and liberal Prime Minister Muhammad Mzali declared readiness to open up the political system, finding a place for opposition parties. The MTI applied for recognition but the regime feared a party which appeared to be trying to claim a monopoly over Islam and refused. In July 1981 religious extremists attacked a tourist camp where French people were drinking during Ramadan and threatened swimmers with vitriol. There followed a sharp crackdown with the arrest of the entire leadership on charges of illegal association and insulting the Government. Sentences of up to 11 years were imposed upon Ghannouchi and 88 others but in August 1984 they were freed on the intercession of the Gulf States. Meanwhile the MTI had not been permitted to contest the elections of November 1981 and had claimed a leading role in the Bread Riots of January 1984. After their release the leaders held a secret Congress in which Ghannouchi was nominated Amir and a clandestine Consultative Assembly (*Majlis al-Shura*) created. In each district an Amil with his own executive office could call upon considerable resources in transport, lodgings etc. Links were established with trade unions and student organisations. The MTI made a deliberate effort to infiltrate the armed forces, young officers were said to be running undercover training camps, and in August 1983 18 officers had been amongst a group of 29 jailed for defaming Bourguiba. Their publications remained banned. In May 1985 in common with the rest of the opposition, they boycotted the elections. The MTI was divided between advocates of the *Shariah* and those of concentrating upon Human Rights but in June 1985 a leadership reshuffle was regarded as a victory for the more militant group. A new Politburo was headed by Ghannouchi with Abd al-Fattah Mourou as Secretary-General, Hammadi al-Jibali in charge of political relations, Habib al-Lawz Islamic matters and Habib al-Suwaysi, Information. They applied again for registration and in a meeting in October Mzali indicated that it might be possible but no organisation could claim a monopoly over Islam or use it as a political weapon. In 1986 Ghannouchi stated that the MTI had reached the stage achieved by the Egyptian Muslim Brotherhood in the 1940s and there was still a great distance to go. They could not contest the elections of November 1986 but claimed that Independents supporting them won 13% of the votes overall with 30% in some districts. In the spring of 1987 several hundred militants, including Ghannouchi, were arrested setting off attacks on tourists and by June the figure had reached 1,000 with the police twice having to use armour and helicopters against rioters: on one day ten simultaneous demonstrations were organised in different towns. In August bombs in hotels in Monastir and Sousse injured 13 tourists. In September 90 (40 *in absentia*) were charged with plotting with a foreign power, presumed to be Iran with which relations had been broken off, to overthrow the State. Saudi Arabia refused to extradite Mourou who had taken refuge in the Kingdom. The judge was normally the Prosecutor General and few thought the charges proven but 7 (5 *in absentia*) were sentenced to death, 16 acquitted and the rest, including Ghannouchi received sentences up to life imprisonment. Riots were expected and troops put on standby as Bourguiba appointed the tough General Ben Ali as Prime Minister with orders to organise a retrial to produce more death sentences. The MTI naturally welcomed Ben Ali's take-over and he quickly released 600 prisoners although Ghannouchi was not freed until May 1988. Ben Ali moved to conciliate Muslim opinion, introducing prayer on the television, increasing religious education and going to Mecca. In September Mourou and Jibali returned from exile, were sentenced to five years' imprisonment and immediately released. Ben Ali brought the MTI into the National Pact but refused to recognise a party based on religion. In the hope, therefore, of being able to contest the elections of March 1989 the MTI changed its name to the Nahdah.

MOUVEMENT NATIONAL ALGÉRIEN

In 1954 the Algerian nationalist party, the Mouvement pour le Triomphe de la Liberté et de la Démocratie, split with many of its members disagreeing with its founder Messali Haj who wished to impose unquestioning obedience upon it and who was prepared to negotiate with the French for concessions. The more militant anti-colonialists eventually became known as the Front de Libération Nationale while those who continued loyal to Messali became the Mouvement National Algérien. When the fighting started after the All Saints' Day Uprising, Messali ordered his representatives in Cairo to negotiate the entry of the MNA *en*

bloc into the FLN but Ben Bella rejected the proposal although individual members such as Ben Yusuf Ben Khedda did join the FLN. Those who did not were savagely attacked. In Kabylia a battle between the two lasted for 48 hours and over 500 were killed while the French stood gleefully by. In May 1957 the FLN massacred over 300 suspected MNA supporters in cold blood at Melouza in South Kabyle on the edge of the Sahara. Some 1,500 members of the MNA then took service under the French, calling itself the Armée Nationale Populaire Algérienne. There were also clashes in France between members of the two groups and several hundred were killed in Paris alone. President de Gaulle bowed to the insistence of the FLN that the MNA should be excluded from the Evian talks and took no action when many who had fought for France were slaughtered after independence.

MOUVEMENT POPULAIRE (Morocco)

al-Harakah al-Shaabiyyah. After Morocco had regained its independence in 1955 the Berbers of the Riff and Atlas Mountains who had, as the Armée de Libération Nationale, constituted the armed resistance to the French, resented the pretensions of the largely Arab and urban Istiqlal Party to a monopoly of power. Their dissatisfaction at the Government and their simultaneous loyalty to the Monarchy were shown by the brief revolt of Addi ou Bihi in January 1957. In November 1957 two of the former leaders of the ALN, Mahjoubi Ahardan and Dr Abd al-Krim Khatib, announced the formation of the Mouvement Populaire to put forward the needs of peasants and tribesmen. The new Party had the tacit support of Muhammad V, who saw it as a useful link between the Palace and the people, and of the many Berber officers in the army so the Istiqlal failed to prevent its legal recognition in February 1959. Its Constituent Congress in November 1959 urged "Islamic Socialism", more social services in rural areas and a more equitable distribution of government development funds between town and country. It stressed its loyalty to the Monarchy and Berber traditions. As a Peasant Party, the MP was unique in the Arab world. In the communal elections of May 1960 it did well in its own areas but won only 7% of the seats. When Hassan II formed his own Cabinet in June 1961 he included both Ahardan and Khatib. In the spring of 1963, at the request of the King, the MP formed part of the government coalition, the Front pour la Défense des Institutions Constitutionelles, providing about 42 of its 69 seats. It was rewarded by further government posts while General Oufkir, himself a Berber, ensured the appointment of local Caids who were MP supporters. In 1965 after the King had dissolved Parliament, the MP split with Ahardan remaining in the Government while Khatib went into opposition. After each had declared the other expelled, Khatib in 1967 formed the Mouvement Populaire Démocratique et Constitutionelle. In the 1976 local elections the MP won 1,045 seats with 7.5% of the vote. The mainstream continued in government, with 44 Deputies elected and 4 Cabinet positions after the 1977 polls. It accepted two seats on the Defence Council set up in March 1979. In 1982, attempting to broaden its appeal, the MP started a newspaper in French. In the local elections of June

1983 the MP won 1,900 seats with 12% of the popular vote. In November when Karim Lamrani formed an all-party government to conduct elections, he included repesentatives of the MP. In the parliamentary elections of September 1984 the MP increased its total to 47 (31 directly with nearly 16% and 16 indirectly elected), making it the third largest party. However when Lamrani reshuffled his Cabinet in April 1985 he apparently did not offer the MP the portfolios to which they felt entitled and they refused to serve. In October 1986 internal disputes led to an Extraordinary Congress in which Ahardan was replaced by an 8-man collective leadership under Muhammad al-Ansar. Ahardan subsequently set up the Mouvement National Populaire which began with 12 Deputies who defected from the MP. Improved in municipal elections October 1992 the MP took most of the 22% of votes cast for Berber candidates. In parliamentary elections June 1993 the MP formed part of the alliance of pro-Government parties while the MNP refused to join either Bloc. After direct and indirect elections, the MP ended with 51 seats and the MNP with 25. Dr Khatib's MPDC never flourished, winning only two seats in 1977, none subsequently. He retired handing over leadership to Ashur Bekkai.

MOUVEMENT POUR LA DÉMOCRATIE EN ALGÉRIE

In exile Ahmad Ben Bella conducted a propaganda campaign against the Algerian Government and in May 1984, 265 of his supporters held the founding Congress of the Mouvement pour la Démocratie en Algérie near Paris. Ben Bella, unwelcome in France, sent a taped message denouncing President Chadli as a fascist, calling for multi-party democracy, and declaring Algeria part of the "Arabo-Islamic International". The following year 19 supporters of Ben Bella were sentenced to up to 13 years' imprisonment for endangering national security and a further batch was jailed in January 1986. In March 1990 the MDA was legalised and Ben Bella returned home in the summer. The MDA strongly supported Saddam Hussain after his invasion of Kuwait. It had boycotted the local elections of June 1990 but, hoping to attract moderate Muslims away from the Front Islamique du Salut, it put up over 360 candidates for the parliamentary elections of December 1991. None were successful. The MDA refused to accept the legality of the subsequent military take-over and refused to participate in discussions with the new regime. There was often dissent within the Party because of the dictatorial methods of Ben Bella.

MOYNE ASSASSINATION (1944)

In February 1941 Lord Moyne became Colonial Secretary and during his year-long tour of office he was suspected by the Zionists of favouring, and possibly even arming, the Arabs against them. In particular he held up the raising of a Jewish army and acted against illegal immigration. In 1942 he said that the modern Jews were not the descendants of the ancient Hebrews and had "no legitimate claim" to Palestine. In January 1944 he became Minister of State resident in Cairo and was there during the meeting which produced the Alexandria Protocol with its commitment to help the Arabs of Palestine secure the provisions of the MacDonald White Paper which was held in detestation by the Zionists. The same year saw the start of Jewish terrorism associated with the Stern Gang which specialised in the murder of British officials. An attempt on the life of Sir Harold MacMichael, the High Commissioner and his wife failed in August. The Stern Gang, in which the future Israeli Prime Minister Yitzhak Shamir was a leading member, then determined to kill Lord Moyne whom they saw as responsible for the policies of London, as a warning to his successor and as a chance to gain publicity. It is, however, also possible that they had some hopes that the Egyptians would be blamed. On 1 November Moyne and his chauffeur were shot outside his residence in Cairo. Dr Weizmann stated that the murder was a great blow to Zionism for this killing of a personal friend greatly upset Winston Churchill previously a strong supporter and he took no further measures to help it during his period in office. He took a close interest in securing the execution of the assassins which took place in March 1945 after a trial in an Egyptian court.

MUAWAD, Rene Anis (1925–89)

Lebanese President. He was a Maronite born in Zghurtah into a family allied to that of President Sulayman Franjiyah with whom he had to flee to Syria after members of a rival clan were murdered at church. After taking a Law Degree from the Jesuit University he was elected for Zghurtah in 1957. Muawad worked for President Fuad Shihab who used him for confidential missions and whose views that Lebanon was essentially an Arab country where Christians and Muslims had to co-operate he retained all his life. He first became a Minister in 1961. After the outbreak of civil war in 1975 he continued to try to work with the Muslims and with the Syrians and did not, unlike many other Maronites, look to Israel for support. In 1978/9 he was sent by President Elias Sarkis round the Arab world to plead for help to restore government authority in Southern Lebanon. In 1980 as Minister of Education he tried to get the school system working again. During the rest of the decade he made frequent visits to Damascus. A pragmatic, uncharismatic figure, he was scarcely known when, following the Ta'if Parliament on November 5 1989 Muawad was elected President at a meeting of the surviving members of the 1972 Parliament on a disused airfield near the Syrian frontier. It was said, not least by General Michel Aoun with whom he had to compete for the loyalty of the Christians, that he had been chosen by the Syrians and the Saudis, who had made the necessary funds available and that he was merely a puppet. He announced his determination to restore national unity and asked Aoun's rival Dr Salim al-Hoss to form a Cabinet. On November 22 an enormous bomb was exploded as the President's motorcade was passing and he and 17 others were killed instantly. There was a general feeling that he would have made a good President and he was sincerely mourned. He was a man of considerable culture with a wide knowledge of Arabic literature.

MUBARAK, Husni (1928–)

Egyptian President. Born in a small Delta village, the son of a court official, he graduated from the Air Force Academy in 1952. After commanding a bomber squadron in the Yemen War, he was appointed an instructor at the Academy before spending a year at the Russian Military. He returned speaking the language fluently but with a stong dislike of the Russians. In 1967 he was appointed to command the Academy and in 1969 Chief of the Air Staff. In 1972 he was appointed Commander of the Air Force and planned the strikes that were essential to the early Egyptian successes in the October War. There was surprise, however, when in April 1975 Anwar Sadat named him as Vice-President as he appeared to have little political qualification for the post apart from being anti-Russian. He was at the President's side when Sadat was murdered and was quickly sworn in as his successor. Saying that he would not be "merciful", he authorised over 4,000 arrests and succeeded in averting any threat to national stability. He launched no sweeping changes although he gave a little more democracy, attempting to end the divisiveness of recent years, freeing political prisoners such as Haykal and Sadawi, beginning a dialogue with the opposition. He also stamped down on some of the worse instances of corruption. Soon he was seen as a modest, sane and hard-working leader after the dreams of Nasser and the illusions of Sadat, to whom he was always careful, early years, to pay tribute. In 1982 Mubarak instituted two reshuffles to correct inequality and improve economic performance. He succeeded in arresting economic decline and tried to deal with the poverty which the so-called Bread Riots of 1977 brought to the surface. However, this was a problem that required money from the IMF and they were opposed to subsidies. With graduates no longer guaranteed government jobs there were problems with unemployment. Sadat had left Egypt at peace with Israel but at war with itself. There was internal insecurity, with the intelligentsia opposing peace with Israel and Egypt's consequent isolation. Egypt was seen as being of little account as it did nothing to defend Arab rights in the Lebanon (beyond recalling its ambassador from Tel Aviv) and the Palestinians were able to persuade Egypt's people of the benefits of peace. This led to a rise of Islamic Fundamentalism which had to be appeased without upsetting the Copts. There were some arrests in 1981/2 but later Mubarak tried to co-opt them as part of a policy involving as many elements as possible in decision-making. In 1984 Mubarak clearly wanted fair elections to give him a genuine mandate. He cleansed the National Democratic Party and issues were freely discussed but the opposition was not allowed to draw up joint lists. He won 75% of the vote in a 43% turn-out and his position was clearly unstable. He was shaken by the Gizeh Mutiny and by the possibility that Abu Ghazala would take over. In 1987 the election was held to be illegal by the Supreme Court. March 1992 saw a plot by Islamic Fundamentalists to overthrow the Government and 28 were arrested. In July Mubarak introduced strong anti-terrorist legislation after Dayrut, and tried to assert that the Islamic problem was more to do with law and order rather than being about social and economic issues. He tried to divide the moderates from hard-core extremists by getting the media to give them more space and setting up a committee to study the *Shariah*, but these concessions merely made them demand more. In December 1992 there was a major crackdown and in May 1993 19 fundamentalists were imprisoned for attempted murder, one a member of the Presidential Guard. In July 1993 441 out of 454 deputies signed a petition supporting a third six-year term. Only the five-member Union Progressive Party did not and Muslim Brothers which in fact had no MPs. One of Murbarak's first moves was to reassure Israel that the death of Sadat did not mean the end of peace, but he always refused to go there. He had to be careful at first because the evacuation of Sinai under the Egyptian–Israeli Peace Treaty was not complete and he withdrew the Egyptian ambassador after Sabra. Relations worsened over Taba. Mubarak was able to make the rest of the Arab world feel that they needed Egypt and he stopped Sadat's personal abuse of leaders. He was seen, however, as too subservient to the US especially as he took no action after an Egyptian aircraft was forced down after the *Achille Lauro* hijacking. The Mubarak Initiative of February 1985 was received more favourably by Israel than by the PLO. He suggested a first-stage dialogue between the US and a joint Jihad–Palestine delegation. He enjoyed better relations with Arafat who had quarrelled with Assad. In August 1984 he restored relations with Reagan and improved dialogue with Qadafi (in August 1992 he tried to mediate over Lockerbie). In 1982 he signed the Integration Charter with Sudan but relations later became extremely bad over Halaib and accusations that Sudan was supporting Islamic Fundamentalists. In March 1983 he attended a non-aligned meeting in Delhi. He played a key role in a rally opposed to Saddam's occupation of Kuwait which led to the Damascus Declaration. In February 1993 he was active in Arab diplomacy in Africa in an attempt to improve the economies of African countries and see that African voices were not drowned in the new world order. Much of early 1993 was spent in an attempt to get the Middle East peace process restarted and he mediated successfully after visiting London, Paris and Washington, meeting Arafat, Assad and Rabin and securing agreement on East Jerusalem participation and land for peace. He was not reluctant to blame Iran for terrorism and in May 1993 toured the Gulf in an attempt to strengthen co-operation between the Gulf states. He is a stocky and laconic man, early on regarded as slow and thick-headed. He is a squash player, reader of military history, inscrutable and extremely quiet. He is said to be a dull conversationalist. He is considered shrewd and shows little emotion in public. There has never been any suggestion of nepotism or corruption. He is a hard worker, making frequent visits to factories. He adopts a pious stance and shuns sycophants. He ignores the so-called smart set and lives an unostentatious and quiet life with his half-Welsh wife. In the summer of 1992 he indicated that his family wanted him to retire.

MUBARAK PEACE INITIATIVE (1988)

In December 1987 the *Intifadah* began and at least one Palestinian a day was being killed and several more injured by the Israeli security forces. On 22 January

1988 Husni Mubarak put forward a call for a halt to all forms of violence for six months during which the Israelis should cease settlement activities in the Occupied Territories. The political rights of the Palestinian people and their basic freedoms should be respected and their security guaranteed by "a suitable international force". He emphasised that it was essential to resume the peace process. Violence continued but a month later the Shultz Initiative did attempt to start peace talks in December 1988.

MUBARAK PEACE INITIATIVE (1989)

In an attempt to conciliate world opinion, upset by the brutality with which the *Intifadah* was being repressed and urged by the new Bush administration, Israel in April 1989 grudgingly put forward the Shamir Plan which envisaged elections in the occupied West Bank and Gaza. The proposals attracted little support either from the Palestinians or from even more hardline members of his own party and there was no progress towards peace until in mid-September, attempting to restart the process, President Mubarak put forward ten points which, he stated needed clarification. Having cleared them with the Americans, he suggested: there should be preparations for the elections by a joint Israeli-Palestinian committee over a period not exceeding two months; Israel should pledge itself in advance to accept the result of the election; there should be freedom to campaign before and during the elections under the supervision of international observers; elected representatives should have total immunity; Israeli forces should withdraw from the election areas; Israel should promise to hold talks on the final status of the Occupied Territories in less than five years; all Israeli settlement in the Territories should cease; no Israeli should enter the Territories on Polling day; East Jerusalem (ruled out by Shamir) should be included and Israel should affirm its commitment to the principle of exchanging land for peace. The Americans should guarantee these provisions and the elections should lead not to an "interim settlement" as proposed by Shamir but straight to a final settlement based on Resolution 242 and Resolution 338. Although the Israeli Deputy Prime Minister Shimon Peres supported the Initiative, it was opposed by Shamir. The Americans tried to help with the Baker Proposals in October, suggesting Palestinians with whom the Israelis might talk, but these were rejected by Shamir and by the Palestine Liberation Organisation as it had not been recognised as the sole representative of the Palestinian people although Yassir Arafat had approved the Mubarak Proposals.

MUHAMMAD, Ali Nasir (1939–)

Prime Minister then President of South Yemen. He came from the Hassani tribe of Dathinah and in 1959 after training as a teacher in Aden, was appointed to a primary school in his native Mudiah. Soon afterwards he joined the Arab Nationalist Movement and formed a secret cell which later became active as part of the National Liberation Front. When the area achieved independence in November 1967 he was appointed Governor of the Red Sea Islands. In the following April he became Minister of Local Government under President Qahtan al-Shaabi. When Qahtan was overthrown

and a new government formed under Muhammad Ali Haytham, Ali Nasir retained his post until he became Minister of Defence at the end of 1969. He made numerous visits to other Arab countries but his main work consisted of purging the army and ensuring its control by the Party. By August 1971 he had effectively destroyed the influence of Haytham, a former Defence Minister and a fellow Dathini, in the armed forces and amongst his local tribesmen and he joined with Salim Rubai Ali and Abd al-Fattah Ismail to oust him. Ali Nasir himself became Prime Minister and a member of the five-man Presidential Council. He insisted on unswerving adherence to socialist principles, heading the Government during a period of stamping out local business enterprise and he hailed the nationalisation of privately-owned dwellings without compensation as "a triumph for the Revolution". He played a leading part in the formation of an indoctrinated Party Militia which acted as propagandists and spies. With Ismail he worked to undermine Ali whose place he took when the President was shot after a summary court martial in June 1978. He continued as Prime Minister after handing over the Presidency to Ismail in December 1978. Then, realising that Ismail had a power-base in the Party, Ali Nasir worked to strengthen the Government as his own fief, helped by the President's lack of interest in practical administrative work. He created and chaired a new Committee for State Security. In foreign affairs South Yemen was completely aligned with the Soviet Union, Prime Minister Kosygin became the most senior Russian ever to visit Aden and gave the country observer status at COMECON. Ismail went to Moscow, signed a Twenty-year Friendship Treaty and endorsed the Russian invasion of Afghanistan. A military agreement was made with the new communist government in Addis Ababa. Support for the left-wing National Democratic Front was a major cause of a second war with the YAR in which only Arab League intervention saved the North from a severe defeat. The isolation in the Arabian Peninsula caused by these moves seems to have worried Ali Nasir and some of his colleagues and in April 1980 Ismail was "persuaded" to resign. Ali Nasir resumed the Presidency and one of his first moves was to go to Saudi Arabia where he showed his Muslim credentials by visiting Mecca where he performed umrah. After a prolonged internal struggle extreme left-wing Ministers were dismissed or moved to positions of lesser importance. Although in August 1981 a Tripartite Pact was signed with Libya and Ethiopia, this was of far less significance than the beginning of a closer relationship with the North. After a visit to Aden by President Ali Abd Allah Salih in December 1981, a decision was made to expedite the process of unification and the NDF abandoned to its fate. The following year support for the rebels in Dhufar and the hostility to Oman which had endured since independence were ended with an agreement to establish diplomatic relations. South Yemen established a working relationship with the Islamic Revolutionaries of Iran, agreeing to process its oil at the Aden Refinery. Aid from the West was welcomed. In March 1983 a Supreme Yemeni Council, chaired by the two Presidents was established to hold regular meetings on the practical details of unification. In internal matters some state controls of business and agriculture were relaxed and life became easier for ordinary citizens. Early in 1985 Ismail returned from exile in Eastern Europe, clearly worried by Ali Nasir's departure from rigid Marxist orthodoxy, and started to gather support in the Party hierarchy. Worried by the weakening of his position Ali Nasir determined in January 1986 to arrest or kill his opponents at a meeting of the Politburo. He was only partially successful and set off a brief but intensive civil war in which thousands were killed. Despite the support of the Dathini tribes, the navy and some of the Party Militia, Ali Nasir was defeated and fled to Ethiopia. He later moved to North Yemen where, he claimed, 30,000 Southerners, half of them armed men, rallied to his cause. Salih, however, restrained them from cross-border incursions. Denounced as "The Great Traitor", Ali Nasir was arraigned in his absence in December 1986 on treason charges. A year later, despite international appeals for clemency, he was sentenced to death.

MUHAMMAD V (1910–61)

Sultan and later King of Morocco. Although the third son of Sultan Yusuf, on his father's death in 1927 he was chosen by the French authorities as his successor because they believed him timid and malleable. There was a Regency until he came of age in 1930. The French kept him remote from power, gave him no training in statecraft and one of his few functions was as President of the Council for Islamic Education: he had himself received such an education but he set up a school within the Palace to give a Western education to his two sons and three daughters. He held himself aloof from the growing activities of young nationalists such as Allal al-Fassi and refused publicly to denounce the Berber Dahir which was seen by them as an affront to Moroccan and Islamic dignity. He was deeply embarrassed when in May 1934 nationalists hailed him as King and their leader towards independence. He regarded General Nogues, Resident General from 1936 to 1943, as a personal friend and called for loyal support for France after its defeat in 1940. He accepted the allegiance of Nogues towards Vichy, allowed French military units to masquerade as forestry officials and he helped to keep the country quiet by greatly increased contact with the tribes. He refused to apply the Vichy anti-Jewish laws in his country. He welcomed the Allied invasion of November 1942 and in January 1943 he received Churchill and Roosevelt, the first time that he had been allowed to meet foreigners without the supervision of a French official. At the Anfa Meeting of January 1943 Roosevelt appears to have indicated that the Americans would support Moroccan independence. Thereafter the Sultan gave discreet encouragement to the newly founded Istiqlal Party although he refused publicly to endorse its demand for independence. In April 1947 his Tangier Speech, emphasising Moroccan unity and solidarity with the Arab and Islamic world, showed that he was no longer a puppet of the French but was transforming himself into the national leader. It did, however, alarm the colons so that they brought pressure on Paris for the replacement of the relatively liberal Resident General Labonne by bullying reactionary Marshal Juin

who was sent to bring the Sultan to heel: soon after his arrival Juin ordered his officers to study the possibility of replacing the Alawite dynasty with an Idrisi Sharif. Assisted by his son, the future Hassan II, the Sultan travelled incessantly around the country, deliberately seeking support amongst the Berbers, subsidising potential leaders and using his religious authority to discredit the *marabouts* and *tariqahs* who were providing in the *Bled* invaluable support for the French who still regarded nationalism as a purely urban phenomenon. In October 1950 Muhammad went to Paris where he failed to secure the Government's recognition of Moroccan sovereignty. As the Sultan refused to sign decrees banning Istiqlal or dismissing Caids sympathetic to it, "the Strike of the Dahirs", Juin, disregarding the Fez Treaty which committed France to the protection of the Sultan, mobilised against him traditional religious and tribal authorities headed by Sharif Abd al-Hayy al-Kattani and Thami al-Glawi, Pasha of Marrakesh. In December Muhammad had a bitter quarrel with Glawi who insulted him as the "Sultan of the Istiqlal" and was banned from the Palace. In February 1951 the French organised the tribes to threaten to depose the Sultan and Juin gave an ultimatum that he would not protect him unless he repudiated the Istiqlal; Muhammad gave way to *force majeure*. In August 1951 Juin was replaced by another soldier, General Guillaume but relations did not improve. In March 1952 the Sultan transmitted to President Auriol of France a memorandum in which he requested a revision of Franco-Moroccan relations, which should be preceded by the end of the state of emergency, the recognition of the right of Moroccans to form trade unions, and his own formation of a government to conduct negotiations: the proposal received a refusal six months later. In December the situation was worsened by violent riots in Casablanca followed by a savage repression and the formal banning of Istiqlal. The French settlers in Morocco were by now determined to get rid of Muhammad and had strong support from the recently reappointed French Foreign Minister Georges Bidault. Glawi toured the country organising a petition which was signed by over 250 Pashas and Caids calling for the deposition of the Sultan on the grounds that he had broken his commitments to the Muslim religion and the Moroccan people by his support for illegal extremists. On 15 August 1953 Glawi organised the proclamation of the elderly, pious Muhammad ben Arafa, a grandson of Muhammad IV, as Imam, nominally to provide respectable religious leadership. Guillaume declared that this would not satisfy the tribes who were determined to oust the Sultan and France could not use force against its loyal friends. On 20 August, having surrounded the Palace with tanks, he advised the Sultan to abdicate to save the dynasty and his own life. The Sultan refused whereupon, according to Hassan, a gendarmerie officer put a gun in his back and bundled him into a vehicle without allowing time to say farewell to his womenfolk or bring luggage and he was deported, with his two sons, to Corsica. Joined by others of the family, they were then confined to a hotel, where they had to pay all expenses, including those of their jailers. At the end of January 1954 they were transferred to Madagascar while a final residence for them was prepared in Tahiti. The Spanish, who had not been consulted despite their Protectorate over part of Morocco, refused to recognise Ben Arafa who had been installed as Sultan but who lacked any credibility. The exiled Sultan was everywhere regarded as the leader of his nation and there were even reports that his face had been seen in the moon. Violence spread throughout the country with attacks upon his opponents and upon French settlers and in two years and in 6,000 incidents, 700 people including 100 Europeans lost their lives. Morocco was moving towards chaos as the colons, fearing a sell-out, turned on their own government while the Berber Armée de Libération Nationale was seizing control in the mountains and strikes closed down the cities. Nationalists were unanimous that the return of Muhammad V was the prerequisite to any settlement. In August 1955 Prime Minister Fauré summoned to Aix-les-Bains a Conference of all shades of Moroccan opinion which convinced him to remove Ben Arafa and bring the exiled Sultan back to France. This was followed by the Antsirabe Accord in which the French representative General Catroux accepted the principle of a free sovereign Morocco. On 31 October the Sultan returned to France and the following week a meeting with Foreign Minister Pinay at La Celle St Cloud led to his return to Rabat on 16 November amidst wild rejoicings. He had already pardoned Glawi who had been photographed kissing his foot and his first demand was that there should be no reprisals upon his former opponents. The Sultan was confronted by problems urgent and numerous. He had to restore order, secure the independence and unity of the country and create new political and administrative structures. Independence was recognised by a Treaty with France signed on 2 March 1956, Spain relinquished control of its zone the following month and in October an agreement put an end to the international status of Tangier. Morocco had no tradition of sharing power, devolved government or party politics, and the Istiqlal, considering that it had played the major role in winning independence, expected to dominate the country. Muhammad, aiming to establish national unity by balancing Arab and Berber, town and country, bourgeoisie and trade unions, determined to be above the control of any one group. In October 1955 he formed the country's first Cabinet with advisory and administrative functions under the non-party Mubarak Bekkai which included representatives not only of the Istiqlal but of the smaller Parti Démocratique de l'Indépendence and representatives of other interests. He considered essential to exercise personal authority over the security forces so he made his son Hassan Chief of Staff of the new national army with a minimum of senior officers between him and the battalion commanders while units were without a territorial basis and kept busy on road-building and similar tasks. The army aided by the personal prestige of Muhammad helped to defuse the tribal troubles in the Riff and the Atlas that had been caused in part by the imposition of Arab officials, often linked with the Istiqlal, in Berber areas. The Sultan had from the moment of his return declared his commitment to democratic government and in August 1956 he announced the first move towards it, nominating a 76-

member National Council based on geographical, cultural, economic and professional units with power to discuss legislation, approve the budget and question Ministers. The following year to show that his position was that of the leader of a nation state rather than that of the spiritual head of a collection of tribes he changed the title of Sultan for that of King. He emphasised the national aspect by assuring the local Jews that they had nothing to fear and that "Morocco has need of all its citizens". In May 1958 he issued a Royal Charter which proclaimed the eventual objective of a constitutional monarchy with the King, the symbol of the nation, sharing legislative power with a fully elected National Assembly. In a move towards that goal, administration would be based no longer on tribal but on regional units. He outlined also a code of civil liberties which was elaborated in another Charter in November and which was formalised after his death in the Fundamental Law. During 1959 the National Council was allowed to lapse but in May 1960 the country voted for the first time in regional and communal elections. In the same month he promised that a Constitution would be issued before the end of 1962 and he appointed in November a 78-member Council to prepare a draft. There were during all this time far-reaching reforms in education, particularly of girls, and agriculture with Operation Plough aimed at a fairer distribution of land as well as in administration and justice with trial by jury for the first time in Morocco. After the worst earthquake in African history killed 12,000 of the 40,000 inhabitants of Agadir, the King pledged his personal fortune as collateral for a loan for rebuilding. The Istiqlal was never happy at sharing power and pressured the King into first dropping the PDI from the Bekkai government and then into accepting an almost entirely Istiqlal Cabinet under Ahmad Balafrej. To prevent eclipse by a monolithic party the King encouraged the younger and more left-wing elements to split away to form the Union Nationale des Forces Populaires. After a prolonged crisis Balafrej was brought down and the King formed a government of his critics under Abd Allah Ibrahim, giving them the tasks of organising the communal elections and solving economic problems. In February 1960 after an attempt on the life of the Crown Prince there was a dispute between the King and his Prime Minister over the investigation and control of the police so in May Muhammad took the surprising step of forming a Cabinet with himself as its head and his son as his deputy effectively running the administration. Throughout his reign the King conducted a foreign policy that avoided attack from radical Arab and African nationalists at home and abroad. He spent a month touring the Arab states and welcomed Nasser as a member of the Casablanca Bloc which he formed as a counter to the pro-Western Brazzaville Bloc. Declaring that "North African unity is one of our most cherished hopes", he permitted the use of Moroccan territory by the insurgents fighting the Algerian War of Independence. Despite this, the kidnapping of Ben Bella on an Air Maroc aircraft, after having been his guest, the presence of French troops, French nuclear tests in the Sahara, the granting by Paris of independence to Mauritania which he claimed part of historic Morocco, the King remained on good terms with

France and de Gaulle mourned him as a "companion and friend". On the world stage Muhammad saw Morocco as a "hyphen", linking the West with Islam, Arabs and Africans. From the beginning of his reign he wished to get the Americans out of Nouaceur and the other bases that they had been granted while Morocco had been under French rule. Otherwise his relations with Washington were good and he received aid but he also established diplomatic links with Moscow and Peking and welcomed President Brezhnev. When on 6 February 1961 he unexpectedly died while receiving minor surgery for a nasal complaint the country was grief-stricken and stunned. Throughout his reign, in difficulties he kept his dignity, his sense of honour, responsibility and justice, never sinking to pettiness or intrigue and in success he showed moderation and a lack of vindictiveness. His private life remained private; his wife never appeared in public and his eldest daughter Lalla Aisha acted as his official hostess. He was keen on sports, particularly riding, tennis and bowls.

MUHAMMADI, Driss (1912–69)

Moroccan politician. He came from a modest family in Meknes and received a religious education. In 1936 he joined the civil service and in his spare time studied for the bar. In 1941 he left government service to set up in practice in Meknes where he became noted for defending people accused of political offences. He was a founder-member of the Istiqlal Party and was also involved in organising nationalist youth groups. He spoke Berber and was active in spreading nationalist ideas amongst the tribesmen. In 1952 he was imprisoned for two years, accused of involvement in riots in Casablanca. In December 1955 he was appointed Minister of State, charged with negotiations with France, in the first independent government. In May 1956 he was appointed Minister of the Interior at a time of Berber unrest. His first action was to demand the surrender of unauthorized weapons and he then played a major part in bringing the Berber guerrillas of the Armée de Libération Nationale into the framework of the new state. Muhammadi then embarked upon a purge of suspect officials, replacing them with Istiqlal loyalists. This caused further unrest, such as the revolt of Addi ou Bihi, which was firmly crushed. He was then largely responsible for preparing for the first elections which involved dividing the country into communes and drafting electoral laws. When the Istiqlal split, Muhammadi adhered neither to the old guard around Balafrej nor to Ben Barka and the others who were to form the Union Nationale des Forces Populaires. Balafrej discouraged Muhammad V from appointing Muhammadi as his successor when he resigned in November 1958 but the King insisted that the new Prime Minister Abd Allah Ibrahim should give him back the Interior Ministry with its vital function of controlling the police. When the King assumed the Premiership in May 1960 Muhammadi was sent to the Foreign Ministry but he remained there only until October when he retired into private life after a quarrel with Allal al-Fassi who accused him of showing insufficient zeal in pursuing an irredentist claim to Mauritania. In 1963 when Hassan II divested himself

of the Prime Ministership he appointed Muhammadi as Director-General of the Royal Cabinet with the task of acting as intermediary with the political parties. After the King had suspended the Constitution and resumed the Premiership in June 1965 Muhammadi was effectively his deputy and the second most powerful man in Morocco. He retired in January 1969 because of ill health and died two months later. A French journalist who knew Muhammadi described him as resembling a Sicilian bar-owner as shown in an American film; fat, jovial and witty but with great cunning and adaptability.

al-MUHAYSHI, Umar Abd Allah (1941–84)

Libyan politician. He came from an upper middle-class family of Circassian origin, the son of a former Ottoman official. Born in Misurata, he attended the high school there, joining the cell of student nationalists set up by his classmate Muammar Qadafi. Like other future members of the Revolution Command Council he was encouraged by Qadafi to become an army officer as a preparation for playing a role in the revolutionary transformation of the country. On 1 September 1969 Qadafi sent Muhayshi, then a Captain, from Benghazi to take over a key barracks in Tripoli. In January 1970 he was nominated Minister of Economy and Industry. He created the Libyan Industrial Corporation, grouping all state-run industries under his own direction. He was particularly keen in establishing a great steel complex in his home town of Misurata and on making technical agreements with other Arab states. Later in the year he was transferred to the Finance Ministry but resigned without any reason being given shortly afterwards. In 1971 he was the Prosecutor when the former King Idris was sentenced to death and three former Prime Ministers to jail for corrupting Libyan life. In 1972 he headed the Libyan team handling negotiations for a merger with Egypt and the following year he accompanied Qadafi on a prolonged visit to Cairo trying to force it through. During the October War he acted as Libyan liaison officer at the headquarters of President Sadat with whom he established close relations. In November 1974 he returned to the Cabinet as Minister of Planning. In this capacity, with many technocrats, he resented the use of national resources for an enormous arms deal, put by some contemporary estimates at $12,000 million with the Soviet Union and the large sums handed out to international terrorists and with the support of some other RCC members, including Abd al-Munim al-Huni he urged Qadafi to change his ways or resign. Meeting no response he formed a conspiracy with possibly 30 army officers to seize power: Cairo reported that 125 officers were arrested. It is possible that in this he received the encouragement of Sadat, anxious to divert Qadafi's attention from his peace negotiations but that the Egyptians came to fear the consequences of being involved in a coup and warned Qadafi and at the same time told Muhayshi that they were doing so in order to give him the opportunity of flight which he took in August 1975. After escaping to Tunisia which refused to hand him back, he took refuge in Cairo where he gave a press conference accusing Qadafi of being a despot who spread intellectual terrorism in Libya. Later he was the first to suggest that his old friend was a dangerous psychopath. The enraged Qadafi sent a hit-squad to kill Muhayshi but it was caught by the Egyptian police in March 1976. In August in Khartoum he joined President Nimeiri in calling for a revolution in Libya and in December 1976 he was sentenced to death *in absentia*: 22 officers accused of backing him were executed in April 1977. Muhayshi set up the Libyan National Democratic Movement with financial support from Saudi Arabia although it had little support within the country. In April 1982 he with al-Huni and the former Prime Minister Abd al-Hamid Bakkush, whose imprisonment he had secured in 1971, was a founder-member of the Front for the Liberation of Libya. Muhayshi was described as an intense, nervous man and after 1981 he was treated in Saudi Arabia and Morocco for a mental breakdown. In 1984 at the time of the *rapprochement* between Libya and Morocco which resulted in the Arab–African Union he was handed back by the Moroccans with a promise of safe conduct but was reported to have been kicked to death in the presence of Qadafi.

al-MULQI, Fawzi (1913–62)

Jordanian Prime Minister. He was of Syrian origin, born in Irbid and studied at the American University of Beirut and Edinburgh University, the first Jordanian Prime Minister to have been educated abroad. He worked as a teacher but during the war was Food Controller in Trans-Jordan. He served King Abd Allah as Foreign Minister and took part in the negotiations with Israel that led to the Shunah Agreement. He was later Minister of Defence and Ambassador in London where he became a confidant of King Hussain who was then at Sandhurst. In May 1953, the Regency ended and Hussain, assuming full power, dismissed the veteran conservative Prime Minister Tawfiq Abu al-Huda and appointed Mulqi to introduce more liberal measures. He formed a Cabinet that included members of the opposition and independents, suspended emergency regulations and released political detainees. The regime had not been popular and the British connection subject to much criticism but Mulqi greatly improved its standing by amendments to the Constitution, a General Amnesty Law, a Land Distribution Scheme and relaxing controls on the press and political parties. There was some feeling in Palace circles that Mulqi had weakened the Government's ability to act in a crisis and that the country was not ready for democracy. The Assembly sent a telegram to Moscow thanking it for pro-Arab statements and the Jordanian Communist Party, although banned, appeared to be gaining influence. Taking advantage of the new freedoms demonstrations against the British connection were organised throughout the country and in May 1954 Mulqi suddenly resigned, making way for the return of Abu al-Huda. No reason was given but his Minister of the Interior Hazza al-Majali recorded that it was on the instructions of the King. Mulqi, appointed Chief of the Royal Court, remained close to Hussain. In April 1957 after he had dismissed the government of Sulayman al-Nabulsi the King asked Mulqi to form a Cabinet but he refused.

MULTI-NATIONAL FORCE (Lebanon)

The Israeli invasion Operation Peace for Galilee of June 1982 and the subsequent Beirut Siege resulted in about 12,000 Palestinian guerrillas being shut up in the capital. An American envoy Philip Habib secured an agreement between their leaders, the Israelis and the Lebanese Government that a Multi-National Force should be landed to supervise their withdrawal and protect the now-defenceless population of Muslim West Beirut and the refugee camps. This Force was not under the auspices of the United Nations. On 25 August French and Italian soldiers and American marines arrived. The guerrillas were safely embarked and on 10 September the Multi-National Force started to leave despite an understanding that they would remain at least another fortnight and the protests of the Prime Minister Shafiq al-Wazzan that their presence was still necessary. On 14 September the President-elect Bashir Gemayel was assassinated and on the evening of 16 September the Maronite Lebanese Forces began the Sabra-Chatila Massacre. On 20 September the Lebanese Cabinet formally requested the return of the MNF, the Israelis withdrew from West Beirut and on 29 September 1,500 American troops deployed around the airport while 1,800 Italian and 2,400 French soldiers were within West Beirut. In February 1983 they were joined by a small British contingent of 100 men. President Reagan promised that American forces would remain until all foreign troops had left Lebanon. The MNF had no headquarters, no unified command and no rules of engagement and was therefore incapable of fighting; it was hoped that its mere presence would provide security. However in August 1983 the Shiah Amal militia attempted to expand its area of control and came into conflict with the Lebanese Army. The Americans were caught up in the fighting and suffered casualties. The following month fighting between the Lebanese Forces and the Druzes for the Shuf overflowed into the capital and both the French and Americans suffered losses. On 23 October extreme Shiahs carried out suicide attacks on the American and French compounds with lorries filled with explosives. The Americans had 241 killed and the French 57. Fighting between Amal and the army continued and it was clear that the MNF could not play a useful role without becoming deeply involved in local politics. On 7 February 1984 President Reagan ordered the Marines to leave and their example was followed by the other contingents. The French left about 50 observers behind but they were withdrawn during the following 18 months.

MULTI-NATIONAL FORCE AND OBSERVERS

The Egyptian–Israeli Peace Treaty of 1979 provided for the evacuation of Israeli forces from the whole of Sinai by the end of April 1982. The previous spring the two countries agreed on the establishment of a neutral body to supervise security in Sinai after the withdrawal. With some difficulty a force of 2,600 men was established, about half of them American. Fiji and Colombia each provided an infantry battalion, France, Australia and New Zealand aircraft, the UK administrative support and base security, the Dutch military police and signals, the Italians ships and Uruguay transportation. Norway sent a small staff and the first commander of the force, General Bull-Hansen. Its headquarters was established in Rome and costs paid by Egypt, Israel and the USA. The force kept a low profile and avoided confrontations but suffered the loss of 250 American soldiers when a Douglas DC8 crashed on its way home in December 1985.

MUNICH OLYMPICS MASSACRE

On 5 September 1972, shortly before dawn, eight Palestinians belonging to the Black September Organisation broke into the building at the Munich Olympic village occupied by the Israelis, killing two athletes and taking a further nine hostage. The West German Government offered a large ransome but the terrorists demanded the release of 200 Palestinians from Israeli jails and safe passage for themselves and their hostages to a friendly country. They were taken to the airport, expecting a flight to Egypt but instead were ambushed by West German policemen. In a shoot-out five terrorists, the nine hostages and a policeman were killed. Three terrorists were captured. The Games were put back a day for a memorial service. The unsubtle methods of the German police were criticised but there was international condemnation of the attack. King Hussain, whom Black September aimed to assassinate, called it "a disgraceful crime engineered by sick minds" and the Palestine Liberation Organisation denied any responsibility.

al-MUNLAH, Saadi (1895–?)

Lebanese Prime Minister. A Sunni Muslim, he came from a prominent family in Tripoli and studied in Istanbul. He was a landowner with industrial interests including a soap factory when he was elected a Deputy in 1943. He was a supporter of Abd al-Hamid Karami and served in his Cabinet and in that of Sami al-Sulh. In May 1946 the President Bishara al-Khouri, looking for a pliable Prime Minister, appointed Munlah. His administration saw the final evacuation of all French and British troops but was not otherwise a success and he resigned in December amidst allegations that he was using government funds to buy support. He withdrew from politics and did not contest the 1947 or 1953 elections. He concentrated on his business activities, becoming Chairman of the Electricity Company. Later he was Chairman of the Board for Tripoli International Fair. A bachelor, he was said to be most genial but not highly intelligent.

al-MUNTASIR, Umar Mustafa (1939–)

Libyan "Prime Minister". He came from a patrician family of Misurata and was educated at Victoria College, Alexandria and the American University of Beirut. Muntasir entered the oil industry as an accountant, working for Mobil but at the same time, as a member of the Arab Nationalist Movement, was involved in illegal organisation of the workers for which he was imprisoned in February 1969. Freed after the Revolution, he was appointed Director-General of the economics division of the Ministry of Petroleum. He represented Libya at OPEC meetings. He was then made Chairman of the American Oasis Oil Company

until in 1975 he was appointed Managing Director of the National Oil Corporation. From 1979 until 1987 he was in charge of Heavy Industry, becoming associated with several grandiose and expensive projects but establishing good contacts with Western businessmen. In March 1987 he was elected Secretary-General of the General People's Committee – effectively Prime Minister. His Cabinet were mostly technocrats although his Minister of Health had been accused in Germany of torturing anti-regime students. He was generally seen as a moderating influence on Colonel Qadafi, persuading him to write off the adventure in Chad and to tone down verbal hostility to the West. He relaxed state controls and allowed a measure of private enterprise and in June 1988 proposed a law which extended human rights. He played a part in the negotiations that restored relations with Tunisia and led on to the formation of the Arab Maghreb Union. In July 1990 he signed an agreement with Sudan by which the two countries would merge after four years. In October 1990 he was moved to a new portfolio which combined planning and the economy, but in November 1992 he was made Foreign Minister in order to improve relations with the Western powers at the time that they were demanding the hand-over of the two men suspected of the Lockerbie bombing: his predecessor Ibrahim Muhammad Beshairi had been Chief of Intelligence at the time of the outrage. In December 1993 he urged Dr Butros-Ghali to call for their trial in a neutral country and in May 1994 he was reported to be negotiating in Paris.

MURAD BEY (1801–?)

Ruler of Egypt. He was a Mamluk in the service of Abu al-Dhahab who promised him the immensely rich wife of the former *Shaykh al-Bilad* Ali Bey; when therefore in 1773 Ali attempted to return from Syria, Murad led the army that defeated and killed him. In 1775 he was with Abu Dhahab campaigning in Syria and when his master died Murad brought the troops back to Egypt. He and his partner Ibrahim Bey seized power and ruled jointly. The wily, politic Ibrahim worked very well with the impulsive, headstrong Murad who looked after the military matters while Ibrahim ran the country. In 1777 Murad became worried by the increasing support for Ismail Bey, who led the adherents of Ali Bey and tried to poison him; the rest of the *Diwan* united against him and he and Ibrahim had to flee to Upper Egypt. The following year they succeeded in regaining power. In 1784 Murad quarrelled with Ibrahim, expelled him and ruled on his own but a few months later they were reconciled. In 1786 the Ottoman Sultan determined to bring Egypt under control and sent a strong army which defeated Murad and he and Ibrahim again had to escape to Upper Egypt. In 1791 the Turks withdrew their troops which were needed against the Russians and Ibrahim and Murad had little difficulty in regaining their old position. Murad founded an arsenal and the first Nile flotilla. When Bonaparte advanced on Cairo Murad, on 21 July 1798, led a series of reckless cavalry charges against him at the Battle of the Pyramids. He then fled to Upper Egypt for the third time in his career and carried on a guerrilla campaign which took him to the outskirts of Cairo. After the al-Arish Convention he negotiated with the French who recognised him as Governor of Upper Egypt. Shortly afterwards he died of the plague. Murad was a large man with a thick blond beard and shaggy eyebrows, immensely strong and reputedly able to decapitate an ox with a single stroke. As a commander in the field his method was to charge and then if necessary run. He had all the virtues and vices of a Mamluk, by turns prodigal and rapacious, treacherous or quixotically loyal, kindly and cruel, capable of surprising acts of justice or injustice but always haughty and of commanding personality.

al-MURSHID, Sulayman (c. 1908–)

Alawite "Mahdi". Murshid was a penniless, illiterate, epileptic shepherd boy from a remote Alawite village who claimed to have received messages about the approaching end of the world. He won a reputation as a miracle worker by such tricks as moving by night with paint on his boots and came to be regarded as divine by at least 40,000 of his compatriots. By brigandage and by drug-running he became immensely rich and after twice falling foul of the French reached an accommodation with them, as they found him useful in maintaining the separatism of the Alawites. Sir Edward Spears heard that Syrian government forces sent against him were supplied by the French with defective ammunition to give his followers a reputation for invulnerability. Murshid grew enormously fat and took 13 wives from notable families. In 1943 he was elected to Parliament and at first worked within the national framework but later reverted to separatism. When Syria became independent an inquiry was instituted into the lands that he had acquired and troops sent to take them over. One of Murshid's wives mobilised his followers for resistance but was defeated: Murshid shot her for getting him into trouble. In November 1946 he was hanged in Damascus and his loot used to found a hospital.

MUSCAT SECURITY CONFERENCE (1976)

On 25 and 26 November 1976 the Foreign Ministers of the Arab Gulf States and Iran met in Muscat to discuss security and economic co-operation. Iraq having tried to get the Conference postponed as "premature", decided at the last moment to attend. Five working papers on defence put forward by Iran, Iraq, Kuwait, Oman and the UAE showed a wide divergence of views from a comprehensive defence alliance suggested by Iran to a complete rejection of the need for one by the UAE. The Omani recommendations were the most generally acceptable, although Iraq, which wanted recognition for its own special police role, called for changes. It was agreed that the meeting had failed to achieve anything, the Chairman, Qais Abd al-Munim Zawawi of Oman, said that there was "a situation, or better an atmosphere" which did not make defence co-operation possible at the moment. The Arab Gulf States learned the lesson that if they wished to set up an organisation for co-operation they should do so when their large neighbours were busily committed elsewhere: the Iran–Iraq War provided the opportunity for the establishment of the Gulf Co-operation Council.

MUSLIM BROTHERHOOD

In 1928 a primary school teacher in Ismailiyyah, Hassan al-Banna started a Society for the Prevention of Sin which was to become the Muslim Brotherhood. He defined the movement as "not a benevolent society, not a political party . . . (but) a new soul to give life by means of the Qur'an". It was based on "science, education and a spirit of militancy which are the pillars of the Islamic mission". He saw it as "a doctrine and a nation", a complete civilisation, calling for a religious renewal through a return to the theocratic state of the "pious ancestors". The Brotherhood demanded the reintroduction of *Shariah* law, that its members should speak only Arabic at home, Islamisation of the civil service and the abolition of co-education. Western civilisation was as great an evil as British occupation. In addition to being a compelling speaker, al-Banna was a brilliant organiser, training missionaries who set up hundreds of cells (eventually 2,000 in Egypt) which arranged literacy classes and screened potential recruits for their moral character and physical fitness. Members took financial responsibility for one another and, taking a personal oath to al-Banna, submitted their diaries to their shaykh for inspection. Al-Banna thus controlled much of the private life of a membership conservatively estimated at a half a million, many of them middle-class intellectuals. The movement trained workers to develop new skills in its own factories, brought electricity to villages, built schools and hospitals and ran its own publishing house. There was a female branch, the Muslim Sisters, but it took no part in public life or mixed social events although it encouraged its adherents to train as doctors or teachers. In its early days it was not directly political although it was the first organisation in Egypt to put forward plans for comprehensive social reforms. It stood aside from party strife, holding that Islam already contained all that was best in democracy, fascism and communism and none of their defects. It was helped by the inertia of al-Azhar, the lack of interest by politicians in social reform and the disparities of wealth accentuated during the war. Al-Banna had said "my religion is my first country" and it was in the name of pan-Islamic solidarity that the Mufti of Jerusalem, Haj Amin al-Hussaini in 1936 appealed for help against the Zionists and the British. From then onwards the Brotherhood became political and some of its original members defected. King Farouq maintained discreet contacts with it, hoping to use it against the Wafd which it regarded as too nationalistic. Al-Banna instructed his followers to "detest the British Empire so that they will be confronted with hearts that hate, tongues that curse and hands that kill". In 1941 in what they called "the first persecution", several of the leaders including al-Banna were arrested as security risks, believed to be in touch with German intelligence. After their release they set up an inner secret organisation (*al-Nizam al-Khass*), with members taking an oath on the Qur'an and a pistol and being trained by sympathetic officers, possibly including Lieutenant Nasser in street-fighting: twice Brotherhood members failed to kill Nahhas Pasha. Relations were cemented with the Yemeni Ahrar and with disgruntled young officers through Anwar Sadat. After the early 1940s the Brotherhood opposed every government and party and could properly be regarded as subversive, although it put up unsuccessful candidates in the elections of 1943 and 1945. There were almost daily street clashes and demonstrations and in 1948, after some of its members fought in the Palestine War in organised units better equipped than those of the Egyptian army, it appeared that the Brotherhood was trying to overthrow the regime and re-establish the Calpihate. In December 1948 they were outlawed by Nuqrashi Pasha and the take-over of their assets showed the gigantic organisation that had been established almost single-handedly by al-Banna. Later that month one of its members assassinated the Prime Minister and there followed a savage repression under his successor Abd al-Hadi Pasha, in the course of which al-Banna was murdered by government agents. The persecution ceased when the Wafd came to power in January 1950 and the Government, reassured by the election of the obviously moderate Hassan Hudaybi as Supreme Guide (*Murshid al-Amm*) allowed the Brotherhood to resume its religious but theoretically not its political activities. They played a prominent part in the attacks on the British in the Suez Canal Zone and in the burning of Cairo on Black Saturday. They welcomed the July Revolution and, as a religious organisation, were not dissolved like the political parties. However their attempts to secure a leading role in the new regime, for example presenting a list of approved Ministers and policies, were frustrated and many of their members were wealthy peasants who resented land reform: relations rapidly deteriorated. After student clashes with the official Liberation Rally in 1954 the leaders were imprisoned but the Brotherhood, under the patronage of General Neguib was permitted to survive as a non-political body. Angered by the Anglo-Egyptian Treaty that Nasser had signed, on 26 October a Muslim Brother fired eight shots at him at point-blank range. Nasser himself reported that 18,000 of the Brotherhood were subsequently arrested, many were sentenced to long prison terms and seven including Hudaybi to be hanged, although the Supreme Guide was reprieved. The repression led to attacks on Egyptian Embassies in Muslim countries. Many sought refuge abroad, particularly in Jordan and the Gulf. Most were released as Nasser felt that he needed their support against the Egyptian Communist Party but in 1965 he claimed that they were again plotting against him, backed by Saudi Arabia which was opposing him in the Yemen War. According to his figure 400, according to theirs 40,000 were imprisoned and several, including the theorist Saiyyid Qutb were hanged. The Brotherhood lay low until the death of Nasser but then rallied to Sadat in his conflict with the pro-Moscow Ali Sabri. In general the more moderate, led by the *Murshid* Umar al-Tilimisani who had succeeded Hudaybi in 1973, favoured his regime and that of Mubarak while the more fanatical, inspired by Qutb, split off into small groups such as *Tafkir wa-al-Hijra*. The ban on them was not removed, indeed as late as February 1992 a court refused to lift it, but members contested elections either as independents or as members of other parties. It was estimated that standing alone in a free poll the Muslim Brothers would attract at least 25% of the votes. In 1984 they co-operated with the New Wafd winning 10 seats and in 1987 they claimed that 36 out of the 60 Deputies of the Socialist Labour Party were supporters of the Brotherhood. In 1990 they boycotted the election. They were very strong amongst the educated classes, sometimes winning all the seats in polls for syndicates of doctors and engineers, cultivating contacts with diplomats and maintaining their own network of clinics and other social services. They opposed the ulema of al-Azhar as "co-opted Islam" and continued to call for the *Shariah*. No new *Murshid* was elected after the death of Tilimisani in 1986 but the oldest member of the Guidance Council, Muhammad Ahmad Abd al-Nasir acted as leader. The Muslim Brotherhood was by no means confined to Egypt. A branch was formed in Aleppo in the mid-1930s and there were several groups in Syria and Lebanon. Professor Mustafa Sibai, the leader, was a prominent figure and in December 1949 was considered a possible Prime Minister. Later he was one of the main opponents of union with Egypt and upon the formation of the United Arab Republic their organisation, the Islamic Socialist Front was banned and its leaders exiled. They held the Baath Party with its Alawite leadership in particular abhorrence and in the 1970s they brought the country to the verge of civil war, until their Hama Uprising was bloodily repressed. Thereafter membership was a capital offence and several thousand were executed. They were also repressed in Iraq after the fall of the Monarchy. al-Banna never formed a branch in the Sudan but a local one, the *Hariqat Tahrir al-Islami* came into being in about 1947 with the aim of purifying the Westernised élite. In 1954 this group changed its name to the Muslim Brotherhood. Led by Hassan al-Turabi they were a moderating force under Nimeiri and a dominating one under his successors. In Libya three members of the Brotherhood were in 1984 convicted of attempting to kill Qadafi who claimed that they were agents of the British or the CIA. There are Muslim fundamentalist groups throughout North Africa such as the Islamic Liberation Party and in Turkey. It has never been clear whether these have any organisational links with Cairo and with each other or whether they merely share broadly similar ideals. It is also uncertain to what extent they benefit from Saudi Arabian patronage. During the *Hajj* of 1393 (February 1973) there was a meeting in Mecca of Muslim leaders including Turabi and Rashid Ghannouchi which discussed accepting the overall leadership of Hudaybi. In the event the Lebanese, Jordanian and Gulf representatives accepted; the Syrians were split and the Iraqis, Sudanese and Tunisians refused.

MUSLIM BROTHERHOOD (Syria)

Some fundamentalist groups began in Aleppo in the mid-1930s and in the following decade they were brought together with other groups in Damascus by Mustafa Sibai who had studied at Al-Azhar and had come under the influence of Hassan al-Banna. Their membership was drawn mostly from small shopkeepers and artisans and they were hampered by the local tradition of secular nationalism and by the religious diversity of the country. They were never, therefore, a highly-organised, paramilitary group as was the Muslim Brotherhood in Egypt. In 1947 they had some success in Damascus in the elections and later they opposed Husni al-Zaim and his intrigues with the Hashemites and his foreign-inspired reforms. After his overthrow they organised as a political party, the Islamic Socialist Front and Professor Sibai became such a prominent figure in Parliament that in December 1949 he was considered a possible Prime Minister. In January 1952 the Shishakli government ordered the dissolution of the Brotherhood, closing its offices and schools as part of the programme of removing all alternative leadership to that of the President. Later Sibai was one of the main opponents of the union with Egypt, where the Brotherhood was being persecuted and upon the formation of the United Arab Republic the ISF was banned and its leaders exiled. After the break-up it re-emerged and soon was involved in a struggle with the Baath Party whose Alawite leadership it held in particular abhorrence: as early as 1948 one of its members had knifed Hafiz al-Assad in a student brawl. By this time their membership was largely composed of students and members of the professions. In April 1964 there were two days of street fighting in Hama in which about 70 of the Brotherhood were killed. Their leader Isam al-Attar was exiled and settled in Germany from where his virulent publications were smuggled into the country. His closeness to the Movement added to Assad's distrust of Yassir Arafat. In the 1970s, having formed a secret strike force the *Kataib Muhammad*, estimates of whose numbers ranged from 400 to 7,000, they brought the country to the verge of civil war, carrying out hit and run killings of government and party officials, always prepared to lose their own lives. In addition nine Russian officers were killed and a bomb exploded at the Aeroflot office. In June 1979, helped by a sympathetic army officer they mowed down Alawite cadets at the Aleppo Artillery School; some reports put the number of dead at over 80. In June 1980 they only just failed to kill the President after which his brother Rifaat al-Assad took his special forces to storm the prison at Palmyra where Brotherhood members were detained: about 500 died in their cells. In July 1980 membership of the Brotherhood was made a capital offence. At a meeting in Aachen al-Attar was replaced by a triumvirate led by Ali al-Bayanuni. The tolerance shown to them by Jordan caused several incidents between the two countries and other opponents of Syria such as Saddam Hussain, the CIA, Israel and the Lebanese Christians were accused of supporting them. In February 1982 there was a showdown in the Hama Uprising where fighting lasted for a fortnight in which opponents of the regime claimed that 20,000 were killed. After this several thousand members were believed to have been executed and at the Baath Congress of 1985 it was claimed that the Muslim Brotherhood had been exterminated.

MUZAFFAR Pasha (c. 1840–1907)

Mutasarrif of Lebanon 1902–7. He was the son of a Pole who had embraced Islam but he himself reverted to Catholicism. He was educated at St Cyr, served in the Ottoman army, becoming a Marshal: at one time he commanded the Imperial Stud. He was mentioned as a possible Mutasarrif in 1883 but was only appointed the sixth Mutasarrif in 1902. He arrived with ambitious

plans for reform, including the election of shaykhs by secret ballot but nothing came of them. He tried to introduce financial discipline into the administration but backed down in the face of opposition. He worked to maintain a balance between the communities but this upset the Maronites who expected to be dominant. He was intelligent, well-meaning and well-educated with personal integrity, tact and kindness but he lacked the special qualities needed to govern an unruly province. He lacked strength of personality and ended as a puppet in the hands of local politicians, Consuls and above all of his family who exploited his position for corrupt gain. He died in office.

MZALI, Muhammad (1925–)

Tunisian Prime Minister. Born in Monastir, he was at Sadiqi College before taking a degree in Philosophy from the Sorbonne. In 1947 he joined the Neo-Destour but does not appear to have played any significant role in the struggle for independence. In 1950 he became a teacher at Zaytuna University and at Sadiqi while working as a Post Graduate in Higher Literary Studies. He founded an influential cultural review, *al-Fikr*, which urged openness to the West while stressing that it was essential to maintain an Arab–Islamic identity and the unique authenticity of the Tunisian personality. At the same time he became perhaps better known as a footballer. Mzali then embarked on a civil service career mainly in educational and youth matters and was also President of the Tunisian Olympics Committee, organising the Mediterranean Games of 1967. He was elected to the National Assembly and in 1964 to the Central Committee of the Parti Socialiste Destourien and appointed Director-General of Radio and Television. In April 1968 when Ahmad Mestiri resigned from the Government in protest at the socialist measures of Ahmad Ben Salah, Mzali replaced him at the Ministry of Defence; he was transferred to Youth and Sport in November 1969. During the 1970s he held the Ministries of Public Health and then Education. In April 1980, after the rigid and uninspiring Hedi Nouira had had a heart attack, Mzali was chosen by Bourguiba to succeed him as Prime Minister and Secretary-General of the PSD. The appointment was seen as bringing in a breath of fresh air for Mzali, unlike his predecessor and most of the Government, was a politician rather than a technocrat, anxious to attract the legitimate opposition, students and the Trade Unions. He made every effort to explain his policies and determined not to make violence the only possible form of protest. Torture and the police presence on the University campus were ended, nearly 1,000 trade unionists, including their leader Habib Achour, held since Black Thursday, were released and the Party grip on their organisation relaxed. Opposition groups were allowed firstly to publish their own newspapers and then had their "movements" officially recognised and brought in to the political system. Mzali faced economic problems, unemployment, inflation and a drop in earnings from oil and phosphates which he tried to solve with a mixture of 1960s socialism and 1970s liberalism. In February 1981 a new Five-Year Plan, aiming to revitalise the phosphate industry and developing agriculture and fishing, tourism and textiles anticipated

25% of the investment coming from abroad – mostly from Arab sources while Nouira had relied on European. The Plan aimed to create 300,000 new jobs, reducing the pressure on Tunisians to seek work abroad and to reduce the imbalance between the rich Northern provinces and the rest of the country. Mzali showed immense energy, once opening seven factories in a day, as well as a school and an incubator and giving three interviews. In the spring of 1981 Mzali had to bow to a wave of strikes by permitting pay rises of 20% and promising to hold down prices. In July 1981 he legalised the Tunisian Communist Party but cracked down on the Mouvement de la Tendance Islamique whose leaders were imprisoned. This by no means ended the threat from Muslim fundamentalists and later arrests showed that they had infiltrated the army. In October, to the extreme annoyance of PSD diehards, Tunisia had the freest elections in its history with the opposition leaders given access to the state-controlled media but the result was an embarrassment since the Government was declared to have won all the seats with 95% of the vote: there were few who did not believe the result fraudulent. On taking power Mzali had said that he needed five years to rejuvenate the country but after two and a half years there was a feeling that politically nothing was happening and that he was hovering indecisively between repression and reform while inflation rose rapidly, causing small businesses to close. He did win considerable support by welcoming the leaders and fighters of the Palestine Liberation Organisation after their expulsion from Lebanon. In the first half of 1983 there were strikes which caused sharp differences within the Government over the budget: the Finance Minister Mansur Mualla gave priority to financial stability while Mzali wanted concessions for social peace. It was not until June that the Prime Minister prevailed and later in the year he gave further indications of political liberalism by appointing the first ladies to the Cabinet, one of them his own wife Fathia. He dismissed his Economy Minister, leaving himself without expert advice. He also managed, with the help of Mme Bouguiba, to get rid of Muhammad Sayah, the SPD hardliner who abhorred a multi-party system and in November the two opposition "movements" were recognised as legal political parties. In the meanwhile, in February 1983, he had called for closer co-operation of Maghreb states, beginning in March with a Treaty of Fraternity and Concord with Algeria. In June he led a delegation which included representatives of Morocco and Algeria to Brussels to negotiate with the EEC. He had to reassure the touchy Qadafi that Libya was not being excluded and in July he took his Cabinet to Tripoli for a joint session. Despite that relations between the neighbours were at times very bad and more than once they appeared on the verge of war. Mzali tried several times in 1984 and 1985 to organise a Maghreb Summit but was always frustrated as Algeria demanded the participation of Polisario which Morrocco refused to countenance. The trade deficit rose, the national debt doubled between 1980 and 1984 and, under pressure from the IMF, in October 1983, Mzali announced the removal of subsidies on essential foodstuffs which had kept wages low and enabled new Tunisian industries to compete: prices would double from the new year. He obviously had not

grasped the difficulties of the young unemployed and at the end of December Bread Riots broke out which nearly toppled the regime. Bourguiba personally rescinded the price rises, giving the impression that Mzali was to blame. It appeared that Mzali might fall but instead Bourguiba dismissed his rival Driss Guiga from the Interior Ministry which he assigned to the Prime Minister whom he endorsed as his heir. The fundamentalist MTI, which Mzali again refused to legalise, grew in strength, particularly amongst students and there were frequent disorders, intensified by Mzali's efforts to change the educational system by intemperately substituting Arabic for French. There were also troubles with the trade unions, increasing after Qadafi expelled large numbers of Tunisian workers: Mzali took over union offices by force. As Bourguiba appeared to be sinking into senility politics became an unedifying struggle between factions supporting Mzali, Mme Bouguiba, Bourguiba Junior and Muhammad Sayah who was intriguing against the Prime Minister for control of the Interior Ministry. Municipal elections in May 1985 were boycotted by the opposition, ending any appearance of a liberal regime. In January 1986, at a time of acute financial crisis and after months of rumours of financial scandals, two senior officials were arrested for corruption. Bourguiba bestirred himself and dismissed his wife from his palace and his son from his ministry and followed this by a series of changes, removing supporters of Mzali, including taking the Interior from him and assigning it to Colonel Ben Ali. In June, at the Party Congress, Bourguiba spoke of Mzali as "my son who has my confidence now and in the future" and three days later he dismissed Mme Mzali from the Cabinet. Twelve days later he signed a decree unceremoniously and without notice ejecting the Prime Minister who only heard through the media. Mzali's supporters were ousted from office and two of his sons and a son-in-law imprisoned. He himself, after once failing, managed to escape to Algeria reportedly with a false moustache and disguised as a grocer. He was sentenced *in absentia* to a year's imprisonment for crossing the frontier illegally and later to fifteen years' for embezzlement. In exile he wrote many witty articles about Bourguiba and Tunisian politics and was said to live on money provided by Kuwait.

MZALI, Muhammad Salih (c. 1896–)
Tunisian Prime Minister. He trained as a lawyer in Lyons and in 1918 entered government service, being for many years Caid of Bizerta until he was dismissed by the Vichy Government. In 1921 he published a book calling for critical self-examination and an end to fatalism and ignorance of economic facts. He was a member of the Chenik Cabinet and was one of the three Ministers arrested with the Premier in March 1952. When in March 1954 the Bakkush government lost the confidence of the French in addition to that of the Bey Muhammad al-Amin, Mzali agreed to form a government. He included several moderate nationalists but was unable to get any of the Neo-Destour to join – Bourguiba dismissing him as "an adventurer". *Fellagha* activities started and in 6 months 74 civilians were killed. The conservative French Government of Laniel

was replaced by the progressive one of Mendes-France who instead of continuing the policy of granting minor reforms while trying to crush the nationalists by force, determined to try a new approach in Tunisia. Mzali who had several times requested to resign was allowed to do so in August 1954. After independence he was sentenced to 10 years' imprisonment by a special court but was released after serving little more than two years.

al-NABHANI, Sulayman b. Himyar (c. 1914)

Omani tribal leader. He succeeded his father who had played an important part in the insurrection against Faysal b. Turki Al Bu Said as *Tamimah* (paramount chief) of the Bani Riyam and generally acknowledged leader of the Ghafiri faction. He assumed the title of "King of the Green Mountain" and attempted to establish relations with foreign powers, succeeding only with Saudi Arabia. In April 1950 he unsuccessfully asked the British to recognise his independence and he also attempted to negotiate independently with oil companies. The explorer Thesiger found him "a powerful if not very congenial figure . . . not a tribal shaykh ruling by consent but an autocrat accustomed to obedience". He was reputed to exercise *droit de seigneur* and his walking-stick outside a door was an instruction to a husband to stay away. He played a prominent part in the election of Ghalib b. Ali al-Hinai to the Imamate in 1954. When the forces of Sail b. Taymur Al Bu Said entered Inner Oman, Bin Himyar, abandoning the Imam, submitted and spent some time in Muscat as a "guest" of the Sultan. When Talib started the rebellion in June 1957 Bin Himyar escaped to join him. His fort was utterly destroyed by the RAF but he spent the next 18 months as one of the leaders of the rebels on Jabal Akhdar. In January the British stormed the Mountain and Bin Himyar escaped to Saudi Arabia and was still living in Dhahran over 30 years later. In appearance he resembled a caricature of a fictional bandit.

al-NABULSI, Sulayman (1910–76)

Jordanian Prime Minister. He was born in Salt and educated at the American University of Beirut before becoming a bank official. He took an early interest in politics, leading the *Faysali*, a group of young men opposed to the patriarchal rule of Amir Abd Allah and his reliance on the British. In February 1947 he was appointed Minister of Finance in the Cabinet of Samir al-Rifai, holding the office with one interruption for over four years. In 1953 Nabulsi became Ambassador to London where his anti-British views and left-wing attitudes were very noticeable; he resigned after five months. He returned to Jordan in 1954 and his supporters were legalised as the National Socialist Party which aimed to liberate politics from the control of the Palace, replace the British connection with close links with the anti-imperialist Arab states and work for greater equality at home. Nabulsi established good relations with President Nasser and led the opposition which frustrated the desire of King Hussain to join the Baghdad Pact. The elections of October 1956, the most

democratic ever held in Jordan, made the NS the largest party and Nabulsi became Premier and Foreign Minister. His Cabinet was a coalition that included a communist and, as Deputy Foreign Minister, a member of the Baath who was reputed to make frequent visits to Damascus from which he returned with suitcases full of money. Nabulsi agreed to the establishment of a Unified Military Command which put the Jordanian and Syrian armies under the Egyptian General Abd al-Hakim Amer. Almost immediately afterwards the Suez War erupted and Nabulsi wished to break diplomatic relations with Britain and France but was prevented from doing so by the King. Nabulsi succeeded, however, in abrogating the Anglo-Trans-Jordanian Treaty and negotiated the replacement of the British subsidy by Egypt, Syria and Saudi Arabia. He denounced the Eisenhower Doctrine, although it was welcomed by Hussain, and invited the Russian news agency TASS to open an office; the King published a letter to his Prime Minister warning of the dangers of communist infiltration but the Cabinet voted for diplomatic relations with Moscow and to recognise Red China. Tension mounted early in April 1957, the Government refused to repress anti-monarchist demonstrations and what later appeared to have been an attempt at a coup by the Chief of Staff Major-General Ali Abu Nuwar only just failed. For the only time in Jordanian history the Government considered itself rather than the King the principal decision maker. On 10 April Hussain demanded the resignation of Nabulsi who, despite a telegram from Nasser telling him to remain in office, complied but frustrated attempts to form a new government. Revolution was finally prevented by the firmness and courage of Hussain in the Zerka Incident and a compromise Cabinet was formed under Hassan al-Khalidi with Nabulsi as Foreign Minister. After a week when the situation had become more stable Khalidi gave way to the firmer Ibrahim Hashim and Nabulsi was dismissed and put under house arrest. In August 1961 he was released and after a brief period of detention in 1963 during a security scare was appointed a Senator. In April 1968 he put together a National Front to support the Palestinians whose militancy was growing after the June War and backed them during Black September. Later he criticised the King for inactivity in the October War. Nabulsi was an intriguer and an opportunist rather than an extremist but was not a strong enough character to control the forces that he let loose.

NAHDAH (Tunisia)
President Ben Ali was determined that no political party could claim a monopoly of Islam of which, he said, that State was the trustee for all its citizens. He therefore refused to register the Mouvement de la Tendance Islamique, a moderately fundamentalist group whose leader Rashid Ghannouchi stressed the democratic features of Islam. In February 1989, in order to contest the parliamentary elections due in April, the MTI changed its name to al-Nahdah (Renaissance) and applied for recognition. No reply was received but its leaders stated that three-quarters of the 114 Independent candidates were members or sympathisers. Although they won no seats they took 15% of the national vote (up to 30% in some parts of Tunis), making them the third largest group. In June 1989 they applied again for registration which was refused because Ghannouchi and the Secretary-General Abd al-Fattah Mourou had criminal records. In July Ben Ali issued an amnesty which wiped out 5,164 convictions, mostly for political offences. In December the Nahdah was again refused registration but allowed to publish a newspaper, al-Fajr which was edited by Hamadi al-Jabali. That winter there were frequent clashes as militant Muslim students tried to dominate the Universities: many were drafted into the army. During 1990 the chief Nahdah spokesman Ali Laaridh, who had been sentenced to death under Bourguiba, was arrested on at least four occasions for criticising the Government. The legal opposition parties were compromised by the frequent attempts of Ben Ali to secure their co-operation and Nahdah appeared the only genuine opposition. Al-Fajr was temporarily suppressed for publishing an article in which Ghannouchi called for jihad. They boycotted the local elections of May 1990 but were inspired by the victories of the Front Islamique du Salut in Algeria the following month. After the Iraqi occupation of Kuwait some led by Ghannouchi strongly supported Saddam Hussain, to the annoyance of the Saudis from whom they had obtained some financial support, while others under Mourou were more moderate. They organised frequent demonstrations and early in November Laaridh claimed that 200, including himself, had been arrested: government reports that arms and explosives had been seized were indignantly denied. At the end of the month there were further arrests of some 70 including 30 members of the security forces led by Muhammad Lahbib Lassoued, a 32-year-old engineer who stated that he had been a member of Nahdah but had left it to form the Commandos of Sacrifice because it had refused to countenance violence. In December another 102 were accused of trying to set up an Islamic state by force which involved sabotage and murder. In January 1991 demonstrations against the arrests were dispersed with tear gas. In the same month Mourou and Jabali declared that Nahdah wished to operate as a legal party and published a list of the 60 members of its Consultative Council to show that it was not clandestine. In February after a demonstration against the Gulf War there was an attack on a local office of the government Rassemblement Constitutionnel Démocratique Party in which a caretaker was deliberately burned to death. Three men arrested claimed membership of Nahdah

which was denied by the organisation: they were hanged in October. In March there had been further arrests after a raid on the headquarters of the Students Union which had been set up by the MTI in 1985 and which claimed the support of at least half the student body. Mourou and two other members of the executive committee resigned in protest against the violence of irresponsible youth and six of the other ten members were arrested. In May a further 300, including 100 of the security forces were arrested. Most were dealt with quietly in civilian courts, getting sentences of up to five years' imprisonment for such crimes as holding illegal meetings or distributing pamphlets but two major trials of 279 militants (55 in absentia) began in July 1992. They were accused of a "diabolical plot" to shoot down the presidential aircraft and seize power in the subsequent power vacuum. At the trials there were allegations of torture. Despite prosecution demands for death sentences of the first batch of 171 brought before a civilian judge with military assessors, mostly alleged Nahdah members, 35 including Ghannouchi were sentenced to life imprisonment, nine acquitted and the rest given sentences of from one to 24 years. Eleven of the second batch, the 108 followers of Lassoued, tried by a military tribunal, received life sentences. The absence of death sentences was attributed either to an unwillingness to create martryrs or to offend the EC. There were no demonstrations after the trials and the claim of Ben Ali that Nahdah had been crushed appeared justified. Relations with the Sudan, accused of training Islamic terrorists, had deteriorated during the struggle and in October 1991 Tunisia recalled its Ambassador from Khartoum, formally severing relations in August 1992. Nahdah was seen as probably the most progressive of the North African fundamentalist movements.

al-NAJAH UNIVERSITY SIEGE (1992)
In July 1992, six armed men entered the campus of Al-Najah University in Nablus to demand support for mainstream nationalist candidates against those of Hamas in a forthcoming student election. Israeli troops surrounded the buildings and demanded their surrender. Two hundred students barricaded themselves in the University to support the gunmen, about a hundred notables went on hunger strike and the Israeli army sealed off Nablus. Yitzhak Rabin, who had just become Prime Minister, committed to achieving Palestinian autonomy within nine months, was anxious to avoid a bloody clash, particularly as the American Secretary of State Baker was about to arrive to discuss the resumption of the Washington Peace Talks. Palestinian leaders such as Faysal al-Hussaini were also anxious to show their capacity for leadership and for calm. As a result of negotiations, after four days, it was agreed that the six gunmen should leave the campus in safety and be handed over to the Red Cross. They would then be expelled to Jordan and not allowed to return for three years. The solution, a rebuff to Israeli hardliners, gave hope that a new spirit had arisen in which Israelis and Palestinians could settle problems by negotiation.

NAJRAN–ASIR DISPUTE
In the seventeenth century after they had expelled the Turks for the first time, the Zaidi Imams brought most

of South West Arabia from Asir to Hadhramawt under
at least nominal control. After a few decades local governors asserted their independence. In about 1750 a
Sharif named Muhammad b. Ahmad b. Khairat, whose
grandfather had fled there from Mecca, was appointed
Governor of Abu Arish by the Imam al-Mahdi. He
immediately revolted and fought off several attacks to
reduce him to obedience. Slightly later Shaykh
Makrami who had been appointed Governor of Najran
also threw off his allegiance to the Imam. In about 1763
a group of Asiri tribal leaders, including Muhammad
b. Amer Abu Nuqtah, became Wahhabis and their local
opponents made nominal submission to the Imam in
return for help. After several years warfare, the Wahhabis subjugated all of Asir but in 1805 Sharif Humud
managed to re-establish an independent Amirate at Abu
Arish. In 1811 he allied with the forces of Muhammad
Ali Pasha and the whole area down to Mokha passed
under Egyptian control. In the early 1830s while
Muhammad Ali was preoccupied with Syria, an alliance
of Sharif Humud and the tribal leader Ibn Mujathil re-
established the independence of Asir. It lasted only a
few years before the Egyptians returned but they withdrew again in 1840. The area was then dominated by
an alliance between Sharif Hussain b. Ali Haydar of
Abu Arish and Ayidh Ibn Miri until the Turks succeeded in imposing direct rule over both Asir and
Yemen in the 1850s. Meanwhile a religious leader of
Moroccan origin, Saiyyid Ahmad Ibn Idris had established a *zawiah* in Sabiyah which exercised considerable
influence over the tribes. This influence was mainly
religious until at the beginning of the twentieth century
his great-grandson, Muhammad b. Ali al-Idrisi used it
to build for himself an independent Amirate. In 1910
he revolted openly and later received help from the
Italians during the Italo–Turkish War. In 1911 he allied
with the Imam Yahya who was also fighting for independence from the Turks. Both achieved their aim but
rivalry broke out between them in which the Idrisi, who
had formed an alliance with the British who gave him
generous financial aid, gained the advantage over the
Imam who had refused to do so. He won control of
the Tihamah as far south as Hodeidah. However both
King Hussain of the Hijaz and Ibn Saud were by now
taking an interest in Asir. In 1923 Muhammad b. Ali
was succeeded by his son Ali b. Muhammad al-Idrisi
and the Imam took advantage of the weakness of the
new ruler to regain the Tihamah as far north as Midi.
The ruling family split, Ali was replaced by his uncle
Hassan b. Ali al-Idrisi and sought the help of the
Imam. Hassan thereupon, by the Mecca Agreement,
ceded sovereignty over Asir to Ibn Saud who, in November 1930, formally declared Asir part of his
Kingdom. In 1932 Hassan revolted to regain his independence but was defeated and took refuge with the
Imam who then asserted his own claim to sovereignty
over Asir. Najran had in the meanwhile enjoyed local
independence and in 1870 Joseph Halévy, a French Jew
who had been the first Westerner to visit the area since
the Roman invasion of 24 BC, found it peaceful and
prosperous. In the early 1930s, however, factions had
developed seeking support from either the Imam or Ibn
Saud. In April 1933 the Yemeni Crown Prince Ahmad
occupied Najran. This and the repetition of the Imam's

claim to Asir led in the spring of 1934 to the Saudi–
Yemeni War in which the Amir Faysal advanced
through the Tihamah to capture Hodeidah. The Iman
sued for peace and in the Ta'if Treaty of May 1934 had
to renounce his claim to Najran and Asir. After the
overthrow of the Imamate in 1962 the Saudis gave
assistance to the Imam Badr whereupon Marshal Sallal
resurrected the Yemeni claim to Najran and Asir which
were serving as bases for the Royalists in the Yemen
War. During the fighting the Egyptians bombed both
areas and attacked Najran with poison gas. After the
National Reconciliation ended the fighting, the Yemen
Republic became financially dependent upon Saudi
Arabia and in March 1973 on a visit to Riyadh, the
Prime Minister Abd Allah al-Hajri formally declared
the continuing validity of the Ta'if Treaty. The Yemeni
Government has not since then made any claim upon
Najran and Asir, although individual politicians have
done so, and there have been disputes over the actual
details of the frontier which became infested with smug-
glers and under which there was believed to be oil.
There were also occasional rumours of armed clashes
between Saudi and Yemeni border guards.

NAMI, *Damad* Ahmad (c. 1880–?)

Syrian Head of State. He was a Circassian aristocrat
whose family had settled in Beirut after the Russian
conquest of the Caucasus. He was educated at the
Military College in Istanbul and in Paris and acquired
the title *Damad* (Son-in-law) through marriage to a
daughter of Sultan Abd al-Hamid. He had connections
with leading French Freemasons but played little part
in public life. In the troubled period of the Druze Revolt
the French tried to work through Subhi Barakat but
found him impossible. They then tried the *Damad* who
was believed honest and conciliatory and appointed
him Prime Minister at the end of April 1926. He
included three leading nationalists in his Cabinet and
called for a Constitution, a Treaty with France rather
than a Mandate, Syrian unity, gradual evacuation of
French troops, currency reform, membership of the
League of Nations and an amnesty. He worked con-
scientiously for peace and on French instigation asked
the rebels to lay down their arms. The three nationalist
Ministers refused to concur, were arrested and taken
into exile and replaced by men subservient to the
French. In November 1926 internal disputes led to a
further Cabinet reshuffle. The *Damad*, as an outsider,
was never popular with the Damascenes and there was
much resentment at the regal state which he kept so he,
rather than the French, became the target of nationalist
venom. British diplomats believed that some of the
press attacks on him were orchestrated by the French
to distract attention from themselves. Early in 1928
the French were considering a fresh start with a new
Constitution and possibly a monarchy. The *Damad*'s
open ambitions for a throne provided a pretext for the
French to drop him on 2 February on the grounds that
his government "did not possess sufficient confidence
to preside over elections with complete disinterest".
However in June 1932 he was a candidate for the Presidency but the French preferred Muhammad Ali al-
Abid. A Foreign Office report of 1939 reported that he
still hoped for a throne but "has far less political influ-

ence than he thinks. Well meaning, perhaps a little fatuous".

al-NAMSAWI, Umar (1806-?)

Governor of Mount Lebanon. A Croat, he was born Michael Lattas and took the name of Umar when he became a Muslim. He co-operated with the Allies in the operations that led to the evacuation of Syria by Ibrahim Pasha and after the collapse of the regime of Bashir III Shihab he was installed as Governor of the Mountain. His main concern was to prevent a Shihab restoration and he settled himself in their palace and showed special favour to all their opponents, particularly the feudal aristocracy. He used them to compel the peasantry to sign documents denouncing the Shihabs and praising his own administration. The Maronites were unwilling to do this and sought the protection of France. The Druzes, on the other hand, supported the Governor and obtained the backing of Britain. The Druzes, however, came to resent the Pasha's attempt to establish firm government and turned against him; he arrested their leaders by treachery and hoped to rely upon the Maronites. He decreed that taxes should no longer be collected by the feudal lords but by agents of the Porte and relied upon Albanian troops who were little better than bandits. The European Consuls in Beirut protested constantly to Istanbul about the chaos in Lebanon caused by his proceedings. In November 1842 the Druzes revolted and besieged Umar Pasha in Bayt al-Din. The Ottoman Governor of Damascus came to his relief but dismissed him from the post which he had held for less than a year. The Powers urged that a new form of government be created for the Mountain and Prince Metternich negotiated a settlement that led to the establishment of the Dual Kaymakamate.

NAQQASH, Alfred (1887-1978)

Lebanese President. A Maronite from a prominent family, he studied Law at the Jesuit University in Beirut and in Paris. He then settled in Egypt where he practised law until he returned to Beirut where he made a career in the judiciary. He was President of the Court of Appeal and had played no part in politics when in April 1941 popular unrest caused President Emile Edde to resign. General Dentz, the High Commissioner who served the Vichy Government appointed Naqqash executive Head of State and when in the summer the Free French took over they considered him so useful that they maintained him in office. In November General Catroux proclaimed the formal independence of Lebanon and appointed Naqqash as President. The choice of Naqqash was opposed by the Maronite Patriarch who considered him too close to the Jesuits. He was not a strong personality and in general did little more than carry out the instructions of French officials. In April 1942 he threatened to resign unless more were done to implement promises of independence but he was not taken seriously. Sir Edward Spears found him "a polite and well-bred man" but ludicrously timid. In March 1943 he was replaced by Ayyub Thabit at the head of a caretaker administration to prepare for elections. Naqqash was elected a Deputy for Beirut but achieved little prominence as a politician although he

did serve as Foreign Minister for two years under Camille Chamoun. He failed to be re-elected in 1957, retired from politics and became a successful banker. Naqqash was a keen tennis player.

al-NASHASHIBI, Raghib (c. 1880-1951)

Palestinian politician. The Nashashibis were one of the three most important families in Jerusalem and Raghib trained as an engineer in Istanbul. Standing on an anti-Zionist platform he was elected MP for Jerusalem in the Ottoman Parliament and served in the Turkish army. He was a member of the General Syrian Congress at which the Amir Faysal was elected King. In 1920 when the British dismissed Musa Kazim al-Hussaini, the head of a rival family, from the post of Mayor of Jerusalem, Nashashibi was appointed to succeed him: the Hussaini family already held the office of Mufti and the Government wanted to avoid the concentration of too much power in their hands. In March 1921 despite the opposition of Nashashibi, Haj Amin al-Hussaini succeeded as Mufti and thenceforth their mutual hostility prevented the Arabs of Palestine from ever establishing a united front against either the Mandate or the Zionists. Nashashibi lost influence on the Supreme Muslim Council but succeeded in winning the support of local mayors. In 1934, however, disgust, particularly amongst the Jews, at the corruption of his administration led to his defeat as Mayor of Jerusalem by Dr Hussain al-Khalidi. He tried to rebuild his following by forming the National Defence Party. In 1936 as head of this Party he became a member of the Arab Higher Committee and supported the Arab Rebellion in its early days. In 1937 he resigned, disgusted by the terrorism practised by followers of the Mufti. There was then very considerable fighting between adherents of the two factions. Nashashibi established close relations with another arch-enemy of the Mufti, the Amir Abd Allah of Trans-Jordan and like him, saw that it would be possible to profit from the partition of Palestine proposed in the Peel Report. Early in 1939 he was a delegate to the London Palestine Conference. During the 1940s Nashashibi was not very active politically and his support ebbed away as he was seen as little more than the Palestinian henchman of the Amir Abd Allah. In 1948 he supported the union of the West Bank with Trans-Jordan and became Governor of Jerusalem under the new regime. He later held portfolios in Cabinets in Amman and was Custodian of the Holy Places.

al-NASIRI, Muhammaad al-Makki (c. 1904-)

Moroccan nationalist leader. He came from a leading family in Sale and studied at Cairo University and in France. He worked with Shakib Arslan and spoke against the Berber Dahir at the Jerusalem Islamic Congress in 1931. He was one of the signatories of the Plan de Réformes of 1934. In 1936 he was exiled from the French zone and came into further prominence by his attacks on French policies and upon *tariqahs* in mosque sermons in Tetuan. He stressed the comparative benevolence of the government of General Franco and, with financial support from the Spanish authorities, founded in 1937 the Maghreb Unity Movement. The Spanish appointed him Director of the Khalifal Institute in

Tetuan where he remained until 1946 when, his relations with the Spanish having deteriorated, he moved to Tangier. He later welcomed the visit of Muhammad V to Tangier and then travelled widely promoting the Moroccan cause in all independent Muslim countries. In 1951 he signed the manifesto of the Moroccan National Front. He remained politically active after independence but was never really important owing to his failure to attract followers. He was described as resembling Savonarola, a good scholar and an eloquent speaker.

NASSAR, Fuad (c. 1912–76)

Jordanian Communist leader. A Christian, he was born in Nazareth and involved from an early age in anti-British and anti-Zionist activities, working with the military side of the Arab Higher Committee. After the collapse of the Arab Rebellion in 1939 he fled to Iraq, returning to Palestine in 1943. He was a member of the Palestine Communist Party and when the Jordan Communist Party was founded in 1951 he was its First Secretary-General. The Party was immediately declared illegal and Nassar sentenced to ten years' imprisonment but he was released in 1956 when Sulayman al-Nabulsi led a left-wing government. He went to Eastern Europe where with Khalid Bakdash and other exiled communists he tried to fit nationalist revolts such as those in Algeria and Aden into a Marxist framework. In April 1965 when King Hussain was wooing Russia, Nassar and other communists were formally amnestied. Subsequently he was active in the Palestine Liberation Organisation.

NATIONAL ALLIANCE FOR NATIONAL SALVATION (Sudan)

Early in 1985 when the government of President Nimeiri had reduced the Sudan to economic chaos, crippling strikes, a reign of terror due to the arbitrary application of the *Shariah*, an unpopular foreign policy and a civil war in the South, representatives of the middle-class professional organisations, secular intellectuals, the trade unions and the students formed an alliance to bring about its overthrow. They were joined by the surviving remnants of the banned political parties, the Umma, the Democratic Unionist Party, and the Sudanese Communist Party. They issued a Charter which called for a three-year transitional period during which the 1956 provisional constitution, as amended in 1964, would replace that imposed by Nimeiri. Basic freedoms would be restored and "decadent" institutions of the Nimeiri regime would be abolished. There should be regional self government for the South and a non-aligned foreign policy instead of "dependence on world imperialism". The National Islamic Front refused to sign the Charter which they saw as relaxing *Shariah*. The general strike organised by the Alliance played a major part in the overthrow of Nimeiri as the army refused to repress it and then General Siwar al-Dhahab headed a Transitional Military Council which accepted the Alliance as the civilian representatives of the nation and appointed its leader Dr Jazuli Dafallah as Prime Minister. A general election was announced and the political parties resumed their individual existence leaving the Alliance a hetero-geneous collection of splinter groups such as the Nuba Mountains Union, Nasserists, the Workers and Farmers Party, the Islamic Socialist Party and the Socialist Labour Party. After the election its leader Dr Khalid Yagi briefly served in the Cabinet of Sadiq al-Mahdi as Minister of Peace and Unity. The Alliance was not represented in later governments but it did not align with any of the major parties, opposing dealings with the IMF and calling for resistance to imperialism. There were suggestions that some of its members were intriguing with former associates of Nimeiri or plotting with the army to overthrow the Government. Like the parties it was banned by General Bashir.

NATIONAL BLOC (Syria)

Kutlah al-Wataniyyah. In 1924 Dr Shahbandar and Faris al-Khouri founded the People's Party to crystallise opposition to the French Mandate but it was banned after less than a year for giving open support to the Druze Revolt. The Revolt showed that the French could not be expelled by force and many nationalists were exiled or imprisoned. After an amnesty in 1928 a group came together to achieve independence by political action and gradually coalesced into the National Bloc. It was never a monolithic organisation but a number of leaders and their clients. Thus Ibrahim Hananu, perhaps the leading spirit, represented the notables of Aleppo, Jamil Mardam the landowners and Lutfi al-Haffar the merchants of Damascus, Hashim al-Atasi the notables of Homs, and Faris al-Khouri the lawyers and Christians while later Shukri al-Quwatli stood for the pre-war freedom movement. Despite French opposition it was the most effective group in the Constituent Assembly of 1928 and able to elect Atasi as President of the Assembly. Its principal demand was for an agreement with France similar to the Anglo-Iraqi Treaty of 1930. It opposed French suggestions of a monarchy and was in general pre-occupied with local problems, particularly the establishment of a unitary state, rather than those of the Arab world as a whole. At this time the Bloc had a paramilitary youth movement and was active in developing industries and utilities under nationalist control; the fez was adopted as its symbol. In a conference in Homs in 1932 it established its formal organisation. Early in 1936 demands for a Treaty rose to a crescendo with strikes and agitation and many of the leaders of the Bloc were arrested. After a brief period they were released and headed the delegation that negotiated the Franco-Syrian Treaty of 1936. In the elections of November 1936 it won a large majority and Atasi became President of the Republic and Mardam Prime Minister. However it soon started to lose prestige for the French Chamber refused to ratify the treaty and there were difficulties in the Druze and Alawite areas as well as the emotion caused by the Alexandetta question. In order to secure ratification Mardam made concession after concession and came under attack from the more extreme nationalists like Shahbandar who had been in exile but resented his exclusion from the leadership and also from Quwatli who resigned from the Cabinet. Those who remained in power lost touch with the grass roots and Mardam was a poor administrator and never had a free hand owing to French restrictions. The National Bloc

Government fell apart. In July 1939 the French suspended the Constitution and ended political life. When it was restored in 1943 the Bloc won an overwhelming majority and Quwatli became President of the Republic. It provided the Government during the years in which independence was achieved but then split into factions – the National Party led by Quwatli and the Damascenes and the People's Party under the Aleppans Nazim al-Qudsi and Rushdi al-Kihkya.

NATIONAL CHARTER (Egypt) (1962)

After the break up of the United Arab Republic President Nasser determined on a new beginning. He designated 250 persons to form a preparatory committee to organise a National Congress of Popular Forces which consisted of themselves, 379 peasants, 300 labourers, 150 representing "national capital", 461 representing government officials, professional bodies and women, and 210 professors and students. The Congress opened on 21 May 1962 and Nasser spent five hours reading to it the ten Chapters of the draft National Charter which set out details of the national aims of freedom, "scientific socialism" and unity. It also embodied the principles of Islam and Arab unity and seemed to some extent to have been influenced by the ideas of Young Egypt of which Nasser was once a supporter. Socialism was declared "an historical inevitability imposed by reality" but it rejected the Marxist concept of class struggle. The basic infrastructure of the economy should be in public ownership but this did not mean the nationalisation of all forms of production or the abolition of private property or the right of inheritance. Land ownership was permitted within limits but required restrictions to prevent it from developing into "feudalism". Priority should go to the development of heavy industry but not carried to the Stalinist extent of starving consumers. Western-style democracy was the dictatorship of capital. Imperialism in all forms had to be opposed because it was an affront to human dignity and Egypt would support every "nationalist popular progressive movement". Arab unity could not be imposed but had to have a popular basis. There should be freedom of speech and of the press (a provision consistently ignored) and of worship with warnings against its exploitation by "reactionary elements" (Nasser was engaged in a struggle with the Muslim Brothers). Socially there should be equality of opportunity. There was a need to restrict population growth. The Charter is a key document for the understanding of Nasser's political thought and of his aims for Egypt and the Arab world. In order to assist in bringing about these ideals, a new political structure, the Arab Socialist Union, was to replace the National Union, from which it differed in the provision that at every level half the seats were to be filled by peasants and workers. There should be collective leadership with a Presidency Council of twelve members. The draft was approved as it stood, after the only lively political debate of the Nasser years, not merely in the Congress but on television and in professional groups, on 30 June.

NATIONAL CHARTER (Jordan)

In April 1988 the stern repression of the government of Zaid al-Rifai set off riots in Southern Jordan which led King Hussain to decide upon a series of measures to liberalise the political system. After meetings with regional leaders he set up a Commission under the former Prime Minister Ahmad Ubaydat to draw up a Charter for "full participation" of the people in a regime of "responsible freedom".

NATIONAL BLOC (Lebanon)

Al-Kutlah al-Wataniyyah. The National Bloc came into existence in 1930s and consisted of the partisans of the President Emile Edde and those who hoped for favours at his hands. It had no systematic programme or doctrine beyond the necessity of maintaining Maronite predominance and the realisation that this could best be done in alliance with the French mandatory authorities. After independence the Bloc tried to present itself as a national political party but it could never claim more than about 7,000 members in the Mountain, 3,000 in Beirut and 1,500 in the rest of the country. After 1949 when its founder died his son Raymond Edde succeeded him as leader. Elections brought it between two and six Deputies. Its main planks were always unrestricted free enterprise and the maintenance of the sectarian arrangements of the National Pact. The Party took little interest in Arab issues except insofar as they affected Lebanon. It opposed, therefore, the settlement of Palestinian refugees. It always took a strongly pro-Western stance in international affairs.

NATIONAL CHARTER (Jordan)

On 9 June 1991 the 40-page document was published as an attempt to reconcile Palestine nationality with Jordanian citizenship and which reflected the need for support following the Gulf War. The wording of the document suggested some form of unity between Jordan and an independent Palestinian state, possibly a confederation: "Arab Palestinian identity is an identity of political struggle and is not in contradiction with the Jordanian–Arab identity". The Charter led to the drafting of a law allowing political parties that had been banned since 1957. It reaffirmed the *Shariah* and put a restriction on the prerogatives of each branch of government and guaranteed the separation of powers and human rights. "Pluralism is the only guarantee against dictatorship" – no single party can claim to posses the truth.

NATIONAL DEFENCE PARTY (Palestine)

Hizb al-Difa al-Watani. The National Defence Party was constituted in Jaffa in December 1934 under the leadership of Raghib al-Nashashibi as a means of organising opposition to his political and family foe the Mufti, Haj Amin al-Hussaini. Apart from his personal following much of its support came from the rural areas and from Christians. Its goal was defined as the achievement of Arab sovereignty and it understood that this could best be brought about by co-operation with the British authorities and in its early days it sought good relations with the Jews. The Party also cultivated another sworn enemy of the Mufti, the Amir Abd Allah of Trans-Jordan. In 1934 the Party was prepared to accept the British offer of a Legislative Council. In April 1936 Nashashibi was one of the original members of the Arab Higher Committee but the Party was weakened by its ambivalent attitude towards the increasing violence of the Arab Rebellion and in July he and his Party officially left the AHC. The equivocal nature of its policies was also made apparent by the publication of the Peel Report with its recommendation of partition and the unification of the Arab area to Trans-Jordan: the Party publicly opposed while Nashashibi privately supported it. Early in 1939 the Party was represented by its leader at the London Palestine Conference and later in the year, unlike the AHC, declared its readiness to co-operate in fulfilling the MacDonald White Paper. The Party announced its support for Britain during the war but gradually faded away until by 1945 the British had come to regard the Istiqlal Party as its best friend amongst the Palestinian Arabs.

NATIONAL DEMOCRATIC FRONT (Yemen)

As part of his campaign to build a centralised state and weaken the preponderance of the great tribal leaders, Colonel Ibrahim al-Hamdi did not discourage the emergence of small left-wing groups, some of them affiliated to the Arab Nationalist Movement, others to the Baath and the Communists. In 1976 such bodies as the Revolutionary Democratic Party, the Organisation of Yemeni Resisters and the Labour Party came together as the National Democratic Front calling for a democratic state with control of the economy, land reform and opposition to the dominance of Saudi Arabia. They were anxious to collaborate with Hamdi who appeared to be working along similar lines. Their leader was Sultan Ahmad Umar, a graduate of the American University of Beirut who had written a book on socio-economic reform. They were mostly Shafais and received discreet encouragement from Aden. After the murder of Hamdi, one of his closest associates, Major Abd al-Aalim, a Shafai of leftist leanings, fled to Hujariyyah and started a revolt. This was quickly put down by Ali Abd Allah Salih but the remnants regrouped in Aden within the NDF, receiving radio facilities there and participating in the inaugural meeting of the Yemeni Socialist Party in October 1978. Relations between Aden and Sanaa were extremely bad and the NDF was given bases near the frontier from which they could raid into the North. These incursions, and Salih's ripostes to them, escalated into actual war in February 1979 during which the NDF overran the frontier towns of Harib, Baydha and Qatabah. The cease-fire the following month provided for a union between North and South in which the NDF hoped for a major role. There was no apparent progress towards union and the NDF impatiently resumed guerrilla activities. In January 1980 Salih, temporarily on bad terms with Saudi Arabia, met Umar who claimed that there had been agreement on most of their demands. In December 1980 Salih attacked them, driving them all south of the border. They soon launched a counter-offensive and claimed to have overrun all the Shafai areas, establishing their own administration including hospitals and schools there. At this time they had a hard core of perhaps 1,500 militants but they could rely on armed support from another 8,000 tribesmen, making their forces roughly the same size as the Yemeni army. Their arms were believed to come from Libya. The principal supporter of the NDF, described by the Yemeni Prime Minister Abd al-Krim al-Iryani as "a 100% Marxist-Leninist Party" had been Abd al-Fattah Ismail and after his overthrow support for their cause was a matter of contention between his more pragmatic successor Ali Nasir Muhammad and the more radical doctrinaires. In December 1981, while Muhammad was in the ascendant, Salih visited Aden and agreed to increase the momentum towards union. They also agreed not to support one another's dissidents. Early the following year Salih launched an all-out offensive during which the NDF showed its possession of sophisticated weaponry by shooting down aircraft with missiles. Deprived of support from Aden, which anyway was too devastated by flooding to intervene, they were crushed and in May Salih offered the remnants amnesty and reincorporation in the YAR.

NATIONAL DEMOCRATIC PARTY (Egypt)

Hizb al-Watani al-Dimuqrati. In October 1975 Anwar Sadat permitted the emergence of left, right and centre platforms within the only legal party, the Arab Socialist Union. The first to be organised was the Centre, the Social Democrats, supporters of the Government, led by the President's brother-in-law Mahmud Abu Wafia who outlined its objectives as adherence to socialism, faith in God and social justice to raise the standards of the people, justice in distribution of national wealth, selfless work for the people and supremacy of law. As the Egyptian Arab Socialist Organisation or Misr Party, led by the Prime Minister Mamduh Salim, it won 280 out of 360 seats in the general election of October 1976. In July 1978 Sadat announced his intention of forming his own National Democratic Party which was joined by nearly all the parliamentary representatives of the ASU which was later formally dissolved. The NDP took over its assets and was always better financed than the other parties with a grip on the media and the support of local officials. This gave it a predominance so that it differed little from a single official party and a law that a party had to win 8% of the votes to secure representation in the Assembly made things still more difficult for the opposition. The principal duty of the NDP was to legitimise, articulate and enact measures devised by the President and act as a link between the masses and the political élite. It claimed 1.4 million members. In the election of June 1979 it won 302 out of 362 seats. Sadat retained the presidency of the Party until his assassination when it was assumed by Mubarak who had been in charge of the organisation since 1980. The Secretary-General was Fikri Makram Ubayd. The NDP fought the 1984 election on a programme of scientific planning, raising the standard of living, ideology giving place to specific issues such as industry and agriculture. It promised to strengthen the public and provide a healthy climate for the private sector. It resisted other parties' demands for revision of the Constitution saying that democracy depended upon the behaviour of the Government rather than on written rules. It received 73% of the valid votes and won 390 out of 448 seats. In the 1987 elections the NDP reiterated democratic socialism, the creation of a "modern state based on science and faith", Islamic law forming "a principal source of legislation", and a free press regarded as the fourth pillar after the legislative, executive and judiciary. It took 347 seats against 60 for the joint opposition list and 36 for the New Wafd but the result was later held to be illegal and further elections were held in November 1990. These were boycotted by the other major parties except for the National Progressive Union Party leaving the NDP to face only about 100 representatives of minor groups and 2,000 Independents, at least half of whom were government supporters. It won 348 seats and was assured of the support of 56 nominal Independents.

NATIONAL FRONT (Sudan)

Al-Jabhah al-Wataniyyah. There have been three groups using this name in the Sudan. The first was formed in August 1949 with the backing of Saiyyid Ali al-Mirghani, calling for unity with Egypt. It was more nationalist than the Ashiqqa, demanding dominion status under the Egyptian crown rather than complete incorporation. One of its leading members was Mirghani Hamza, an engineer. It boycotted the elections for the Legislative Assembly but participated in the Constitutional Amendment Commission of 1951. It served in the first government after independence but after the Prime Minister Ismail al-Azhari disavowed union with Egypt, it became the nucleus of the People's Democratic Party. The second National Front was set up in November 1960 after a protest by Azhari and Saiyyid Siddiq al-Mahdi at the military regime of General Abboud and called for the restoration of the 1956 Constitution and for elections. It was supported both by the Islamic Charter Front and the Sudanese Communist Party. In June 1961 its leaders Azhari, Abd Allah Khalil, Muhammad Ahmad Mahjoub and Abd al-Khaliq Mahjoub were sent into detention in Juba where they remained until January 1962. After the overthrow of Abboud some of the leaders of the Front issued a National Charter which served as a programme of action for the government of Sirr al-Khatim al-Khalifah which some of them entered. The third National Front was established in opposition to Nimeiri soon after his take-over. It consisted of a coalition of the leaders of the traditional parties, the Umma led by Sadiq al-Mahdi, the National Unionist Party, led by Yusuf al-Hindi, and the ICF under Hassan Turabi. It declared two major aims, the revival of Islam in a modern progressive state and the guarantee of democratic rights. In January 1973 the Government claimed to have averted a "naïve and low-level" plot by NF leaders to assassinate the President and in September 1975 another plot failed. Mahdi and Hindi were in exile, receiving encouragement from Libya, Ethiopia and Iraq. Training camps for guerrillas were set up abroad and in July 1976 2,000 exiles based in Libya, strengthened by some mercenaries, infiltrated back into Khartoum. It was hoped that there would also be a military mutiny and a civilian uprising. An attempt to seize Nimeiri at the airport as he returned from state visits to Paris and Washington was frustrated by his early arrival but the insurgents seized Omdurman Radio and the army HQ and there was serious fighting for 24 hours in the course of which

an estimated 1,000 people were killed. There was no mutiny nor popular rising in their support. Later 81 people were executed without the possibility of appeal and Mahdi and Hindi were sentenced to death *in absentia*. Egypt and Saudi Arabia promised help against any further attempts to overthrow the regime. Nimeiri then made considerable changes to give his government a more democratic appearance and the NF started to split. During 1977 Mahdi and Turabi were reconciled with Nimeiri while Hindi remained in exile. The National Reconciliation effectively brought the NF to an end although some 3,000 dissidents giving allegiance to Hindi continued to resist for some years in Libya and Ethiopia.

NATIONAL FRONT FOR THE SALVATION OF LIBYA

After the call by Qadafi for a Libyan Cultural Revolution a series of senior figures sought refuge abroad and attempted to organise opposition groups. In 1975 two of his closest associates, Umar al-Muhayshi and Abd al-Munim al-Huni, having failed to overthrow him in a military coup, set up the Libyan National Rally which was allowed to broadcast from Cairo. This later merged with the Libyan Democratic Front, founded by the former Prime Minister Mahmud al-Maghribi to form the Libyan Democratic National Rally. Meanwhile Abd al-Hamid Bakkush who had been Prime Minister under the Monarchy had founded the Libyan Liberation Organisation. These groups were largely ineffective, confining their activities to occasional propaganda as were the Libyan National Movement which was financed by the Baath Party of Iraq and the monarchist Libyan Constitutional Union, based on Manchester. More important than any of these was the National Front for the Salvation of Libya founded in October 1981 by Muhammad Yusuf Mughariaf who until his defection had been Ambassador in India. He had been a lecturer at Benghazi University when 10 students were hanged for opposing government control of their union. The NFSL published an English-language newspaper and broadcast from Omdurman where President Nimeiri made it welcome as a reprisal for Qadafi's support of the Sudanese opposition. In April 1982 Muhayshi, Bakkush and Mughariaf met in Mogadishu and agreed to collaborate. In January 1983 Mughariaf claimed that two Colonels supporting his organisation had been shot for attempting a coup: there were regular rumours of plots to assassinate Qadafi. In March 1983 the NFSL petitioned the Delhi Non-Aligned Conference for moral support. The NFSL publicised atrocities within Libya and organised demonstrations in European cities. Their activities incensed Qadafi who demanded the killing of "stray dogs" and exiles were murdered in several countries although the attempt in Cairo on Bakkush held up the Libyans to international condemnation and ridicule. In the course of a demonstration outside the Libyan Embassy in London in April 1984, a diplomat fired a shot from within which killed a policewoman, leading to the breach of diplomatic relations between London and Tripoli. Consisting mainly of professional people and students, the NFSL preached no particular ideology beyond a desire to make Libya a Western-style democracy, uniting Muslim and liberal opinions. It was believed to have help from the Americans and money from Saudi Arabia. It had a military wing, the General Command of the Salvation Corps under a former senior officer Ahmad Ahwas who was killed in an attack on Qadafi's bunker in May 1984. The NSFL in 'Communique Number One' claimed responsibility but, although there were up to 4,000 arrests the incident showed that the people were either too cowed or too contented to seize the opportunity to get rid of the regime. The survivors were hanged in front of the TV cameras. In March 1984 Qadafi had ordered the bombing of Omdurman to silence its radio but the following year, after the overthrow of Nimeiri, he succeeded in doing so with a large sum to the successor regime: Saddam Hussein took over as chief patron of the Libyan opposition. President Hissene Habre gave training facilities to disgruntled Libyan soldiers captured in Chad to reform, with American help, as the Libyan National Army: after they had been forced to leave Chad, 350 of them under Colonel Khalifah Haftar were taken to the USA in May 1991. Meanwhile in January 1987 eight opposition groups meeting in Cairo under the chairmanship of Huni agreed to co-ordinate their activities but in July he met Qadafi leading to a split in the movement. Much of the activity of the Libyan opposition was purely verbal – during 1989 Maghariaf proposed that the remaining nine members of the Revolution Command Council should form a transitional government to prepare for elections for a Constituent Assembly and nine groups formed a Democratic Alliance under Mansur Kikhia but growing Islamic fundamentalism within the country presented a greater threat to the regime. The third National Congress of the opposition was held in Dallas in April 1992. Algeria, incensed by Qadafi's support for the Front Islamique du Salut started to help his opponents. In October 1993 Bakkush claimed that a military rebellion in Eastern Libya, which was reported to have been crushed by bombing and by the Revolutionary Committees had been organised by his faction. Qadafi's deputy, Major Jalloud was reported under arrest and in March 1994 55 officers were sentenced to death. The external opposition was shaken by the mysterious disappearance of Kikhia on a visit to Cairo in December 1993.

NATIONAL GUIDANCE COMMITTEE
(West Bank)
After the signature of the Camp David agreements between 100 and 150 leading residents, mayors, journalists, teachers and representatives of religious, professional, trade union bodies etc., of the occupied West Bank held a meeting in Bayt Hanina on 1 October 1978. They rejected the proposed autonomy with demands for full self-determination, the withdrawal of Israeli troops and the re-establishment of Arab sovereignty over East Jerusalem and declared that there could be no substitute for the Palestine Liberation Organisation, whose local branch, the Palestine National Front, had just been outlawed by the Military Governor. They established a committee, on which the Mayor of Nablus Bassam Shakaa was the most prominent member and on which radicals supporting the Popular Front for the Liberation of Palestine and

the Democratic Front for the Liberation of Palestine had more influence than more moderate adherents of Fatah or links with Jordan. It issued a statement reaffirming the right to "resist Israeli rule by all ways and means", condemned new settlements, the closure of educational institutions and other "measures of collective punishment". The NGC attempted to co-ordinate the resistance to the occupying forces. The group was always short of money as funds from nationalists abroad were channelled through the PLO which retained them for its own purposes. Some leaders of the NGC were deported from their homeland, others put under house arrest and there were attempts to murder others such as Shakaa. After the establishment of Civil Administration in November 1981 the NGC was officially outlawed and the next major wave of unrest took place under different leadership.

NATIONAL PARTY (Syria)
al-Hizb al-Watani. The National Bloc which had led Syria to independence broke up once it had been achieved. The ruling group, based on Damascus, constituted itself in August 1947 the National Party under the leadership of the President Shukri al-Quwatli, Jamil Mardam, Sabri al-Assali and others. It exploited Arab nationalism but had no particular programme or organisation and was little more than an instrument for furthering political careers. It was successful in the 1947 elections and was the ruling party at the time of the coup of Husni al-Zaim who dissolved all political organisations. The Party, and its rival People's Party were revived after the coup of Sami al-Hinnawi and were again banned by Adib al-Shishakli in November 1951 re-emerging after his overthrow. Both opposed military rule but found it difficult to co-operate as each was preoccupied with defending its own fief. The principal difference between them was on foreign policy for while the Shaabists favoured close relations with Iraq, the National Party leaned towards Egypt and Saudi Arabia but Sabri al-Assali while Prime Minister removed even that difference. Contesting the freely-conducted elections in the autumn of 1954 it gained only 19 seats out of 142 but provided in Faris al-Khouri the leader of a brief and unstable coalition which ended in splitting the Party. In August 1955 the two conservative parties collaborated to secure the defeat of Khalid al-Azm in the Presidential election but soon quarrelled over offices and their feuding made possible the rise of more left-wing parties such as the Baath. They were swept willy-nilly into union with Egypt during which all parties were banned and never really recovered after it broke up.

NATIONAL PROGRESSIVE FRONT (Syria)
After years of struggles within the Syrian Baath Party were ended by the victory in 1970 of Hafiz al-Assad, the new President felt the need to widen his basis of support by giving other left-wing groupings some formal share of power although most of them were already unofficially represented in the Government. After a year of bargaining the Charter of the National Progressive Front was signed in March 1972. This provided for an 18-man central leadership composed of the President, nine other members of the Baath and two

representatives each of four other groups, the Syrian Communist Party, the Arab Socialist Union (an insignificant group of Nasserists), the Socialist Unionists (also Nasserists) and the Arab Socialist Party. The leadership would be concerned with internal and external political issues but political activity amongst the armed forces and students would remain a monopoly of the Baath. Their inclusion in the NPF gave the Communists a formal legitimacy but it led to a split in their ranks, and also those of the Socialist Unionists which left the Baath more dominant than ever. The Front enabled the Baath to share responsibility for unpopular decisions. Only parties belonging to the NPF were allowed to contest elections. In 1977 36 independent candidates were allowed to be elected in addition to the 159 NPF members. In November 1981 the Communist Party presented a separate list of candidates, all of whom were defeated, and there were no independents. In the election of 1986 the Communists stood as part of the NPF, being given 9 seats while the Independents were allowed to take 35.

NATIONAL PROGRESSIVE UNION PARTY (Egypt)

Hizb al-Tagammu' al-Taqaddumi al-Wahdawi. In October 1975 Anwar Sadat permitted the formation within the only legal party, the Arab Socialist Union of three platforms representing the right, left and centre streams of opinion. The left, the National Progressive Union, was led by the former Free Officer Khalid Mohieddin and Dr Rifaat al-Said, a Marxist journalist. In the general election of October 1976 it nominated 61 candidates, winning four seats and the following month was permitted to register as a political party separate from the ASU. Stressing that it was not Marxist, although it certainly had some amongst the leadership including those who had supported Ali Sabri, it recruited amongst the industrial workers of Cairo and Alexandria and had a considerable following of intellectuals, "enlightened" Muslims who did not wish to impose Islam by law, Pan-Arabists and Copts. It stood for state ownership of industry, free trade unions, the exclusion of foreign investment from key industries, the end of dependency upon America and greater support for the Palestinians, whose flag it flew outside its Cairo HQ. It was alone amongst the parties in opposing the bilateral Egyptian-Israeli Peace Treaty and it attacked the corruption and lack of overall planning that followed the *Infitah* (Open Door) policy. In May 1978 Sadat "invited" the Party to dissolve itself and upon its refusal encouraged the formation of the "loyal" left wing Socialist Labour Party to draw support from the NPUP. The NPUP itself was harassed by the Government, its newspaper *al-Ahali* frequently confiscated and it lost its two seats in the general election of June 1979. Some of its members were arrested in Sadat's purge of September 1981 but were released by Mubarak. It contested the elections of May 1984 but although the only party to emphasise social welfare, attracted only 4.2% of the votes, failing to win a seat. In 1985 it claimed a membership of 170,000. For the 1987 election the NPUP tried to form a united opposition to the Government National Democratic Party but was unable to reach agreement with the New Wafd.

Attracting only 2.2% it won no seats. Unlike the rest of the opposition, the NPUP contested the elections of November 1990 in which six of its candidates including Mohieddin were returned.

NATIONAL RECONCILIATION (Sudan) (1977/8)

The failure of the National Front attempt to seize power in July 1976 showed that it could only hope to prevail with the help of foreign forces while at the same time its near-success made it clear that President Nimeiri needed the support of Egypt to stay in power indefinitely: this situation inevitably meant interference by outsiders in the affairs of the Sudan. Nimeiri therefore made various changes to give his regime a more democratic appearance. He also cemented relations with Saudi Arabia which had sympathies with his opponents in the banned Islamic Charter Front. In April 1977 he was re-elected for a second six-year term after gaining 99.1% of the votes in a referendum and felt strong enough to offer his opponents the opportunity of returning from exile and prison to participate in political life. In July he met the NF leader Sadiq al-Mahdi secretly, then issued a general amnesty and released several hundred political detainees. The leading exiles, apart from Sharif Yusuf al-Hindi agreed to join the Central Committee of the Sudan Socialist Union, giving up their hopes of reviving their old parties. There were expectations that Saiyyid Sadiq might become Prime Minister. Some NF training camps in Libya were wound up. Promises were made that the security apparatus would be curbed, that the press would have more freedom, that civil liberties would be respected and that there would also be fair elections to all posts. Nimeiri also promised a foreign policy less linked to that of Egypt and the USA. In April 1978 a further agreement was signed in April by Hindi and others in which the Government agreed that the constitution provided for freedom of movement, of expression, the right of all to participate in public life, the autonomy of the judiciary and the opening of the SSU in which all posts should be filled by election to all citizens. In the event these guarantees were not honoured and Saiyyid Sadiq resigned from the SSU in protest in October 1978; he was particularly angered by Nimeiri's complete support for the Camp David Agreements. Hassan Turabi, leader of the ICF became Attorney-General and took the opportunity to put forward a long-term project for introducing *Shariah* and the establishment of an Islamic state. Sharif Hindi remained in exile until his death.

NATIONAL SOCIALIST PARTY (Jordan)

In Trans-Jordan prior to 1948 there were no political parties based on ideology but this situation changed when the population was augmented by better-educated Palestinians. In October 1950 Sulayman al-Nabulsi asked for a licence to form a party but this was not permitted to operate freely until July 1954. The National Socialists, non-Marxist in that they did not call for the class war, shared many of the ideals of the Baath, a unified Arab state as Jordan could not exist alone, the narrowing of gaps between rich and poor, and regarding feudalism and imperialism as "the source of all our miseries". Its members, prosperous but progressive businessmen and liberal professionals, rejected the resting of Jordan on Hashemite traditions and royal despotism. It was prepared to co-operate with the Jordanian Communist Party and had about a quarter of the members in the second and third Parliaments although it lost heavily in the elections for the fourth which were rigged by Tawfiq Abu al-Huda. It opposed the payment by London of the subsidy for the Arab Legion into an account administered by British officers instead of into the Jordanian Treasury and vehemently attacked the Baghdad Pact. The elections of October 1956, the freest held in Jordan, made the NS the strongest party and King Hussain asked Nabulsi to form a Cabinet which he did with members of his own party in the key ministries but with others given to a Baathist and a communist. The Ministry became increasingly revolutionary, seeking support from other Arab states but the dismissal of Nabulsi in April 1957 followed by the Zerka Incident resolved the struggle in the King's favour. Martial Law was proclaimed at the end of the month and all parties banned.

NATIONAL UNION (Egypt)

al-Ittihad al-Qawmi. By the end of 1956 it was clear that the Liberation Rally was ineffective in organising popular support for the policies of President Nasser. A new Constitution required the election of a National Assembly and the National Union was created to select candidates and exclude all who were deemed "imperialist agents, reactionaries and opportunists". More than half the 2,500 candidates who presented themselves for the 350 seats were declared disqualified by a committee presided over by Abd al-Latif al-Baghdadi. All citizens were potential members, although they had to apply and pay a small subscription and it was theoretically a pyramid, based on units in every village but Nasser as its Chairman, Sadat as its Secretary-General and Ministers dominated its executive committee. Its slogan was "Socialism, Co-operativism and Democracy" and it was to be a "school" for "liaison between the Government and the people" and end all forms of exploitation. It was never consulted on major matters of policy. After the formation of the United Arab Republic Kamal al-Din Hussain was put in charge of organising an elaborate secretariat for the Egyptian Region and Abd al-Hakim Amer was ordered to give priority to extending it throughout Syria, where, as in Egypt, no other party was permitted. In 1959 the ownership of all newspapers and periodicals was transferred to the National Union. After the Syrians broke away, in October 1961 Nasser dissolved the National Union, declaring that it had been infiltrated and paralysed by the forces of reaction. It was replaced by the Arab Socialist Union.

al-NAYIF, Abd al-Razzaq, Colonel (1934–78)

Iraqi Prime Minister. He was born in Ramadi and graduated from the Military Academy in 1953. After Staff College he became an instructor and staff officer until 1964 when he was posted to Military Intelligence as Deputy Director. He was the chief liaison officer between President Abd al-Rahman Arif and Prime Minister Tahir Yahya and the intelligence service, res-

ponsible for keeping them informed of plots. He conspired with Colonel Ibrahim al-Daud, Commander of the Republican Guard to seize power but, feeling it necessary to have some form of political façade, allied with military members of the Baath such as General Ahmad Hassan al-Bakr. On 17 July 1968 in a palace coup rather than a revolution they took power with Nayif as Prime Minister heading a Cabinet which was a mixture of members of the Baath and independents: Daud was Minister of Defence and Bakr President. Nayif declared that socialism had twice failed, that the country had been plagued by corruption, chaos, economic deterioration, exorbitant prices and espionage. Some supporters of President Nasser and some left-wingers were arrested. Those responsible for defeat in the June War would be identified and the Iraqi forces strengthened. Nayif was vaguely pro-Western and also inclined to co-operate with President Nasser while the Baath opposed these policies on ideological grounds. A fortnight after the coup, taking advantage of the absence abroad of Daud, which left his ally the Chief of Staff Hardan al-Takriti in charge of the forces, and having secured the support of key commanders, Bakr invited Nayif to lunch after which he was arrested at gunpoint by Saddam Hussain and placed on an aircraft to Morocco. Subsequently he took Jordanian nationality and travelled between there and London. The Iraqi Government regarded him as dangerous and in July 1970 condemned him to death; in February 1972 in London he survived a murder attempt in which his wife was wounded. On 9 July 1978 he was shot outside the Intercontinental Hotel in Park Lane and died in hospital the following day. Iraqi diplomats suspected of helping the killers were expelled. His two assassins claimed that he was an enemy of the Palestinians – one was condemned to life imprisonment while the other, who pleaded guilty, received a lesser sentence.

NAZIR, Hisham (1932–)

Saudi Arabian Oil Minister. A member of a distinguished Hijazi family, he was educated at Victoria College, Alexandria before taking a degree in political science from the University of California, Los Angeles. He entered government service as a legal adviser in 1958 in the Petroleum Department which was then under the supervision of Prince Faysal who spotted Nazir's ability. In 1960 he was appointed assistant to Abd Allah al-Tariki and thus was associated with OPEC from its beginning. When Ahmad Zaki Yamani succeeded Tariki as Minister of Oil in March 1962, Nazir became Deputy Minister. Obviously a highly efficient technocrat he was President of the Central Planning Organisation, and with the full support of the King, produced the first Five-Year Plan in 1970. He became Minister of Planning in October 1975 and replaced Yamani in December 1986. A quiet, courteous, rather shy man, he avoided the flamboyant attitudes of his predecessor and took pains not to antagonise the Royal Family. Nazir was soon on friendly terms with the future President Bush and the future Secretary of State Baker, men with oil interests in Texas that were threatened by low prices. At the same time he believed that excessively high prices would damage the world economy and in particular developing countries. He was forced to back down in the face of the more aggressive approach of Iraq and Iran in the summer of 1990 but after the invasion of Kuwait, supervised a great increase in production. He published numerous studies on petroleum questions.

NEGUIB, Muhammad, General (1901–82)

Egyptian President. His father was an army officer of peasant descent and his mother Sudanese, he was born in Khartoum and educated at Gordon College. He was commissioned in 1918 and spent his early service in the Sudan where he became involved with the nationalist White Flag League and was recalled to Egypt. He took Degrees in Law and in Political Science and founded and edited an army journal in which he advocated military training in schools and conscription. Neguib served in the Frontier Corps and attended Staff College in England. In 1942 he wished to resign after the humiliation of King Farouq in the Abdin Incident. As a Brigadier he fought in the Palestine War, showing exceptional courage and being three times wounded. He then commanded the Senior Officers School and the Frontier Corps and was appointed Inspector-General of Infantry. He was admired throughout the army for his leadership and integrity and in January 1952 he infuriated the King by accepting nomination as President of the Officers Club, easily defeating a royal nominee, notorious for incompetence and corruption: Farouq declared the election invalid and subsequently refused to accept Neguib as Minister of War. According to his own and some other accounts he had been approached in 1949 by two younger officers, Majors Amer and Nasser, learned of dissatisfaction in the army and accepted the chairmanship of the Free Officers: according to other accounts, such as that of Sadat, Neguib was only their third choice for a titular leader and knew nothing of their plans until just before the July Revolution in which he played no personal part. He then issued proclamations, assumed the post of Commander-in-Chief, approved the appointment of a new Cabinet under Ali Mahir, supervised the dignified departure of the King and appointed a Council of Regency. The Revolutionary Command Council set up committees for land reform and the investigation of corrupt politicians and his unwillingness to implement these measures led to the resignation of Ali Mahir on 7 September 1952: Neguib replaced him as Prime Minister at the head of a Cabinet otherwise composed of civilians. In December the RCC proclaimed him "Leader of the Revolution" and on 18 June 1953, President of the Republic. He continued as Prime Minister but had to bring some officers, including Nasser, into the Government. Neguib's greatest success during this period lay in the conclusion of the Anglo-Egyptian Agreement on the Sudan. Extremely popular there and sensitive to the aspirations of its people, he realised that Sudan would be a more reliable custodian of the Nile waters as a friendly independent state than as a sullen province of Egypt. He reached an agreement with Abd al-Rahman al-Mahdi that cut the ground from under the feet of the British who had relied upon the Saiyyid's unwillingness to compromise with Egypt. He was less successful in dealing with the problem of the Suez

Canal Zone and in May 1953 talks were broken off. Domestically he thought that once the worst rascals had been swept away Egypt would become and stay a genuine democracy. In January 1953 all former political parties were dissolved and the Liberation Rally set up under his chairmanship. He was exceptionally popular, touring widely, fraternising with the Copts and Jews, and with his pipe, was seen as a benevolent, smiling, cunning but kindly old uncle; he made the Revolution acceptable. Sadat said that the RCC "built a legend around him but he was simply a puppet" but, relying upon his popularity, Neguib started to complain that decisions were taken behind his back and to demand a veto over them and over military and political appointments. He felt that the officers should make way for politicians – a view uncongenial to Nasser and others who wanted a tight, harsh, efficient military oligarchy. On 23 February 1954, after the RCC had banned the Muslim Brothers after a clash between its supporters and members of the Liberation Rally, Neguib resigned in an attempt to force Nasser's hand. Despite his peasant cunning, however, he was no match for his opponent as a conspirator. Neguib was put under house arrest but there were widespread demonstrations in his favour and the possibility that some of the army, particularly the cavalry under the influence of Khalid Mohieddin, would restore him by force. Neguib had been due to go to Khartoum for the independence celebrations and the Sudanese also demanded his release. After two days an arrangement was made by which Neguib resumed the Presidency, saying that this was on the understanding that parliamentary life would be restored after free elections, while Nasser became Prime Minister. Neguib went to Khartoum but encountered a violent demonstration by the Ansar. On 9 March Nasser who had used his ten days as Prime Minister to purge supporters of Neguib from the army and trade unions, restored the office to the President. The difficulties with the RCC did not decrease and a period of unrest showed that his popularity with people, who saw him as standing for democracy was ineffective against the force of the army. Members of the Liberation Rally were dragooned into demonstrating against him. Neguib had a nervous breakdown and was forced to resign as Prime Minister on 17 April. He was also dropped from the RCC but continued as titular President while all power passed into Nasser's hands. He played no part in the renewed negotiations for the Anglo-Egyptian Treaty which led to the British withdrawal from the Canal Zone. On 26 October a Muslim Brother attempted to assassinate Nasser and the RCC, claiming that Neguib had known of the plot, removed him from the Presidency. He was placed under arrest in a suburban villa where he was kept for sixteen years, being released by Sadat after Nasser's death. He took no part in politics and was given a military funeral led by President Mubarak. He published his memoirs.

NEO-DESTOUR (Tunisia)

By the early 1930s the Destour Party, the only group that sought Tunisian independence, appeared traditionalist, middle class, confined to the capital and inactive; it was clearly making little impact upon the French authorities. In 1932 a group of dynamic young,

Western-educated provincials, led by Habib Bourguiba and Mahmud Materi started a newspaper, *L'Action Tunisienne* to demand more vigorous policies and in March 1934, meeting at Kassar Hallal, they formed a breakaway group which they called the Neo-Destour. Materi was elected President and Bourguiba Secretary-General. They started a noisy propaganda campaign for independence and a constitution and set out to organise support groups throughout the country: though mostly secular in outlook, they used Islam to attract the uneducated. In September 1934 the leaders were sent into forced residence in the South. The French Popular Front Government of 1936 released them and they resumed their campaign, paying particular attention to the organised workers whose leaders, Farhat Hashid, Habib Achour and Ahmad Tlili also held high rank in the Party. In July 1937 the former leader of the Destour, Shaykh Abd al-Aziz al-Thaalibi returned from exile and tried to reassert the supremacy of his brand of bourgeois and Islamic nationalism. Neo-Destour militants broke up his meetings and the older group lost its credibility. By the end of 1937 Neo-Destour claimed 400 branches, a youth wing and paid organisers. In March 1938 the Central Committee decided to embark on a campaign of civil disobedience and illegal demonstrations. Materi disapproved and resigned but Bourguiba and others were jailed and the Party officially banned after some bloody riots on 9 April that were later commemorated as "Martyrs' Day". They had, however, prepared for this to happen and a "second wave" of leaders, such as Dr Thameur and Taiyib Slim were able to maintain a clandestine organisation. When they in turn were caught, a "third wave" took over. During the war the imprisoned Bourguiba insisted that the nationalists should not collaborate with the occupying Germans and Italians and after his release he continued anxious to co-operate with the French to obtain independence: rejected, he spent much of the late 1940s abroad while Salih Ben Yusuf organised the Party as Secretary-General. In September 1946 the Neo-Destour agreed to work with the moderate nationalists for independence, an extremely important decision as it reversed the previous policy of militancy and exposed it to accusations of treachery from extremists. In August 1950 Ben Yusuf was the first Party member to accept government offices, becoming Minister of Justice in the Cabinet of Muhammad Chenik. In January 1952 the French launched a new crackdown and most of the Neo-Destour leaders escaped abroad. Those who remained underground started a campaign of violence against French settlers and government institutions and the *Fellagha* leaders were closely linked with the Party. In July 1953 the Neo-Destour was suspected of murdering the Crown Prince, Izz al-Din. In July 1954, seeing no other way to end the bloodshed, the French Prime Minister Pierre Mendes-France made the Carthage Declaration in which he accepted the principle of Tunisian autonomy and the following month a government under Tahar Ben Ammar was formed to negotiate the details. The *Fellagha* laid down their arms at the behest of the Party. The Government contained several leading Neo-Destour figures including Mongi Slim who played a leading part in settling the terms of the Franco-Tunisian

Autonomy Agreeement which was signed in June 1955. Although it appeared to link Tunisia inextricably to France, Bourguiba who had returned the previous month urged its acceptance but Ben Yusuf who remained in Cairo vehemently opposed it as a capitulation to colonialism. Bourguiba persuaded him to return for a brief show of reconciliation but Ben Yusuf demanded a public debate within the Party. He was, however, outmanoeuvred by Bourguiba who had won the support of the Trade Unions under Ahmad Ben Salah in the Sfax National Congress and was deprived of the Secretary-Generalship. Ben Yusuf launched a terrorist campaign, was defeated and went into exile, leaving no possible challenger for Bourguiba. After complete independence was obtained in March 1956 elections were held for a Constituent Assembly in which practically all the seats were won by the Neo-Destour. The Party, enjoying overwhelming legitimacy from its role in the struggle for independence, now had to change from a war machine to an instrument for progress. Tunisia, effectively a one-party state, although there were a few legal communists until the Tunisian Communist Party, was banned in January 1963. In 1956 the Party defeated a challenge from Ben Salah, which claimed for the Unions equality in economic policy making and thenceforward Union leadership lost its independence but was brought into the highest Party levels. The Neo-Destour was the first Arab political party, unlike the Wafd, cohesive, disciplined and without local barons. It was strongly centralised with at the base about 2,000 local or professional cells, directed by an elected committee which took orders from the centre and controlled all political activity in its own sector. The veteran nationalist Ben Sulayman said that the Tunisian people had no voice in any matter – all it had to do was listen and applaud. Cells were expected to mobilise and educate their members rather than make proposals for national policy. The cells were grouped in 36 regional federations each with a committee elected by delegates from the cells. The central organisation consisted of the National President, Bourguiba, elected directly by Party members, the Political Committee of 10 elected by general vote, although members could be co-opted and a National Council, which rarely met, of the 36 regional chairmen with another 20 elected. There was also a National Congress of one representative from every cell which met only in 1959 and 1964. The Political Committee was all-powerful and its Secretary-General was responsible for Party discipline. No opposition was permitted. Membership was obligatory for all important posts inside and outside government. The Party also had feminine and youth groups, leadership and propaganda schools and *al-Amal*, the most important newspaper in the country. In foreign policy the Neo-Destour was usually friendly with the West and more interested in Africa, particularly the Maghreb, then in the Arab world. It was officially socialist but "Destourian Socialism" was never authoritatively defined until the Party in October 1964 held its seventh (Bizerta) Congress from which it emerged as the Parti Socialiste Destourien.

NEUF HISTORIQUES (Algeria)

After 1945 there were in Algeria and amongst Algerians abroad a considerable number of competing nationalist groups. Many of the younger men, disillusioned with the leadership of Messali Haj formed the Organisation Spéciale which was committed to obtaining independence by force. After the OS had been broken up in 1950 some of its former escaped to Paris or Cairo while others remained underground in Algeria. In March 1954 Muhammad Boudiaf arranged for a meeting in Switzerland of a group which constituted itself the Comité Révolutionnaire d'Unité et d'Action to plan a revolution. It is not clear whether its nine original members, later hailed as the Historic Chiefs, were present on this occasion or whether some were later co-opted. Their average age was 32 and all were literate although none would have been regarded as an intellectual. Of the nine three, Mustafa Ben Boulaid, Murad Didouche and Larbi Ben M'hidi were killed in action during the Algerian War of Independence, three, Muhammad Khidr, Belkasim Krim and Muhammad Boudiaf were killed by their fellow-Algerians for political reasons and three, Ahmad Ben Bella, Hocine Ait Ahmad and Rabah Bitat were, in 1993 still alive.

NEW WAFD (Egypt)

The original Wafd was dissolved with all the other pre-Revolutionary parties in January 1953 when Nasser introduced the single-party rule which lasted until 1976 when Sadat recognised the three "platforms" that had been officially formed within the Arab Socialist Union as separate political organisations. In May 1977 12 groups claiming to represent 5,000 former members decided to reform the Party and chose as their Presidents the former Secretary-General Fuad Siraj al-Din and Ibrahim Farraj, another pre-Revolution Minister. In February 1978 22 members of the National Assembly applied for registration as the New Wafd, the first freely constituted party to come into existence since 1952. Siraj al-Din declared that the real Egyptian Revolution had been the struggle of Zaghloul and the Wafd against the British while the July Revolution had been merely a military coup. In May the angry Sadat, ordering the "Party of the Pashas" to "stand aside", called a referendum on whether those holding to "atheist ideologies" or "responsible for corrupting public life" before 1952 should be allowed to take part in politics. He received the customary 98.29% vote and in June the New Wafd decided to disband in protest although some of its members continued to sit as Independents until they lost their seats in the general election of June 1979. Wafdists continued to criticise the regime over its policies towards Israel and towards the economy and its tolerance of corruption in its weekly newspaper and there were reports that the Party was regrouping under younger leadership, some of whom were rounded up in the purge of September 1981. In January 1984 the Supreme Court ruled that the New Wafd had not been legally dissolved, merely suspended, so was entitled to participate in the forthcoming general election. The following month Siraj al-Din was legally rehabilitated enabling the Party to claim continuity from its heroic days. Seen as centre-right, drawing its membership from middle-level civil servants and landowners, the New Wafd campaigned in May in alliance with the Muslim Brothers which, as a banned organisation, could not put forward its own candidates. It waged a sophisticated campaign on a programme of liberal-democratic socialism, balance between public and private sectors, a parliamentary rather than a presidential system, encouragement of competition, neutrality between the Super-Powers and it won 15% of the vote and 57 seats making it the sole opposition party. In addition it claimed to be the only party with roots in the nation as all the others had been created by Sadat. The New Wafd absorbed the National Front Party which had been refused permission to register. In the April 1987 election it refused to join the other opposition parties and the Muslim Brothers, fought on its own and still won 36 seats. It also did not join the other parties in voting for the re-election of President Mubarak on which it abstained. In the November 1990 general election the Party officially abstained, declaring the need for a new Constitution but 14 members were returned as Independents. The New Wafd denounced the occupation of Kuwait by Saddam Hussain before the Egyptian Government did so and it endorsed the sending of troops. Later it supported the Madrid Peace Conference. The New Wafd claimed 500,000 registered members and published its own newspaper *al-Masr al-Jadid*.

al-NIHAYYAN, Zaid b. Sultan (c. 1915–)

Ruler of Abu Dhabi and President of the United Arab Emirates. A son of Sultan b. Zaid al-Nihayyan who came to power by murdering his brother and was in turn murdered by another brother, Zaid as a boy was brought up in the desert out of the reach of his uncle. When the usurper was murdered in 1927 and Zaid's elder brother Shakhbut b. Sultan al-Nihhayan became Ruler their mother induced all her sons to take an oath of loyalty to him. Zaid observed this with exemplary fidelity for over thirty years serving as his brother's deputy, usually in the interior where he showed all the qualities, generosity, courage, endurance, sense of social justice and skill in falconry and wrestling most admired by the bedouins. He was also noted for his readiness to listen and ability to settle apparently intractable disputes. He was involved in several skirmishes against the tribal levies of Shaykh Rashid al-Maktum during the Abu Dhabi–Dubai War of 1945 to 1949. In 1952, believing that oil would be found in the area, the Saudis sent troops to the Buraymi Oasis and brought intense pressure, including the offer of the largest bribe in history, upon Zaid to admit their sovereignty but, with British support, he remained steadfast for over four years until they were expelled. In 1960 oil was found in Abu Dhabi, then a wretchedly poor village of *barastis* without schools, hospitals and even roads. Money started to flow in but Shaykh Shakhbut was deeply suspicious of the possible effects of rapid social change and of the motives of the numerous foreign businessmen who poured in, anxious to help him to spend his new wealth and he was unwilling to initiate the development schemes that the British considered essential to the security of the area. They therefore threatened Zaid that unless he deposed his brother, they would replace him themselves with another branch of the family and, after much hesitation, he agreed to do so in August 1966. The result of the change of Ruler was the extremely rapid transformation of Abu Dhabi into an ultra-modern city with many prestige projects including an international airport and an industrial complex at Ruwais. Although himself barely literate, Zaid realised the importance of education founding many schools and a University at al-Ayn which he always regarded as his home. Through his shrewdness, his generosity and his unwillingness to refuse requests, which were often imposed upon him in the early days, but he did much to help less fortunate Arabs through the Abu Dhabi Fund for Arab Economic Development. He was also a lavish supporter of Muslim causes world-wide. He brought back members of the Al Nihayyan who had been in exile and potentially dangerous during the reign of Shakhbut and also gave important responsi-bilities to talented outsiders with University degrees. In 1968 as the British announced their impending with-drawal from the Gulf, Zaid realised the vulnerability of very small, very rich states and started work to unite them making the Simayh Agreement which provided for a federation of Abu Dhabi and Dubai. The Dubai Agreement, signed a week later, provided for the creation of a Federation of Arab Emirates comprising nine states but internal jealousies showed that it would be unworkable although a meeting of the Rulers in Abu Dhabi in October 1969 agreed that Shaykh Zaid would be its President. The hope of a Federation collapsed in the autumn of 1971 after Bahrain and Qatar declared their independence and a smaller union of the seven former Trucial States came into existence in December as the United Arab Emirates with Zaid as President. For the next two decades his primary object was to hold the Union together until it should become unthinkable for the individual members to think of secession. In order to accomplish this Zaid was pre-pared to pay very much more than Abu Dhabi's fair share of the administrative costs and to accept the prac-tical equality of Dubai despite its minimal contribution to Union funds. His attempts to centralise authority, however, led to the Unification Crisis of the summer of 1976 during which he announced his readiness to leave office. The other Rulers feeling that he was indis-pensable agreed to constitutional changes which strengthened his powers. Al-Nihayyan's Presidency of United Arab Emirates gave him international standing. He ended the Udayd dispute with the Kingdom of Saudi Arabia and established good relations with Iran. The first meeting of the Gulf Co-operation Council in May 1981 was in Abu Dubai. He was concerned to end the isolation of the People's Democratic Republic of Yemen. In February 1988 he went to Tehran as rep-resentative of the Gulf Co-operation Council to try to mediate between Iran and Iraq. He was generally considered a moderate in OPEC although not always prepared to follow the Saudi line. He was a strong supporter of the Palestinians. He was the first to announce the oil boycott of the US after the June War. Always ready to try to mediate or give financial assist-ance, like Ibn Saud he was able to operate as bedouin tribal leader and international statesman. In public Al-Nihayyan is very dignified and aloof but in private is jovial and relaxed. He is very hard-working but goes in for long holidays in desert camps. He is an enthusiastic falconer. A pious Mulism he is nevertheless a tolerant man.

NIMEIRI, Jafar Muhammad (1930–)

Sudanese President and Prime Minister. The son of a door-keeper, he was educated at Wad Madani and at Hantoub Secondary School where he showed more aptitude for football than for academic studies. He graduated from the Military College in Khartoum and received further training in Egypt, West Germany and the USA. He took part in an attempted coup against the military regime of General Abboud and was impris-oned. In December 1966 he was again arrested after another unsuccesful conspiracy. He later fought in the South against the Anya Nya guerrillas and then com-manded the School of Infantry. In May 1969, as a Colonel, he was the most senior of a group of young officers which overthrew the elected government of Muhammad Ahmad Mahjoub and assumed the Chair-manship of the Revolutionary Command Council. He appointed himself Major-General, Commander-in-Chief and Minister of Defence. He expressed admir-ation for the achievements of Egypt's July Revolution and declared Sudan on the road to socialism. He aimed to weaken the traditional leadership; the National Assembly and all political parties were dissolved and their leaders imprisoned. Nimeiri appointed as Prime Minister Babikr Awadhallah, who was well known for his left-wing sympathies and a mainly civilian Cabinet which included at least two avowed members of the Sudanese Communist Party while two of their allies were on the RCC. Among the first acts of the new regime were to recognise East Germany, send a military delegation to Moscow, and declare that it would not resume relations with the USA or West Germany. Large and foreign-owned businesses were nationalised. Nimeiri expressed willingness to grant regional autonomy to the South. At the end of October, after Awadhallah had made a speech in East Berlin about the indispensability of communist leadership, Nimeiri dismissed him and himself became Prime Minister. He visited Moscow as he still needed communist support for there were two plots against him reported before the end of the year and early in 1970 the Ansar rose and were bloodily crushed at Aba Island. He toured Eastern Europe, visited Peking, and there were reports that there were 3,000 Russian military advisers in Sudan. Nimeiri had attended the Rabat Summit in December 1969 and had begun discussions with Nasser and Qadafi, both noted for their harsh treatment of their own communists, for the formation of a Feder-ation of Arab Republics. He aspired to a leading role in Arab affairs and showed considerable personal courage in bringing about a cease-fire during the fighting in Amman in Black September. Nimeiri, having used the communists, became doubtful of their ulti-mate loyalty, started purging them from key positions in the army and in May 1971 announced the creation of a single legal party, the Sudan Socialist Union, in which they would be absorbed. The SCP leader Abd al-Khaliq Mahjoub and his supporters on the RCC such as Colonel Babikr al-Nur conspired against Nimeiri and on 19 July 1971 they succeeded in arresting him and announcing a new "national democratic front". On 22 July units loyal to Nimeiri overpowered the plotters who were shot after summary courts martial. Nimeiri called for an immediate round-up of all communists, ordered out several Russian diplomats and military advisers, denounced the "new imperialists" and visited Saudi Arabia where he established friendly links with King Faysal. Later he resumed diplomatic relations with the USA, restored some British property nationalised after his take-over and visited London. In March 1973 after the murder of the American Ambassador, Nimeiri closed the office in Khartoum of the Palestine Liberation Organisation. He had already broken with Iraq which had supported the coup of July 1971, and with Libya and Egypt after preventing Libyan aircraft overflying Sudan to assist Idi Amin of Uganda. Sudanese troops confronting the Israelis on the Suez Canal were withdrawn. At home there was little further mention of socialism, the RCC disappeared and Nimeiri sought to establish the legitimacy of his regime by holding a referendum on his nomination as President which was approved in October 1971 by 3,800,000 votes to 56,000 and issuing in January 1972 the draft of a permanent constitution which listed the national aims of liberation from economic exploitation, bureaucratic coercion, sectarian and tribal duress, amendment of obsolete laws, the eradication of backwardness, agrarian reform, sexual equality and family welfare through education, health and social security services. This came into effect the following year and a new People's Assembly with all members nominated by the SSU was opened in October 1972. Early in 1972 Nimeiri achieved a major success in ending the guerrilla warfare in the South by concluding the Addis Ababa Agreement which set up an autonomous regional government and included a general amnesty: until the agreement was broken by Nimeiri there was no further trouble in the South. Nimeiri profited from the good relations that he had now established with the West to borrow money to launch over ambitious, ill conceived and worse executed schemes of development, aimed at turning the Sudan into "the bread-basket of the Arab world". The national debt doubled in a year and in a decade Sudan was one of the world's most heavily indebted states, owing $9,000 million upon which its import earnings of $800 million unable to cover the interest. In the event it was estimated that only $2,000 million was actually spent on development as international businessmen moved in and there were rumours of corruption involving members of the President's family. Shortage of foreign currency meant lack of equipment and of spare parts and further loans had to be sought. In May 1979 after an agreement with the IMF there were riots against the consequent increase in prices. The former politicians continued their opposition, old opponents like Sadiq al-Mahdi and Yusuf al-Hindi and the Muslim Brothers all uniting in the National Front which received the backing of Nimeiri's external foes, in particular Libya. There was a series of plots; one to kill the President in January 1973 involved communists and Islamic fundamentalists while another in September 1975 by a small group of army officers succeeded in seizing the radio station but was unable to profit further because its

leader had lost the draft of his speech. Ten people were killed in the fighting after which the constitution was amended to confer new powers on the President. In July 1976 there was a major attempt to overthrow the regime when some 2,000 men armed by Qadafi infiltrated into Khartoum hoping to promote a civilian uprising and a military mutiny co-ordinated by the National Front; it only failed after heavy fighting in which an estimated 1,000 people were killed. Subsequently 81 people were executed. For protection against Libya, with which he broke off relations, Nimeiri drew very close to Egypt, signing first a defence pact and later in 1982 an Integration Charter which was to lead to eventual union of the two states. He was one of the few Arab supporters of Anwar Sadat after the signature of the Camp David Agreement and worked hard to end the consequent boycott of Egypt. He also signed a defence agreement with Saudi Arabia which he gratified by summoning the Taizz Conference, an attempt to wean Somalia and South Yemen away from their dependence on the Soviet Union, and also by imposing restrictions on alcohol and gambling but later his pro-Egyptian stance weakened this alliance. Following the fall of Haile Selassie, Nimeiri supported insurgents against the pro-Russian regime in Addis Ababa. He expelled the remaining Russian technicians and sought arms from France and America. It was reported that he was willing to stockpile arms for the American Rapid Deployment Force. After his re-election as President in April 1977 by 99.1% of the votes cast in a 98.3% poll, Nimeiri contrived to win over some of his exiled opponents in the National Reconciliation by promising greater democracy. There were still minor attempts at coups in December 1977, February 1978 and March 1979 after which he broke off relations with Iraq. Another conspiracy in March 1981 led to 10,000 arrests and quarrels with Syria and Russia. The Reconciliation did not last and some, such as Sadiq al-Mahdi, who had returned soon withdrew their support. Nimeiri reshuffled his Ministers several times a year to prevent them from establishing power bases or to use them as scapegoats. After riots over the removal of subsidies in November 1981 and in January 1982 there were large-scale dismissals of Ministers and SSU officials. Once, briefly, he handed over the Premiership to Rashid al-Tahir (Bakr) but he was never willing to share power with anyone of real substance. He quarrelled with long-time supporters of his regime such as Mansur Khalid who held him to ridicule in a savagely-written book and with senior army officers, many of the most able of which were retired. In 1978/9 Nimeiri was President of the Organisation of African Unity and made genuine efforts to settle disputes amongst its members, trying, for example, to mediate in the question of the Western Sahara. In May 1980 he was re-elected President, stating that it would be his final term but by now there were questions about his physical health and even his mental stability. He appeared to suffer from megalomania, promoted himself Field Marshal, hounded civil servants and judges over minor decisions and even personally sacked the coach of a football team. Hopes that the discovery of oil and the development of the Jonglei Canal would bring great wealth were disappointed, inflation soared and natural disasters caused widespread famine in which it was conservatively estimated that 500,000 died. Epidemics killed large numbers of children, particularly in the South. Bankruptcy threatened and, exploiting the hostility of Qadafi, Nimeiri called desperately for more Western aid: Sudan received more from America than any country in Africa apart from Egypt but only succeeded in misusing it. In December 1984 the US suspended $184 million in economic aid on the grounds of the mismanagement of the economy. While refugees flooded in from civil wars in Chad, Ethiopia and Uganda, many of the best educated Sudanese sought jobs abroad. Nimeiri was essentially a juggler who hoped by frequent administrative changes the right solution would emerge. The elected Regional Government in the South, while hardly ideal, was not unpopular locally but in 1982 Nimeiri decided to replace it by the redivison of the area into three provinces ruled by officials appointed from Khartoum. This, coupled with the fact that the South was obviously not receiving its fair share of development and even its oil was to be used for the benefit of the North, set off a rebellion – Anya Nya II. In the face of Southern revolt and Northern dissatisfaction at economic conditions, Nimeiri decided, with the advice of one of his closest confidants, Dr Hassan Turabi the leader of the Islamic Charter Front, to seek a new legitimacy through emphasis on Islam. In the September Laws of 1983 he decreed a revision of the country's legal code to link it to the *Shariah*. Although Nimeiri had once been known as a very hard drinker, he ordered that all alcohol should be dumped in the Nile. Criminals had their hands or feet amputated in public and on television and, according to Sadiq al-Mahdi, 200 people were mutilated in a single year – more than had suffered in Saudi Arabia in a quarter of a century. The introduction of Islamic taxation threw state finances into even deeper confusion. The September Laws made reconciliation with the South impossible and even devout Muslims opposed Nimeiri's interpretation of *Shariah*: one of the most repected, Mahmud Taha being hanged for his criticism. There was an atmosphere of terror as people were rounded up for these punishments upon scanty evidence, often merely denunciations, particularly during the application of martial law from April to September 1984. Nimeiri had two books published in his name – "The Islamic Way – Why" (*al-Nahj al-Islami li-Madha*) and "The Islamic Way – How? (*al-Nahj al-Islami Kayfa*). In July 1984 he carried his Islamic pretensions further by proposing to assume the title of Imam and demanding that officers should make *baya* to him personally. This did not, however, stop him from ingratiating himself with the US authorising the conduct of Operation Moses – the large-scale movement of Ethiopian Jews to Israel for which he is said to have received the larger part of $56 million paid to Swiss accounts. He was also said to have accepted money to permit the dumping of atomic waste in the desert. Discontent amongst the professional classes was shown by a series of strikes including ones by judges and doctors as they joined the students (the University was frequently closed) and the economically deprived in hostility to the regime. There were reported to be 35,000 malnourished children in Khartoum alone but

Nimeiri, saying "why do Sudanese need three meals a day?" increased the prices of bread, sugar and petrol by up to 100% at the behest of the IMF. There were five devaluations in three years. Nimeiri suddenly blamed all that had gone wrong on the Muslim Brothers and imprisoned their leaders including Turabi: the judge who had imposed amputations and 11 Ministers were dismissed. He then appointed General Siwar al-Dhahab Commander-in-Chief and Minister of Defence and departed on state visits to the USA and France. There was a spontaneous rising against him which the army declined to repress. A rally called by the SSU attracted less than 3,000 and showed that he had no popular support. Nimeiri, by then in Cairo, was unable to return home. The Egyptian Government refused to extradite him but kept him under observation and restricted access to him. His regime had lasted longer than any other since independence but had shown that neither the military nor politicians could satisfactorily govern the Sudan and he, like most other rulers, left the country worse off than he had found it. In the spring of 1989 as the government of Sadiq al-Mahdi stumbled from on crisis to another there were demonstrations in Khartoum calling for his return to power and after the take-over by General Bashir, Nimieri was said to be collecting his luggage in expectation of return. Disappointed he was said in November 1990 to be seeking Saudi and Ethiopian aid to overthrow Bashir.

al-NIMR, Abd al-Halim (c. 1912–60)
Jordanian Prime Minister. He came from Salt and after secondary education there graduated in Law from Damascus University. He was a founding member of the National Socialist Party of his relative Sulayman al-Nabulsi. He was Minister of Defence and the Interior in Nabulsi's Cabinet which was dismissed by King Hussain on 10 April 1957. The King, regarding Nimr as more moderate, then asked him to form a Cabinet but under pressure from his old colleagues, Nimr insisted that it should include some regarded by the King as communists. Hussain then asked Said al-Mufti to become Prime Minister but army officers led by Major-General Ali Abu Nuwar demanded that Nimr should take office with a programme of federal union with Egypt and Syria, opposition to foreign pacts, rejection of the Eisenhower Doctrine, respect for civil liberties and cleansing the administration. The King then asked Nimr to form a Cabinet which he did but before it could be presented to the Assembly Hussain had routed the conspirators against him in the Zerka Incident and appointed Hussain Fakhri al-Khalidi as Prime Minister. Nimr left politics and returned to his farm. He was much loved locally.

NIXON DOCTRINE
In July 1969, following the British decision to withdraw their forces from the Gulf, President Nixon made it clear in a speech in Guam that the US, deeply entangled in Vietnam, was not prepared to be the world policeman. He declared that the US would protect its allies against Russian aggression but that otherwise they must develop their own defensive arrangements. Special assistance would be given to selected states – in the

Middle East to Israel, Iran and Saudi Arabia. It became clear that the interests of Iran and Saudi Arabia were not identical and after a visit to Tehran in May 1972 Nixon decided that Iran was the more important. He ordered that the Shah should be allowed to buy whatever military equipment he wished. The Pentagon disapproved of this "blank cheque" but was overruled by the President and Secretary Kissinger. Saudi Arabia, a target of the Jewish lobby, was not given equal access to American weaponry. The rise in the price of oil after 1973 meant that Iran could spend enormous sums on equipment often too sophisticated for its personnel to use effectively. An objective of the Nixon Doctrine had been to cut the number of American service personnel abroad: in fact it had the opposite effect for a Senate report of 1976 showed that there were 26,000 American technicians in Iran.

NOUACEUR (Morocco)

In November 1941 American forces landed in Morocco, then ruled by the Vichy French. Combat troops were withdrawn a year later but several bases were maintained. In December 1950 within the framework of NATO the French agreed to continued use by the American Strategic Air Command of Sidi Sliman near Meknes, Ben Guerir near Marrakesh, Ben Sliman (Boulhaut) between Rabat and Casablanca and Nouaceur near Casablanca. They also had a naval air station at Port Lyautey and at the time of independence there were about 7,500 American military personnel and the same number of civilians at these bases. The bases brought about $50 million a year into the local economy. King Muhammad V who had not been consulted about the installation of these bases on Moroccan soil stated in March 1956 that the agreement made by France for their presence was invalid but he made no immediate demand for their removal. The problem was complicated by the continued involvement of the French. Disputes arose, however, between Moroccan workers and their American employers and the existence of the bases was taken up by left-wing politicians. Preliminary negotiations in May 1957 brought no results but were revived when the King visited Washington in November 1957 ending with a vague declaration of respect for the sovereignty of Morocco. During 1958 several incidents, including the belief that Nouaceur had been used as a staging post for the landing of troops in Lebanon, showed American lack of respect for Moroccan susceptibilities and in August the Minister of State for Foreign Affairs Muhammad Boucetta called for the evacuation of all foreign troops. In October 1959 the Prime Minister Abd Allah Ibrahim failed to obtain Washington's agreement to evacuation after two years although he did get a renewed assurance of recognition of Moroccan sovereignty. Two months later President Eisenhower visited Morocco and agreed to the evacuation of Boulhaut in 1960 and the rest over a four-year period. A follow-up agreement was negotiated by Hassan II and President Kennedy in March 1963 and the bases were handed over by the end of the year. Some naval elements remained at Kenitra (Port Lyautey) until 1978. In May 1982 a new agreement allowed the US to have transit use of certain airports, on which they would be authorised to con-struct facilities, during emergencies or for periodic training but they would not permanently station troops in Morocco.

NOUIRA, Hedi (1911–93)

Tunisian Prime Minister. He was born in Monastir which was also the birthplace of Bourguiba to whom he was always loyal and who was to refer to him as "my comrade in battle and my main collaborator". After schooling in Sousse, he took a degree in Law at the Sorbonne and a Diploma from the Sciences Politiques. Nouira was profoundly affected by his period in Paris, marked all his life by a French culture with a Cartesian belief that problems could be resolved by logic. Nevertheless he was a founder-member of the Neo-Destour, serving on its Politburo and also as Secretary-General of its allied trade union, the CGTT. Nouira was amongst the nationalist leaders arrested in April 1938, removed to France after the outbreak of war, and released by the Germans when they overran Vichy. Bourguiba then appointed him Assistant Secretary-General of the Party in charge of youth work. Seen as one of the Party's leading intellectuals, he was responsible for producing a French language newspaper. In January 1952 when Salih Ben Yusuf fled to Cairo, Nouira became Secretary General of the Neo-Destour and in April he refused to join the government of Salah al-Din Bakkush. Later in the year he was briefly confined in a concentration camp in the South. In May 1953 he was again arrested, charged, with Muhammad Masmoudi, with the murder of the moderate Vice-Chairman of Tunis City Council: the case was not proved and he was released. In 1954, strongly disapproving of the linking of the Party with the terrorist campaign of the *Fellagha*, he resigned the Secretary-Generalship and went into legal practice. In August 1955 when Tahar Ben Ammar formed a Cabinet to negotiate over autonomy for Tunisia, Nouira served as Minister of Commerce. As Finance Minister in the first government after independence his main achievement was founding the Central Bank of which he himself became Governor. Nouira held the post for twelve years during which he played a large part in building reserves, protecting the currency and keeping prices stable. He vainly opposed the socialist measures being taken in the 1960s by Ahmad Ben Salah after whose fall in November 1968 he became firstly Assistant Secretary-General of the Parti Socialiste Destourien and then a Minister of State with a seat in the Cabinet. Now clearly one of the most important men in the country, he was appointed Minister of the Economy in June 1970, interim Prime Minister while Bahi Ladgham was dealing with the aftermath of Black September and Prime Minister in November. Promising stability and economic liberalism, he appointed a Cabinet mainly of moderate technocrats. The situation in agriculture was difficult as the peasants had to struggle to recover from the policies of Ben Salah so Nouira concentrated on creating labour-intensive industries. In 1972 tax measures were introduced to encourage exports and lures set for foreign capitalists: an average of two factories a week were opened in the years 1973 to 1978, doubling the industrial sector. Small businesses prospered and Tunisia had the highest *per capita* income in

Africa outside the major oil states. Tunisia's small oil industry benefited from the price rises of 1973. In 1973 the President made Nouira the first recipient of the "Bourguiba Medal of Merit" for saving the country from bankruptcy and re-establishing confidence. The liberalism shown in the economic sphere was not extended to that of politics. As early as 1971 Ministers resigned at the lack of progress towards democracy and they and other critics were routinely expelled from the Party. The Monastir Congress of 1974 showed that there would be no departure from autocracy. The Party of which he was already Secretary-General, formally confirmed him as Bourguiba's designated successor. The extent of Nouira's influence over the President had been shown earlier in the year when, after Muhammad Masmoudi had persuaded the President to agree by the Jerbah Declaration to unity with Libya as the Arab–Islamic Republic, the Prime Minister who had not been consulted, prevailed on Bourguiba to disavow his signature. Thereafter he was faced with the persistent hostility of Qadafi who in 1976 attempted to have him kidnapped or murdered. In foreign affairs Nouira saw the role of Tunisia as a link between Europe, the Eastern Arabs and Africa. In 1976 the economic situation started to deteriorate because, in order to boost exports which were threatened by the development of the EEC, wages had been kept low while inflation was running at 14% and unemployment was made worse by the expulsion of 200,000 Tunisian workers from Libya who joined others in flooding to the towns. Strikes started, even amongst the magistrates, and were broken by the police as was unrest at the Universities. Nouira complacently put these down to "the troubles of growth" and had no idea of defusing criticism other than by stifling it: "too much freedom would carry off all our good work" and he refused a multi-party system saying that the PSD represented all shades of opinion. In October 1977 there was a sit-in in a textile factory which Nouira saw as a trial of strength, sending in troops to assist the police for the first time in a decade. Despite the personal intervention of Bourguiba, he refused to be reconciled with his old colleague Habib Achour and may have been involved in an attempt on the life of the trade union leader. Cabinet Ministers who favoured concessions to the unions were dismissed and students were imprisoned. In January 1978 Black Thursday saw the worst violence since independence but Nouira continued to set his face against concessions. In April 1978 he rejected proposals for a National Pact. In June 1978 he appointed Hedi Bakkush to rejuvenate the Party but he refused, still, to allow either criticism within it or the creation of other parties and this closure of political life drove the discontented, as they were doing in Iran, to use the mosque as a platform and proved a great stimulus to Islamic fundamentalism. In elections held in November 1979 a choice between two candidates, both nominated by the PSD, was permitted but a third of the population of the capital did not bother to vote. During 1979 he broke off relations with Egypt after Camp David and offered Tunis as headquarters for the Arab League. In January 1980 the Government was shaken by the Gafsa Raid and at the end of February Nouira had a heart attack, retiring the following month. He played no further part

in politics. All agreed on his competence but he was uninspiring and unable to communicate with ordinary people, relying on discreet back-room arrangements. His loyalty, added to his lack of charisma, made him no challenger to Bourguiba who could leave him to run the details of government. He was said to have kept a daily diary since childhood and his main hobby was watching football.

NOVEMBER REVOLUTION (Iraq) (1963)

After the Ramadan Revolution the Baath gained a dominating role in the Government with 16 out of 18 members of the National Council of the Revolutionary Command and key Ministers. The President Marshal Abd al-Salam Arif appeared little more than a cypher. The Baath drove towards one-party rule, was outmanoeuvred by President Nasser in the Unity Talks, failed to settle the Kurdish Revolt (I) and finally split into competing factions. Its militia, the National Guard, led by air force Colonel Mundhir al-Wandawi, got out of hand and terrorized Baghdad, arresting and torturing opponents, insulting officers, establishing roadblocks and breaking into government buildings. Moderate Baathists, including the Prime Minister General Ahmad Hassan al-Bakr, the Defence Minister Colonel Salih Mahdi Ammash, the Chief of Staff General Tahir Yahya and the air force commander Brigadier Hardan al-Takriti united with Arif in determination to bring it to heel. On 1 November the Government gave Wandawi a sinecure diplomatic post in Damascus but he refused to go. The Baath extremists called an "Extraordinary Regional Conference" to expel the moderates but it was interrupted by armed officers and the participants sent out of the country at gunpoint. On 13 November Wandawi and another pilot seized an aircraft, bombed the airbase and fired a rocket into the President's bedroom and the National Guard occupied public buildings. The founder of the Baath Michel Aflaq and the Syrian President Amin al-Hafiz went to Baghdad in an unsuccessful attempt to reconcile the warring party factions and then the Government launched an all-out attack on the National Guard which was effectively destroyed in a single day's fighting on 18 November 1963. Three months later Arif felt strong enough to discard the moderate Baathists and remained in effective control of the country until his death in 1966.

NU'MAN, Ahmad b. Muhammad (c. 1910–)

Prime Minister of Yemen. He was descended from a very prominent family of Shafai shaykhs of Hujariyyah which had long played a political role on the frontier between the British in Aden and the Turks in Sanaa. They also owned a great deal of land. After a traditional education in Yemen he went to al-Azhar in 1937. When he returned Crown Prince Ahmad, then Viceroy of Taizz, appointed Nu'man Director of Education after which he was generally known as al-Ustadh, the Professor. Nu'man also served as tutor to Ahmad's son Badr and hoped to imbue him with liberal principles. For a while Ahmad encouraged talk of reform but then became alarmed that the ideas advocated by Nu'man and his close friend Muhammad Mahmud al-Zubayri might harm the dynasty. The two fled to Aden in 1944 and founded there the Young Yemeni Movement, the

Ahrar, of which *al-Ustadh* was President. They conducted a propaganda campaign and also entered into a conspiracy to establish a constitutional Imamate under Saiyyid Abd Allah al-Wazir. In February 1948 Imam Yahya was murdered, al-Wazir seized power and nominated a Cabinet in which Nu'man was Minister of Agriculture, the first Shafai to hold Ministerial office. Ahmad succeeded in overthrowing the usurping regime and Nu'man and those of the Ahrar who were caught were imprisoned in Hajjah jail from which they exchanged with the Imam verses and letters of political advice. *Al-Ustadh* was released after seven years but, realising that Ahmad feared his influence upon Badr, deemed it wise to flee to Cairo where he joined Zubayri in restarting their old newspaper *Sawt al-Yaman* attacking the despotic Imamate. During a *rapprochement* between Nasser and Ahmad, Nu'man moved to Aden but after Yemen's relations with Egypt cooled and those with the British became closer, Nu'man was expelled in July 1960. He returned to Egypt, resumed his campaign and when the monarchy was overthrown in September 1962 he became Minister of Local Government under the Republic. He soon came to feel that Marshal Sallal was aiming at a military dictatorship, was doing nothing for the Shafais and allowing Egyptian influence to become predominant so he obtained a post abroad as Permanent Representative to the Arab League. In 1964 he was made Vice-President of the Executive Council and Chairman of the Consultative Council, posts which he resigned with his closest friend Abd al-Rahman al-Iryani and Zubayri after the intransigence of Sallal and the Egyptians wrecked the attempt to make peace at the Erkowit Conference in November 1964. In April 1965 the murder of Zubayri shook Sallal and his regime and Nu'man agreed to become Prime Minister on condition that a peace conference be held and Presidential powers reduced. He formed a Cabinet of nine Shafais and nine Zaidis and included some Baath members notably Muhsin al-Ayni at a time when the Party was on bad terms with Nasser. As a traditional Muslim grandee he was acceptable to King Faysal and he put out feelers to other Arab states to lessen dependence upon Egypt. With the same motive he called a tribal conference at Khamir to discuss the establishment of a national army, a new Constitution and a peace settlement. He had been in office only ten weeks when, without consulting him, Sallal established a Supreme Military Council whereupon Nu'man resigned. Sallal wished to arrest him but the Egyptians gave him refuge. In September 1966 he joined a delegation led by his successor as Prime Minister, General Hassan al-Amri petitioning Nasser for the removal of Sallal and was detained with the other members. The Egyptians, however, refused to send him home for trial on treason charges. When the Egyptians withdrew from Yemen in October 1967 he was released but went to Beirut in an attempt to make peace with the Royalists. When Sallal was ousted the following month Nu'man became a member of the three-man Presidency Council but quickly resigned as he thought that the new regime was not serious about making peace. He remained abroad but after the National Reconciliation of 1970 he became a member of the Presidency Council. In May 1971 he was again Prime Minister. By then old and ill

he felt incapable of coping with the chaotic financial situation, the corruption and inefficiency and the rivalry between military and civilians as they competed for scarce resources and he resigned after ten weeks. His son Muhammad Ahmad was an extremely active and able politician, holding such posts as Roving Ambassador and Foreign Minister. In June 1974 he was murdered in unexplained circumstances. Around the same time Iryani was overthrown and went into exile and Nu'man went as well, playing no further part in politics. *"Al-Ustadh"* was an honest, greatly respected man, too much an idealist to be a practical politician and he lacked the cynical toughness necessary to govern the Yemen.

al-NUR, Babikr (?–1971)
Sudanese Minister and conspirator. When General Nimeiri seized power in May 1969 Nur, a Lieutenant-Colonel was the second most senior member of the Revolutionary Command Council. In a Cabinet reshuffle in July 1970 he was appointed Assistant Premier for Economy and Planning but he was dismissed in November with his close associates Major Faruq Uthman Hamadallah, Minister of the Interior, and Major Hashim al-Atta, Assistant Premier for Agriculture, who were also members of the RCC. Nimeiri stated that they had been sacked for leaking confidential information to the illegal Sudanese Communist Party of which they had long been known to be supporters. On 19 July 1971 Atta took Nimeiri prisoner and announced that he and other "Free Officers" proposed to establish a democratic political system which would be a front of peasants, workers, soldiers, "free officers", "national capitalists" and intellectuals. The South would be given regional autonomy and the "popular organisations" banned by Nimeiri would be free to operate again. The old RCC was corrupt and a new one headed by Nur and including himself and Hamadallah would guide Sudan towards democratic socialism. Russia and Iraq congratulated the new regime. Nur and Hamdallah, who had been in London, left for Khartoum on a BOAC aircraft which was forced down by the Libyan authorities who detained them until Nimeiri had regained power in a counter-coup and then handed them over to him. It was generally believed that the British, anxious to prevent a communist state in the Sudan, had passed on information about the flight. Despite a British plea for clemency all the leaders of the coup were shot. Nur claimed that he had no advance knowledge of the plot. Russian protests at the executions led to a deterioration in relations while those with Iraq were severed. About 1,000 communists were rounded up and their leaders including Abd al-Khaliq Mahjoub, hanged. After his resumption of power Nimeiri started to move to the right, both in domestic and foreign affairs.

NUSSAIBAH, Sari (1950–)
Son of Jordanian Defence Minister and Ambassador to London. He was educated at Oxford and is married to a Briton. He taught Philosophy at Bir Zeit and wrote on Arab–Israeli coexistence. He was imprisoned during the Gulf War for three months accused of passing information to Iraq, although the case was never proved.

OAPEC

Prior to the June War of 1967 the Gulf oil-producing states had refused to allow their oil to be used as a Pan-Arab weapon against Israel but public emotion during the conflict compelled them to sacrifice their own interests and proclaim an embargo on exports to supporters of Israel. At the Khartoum Summit the producers had to promise to subsidise Egypt, Jordan and Syria in return for general consent to their resuming supplies. Immediately afterwards the most conservative oil states, Saudi Arabia, Kuwait and Libya under King Idris decided to form the Organisation of Arab Petroleum Exporting Countries to keep Arab oil out of politics. Unlike OPEC which was solely concerned with co-ordination of policies in the export of a single commodity, OAPEC aimed ultimately at the integration of its members' economies in what was called by Ahmad Zaki Yamani "an EEC of the Arab oil producers". Membership was confined to those states in which oil "constitutes the basic source of national income" – thus excluding radicals such as Egypt and Algeria but including Iraq which declined, however, to associate with "a club of conservatives". An inaugural meeting was held in Kuwait in September 1968. Yamani was appointed Acting Secretary-General. The non-political stance of OAPEC was transformed after the Libyan Revolution as Qadafi saw it as a weapon in his struggle against the oil companies. During 1970 Algeria and then Abu Dhabi, Bahrain, Dubai and Qatar were admitted and agreement was reached to establish a jointly-owned tanker fleet. In 1971 Iraq joined and the constitution was amended to admit Syria and Egypt. Oman has refused to become member. An OAPEC meeting in Kuwait after the outbreak of the October War launched the Oil Weapon with the announcement that members would cut production by 5% a month. Based in Kuwait, OAPEC has organised numerous conferences on technical matters, training, information policy, etc. and put out numerous publications. A Judicial Board settles disputes amongst members. It has also financed development projects of which a dry dock in Bahrain was the most important. The political nature of the Organisation was shown by the suspension of Egyptian membership after the Camp David Agreement. Tunisia which had joined in 1982 withdrew in 1986 as its production hardly justified its membership costs.

OCTOBER RIOTS (Algeria) (1988)

At the end of July 1988 a wave of strikes showed popular discontent at the economic situation. The fall in oil revenues by 40% in two years led to a reduction in food imports as the Government refused to reschedule its debts. A consequent shortage mainly affected the poor with meat costing £20 a kilo whereas wages were £100 a month. Unemployment was reckoned at 40% for the young and 65% of the population was under 25. Three million people were crammed into Algiers which had accommodation for 800,000. At the same time liberalisation of the once strictly controlled economy and corruption in the ruling Front de Libération Nationale meant that some were acquiring enormous wealth which they flaunted in a provocative manner. In late September President Chadli broadcast that there existed "a deep and permanent crisis" as corrupt officials refused to implement the reforms that he ordered. On the night of 4 October children started to riot and this led to a spontaneous explosion of anger that lasted throughout the following day. There were attacks on Party and government offices and symbols of wealth such as expensive shops and airline offices which were looted and cars overturned amidst shouts of "Young People rise up!". The exiled Ben Bella said that the people were yearning for "bread, freedom and democracy" but with most of the rioters under 20, some as young as 12, many of their actions appeared motivated by vandalism rather than politics although later Muslim fundamentalists such as Ali Belhadj claimed leadership. On 6 October Chadli imposed a state of siege and the troops behaved with extreme ferocity with tanks firing live ammunition at crowds of young people, killing an estimated 200 while 900 were arrested. The following day the riots spread to other cities, with further deaths. Chadli held a meeting with several Imams, including Belhadj, but it was not until 10 October, after rumours that he was dead or deposed, that he made any public statement, promising unspecified reforms with a referendum on restructuring relations between the legislative and executive authorities. Violence continued, but on 12 October, in what was seen as a gamble, he lifted the state of siege. Large quantities of previously scarce food were made available at half the pre-riot prices. Official casualty figures were 180 killed although unofficial estimates were as high as 500. Some 3,500 were detained although 500 minors were released without charge: damage was put at $250 million. Chadli used the riots, which many compared to the *Intifadah*, to show the FLN apparatchiks that they could not cope with the situation and he proceeded to introduce reforms which brought about firstly their downfall and then his own.

OCTOBER WAR (RAMADAN WAR, YOM KIPPUR WAR) (1973)

After the disaster of the June War which left Israel in occupation of Sinai, Nasser promised that every inch of Egyptian territory would be regained but the War of Attrition left the situation unchanged. Sadat upon inheriting the Presidency swore that the matter would be resolved in 1971 but that year ended with him feebly blaming an unexpected fog on the battlefield and considerably damaged credibility. The Jarring Mission produced no result, a Summit Meeting between Nixon and Brezhnev in May 1972 scarcely mentioned the Middle East and it appeared that there was a general acceptance of a stalemate. Egypt was being crippled by defence expenditure and there was a sense of humiliation in the army and people. The Israelis were starting to build an entire city, Yamit, on Egyptian territory as well as increasing settlement on the West Bank. Sadat determined to break the deadlock and compel the Super-Powers to pay attention to the area. He aimed also to shatter the Israeli theory that they enjoyed permanent military superiority which led them to believe that the obvious build-up of Egyptian and Syrian troops at the beginning of October 1973 were simply manoeuvres. The Israelis also believed that the Egyptian army would be unable to break through the strongly-fortified Bar-Lev Line along the Suez Canal. At 1400 hours on 6 October Egypt and Syria launched simultaneous attacks, achieving complete surprise. Employing high-pressure hoses the Egyptians swept away the sand rampart of the Bar-Lev and within an hour had brought across 14,000 men and stormed the first fortress. They had also designed new bridges and assembled ferries and after 24 hours the force in Sinai numbered 100,000 men, 1,000 tanks and 13,500 other vehicles. The Egyptian air force gained at least equality over the battlefield. In the meanwhile the Syrians had advanced into the Golan Heights and helicoptered troops had captured an Israeli post on Mount Hermon. The Israelis were able to mobilise very quickly because the Yom Kippur Holiday meant that most men were at home and by 8 October halted the Syrian advance. Two days later they had regained most of the Golan but the Syrians, joined by Iraqi, Jordanian and Moroccan troops prevented them from advancing more than 15 miles towards Damascus. By 17 October there was an effective cease-fire with little movement on either side. There were heavy casualties on this front with the Syrians losing perhaps 3,000 dead and over 1,000 tanks while the Israelis had nearly 800 killed and lost 250 tanks. The Syrian navy was obliterated. In Sinai the Egyptians had by 9 October three major bridgeheads, the Second Army in the north opposite Qantara and in the centre opposite Ismailiyyah and the Third Army opposite Port Suez. The Israelis were in disarray but despite the demands of his officers, Sadat refused to go beyond his original plan and authorise an attempt to seize the strategic Gidi and Mitla Passes in Central Sinai. The Egyptians were receiving strong moral support from Russia, China and much of independent Africa while the Arab states were beginning to unloose the unknown potential of the Oil Weapon. They were also having some weapons replaced by Russia although the quantity was small in comparison with the amount

that the Israelis were getting from the Americans who believed that there was a real possibility of their being defeated. On 15 October it was stated that American service personnel were in the country maintaining newly arrived jet fighters and that heavy freighters were leaving the US base in the Azores every 15 minutes and American spy-planes provided battlefield information. The division between the Super-Powers meant that the Security Council could take no action. On 16 October, in a brilliant thrust in the gap between the Egyptian Second and Third Armies, General Sharon managed to get across the Suez Canal a small force which the Egyptians were unable to destroy. Sadat had frittered away the reserves that should have been kept for an emergency. The Israelis overran the missile batteries west of the Canal and so regained air superiority enabling them to increase the forces in the Deversoir area to three divisions which started to move southwards, cutting off the Egyptian Third Army. The Russians who had obstructed attempts to bring about a cease-fire while it had appeared that the Arabs were winning, were now anxious for one and after a visit to Cairo by Prime Minister Kosygin and one to Moscow by Secretary of State Kissinger the Security Council on 21 October passed Resolution 338 calling for a cease-fire within 12 hours. Egypt and Israel concurred although Syria, which heard of the Egyptian acceptance on the radio, held out for a further two days. At this time Israel controlled about 1,200 km the west bank of the Canal and Egypt 500 km the east. The Israelis almost immediately broke the cease-fire so as to complete the encirclement of the Third Army, cutting off its 45,000 men from their supplies of food and water and also bombing Port Said. Sadat appealed for American and Russian troops to supervise the cease-fire but Washington brusquely refused. The Russians appeared likely to comply whereupon the Americans put their forces, including the nuclear strike force, on world alert making it clear that they were prepared to go to war to prevent the arrival of Russian troops in the Middle East: in their anxiety to help Israel they did not see fit to consult in advance their NATO allies who would perforce have been involved in the hostilities and they subsequently complained about the lack of enthusiasm for their policies shown by European states. The Security Council passed on 25 October Resolution 340 which set up UNEF (II) to supervise the cease-fire. There were no more serious incidents and a meeting on 11 November at Kilometre 101 started the disengagement process. During the fighting on this front the Egyptians lost perhaps 12,000 killed, 8,000 taken prisoner, about 800 tanks and nearly 200 aircraft: the Israeli figures were about 2,000 killed, 240 prisoners, 700 tanks and about 100 aircraft. More tanks were involved than at the Battle of El-Alamein or in any single action on the Russian Front in World War II. For the first few days the Egyptians avoided the absurd claims of successes that had made them ridiculous in the June War but after Sharon had crossed the Canal they concealed the truth. Despite the defeats of the final days the Arabs saw the crossing of the Canal as a triumph: the famous writer Tawfiq al-Hakim saw it as "a spiritual crossing to a new stage in our history". They saw themselves as the victors for they had shown that they could plan a major war and considered that they had ultimately failed only because of the speed and extent of American equipment made available to the enemy. They no longer saw Israel as invincible. The Israelis themselves lost some of their self-confidence as a result of the intelligence and military failures of the first few days. The reputations of Golda Meir and Moshe Dayan were damaged and both left office not long afterwards. Sadat, on the other hand, won an immense prestige and popularity which he was able to use in a campaign of de-Nasserisation. Assad never forgave him for accepting the cease-fire without consulting his allies but the Syrians never realised how limited the original Egyptian objectives had been and that Sadat had never aspired to total victory. The future President Husni Mubarak made his reputation as the architect of the greatest successes ever achieved by an Arab air force. General Saad al-Din Shazli who had done the actual planning of the crossing was made a scapegoat by Sadat and subsequently wrote a book about the war. Use of the Oil Weapon led to a huge increase in the price of petrol and in the consequent wealth and importance of the Gulf States but it had not forced policy changes on the industrialised world. Many African states broke off diplomatic relations with Israel and some did not restore them for many years. The success of Russian missiles against Israeli tanks surprised military experts. A further cease-fire was signed at Kilometre 101 on 9 November but an attempt to reach an overall settlement at the Geneva Peace Conference in December failed and the way was left clear for complete American domination of the peace-making process with the full assent of Sadat.

OIL WEAPON
During the Suez War King Saud ordered that no oil should be sold to Britain and France but the decision was ineffective because other OPEC countries continued or increased production and the oil companies were able to divert supplies from elsewhere. The creation of OAPEC in 1968 provided the machinery for the Arab oil-producing states to enforce a common policy. King Faysal announced on several occasions that he would use oil as a weapon to pressure the main consuming countries, the West and Japan to take a line more sympathetic to the Arabs in their dispute with Israel. OPEC met on 15 September 1973 and decided to demand a price rise at a meeting with the companies in Vienna on 8 October. On 6 October Egyptian and Syrian forces crossed the cease-fire lines to set off the October War. Led by Shaykh Yamani the Arabs demanded $6.00 a barrel, double the existing rate. The companies offered $3.50 and with the producers insisting on a minimum of $5.12 the talks broke down. Meeting in Kuwait on 16 October the Arab Gulf states and Iran rejected calls from Iraq and Libya to nationalise all American oil interests, withdraw financial reserves from that country and break off diplomatic relations. They did decide, however, unilaterally to raise the price of crude to $5.19 and the companies had no choice but to comply; this was an historic step which altered economic relationships between producers and consumers throughout the world. Libya raised the price of its oil even more steeply. The following day OAPEC

decided to cut production by 5% a month until Israel withdrew from the territories occupied after the June War but the Ministers declared that this should not affect friendly states. The Arabs then decided, in addition, to cut all oil exports to the USA and to Holland which had been notorious for support of Israel. An OAPEC meeting in Kuwait on 4 November ordered further cuts in production by 25%, extended the ban to Portugal and frightened the Danes into reversing a pro-Israeli statement. An even greater success was causing Japan, which felt the need for oil more acutely than any other country, to reverse its previous subservience to the dictates of American foreign policy and openly criticise Israel: subsequently the Miki Mission secured the reclassification of Japan as a friendly country. The price of oil on the stock market had now risen to about $20 a barrel and there was petrol rationing in Scandinavia. Gradually more exemptions were permitted and the cut for December was not applied to the European Community apart from Holland. In that month first Iraq and then the rest of OAPEC decided to increase production and also an OPEC meeting in Tehran decreed a new price of $11.65 a barrel. In January 1974 Yamani said that he knew that the ban on sales to America and Holland had been ineffective but it had served its purpose as a political protest. In March the embargo on the USA was lifted but the solid front was dissolving with Libya and Algeria continuing the boycott while Saudi Arabia increased production to meet American needs. The use of the oil weapon in 1973 left open the question of its potential power. Certainly it had the effect of raising prices but politically it secured little more than verbal expressions of support for the Arab cause or condemnation of Israel. Also, despite some wild talk in America of seizing the oilfields by force, it was not put to the test of facing retaliation. There was always the likelihood that ultimately each producer would put its own national interests first and later the weapon was blunted by the enormous increase in non-OPEC sources such as the North Sea.

OKASHA, Sarwat (1921–)
Egyptian Minister. The son of a General, he entered the cavalry and fought in the Palestine War. He then joined the Free Officers, providing a valuable contact with the Wafd, the editor of whose newspaper, his brother-in-law who was able to warn him that King Farouq was preparing to pounce upon them. He wrote several accounts of the July Revolution in which he was closely involved. Okasha had by then won a degree in Art from Cairo University. He was put in charge of a magazine published by the Revolutionary Command Council but quarrelled with the Minister of National Guidance, Salah Salim and was sent as Military Attaché to Paris. Later he was Ambassador in Rome before, in 1958, being recalled to become Minister of Culture. Okasha achieved some success in mobilizing the intellectuals to provide a theoretical basis for an ideology of Arab socialism. He created a Centre for Political Studies, reorganised the press and was involved in the reform of al-Azhar. He led the international effort to save the temples of Abu Simbel from being submerged by the Nile as the building of the Aswan High Dam

progressed. He was also involved in restoring relations with France after the Suez War. In 1962 he quarelled with Nasser whom he failed to convince that culture could not be spread by press and radio like propaganda. He became chairman of the National Bank, a member of the Executive Board of UNESCO and was awarded a Doctorate by the Sorbonne. In 1966, reappointed Minister of Culture he was responsible for the Tutankamun exhibitions in many capitals. In 1971 when the Ministry of Culture was amalgamated with that of Information, Sarwat was dropped from the Cabinet but appointed an assistant to the President. He lost this post in June 1972 and devoted himself to Art History, publishing numerous works including translating Ovid into Arabic.

OPEC

Before the Second World War the situation in the oil industry was less favourable to the host states than to the international companies which had been given large, long-term concessions with numerous privileges in matters of taxation and extra-territorial rights. The experience of Dr Musaddiq showed that an individual producing country, even one as important as Iran, could not really win a confrontation with the companies while there were numerous other states eager to sell as much as possible. The companies fixed the price of crude amongst themselves without consulting the host states and in February 1959 unilaterally reduced it by 10%, causing severe problems for the budgets of several countries including Saudi Arabia. This led its Oil Minister, Abd Allah al-Tariki to play the leading part in summoning the First Arab Petroleum Congress in Cairo in April 1959 which was attended also by representatives of Iran and Venezuela. It called for periodic renegotiation of agreements but in August 1960 the companies made another unilateral cut, this time of up to 6%, reducing the price to below the level of 1953. The Iraqi Oil Ministry invited delegates from Saudi Arabia, Iran, Venezuela, Kuwait and Qatar to a conference in Baghdad which resolved to adopt "a united front against companies that reduced prices unilaterally and without consultation". It decided to establish a permanent Organisation of Petroleum Exporting Countries with a secretariat. This would resist attempts to divide the producing countries which demanded consultations with the companies on pricing and production levels. The supreme body was to be a Conference scheduled to meet at least twice a year. Additional countries – Algeria, Ecuador, Gabon, Indonesia, Libya, Nigeria and the UAE – joined later. Membership was restricted to countries for which oil was the main source of income thus excluding states such as Egypt, Syria or indeed the UK. In 1968 the conservative Arab governments formed OAPEC to keep oil out of politics but later this objective was transformed by the admission of the radical states. When OPEC was unanimous it proved strong enough to enforce its will upon the companies which, denied support by their governments, surrendered to an ultimatum to sign the Tehran Oil Agreement of 1971. In the same year the Beirut OPEC meeting called for effective participation in the management of oil resources. The shift of power to the OPEC states from the companies was confirmed by the dictation of the Geneva Oil Agreement and the enormous prices rises that followed the October War of 1973 which took crude from $3.01 to $11.65 in three months. This proven ability of OPEC to set the price of oil led to divisions amongst its members for the rest of the decade. The "Moderates" – states with large reserves and manageable needs – argued that the price should not rise too steeply otherwise consuming countries would seek alternative sources and methods of power and also, if the economies of the Western states were ruined, the oil countries would hold enormous sums of cash with nothing to buy. This group was led by the Saudi Shaykh Yamani. The "Radicals" – states with ambitious programmes of development for which they needed large sums, preferred as much money as possible as soon as possible. This group was led by Algeria, Iran, Iraq and Libya. Prices rose regularly and in June 1980 reached $32.00. The summit planned for Baghdad in November had to be postponed owing to the Iran–Iraq War but both countries attended a meeting in Bali which raised the price to $41.00. At this and subsequent meetings the chair of the Iranian representative who had been kidnapped by the Iraqis was filled with his likeness cut from cardboard. Saudi Arabia disapproved of spiralling prices and increased production to force them down, acting as a "swing producer", raising or cutting output to meet market demands. By 1980 OPEC's share of world production had fallen from the peak of 55.5% in 1973 to 45% and was to fall to 30.9% in 1987. To maintain the price an emergency summit in Vienna agreed in March 1982 to impose an overall production ceiling of 18 million barrels a day but it proved impossible to enforce the necessary cuts. Unanimity crumbled as states desperate to sell offered inducements, barter arrangements, etc. while non-OPEC states increased production. Ecuador in October 1985 became the first country to leave OPEC, albeit temporarily, when refused a larger quota and Iraq, denied parity with Iran, refused to co-operate. By the beginning of 1986 the price had declined to $10 a barrel and OPEC appeared on the verge of collapse: while able to domineer over the companies, it found itself the slave of the market. The OPEC meetings of the next three years normally ended with some form of agreement which was in practice little observed. After the Iraqi invasion of Kuwait, a meeting in December 1990 decided effectively to suspend quotas and OPEC production soared from 21 million barrels a day to 23 despite the disappearance of the 4.5 million alloted to Iraq and Kuwait. Saudi Arabia increased its production from 4.4 mbd to 8.5 million, over a third of the total. In March 1991, still meeting without Iraq, it was decided to reduce production – a decision seen as a victory for the Saudis. In February 1992 production was at its highest level for a decade and there were proposals to reduce it by about 6% to 23 mbd but the Saudis said they would not cut unless other countries guaranteed not to exceed their quota but both Russia and Iran sold all that they could while Kuwait pleaded that its need for reconstruction made it a special case. Haggling in February 1993 appeared to end in an agreement to keep output below 24 mbd which would stabilise prices at $18 a barrel – $3 less than six months earlier – but cheating continued to the extent of a million barrels a day. In May Kuwait threatened to leave OPEC unless its quota were increased from 1.6 mbd to 2 mbd. The situation was further complicated by the possibility that Iraq might reach agreement with the United Nations to sell the $1,600 million worth of oil that it was authorised to do under the Resolutions (Security Council) after Operation Desert Storm. In July the Saudi Oil Minister Hisham Nazir openly accused Iran of exceeding its quota to split OPEC while its President Jean Ping of Gabon tried to mediate. The permanent HQ of the Organisation was established in Vienna. Various departments, energy studies, statistics, public information and legal have been created. In 1976 it created a Fund for International Development with an initial capital of $800 million which has financed projects in 90 countries with grants and loans.

OPEC MINISTERS KIDNAPPING (1975)

On 21 December 1975 five men and a woman with sub-machine-guns and grenades broke into the building in Vienna where the OPEC Oil Ministers were meeting and took 90 hostages including eleven Ministers. The best known of those seized were Ahmad Zaki Yamani, Belaid Abd al-Salam of Algeria and Jamshid Amouzegar of Iran. In the attack three people were killed and a guerrilla was amongst those wounded. The kidnappers, calling themselves "The Arm of the Arab Revolution", demanded a bus to the airport and the reading of a lengthy communiqué on Austrian Radio, failing which they would blow up the building with all the hostages. Their demands were met and all the Austrian hostages and residents were released. The remaining 35 were taken to Algiers where all the non-Arab Ministers except Amouzegar were released in return for another radio communiqué demanding no compromise with Israel, nationalisation of oil and the unification of Iraq, Syria and the Palestinians to launch a war of liberation. They then flew to Tripoli where more were freed and another communiqué broadcast. The terrorists apparently planned a propaganda tour of Arab capitals but none would receive them and they returned to Algiers where they surrendered and released the remaining hostages. The kidnappers were allowed to go to Libya. The attack was condemned by Abu Iyad and Abu Lutf on behalf of the Palestine Liberation Organisation and the Popular Front for the Liberation of Palestine denied involvement. It was believed that the operation had been planned by Wadei Haddad and this was rendered more likely by the international nature of the terrorists, certainly including West Germans and probably the notorious Venezuelan "Carlos the Jackal".

OPERATION ACCOUNTABILITY (1993)

On 16 February 1993, the anniversary of the murder of the Shiah leader Abbas Mussawi and his family by Israeli forces, Hizbullah militiamen launched attacks on four posts in the Security Zone occupied by Israeli-paid South Lebanon Army, ending several months of inactivity. Rockets were also fired into the Zone hitting its main town Marjayun and the Israelis retaliated with artillery and helicopters. Prime Minister Hariri called on the Lebanese people to assist the militiamen against Israeli aggression and complained to the UN about the

death of civilians. As the 20 April date for the resumption of the Washington Peace Talks approached, there was an escalation of attacks on Israeli and SLA patrols in which three Israeli soldiers and an SLA gunman were killed and on 21 April there was a rocket duel during which Galilee was hit. In May the guerrillas showed a new mobility with Sagger missiles acquired from Syria moved around by motor cyclists. An Israeli major was killed and UNIFIL was in danger from both sides. Before the 15 June date for the resumption of peace talks, there were several bomb and machine-gun attacks on Israeli and SLA patrols and retaliatory shelling. On 8 July a new cycle of violence began as the Popular Front for the Liberation of Palestine (General Command) claimed the killing of two Israeli soldiers and more were killed in the next few days bringing the total to twelve. Israel moved up artillery reinforcements, staged mock air raids and threatened Syria. Clashes continued leading to the death of three more Israeli soldiers and on 23 July the Israelis launched Operation Accountability, a prolonged artillery attack on towns and villages inside Lebanon. In an attempt to isolate the guerrillas, civilians in a nine-mile strip north of the border were warned that they should flee and after three days of practically non-stop attack, some 250,000 out of a population of 800,000 had done so, 53 civilians including small children had been killed and 254 wounded. Twenty villages were almost destroyed and the population of Nabatiya was reduced from 50,000 to less than 20,000. Prime Minister Rabin candidly admitted that his strategy was to create a refugee crisis in Beirut and to force the Lebanese and Syrian Governments to put pressure on Hizbullah. In the heaviest air raids since 1985 a UNIFIL post was bombed, Beirut airport was buzzed and Israeli warships shelled Tyre and Sidon. A training camp near Tripoli was attacked by Israeli commandos. International opinion, even in the US, condemned Israeli savagery in deliberately targeting civilians and praised Syrian restraint after five of its soldiers had been killed. Hizbullah continued rocket attacks, killing another Israeli soldier and in Qiryat Shemona in Northern Israel two civilians were killed. On 27 July Israel stepped up its blitz, hinted at the possibility of an invasion and the area appeared on the brink of all-out war: Lebanon demanded a meeting of the Security Council. Correspondents were horrified at the sight of babies mutilated with shrapnel and old people with their skin burned off by phosphorus shells. After a week the estimate of killed had risen to nearly 150 with over 500 wounded and up to 500,000 refugees. Hizbullah offered to halt rocket attacks on Galilee if Israel stopped its bombardment but the Israeli Government insisted that it would negotiate only with the Lebanese Government which refused to curb Hizbullah until Israeli troops left its soil. The US Secretary of State Warren Christopher was due in the Middle East for talks about the peace process which was seen as blocked by the refusal of the Arabs to talk while attacks on Southern Lebanon continued and the Americans brokered a cease-fire which came into effect on 1 August. There was an understanding that the guerrillas would no longer fire rockets into Galilee although they would be free to attack in the Security Zone. On 2 August the Lebanese army started to move into the frontier area to collaborate with UNIFIL watching the guerrillas. Refugees started to return but Hariri estimated that 1,500 houses had been destroyed and 15,000 damaged in 120 villages. The Arab League agreed to provide $500 million for rebuilding. Although at the time of Operation Accountability the ruthless ferocity of Prime Minister Rabin appeared to have destroyed the peace process it was eventually seen to have contributed to it as his people were prepared to trust him when he signed the Israeli–PLO Agreement. On the ground the guerrillas continued active: on 6 August rockets were fired into the Security Zone where a fortnight later 9 Israelis were killed and four wounded in a major incident.

OPERATION MAGIC CARPET (1948–50)
(Yemen)

At the time of the proclamation of the State of Israel there were in the Yemen approximately 50,000 Jews who claimed that their ancestors had fled there at the time of the destruction of the Temple by Nebuchadnezzar. They made an agreement with the first Zaidi Imam by which they would pay the poll tax (*jizyah*) in return for protection and this pact lasted for a thousand years. Some were agriculturalists but many lived in Sanaa where they monopolised many crafts, in particular metal working. They were not persecuted but subject to certain restrictions to emphasise their inferior status. In December 1947 there were major riots, in the course of which 78 Jews and 33 Arabs were killed, in Aden in protest against the British policy in Palestine which was seen as pro-Zionist. These events were exploited by Zionist propagandists in the USA to alarm the Jews of Yemen who were also impressed by the identification of the Israeli leader David Ben Gurion as a new King David. The American Joint Distribution Committee persuaded the British to allow the setting up of a transit camp in Aden from which American civil aircraft transported Yemeni Jews to Lydda. The Aden Protectorate rulers collaborated in return for transit fees. The first aircraft left on 15 December 1948 but the operation was on a small scale until in the summer of 1949 the Imam Ahmad stated that he had no objection to the departure of the entire community. He stipulated only that they had to sell their property, giving them no right to return, and teach their trade to a Muslim. There was then a flood of immigrants and by the time the Operation ended in September 1950 over 45,000 Yemeni Jews reached Israel. It was estimated that about 1,500 Jews preferred to remain in Yemen.

OPERATION MOSES (Sudan) (1984/5)

The Falashas were an Ethiopian group, numbering over 25,000 people, who practised a form of Judaism. They claimed to be the descendants of the retinue of Menelik, the son of King Solomon and the Queen of Sheba. They lived separately from other Ethiopians, whom they did not allow into their villages and were so isolated that they believed themselves the only Jews in the world. In 1975 the Israeli Government accepted a ruling of the Sephardic Chief Rabbi that they were Orthodox Jews, entitled to residence in Israel. In 1984 Ethiopia was devastated by famine as well as by civil war and the plight of the Falashas attracted the concern of Zionists

in the US and of Israel which was anxious for immigrants to settle upon the occupied West Bank. Arrangements were made by the CIA and Mossad with the government of General Nimeiri to bring them from their homes in Western Ethiopia to the Sudan from where they were secretly airlifted to Israel. Some 8,000 or 10,000 Falashas were transported and it was stated that the Sudanese Government was rewarded with $56 million, most of which went into the private pockets of the President and his associates. When this collusion became known it caused great indignation in the Sudan and in the Arab world and was one of the main causes of the overthrow of Nimeiri in April 1985. Subsequently the First Vice-President Major-General Umar Muhammad al-Taiyib was charged with receiving a bribe of $2 million for facilitating Operation Moses and was condemned to 20 years' imprisonment in addition to the two life sentences and fine of nearly $9 million that he had received for abuse of power, theft and blackmail.

OPERATION PEACE FOR GALILEE (1982)

Code name for the Israeli invasion of Lebanon. After the outbreak of the Lebanese civil war in 1975 the country had on its territory Syrian troops and Palestinian guerrillas acquiring the upper hand over the traditional Maronite leadership. The Israelis wanted these forces removed and they wanted also a Security Zone some 40 km wide along their northern frontier to prevent rocket attacks on settlements in Galilee. In August 1981 after a convincing electoral victory Menachem Begin reformed his Cabinet bringing in the aggressive and ambitious General Ariel Sharon as Minister of Defence. Sharon boasted that Israel was the "world's fourth largest military power" and entitled to a sphere of influence stretching from North Africa to Pakistan. The first step would be to change the map of the Middle East by turning Lebanon into an Israeli satellite ruled by its ally Bashir Jumblatt. In Washington which regarded all foreign policy issues as part of the cold war against Russia it was easy for leaders such as President Reagan and the Secretary of State General Haig, who were already notorious for their pro-Israeli sentiments to see the Syrians and Palestinians as Russian surrogates. On 20 May 1982 Sharon saw Haig alone and almost certainly received his support for an invasion of Lebanon. Only a pretext was now needed and this was provided on 3 June when a Palestinian shot and wounded the Israeli Ambassador in London. There followed two days of intensive bombing of Lebanon before on 6 June about 90,000 Israeli troops crossed the frontier. Within a day they had overrun most of the Security Zone and total control of the air enabled them to shower military and civilian targets throughout the country with phosphoros, fragmentation, suction and cluster-bombs and other examples of the latest American military technology. In a brilliantly-planned campaign they advanced in three columns, one went rapidly up the coast, leapfrogging hostile positions while a second went more slowly through the mountains and a third operated in the east to outflank the Syrians. On 9 June the Israelis knocked out the batteries that had led to the missile crisis of the previous year, heavily defeated the Syrian air force shooting down 47 of their jets without loss and then won a tank battle. On 11 June the Syrians sought a cease-fire. None of the other Arab states showed the least inclination to become involved in a war with Israel and even Qadafi did little more than advise the Palestinians to commit suicide rather than surrender. It was assumed by most of the army and even by the some of the Israeli Cabinet, which Sharon had misled about his ultimate intentions, that the invaders would halt as they had done in 1978 but they swept on to encircle Beirut which they did on 13 June. These operations, followed by the brutalities of the Beirut Siege and the subsequent Sabra–Chatila Massacre caused distress to some Israeli army officers and to many ordinary citizens because for the first time it did not appear as if the country was fighting a just war in self-defence and they were unable to condone acts of barbarism against unarmed civilians. It was officially stated that Israeli casualties were 344 killed and 2,000 wounded while an estimated 20,000 Lebanese and Palestinians, mostly civilians, were killed, 30,000 wounded and 600,000 made homeless. As a result of American mediation, a Multi-National Force supervised the evacuation of about 12,000 Palestinian guerrillas, many of whom later returned. The Syrian grip on Lebanon was, if anything, strengthened and even the Christians rejected the idea of becoming Israeli allies. The war was an embarrassment and even humiliation for the Soviet Union which, preoccupied by the approaching death of Brezhnev and events in Poland and Afghanistan, could do no more than utter a few bleats of protest. Increasing dissatisfaction both in the army and at home led to a unilateral withdrawal by the Israelis in September 1983 to the Awali river and a complete evacuation in the summer of 1985.

OPERATION PLOUGH (Morocco)

In 1957 King Muhammad V, himself driving a tractor, inaugurated an ambitious programme to increase agricultural production. Government rural mobilisation centres purchased tractors, fertilisers and improved seed which were made available to peasant farmers. Nearly 600 local committees were formed to manage the new lands of which 160,000 hectares were reclaimed in the first season. The Deputy Prime Minister, Abd al-Rahim Bouabid, declared that the scheme would play an important part in integrating remote or backward communities into the new nation. The Union Marocaine des Agriculteurs was also inaugurated by the King. In the second year it was planned that three times as much new land should be brought into cultivation but weather and technical difficulties arose. Operation Plough was also hampered by the innate conservatism of the farmers and by becoming enmeshed in party political struggles over funding. A severe drought in 1961 effectively ended what had been designed as a radical attempt to raise standards in the countryside.

ORGANISATION SPÉCIALE (Algeria)

In 1947 some of the younger members of the Mouvement pour le Triomphe de la Liberté et de la Démocratie, considering its leader Messali Haj too willing to compromise with French colonialism, decided to set up an Organisation Spéciale to prepare for an inevitable armed confrontation. It was given impetus by the transparent fraud of the April 1948 elections. Members were carefully vetted and took an oath on the Qur'an before being trained by Ait Ahmad in guerrilla tactics, sabotage and supporting skills such as radio operating. Possibly 2,000 members were organised into small cells. The OS was based mainly in the Oranie but it established links with a similar underground movement, led by Belkasim Krim in Kabyle. In the winter of 1948/9 it was felt that the OS should be headed by an Arab rather than a Berber and Ahmad Ben Bella replaced Ait Ahmad. The OS was hampered by lack of money and started to obtain it by raids, the most famous of which was on the Post Office at Oran in April 1949. Subsequent investigations enabled the French to penetrate the Organisation, many of its leaders, including Ben Bella, were arrested and it effectively ceased to exist. Many of its members, however, kept in touch and formed the nucleus of the Front de Libération Nationale: the Neuf Historiques had all been in the OS.

OSIRAK RAID (1981)

Israel was determined that its reactor at Dimona should be the only one in the Middle East capable of producing nuclear weapons. In about 1974 Iraq with French aid obtained in exchange for oil started a programme called Tammuz. In the summer of 1980 France was reported to be supplying the highly enriched uranium which could make the plant operational by the end of the year. After the outbreak of the Iran–Iraq War there were two attacks on the reactor which led to the departure of many of the foreign technicians and delayed the expected date of completion until the late summer of 1981. In January 1981 the International Atomic Energy Agency stated that its inspection had shown no evidence that Iraq was making weapons at the Osirak reactor ten miles south-west of Baghdad and this was confirmed by its French builders. It was also noted that Iraq, unlike Israel, had signed the Nuclear Non-Proliferation Treaty. In the summer of 1981 the Israeli Prime Minister Menachem Begin was fighting a difficult election campaign and his need to show strength had already led to the missile crisis with Syria. In the early evening of 7 June 8 F-16 fighter-bombers escorted by 6 F-15 interceptors attacked the reactor with 2,000-pound bombs causing extensive damage and the deaths of a French technician and an Iraqi in an attack of extraordinary accuracy. The Iraqis were taken totally by surprise. The Israelis claimed that they had refuelled in mid-air but it is more likely that they had been granted facilities in Iran. The US Government at first condemned the raid and protested at the use of American aircraft but otherwise confined their response to suspending the supply of further aircraft for a few days. They did not veto the Security Council Resolution 487 which strongly condemned the raid as the Iraqi delegate had agreed to withdraw a call for sanctions. The General Assembly declared the raid a serious threat to the IAEA by 119 votes to those of Israel and the USA. The raid was condemned by most European countries and rallied Arab support behind Iraq. France offered to build and Saudi Arabia to pay for a new reactor. Later the Director-General of the Israeli Foreign Ministry said that his Department had not

been informed in advance of the raid and had had
difficulty in finding justification that would satisfy the
outside world. The plant was not rebuilt during the war
but in March 1990 the arrest of smugglers of nuclear
triggers suggested that Saddam Hussain had not abandoned his desire for nuclear weapons and this was
confirmed by discoveries made after his defeat in the
Gulf War. A possible result of the Osirak Raid was to
divert Iraq attention from nuclear to chemical weapons
which were less easy for hostile intelligence forces to
uncover.

OSMAN, Amin Pasha (1899–1946)

Egyptian politician. He qualified as a barrister at the
Inner Temple in London and married an English lady.
He practised in Cairo and was also a financial expert.
Osman was Secretary-General of the delegation that
negotiated the Anglo–Egyptian Treaty of 1936 after
which he received an honorary knighthood. He acted
as an intermediary between the British Embassy and
Nahhas Pasha, ascertaining his willingness to take
power after the Abdin Incident of 1942. In 1943 Nahhas
appointed him Minister of Finance. He was regarded
as the most pro-British of all Egyptian politicians,
declaring that the partnership was like a Catholic marriage and could not be dissolved even if Britain wished
it. He headed an appeal to build a War Memorial at
El-Alamein and formed a Revival League pledged to
friendship with Britain. On 6 January 1946 he was murdered. His funeral was accompanied by student
demonstrations against the Government. Anwar Sadat,
who had been involved in planning the killing, was
arrested but finally acquitted in July 1948.

OU aL-HAJ, Mohand (1912–72)

Algerian politician. Born Makrane Belhaj in Kabyle,
before the outbreak of the Algerian War of Independence he was a landowner and merchant. He joined
the Resistance in November 1955 and remained in
Wilaya III, Grand Kabyle, throughout the fighting, succeeding Colonel Amirouche as its commander in April
1959. In July ou al-Haj survived a major offensive by
General Challe by splitting up his forces into groups of
10 or 20 men who hid in caves or trickled through
enemy lines. The French claimed that 3,700 of the
enemy had been killed, captured or wounded. The following year ou al-Haj was promoted Colonel. In June
1962 in the struggles after independence ou al-Haj and
his 1,000 fighting men allied with his fellow Berber
Bilkasim Krim and the Gouvernement Provisoire de la
République Algérienne against Ben Bella and Boumédienne. He succeeded in making his peace with them,
became a Deputy and remained as commander of
Kabyle. In September 1963 he joined Ait Ahmad in a
Berber rebellion. Ben Bella accused him of collusion
with Morocco at the time of the Tindouf Dispute and
ou al-Haj rallied to the Government but was stripped
of his command. He remained the principal spokesman
for the Berbers and extremely popular in Kabyle. He
became a member of the Politburo of the Front de
Libération Nationale in April 1964. He joined Boumédienne after the coup of June 1965 and continued to
hold high office in the FLN. In December 1967 after

the failure of the Zbiri coup he left the Government
and apparently withdrew from public life.

OUDJDA DECLARATION/ARAB – AFRICAN UNION (1984)

For the first decade after Qadafi seized power relations
with Morocco were generally bad. He had publicly
regretted the failure of the Skhirat attempt on the life of
Hassan II, condemned the King's pro-Western foreign
policy and provided arms and diplomatic support for
the Polisario fighters in the Western Sahara. Morocco
had riposted by having a special radio transmitter
beamed at Libya on which, for 24 hours a day, there
was nothing but the yapping of dogs. In 1981 Morocco
agreed to refrain from condemnation of Libyan activities in Chad in return for a promise to an end for help
to Polisario. This agreement was confirmed when in
1983 Qadafi made his first visit to Rabat since 1969. In
January 1984 a joint commission agreed to increase
economic co-operation, create a joint bank and open
Libya to Moroccan investment and labour: 14,000 Moroccans found jobs there within months. This was
followed in August by a meeting at Oudjda where a full
union of the two countries was announced. Any Arab
or African state, not merely those in the Maghreb,
might join the Arab–African Union provided that the
two original members agreed. It was to be a federation
in which both countries retained their sovereignty, with
a joint presidency which alone had the power to make
decisions and an Executive Council of both Cabinets to
implement them. There was to be a rotating secretariat
headed by a Secretary-General and an Assistant who
would not come from the same country. There was also
to be a joint legislature of equal numbers from each
"Parliament" and four councils dealing with defence,
economic, political and cultural matters. And a
common approach to foreign policy but either partner
might make a treaty with another state without prior
agreement. An attack on one would be regarded as an
attack on the other. There would be combined development in trade, agriculture and social affairs, exchange
of teachers, establishment of common Universities, cultural centres and research projects. A Federal Court
would be constituted. The King declared on television
that the initiative had been his and that Qadafi had
been "dumbfounded". The avowed object of the union
was the preservation of Islamic moral and spiritual
values and of the Arab national identity but it had the
more practical effects of signalling an end of Libyan
isolation, Moroccan independence of the United States,
and a mutual dislike of Algeria. It was overwhelmingly
approved by a referendum in each country but in practice it had little meaning. Nigeria and Madagascar,
mentioned as possible recruits, did not apply. During
1985 the two leaders were frequently in touch by telephone and Qadafi gratified the King by cancelling a
meeting of Arab and African Ministers which Polisario
was set to attend. In July a joint Assembly of 60 Moroccan and 60 Libyan-parliamentarians worked out
procedures for closer co-operation and established a
secretariat with committees to co-ordinate policies. In
August 1986, however, after a joint Libyan-Syrian communiqué had characterised his meeting with the Israeli

Prime Minister at Ifrane as "treason", King Hassan declared the Oudjda Act abrogated.

OUDJDA GROUP (Algeria)

Colonel Boumédienne as Chief of Staff of the Armée de Libération Nationale formed at his headquarters in Oudjda a group of able and ambitious young officers that he trained to play a major political role after independence had been gained. They were all elected to the National Assembly and Boumédienne insisted that some of them should have Cabinet posts to support his interests. In three reshuffles in three years Ben Bella managed to oust Ahmad Madaghri from the Ministry of the Interior and Ahmad Kaid from Tourism and demote Sharif Bilqasim but his attempt to dismiss Abd al-Aziz Bouteflika from Foreign Affairs led to the coup by the Oujda Group in which he was overthrown. Subsequently all were members of the new Revolutionary Council and given important Ministerial or Party office. Kaid and Bilqasim subsequently quarrelled with Boumédienne and were dropped, Madaghri remained in office until his death while Bouteflika was still Foreign Minister when Boumédienne died fourteen years later. Ali Mendjli who was regarded as one of the Group and who had represented Boumédienne at the Evian negotiations was only given titular posts in the National Assembly.

OUFKIR, Muhammad (1920–72)

Moroccan Minister. The son of a Berber tribal leader who was made Pasha of Bou Denib by the French for his services in helping to pacify the area, he was educated in Azrou College, the school for Berber tribal notables and at the Military Academy at Dar al-Bayda. Oufkir fought with great distinction in Italy where he was selected to carry the *Tricolor* into Rome, France, Germany and Indo-China where he was decorated twelve times and twice wounded. He was later on the staff of the French Resident General of Morocco and was deputed to put pressure on the puppet Sultan Muhammad ben Arafa to abdicate in 1955 and to retrieve the letter in which President Coty had promised him the unchanging support of France. After independence he led one of the columns that crushed a tribal rising in the Riff in 1958, pitilessly destroying rebel villages. In July 1960 he was appointed Director of National Security and in 1964 Minister of the Interior.

He dealt ruthlessly with all opposition and victims frequently accused him of being personally active in their being tortured. After the Agadir Earthquake he cut off the hands of hundreds of looters and shot the ringleaders. In March 1965, almost single-handed, he put down a riot in Casablanca, landing by helicopter at a besieged police station and scattering the crowd with a machine-gun. In October 1965 the opposition leader Mehdi Ben Barka disappeared in Paris and it is believed that Oufkir himself cut his throat after torturing him. He was publicly accused of the kidnapping by General de Gaulle who demanded his dismissal which King Hassan II refused. France withdrew her Ambassador from Rabat and Oufkir was sentenced *in absentia* to life imprisonment. He was an extremely efficient Minister under whom the public services worked smoothly and he was constantly touring, talking to workers and peasants. He worked with Mahjoubi Ahardan to see that local power was in the hands of loyal Berber caids. Oufkir organised the referendum of August 1970 which approved the new Constitution by such an improbable majority that in some provinces there was not a single contrary vote. After the attempt on the life of the King by army officers at Skhirat in August 1971, Oufkir was transferred to the Ministry of Defence to purge the armed forces which he did with his accustomed ferocity. He was probably now more powerful than the King but after the attempt to shoot down the Royal Boeing in August 1972, Oufkir was himself accused of planning the conspiracy. The same night it was announced firstly that Oufkir had committed suicide "out of shame at his failure to protect the King" and later because his complicity had been uncovered. In retrospect it was seen as suspicious that he had not been amongst those senior officers killed at Skhirat. The affair remains a mystery – had Oufkir turned against the Monarch that he had served so well and if so why? He was already practically all-powerful and was unlikely to have cared for the trappings of Head of State; also if he had been involved in the plot, it is unlikely that it would have failed. It is more probable that the Court seized the opportunity of ridding itself of an over-mighty servant, one whose continuance in office led to losses of foreign aid. His family were imprisoned and not released until 1992. In person Oufkir was tall and thin with snake-like features always concealed behind dark glasses which are said to have proved the inspiration for a series of "goggle-heads" by the sculptor Dame Elisabeth Frink.

PALESTINE ARAB PARTY

In December 1934 Raghib al-Nashashibi organised his followers as the National Defence Party and his arch-opponent, the Mufti Haj Amin al-Hussaini determined to do the same. A Congress held in Jerusalem at the end of March 1935 attended by about 1,500 people resolved to form the Palestine Arab Party. The President was the Mufti's kinsman and close associate Jamal al-Hussaini and the Vice-President a Greek Catholic from Jaffa. Its formal objectives were to maintain the Arab character of Palestine, to resist the implementation of the Balfour Declaration and to improve the lot of the Palestinians. It did not feel that this could be done in co-operation with Britain so it maintained a stream of protests, often violently worded, to the Palestine Government and the League of Nations. It called constantly for help from the rest of the Arab and Muslim world and the Mufti worked hard to establish himself as an international figure. Early in 1936 it did not reject out of hand proposals for a Legislative Assembly and later in the year took a leading part in the formation of the Arab Higher Committee. When the AHC was banned, the Hussainis fled into exile and there was a feeling that the time for purely political activity had passed. The Party disintegrated despite the loyalty of individuals to the Mufti.

PALESTINE ARMED STRUGGLE COMMAND

Early in 1969 leaders of Palestinian *fedayin* groups decided to improve the co-ordination of their actions. Those that joined the Palestine Armed Struggle Command included Fatah, Saiqa, the Arab Liberation Army, the Palestine Liberation Army and the Popular Democratic Front for the Liberation of Palestine. Later the Popular Front for the Liberation of Palestine – General Command came in. The Popular Front for the Liberation of Palestine, suspected of claiming credit for operations carried out by others, refused to join. A few operations combining several guerrilla groups did take place, for example a rocket attack on Eilat in April 1969 and several raids later in the year on Israeli military installations but were probably greatly exaggerated. Occasionally, too, several groups combined to discipline mavericks. The PASC sometimes acted as a single force to perform police functions and man roadblocks, particularly in Beirut. In general, however, it was dominated by Fatah and other organisations co-operated or not as it suited them or their external backers. It does not appear to have remained in existence, even on paper, for long.

PALESTINE COMMUNIST PARTY

The first meeting of the Palestine Communist Party seems to have been in September 1922 with an entirely Jewish membership. As none of its leaders spoke Arabic it had no contacts with the majority of the population and its opposition to Zionism led to its members being banned from the *Histadrut* trade union. Moscow kept demanding a predominantly Arab party and in the late 1920s some Palestinians were sent to Russia for indoctrination. There were publications in Arabic but all those for Jews were in Yiddish until 1930. The Party supported Arabs against the acquisition of land by Zionist agencies but many Jews resented taking second place and most of the Haifa branch was expelled in December 1929. In October 1930 Moscow dissolved the PCP Central Committee and appointed a new one with a majority of Arabs. In 1934 Radwan al-Helou ("Musa") returned from Moscow and started to organise Arab cells in the trade unions. Musa formed alliance with the nationalist leaders such as the Mufti Haj Amin al-Hussaini despite Russian denunciations of them as Fascists and in 1937 Jewish communists attempted to set up their own party. Musa prevented this but shortly afterwards the British imprisoned him for his nationalist activities, keeping him in detention until Russia joined the war, when the PCP was allowed to operate more openly. Under Russian direction it was the only Arab group not to oppose the partition of Palestine. After 1948 a separate legal Israel Communist Party came into existence while Musa and others went to the West Bank where they shared the fortunes of the Jordan Communist Party which, after some minor successes, was formally banned in 1957. The ban continued after the Israeli conquest of the West Bank. In 1970 many of them joined the short-lived al-Ansar Organisation which was designed by the Russians to get inside the Palestine Liberation Organisation but failed to do so. Musa died in 1975. A group calling itself the "Palestinian Communist Organisation in the West Bank" was apparently tolerated as it followed the Soviet line of accepting the recognition of Israel and it played some part in the Palestine National Front. In August 1981 Muslim fundamentalists attempted to assassinate Bashir Barghuthi, one of its leaders and the editor of its newspaper. The Russians had discouraged the formation of a Palestinian party distinct from that of Jordan because it would appear to be recognising the separation of the West Bank but in February 1982 they changed policy and permitted the formation of a new PCP. It probably had about 200 members on the West Bank and abroad. It supported the moderate group in the PLO but was not accepted as a full member of the organisation until the "Reconciliation Congress" of the Palestine National Council in 1987. Its official leader was Sulayman Najjab.

PALESTINE CONCILIATION COMMISSION
In December 1948 General Assembly Resolution 194 created the Palestine Conciliation Commission to work for a peaceful settlement after the Palestine War. It replaced the Acting Mediator, Dr Ralph Bunche and arrived in the area in January 1949. Its tasks included the preparation of recommendations on Jerusalem, on economic development and the refugee problem. The permanent members of the Security Council nominated representatives of the USA, France and Turkey. It took a major initiative in calling the Lausanne Talks in the spring and summer of 1949 which broke down without even agreeing on an agenda. In the late 1950s the PCC tried to find a formula for settling the problem of Palestinian refugees, of which it put the number at 711,600: some were to return to their homes, a second group to settle in different Arab countries and the remainder in third countries. At the invitation of the PCC Dr Joseph E. Johnson of the Carnegie Foundation made an investigation and submitted a report in October/November 1961 and a final report in September 1962. He declared that the situation would persist for at least a decade. Neither side found his proposals acceptable and nothing happened. Although it was not dissolved, the PCC lapsed into inactivity, apart from submitting an annual report to the General Assembly.

PALESTINE LIBERATION FRONT
Jabhat al-Tahrir al-Falastiniyyah. The Popular Front for the Liberation of Palestine – General Command under the leadership of Ahmad Jibril had close links with the Syrian Government and refused to fight against their forces in Lebanon. This led to a split in the PFLP – GC with a group led by Talat Yaqub breaking away to form the Palestine Liberation Front. This new group, supported by Iraq, replaced the PFLP – GC as members of the Rejection Front. In July 1978 it was reported to have been involved in the kidnapping of 40 UNIFIL soldiers in South Lebanon which was followed by clashes with Fatah in which more than 50 people were killed. A large part of the PLF then split away under the leadership of Abu al-Abbas to form a pro-Arafat faction. Shortly afterwards his headquarters in Beirut was blown up, it was believed by Jibril, with about 200 deaths. It specialised in raids into Israel – one on Nahariya in April 1979 leading to reprisal bombing of refugee camps. The PLF became notorious through the *Achille Lauro* Hijacking in 1985. In June 1990 its attack on Israeli beaches which Arafat refused specifically to condemn, led to the breaking off of talks between the American Government and the Palestine Liberation Organisation.

PALESTINE LIBERATION ORGANISATION
The Cairo Summit of January 1964, on the initiative of President Nasser, decided to create an organisation to represent the Palestinians at the Arab League and other meetings and Ahmad Shuqayri was put in charge of

making the necessary arrangements. A founding meeting of 400 mainly middle-class delegates from throughout the Arab world met in Jerusalem in May, established the Palestine National Council and adopted the Palestine National Covenant. The Alexandria Summit in September recognised the Palestine Liberation Organisation as "the sole legitimate representative of the Palestinian people" and called for the creation of a Palestine Liberation Army. Although there were contributions from individual Palestinians and also from various states the PLO was mainly financed by the Arab League then firmly under Egyptian leadership. In April 1966 Wasfi al-Tall accused the PLO of being under communist influence and arrested 200 members including the office staff in Amman. In Cairo an Executive Committee controlled a Research Centre, a Military Council, an Information Council and a series of Departments such as those for Political, Military, Administrative, Cultural, International and Social Affairs, Unions, Radio and the National Fund. Shukayri proved an inefficient administrator of this ponderous bureaucracy and his pretensions and demagoguery alienated many Arab states so in December 1967 he was forced to resign, being replaced by a leftish lawyer Yahya Hammouda. In-fighting brought a transfer of power from the old bourgeoisie to the guerrilla groups and a meeting of the PNC in Cairo in July 1968 amended the constitution of the PLO, creating a Central Council, representing the commando organisations, between the Executive Council and the PNC whose authority it enjoyed when the main body was not in session. A struggle for power between the various guerrilla groups resulted in the emergence of Fatah as the most powerful and in February 1969 its leader, Yassir Arafat was elected as Chairman of the Executive Council. This led to considerable friction between the EC and the PLA and some other groups such as the Popular Front for the Liberation of Palestine which claimed parity with Fatah. The close relationship of Fatah with Egypt and Saudi Arabia led to Syria and Iraq creating guerrilla groups under their own control, Saiqa and the Arab Liberation Front while even the Russians set up the Ansar Organisation. There was friction with King Hussain who continued to assert sovereignty over the West Bank even after it had been conquered by the Israelis in the June War. The PLO committed itself to rejection of Resolution 242 and called for an independent Palestine in which Muslims, Christians and Jews could live together. The success of the guerrillas in the Battle of Karamah made the PLO so self-assertive that it appeared to aspire to the control of Jordan until it was defeated in heavy fighting in Black September 1970. The majority of the *fidayin* then moved to Southern Lebanon where once again it attempted to act as an independent power, causing great resentment particularly amongst the Maronites although it had support from the Sunnis and the followers of Kamal Jumblatt: President Franjiyah called it "an army of occupation". Although it had had to accept some restrictions upon its activities in the Cairo Agreement of November 1969 it continued to raid into Israel although it officially condemned aircraft hijackings as harmful to the Palestinian cause. The PLO declared in 1974 that operations would be restricted to Israel and the Occupied Territories. In September 1974 suspicions that Arafat was engaged in negotiations which might lead to some compromise that did not bring about the total elimination of Israel led to a serious split when Habash formed the Rejection Front of radical factions which determined to boycott the Central Council but not the PNC. The Rabat Summit of October 1974 ended claims by Hussain to speak for Palestinians and recognised the right of the PLO to establish an independent state on all liberated Palestinian territory as the sole legitimate representative of its people. Israel, obediently followed by the USA, still utterly refused to recognise the PLO as a valid interlocutor or to consider the creation even of a Palestinian mini-state on the Occupied Territories. In November 1974 the PLO was invited to take part in a UN debate on Palestine and Arafat appealed to the General Assembly for support in his "olive branch and freedom fighter's gun" speech. This was followed by Resolution 3236 which affirmed the right of the Palestinians to national independence and sovereignty and granted the PLO observer status at the UN. Subsequently the PLO was admitted to other international organisations such as the Non-Aligned Movement and eventually in 96 countries its representatives were given diplomatic status. In September 1976 it became a full member of the Arab League. In the meanwhile the PLO had become deeply enmeshed in the fighting in Lebanon and after the Ayn al-Rummanah Massacre in April 1975 was engaged in all-out war against the Maronites to support whom the Syrian army entered the country in June 1976. This led to a split in the PLO with Syrian-backed factions such as Saiqa refusing to join the others in opposing their presence. In 1977 the new administration of President Carter said that the Palestinians had a right to be represented at peace talks but that they had to accept the right of Israel to exist but the PLO claimed that it alone could represent them and Begin refused to talk to them even if they did accept Israel. That the PLO had the support of the Arabs of the West Bank was, however, made clear in the municipal elections in April 1976 where their followers won most of the major towns. The following year the PLO denounced the "capitulationism" of Sadat and the withdrawal of Egyptian support meant that Fatah became mainly dependent upon Saudi Arabia and the Gulf States while other groups continued to be financed by Syria and Iraq. This led to internecine fighting with moderate PLO officials such as Said Hammami being murdered by the followers of Abu Nidal who was one of the few Palestinian leaders who did not attend the meeting in Algiers in February 1978 which set up the Steadfastness Front. The Venice Declaration, following the statement of the British Foreign Secretary Lord Carrington, that the PLO was not "a terrorist organisation as such", that it should be associated with the peace process showed its growing acceptability and this was confirmed by the denunciation of its moderation by Qadafi. The PLO maintained its strong presence in South Lebanon from which it launched frequent attacks on Israel which led in June 1982 to Operation Peace for Galilee in the course of which the Israelis claimed to have killed over 1,000 commandos and captured 6,000 to whom it denied prisoner-of-war status. In August over 12,000

Palestinian fighters were evacuated from Beirut, their military infrastructure smashed, and were dispersed amongst several countries. Their head-quarters was established in Tunis. Many, perhaps 7,000, returned to Lebanon the following year but in May 1983 there was a major revolt against the leadership of Arafat who was expelled from Syria and after heavy fighting within the PLO, evacuated from Lebanon in December. His subsequent *rapprochement* with Mubarak and Hussain led to demands for his resignation and a further split in the PLO with the foundation in March 1985 of the radical Palestine National Salvation Front. The Damascus-based National Alliance consisted of Saiqa, Fatah – Revolutionary Council, Popular Front for the Liberation of Palestine – General Command and the Palestine Popular Struggle Front attacked the "capitulationism and deviationism" of Arafat who was supported the PFLP, the Democratic Front for the Liberation of Palestine, the Palestine Communist Party and the Palestine Liberation Front. After the Amman Accord Hussain tried to put together a joint negotiating team of Jordanians and Palestinians not actually members of the PLO and appeared to be having some success when the British Government agreed to receive them but the meeting was aborted when the Palestinians refused to sign a document renouncing terrorism. There were at this time particularly serious terrorist incidents including the hijacking of the *Achille Lauro*. The Syrian attempt to wipe out the pro-Arafat wing of the PLO by instructing their subsidised Amal militia to attack Palestinian camps in Lebanon such as Burj al-Barajinah in 1985/6 caused the guerrilla groups to draw together as Presidents Chadli and Ali Nasir Muhammad attempted to mediate. At the same time it improved their relations with King Hussain but, exasperated by Arafat's refusal to condemn terrorism or accept Resolution 242, Hussain denounced his alliance with the PLO in February 1986. This, following further mediation by Algeria and Libya, made possible a general reconciliation of most factions in the Algiers meeting of the PNC in April 1987. In September 1987 under Zionist pressure Congress demanded the closure of the PLO observer mission to the UN: the State Department resisted this as illegal but the office in Washington was closed. In October 1985 the PLO offices had been attacked in the Tunis Bombing by Israeli aircraft with American support in a raid in which 60 people were killed and later relations between the Palestinians and their hosts deteriorated to the extent that Arafat, in October 1987, transferred the military HQ to Baghdad leaving a reduced staff in Tunis. A month later the start of the *Intifadah* showed the strength of the support of the people in the Occupied Territories for the PLO and until his murder by the Israelis in April 1988 some of the actions were co-ordinated by Abu Jihad. In July 1988 King Hussain formally renounced all claims on the West Bank which thus under international law was without a sovereign. The PLO finally adopted the concept of two states in Palestine and at the Palestine National Council – Algiers Meeting in November 1988 declared an independent state of Palestine, accepted Resolution 242, thus admitting the right of Israel to exist, and formally renounced terrorism. These points were reiterated the following month by Arafat, addressing the UN in Geneva and inviting the "leaders of Israel" to join in reaching a peace settlement. Finding itself isolated, the US agreed to open direct talks with the PLO and a further sign of acceptance was an official visit by Arafat to Paris in May 1989. As the *Intifadah* continued there were increasing signs that local bodies such as Hamas rather than the PLO were in charge of events and the breaking off of talks by the Americans after an attack by the PLF on an Israeli beach was a further blow. The enthusiasm of its support for the Iraqi annexation of Kuwait was also bound to lose it support. In the 1980s the PLO, including the guerrilla organisations, was an extremely wealthy body with an income variously estimated at between $100 million and $1,000 million a year, although it was probably $240 million. The 700,000 Palestinians working in the Gulf had 5% of their salaries deducted by the host governments and forwarded to the Palestinian National Fund which was augmented also by donations from Arab states and wealthy individuals, property in major centres throughout the world, farms, factories, a bank, various businesses and, some alleged, drug-running. "Martyr's Families" and disabled fighters received generous pensions and officials and guerrillas were well paid with ample expenses. In December 1990, four months after the invasion of Kuwait, the PLO had lost half its income – $2 billion in revenue – when the Kingdom of Saudi Arabia and Kuwait curtailed its contributions. Even Iraq stopped. For economic reasons the PLO closed its offices in Norway and Denmark. In April 1991 the Central Council meeting in Tunisia discussed tactics for a possible peace conference. The PLO was anxious to improve relations with Syria. In May 1991 it invited the Palestine National Salvation Front for reconciliation talks in Tunis – the first PLO delegation to Damascus in 1988. The PLO was reported to have had 6,000 men in South Lebanon but was losing ground to the Lebanese army. In July it was humiliated by having to hand over weapons to the Lebanese army having held out for only four days. It had in any case been ineffective since it rarely got through the Security Zone. Some PLO leaders started to think that commando action was futile – that they were in fact too weak for such tactics and that it would perhaps be better to negotiate if even for limited autonomy. In July preparations commenced for an ANC meeting amid considerable speculation on who would attend. Fysal questioned whether the PLO alone could designate the delegation for a peace conference; Hussain insisted that Baker have a letter of accreditation from Tunis. Fatah wanted talks. Kaddoumi took a hard line – no talks. The PFLP and DFLP were divided. Some members left and joined Hizbullah. In June 1991 the PLO agreed to pull out of South Lebanon and this was completed by February 1992. In November 1991 it was reconciled with Syria after eight years. The People's Party and DFLP called for more collective leadership and the appointment of a Deputy. It was clear after the disappearance of Arafat in April 1992 that since the murder of Abu Jihad and Abu Iyad, Arafat had no successor. Moreover, virtually all the PLO's funds were in Arafat's name in Swiss banks. In May 1992 the PLO requested a confederation with Jerusalem but Hussain was cool. The Palestine

National Council had 450 seats with 180 reserved for West Bankers who were unable to take them because of the law against meetings. The 80-member Palestine Central Command acted as liaison between its Executive Committee. In December 1992 it said it would not take part in peace talks until 400 Hamas were returned. In January 1993 the Law of Contacts was repealed but Rabin said he would not negotiate with the PLO. In March 1993 the British Government resumed ministerial contacts and in April so did Washington. In July there were discussions with Jerusalem about future relations and six committees were formed. In the 18-man Executive which acted for the Palestine National Council five opposed Arafat over the peace signing. In June 1993 Arafat talked of resigning after charges of corruption were levelled at him. Officials had said that they had suspended payments to 30% of its 5,000 employees and in August the PLO sold property to raise around $125 million needed for unpaid salaries, pay for the army, pensions and welfare payments. It had 100 missions worldwide, 75 of them embassies. In August the veteran Shaffiqal-Hut withdrew from the executive saying that it was being wrecked by problems over leadership, peace talks and finance, and appealed for a meeting of the Palestine National Council. In August the well-known poet Mahmud Darwish resigned from the Executive. At the end of the same month came the revelation that the PLO had been holding secret talks in Norway and at the end of September, the Charter against Israel was declared dead. Only nine of the 18-strong Executive voted for the proposal. Four voted against: five either resigned, boycotted the vote or were ill. Following the signing Israeli Minister Yossi Sarid said there had been no PLO violence. There was talk within the PLO of its dissolving itself in preparation for government. It requested $11.6 billion from the World Bank over seven years. The bank estimated that $3 billion would be needed over five years.

PALESTINE NATIONAL COUNCIL ALGIERS MEETING (1988)

In November 1988 the Palestine National Council met in Algiers with the object of supporting the *Intifadah* and trying to start a dialogue with the USA which had refused to talk to the Palestine Liberation Organisation as a "terrorist organisation". The groups that did not participate were Saiqa, the Popular Front for the Liberation of Palestine – General Command and the Fatah Revolutionary Command. The Council paid tribute to the "titanic" struggle of those in the Occupied Territories and called for the escalation of their efforts and for support from other Arab countries. It declared the right of the Palestinians to a land of their own and proclaimed the existence of a democratic, parliamentary State of Palestine with Jerusalem as its capital. A Provisional Government would be announced as soon as possible. It would co-exist with its neighbours. The Palestinian Republic was recognised by all Arab states except for Syria. The Council called for an international conference to discuss a peace settlement on the lines of Resolution 242 and Resolution 338. It demanded the withdrawal of Israeli troops and settlers from all the territories occupied in the June War including East

Jerusalem and that the territories should be placed under the supervision of the United Nations for a limited period. There should be a settlement of the refugee problem. At a subsequent press conference Yassir Arafat specifically recognised the right of Israel to exist for the first time and also "renounced" terrorism. Nevertheless the US refused to allow him a visa to address the UN in New York and the General Assembly had to meet in Geneva. Later the Americans accepted the disavowal of violence and opened a dialogue with the PLO which continued until June 1990 when Arafat refused to condemn an unsuccessful raid by the Palestine Liberation Front on an Israeli beach.

PALESTINE NATIONAL COUNCIL

In 1963 Ahmad Shuqayri was recognised by the Arab League as the chief spokesman for the Palestinian people and his position was formalised at the Cairo Summit of 1964 which approved the creation of the Palestine Liberation Organisation. He arranged for the creation of as representative as possible a body of 422 members, half of them from Jordan, as the Palestine National Council. The founding conference, held in Jerusalem in May/June 1964, declared itself the sovereign body of the PLO, the sole legitimate representative of the people, appealed for military volunteers, established the National Fund to which all should contribute and adopted the Palestine National Covenant despite the unwillingness of King Hussain to let it operate on his territory. The *second* Congress held in Cairo in May/June 1965 called for the gathering of all factions in a single organisation. The *third* Congress met in Gaza at the end of May 1966 at a time of bitter exchanges between the King and his Prime Minister Wasfi al-Tall and Shuqayri who gave free rein to those opposed to Hussain. The *fourth* Congress in Cairo in July 1968 rejected Resolution 242, pledged itself to the destruction of Israel by armed struggle and also amended the constitution of the PNC so that henceforth it consisted not of individuals but of representatives of the various guerrilla organisations, 38 members from Fatah, 10 from the Popular Front for the Liberation of Palestine, 20 from the Palestine Liberation Army as against 20 civilians from the PLO and 2 independents. Shuqayri was dismissed, and replaced by Yahya Hammouda, a leftist lawyer. The *fifth* Congress in Cairo in February 1969 rejected all foreign intervention in attempting to solve the problem, pledged to intensify guerrilla activity under a unified command and elected Yassir Arafat as Chairman. This show of Fatah predominance led to a boycott by the PFLP and PLA. The *sixth* assembly, in Cairo in September 1969, increased membership to 112 in the hope of satisfying all groups but the PFLP, demanding parity with Fatah, continued its boycott. Meeting before the conclusion of the Cairo Agreement it condemned the hostility of the Lebanese Government. The *seventh* council, meeting in Cairo at the end of May 1970 urged the unity of all guerrilla groups and deplored wasteful competition between them. The Council meeting in Cairo in March 1971 refused to demand the overthrow of Hussain after Black September and expressed opposition to aircraft hijacking. It approved an "Arafat Plan" for greater unity but did nothing to implement it, reaffirmed previous statements

and rejected any idea of a "mini-state" and increased its membership to 151 of whom 85 were representatives of guerrilla organisations, 25 of labour groups and 41 "independent". This Congress, the *eighth*, was dubbed "a complete failure" by the radical leaders George Habash and Nayif Hawatma. In July of the same year the PNC again met in Cairo and called upon all Arab states to put pressure on Hussain "to prevent any further massacre" of commandos. This *ninth* session was the first in which all commando organisations took part. The *tenth* Congress, expanded into a Popular Congress attended by over 500, met in Cairo in April 1972 to denounce Hussain's United Arab Kingdom Plan. Shuqayri called the US "a real enemy of all the Arabs" and demanded a boycott of their goods and a breach of diplomatic relations and asked that these measures be extended to Jordan. It called for unification of the groups which would be allowed ideological independence and internal autonomy. The *eleventh* Congress took place in Cairo in January 1973 and was marked by disputes over the role of the PLA and calls for greater financial support from the oil states. The *twelfth* in Cairo in June 1974 adopted a 10-point programme which included a resolution to set up a Palestinian authority on "every part of territory which is liberated", to help Jordanian democrats to take power and struggle in unity with Palestinians, to work with socialist states and promote unity between the frontline countries as a step towards Arab unity. The more radical groups, the PFLP, the Popular Front for the Liberation of Palestine – General Command and the Arab Liberation Front walked out as there was no firm commitment to no negotiations with Israel. The *thirteenth*, the last held in Cairo before Camp David ruled it out as a venue, in March 1977 agreed in a 15-point programme that in principle political negotiation might be used along with the armed stuggle as a means of gaining all Palestinian territory for a Palestinian state although it did not actually rule out a state on part only of the territory. It claimed the right to bases in Lebanon within the framework of the Cairo Agreement and to participate as an equal in negotiations on the area. This Congress seemed to confirm the leadership of Arafat but the next, the *fourteenth*, held in Damascus in January 1979 at a time when the Palestinians were split into groups supporting Syria and Iraq, objected to his "autocratic rule" and there were angry debates over the composition of the Executive Committee. The Rejection Front, led by Habash still remained aloof. The *fifteenth* Congress, held in Damascus in April 1981 was again marked by acrimony over the membership of the Executive Committee but ended with a strengthening of Fatah. The *sixteenth* Congress in Algiers in February 1983 was attended by 380 members. It rejected the Reagan Plan and was still not prepared to recognise the right of Israel to exist or to accept Hussain as having any authority to negotiate on behalf of Palestinians. After several postponements the *seventeenth* Congress, met in Amman in November 1984, boycotted by pro-Syrian factions. Amongst them was the Speaker, Khalid Fahoum who declared that there was no quorum but this difficulty was overcome by Arafat's co-opting loyalists to provide one. Challenged, he dramatically resigned but was "persuaded" to continue in office.

The session was addressed by Hussain who urged acceptance of Resolution 242 and the exchanging of peace for territory. The PNC agreed to study his proposals. The terrorist, Ahmad Jibril was expelled. The PNC decided to move its headquarters to Amman from Damascus but relations with the King soon deteriorated and the *eighteenth* session was held in Algiers in April 1987. This was later referred to as the "Reconciliation Congress" when former dissidents like the PFLP rejoined the mainstream and others, such as the Palestine Communist Party were admitted for the first time while only Syrian-backed factions, Saiqa, the Fatah rebels and Abu Nidal remained aloof. The PNC continued to reject Resolution 242 and all peace initiatives based upon it and called for an international conference which should be attended by the PLO as an equal participant. Friendly messages were sent to Walid Jumblatt and Hizbullah and conciliatory remarks made about Jordan but criticism of Egypt led to the closure of PLO offices there. It was attended by other nationalist movements such as Polisario. The *nineteenth* session, the Palestine National Council Algiers Meeting of November 1988 took the historic steps of proclaiming a Palestine Republic, accepting Resolution 242 and thereby the existence of Israel, and renounced terrorism. In January 1990 Habash called for a meeting of the PNC to discuss what had been achieved by these concessions. In April 1991 discussion started on electing members from the West Bank and Gaza. Hamas said it would not participate unless given half the seats – 452 members. In September 1991 at the twentieth meeting in Algiers Arafat proclaimed his "readiness" to wotk with the US on a peace conference but repeated his commitment to an independent Palestine with Jerusalem as the capital. There was a feeling that the PLO should take part in a peace conference but could not be expected to set the terms. Arafat agreed to drop the claim to nominate the Palestine delegation and was prepared to attend as a joint delegation with Jordan after the US guaranteed that they would be recognised as a distinct group. Arafat was anxious to keep unity but Hawatma and Habash saw it as a sell-out. Arafat objected to delegates having armed bodyguards while they spoke and said he should be the only one there with a gun. Saiqa and the Popular Front for the Liberation of Palestine – General Council boycotted his speech. Faysal al-Hussaini and Hnan Ashrawi put in a clandestine appearance. Haddoumi said he believed that the US was sincere. There was general support for the Arafat line. He made no reference to the possibility of continuing the armed struggle. He said he was ready to accept land for peace. He wanted an end to settlements and an end to Israeli occupation in return for Israel's commitment to Palestine's self-determination and rights in Jerusalem.

PALESTINE NATIONAL FRONT
In August 1973 nationalist leaders on the West Bank set up a coalition to act as the internal representative of the Palestine Liberation Organisation. It rejected any Jordanian role in any negotiations. Supposedly non-partisan and including many mayors, it had a strong communist element. After the October War it supported the Russian line of involvement in the Geneva Peace Conference which implied acceptance of Resolution 242 and a "two-state" solution. It co-ordinated the resistance and called effective strikes. The PNF won a notable triumph in the municipal elections of April 1976, winning control of the major towns and displacing pro-Jordanian mayors. The fourteenth session of the Palestine National Council in January 1979 called for its strengthening but in practice it became enmeshed in the internal politics of the PLO with radical groups such as the Popular Front for the Liberation of Palestine trying to use it to prevent Fatah from increasing its influence in the Occupied Territories. The PNF was finally crushed by the Israelis during the crackdown after Camp David.

PALESTINE NATIONAL SALVATION FRONT
In February 1985 King Hussain and Yassir Arafat signed the Amman Accord which provided for a joint peace-negotiating team leading to some form of confederation. It was denounced by the Syrians who the following month in Damascus induced the more radical groups subject to its influence to form a Front to oppose it. These were the Popular Front for the Liberation of Palestine, the Popular Front for the Liberation of Palestine – General Command, al-Saiqa, Fatah Revolution Council and the Popular Struggle Front. Syrian use of Amal to attack supporters of Fatah in refugee camps such as Burj al-Barajinah caused revulsion amongst Palestinian former clients and in February 1986 Hussain said that Arafat was not keeping his word, subsequently expelling Palestine Liberation Organisation representatives from Jordan. At the Algiers meeting of the Palestine National Council in April 1987 there was general reconciliation of guerrilla factions and George Habash, regarded as the leader of the NSF, said that effectively the Front had ceased to exist.

PALESTINIAN NATIONAL COVENANT
The inaugural meeting of the Palestine National Council in Amman in 1964 adopted as a Constitution a document drafted by its Chairman Ahmad Shuqayri. Influenced by the ideas of Nasser it declared that "Palestine is an indivisible part of the Arab homeland" and that Arab unity and the liberation of Palestine were complementary aims. There was a need to "forge a Palestinian consciousness" in the present generation. People born before the "Zionist invasion", even Jews, were Palestinians. Armed struggle was the only method of liberation. The State of Israel was "entirely illegal" and Zionism was racist, imperialist and fascist. The fight against it would be conducted by the Palestine Liberation Organisation which would co-operate with all Arab states but would not interfere in their internal affairs. The Covenant could be amended only by a two-thirds majority of the PNC. There were some changes made in 1968 and in May 1989 Yassir Arafat stated that the resolutions of the Palestine National Council Algiers Meeting of November 1988 with its proclamation of a Palestinian State and acceptance of Resolution 242 had rendered the Charter obsolete. The anti-Zionist rhetoric was renounced in the Israel–PLO Agreement of 1993.

PAN-ARAB DECLARATION (1980)

On 8 February 1980, the anniversary of the seizure of power by the Baath Party in 1963 Saddam Hussain put forward a bid for leadership of the Arab World. Addressing a mass rally he read out an 8-point declaration, pausing after each one to ask the crowd whether it agreed. The first rejected the presence of any foreign forces on Arab soil and then demanded the isolation of any government that permitted it. Secondly the banning of the use of armed force between Arab states. Thirdly the banning of the use of force between the Arabs and neighbouring states (not including "the Zionist entity" which was not a state) except in self defence. Fourthly the solidarity of the Arab states against any aggression against any of them by an outsider. Fifthly, the commitment of the Arab states to international law on the use of water and airspace. Sixthly the Arabs should remain completely neutral in any war outside their area. Seventhly the Arabs should co-operate for development despite political differences and should work towards economic integration. Finally Iraq declared its readiness to be committed to these principles and to discuss them with their Arab brothers. Points one and six were seen as criticism of Oman, Egypt and South Yemen and points three and five as possibly an approach to Iran for some kind of non-aggression pact. The final point was amplified into a call for a special Summit under Iraqi chairmanship. Syria which declared it would boycott the proposed Summit and South Yemen rejected the Declaration as anti-Soviet in that it did not differentiate between Russian and American bases. Other states gave tepid approval but the Summit never took place.

PARTI DE L'UNITÉ POPULAIRE (Tunisia)

In 1980 a split occurred in the illegal Mouvement de l'Unité Populaire, led by the exiled Ahmad Ben Salah between his radical followers abroad and a more moderate "internal" group led by Muhammad Belhadj Amor which became known as MUP-2. In January 1981 the MUP-2 was refused permission to form a party but it was allowed to participate in the elections of November 1981 as a "movement". It gained, however, less than 1% of the votes. In November 1983 MUP-2 received full legal recognition as a party and in 1985 renamed itself the Parti de l'Unité Populaire. As 10 of its proposed 30 candidates for the parliamentary elections of November 1986 were declared ineligible, the PUP refused to contest any seats. The PUP welcomed the seizure of power by Ben Ali and participated in the discussions for a National Pact. It refused an invitation to collaborate with the Tunisian Communist Party in the parliamentary elections of April 1989 but later formed a left-of-centre alliance with it and the Mouvement des Démocrates Socialistes. In August 1989 Jalloul Azzouna, leader of a splinter group of the PUP, was sentenced to one year's imprisonment for disparaging the President and for distributing a press statement without registering it: this was the first political trial under the new regime.

PARTI DÉMOCRATIQUE DE L'INDÉPENDENCE (Morocco)

Hizb al-Shura wa al-Istiqlal. In 1937 the French banned the National Action Bloc and the nationalist movement divided into two clandestine groups. The larger, traditionalist, Islamic and monarchist followed Allal al-Fassi and later emerged as the Istiqlal Party. The smaller, more modernist democratic and republican, recruited mainly from bourgeoisie with a French education, was led by Muhammad Hassan al-Wazzani who organised it as the Parti Démocratique de l'Indépendence in 1946. While Wazzani was in exile the PDI was led by Abd al-Qadir Ben Jalloun, a Casablancan lawyer. It did not reject the hope of reform by negotiation and in September 1947 a delegation, received by Marshal Juin, the Resident General, requested the end of the Protectorate, a Constituent Assembly and a new relationship with France. His refusal led the Party to improve relations with Muhammad V and in April 1951 it joined other groups, including from the Spanish Zone in a National Front. After the exiling of the Sultan in August 1953 the French tried to encourage it in order to prevent the Istiqlal from posing as the sole nationalist party and two of its leaders visited the Sultan in Madagascar to warn him against an Istiqlal monopoly. After independence the PDI had six Ministers in the Bekkai Cabinet compared with nine from istiqlal. Its strength was then estimated at about 150,000. The rivalry between the two became acute although there was little ideological difference except that the PDI put less stress on national discipline and the need for a strong state than on democratic liberty. In January 1956 there was a shoot-out between militants of the two parties in Suq al-Arba. In a government reshuffle in October 1956 Istiqlal insistence led to the elimination of PDI Ministers. In February 1958 the Government restricted public meetings of the PDI and suspended its newspapers. In 1959 the Party split with its younger and more left-wing members joining the new Union Nationale des Forces Populaires while the original members renamed their group the Parti Démocratique Constitutionel. It joined the Front pour la Defense des Institutions Constitutionelles, the supporters of the King set up to contest the 1963 elections. The PDC never attracted much support, winning only two seats in the August 1970 parliamentary elections and by the 1980s ceased to figure in lists of significant political parties.

PARTI DU PROGRÈS ET DU SOCIALISME (Morocco)

After the Moroccan Communist Party was declared illegal in 1959 its leader, Ali Yata, made several attempts to revive it under different names. In August 1974 when Hassan II was trying to consolidate national unity in support of his claim to the Western Sahara, Yata who had already toured the Communist Bloc to put Morocco's case, was allowed to form the Parti du Progrès et du Socialisme dedicated to "scientific socialism". Its first Congress in February 1975, attended by representatives of Eastern Europe, the Baath Party and the Palestine Liberation Organisation, demanded nationalisation of the main sectors of the economy and foreign property, reform of the agricultural system, control of prices, more Arabisation of education and the formation of a coalition government to supervise free elections. It declared Morocco not yet ready for a socialist revolution. In the parliamentary elections of

June 1977, although it contested half the seats, Yata was the only one of its candidates elected; it took 2.3% of the votes. At its Second Congress in February 1979 850 delegates called for a National Coalition Government, a non-aggression pact with Algeria and Mauritania to end the war with a united Maghreb. The PPS was represented on the all-party National Defence Council. In the referendum of June 1980 the PPS voted against the extension of the life of the Assembly from four to six years. In the local elections of June 1983 its share of the poll fell to 1% and it complained of fraud. Early in 1984 the King blamed communists and Islamic fundamentalists for riots in the steel town of Nador in which the number of dead varied from an official 29 to an opposition 240: some PPS members were jailed for up to five years. In the parliamentary elections of September 1984 it again took 2.3% with over 100,000 votes and won a second seat. The PPS claimed a membership of 40,000 although most estimates put it below 4,000, mainly in the Trade Unions and amongst students. It published two newspapers but unlike the other opposition parties it did not have its own trade union movement. Although it frequently attacked government policies, the PPS remained tolerated because it never attacked the person of the King or his policies in the Western Sahara. In 1991, however, after one of its activists had died in prison, it denounced an "administration that perpetuates the habits of the Middle Ages". During the Gulf Crisis of 1990/1 the PPS was the only party not to take a pro-Iraq stance. In May 1992 the PPS formed a Democratic Bloc with the Istiqlal and the Union Socialiste des Forces Populaires, issuing a Charter which demanded more democracy and an end to corruption. Unlike its partners it participated in the referendum on a new Constitution, supporting the proposals. The following month it improved its vote in the municipal elections. In the preparations for the parliamentary elections of June 1993 the PPS failed to reach agreement with its partners of the Democratic Bloc over a joint programme and the division of seats so it stood on its own, trebling its wins in the direct elections from two to six. The indirect elections brought it a further six and Ali Yata, again differing from his partners, expressed willingness to collaborate with the Government.

PARTI POPULAIRE SYRIEN (Lebanon)

Al-Hizb al-Suri al-Qawmi. In 1932 Antun Saadeh formed a secret organisation of five members, bound to him by a solemn oath, to recreate the historic Syria from the Tigris to the Mediterranean. Saadeh rejected both communism and democracy and declared that the duty of government was to protect the interests of the people rather than allow them to rule themselves: this he termed "symbolic democracy". Private capital should not be nationalised but controlled by the State and trade unions should be banned. As his following grew it was organised on Fascist lines with a Supreme Leader, a strict hierarchy, salutes and a swastika-type emblem. There was emphasis on discipline and dedication, members needed permission to emigrate or marry a foreign girl, and the group created the first paramilitary youth organisation seen in the Lebanon. It had branches in Syria, Egypt and Palestine but,

seeing itself as representing a Syria that had existed long before Islam and the Arab invasion, took little interest in Arab causes. The membership came mostly from students and the professional classes and the leaders professed not to know the religion of their supporters, although Jews could not be regarded as part of the Syrian nation. The group was so successful in maintaining its secrecy that the French did not learn of its existence for three years by which time it had several thousand members. It surfaced at a rally and shortly afterwards Saadeh was imprisoned, taking the opportunity to write a book setting forth his "scientific" doctrines. Alarm at its strength caused the Maronite Pierre Gemayel to form another youth movement, the Kataib on similar lines. In 1938 Saadeh went to Brazil and was absent for nearly ten years while the Party was led by Georges Abd al-Massih who was subsequently imprisoned by the Vichy authorities. Later, in Aleppo, he was sentenced to death for working for the Germans but was reprieved. After Lebanon had become independent the Minister of the Interior, Camille Chamoun licensed the PPS to operate legally provided that it dropped "Syrian" from its title. Saadeh resumed leadership in March 1947, refused to accept the omission of "Syrian" and the Party became the Syrian Social National Party.

PARTI SOCIALISTE DESTOURIEN (Tunisia)

In the years immediately after independence the Neo-Destour established itself as the sole party with a firm grip on the machinery of state, the trade unions, universities, the press etc. The electoral system of large constituencies favoured central control at the expense of regional leadership. It was, however, unclear about its doctrines and "Destourian Socialism" remained undefined enabling Ahmad Ben Salah to nationalise land and industries. This clear left-wing stance was marked when the seventh, the Bizerta Congress of October 1964, was officially dubbed the Congress of Socialism and the name of the Party changed. Bourguiba in a three-hour address declared a free economy inadequate for a developing society although private ownership was not totally condemned. The Political Committee was enlarged from 15 to about 50 to include regional representatives and about 10 members of this body would be selected by the President to form a Central Committee. The Central Committee included Ministers thus officially tying party and government together and the Party was declared "the motor of the state". Later Bourguiba was to say that the state was "the instrument implementing the Party's historical message". The leaders of the trade union movement were similarly co-opted and lost much of their autonomy. During the struggle for independence the Neo-Destour had aimed at mass membership to impress the French but the Parti Socialiste Destourien wished to constitute an élite. No great ideological commitment was required, applicants for membership were not even screened but after three years of showing willingness to do Party work they might be promoted "militant" – a prerequisite for office. The SPD had its own militia and organisations for women, students, etc. and provided favours, such as scholarships and local office, in return for obedience. The increasing momentum of Ben Salah's reforms divided the Party which in September 1969 expelled him. This was followed by the rise of a liberal group, led by Ahmad Mestiri, which complained that the regime was too authoritarian and that the 400,000 ordinary members, in about 1,400 branches, had little chance of making themselves heard and were confined to rallying support for the Government's decisions. Muhammad Sayah, Director of the Party, had great influence through his power to expel dissenters. Bourguiba gave some indications of readiness to reform but when the Monastir Congress of October 1971 endorsed the liberals, giving the most votes to Bahi Ladgham and Mestiri, he refused to appoint them to the Central Committee. Promises that posts in the PSD would be filled by election rather than nomination were not kept. In May 1973 Bourguiba decreed that non-members of the PSD should be expelled from the National Assembly. Before the Monastir Congress of 1974 four former Ministers were purged and during it Bourguiba reasserted his complete control being acclaimed Party President for Life and appointing all the members of the Politburo. His nominee, the Prime Minister Hedi Nouira became Secretary-General of the Party which became less socialist, encouraging private enterprise although the State kept control of key sectors. By 1978 it was clear that the Party was becoming ossified, no longer attracting the young while the trade unions under Habib Achour asserted their independence in a struggle that culminated on Black Thursday and Nouira gave Hedi Bakkush the task of rejuvenating it. In the Congress of September 1979 the Party Treasurer Abd Allah Farhat intrigued to get his own supporters into key posts and was dismissed. A major change was that the voters in the parliamentary elections of November 1979 had, for the first time, a choice between two candidates although both had to be members of the Party. Although some Party stalwarts were replaced by younger blood, such was the general lack of enthusiasm that in Tunis 32% of the electorate did not bother to vote. In April 1980 the new Prime Minister Muhammad Mzali took over as Secretary-General and moved Sayah out of the Party organisation. Against the opposition of the diehards, although with the endorsement of Congress, two-thirds of whose delegates were attending for the first time, other parties were allowed to contest the elections of November 1981 although massive fraud prevented them from winning any seats: 95% were declared to have supported PSD candidates. By 1984, although the official membership was 750,000, it was becoming clear that the young were turning from the secular Westernised ethos of the PSD towards Islam and Arabism. In May 1985 the opposition boycotted the local elections which nevertheless brought in 70% new councillors with a high proportion of youngish graduates. At the Twelfth Congress of June 1986, Bourguiba, so frail that he had to be supported and prompted throughout his speech, declared that he had personally checked the credentials of candidates for the Central Committee as an anti-corruption measure and his list of 80 was elected by acclamation. He also nominated three Assistant Secretaries-General, the Interior Minister General Ben Ali, his now closest associate Mansur Skhiri and his personal physician Amor Chadli. He endorsed Mzali as

his "son" and successor but three weeks later replaced him by Rashid Sfar. The legislative elections of November 1986 were boycotted by the opposition: 15 Independents who stood were all defeated. After taking power in November 1987 Ben Ali became Secretary-General, and cut the Politburo from 20 to 12, omitting many veterans. Bakkush, now Prime Minister, said that the Party would be reformed to take a leading role and in February 1988 its name was changed to the Rassemblement Constitutionel Démocratique.

PASSFIELD WHITE PAPER (1930)
Following the Wailing Wall Incident of August 1929 and the subsequent Shaw and Hope Simpson Commissions, the British Government found it necessary to set out its policy with regard to Palestine. This was drafted by the Colonial Secretary Lord Passfield and issued simultaneously with the Hope Simpson Report in October 1930. The White Paper, reaffirming the Churchill White Paper, stressed that international obligations compelled the Government to observe the terms of the Mandate and entailed equality of obligations to Arabs and Jews. It said rather plaintively that "it is too much to hope that any declaration of policy will fully satisfy the aspirations of either party . . . HMG have received little assistance from either side in healing the breach between them". There should be co-operation with the Jewish Agency which might offer advice but could not expect to share in the government of Palestine. It accepted the Hope Simpson view that there was little agricultural land available for new immigrants and his criticism that the Jewish refusal to employ Arabs was contrary to the Mandate. Unrestricted immigration would be contrary to the interests of both communities. Transfers of land would be more strictly controlled. Passfield announced the intention of setting up a Legislative Council of 22 Members of whom 12 would be elected. British police and military personnel would be increased. There was a great deal of opposition to it, both from Zionists and from lawyers who held that it was incompatible with Britain's obligations under the Mandate and it was effectively withdrawn after what became known as the "Black Letter" from the Prime Minister Ramsay MacDonald to the Zionist leader Chaim Weizmann saying that no real changes in policy were contemplated.

PATRIOTIC UNION OF KURDISTAN
After the collapse of the Kurdish Revolt (II) and the disintegration of Kurdistan Democratic Party in March 1975 the left-wing leader Jalal Talabani set out to build a new organisation amongst the exiles. In June 1976 he established the Patriotic Union of Kurdistan in Damascus where the Government was happy to support opponents of the regime in Baghdad. It consisted of some Marxist-Leninists (the Komala), some milder socialists and Talabani's personal following. The Komala had members within Kurdistan and started fighting against Baghdad's policy of mass deportations of Kurds late in 1976. In 1977 Talabani moved his HQ into Kurdistan, receiving supplies from Syria by way of Turkey. Soon he was quarrelling with the KDP which had been revived under the sons of Mulla Mustafa Barzani. In the spring of 1978 KDP guerrillas defeated

800 *Pesh Mergas* of the PUK and hanged their leaders. Some of the socialists then split away to form the Socialist Party of Kurdistan–Iraq. Talabani managed to re-establish his authority in Sorani-speaking areas and formed an alliance with the Democratic Party of Iranian Kurdistan led by Abd al-Rahman Qassimlu who was at war with the Barzanis. In 1980 the PUK formed part of a National Democratic Front with Arab opponents of the Government, the Iraq Communist Party and the SPK-I but its two partners then formed a second National Democratic Front with the PUK's foes, the KDP. The PUK thereupon attacked the SPK-I, killed hundreds of its members and drove the remnants up to the north-east frontier area. When, during the Iran–Iraq War the Barzanis with Iranian support invaded Iraq in 1983 the PUK resisted them. This led to a reconciliation with Baghdad but prolonged negotiations broke down early in 1985 and new fighting broke out; the PUK attacked an army garrison and kidnapped two Russian technicians. The PUK received some help from Syria and perhaps from Libya, sent its wounded to Iran for treatment and enjoyed good relations with the Turkish Kurds. This alarmed Ankara which co-operated with Baghdad against the PUK. Tehran, meanwhile, arranged for the PUK to be reconciled with the KDP and for it to establish connections with the Shiah al-*Dawah* Party. Talabani later declared that the Union controlled large regions of Kurdistan but the end of the war freed the Government to concentrate on bringing the area under control and little was heard of the PUK.

PEACE DAY (1987)
The beginning of the *Intifadah* had a powerful effect on the previously largely quiescent Arab population living within the pre-1967 boundaries of Israel. Tawfiq Zayad, the communist mayor of Nazareth was one of the leaders who called for a general strike as a display of solidarity against "Israeli barbarism in the occupied territories". The strike on 21 December 1987 was almost universally observed. Demonstrators called for the peaceful resolution of the Arab–Israeli conflict through the auspices of an international conference to be attended by all parties to the dispute including the Palestine Liberation Organisation, Israeli withdrawal from the West Bank and Gaza and the establishment of an independent Palestinian state in those territories.

PEEL REPORT (1937)
In August 1936 after the start of the general strike which preceded the Arab Rebellion the British Government appointed a Royal Commission "to ascertain the underlying causes of the disturbances", to enquire whether the obligations under the Mandate to Arabs and Jews were being implemented and whether either community had legitimate grounds for complaint, and if so to make recommendations. The Chairman was Lord Peel, a former Secretary of State for India, there were two judges, a former Indian Governor, but perhaps the two most influential members were Sir Horace Rumbold, a former Ambassador to Berlin and Professor Sir Reginald Coupland, an eminent historian of colonial administration. The Commission spent three months in Palestine with its deliberations reputedly "bugged" by the Zionists and at first the Higher Arab

Committee, guided by the Mufti Haj Amin al-Hussaini refused to testify before it; only at the last moment did it bow to the urging of the independent Arab rulers and give evidence. The Report stated that the underlying causes were "the desire of the Arabs for national independence and their hatred and fear of the establishment of the Jewish national home". Subsidiary causes were the public excitement arising from the achievement of independence by other Arab lands, worldwide pressure on behalf of the persecuted Jews of Europe, the greater access to Whitehall believed to be enjoyed by the Jews, purchase of Arab land by Jews, growing distrust of London and the provocative language of irresponsible Jews. There was disbelief in the promise that the Mandate would lead the Arabs to independence. The second part of the Report contained detailed recommendations in such fields as administration, agriculture, finance, education and immigration which should be regulated not only by economic capacity but by political considerations. It should be limited to 12,000 families a year, not necessarily all Jewish. The third section, recognising "the irreconcilable conflict between the aspirations of Arabs and Jews", recommended "drastic treatment" – "Partition seems to offer at least a chance of ultimate peace. We can see none in any other plan". The Mandate should continue over a corridor from Jaffa to Jerusalem and contain the Arab towns of Bethlehem, Ramla and Lydda. The coastal plain and the districts of Haifa and Galilee should be a new Jewish state. The rest, including Gaza and the Negev, would be united with Trans-Jordan. This arrangement would necessitate the transfer, perhaps compulsorily, of nearly 300,000 Arabs from the Jewish to the Arab area. The proposal was instantly rejected by the Arabs of Palestine who demanded independence and the end of the Mandate and by other Arabs such as Ibn Saud who had advocated co-operation with the Commission while the potential beneficiary, Amir Abd Allah, half-heartedly went along with the rest. The Jews were non-committal, requesting further information on the Government's intentions. The Peel Commission was perhaps the strongest ever appointed and its Report was a document of intellectual distinction. It was the first time that the possibility of Partition had been officially discussed. The Foreign Office and the Colonial Office considered the scheme for Partition likely to be unworkable and to cause more problems than it solved. The following year the Woodhead Commission was sent to work out the practical details.

PENINSULA SHIELD
The Gulf Co-operation Council established a Military Committee and the Chiefs of Staff of the six members first met in September 1981. After the AWACS Deal Saudi Arabia was in a position to co-ordinate possible military operations on behalf of its partners. In October 1983 the six rulers watched joint exercises held in Abu Dhabi to demonstrate the feasibility of co-ordinating their armed forces. The following year a fortnight of exercises in north-eastern Saudi Arabia involved 10,000 men including parachute drops, night attacks and air strikes. At the GCC Summit Meeting at Kuwait immediately afterwards it was decided that most of the

troops should be kept permanently together, under the command of a Saudi General and based on King Khalid Military City at Hafr al-Batin. Owing to practical difficulties of uniting the forces, the Secretary-General Abd Allah Bishara said that it would be largely symbolic and Sultan Qabus Al Bu Said, the only Ruler with army training and experience admitted, "we do not have the army that can defend the security of the Gulf". Moulding the armed forces of the member states into a credible unit would have demanded complete restructuring and by removing them from their role of internal security would possibly have endangered some of the ruling families. Some steps were made towards co-ordination in arms procurement and there were discussions of a local arms industry. After the Iraqis invaded Kuwait the Peninsula Shield contingent was subsumed in the larger allied forces. In February 1991 there were discussions about involving Iran in future security arrangements and the Damascus Declaration envisaged defence of the area being undertaken by Egyptian and Syrian troops paid for by the Gulf States. In August 1991 the Chiefs of Staff met in Muscat and agreed in principle to set up a new joint defence force.

PEOPLE'S PARTY (Syria)

Hizb al-Shaab. After the overthrow by the French of the government of King Faysal his most ardent supporters went into exile. Many of them were amnestied and returned in 1924 and organised themselves around Dr Shahbandar and Faris al-Khouri to form the People's Party. They demanded the recognition of Syrian sovereignty, its right to democratic government, its unification within its natural boundaries and the guarantee of human rights including compulsory education. It also demanded independence for all Arabs. It strongly opposed the collaborationist government of Subhi Barakat. The Party received financial support from the Syro-Palestinian Congress in Cairo. By June 1925 it claimed 1,000 members, mostly from the educated classes in Damascus. It was not a monolithic party but consisted of groups following individual leaders. The following month the Druze Revolt erupted and the People's Party, giving it full support, was banned by the French. Some of its members, however, including Khouri, and Lutfi al-Haffar were members of the Cabinet of the *Damad* Ahmad Nami. They and other People's Party members were later amongst the leaders of the National Bloc. Its name was later assumed by a second People's Party in 1948.

PERIM

Perim, known in Arabic as Mayun, is a small island in the Bab-al-Mandab about 1 mile off the Arabian coast and 11 miles from Africa. As it dominates the entrance to the Red Sea it has great strategic importance but is completely without fresh water. Albuquerque the Portuguese leader considered fortifying it in 1513 but had to reject the idea. In 1799 after Bonaparte's invasion of Egypt it was briefly occupied by the British but they were compelled by the lack of water to move to Aden. In 1857 as the building of the Suez Canal was starting, the British feared that Perim might be annexed by the French. Learning that a warship charged with this mission was putting into Aden, the Resident there,

according to a legend strongly denied officially, made its officers drunk and had the British flag planted there before they could return to sobriety. A lighthouse was erected. In 1881 a London businessman obtained permission to start a coaling station there and this provided formidable competition for Aden, acquiring a larger share of the business within a few years. Perim also achieved further importance as a centre for pearl fishing and of a cable network. In October 1914 the British feared that the Turks occupying Shaykh Said on the mainland would attempt to capture Perim so they launched a pre-emptive attack, destroying enemy positions. The Turks reoccupied Shaykh Said and, having on several occasions bombarded the island, attempted a night attack in June 1915. This was repulsed without difficulty. By 1935 the shift to oil fuel destroyed the prosperity of Perim and the coal company left, followed by the Cable and Wireless. The island was left virtually uninhabited except for a few fishermen, a detachment of police and the two lighthouses. The manager of the coal company had administered the island and this responsibility was taken over by the Aden Police Commissioner who was represented by a local Arab agent. Perim was bombed several times by the Italians in 1940/1. In 1971, after it had become part of the new state of South Yemen, it was said to have provided a base from which Palestinian guerrillas attacked an Israeli tanker.

PETROMIN

The General Petroleum and Mineral Organisation of Saudi Arabia was created on the initiative of the Oil Minister Shaykh Yamani in 1962 with the task of developing and exploiting the petroleum resources in the national interest, particularly marketing oil and natural gas on an international scale, processing within the country and participating in the international energy transport industry. Wholly owned by the Government, it worked in partnership with ARAMCO. In 1967 it started operating a new refinery built by the Japanese near Jiddah and took over the marketing of petroleum products within the Kingdom. The First Five-Year Plan of 1970 put Petromin in charge of diversification and its first project was the Saudi Fertiliser Plant, in which it took 51% of the shares and sold the rest to the Saudi public. It built a series of major refineries and a pipeline which made possible the Yanbu and Jubayl Development Schemes. It was also responsible for gathering the 3,000 cubic feet of gas a day which previously had wastefully been burned off. There were demarcation disputes between Abd al-Hadi Tahir, the Governor of Petromin and the Planning Minister Hisham Nazir. In December 1975 after the creation of a new Ministry of Industry and Power, Petromin's functions were restricted to marketing, refining, distribution and transport of oil internally and abroad and to control of some technical companies. Petromin was much concerned with the technical training of Saudi nationals, setting up a University at Dhahran and Industrial Training Centres in other cities. Amongst other activities was prospecting for gold. In 1987 many of the operating parts were given a large measure of autonomy while remaining under the umbrella of Petromin.

PHILIPPEVILLE MASSACRES (1955)

After the initial surprise of the All Saints' Day Uprising, the Algerian War of Independence made little progress in the next eight months. The commanders of the *wilaya* covering North Constantine, Yusuf Zightut and Lakhdar Ben Tobal, determined to provoke by an atrocity the French colon population into a reaction against the Muslims that would provide the Front de Libération Nationale with new recruits. In August 1955 there was a series of concerted attacks on European communities in the neighbourhood of Philippeville. At a mining centre FLN guerrillas joined by frenzied crowds killed babies by bashing their heads against walls, disembowelled women and kicked old ladies to death. French soldiers arriving upon the scene opened fire at random upon Muslims, killing so many that bulldozers had to be used to shovel the bodies into graves. The Governor-General, Jacques Soustelle, stated that 71 Europeans and 52 Arabs were killed by the FLN and 1,273 "insurgents" died at the hands of the security forces: the FLN claimed that over 12,000 Muslims had been killed. Soustelle himself who had gone to Algiers hoping to end the fighting by liberal concessions which would enable the two communities to live together came to the conclusion that it could only be ended by force and that thenceforth there was "an abyss through which flowed a river of blood" between them.

POPULAR FRONT FOR THE LIBERATION OF OMAN

By the summer of 1974 in the hope of getting financial aid, the government of South Yemen started to abate its hostility to the rich oil-states of the Gulf and dropped its previous commitment to overthrowing their regimes, where anyway there was little enthusiasm for revolution. In August the Congress of the Popular Front for the Liberation of the Occupied Arab Gulf meeting in Aden was instructed to change its name and confine its activities to prosecuting the Dhofar Rebellion. The fighting there had turned in favour of Sultan Qabus b. Said Al Bu Said and the insurgents controlled only an 80-km strip east of the Yemeni frontier. Its fighting strength was probably about 800 militants supported by a "militia" of about 1,000. Arms were received from China after Russia saw more advantage in trying to conciliate the Shah whose troops were assisting the Sultan but the PFLO depended entirely on Aden especially after the winter of 1975/6 when its last units were driven from Dhofar. The hardcore had established hospitals and schools, for which children were kidnapped and brought across the frontier, on Yemeni territory and claimed to rule over 3,000 refugees, although the number constantly diminished in response to amnesties offered by the Sultan. They carried out sporadic raids, sometimes assisted by Yemeni soldiers. In July 1982 the leaders tried without success to bring in non-Marxists to form United Oman National Front, abandoning revolutionary rhetoric, focusing on democracy and no longer calling for the overthrow of the Sultan. The normalisation of relations between Aden and Muscat still further weakened the remnant which was reduced to a small group begging for Syrian money.

POPULAR FRONT FOR THE LIBERATION OF PALESTINE

The June War of 1967 led many Palestinians to feel that they could not rely on the armies of the Arab states to regain their rights but had themselves to play the leading role in the struggle. In the winter of 1967/8 various groups such as the Palestine Liberation Front, the Return Heroes Organisation and the Vengeance Youth Organisation came together under the leadership of George Habash, Wadia Haddad and Nayif Hawatma to form the Popular Front for the Liberation of Palestine, pledged to use revolutionary violence to "transform Palestine into an inferno which burns the invaders". Every Palestinian had a part to play in the resistance and every Arab a duty to oppose world imperialism. The liberation of Palestine should thus proceed hand in hand with a struggle for a people's revolution throughout the Middle East. Its first demand was the dismissal of Ahmad Shuqayri. The PFLP contained many former members of the Arab Nationalist Movement who had strong right-wing views and from the earliest days there was strife between them and the Marxist-Leninists led by Hawatma who at the first congress in August 1968 succeeded in committing the PFLP to "scientific socialism". This led to the breakaway of the followers of Ahmad Jibril to form the Popular Front for the Liberation of Palestine – General Command. The ideological debate continued however, and the decision that the PFLP was a nationalist group, borrowing a few slogans from Mao Tse Tung and Che Guevara, rather than a socialist movement caused Hawatma to split away to form the (Popular) Democratic Front for the Liberation of Palestine. There was fighting between the groups and Fatah had to intervene to prevent the liquidation of the leftists. Habash announced his own conversion to Marxism but hostility between the groups persisted for several years. The PFLP engaged in guerrilla skirmishes within the Occupied Territories but its originality lay in the realisation that activities outside Palestine attracted far more international attention and, through the television screen, would become known in households throughout the world. The PFLP was also the first commando organisation to recruit women in substantial numbers. It initiated a series of aircraft hijackings of which that of an El Al plane to Algiers in August 1968 was the first while an attack on an El Al aircraft at Athens in December led to the Beirut Airport Attack – a warning to Arab states to keep guerrillas under control. Then two by Leila Khalid attracted great publicity while the destruction of four aircraft at Dawson's Field was even more spectacular. The Egyptian Government condemned the PFLP as responsible for the tragedies of Black September and also for claiming credit for successes actually achieved by other groups. The close links of the PFLP with South Yemen and its hostility to the Saudi regime was shown by the attack on an Israeli tanker in the Coral Sea Incident in June 1971. The PFLP declared its intention of making "the world a theatre of commando operations" but Russian and Chinese leaders urged Habash to call a halt which he did in a press conference in Beirut in March 1972. This led to the defection of Haddad who continued his terrorist activities. At the same time, with Syrian support, the Popular Revolutionary Front for the Liberation of Palestine broke away under Abu Shihab. The PFLP maintained links with international terrorist organisations as was shown in the Lydda Airport Attack in May 1972. The PFLP was anxious to be regarded as the equal of Fatah and as early as February 1969 boycotted the Palestine National Council when refused equal representation. In August 1974, accusing Yassir Arafat of opening secret links with the Americans in the hope of a negotiated peace, Habash withdrew the PFLP also from the Executive Committee of the Palestine Liberation Organisation and set up the Rejection Front. The PFLP gave strong support to Kamal Jumblatt and other leftist leaders during the early part of the fighting in Lebanon. About this time an Israeli estimate put its full-time fighting strength at between 500 and 1,000. In 1983 after the split in Fatah the PFLP and the DFLP decided to reunite but this did not last long. Habash moved closer to Syria and followed its denunciation of the Amman Accord by the formation in March 1986 of the Palestine National Salvation Front – an alliance of radical and pro-Syrian groups. Later Habash criticised Syria for allowing its surrogate Amal to attack Palestinian camps and the breakdown of negotiations between Arafat and King Hussain led to the PFLP's rejoining the mainstream PLO which it did at the Algiers meeting of the PNC in April 1987. The PFLP, unlike the DFLP, accepted the decisions of the Palestine National Council Algiers Meeting of November 1988 but came to consider that there had been insufficient return for the concessions made there. It moved therefore, once more into opposition to Fatah and early in 1990 allied with Hamas to prevent Fatah from dominating the *Intifadah*. In November 1990 the PFLP claimed responsibility for an attack in Northern Israel. In September 1991 the Isaelis announced that they had rounded up 450 activists and uncovered a cache of weapons and dollars together with a clandestine printing press. It was claimed that the PFLP had killed 20 of their own members whom they had suspected of collaboration. In October 1991 the PFLP opposed the Madrid Conference and took part in the Ayn Halwah mutiny that tried to unseat Arafat. Their radio station in Damascus frequently attacked him. In January 1992 alleged members were rounded up to placate settlers after it was said that the PFLP had attacked Israeli vehicles. In April the PFLP announced they were prepared to accept confederation with Jerusalem after independence.

POPULAR FRONT FOR THE LIBERATION OF PALESTINE – GENERAL COMMAND

In 1959 Ahmad Jibril founded a small group, the Palestine Liberation Front, to carry out terrorist operations against Israel. In 1967 he merged it into the Popular Front for the Liberation of Palestine but the following year Jibril considered its leader George Habash too involved in Marxist ideological matters so he broke away to form the PFLP – General Command which aimed at military efficiency rather than political sophistication. It joined the Palestine Armed Struggle Command. Organised into small cells it specialised in suicide missions into Israeli territory and attacks upon aircraft. Its first known operation was an attack on an Israeli bus in May 1970 when eight schoolchildren were killed and in 1972 its attack upon an Israeli bus provided a pretext for a major incursion into southern Lebanon. Its most notorious action was the seizure of a block of flats at Qiryat Shemona in April 1974 which led to a shoot-out in which the three guerrillas involved and 18 Israelis were killed. Later that year it joined the Rejection Front. In July 1975 it claimed responsibility for a bomb in Jerusalem which killed 14 and wounded 78. Although it took arms and money from anyone who would supply them, the PFLP-GC was generally pro-Syrian and worked closely with its Saiqa organisation. It was not represented on the Council of the Palestine Liberation Organisation and often ignored its decisions, for example it refused to freeze its operations in Lebanon. Jibril refused to join other Palestinian groups in fighting Syrian troops in Lebanon and this led to a split amongst his followers with a pro-Iraqi faction led by Abu al-Abbas forming a new Palestine Liberation Front in April 1977. In May the PFLP-GC was formally expelled from the Central Council of the Rejection Front. The PFLP-GC, financed by Libya and Syria, continued its operations and after the Iranian Revolution established close links with Iran and its allies such as Hizbullah. In June 1982 its members did not distinguish themselves in the fighting of Operation Peace for Galilee. In the autumn of 1983 the PFLP – GC fought against Yassir Arafat during the Fatah mutiny in Lebanon. In May 1985 it exchanged 3 captured Israeli soldiers for a large number of Israeli hostages and prisoners including the Japanese survivor of the Lydda Airport Attack. A spectacular exploit was the use of hang-gliders to attack Israel and kill six soldiers in late 1987. The PFLP – GC had joined the Palestine National Salvation Front on its formation in March 1985 and in April 1987 it did not take part in the general reconciliation of guerrilla factions at the Palestine National Council meeting in Algiers. In December 1988 the PFLP-GC was accused of placing the bomb that destroyed an American airliner over Lockerbie. As Qadafi became more anxious for acceptance by the West, he cut off his subsidy, reckoned at $4 million a month, to the PFLP-GC which was forced to rely on Iranian money. Jibril's alliance with Hizbullah as it fought against the Syrian-backed Amal for the allegiance of the Lebanese Shiah brought the group near to another split which was only averted by a division of authority. Jibril was left in command of military operations in the Lebanon while his more moderate deputy Talal Najih took charge of political leadership. In November 1989 the PFLP-GC was estimated to have between 800 and 1,000 members, mostly in Syria and Syrian-controlled Lebanon. In 1988 a network of 16 agents operating in Germany was rounded up. One was a known bomb-maker. In November it called for mourning after the PNC Algiers Meetings recognised Israel. In May 1991 the PFLP-GC said that forces in Lebanon would disarm like other militias. In July it claimed responsibility for a series of attacks on Israeli positions in Gaza. The PFLP-GC ran Sawt al-Quds radio in Damascus – more powerful than Arafat's transmitter in Baghdad – and attacked him for his readiness to talk to the the the Israelis. The PFLP-GC's killing of 2

Israeli soldiers in South Lebanon set off the cycle of events that led to Operation Accountability in 1993.

POPULAR FRONT FOR THE LIBERATION OF THE OCCUPIED ARAB GULF

At its Zinjibar Congress of March 1968 the National Liberation Front which had seized power in South Yemen declared that its revolution would not be regarded as complete until it had spread throughout the Peninsula. The United Arab Emirates was derided as "a creature of Anglo-American Imperialism and Iranian-Arab reaction" and the "fake independence" of Bahrain and Qatar denounced. Financial and military support was provided for the Dhofar Liberation Front which had started the Dhofar Rebellion mainly as a tribal protest against the refusal of all reform and development by Sultan Said b. Taymur Al Bu Saidi. This aid was used as a lever to transform the DLF into a Marxist-Leninist revolutionary organisation to join which pressure was brought on radical nationalists in the other Gulf states. At its second Congress in Hamrin in Central Dhofar in September 1968 the DLF renamed itself the Popular Front for the Liberation of the Occupied Arab Gulf and called for "organised revolutionary violence" as a road to "scientific socialism". A 25-man General Command was set up with Muhammad Ahmad al-Ghassani as Secretary-General. The Central Committee was in Aden where it had its own radio and there were offices in Bahrain, Kuwait, Qatar, the UAE and later Libya. It had close relations with the Popular Front for the Liberation of Palestine. Iraq provided money, China weapons and the PDRY, Russia and Cuba military training and political indoctrination. Many of the original dissidents fell away as the leaders reviled Islam and attacked tribal loyalties. The PFLOAG was effective only in Dhofar where it had a hard core of about 2,000 highly-motivated fighting men and a further 4,000 armed supporters. The Sultan was unwilling either to spend money on crushing the rebellion or to conciliate the insurgents by political reforms and by the end of 1969 they ruled all Dhofar except for a heavily fortified enclave around Salala. They ran their own schools orientated towards the teaching of Marxism, clinics, and ruthless "People's Courts" which normally executed any accused without trial. People were tortured for refusing to abandon Islam or tribal traditions. Particular emphasis was laid on the rights of women. In July 1970 Qabus b. Said Al Bu Saidi took power and immediately set out to win over the dissidents by promises of reform, development, amnesty, financial support for those who surrendered, and, at the same time greatly augmented the fighting strength of his own forces. The Third Congress of the PFLOAG in Rakhyut in June 1971 put forward a 29-point programme but could not compete with the solid benefits provided by the Sultan's use of increasing oil revenues. Attempts at rebellions in other parts of Oman were suppressed. The war turned against the PFLOAG and by the summer of 1974 they were confined to a small area in Western Dhofar. The Aden Government under Salim Rubai Ali, in desperate financial straits, was anxious to gain economic support from the Gulf States and dropped all attempts to subvert them. The PFLOAG was therefore instructed to restrict its activities to Dhofar and to rename itself the Popular Front for the Liberation of Oman.

POPULAR STRUGGLE FRONT (Palestine)

In July 1968 a small left-wing group led by Bahjat Abu Gharbiah and Dr Samir Ghosha broke away from the main Fatah and received the patronage of Iraq, co-operating closely with the Baghdad-sponsored Arab Liberation Front. In July 1973 it announced that it had rejoined Fatah and would merge its fighting men, who probably never exceeded 100, with the military wing of Fatah, *Asifa*. A year later it broke away again, joining the Rejection Front. The PSF continued outside the mainstream, joining the Palestine National Salvation Front upon its formation in March 1985. At the 1987 meeting of the Palestine National Council in Algiers it took part in the general spirit of reconciliation.

PRESIDIOS TROUBLES (1987)

The Presidios of Ceuta and Melilla on the North coast of Morocco have been held by Spain since the sixteenth century. Ceuta, covering with its hinterland an area of just under twenty square kilometres had a population of about 70,000 while Melilla in just over twelve square kilometres had about 60,000 of whom 27,000 were Muslims. After the other Spanish possessions in North Africa, Ifni and the Western Sahara had been handed over to Morocco the Presidios continued to be ruled from Madrid, although the Moroccans had raised the question at the UN in January 1975 and there had been some bombs later in the year. Moroccans pointed out the inconsistency between Spain's demands for the return of Gibraltar and its refusal to return the Presidios. There were demands for their liberation by politicians such as Muhammad Boucetta but official relations between the two states were good and in 1984 they had held joint manoeuvres. In 1985 Madrid gave certain legislative powers to provincial assemblies but not to the Presidios. It also joined the EEC and consequently promulgated a law regulating the position of non-citizens. Many Muslims in Melilla, although their families had been resident for generations, were technically illegal as they had never formally applied for Spanish citizenship: they were given until 1 April 1986 to regularise their position. Some were granted citizenship and a census started of Muslim residents. A 35-year-old economics graduate from Malaga University, Aomar Muhammad Dudu set up an organisation to demand full citizenship and denounce "South African style laws". There were protest strikes by Muslims early in 1986 which were dealt with brutally and in June a riot as Christians attacked Muslims applauding the opponents of Spain in the World Football Cup. In September Dudu was appointed an adviser to the Spanish Government but after a general stike in Melilla, he defected to Morocco. In February 1987 there was a weekend of violence with one demonstrator killed, 70 injured and 40 arrested. Madrid brought in more Civil Guards, appointed a hard-line Governor and refused to consider the creation of a joint committee with Morocco to study the problem. On Throne Day in March Hassan II publicly received the allegiance of Dudu and referred to "our faithful subjects in our two cities of Ceuta and Melilla". There were further riots and arrests in June but neither Spain nor Morocco wanted a confrontation as they were negotiating over fishing rights and Hassan had made an application to join the EEC. In July Spain gained an extension of a favourable fishing treaty while Morocco received free transit for goods across Spain. In September 1989 Hassan paid his first official visit to Spain since independence and said that he would maintain Morocco's claim but not to the extent that it would cause "fever" between the two countries: he signed a five-year military agreement and arranged for an annual meeting of Prime Ministers. In August 1990, Boucetta threatened to liberate by force the last vestiges of colonialism in Africa but by then the main problem between the two countries concerned illegal immigration.

QADAFI, Muammar (c. 1941)

Libyan "Leader, Thinker and Symbol". Born in a tent in the desert near Sirte, he came from a bedouin family with no identification with any of the three provinces and a record of resistance to the Italians; his grandfather had been killed in 1911 and his father and uncle were later condemned to death but reprieved. He went to a Qur'anic school at Sirte and throughout his life remained influenced by the religious teaching that he had received; he once said that everything including the atom bomb could be found in the Qur'an which, although a pious Muslim, he often used as a political tool, interpreting it to justify his own theories. He was at the same time captivated by the image of Nasser projected by *Sawt al-Arab*. In 1956 his family moved to the Fezzan where he attended Sabhah School where he formed a nationalist group amongst his schoolfellows who included Abd al-Salam Jalloud. He was expelled for leading a demonstration and finished his education at Misurata where he founded another group which included Umar al-Muhayshi whom he encouraged to join the army as he was convinced that civilians could never bring about the revolution he regarded as essential. He himself joined the Military Academy in 1964 and attended part-time courses in history and geography at Benghazi University although he did not take a degree. He spent several months in 1966 at Beaconsfield on a signals training course. During 1969, by then a Captain, he made plans for a military coup which twice had to be postponed and then had to be hurried through on 1 September to pre-empt the possible abdication of King Idris and a take over by Colonel Abd al-Aziz al-Shalhi. Although he personally broadcast the news he remained anonymous for over a week and the names of the members of the Revolution Command Council were not revealed. No programme was published and there was an impotent civilian Cabinet and an invisible RCC which a provisional constitution published in December 1969 had declared "the highest authority": the arrest of two ministers in the same month added to the confusion. In January 1970 Qadafi assumed the Premiership giving 8 out of 13 portfolios to officers. His first objective was the complete withdrawal of foreign troops which was achieved when the Americans left Wheelus air base in June 1970. He also ended arms contracts with British companies. Declaring "he who engages in party politics commits treason", he abolished them in the name of national unity. The Sanusi *tariqah* was also banned. The 25,000 remaining Italians and Jews were expelled and their property confiscated: the Italian Government needing

Libyan oil made no protest. Arab specialists replaced foreigners and Western script was banned in public signs and official publications. Foreign banks were nationalised and, with a shrewd strategy of picking off the weakest without alternative sources, the oil companies were brought to heel leading to an enormous increase in Libyan revenues. There were show trials of over 200 members of the *ancien regime*. Showing what Hassanain Haykal called "a terrifying innocence of the real world", Qadafi declared that his attitude towards states would be determined by their stance over Palestine and he attempted to buy nuclear weapons from China. He saw himself as the successor of Nasser, a philosopher-leader of the Arabs, needing a larger stage than Libya to display his talents. He rushed into the Federation of Arab Republics in which he was soon quarrelling with his Sudanese partners whom he considered too tolerant of communism: he was angered by the lack of enthusiasm shown by Sadat and tried to enforce unity with a "holy march" after behaviour in Cairo which led to serious questioning of his sanity. Believing that Israel could be defeated by uniting Libyan money with the manpower of another state, Qadafi was over the next fifteen years to propose union with Tunisia (Arab–Islamic Republic, 1974), Algeria (Hassi Masaoud, 1975), Syria (Libyan–Syrian Union, 1980), Morocco (Oujdah Declaration, 1984) and even Chad. While calling for Arab unity he quarrelled with other leaders, calling for the execution of King Hussain for Black September, publicly regretting that Hassan II had survived the Skhirat Attempt and insulting King Faysal as "nothing but an oil merchant". He briefly broke off relations with Baghdad after the signature of the Iraqi–Soviet Treaty but at the same time sent Jalloud to Moscow: he saw Russia's role in the Middle East as an arms supplier without political influence. Qadafi condemned Sadat for accepting a cease-fire in the October War and offered personally to lead the Egyptian army to victory. After much criticism of the lack of activity by the Palestine Liberation Organisation he funded the terrorists Ahmad Jibril and Abu Nidal. Libya gave heroes' funerals to the terrorists killed in the Munich Olympics Massacre. In December 1971 he had taken over the assets of British Petroleum as a reprisal for the Iranian occupation of Abu Musa Island in the Gulf and he was consistently hostile to the British, assisting Irish terrorists, the Argentinians in the Falklands War and the miners in their strike of 1984/5. In March 1973 the Irish navy intercepted a load of arms and later that year he tried to persuade an Egyptian submarine officer to sink the British liner

336

Queen Elizabeth II. His support helped the blood-thirsty Idi Amin to stay in power in Uganda. At home meanwhile he was attempting to refashion Libya as an idealised version of Egypt under Nasser, founding in June 1971 the Arab Socialist Union with doctrine based on Islam rather than Marxism. He declared it intolerable that one person should own a company and merchants were "unproductive exploiters". During 1971 Qadafi resigned twice and survived at least one assassination attempt and in July 1972 he handed over the Premiership and in April 1974 ceremonial and administrative duties to Jalloud who was to supervise domestic affairs while he himself concentrated on preparing a transformation of Libyan society. This bore fruit in his Zuwarah speech of April 1973 which launched the Libyan Cultural Revolution with a network of People's Committees to build a new form of democracy, returning to the Qur'an and rejecting all imported ideologies whether capitalist or communist. His zeal was such that in June he interrupted Tripoli Radio to tell the people to take over the studio along with schools and hospitals. His Utopian ideas, that the people should rule themselves without institutions, that necessities such as food, transport and lodging should be free, with no one having more or less than they needed, that there should be no "workers" only "partners in production" and that money, school curricula, embassies and the armed forces should be abolished, were developed in the Third Universal Theory, the *Green Book* and at the Sabhah Congress: he spent huge sums paying for conferences at which they were applauded as exceeding the wisdom of Plato and Aristotle. However by 1977 the Libyan development budget was, *per capita*, four times higher than any other Arab state, major industrial projects such as steel mills at Misurata and a petrochemical complex at Ras Lanuf were under way, the number of University students had risen from 3,000 to 20,000 and the bedouins had been settled: the poor benfited but the middle class was destroyed. There had also been a very real improvement in the status of women who, despite opposition from the ulema, were, as "revolutionary nuns", enlisted in the army. In August 1975 Qadafi had survived a military coup after which two of his oldest allies, Umar al-Muhayshi and Abd al-Munim al-Huni went into exile, forming opposition movements: only 4 of the original RCC were now left. Qadafi was paranoid about his foreign-based opponents, demanding that they be hunted down as "stray dogs". Fanaticised Revolutionary Committees sniffed out heretics at home and in April 1977 in the first executions for political offences since independence five students were publicly hanged and 22 officers reported shot. There were frequent rumours of military plots and assassination attempts. In the late 1970s and early 1980s Qadafi was found to be financing subversive movements in Brittany, Corsica, Somalia, Eritrea, Niger, Gabon, Kenya, Botswana, Mozambique, Curaoa, Martinique, Malta, Iran, the Philippines, Tonga, Thailand and New Caledonia and President Ford remarked that Tripoli was the capital of world terrorism. His meddling drove neutral countries into the arms of his enemies. In 1974/5 he was said to be collaborating with Pakistan in a search for an "Islamic Nuclear Bomb". In 1976 he spent $200 million in an attempt to overthrow President Nimeiri who later remarked that Qadafi had "a split personality – both of them evil". He eagerly supported the Polisario guerrillas against Morocco. In 1977 the Egyptian–Libyan Border Clashes almost escalated into full-scale war. Isolated in the Arab world, Libya drew closer to Russia, making huge purchases of arms, accepting some 2,000 military advisers, talking of joining the Warsaw Pact and boycotting the Ta'if Islamic Summit which was to condemn their actions in Afghanistan. He was able to regain some friends after Sadat had visited Jerusalem by chairing the meeting that led to the formation of the Steadfastness Front. Libyan interference in Chad in pursuit of a Greater Libya which would include most of the Sahara, however, brought Qadafi new foes while his vehement support for Tehran in the Iran–Iraq War angered not only Baghdad but the Gulf States. In 1980 Tunisian dissidents trained in Libya attempted to overthrow their government in the Gafsa Raid. Qadafi, declaring that Libya had lived for 5,000 years without petrol, frequently threatened to cut off supplies to the West where anger mounted at the terrorist activities of his agents. Italy was threatened with war if compensation was not paid for the years of occupation and Portugal ordered to give independence to Madeira: Britain and France were to surrender all their islands. In August 1981 Libyan aircraft were shot down by Americans in the Sirte Gulf Incident after which Qadafi took the lead in forming the pro-Russian Tripartite Pact with South Yemen and Ethiopia. The Americans imposed trade sanctions on Libya in March 1982 and tried unsuccessfully to persuade their friends to do the same. During the Beirut Siege he advised Palestinian leaders to commit suicide rather than withdraw, demanded that the Arabs should send ten divisions to the front and withdraw all money from American banks: he was subsequently the only leader to boycott the Fez Summit which tried to form a common plan of action. Qadafi had constantly reshuffled the pack of his friends and enemies but since coming to power Morocco had been his constant target but in 1983 he suddenly went to Rabat and asked for unity. His unpredictability increased and he took to visiting foreign capitals uninvited or with minimal notice, attired in theatrical robes and guarded by a troop of beautiful women with machine-guns, frequently calling for revolution against neighbouring states: it became increasingly difficult to determine whether he was a figure of menace or of fun, particularly as he declared that he resigned every two months and had "no wish for command". Despite some financial stringency caused by the fall in oil prices and attempts to apply his economic theories, in furtherance of his doctrine that no country which had to import food could be really independent, Qadafi in 1983 committed vast sums to the Great Man-Made River Project which he saw as one of the wonders of the world. The lawlessness of his agents was demonstrated in 1984 when, after the explosion of bombs in Manchester, one killed a policewoman in London and an attempt to murder the former Prime Minister Abd al-Hamid Bakkush in Cairo ended in farce. President Reagan, calling him "the most dangerous man in the world" and "a flaky barbarian" responsible for 800 terrorist actions, said that he spent

$100 million a year on terrorism including attempts to persuade Red Indians and Black Muslims to revolt. Upon the overthrow of his enemy Nimeiri in April 1984 Qadafi, who two months earlier had been accused of bombing Omdurman, went uninvited to Khartoum, offering the successor regime $3,000 million for immediate union and joint action to overthrow President Mubarak. There had been reports in 1979 and 1980 of dissident officers being executed but in May 1984 there was a prolonged assault upon Qadafi's bunker in a barracks in Tripoli which he blamed upon British-trained Muslim fundamentalists. There were some summary executions and thousands of arrests but it was significant that while the outcome was in the balance, there was no popular rally to help his opponents. The Americans, without producing evidence, blamed the Rome and Vienna Airport Attacks at the end of 1985 upon Qadafi, severed economic relations and froze Libyan assets, and for three months their warships prowled off the Libyan coast seeking a pretext for an assault. An explosion in a Berlin nightclub served and in the Tripoli Bombing on 15 April about a hundred civilians, including a baby said to be Qadafi's adopted daughter, were killed: his house had been specifically targeted and later preserved as a museum. For some weeks Qadafi did not appear in public, leading to rumours that he had had a breakdown or was on drugs while the Americans vainly hoped that threats of further attacks would cause a rising to overthrow him. During 1987 Qadafi ardently sought a union with Algeria which, however, preferred the looser link of the Arab Maghreb Union and the following year, in a characteristic reversal of previous attitudes, he was reconciled with Mubarak whom he hoped would serve as a guarantor of his respectability after he had withdrawn from Chad and loosened links with Russia which was demanding payment of its debts. It was, however, difficult for him to realise that the world had changed as a result of the end of the cold war to live down the rhetoric of his earlier years. He criticised the Iraqi invasion of Kuwait, particularly as its obvious result would be to increase American influence in the area. In October 1991 Britain, France and the USA demanded the handing over of two Libyans accused of the destruction of an airliner over Lockerbie and when Qadafi refused, imposed sanctions which caused hardship and consequent dissatisfaction. There was a rise of Islamic militancy which led to hundreds being imprisoned and, although Qadafi had always opposed official religion, introduction of the *Shariah* in February 1994 and the empowerment of Imams to issue *fatwas*. There were rumours of an army rebellion in October 1993 and the subsequent arrest of Jalloud. With his actions based on whims, Qadafi never lost his ability to astonish: he announced that the capital would be transferred to a fly-blown oasis deep in the interior, he personally drove a bulldozer to knock down a prison and in June 1993 he allowed Libyan pilgrims to visit Jerusalem. He has a mischievous sense of humour: in July 1991 he declared that having been born an Italian subject, he might stand for Italian President to clear up the corruption in Rome. He works immensely hard, several times on the verge of a breakdown, in a tent in a barracks. There he receives numerous journalists, almost always succeeding in charming them, particularly American ladies. His first wife was the daughter of a general and his second is a nurse of tribal origin who had attended him during appendicitis: he has six children. He has a childlike need to attract attention and he succeeds to the extent that no other country with a population of three million has figured so frequently in newspaper headlines all over the world.

al-QADAFI, Wanis (1921–)

Libyan Prime Minister. He had been President of the Cyrenaican Legislative Council, an Ambassador and Foreign Minister before being appointed to succeed Bakkush as Prime Minister in September 1968. It was felt that someone "safer" and less dynamic was required and for the year that he remained in office, Qadafi made mild attempts at reform. He described his foreign policy as moderate and constructive. He carried through a major arms deal, involving Chieftain tanks, with Great Britain but also called for the removal of Western bases. His demand for an increase in oil prices was overtaken by the Revolution on 1 September 1969. In November 1971 he was sentenced to two years' imprisonment for corruption and ballot-rigging.

QAISSUNI, Abd al-Munim (1916–)

Egyptian Minister. He trained at Cairo University and the London School of Economics where he was awarded a doctorate. He worked briefly in Barclay's Bank in London before becoming a Lecturer in Economics at Cairo University in 1944. He then held a series of economic posts including the Directorship of the Middle East Department of the IMF before becoming Minister of Finance in 1954. Under various titles, including Deputy Prime Minister, Qaissuni controlled economic affairs for most of the Nasser period. In November 1955 he obtained the support of the World Bank for financing the Aswan High Dam – the US would provide $56 million – although the agreement was later cancelled by the American Government. After the Suez War he negotiated an agreement which provided for the release of sterling blocked in London in return of payment of compensation for sequestered property. In 1957 he made an economic agreement with Syria that was the first step towards the formation of the United Arab Republic. In 1960 he was put in charge of the over-optimistic first Five-Year Plan. He also nationalised the two principal banks and other firms to break their monopoly and gain control of funds for investment. In April 1962 he led another mission to the US obtaining loans for a power station and railways and a promise of grain for the next three years. In September 1966 when Nasser dismissed the pro-Western and financially orthodox Prime Minister Zakariah Mohieddin, Qaissuni also lost his job but in 1967 he was brought back into the Cabinet to cope with the financial consequences of the June War. In 1971 he became Chairman of the Arab International Bank which was created in the hope of attracting money from the Gulf and other businesses but in November 1976 when Sadat wanted Western economic help that was conditional upon fiscal restraint he brought back Qaissuni as Deputy Prime Minister for Financial and Economic Affairs. His cutting of subsidies and raising of taxes sparked off the Bread Riots of January 1977 for which he took full responsibility. Even so the domestic deficit soared. In May 1978 he opposed the financial policies of the Prime Minister Mamduh Salim in raising salaries irresponsibly and resigned, rejoining the AIB. He remained, however, close to Sadat and, as Egypt's most respected economic expert, continued to be consulted.

QALQILYA, Battle of (1956)

In September 1956 there was an escalation of clashes between raiders from Jordan and the Israeli security forces. On 10 September 6 Israelis were killed and the following evening the Israelis attacked the Jordanian police post at Rahwa, killing 5 policemen, 10 soldiers and 10 members of the Arab Legion coming to the rescue. The police post and a school were blown up. The next day 3 Israeli Druze guards were killed in the Negev. The following night 9 Jordanian policemen and 2 civilians were killed when the Israelis blew up a post at Gharandal, 45 miles north of Aqaba. On 23 September 4 Israeli archaeologists were killed near Jerusalem and 2 other civilians lost their lives in a separate incident. This was followed by a major reprisal on 25 September when 5,000 Israeli troops attacked the police post at Husan, 4 miles west of Bethlehem. After heavy fighting in which 37 Jordanian soldiers and policemen were killed, the post was destroyed. The Jordanians claimed to have killed 90 Israelis but Tel Aviv admitted only 9 killed and 8 wounded. UNTSO condemned Israeli aggression, causing an Israeli boycott of its proceedings. While the UN was discussing these violations of peace, on 4 October 5 Israelis were killed in an ambush on the Sodom–Beersheba road and later two more were killed near Peta Tikvah. The Israelis then on 9 October launched a major attack on Qalqilya police fort, 20 miles north-east of Tel Aviv, with 2 infantry battalions with armour and artillery support. After a 3-hour bombardment there was hand-to-hand fighting. General Burns of UNTSO called for a cease-fire which the Israelis refused until they had stormed the barracks, blowing it up with its ammunition and petrol dumps. A Jordanian battalion coming to help was ambushed and an Israeli company was cut off, having to be rescued with air support. King Hussain arrived from Amman, took part in the fighting and called for the intervention of the RAF. Burns said that 48 Jordanian soldiers were killed and the Israelis admitted losing 18. The King went to Baghdad and asked for some Iraqi troops to be sent into Jordan: the British stated that if Israel took any further military action against Jordan they would assist the King. This complicated relations between Britain and Israel which were already starting to plan the collusion that led to the Suez War.

QARU AND UMM AL-MARADIM

The ownership of these two small uninhabited islands has been disputed between Kuwait and Saudi Arabia. Qaru is about 25 miles from the coast, with a diameter of 200 yards and is about three feet above sea-level. In 1949 the Kuwaiti Government included it in a concession granted to Aminoil although no exploration followed. When in 1966 it was decided to divide up the Neutral Zone (Saudi Arabia–Kuwait) the Kingdom claimed that the islands should be included in the area delimited but Kuwait objected that they had always been recognised as Kuwaiti. In June 1977 Kuwait officially denied a report that they had been occupied by the Saudis. Both governments have kept silence over the matter but it is probable that some private agreement was reached between them. The islands were occupied by the Iraqis in August 1990 and were later the first part of Kuwaiti territory to be liberated – by Saudi soldiers.

al-QASIMI

Ruling family of Sharjah. In the first half of the nineteenth century Sharjah was part of the area ruled by Sultan b. Saqr al-Qasimi but he left the administration of the town in the hands of his son Saqr. In 1840, encouraged by Maktum b. Buti al-Maktum of Dubai, Saqr revolted against his father but although defeated was allowed to continue in power. In 1846 he was killed in action against the Shaykh of Umm al-Qaiwain. He was succeeded by his brother Abd Allah who was killed fighting against Hamriyyah. He was followed by another brother Khalid who became chief of the weakening confederation upon the death of Sultan in 1866. Khalid was killed in single combat by Zaid b. Khalifah al-Nihayyan of Abu Dhabi in 1868 as they duelled in front of their armies. The next Shaykh was yet another son of Sultan, Salim, born about 1825 and the son of a slave. Salim was mainly interested in learning and religion and neglected his duties so the Shaykhdom continued to decline while the fortunes of Abu Dhabi under its vigorous ruler increased. In 1869 his nephew Humaid b. Abd Allah al-Qasimi, Governor of Ras al-Khaymah, declared his independence and after the Political Resident had forbidden an expedition by sea to bring him to heel, Salim accepted the position. In 1883 after a reign of 15 years Salim was ousted by his 20-year-old nephew Saqr, the son of his predecessor Khalid. According to British reports Saqr was "weak, miserly and uxorious; in public business he was apathetic and seemed incapable of exertion; he forfeited the respect of other Trucial Shaykhs by his general insignificance both as a man and as a ruler". In general he was treated with contempt by his subjects who declined to pay their taxes. His state crumbled with Fujairah becoming practically independent under Humaid b. Abd Allah al-Sharqi and after a vain attempt to reduce it to obedience, Saqr washed his hands of the matter. Hamriyyah also was lost. In 1900 on the death of Humaid b. Abd Allah of Ras al-Khaymah, that area reverted to the control of Sharjah but in 1909 Saqr appointed Salim, the uncle that he had replaced, as its Governor and it escaped his rule once again. Saqr also lost the hereditary influence that the Shaykhs of Sharjah had enjoyed in the interior. Saqr died in April 1914 and despite an attempt by the elderly Salim to regain the throne, Khalid b. Ahmad of another branch took power. He was mercenary and unpopular as a usurper. The decline continued with the formal recognition of the loss of Hamriyyah and of Ras al-Khaymah, which led to the assignment of the Tunbs to Ras al-Khaymah while Sharjah kept Abu Musa. Khalid was marginally a stronger ruler than his predecessor and his attempts to collect taxation were resented. In 1924 he built a large fort that overlooked the houses of his people in a way that caused offence and there was a general rising against him. Khalid held out in the fort for nine days before abdicating and going into exile in Dubai. He twice attempted to regain the throne but later acted as Regent of Kalba. He was formally reconciled with his successor in 1943. His successor was Sultan b. Saqr, grandson of the Khalid who had been killed in single combat in 1868. During the early years of his reign there was a period of depression caused by world conditions and the decline of the pearl trade and accentuated by the silting up of Sharjah creek. Sultan's demands for money led to the emigration of half the population and he lost influence with the tribes as he was unable to provide the customary subsidies. The British regarded him as not especially intelligent and thoroughly untrustworthy. In 1927 he blinded and tortured suspected adherents of the ousted Khalid. This led to a brief civil war until the British threatened to stop his pearling fleet from putting to sea. He was believed to have been involved in the murder of Hamad b. Ibrahim al-Mualla of Umm al-Qaiwain. However in 1932 he agreed to the British establishment of a landing ground in return for a subsidy which he failed to share with his family as custom demanded. In 1936 he granted an oil concession which greatly increased his income, some of which he spent on education, the first Trucial Chief to do so. In 1939 he went to war with Said b. Maktum al-Maktum after the leaders of the Dubai Majlis had taken refuge in Sharjah. In his last illness Sultan appointed his brother Muhammad to act for him and after his death in a London nursing home in May 1951 Muhammad attempted to retain power. After some weeks of negotiation he agreed to hand over to his nephew Saqr b. Sultan. Saqr, who was born in 1924, proved the first really strong leader for many years. Soon after his accession he had the headman of Kalba murdered and then with the consent of the other Trucial Shaykhs reannexed the area. He regained Diba and much of the influence lost by his predecessors in the interior. His rule was harsh and authoritarian, but he became popular because of his evident sympathy with Arab nationalism. His first official act had been to ask the British for a school and he accepted an Egyptian educational mission, causing the British to worry about the real strength of his links with Nasser: it was even thought possible that he was trying to enlist help from the Arab League as a preliminary to a declaration of independence. In that case he might have closed down the British base which was going to be of vital importance if Aden were ever lost. In 1965 the British invited him to a discussion at the Agency and, after arresting him, put him on an aircraft for Cairo. The British claimed that the action had been taken at the request of his family because of his drunkenness and corruption. His first cousin, Khalid b. Muhammad, who had previously been approached by the British, assumed the throne. Khalid, born in 1927, had been a paint merchant in Dubai. He was anxious for modernisation and despite the lack of oil money was able to introduce electricity and some irrigation. Kind, mild, unassuming and good-natured, he was, however, weak and indecisive and was felt not to stand up sufficiently for the

rights of his state. Despite Sharjah's historic claims to the leadership of at least the northern part of the coast, he was prepared to accept a position subordinate to that of Abu Dhabi and Dubai in the establishment of the United Arab Emirates. He was nominated for Vice-President but failed to attract sufficient support. Even worse he acquiesced in the Iranian invasion of Abu Musa, accepting a subsidy in return. In July 1970 there was an attempt to kill him by placing explosives under his car. In January 1972 Saqr b. Sultan, with arms and money provided by Iraq, returned and attacked the palace. The coup failed, owing to the intervention of the Trucial Oman Scouts but Khalid was killed in the fighting. After some detention in Abu Dhabi, Saqr went into exile in Cairo. Khalid was succeeded by his younger brother Sultan b. Muhammad al-Qasimi.

al-QASIMI, Saqr b. Muhammad (al-QASIMI, Saqr b. Muhammad)

Ruler of Ras al-Khayamah. He was the son of Muhammad b. Salim al-Qasimi who had renounced the Shaykhdom in favour of his brother Sultan in 1919. Saqr spent his early manhood as a farmer, a merchant and as a judge in the family court. He deposed his uncle Sultan, a grasping, truculent man, with British blessing in March 1948 and quickly showed his intention of becoming a strong ruler by blinding one headman and kidnapping and threatening to kill the young son of another. He had difficulty in persuading oil companies, then actively seeking concessions in neighbouring states, to take an interest in Ras al-Khaymah but early in 1964 he did a deal with two independent American groups and then had some money available for modernisation. He showed particular interest in education, sending all his sons and even a daughter to Universities. In 1966 Saqr became the first elected President of the Trucial States Council. He took an active part in the discussions over the Dubai Agreement of 1968 and during the abortive attempt to establish the Federation of Arab Emirates he generally sided with Qatar and Dubai against Bahrain and Abu Dhabi. He refused nomination as Vice-President of the Supreme Council and accused the British of interference, opposing any request to them to reverse their decision to withdraw from the Gulf. Despite British advice he refused to hand over Tunb to the Iranians and ordered active resistance. This defiance made him a popular hero. He refused to join all the other Trucial Shaykhdoms in forming the United Arab Emirates but found himself under strong pressure both from the Saudis and from his own people to become a member. Influenced also by his continued failure to find oil, he applied for membership in February 1972. Once inside he proved a prickly member, opposing the hegemony of Abu Dhabi and Dubai, demanding major portfolios in the Federal Government for his subjects and more expenditure of Federal money in his territory. In 1977 Saqr attempted to open a casino but desisted after Saudi objections.

al-QASIMI, Sultan b. Muhammad (1939–)

Ruler of Sharjah. He was the son of Muhammad b. Khalid al-Qasimi who ruled the Shaykhdom briefly in 1951 and 1952 and the younger brother of Khalid who became Shaykh in 1965. Sultan took a degree in Agriculture from Cairo University and then taught at the Sharjah Technical Training School before becoming Minister of Education in the first Cabinet of the UAE in December 1971. The following month Khalid was killed in an attack on the palace by his deposed predecessor Saqr b. Muhammad and Sultan was electe to succeeded him. Al-Qasimi co-operated with Zaid, his strongest ally, to strengthen central government. In 1973 Zaid was a member of a committee that recommended a united defence force. Not having ruled before and not being a separatist on 4 November 1975 he abolished the flag, local departments of police, justice, public security and communications. He ended frontier disputes with Ajman, Fujayrah and Dubai. In November 1976 after crisis over Zaid's re-election rulers agreed to contribute to the federal budget and the Sultan chaired the budjet committee. Eager to attract investment in Sharjah he tried to encourage oil explorations. In June 1987 his older brother Abd al-Aziz, head of the national guard, deposed him. Zaid is said to have given his approval but Fahd warned that this would lead to instability. The Sultan was accused of wasting money and of getting into debt. Al-Qasimi spends much of his time travelling. He has a Ph.D. from Exeter University and writes local history. He has been accused of "extravagance and corruption" and of wasting money on "imaginary projects" including funding a new covered suq, an unfinished TV station and museum and subsidising a local paper. Dubai became worried that a neighbouring ruler had been overthrown so easily and so gave support to the Sultan. Sharjah had outstanding debts of over $600 million. He was in the UK when he was deposed and flew back to Dubai. The Supreme Council of UAE reinstated the Sultan. Abd al-Aziz was made Crown Prince and given a seat on the Supreme Council. In July 1987 the Sultan set up an Executive Council comprising the heads of departments and selected individuals. He also signed an agreement rescheduling Sharjah's debts.

QASSIM, Abd al-Krim (1914–63)

Iraqi Prime Minister. He was born in Baghdad, the son of a carpenter and trained as a teacher before going to the Military Academy from which he graduated in 1934. He fought in the Palestine War, attended courses in England and was a protégé of Nuri al-Said. However in the summer of 1954 he joined the small group of Free Officers plotting the overthrow of the Monarchy and as a Brigadier the most senior officer, was acknowledged as their leader. He played a major part in planning the July Revolution of 1958 although he did not arrive in Baghdad until it had taken place. Qassim neither set up a Revolutionary Command Council nor became President as had been expected but instituted a Council of Sovereignty taking for himself the posts of Prime Minister, Minister of Defence and Commander-in-Chief. He appointed Colonel Abd al-Salam Arif as his Deputy but otherwise the Cabinet consisted of civilian politicians representing all groups, leaving many of his original Free Officer colleagues feeling that they had been deceived. Qassim was genuinely concerned with the problems of the poor and his first measures were social reforms. Rent and price control, enforce-

ment of social security laws, the creation of labour exchanges and orphanages and, above all, drastic agrarian reform were begun within weeks. Later there were measures to raise the status of women and a great expansion in education and housing. Trade Unions were permitted. Army pay was substantially increased. More controversial, however, was the question of whether there was to be the immediate unity with Egypt which was demanded by Arif who, when he found that Qassim, unwilling to be subordinated to Nasser, was hesitating, clearly challenged his leadership. Arif was imprisoned and then Qassim had to survive an attempted coup by Rashid Ali al-Gilani and then the pro-Nasser Mosul Uprising of March 1959. In October 1959 members of the Baath attempted to assassinate him; he spent two months in hospital. It appeared that Qassim's only friends against pan-Arabism were the communists and the Kurds as Radios Baghdad and Cairo traded insults. Relations with the communists cooled after the Kirkuk Killings of July 1959 and the refusal of their demands for Cabinet places but basically they and Qassim depended upon one another and neither had many other friends. In 1960 he licensed some political parties but he never attempted to form one of his own, preferring to surround himself with officers and technocrats and to attempt to manipulate existing forces. The Provisional Constitution after the Revolution foreshadowed a partnership of Arabs and Kurds but nothing happened and the Kurds pressed for greater autonomy. In the summer of 1961 muddled intrigues and government intervention in support of the tribal enemies of Mulla Mustafa Barzani set off the full-scale Kurdish Revolt (I) which proved a terrible drain upon resources; Qassim also blamed the army for inefficiency in suppressing it and purged 2,000 officers, causing great resentment. Qassim's foreign policy was equally unsuccessful. In March 1959 Iraq withdrew from the Baghdad Pact, offending its former partners, especially Turkey and Iran which later gave help to the Kurdish rebels. Qassim had a further quarrel with Iran over the Shatt al-Arab, his claim to the province of Khuzistan with its Arab majority and his insistence that the Gulf was Arab and not Persian. Russia signed a technical and economic agreement and sold him arms but disapproved of his erratic conduct towards the Iraqi Communist Party and the regional instability caused by the fighting in Kurdistan while the West thought him excessively pro-Moscow. Qassim's natural allies, Egypt and Syria were antagonised by his treatment of his local pan-Arabs. In July 1961 a few days after Kuwait had become independent Qassim, without warning either his Ministers or the army, declared that it was historically part of Basra Province and there were fears that he would invade to enforce the claim. The poor of Baghdad, promised the wealth of Kuwait, applauded but internationally it made him ridiculous. The Kuwaitis requested British protection and troops, later replaced by Arab contingents, arrived but no attack came. Kuwait was admitted to the Arab League showing Qassim's isolation which was enhanced when he withdrew Ambassadors from the numerous states which recognised Kuwait. Protracted negotiations with the Iraq Petroleum Company which Qassim handled with acerbity ended in Public Law 80 of December

1961 by which the Government appropriated 99.5% of the area for which the Company held concessions: the immediate result was a large fall in production and consequent diminution of revenue for Iraq and increased hostility from the West. By the end of 1962 Qassim had few friends abroad or even at home. Shaykhs and landowners were outraged by the land reforms, Muslims offended by Qassim's evident lack of interest in Islam and reliance upon communists, politicians upset by his apparent lack of a political creed and failure to advance consistently in any particular direction and intellectuals by the denial of civil liberties, the antics of the People's Court of Fadhl al-Mahdawi and a cult of personality carried to a ludicrous extent. The shirt he was wearing during the assassination attempt was treated as a sacred relic. Every day the newspapers all carried the same photograph with the title "The Honest Leader" and carried all his speeches in full – often there was space for little else as each lengthy oration was serialised. One which covered ten pages of print developed the theme that one hour of work was better than a thousand hours of talk. Qassim became more and more arbitrary, unpredictable, incoherent and aloof, unable to look facts in the face. A bachelor who neither smoked nor drank, he lived alone in the heavily-fortified Ministry of Defence surrounded by photographs of himself and tape recorders repeating his old speeches, emerging occasionally to roam incognito round the streets at night, listening to people as the Caliphs had done, or to arrive, surrounded by gunmen, unexpectedly at an Embassy reception. In the winter of 1962/3 discontented officers, the Baath, pan-Arabists and Kurds came together to plan his overthrow. In the Ramadan Revolution in February the Defence Ministry was stormed and after pleading for his life, Qassim was taken to the TV studio and shot; his battered body was frequently shown on the screen before being buried in a secret grave to prevent his tomb or remains from being venerated by the poor who genuinely mourned him. He was a tall, lanky man with a pleasant smile who lacked the ruthlessness of his successors and no one ever suggested that he was guilty of financial wrongdoing.

QASSIMLU, Abd al-Rahman (?–1989)
Kurdish leader. Democratic Party of Iranian Kurdistan. Lectured at Sorbonne. Complained people ignored Kurds because did not hijack aircraft. Took assistance from Iraq. Fought against Barzani Kurds Murdered by Iranian agents.

al-QAWD, Abd al-Majid (1943–)
Libyan "Prime Minister". Born in Gharian, he studied at the University of Libya and Stirling University, getting a degree in Engineering and a diploma in Town Planning. Upon his return he was appointed Chief Engineer of Tripoli and, after the Revolution, its Mayor. From 1972 he was Minister in charge of land reclamation and played a leading role in the Green Revolution, confiscating land not in use for cultivation under government control. He travelled widely, even visiting the Antipodes in search of expertise and, with an American company, established hydroponic farms. Qawd was briefly involved with Atomic Energy before

returning to Agriculture. In May 1990 he put forward plans for settling a million Egyptians on land to be reclaimed in Southern Libya under the Great Man-Made River scheme. In January 1994 when the country was suffering from sanctions imposed by the West for failing to hand over those suspected of the Lockerbie Bombing, he was named as Secretary-General of the General People's Congress, effectively Prime Minister in succession to Abu Zaid Durdah.

al-QAWUKJI, Fawzi al-Din (c. 1888–?)
Arab nationalist leader. Of Turcoman origin, he was born in Tripoli, Lebanon and joined the Ottoman army, being at the Military Academy with Nuri al-Said and was probably like him a member of the secret nationalist officers group, the Ahd. He deserted to join the Arab Revolt and fought for the Amir Faysal against the French. Qawukji then served as a captain in the auxiliary forces raised by the French in Syria, gaining the Legion of Honour as an intelligence officer, but deserted during the Druze Revolt, raising a bedouin force that massacred the police at Hamah and he continued fighting long after most had surrendered. He was condemned to death by the French but took refuge with Ibn Saud who made him Director-General of Military Organisation. He proved efficient at raising and training a modern army. In May 1931 he was dismissed amidst rumours that he had been bribed to try to bring about a Sharifian restoration and he was later arrested on suspicion of involvement in the raid of Ibn Rifada. After his release Qawukji went to Baghdad where he taught at the Military Academy, inspiring many young nationalist officers. In July 1934 and April 1935 he visited Palestine, hoping to organise simultaneous revolts there and in Syria. During the Arab Rebellion in Palestine in the summer of 1936, he raised a volunteer force and tried to unite the various groups under his command. After some skirmishes in the hills, during which he showed qualities of ruthlessness and dash, the Rebellion collapsed in October and he escaped back to Iraq. When fighting started again he hoped to return but the Prime Minister Hikmat Sulayman exiled him to Kirkuk. In 1939 he was reported to be trying to enlist the Shammar tribe to attack the French in Dayr al-Zawr. In 1941 he worked closely with Rashid Ali al-Gilani and commanded the force that tried to hold up the British at Rutbah. Qawukji managed to escape to Berlin where he was employed in one of the Arab offices working for the Axis. When the Third Reich collapsed he was detained by the Russians but was released and went to France. He returned to the Middle East in 1947, settling in Syria where he acquired considerable influence in the army through his association with Akram Hawrani and Adib al-Shishakli. In January 1948 he was appointed by the Arab League as Commander-in-Chief of the Arab Liberation Army which later failed to achieve any substantial success in the north of Palestine before being driven back over the frontier into Lebanon in October. Qawukji remained in Syria as a mentor for politically-minded officers. His admirers saw him as "The Arab Garibaldi" while many others regarded him as a thug and a charlatan.

QIBYA, Destruction of (1953)

From the Rhodes Armistice of April 1949 until January 1953 there was little trouble on the Israel–Jordan armistice line but in that month the Israelis started to take reprisals against the activities of "Arab marauders". On 13 October 1953 the Israelis complained that Arab infiltrators had thrown a grenade in a village, killing a woman and two children. The Jordanian authorities tried to find the offenders but were unsuccessful. The following night a large Israeli force attacked the village of Qibya, a mile inside Jordan which was defended by a small detachment of National Guard. After the Arabs ran out of ammunition Israelis sappers went in and blew up 42 houses and all the public buildings. During the fighting old men, women and children had been sheltering in the houses and the Israelis fired upon those that attempted to leave. Later 66 bodies, three-quarters of them women and children, were found in the rubble. There was a strong force of the Arab Legion under a British officer not far away but owing to lack of information it did not intervene; this caused a political storm. From the precision of the Israeli operation it was inferred that it had been long planned and awaited only a pretext.

QIFL HARIS INCIDENT (1989)

During the Intifadah a group of about 30 armed Jewish settlers on the West Bank entered the Arab village of Qifl Haris on the pretext of visiting the tomb of the Prophet Joshua. Claiming that they had been attacked by villagers with stones they opened fire indiscriminately killing a girl of 13 and wounding a 16-year-old boy. They started fires, killed animals, broke windows, destroyed cars and shot bullets through water tanks. At least 20 settlers were later arrested. The Israeli Defence Minister Yitzhaq Rabin denounced "indiscriminate punitive action" as "an offence to Jewish values". It was not clear whether the incident was caused by anger at the continuation of the Intifadah or was a deliberate attempt to frustrate the Shamir Peace Plan then under discussion.

QIRYAT SHEMONA KILLINGS (1974)

On 11 April 1974 three guerrillas of the Popular Front for the Liberation of Palestine – General Command shot their way into a block of flats in the Galilee village of Qiryat Shemona about three miles from the Lebanese frontier. They took hostages but were surrounded by Israeli troops and held out for 4 hours before blowing up the building. The three guerrillas were killed and so were 18 Israelis (eight civilian adults, eight children and two soldiers), some of whom died after jumping from windows. The Israelis as a reprisal attacked six villages in Lebanon, killing a woman and child and blowing up houses. The Lebanese Government complained to the Security Council which passed a unanimous Resolution condemning Israel. An American attempt to link this with a mention of Qiryat Shemona was defeated.

QUBAR, Abd al-Majid (1909–)

Libyan Prime Minister. He came from a distinguished family of Gharian and although his father had been hanged by the Italians, Qubar held various administrative posts under the colonial regime. He was elected to the first Libyan Parliament and was its Speaker when he succeeded Ben Halim as Prime Minister in May 1957. He stated that he would continue the policies of his predecessor but he took very many more pains to conciliate the clique around King Idris. In foreign affairs his main anxiety was to offend no one, keeping out of disputes such as that between Egypt and Tunisia and those that followed the July Revolution in Iraq and the American landing in the Lebanon. At the same time, without upsetting Arab nationalists, he proved clever at attracting financial gifts from the West. He declined Soviet aid which would have given Moscow a foothold in the country. He protested against French nuclear tests in the Sahara. The first big oil strikes took place during his premiership. In home affairs he was easy-going and conciliatory, loath to interfere even with inefficiency or corruption which started to multiply with the dramatic increase in revenues and the subsequent expansion of bureaucracy. This led to his downfall after the longest rule of any Libyan Prime Minister. A contract for building a road to the Fezzan had been awarded to a member of the royal family who subsequently received many times the sum agreed in payment. Qubar had allowed a relatively free election and there was criticism of him in Parliament which he mishandled. In order to stifle further discussion he asked for a dissolution of Parliament which the King, already worried about corruption, refused to grant. Qubar therefore resigned in October 1960.

QUTB, Saiyyid (1906–66)

Egyptian religious and political thinker. Saiyyid Qutb Ibrahim Hussain Shadhili came from a family of rural notables in the Asyut area, his father had been a prominent supporter of Mustafa Kamil, and he remained throughout his life influenced by his upbringing in a village. He received a modern primary, not a Qur'anic education and in 1921 went to Cairo for secondary education. In 1925 he started training as teacher, then became an elementary school inspector and in the late 1930s transferred to Ministry of Education in Cairo. During this time he had a parallel career as a journalist and literary critic; he was much influenced by the modernist poet Abbas Mahmud al-Aqqad and politically he supported the Wafd. In October 1947 he established a journal *Al-Fikr al-Jadid* (New Thought) in which he made a detailed examination of the causes of poverty, pressed for labour legislation, the establishment of co-operatives and the possibility, like Abduh of modernising Islam. Qutb was in 1948 sent for further training in the USA but he returned in 1951 so anti-Western that he had to leave government service. After the July Revolution he joined the Muslim Brothers and was said to have become cultural adviser to Revolutionary Command Council, living in an army barracks. When the Muslim Brothers quarrelled with the RCC early in 1954 Qutb was one of the members who was briefly imprisoned. Upon his release he was chosen by the Supreme Guide, Hassan Hudaybi to be editor of the Brotherhood's newspaper. In October 1954 after a member of the Brotherhood had attempted to kill Nasser Qutb was arrested, tortured and in July 1955 sentenced to 25 years' hard labour. As he had consumption he spent most of the sentence in the concentration camp infirmary. There he wrote *Fi Zilal al-Qur'an* (In the Shadow of the Qur'an) – 30 part commentary on the Holy Book. In this and a subsequent work Ma'alim fi al-Tariq (Signposts along the Way) he attacked nationalism, Arabism and socialism, the very fundamentals of Nasserism which he saw as Pharaohism. In a clear, concise and logical way he argued that nationalism had been created by imperialists to divide the Muslims whose true homeland (*Watan*) was where Islam was supreme. All other governments, even those calling themselves Islamic, were illegitimate as God alone, and not the people, was the source of sovereignty and they should be strongly resisted with whatever personal sacrifice was needed. Those who did not accept this (and indeed practically everyone he disapproved of) was in a state of *Jahiliyyah* (ignorance) comparable to that of the Arabs before the revelation of the Prophet. His guards were certainly in this condition for they had forgotten God and worshipped Nasser and the state. Solidarity based on a common nationality was meaningless and he saw himself as a revolutionary leading forward to Islam, a classless society of brotherhood and justice, and not as a reactionary trying to return to an idealised past. Qutb attempted to raise the intellectual level of religiosity by attacking the popular belief in Satans and *jinni*. He declared that women should not compete with men but they had qualities which supplemented them as guardians of morality and "manufacturers of humanity" (Qutb remained a bachelor). Nasser had reduced the ulema of Al-Azhar to impotence and they roundly condemned Qutb as a blasphemer and a Kharijite. He also attacked the Jews as being responsible for materialism, animal sexuality, destruction of the family and the dissolution of society. In May 1964 he was released "for reasons of health", perhaps at the request of the visiting Iraqi President Abd al-Salam Arif or perhaps as a trap. In August 1965 Qutb was charged with plotting to kill Nasser and some film stars and popular singers and in court he made no attempt to deny the charges but claimed that the actions were justified. He was accused of working for the Saudis, then opposing Egypt in the Yemen War. He was sentenced to death on 21 August 1966 and despite worldwide pleas for mercy was hanged a week later. Seeing Islam as in permanent struggle, both against the West and against lukewarm fellow citizens, his writings and his death provided an inspiration for the fundamentalists such as those of *al-Takfir wa al-Hijrah* later opposing Presidents Sadat and Mubarak.

al-QUWATLI, Shukri (1892–1967)

Syrian President. He came from one of the richest landowning families in Damascus and was educated at an élite school there and at the Administrative College in Istanbul. He served briefly in the Ottoman bureaucracy, found his way blocked by increasing Turkification and retired to administer his estates. He was an early nationalist and a leading member of al-Fatat. During the war he survived torture and a death sentence from Jamal Pasha, managing to join the forces of Faysal, seeing active service. He failed to be elected to the General Syrian Congress but held a post in the Government. When the French overran Syria Quwatli was sentenced to death but escaped to Egypt where he

became extremely active in the Syro-Palestinian Congress travelling widely to campaign against the Mandate. Paris regarded him with Shakib Arslan as the most dangerous of the exiles. During the Druze Revolt he was active in supplying the insurgents with arms and money, some of which he was accused of pocketing. It was not until July 1930 that he was able to return to Damascus. His family was the Damascus agents of Ibn Saud with whom he maintained close relations throughout his life and to whom he sent some of his nationalist friends to serve as administrators. He immediately became one of the leaders of the more intransigent wing of the National Bloc and was active in the General Strike of February 1936 although he was not arrested. The British Consul commented that he was "a sincere extremist as long as his personal safety was not involved". When Jamil Mardam formed a National Bloc government in December 1936 Quwatli was appointed Minister of Finance and Defence, a post he used to smuggle help to the guerrillas of the Arab Rebellion in Palestine. In March 1938 he resigned from the Cabinet stating that Mardam was making too many concessions to the French in the hope of getting ratification of the Franco-Syrian Treaty. An anti-Zionist, he cultivated friendly relations with the Germans and Italians and also organised support for Rashid Ali al-Gilani. In July 1940 after the murder of Dr Shahbandar the Bloc leaders Mardam, Lutfi al-Haffar and Saad Allah al-Jabiri fled abroad, leaving Quwatli dominant amongst the nationalists, a position he consolidated by the vehemence with which he denounced the food-shortages and the Mandate which he claimed had lapsed with the League of Nations. When the British and Free French took over Syria he withdrew for a year to Mecca. In August 1943 after elections had produced a great majority for the Bloc, Quwatli became President and appointed a strongly nationalist Cabinet. Despite the De Gaulle–Lyttelton Agreement which promised independence for Syria, the French were most unwilling to leave and Quwatli showed considerable adroitness in using the British against them. He also declared that he would rather see a Syrian Soviet Republic than continuation of French rule. Once they had left Quwatli proved unequal to the task of building a modern democratic state, even if he had wished to do so. He failed to provide any sense of national direction and presided over a period of factionalism and corruption that discredited parliamentary rule. The veteran journalist Muhammad Kurd Ali wrote that his most ardent supporters were traitors and thieves to whom he granted concessions and appointments even if they were illiterate. In November 1947 he managed to procure an alteration of the Constitution to enable him to serve a second term. The failure of the Syrian army in the Palestine War gained his regime widespread unpopularity and when it was overthrown by the coup of Husni al-Zaim in March 1949 there was general rejoicing. Quwatli, ill at the time, refused to resign but after intercession of King Farouq and Ibn Saud, was allowed to go into exile. He spent much of the time in Alexandria while his supporters, in particular Sabri al-Asali, convinced many people that Quwatli was the only real alternative either to rule by Colonels or absorption by the Hashemites, whose enemy he had long been. After army rule had ended and the aged Hashim al-Atasi had declined a further term as President, Quwatli, upon his return from exile, was re-elected in preference to Khalid al-Azm in August 1955. At home he was little more than a figurehead with vague aspirations for all-party national government but he was unable to win support from the more dynamic political elements such as the Baath and the Communists. Abroad, where it was generally believed that he was still on the Saudi payroll, he took an anti-Hashemite and anti-Western attitude, meeting Nasser and King Saud in March 1956 to agree on unified foreign, military and economic policies. Quwatli was on a visit to Moscow at the time of the Suez War and persuaded the Russians to emphasise their support for Nasser and to provide Syria with arms and economic aid. Though sympathetic to Communists abroad, he was frightened of those at home and was one of the first to advocate union with Egypt to prevent them from taking over. When the United Arab Republic was formed Quwatli effectively retired from politics with the honorary title of "First Arab Citizen". Not a man of great intellectual capacity, Quwatli was a master of manipulation and patronage politics. He was a fine orator and an impressive figure. He was known as "The Camel" because of his tenacity and nasty temper when aroused.

RABAT ISLAMIC SUMMIT (1969)

There was outrage in the Islamic world at the burning of Al-Aqsa Mosque, its third holiest shrine, in Israeli-occupied East Jerusalem by a mentally deranged Australian in August 1969 and this led to the first major meeting of Muslim leaders in Rabat from 22 to 25 September. In addition to six Arab Heads of State it was attended by the Shah, the Presidents of Pakistan and Somalia, the Prime Ministers of Afghanistan and Malaysia and representatives of the other Arab countries except Syria and Iraq, five African states, Turkey and Indonesia. After stating that "the unity of their religious faith" made close co-operation in most fields necessary to preserve their values, they condemned the burning of the Mosque, resulting from Israeli occupation and demanded a return to the pre-June War status of the city which they called upon the Great Powers to help to liberate. It was resolved to hold a meeting of Foreign Ministers in Jiddah in March 1970 to discuss the results of the Summit and establishment of a joint secretariat. Twenty-two countries attended the Jiddah meeting which was to lead to the creation of the Islamic Conference Organisation in May 1971.

RABAT SUMMIT (1969)

The fifth Summit assembled in Rabat on 21 December 1969 primarily to discuss mobilisation of all resources to expel Israel from the occupied territories. It was attended by Kings Hassan, Faysal and Hussain, Presidents Nasser, Nimeiri, Boumédienne, Helou, Qadafi, Iryani and Ali, Amir Sabah al-Salim al-Sabah, Tayib Slim, Hardan al-Takriti and the Syrian Interior Minister. Yassir Arafat made his first appearance. Nimeiri, as chairman of the preceding Khartoum Summit gave the opening address attacking the US and praising France and the socialist countries. The Egyptian War Minister General Muhammad Fawzi stated that his army would not be ready for war in the near future and needed more resources even to stand on the defensive: the lack of enthusiasm that his demands evoked caused Nasser to threaten to walk out. Takriti put forward a seven-point plan for mobilisation which was rejected. Both Yemens then demanded discussion of the al-Wadiah Dispute with Saudi Arabia and Faysal threatened to walk out: the conference agreed to set up a committee to study the matter. The Rabat Summit was clearly a failure.

RABAT SUMMIT (1974)

After being postponed from April 1974 and then from September the seventh Summit was held in Rabat from 26 to 29 October and had been preceded by a meeting of Foreign Ministers. Libya and Iraq sent representatives but otherwise Heads of State led their delegations. The main topic was the status of the West Bank and King Hussain started by arguing that if Israel were to withdraw as required by Resolution 242 the territories would legally revert to the previous holder, Jordan, which still paid the salaries of officials there. Yassir Arafat asked the King to recognize that the Palestine Liberation Organisation was the sole and legitimate representative of the the Palestinian people. The Summit then agreed to form a Committee of Kings Hassan, Faysal and Hussain, Presidents Sadat, Assad and Boumédienne and Arafat to reconcile the two positions but in fact they all supported Arafat and Hussain gave way. The cutting of the link between Jordan and the West Bank was strongly supported by Sadat who probably saw it as facilitating his own making of a peace settlement with Israel. The uncritical support of the Americans for Israel was deplored. The final Resolution asserted the rights of the Palestinians to return to their homeland and establish a national authority under the leadership of the PLO which all Arabs should support and in whose affairs other Arab states should not interfere. The Summit was a clear defeat for Hussain who on his return home dissolved his Parliament because half of the members represented the West Bank and reduced the number of Palestinians in the Cabinet: thereafter relations with Arafat were variable but never easy. The Israelis had consistently refused to negotiate with the PLO so now had no one with whom they could discuss the West Bank apart from Sadat who had little influence on the ground compared with Jordan. The Rabat Summit took other decisions which were not published but reportedly included the setting up of the Arab Military Industries Organisation and a defence fund from which the front-line states would benefit.

RABIGH CRISIS (1916/17)

On 10 June 1916 Sharif Hussain of Mecca set off the Arab Revolt but although Mecca itself, Jiddah and subsequently Ta'if, were liberated, there was no progress outside this small area. The attack on Medina by Sharif Faysal failed and there were at least 9,000 Turkish troops there who were then available to advance on Mecca and extinguish the revolt. As it was the dry season such a large force could not march by the inland route but would have to come down to the Red Sea coast at Rabigh. It was unlikely that the Arabs would be able to hold them off and the question arose of sending Allied troops to defend the town. The British, under pressure from the Indian Government, thought it undesirable that Christian troops should campaign in the Holy Land and although the French had Algerian *goums* available, the British were not prepared to let them have exclusive credit for rescuing the Arabs and considered whether it might not be preferable to allow the Revolt to collapse. In October, however, two Egyptian companies with British officers were sent but this was clearly not enough. The Qadi of Mecca issued a *fatwa* that Christian troops would be acceptable but the General Staff in London exaggerated the number that would be required and was adamant that they could not be spared. More Egyptian and a few British were sent and also some aeroplanes. A further British Brigade was held in readiness for a written request for their dispatch from the Sharif. In the event in January 1917 the Arab troops went on the offensive and freed Wijh and the crisis was over. In March the Turks made a half-hearted attempt to advance on Rabigh but were easily beaten off by Arab forces with some help from the British aircraft.

RABTA

Rabta, about 50 miles south-west of Tripoli was a chemical plant built by West Germans. In December 1987 the Americans alleged that it was producing chemical weapons which Qadafi might use for his adventure in Chad or supply to terrorists. In June 1988 his Great Green Document banned chemical weapons (and also housemaids) and in October he invited journalists to Rabta which he said was producing only medicines. Although the CIA said that it was defended by Soviet missiles in December President Reagan spoke of the possibility of destroying it as production was expected soon to begin. The Americans complained that European and Japanese businesses were helping the Libyans and in October 1989 the German Public Prosecutor said that he was investigating reports that there were companies helping Libya to build rockets with a range of 720 km. Early in March 1990 the US estimated that Rabta had produced 30 tons of mustard gas, enough for 150 bombs, and that output was being increased and did not rule out a pre-emptive attack. A few days later the factory was destroyed by a fire in which at least two people died. Libya blamed American and Israeli sabotage and Qadafi threatened economic sanctions against Germany. Several Arab countries condemned aggression against Libya but there were suggestions that the fire had been organised or faked to head off an American strike. In March 1991 the Libyans denied American allegations that the plant was being rebuilt. In 1992 five German businessmen were convicted of selling equipment for the building of Rabta and in February 1993 Bonn banned two companies from supplying certain materials to Libya. There were allegations that a similar plant was being built at Tarhunah by a Thai company.

RAJAB, Muhammad Zaruk (1940)

Libyan "Prime Minister". Born in Benghazi he studied at the University there before qualifying as a chartered accountant in the UK. He then lectured on accountancy at the University of Libya. He was Head of the Audit Division of the Treasury when in July 1972 he was appointed Minister of Finance in the Cabinet headed by Abd al-Salam Jalloud. In the following years when the price of oil made Libya extremely rich Rajab often travelled abroad providing money to developing countries in return for political support. In August 1975 he announced that Libya had spent $7.020 million since the Revolution on social and economic development projects. When in March 1977 the Sabhah Congress abolished ministries, Rajab remained in charge of finance as Secretary of the relevant Committee of the General People's Congress. In January 1981 Rajab was put in charge of the Secretariat of the Committee and in January 1984 he succeeded Jadullah al-Talhi as Secretary-General of the GPC, in effect Prime Minister. Shortly afterwards there was a crisis in relations with Britain after a woman police constable in London was killed by a Libyan diplomat. He was in office during a period of unrest, during which several students were hanged: there was a rise in Islamic militancy and in May 1984 a major attack on Qadafi's HQ. Quarrels with Egypt and Tunisia led to the deportation of their citizens. In September 1986 Rajab went to Ankara with which relations had become strained owing to Libya's failure to pay Turkish firms at least $400 million owed for goods and services: he secured some agreements on economic co-operation. In March 1986 Rajab was replaced as Prime Minister by Talhi. In May 1988 he was appointed Governor of the Central Bank.

RAMADAN REVOLUTION (1963)

By the end of 1962 the erratic, authoritarian and irresponsible rule of General Abd al-Krim Qassim had, with the exception of the very poor, alienated people of every class and opinion. A conspiracy against him was formed by pan-Arabists such as his former deputy Colonel Abd al-Salam Arif, military supporters of the Baath such as Colonels Ahmad Hassan al-Bakr and Tahir Yahya and representatives of the Kurdish rebel leader Mulla Mustafa Barzani. At the end of December 1962 the bodyguards of Qassim's cousin and close associate Colonel Fadhl al-Mahdawi beat up students who had teased his son and this led to a series of student strikes which attracted public sympathy. The projected coup had to be several times postponed because the conspirators feared that it had been betrayed but it took place in the early morning of Friday, 8 February 1963 (14 Ramadan). Qassim's headquarters in the heavily fortified Ministry of Defence was bombed and then attacked by tanks for about ten hours while the Baath militia prevented the communists from coming to Qassim's assistance. Qassim, Mahdawi and a few others held out for a further twelve hours before surrendering. They were taken to the Broadcasting House where they met Arif and Bakr and pleaded for their lives. They were machine-gunned and their bodies shown on television.

RAPID DEPLOYMENT FORCE

In July 1977 President Carter ordered officials to prepare a study of the American ability to react quickly to an emegency to protect the oil of the Gulf area and early in 1979 the Iranian Revolution and a brief war between North and South Yemen led to a further review of strategic needs undertaken by the National Security Adviser Brzezinski. A team sent to the area to request access to facilities was successful in Oman, Somalia and Kenya and obtained a promise of co-operation from Egypt. There were already a major base at Diego Garcia, naval facilities in Bahrain and transit stopovers in Morocco. At the end of 1979 Russian troops moved into Afghanistan and in January 1980 the Carter Doctrine pledged to fight if necessary to prevent "any outside force" from attempting to gain control of the Gulf. Plans were announced to build up a Rapid Deployment Force for use outside the NATO area. The RDF, renamed US Central Command in 1983, claimed to be able to deploy an air force fighter squadron and a battalion of 800 paratroopers with bomber support within 48 hours if invited and given five days' notice and over 3,000 men within a week. It was considered that this could act as a "trip-wire" to forestall Soviet aggression. Most Gulf states, while anxious to have American protection preferred that it should remain "over the horizon", the Saudis in particular considering it more likely to provoke than to restrain the Russians whom anyway it thought unlikely to invade the area. There were also discussions about the possibility of the RDF's intervention in reaction to a coup in a friendly state although many Arabs thought that given the unpopularity of the Americans an intimate alliance with them might actually cause dissension. There were also fears that the RDF might be used to seize rather than defend the oilfields as Kissinger had once suggested. The Gulf Co-operation Council set up its own RDF. The Americans conducted joint manoeuvres with Oman and Egypt which provoked controversy and spent large sums on improving airfields and ports. The American force was greatly increased under Reagan and the total strength of USCENTCOM was nearly 300,000 men, mostly based in the US, and included aircraft carriers.

RASLAN, Mazhar (c. 1883–?)

Chief Minister of Trans-Jordan. He was born in Homs and after training in Istanbul, entered Ottoman service. During the war he was *Kaimakam* of Mosul but having long held Arab nationalist views, entered the service of the Amir Faysal in Damascus as Director of Education. He was later *Mutasarrif* of Dayr al-Zur and then of Salt. He was holding that position in 1921 when the Amir Abd Allah arrived in Ma'an; at first Raslan said that he would resist a further advance but then rallied to him. He was appointed Chancellor and Treasurer but after a few months in August 1921 when the aggressive nationalism of Rashid Tali appeared likely to endanger the state, Raslan, more moderate although also a member of the Istiqlal Party, replaced him as Chief Minister. He worked well with T. E. Lawrence who was then representing Britain but when in March 1922 it was felt that a stronger leader was necessary, he was replaced by Ali Ridha al-Rikabi under whom he accepted a post. In February 1923 he was again Chief Minister but was removed in September after failing to cope with the Adwan Rebellion. He was appointed Minister of Finance but the following year returned to Syria. He was implicated in the Druze Revolt and had to escape abroad but in 1928 returned and became Deputy for Homs. He later served in various Syrian Cabinets such as those of Haqqi al-Azm,

his old Istanbul friend Lutfi al-Haffar, and Sa'd Allah al-Jabiri but was never a major figure. He was regarded as a typical old-fashioned Ottoman official, courageous but slow-witted but although a strong nationalist, never doctrinaire.

RASSEMBLEMENT CONSTITUTIONNEL DÉMOCRATIQUE (Tunisia)

In February 1988, three months after the overthrow of its founder President Bourguiba, the Central Committee of the ruling Parti Socialiste Destourien determined to change its name to the Rassemblement Constitutionnel Démocratique: the 'Socialiste' adopted at the time of Ben Salah was clearly out of line with policies in the twenty years since his fall. In July at the first Congress attended by more than 2,000 delegates, President Ben Ali warned that it would have to compete in a multi-party democracy and said that in future the Central Committee would be at least partially elected; he actually nominated 122 out of 200. The Secretary-General would no longer sit in the Cabinet. The Politburo was cut from 12 to 6 leaving only 2 Bourguiba associates. Ben Ali tried to form a united front with the opposition parties for the parliamentary elections of April 1989 but they declined to co-operate and put up their own candidates. The RCD won 80% of the vote and all the seats although over 100 of the 125 Deputies were elected for the first time, thus bringing in new blood. In March 1990 Ben Ali offered the opposition one-third of the seats in the forthcoming municipal elections but they preferred to boycott the poll. The result, described as "meaningless" by the opposition, gave the RCD control of 245 out of the 246 councils with all but 34 of the 3,774 seats in a 78% turn-out. In August, after the occupation of Kuwait by Iraq, the Politburo declared that there was no justification for the deployment of foreign troops in Arabia and expressed sympathy with Saddam Hussain. After making enemies by his attitude during the Gulf War Ben Ali was extremely anxious to give an impression of democracy and when there were nine by-elections due in October 1991 he offered the seats to the opposition without contest. They were unable to agree amongst themselves so RCD candidates stood unopposed and maintained the Party's monopoly in Parliament. The high turn-out, 90% in some areas, was seen as a sign of popular support against the Islamic militants of Nahdah. The RCD claimed 1,600,000 members of whom 60,000 were elected cadres. The Second Congress, the "Congress of Perseverance", was held at the end of July 1993 with Ben Ali calling for political pluralism and competition, warning that this could lead to multi-party government. For a new Central Committee 60% of the delegates were elected. Before the poll in March 1994 great efforts were made organise female voters and the number registered tripled; they were encouraged to see Ben Ali as a force for stability and a guard against Islamic extremism. The election was fairly conducted, the opposition given funds and access to the media but remained disorganised and, in a turn out of more than 95% the RCD won 98% of the votes and all the seats.

RASSEMBLEMENT NATIONAL DES INDÉPENDENTS (Morocco)

In the municipal elections of November 1976 Independent candidates won 8,600 seats out of the 13,500 contested and in the parliamentary elections of June 1977 Independent candidates won 140 out of 264 seats. Most of them had described themselves as "unconditional" supporters of Hassan II: "Hassanism is our doctrine". Many of them were young technocrats without any personal power base of their own but enjoyed the backing of local officials: the long-established Istiqlal Party sneered that they were "a trunk without roots which would be blown down at the first storm". In October 1978, at a Congress attended by 3,500 delegates, the Prime Minister Ahmad Uthman, in order to give them cohesion, announced the formation of what he called a mass movement rather than a political party "to inject enthusiasm into the masses" and mobilise the nation's youth. When in March 1979 Maati Bouabid formed a government it included eight Ministers and two Secretaries of State from the RNI which also had two representatives on the National Defence Council. In November 1980 a Cabinet reshuffle removed all of its RNI Ministers. In 1981 the RNI split with 61 deputies under Abd al-Hamid Kasimi hiving off to form the Parti National Démocrate. The PND consisted mainly of aristocratic landowners leaving the majority of the RNI urban entrepreneurs, anti-socialist and pro-Western. In April 1983 Uthman called the RNI "HM's Opposition", loyal but critical of the way that the Government was run, waste and corruption and neglect of industry engendering a lack of confidence. In the municipal elections of June 1983 the RNI took 14% of the votes, making it the fourth largest party. In November 1983 both Uthman and Arsalan al-Jadidi who had given up the Ministry of Labour to lead the PND became Ministers of State in the government that Lamrani formed to conduct parliamentary elections. In the poll in September 1984 the RNI emerged as the second largest group with 39 Deputies directly elected and a further 22 indirectly. The figures for the PND were 15 direct and 9 indirect. In the communal elections of October 1992 the largest number of seats was won by Independents with no party affiliation but the RNI was the most successful of the organised parties with 18% of the votes and 21% of seats. The parliamentary elections of June 1993 were fought mainly between two groups of parties – one pro-government and the other opposition – but the RNI refused to ally with either. It emerged with its number of directly elected Deputies down to 28 and the indirect round brought it only a further 13. Nevertheless the RNI appeared able to join either group of parties to form a majority government but no agreements were reached and the government of Karim Lamrani continued in office.

RASSEMBLEMENT POUR LA CULTURE ET LA DÉMOCRATIE (Algeria)

In 1989 the Front de Libération Nationale lost its monopoly and about 50 political parties were founded within a year. One of the most significant of these was the Rassemblement pour la Culture et la Démocratie founded by Said Saadi mostly from Berbers who had been supporters of the Front des Forces Socialistes. It was strongly secular and although possibly technically illegal as based on regionalism, the Government was glad to recognise it as a potential ally against the Front Islamique du Salut. Its inaugural Congress in December 1989 was attended by 1,000 delegates. In the communal elections of June 1990 it came third after the FIS and the FLN, winning one provincial council and over 80 municipalities. During the parliamentary elections of December 1991 the RCD made the first television broadcasts in Berber, attracting 200,000 votes. It won no seats on the first round but although it could expect four on the second, it called for the cancellation of elections and even a military take-over to prevent the Islamic state that would follow a FIS victory. Saadi, born in 1947, with a long record of refusal to compromise which had led to several terms of imprisonment, was seen by Boudiaf as representing a new generation and a potential Prime Minister but relations were bad between the RCD and the Belaid Abd al-Salam who accused it of "laico-assimilationism". Several hundred RCD councillors resigned in protest against his policies in March 1993 and the Party refused to talk even to non-militant Muslim groups. Saadi spoke of an Autonomous Kabyle Republic and called for a boycott of government schools, alleging that they were controlled by fundamentalists. The RCD was one of the few parties which did not boycott constitutional talks in January 1994. Later that month Rashid Tigziri, one of its leaders was assassinated, probably by fundamentalists.

REAGAN PLAN (1982)

In June 1982 the Israeli aggression against Lebanon, Operation Peace for Galilee caused new dangers in the Middle East and also led to the appointment of a new US Secretary of State, George Shultz who was more even-handed than the strongly pro-Israeli Haig. Shultz gave the region his first attention. On 1 September, as the Palestinian guerrillas were being withdrawn from Beirut, President Reagan put forward a Plan "for a fresh start" building on Camp David. He urged Israel to understand that it could only have peace if it acted with magnanimity and justice and the Arabs to accept the reality of Israel and to see peace could only be achieved through genuine negotiation. There should be a five-year period during which there should be "a peaceful and orderly transfer of domestic authority from Israel to the Palestinian inhabitants of the West Bank and Gaza" with due regard for Israel's security. The US would support neither an independent Palestinian state nor Israeli annexation, considering that these areas should be linked with Jordan. Jerusalem should stay united but it would be necessary to negotiate upon its future status. There should be no further Israeli settlements in the occupied territories. The conflict should be settled on the basis of exchanging territory for peace. Reagan regarded Resolution 242 as the "foundation stone" of American peace efforts and added that its "commitment to the security of Israel is ironclad". For the Plan to have any success it needed Israeli acceptance, but, confident of the power of the Zionist lobby to prevent any real pressure upon him, Prime Minister Begin rejected it and continued building settlements. He declared that a self-governing Palestinian entity "would endanger our very existence". The Plan needed also the help of Bashir Gemayel but he was killed before taking office. It needed the withdrawal of Syrian troops from Lebanon which Hafiz al-Assad refused to countenance. It needed Palestinian acceptance of King Hussain as their representative, a role that he had renounced in the Rabat Summit of 1974. Hussain welcomed the Plan which was widely seen as an attempt to reconcile the legitimate needs of Israeli security with the legitimate rights of the Palestinians. Ten days after Reagan's speech the Arabs put forward their own peace proposals at the Fez Summit.

REFORM PARTY (Palestine)

Hizb al-Islah. In 1934 Dr Hussain Fakhri al-Khalidi defeated Raghib al-Nashashibi in the election for Mayor of Jerusalem and the following year he determined to organise his followers as a political party. As he had won thanks to the support of Jewish voters he had pledged to work for a compromise solution to the Palestine question but when the Reform Party was constituted its programme called for the independence of the country within Arab unity and resistance to the Jewish National Home by all means. Independence should come step by step and it therefore supported a Legislative Assembly. The Party also established links with the Amir Abd Allah of Trans-Jordan. When the Arab Higher Committee was established in April 1936 the Reform Party was represented on it. After the banning of the AHC and the exile of Khalidi in September 1937 the Reform Party practically ceased to exist as an effective force but after his return the name was preserved to give him the status of a Party Leader.

REJECTION FRONT

The Geneva Peace Conference in the winter of 1973/4 had been attended by representatives of Egypt, Jordan and Israel as well as those of the USA and USSR and had been followed by the Egyptian–Israeli agreement at Kilometre 101. Subsequent talks between King Hussain and President Sadat made the Palestinians feel that the fate of their country would be settled over their heads. The more radical elements were further alarmed by a visit of Yassir Arafat to Moscow, which had always recognised Israel within its pre-1967 boundaries, and suspicions that he was in secret contact with Washington and would agree to representation at resumed Geneva talks on the basis of Resolution 242. In September 1974 George Habash refused to accompany Arafat to Moscow and declared that his Popular Front for the Liberation of Palestine would leave the Palestine Liberation Organisation rather than agree to any talks which did not envisage the total elimination of Israel. He "rejected a Zionist presence even on one square inch of Palestine". His Rejection Front was joined by the Popular Liberation Front – General Command of Ahmad Jibril, the Popular Struggle Front and the Arab Liberation Front. It boycotted meetings of the Palestine Central Council but participated in those of the Palestine National Council. The Tripoli Declaration of December 1977 appeared to have reunited most of the Palestinian factions with all of them accepting the Habash rejection of any idea of a peaceful settlement

with the "three noes" – no negotiation, no peace with Israel and no recognition of Israel.

REPUBLICAN BROTHERHOOD (Sudan)

Ikhwan al-Jumhuriyyin. This was a small group, never more than 1,000, of intellectuals founded in 1945 by Mahmud Muhammad Taha who advocated a modernised form of Islam. They then advocated a Federal Republic, independent of both Britain and Egypt. It was very active but was never strong enough to organise as a political party or pose a serious challenge to the more traditional Islamic Charter Front or to the religious leaders who dominated parties such as the Umma or the National Unionists. After 1967 the Brotherhood called for recognition of Israel. It stood for Islamic socialism and the rights of women. It held that the Qur'an and the *Sunnah* were the true source of law and the *Shariah* codified by jurists many years after the death of the Prophet, was merely one means of interpreting it and particularly that the version imposed by President Nimeiri was wrong. They therefore opposed his September Laws of 1983, particularly their application to the South. Their leaders were imprisoned for 18 months but after their release continued their campaign. In January 1985 Taha was hanged after a trial later held to have been illegal. Subsequently little was heard of the group.

RESOLUTION 242 (SECURITY COUNCIL) (1967)

In November 1967 the Security Council discussed the means of settling the Middle East after the June War. It became clear that Resolutions submitted by the Russians, the Americans and the Third World could not command general acceptance but on 22 November the Council unanimously passed a British-drafted Resolution "emphasising the inadmissibility of the acquisition of territory by war and the need to work for a just and lasting peace in which every state in the area can live in security". It called for "withdrawal of Israeli armed forces from territories occupied in the recent conflict" – a deliberately ambiguous phrase as it omitted either "all" or "the" from before "territories", thus leaving open the possibility of discussion about future frontiers. It further called for the termination of states of belligerency and acknowledgement of the sovereignty and independence of each state in the area "within secure and recognised boundaries". It affirmed the necessity of guaranteeing freedom of navigation through international waterways, demilitarised zones and "a just settlement of the refugee problem". This last concept was unacceptable to the Palestinians who urged that the problem was not about refugees but about their right to an independent existence. The Secretary-General was requested to send a special representative to the area and this led to the Jarring Mission. Syria immediately rejected the Resolution but King Hussain accepted it and eventually persuaded President Nasser to do the same. Israel insisted on direct negotiations with the Arabs, knowing that none of their leaders could agree to this. Eventually Resolution 242 was either formally or tacitly accepted by all the states concerned and formed the basis of all subsequent attempts to secure a peace settlement between the Arabs and Israel but the Palestinians remained adamant in rejecting it until it was endorsed by Yassir Arafat at the Palestine National Council Algiers Meeting of November 1988: even then extreme sections such as the Popular Front for the Liberation of Palestine held out against it.

RESOLUTION 338 (SECURITY COUNCIL) (1973)

The October War began on 6 October 1973, the Security Council was unable to agree on 8 October and 9 and by 10 October the Americans and Russians were heavily involved in rearming their protégés. Oil supplies to the West were cut. By 17 October there was a practical cease-fire on the Golan Heights and the Israelis had already crossed the Suez Canal. The Russian Prime Minister Alexei Kosygin visited Cairo and when he had returned home Secretary of State Henry Kissinger went to Moscow on 20 October and messages were exchanged between Presidents Nixon and Brezhnev. The Super-Powers agreed on a joint Resolution which was submitted to an extraordinary session of the Security Council at 10 p.m. on 21 October and passed unanimously although China did not vote, two hours later. Resolution 338 called for a cease-fire within 12 hours, an immediate start on the implementation of Resolution 242 "in all of its parts" and "decides that, immediately and concurrently with the cease-fire, negotiations start between the parties concerned, under appropriate auspices aimed at establishing a just and durable peace in the Middle East". Egypt, Israel and Jordan accepted the Resolution while Iraq, Libya and the Palestine Liberation Organisation rejected it: Syria accepted it on 24 October. In the meanwhile the cease-fire had been broken on the Canal Front and Resolution 339 of 23 October urged that forces be returned to their original positions and requested the Secretary-General to send observers. The Egyptians asked for American and Russian troops to supervise the cease-fire: the Americans refused and put their forces on worldwide alert to prevent the dispatch of a Russian contingent. On 25 October the Security Council adopted Resolution 340 which repeated the demand for the return of troops to their positions of 22 October and decided to set up a United Nations Emergency Force (UNEF) of personnel drawn from states other than the five permanent members of the Security Council.

RESOLUTION 465 (1980)

On 1 March 1980 the Security Council passed unanimously Resolution 465 deploring the refusal of Israel to co-operate with the Commission to examine illegal settlements in the Occupied Territories and deploring official support of settlements in Arab territories including Jerusalem which needed protection because of its "unique spiritual and religious dimension". The Resolution declared that this was bound to hamper any search for peace. It further determined that "all measures taken by Israel to change the physical character, demographic composition, institutional structure or status of Palestinian and other Arab territories occupied since 1967, including Jerusalem, have no legal validity and that Israel's policy and practices of settling parts of its population and new immigrants

in those territories constitute a flagrant violation of the Fourth Geneva Convention". It called upon Israel to dismantle existing settlements and not to build any more in the Occupied Territories including Jerusalem. The American failure to veto this Resolution outraged the Israeli Government and its supporters in Washington who made their displeasure felt to President Carter who had to issue a hasty statement that he had not understood that the Resolution included Jerusalem and that it marked no change in the American commitment to Israel.

RESOLUTION 509 (1982)

7 June. Demands that Israel unconditionally withdraws fom Lebanon. Repeats 508 of 5 June which calls for end of all military acivities within Lebanon and across the border. Calls on all to report their acceptance within 24 hours.

RESOLUTION 521 (1982)

Following the Sabra-Shatila Massacre the Security Council declared itself "appalled at the massacre of Palestinian civilians". It authorised the Secretary-General immediately to increase the number of UN observers in and around Beirut from 10 to 50 and insisted that there should be no interference with them. It requested the Secretary-General to consider, with the Lebanese Government, the deployment of additional UN forces to protect the civilian population.

Reaffirmed 512 and 513 about civilian population.

RESOLUTION 681 (Security Council) (1990)

After his invasion of Kuwait, Saddam Hussein declared that its future could only be considered in the context of other Middle Eastern problems, in particular that of Palestine, which should be discussed at an international conference. This was adamantly resisted by the Americans who saw this as a "reward" for Saddam's aggression and as unacceptable to the Israelis who refused a peace conference. The Americans were, however, worried about alienating the Arab members of the coalition against Iraq and after prolonged diplomatic discussions agreed not to veto a Security Council Resolution which condemned Israeli actions in the Occupied Territories and Jerusalem, including deportations of Palestinians, and requested the Secretary-General to "monitor and observe" events there. It called further for a peace conference "at an appropriate time". Resolution 681, drafted by Finland, was passed unanimously on 20 December 1990. This was the third time since the Temple Mount Massacre that the Americans had not vetoed an anti-Israel Resolution. After the defeat of Iraq the Americans took the lead in the diplomatic activities which led to the meeting of the Madrid Peace Conference in October 1991.

RESOLUTION 3236 (GENERAL ASSEMBLY) (1974)

At the Rabat Summit in October 1974 King Hussein renounced sovereignty over the West Bank. On 13 November 1974 when Abd al-Aziz Bouteflika was President of the General Assembly Yassir Arafat was invited to speak on the first day of a debate on Palestine. He was received as a Head of State and given a standing ovation before and after his address, during which he used his famous phrase about "the gun and the olive branch" and spoke of the Palestinians' dream of their own homeland while accepting the right of Israel to exist. On 22 November by 89 votes to eight (Israel, the USA, some Latin American states, Iceland and Norway) with 37 abstentions (including the European Community) the General Assembly passed Resolution 3236 which recognised that the Palestinian people were entitled to self-determination and to return to their homes and properties, declared them a principal party in any Middle Eastern peace settlement and appealed to all states to help them to regain their rights. It also requested the Secretary-General to establish contacts with the Palestine Liberation Organisation "on all matters concerning the question of Palestine". This was followed by another Resolution (3237) adopted by 95 to 17 (the previous eight plus some EEC countries and Canada) with 19 abstentions to grant the PLO observer status at the UN. The Israeli delegate described the Resolutions as "utterly contemptible".

RESOLUTION 3379 (GENERAL ASSEMBLY)
1975

In November 1975 the General Assembly passed a series of motions concerning apartheid in South Africa whose "unholy alliance" with Israel was condemned in Resolution 3151. On 10 November after a week of debate three Resolutions supporting the Palestinians were passed. Resolution 3375 called for a "guarantee of their inalienable rights" and for their participation in any peace conference and 3376 called for the establishment of a 20-nation committee to draft a programme for their self-determination. Most controversial was Resolution 3379 previously passed by the Social, Humanitarian and Cultural Committee which described Zionism as "a form of racism and racial discrimination", aiming at "the repression of the dignity and integrity of the human being". Speakers pointed out that Israel had been created for Jews alone and that Jews, wherever they had been born, were entitled to settle there. A Western-sponsored motion moved by Belgium to postpone consideration for a year was rejected by 67 votes to 55 with 15 abstentions and the Resolution itself was then passed by 72 votes to 35 with 32 abstentions. Russia, its satellites, all the Arab states and most of the developing nations voted in favour. The passing of the Resolution was greeted with extreme indignation by America where the Senate called for a reassessment of further participation in the General Assembly after this "infamous act". Israel, which said that the UN was "on its way to becoming the world-centre of anti-Semitism", actually found in the Resolution a convenient pretext for demanding the exclusion of the UN from subsequent peace negotiations. In September 1991 when President Bush was preparing to convene the Madrid Peace Conference and was also under Zionist pressure to guarantee a loan of $10,000 million for settling Russian Jews on the occupied West Bank, he called for the cancellation of Resolution 3379. This took place in December 1991 by 111 votes to 25 with 13 abstentions and 12, including Morocco, Egypt and Tunisia playing no part. Kuwait, Bahrain and Oman voted for repeal while in addition to the other

Muslim countries Cuba and Sri Lanka voted for its retention.

RESOLUTIONS (SECURITY COUNCIL) AFTER OPERATION DESERT STORM

After their defeat in Operation Desert Storm the Iraqis, on 3 March 1991, accepted a cease-fire. On 3 April the Security Council passed by 12 votes to 1 (Cuba) with China, Ecuador and Yemen abstaining Resolution 687 which laid down its formal terms. This Resolution with 34 points and 3,900 words, the longest in UN history, was accepted by Iraq on 5 April. Iraq was to hand back prisoners of war (45 were quickly returned). Its military aircraft were grounded. It was to provide information about minefields. Procedures for avoiding accidental clashes were established. Iraq was to adhere to all the Kuwait Invasion Security Council Resolutions. Furthermore it was to accept, under international supervision, destruction or removal of nuclear, chemical and biological weapons and missiles with a range greater than 150 km. Iraq was to submit within 15 days a list of locations, types and quantities of weapons of mass destruction. Within 45 days the Secretary-General would set up a Special Commission (UNSCOM) to make on-site inspections and destroy these weapons within a further 45 days. The UN was to develop a plan for future monitoring of Iraqi compliance: this was regarded as "a step towards the goal" " of making the Middle East free from weapons of mass destruction. A further provision was for Kuwait–Iraq Frontier Delimitation for which a Commission was established. The UN would set up UNIKOM to monitor a demilitarised zone extending 10 km into Iraq and 5 into Kuwait: the Resolution "noted" that this would allow the Allies to move their troops from Iraq. Iraq was to restore all loot (some of it appeared in a London auction house in 1993) and pay compensation for damage caused: Iraq was declared "liable under international law for any any direct loss, damage, including environmental damage and depletion of national resources or injuries to foreign governments, nationals and corporations as a result of its unlawful occupation of Kuwait". These reparations were to come out of a fund to be created on a percentage of oil revenues which would be administered by a Commission. Payments were to take account of the needs of the Iraqi people, its economy and foreign debts. Sanctions on the import of food were lifted and restrictions eased on essential civilian needs. A Committee could lift the embargo on specific Iraqi exports so that it could buy essential supplies. The Security Council would review the embargo every 60 days and the ban on exports would be lifted after weapons had been removed. Iraq's assets abroad were unfrozen and not included in the compensation fund. The arms embargo was to continue but would be reviewed on 1 August if there had been full compliance with other clauses. Iraq was not to sue anyone for failure to observe contracts as a result of sanctions. Iraq was to co-operate with the Red Cross on the repatriation of Kuwaitis and other missing foreigners: in May 1993 620 Kuwaitis were still unaccounted for. Iraq was to pledge not to support international terrorism. French efforts on "political and moral grounds" to insert some protection for the Kurds who were then being harried by the Iraqi army were rebuffed by the US, China and Russia as an internal matter. The Iraqis were given to understand that they would be treated with greater leniency if they got rid of Saddam Hussain.

Resolution 688 of 5 April condemned repression of the Iraqi civilian population and demanded that Iraq end it immediately. It expressed the hope that an open dialogue would take place to ensure that the human and political rights of all Iraqi citizens were respected as repression threatened international peace. In effect it told the Iraqi Government to be nice to its people which historically it had never done. This interference in the internal affairs of a member-state of the UN was unprecedented and caused some misgivings. No sanctions were stipulated but the Resolution was interpreted, somewhat dubiously according to International Law, as authority to declare "No-fly Zones" to protect the Kurdish Federated State and later the Shiah Uprising. Iraq's failure to observe this Resolution was given as a reason for refusing to lift sanctions.

Number 689 of 9 April laid down particulars of the military zone on the frontier between Kuwait and Iraq and the functions of UNIKOM.

Number 692 of 20 May established a compensation fund for victims of Iraqi aggression into which a percentage of the receipts of oil exports would be paid. A body was set up in Geneva to decide how much should be paid. Iraq denounced this Resolution and refused to sell any oil.

Number 699 of 17 June, passed unanimously, decreed that Iraq should bear the cost of destroying its weapons of mass destruction.

Number 700 of 17 June laid down guidelines to facilitate the implementation of an international arms embargo.

Number 705 of 15 August directed Iraq to start a war reparations fund paid for by up to 30% of future oil revenues. In March 1993 the UN estimated that there might be 1,200,000 claims totalling $100,000 million.

Number 706 of 15 August passed by 13 – 1 (Cuba) with Yemen abstaining laid down that to implement 692 and 705 Iraq would be authorised to sell $1,600,000 worth of oil. The proceeds which would be distributed under UN supervision would be used 30% for the compensation fund, 30% for UNSCOM and the rest for humanitarian relief. Iraq rejected this Resolution.

Number 707 of 15 August reinforced the demand in Number 687 and condemned the Iraqi failure to disclose full details of its chemical, biological and nuclear weapons programmes, ordering it to provide complete access to UNSCOM.

Number 712 of 19 September passed by 13 – 1 (Cuba) with Yemen abstaining, approved plans put forward by Secretary-General Perez de Cuellar for a mechanism to sell oil as decreed in Number 706. A series of talks, the most recent in July 1993, broke down without agreement on both the principles and the methods of implementing this. As the price of oil was depressed, other Arab states were not keen to see this amount of oil come on the market.

Number 715 of 11 October put most of Iraqi industry, military and civilian under permanent UN supervision.

As the Iraqi Government made no effort to co-operate, the Security Council on 2 October 1992 passed Resolution 778 impounding most of the country's oil-related assets to buy food and medicine for the Kurds and pay compensation to war victims. The assets were worth about $500 million, mostly in the USA. China abstained on this Resolution.

REVOLUTIONARY COMMAND COUNCIL (Egypt)

After the success of the July Revolution, the Executive of the Free Officers emerged into the open as the Revolutionary Command Council and declared its intention to "cleanse the nation of its tyrants and to reform the constitutional life of the country". It pledged an end to imperialism, feudalism and monopoly and the establishment of a powerful army, social justice and a sound democracy. Chaired by General Neguib, its membership was that of the original Executive with the addition of Colonels Ahmad Shawqi, Kamal Rifaat and Lutfi Wahid. It quickly abolished the monarchy and confiscated its property, removed many senior officers, ordered political parties to purge their ranks, promised general elections in February 1953 and passed an Agrarian Reform Law which limited holdings to about 200 acres. Its members toured their home districts, preaching self-sacrifice, settling feuds, organising medical missions and literacy classes. At the same time it showed readiness to use force, hanging two workers after the Kafr al-Dawar Riot, sentencing a recalcitrant landlord to life imprisonment and later cracking down on the Muslim Brothers and the Egyptian Communist Party. Some of these measures, and indeed whether the King should be executed, were settled after genuine debate and a vote within the RCC. Several members have written memoirs which show frequent bickering and walkouts. In September Neguib took over as Prime Minister, heading an otherwise civilian Cabinet. Three RCC members formed the Tribunal established to judge corrupt politicians. After having at first allowed political parties to proliferate, in January 1953 the RCC abolished them all, setting up the Liberation Rally which served to clear out antagonistic elements in trade unions, student organisations etc. At first the RCC had appeared content to be the power behind the scenes but in February 1953 it assumed power to rule by decree for a transitional period of three years and one of the Eleven Rules of Government described the RCC and the Council of Ministers as jointly composing an Executive Council to consider general policy and to which each Minister was formally responsible. This institutionalised its control over both the formation and execution of policy. While the popular Neguib acted as front man, the RCC came increasingly under the control of Nasser who held no official position until June 1953 when he became Deputy Prime Minister: other RCC members took over the key portfolios of the Interior, War and National Guidance. The RCC was developing into a military dictatorship so Neguib, wishing to restore some democracy, found himself isolated within it and was finally removed in November 1954. From early days members, and later some as prominent as Khalid Mohieddin and Salah Salim, who had differences with Nasser, were removed from the

RCC and by the time it formally ceased to exist in January 1956 only six of the original fourteen members remained active in government.

RHODES ARMISTICE (1949)
The last fighting in the Palestine War had been between the Israelis and Egyptians in Sinai at the end of 1948 and peace negotiations began between these two Powers in Rhodes on 13 January 1949 under the chairmanship of the Acting UN Mediator, Dr Ralph Bunche. The two delegations did not meet face to face and the Mediator had to move from one to the other in separate suites in the same hotel. There were considerable disagreements about strategic locations on the cease-fire line and over the fate of Beersheba but a compromise agreement was signed on 24 February which left Beersheba with the Israelis, the Gaza Strip with the Egyptians and the strategic location of al-Awja was to be demilitarised. It was stressed that the delimitation was "not to be construed in any sense as a political or territorial boundary" or "an ultimate solution to the Palestine question" but was merely valid for the period of the Armistice. Neither would undertake aggressive action against the other. An Israel–Lebanon armistice was signed on 23 March at Ras al-Naqura on the frontier between them, restoring the previous border between Lebanon and Palestine with a small demilitarised zone. The Armistice between Israel and Jordan was secretly negotiated at Sunah but was formally signed at Rhodes on 3 April. The Armistice between Israel and Syria, hampered by internal instability, was the most difficult to negotiate but an agreement to restore the pre-war frontier with some demilitarised zones was signed near Mahanayim on 20 July 1949. No armistice was signed between Israel and Iraq.

RIAD, Abd al-Munim, General (1919–69)
Egyptian soldier. Born in Tanta, he graduated from the Military Academy in 1938 as a specialist in anti-aircraft gunnery and had further training at Woolwich. He fought in World War II and in the Palestine War. After 1952 he commanded the anti-aircraft school and held posts on the General Staff. In March 1964 he was appointed Chief of Staff to the Unified Arab Command established after the Cairo Summit of 1964 and later attended a Chief of Staff's course in Moscow. Before fighting broke out in the June War of 1967 he went to Amman to assume command of the Jordanian army as had been agreed by King Hussain. He was unwilling to consult the experienced Jordanian General Habis al-Majali and took his orders directly from Cairo despite insecure communications. Believing Egyptian propaganda reports that they were advancing towards Hebron to cut off the Negev from Tel Aviv and that 75% of Israeli aircraft had been destroyed, he overruled Jordanian objections and abandoned the original Jordanian plan of seizing West Jerusalem as a bargaining counter, which could easily have been done. Instead he launched an attack on a wide front which was defeated, leading to the loss of the West Bank from which he insisted upon retreating despite the protests of the King. At the end of the war he was appointed Chief of Staff of the Egyptian Armed Forces in succession to General Muhammad Fawzi with whom he worked to reorganise

and re-equip them. In July 1968 he accompanied President Nasser to Moscow for talks on military aid. While inspecting positions on the Suez Canal he was killed in an artillery bombardment. Riad was regarded as one of the ablest Arab generals, and, a very sociable bachelor, was a man of exceptional charm. He was so popular that politicians feared that the army might carry out a coup to make him Head of State.

RIAD, Mahmud (1917–92)
Egyptian Minister and Secretary-General of the Arab League. He came from a middle-class family and at the time of the expansion of the Egyptian army, joined the Military Academy in the same term as Nasser. He also took a degree in International Law and fought in the Palestine War. He then led the military section of the Egyptian delegation to the Rhodes Armistice, remaining in charge of Palestine affairs in the War Ministry. Riad was a member, although not one of the leaders, of the Free Officers. In 1952 he left the army as a Colonel and headed the Palestine Desk in the Foreign Ministry. In 1954 he took part in the Sarsank Meeting when the Egyptians tried to woo the Iraqis from their commitments to the West and the next year was sent as Ambassador to Damascus. There he was an extremely successful envoy, defeating supporters of Syria's joining the Baghdad Pact, winning allies in the army and the Baath Party, negotiating a Unified Military Command, organising public opinion against Britain and France in the Suez War and warning of the difficulties of the formation of the United Arab Republic. For the next three years he was Presidential Adviser on Foreign Affairs before in 1962 he was appointed Permanent Representative at the UN. During this time he was active in the Arab nationalist and Non-Aligned Movements making Egypt a major participant on the world stage. In 1964 he was appointed Foreign Minister, holding the post, latterly with the title of Deputy Prime Minister, until 1972. Riad worked closely with India and Yugoslavia to harvest the advantages of "positive neutrality". He persuaded most of the African and communist states to break off diplomatic relations with Israel. His immense knowledge of the Palestine problem was of value in the drafting of Resolution 247 which accepted the existence of Israel in return for its evacuation of conquered territories, in the Khartoum Summit of 1967 when the rich oil states were persuaded to subsidise Egypt and in the attempts to reconcile King Hussain and the Palestine Liberation Organisation. Riad also negotiated the Egyptian withdrawal from the Yemen War. He worked well with the Russians during the War of Attrition and with the Americans over the Rogers' Plan. Riad also took unprecedented steps to ensure that Egyptian diplomats received adequate training. In June 1972 he was unanimously elected Secretary-General of the Arab League where his great experience enabled him to prevent disputes between the Steadfastness Front and the "moderates" from destroying the organisation although there were some boycotts such as that of Iraq and Libya of the Algiers Summit of 1973. He was unable, however, to ward off a major split after Sadat had made the Camp David Agreement with Israel. Although he had personally opposed this policy, Riad declared the sub-

sequent Baghdad Summit illegal as he had not issued the invitations and he resigned when the decision was taken to move the League headquarters to Tunis. He was never as close to Sadat as he had been to Nasser and was to be as an unofficial councillor to Mubarak, whom he helped to bring Egypt back into the centre of Arab affairs. His influence was seen during the crisis that followed the invasion of Kuwait by Saddam Hussain and in the organisation and proceedings of the Cairo Summit of August 1990. He was also often asked for advice by Palestinian leaders. He wrote useful memoirs, *The Struggle for Peace in the Middle East* and other books. He was a highly skilled diplomat and a pleasant companion.

RIFAH KILLINGS (1956)

Rifah was a refugee camp with a population of about 32,000 in the Gaza Strip which was overrun by the Israelis during the Suez War in 1956. It had previously served as a base for *fidayin* raids across the armistice lines. On 12 November the Israelis sent loudspeaker vans around the camp calling upon the men to gather at designated points for screening. According to Palestinian sources insufficient time was given and with many people running towards the points, Israeli soldiers panicked and opened fire. The Israelis said that the Arabs were killed in the course of resistance to screening. The Director of UNWRA put the number of deaths at 111.

al-RIFAI, Samir (c. 1896–1965)

Jordanian Prime Minister. A Circassian, he was born in Safad, educated at an Anglican school and went to Trans-Jordan as a civilian employee of the RAF. He moved into the service of the Amir Abd Allah and became one of his most confidential staff. In October 1944 he became Prime Minister but was replaced in May 1945 by Ibrahim Hashim whom he in turn succeeded in February 1947 after the holding of the first parliamentary elections. Abd Allah made use of him in his most secret dealings with regard to Palestine; at the London Conference in the autumn of 1946 he publicly stood firmly with the rest of the Arab delegates against partition but privately put forward his master's support for it to British officials. In December 1947 Rifai was replaced as Prime Minister by Tawfiq Abu al-Huda but, as Minister of the Royal Court, he was still one of the King's closest advisers. In 1949 he interpreted for Abd Allah at meetings with Jewish businessmen about joint enterprises and with politicians about access to the Mediterranean. In December 1950 he became Prime Minister again after Said al-Mufti had refused to hold peace talks with Israeli leaders; Rifai held several secret meetings with representatives of Ben Gurion the following spring. He was still in office when the King was assassinated but gave way to Tawfiq Abu al-Huda who was considered more capable of surmounting the crisis. When Abu al-Huda's health gave way, Rifai succeeded him as the strong man of the "Palace politicians" and in the crisis of January 1956 once again became Prime Minister. He proclaimed martial law but defused popular anger by declaring that there was no possibility of Jordan's adherence to the Baghdad Pact. In March, on behalf of King Hussain, he formally notified Glubb Pasha of his dismissal as Commander of the Arab

Legion, brushing off British complaints by stating that it was merely an internal matter. Despite differences with the King who appeared to him to be falling under pro-Nasser and anti-British influences he remained in office until May when Hussain decided to try to conciliate public opinion by the appointment of Said al-Mufti. In April 1957 at another time of crisis, following the dismissal of the popular Sulayman al-Nabulsi, partly at Rifai's urging, and the Zerka Incident, Hashim became Prime Minister to cope with internal affairs with Rifai as his Deputy in charge of Foreign Affairs. He obtained American aid but refused to receive an envoy to explain the Eisenhower Doctrine. He thus greatly strengthened the country's external position and by the end of the year was able to say that the country could now withstand the opposition of Egypt and Syria. After the formation of the United Arab Republic he went to see King Saud in the hope of countering it by a monarchical union with the Kingdom and Iraq. This failed but when in May Hashim went to Baghdad as Deputy Prime Minister of the newly-created Arab Federation consisting merely of Jordan and Iraq, Rifai once again became Prime Minister. He was thus in office during the crisis that led to the arrival of British troops in July 1958. In March 1959 he accompanied the King to Washington in a visit which marked the formal transfer of Jordan from British protection to that of the United States. Two months later, Hussain again tried to introduce more liberal policies and Rifai was regarded as too old, too authoritarian and too conservative to carry them out. He was therefore replaced by Hazza al-Majali and became President of the Senate and later of the newly-founded University. He became Prime Minister in March 1963 at a time when there was a possibility of a new Arab Union of Egypt, Syria and Iraq: his appointment was a signal that Jordan would not join. Students rioting to demand a Prime Minister who would improve relations with other Arab states were firmly repressed but there was a vote of no-confidence in his government and he remained in office for less than a month. Rifai was universally regarded as a man of principle, firm and formidable, indifferent to public opinion. He was wont to give Parliamentarians firm lectures on good behaviour. In foreign affairs he showed statesmanlike qualities of flexibility, moderation and inventiveness.

al-RIFAI, Zaid (1936–)

Jordanian Prime Minister. He was the son of the Prime Minister Samir al-Rifai and educated at Victoria College in Alexandria where he formed a close friendship with his classmate the future King Hussain and at Harvard and Columbia where he took degrees in political science and international law. Rifai joined the diplomatic service, holding posts in Cairo, Beirut and New York before returning to Amman where, working with Hazza al-Majalli, he very nearly shared the fate of the Prime Minister. A series of Court posts, including that of Private Secretary, emphasised his intimacy with the King whom he warned against participation in the June War and later advised to take a firm line with the Palestinian guerrillas who were flouting the authority of the Jordanian Government. In June 1970 they ambushed the car in which Hussain and Rifai were travelling. He was regarded as one of their major opponents and the Black September Organisation sentenced him to death. In December 1971 while he was Ambassador in London, 30 bullets were fired into his car and nearly every bone in his right hand was smashed. The suspected assassin, an Algerian, escaped. In March 1972 Rifai was recalled as Political Adviser to the King in which post he showed great skills in diplomacy and public relations at a time when Hussain was seeking military and economic aid from the USA, had difficulties with the Palestinians and few friends amongst the Arab states. In May 1973 Hussain appointed him Prime Minister and Rifai formed a Cabinet, a mixture of politicians and technocrats, mostly young, almost half Palestinians. He himself retained responsibility for Foreign Affairs and Defence. An amnesty for guerrillas was announced. After a break of 17 months relations were restored with Egypt and Syria in time for the October War during which Jordan sent troops to the Syrian front. After it Rifai was deeply involved in all the diplomacy associated with Henry Kissinger whom he had known at Harvard. He attended the Rabat Summit of October 1974 when Hussain renounced sovereignty over the West Bank and arranged the consequent revision of the Constitution. Rifai then reformed his Cabinet reducing the number of Palestinians. Relations with the Palestine Liberation Organisation were never easy and Rifai several times had to deny secret dealings with Israel. Relations with other Arab states were generally good, there were frequent exchanges of visits, and Jordanian troops were sent to assist Sultan Qabus Al Bu Said in the Dhofar Rebellion. After a visit by Hafiz al-Assad a high-level committee was created to co-ordinate policies and later a joint military command was set up: total unity was perhaps only prevented by an unwillingness to alienate Egypt completely and reservations on the part of the Jordanian army but co-operation between the two reached unprecedented levels and this was largely ascribed to the efforts of Rifai. The Americans made difficulties over requests to supply weapons and the Jordanians threatened to make approaches to Russia, receiving a visit from the Soviet Deputy Defence Minister. Rifai showed little enthusiasm for the Sinai Agreement. It was a time of considerable prosperity, foreign aid was generous, the development plan reached most of its targets and there appeared the possibility that the country would be self-supporting by 1980. Many businesses, affected by the fighting in Beirut, moved to Amman. In February 1976 Rifai postponed elections indefinitely because of the changed status of the West Bank and the following month he accompanied the King to Australia and Japan. In July, stating that he had "worked continuously" for three years and needed a rest, he resigned. In the spring of 1985 the King was actively engaged in a search for peace in collaboration with the Americans and Yassir Arafat, then the *bête-noire* of the Syrians, and this led to bad relations with Damascus. In order to improve them without upsetting the Americans and also to restore the economic situation, the King again turned to Rifai who became Prime Minister on 5 April. He embarked on wide-ranging measures to stimulate local industry and promote exports. In February 1986 the King repudiated an agreement with Arafat who had been unable to convince his followers to accept Resolution 242 and expelled the PLO representative Abu Jihad amidst talk of collusion with Israel. A *rapprochement* with Syria enabled the King to pay his first visit since Rifai's last term of office but closer relations were difficult while Jordan supported Baghdad in the Iran–Iraq War: Rifai tried without success to reconcile the hostile Baathist regimes. In order to placate Syria, Rifai tried to weaken Arafat by appealing over his head to the West Bankers but this tactic failed. The American Congress blocked Jordan's attempt at obtaining more up-to-date missiles and fighter aircraft and was unmoved at threats to turn to Russia: they also demanded that Jordan should negotiate directly with Israel, refusing the international conference that Hussain desired. In July 1988 the King ended legal and administrative ties with the West Bank and this was seen as due to the influence of Rifai. Preparations were made for elections under a new law which enabled the Government to rule out candidates simply by a police statement that they were "affiliated with illegal political parties". There was little popular participation in public life and for the first time for years there was internal unrest with 3 students killed at Yarmuk University in May 1986. The press was strictly controlled, 5 journals were banned in 1988, newspaper licences could be revoked at any time and the Government bought controlling shares in publishing. Rifai treated Islamic fundamentalists with scant courtesy and despite his successes abroad, he had few friends at home. He was warned as he grew increasingly intolerant of dissent, that he and the King were out of touch with the people and that rioting was the only way in which opinions could be expressed. Corruption spread and the people were frightened of officials. The economy resisted improvement, aid was curtailed owing to the declining revenues of the oil states. In April 1989 the World Bank and the International Monetary Fund in return for rescheduling debts of $8.3 billion insisted on cuts in subsidies that meant that the prices of essential commodities rose between 15 and 50%, and this led to rioting in Southern Jordan, traditionally the most loyal area of the country. Ten people were killed and at least a hundred injured. Rifai, in the tradition of Jordanian Prime Ministers, offered himself as a scapegoat to deflect criticism from the Monarchy and resigned. He was married to the daughter of the former Prime Minister Bahjat al-Talhuni, another member of the the inner circle around the King. Rifai was tough, loyal, autocratic, a quick-witted manipulator, urbane, cultured, rather flamboyant with his large cigars and a keen sportsman, fond of water skiing and tennis.

al-RIHANI, Amin (1876–1940)

Lebanese/American writer. A Maronite, he was born at Freike 30 km west of Beirut and given a French education. He moved with his family to New York in 1888 and spent some time there in poverty, including employment in a theatrical troupe which went bankrupt. Rihani studied law in the evenings while doing menial tasks by day but in 1898 his health deteriorated and he returned to Lebanon where he spent most of the rest of his life. He offered himself as a bridge betweeen East and West seeing the advantages and drawbacks of both cultures. Rihani was also a mystic and poet and wrote in an ornate style partially modelled on Arabic verse forms. He advised various Arab leaders on how to deal with the Western Powers and was active at the Versailles Peace Congress and the Uqayr Conference of 1922. Most unusually for a Christian he received a piece of the *Kiswah*, the covering of the Ka'aba from King Hussain, but his main role was awakening the world to the importance of Ibn Saud, then widely believed to be a mere bedouin chief, even, according to the Consul in Aden, the only American official then resident in the Peninsula, "a member of the Shiah or Persian sect of Islam". In 1925 he attempted to mediate between them and for Ibn Saud, Rihani was a valuable source of information about the outside world. Rihani's three main travel books, written he said "to be of service to the Arabs" were the only generally available source of information on other rulers such as the Imam Yahya and Muhammad Ali al-Idrisi. He married an American painter who refused to live in Lebanon.

al-RIKABI, (Muhammad) Ali Ridha (c. 1860–1942)

Prime Minister of Syria and Chief Minister of Trans-Jordan. He came from a distinguished Damascus family and was educated in Istanbul. He was an early member of the Ahd, the secret group of Arab nationalist officers. Rikabi became a General, and was Governor of Medina. He was transferred to Damascus and in May 1917 was said to have met the Amir Faysal and T. E. Lawrence to arrange his defection to the Allies. Early in 1918 the Ottoman Government sent him to Switzerland to see if it would be possible to make a separate peace. After his return he deserted and subsequently re-entered Damascus with the forces of Faysal who made him Military Governor and later Prime Minister. In May 1920 he was thought too ready to compromise with the French and was replaced. Unlike other officials he did not leave Damascus when the French entered and was subsidised by the new regime. Later he moved to Trans-Jordan where his experience, forceful character and efficiency (Rikabi was said to be able to spot a discrepancy in accounts at a glance) made a good impression upon British officials. In March 1922 they secured his appointment as Chief Minister. In October 1922 he accompanied the Amir Abd Allah to London, remaining to negotiate the first agreement to regulate the status of the country. He was greatly feared by Abd Allah, to whom he had no particular loyalty and who suspected that he had ambitions to become Amir and he was disliked by local officials for his arrogance. He thus did not receive sufficient support to solve the problems of a newly-created country and resigned, going to Palestine in the hope of making a career there. In April 1924 the British insisted upon his reinstatement because they considered that only he had the strength to impose some measure of financial discipline on the Amir and to restrain the aggressive nationalists who were making trouble with the French in Syria. Rikabi pledged to end corruption, make appointments on merit and work for constitutional government but then started to complain about heavy-

handed British control. In June 1926, just after he had toured the frontier, a raid occurred and he was dismissed to appease the French. He made his peace with them and returned to Damascus where he was involved in forming a Monarchist Party, probably himself aspiring to the throne. Soon afterwards he became senile and played no further part. Philby, with whom he had clashes, saw him as "the ablest of the men surrounding Abd Allah . . . a dynamic personality ever seeking new spheres, moral or material to conquer" but a report from an official in Damascus described him as vengeful, avaricious, unscrupulous and "past-master of Turkish methods of intrigue".

al-RIMAWI, Qassim (c. 1915–82)

Jordanian Prime Minister. He was born in Ramallah and took a doctorate in Law from the American University of Beirut. Rimawi was active in nationalist politics in Palestine before 1948 and subsequently represented Ramallah in the Jordanian Parliament. He was appointed Minister of State for Municipal and Rural Affairs in 1962 in the Cabinet of his close friend Wasfi al-Tall. He held the same post in Tall's government of 1965 until he became Speaker of the Chamber in April 1967. He was Deputy Prime Minister in the Cabinet of Abd al-Hamid Sharaf upon whose totally unexpected death on 3 July 1980 he was appointed caretaker Prime Minister. He held the office until Mudar Badran formed a government on 28 August.

RISHON LE ZION KILLINGS (1990)

On 20 May 1990, at a time when the *Intifadah* seemed to be losing some of its impetus, a 21-year-old Israeli armed with an Uzi sub-machine-gun approached the "slave-market" where Palestinian labourers waited in the hope of getting a day's work and ordered them to sit down. As he was wearing army trousers and as such conduct from Israeli soldiers was not unusual they obeyed. He thereupon opened fire upon them indiscriminately killing seven and wounding eleven others. The massacre set off three days of riots in which a further 13 Palestinians were killed by the army. The murderer was brought to trial in December but claimed that he had been temporarily insane.

ROGERS' PLAN (1969)

William P. Rogers was appointed Secretary of State by President Nixon in January 1969 and soon found himself involved in an escalating crisis in the Middle East. The June War of 1967 was followed by a period of comparative calm but in March 1969 a series of heavy artillery duels took place across the Suez Canal, the east bank of which was occupied by the Israelis. These were followed by Israeli air incursions and on 22 April the UN Secretary-General U Thant declared that "a virtual state of war" existed. There were also clashes on the Syrian and Jordanian fronts and raids by Palestinian guerrillas. In June Rogers put forward a twelve-point plan which included an end to the state of war between Egypt and Israel, aid to guerrillas, and hostile propaganda. Israel would evacuate occupied Egyptian territories which would be demilitarised. Navigation through the Canal and the Gulf of Aqaba should be unrestricted. Gaza should be placed under the supervision of Dr Gunnar Jarring who would decide its future after discussions with Egypt, Israel and Jordan. Jerusalem should be kept unified. A settlement should be reached over the fate of Palestinian refugees, not more than 10% of whom could be repatriated. Direct Arab—Israeli contacts should be started. A final settlement should be guaranteed by the United Nations. The Plan was almost immediately rejected by President Nasser as an attempt to divide the Arabs and liquidate the question of the Palestinians without reference to them. Instead he declared a "War of Attrition". The Russians declined to support the Plan and the Israelis refused to evacuate conquered areas. Fighting continued and on 7 September the Israeli Chief of Staff stated that there had been 1,000 aircraft sorties into Egypt in the previous 50 days. In October Rogers put forward a revised version for indirect talks, such as those employed in the Rhodes Armistice under the auspices of Jarring, that Egypt and Israel should agree on a timetable for the withdrawal of Israeli forces, that the state of war between them should end, that secure and recognised borders should be agreed, that Gaza should be demilitarised under an interim UN administration, the Tiran Straits should be an international waterway and a "fair settlement" should be agreed by both sides. In November the Egyptian Foreign Minister Mahmud Riad finally rejected the "principle of a piecemeal settlement" while the Israelis stated that there should be "a directly negotiated peace" without interference from states outside the area. The Russians rejected it as anti-Arab. At the same time Rogers made separate proposals for a peace settlement between Jordan and Israel on the basis that the two should negotiate procedures for an Israeli evacuation of the West Bank, prohibition of violence from one territory against another, an agreed permanent frontier, negotiations over a unified Jerusalem and over Gaza, the Gulf of Aqaba to be an international waterway, the refugees of 1948 should be given the choice of repatriation or resettlement in Arab countries with compensation from Israel and formal recognition of each other's sovereignty. Jordan accepted the proposals but they were rejected outright by Israel. The following summer Rogers' Plan II met with more success.

ROGERS' PLAN (II) 1970

After Israel and Egypt refused to accept Rogers' Plan (I) of 1969 the war of attrition between them intensified. Installations near Cairo were bombed, 70 workers being killed in an attack on a factory and 46 children in a raid on a primary school. In order to defend Cairo in March 1970 Russian SAM missiles and their crews arrived in Egypt and in April the Israelis claimed that Russian pilots had been in action against their aircraft, some of which were flown by American citizens. The Israelis invaded Lebanon, raided Jordan and bombed a camp near Damascus. The threat of further escalation involving the Super-Powers was obvious and on 25 June the US Secretary of State William P. Rogers announced a new peace initiative. He called for a cease-fire for three months, starting on 1 July, during which the UN mediator Gunnar Jarring would negotiate the withdrawal of Israeli forces from the territories occupied in the June War. All concerned would undertake to uphold

Resolution 242 and would pull back forces 20 km from their present positions and this would be supervised by the UN. The proposals were rejected immediately by the Palestinians, Syria which called them "hateful", Iraq and Algeria. Four days later Mrs Golda Meir denounced them as "a trick" but accepted them on 31 July after "clarifications" that it would not have to abandon all conquered territory or accept the return of too many refugees. After a long visit to Moscow, during which fighting continued, President Nasser had already accepted the Plan with slight modifications on 23 July; his reasons were tactical, securing a breathing space while he completed his deployment of missiles. He was immediately followed by King Hussain. On 7 August a cease-fire came into effect with Egypt and Israel agreeing to stop all incursions and refrain from strengthening their forces within zones of 50 km east and west of the cease-fire line. This could be verified by limited reconnaissance flights. Despite constant allegations of infractions the cease-fire was renewed for three months in November 1970 and in February 1971 President Sadat agreed to a further month but in March refused a prolongation. In the meanwhile Palestinian frustration at the cease-fire had led to Black September.

ROME AND VIENNA AIRPORT ATTACKS (1985)

On 27 December 1985 four terrorists threw grenades and fired indiscriminately at the El Al and TWA check-ins at Rome airport. Italian and Israeli security guards returned fire, killing three of the gunmen and wounding the fourth who was captured. In the firing 13 passengers were killed and 75 wounded. The attackers were found to have been drugged and the survivor, who carried a forged Moroccan passport, claimed that they had intended to take control of an aircraft and crash it on Tel Aviv. Approximately five minutes after the start of this incident another three gunmen with grenades and automatic rifles attacked the El Al check-in at Schwechat airport Vienna. Three passengers were killed and 30 wounded. The terrorists commandeered a car and escaped in the direction of Czechoslovakia but were caught by the Austrian police who killed one of them and captured the other two. They, also, had intended to crash an aircraft on Tel Aviv. The Palestine Liberation Organisation denied any involvement and it was generally believed that the attacks had been planned by Abu Nidal. The Reagan Administration, however, was itching for a pretext to take action against Qadafi and claimed to have evidence that, despite his denials, he had been responsible. In January 1986 American citizens were ordered to leave Libya and American warships "trailed their coats" near Libyan waters but failed to provoke an attack. Attempts to persuade the Europeans to join in sanctions against Libya were equally unsuccessful.

ROSEIRES DAM/KENANA SCHEME (Sudan)

The dam at Roseires on the Blue Nile about 400 miles south east of Khartoum was primarily designed to store water for the irrigation of 1.5 million acres in the Kenana area and was planned by British and French consultants in 1955. Built at a cost of Sud20 million by an Italian consortium, it was inaugurated by President al-Azhari in December 1966. Arrangements were subsequently made for it to generate electricity and for a further area at Rahad to be irrigated at an estimated cost of Sud180 million. This was seen as part of a vision of Sudan as the bread-basket of the Arab world. The World Bank and Arab sources provided support and it was hoped to settle 14,000 families on 290,000 acres growing cotton and groundnuts. Poor decision-making and bad administration prevented the scheme from becoming a success and foreign funds dried up. In 1971 the British Lonrho Company proposed that sugar be grown at Kenana and it was hoped to produce 350,000 tons a year. The original estimated cost was $180 million but when it actually came into production in 1981 it was estimated to have cost nearly $1,000 million, mainly subscribed by the Saudi and Kuwaiti Governments. The Sudan Government held a 33.5% share. In 1983 a 10-year improvement plan was announced but it had to be drastically reduced as a result of Sudan's inability to pay its debts. After the fall of Nimeiri more credit became available. In May 1988 the World Bank agreed to provide additional funding to rehabilitate the irrigation network. A further scheme to plant another 6,000 acres of sugar cane at a cost of $50 million was announced in 1991. It had been hoped that sugar production would be a major hard currency earner but in fact all produced was consumed locally.

ROYAL BOEING, Attempt upon (1972)

On the afternoon of 16 August 1972, the Boeing 727 bringing Hassan II home from a private visit to France was accosted over the sea by four Moroccan Air Force F-5 fighters which ordered it to land at Kenitra military base instead of at Rabat; they opened fire when it refused. Two out of three engines were wrecked. Hassan, posing as the wireless operator contacted the attacking aircraft and declared that the pilot had been killed and the King and the co-pilot seriously wounded. They received permission to proceed to Rabat where the aircraft landed safely despite a smashed undercarriage and were greeted by rumours that the Royal Boeing had crashed into the sea. As the King was leaving the airport the fighters returned and machine-gunned buildings there, killing 8 and wounding 47 including Ministers who had come to greet him. One pilot who had parachuted into the sea was captured and two others who had sought political asylum in Gibraltar were handed back. Their testimony was said to have implicated the Defence Minister General Oufkir whose death took place a few hours after the failure of the attempted assassination. In October 220 officers from Kenitra were put on trial and 11 officers sentenced to death, 32 received prison sentences and the rest were acquitted.

RUSSO–EGYPTIAN TREATY OF FRIENDSHIP (1971)

During the War of Attrition Russia had contributed to the defence of Egypt in a way that it had never previously helped a non-communist state. According to Sadat, Nasser twice asked for a formal Treaty of Friendship but was refused. In January 1971 President Nikolai Podgorny visited Egypt for the ceremonial opening of the Aswan High Dam and was assured by Sadat that "our friendship is for ever". In April, after a visit to Tripoli where he met the strongly anti-communist Qadafi, Sadat announced that they planned to establish a Federation of Arab Republics. The most pro-Russian of Nasser's entourage, Ali Sabri was so opposed to this conception that he conspired to overthrow the President and was imprisoned. At the same time William Rogers became the first Secretary of State since 1953 to visit the Middle East and the Russians feared that Sadat might be interested in an American-brokered settlement. Podgorny hurriedly returned on an ostensibly private visit and apparently demanded that Russo-Egyptian relations be formalised for if Russia were committed to defend Egypt it required some control over its policies. Some thought that the very speed with which Sadat concurred showed that he did not take very seriously the Treaty which was signed on 27 May for the development of friendship in the political, economic, scientific, technical and cultural fields on a basis of non-interference and equality. They would consult regularly on all important matters and would co-ordinate their stands in the event of a threat to peace. Military co-operation would continue and the Russians would provide equipment and training. Neither side would join any pact directed against the other. The Treaty would be valid for 15 years and would be renewable for periods of 5 years. A communiqué condemned Israel's "expansionist programme which threatened world peace", reaffirmed Resolution 242, criticised imperialists and called for the banning of nuclear weapons. The Treaty was similar to those signed with Russia's European satellites. The Russian Ambassador mentioned that Egypt had received $720 million in the past decade and might look forward to a further $500 million in the next five years. In February 1972 Sadat paid his third visit to Moscow in the 18 months of his Presidency and his request for offensive weapons was apparently rebuffed. On 18 July 1972 he announced that he no longer required the services of the Russian military mission whose 15–20,000 personnel left within a month. The reasons that he gave were their failure to provide offensive weapons needed to carry the war to Israel, failure to keep promises on the quantity and delivery date of weapons and "excessive caution" in imposing conditions on their use. It is more probable that his reasons were dislike for the Russians on the part of his officers and on that of his Arab allies such as King Faysal and the need to bolster his personal prestige by a gesture as dramatic as that of Nasser in nationalising the Suez Canal. He also presumably hoped from some reward from the Americans although he had not bargained with them in advance. The Russian navy retained the use of Alexandria and after a visit of the Egyptian War Minister to Moscow at the end of February 1973 arms supplies were resumed. During the October War the Russians put support for Egypt above their desire for détente with the US but found themselves frozen out of the Geneva Peace Conference after which Sadat made no secret of his preference for dealing with the Americans. On 14 March 1976 he called for the termination of the Treaty on the grounds that the Russians in their own interests were opposing moves towards peace and the economic, social and political reforms involved in the *Infitah*. They had refused to reschedule Egypt's civil debt of $1,500 million and military debt of $4,000 million upon which they were even demanding interest. Finally they had prevented India from selling the spare parts without which some of his aircraft were no more than scrap. The Russians, faced with the loss of a position that they had paid dearly for 20 years to attain were bitterly angry but could do nothing.

RUSSO-IRAQI TREATY (1972)

By the early 1970s Russia had become the main source of arms for Iraq from which it accepted payment in oil on favourable terms. Iraq felt isolated as it was on bad terms with all its neighbours and in February 1972 Saddam Hussain visiting Moscow called for "a solid strategic alliance" between the two. In April Prime Minister Kosygin visited Baghdad and signed a 15-year Friendship Treaty with President Ahmad Hassan al-Bakr. It closely resembled the Russo-Egyptian Treaty of 1971 and contained 14 clauses. It guaranteed that neither would join an alliance directed against the other and provided for immediate consultations if there were a threat to peace involving either participant. Stressing "permanent, unbreakable friendship" it called for constant co-operation in the development of political, military, industrial, scientific and cultural relations. Both would wage an "unrelenting struggle against imperialism and Zionism" and would support "just struggles". It would be renewable for five-year periods after its expiry in 1987. The Treaty, bringing Soviet influence to the Arabian Peninsula and the Gulf caused great alarm in those areas and it was thought that the Russians would find Iraq a more stable and reliable ally than Egypt or Syria. Libya withdrew its Ambassador in protest. In fact, particularly after the start of the Iran-Iraq War, there were substantial political differences between Moscow and Baghdad but the Treaty was duly renewed in April 1987.

RUWAIS DEVELOPMENT SCHEME

Following the success of the Jabal Ali Development scheme created by his rival Shaykh Rashid al-Maktum of Dubai, Shaykh Zaid al-Nihayyan announced plans for a site for heavy industry at Ruwais, 250 km west of Abu Dhabi. In 1979 the General Industries Corporation was set up to co-ordinate non-petroleum development and factories built to manufacture, paper-bags, bricks, concrete blocks, fertilisers and animal feed. A 120,000 barrel a day refinery came on stream in 1981 and Ruwais also acted as a terminal for natural gas from offshore fields. A plan to produce steel was postponed because of lack of funds. The site was officially opened by Shaykh Zaid in March 1982. Later a bottling plant for Coca-Cola and a plant to manufacture polyurethane blocks were opened.

al-SAAD, c. 1860–1942

Lebanese Prime Minister and President. He came from an aristocratic Maronite family and after education by the Jesuits in Beirut, entered the Ottoman administrative service. He rose to become Vice-President of the Lebanese Council and to act as *Mutassarif* during vacancies. He had considered that the modernisation by the Young Turks made the old special position of Lebanon out of date but none the less was exiled to Adana during the war. When an Arab government representing Faysal was proclaimed in Beirut, Habib Pasha was appointed Governor of Mount Lebanon but he was expelled by the British after a few days and replaced by a French colonel. When the French took over Lebanon they appointed him President of the Administrative Council and he was said to have denounced to them colleagues regarded as sympathetic to Syrian unity under King Faysal; he worked closely with the Maronite Patriarch in organising demonstrations against unity with Syria. He became so partisan that his house was attacked by the Druzes. He was regarded as an expert in fixing elections and was himself the first President of the Representative Council established in May 1922. He intrigued successfully to cause friction between French officials and succeeded in ousting those who opposed him. In August 1928 after his relative Bishara al-Khouri lost a vote of confidence, Habib Pasha became Prime Minister. He announced a programme which included major irrigation projects and did much to rebuild South Lebanon which had suffered in the Druze Revolt but was quite incapable of making essential cuts in expenditure or of coping with the factional strife in the Assembly. He resigned in May 1929. In January 1934 when a new High Commissioner wanted to introduce a new Constitution he appointed Saad as interim President of the Republic for one year as he was regarded as too old to be a nuisance. His term was subsequently extended for another year after which he retired. He was typical of the old-fashioned Turkish-trained officials who had administered the Ottoman Empire in its last years, wily, anxious to avoid committing himself, unscrupulous and governed by a strange mixture of self-interest and genuine patriotism.

al-SAADAWI, Nawal (1930–)

Egyptian feminist leader. Although born in a village she took degrees in medicine from Cairo and Columbia Universities. After practising as a psychiatrist in rural Egypt she joined the Ministry of Health of which she became Director and Chief Editor of a health journal.

In 1971 she was dismissed for writing *Women and Sex* which enraged religious and political authorities throughout the Arab world and was banned in many countries including Saudi Arabia. She then spent three years on a research project involving women and neurosis before becoming a UN Adviser on Women's Programmes for the Third World. Two marriages failed because of her independence. She set forth her views in nearly 30 works of fiction and social research, winning a reputation as the most outspoken and controversial Arab female writer. Her books had to be published in Lebanon and some could not be sold in Egypt in Arabic. She founded the Arab Women's Solidarity Association which was accused of promoting sexual permissiveness. Saadawi opposed the veil, the belief that virginity at marriage was important only for girls, female circumcision and the absolute right of a husband to a divorce. In 1981 she wrote that all political parties were puppets of Sadat and so Egypt was not a democracy, particularly as half of society was not free: she was imprisoned for three months until released by Mubarak. Later the ulema were infuriated by her *Fall of the Imam* and declared that she deserved death; she had to be protected by the police. In January 1991 Saadawi led the Women's Initiative for Peace in the Gulf, going to Baghdad and criticising the Allies for not wanting a diplomatic solution. She opposed both the Iraqi occupation of Kuwait and the use of troops to expel them. The AWSA was closed down. She later campaigned for the punishment of the US for war crimes. Saadawi, who confessed that ever since childhood she had loved demonstrations, saw life as a passionate struggle against injustice. Her novels were highly regarded in the West and she received major literary awards.

SAADEH, Antun (1904–49)

Lebanese political leader. A Greek Orthodox, he was born in Brazil, the son of a scholar who wrote an English–Arabic dictionary, and received part of his education in Germany. In the late 1920s he went to Damascus where he worked as a journalist. He then moved to Lebanon where he hung around the American University of Beirut giving private lessons in German, often passing for a member of the Faculty. Saadeh exercised a considerable fascination over a number of students and in 1932 he founded a secret organisation with the aim of removing all vestiges of foreign domination from the area and recreating a secular Syrian nation. Five members, later reduced to two, bound themselves by a solemn oath to follow his leadership.

With great eloquence and total conviction he stressed youth, discipline, idealism and the role of The Leader and attracted young intellectuals beyond the University, forming the first para-military organisation in Lebanon. His followers emerged as the Parti Populaire Syrien, holding a congress in 1935. Saadeh petitioned for a union of Lebanon and Syria and was sentenced to six months imprisonment. In jail, like Hitler, he wrote a book *The Rise of Nations (Nushu' al-Umam)* setting out his political creed. He declared that science showed that the nation is the fundamental unit of human history, obeying no authority but its own. He preached "an indissoluble bond" between the land of Syria which spread west from the Tigris and included Cyprus, and its inhabitants which made them different from any other people on earth. A common language gave them no particular links with the Arabs who had arrived on the scene when the Syrian nation had already long been in existence. There was no difference between Christianity and Islam as both were based on submission to the will of God. What was good for religion was not necessarily good for the nation so there should be complete separation of Church and State. Democracy was corrupt and wasteful and should be replaced by "an aware and excellent élite who will personify the people, leading them to justice and love" with fundamental economic and social reforms. The good of Society should take preference over individual rights. Alarm at Saadeh's views and the following that they attracted caused the Maronite Pierre Gemayel to form another youth movement, the Kataib to oppose them. Towards the end of 1938 Saadeh visited Italy and Germany before going back to Brazil where he spent the war, according to the French, subsidised by the Nazis. In March 1947 he returned and resumed his agitation for a Greater Syria. He renamed his party the Syrian Social National Party. In the summer of 1949 armed clashes took place between his followers and those of Gemayel, culminating in an armed attack on the PPS newspaper, with the support, Saadeh alleged, of the Lebanese Government. The police then raided his offices, claiming to have discovered plans to seize power with Zionist support. Saadeh fled to Syria where he was originally welcomed by Marshal Husni al-Zaim who gave him weapons. Saadeh declared war on the Government of Lebanon from the "HQ of the First Popular Social Revolution" and his followers started to attack across the frontier from Syria. Shortly afterwards Zaim struck a bargain with Beirut and handed over Saadeh. In less than 24 hours he was court-martialled and shot. He was a man of great magnetism and inspired complete devotion and was seen as a martyr by his supporters who mourned him as "The Führer of the Syrian Nation". His ideas were a strange mixture of romanticism, authoritarianism, pseudo-science, modernism and notions taken from Marx and Hegel.

al-SABAH, Jabir al-Ahmad (1926–)

Ruler of Kuwait from January 1978. The son of Shaykh Ahmad b. Jabir al-Sabah he was educated by tutors and at the Mubarakiyyah School. In 1949 he was appointed Head of Security at Ahmadi which brought him into close contact with the Kuwait Oil Company. He held this post until 1959 when he was put in charge of the Department of Finance and was responsible for the provision of the welfare state, oil policy and the building of a large-scale bureaucracy as well as for the establishment of pioneering the Kuwait Fund for Arab Economic Development. In 1962 when Ministries were established he continued in office and was also Minister of Commerce. During this period he had a struggle to assert financial control over senior members of the family with agendas of their own. On the death of Shaykh Abd Allah al-Salim al-Sabah in November 1965 he became Prime Minister and later Crown Prince. His first official tour abroad was to China and Russia. During the reign of Sabah b. Salim al-Sabah he played a large part in the formulation of policy in particular in financial and oil matters and in support for the Palestinians, and was the first effective Ruler for some years. In 1976 he resigned when the Assembly demanded political parties and made difficulties over the budget. The Amir dissolved the Assembly and reinstated Jabir who succeeded as Amir on 31 December 1977. He said his objective was to keep Kuwait "an oasis of love, security and prosperity" but always stressed the need for strong leadership and respect for authority. Hard working, with meticulous attention to detail, particularly in money matters, he has maintained stability in Kuwait. He has stayed calm during a series of crises such as the Iranian Revolution, which caused the stirring of consciousness amongst the Shiah; the Iran–Iraq War, in which he gave financial but not military support; the Manakh Scandal; the 1983 bomb attacks (consistently refused to release *Dawah* despite the 1988 hijacking); and the decline in oil prices, when he had tp preside over a period of consolidation. He supervised a policy of investment abroad so that profits earned there exceeded oil revenues. He has always been active in foreign policy, mediating during many disputes such as the 1979 war between the Yemens. He has avoided any commitment to the Super-Powers and paid State Visits to Eastern Europe. He condemned Camp David, US policies in Lebanon and refused to accept a US Ambassador who had served in Jerusalem. In 1981 he was active in the foundation of the Gulf Co-operation Council. Despite the Constitution, elections were not held until 1981,when Kuwait was worried over the Iran–Iraq War, Manakh and local fundamentalism. In 1984 al-Sabah negotiated an arms' deal with Russia after the US refused to sell missiles to Kuwait and he also applied to Russia for re-flagging during the War of the Tankers.

In 1985 he was injured and one of his bodyguards killed in an attempt on his life by al-*Dawah*. In July 1986 he said that the National Assembly was shaking national unity and dissolved it. He also introduced censorship, contrary to the Constitution which also provided for elections after two months. The nationalisation of the oil industry was his idea. He was unwilling to increase the number of foreign workers. In late 1989 there were demands for the return of elections and these were held in June 1990, but were largely boycotted as the Assembly was expanded to take in 25 nominated members. Al-Sabah's brother was killed defending the palace in another violent attack as he went into exile in Ta'if. He appeared traumatised and spent much time in seclusion, making no public speeches for three weeks. After returning he made no attempt to incorporate the patriotic opposition in a government of national unity. In March 1991 96 prominent citizens issued a call to the Amir for political reform including wider representation in the Cabinet, a free press, reforms to end corruption and an independent judiciary. In April 1991 he promised elections for the following year and consider votes for women, but he delayed elections feeling that his family was disunited and held a number of show trials. In December 1991 hundreds of Biduns were deported. Anxious to retain Western troops he signed the Damascus Declaration but did not seriously implement it. In February 1992 he was pro-Iran. By April 1992 the Prime Minister was the only popular member of his family but the Amir refused to allow a non-royal Prime Minister. In September 1992 there were 278 candidates for 50 seats in 25 constituencies with an electorate of 81,000. Critics of the Government won 35 seats and the opposition demanded that half the Government be chosen from the Assembly. After the end of the Iran-Iraq War former parliamentarians campaigned for reforms but demonstrations were crushed brutally. Uncharismatic, dour, reclusive, rarely speaking in public, al-Sabah rarely gives interviews and when he does appears to mumble. He has a modest lifestyle and is said to go to bed at 9 pm. He did not indulge in flashy cars when young, does not smoke or drink but is a keen gardener. He has three permanent wives with a rotating fourth every few months. His wives never appear in public. He is said to have at least 30 children. His personal wealth is estimated at over $5,000 million.

al-SABAH, Saad b. Abd Allah (?1930-)

Kuwaiti Prime Minister. The son of Shaykh Abdallah b. Salim al-Sabah by an African wife, he was educated at the Mubarakiyyah School before joining the police. After further training at the British Metropolitan Police College at Hendon he became Deputy Head of the force and in 1961 Chief of Police and Public Security. In 1962, when the Ministry of the Interior was created, Saad was appointed to head it. He added the Ministry of Defence in 1964 and held both offices until January 1978 when he succeeded Jabir al-Ahmad al-Sabah as Crown Prince and Prime Minister. He was much more articulate and outgoing than the Amir. After the invasion he went into exile and was said to have promised an early return to the 1962 Constitution and also to have drawn up plans for deporting 200,000 Palestinians – some of whom had been collaborating with the Iraqis. March 1991 he imposed a martial law administration and three weeks after liberation resigned following public dissatisfaction at the slowness of the process of cleaning up, but was reappointed. In June 1992 he ruled out friendly relations with countries that had sided with Iraq. He said he would not obstruct investigation of events leading to and following the Iraq occupation. He resigned after the October 1992 election at which the majority of seats were won by his critics. He was said to be unwilling to resume because of the lack of support and the difficulty of forming a government but eventually reformed with double the previous number of critics. His new government outlined a pro-

gramme which included improving security by alliance with the West, obtaining the release of those held in Iraq, establishing the demarcation of the frontier, and diversifying the economic base away from oil. He supported votes for women but said it would be up to the new Assembly to decide. His son and nephew were reported to have been involved in the torture of Palestinians. His wife was said to have been involved in the Manakh scandal and there were objections (1977) and over unpaid bills.

SABHAH CONGRESS (Libya)

In his Zuwarah speech in April 1973 Colonel Qadafi announced the Libyan Cultural Revolution which swept away the past and in his *Green Book* he laid down a blueprint for the future. This was inauguarated at a meeting of the 970-member Libyan General People's Congress at Sabhah in February and March 1977. The Sabhah Declaration swept away all conventional institutions of government, Ministers, classes, tribes, political partics, even the army as armed defence was deemed the responsibility of all citizens, male and female. The state itself was abolished, being replaced with a new concept of "massdom" (*Jamahariyah*) – a direct grass-roots democracy in which decisions were to be taken collectively by society as a whole. "Undisputed power" was to be exercised by the people acting through People's Congresses which did not represent the people but were the people. Qadafi declared democracy to be "the people's supervision of itself". The Revolution Command Council was replaced by a General Secretariat which happened to consist of the same five officers and the Cabinet by the General People's Committee which was headed by Abd al-Ati al-Ubaydi. The Qur'an would be the "code" of the new Libyan society. These proceedings, termed by the ex-Prime Minister Major Jalloud "the first time in the history of the world that a ruler has handed over power to the people" must have aroused some scepticism in the Guest of Honour, the authoritarian communist Fidel Castro. The Libyan press applauded "greatest event in the history of world" and throughout the proceedings the town was decorated with slogans to the effect that the Arabs had invented socialism and that Nasser had personally declared Qadafi his true heir.

SABIC

For over thirty years the natural gas which is a by-product of oil extraction was flared off as being of no value. By the early 1970s technology existed to capture and exploit it as a cheap source of power. The Saudi Basic Industries Corporation was set up by the Government in 1976 to foster a petrochemical industry and others based on oil through joint ventures with foreign partners and also to market their products. Another major objective was the training of a Saudi managerial class. Its original capital was 10,000 million Saudi riyals. SABIC played a major role in the Yanbu and Jubayl Development Schemes. In 1984 30% of the shares were sold to Saudi nationals. Petrochemical exports ran into problems of protectionism, especially in the European Community. By 1990 SABIC grouped 15 modern industries including fertilisers, plastics, gases and oil and steel in 33 plants. It participated in ventures in other states of the GCC and opened offices in commercial centres thoughout the world, particularly in the Far East. It paid special attention to pioneering ultra-modern technology. The fact that the Minister of Industry and Electricity was its chairman showed the importance of its role in Saudi development. Its staff was about 8,000.

SABRI, Ali (1920–91)

Egyptian Prime Minister and Vice-President. He came from an upper-class family, related to that of Queen Farida, was educated at a Jesuit School and an American College and graduated from the Air Force Academy in 1940. His brother Zhulfiqqar was the pilot who attempted to fly General Aziz Ali al-Misri to join the advancing forces of Rommel. Both saw action in the Palestine War. Neither of the brothers was a member of the original Free Officers but they were in contact with them. At the time of the July Revolution of 1952 Ali Sabri was a Wing Commander in Air Force Intelligence and had close relations with the American Embassy which he was able to reassure that the coup was not directed against Western interests. Later he went to Washington in an unsuccesful attempt to purchase arms. Nasser then appointed him as Director of the Presidential Office and for many years regarded him as one of his closest collaborators. Sabri supervised the Higher Council for Art and Letters, directing the activities of intellectuals into channels approved by the regime. He took part in negotiations for the Anglo-Egyptian Treaty of 1954 and was used in the secret diplomacy that led to the foundation of the Non-Aligned Movement. After the nationalisation of the Suez Canal he was sent to London to argue that Egypt wished to be conciliatory and at the UN he worked with Khrishna Menon to win over uncommitted delegations. In 1957 he became Minister of State for Presidential Affairs, a post he held throughout the period of the United Arab Republic. After the dissolution of the Union, he was effectively Prime Minister although he did not receive the formal title until 1964. The break-up had facilitated the introduction of socialism in Egypt and Sabri pushed ahead with nationalisation of essential and foreign-owned industries. He was a poor administrator, unwilling to take decisions, tolerant of corruption and inefficiency, and he had to admit that under the Five-Year Plan the only real increase had been in the number of bureaucrats. He presided over a period of growing intimacy with the Communist powers, visiting Peking, acting as host to Khruschev and signing in Moscow agreements for new debt schedules and new loans. His activities led to the belief that he was strongly socialist though it is possible that he was merely used by Nasser who knew that he had no real sympathy for communism but saw the Soviet Union as the Super-Power most likely to help Egypt. His period of office saw the commitment of Egypt to the expense of the Yemen War. In September 1965, the President, aiming at better relations with America and an improved economy, replaced Sabri with Zakariah Mohieddin. Sabri was appointed Secretary-General of the Arab Socialist Union which he determined, lacking other support, to make his power-base. He organised it into cadres on Russian lines and

tried to win it the power to supervise the work of the bureaucracy, the trade unions and even the armed forces. He wrote extensively and set up subsidiary organisations such as the Socialist Youth Organisation and the Higher Institute of Socialist Studies. After the June War he was put in charge of rebuilding the Suez area while Nasser himself took over the ASU. In January 1968 Sabri returned to his former post. In January 1969 Sabri was appointed a member of the newly created National Defence Council but in July, returning from a three week visit to Moscow, he was caught smuggling luxury goods. It is probable that this merely provided a pretext for his dismissal from his post in the ASU and that the real reason was either that he had not been discreet in Russia or that Nasser feared his attempts at politicisation of the army or as a gesture to the Americans after the rejection of the Rogers' Plan (I). In September Sabri was reported to be under house arrest but in the summer of 1970 he reappeared on the Executive of the ASU and as the President's Adviser on Air Force matters with the rank of Lieutenant General, accompanying Nasser to Moscow. In October the new President, Anwar Sadat appointed him one of the two Vice-Presidents, as a signal that there would be no change in basic policies, and in December he made his third visit to Moscow in a year. In May 1971 he was abruptly dismissed by Sadat, accused of attempting to sabotage the formation of the Federation of Arab Republics and of being a Soviet agent; his real crime was attempting to build a power centre under his own control to dictate policy to the President. In December he was condemned to death but the sentence was commuted to life imprisonment. He refused to petition Sadat for clemency and remained in jail until May 1981. After his release he took no part in politics. Sabri was a prudent, intelligent man of files but unattractive and unscrupulous and he rarely had a good word for anyone.

SADAT, (Muhammad) Anwar (1918–81)

Egyptian President. He was born in the Delta village of Mit Abu al-Kum which with its embodiment of traditional Egyptian Muslim society and values remained important to him throughout his life: as President he was to talk of Egypt as "one big village". His father, of peasant stock, was an army clerk who spent much time in the Sudan, marrying a Sudanese wife. In 1925 the family moved to Cairo where Sadat was educated. The expansion of the army that followed the Anglo-Egyptian Treaty of 1936 enabled youth of his background to become officers and he was commissioned in 1938. His first posting was to Manqabad in Upper Egypt where he and his contemporaries Lieutenants Nasser and Zakariah Mohieddin agreed on the need to end British domination. Sadat joined Young Egypt and the Muslim Brotherhood, worked with a German espionage group and attempted to take the veteran nationalist General Abd al-Aziz al-Misri to join Rommel. In October 1941 he was dismissed from the army and imprisoned. In October 1944 he escaped and worked as a garage mechanic until a general amnesty at the end of the war. Having been involved in an attempt on the life of Nahhas Pasha, in January 1946 he was implicated in the murder of the pro-British politician Amin Osman

Pasha and imprisoned until he was put on trial in January 1948. After eight months he was acquitted. Sadat had made a traditional arranged marriage with a relative from the village who, while he was in jail, was supported by his army friends. After his release he divorced her, married the well-educated half-English Jihan and worked as a provincial journalist. In January 1950 he was reinstated in the army in his former rank of captain, was brought by Nasser and Amer into the Free Officers and during the July Revolution read on the radio the proclamation of General Neguib that the army had taken power. Sadat was the first participant to write an account of these events in *Revolt on the Nile*. He was made a member of the Revolutionary Command Council and his main task was liaison with the Muslim Brotherhood. Sadat was also editor of the official newspaper *al-Jumhuriah*. He was not a member of the inner circle and for over a year was the only RCC member without government office until he was made Minister of State in September 1954. When the National Union was established as the only official party in 1957 Sadat was its Secretary-General and threatened the communists to "torture them out of existence", later justifying this in a loud exchange with Khruschev. He was already Secretary-General of the Islamic Conference, chaired its first meeting in Mecca in 1955 and, as the Free Officer most identified with Islam, took part in much diplomacy with Muslim countries. He was particularly concerned with the Arabian Peninsula and bore a considerable responsibility for the train of events that led to Egypt's involvement in the costly Yemen War which he had forecast would be "a picnic on the Red Sea". Sadat may have been influenced by the fact that the revolutionary leader Abd al-Rahman al-Baydani was married to a sister of his own wife Jihan. In March 1958 when Nasser appointed the National Assembly of the United Arab Republic, Sadat was elected its Speaker, continuing to hold, after the break-up of the Union, a post which gave him a good knowledge of what was happening in the countryside. Sadat was one of the five members of the Presidency Council set up in 1962 and in 1964 was one of seven Vice-Presidents. When Nasser decided to have a single Vice-President in December 1969 he chose Sadat rather than the abler Ali Sabri who was building an independent power centre within the Arab Socialist Union for the tactical reason of playing off the Assembly against it. During the 1960s Sadat was regarded as a loyal, almost subservient and not over intelligent adjutant to Nasser who did not seek his views on matters of policy. Sadat in his memoirs *In Search of Identity* gives a not very credible account of himself as the voice of conscience and common sense behind the scenes. The zest with which he undid much of his predecessor's work showed the *fellah* characteristic of riding out humiliation until able to hit back. When Nasser died on 28 September 1970 it was said that on his deathbed he had nominated the right-wing Zakariah Mohieddin as his successor but this choice would have angered Sabri and the left who did not feel strong enough to make their own bid and would also have upset the Russians whose military aid was still regarded as essential in the aftermath of the War of Attrition. As a compromise the Higher Executive Committee of the

ASU therefore nominated Sadat and he was unanimously elected by the National Assembly and endorsed by 90% in a referendum. Sadat chose as his Vice-Presidents Sabri and the pious conservative Hussain al-Shafai and appointed the first civilian Prime Minister since the Revolution – the veteran diplomat Mahmud Fawzi. Sadat pledged himself to continue the work of Nasser in strengthening the armed forces to regain Sinai and supporting Arab unity, non-alignment and socialism but started to release some political prisoners and decentralise power. He also agreed to union in the Federation of Arab Republics with the strongly anti-communist Qadafi and proposed reopening the Suez Canal by some sort of agreement with Israel. These projects alarmed Sabri and the Minister of the Interior Sharawy Jumaa who appeared about to launch a coup. Having assured himself of the loyalty of the army, Sadat in the May Corrective Revolution arrested his political opponents. He also carried out a drastic purge of the ASU and personally set fire to heaps of tapes of intercepted telephone calls. He asked the Assembly to draft a permanent Constitution to replace the series of interim ones since 1952 and changed the title UAR back to Egypt. These bold measures ended the impression that Sadat was an indecisive lightweight and added greatly to his prestige which increased still further when he vowed to regain Sinai in this "Year of Decision". He reassured Moscow after the imprisonment of its favourite, Sabri, by signing the Russo–Egyptian Treaty of Friendship in the same month but he also grew more intimate with King Faysal and the anti-communist Nimeiri. The end of 1971 without any move against Israel caused rioting and made Sadat's promises look absurd so he replaced Fawzi with a technocrat, Aziz Siqdi, who was instructed to prepare Egypt for war. In July 1972, having been to Moscow for arms and returned almost empty-handed, Sadat, with the dramatic flourish that was to distinguish so many of his major actions, dismissed the 15–20,000 Russian advisers, who, he claimed were hampering his preparation for battle. There was widespread surpise not merely at the move but at the fact that he had not in advance obtained concessions from the Americans as a reward for it and continued to criticise them. When 1972 also ended without military action there were student riots which Sadat blamed on the "adventurous left", purged the ASU for the third time and bullied the press. He had some difficulties in fending off the ardent desire of Qadafi for union and was prepared to use force to prevent the arrival of Libyans to demand it. In March 1973 Sadat assumed the Premiership and the title of Military Governor-General to concentrate all resources for the crossing of the Canal. When he launched the October War, he achieved complete surprise and the first victories by Arab troops over Israelis. Pursuing the limited political objective of breaking the stalemate and compelling the Super-Powers to make a renewed intervention for peace in the Middle East, Sadat did not attempt a major victory by a dash for the mid-Sinai passes and, after the Israelis had crossed the Canal he militarily mishandled the situation. He also antagonized Hafiz al-Assad in conjunction with whom he had started the war by ending it without consulting him. Nevertheless the Egyptians had erased memories of the humiliation of the June War, showing themselves capable of military planning and leadership and although the war ended with the Israelis 60 miles from Cairo, politically it had been a success with the convening of the Geneva Peace Conference. This showed that Sadat proposed to rely exclusively upon the Americans who, he said, held 99% of the cards: he appears to have sensed that Russia, economically weak and over-extended by worldwide interests, was no long a Super-Power. He put excessive trust in Kissinger, referred to by Sadat as "my friend Henry" who negotiated the Kilometre 101 and Sinai Disengagement Agreements. To prepare for a more general peace settlement Sadat, at the Rabat Summit played a leading part in ending the claim of King Hussain to speak for the Palestinians. In Egypt the crossing was seen as Sadat's victory and the start of a new era. He felt strong enough to end censorship and promised a more liberal society, based on faith and science, in the "October Paper" of April 1974. One of the most striking measures to implement this was the policy of the "Open Door", (Infitah), which encouraged private enterprise at the expense of state industries. In September Sadat appointed the economist Dr Abd al-Aziz al-Hijazi as Prime Minister to prepare plans for foreign investment and lifting of import restrictions which, however, brought in luxuries rather than investments. Infitah therefore caused rises in the cost of food and social divisiveness which saw 500 new millionaires in a year. There were riots which Sadat blamed on communists to counter whom he released Muslim Brothers imprisoned by Nasser and replaced Hijazi by a policeman Mamduh Salim. At the same time in April 1975 he appointed a single Vice-President, Air Marshal Husni Mubarak. Economic liberalisation was accelerated despite its unsatisfactory results and was accompanied by relaxation of the discipline imposed by a single political party. In October 1975 Sadat permitted the creation of three separate platforms within the ASU which after the elections of October 1976 were allowed to become independent parties. This system did not work to his satisfaction and, galled by the attacks of the the National Progressive Union Party, Sadat firstly formed his own party, the National Democratic Party and then encouraged some of its members to form a "loyal" opposition, Socialist Labour Party. Sadat conducted vigorous personal diplomacy, telling the Oil States that it was their duty to give financial support to Egypt and also visiting Paris, London and Tehran for technical help. He met President Ford in Salzburg and Washington and, after a visit from Brezhnev was curtly postponed, he repudiated the Friendship Treaty and Egypt's debts to Russia. In June 1975, on what he said was the proudest day of his life, he reopened the Suez Canal with the great pomp that he increasingly showed. In common with many of his countrymen he felt that Egypt had done enough for the Palestinians with whose leaders his relations were extremely bad even before he closed their radio in September 1975. He felt also that the recovery of most of Sinai was no nearer despite the intolerable financial burden, absorbing one third of the GNP, that Egypt bore in maintaining large armed forces. He felt that though these forces were swollen for pan-Arab rather than for purely Egyptian interests that the wealthy Arab states were not bearing their share of the burden. Egypt had recourse to international bankers under whose pressure subsidies on basic foods were cut, setting off the Bread Riots of January 1977 in which troops had to fire upon the people for the first time in 25 years. In November Sadat made another of his dramatic gambles, declaring that in the interests of peace he would even go to Jerusalem. Begin, forewarned, issued an invitation and, after a delirious welcome, Sadat delivered an eloquent plea for reconciliation in his Knesset Speech. He called for legitimate rights for the Palestinians but, at the request of his hosts, did not mention the Palestine Liberation Organisation by name. He received an equal reception on his return to Cairo. The Sadat Peace Initiative came to nothing: there was no tangible response from Israel and the main result was to alienate even the moderate Arab states; the more intransigent issued the Tripoli Declaration which condemned him for breaking Arab solidarity. The new American President Jimmy Carter gave a fresh impetus towards peace by becoming personally involved in the process and in September invited Sadat and Begin to Camp David where agreements were made that the Israelis should withdraw from Sinai and that the "legitimate rights" of the Palestinians should be recognised. The Egyptian Foreign Minister resigned in the middle of the discussions, appalled at the concessions that Sadat, underestimating Israel's determination to keep its conquests and relying upon American support, was prepared to make: Carter subsequently said that he felt that Sadat had trusted him too much. Sadat and Begin shared the Nobel Peace Prize. After prolonged negotiations during which Begin's good faith became more and more doubtful, the Egyptian–Israeli Peace Treaty was signed in March 1979 by which although the Egyptians were to regain the whole of Sinai the problem of the Palestinians was shelved. The isolation which this brought upon Egypt was shown by condemnation at the Baghdad Summit and its expulsion from the Arab League. Sadat was impenitent, bandying vulgar abuse with other Arab leaders, "the dwarfs", and declaring that they needed Egypt more than Egypt needed them. Egypt having previously alienated the Eastern Bloc was now completely dependent upon the Americans who gave it more aid than they gave even to Israel – $1,000 million in 1978/9. In return he made available facilities for their forces, including a base which they used in the abortive attempt to rescue hostages held in their Embassy in Tehran. He also expelled the Russian Ambassador. The breach with the Muslim world, added to resentment at the growing corruption that stemmed from Infitah gave a great impetus to Islamic fundamentalists and groups such as Takfir wa al-Hijrah had frequent clashes with the police during 1978/9. In January 1980 in his Law of Shame Sadat apparently sought to forbid all opposition and even criticism and increasing repression showed the hollowness of his commitment to democracy and that his popularity was ebbing. A two-tier Egypt was taking shape with the "fat cats" contrasting with increasing urban squalor as the soaring birth rate drove people into cities where the amenities were swamped. Sadat, by now a self-satisfied autocrat with a ludicrous personality cult, insisted on being at the centre of everything and so was blamed when things went wrong. Intoxicated with the adulation of the Western press, he was surrounded by courtiers rather than advisers. The people no longer believed in him and there was a deep dislike for Jihan Sadat and for other members of his family – his brother Esmat who had been a bus driver was now a millionaire and was later sentenced to jail for corruption. Sadat became involved in a quarrel with the Coptic Pope who was confined to a monastery and his powers passed to a committee. In April 1980 Sadat presented a new Constitution which empowered him to serve further terms as President and took over the Premiership from the loyal technocrat Mustafa Khalil whom he had appointed to symbolise yet another new beginning after Camp David. Despite the frequency with which he announced grandiose schemes, he took no interest in the details of administration. In September 1981 Sadat ordered the arrest of over 3,000 of his critics, religious, secular, left and right. On 6 October 1981, reviewing the army on the anniversary of the Crossing, he was assassinated by military members of the fundamentalist group *Jihad*. His death was mourned more in the West than in Egypt and his successor undid much of his work as he himself had undone that of Nasser. He genuinely saw himself as the patriarch of a village and Ministers, soldiers and workers were all addressed as his "sons". He wished the people to be free from police intimidation but was hypersensitive when they criticised him. His style of government was dictatorial, backed by a referendum with a routine favourable vote of at least 95%. He was quixotic, accepting attack at home and abroad for giving refuge to the dying Shah, and was a pious Muslim. In later years his vanity made him ridiculous as he appeared in ever more splendid uniforms with more decorations and titles. He enjoyed appearing on the international stage. Sadat could be rash, his actions that led to the Larnaca Airfield shoot-out and subsequent vilification of President Kyprianou were most unwise, but he compelled attention with a series of successful gambles. A decade after his death his reputation started to recover and people realised that with all his faults he had ended the most oppressive features of Nasserism.

SADAT PEACE INITIATIVE (1977/8)

In 1973 Anwar Sadat suddenly launched the October War to prevent the stalemate in the Middle East from hardening into a permanent settlement. This brought about the Geneva Peace Conference which achieved nothing although American assistance led to the Sinai Disengagement Agreement of 1975. By 1977 there was a renewed stalemate which Sadat thought to break but a renewed war would be too risky. Elections had brought a new American President in Jimmy Carter who was interested in peace in the Middle East and a new Israeli Prime Minister in Menachem Begin who was not vulnerable to attacks of being too soft towards the Arabs. Sadat therefore decided to break the deadlock by peace negotiations and secret soundings were made through the Romanian President Ceausescu and in a meeting in Tangier between one of his closest associates and the Israeli Foreign Minister Moshe Dayan. In September Secretary of State Vance and

the Russian Foreign Minister Gromyko called for a reconvening of the Geneva Conference not later than the end of the year. Commending this, on 9 November, Sadat told the Egyptian Assembly that if it would prevent one of his "sons" from being wounded, he would he was prepared to go to the ends of the earth or even to Jerusalem. Two days later Begin said that he would be welcome. On 16/17 November in Damascus Sadat failed to win the support of Assad for his venture and much of the Arab world, apart from Morocco, Sudan and Oman was also hostile. The Egyptian Foreign Minister, Ismail Fahmi refused to accompany the President and resigned, his designated successor refused to take office and Butros Butros-Ghali was appointed Acting Foreign Minister. On 19 November Sadat delivered his Knesset Speech in which he declared that he would accept the right of Israel to exist in return for a withdrawal from the Occupied Territories and Palestinian self-determination. On his return he called for a conference in Cairo to draw up guidelines for a reconvening of Geneva so that it would not collapse over procedural matters and invited the US, the USSR, Israel, Syria, Jordan, Lebanon, the Palestine Liberation Organisation and the UN. He then proceeded to break off relations with Syria and the PLO and to insult the Russians so that none of these would attend the Conference: Lebanon with Syrian troops on its soil refused to attend and Jordan declined to be the only participating Arab state. Five states, Syria, Libya, Algeria, South Yemen and the PLO, opposed to the initiative met on 2 December and issued the Tripoli Declaration which led to the establishment of the Steadfastness Front and the breach of diplomatic relations with Egypt. Cyrus Vance visited Syria, Lebanon and Jordan in an unsuccessful attempt to persuade them to attend the Conference which assembled on 14 December. The Egyptians led by Ismat Abd al-Majid and the Israelis restated their declared positions and there was a dispute over whether there should be a name-plate in front of the vacant seat assigned to the Palestinians and there were disagreements over whether peace or withdrawal should first be discussed and whether a peace treaty or a peace agreement should be sought. The Conference adjourned on 22 December for a summit between Sadat and Begin at Ismailiyyah at which no compromise could be found and the Conference was formally concluded on 26 December. It had been agreed that political and military committees should be set up but although these met in January there was no further progress towards peace, the subsequent Begin Proposals for the Occupied Territories were judged inadequate, until Carter hosted the meeting at Camp David. Although the "electric shock" on which he had gambled produced no concrete results it did increase Sadat's standing within Egypt and enabled him to make further reforms.

SAINT JEAN DE MAURIENNE AGREEMENT (1917)

The Sykes–Picot Agreement arranged the post-war distribution of the territories of the Ottoman Empire between the Allies, Britain, France and Russia and gave nothing to Italy which was not then fully at war. The Italians later demanded their share and Lloyd George,

Ribot for France and Boselli for Italy met in a railway carriage on the Franco–Italian frontier in April 1917. Russia where the Revolution had started was not represented. It was decided that the Arab areas should still be divided in the manner already agreed and that Italy's portion should be in Anatolia with trading rights in Alexandretta, Haifa and Acre.

al-SAIQA

Literally "Lightning bolt". After the June War the Syrian Baath Party, and in particular Salah Jadid, decided to form its Palestinian adherents into a guerrilla force under its own control as a counterbalance to Fatah. Its unique character was shown by the fact that it did not have "Palestine" in its title: it saw the Palestinian struggle as part of a wider Arab one under Syrian leadership. It resisted the attempt of Fatah to dominate the Palestine Liberation Organisation and allied with the Popular Front for the Liberation of Palestine against it. Saiqa's first operations were launched from Jordan where it established bases and when it became clear that King Hussain was determined to restrict guerrilla activities, it attempted to organise a coup against him. After Black September its main bases were in Southern Lebanon where its Syrian support prevented any army action against it. However it became involved in internal Syrian politics and Hafiz al-Assad arrested several of its leaders. On 28 September 1973 two armed men, calling themselves "Eagles of the Palestinian Revolution" took hostage some Soviet Jews going by train from Czechoslovakia to Austria en route for Israel and an Austrian customs official. Their demand for the closure of a Jewish transit camp in Austria was accepted by Chancellor Kreisky, to the fury of Golda Meir. The guerrillas, later revealed to be members of Saiqa, and the hostages all went free. Saiqa did not join the Rejection Front in the autumn 1974 and was regarded as one of the mainstream groups supporting Yassir Arafat. Saiqa members consistently put their obligations to Syria above relations with other Palestinian groups and after the Syrians went into Lebanon in 1976, Saiqa fought on their side against Fatah although their leader, Zuhair Muhsin, a former Syrian officer, was also the head of the Military Department of the PLO. Subsequently it made its peace with the main organisation and carried out minor attacks within Israel and against Jewish interests in Europe. In June 1979 Muhsin was murdered in Cannes and replaced by Isam al-Qadi. In July four "Eagles" stormed the Egyptian Embassy in Ankara, killing two Turkish security guards. At this time Israeli sources estimated its fighting strength at 2,000 but it had little support amongst the Palestinian people. After the outbreak of the Iran–Iraq War, Saiqa supported the Shiah militias in Lebanon against the Iraqi-backed Arab Liberation Front. In February 1981 when Syrian–Jordanian relations were tense, "Eagles" kidnapped the Jordanian Military Attaché in Beirut and later, still obedient to Syria it opposed the Fahd Plan. When Syria turned against Arafat because of his search for a "two-state" solution, Saiqa inevitably followed its lead and joined the Palestine National Salvation Front. It joined the other Damascus-based groups to form the anti-Arafat National Alliance and it remained aloof from the general reconciliation that took place at the Algiers meeting of the Palestine National Council in April 1987.

SAKIET SIDI YUSUF BOMBING (1958)

In the early stages of the War of Algerian Independence considerable numbers of nationalist guerrillas were based in Tunisia. Despite the construction of the Morice Line some still succeeded in reaching Algeria. In January 1958 an unusually strong force ambushed a French patrol killing 15 soldiers and a French aircraft was shot down by machine-gun fire from the Tunisian village of Sakiet Sidi Yusuf which had a population of 3,300 and which appeared to contain a strong concentration of guerrillas. On 8 February fire from Sakiet brought down a second aircraft and three hours later a squadron of American-built bombers attacked the village, destroying a school and a hospital. The suq was crowded because of market day and 80 people were killed. It appeared that the raid had been ordered by French generals in Algiers without consulting the Government. President Bourguiba immediately ordered the evacuation of all French troops and appealed to the UN. The US and the UK sent a "good offices" mission to improve the relations between France and Tunisia. This interference by outside powers infuriated many right-wing French politicians and officers and contributed to the fall of the Cabinet of Felix Gaillard. A month-long political crisis was ended by the coup which brought General de Gaulle back to power.

SALAFIYYAH

The Arabic term salaf, often translated as "the pious ancestors" is used to describe the Companions of the Prophet and the next two generations when, it is held, Islam was practised in its pristine purity. A return to these golden ages was preached intermittently for centuries, most notably by Muhammad Ibn Abd al-Wahhab whose ideas influenced the Moroccan Sultan Sulayman. Later the early traditions were drawn upon by Muhammad Abduh to argue that they in no way conflicted with scientific progress or even democracy. His doctrines, developed by Rashid Rida, were influential in the Eastern Arab world, India and Indonesia. In North Africa intellectual Muslims were also attracted by the attack on "saint-worship", as practised by the tariqahs which were generally encouraged by the French administration. In Algeria these ideas were combined with nationalism by Abd al-Hamid Ben Badis. In Morocco they had earlier been taken up by Abu Shuaib al-Dukkali who passed them on to Mulai Larbi al-Alawi who both vehemently attacked the tariqahs. This assertion of Islamic identity, at the time that it appeared under threat through what were perceived as the attempts of the French in the Berber Dahir to spread Christianity did much to awaken Moroccan nationalism. The leaders of a neo-Salafiyyah movement were the young alims Allal al-Fassi and Muhammad Lyazidi who were later to be the leaders of the Istiqlal Party demanding independence from France. They rejected the idea of a secular state, aiming at the reformation of society through correct Islamic education. This would need the formation of political parties so that the community could gain its ends by legal means.

The revival of a universal Caliphate was rejected in favour of nationalism based on religion. The Arabic language should become the common language of all Muslim countries, the *Shariah* should be the basis of legislation, reinterpreted where necessary, not by the ulema, but by elected representatives of the people. The Sultan Muhammad V supported the attack on the *tariqahs* and tried to order that no *zawiahs* should be founded without his permission; the French, however, refused to publish this decree.

SALIM, Gemal (1917–1968)

Egyptian politician. Born in Port Sudan, he joined the air force eventually becoming a Wing Commander. He was influenced by the Socialist ideas of Ahmad Hussain and may have been a member of Young Egypt. A serious plane crash kept him out of the Palestine War but while in an American hospital he read widely on political and economic questions. Salim was a member of the original executive of the Young Officers and during the July Revolution went with his brother Salih Salim to win over the important garrison at al-Arish. He advocated that King Farouq should be put on trial and executed. He was a member of the Revolutionary Command Council and was put in charge of agrarian reform, in which he was advised by two left-wing economists. When the officers entered the Cabinet, he was appointed Minister of Communications. He was perhaps the most socialist and technocratic of the officers and took a leading part in harassing General Neguib who wanted a return to civilian politics. In 1954 he chaired the Court which punished the Muslim Brothers after one of them had attempted to kill Nasser. In August 1954 he became Deputy Prime Minister and pressed hard for industrialisation and in particular for the construction of the Aswan High Dam. In June 1956 he was dropped from the Government. When the British were planning the Suez War they considered Salim as a possible replacement for Nasser. Salim was never close to Nasser and Sadat said that he was hot-tempered, extremely nervous and of completely unbalanced character who attempted to ride roughshod over his colleagues. He was unpleasantly sarcastic and capricious, and suffered from chronic ill health, possibly augmented by addiction to hashish.

SALIM, Salah (1916–62)

Egyptian politician. Born in Port Sudan, he became an artillery officer. He was one of the officers who were greatly angered by the humiliation of King Farouq in the Abdin Incident of January 1942 and became strongly anti-British. During the Palestine War he served with Nasser and also passed ammunition to the Muslim Brothers who were fighting the Israelis more effectively than were some army units. With his brother Gemal Salim he was a member of the original executive of the Free Officers in November 1949. He was later a Major at GHQ, working closely with the Chief of Staff and an instructor in tactics at Staff College. Before the July Revolution he was sent with his brother to Sinai to secure the allegiance of the important garrison at al-Arish and later he urged the execution of the King. He became a member of the Revolutionary Command Council. In January 1953 he went to the Sudan to

disprove the British contention that the Southern Sudanese opposed independence because it would mean links with Egypt and he assisted Ismail al-Azhari to establish the National Unionist Party. In June 1953 when the Free Officers took Cabinet posts, Salim was made Minister of National Guidance and of Sudanese Affairs. In February 1954 his justification of the dismissal of General Neguib and his willingness to use force against his supporters led to his being man-handled by angry students. In the summer of 1954 he was sent to Iraq to dissuade Nuri al-Said from forming an alliance with the West but his mishandling of the Sarsank Meeting contributed to the growth of hostility between Egypt and Iraq. During the winter he visited several Arab countries in an unsuccessful attempt to enlist them in a defence union directed against the Baghdad Pact. In April 1955 he accompanied Nasser to the Bandung Conference. After his return his contacts with the Russian Ambassador set in train the events that led to the Czechoslovak Arms Deal. He produced a crack-brained scheme for two Sudanese republics each with its own President, parliament and army with a federal President who should be alternately Sudanese and Egyptian. It became clear that his attempts to destabilise the regime of Ismail al-Azhari which had turned against union with Egypt by massive bribery and wooing the Southern tribes, in the course of which he engaged in tribal dancing clad only in underpants, earning international ridicule as "the Dancing Major", had failed and in August 1955 Nasser dismissed him. Subsequently he became a columnist. Before the Suez War he went, with Field Marshal Amer to Nasser in a state of near panic to urge acceptance of the Allied ultimatum and was put briefly under house arrest. Later he opposed the creation of the United Arab Republic. He was eloquent and energetic but known for excitability, truculence and exhibitionism and Nasser privately referred to him as "Major Balloon – when you prick him there is nothing inside".

SALLAL, Abd Allah (1917–)

President of Yemen. He came from a non-tribal Zaidi family being the son of a blacksmith. He was trained as an army officer in Baghdad and shortly after his return in 1939 was briefly imprisoned as a warning against political activity. On his release he resumed his army career and took an active part in the coup of February 1948 in which Abd Allah al-Wazir seized power after the murder of the Imam Yahya. Sallal spent the next seven years in prison, part of the time in chains in an underground cell before he was released at the request of the liberal-minded Crown Prince Badr. He was put in charge of the port of Hodeidah and in about 1959 made contacts with Egyptian Intelligence. In March 1961 the Imam Ahmad was nearly assassinated in Hodeidah and Sallal, suspected of involvement, was dismissed. Ahmad, however, allowed Badr, who still trusted him, to make him chief of his personal body-guard and he became Chief of Staff upon the accession of the new Imam in September 1962. A week later Badr was overthrown by a group of young officers with Egyptian support. It seems that Sallal was not involved in the coup but the young officers, recalling the precedent of General Neguib, felt that a senior officer was needed as Head of State. Sallal became President, quickly promoted himself Field Marshal and determined to rule. He had no ideology and contented himself with vague statements about eliminating social and political injustice and playing a full part in Arab affairs in unity with Egypt. He got rid of potential rivals, quarrelling with his Deputy Abd al-Rahman al-Baydhani who fled into exile. He alienated the Shafais by refusing them all concessions and was despised by the Zaidi tribes because of his mean birth. He became immensely unpopular, generally regarded as a bully and an intriguer, motivated purely by self-interest. There were several attempts on his life. As Royalist resistance, leading to the Yemen War grew, he became entirely dependent upon the Egyptians to the extent that he was regarded merely as their puppet. They regarded him with contempt, even censoring his speeches. Sallal called for all-out war against Saudi Arabia which was supporting the Royalists, proclaiming a Republic of the Arabian Peninsula and demanding the return of Najran and Asir which had been recognised as part of the Kingdom by the Taif Treaty of 1934. Initially he wooed the West, and succeeded in gaining recognition from Washington although it was refused by London. He had to rely upon the Russians, through the Egyptians, for arms. He made several attempts to secure constitutional legitimacy, the first in April 1963 made him President, Commander in Chief and Chairman of the all-powerful Presidential Council. He was, however, extremely inefficient and Nasser, visiting Sanaa in April 1964 was horrified at the administrative chaos. He compelled Sallal to revise the form of government, creating the post of Prime Minister which went to General Hamud al-Jaifi. Stripped of most of his power, Sallal spent several months abroad, mainly in Cairo although he also visited Moscow where he signed a five-year Friendship Treaty, and Peking. At the Erkowit Conference of November 1964 moderate Royalists and moderate Republicans attempted to reach a peace settlement that would involve the stepping-down of both Badr and Sallal but this was wrecked by the President's intransigence, causing a split in the Republican ranks. In April 1965 the regime was shaken by the murder of Muhammad Mahmud al-Zubayri and Sallal was forced to replace the hard-line Prime Minister General Hassan al-Amri by Ahmad Muhammad Nu'man who stood for a policy of peace through negotiations with the tribes rather than by repression. The Khamir Conference produced a Constitution under which an Assembly would be able to dismiss the President and a People's Army which would reduce dependence upon Egypt as well as peace proposals. In order to frustrate this Sallal created a Supreme Military Council without consulting his Prime Minister who promptly resigned. General Amri again became Prime Minister and shortly afterwards Sallal left for Cairo where he remained for most of the next year. The Egyptians, at this stage anxious for peace, saw Sallal as a barrier to it and kept him under a measure of restraint. During his absence opposition grew to Sallal and the policy of subservience to Egyptian interests that he represented. In August 1966 when the Egyptians had decided against a settlement, they announced that Sallal would return and Amri, who had moved towards the

moderate Republicans, occupied the airfield to stop him from landing but was compelled by superior Egyptian forces to desist. Amri went to Cairo to protest and was detained there although the Egyptians refused Sallal's demand to return him for trial on charges of treason. In defiance of his own Constitution, the President appointed himself Prime Minister and conducted a savage purge: amongst the 15 public executions were those of a Vice-President, a Deputy Chief of Staff and a former Minister and there were reports that many of the thousands arrested were tortured. Sallal made a final attempt in January 1967 to win support by forming a Popular Revolutionary Union "to embrace the whole people" on the lines of Nasser's Arab Socialist Union but it was generally ignored. After the defeat of Nasser in the June War the Arab Heads of State at the Khartoum Summit in August 1967 agreed that the Egyptian troops should leave Yemen and that a Tripartite Committee should endeavour to make peace. Sallal refused to meet them and arrested five of his Ministers who urged that he should. He had now no support at home or abroad and at the beginning of November left for Baghdad and Moscow. In the early hours of 5 November he was ousted in a coup, bloodless because nobody lifted a finger to defend him. Nasser contemptuously refused him refuge in Cairo and he settled in Baghdad on a pension from the Iraqi Government. For a while he intrigued hopefully but it was clear that no one in Sanaa wanted him back in power. In October 1981 he returned and lived quietly without playing any part in political life. Sallal was a short, swarthy, black-jowled man, usually looking crumpled and untidy. He had an acid wit and many of his remarks rang round the capital.

SALZBURG MEETING (1975)

In March 1975 the efforts of Henry Kissinger to bring about disengagement in Sinai appeared stalled and President Ford, criticising Israel's lack of flexibility, announced a "total reassessment" of American Middle East policy. He declared that the US "will not tolerate stagnation and stalemate in our search for a negotiated settlement". On 1 June after a visit to NATO HQ in Brussels, he and Kissinger met Anwar Sadat, who was on a state visit to Austria, Husni Mubarak and Ismail Fahmi in Salzburg. President Assad declined to participate. No official communiqué was issued but it was understood that it was agreed that a $2,000 million international development fund would be set up to help Egypt and that Sadat would guarantee to keep the peace for another three months in order that Kissinger might recommence his "step by step" diplomacy and bring pressure on Israel to agree to a withdrawal behind the strategic passes in Sinai. The Sinai Disengagement Agreement was signed at the beginning of September.

SAMU, Destruction of (1966)

In the autumn of 1966 the Syrian government, led by the bellicose Yusuf al-Zuayyin encouraged Palestinian guerrillas to raid into Israel and also shelled Jewish settlements from the Golan Heights. As a reprisal for the Syrian actions the Israelis attacked the undefended Jordanian village of Samu about ten miles south of Hebron and four miles from the border with the Negev.

A mechanised infantry brigade supported by tanks and aircraft made this the largest military operation since the Suez War. Several civilians were shot in cold blood and 40 houses dynamited. A Jordanian force advancing to the rescue ran into an ambush and in four hours fighting lost 21 killed: the Israelis admitted one killed. The Israelis were censured by the Security Council. Egypt, Syria and the Palestine Liberation Organisation, however, all criticised Jordan and their radios called for the overthrow of King Hussain. There were riots in West Bank towns, and Syrian troops entered Jordan and killed a border guard causing the expulsion of their Ambassador from Amman. The incident effectively divided the Arabs, showed the futility of the Unified Arab Command and convinced Hussain that the Israelis were less interested in his efforts to restrain the *fedayin* than in looking for a pretext to annex the West Bank: his view that the Israelis would attack whatever he did led to the fatal decision not to opt out of the June War.

SAN REMO CONFERENCE (1920)

In April 1920 the Allied Supreme Council, led by Lloyd George, Millerand and Nitti met to discuss problems, amongst which was a peace treaty with the Ottoman Empire which had been left over from the settlement at Versailles. The Americans were not represented and dropped out of Middle East peace-making. The League of Nations had laid down the principle that territories taken from the old Empires should not be treated as colonies by the victors but as Mandates, "a sacred trust of civilisation", and helped to advance until they were ready for full independence. The decisions reached at San Remo followed broadly those of the Sykes–Picot Agreement. Mandates for Syria (less Palestine and a vaguely defined area East of the Jordan) and Lebanon were assigned to France while Iraq and Palestine went to Britain which accepted the commitment to "recognise the historical connection of the Jewish people with Palestine". The Arabs saw the decisions of the Conference as a clear breach of the terms laid down in the Hussain–McMahon Correspondence while the Zionists were pleased. At the same time a further agreement was reached allowing the French a quarter of any oil found in Mesopotamia and a pipeline from there across to the Mediterranean. The Conference transformed the rough demarcation lines between British and French occupation zones into political boundaries scarcely changed today. It also paved the way for a transition from pan-Arab nationalism to a nationalism of individual states.

al-SANUSI, Hassan al-Rida (1928–92)

Libyan Crown prince. The childless King Idris was predeceased in 1955 by his brother Muhammad whom he had chosen as his successor. Muhammad's eldest son Sadiq had been implicated in the Shalhi killing and was passed over in favour of Hassan whom the King regarded as pious and uncorrupt. Hassan had studied at a local religious school and at al-Azhar. His health was poor and he spent much of 1957/8 in Sweden under medical care. He married into a leading Tripoli family to cement the union with Cyrenaica. In 1962 he acted as Regent while Idris made the *Hajj*. In 1963 he repre-

sented the King at the foundation meeting of the Organisation of African Unity and later he stood in for him at Arab Summit conferences. Hassan, nicknamed "the man with no shadow", was weak and ineffective and endeavoured to keep out of politics although he later claimed to have attempted to prevent corruption. Demonstrations in March 1964 against the King's abdication were dictated at least as much by doubts about the qualities of his successor than by affection for Idris. Hassan himself on more than one occasion asked to be passed over for the throne. In September 1969 when the imminent abdication of the King seemed certain, it appears that the Shalhis were planning a coup to establish a government which would have the backing of Nasser but were forestalled by the take-over by Qadafi. Hassan who was Regent at the time formally abdicated on behalf of his uncle. After being under arrest for two years he was brought to trial on charges of corruption and sentenced to three years imprisonment in November 1971. After his release he was under house arrest. In 1984 he, his wife and their eight children were thrown out of their house and forced to watch it being burned down. They then lived for two years in a beach cabin. In 1988 he had a stroke and was allowed to move to London where he lived in poverty in a 2-bedroom flat. It is not clear whether he was regarded as succeeding Idris as leader of the Sanusi *tariqah*. His heir was his son Mahdi who lived in Jordan.

al-SAQISLI, Muhammad

Libyan Prime Minister. He came from an old Benghazi family and after a legal training went into exile in 1920 with Idris al-Sanusi to act as his clerk. When in September 1949 after the expulsion of the Italians a government was set up in Cyrenaica, Saqisli was the first Minister of Justice. The first Prime Minister, Umar Mansur al-Kikhya proved quite incapable of working either with the British administrators or with his Arab colleagues and in March 1950 after the National Congress had passed a vote of no-confidence in him, Saqisli succeeded as Prime Minister. He appointed a committee to recruit a civil service but of 1,500 posts qualified Cyrenaicans were found for only 1,100 and 250 Britons had to be retained. Saqisli sent able young men abroad for training, contributing to the country's financial problems already caused by creating an infrastructure. He had to raise customs duties, leading to an unpopular rise in the cost of living. At the same time his conservative policies alienated the young who provided a noisy minority in the Cyrenaica Assembly elected in June 1950. After several disputes Saqisli prorogued it *sine die* in April 1951 after his proposals for trading with Israel were defeated. After the provinces of Cyrenaica, Tripoli and Fezzan were formally united in December 1951 the post of Cyrenaican Prime Minister was abolished but Saqisli kept much of his powers as Provincial Governor. He was a strong advocate of regional autonomy, resisting the centralising efforts of the Libyan Prime Minister Mahmud Muntasir, regarding himself as responsible only to the King as Amir of Cyrenaica. He was always very close to the King, becoming Chief of the Royal Diwan in February 1953. When the Muntasir government fell in February 1954 over the question of relations between the centre and the provinces, Saqisli became Prime Minister and Foreign Minister. The King had dissolved the Tripolitanian Assembly for its failure to co-operate with the executive but this decision was declared illegal by the Supreme Court. This decision was presented as a blow at royal authority and Saqisli resigned in April. He was described as a strong and meticulous man of great integrity but inflexible and over-legalistic.

SARRAJ, Abd Allah (c. 1870–)

Chief Minister of Trans-Jordan. He was a Hijazi of noble family who became a Mufti in Mecca and subsequently Minister of Justice in the first government established by King Hussain. A British report described him as a tall spare man with a short grizzled beard and a reputation for ability and fair dealing. After the Hijaz was conquered by Ibn Saud, he moved to Trans-Jordan where the Amir Abd Allah appointed him Chief Justice. In February 1931 after clashes with the Legislative Council had led to the fall of the government of Hassan Khalid Abu al-Huda Sarraj became Chief Minister. His period of office was uneventful and he was dismissed in November 1933 after further disputes between the Legislative and Executive Councils.

SARSANK MEETING (1954)

In 1954 the new Eisenhower government revived the Middle East Command Proposal to prevent Russian expansion into the area. Iraq, under Nuri al-Said was willing to ally with the West but Nasser saw this as compromising the neutrality of the Arab League and also, by making Baghdad the only recipient of modern weapons, as giving it predominance in the area. He therefore sent his expert on inter-Arab relations, Major Salah Salam to see Nuri and the Regent Abd al-Illah. They met at Sarsank in the Kurdish mountains in August. The Iraqis stressed their vulnerability to Russian or even Turkish aggression and to internal communism. Salam suggested a stronger and more united Arab League and that local communism would be stimulated by closer links with the interfering West. Nuri appeared to agree, said that he wished to do something for Palestine and would visit Cairo shortly. Subsequently Salam said at a press conference that "if two or more Arab peoples wish to unite in some form, Egypt does not object". This appeared to approve of the Regent's aspiration to annex Syria and caused uproar there. He also reported that Egypt and Iraq had agreed to strengthen the Arab Collective Security Treaty, in consultation with Britain and America, before putting the matter to other Arab states. It was not clear whether Iraq had promised not to join a non-Arab military organisation or whether Salam had agreed to its joining Turkey and Pakistan. Nuri's visit to Cairo the following month showed that no substantive conclusion had been reached at Sarsank and Iraqi–Egyptian relations rapidly deteriorated into overt hostility.

SARTAWI, Isam (1936–83)

Palestinian leader. He was born in Acre and became a successful surgeon. In 1967, abandoning a research programme in America, he joined Fatah and took part in guerrilla operations. Sartawi was always regarded as particularly close to Yassir Arafat. Later he became convinced that the Palestinians could only regain their rights by negotiations with the Israelis. He made strenuous efforts to win over moderates of both sides and held numerous meetings with Israeli "doves". Based on Paris he was indefatigable in trying to persuade political leaders such as the Austrian Chancellor Bruno Kreisky to help with a peace settlement. Sartawi realised that the Americans would not deal directly with the Palestinians until they had recognised the right of Israel to exist in peace but he argued that statements made by the Palestinian Liberation Organisation constituted *de facto* recognition of Israel within its 1967 borders and also renunciation of terrorism. He said that Abu Nidal should be put on trial by the PLO as a proof of their sincerity. His activities were disavowed by official leaders of the PLO such as Abu Lutf although not by Arafat. In February 1983 the Palestine National Council opposed the Reagan Plan and showed little enthusiasm for the Arab proposals set out at the Fez Summit. Sartawi was not allowed to speak and resigned in protest. On 10 April, attending an international socialist conference in Portugal, he was murdered. Abu Nidal claimed responsibility, saying that Sartawi had worked for the CIA, Mossad and the British. There were numerous tributes to his courage and integrity, as well as his eloquence and good humour, paid by European leaders as well as by his Israeli contacts.

al-SAUD, Khalid b. Sultan (1949–)

Saudi General. The son of Prince Sultan, for thirty years Minister of Defence, he graduated from Sandhurst in 1968. He subsequently attended courses at the American Artillery School at Fort Worth, specialising in missile and electronic warfare, at the General Staff College at Fort Leavenworth where he took a Masters degree in Military Science, in Air Warfare, and in international defence management at the American Navy Postgraduate School, Monterey. He also took a Masters Degree in political science from Auburn University, Montgomery, Alabama. His brother, Prince Bandar, was the extremely influential Ambassador in Washington. During Operation Desert Storm, with the rank of Lieutenant-General, he was nominally Commander of all the non-American troops although in practice the British and French forces dealt directly with General Schwarzkopf. He had however, an important part to play in the early stages of the fighting which took place with bombing and missiles and in the Saudi victory at Khafji. His Saudi forces were amongst the first into Kuwait and he was present with Schwarzkopf when the Iraqi generals accepted the cease-fire terms. He was decorated by the British and American Governments. In September 1991 Prince Khalid suddenly retired, receiving promotion to full General. There were rumours that, exemplifying the American way of life, he was unpopular amongst traditionalists and that he was involved with a newspaper *al-Hayat* which had been running liberal articles disrespectful to King Fahd. Later there were allegations that he had improper ties with arms dealers and in particular was connected with bribery which had secured contracts for Westland helicopters as part of the Yamamah Deals and that large sums for supplies had vanished during the Gulf War.

al-SAUD, Saud al-Faysal (1940–)

Saudi Minister. The fourth son of King Faysal, he was born in Riyadh in 1940 and like all his brothers was sent abroad for higher education. After a degree in economics from Princeton he returned to work in Petromin. He was deeply involved in the drawing up of the first Five-Year Plan and the consequent diversification of the Saudi oil industry. He became Deputy Minister under Shaykh Ahmad Zaki al-Yamani and was generally regarded by foreign diplomats and businessmen as one of the ablest men in the Kingdom. Immediately after the assassination of his father he was appointed Minister of Foreign Affairs, a field in which King Khalid had limited experience and was prepared to leave to his nephew. Saud always accompanied the King on state visits and went many times to America where his charm, good looks and fluent English, he was extremely successful in putting the Arab case on television. He was particularly involved in trying to bring peace to the Lebanon and played a major role in the Riyadh Summit of 1976 which arranged for the setting up, with Saudi financial backing of the Arab Deterrent Security Force and in the arrangements for the Ta'if Parliament of 1989. He was also deeply involved in the search for a solution to the Palestine problem and played a part in the drafting of the Fahd Plan in which for the first time Saudi Arabia took the lead in suggesting a policy for all the Arab states. After the invasion of Kuwait by Saddam Hussain the good relations that he had cultivated with foreign powers, both Arab and Western, were important in rallying support for the Kingdom and in keeping together the allied forces that were victorious in Operation Desert Storm. With his brothers he was instrumental in setting up the richly endowed charitable foundation which made grants for religious and scholarly purposes. A cultured man, he was one of the few Amirs who in *Who's Who* gave reading rather than falconry and riding as his favourite pastime. By the late 1980s he was generally considered to be the most likely to be the first of the grandsons of Ibn Saud to become King.

al-SAUD, Talal b. Abd al-Aziz (1931–)

He was the twenty-third son of Ibn Saud and spent some of his youth in Beirut where he had inherited money from his mother and married a daughter of the Lebanese Prime Minister Riad al-Sulh. Talal was regarded as one of the ablest and most sophisticated of the sons of the King and at the age of 19 was appointed Comptroller of the Royal Household. He was the first to apply for permission to go into business, starting a cement factory. In 1953 he was appointed Minister of Communications but quarrelled violently with his elder brother Mishaal, the Minister of Defence and Aviation and was sent as Ambassador to Spain and France where he appears to have absorbed ideas about constitutional government. Returning in 1957 he built up a following amongst the younger princes whom he inspired with ideas of reform and also amongst educated commoners. Feeling that King Saud who had been forced to hand over power to his brother Faysal was the more likely to

make radical changes, Talal supported him and was made Minister of Finance in December 1960 when Saud resumed control. Talal publicly called for a National Assembly with two-thirds of its members elected and the rest nominated. Saud made no effort to modernise the political system which under his incompetence slipped into chaos. Talal attempted to restrain the King's extravagance and failing, resigned. He sought an ally in Nasser who had been attacking the Saudi Government. In August 1962, arriving in Beirut from Europe, Talal was informed that his passport had been revoked and his homes searched for subversive material. He then broke all precedent by holding a press conference in which he aired differences within the Royal Family, proclaimed himself a "Fabian socialist", called for left-wing measures, renounced his title and then sought political asylum in Cairo from where he broadcast attacks on his brother. He spoke of the "Free Princes" and predicted the breakup of the Kingdom. Although Talal had no political organisation, evidence of a split in the Royal Family may have helped to convince Nasser that it would be safe to go ahead with plans for a revolution in Sanaa. Bombing of Saudi territory by the Egyptians during the Yemen War shocked Talal and, admitting his errors, he returned in February 1964. He went into business, playing no more part in politics although in 1979 he was appointed Special Envoy to UNESCO.

SAUDI FUND FOR DEVELOPMENT

The Saudi Fund for Development was set up by King Faysal in 1974 to help finance projects in the "Third World". It gives assistance either by grants or loans and is particularly concerned with airports, electricity, road-building, railways, water and agriculture. Importance is attached to transfer of skills and technology to the recipient countries. Until Camp David Egypt was its major beneficiary but North Yemen in less than a decade received 50 schools, 20 medical centres, 26 mosques, and 35 urban water projects. Its original capital of 10,000 million Saudi riyals was nearly exhausted by 1979 but in 1981 it was increased 25,000 million, making it the largest of any Arab fund. In its first decade the Fund disbursed $5,684 million to finance 266 projects in 59 countries, constituting a valuable support for the Kingdom's diplomacy. In the 1980s an increasing proportion of aid went to non-Arab countries, particularly in Africa and Latin America but a major dam was built in Pakistan. A weakness of the Fund has been a lack of expert staff of its own which it has tried to overcome by working with other international agencies.

SAWT AL-ARAB

In May 1953 General Neguib inaugurated "The Voice of the Arabs" on Cairo Radio to broadcast propaganda for an hour a day. It proved extremely successful and after a year was putting out programmes on both medium and short waves for four hours a day. It had also started its first foreign language service – in Swahili attacking the British who were then trying to repress Mau Mau in Kenya and thus was one of the factors which helped to convince London that Nasser was implacably hostile. The invention of the transistor set meant that it could spread its message everywhere and the sight of a peasant ploughing with a set strapped to his camel or oxen became common. Its presenter, Ahmad Said became an international figure with his witty but virulent attacks on the enemies of the regime and the destruction of Cairo Radio was one of the first British objectives in the Suez War. It did much to mobilise hostility to the Baghdad Pact and called for the murder of King Hussain and Nuri al-Said. Fadhl Jamali said that it played a primary role in the overthrow of the Iraqi Monarchy. It called for a rising of the Muslims against President Chamoun. *Sawt al-Arab* was important in stirring up revolution in Aden and in Yemen. By 1963 Cairo was transmitting 755 hours a week in 24 languages, putting out more broadcasts than any service apart from the BBC, Voice of America and Radio Moscow. During the June War it made itself ridiculous by boasting of unbelievable victories and never recovered its former credibility, particularly after Ahmad Said fell from favour in 1968.

SAYAH, Muhammad (1933–)

Tunisian politician. Born in the Sahil, he was educated at Sadiqi College and Tunis University. While still a student he attracted the attention of Bourguiba, who came from the same area, and in 1960 was appointed Secretary-General of the Students' Union (UGET). In 1962 he was put in charge of the bureaucracy of the Neo-Destour Party and of its newspaper *L'Action*. In November 1969 he became Secretary of State for Information but his involvement with Ben Salah led to his being demoted in July 1970 to Permanent Representative to the UN in Geneva. During his tenure Bourguiba went to Switzerland for medical treatment and Sayah seized the opportunity to regain favour. In October 1971 he returned to the Government as Minister of Public Works and Housing. In June 1973 he resumed his old post as Director-General of the Party and later in the year was given a supervisory role in the office of the Prime Minister, Hedi Nouira. He organised a party militia which dealt roughly with dissidents and he so managed the Monastir Congress of 1974 that it was a complete triumph for Bourguiba. He was also responsible for the punishments that followed the riots of Black Thursday in 1978. In 1979, when Chadli Klibi moved to the Arab League, Sayah succeeded him as the editor of the official history of the Party and the definitive volumes of the speeches of Bourguiba: this he did in a way that exalted Bourguiba at the expense of other nationalist leaders. He also held Ministerial posts in Planning, Housing and Equipment and Supply while continuing to run the Party machinery. His authoritarian views brought disputes with the more liberal Prime Minister Muhammad Mzali but Bourguiba was content to let them balance each other until November 1983 when Mzali with the help of Mme Bourguiba managed to post Sayah as Ambassador to The Hague. Two months later the Bread Riots rocked the regime and Mzali felt the need of the alliance of a tough-minded disciplinarian and brought back Sayah as Minister of Equipment and Housing. Sayah, in alliance with Bourguiba Junior and opposed by Mme Bourguiba, was now seen as a possible candidate for the succession in competition with Mzali with whom he struggled for

control of the Interior Ministry. His claims appeared still stronger after Mzali was replaced by the colourless Rashid Sfar who appeared to have neither the wish nor the charisma for the Presidency. Early in 1987, as Islamic militants were struggling for control of the Universities, Sayah was moved to the Education Ministry to keep them in check and given the superior rank of Minister of State. One of the first acts of Ben Ali upon seizing power was to arrest Sayah, whose political career, dependent upon the favour of Bourguiba, was effectively over although he was quickly released to house arrest.

SECTEURS DE MODERNISATION DU PAYSANNAT (Morocco)

In 1945, under the inspiration of Jacques Berque, then a civil administrator and later the most influential French sociologist on the Arab world, the Protectorate authorities in Morocco announced measures that they hoped would lead to a total transformation of rural life. Whole areas were to be developed as complete units rather on the lines of a Soviet *Kholkhoz*. Peasants would be told what to cultivate so that instead of their all growing corn, the totality of the needs of the community would be produced. At the centre of each Secteur there would be a school, an infirmary, workshops, craft schools and even a sports ground. Each Secteur would have a French director assisted by an elected *jemaa* of local notables which was seen as the germ of regional self-government, freed from possible oppression by tribal leaders. Enthusiasts compared the creation of the SMP with the Czar's emancipation of the serfs in 1861. Each Secteur was complete in itself but there was a central council to co-ordinate their activities. By 1955 57 SMPs had been established. Membership was compulsory and in some cases imposed by force. The scheme was opposed by the colons, influential in Paris and Rabat, as threatening their economic predominance and by some administrators as creating rival centres of authority and the *fellahin*, not fully consulted, were apathetic and failed to play their part in management. It had been an inspiring ideal but failed to take account of realities. Some economic progress was made but there was no social transformation and the experiment was moribund before the end of the Protectorate.

SECURITY ZONE

It was a long-standing desire of the Israeli Government to dominate an area inside Lebanese territory immediately north of their frontier so as to control the Litani River and to deny its use to Palestinian guerrillas. After their invasion of Lebanon in 1978 when compelled by Resolution 425 to withdraw they handed over an area 9 miles deep, 50 miles long, covering 440 square miles, not as they should have done to UNIFIL but to their puppet South Lebanon Army. This mercenary force under Major Saad Haddad was unable to prevent its occasional use for rocket or artillery attacks on Northern Galilee so its reconstitution as a reliable buffer was one of the publicly proclaimed objectives of the second major invasion, Operation Peace for Galilee in June 1982. When they withdrew again after three years once again the SLA was put in charge with a force of some 1,000 Israeli soldiers to supervise them.

The population of about 150,000, mainly Shiah was subjected to strict security regulations – for example, each car driver had to have a passenger to prevent suicidal ramming of Israeli vehicles. All vehicles had to stop 100 yards away from a moving Israeli vehicle or risk being shot. Despite this there were constant incidents and 60 Israeli soldiers were killed in six years. UNIFIL personnel stationed in parts of the area were systematically obstructed and sometimes attacked. People suspected of hostility to the Israelis were tortured in the notorious Khiam Prison. After November 1983 all visitors from other parts of Lebanon had to have passes to visit the area. In September 1984 a Security Council Resolution calling upon Israel to lift these restrictions and observe the 1949 Geneva Convention with regard to treatment of civilians under occupation was vetoed by the USA. As part of the policy of attaching the area to Israel, villagers were compelled to sell their produce there and the occupying authorities set up a form of civil administration with which the population refused to co-operate. In April 1989 the Israelis formally annexed 40 square miles of Lebanese territory. In November 1990 after the defeat of General Aoun the Lebanese Government declared its wish to extend its authority throughout the country but Moshe Arens, the Israeli Defence Minister, said that this could not be tolerated and that the Lebanese army would not even be allowed into Jezzine, several miles outside the Security Zone. However the withdrawal of the militias from Beirut meant that considerable numbers of fighting men from Hizbullah and other groups moved into the Security Zone and there were further clashes. At this time it was reckoned that there were still 3,000 SLA mercenaries and 1,000 Israelis still attempting to control the area. In July 1991 the Lebanese army established a presence in much of the South which it had been unable to do since 1975 but the Israelis moved up tanks and artillery to prevent their entry into Jezzine. In April 1992 after two Israeli soldiers had been killed in a Hizbullah ambush, Prime Minister Shamir vowed to keep the Zone but his successor Rabin indicated that it could be evacuated if the Lebanese Government signed a peace treaty, if it had an army capable of preventing cross-border attacks and if it integrated the SLA gunmen into its regular forces. On becoming Prime Minister Rafiq Hariri declared that the Lebanese Government was under no obligation to restrain attacks on Israel while part of its territory was occupied. After a series of attacks by Hizbullah on Israeli and SLA personnel, interspersed with rocket attacks on Galilee, the Israeli Government in July 1993 launched Operation Accountability, a ruthless bombardment of civilian villages outside the Zone in a deliberate plan to force their inhabitants to flee. Through American mediation an agreement was reached by which Hizbullah halted attacks on Israel proper but was free to continue operations in the Zone. Two retired Israeli generals called for evacuation of the Zone on military grounds and Rabin said that if there were no attacks for about nine months he would be willing to do so. However incidents continued and in August nine Israeli soldiers were killed in an ambush.

SEPARATION STATEMENT (1988)

By mid-1988 King Hussain realised that his attempt to "buy" the loyalty of the inhabitants of the West Bank by his West Bank Development Plan of 1986 had failed. The outbreak of the Intifadah in December 1987 showed that he could not compete with the influence of Hamas and his closest advisers such as the Prime Minister Zaid al-Rifai urged him to devote all his attention and resources to the East Bank. On July 28 he cancelled the Development Plan and two days later dissolved the Chamber of Deputies in which West Bankers had continued to be represented. On 31 July in a televised speech the King severed all legal and administrative ties stating that his goal was to "enhance Palestinian national orientation and highlight Palestinian identity". Some 18,000 teachers, health workers, municipal employees would be retired and receive pensions: most of those retired had also received salaries from Israel. The Supreme Committee for West Bank Affairs was and the Ministry for Occupied Territory Affairs were abolished and their functions transferred to a new department in the Foreign Ministry. On 20 August the Prime Minister ordered that those living on the West Bank would no longer be Jordanian citizens although they could obtain temporary passports: East Bank residents of Palestinian origin were not affected. The Government stressed that it was not building a wall along the Jordan for trade continued and the 3,000 civil employees paid by the Ministry of Religious Affairs were exempted "to preserve Islamic cultural presence in the occupied Palestinian territory" continued to give Jordan a significant presence in Jerusalem and other religious centres.

SEPTEMBER LAWS (Sudan) (1983)

In the early 1980s opposition grew to the regime of President Nimeiri. The disastrous economic situation caused serious strikes in the North and his decision, contrary to the Addis Ababa Agreement of 1972, to divide the South into three Regions and to move Southern troops to the North led to armed unrest there. He was particularly incensed by a strike of judges, after which, contrary to the constitutional guarantee of judicial independence, he removed in June 1983 42 of their number as drunken, corrupt or lazy. Determined to rally support from the Muslim North and from conservative Arab countries, in September he announced, without notice, a revision of the country's penal code to link it "organisationally and spiritually" with the *Shariah*. This was probably the only way in which he could claim legitimacy for harsh repression. He released 13,000 prisoners, held under former laws stating that their convictions were no longer valid. He banned alcohol and large stocks were dumped in the Nile. Gambling was also prohibited. Theft, adultery and murder were to be judged according to the *Shariah* and the Qur'anic penalties, (*hudud*), cutting off of hands and feet and stoning to death were to be enforced. The move was strongly supported by the leader of the Islamic Charter Front, Dr Hassan Turabi but opposed by other Muslim leaders such as Sadiq al-Mahdi who was imprisoned and Mahmud Muhammad Taha who was later hanged. These punishments were enforced with a ferocity; people accused of stealing

more than £100 could lose an arm and a leg, punishment not shown in other countries such as Saudi Arabia
and Pakistan which also used the Code, and some 150
people were condemned to public execution or amputation, some shown on television. The application of
religious taxes such as *zakat* threw revenue-collection
into chaos and aggravated an already desperate financial
situation: it also frightened off potential foreign investors. After a wave of strikes, in April 1984 Nimeiri
proclaimed a state of emergency and the full implementation of his version of *Shariah* by special courts. There
was an atmosphere of terror as people denounced by a
neighbour might be punished without proper trial and
a man speaking to a woman could be condemned for
"suspected intended adultery". Nimeiri came to regard
himself as a religious as well as a military leader and in
July had himself proclaimed Imam so that opposition
became heresy as well as treason. After intense pressure
from friends at home and abroad in September Nimeiri
ended the state of emergency and the special courts
proclaiming that "society had been purified of corruption and immorality". Although in theory *Shariah*
applied to Muslims in the South and a court was established in Juba in February 1984, in practice it did not
operate although Christians and pagans feared that it
might. Foreigners were supposed to be exempt but in
June 1984 an Italian was flogged, imprisoned and
deported for having alcohol. The September Laws were
one of the main reasons for the overthrow of the regime
in April 1985 as they had divided the North and stimulated revolt in the South. The successor regime felt
unable to abolish them but they were no longer strictly
enforced.

SERFATY, Abraham (1926–)

Moroccan dissident. He was born in Casablanca into a
Jewish family which had returned to Morocco after
making a fortune in Brazil. He trained at the École des
Mines in Paris where he made many contacts with
extreme left-wingers. In 1952 he was involved in bloody
riots in Casablanca but the authorities insisted on treating him as an alien so he was expelled to France rather
than imprisoned in Morocco. After independence he
returned and worked under Abd al-Rahim Bouabid,
the Minister of the Economy. In 1960 he was appointed
to a senior post in the extremely important nationalised
phosphates industry. In 1967 after a strike in the Khourigba mines in which he had supported the workers he
resigned and although he later did some work as a
mining engineer he spent most of his time as a political
agitator. He became a friend of Naif Hawatmah and
other extremists and he established a clandestine organisation, *Ila al-Amam* (Forward), far more radical than
the communist Parti du Progrès et du Socialisme. In
January 1972 Serfaty was arrested for running a pro-
Mao journal and was tortured. He escaped but in September 1973 was sentenced *in absentia* to life
imprisonment for involvement in the March Plot threatening state security. He took refuge with a French
teacher whom, as a result of the intervention of President Mitterand, he was allowed to marry in jail in
1986. In November 1974 most of *Ila al-Amam* including
Serfaty were captured and he was again tortured. After
a trial in Casablanca, Serfaty and 44 others were sen-

tenced to life imprisonment. He admitted that he was
a Marxist-Leninist but denied that there had been a
plot to set up a republic of which he would have been
President. Moroccan barristers refused to defend him
because of his attitude to the Western Sahara War. He
was imprisoned in Kenitra and was not included in
the amnesty granted to his comrades in 1984. After the
release of Nelson Mandela, Serfaty was Africa's longest-
serving political prisoner. In September 1991, after a
threat of a hunger strike, he was released, it was said at
the request of Yassir Arafat. Despite his protests he was
expelled to France.

SÈVRES ACCORD (1956)

At the Chequers Meeting of 14 October 1956 French
officials had proposed to Prime Minister Eden that
Britain and France should collude with Israel to bring
down Nasser; he accepted the idea and drew up a plan
with Prime Minister Mollet, agreeing that an Israeli
attack on the Suez Canal would provide the ideal
pretext for intervention. On 22 October Prime Minister
Ben Gurion and Defence Minister Dayan came to
Sèvres in great secrecy to say that Israel was unable
to attack Egypt on its own without the help of French
fighter aircraft and British bombers. Foreign Secretary
Selwyn Lloyd then arrived. An accord was reached by
which Israel would attack Egypt on the evening of 29
October. The following day Britain and France would
appeal for a cease-fire and the withdrawal of Egyptian
and Israeli forces to ten miles back from the Canal so
that the Allies could ensure its safety by a temporary
occupation. If either rejected the appeal or failed to
comply within 12 hours, the Allies would intervene by
force. If Egypt refused, air attacks would start on 31
October. Israel would not attack Jordan but if Jordan
attacked Israel, Britain would not intervene. Israel
would be allowed to occupy Sharm al-Shaykh on the
eastern coast of the Sinai Peninsula. (These terms are
taken from the memoirs of Dayan – Eden was horrified
that they had been recorded in writing and sent FO
officials back to Paris to ask for destruction of the
record: this was refused but the British official copy
has disappeared.) The Accord was approved by Eden
without consultation with the full Cabinet.

SÈVRES, Treaty of (1920)

At the San Remo Conference in April 1920 the Allies
laid down the terms that they would dictate to a
defeated Ottoman Empire. These were reluctantly
signed by Turkish representatives at Sèvres in August.
They provided for the dismemberment of the Empire.
Turkey had to renounce all rights in its former Arab
provinces of Syria, Iraq, Palestine, the Hijaz and Egypt.
In addition it had to recognise the British annexation
of Cyprus and Smyrna would remain nominally under
Turkish sovereignty but would be administered by
Greece. Armenia would be independent. A Commission would study the wishes of the Kurds, and if
they wished for independence Turkey would not demur.
These two buffer states would serve British strategic
interests. A Commission would control the Straits and
ensure the protection of minorities in Constantinople.
News of the Treaty was greeted with national mourning
in Turkey. The nationalists led by the Ghazi Mustafa

Kemal refused to accept it and after defeating a Greek invasion, assumed power in the new capital of Ankara. The peace treaty was renegotiated and signed at Lausanne in 1923.

SFAR, Rashid (1933–)
Tunisian Prime Minister. Born in Mahdia, he attended school in Sousse before going to the École Nationale des Impôts in Paris. He then became a tax inspector, Director of the Tobacco Monopoly, Director of Taxation and held senior posts in the Ministries of Education and Finance before, in 1977, joining the Cabinet as Minister of Mines and Energy. He was elected to the National Assembly and the Politburo of the Parti Socialiste Destourien as its Treasurer in 1979. Seen as a strong supporter of the financial orthodoxy of Hedi Nouira, Sfar held the Ministries of Defence, Health, Economy and Finance before Bourguiba appointed him Prime Minister in July 1986 on the sudden dismissal of Muhamad Mzali. He also became Secretary-General of the PSD and presumptive successor to the President but, having the support of no political faction and no ascertainable views on political or social matters, was generally seen as a transitory figure, perhaps preparing the way for Bourguiba Junior. His Cabinet was chosen by the President who appeared to make the main decisions while Sfar acted as spokesman and co-ordinator. He was, however, competent at financial management as he faced a financial crisis with huge public debt which had doubled between 1980 and 1984, demanding 23% of export earnings for its servicing, and oil revenues halved leading to an acute shortage of foreign currency; he had already in December 1985 introduced an austerity budget. Blaming his predecessor for failing to take unpopular measures, he immediately devalued the dirham by 10%, made stringent cuts in government expenditure, introduced VAT, proposed to phase out food subsidies and dismissed for corruption the Governor of the Central Bank. All senior officials were ordered to declare their incomes upon entering or leaving a post and there was a witch-hunt of Mzali supporters. In November there were parliamentary elections but, as they were boycotted by the opposition, the PSD won all the seats. There was rigid restriction of the press and human rights leaders such as Khamis Chamahri were arrested. The main threat, however, came from the militants of the Mouvement de la Tendance Islamique of whom about 1,000 had been arrested by June 1987 while Sfar tried desperately to conciliate the moderate opposition. He also introduced the Seventh Plan primarily aimed at job creation and rural development in previously unfavoured areas to prevent the drift to the towns. Sfar, respected by international financiers, obtained two large loans from the World Bank. Sfar saw a Maghreb Common Market as an economic necessity, visiting Morocco and Algeria to sign trade agreements. In October 1987, after the trial of MTI leaders, riots were expected and the need felt for a stronger hand: General Ben Ali therefore took over as Prime Minister. Honest, colourless, cold and distinguished-looking, Sfar was described as resembling "un clubman britannique".

SFAX CONGRESS (1955)
The Franco-Tunisian Autonomy Agreement of June 1955 caused a deep split in the Neo-Destour. Although it gave less than full independence it was commended by Bourguiba as a stepping-stone towards it but vehemently opposed by the former Secretary-General of the Party Salih Ben Yusuf who was thereupon expelled by the Politburo by its Bourguibist majority. As Ben Yusuf's strongest support lay in the capital, a Congress was called for 15 November in Sfax where, as he came from Jerbah, he and his adherents would be unpopular. When he foresaw that he would lose, Ben Yusuf called for a boycott, arguing that only he as Secretary was empowered to convoke a Congress but 1,260 of the 1,314 delegates participated. At the Congress Bourguiba stole Ben Yusuf's thunder by suggesting that total independence might soon be attained by negotiation for which he was the best qualified person. Ahmad Ben Salah, promising progressive economic and social policies, put the massive trade union strength behind Bourguiba. Ben Yusuf refused to appear. The Congress approved "without reserve" the policies of the Politburo since 1952 and elected Bourguiba's list of supporters to a new Politburo. Ben Yusuf attempted to reverse the decisions by setting up a rival party and then by violence but the Sfax Congress showed the mixture of tactical skill and overpowering authority that had led to the dominance of Bourguiba.

SHAAB Party (Trans-Jordan)
In his early years as Amir of Trans-Jordan Abd Allah worked with the Istiqlal Party which opposed the Mandates held by European States and aspired to a union of independent Arab states. Political necessity, however, compelled the Amir to accept the Mandate and to consolidate in Amman. As a support he encouraged the foundation in 1927 of the *Shaab* Party, a purely Trans-Jordanian grouping which opposed the influence of Arab "foreigners" in local affairs. It maintained friendly relations with the Amir's Palestinian adherents, the National Defence Party of Raghib al-Nashashibi. Little more than a grouping of Abd Allah's adherents, it lacked a mass following and was scarcely a political party although officially recognised as such in May 1947.

al-SHAABI, Faysal Abd al-Latif (c. 1937–70)
Prime Minister of South Yemen. He came from a family of tribal notables and after schooling in Aden, took a Degree in Commerce from Cairo University. He was then employed in the Ministry of Commerce of the Federation of South Arabia. He had numerous personal grievances, especially against the Sultans of Lahej over land disputes. While in Cairo he came into contact with the Arab Nationalist Movement and founded a cell of supporters in Aden which became one of the groups that merged in 1963 to form the National Liberation Front. Faysal became a member of its executive at its First Congress in Taizz in June 1965. He was one of the main organisers of terrorism in Aden, reputedly killing Britons and Arabs, including many members of the rival nationalist organisation the Front for the Liberation of Occupied South Yemen with his own hands. He maintained some links with the British,

reassuring them that their withdrawal would not lead to Egyptian domination of Aden. In August 1967 he played a large part in ensuring that the western states of the Federation fell under NLF rather than FLOSY control. When his cousin Qahtan al-Shaabi formed the first independent government in November 1967, Faysal became Minister of Trade and the Economy. He soon resigned this and took charge of Party affairs and to act as the President's deputy. In June 1968 the army, fearing a coup by the left wing of the Party, offered to arrest them but Faysal contemptuously declined. In February 1969 he became Foreign Minister at a time of acute tension with Saudi Arabia and North Yemen. He visited Kuwait, trying to obtain financial aid in a desperate economic situation. In April 1969 criticism of his combining the offices of President and Prime Minister led Qahtan to divest himself of the latter which he entrusted to Faysal. In June 1969 both were deposed in the Glorious Corrective Move by the leftist group. Faysal was dismissed from the Party, accused of isolating it from the People and causing dissension. In March 1970, amidst rumours of counter-coups, he was arrested and in April shot, officially "while trying to escape".

al-SHAABI, Qahtan b. Muhammad (1920–81)

First President and Prime Minister of South Yemen. He came from a family of tribal notables in Lahej and, after schooling in Aden, studied agricultural engineering in Khartoum. In 1955, as an Agricultural Inspector in Lahej he was an early recruit to the South Arabian League. In 1960 he defected to the Yemen and, alienated by the conservatism of the SAL, started to form a more left-wing liberation movement according to the philosophy of the Arab Nationalist Movement. He saw it as essential to mobilise the tribal hinterland and not merely the urban proletariat that followed Abd Allah al-Asnaj and the People's Socialist Party. He advised the Imam Ahmad and later the Republican leaders on Southern affairs and also spent much time in Cairo where he published a newspaper. He was put in charge of the shadowy, ineffective Arab Liberation Army because the Egyptians saw him as a more effective leader of terrorists than Asnaj. He emerged as the leader of the National Liberation Front at its first Congress in Taizz in June 1965. The Egyptians who were paying both the NLF and the Organisation for the Liberation of the Occupied South brought pressure upon the two to unite as the Front for the Liberation of Occupied South Yemen in January 1966. Qahtan who refused to accept this was detained in Cairo although in August he agreed to some form of merger and for this he was disavowed by the "second-level leadership" of the NLF and briefly expelled from the Party. He was reinstated as leader, partly because he was the only member of the Executive over 40 years of age and thus had sufficient seniority to make a credible President. In August 1967 the NLF which had been fighting FLOSY for control of the hinterland as the Federation of South Arabia crumbled, captured Zinjibar where Qahtan held a press conference in which he expressed his willingness to hold talks with the British about taking over the government and with FLOSY to permit their living in peace under his regime. In October he returned to Cairo to hold talks with FLOSY while his supporters smashed them on the ground. In November he headed an NLF delegation to Geneva for the formal take-over of sovereignty from the British. On 30 November he proclaimed the independence of the new state with himself as President, Prime Minister and Commander-in-Chief. He at once declared South Yemen a unitary state, abolished the old shaykhdoms and attempted to stamp out tribal blood feuds. Other Parties were banned, a State Security Supreme Court established a firm grip, some purges were carried out and former rulers and officials put on trial. An attempted invasion of Bayhan and a rising in Yashbum were savagely crushed. Relations with Great Britain became icy as advisers were expelled and offers of aid rejected as inadequate. Arms were obtained from Russia. Nevertheless three months after independence a split emerged between the faction of Qahtan and his cousin Faysal b. Abd al-Latif al-Shaabi who wished to tackle immediate problems by retaining elements of the past and building upon them and the followers of Abd al-Fattah Ismail who called for all-out revolution and its export to neighbouring states. At the Zinjibar Conference of March 1968 the extreme left prevailed but the President turned the tables by arousing fears in the army of further purges and used it to arrest his opponents. He had, however, himself to move leftward to outflank them and talked of the socialist road, started a redistribution of land and set up National Organisations to regulate imports and processing. He was anxious to avoid unrealistic dogmatism and to encourage the investment of local and foreign capital. He played an active role in foreign affairs, visiting Moscow, Cairo, Damascus, Algiers, Baghdad and North Korea. He called on the Saudi people to oust their King and provided bases from which the Chinese could help left-wing rebels in Dhufar. Relations with Sanaa were good when it appeared that the radicals might triumph there but deteriorated into a war of words as the government of President al-Iryani moved to the right. As his domestic leftists regrouped he attempted to win some of them over by socialist measures and taking their leaders into his Cabinet. In June 1969 a trivial dispute over the posting of an officer led to an angry quarrel with his Minister of the Interior Muhammad Ali Haytham whom he dismissed. Haytham who had considerable influence with the army and the tribes joined forces with the left wing and Qahtan was deposed bloodlessly in the Glorious Corrective Move in June 1969. He was detained for some time but then released and lived quietly in Aden until his death was announced "with profound regret" by the Government. He was given a state funeral with religious rites. A dour, intense, prickly man, with a strong sense of national and personal assertiveness, Qahtan was a socialist in the Nasser sense, never a Marxist but an authoritarian egalitarian. In May 1990 he was officially rehabilitated and the Government declared that his deposition had taken place "in the absence of true democracy".

al-SHAALAN, Nuri (c. 1855–1942)

Tribal chief. As Shaykh of the Rwala tribe of about 7,000 tents, he was regarded as an Amir, the equal almost of the Sharif of Mecca, the Ruler of Jabal

Shammar or Ibn Saud. In order to attain this position he had had to kill two of his brothers, both of whom had tried to kill him, and fight innumerable battles. His tribe was dependent upon markets controlled by the Turks and in the early years of the century he collaborated with them, assisting them against the Druzes and receiving large gifts. His son Nawwaf, however, more intelligent and better educated, had strong sympathies with the Arab nationalists after the Young Turks came to power and had much influence over his father. In 1910 Nawwaf wrested the Jawf oasis from Saud b. Abd al-Aziz al-Rashid. An incorrigible intriguer, Nuri did all that he could to hamper the extension of Turkish influence amongst the desert tribes or the construction of the Hijaz Railway. In 1911 he was invited to Damascus and detained there for almost a year. After the outbreak of war he hampered the Turkish campaign against Egypt by obstructing their search for camels and he maintained a friendly correspondence with Sharif Hussain. He hesitated to join the Arab Revolt, however until it was clear that it was completely successful and it was less than a month before the liberation of Damascus that he entered the camp of the Amir Faysal. He was described at this time as a true bedouin, unkempt, rarely changing or cleaning his clothes but Lawrence wrote "he had none of the wheedling diplomacy of the ordinary Shaykh; a word and that was the end of the opposition or of his opponent. All feared and obeyed him". Realising that the French were determined to rule Syria, Nuri let them know that he would be prepared to collaborate. In return he received a palace in Damascus, great wealth, aerial assistance against trouble-makers in his own tribe and appointment as a Parliamentary Deputy. He assisted the French in the Druze Revolt. A British Consulate report of 1936 described him as "a treacherous blackguard who has committed enough crimes to merit being hanged many times over ... Superlative ruffian, completely and frankly venal; boasts of having sold himself in turn to Turks, Arabs, British and French. Still for sale, but today not worth his price". He had lost much influence to his grandson Fawwaz who had married his sisters to Ibn Saud and Crown Prince Saud.

SHABWA DISPUTE
Shabwa, now a small group of hamlets in the desert some 200 miles north-east of Aden, was once a flourishing walled holy city, a centre of the incense trade and the reputed capital of the Kingdom of Sheba. It was not visited by a European until the late 1930s until which time the local tribes had no connections with the government either of Sanaa or Aden. In 1936 the explorer Philby with an armed Saudi escort arrived and the tribes, fearing annexation to the Kingdom and envious of the advantages that the Hadhramawt, in which it was an enclave, were receiving from pacification, asked for links with the British. The Imam Yahya claimed that Shabwa was part of the territory of his Himyaritic ancestors and protested vehemently with Italian support. The British therefore did not build a post in Shabwa but established one about 55 miles to the north at Husn al-Abr. In the autumn of 1938 the Imam sent a force under the Governor of Harib, Ahmad Nasir Gardai to occupy Shabwa. In turn the

British sent a Political Officer who raised a local force of 200 men and with air support, forced the Yemenis to withdraw. In deference to the continuing Yemeni claim, the British did not remain and permitted no one to visit the area. The Qardai regarded themselves as humiliated and one of their tribesmen was later on the actual assassination of the Imam. After the war there were rumours that oil was to be struck at Shabwa and the Imam Ahmad seeing the British plan to build a road across Awlaqi country as a move towards exploiting the deposits, embarked upon a large-scale campaign of subversion in the Aden Protectorate. No demarcation of frontiers took place and was still vague when oil was discovered there in the mid-1980s. The realisation that it would have to be either shared or fought over played an important part in bringing about the union of North and South Yemen.

SHADWAN ISLAND, Battle of (1970)
Shadwan is an island about 10 miles long at the entrance to the Gulf of Suez. It had radar installations which enabled it to monitor all Israeli air and naval movements in Sinai during the War of Attrition. On 22 January 1970 Israeli troops landed on the island by helicopter meeting fierce hand-to-hand resistance in which the Egyptians lost about 30 men killed while they claimed 55 Israelis killed or wounded. The Israelis put their own losses at 3 killed and 6 wounded. Two Egyptian patrol boats coming to the rescue were sunk by Israeli aircraft with a further 40 sailors drowned. There were reports that the Israelis had intended to remain in occupation but Nasser told the Russians that he would have no option but to launch a major operation to recapture it. Moscow thereupon used the "hot line" to Washington which brought pressure on the Israelis to withdraw which they did after an occupation of 32 hours, taking with them 62 Egyptian prisoners and a British-made radar unit and other military equipment. The rest was destroyed. Two days later an Egyptian ship taking supplies to Shadwan was disabled by Israeli air attack. This was the second time within a month that the Israelis had carried off a complete radar station for on 26 December 1969 they had landed by helicopter at Ras Ghalib on the west coast of the Gulf of Suez. The seven-ton piece of Russian equipment proved of great interest to the US Strategic Air Command but was subsequently returned. Two Egyptian soldiers were killed and four taken prisoner in the operation.

al-SHAFAI, Hussain Mahmud (1918–)
Egyptian Vice-President. The son of an irrigation official, he was commissioned in the cavalry in 1938. He had strong sympathies with the Muslim Brothers. After fighting in the Palestine War, he was one of the original Free Officers. Shafai, as a colonel commanding a tank regiment, played an essential part in the July Revolution when his men seized strategic points in Cairo. Later he preached in the mosques, emphasising the Islamic nature of the new regime. He was a member of the Revolutionary Command Council and was one of the few cavalrymen to support Nasser against Neguib, after whose fall he was Minister of War, employed in a purge of officers. In October 1954 he was a member of the Tribunal that repressed the Muslim Brothers after

the attempt on Nasser's life. From 1954 to 1961 he was Minister of Social Affairs, later combined with Labour and Waqfs. In August 1961 he was appointed one of the Vice-Presidents of the United Arab Republic, retaining the title after Syria split away in October when he was put in charge of religious affairs. In January 1963 he chaired a Tripartite Committee set up to elaborate an ideology for the new Arab Socialist Union. In March 1964 he was appointed one of the Deputy Prime Ministers. After the defeat in the June War he presided over the Court that condemned several senior figures to long terms of imprisonment for plotting against Nasser. In November 1967 Shafai was sent to see King Faysal to arrange for the replacement of the Yemeni leader Marshal Sallal. He was still Deputy Prime Minister for Religious and Social Affairs when, in October 1970, the new President, Anwar Sadat appointed him and Ali Sabri as Vice-Presidents, an office he held alone after the arrest of Sabri in May 1971. He left office in April 1975, reportedly after differences with Sadat who wished also to emphasise that Mubarak was his preferred successor. Later, he with old comrades of the Free Officers, criticised the Camp David Agreement as isolating Egypt from the rest of the Arabs. Shafai was described as an extreme conservative, so religious that he was more like an *alim* than a revolutionary leader. Colourless and self-effacing, he was never personally close to Nasser, but served him loyally and with Sadat was the only original member of the RCC to be still holding office when the President died.

SHAHBANDAR, Abd al-Rahman (1882–1940)

Syrian political leader. He came from a prosperous merchant family of Damascus and he later married into the distinguished al-Azm family. While still a schoolboy he was in trouble for nationalist activities. He trained as a doctor at the Syrian Protestant College and was so brilliant that he was asked to stay a further two years and teach. In 1906 he returned to private practice in Damascus. Originally he supported the Revolution of the Young Turks but turned against it when it imposed Turkification. After the outbreak of war Shahbandar went to Basra and offered his services to the British and was sent to Cairo where he worked as an army doctor. In May 1916 Shahbandar was condemned to death *in absentia* by a Turkish Court Martial. He worked closely with the Arab Bureau, assisting a propaganda journal *al-Kawkab*. He was the leader of the group to whom the Declaration to the Seven promising independence for the Arabs was made. He returned to Damascus soon after its liberation and, always more interested in a united Syria than in Pan-Arabism, founded the Syrian Unity Party. The Amir Faysal put him in charge of preparing Syria's case for the King–Crane Commission, used him for liaison duties with the British and later made him Foreign Minister. Shahbandar was prepared to accept a French protectorate "rather than fall into the bottomless pit to which (our) unguarded steps would lead (us)". When the French invaded, however, he fled to Cairo and was for the second time sentenced to death *in absentia*. He was extremely active in the disputes that surrounded the Syro–Palestinian Congress before taking advantage of an amnesty to return home in 1921. He formed a

nationalist group, the Iron Hand Society, which the French broke up in April 1922, sentencing Shahbandar to 20 years' imprisonment on Arwad Island off Tartus. He was released after 17 months and went to London where his reception by Tory MPs confirmed French suspicions that he was a British agent. He returned to Syria in 1924 and founded the People's Party the following year. When the Druze Revolt started Shahbandar had a secret meeting with Sultan al-Atrash, undertaking to spread the rebellion to Damascus and later the two men headed a "government" in the mountains. When the Revolt was crushed he fled to Cairo and was again condemned to death *in absentia*. He was not on the amnestied list of 1928 and so remained abroad while the National Bloc arose under new leaders. In exile he established close ties with the Amir Abd Allah but quarrelled bitterly with the faction of Shukri al-Quwatli which looked towards Ibn Saud. He hoped to be amnestied in order to take part in the negotiations for the Franco-Syrian Treaty of 1936 but Paris would not accept him. In April 1937 he was allowed to return, receiving a great popular welcome but immediately attacked the government of Jamil Mardam for having given away too much to the French over the Treaty and over Alexandretta. Early in 1938 Mardam sent Shahbandar into forced residence in Bludan and after his release he was kept under surveillance. When the Mardam government fell in March 1939 Shahbandar appeared to be the leading nationalist. He worked for a confederation of Syria, Palestine and Trans-Jordan under the Kingship of Abd Allah with British support. Relations with the National Bloc leaders became so bad that when in July 1940 Shahbandar was assassinated its leaders fled to Baghdad. The killers were put on trial in December and confessed that their motive had been religious as they blamed Shahbandar for the decline of Islam. Six were executed and others imprisoned. Shahbandar was an ardent patriot, highly intelligent, sincere, perhaps the most inspiring orator in the country but inflexible, self-righteous and convinced that he alone represented Syrian nationalism.

al-SHALHI

A Libyan family that acquired great influence and wealth under the Monarchy of Idris. Ibrahim al-Shalhi, born 1899, a member of a family that had originated in Algeria, started to work for Idris at the age of 14 and went into exile in Egypt with him in 1922. He became his most trusted adviser, maintaining the position when Idris became King and was always intensely loyal to his master. Officially Chief of the Royal Estates, Shalhi had far more influence than any Prime Minister although he was always helpful and courteous to politicians and officials. He advanced the careers of young men of ability such as Ben Halim and the business interests of his friends, even those involved in corruption such as that which brought down the government of Qubar. In October 1954 he was murdered by a 19-year-old prince, grandson of Ahmad al-Sanusi who believed that the claims to the throne of his branch of the family were being jeopardised by Ibrahim's support for Hassan al-Ridha al-Sanusi. The Prince was executed and his body displayed at the scene of the crime while seven young Princes were exiled to the Sahara and all members of the family, apart from those in direct line of succession, were stripped of their privileges and banned from official posts. This harsh reaction shows how deeply Idris was distressed by the murder of his best friend by a nephew of the Queen, some said that he never recovered; he adopted Ibrahim's sons as his own responsibility. The eldest, Busayri, was appointed Superintendent of the Royal Household where he had the same influence a his father, able to make or break Prime Ministers. Busayri, despite education at Exeter University and marriage to an Englishwoman, was regarded as anti-British and cultivated good relations with Egypt. Another son, Umar, (born 1934), became the most important businessman in the country with commissions on most major deals and investing huge sums abroad while a third, Abd al-Aziz, as Director of Military Operations controlled the Cyrenaica Defence Force and was involved in enormous contracts such as one to buy missiles from the UK. Busayri was killed in a car crash in 1964 but his place as chief adviser was taken by Umar, a man of great intelligence and drive. To give Umar tribal backing the King insisted that his Prime Minister Maziq should give him his daughter although she was already betrothed; people were shocked at the ostentatious wedding which cost £10 million. It is appears that Colonel Abd al-Aziz, knowing the intention of Idris to abdicate, was planning a military coup in conjunction with Nasser, who had been receiving Libyan subsidies since the June War and with whom he had established a close relationship, to preserve the position of the family and prevent the succession of the unpopular and ineffective Crown Prince: he got young officers of dubious loyalty out of the way on courses in England and issued ammunition to selected units. At the time that Qadafi overthrew the Monarchy, Umar Shalhi who was abroad with the King, went to London where he attempted without success to persuade the British Government to intervene. He later organised and financed a coup by mercenaries to oust the new regime and liberate his brother Abd al-Aziz from prison. The plot failed as the British, American and Italian governments feared the consequences of the overthrow of the anti-communist Qadafi. Umar was sentenced *in absentia* to life imprisonment but continued to live as a prosperous businessman in Switzerland.

SHAMIR PLAN (1989)

The newly-formed administration of President Bush was less uncritically pro-Israeli than that of Reagan and brought strong pressure on Prime Minister Shamir to make concessions in return for peace. On a visit to Washington in April 1989 Shamir put forward a plan proposing free elections in the West Bank and Gaza to form a delegation, who should not be members of the Palestine Liberation Organisation, to negotiate an "interim settlement" when a "self-governing administration" might be established. This interim period would be an "essential test of co-operation and co-existence" after which there would be negotiations for a "final settlement" in which Israel would discuss any option including Palestinian autonomy. The Plan was qualified by a clause which stated that Israel's readiness to proceed with elections in the occupied territories was conditional upon simultaneous progress towards peace between Israel and its neighbours. This unrealistic proviso effectively ruled out any practical result. Even so the Plan was attacked by the more hard-line members of his Likud Party and on 5 July Shamir was forced to modify it by excluding the Arab inhabitants of East Jerusalem and clearly stating that neither was the PLO a viable partner for negotiations nor was the eventual establishment of a Palestinian state acceptable. The existence of the Shamir Plan enabled the Israeli Government to discount the Baker Proposals as unnecessary.

SHARAF, Abd al-Hamid (1939–80)

Jordanian Prime Minister. He was born in Baghdad where his father Sharif Sharaf, a leader of tribesmen in the Arab Revolt singled out for praise by T. E. Lawrence, had fled after the Hashemites had been driven from the Hijaz. Sharaf was appointed by Rashid Ali al-Gilani as Regent of Iraq in 1941 and was subsequently exiled to Rhodesia then imprisoned in Iraq until 1947. His family spent the war in Berlin and Istanbul before being invited by King Abd Allah to live in Amman where he gave them a villa in the palace grounds. Abd al-Hamid attended an English school and an Islamic College before going in 1955 to the American University of Beirut. There he became involved with ardent Arab nationalists, writing pamphlets and editing a newspaper. This angered King Hussain who had him briefly imprisoned. Having taken a degree in philosophy and later in international law he left the Arab nationalists as they became more socialist and was reconciled with the King who appointed him Director of Arab Affairs at the Foreign Ministry. In 1963 he was Assistant to the Director-General of Broadcasting before in 1965 he entered the Cabinet of Wasfi al-Tall as Minister of Information and Culture. Sharaf founded a national gallery and the first TV station and did much to increase public interest in drama, art and folklore: he was an enthusiast for the cinema. After the disaster of the June War in 1967 he was appointed Ambassador to Washington where he also took a Doctorate at Georgetown University. After a very successful period there he was recalled in 1976 to become Head of the Royal Diwan, principal adviser to the King whom he helped with the difficult decision to put Arab solidarity above relations with the West after the Camp David agreements. In December 1979 he was appointed Prime Minister amidst general feelings that this represented a fresh start: the King spoke of a "new leap forward in all fields". Sharaf appointed a Cabinet of young newcomers, including the first woman Minister. He spoke of "respect for all", made himself readily accessible and declared his intention to ensure dialogue with the public and their participation in decentralisation to improve education, welfare, female rights, labour legislation and press freedom. Aiming to make Jordan a model for the Arab world he endeavoured to give the country a new radical, social-reforming face: in this he was helped by his close relationship with the King to whom he appeared a partner rather than a servant. Political parties, however, were still banned and parliamentary government awaited the solution of the

Palestinian problem although he enhanced the powers of the National Consultative Council. He worked for better relations with the Palestinians, criticising the American attitude towards them as too simplistic. On 3 July 1980 Sharaf died suddenly of a heart attack, greatly mourned at home and abroad. He was a tall, aristocratic, elegant man, calm, unpompous and informal. In a depressing period he had given hope for a better future.

SHARM AL-SHAYKH

Sharm al-Shaykh is a small bay on the east coast of the Sinai Peninsula from which it is possible to control the Straits of Tiran, the 800-yard wide entrance to the Gulf of Aqaba. In 1954 it was fortified by the Egyptians with coastal guns in order to blockade the Israeli port of Eilat and its capture was one of Israel's main military objectives in the Suez War. They delayed acceptance of a cease-fire until the garrison of 1,200 men had been overwhelmed; over 100 Egyptians were killed. It took immense American pressure and an agreement by Nasser that it should be occupied not by Egyptian troops but by UNEF to get the Israelis to withdraw at the beginning of March 1957. In the next decade the population of Eilat trebled, oil could be imported from Iran and there was even talk of a rival to the Suez Canal across Israeli territory. In May 1967 Nasser ordered that UNEF should be withdrawn and Egyptian troops reoccupied Sharm al-Shaykh. On 23 May Nasser announced that the Straits would be closed to Israeli shipping. Some mines were laid. On the same day the Israeli Prime Minister Levi Eshkol stated that closing the Straits would be "an act of aggression" against Israel and President Johnson denounced it as "illegal". The June War started on 5 June and two days later Sharm al-Shaykh was captured by Israeli parachutists. They remained there until after the signature of the Egyptian–Israeli Peace Treaty of March 1979 in which freedom of navigation in the Straits was guaranteed.

SHATT AL-ARAB DISPUTE

The Shatt al-Arab is formed by the junction of the Tigris and the Euphrates at Qurna and flows for over a hundred miles to the Gulf. It is augmented by rivers such as the Karen from Iran and on its banks were the main ports of Iraq and Persia, Basra and Muhammarah, respectively 70 and 50 miles from the open sea. A sand bar near the mouth restricts the size of the shipping that may use it. The boundaries between Ottoman-ruled Iraq and Persia were not precisely defined although the Erzerum Treaty of 1847 recognised Persian sovereignty over Muhammarah, Abadan island and the eastern bank and allowed free navigation on the river. The fact that the international frontier was not, as normally in water boundaries, stipulated as the *Thalweg*, the middle of the deepest channel, was not important until the discovery of oil in Persia in 1908; the country's main port was legally cut off from the sea at a time when vast amounts of equipment had to be imported. In 1913-14 an Anglo-Russian commission surveyed part of the frontier and it was agreed that anchorage of Muhammarah should be assigned to Persia. After the strong-minded Reza Pahlavi became Shah there were constant incidents as the Persians often aggressively ignored the Iraqi river authorities and complained that tolls collected were not used as stipulated for improving navigation but disappeared into the Treasury in Baghdad. At the end of 1934 the dispute was referred to the League of Nations which failed to produce a settlement. In 1937, however, Iran and Iraq about to become partners in the Saadabad Pact signed a Treaty that the waters out to the *Thalweg* off Abadan, the oil refinery, should be recognised as Persian and that elsewhere ships should fly the Iraqi flag and carry Iraqi pilots. After the war Iran and Iraq were allies in the Baghdad Pact until it was denounced by Abd al-Krim Qassim in March 1959. Later that year he appeared to threaten action to reassert Iraqi sovereignty over the waters off Abadan; the Shah moved troops to the frontier and Qassim had to back down looking foolish. The two governments were thoroughly suspicious of each other and the Shah seized the opportunity of the Kurdish Revolt (I) to encourage rebels against his neighbour which, in return penalised any reference to the "Persian" Gulf and laid claims to the province of Khuzistan with its Arabic-speaking population. In April 1969 there was considerable tension as minor incidents escalated with both sides appealing to the UN while Arab monarchs attempted to mediate. The Shah renounced previous agreements, stated that he would use force to assure the *Thalweg* and refused to pay tolls. On 30 November 1971 Iraq broke off relations with Iran which had just annexed the Tunb and Abu Musa islands and did not resume them for two years. In January and February 1974 soldiers on both sides were killed in border incidents. The Shah encouraged Mulla Mustafa Barzani to launch the Kurdish Revolt (II) which he supplied with money and arms until March 1975 when he abandoned it in return for the Algiers Pact in which Saddam Hussain formally recognised the *Thalweg* as the international frontier. This was not challenged until September 1980 when, assuming Iran reduced to impotence by the Islamic Revolution, Saddam started the Iran–Iraq War in the course of which the Shatt al-Arab became unusable and all installations on it were destroyed. In October 1982 Saddam, facing defeat, stated willingness to revert to the Algiers Pact in return for peace but Khomeini, intent on his overthrow, refused. In August 1990 after invading Kuwait, Saddam, desperate to neutralise Iran, formally accepted the Algiers Pact as still valid.

SHAW REPORT (1930)

The Wailing Wall Incident of August 1929, the first serious clash between Arabs and Jews cost over 250 lives and the British Government appointed Sir Walter Shaw, former Chief Justice of the Straits Settlements, to chair a Commission of an MP from each of the three major political parties to report upon its causes. The Report published in March 1930 declared that the attacks upon the Jews had not been pre-meditated or organised and were not directed against the British authorities. Charges that the Mufti, Haj Amin al-Hussaini was responsible were not substantiated. No blame rested on the Government or the police. Shaw saw the cause as disappointment amongst the Arabs that their political and national expectations had not been met and fear for their economic future. He recommended

Commissions of Investigation into the organisation of the police and into immigration. He recommended that the Government should clearly state its policy on Jewish immigration and that the eviction of rural Arab landowners should be stopped until an agricultural survey had been held to ascertain whether the country could support a larger population. The League of Nations should be asked to investigate rights at the Wailing Wall. The Zionist Organisation should be reminded that it did not participate in governing the country. The Labour Party MP dissented from some of the conclusions, attaching more blame to the Mufti and the Government of Palestine. The Report was received with disappointment by the Jews and led to the Hope–Simpson Commission and the Passfield White Paper.

SHIAH UPRISING AND THE PUNITIVE CAMPAIGN (Iraq) (1991–3)

Before it became clear that Operation Desert Storm would be such an overwhelming success, the Americans encouraged the Kurds of Northern Iraq and the Shiah of the South to rise against Saddam Hussain. On 3 March 1991 the Iraqi Government accepted cease-fire terms and immediately the Shiah succeeded in seizing the main southern cities of Basra, Najaf, Karbala, Nasriyyah and Diwaniyyah. By then, however, the Americans had come to fear that the breakup of Iraq would cause more instability and the spread of Iranian influence and saw the best solution as the overthrow of Saddam by a Sunni junta. Reluctance to support the Uprising was increased by the claim of the extremist religious group al-Dawah, based in Iran, that they were leading it and by evidence of fanaticism such as attacks on Basra hotels which sold alcohol. The Americans accepted the surrender of many of Saddam's hated Republican Guards to save them from lynch mobs. The Shiah Spiritual Leader, Ayatollah Abu al-Qasim al-Khuei sent his son to tell General Schwarzkopf that the insurgents were aiming for democracy not Shiah rule but was warned against escalation which might prejudice an army coup in Baghdad. The Iraqi Government therefore had a free hand to repress the revolt which they did in a fortnight with the utmost brutality and there were reports of officials cutting off heads with swords, patients being thrown out of hospital windows and of nerve gas being used in Karbala. Unlike the Kurds, the Shiah had no real organisation and their brethren in Baghdad never became involved. Ayatollah Khuei was kidnapped and taken to Baghdad where he was compelled to condemn the Uprising on TV. By the end of March it is possible that 250,000 had been killed, 10,000 had taken refuge in Iran and thousands more pinned down in Marshes as the Kuwaiti and other Arab governments were unwilling to admit Iraqi Shiah and UNIKOM was unwilling to accept responsibility for them. On 3 April the Iranian President Rafsanjani accused the US of indifference to these horrors and to the apparently deliberate destruction of the Shiah heritage. Najaf and Karbala were shut off for six months while there was systematic looting of the Holy Places, looting, burning of libraries, bulldozing of cemeteries and the imprisonment of 500 ulama in Najaf alone. Unrest continued and in January 1992 76 were executed

for an anti-Saddam riot in Karbala. The Government then began a Punitive Campaign (Hamlah al-Tadibiyyah), using about 75,000 troops with air support, against the Shiah tribes living in the 6,000 square miles of the Marshes. During December 1991 and January 1992 it was estimated that 70 villages had been destroyed and their residents transported to camps in the north. After the withdrawal of UN personnel and relief workers at the end of June 1992, it appeared as if Baghdad was repeating the Anfal Campaign in which parts of Kurdistan had been systematically depopulated. Parts of the Marshes were drained by the work on the Third River, making life impossible for villagers dependent upon their water buffaloes, streams were poisoned and exits were mined. In August 1992 the Americans, without reference to the Security Council, imposed a no-fly zone for Iraqi aircraft south of 32nd parallel despite reservations on the part of its Arab allies. They were supported by British and French aircraft and in the first 12 hours 100 sorties were flown. They were not allowed to attack Iraqi troops on the ground and the burning of villages continued with widespread torture and other appalling atrocities. In December, after the Allies had flown 7,500 sorties, an Iraqi plane was shot down in the no-fly zone and in January 1993, possibly hoping to exploit the change over of American Presidents or to divert attention from economic hardships, Saddam Hussain positioned anti-aircraft missiles in the zone. After he had refused to move them, on 13 January 1993 in what the Americans called "a spanking, not a real beating" the sites were attacked by fighter aircraft. Progress on the Third River dried out large areas of the Marshes increasing the hardships of the inhabitants, 350,000 of whom were said by the Iraqi opposition to to be starving and in March there was a suggestion that aircraft might breach the dykes that were holding back the Great Rivers. In July American aircraft, still patrolling the no-fly zone fired at Iraq radar but a new offensive started on land and the United Nations High Commission for Refugees reported that 150 people a day were escaping from the Marshes, adding to the 15,000 already waiting to cross into Iran.

SHIHAB, Amir Khalid (1892–?)

Lebanese Prime Minister. A Sunni Muslim member of the famous Shihab family he was born in Hasbayya and went to a Christian College in Damascus but had no higher education. He was elected a Deputy in 1922 and was a member of the committee which drafted the Constitution in 1926. The following year he was Minister of Finance in the first government of Bishara al-Khouri. The Amir was known to be pro-French and in 1936 was considered as a candidate for the Presidency. He was Speaker of the Chamber of Deputies before becoming Prime Minister in March 1938. The Shihab government lasted only until October when it fell apart with Ministers mainly concerned with pursuing their own interests. In March 1943 he was one of the three Ministers in the government of Ayyub Thabit which had been set up to supervise elections. After the war he was Ambassador to Jordan until in 1952 the new President Camille Chamoun, whose first Ministerial post had been in Shihab's 1938 Cabinet, found it difficult to find a Sunni Muslim to take office after the dramatic events of the resignation of Khouri. His choice eventually fell on Shihab who formed a Cabinet of three government officials in October. He empowered to rule by decree for six months and embarked on a series of drastic reforms, altering the administrative system, dismissing officials, changing the electoral law by reducing the number of Deputies, giving the vote to women, and tightening the grip of the government auditing authorities. His Ministry created a Development Board and accepted American money for irrigation and a survey of a project to increase use of the Litani River. Attempts were made to spread taxes more fairly and develop tourism. As a government of functionaries it was, however, unpopular amongst politicians and Shihab resigned in April 1953 to avoid an Assembly vote of no-confidence. Shihab continued in politics and also was active in business. Shihab was respected as a bold and energetic man but had little time for wooing supporters.

SHIP OF RETURN (1988)

The Israeli Government, contrary to international law and Security Council Resolutions 607 and 608 expelled Palestinians from the West Bank for political activities. Some Palestinians determined to follow the famous example set by the Zionists in 1947 when they won a great propaganda victory by loading the ship *Exodus* with victims of the Holocaust and sailing it to Palestine. The Palestinians hired a ship, the *Silver Paloma*, and announced that it would sail from Athens with 135 deportees on 10 February 1988. Large numbers of journalists arrived to see the event but the Israelis brought such intense pressure on the owners of the ship that they withdrew their agreement. The Palestinians subsequently found four other ships but the same thing happened. Later the Palestinians were about to buy a rusty old ferry in Cyprus when it was withdrawn from the market and the Palestians dealing with the purchase murdered in a car bomb explosion. Then it was announced that a ship would sale from Larnaca but before it could do it was blown up. The Israeli Defence Minister Yitzhak said that the Government had been determined that the Palestinians would not achieve their purpose.

SHKAKI, Fathi (1951–)

Palestinian leader. Born in Rafah refugee camp in the Gaza Strip, he studied medicine at Cairo University where he was influenced by militant Islamic groups such as Takfir wa al-Hijrah and the writings of Saiyyid Qutb. In 1979 he published *Khomeini, the Islamic Solution and the Alternative*. In 1981 he returned and practised in a hospital in East Jerusalem. Shkaki started to gather followers who later became known as the Islamic Jihad and, regarded by the occupation authorities as particularly dangerous for combining religion and nationalism, was in 1983 imprisoned for a year. He was rearrested in 1986 and deported to Lebanon in 1988. After a visit to Tehran where he was greatly impressed by the Ayatollah Khomeini, he settled in Damascus. He ordered numerous terrorist operations but denied any attacks on Israelis outside Palestine. Shkaki received financial backing from Iran and worked closely with Hizbullah. He is described as cheerful and gently courteous.

SHTAURA COUNCIL MEETING (1962)

After the breakup of the United Arab Republic there were strong disagreements in Syria between those who wanted some sort of federal union with Egypt and those who, like Akram al-Hawrani totally opposed any relations with President Nasser. Violent polemics were exchanged between Syrian anti-Nasserists and the Egyptian propaganda machine and on 21 July 1962 the Syrian Government claimed to have uncovered a plot hatched by the Egyptian Embassy in Beirut for its overthrow. An appeal was made to the Arab League and a Council Meeting took place in Shtaura beginning on 22 August. The Iraqis did not attend. Nasser, deliberately provocative, was represented by three pro-Union Syrians who had remained in Cairo. The Syrians presented a "Black Book" of evidence of crimes committed by the Egyptians during the Union and within Egypt itself. The Egyptians accused the Syrians of torturing nationalists and serving imperialism. The Syrians countered by alleging that Nasser was conspiring with the Americans against the Palestinians. The Saudis and Jordanians also complained of Egyptian meddling and intrigue. The Egyptians walked out and the meeting adjourned without taking any decisions in such uproar that the police had to be summoned. During the Unity Talks of March 1963 it was agreed to expunge all mention of the Shtaura Meeting from Arab League records.

SHULTZ INITIATIVE (1988)

The outbreak of the Intifadah in the winter of 1987/8 led Secretary of State Shultz to put forward proposals for a settlement of the Arab–Israeli dispute. In February 1988 he suggested that this might be on a basis of Palestinian autonomy in an entity linked with Jordan and that this should be negotiated through a joint Jordanian–Palestinian delegation. Direct talks should start in December 1988. There would be a transition period of three years during which a permanent settlement could be reached. The Israeli army would retain responsibility for the defence of the Occupied Territories but would withdraw from certain parts which would be policed by Jordanians. Elections for Palestinian officials would be held during 1989. Israeli settlers might remain but would be subject to the Palestinian authorities. Shultz was prepared to accept an international conference on the Middle East – an idea long resisted by Israel and the US. The Shultz Plan was a slightly new version of the traditional American policy of working through King Hussain but it was obvious that he had no control over what was happening in the West Bank and Gaza and that the Palestine Liberation Organisation had to be treated as an independent actor. This was stressed by Arab Leaders at the Algiers Summit in August. The Israeli Government under Shamir was not prepared to concede territory for peace so the Shultz initiative was satisfactory to neither party.

SHUNAH AGREEMENT (1949)

Shunah in the Jordan valley was the favourite winter residence of King Abd Allah and in March 1949 was the scene of a series of secret meetings continuing over five nights with the Israelis to negotiate the armistice for which official meetings were being held in Rhodes. The Israeli delegation, led by the Acting Foreign Minister Walter Eytan included Yigael Yadin and Moshe Dayan. All the Jordanian Cabinet, headed by Tawfiq Abu al-Huda were originally present but the leading parts were later played by Fawzi al-Mulqi and Samir al-Rifai. After denouncing his Ministers to the Israelis, stating that they and the Egyptians had forced him into war, Abd Allah himself withdrew. Frontiers were specified but were arbitrary and not clearly demarcated nor expected to be permanent. In Jerusalem there was to be a stand-still where the fighting had stopped. It was agreed that the Iraqi troops in the Janin-Tul Karm-Nablus area should be replaced by the Arab Legion and thus effectively annexed to Trans-Jordan which acquired an extra 2,100 square miles of territory. In the south the frontier was to follow the old line between Palestine and Trans-Jordan and thus gave Israel the Negev which they had not fully occupied and which had not been assigned to them in the UN Partition plan. Israel there and in Western Galilee added another 2,380 square miles, thus increasing its area by more than 30%. A map was drawn by a British Brigadier, who represented Glubb Pasha, and Yadin and initialled by the King. It was then taken to Rhodes and signed as if it had been drawn up there. Abd Allah managed to keep his dealings secret from his people and the fact that some of them became known caused a political crisis in November–December 1951 which led to the dismissal of his Prime Minister Said al-Mufti.

SIBAI, Yusuf (1917–78)

Egyptian writer and politician. Coming from an aristocratic family, he served in the cavalry and retired as a colonel. He taught military history at Staff College and was in charge of the Army Museum. In 1957 he was appointed Secretary-General of the Higher Arts Council and worked with Sarwat Okasha to mobilise the support of intellectuals for the regime and also to repress its critics, preferring ideological correctness to literary merit. He was also Secretary-General of the Afro-Asian Peoples' Solidarity Congress which was set up in 1957 to encourage anti-colonial movements. Sibai was also Secretary-General of the Egyptian Writers' Association. He founded the Short Story Club and wrote bitterly realistic novels about the poorer quarters of Cairo. He also wrote several film scripts. In March 1973 Sadat made him Minister of Culture to which in August 1975 he added the portfolio of Information. In March 1976 he replaced Ihsan Abd al-Qaddus as Chairman of *al-Ahram* from which he started to purge left-wing journalists. He was a close friend of the President whom he accompanied on his Knesset visit to Jerusalem and also to Europe and America. On 18 February 1978 while attending a conference of the Afro-Asian Congess in Nicosia he was murdered by two Palestinians in the Hilton Hotel. Sadat's impulsive action in attempting to seize the killers led to the Larnaca Airfield shoot-out in which 15 Egyptian commandos were killed and a breach of diplomatic relations between Cairo and Nicosia. Although the Palestine Liberation Organisation officially denounced the murder

as "criminal and cowardly" there was a further deterioration in relations between the Egyptians and Palestinians as crowds at his funeral called for revenge. His murderers received death sentences which were later commuted to life imprisonment.

al-SIBSI, Baji Qaid (1926–)

Tunisian politician. He came from an aristocratic family of Turkish origin and was educated at Sadiqi College before taking a degree in Law at the Sorbonne, where he was Vice-President of the North African students. In 1950 he met Bourguiba, was captivated by him, worked in his office and gave his legal services to arrested nationalists. After independence he was Director firstly of Tourism and then, after there had been a plot against the life of the President, of Police. In 1965 Sibsi was made Minister of the Interior where his position, caught between the socialism of his colleague Ahmad Ben Salah and the landed interests represented by Mme Bourguiba, was often very difficult. He was a member of the Politburo of the Parti Socialiste Destourien and of the National Assembly. In the major government changes of November 1969 Sibsi moved to the Defence Ministry but only nine months later went as Ambassador to Paris. In October 1971 after the Monastir Congress in which liberals such as Ahmad Mestiri and Bahi Ladgham were ousted by the supporters of autocracy, Sibsi resigned his post. In 1974, having signed a memorandum condemning the exclusion of the Central Committee from making any decisions about the forthcoming Congress, he was expelled from the Party. Alarmed that Sibsi might join the Mouvement des Démocrates Socialistes that Mestiri was projecting, the new comparatively liberal Prime Minister Muhammad Mzali coaxed him back into the PSD, made him a Minister of State and a member of the Party Politburo. In 1981 he became Foreign Minister and was regarded as a possible future Prime Minister. He held the office for a very active five years, greatly preoccupied with the antics of Qadafi whose attitude to Tunisia varied between ardent wooing and threats of war and who in 1982 three times, uninvited, visited the country. In 1985 Sibsi had to seek the support of other Arab countries after Qadafi had expelled large numbers of Tunisian workers in an attempt at coercion. In 1982 Sibsi took Tunisia into OAPEC. In November 1982 he called for a People's War against Israel as conventional wars had failed and declared that he would reconsider relations with any country, including the USA, that supported Zionism: the following year he claimed that he had given Secretary Schultz an "earful" of criticism, demanding a more balanced attitude. He was very active in North African affairs, particularly friendly with Hassan II who used him as a go-between in relations with Algeria. He was regarded as a protégé of Mme Bourguiba and in September 1986, after her disgrace, was removed from the Foreign Ministry and sent as Ambassador to Bonn. Bourguiba had called him "a man for delicate and difficult missions" and he was regarded as conciliatory but not weak, reputedly fond of intrigue. In appearance, fair haired with blue eyes, he was normally taken for a European.

SIDQI, (1930–)

Egyptian Prime Minister. Educated at the Sorbonne. Professor of General Finance at Cairo University from 1958 to 1973. Cultural Attaché in Paris from 1973 to 1980. He was appointed President of the Government Advisory Commission for Economic and Financial Affairs 1980–5 and President of the Government Audit Office 1985–6. He became Prime Minister on 9 November 1986.

SIFI, Mokdad (1949–)

Algerian Prime Minister. Born in Tebessa. He was Cabinet Secretary under Ghozali and became Minister of Equipment in July 1992. He survived an assassination attempt in early 1993 and was appointed Prime Minister after hard-liner Malik had been dismissed. His appointment was welcomed by FIS.

SILWAN EVICTIONS (1991)

Silwan was a village within the Jerusalem city limits, entirely inhabited by Arabs. In October 1991 at least 50 armed Jewish settlers broke into and seized at least seven houses, claiming to have bought the properties from the Israeli authorities. The police then forcibly evicted the settlers from all but one house where several members of the Knesset and one Jewish family were permitted to remain. The police then sealed the houses to prevent the Palestinian occupants returning to their homes. The Arab Mukhtar stated that 17 Palestinian families had received eviction notes from the Occupation authorities in charge of "absentee property". On 8 December the Shamir Cabinet, overriding its own chief legal officers and in breach of international law, decided to allow Jewish settlers to move in as long as they held documents "valid under Israeli law". Six Palestinian families were then expelled from their homes by settlers and police. Later in the month a mixed crowd of 3,000 Jews and Arabs demonstrated in a protest march but the incident showed the complete disregard of the Occupation authorities for the rights of West Bank Arabs.

SINAI DISENGAGEMENT AGREEMENT (1975)

The Disengagement Agreement signed at Kilometre 101 in January 1974 left the Egyptians in occupation of a narrow strip, about six miles wide, along the east bank of the Suez Canal. After intense diplomacy by Dr Kissinger, who made six visits to Egypt in a fortnight, an agreement was signed in Geneva on 4 September 1975 which provided for the withdrawal of Israeli troops from a further 1,000 square miles, a strip between 12 and 26 miles wide, while leaving 95% of Sinai under their occupation. The territory returned included the Abu Rudais oilfields which were transferred to joint Egyptian–UN administration. Between the two armies there would be a buffer zone behind which would be a further strip in which it was agreed that neither side would maintain more than 8,000 men or weapons which could reach the other. The Israelis would withdraw to the eastern end of the strategic Mitla and Gidi passes which were to be demilitarised and a maximum of 200 US civilians stationed there to monitor two electronic stations, one operated by Egyptian and the other by Israeli personnel. The Egyptians would permit the passage of non-military cargoes to and from Israel through the Suez Canal which had been reopened in June. Other clauses stated that the Agreement was a first step towards a just and durable peace, based on Resolution 338, agreed that there should be no use of force or blockade and reaffirmed the "essential" role of UNEF. It was expected that Egypt would receive between $1,500 million and $2,500 million in aid, mostly from the USA and the Americans promised to try to bring about a peace settlement between Israel and Syria. Sadat achieved the main objectives for which he had launched the October War – the full involvement of the US in peace-making. The Israelis were promised compensation of $350 million a year for the loss of Abu Rudais and that the Americans would make oil available if the Israelis could not buy it on the open market. Congress would be asked for $2,500 million in aid and military supplies would be maintained to ensure its military superiority. A Memorandum of Understanding pledged that the US would be "fully responsive" to Israeli needs, that it would not negotiate with the Palestine Liberation Organisation and that they would consult in the event of Russian intervention in the area. Nevertheless Begin and the Likud Party voted against the Agreement which was also denounced by Iraq, Libya, Syria and the Palestinians while the Russians, alarmed at American dominance, refused to attend the signing ceremony. President Ford hailed the agreement as "one of the most historic achievements of the decade, perhaps of the century". After the Egypt–Israel Peace Treaty of 1979 the rest of Sinai reverted to Egyptian rule.

SIRAJ AL-DIN, Fuad (1906–)

Egyptian politician. The son of a large landowner, he joined the Wafd in which, as Secretary-General after the departure of Makram Ubayd he was the acknowledged successor of Nahhas. With his great belly, pendulous jowls and perpetual cigar, he symbolised all that was worst in pre-Revolutionary Egypt but he was a consummate politician, cunning, strong, highly competent, witty and demagogic. He was believed to have assisted Mme Nahhas in "rigging" the Alexandria Cotton Exchange. As Minister of the Interior he tried to distract attention from corruption and incompetence by winning over the Muslim Brothers and encouraging attacks on the British in the Suez Canal Zone. Convinced that the anti-British reaction would help his party, he ordered policemen to fight to the death against British tanks in the Ismailiyyah Massacre in January 1952. The popular indignation led to the burning of Cairo on Black Saturday, which engaged on private business, he delayed efforts to stop; some even alleged that he had instigated the trouble to discredit King Farouq. He was dismissed and went off to Europe from which he hurried back after the July Revolution, hoping to be appointed Prime Minister. He tried to prevent agrarian reform and was arrested in September but released in December. He was arrested in September 1953 and in January 1954 was sentenced to 15 years' imprisonment for having "thrown the nation into the battle of the Canal" with insufficient preparation and negligence on Black Saturday. General Neguib later said that the sentence was "a blunder and an injustice". Stephens says he was arrested again in autumn 1962. In 1974 his political rights were restored. In February 1978 after Sadat had permitted the formation of political parties the New Wafd chose Siraj al-Din as its President and he declared that the real revolution had been the Egyptian Uprising of 1919 while that of 1952 was merely a coup. Sadat replied by denouncing him as a "feudalist" and a "cadaver" and in May 1978 insisted on a referendum, one of the main targets of which was Siraj al-Din on the question of whether those responsible for "corrupting public life" before 1952 should be allowed to hold office or be published in the media. It was announced that 98.29% had voted and approved it and he was duly banned. In September 1981 when Sadat carried out a major purge of the opposition, Siraj al-Din was amongst those arrested but he was released by the new President Mubarak.

SIRTE GULF INCIDENT (1981)
In the late spring of 1981 relations between Washington and Tripoli deteriorated rapidly and in May the Americans having expelled all Libyan diplomats, advised their 1,500–2,000 citizens to return home. In June the State Department declared that it would help any country attacked by Qadafi and in July the press reported that the CIA was planning to murder him. In August the American Sixth Fleet was ordered to undertake manoeuvres inside the Gulf of Sirte, an area which since 1973 Libya had claimed as its territorial waters, with the intention of provoking an incident. In 1976 Libya had submitted a document to the UN declaring the whole area within a line from Benghazi to Misurata, rather than the normal 12-mile limit was the maritime boundary. On 19 August when the Fleet was about thirty miles from the Libyan coast, two Russian-built Libyan fighter aircraft came to investigate. One fired a missile whereupon both were shot down by American fighters. Qadafi complained to the UN and threatened to launch a world war and to make the Sirte Gulf redder than the Red Sea with American blood if they ever returned. In December President Reagan stated that a squad of Libyan assassins had been sent to Washington to kill him. Reagan's detestation of Qadafi was to fester and led to the attempt to kill him in the Tripoli Bombing of April 1986.

SIWAR AL-DHAHAB, Abd al-Rahman (1934–)
Sudanese Head of State. He was born in Omdurman with a family background of allegiance to the Mirghani/Khatmiyyah *tariqah* and graduated from the Military Academy in 1958. Later he had further training in Jordan, Britain and Egypt. In February 1983 President Nimeiri appointed him to the Central Leadership of the Sudan Socialist Union as representative of the military. In March 1985 Nimeiri gave him the post of Commander-in-Chief which he had himself held during his sixteen years in power and made him Minister of Defence. Three weeks later, faced by a general strike, the possibility of civilian violence and an army mutiny, in the absence of the President, fifteen officers who were able to assure the loyalty of units in and around the capital established the Transitional Military Council to which they co-opted the leaders of the National

Alliance for National Salvation. Siwar al-Dhahab, the senior, became acting Head of State after overcoming considerable scruples about breaking his oath to Nimeiri. He had no known political affiliations and stated that he would hold power for an interim period while multi-party elections took place. He immediately suspended the Constitution, dismantled the hated security apparatus and abolished the SSU so the general strike was called off despite some reservations on the part of the NANS. He did not repeal the September Laws in which Nimeiri had imposed his version of *Shariah* upon the country but suspended the activities of "decisive justice courts" which had ordereded mutilations and he ended the system of Islamic taxation which had added to the financial chaos. A month before the take-over the country had been declared bankrupt. Some of Nimeiri's henchmen were imprisoned for corruption and the Saudi businessman Adnan Khashoggi was deprived of his stake in the Southern oilfields. The TMC appointed a civilian Prime Minister, Jazuli Dafallah. The new regime faced a series of problems, a civil war in the South in which 10,000 guerrillas were indulging in hit-and-run attacks and which was costing Sud one million a day, famine in the Western and Red Sea provinces and a massive influx of refugees from civil wars in Chad and Ethiopia. Siwar al-Dhahab took personal charge of overseeing famine relief. Relations with the neighbouring states, inherited from Nimeiri, were strained but Siwar al-Dhahab quickly sent two members of the TMC to Libya where they reached an agreement with Qadafi by which neither state would support the other's opponents. An attempt to conciliate Ethiopia was less successful. Egypt, which had had particularly close ties with Nimeiri, refused to extradite him and was alarmed that the coup might lead to an increase in Libyan influence in the Sudan remained aloof, but Siwar al-Dhahab visited Cairo and stated that he would maintain "blood ties of common destiny with sister Egypt". The wooing of Libya and Ethiopia was part of a two-pronged strategy for dealing with the Sudan People's Liberation Movement by cutting off their external support while he made conciliatory gestures such as reversing Nimeiri's decision which had broken up the autonomous Region into three provinces. Siwar al-Dhahab also appointed three Southern Ministers instead of one under Nimeiri, admitted past mistakes by Khartoum and promised economic benefits. A minor military mutiny in September 1985 was mistaken by the Government for "a racist coup" and hundreds of Southerners were arrested. Multi-party elections were held on schedule in March 1986 and after their conclusion Siwar al-Dhahab retired and took no further part in politics. He had performed good service to his country by presiding over a return to democracy and it was hardly his fault that the civilian politicians mismanaged affairs so badly that there was a further military take-over three years later.

SKHIRAT ATTEMPT (1971)
Skhirat, a royal palace on the Atlantic coast of Morocco between Rabat and Casablanca, was the scene of an attempt upon the life of Hassan II on 10 July 1971. About 800 guests including diplomats and political leaders were attending the King's birthday party when

about 1,400 young cadets from the NCO school at Ahermoumou in the Atlas Mountains burst into the palace just after 2 p.m. spraying bullets in all directions. About a hundred people were killed including the Belgian Ambassador, the former Prime Minister Ahmad Bahnini and the Commander of the Air Force and more than 200 wounded. The other guests were forced to lie on the floor for more than two hours. Some details of what happened are obscure. The King, accompanied by the Prime Minister Ahmad Laraki, the Interior Minister General Oufkir and others appear to have taken refuge in a bathroom while some senior officers named on a list were shot. In the confusion the leader of the attackers General Muhammad Madbuh, the Head of the King's Military Household, was killed apparently by accident. The other leader Colonel Muhammad Ababou went off with some followers to take over strategic installations in Rabat and proclaim a Revolutionary Council. After three hours the King emerged and was recognised by the cadets who paid homage to him before he led them in prayer. Many of them were said to have been drugged while others believed that they had come to save the King from a conspiracy. At GHQ in Rabat the Chief of Staff and Ababou were killed. The remaining rebels, leaderless, melted away or surrendered. The King delegated to General Oufkir "all civil and military powers" to restore order. Later four generals and six other officers were executed by firing squad. On the evening of the coup Colonel Qadafi declared absolute support for the coup and that he was putting his forces on full alert to fly them in to fight by the side of the Moroccan people. The King described the leaders as men of limited intelligence, devoid of a political progress and without serious support but the attempt was probably motivated by resentment at the corruption and involvement with foreign financiers amongst those surrounding him. In February 1972 1081 officers and men were put on trial before a civilian, judge on charges of armed rebellion, threatening state security and pre-meditated homicide. One cadet was sentenced to death for shooting the King's ADC, three received life sentences and ten sentences over ten years while over 1,000 were acquitted. Later there were allegations that Oufkir had been involved in the conspiracy but it seems improbable that if this were so, it would have become such a shambles.

SLIM, Mongi (1908–69)

Tunisian nationalist leader and Minister. He came from an aristocratic family of Graeco-Turkish origin and started studying mathematics at the Sorbonne. He switched to law and qualified as a barrister but upon returning home did not practise, instead becoming with Bourguiba and Ahmad Ben Salah one of the founders of the Neo-Destour Party and a member of its original Politburo. In April 1938 he was arrested with Bourguiba after there had been riots in Tunis; he was interned at Ramada in the extreme South. After the outbreak of war the nationalist leaders were transferred to a fortress in Marseilles from which they were freed by the Germans after the occupation of Vichy France. Upon returning home Slim took charge of the Politburo, standing in when Bourguiba was absent. In January 1952 both men were imprisoned. In August 1954 Slim

was appointed Minister of State in the government of Tahar Ben Ammar which negotiated the Franco-Tunisian Autonomy Agreement of which he was one of the signatories. In September 1955 he was moved to become the first Minister of the Interior, where he had the important task of purging pro-French local officials and replacing them with Neo-Destour loyalists. He also played a part in the actual negotiations and in resettling the *fellagha* guerrillas who considered they were owed much for their part in the fight for independence. Slim was able to give invaluable support to Bourguiba in the struggle against Salih Ben Yusuf. Upon the achievement of full independence Bourguiba sent Slim as Ambassador to Washington, a post so important he said, that it could only be occupied by one or other of them, and also as Permanent Representative to the United Nations. In New York Slim became a prominent figure, a close friend of Dag Hammarskjöld, President of the General Assembly in 1961/2 and one of the leading advocates of Algerian independence. He was so well regarded that he was later considered to be a possible successor to U Thant as Secretary-General but in August 1962 he handed over the UN post to his brother Taiyyib Slim and returned to Tunis as Foreign Minister. He was also one of the six members of the Party Politburo. In November 1964 Bourguiba appointed Slim his personal representative, replacing him with his own son but he remained Treasurer of the Party. In September 1966 he was appointed Minister of Justice although he still carried out numerous diplomatic missions. In 1968, while leading the Tunisian pilgrims, he suffered a heart attack in Saudi Arabia. He was ill with hepatitis much of 1969 until his death in October. Slim, a man of great political skill remained a bachelor – for which he was once publicly criticised by Bourguiba.

SLIM, Taiyib (1914–)

Tunisian nationalist leader and diplomat. He was the younger brother of Mongi Slim whom he followed to the Sorbonne and in early membership of the Neo-Destour Party. He remained in France, spreading nationalist propaganda amongst North African students until 1938 when, after the arrest of Bourguiba and his own brother Mongi he returned to Tunisia and started to organise an underground movement. In 1941 he was caught and sentenced to twenty years' hard labour but in 1943 he was pardoned by the new Bey, Muhammad al-Amin. Slim then edited an underground newspaper, was caught by the Free French, accused of collaboration with the Nazis, sentenced to death but escaped to France. He then worked in the Maghreb Bureau in Cairo and travelled widely in independent countries of Asia and Africa setting up offices to represent the Tunisian nationalists. Slim was present at the Bandung Conference in 1955 which established the Non-Aligned Movement. Upon independence he was briefly Head of the Foreign Affairs department of the Council of Ministers, charged with setting up a diplomatic service. He himself went as the first Tunisian Ambassador to London and Scandinavia where he remained until succeeding his brother Mongi as Permanent Representative at the UN in 1962. In January 1967 he was elected Chairman of the UN Development Programme but in October he returned to Tunis to take up the post of

Personal Representative of the President, recently vacated by Mongi, which involved numerous diplomatic missions including a month-long tour of Africa in 1968. Slim represented Tunisia at the Rabat Summit of 1969. In July 1970 he resumed his formal diplomatic career as Ambassador to Rabat but in October he was recalled to become Minister of State. In March 1973 he was sent back to the UN as Permanent Representative, concurrently serving as Ambassador to Canada. He switched posts again, returning as Minister of State from 1976 to 1977 before going back to the UN for the third time. Although he had been elected to the Politburo of the Neo-Destour in 1959, and was re-elected in 1969, his prolonged service abroad meant that he was not an influential figure in the Party. Slim was a man of great sophistication and urbanity.

SOCIALIST LABOUR PARTY (Egypt)

Hizb al-Amal al-Ishtiraki. In November 1978 Anwar Sadat, worried by the genuine opposition of the National Progressive Unionist Party and the New Wafd, declared that "extremists of the Left and Right" were ruining the new democracy that he was trying to introduce and encouraged the formation of "an honest and patriotic opposition". Immediately afterwards the Socialist Labour Party consisting mainly of members of his own National Democratic Party under the leadership of Ibrahim Mahmud Shukri who had been a Minister since February 1977 was recognised. It claimed its origins in the pre-war Young Egypt movement and attracted urban youth rather than labourers. The Party advocated socialism based on Islam rather than Marxism but started to take its opposition role seriously. It contested the June 1979 general election on economic reform, a new wage policy, the break-up of state monopolies into holding companies, end of isolation from the Arabs, balanced relations with the Super-Powers and it won 33 seats becoming the main opposition party. In September 1981 its newspaper *al-Shaab* was closed and the leadership arrested in Sadat's purge but released by Mubarak after his assassination. Shukri promised to co-operate in the new President's campaign against nepotism, to increase production and improve relations with other Arab leaders. In the general election of May 1984 the SLP stood for the amendment of electoral laws, press freedom, less reliance on foreign loans, the need to rectify the imbalance between wages and prices and direct election of the President for a maximum of two terms. It argued that Camp David was not sacred and more effort was required to solve the Palestinian problem. Its symbol was a star. As it had obtained only 7.1% of the votes and 8% was required to enter the Assembly, it won no seats but four of its members were appointed to the Assembly by the President. During the 1984 campaign one of its candidates, a woman, was killed and in 1987 it claimed that 100 of its offices had been raided and 2,000 of its members, including poll watchers had been arrested. Nevertheless, in coalition with the Liberal Socialist Party and with the support of the illegal Muslim Brotherhood, it won a share of a million votes and 60 seats, overtaking the New Wafd as the main opposition party. The coalition supported the re-election of Mubarak. It boycotted the election of November 1990 which it stigmatised as "a theatrical act" because of the inbuilt advantages of the government NDP. In foreign affairs *al-Shaab* was strongly anti-Western and although it condemned the invasion of Kuwait, it opposed going to war to end it. It opposed the Madrid Peace Conference on the grounds that it put the Arabs in a weak position and favoured UN participation. The feeling was that there was a need to end the 13-year state of emergency and that it was time to hold free elections.

SOCIALIST PARTY OF KURDISTAN–IRAQ

After the collapse of the Kurdish Revolt (II) its leader Mulla Mustafa Barzani retired from politics and a struggle developed for leadership of the Kurdistan Democratic Party between his sons Masud and Idris and his former close associate Mahmud Osman, a doctor from Sulaymaniyya. Osman left the Party, taking a splinter group with him and set up the "Preparatory Committee of the KDP" in Damascus in 1976. The following year he moved his HQ into Kurdistan, not far from that of Jalal Talabani and his Patriotic Union of Kurdistan in the southern Sorani-speaking area; the relations between the two were uneasy. After the PUK were defeated by the KDP in 1978 many of their moderate socialist members led by Rasul Mamand broke away and joined Osman in what became known as the Socialist Party of Kurdistan–Iraq. In 1980 the SPK-I formed a "national democratic front" with the Iraq Communist Party and the KDP. Fighting broke out between the SPK-I and the KUP which succeeded in driving its opponents into the north-east where they became dependent upon the KDP and Iran to whose forces they gave some help in the Iran–Iraq War.

SOCIÉTÉS INDIGÈNES DE PRÉVOYANCE (Morocco)

Sociétés Indigènes de Prévoyance, which had been successful in Algeria were in 1917 established in the pacified area of Morocco. Membership was compulsory and contributions were collected at the same time as taxes. The objective was to fix small farmers on the land by protecting them against usury and encouraging mutual assistance. The SIP reached every rural community and by the end of the Protectorate had two million members, some Societies having over 50,000 members. Most advances were in kind, usually in seed and implements, but they could provide cash for development such as irrigation or establishing co-operatives which bought machinery for common use. They served as a vehicle for propaganda for new methods of farming and new crops. Each section had a council with the Caid as Chairman, a French officer as Deputy and a local schoolmaster as secretary; councils were elected after 1946. The local councils came under the control of a central council, chaired by the Grand Wazir, which could provide loans for projects above the competence of a local council. The system was hampered by excessive bureaucracy and lack of enterprise on the part of members but it did much to increase rural prosperity and prevent dissidence.

SONATRACH (Algeria)

In December 1963, eighteen months after independence, the Algerian Government created the Société Nationale pour le Recherche, la Production, le Transport, la Transformation et la Commercialisation des Hydrocarbures to sell and transport the oil in the Sahara. Other nationally-owned corporations set up around the same time, SONAREM for mining, SONACOME for mechanical engineering, SNS for steel and SNLB for cork and wood were of considerable importance but did not have the international or political prominence of SONATRACH. In its first years SONATRACH was headed by Belaid Abd al-Salam who continued to dominate it after his appointment as Minister of Industry and Energy in 1965: his successor was Sid Ahmad Ghozali. In June 1965 it signed an agreement to co-operate with the French company SOPEFAL which increased its participation in petroleum-related activities and shared prospecting over a 70,000 square mile area. It also obtained effective control of all gas marketing within Algeria. In 1966 its activities were expanded to include exploration, production and transport, ensuring state control at every stage of the process. It also started working with American interests, building a 500-mile pipeline at the cost of $70 million. After the June War of 1967 SONATRACH took over the internal distribution networks of British and American companies and the following year those of a further 14 foreign companies. It took over natural gas and set up several mixed companies in which it controlled 51% of the shares. In 1968 some businesses run through Autogestion were put under SONATRACH. SONATRACH entered into partnership with Syria and South Yemen to prospect for oil but these ventures did not prove successful. In 1969 work began on two pipelines linking the oilfields with coastal refineries at Skikda and Arzew and on the creation of a petrochemical industry. At the end of the Three-Year Plan in 1969 SONATRACH was the largest state company employing 8,600 workers and under the next two Plans it was especially favoured by Boumédienne as the spearhead of his drive for industrialisation, receiving 80% of the national investment on heavy industry which was 45% of the total national investment (agriculture received 15%). In July 1970 the Algerian Government unilaterally raised the price of oil from $2.08 to $2.85 backdated to January 1969, contrary to agreements. Boumédienne declared that it was impossible for a country to develop while outsiders controlled its natural resources and in 1970 a further five foreign oil companies were nationalised, bringing SONATRACH's share of the production to 30%. This was extended to over 80% the following year when 51% of all French companies operating in Algeria were taken over: the companies were given $37 million in compensation and charged $80 million in back taxes. In April 1971 a new basic law decreed that the state was to have a majority holding in all future research and exploitation. Two refineries and, at Arzew, the world's largest liquid gas plant were built. By 1973 SONATRACH's staff exceeded 30,000 and in the same year feasibility studies of a gas pipeline under the Mediterranean to Italy were initiated. In 1977, when hydrocarbons provided 90% of Algeria's export earnings, a large-scale development plan, aiming to change 16 million peasants into an industrialised society by the year 2005 was published. Oil production had reached its peak with 1.2 million barrels a day in 1971 after which liquid gas began to surpass it in importance and led to close commercial relations, and some disputes, with the USA, France and Spain with Algeria exporting 40% of the world supply. Further development of SONATRACH, which by then employed 80,000, was financed by foreign loans and in 1979 it borrowed an estimated $3,000 million – 70% of all loans raised abroad. Work started on the Trans-Med pipeline in June 1979 but plans for a similar Gazoduc across Morocco were held up by the dispute over the Western Sahara. Chadli reversed the drive for heavy industry for which his predecessor had condemned the people to low living standards in the hope of a glorious future: he declared that industry was working at only half capacity and that much it was "scrap iron". SONATRACH was split into thirteen separate units of production in which foreigners were invited to invest. In 1983 OPEC assigned Algeria a production quota of 800,000 barrels a day which it was not always able to meet. In 1987 the Ministry of Planning which had closely supervised every detail of the economy was abolished and management of state-owned enterprises was decentralised with each responsible for its annual plan and prices. By 1989 three-quarters of state businesses had become Enterprises Publiques Économiques with their shares and capital held by eight state holding companies, Fonds de Participation, each responsible for a sector of the economy. New laws made it easier for foreigners to participate and was followed by a series of agreements with companies such as Universal and Shell. In 1991 Ghozli, now Prime Minister, was so desperate for foreign currency to relieve a situation that he described as "catastrophic" that he announced proposals to enable foreigners to take majority shareholdings in state enterprises. This policy caused much opposition and was reversed by his successor Abd al-Salam who determined that enterprises should remain 100% state-owned and that they should hold 51% in joint ventures. In the early 1990s the annual profits of SONATRACH exceeded $1,000 million.

SOUMMAM VALLEY CONFERENCE (1956) (Algeria)

Some 18 months after the All Saints' Day Uprising the War of Algerian Independence appeared to making little progress. There was a lack of central leadership with some members of the Comité Révolutionnaire d'Unité et d'Action in exile and little communication between the local military *wilya* commanders and the politicians. On the initiative of Ramdan Abane a Congress assembled in the Soummam Valley in Kabyle. The "externals" including Ben Bella were invited but Abane seems to have made it impossible for them to come. The delegates met on 20 August 1956 and the proceedings lasted for 20 days with the French authorities ignorant that many of their most important adversaries were assembled in one place. There was criticism by field commanders such as Belkasim Krim, Lakhdar Ben Tobal and Larbi Ben M'hidi of Abane, but the latter prevailed. Military ranks were established and the *wilayas* divided into sectors and endowed with political officers. Activities were to be directed by a three-man Comité de Coordination et d'Éxecution to which Abane, Krim and Ben M'hidi were elected and they later co-opted Ben Yusuf Ben Khedda and Saad Dahlab: decision-making was to be collective. A Parliament of 34 elected delegates, the Conseil National de la Révolution Algérienne was supposed to meet regularly but would obviously be unable to do so as it included the "externals" and militants in France. The Congress also produced a 40-page document which declared the CNRA the sole representative of the people. The primacy of the political over the military and the "internals" over the "externals" was made plain. It laid down peace terms such as no cease-fire without recognition of Algerian independence and no separate status for colons or the Sahara. The war was to be conducted ruthlessly and attacks on civilians were not ruled out and the maximum damage done in France itself. The colonialist economy had to be sabotaged and France isolated internationally. There were promises of social reforms affecting women, peasants, students and trade unions which were given representation on the CNRA. The Soummam decisions were rejected as invalid by Ben Bella and his associates and in July 1957 were reversed by the CNRA but they gave a new impetus and a new leadership to the War.

STARK, USS, Attack upon (1987)

When the Iran–Iraq War developed into a virtual stalemate on land the Iraqis launched the War of the Tankers and as it intensified, American warships were sent to the Gulf to restrain Iranian, but not Iraqi attacks on neutral shipping. In the evening of 17 May 1987 the radar of the 3,585-ton American frigate *Stark* identified the approach of a lone Iraqi Mirage F-1 fighter-bomber and although the aircraft had locked its weapons on to the ship, it was assumed its intentions were friendly. The Mirage, however, fired an Exocet missile which smashed into the ship and detonated an enormous fireball which reached a heat of over 180°F, roasted sailors alive and melted metal. Thirty-seven sailors were killed. The Iraqis claimed that the ship had been within the war zone (which the Americans disputed) and apologised for the attack as an accident. The Reagan administration, virulently hostile to Iran, accepted the regrets rather than quarrel with Iraq and the President declared that "Iran is the villain of the piece". The captain of the *Stark* was relieved of his command and an official inquiry showed design faults in the ship and the operation of its equipment.

STEADFASTNESS FRONT

After the visit of Anwar Sadat to Jerusalem, the Arab leaders most opposed to him issued the Tripoli Declaration in December 1977. The signatories, Syria, Algeria, Libya, South Yemen and the Palestine Liberation Organisation constituted themselves the pan-Arab Front of Steadfastness and Resistance to continue confrontation with Israel. The recognition of Syria as "the principal confrontation state" antagonised Iraq until the Camp David Agreement led to a general reconciliation at the Baghdad Summit of November 1978. The Front members generally co-ordinated foreign policy,

supporting the Russians in Afghanistan but it was weakened by quarrels between Qadafi and Arafat. In April 1980 a Foreign Ministers meeting in Tripoli agreed to set up a Supreme Command of Heads of State to meet every six months, a Political Committee of Foreign Ministers to co-ordinate activities against Israel and its main supporter the USA, an Information Committee and a Joint Military Force under a Syrian officer. It also gave its backing to the private quarrels of its members, antagonising Morocco by recognising POLISARIO at the behest of Algeria. Its members also made bilateral agreements – the Libyan–Syrian Union and the Tripartite Pact of Libya, the PDRY and Ethiopia. In November 1980 Front members boycotted the Amman Summit causing its failure. A Summit in Benghazi in September 1981, to which Qadafi had invited the Iranian Foreign Minister, pledged to "pool their resources" to support Libya against "American aggression" in the Sirte Gulf and urged all Arab states to use their economic strength to remove the American military presence from the Middle East. In November 1981 the Front Foreign Ministers met in Aden and agreed to condemn the Fahd Plan which appeared to recognise the right of Israel to exist. Although two of its members were actively engaged in fighting the Israelis during Operation Peace for Galilee, the other three took no positive steps to assist them. At the subsequent Fez Summit the Front was divided with Qadafi staying away, the PLO preoccupied with its own affairs, Syria opposing the Saudi line which was supported by the Yemenis and Algeria, now under Chadli, advising against dividing the Arabs by opposing every suggested initiative. During the crises of 1982/3 there was no meeting of all Front members at any level and in January 1983 Algeria refused to attend a meeting of Syria, Libya and Iran. Subsequently Chadli, amidst gibes from Qadafi that he was a "second Sadat", took an increasingly moderate line inviting Egyptian officials and receiving King Hussain and Arafat after their Amman Accord which had been vehemently denounced by Syria.

STRATEGIC CO-OPERATION AGREEMENT (US–Israel) 1981

In September 1981 Prime Minister Begin, feeling that Israel could not forever depend upon sympathy over the Holocaust and admiration for "the only democracy" in the Middle East, was anxious to find a new basis for relations with the US at a time when he wanted increased financial support. He therefore, during a visit to Washington in September 1981, proposed that Israel should form a strategic partnership with the USA against any advance by the Soviet Union in the area. This accorded well with the obsession of Reagan that Russia was behind all the mischief in the world and controlled the main enemies of Israel, Syria, Libya and the Palestine Liberation Organisation. He saw an agreement, also, as some form of compensation for the recently concluded AWACS Deal with Saudi Arabia. Israel was able to offer prepositioning of arms for the Rapid Deployment Force, escorts and action against the Soviet fleet in the Eastern Mediterranean and intelligence co-operation. The Arab states naturally saw the agreement as being directed against them and Colonel

Qadafi said that it made a third world war imminent. The agreement, signed at the end of November, "builds on the mutual security relationship that exists". It was stressed that it was directed solely against the Soviet Union and "not at any State or group of States within the region". It was vague in terms but provided for joint military exercises, readiness activities and a co-ordinating council. The fact that it was signed by the Defence Ministers, Weinberger and Sharon, and not at higher level showed that the US did not want to make too much of it. Sharon said that there was a secret appendix with economic consequences. A fortnight after signature it was suspended by the US Government as a punishment to Israel for its illegal annexation of the Golan Heights. This led to an almost hysterical speech by Begin in which he stated that Israel was not "a banana republic" but "had survived thousands of years without it and would survive without it for several thousand more" and he abruptly abrogated the agreement.

SUDAN PEOPLE'S LIBERATION ARMY

In August 1983 various groups of Southern Sudanese fighting the government of Jafar Nimeiri united as the Sudan People's Liberation Movement under John Garang who was also Commander-in-Chief of its army. Its first successes, by kidnapping foreign workers, were to stop work on the Jonglei Canal and on the oilfields of the Chevron Company. In December 1984 it achieved further international notoriety by sinking two Nile steamers, killing 150 passengers and capturing 300 including Kenyans and Zairaens. In January 1985 the SPLA launched its first offensive into Equatoria and it had seized most of the three Southern Provinces when in March Nimeiri declared a unilateral cease-fire. In January 1986 the SPLA claimed to have killed 425 soldiers in a year. By this time it was estimated to have 40,000 armed men in the field and realising that the army alone could not defeat it, the government of General Siwar al-Dhahab armed neighbouring Arab tribes. The SPLA besieged many of the principal towns which had to be supplied by air until in August 1986 it shot down a civilian aircraft killing 60 people on the pretext that Khartoum was using it to smuggle weapons. It was estimated that 250,000 people were starving as atrocities were committed by the SPLA against non-Dinkas, by the police who killed any passing Dinka after eight of their number had been blown up by a land-mine and by the tribal militias. The army often went on the rampage, in August 1987 attacking the residential area of Wau, killing 600 and in April burning 40 houses in the town. Food was used as a weapon by both sides, cattle were deliberately killed in addition to those that perished through drought and relief vehicles had to fight their way through ambushes: on one occasion a convoy on what should have been a three-hour journey from Torit to Juba took four weeks and suffered 27 killed while Garang refused to allow food into Juba or Malkala saying that the situation was worse in other places. The SPLA made considerable progress early in 1989, capturing Nasir on the Upper Nile despite the intervention of Libyan aircraft and in February the Southern capital Juba was shelled for the first time. The government of Sadiq al-Mahdi was des-

perate for peace, particularly after an ultimatum from army officers that it should open negotiations within a month. The take-over by General Bashir had little effect in the South where the insurgents controlled 90% of the area apart from the towns. In December 1989 there was heavy fighting in Kosti, little more than 200 miles from Khartoum. In October 1990, anxious to prove that it was not anti-Muslim, the SPLA offered to send some of its men to defend Saudi Arabia against possible attack by Saddam Hussain. In August 1991 it refused to guarantee the safety of the airlift of food to the 300,000 besieged in Juba after the Government misused UN-marked planes to fly in troops and ammunition and later it heavily bombarded the city. During the summer a split developed within the SPLM and one group, the Nasir faction, effectively changed sides and supported the Government. In December there was fighting between the two groups as Garang's Torit faction tried to regain Borr which had been seized by the Nasir group. In January 1992 the SPLA launched a new offensive in Darfur but in March when usually light rains left the roads passable and restricted the growth of the vegetation which facilitated ambushes, the army began its largest attack of the war. There were three prongs, from Wau, from Malakal along the Jonglei Canal and a third along the frontier with Ethiopia which since the fall of Mengistu no longer provided bases for the SPLA. Within weeks the SPLA lost several towns and was driven from its HQ at Torit and then its main supply link with Kenya was lost. The army captured Borr, the Dinka stronghold, and broke out of Juba while leaving in peace the Nasir area of Equatoria. The dissidents had difficulty in feeding their troops and in June the Government claimed that there had been 1,300 defections in ten days and that the opposition ranks were being filled with conscripted children and relying on Egyptian support. The SPLA countered that the Government was receiving logistic support from Ethiopia and men from Iran, six of whom it had captured. In January 1992 Bashir promised to stamp out the SPLA within a year. Garang tried to restore credibility after the abortive Abuja Talks by launching a surprise attack on Juba, threatening to shoot down aircraft bringing in food although in August he was prepared to accept the evacuation of civilians under UN supervision. UN workers had to be withdrawn in October after three of its staff and a journalist were killed in factional fighting. In the same month the Government stated that an entire battalion of Dinkas had defected from the SPLA. In November Bashir predicted the early fall of the SPLA HQ at Kajo Kaje near the frontier of Uganda but called for a new civilian police force to fight alongside the army. In January 1993 the Government claimed successes on the Ethiopian frontier, relieving Nasir but this was followed by a cease-fire for a second round of talks at Abuja. The condition of the non-combatants was appalling with an estimated 1.5 million needing help and 600,000 totally dependent on outside aid but in April relief workers pulled out after threats by Garang whose forces later attacked a relief train. By the end of 1993 the Garang faction held little more than Nimule on the Ugandan frontier and some areas in Equatoria while the Nasir faction, now calling itself SPLM-United held most of the Upper Nile except for

Bor. The Government launched a major offensive to wipe out the remaining rebel strongholds and its reckless bombing was condemned by the US. It appeared that the SPLA was running out of ammunition until new supplies appeared, sent the Government believed, by the Americans through Israel and Saudi Arabia. In mid-March fighting died down as there were peace talks in Nairobi.

SUDAN PEOPLE'S LIBERATION MOVEMENT

President Nimeiri's breaches of the Addis Ababa Agreement and the feeling that the South was being exploited led to the outbreak of renewed guerrilla activity in the area as soldiers mutinied in February 1983, forming Anya Nya II and other groups. In August most of the groups united to form the Sudan People's Liberation Movement under the leadership of John Garang who was also Commander-in-Chief of the Sudan People's Liberation Army. Shortly afterwards the September Laws which imposed *Shariah* upon the country caused more Christians and pagans to support the SPLM which saw itself, not as a secessionist movement to free the South from the domination of Khartoum, but as a national radical movement dedicated to the overthrow of Nimeiri. However, apart from some Christians in the Nuba Mountains it was unable to attract any following outside the South but did manage to get help from the enemies of Nimeiri, Libya and Ethiopia which afforded it a base, a radio station and transit facilities for arms from Russia. In September 1984 Nimeiri, through some of his business associates, offered peace and the appointment of Garang as Vice-Pesident and of six other Southerners as Cabinet Ministers: this merely served to convince the SPLM that it was winning. In March 1985 just before a visit from Vice-President Bush, Nimeiri declared a unilateral cease-fire. Rejecting friendly overtures the SPLM refused to recognise the new government of General Siwar al-Dhahab, demanding immediate abolition of *Shariah* and a constitutional conference. Libya switched sides, urged negotiations and when the SPLM refused, gave the army air support against it. In March 1986 a meeting at the Koka Dam appeared to have arranged for a constitutional conference in Khartoum during the summer. The SPLM ordered a boycott of the elections of April 1986 with the result that voting could take place only in 31 of 68 Southern constituencies. In July Garang met the new Prime Minister, Sadiq al-Mahdi, at the OAU Summit in Addis Ababa but agreement could not be reached because, although Saiyyid Sadiq was willing to modify the September Laws so that they applied only to the North, Garang wanted a uniform legal system throughout the country; he also refused a cease-fire until the state of emergency was ended. In December 1987 it was reported that at a secret meeting in London, the SPLM had ended its insistence that the withdrawal of *Shariah* was a pre-requisite for negotiations but fighting expanded into the Blue Nile, Equatoria and Kordofan Provinces and by mid-1988 it was estimated that 2,000,000 non-combatants were facing starvation and a further 1,000,000 had fled from the South to Khartoum or Ethiopia. The situation was exacerbated by the Government's arming tribal militias

to fight the SPLA and by its denial that the SPLM had genuine grievances, maintaining that it was only trouble making on behalf of Mengistu. In November 1988 the leader of the Democratic Unionist Party, Muhammad Uthman al-Mirghani met Garang in Addis and signed an agreement which, amongst other things, provided for freezing the *Shariah*. The Prime Minister approved and said that there would be peace by mid-December but was not supported by his coalition partners, the National Islamic Front. In May 1989 after a further meeting in Addis, the SPLM proclaimed a 45-day cease-fire. After Saiyyid Sadiq's overthrow in June 1989 there were talks in Addis and Nairobi but they broke down over the issue of the *Shariah* as did further discussions brokered by ex-President Jimmy Carter. In August 1989 talks failed as the SPLM demanded a civilian government in which it would be represented. In February 1991 the SPLM rejected the proposal of General Bashir of a new federal structure of nine states. Early in 1991 the Government presence in the South was restricted to Juba and a few garrison towns which had to be supplied by air but the SPLM suffered a severe blow in May in the fall of Mengistu after which it lost its facilities in Ethiopia and had to import military supplies by train across Kenya from Mombasa. In August 1991 a severe split in the SPLM became evident with the "Torit" faction, mostly Dinka, supporting Garang and his call for a united secular Sudan and a "Nasir" faction, mostly Nuer, led by Riek Machar, who had a doctorate from Bradford and an English wife, and Dr Lam Akol wanting a completely independent South and by the autumn there was vicious fighting between the two factions, causing thousands to flee to Uganda: Amnesty International accused the SPLM of massacring 2,000 civilians. In December after mediation by the National Council of Churches of Kenya the Torit and Nasir factions signed a peace accord which did not, however, end their mutual hostility. Bashir offered an amnesty and in January 1992 his representatives met members of the Nasir faction in Frankfurt. In April when the army launched a major offensive the Nasir faction, now calling itself the SPLM-United, collaborated with it against the Torit. In May, at a time when it was estimated that since 1983 250,000 had been killed and a further 250,000 died of starvation, peace talks were held at Abuja. The two factions initially presented conflicting plans but subsequently united on self-determination. In September 1992 leading members of the SPLM went to Cairo hoping to persuade the Egyptians that they were not anti-Islamic and that the secular SPLM would be less dangerous neighbours than a fundamentalist regime dominated by the NIF. In the autumn the Garang faction was again split when his Deputy, William Nyuon, defected with hundreds of armed men to form another militia which later formed a common front with the SPLM-United. In May 1993 there was an agreement to provide safe havens for non-combatants but it had no effect. In heavy fighting in the summer which the Government said was between the rival SPLMs but in which Garang said that the army was playing a major role, refugees flooded across the border into Uganda: their numbers were estimated at between 1,000 and 3,000 a day and by the end of the year there were some 200,000 displaced persons from the original Southern population of 4.5 million. The Inter-Governmental Authority on Drought and Development, a grouping of neighbouring countries, attempted to mediate and so did former President Carter who in October saw Machar although Garang refused to meet him. In January 1994 after meeting Machar in Nairobi, Garang said that they had agreed upon a cease-fire but Machar said that he did not trust him. By now nearly two million people were hungry and the World Food Program estimated that the Sudan would need 434,000 tons of food, costing $217 million. The Archbishop of Canterbury visited the South without the approval of the Government in Khartoum and in the ensuing diplomatic squabble both Britain and the Sudan recalled their Ambassadors. In February President Moi persuaded Bashir and the insurgent leaders to agree to a meeting the following month at which Garang and Machar agreed on measures for humanitarian relief with the Government representative, the Assembly Speaker Muhammad al-Amin Khalifah. They also agreed to hold proper peace talks in May but the Foreign Minister Hussain Abu Salih said that self-rule for the South would not be granted.

SUDAN SOCIALIST UNION

al-Ittihad al-Ishtiraki al-Sudani. In October 1969, five months after seizing power, Nimeiri declared all political parties dissolved. In May 1971 he ordered the creation of a single party along the lines of the Egyptian Arab Socialist Union and the Syrian Baath, Sudan's partners in the Federation of Arab Republics. There would be room in it for all, except those who "retreated from the path of socialism", and he hoped it would shift membership away from more traditional groups, including the Sudanese Communist Party although most of its members were then supporting him. He aimed that it should serve as his "eyes and ears", that it would settle conflicts internally, indoctrinate the masses and throw up an élite and an ideology. Its founding congress in January 1972 approved a National Action Charter. A Politburo was formed with Nimeiri as its Chairman and he appointed 260 members of its Central Executive Committee. A National Congress was to meet every three years with representatives of provincial Committees and the armed forces. The 1973 Constitution which proclaimed it the "sole political organisation" gave the SSU the power to nominate the President and the drafters of the Constitution, Jafar Bakhiet and Khalid Mansur tried to give it some powers to restrain the Executive. Despite claims of 2 million members in 1974 and 4 million in 1977 and that it was "the soul of the Sudanese people", the SSU appeared to achieve neither genuine support nor a political ideology. Some of its 6,381 basic units existed only on paper, in the countryside it had little effect and in the South it barely existed, being seen merely as an instrument of government. It established "think-tanks" for "scientific socialism" which had little influence, although in 1977 it drew up a Six-Year Development Plan which was accepted by the Government, but its main purpose was to produce cheer leaders and act as a source of patronage for an enormous bureaucracy. In some spheres, such as providing social amenities it confus-

ingly overlapped with the local administration. In January 1975 it was able to secure the dismissal of an unpopular Minister of Finance. When the regime was in real danger during the attempted coup by the National Front in July 1976, the SSU was inactive and Nimeiri attempted to revitalise it by handing over the Secretary-Generalship which he had retained since its foundation to the Minister of Agriculture Major Abu al-Qasim Muhammad Ibrahim. After the National Reconciliation of 1977 the former dissidents Sadiq al-Mahdi, Hassan Turabi, Ahmad al-Mirghani and Clement Mboro were appointed to the Central Committee and there was talk of reform and democratisation of the SSU, elections at every level and its separation from the state but little happened. It provided all the candidates for the general election of February 1978 although choice between them was permitted: it was estimated that 120–140 of the Deputies were genuine SSU while about 70 were really supporters of the banned parties. In August 1979 Nimeiri threatened to dissolve the SSU or dismiss all its leaders for their impotence in confronting a series of strikes but contented himself with replacing Ibrahim by General Abd al-Majid Khalil, the First Vice-President who was seen as his own likely successor. Before the third SSU National Congress at the end of January 1980, which endorsed measures of decentralisation, Ibrahim unsucessfully tried to use his contacts within the SSU to challenge Nimeiri for the Presidency. In June 1981 after a railway strike the SSU was put in charge of the Trade Unions. The SSU again approved all the candidates in the election of December 1981. In January 1982 after riots at the increased price of sugar after the removal of subsidies, Nimeiri dismissed the entire Central Committee including Khalil whose office he assumed and he chaired a working party to carry out reforms. Administration was in the hands of the First Secretary, Badr al-Din Sulayman. In the last months of his regime Nimeiri preferred to rely on the secret police as his main prop and the SSU languished. It did not survive his overthrow.

SUDANESE COMMUNIST PARTY

Extreme left-wing politics were introduced to the Sudan during the war by teachers and students returning from Cairo, abetted by sympathisers in the British army. A communist party was formally organised in 1946, operating through front organisations such as the Anti-Imperialist Front. Led by the exceptionally able Abd al-Khaliq Mahjoub the SCP gained a measure of control over the Sudan Workers Trade Union Federation and other bodies such as the Students' Congress and the Gezirah Tenant Farmers Association. Unlike more doctrinaire communist parties, the SCP declared that it had no conflict with organised religion and practising Muslims sat on its Central Committee. Mahjoub led a staunchly pro-Soviet wing which received financial backing from Moscow and sometimes came into conflict with local interests and later with Maoists. An AIF member won a seat in the general elections of 1953 and 1958. The SCP strongly supported the anti-Westernism of Nasser and in 1958 advocated gradual union with Egypt. Its great opportunity came with the banning of political parties during the Abboud regime for it was the most effective organiser of underground resistance and participated in the National Front. During that time its numbers may have grown from about 750 to nearly 10,000, making it the largest Communist Party in the Arab world. It members, particularly in the professional organisations and the students, played an important part in the 1964 revolution after which it was officially represented in the Cabinet of Sirr al-Khatim al-Khalifah, the first occasion in the Arab world that communists had held Ministries without the label of "Independents". In the elections of April 1965 in the Graduates' Constituencies it won 11 seats out of 15, including the first woman parliamentarian, Fatima Ibrahim, but had no success in the regular constituencies. After the outbreak of the Anya Nya rising in the South the SCP advocated regional autonomy. In December 1965 under the premiership of Muhammad Ahmad Mahjoub the Constituent Assembly expelled its communist members and declared the party illegal. A year later the High Court reversed the decision but in the meantime several of its leaders had been arrested and others dismissed from the army and public services. In November 1965 Abd al-Khaliq Mahjoub narrowly failed to win a seat at Omdurman in a by-election but in May 1967 another leading party member Ahmad Sulayman, a lawyer who had been a Minister under Sirr al-Khatim, was returned for Khartoum North and was permitted to take his seat. When Nimeiri seized power in May 1969 Mahjoub declared his support for the new "progressive, anti-capitalist, anti-imperialist" regime. The SCP was, like the other parties nevertheless formally banned. When the new Cabinet was announced it was headed by a communist sympathiser Babibkr Awadhallah and contained known party members in Joseph Garang and Farouq Abu Isa while Ahmad Sulayman was appointed firstly Ambassador to Moscow then Minister of Industry. Nimeiri wished that its members should be absorbed into his projected Sudan Socialist Union but Mahjoub dissented and was driven into exile while another faction, headed by Ahmad Sulayman continued to serve the regime. Nimeiri, having used the communists to smash the Ansar, became doubtful as to where their ultimate loyalty lay and was angered by their opposition to his policy of union with the strongly anti-communist Qadafi in the Federation of Arab Republics. In November 1970 he dismissed three of their main allies, including Colonel Babikr al-Nur from the Revolutionary Command Council and retired 13 officers suspected of supporting them. In February 1971 he declared that they had tried to sabotage the economy and foreign relations and "ridiculed the army" and that he would "crush and destroy them". In May he dissolved several front organisations including the Sudanese Women's Federation, headed by the Central Committee member Fatima Ibrahim. In July pro-communist officers attempted a coup to install al-Nur as President but their brief success was reversed in a counter-coup. Six officers were shot and civilian leaders, Mahjoub, Garang and Shafai Ahmad Shaykh, the Secretary-General of the SWTUF and a Lenin Peace Prize winner, were hanged. The Russians officially protested at the executions. The Minister of Information stated that at least 3,000 suspected com-

munists had been detained, nearly half being released before the end of the year. The SWTUF was dissolved and a new grouping dominated by the SSU established. Those surviving underground elected Muhammad Ibrahim Nuqud as Secretary-General. Some members joined the National Front but the Party as a whole was not invited to participate in a strongly Islamic grouping. Despite a call published by exiles in Beirut in April 1976 for an uprising, Nuqud was released in August as part of the National Reconciliation but there were waves of arrests in January and June 1977 when the Party was still believed to have some 5,000 members, many of them in influential positions, and to be well organised. Further groups were detained in May 1979 after a series of strikes and two prominent figures were imprisoned after industrial unrest. A further 60 were jailed in January 1981 and in September 1981, after a strike in its traditional stronghold, the Sudan Railways, an estimated 3,000 were rounded up. The SCP resumed its overt existence after the downfall of Nimeiri in April 1985 and won two seats in the elections of April 1986. After the take-over by General Bashir in April 1989 the SCP was again declared illegal and one of its best-known members, "The People's Poet", Mahjoub Muhammad Sharif, was jailed.

SUEZ CANAL

The idea of linking the Mediterranean and the Red Sea by means of a canal was as old as the Pharaohs and in modern times was reconsidered by Ali Bey and then by Bonaparte whose engineers informed him that it was impractical. The introduction of steamships in the late 1820s led to a great increase in travel overland from Alexandria to Suez and also to the pioneering by the British of an alternative route using steamers on the Euphrates. Muhammad Ali resisted pressure for a canal, fearing that it would lead to foreign domination of the country but Ferdinand de Lesseps, who had been French Consul in Alexandria from 1832–37 had won the friendship of his youngest son Said. In 1854 Said, now Ruler, gave de Lesseps a concession to build a canal with the provision that it had to be approved by his sovereign, the Ottoman Sultan. The British, fearing the establishment of a French enclave on the route to India, successfully urged the Sultan to withhold his consent but de Lesseps, a cousin of the Empress Eugenie, had the strong support of the French Government. In 1856 in the name of the Compagnie Universelle du Canal Maritime de Suez de Lesseps received a second concession which included the grant of a strip of land to build a second canal bringing sweet water from the Nile with the Company having the benefit of cultivation in the area free from taxation. Said also promised that conscripted workers would undertake the construction without charge to the Company. The concession was valid for 99 years. The profits were to be divided 15% to the Egyptian Government, 10% to the holders of Founders' Shares and 75% to the purchasers of the 400,000 shares which were offered at 50,000 francs (£2,000) each. More than half were taken up in France, and a quarter by the Egyptian Government but the remaining quarter which de Lesseps had hoped would be bought by business interests in Britain, the US and Russia remained largely unsold until de Lesseps blackmailed Said into taking them up. Digging started in April 1859; 20,000 *fellahin* were conscripted monthly causing great disruption because at any one time 60,000 workers were either preparing to go, working, or recovering. Many, perhaps 100,000, died and the scandal of this *corvée* caused Said's successor, Ismail to pay the Company £3 million in return for its surrendering the right to it. He also had to buy back some of the rights to colonisation along the Sweet Water Canal which had alarmed the British. In March 1866 the Sultan issued a *Firman* approving the concession. In November 1869 the Canal was opened in the presence of European royalty with Ismail, presiding over scenes of vulgar extravagance. It was 101 miles long, 43 feet deep and 796 feet wide at its narrowest point. The original estimate for the construction had been £6 million but in the event the cost was about £16 million of which over £10 million had been paid by the Egyptian rulers, much of it borrowed at exorbitant interest. In 1875, Ismail, deep in debt, had to sell his shares which were bought by Disraeli for just under £4 million, making the British Government, with 40% of the equity, the largest single shareholder. As the Treasury had not the cash in hand, it had to be borrowed from the Rothschilds. Later in order to appease the French, Lord Cromer sold the Egyptian Government's 15% back to the Company for £860,000 so that Milner remarked that "Egypt no longer has any share in the vast profits of the undertaking". As Muhammad Ali had feared the Canal was too important to leave to the Egyptians and it passed under *de facto* British control after the occupation of the country in 1882. Its international status was regulated by the Constantinople Convention of 1888 which laid down that it should be open in peace or war to vessels of commerce or war without distinction of flag. The Canal quickly became profitable and its strategic importance for moving troops was obvious in both world wars, in the first of which the Turks and in the second the Germans tried to seize or disrupt it. In 1923 Egyptian representatives were admitted to the governing board. The Anglo–Egyptian Treaty of 1936 emphasised that the British had special interests in the Canal and provided for the establishment in the Suez Canal Zone of a major military base to which the army of occupation would move from the Delta. The outbreak of war delayed the withdrawal until 1947. After the Egyptian abrogation of the Treaty in 1951 Egyptian militants harassed the British troops and the strife culminated in the "Ismailiyyah Massacre" of January 1952. After the July Revolution negotiations for British evacuation were resumed and the Anglo–Egyptian Treaty of 1954 provided for the departure of all British military personnel by July 1956 although civilian technicians would remain. In the meanwhile the Egyptians had violated the Constantinople Convention by refusing passage to ships flying the Israeli flag or plying to or from that country. This practice was condemned by the Security Council in 1951 and 1954 but a Russian veto prevented any action to end it; an Israeli attempt to force the issue in the *Bat Galim* Affair failed. During 1955 14,666 ships used the Canal. In July 1956, in a deliberately provocative way, Nasser announced the nationalisation of the Canal, setting off the events which led to the Suez War. This resulted in the closing of the Canal, in which 47 ships were sunk, from November until April 1957. One of the pretexts for the Anglo–French aggression had been the fear expressed that the Egyptians were not sophisticated enough to manage the Canal but in fact the 1960s were flourishing years with annual traffic of some 275 million tons bringing in a revenue of over $150 million which now all went to Egypt. The June War of 1967 again closed the Canal, this time for eight years, with Israeli troops along its eastern bank. During this period super-tankers displacing up to 250,000 tons were built to take oil from the Gulf round the Cape of Good Hope to Europe or America. American mediation led to the reopening of the Canal in June 1975 and the Sinai Agreement of September 1975 provided for the passage of foreign-flagged vessels bound for Israel. The Camp David Agreement extended this right to Israeli shipping. Between 1976 and 1980 the Canal was widened and deepened but it faced the competition of an oil pipeline built from Suez to the Mediterranean (Sumed) which could move 1.6 million barrels a day. In 1990 the Canal brought the Egyptian Government $1.77 billion, making it the main source of foreign currency after the export of oil and further plans were being considered for its deepening.

SUEZ CANAL USERS ASSOCIATION

After the nationalisation of the Suez Canal in July 1956 the London Maritime Conference decided that the Waterway was too important to be controlled by a single state and that it should be administered by an international authority. In September, as soon as it had become clear that the Menzies Mission had failed to persuade Nasser to agree to this, the American Secretary of State Dulles suggested the creation of a Canal Users Association would establish an organisation based outside Egypt which would hire pilots, manage technical aspects and receive the tolls of which a fair proportion would be paid to Egypt. It would invite Egyptian co-operation but if this were not forthcoming it would operate without it. The British Government considered it impractical but accepted it as its failure, or the seizure of a ship which had refused to pay the Egyptian authorities would provide an excuse for the use of force. The SCUA depended upon the assumption that the withdrawal of British and French pilots due to take place on 15 September would make it impossible for the Egyptians to operate the Canal but in fact pilots were recruited from Russia and other countries. It also depended upon Egyptian co-operation but when Nasser denounced it as "leading to international anarchy", Dulles said that the Americans did not intend "to shoot their way through the Canal". The Second London Maritime Conference endorsed SCUA although some participants opposed it and it was formally inaugurated by the Foreign Secretary Selwyn Lloyd on 1 October. Committees were set up and Eyvind Bartels, the Danish Consul-General in New York was appointed Administrator. It remained in existence for some months after the Suez War but in May Bartels resigned and it was agreed that each member should make its own arrangements with the Egyptian authorities. SCUA then effectively ceased to exist.

SUEZ CANAL ZONE

The Anglo-Egyptian Treaty of 1936 provided for the evacuation of barracks in Cairo and Alexandria by British troops and their reallocation along the Suez Canal in barracks to be built by the Egyptian Government. In the event the facilities were built at British expense, the move was delayed by the war and the last British units left the Delta in March 1947. The Treaty stipulated that the number of troops should not exceed 10,000 with 400 pilots and an unspecified number of ancillary personnel but the actual number probably reached 80,000. In addition there were many families. There were 150 units, one, the Ordnance Depot at Tel al-Kabir, was 28 miles in circumference. In October 1951 Nahhas Pasha denounced the 1936 Treaty and demanded that the troops should leave the Canal Zone. This was followed by a state of near guerrilla war as militants, particularly from the Muslim Brothers engaged in a series of raids, bombing and abductions. In just over 3 years 47 servicemen were killed and 7 were missing. There were 10 major incidents of arson and over 3,000 cases of theft. The British belief that some of the incidents were organised by the Egyptian army or police led to an attack by the army on a police barracks and the killing of at least 40 policemen in the Ismailiyyah Massacre of January 1952. After the July Revolution negotiations were begun for an agreement on the future of the base and eventually the Anglo-Egyptian Treaty of July 1954 provided for the withdrawal in stages of British military personnel but for the retention of civilian technicians to maintain the base for a further seven years so that it could be reactivated in the event of an attack by an outside power on an Arab state or on Turkey. The last soldiers left in July 1956 leaving behind large quantities of military stores, which, after the Suez War, were seized by the Egyptian army.

SUEZ WAR (1956)

Even before the nationalisation of the Suez Canal the British and French Prime Ministers, Eden and Mollet, saw the overthrow of Nasser as essential for the maintenance of their interests in the Arab world. The London Maritime Conferences gave time for the move of troops to Cyprus and Malta and the preparation of a plan – "Operation Musketeer". The first version which involved a landing at Alexandria and an advance on Cairo was abandoned when the possibility arose of collusion with Israel which was finalised at the Sèvres Accord of 22 October. The Israelis had in recent months become exasperated by the continuing blockade of Eilat and *fida'i* raids and alarmed by the Czechoslovak Arms Deal and the moves towards the creation of a joint Egyptian–Syrian–Jordanian military command, accompanied by threatening speeches. The possibility was discussed of landing at Haifa where there would be no opposition or at Gaza and advancing by good roads across Sinai but this made collusion too obvious. The revised plan was for the destruction of the Egyptian air force by two days of bombing in which it was also hoped to cut off the country from the world by destroying Cairo Radio and international telecommunications links. Individual cities were to be isolated by the destruction of roads and bridges and there was

to be an intensive propaganda campaign to demoralise the armed forces and the people by stressing that the sole enemy was Nasser and not the Egyptian people. This phase could not be prolonged as it would give time for international opposition to rally and was to be followed by parachute and amphibious troops at Port Said and Port Fuad. The Canal would be occupied down to Suez and the Suez Canal Users Association would manage it. The operation, better planned than the Normandy landings of 1944 which provided a model, involved 376 British aircraft and an armoured and an infantry division as well as French forces. Reinforcements were sent to Aden and the Gulf in case of local unrest. If the Egyptian air force fled to Syrian airfields, these would be bombed. It was expected that the Egyptian people would welcome the end of a military dictatorship and that it would be easy to install in Cairo a friendly government, perhaps led by Ali Mahir or a member of the Wafd but there might have to be an interim military administration with which it was assumed willing collaborators would be found. It was seen as vital that the Americans should not find out what was being planned. Nasser was expecting an invasion which he said that he would not resist but would "wait for world opinion to save me" but he did not anticipate collusion with Israel and withdrew some of his troops from Sinai. In the afternoon of 29 October the Israeli paratroopers dropped in Sinai and seized the strategic Mutla Pass. They then attacked in three columns, one by a road deemed impossible along the east coast of Sinai, the second through the centre towards Ismailiyyah and the third, having taken Gaza, along the northern coastal road. The following evening the British and French issued their prepared ultimatum calling on both Israeli and Egyptian forces to withdraw ten miles to opposite sides of the Canal within 12 hours. The Israelis, then more than a hundred miles east of it accepted at once while the Egyptians, who would have had to abandon Sinai, refused. A Security Council Resolution calling for immediate Israeli withdrawal behind the armistice line was vetoed by Britain and France. On the evening of 31 October the British started to bomb Cairo and 50 Egyptian aircraft were destroyed and 40 severely damaged. Some of Nasser's colleagues, particularly the Commander-in-Chief General Abd al-Hakim Amer advised acceptance of the ultimatum but, encouraged by popular support, he determined to resist and ordered the blocking of the Canal and the issue of rifles to civilians. He also ordered back troops from Sinai to defend the Canal; it was said that he had to threaten to resign to compel his officers to obey. On 31 October the Israelis captured an Egyptian warship which had fired on Haifa. On 1 November a Royal Navy cruiser sank an Egyptian frigate in the Red Sea. Early in the morning of 2 November the General Assembly called for an immediate cease-fire, withdrawal to previous positions and the establishment of a UN force to keep the peace. The Egyptians accepted, provided that the Israelis ceased their aggression. The Israelis, determined to occupy Sharm al-Shaykh, pressed on in Sinai mercilessly harrying the retreating Egyptians, many of whom abandoned their weapons and even their boots as they dissolved into a rabble. The campaign lasted 100 hours. Early on the morning of 4 November, just as the Russians were starting to crush an outbreak of democracy in Hungary, the General Assembly again demanded a cease-fire which this time the Israelis accepted. The British Cabinet now no longer had any pretext for intervention as the Canal was in no danger and was deeply divided on whether to call off the landings planned for the early morning of 5 November. However in Eden's eyes the destruction of Nasser was more important than the Canal and by threatening resignation and attempting to pass off the Allied invasion as the vanguard of the UN force he had his way and 600 British paratroopers landed at Port Said and 487 French at Port Fuad which they captured immediately. The Governor of Port Said surrendered but was ordered by Nasser to fight on with the help of local resistance groups. Later that day the Russian Government hinted at sending "volunteers" to assist the Egyptians and at rocket attacks on London, Paris and Tel Aviv: they asked for American co-operation but Washington warned that it would oppose Soviet intervention. Peking reported that 280,000 Chinese had "volunteered" to fight the imperialists. The Israelis who had revoked their acceptance of a cease-fire and captured Sharm al-Shaykh had now attained their main objective and stopped fighting. The next day more British and French soldiers, perhaps totalling 70,000, were landed and after heavy fighting in which civilians joined, captured Port Said and started moving down the Canal. They had reached El-Cap, twenty-five miles south when London accepted a cease-fire. The French reluctantly followed. The main reason for calling off the operation was intense pressure from the Americans, particularly from Eisenhower who felt that he had been deliberately deceived. The venom and self-righteousness with which Dulles pursued his Allies caused a considerable strain on Trans-Atlantic relations. There was also a financial crisis which led to a fall of sterling on the US market and 15% of British gold reserves were lost in a few days. The attack on Egypt was widely felt at home to have been immoral and was bitterly opposed by many who normally supported the Government. King Saud cut off oil supplies to Britain and France and there were further threats that the Americans might do the same. The Russian threat of rocket attacks was not taken seriously by the Allies but won them much credit in the Arab world and distracted attention from their own repression in Hungary; it was noticeable that they made no move until it was clear that the US was opposed to the attack. The advance party of UNEF arrived on 15 November and on 3 December the British announced that they would leave; the withdrawal was completed by 22 December. The Israelis lingered until threats of sanctions forced them to evacuate the Gaza Strip on 7 March 1957: the presence of UNEF lifted off the blockade of Eilat and there were no major incidents on the frontier for a decade. The Canal was reopened in April 1957 at the cost of £10 million and there was no further dispute over its ownership. Egypt restored diplomatic relations with Britain in December 1959 and with France in April 1963. British casualties were 25 killed, 2 missing and 149 wounded. General Dayan put Israeli losses at 172 killed, 817 wounded, 3 missing and 1 taken prisoner. Egyptian casualties were perhaps 1,000 killed in the initial fighting in Sinai and another 1,000 during the retreat and between 750 and 1,000 killed in Port Said. They also lost large amounts of equipment. The Egyptians treated resident British and French civilians without brutality, although some 3,000 were expelled, and protected the local Jewish community in contrast to the Israelis who killed nearly 50 Arab peasants at Kafr Kassim for breaking a cease-fire of which they had not been informed. British equipment in the Suez Canal Zone was seized as war booty and later British and French businesses were taken over. Nasser both gained and lost prestige; personally he had emerged as the "hero-martyr" who had beaten off the attacks of two major Powers but there was no disguising that his troops had proved no match for the Israelis who released more than 5,000 that it had taken prisoner. No Arab state helped the Egyptians, although some volunteers were recruited in Yemen, but some did break off diplomatic relations with the Allies. The career of Eden was finished and his memory tainted by the mendacity that he had displayed, deceiving even his own Ambassadors as well as his friend Eisenhower who, involved in a Presidential election, had from the beginning ruled out the use of force. The moral authority of Britain and France was severely damaged and the consequent diminution of their influence in the Middle East prepared the area for three decades of polarisation between Washington and Moscow.

SULAYMAN, Abd Allah (al-Hamdan) (c. 1887–?)
Saudi Minister. Born in Anayzah, he was the only Najdi amongst the chief administrators employed by Ibn Saud. He was said to have been a coffee-boy and minor clerk in the office of Ibn Saud's Agent in Bahrain before becoming a poorly paid clerk in Bombay for ten years. On the death of his brother who was correspondence clerk to Ibn Saud, he succeeded to the post. By 1928 he was in complete charge of the country's finances, reputedly keeping the Treasury under his bed. A British Minister described him as "excellent as a grand extortioner and evader of liabilities". For many years he was regarded as being after his master, the most powerful man in the country. His relations with his colleagues were often bad but no one doubted his fidelity to the King. He played the major part in administering, supplying and paying the army during the Saudi–Yemeni War and in negotiating with foreign business interests such as ARAMCO, showing a keen interest in development. He was also largely responsible for building the administrative machinery of the state. As money poured in and the King aged, Abd Allah Sulayman was unable to control the extravagance of the Princes (on one occasion having refused to give money to Crown Prince Saud, he had to flee from his wrath from Mecca to Jiddah and even take refuge on a ship in the harbour) and his power decreased. As the Kingdom prospered, he himself became immensely rich and after he left office in August 1954, he was reported to have given four palaces and 750,000 square metres of real estate to the University of Jiddah. His appearance was not impressive but he had a cheerful countenance and a ready tongue. A British diplomat described him as the only Finance Minister of his acquaintance who drank

methylated spirits and it is possible that this indulgence contributed to his decline.

SULAYMAN, (Muhammad) Sidqi, (1919–)

Egyptian Prime Minister. He obtained a Science Degree at Cairo University before joining the army where he obtained further engineering qualifications. He was a highly efficient officer-technocrat and was involved in running the Suez Canal after its nationalisation. He was also a member of the National Production Council and was appointed Secretary-General of the National Planning Council. In 1962 he was appointed Minister in charge of the Aswan High Dam when it was two years behind schedule and still ensured that the first stage was finished on time. He also cut the scheduled time for the second stage by a year and ensured that the new target was met. His work on the Dam involved him in all aspects of agricultural planning and with the handling of large budgets. Sulayman believed in the partnership of state and private capital but was suspicious of the interference of ill-informed politicians. He was described as a tough, practical engineer who worked in his shirt sleeves. He was President of the Soviet–Egyptian Friendship Society and received the Order of Lenin but was still a practising Muslim. In September 1966 Nasser appointed him Prime Minister, replacing Zakariah Mohieddin who had been urging the end of the Yemen War and negotiations with the IMF to ease the economic crisis. It was also thought that Nasser regarded Mohieddin as too independent and had determined to be effectively his own Prime Minister as Sulayman had neither political support nor strong views; he administered the country while the President made policy. Over half the new Cabinet were former officers, many with technocratic backgrounds. Sulayman continued the austerity programmes of his predecessor, limiting government expenditure, demanding longer working hours to the extent of causing labour unrest. He called for expansion of heavy industry and alterations to the educational system to train a better workforce. With Abd al-Hakim Amer he chaired the Supreme Control Commission which purged inefficient managers – 38 out of 48 chairmen of major state organisations were removed. In February 1967 he launched a programme to reclaim over 100,000 *feddans* a year and to increase the income of the *fellahin*. In May 1967 Sulayman became the highest Egyptian official to visit Syria since the break-up of the United Arab Republic when he went to discuss defence arrangements. In the same month he appeared to have persuaded Nasser to open talks with the IMF but these were frustated by the outbreak of the June War, in which although Prime Minister he does not seem to have had an important role. After the defeat Nasser himself assumed the Premiership and Sulayman reverted to Vice-Premier in charge of Electricity, Industry and the High Dam. In April 1969 he headed a committee to popularise contraceptives. In November 1970 he was dropped from the Government but appointed Chairman of the Central Auditing Office. He held this post for some years but resigned in protest at the financial scandals if the Sadat era.

al-SULH, Rashid Anis (1926–)

Lebanese Prime Minister. A Sunni Muslim born in Beirut, he trained as a lawyer at the Jesuit University and became a magistrate. He entered Parliament in 1964, and although he failed to be re-elected in 1968, in 1972 he defeated the Najjadah leader Adnan Hakim. He was a strong Arab nationalist and committed to reform. As a supporter of Kamal Jumblatt he was not a member of the Sunni establishment which was at odds with President Sulayman Franjiyah. In September 1974 the Prime Minister, his distant cousin Taqi al-Din al-Sulh, resigned in despair at the worsening situation caused mainly by the presence of large numbers of Palestinians in the South which infuriated the Maronites and which led to Israeli counter-action which inflamed the Shiah. Saeb Salam refused to take office unless he were given wider powers and the President's son Tony removed from the lucrative Ministry of Communications and Franjiyah had quarrelled with Rashid Karami. The President was pleased to snub them by picking a less prominent Sunni; his choice fell on Rashid al-Sulh who had the added advantage of lacking a substantial power base of his own. Israeli aircraft attacked Beirut and, despite opposition from Pierre Gemayel Sulh tried to arrange for the purchase of anti-aircraft missiles. In January 1975 the Government had a success in stamping out an armed gang in Tripoli but in February fishermen in Sidon rioted against a concession granted to the Maronite leader Camille Chamoun. The army was sent in and there was considerable bloodshed and it was widely felt that Sulh had handled the matter clumsily, allowing it too free a hand; also, owing to the opposition of the President he was unable to dismiss the Maronite General responsible. In April the Ayn al-Rummanah Massacre led Jumblatt to declare that he would boycott any Cabinet which contained representatives of the Kataib Party. Widespread fighting broke out and Gemayel demanded that the army, under its Maronite commander, should intervene while Sulh, supported by Jumblatt considered that it would fight on the Christian side and therefore refused. The Cabinet was so divided that it was unable to meet for a month. Gemayel and Chamoun withdrew their representatives from the Cabinet while other anti-Jumblatt members resigned leaving the Prime Minister helpless. After a bitter attack on the Kataib he himself resigned, saying that there was no longer any possibility of compromise while one sectarian group attempted to impose its will on the country. Sulh played no further part in politics.

al-SULH, Riad (1894–1951)

Lebanese Prime Minister. He was a Sunni Muslim from a prominent Sidon family and his father and grandfather, senior officials under the Ottoman regime, had acquired land. He attended the same Christian school as Bishara al-Khouri and later trained at the Law School in Istanbul. A supporter of Arab nationalism during the war he was exiled to Adana and then, a leading supporter of Faysal, was a member of the General Syrian Congress and Minister of the Interior in the Cabinet of Ali Ridha al-Rikabi. After the French occupied Damascus he went into exile in Egypt, sentenced to death *in absentia*. Sulh was amnestied in 1924 but went into exile again in 1925 until 1929. He was then active at the bar, founded a newspaper with Khayr al-Din al-Ahdab and was regarded as the most important Arab nationalist in the Lebanon, in touch with the nationalists of other Arab countries, such as Shukri al-Quwatli and with the exiles such as Shakib Arslan. A British Consular report of the 1930s described him as "very intelligent, a born politician . . . clever and persuasive and ready to use his own means in the Arab cause". In 1935 he was briefly exiled on the accusation of encouraging a strike in Beirut. He was active at the Bludan Conference of 1937. At this time the French believed he was being subsidised by Mussolini and later he was said to be organising support for Rashid Ali al-Gilani. He was always conciliatory towards the Maronites and maintained friendly links with the Patriarch. He also abandoned his former objective of unity with Syria and, arousing some scepticism, came to accept the validity of an independent Lebanon. This enabled him in 1943 to negotiate the National Pact with Bishara al-Khouri which was to set the pattern of Lebanese politics for the next thirty years and when Khouri was elected President he appointed Sulh Prime Minister. Sulh's popularity and prestige amongst the Muslims ensured their acceptance of the alliance. The new government immediately opened negotiations with the French to bring the Mandate to an end and to rewrite the Constitution but the French Delegate-General Jean Helleu declared that France would not tolerate unilateral changes. Khouri and Sulh persisted and in the early morning of 11 November 1943 both were arrested and imprisoned in filthy conditions in the fortress of Rashayya. Riots paralysed the country and British pressure forced the French to release them 11 days later. Sulh visited most of the Arab capitals and attended the meeting which led to the Alexandria Protocol and the formation of the Arab League. He thus ensured general acceptance at home and throughout the area of the country's Arab status. In January 1945 his government fell. He formed his third Cabinet in December 1946 and was to form another three in the next four years. In alliance with Khouri he rigged the election in 1947 to alter the Constitution to maintain the President in power. He continued to co-operate with Arab states but ensured that Lebanon took no major part in the Palestine War. In 1949 he persuaded the Syrian President Husni al-Zaim to return the fugitive Antun Saadeh to Lebanon and had him shot. His relationship with Khouri began to deteriorate and it was clear that they were competing for power. In February 1951 Sulh resigned to allow a caretaker government to conduct elections. In July he went to visit his old friend King Abd Allah in Jerusalem where he was murdered. There had been an attempt on his life the previous year. It was generally accepted that the killers were avenging the execution of Saadeh but there were some whispers that agents of his former ally Khouri were responsible.

al-SULH, Sami (1890–1968)

Lebanese Prime Minister. A Sunni Muslim, he was born in Sidon where his father, an official in the Ottoman administration was then serving. He was educated at the Ottoman College in Beirut and studied law

in Istanbul and Paris. He then worked in Aleppo as a lawyer for the Baghdad Railway but became suspected of Arab nationalist activities and had to take refuge with the bedouins in the desert. He gave himself up but spent the rest of the war in exile in Turkey with his cousin Riad al-Sulh. He then returned to Damascus and during the reign of Faysal worked for the Hijaz Railway. He came to terms with the French Mandate and held various posts such as President of the Criminal Court before entering formal politics. In July 1942 he formed the first of his seven governments after Ahmad al-Daouq had resigned feeling unable to cope with a food crisis. He stayed in office until the following March when the politically neutral Ayyub Thabit took over to supervise elections. In late August 1945 he again became Prime Minister and later in the year took the Lebanese demand for the evacuation of all French and British troops to the UN; although the motion was vetoed by the Russians the two Powers agreed to comply as soon as possible. The following May Sulh was replaced by Saadi al-Munlah as President Bishara al-Khouri tried to find which was the most pliable of Sunni leaders. The murder of Riad al-Sulh removed a rival and made Sami the leading Sunni politician in Beirut although for the rest of his career he had to face the competition of Saeb Salam. In February 1952 Khouri hoped to rally Muslim support through Sami as he had once done through Riad and appointed him Prime Minister. Sulh later stated that the President had only chosen him because he could find no one else, needed a scapegoat and failed to help him as problems mounted. Sulh took office promising reform such a votes for women, reinforcing the army, safeguarding the rights of workers and economic co-operation with Syria. He was faced with a series of strikes by barristers, journalists, teachers and public works contractors and a refusal by the citizens to pay bills to public utilities. At the same time nearly all the other leading politicians joined in opposition to the corruption, scandals and nepotism surrounding the President. A general strike was called and on 9 September Sulh rose in the Chamber and denounced the President for tolerating a coterie of swindlers. He was instantly dismissed and joined the group calling for the resignation of Khouri. His part in overthrowing Khouri made him the natural ally of the next President Camille Chamoun who appointed him Prime Minister in September 1954. He faithfully carried out the President's foreign policy, praising the Baghdad Pact, an action which lost him much Muslim support. He also called in the Ford Foundation to make recommendations to modernise the bureaucracy but took no action to implement their recommendations. Sulh headed the Lebanese delegation to the Bandung Conference. In September 1955 after strong attacks upon him by the opposition he was replaced by Rashid Karami. In November 1956 after Abd Allah al-Yafi and Saeb Salam had refused to support his policies during the Suez War Chamoun once again appointed Sulh Prime Minister and together they kept Lebanon firmly in the Western camp, refusing to break off relations with Britain and France and welcoming the Eisenhower Doctrine. They made no attempt to appease Nasser to whom much of the Arab world was rallying. In 1957 they successfully rigged the parliamentary elections and there were rumours that Chamoun intended to amend the constitution in order to have a second presidential term. In the summer of 1958 after the formation of the United Arab Republic there was much pressure both from the Muslim community and from outside for Lebanon to identify with the Arab nationalist movement. Chamoun and Sulh in June sealed off the frontier with Syria and called for UN support. Sulh consulted with Nasser's enemy Nuri al-Said and with the Turks and called for American aid. He staunchly supported the President's refusal to resign before the end of his term in September and left office when General Fuad Shihab took over. After two attempts on his life and the bombing of his house he deemed it prudent to go abroad for the next two years. He had lost much of his credibility amongst the Muslims by his loyalty to Chamoun and although he was re-elected a Deputy in 1964 he never held office again. He wrote his memoirs in French and Arabic. Sulh was an efficient man who got things done and at the same time an amiable witty fellow who enjoyed puffing a hubble-bubble with his friends.

al-SULH, Taqi al-Din (1909–88)

Lebanese Prime Minister. A Sunni Muslim he studied literature and history at the American University of Beirut and became a journalist. At the same time he lectured at the French Lycée. He was an adviser to his cousin Riad al-Sulh during the struggle for independence. In 1935 Sulh became Director of the Ministry of Information until 1944 when he transferred to diplomacy, being Councillor at the Embassy in Paris and subsequently at the Arab League. It was not until 1957 that he entered politics as MP for Zahle. He was close to President Fuad Shihab whom he served as a speechwriter and was also Chairman of the Parliamentary Commission on Foreign Affairs. From November 1964 until July 1965 he was Minister of the Interior under Hussain al-Uwayni. He was regarded as a man of conciliation and of great experience so in the crisis that followed the resignation of Amin al-Hafiz in June 1973 he was asked by President Sulayman Franjiyah to become Prime Minister. Sulh formed the largest ever Cabinet, consisting of 22 members, with four Ministers of State, each from a different community, trying to satisfy all parties. Reform was hampered by the President's insistence that his controversial son Tony be kept in the Cabinet but at first the Prime Minister was able to restrain the left by alliance with Kamal Jumblatt, although he was worried by the rising militancy of the Shiah under the leadership of Musa Sadr. He urged all-out struggle against Israel during the October War and later the Israelis continued their attacks on Lebanon. Conflict worsened between the Palestinian guerrillas and the Maronite leaders and Sulh was unable to prevent both sides from building up their armed forces. There was labour and student unrest. Jumblatt quarrelled with the Prime Minister over a question of patronage and his refusal to disarm the Maronites but not other groups. Left with little support, not even that of the Sunni leaders, Saeb Salam and Rashid Karami who were anxious for office, in September 1974 Sulh resigned in despair. In July 1980 he was again appointed Prime Minister but, as he was

known to have close relations with Iraq, he was unacceptable to the Syrians and was unable to form a government. He later went abroad and died in Paris. Sulh apppeared an old-fashioned figure, he was one of the last to wear the *tarboosh*, but in his youth he was a keen footballer and he continued jogging until a great age.

SUMED

After the Egyptian defeat in the June War of 1967 the Israelis occupied the east bank of the Suez Canal which was closed to shipping. Hoping to recover some money from the passage of oil, which had amounted to about 80 million tons of crude a year, the Minister of Industry and Petroleum, Dr Aziz Sidqi put forward a plan for a 40-inch 210-mile pipeline from the Gulf of Suez to the Mediterranean. Its initial capacity was to be 50 million tons a year and the cost was estimated at $175 million. A British firm won the contract for a feasibility study. Tankers displacing up to 312,000 tons would unload at Ain Sukhna, the Suez terminal, while smaller tankers would take on 15,000 tons an hour at Sidi Krer near Alexandria. There would be two storage tank complexes, each holding a million tons and two pumping stations each of 41,000 horsepower. A French-led consortium of 11 European companies signed a contract in December 1969 which stipulated that bidders would provide the bulk of the necessary finance. It was not until November 1971 that it was announced that a banking consortium with members from 8 European countries and Japan had been put together. By 1972 estimates of the cost had risen $330 million and it was arranged that a Swiss bank would collect the tolls on behalf of the creditor banks for 8 years and an unspecified amount would be paid to the Egyptian Government. Oil companies signed contracts to use the pipeline and in September 1973 the construction contract was awarded to Bechtel. Final terms could not be agreed and in December 1973 Abd al-Aziz al-Hijazi obtained support from the oil states of the Gulf. The Sumed Pipeline Company was capitalised at $400 million of which Egypt provided half, $120 million in local currency and $80 million through a loan from the Chase Manhattan Bank. Saudi Arabia, Kuwait and Abu Dhabi each put up $60 million and Qatar $20 million. After revaluation of the dollar Bechtel lost the contract to an Italian group. In December 1976 oil started to flow on a test basis and the project was formally opened in July 1977. The Sumed Company also buys oil on its own behalf at the Suez end and sells it on the Mediterranean. In March 1991 it was decided to increase its capacity from 80 million to 120 million tons.

SUPREME MUSLIM COUNCIL (Palestine)

When the British took over the government of Palestine they decided to adopt a form of the Ottoman system of *Millet* by which each religious community regulated its own internal affairs. In December 1921 it established a Supreme Muslim Council with four members representing various areas indirectly elected by a restricted group. The Chairman was the Mufti of Jerusalem Haj Amin al-Hussaini. It was empowered to administer mosques, religious schools and courts and thus enjoyed considerable patronage. Its members were paid by the

Government but it had also a large income from fees and fines. The Mufti exploited it for political purposes and it took a strongly anti-British and anti-Zionist stance. It was active in pushing Arab claims in the Wailing Wall Incident and in the organisation of the Jerusalem Islamic Congress. The Council then became split between followers of the Mufti and the more moderate supporters of Raghib al-Nashashibi. The Council conducted a vigorous campaign in 1934 and 1935 to discourage Arabs from selling land to Jews, often using its own considerable assets to buy properties. It was dissolved in October 1937 by the Mandate authorities on the grounds that its members were involved in the Arab Rebellion and its functions transferred to nominated officials.

SYRIAN COMMUNIST PARTY

There can have been little communism in Syria at the time of the foundation of the Lebanese Communist Party in 1924 as the leadership of a joint party seems to have been based entirely on Beirut. In 1930 it was joined by a Kurdish law student Khalid Bakdash who was to dominate it for half a century. In 1936 the Popular Front government in Paris tolerated communist activities and the Party was allowed to publish its own newspaper and exchange delegations with the French Communist Party. During the next three years its strength increased from about 200 to about 2,000 members. It was outlawed at the start of the war but again allowed to operate after Hitler's invasion of Russia. In the elections of 1943 Bakdash campaigned on a programme which stressed independence rather than socialism and worked closely with nationalist leaders such as Shukri al-Quwatli. He could also rely on the help of the "Red Millionaire", Khalid al-Azm, several times Prime Minister. When Syria and Lebanon in 1943 determined to achieve independence, the Party divided into national groups although until 1944 it retained a single Central Committee. Bakdash and two others unsuccessfully contested Damascus seats in 1947. Its pro-Soviet line discredited it after Russian support for the creation of Israel, its offices were sacked by a mob, and January 1948 it was dissolved. The military coup of Husni al-Zaim drove it underground. It still managed to operate through front organisations such as the Partisans for Peace and to publish clandestine newspapers. It tended to support the rule of Adib al-Shishakli as it shared his hostility to unity with Iraq and to the Baath with whom it competed for support amongst the intellectuals. After his overthrow the Party was legalised and able to stand in the elections in the autumn of 1954 in which, campaigning with the slogan "Syria is not communist: it is nationalist and Arab and will remain so", Bakdash became the first elected communist Deputy in the Arab world. After the death of Stalin, Moscow relaxed its suspicions of bourgeois nationalists and after the failure of the West to coax Syria into the Baghdad Pact the Russians publicly warned Turkey against interfering with its southern neighbour. This was followed by a substantial arms deal and it was estimated that Damascus spent £100 million on weapons from the Eastern Bloc in three years. This all led to a great increase in support for the local communists, then numbering perhaps 18,000. The murder

of Colonel Malki in April 1955 led an alliance of the communists and the Baath to destroy the Syrian Social Nationalist Party, a strong rival to them both with its message of Syrian rather than Arab nationalism. The influence of the communists was strengthened by the appointment of an avowed supporter, General Afif al-Bizri, as Chief of Staff and with Azm in a series of influential posts, it appeared as if, given additional strength by their discipline and tight organisation, they might take over the country and that this would lead to American and Turkish intervention. Baathist leaders, worried about the extent to which their party had been penetrated by communists, pressed for union with Egypt and the communists found it impossible to oppose a move towards Arab unity and agreed in the hope that a loose federal structure would give them a free hand at home. In the event in the new United Arab Republic all parties were banned and Bakdash fled to Prague from where he carried on a propaganda campaign against Nasser while many of his comrades were imprisoned. After the break up of the Union Bakdash was not allowed to return until 1966 when the left-wing of the Baath had triumphed over the old guard and the left-winger Yusuf Zuayyin included two men regarded as communists in his Cabinet. During the struggle between the civil and military wings of the Baath in the summer of 1970, the Russian Government discreetly protested at government actions against communists, including the alleged torturing to death of a prominent activist. After Hafiz al-Assad seized power in November 1970 he included two known communists in his first Cabinet and the Party formed part of the National Progressive Front which he formed in March 1972. This gave the communists formal legitimacy but brought to a head a long-standing split in their central committee, two members of which led a breakaway group protesting at the "aged leadership" of Bakdash and his loyalty to Russia, which was not taking a pro-Arab line over Palestine. This new faction led by Riad al-Turk went into opposition and he was imprisoned. The mainstream itself was not fully united and in 1975 Bakdash attempted to call a summit of the leaders of all the Middle Eastern communist parties to shore up his position against his deputy Yusuf Faysal. The Party continued, however, as part of the NPF, to share in government, and in 1973 seven and in 1977 six communists were elected to the People's Assembly. In November 1981 the Party presented a list of candidates, headed by Mme Bakdash in opposition to the Baath but they were outlawed and many of them arrested. In 1986 they rejoined the fold and nine were elected. In the early 1990s their strength was estimated at 15,000.

SYRIAN PROTESTANT COLLEGE

American missionaries were first active in Lebanon in the 1820s and they had 15 primary schools operating by 1850. The missionaries became worried that their pupils had to seek further training elsewhere so becoming exposed to "the poisoning influence of a Jesuitical education" in an institution such as St Joseph University. In 1862 they recommended the foundation of a collegiate literary establishment in Beirut. The American Civil War hampered fund-raising, some money having to be raised in England, and then it was not until December 1866 that the College opened under the presidency of Daniel Bliss in hired premises with 16 students. The following year a medical department was opened. Cornelius Van Dyck and his colleagues translated scientific textbooks into Arabic, thus enriching the language. One of the early teachers was Nasif al-Yaziji. In 1873 it moved to its own campus overlooking the Mediterranean. At this period there were some difficulties with the Ottoman authorities for the College had been established without official approval which was not obtained until 1886. After 1879 the College taught in English. Faculties of Pharmacy, Commerce and Nursing were added before in 1920 the College was renamed the American University of Beirut. It was extremely unusual in not teaching Law as the French legal tradition was too strongly entrenched in the Levant. It was also unique in attracting many of the best students from the Arab world, particularly after the breakdown of the old Ottoman system in Istanbul.

SYRO–PALESTINIAN CONGRESS

After the French take-over of Syria in 1920 a group of exiles in Cairo set up an organisation to plan opposition to the Mandate system and put their case to the League of Nations. It was organised and funded by Prince Michel Lutfallah who became President with Rashid Rida as Vice-President. The Secretary was Shakib Arslan. They called a Congress in Geneva which met in June 1921 which was attended by 20 delegates from Syria and 15 from North and South America. They condemned French methods in Syria, the cession of territory under the Franklin–Bouillon Treaty and Zionism. There was no follow-up and the following year the Palestinians, including Musa Kazim al-Hussaini, withdrew, complaining that the organisation took little interest in them and was too close to the Hashemites. The Maronites, too, regarded it as unrepresentative. The Congress started to split with an Arslan group in Europe opposing the Hashemites, supporting Ibn Saud, generally pan-Arab and unwilling to seek British help against the French from Syria. Lutfallah, in Cairo, and Dr Shahbandar were pro-Hashemite and pro-British. The split was given a new impetus with the Druze Revolt of which Shahbandar, now back in Syria, was one of the leaders while the Arslan group had no foothold in the country. Arslan met the newly-appointed High Commissioner Henry de Jouvenel in Paris and made conciliatory proposals such as allowing the French exclusive strategic and economic advantages in return for independence and unity. These concessions were disavowed by the other faction. There were further disputes over funding the revolt. The Arslan group, with the backing of the Mufti, Haj Amin al-Hussaini set up a committee in Jerusalem to channel funds derived from Ibn Saud and contacts abroad but were accused of misappropriating them by the Lutfallah faction. The Jerusalem Committee tried to keep the revolt going long after Shahbandar and others realised that all was lost. By the end of 1927 the Congress was irrevocably split into two impotent groups.

TABA TALKS (1993)

The Israeli–PLO Agreement of 13 September provided that one month after signature talks would start on the machinery for the Israeli withdrawal from Jericho and Gaza. Egypt offered to act as host. Before talks started two Israelis were murdered near Jericho and the opening day was marked by a Hamas ordered strike in Gaza. A General Liaison Committee of Peres and Mahmud Abbas agreed to meet in Cairo every two to three weeks. A committee, headed by Major-General Ammon Shahak, Deputy Chief of Staff, and Nabil Shaath, was formed to discuss arrangements for the withdrawal and the hand-over of security responsibilities. In the first two days they set about finalising an agenda and set up working groups on security and civilian matters and sub-committee on prisoners, deportees and fugitives. The problem of collaborators – perhaps 5,000 – and their families was discussed. The Police Minister Moshe Shahl said that 9,000 Palestinians were being held in army camps in the Occupied Territories and 4,000 in prisons in Israel. Talks were set to be completed by and Israel's withdrawal scheduled to start on 13 December. Withdrawal was to be effected by 13 April 1994. The first prisoner was released after 23 years. A third committee meeting in Washington discussed the holding of elections before 13 July 1994. A fourth committee discussed aid and an Economic Committee was formed. There were differences over the Jericho area. The Palestinians wanted 395 sq km, Israel offered 25. On 20 October difficulties arose over security. Israel demanded the right of hot pursuit. Rabin talked of "the hundreds of details we didn't even imagine" and predicted that talks may not finish on time.

TABIT, Muhammad Mustafa (1939–93)

Moroccan criminal. He joined the police in 1960 and by 1976 he had risen to become police chief in Beni Mellal. There he was involved in a scandal when a young girl threw herself from his office window but nevertheless was promoted to Rabat. In 1983 Tabit was appointed chief of the Special Branch in a district of Casablanca. In March 1993 he was sentenced to death for rape, deflowering virgins, inciting debauchery and abduction. At his trial he claimed to have had sex with 1,600 women in three years but denied having used violence. He also admitted having made 118 pornographic videos involving 518 women without their knowledge. It also emerged that he extracted money from his victims in return for not revealing their shame. His chief was jailed for life for complicity and ten other senior officers received sentences of up to twenty years. As parliamentary elections were due, the case assumed considerable political importance as the opposition used it as evidence of abuse of power and of corruption in high places and hinted that the participation of more important people had been hushed up. The excitement generated was such that it contributed to the postponement of the elections. Despite fundamentalist demands for Tabit's execution by crucifixion or stoning, he was put before a firing squad.

TAFILAH, Battle of (1918)

In January 1918 Auda Abu Tayi advancing in front of the main forces of the Arab Revolt liberated the village of Tafilah about 15 miles south-east of the Dead Sea. He was followed in by Amir Zaid ibn Hussain and Jafar al-Askari with about 60 regular soldiers and 250 tribal irregulars. The Turks gathered a force of about 1,000 regulars to recapture Tafilah but large numbers of local peasants and tribesmen turned out to resist them. Small groups held them off for a while breaking the rhythm of their advance until they reached the point where the peasants, strengthened by some machine-guns were massed on a ridge on their flank. Their fire and spirited charge caused panic and the Turkish commander was killed. The Arabs captured two Turkish guns, 23 machine-guns, 12 officers and over 200 men and the Turks lost about 400 killed. T. E. Lawrence was present but it was essentially an Arab victory.

TAHA, Mahmud Muhammad (1909–85)

Sudanese religious and political leader. He was descended from a family of Sufi Shaykhs and trained at Gordon College as an engineer. In 1930 he joined the Sudan Railways but his main interests were religious and philosophical. In 1945 he opened his own engineering office in Khartoum and in the same year founded the Republican Brothers with ten companions. He produced a new version of the Qur'an which differed from the accepted version. In 1946 he was imprisoned by the British for political agitation for two years and after his release went home to Rufaa and became a Sufi. In 1950 he returned to Khartoum and resumed preaching and political activities, producing scores of pamphlets and books on a wide variety of topics. His most important work, translated into English as *The Second Message of Islam*, argued that some of the *Surahs* revealed in Medina, while a guide to morality, no longer provided a valid social and economic framework. He opposed Islamic fundamentalists, advocated the full equality of women and denounced the imposition in the September Laws of 1983 of the *Shariah* with its consequent mutilations upon the non-Muslim South; this, he said, humiliated the Sudan and distorted Islam. He spent 18 months in jail but continued his activities after his release. In January 1985 he was rearrested, and, after a brief trial, later held by the Supreme Court to have been illegal, was hanged. His organisation, a handful of students and intellectuals, was not large enough to pose a threat to the Nimeiri regime but his execution was probably intended as a warning to more important politicians like Sadiq al-Mahdi. The outrage caused by his execution contributed to the overthrow of Nimeiri which occurred ten weeks later. Eloquent, charismatic, incorruptible he was also tolerant and erudite and immensely respected.

al-TAHIR (BAKR), Rashid (1930–)

Sudanese Prime Minister. He was educated at Hantoub Secondary School in the Gezira and at Khartoum University where he was President of the Students' Union. He was imprisoned under the military regime of General Abboud but, as a representative of the Muslim Brothers, he was Minister of Animal Resources and then of Justice in the government of Sirr al-Khatim al-Khalifah. While in the latter post he and 13 others were arrested after the seizure of 18 tons of Czech weapons which he claimed were for the Eritrean Muslims revolting against the regime of Haile Selassie but which were believed to have been destined for a coup at home. In 1972 he was appointed Ambassador to Libya. When Nimeiri established the Sudan Socialist Union, Tahir was appointed a member of its Politburo. In 1974 he became Speaker of the National Assembly. Following a coup attempt by the National Front in August 1976 Tahir was appointed Prime Minister. The President retained all essential powers, appointing and dismissing Ministers although they were nominally responsible to the PM. After Cabinet reshuffles in February and May 1977, Nimeiri took over as Prime Minister in September while Tahir became Foreign Minister replacing the pro-Western Mansur Khalid. Tahir played an important role in ending a prolonged period of hostility to Libya and chaired the Council of Ministers of the Organisation of African Unity. He was also Vice-President. In June 1980 he was dismissed, reportedly for having opposed close relations with Egypt which had been ostracised by most Arab countries since the Camp David Agreements and also with Ethiopia which was still trying to repress the Eritreans. He continued influential in the SSU and in January 1982 he was a member of the committee appointed to revitalise it. In May 1983 he replaced Hassan Turabi as Attorney-General. In March 1985 it was reported that he had warned Nimeiri that Turabi was preparing a coup. He was appointed Third Vice-President but lost the office when General Siwar al-Dhahab overthrew the regime the following month.

TA'IF GULF FOREIGN MINISTERS' MEETING (1979)

After a meeting in October 1979 of the Foreign Ministers of the Gulf States in Ta'if official statements were not informative. However it later emerged that Kuwait had put forward a proposal for some form of federation along American lines, involving unified policies in foreign affairs, defence, judicial system and oil matters with each state retaining control of domestic matters. There was emphasis on social and economic integration. The results of the initiative were seen the following year in the formation of the Gulf Co-operation Council.

TA'IF ISLAMIC SUMMIT (1981)

The Third Islamic Summit (the first was the Rabat Islamic Summit of 1969 and the second was in Lahore in 1974) assembled in Ta'if from 25 to 28 January 1981. It was attended by 28 Heads of State and ten other political leaders while the principal absentees were Egypt, Iran, Afghanistan and Libya. Representatives of numerous organisations including the United Nations (Secretary-General Kurt Waldheim) were present. The first session was held in the Great Mosque at Mecca and was addressed by King Khalid before moving to Ta'if where opulent new buildings erected for the occasion caused criticism from representatives of poorer countries. A special Mecca Declaration on *jihad* was issued followed by a series of Resolutions. It was stressed that Palestine was the most important of all problems for the Muslim world and pledged mobilisation of all resources to recover Holy Jerusalem. Resolution 242 and the Camp David agreement were denounced. Concern was expressed over the Russian intervention in Afghanistan and the plight of its refugees and also for oppressed Muslims in the Horn of Africa. There was a call for Islamic solidarity, abstention from alliances with outside powers and non-interference with each other. A Committee was established to attempt to mediate in the Iran–Iraq War, another to try to find a just solution to the problem of Eritrea and a third to help the famine in the drought-stricken *Sahil* area of Africa. France was asked to discuss the question of Mayotte with the Comoro Islands. It was agreed to set up an Islamic Court of Justice and an Islamic Centre for the Development of Trade. New centres for the study of Islam should be created in Africa and Institutes for Science and Technology and Education established. The Islamic Development Bank should increase grants to the poorer countries and a project for an Islamic relief agency studied. It was agreed that the Islamic Summit should meet every three years. The Conference showed the dominant position in the Islamic world of Saudi Arabia which announced that it would contribute $1 billion for the development of Muslim countries.

TA'IF PARLIAMENT (1989)

When in September 1988 President Amin Gemayel left office Lebanon had no President as the National Assembly had been prevented from meeting in sufficient numbers to elect a successor. As his last action Gemayel appointed General Michel Aoun as Prime Minister although the government of Salim al-Hoss was still in existence and Lebanon therefore had two Cabinets claiming legitimacy. Neither administered a substantial part of the country which was occupied by the Syrian army which Aoun declared he would expel. In May 1989 at the Casablanca Summit it was agreed to set up a Tripartite Arab Committee to bring about a cease-fire and to arrange for constitutional reform and the election of a new President. Much of the mediation between the warring factions was done by the Assistant Secretary-General of the Arab League Lakhdar al-Ibrahimi and the Saudi Foreign Minister Prince Saud al-Faysal. At the end of September the surviving members of the Lebanese Parliament elected in 1972 met in Ta'if. Out of the original 99, 62 remained – 31 Christians and 31 Muslims including such veterans as Saeb Salam. After three weeks of discussions in which the Kataib leader Georges Saadeh played a useful part a revision of the 1943 National Pact was agreed. The old 6–5 division in favour of the Christians would be replaced by parity with each having half of the 128 parliamentary seats. The President would still be a Maronite and Commander-in-Chief but would lose much of his executive power to the Prime Minister (who would still be a Sunni) and his Cabinet. This went a long way towards meeting Muslim demands without too drastically cutting the privileges of the Maronites. The Shiah retained the Speakership while the Druzes received nothing new. It was further agreed that Syrian troops should be withdrawn from Beirut to Eastern Lebanon two years after the reforms had been implemented and their future status would be agreed between the two governments. This gave their presence in Lebanon the legitimacy that it had lacked since the lapsing of the Arab Deterrent Security Force. The decisions were to be fomalised at a meeting on Lebanese soil which would also elect a President. It was generally believed that the Saudis had paid both the parliamentarians and the Syrian Government liberally for the success of the meeting but many of the Christian deputies, instructed by Aoun to accept no constitutional changes until complete Syrian withdrawal had been agreed, were afraid to return home while Walid Jumblatt and Nabih Berri joined their foe Aoun in declaring the proceedings illegal.

TAIZZ CONFERENCE (1977)

Early in 1977 it appeared that Russia was trying to form a close alliance of its supporters in the Red Sea area, South Yemen, Ethiopia and Somalia, all of which were visited by Fidel Castro. There had also been flights by Israeli aircraft and Ethiopia was putting forward claims on islands regarded as Arab. Alarmed by all of this King Khalid and President Sadat induced President Nimeiri to call a conference to discuss making the Red Sea "an Arab Lake". A meeting took place in Taizz in March 1977 of Nimeiri, Colonel Hamdi, Salim Rubai Ali and Siad Barre of Somalia. It is probable that Saudi Arabia and Egypt hoped for an anti-Russian pact but Ali refused to support the idea. The result was a vague declaration that the Red Sea should be "a zone of peace, free of imperialism and Zionist aggression". Only the YAR talked of an Arab Lake but stressed that this was not aimed at anyone. The project fizzled out. Somalia soon started to align with the West when it received no support from Russia for its claims against Ethiopia over the Ogaden. A Technical Committee set up to exploit the wealth of the Red Sea was established but proved ineffective.

al-TAKRITI, Hardan Abd al-Ghaffar, Air Marshal (1925–1971)

Iraqi politician. The son of a village policeman, born in Takrit, he graduated as an air force officer and later trained in England. In the late 1950s he joined the Baath and took part in the overthrow of Abd al-Krim Qassim bombing the Defence Ministry in the Ramadan Revolution of 1963. He was then promoted to command the air force. He supported President Abd al-Salam Arif in the November Revolution which crushed the extreme Baath and was advanced to be Minister of Defence and Deputy Commander-in-Chief. Early in 1964 Arif felt strong enough to get rid of the remaining Baathists so Takriti was appointed Ambassador to Stockholm. He rallied opposition to Arif amongst Baathist exiles, and was dismissed and went into exile in Egypt until June 1967. Takriti had retained his popularity and contacts with the armed forces and was able to convince President Abd al-Rahman Arif in July 1968 that he should leave office without resistance. Takriti was appointed Chief of Staff and a fortnight later, commanding the army in the absence abroad of the Defence Minister, prevented it from intervening as the Prime Minister Colonel Abd al-Razzaq al-Nayif was arrested. A Baathist Cabinet was established in which he was Deputy Premier and Minister of Defence, using the position to bring the forces under Baathist control. In 1969 he negotiated an arms deal in Moscow. Takriti was soon locked in rivalry with the Minister of the Interior, General Salih Mahdi Ammash as each worked to build up a following in the security forces, possibly with an eye to a coup. In April 1970 President Ahmad Hassan al-Bakr strengthened his own position by making each of them Vice-President but taking away their Ministries. He travelled extensively and represented Iraq at the funeral of Nasser and at the Non-Aligned Conference in Lusaka but during the summer there was a fierce struggle for power within the party as the civilian wing, led by Saddam Hussain tried to dominate the military wing. This culminated in Takriti's refusal to support the Palestinians during Black September and served as a pretext for dismissing him from all his posts on 15 October 1970 while he was on an official visit to Spain. Takriti although appointed Ambassador to Morocco nevertheless returned to Baghdad but was immediately flown out of the country. He went to Algiers and his wife on her way to join him died from a heart attack. On 30 March 1971 while living in Kuwait he was in a car with the Iraqi Ambassador when five waiting gunmen killed him. It was believed that this was done at the behest of Hussain who feared that Bakr might have been considering bringing back Takriti as a counter-weight to himself.

TALABANI, Jalal (c. 1933–)

Kurdish leader. He was a left-wing member of the Kurdistan Democratic Party Politburo and edited its newspaper. As Kurdish hopes in the July Revolution faded in the face of the determination of Abd al-Krim Qassim not to grant them autonomy, Talabani was one of the Party leaders in favour of rebellion. When the Kurdish Revolt (I) got under way he moved to the mountains of Southern Kurdistan, the Sorani-speaking area, where he proved an effective organiser of partisans – ·Persh merga – and also introduced socialist reforms. He served as the representative of Mulla Mustafa Barzani in missions to win support in Cairo, Algiers and Western Europe and negotiated the cease-fire of February 1963 with General Tahir Yahya. During the following year, however, relations between the two men deteriorated, partly because Talabani had personal ambitions to be recognised as the leader of his people but also on political grounds for, as an urbanised intellectual, he deplored reliance upon traditionalist shaykhs. In February 1964 Barzani negotiated a cease-fire with Baghdad without informing the KDP Politburo so Talabani went to Tehran, acquiring arms without the knowledge of Barzani. In the summer Barzani expelled Talabani from the Party, invaded his area and chased him into Iran. A few months later they were reconciled and Talabani then, on behalf of Barzani, undertook the negotiations that led to the Declaration of the Twenty-ninth of June and a general cease-fire. Talabani and his faction of the KDP re-established themselves in their old area of South Kurdistan. After the Baath took power in July 1968 Talabani became their close collaborator and was seen as entirely the Government's man. When in October fighting broke out between his followers and those of Mulla Mustafa the army moved to his support in the heaviest fighting since 1961. After the March Manifesto of 1970 ended the first revolt, Talabani returned to live quietly in the same Kurdish village as Barzani and rejoined the KDP although without any official position. In March 1974 after the outbreak of Kurdish Revolt (II) Talabani went to Damascus as its representative. In July 1975, in the general disintegration after the suppression of the Revolt, Talabani founded and dominated the Patriotic Union of Kurdistan, attacking the "rightist, bargaining, bourgeois, tribalist command" of Barzani, calling on all leftists to overthrow "the bloody dictatorial regime" in Baghdad and receiving aid from Syria and, after the Islamic Revolution, from Iran. The Turks co-operated with Baghdad against the PUK but it devoted much of its activities to fighting the KDP. In 1980/1 Talabani returned to Damascus and contacted Colonel Qadafi and anti-Iraqi Palestinian leaders. In December 1983 Talabani concluded an agreement with Saddam Hussein leading to the Kurds receiving considerable concessions towards autonomy in return for support in the Iran–Iraq War. These were not kept and by 1985 he was again in revolt and made his peace with Tehran. He found it difficult to fight in Kurdistan which was gradually being depopulated by the Government and where the tribes anyway no more relished having their lives controlled by a political party than by a central administration so he spent much time abroad. In May 1988 he was reconciled with Masud Barzani and they agreed to share leadership of a new Iraqi Kurdistan Front. In 1989 Talabani declared in favour of attacks in the Arab cities although he promised that there would be no terrorism outside Iraq and early in 1990 he was still trying to put together an anti-government coalition. Although included in an amnesty in May 1990 he did not return to Iraq, merely paying some clandestine visits. Soon after Saddam's invasion of Kuwait Talabani went to Washington but was rebuffed.

In April 1991, after Operation Desert Storm he went to Baghdad where he was shown on TV kissing Saddam with whom he claimed to have made an agreement for turning Iraq into a democracy with multi-party elections within six months, amnesties for Kurds and Shiah and Kurdish control over Kirkuk. He was criticised the Iraqi opposition for breaking ranks. Talabani was always concerned to reassure Turkey that he sought not independent Kurdistan but autonomy within a democratic Iraq and he had several meetings with President Ozel and he promised that the Iraqi Kurds would not assist the Turkish Kurds who were engaged in a guerrilla campaign against Ankara: he later made several attempts to mediate. In July 1991, Talabani was the first Kurdish leader to be received by a British Prime Minister and also visited Paris and Bonn where he asked for the establishment of a Kurdish Development Bank with assets confiscated from Baghdad. Later in the summer he split with Barzani who was prepared to put faith in an agreement with Saddam as he felt that there was a brief opportunity of obtaining more while the West was interested in the Kurds: he saw Kurdistan as a base for the overthrow of Saddam in alliance with the Shiah. Before the elections of May 1992 he visited Iran and Saudi Arabia to enlist support and at home he proved himself an exuberant, humorous campaigner. His PUK won slightly fewer votes than Barzani's KDP but they agreed to share Cabinet posts equally: neither leader took office considering that it would be more difficult to conduct their diplomatic activities as Ministers of an unrecognised state. Talabani continued to make frequent visits to Turkey and Western Europe. Talabani, regarded as over-excitable but a shrewd tactician, was, in contrast to Barzani, rarely seen in Kurdish national dress.

TALAL (1907–72)

King of Jordan. He was born in Mecca, the son of the Amir Abd Allah who had married his paternal first cousin. While his father went off on the adventure that led to his becoming Amir of Trans-Jordan, Talal was left in the Hijaz and it was not until after its conquest by Ibn Saud that he went to Ammam. There was an attempt to get him into an English University but eventually it was decided that he should go to Sandhurst, the first Hashemite Prince to do so. When he returned it was soon apparent that, as the High Commissioner of Palestine wrote, "his father bullies him intolerably" and that he might become a focus for political malcontents. Talal was given few functions and an allowance so small, according to his son King Hussein, less than £1,000 a year, that he could not afford to heat his house and his daughter died of pneumonia. His house was watched and visitors made aware of the displeasure of his father. In 1937 the Commander of the Arab Legion reported that Talal's hatred for his father extended to Abd Allah's friends the British. Although Talal had been appointed Crown Prince, the Amir considered him unfit to succeed and with the agreement of the British Resident, Sir Alec Kirkbride, signed in January 1941 a secret decree setting him aside. He tried also to arrange a union with Iraq whose young King Faysal II would eventually rule both countries. In these circumstances Talal's natural melancholy degenerated into schizophrenia and he was actually undergoing treatment in Switzerland at the time of Abd Allah's murder in July 1951. For some weeks it appeared that he might be passed over in favour of his brother Naif who had been appointed Regent but certificates were received from doctors that Talal had recovered. The Prime Minister, Tawfiq Abu al-Huda ensured that Talal should return as King in September. In November 1951 he broke family tradition by a visit to Ibn Saud and relations cooled with Britain and Iraq. In February 1952 a more liberal constitution was promulgated declaring that sovereignty lay with the people and not with the ruler and making the executive subordinate to Parliament. However, although Talal behaved normally in public, violence in private, including an attempt to kill the Queen who was in hospital having given birth to a child, made it more and more clear that he was unfit to rule. In August 1952 Abu al-Huda arranged for him to be examined by two Egyptian and three Jordanian specialists. In a secret session their recommendation that he be deposed was accepted by the Jordanian Parliament. Talal said "I had expected it" and went into exile. He lived on an island in the Bosphorus, rarely seeing anyone. Ordinary Jordanians, amongst whom he was very popular, believed that his deposition was the result of a British plot. Glubb wrote, "he was of acute intelligence, outstanding personal charm, faultless private morals, and inspired by a deeply conscientious wish to serve his people" and that he had appeared ideally fitted to be King.

al-TALHI, Jadullah Azzuz

Libyan "Prime Minister". After taking a degree in Geology from Louvain University, he worked in the Ministry of Mines until in July 1972 he was appointed Minister of Industry and Mineral Resources. In February 1974 he accompanied the Prime Minister, Abd al-Salam Jalloud on a visit to Paris in which they attempted to get arms and assistance to develop nuclear power in return for a guaranteed supply of oil. Talhi proved energetic in establishing new ventures, claiming in October 1975 that $420 million had been invested in the preceding year. When in March 1977 the Sabhah Congress abolished ministries, Talhi remained in charge of Industry and Mineral Resources as Secretary of the relevant committee of the General People's Congress. In March 1979 he succeeded Abd al-Ati al-Ubaydi as Secretary-General of the General People's Congress, in effect Prime Minister. His period of office was difficult for Colonel Qadafi was encouraging extreme revolution with students taking over schools and Embassies. Qadafi was conducting violent feuds with Jordan, Sudan, Saudi Arabia and others and meddling abroad in support of terrorist groups. Nearer home Qadafi was alternately threatening Tunisia with war or pressing it for union. Talhi led a delegation to China in August 1982. In February 1984 he handed over the Premiership to Muhammad Rajab, assuming the extremely trusted post of head of Qadafi's personal secretariat. In March 1986 he was recalled as Prime Minister but a year later was appointed Foreign Minister under Umar Muntasir. He was again regarded as the moderate face of revolutionary Libya, trying to reassure Arab states that Qadafi was not plotting against

them. In September 1987 he went to Baghdad and restored diplomatic relations which had been broken off in 1985. He was also involved in the negotiations that led to the establishment of the Arab Maghreb Union. Talhi led the talks that resulted in the end of the Libyan adventure in Chad. In January 1989 at the Paris Conference on Chemical Warfare he denied as a "vile calumny" American allegations that Libya was manufacturing chemical weapons at Rabta and in January 1990 he complained at the UN against the extension of American sanctions. In October 1990 he was moved to the Ministry of Strategic Industries, responsible for oil refining, petrochemicals and the vast iron and steel complex at Misurata which he endeavoured to develop despite financial and other difficulties. In January 1994 he was put in charge of the Great Man-Made River Project.

al-TALHUNI, Bahjat (1913–)

Jordanian Prime Minister. He was born in Maan, studied law at Damascus University, and served as a judge at Karak from 1938 until he became President of the Court of Appeals in 1952. A year later he entered the Government as Minister of the Interior and then of Justice before in 1954 being made Chief of the Royal Cabinet where he played an essential role behind the scenes. In April 1957 he was sent by King Hussain to demand the resignation of the Prime Minister Sulayman al-Nabulsi. In the crisis following the assassination of Hazza al-Majali in August 1960 Hussain, confident of Talhuni's total loyalty, appointed him Prime Minister. He managed to stabilise the situation and improve relations with other Arab states, particularly Egypt. In September 1961 elections in which two-thirds of the candidates were unopposed, took place without incident and the new Assembly gave the Government a vote of confidence. The economy improved. Talhuni was not a particularly competent administrator and his leadership was lacklustre so in January 1962 Hussain determined to make a fresh start and replaced him with Wasfi al-Tall. In 1964 Hussain decided to end his support for the royalists in the Yemen War and seek reconciliation with Egypt so in July he brought back Talhuni to execute these policies. This administration only lasted six months before the King decided again to turn to Tall. In October 1967 Talhuni succeeded Saad Jumaa and had to cope with the problems arising from the new influx of Palestinian refugees and their increasing militancy. In August 1968 Talhuni declared that they had a legal right to resist Israeli occupation, and in September the King in an open letter, assured him that he was "the best man to continue shouldering the trust of government for long periods to come" and agreed with him. They toured several Arab countries together trying to get united action after frequent Israeli raids. In January 1969 he signed the first Jordanian trade agreement with the Soviet Union. In March Talhuni was replaced as Prime Minister by Abd al-Munain al-Rifai amidst suggestions that he was too sympathetic to the Palestinians, for whom he pledged full support in April. The following month he led a parliamentary delegation to Moscow. In June he was appointed Chief of the Royal Cabinet and on 12 August he resumed office as Prime Minister, told by the King that the country's first objective was the "liberation of the occupied territories"; there was also a need to improve relations with Egypt which was regarded as Talhuni's specialty. Talhuni made a series of visits to Arab capitals trying to organise joint action after the burning of the al-Aqsa Mosque in Jerusalem. In October there were rumours that he was about to be replaced by Tall but he won a vote of confidence in November. In June 1970 the King thought that the Abd al-Munim al-Rifai would be more successful at dealing with the worsening crisis with the Palestine Liberation Organisation so he appointed him to replace Talhuni who became Chairman of the national airline.

TALI, Rashid (1873–1926)
First Administrative Secretary and President of the Council of Advisers of Trans-Jordan. A Lebanese Druze he studied in Constantinople in the 1890s and was later a member of Fatat, the group of young nationalists. He rallied to the Hashemites and served Faysal when he was King of Syria. He was subsequently sentenced to death by the French. He took refuge in Trans-Jordan and when the first administration was established there in April 1921 he was appointed to head it. A member of the Istiqlal he was primarily concerned with Arab unity and had, therefore, no real interest in the new state as such. Tribal shaykhs complained that all his attention was devoted to the problems of Syria and threatened to remove him by force. At the same time he alienated the British by demanding that the subsidy for the armed forces should be paid to his government instead of to the British Commandant. The Amir Abd Allah found his aggressive nationalism, although often an embarrassment, a convenient excuse for sometimes failing to comply with British wishes. In June 1921 General Gouraud, the French High Commissioner in Syria was ambushed, it was suspected by nationalists who had crossed the border from Trans-Jordan. The High Commissioner in Palestine, Sir Herbert Samuel, demanded that they be surrendered and when this was not done, insisted upon the dismissal of Tali which occurred in August. He remained for some time in Trans-Jordan but the British ensured that he never received another appointment.

TALIB, Naji (1917–)
Iraqi Prime Minister. A Shiah, he was born in Nasiriyyah of which his father was Mayor and Member of Parliament and trained as an officer at Baghdad Military Academy and Sandhurst. He attended Staff College in England, was Military Attaché in London and subsequently Director of Military Intelligence and of Military Training and Commander of Basra garrison. He joined the Free Officers in 1955 and used his position to accumulate secret stocks of ammunition. Talib took part in the July Revolution and was appointed Minister of Social Affairs. A moderate pan-Arab and a known sympathiser with the Baath, he resigned in February 1959 as Abd al-Krim Qassim moved close to the communists. After the October 1959 attempt on Qassim's life Talib fled to Lebanon but despite making propaganda against the regime was allowed to return late in 1961. He was a Minister in the Baath Govern-

ment of 1963 and was Foreign Minister in that of General Tahir Yahya before becoming Prime Minister in August 1966. He was regarded as moderate, conciliatory and not unacceptable to any faction, and he formed a Cabinet of seven soldiers and twelve civilians, mostly apolitical officials. President Abd al-Rahman al-Arif gave General Talib an ambitious programme including the reconstruction of Kurdistan, creating national unity, social justice, development of deserts, reform of the education system, making a reality of the Arab Socialist Union and holding general elections to create a constitution while maintaining the alliance with the USSR. Within three months there were rumours of his resignation because of differences with the President and the impossibility of forming a Cabinet which represented all groups. Talib, acting as Minister of Petroleum, conducted prolonged negotiations with the Iraq Petroleum Company over oil royalties which also involved Syria which had blocked the pipeline greatly reducing Iraqi revenues. He made no progress with solving Kurdish or constitutional problems which were becoming acute. He was unwilling or unable to make any move towards Arab unity. In May 1967 as he had still failed to form a satisfactory Cabinet the President himself determined to take over the Premiership with Talib as one of four Vice-Premiers. In June 1969 a Lebanese businessman declared that both Arif and Talib had been agents of the CIA.

al-TALL, Abd Allah (1918–)
Jordanian military conspirator. He was a member of a notable family of Irbid and after secondary education there became a customs officer before, at the beginning of the war, enlisting in the Arab Legion. He rose rapidly and at the start of the Palestine War was commanding a company in Jerusalem. King Abd Allah, impressed by his skill and courage in action, ordered his promotion despite the reservations of Glubb Pasha. According to his memoirs, Tall started to contact fellow-officers with the intention of organising a coup to introduce radical reforms. He was well aware of the King's secret dealings with the Israelis for he had been present at some of the meetings that led to the Shunah Agreement. After the Rhodes Armistice Tall was appointed Governor of Jerusalem, giving up his military command. He started to put together a conspiracy of Palestinians discontented with the incorporation of the West Bank into the Hashemite Kingdom, members of the Baath and of the Jordan Communist Party. He also contacted the Egyptian Government and President Husni al-Zaim of Syria who resented the aggrandisement of Abd Allah which they saw as the reward for collusion with Israel. He also tried to involve Crown Prince Talal who was at odds with his father but ultimately, as a town-bred intellectual, he failed to get the support of the fiercely loyal bedouin officers. At the end of 1949, despairing after the overthrow of Zaim by the pro-Hashemite Sami al-Hinnawi of the Syrian help that he saw as essential, he fled to Cairo taking stolen documents which showed the King's dealings with Israel. There he allied with the Mufti, Haj Amin al-Hussaini and made propaganda accusing the King and Glubb of treachery. He was sentenced to death in absentia for involvement in the murder of Abd Allah but he strenuously denied impli-

cation and in 1965 he was granted a pardon and allowed to return.

al-TALL, Wasfi (1920–71)

Jordanian Prime Minister. He was born in Irbid, the son of a famous poet, and after taking a degree from the American University of Beirut worked as a teacher in Salt until 1943 when, having been turned down for the Arab Legion, he joined the British army. He commanded British troops in Galilee and ended as a Captain in military intelligence, before going to London where he worked under Musa al-Alami presenting the Arab case on Palestine. During the fighting he spent a brief period in the Syrian army, alongside Fawzi al-Qawukji before returning to Amman where he rose to Assistant Director in the Income Tax Department and Director of the Press Bureau. He spent the years 1955–7 as Counsellor in Bonn, then after some months as Chief of Royal Protocol was appointed Chargé in Tehran. In 1959 at a time when relations with Egypt were extremely bad, Tall was put in charge of propaganda, replying in kind to the vituperation of *Sawt al-Arab*. At the end of 1960 when joint hostility towards Egypt led to a restoration of relations with Iraq, Tall became the first Jordanian Ambassador to Baghdad since the killing of Faysal II. While revolutionary Arab nationalism was sweeping through the area Jordan, under conservative Prime Ministers such as Samir al-Rifai seemed to be making progress neither towards liberalism nor development, so in January 1962 King Hussain decided on a "new phase". Tall, appointed Prime Minister, formed a new type of Cabinet of youngish intellectuals, none of whom had ever held office before and so were untainted by corruption. Tall spoke of "a new frontier" and launched an ambitious Seven-Year Plan to raise the gross national product by 70% in ten years through a system of "welfare capitalism" that would make the state economically viable. Fairer elections produced a more representative Parliament and political prisoners were released. However Tall caused difficulties for Jordan by pushing the King into support of the Royalists in the Yemen War, isolating the country at the time that the Unity Talks between Egypt, Syria and Iraq were taking place in Cairo and on 27 March 1963 he resigned. In February 1965 he returned as Prime Minister after Bahjat al-Talhuni had resigned. In March 1966 he criticised Arab disunity over Palestine. He was a strong, competent administrator who was said to know every tribal notable, and possibly every camel, in the country. In the spring of 1966 he cracked down on left-wing dissent and there were numerous arrests. Tall also strongly opposed the pretensions of Ahmad al-Shuqairi and the Palestine Liberation Organisation and refused to be browbeaten by the Syrians: when they announced they would close the frontier, Tall threatened to reopen it by force. He worked closely with the Saudis and was denounced by President Nasser, whose meddling in Jordanian affairs he refused to countenance, as a "super-imperialist" and an agent of the CIA who had handed over secret documents on Arab planning. In return he attacked Nasser for wrecking Arab unity to escape from his responsibilities for acting against Israel and hiding behind the skirts of UNEF. Early in 1967 a man sent from Syria to murder him was arrested. In March he resigned as the King hoped to improve relations with Egypt and also because some of his Ministers had to leave the Government in order to contest elections. He strongly advised Hussain not to become involved in the June War but then was adamant that the Israeli occupation of the West Bank should not be recognised and that the army and the PLO should be united to regain it. At the same time he was insistent that the guerrillas had to be under the control of the Jordanian Government from whose territory they operated thereby exposing it to consequent Israeli reprisals. After an uneasy truce between the Government and the PLO after Black September Tall was appointed Prime Minister on 28 October with the programme of restoring relations with the *fedayin*, co-operation with other Arab states to regain the occupied territories and overhauling the Government. Yassir Arafat attacked the appointment, convinced that Tall intended to liquidate the guerrillas and for some months talks and clashes alternated. In January 1971 Tall stated that Jordan would recognise Israel if it withdrew from the occupied territories and implemented Resolution 242 but until then it was necessary to increase the armed forces and he would support guerrilla activities outside Jordan. In June Tall was ordered by Hussain to take "resolute action" against those plotting to establish a separate Palestinian state and he replied that he would "chop off the hands which are reaching out to dismantle Jordan's national unity and integrity". A major offensive followed in which Tall said that 2,300 guerrillas were killed and all their bases liquidated. Jordan was completely isolated, Syria closed its frontier and Colonel Qadafi threatened to send troops. On 28 November on a visit to Cairo to attend an Arab League Defence Council meeting on mobilisation against Israel, Tall was murdered in the Sheraton Hotel by four gunmen who claimed to be members of the Black September Organisation. One of the killers licked up his blood. All the Arab states except Libya sent condolences. The four Palestinians, defended by leading lawyers from several Arab countries, were put on trial in Cairo but freed on bail and subsequently allowed to leave Egypt. Tall, a very strong personality, was loyal and patriotic but tough rather than conciliatory. He was incorruptible, never hesitated to speak his mind to the King or anyone else and was trusted by the army and the people. In his British army days he had taken to smoking a pipe, without which he was rarely seen.

TANGIER CONFERENCE (1958)

In April 1958 an unofficial conference was held in Tangier of leading members of the Moroccan ruling party, the Istiqlal, the Tunisian ruling party, the Neo-Destour, and the Algerian Front de Libération Nationale which was heading the fight for independence – Ahmad Balafrej, Bahi Ladgham and Farhat Abbas headed the delegations. The final communiqué called for the establishment of an Algerian Government in exile, the establishment of a Maghrebi Federal Union and the evacuation of all foreign troops. It recommended that North African governments should not commit themselves separately in foreign relations or in defence plans before the Federal Union came into existence. The Gouvernement Provisoire de la République Algérienne was set up five months later and was recognised by the other two governments.

TANGIER SPEECH (1947)

On April 1947, as Muhammad V prepared to make the first visit to Tangier by a Moroccan Sultan since 1889, a clash occurred in Casablanca in which over 100 people were killed or injured in an affray after French Senegalese soldiers had molested Arab women. The French authorities made no effort to punish the men involved. The speech that the Sultan was to deliver had, according to protocol, been previously approved by the French Resident General Eirik Labonne and distributed to the press. Greatly moved by the Casablanca carnage, he pointedly omitted a paragraph which thanked France for its civilising mission in leading the country to prosperity and progress. Furthermore he spoke for the first time about "the legitimate rights of the Moroccan people" and in a subsequent statement to the press he declared his desire to strengthen his country's ties with the Arab countries of the East and the Islamic world generally. He praised the growing importance of the Arab League. As the Sultan had previously held himself aloof from the nationalist movement, apparently concurring in a ban on the **Istiqlal** Party, his declaration that links with the Arab world were permanent and those with France only transitory caused consternation in colonialist circles. The relatively liberal Labonne was replaced by the harsh racist Marshal Juin. For the Moroccan people the mere visit of their Sultan to Tangier reaffirmed the unity of the country and his speech showed that he was no longer a colourless puppet but their national leader.

TAPLINE

Soon after ARAMCO had started producing large quantities of crude it became obvious that the cost of transporting it to Western Europe would be greatly reduced by delivering it to the Mediterranean, cutting out 3,500 miles by tanker and the expensive transit of the Suez Canal. During the war the US Government proposed to finance and control such an undertaking but this was resisted by the oil companies which set up the Trans-Arabian Pipeline Company, owned by the participants in ARAMCO. The pipeline, 1,070 miles long, and requiring great technical innovations and specialised equipment, was a major engineering feat. A workforce which at one time numbered 15,000 Saudis and 2,000 Americans, laying 265,000 tons of 30- and 31-inch steel pipes had to be maintained in the desert. There were five pumping stations between Ras al-Mishaab on the Gulf coast and Sidon and the construction took three years before the first tanker was loaded on the Mediterranean in December 1950. Its initial capacity was 15.5 million tons a year, taking about one-third of ARAMCO's production. The Lebanese, Syrian and Jordanian Governments profited through transit royalties and cheap oil. The pipeline was, however, extremely vulnerable and in May 1969 a section passing across the Golan Heights was blown up by the Popular Front for the Liberation of Palestine and was out of operation for 112 days. A year later it was damaged in Syria where the government of Nur al-Din al-Atasi said that it would be too dangerous to have it repaired. The

Saudis who were losing $200,000 a day, stated that it had been sabotaged and imposed trade sanctions on Syria and threatened to cut subsidies to Jordan and Egypt. The three "transit countries" were losing $10,000 a day. In January 1971 the Syrian Government agreed to repairs and transit royalties were increased. The closure of the Suez Canal led to the development of "Super-tankers" which proved more economical than the Tapline and its importance still further declined after the outbreak of the Lebanese civil war and the Israeli invasion. The Saudi Government when it bought out ARAMCO declined to take over Tapline. There were difficulties over payment of oil for the Lebanese refinery at Zahrani and in September 1983 Tapline gave notice that it would cease operating in Lebanon and Syria. In 1984 its installations were taken over by the Governments.

al-TARIKI, Abd Allah b. Hamud (1919–)

Saudi Arabian Oil Minister. He was born in Zilfi, the son of a Najdi camel driver and at the age of six persuaded his father to let him go to Kuwait to attend school. As the country was still insecure they had to travel by night with the young Abd Allah in a saddlebag. At the age of eleven he started to earn his living, going off alone on a boat to Bombay to work for an illiterate Arab merchant. His next employer was so impressed with his abilities that he sent him back to Najd with a recommendation to Abd Allah Sulayman who was effectively Chief Administrator for Ibn Saud. Sulayman sent Tariki to school in Cairo where he distinguished himself as a scholar and sportsman, winning a scholarship to Cairo University and then to the University of Texas where he took a degree in petroleum engineering. He then joined ARAMCO, working for them in Texas and California. Although he had married an American he was not happy there, finding himself the victim of racial prejudice and he returned to Saudi Arabia where he was welcomed as one of the first young technocrats. In 1949 he joined the Ministry of Finance and Abd Allah Sulayman sent him to Dammam to supervise the financial relations between ARAMCO and the Government. Regarded as one of the Arab labourers rather than as one of the American managers he became convinced that the Company was unfair, refusing to share the benefits but keeping the price of oil artificially low, fixed by private agreement between the producers and not by its market value. Also it did not take into consideration the long-term interests of the country which included Arab participation in management and investment downstream. In December 1954 he was appointed Director General of Petroleum Affairs and when this became a full Ministry in December 1960 he continued to head it. He was the first to advocate a pipeline, built as an inter-Arab enterprise, linking the Gulf with the Mediterranean with feeder lines coming in from Iraq and Qatar. In April 1959 with the Iraqi Dr Nadim Pachachi he played a leading part in convening the First Arab Petroleum Congress in Cairo. He had already been in touch with the Ministers of the non-Arab producers, Iran and Venezuela and was the leading force in bringing them all together in Baghdad in September. As a result of this conference, OPEC was created. Tariki was now a major international figure but at home he became a strong critic of concentrating all power in the hands of the Royal Family, calling for more participation by the newly educated classes. He was impressed by the anti-imperialism and egalitarianism preached by Nasser and associated with the Princes like Talal b. Abd al-Aziz al-Saud who were critical of the maladministration of King Saud. In March 1962 after an argument with the Prime Minister Prince Faysal about the award of a contract to a Japanese company, he was dismissed and went into exile in Beirut. He later settled in Kuwait where he acted as an adviser to its government and those of Egypt and Algeria on oil matters and published a journal. He came to be an advocate of nationalisation of the oil companies. After the death of Faysal he was reconciled with the Royal Family. Extremely honest but impetuous and quick-tempered, he was the pioneer of the concept of Arab participation in the oil industry from the well to the car and also of price-fixing and regulating production levels by the producing-countries. Seeing the Middle East as eventually a single economic unit, Tariqi was an advocate of diversification, particularly into heavy industries such as steel, prepared to sacrifice short-term profit for long-term development. He sent large numbers of Saudis abroad for technical education. He continued at heart to regard himself as a bedouin and was a successful breeder of horses.

TAZMAMART

In August 1973 63 Moroccan military personnel involved in the Skhirat and Royal Boeing attempts were taken to a secret prison at Tazmamart on the foothills of the Saharan side of the Atlas. They were confined to underground cells, two metres square with no light, little ventilation and stone platforms for beds. They never left their cells nor saw sun for eighteen years and, with no medical attention, 33 died. In 1991 letters smuggled out led to their cause being taken up by humanitarian organisations and they were released. Most had health problems and had shrunk between three and six inches in height. Nothing was done for them on their release and they remained without civil rights. Hassan II originally denied the existence of Tazmamart but later conceded that it had in fact existed.

TEHRAN OIL AGREEMENT (1971)

The decade that followed the foundation of OPEC saw increasing confidence amongst the member states that if they acted together they could coerce the oil companies into making concessions. The revolutionary government of Qadafi was the first to make a challenge and succeed in winning very much more favourable terms in August 1970. In December an OPEC meeting in Caracas adopted resolutions which called for a minimum 55% tax rate, elimination of disparities and a uniform increase in prices, deciding to entrust subsequent negotiations to a group of Gulf producers due to meet the representatives of 22 companies in Tehran in January 1971. Led by Shell, the "Majors" and the "Independents" also formed a joint negotiating body and set about trying to obtain some support from the American and British Governments which, however, advised them to submit. When negotiations started the companies, faced with an ultimatum that there would

be a complete embargo on exports unless they gave way, failed to maintain a united front and had to accept an agreement which raised the price of Gulf oil from $1.80 a barrel to $2.10 with an annual increase of 5 cents. There was to be a further increase of 2% annually to cover inflation and a new system of payment taking account of gravity differentials. The tax rate was raised to 55% and the agreement was to run for five years with the Gulf states undertaking to refrain from leapfrogging if other OPEC members attained higher prices. Shortly afterwards the Tripoli Oil Agreement gave Libya even more favourable terms. The unity of OPEC members, only Indonesia had abstained, showed that the balance of power had shifted from the oil companies to the producers. The Agreements also showed the link between oil, Middle East politics and the "energy crisis".

TEMPLE MOUNT MASSACRE (1990)

On the morning of 8 October 1990 Palestinians, warned that Jewish fanatics, the Temple Mount Faithful, were proposing to lay the corner stone to start rebuilding Solomon's temple on the site of the Al-Aqsa Mosque, gathered to defend the third holiest site in Islam. There are contradictory accounts of what actually happened but the Palestinians threw stones to which the police replied with unprecedented ferocity, shooting for over an hour at the crowd. At least 21 people were killed, some shot in the back while running away and one body was found to have been hit by 14 bullets; over 120 were injured. The statement of the Israeli Government that the Palestinians had prepared rocks and sticks to throw at worshippers at the Wailing Wall was almost universally regarded as untrue. An official Israeli inquiry admitted that the police had been "out of control" and fired "indiscriminately", but said that the shooting had been justified. One hundred and twenty Palestinians, including Faysal al-Hussaini were immediately arrested. The Bush Administration was angered that the incident was exploited by Saddam Hussain to distract attention from his annexation of Kuwait and did not veto Security Council Resolution 672 which strongly condemned the killings and requested the UN Secretary-General to send a mission to investigate. The Israeli Government denounced the Resolution as "totally unacceptable" because it rejected its Jerusalem Annexation and did not condemn the Palestinians and refused to receive the mission. The massacre, at a time when the *Intifadah* seemed to have lost much of its momentum, caused a new upsurge of violence in the Occupied Territories. In July 1991 an Israeli judge criticised some of the actions of the police and the veracity of some of their accounts.

TEMPLER MISSION (1955)

In December 1955, at the invitation of King Hussain, the Chief of the Imperial General Staff, General Sir Gerald Templer visited Amman to discuss the adherence of Jordan to the Baghdad Pact. In return the British would increase the subsidy for the Arab Legion from £10 million to £16,500,000 which would have allowed it to increase its strength by a fourth infantry brigade and new tank and artillery regiments. The British would also give an interest-free development loan of £2,000,000 and provide military hardware. He attended a Cabinet meeting on 13 December to put forward these proposals but four Ministers, all Palestinians, insisted that the Egyptian Government should be asked its views on the negotiations. This was refused and they resigned and so immediately afterwards did the Prime Minister Said al-Mufti. Hazza al-Majali formed a new Cabinet to take Jordan into the pact but, spurred on by Saudi and Syrian money and furious propaganda from *Sawt al-Arab* (Nasser who understood that the British had promised him that they would not try to recruit any further Arab states into the Pact was particularly incensed), widespread rioting broke out. In Amman 10,000, including many children led by their teachers, took to the streets and a Legion officer was killed. In Nablus crowds demanded the dismissal of Majali and that Palestinians should break away if Jordan adhered to the Pact. In three days of disturbances in Jerusalem three people were killed and the Turkish Consulate stormed. The French and American Consulates and UNTSO headquarters were also attacked. In Bethlehem two were killed. Majali resigned to enable elections to be held to decide whether or not the people wished for alliance with the West; the victory of Sulayman al-Nabulsi made it clear that they did not.

al-THAALIBI, Abd al-Aziz (c. 1875–1944)

Tunisian nationalist leader. The son of an Algerian notary public he received a traditional Islamic education, graduating from the Zaituna where he had already published a journal. He was an early associate of the Khalduniyyah. He then spent some years in Constantinople and Cairo where he was greatly influenced by his friendship with Muhammad Abduh and Rashid Rida. In 1901 he returned to Tunis, started a newspaper and became the centre of a group which saw modernisation as a means of strengthening Islam. In 1904 he published *L'Esprit libéral du Coran* – a plea for co-operation with the French. Later his followers merged with the Western-educated group around Bashir Sfar and Ali Bash Hamba to form the Young Tunisians. In 1911 he founded a new Arabic newspaper devoted to Islamic unity. In 1912 when the French, blaming them for the Jellaz Affair and the subsequent boycotts banned the Young Tunisians, Thaalibi was ordered into exile. He was allowed to return shortly before the war in which he played no part beyond being in clandestine contact with other nationalists. In July 1919 he went to Paris hoping to lobby French politicians and the Versailles Conference but was rejected as having no official status. In 1920 he published *La Tunisie Martyre* – an idealised portrait of the past which presented the country as the centre of a brilliant culture. It accused the French of stealing land, trying to kill off the Arabs or brutalise them through conscription. The book became a standard text for nationalists. In the same year he led a delegation to the Bey Muhammad al-Nasir calling for the restoration of the Constitution of 1861. He was arrested by the French who decided to release him after nine months rather than risk the embarrassment of a trial. He emerged as the leader of the Destour Party but in 1923, disgusted by their factionalism and the lack of support from the Bey Muhammad al-Habib, went abroad. He travelled widely and in 1931 was one of the

principal figures at the Jerusalem Islamic Congress. In July 1937 Thaalibi returned to Tunisia but found himself out of touch with recent events. The Neo-Destour which had been formed in 1934 accused him of being more interested in Pan-Islam, the Salafiyyah Movement and the unity of the Maghreb rather than in the specific problems of Tunisia. A series of meetings at which he tried to reassert his leadership were systematically broken up by Neo-Destour supppporters and he had the humiliation of having to ask the French police for protection. He quickly went back into exile.

THABIT, Ayyub (c. 1882–?)

Lebanese Head of State. A Protestant, he trained as a doctor although he rarely practised. In the USA before and during the First World War he was the leader of the League for the Liberation of Lebanon and Syria and a strong supporter of the Allies. He, like Emile Edde, saw French protection as the only guarantee for an independent Lebanon and he rejoiced in their victory over the Syrian nationalists at Maysalun. In 1922 the French authorities in Beirut sent him to Paris to counter the arguments of other Lebanese that more powers should be given to local Parliamentarians. In January 1928 he was Minister of the Interior and of Health in the four-man Cabinet formed by Bishara al-Khouri and attempted to improve their administration. He was regarded as an energetic, outspoken and honest man, particularly useful as representing a religious minority but still a strong Lebanese Christian nationalist. In 1934 he was considered as a candidate for the Presidency but ran out of money and was unable to finance a campaign. From January 1936 until the post was abolished the following year on the restoration of constitutional government, he was Secretary of State with full executive powers subject to a French Adviser. In March 1943 when the Constitution was again restored he was made Head of State for three months to supervise elections. Most unwisely he took the partisan step of enfranchising by Decree all Lebanese *émigrés* who had not adopted foreign nationalities. This would have increased the Christian representation in the Chamber by 50%, ensured the election of his ally Emile Edde, and caused uproar amongst the other religious groups and in neighbouring Arab states. He was forced out of office and replaced by Petro Trad.

al-THANI, Abd Allah b. Jasim (c. 1870–1956)

Shaykh of Qatar 1905–49. Abd Allah's father Jasim b. Muhammad al-Thani became the dominant force in the area in the early 1870s although at the time of the clash with the Turks in 1893 he had sheltered behind the nominal authority of his brother Ahmad who was officially Governor of Doha. In December 1905 Ahmad was killed by a servant and his son Ali was too young to succeed him. Jasim's eldest son Khalifah was believed implicated in the murder so the title devolved upon the unwilling Abd Allah who would have preferred to remain a pearl trader. Jasim continued all-powerful in the background and it was not until after his death in July 1913 that Abd Allah exercised any independent authority. He was not, however, in a strong position. The sons of Ahmad and his own brother Khalifah intrigued against him and their lawlessness made it difficult to collect revenue. In 1915 the small Turkish garrison in Doha surrendered as a result of its isolation. In November 1916 Abd Allah signed a Treaty with Sir Percy Cox in which he accepted the same obligations as bound the Trucial Shaykhs, promised not to grant concessions without British consent, banned the trading of arms except through the Muscat warehouse and became responsible for the security of a post office; in return he was assured of protection by land and sea. In fact the end of the threat posed by an Ottoman presence in the Lower Gulf meant that Britain had minimal interest in Qatar and refused to support Abd Allah in his family quarrels. They declined also to guarantee him against Ibn Saud whose refusal to accept the frontier between their states posed a menace in the background although generally their relations were friendly partly because both were hostile to Abu Dhabi and Abd Allah had Wahhabi sympathies: when there were difficulties Ibn Saud exploited the differences in the Al Thani family. He advised Abd Allah to deal with an American oil company but the British insisted that any concession should be given to the Anglo-Persian Company. In 1935 Abd Allah assigned them exclusive rights for 75 years in return for 400,000 rupees on signature and then annual payments. Part of this money had to go as tribute to Ibn Saud. Oil was in fact found in 1939 but not exploited until 1949. Qatar had really no government, Abd Allah opened a school but could not afford to maintain it and was unable to support a hospital. He asked India for armoured cars and machine-guns but was refused on the grounds of his weakness and backwardness. In 1937 the old troubles with Bahrain over Zubarah were revived when Hamad b. Isa al-Khalifah planted a flag there. Abd Allah decided to crush the local Naim tribesmen and the British stopped Hamad from intervening. Abd Allah built a fort to which Bahrain replied with an economic boycott that caused great hardship, particularly in wartime, and led many Qataris to emigrate. In July 1939 there was a second quarrel with Bahrain over the ownership of Hawar which the British awarded to the Al Khalifah. Abd Allah never accepted this. Shortly afterwards he handed over most of his powers to his son Hamad, who, however, died before him in 1948. Abd Allah, regarded as a wise and God-fearing Shaykh of the old type, died himself just before the influx of oil money which caused problems with which his immediate successors were unable to cope.

al-THANI, Khalifah b. Hamad (1933–)

Shaykh of Qatar. When the Qatari Government was set up he held many posts including Director of Police, Director of Education, Minister of Finance and Petroleum and Prime Minister before overthrowing his cousin and becoming Ruler in February 1972. He established the State Advisory Council and reformed the corrupt practices of his family, for example, ending the practice of the Shaykh personally receiving one-quarter of oil revenues. As Chairman of the Committee which in 1968 discussed the idea of a union of the nine Gulf states he proposed a common market and was an active worker for the Federation of Arab Emirates. In January 1976 he tried to mediate between Egypt and Syria. He revived the Qatari claim to Hawar. He is not overstrict – Wahhabism in Qatar allows women to drive. He has established himself as a modern business executive. He is a very hard worker, often working 12 hours at a stretch. He is reputed personally to sign cheques of more than $5,000. Decisive, forthright and cautious, he has total control of the state and full knowledge of what is going on.

al-THANI, Jasim b. Muhammad (c. 1825–1913)

Effective Ruler of Qatar from about 1870 until 1913. A crafty, enterprising, ruthless but occasionally rash leader, he dominated his country despite enormous difficulties. The Turks who ruled Hasa Province after 1871 considered that Qatar was part of this area. The founder of the dynasty, Muhammad b. Thani al-Thani would never accept this but his son Jasim was prepared to do so to avoid British maritime control and also to keep Bahrain at bay. He was later given the official rank of *Kaimakam* and tolerated a Turkish garrison as long as it did not attempt to interfere in local matters outside Doha. From 1876 until 1890 he carried on a desultory war with Zaid b. Khalifah al-Nihayyan of Abu Dhabi over Udayd in the course of which in 1888 he raided into the Liwa. The Abu Dhabi counter-strike neared Doha and in the course of the fighting Jasim's son Ali was killed. He attempted to get Muhammad b. Abd Allah al-Rashid to avenge him but the British brought pressure upon the Turks to prevent this intervention. In 1878 with British acquiescence he destroyed Zubarah after the inhabitants had committed an act of piracy. In 1880 he incited bedouins to attack Bahrain but desisted after a British warning. In 1881 Jasim, determined to monopolise the pearl trade which was bringing him considerable wealth, started to harass Indian merchants and in 1882 he formally expelled them from Doha. The British demanded compensation and their reinstatement under threat of bombardment. The Turks protested but London informed Constantinople that it did not acknowledge any Ottoman standing in the matter. In 1886 Jasim ostentatiously left Doha, having arranged for the Indians to be beaten up in his absence. Although he well understood the advantages to be gained from playing off the Turks against the British, he frustrated their attempts to establish any formal administration. In 1887 and again in 1889 when they wished to open a customs house in Doha he presented his resignation as *Kaimakam*, making it clear that Qatar was ungovernable without him; his resignation was refused and the project dropped. In 1893 the Turkish Governor of Basra visited Qatar and summoned Jasim to meet him. When Jasim refused, the Governor treacherously imprisoned his brother Ahmad who was acting as intermediary and attempted a surprise attack on Jasim's camp. The result was heavy fighting in which at least 100 Turks and 400 Arabs were killed. The dispute was finally settled by the Naqib of Basra who arranged for the return of captured Turkish weapons and a general amnesty. Jasim was allowed to resign as *Kaimakam* in favour of his brother Ahmad but continued to dominate events. During the crisis Jasim applied for British protection but although the Government of India was agreeable, London refused. Nevertheless he repeated the request on several occasions with similar results. Jasim continued to welcome dissidents against the Bahraini Government and in 1888 was warned by the British against rebuilding Zubarah as a base for them. In 1895, with Turkish consent, he ignored all warnings and encouraged rebels to invade Bahrain. The British intervened, destroyed their warships, ordered Jasim to pay a fine and when he refused, destroyed his fleet as well. A Turkish protest to London was ignored. Jasim had sympahies with the Wahhabis and in 1905 was prepared to welcome Ibn Saud, for whom he had often acted as an intermediary with India, to Doha. Ahmad, however, opposed this so strongly that the matter was dropped. In the same year Ahmad, then aged about 45 and described as extremely astute, strong and clever, was murdered by a servant with a personal grudge. Jasim's son Abd Allah b. Jasim al-Thani was appointed to succeed him as Governor but the old Shaykh continued to be the leading figure. A British visitor at this time described him as "a typical patriarch of the ancient type" with a long white beard, vigorous in mind and body and frequently roaring with laughter. Although he was reputed to have had 100 wives, he proudly introduced his youngest son then aged six. His best epitaph was spoken by his brother Ahmad "he plotted a new project every day of his life".

THIRD RIVER

Work started in 1953 to desalinate 15,000 sq km between the Tigris and the Euphrates. Eighty tons of salt a year would be removed from the earth for ten years and 15,000 sq km of arable land would be reclaimed. Six thousand men worked around the clock.

In December 1988, after the Anfal campaign, Saddam Hussain attended a conference in Basra on a plan of action for the Marshes. Draining the Marshes would make control of the land easier. Hussain Kamil Hassan, brother-in-law of Saddam Hussain and Minister of Military Industry, described the process as "drying the marshes by military industrialisation". Saddam Hussain announced that a canal was to be built between the Tigris and the Euphrates – the Leader's River – to be ready by September 1992. A 30-foot-high statue of Hussain was constructed with hand oustretched towards the river. Five-hundred and sixty-five km long, 8 metres deep, 90 metres wide at the south end and tapering to 36 metres at the north and navigable by large ships, it started at al-Mahmudiyyah, 30 km south of Baghdad and ended at Qurnah. Two million cubic metres of earth had to be moved to cut the last 5 km section. There were five road and one rail bridges. It could transfer water from the Tigris to the Euphrates if Turks cut off supplies. Work halted in 1986 but resumed in May 1992 and despite sanctions it was inaugurated in December 1992, trumpeted as an example of Iraqi achievement. A Fourth River, from Kut to Basra, some 190 km, is also planned – the "Loyalty to the Leader River" or Umm al Ma'arikah. The River Banks Project is constructing huge embankments (25 metres wide at the bottom, 6 metres wide at the top and five metres high) that block water from the Tigris and the Euphrates into the Marshes. The Euphrates is now flowing uselessly into Khaw al-Zubayr.

THIRD UNIVERSAL THEORY (Libya)

In July 1972 Colonel Qadafi resigned the Prime Ministership in order to have more time for the formulation of an ideology for the Revolution and in September he founded the Higher Council for National Guidance. In October he developed the positive neutralism between the Super-Powers practised by Nasser into rejection of both capitalism and communism: the one put the good of the few above that of the community while the other stunted individual development. In May 1973 he expounded his "Third Theory" on which both his foreign and domestic policies were based: "religion and nationalism, the only driving forces that since creation have stirred, and always will stir mankind – not sex as some would have us believe". Islam, and he appeared to regard all monotheists as Muslims, provided for social justice, the well-being of the individual within society and denied the existence of social classes. There should be private ownership but an equitable distribution of wealth, not merely within each nation but between nations. Islam provided for consultation between the rulers and the people. Libya was to be a model which would lead first to Arab, then to Muslim then to universal union. Qadafi spent large sums publicising these ideas which he developed further in *The Green Books*.

TINDOUF DISPUTE

It was not until 1933 that some parts of Morocco finally submitted to the French in a campaign which culminated in the battle of Jabal Sagho. At the same time Tindouf, which was known to have important mineral deposits was occupied by French troops from Algeria. Paris decided that Tindouf should henceforth be regarded as absorbed into Algeria, part of Metropolitan France, rather than into Morocco, a Protectorate, despite overwhelming historical evidence that the local tribes had paid *Zakat* to strong Sultans such as Hassan I. When Morocco regained its independence in 1956 it demanded the return of Tindouf. Despite the help that the Moroccans had given them in their own struggle for independence, the new Algerian Government also refused to agree to frontier rectification. In October 1963 Moroccan troops marched on Tindouf but Hassan II halted them four kilometres away saying that he was unwilling to "humiliate a brother nation" and poison relations for years. He feared also that a heavy Algerian defeat might have caused the intervention of Russia and consequently of America. The Algerians were unable to defend so distant an outpost and instead occupied some Moroccan territory near Figuig. Haile Selassie of Ethiopia, acting on behalf of the OAU, intervened and Hassan and Ben Bella met in Mali and agreed on a cease-fire. Both armies felt that they had been let down by their politicians. An Arbitration Commission was established but failed to satisfy both sides but tension relaxed. In January 1969 President Boumédienne paid the first Algerian state visit to Morocco and signed a twenty-year Treaty of Friendship at Ifrane; no mention was made of the frontier dispute. In May 1970 the King and Boumédienne signed in Tlemcen an agreement to set up a commission to mark a precise line, based on a French map and also to set up a joint Algerian–Moroccan company to mine the iron-ore deposits of Tlemcen. The communiqué also said that the two countries had agreed to co-ordinate action "to liberate and assure the decolonisation" of the Spanish Western Sahara: it appears that Hassan understood that he had obtained Algerian support for Moroccan ambitions there in return for abandonment of Moroccan claims on Tindouf. In June 1972 Hassan and Boumédienne signed a further agreement in Rabat defining the frontier and providing for joint exploitation of the minerals. Later Tindouf became a sanctuary for Polisario guerrillas and mercenaries fighting the Moroccans and was several times threatened with reprisal attacks.

TLILI, Ahmad (1916–67)

Tunisian nationalist and trade union leader. Born at Gafsa, he attended Sadiqi College and in 1937 he joined the Neo-Destour. He played a key role in recruiting tribesmen into trade unions which operated in conjunction with the Party and he was the local leader of both groups. He was also deeply involved in clandestine activities and was imprisoned from 1952 to 1954. Had he not been in jail he might well have succeeded Farhat Hashid as leader of the Trade Union Movement (UGTT) when the latter was murdered by French extremists but upon his release he became Treasurer of the Party and a member of its Politburo. In 1956 he replaced Ahmad Ben Salah as General Secretary of the UGTT. Tlili was elected Vice-President of the anti-communist ICFTU and worked to prevent the All Africa TU Federation from affiliating with the communist-controlled WFTU. He was also from 1959 First Vice-President of the Bureau of the National Assembly. In March 1963 Bourguiba criticised the UGTT for divergence from the Party in its opposition to the economic policies of Ben Salah by demanding that wage increases should follow the price rises caused by devaluation and Tlili was replaced by Habib Achour although he remained a member of the executive. Achour in his turn tried to obtain greater autonomy for the Movement and in July 1965 was arrested and expelled from the Party. Tlili defied the Government by going to an Amsterdam congress of the ICFTU claiming that he, rather than the official delegate, truly represented Tunisia and expounding his views and those of Achour. They were both "excommunicated" from the Party for "acts of insubordination designed to discredit our republican regime". Tlili spent 18 months in exile in Europe and America before returning home in March 1967 to be reconciled with Bourguiba who had just had a heart attack. At the beginning of June Tlili was "reintegrated" in the Party but was already under treatment for cancer of which he died later in the month.

TRAD, Petro (1877–1948)

Lebanese Head of State. A Greek Orthodox of wealthy family, he studied law at the Jesuit University in Beirut and in Paris. He returned to practise law in Beirut and in 1913 with some friends wrote a letter urging France to take Greater Syria under its protection. The letter fell into the hands of the Ottoman authorities and Trad had to flee to France where he spent the war. He was condemned to death *in absentia*. He returned to Beirut with the French and made a considerable fortune as a lawyer, being Chairman of the Bar, and as a businessman. Trad was one of the architects of the Constitution of 1926. He was one of the most respected of the pro-French politicians and a member of the Chamber of Deputies over which he presided in 1937. In July 1943 Ayyub Thabit, who had been appointed interim Head of State in order to supervise elections, proved to be so partisan that he had to be dismissed and Trad succeeded him for three months until the Chamber assembled and elected Bishara al-Khuri.

TREATY OF FRATERNITY AND CONCORD (1983)

Early in 1983 there was a clear need for the North African countries to co-ordinate their policies in negotiations with the EEC and in coping with the rising strength of Islamic fundamentalism. In March 1983 Colonel Qadafi threatened to make trouble in both Algeria and Tunisia if they did not implement past agreements to unite with Libya. Later that month President Chadli visited Tunis and signed a Treaty settling all outstanding differences and proposing large-scale development plans in frontier areas to form links between them. Neither would join anything directed at the other nor allow forces hostile to the other to operate from its territory. In May Bourguiba went to Algiers and was joined by President ould Haidallah of Mauritania. Bourguiba said that the alliance was "the spinal column of the Maghreb" which others might join and there were discussions of a North African Summit but Algeria refused to hold one unless Polisario were invited and Morocco would boycott it if they attended. After that there were frequent meetings between Algerian and Tunisian Ministers, setting up a joint bank, a development company, etc. In December Mauritania adhered to the Treaty and Qadafi applied to join but Chadli said that this could not be done until the frontier between them had been delimited. During 1984 Tunisia generally followed the Algerian line in foreign affairs and in May when Qadafi threatened to attack Tunisia, Algeria warned him off. In August Morocco and Libya agreed, in the Oudjda Declaration, to form their own Arab–African Union. In January 1985 a New Mauritanian Government, although less hostile to Morocco, reaffirmed its membership. The group generally worked together until February 1989 when it was subsumed into the Arab Maghreb Union.

TRIPARTITE PACT (1981)

In the summer of 1981 tension between Libya and the USA was building up to the Sirte Gulf Incident of 19 August. At the same time the PDRY and Ethiopia, the other pro-Russian states, felt threatened by the American build-up in the Indian Ocean at Diego Garcia and Somalia and by the close co-operation of Egypt and Oman with the newly created Rapid Deployment Force. With Russian encouragement Qadafi took the initiative and with Ali Nasir Muhammad and Colonel Mengistu signed a pact in Aden on 19 August. They agreed "to resist and foil the conspiracies of imperialism, Zionism and reactionary forces", condemn Western bases, the Camp David Agreement and South Africa. They would stand together in defence and security matters. A Supreme Council of the three leaders was established with Committees of their Foreign and Economy Ministers. Qadafi said that it would "enable us to liberate the

Arabian Peninsula and challenge the US" and some neighbouring countries were alarmed. In fact it was largely symbolic as the three countries were already allies. The most practical outcome was a grant of $400 million from Libya to the PDRY.

TRIPOLI AGREEMENT (1972)

Throughout 1972 relations between North and South Yemen were plagued by a series of frontier clashes which at the end of September became a full-scale war involving tanks and aircraft. The Arab League sent a mission which on 13 October announced that both sides had agreed to an immediate cease-fire. Their Prime Ministers were to meet in Cairo on 21 October to settle the points of conflict. On 28 October Muhsin al-Ayni for the North and Ali Nasir Muhammad for the South signed an agreement to unite their countries with a single flag, capital, legislature, executive and judicial authorities. The two Heads of State would meet the following month to decide upon procedures. On 28 November in Tripoli in the presence of Colonel Qadafi, who claimed it as a success for himself, Abd al-Rahman al-Iryani and Salim Rubai Ali signed a formal agreement providing for the immediate drafting of a constitution and a timetable which could lead to the creation of a unified state within a year. This would be based on Islam and socialism derived from Islamic sources and would struggle against the Imam, old and new colonialism and Zionism. Seven executive committees would be set. In fact with the YAR dependent upon Saudi Arabia and the PDRY upon Russia, both of which feared that its protégé would be submerged in the other, the agreement was never implemented. Despite the strong commitment to unity of Iryani he was never able to convince the conservative ulema and tribal leaders.

TRIPOLI BOMBING (1986)

During 1985 President Reagan, deeply affronted by the TWA hijacking and the *Achille Lauro* hijacking and under domestic pressure to take action, determined to hit at one of the states he accused of sponsoring terrorism. This would have a further advantage in showing that alliance with Russia was no protection. Syria and Iran presented more difficult and dangerous targets than Libya for whose Colonel Qadafi he had anyway nourished an obsessive personal hatred since 1981, calling him "a flaky barbarian". Preparations were made for an attack as soon as a pretext presented itself. Three times in 1985 Qadafi complained to the UN about American aggression: he also said that "we are capable of exporting terrorism to the heart of America" and called upon the Red Indians and Black American soldiers to revolt. There were reports that the Egyptians were offered money to attack Libya. In November 1985 a secret CIA plan to topple Qadafi was leaked to a Washington newspaper. In December there were the Rome and Vienna Airport Attacks which were generally believed to be the work of Abu Nidal although it suited Reagan to hold Qadafi responsible. In January 1986 American citizens were ordered to leave Libya under pain of imprisonment upon their return. The American Government imposed sanctions on Libya and was angered that European countries refused to comply. In

late January and early February a large American fleet, including three aircraft carriers, manoeuvred off the Libyan coast hoping to provoke an incident and on 24 March a pretext was found to sink three patrol boats, killing at least 50 sailors, and bomb coastal radio stations. On 5 April 1986 a bomb exploded in the LaBelle discotheque in West Berlin killing one off-duty American serviceman and a Turkish woman, injuring 200 others including some 60 Americans. The State Department claimed that there was "irrefutable evidence" based on telephone intercepts that the crime had been planned by the Libyan Embassy in East Berlin although it appeared more probable that agents of Iran or Syria had been involved. Although the German Government expelled some Libyan diplomats, no other European government was convinced of Libyan guilt apart from that of Margaret Thatcher who had her own reasons to gratify the Americans. A force of 24 F-11 fighter-bombers, supported by flying radar stations and flying petrol stations took off from Suffolk and had to skirt France and Spain which would not allow it to cross their territory. Libya was taken completely by surprise with its cities not blacked out and its defences unattended although a warning was received from Malta that a force was on its way. While aircraft from carriers in the Mediterranean attacked Bengahzi the main force bombed Tripoli at 2 a.m. local time on 15 April in a raid that lasted eleven minutes. The main target was the Azizya Barracks where Qadafi lived but he was unharmed although his 16-month-old adopted daughter was killed and his two young sons badly injured. American figures put the killed at 36 while journalists estimated the figure at over a hundred with a further thirty in Benghazi where fragmentation bombs were used. Despite claims of "a surgical strike", the damage was widespread, the French Embassy a considerable distance from the target being hit as were other diplomatic buildings. Few credited the statement of Secretary Shultz that Qadafi had not been directly targeted. One aircraft was shot down but the Libyans were humiliated by the ineffectiveness of their defence and the lack of support that they received: condemnation of the Americans was purely verbal and OPEC refused to boycott them. Hassan II, bound to Libya by the Oudjda Declaration, called for an Arab Summit but found no agreement even on where it should assemble. The Americans, who were probably hoping to set off a military uprising, at first alleged that the civilians had been killed in an attempted coup. Qadafi was profoundly shaken and did not appear in public for two days. He planned a reprisal missile attack on American bases in Crete but eventually settled for a few missiles fired from a warship at the Italian island of Lampedusa while two Britons and one American from the Hostages in Lebanon were killed by his supporters. Liberal opinion was shocked at the brutality of the American action which the French Prime Minister Jacques Chirac stigmatised as "totally and utterly unproductive". Late in 1985 Qadafi had appeared to be tottering towards collapse but the bombing restored his credentials as a revolutionary leader. He turned his ruined quarters into a museum and built a monument to his "victory" depicting an immense fist holding the wreckage of an American aircraft that had been shot down.

TRIPOLI CHARTER (1962) (Algeria)

The Evian Agreement of March 1962 provided for a cease-fire to be followed by a referendum on independence for Algeria at the beginning of July. It also provided for the release of the five leaders who had been kidnapped in October 1956. In order to integrate the Gouvernement Provisoire de la République Algérienne, in which they had nominally held posts, the military who had spent the war in Morocco or Tunis, and the men who had actually done the fighting in Algeria, the Conseil National de la République Algérienne held a session in Tripoli in June with the objects of defining an ideology and a programme for the future state and to provide it with governing institutions. A 20-page programme, drafted by four intellectuals with the encouragement of Ben Bella, was adopted. It criticised Evian as providing a platform for neo-colonialism and the wartime leadership of the Front de Libération Nationale which had left a gap between it and the masses, as, dominated by paternalistic petit-bourgeois, it had not looked beyond independence. In order to continue the revolution by non-violent means the FLN would become a political party which would remain distinct from the state. There was no definite commitment to single-party rule. The new state would adopt socialist principles with the main methods of production in government hands to facilitate rational planning in which the workers would participate. Credit and foreign trade would be nationalised. Agrarian reform would come through expropriation of colon estates which would be organised as "production co-operatives". Culture was to be "national, revolutionary and scientific" and modern progressive Islam was to be a central component of the Algerian personality. Islam was not to be used for demagogic purposes or as a barrier to progress. There was a need for a "conscientious vanguard" of peasants, workers, youth and revolutionary intellectuals. Women were to have the full rights of citizens, illiteracy and bad housing would be ended. Part of the army should become officials of the FLN while the rest should form the nucleus of a new national army which would have social service functions in contributing to the reconstruction of the country under the leadership of the Party. Foreign policy would be anti-imperialist with support for nationalist movements. The problem of governing institutions led to a split as the GPRA expected to continue in office while Ben Bella wished to substitute for it a Political Bureau consisting, in his original draft, of the imprisoned leaders and one other. Ben Khedda, the President of the GPRA stormed out of the Conference and the issue was later solved by the adherence of most of the military to the Politburo. After independence the Tripoli Charter was updated by the Algiers Charter of April 1964.

TRIPOLI DECLARATION (1977)

After the visit of Anwar Sadat to Jerusalem and his speech to the Knesset the Arab leaders who most strongly opposed his initiative met in Tripoli on 2 December 1977. These were Assad, Boumédienne, Qadafi, and Abd al-Fattah Ismail while Bakr sent a representative who, after failing to assert leadership at the expense of Syria, walked out claiming that an even stronger line should be taken. The Palestinians were represented by Yassir Arafat, George Habash, Abu Ayad, Ahmad Jibril and Nayif Hawatmah. Their Declaration condemned Sadat for "a flagrant violation of the principles and aims of the pan-Arab struggle" and services to Zionism and American imperialism designed to eliminate the possibility of a peace which would ensure Palestinian rights, isolate the Arabs from African non-aligned and Islamic countries and damage their relations with the Socialist Bloc. It was decided to freeze all relations with Egypt while saluting its betrayed people and to ask all Arab states to provide financial and military assistance to Syria which was now the principal confrontation state. This led to the establishment of the Steadfastness Front with whose members Sadat broke off relations. Libya and Syria deposed him from the Presidency of the Federation of Arab Republics whose headquarters would be moved from Cairo to Tripoli.

TRIPOLI OIL AGREEMENT (1971)

By the time that Colonel Qadafi seized power Libya was the third largest Middle Eastern oil producer, behind Saudi Arabia and Iran, supplying Germany with 45% of its requirement, Italy with 28% and the UK with 22%. King Idris had demanded from the oil companies an increase of 10% in the posted price and was due to receive an answer on the day that the Revolution occurred. The new regime announced "no spectacular changes" but that it would demand "more effective control" over production. In Libya concessions were held by both "Major" and "Independent" companies and the Government played off one against the other. While the Majors had numerous alternative sources, some of the Independents, particularly Occidental, drew most of their production from Libya. The former Prime Minister, Mahmud al-Maghribi, in charge of negotiations, ordered Occidental and other independents to reduce production at a time of international shortage. Esso also had to cut but could make up the shortfall whereas Occidental lost nearly half its output. Occidental was then threatened with a take-over and gave way at the end of August 1970, immediately increasing the price of $2.23 by 30 cents a barrel. Accepting also a revision of the former 50-50 sharing formula it agreed to pay taxes of 58% and had its full quota restored. The other Independents were compelled to accept similar terms and with half Libya's production covered by the revised terms, the Government felt strong enough to force the Majors into line. Some of them had been prepared to defy the Libyans and if necessary lose their concessions but were dissuaded by the British and American Governments. The Tehran Oil Agreement of February 1971 proved that the balance of power had shifted from the companies to the host countries and further negotiations took place in Tripoli with Libya acting for the three other countries which exported via the Mediterranean – Algeria, Iraq and Saudi Arabia. Abd al-Salam Jalloud adopted threatening tactics against the representatives of the 15 companies concerned. On 2 April 1971 a five-year agreement was signed which raised the posted price to $3.45 with annual increases in line with inflation and fixed the tax at 55%. It was estimated that Libyan oil revenues would be increased by 50% to about $2,000 million.

TRIPOLI SUMMIT (1970)

From 20–22 June 1970 Colonel Qadafi acted as host at a Summit which coincided with celebrations of the American evacuation of Wheelus airbase. It was attended by King Hussain, Presidents Nasser, Atasi, Helou, Iryani and Bakr and representatives of Morocco, Tunisia, Sudan, Algeria and Kuwait. Saudi Arabia, angered by the Syrian cutting of Tapline and threatening to cut subsidies to Egypt and Jordan unless it were repaired, was absent. There was substantial agreement with Qadafi that the Arabs had to choose between war and capitulation, that each Arab state had to make either a military or financial contribution or both, that unity of guerrilla organisations should be achieved and a government in exile created. There was unanimous agreement that war was the only way to liberate the occupied territories, that the USA remained "hostile" to the Arabs and that there was "dereliction of duty" in the Arab world concerning the battle with Israel. It was also agreed to set up a four-state committee to mediate in the crisis between Jordan and the Palestine Liberation Organisation that was about to deteriorate into the bloodshed of Black September.

TRIPOLI SUMMIT (1971)

The Cairo Summit of 1970, during Black September, had arranged a cease-fire between the Jordanian Government and Palestinian guerrillas but fighting between them broke out again. There was great indignation in the Arab world: Sadat called King Hussain "a traitor" while Syria closed its frontier. On 19 July 1971 Colonel Qadafi invited the nine Heads of State that had signed the cease-fire agreement, with the exception of Hussain to consider whether the position of the guerrillas had become so serious as to "call for direct intervention by force". Only five, Presidents Sadat, Nimeiri, Assad, Iryani and Ali met in Tripoli on 30/31 July. They issued a six-point schedule of decisions, pledging continued support for the Palestinian revolution "morally, materially and militarily" to ensure their right to self-determination and to operate from Jordanian territory if the Amman Government persisted in refusing to implement cease-fire agreements.

TUNIS, Bombing of (1985)

After the Beirut Siege of 1982, the Palestine Liberation Organisation moved its headquarters to the small town of Hammam-Shott near Tunis. Upon their arrival, they were welcomed by Bourguiba and the entire Cabinet who said that their 1,000 fighters would have the same status as the Algerians had done during the Algerian War of Independence. In the summer of 1985 Tunisian relations with Libya had been broken off after Qadafi had brutally expelled thousands of migrant workers and his diplomats were accused of posting letter-bombs to Tunisian journalists. He threatened force and the Americans indicated that they would protect Tunisia. On 25 September 1985 three Israelis were murdered in the Larnaca Yacht Killings, for which the PLO denied responsibility. When, on 1 October Hammam-Shott was bombed with the loss of 45 Palestinian and 20 Tunisian lives, with 100 wounded, it was at first assumed that the Libyans had done it. It then became clear that the bombs had been dropped by about eight Israeli Mirage aircraft, refuelled in flight by the Americans, as a reprisal for Larnaca. President Reagan said that the Israeli action had been "a legitimate response" but expressed regret at the loss of Tunisian, but not apparently Palestinian lives. He did not, however, veto a "vigorous" condemnation by the UN which said that the Tunisians were entitled to reparations. Yassir Arafat had been away at the time but the Israeli Chief of Staff, General Moshe Levi, stated that he had been a primary target.

TUNIS SUMMIT (1979)

The Baghdad Summit of 1978 had decreed that a meeting of Heads of State should be held annually in November but the following year, as that date approached, none of the major countries showed any particular enthusiasm. The Lebanese President Elias Sarkis, however, was anxious that his government should not be solely dependent upon Syria and that a wider forum should discuss the situation in the south of the country where the activities of Palestinian guerrillas brought Israeli reprisals. The Steadfastness Front hoped to push reluctant states like Saudi Arabia into a stricter boycott of Egypt after Camp David while the Gulf States hoped for commitments to their security after the Iranian Revolution. It was therefore decided to hold the Summit and Tunis, now the seat of the Arab League was chosen for the venue. Fourteen out of 22 Heads of State attended including President Nimeiri who had been regarded as pro-Egyptian. Saddam Hussain called for the use of economic strength against the enemies of the Arabs, an economic summit to reduce excessive differences in wealth between Arab countries and support for the Palestinians in Lebanon. Libya wanted support for Iran against the US: this was rebuffed although the Iraqi proposals were adopted. No real progress was made on Lebanon and it was vaguely hoped that its Government and the PLO could sort things out between themselves but $2 billion, half of it for the south, would be paid to Lebanon over five years. Syrian calls for a total economic, financial and travel boycott were rejected. The US was condemned more harshly than usual for its "hostile" policies. The request for audience by an Iranian delegation was refused at the insistence of Iraq backed by Saudi Arabia. There was no social contact between Saddam Hussain and Hafiz al-Assad. This tenth Summit showed half-hearted unity against Egypt continued but was unable to produce substantial results; Camp David was denounced but no alternative suggested.

TUQAN, Ahmad (1903–81)

Jordanian Prime Minister. The Tuqans had been one of the dominant families in Nablus since the early middle ages and held high offices under the Ottomans and the British mandate, at which time some of them established close links with the Amir Abd Allah. Ahmad Tuqan, after studying at Oxford, entered the Education Department until the annexation of the West Bank to

Jordan where he became Minister of Education. Between 1954 and 1963 he worked for UNESCO dealing with the provision of schooling for children in refugee camps. He then returned to Jordanian politics, holding the Ministries of Defence and Foreign Affairs and the Deputy Premiership until in the crisis of Black September 1970 Tuqan, who as a Palestinian undoubtedly loyal to King Hussain, was acceptable both to the army and to the guerrillas was given the key post of Chief of the Royal Court. When the newly-appointed Prime Minister Brigadier Muhammad Daoud defected, the King decided to end the brief experiment with military government and appoint a civilian to deal with the new Truce Supervisory Commission. Tuqan was therefore named Prime Minister although absolute powers were held by the Commander-in-Chief Field Marshal Habis al-Majali. After a month during which the guerrillas were defeated and a truce arranged, Tuqan made way for the stronger Wasfi al-Tall but remained a close adviser of the King as Court Minister.

TURABI, Hassan Abd Allah (1930–)

Sudanese religious and political leader. Born in Kassala, a descendant of religious leaders of the Funj period, he graduated from the Law Faculty of Khartoum University where he was an active supporter of the Muslim Brothers. He then took higher degrees in London and Paris. He returned in the early 1960s, married the sister of Sadiq al-Mahdi and taught in the Law Faculty of which he became Dean. In 1965, deeply shocked by the fate of Saiyyid Qutb, he resigned to become leader of the Islamic Charter Front and a member of the Constituent Assembly. He was a strong advocate of the outlawing of the Sudanese Communist Party and of the introduction of the *Shariah*. Turabi was involved in the drawing up constitutions in the Gulf States. At home he opposed the alliance of Nimeiri with the SCP in order to defeat the traditional parties and was imprisoned for six years. He was a member of the National Front formed by Saiyyid Sadiq and with him took part in the National Reconciliation of 1977/8. He became a member of the Central Committee of the Sudan Socialist Union, through which he hoped to build an Islamic state under government patronage. After the Iranian Revolution he went to Tehran but received no help and returned disillusioned at the conflict between traditionalists and fundamentalists. Turabi became one of Nimeiri's closest advisers, being appointed Attorney-General through which office he dominated a committee set up for the Revision of Constitutional Law. He proposed banning of liquor sales to Muslims, mandatory collection of Qur'anic taxes such as *zikat* and the introduction of Qur'anic punishments and Islamic banking. For some years Nimeiri was hesitant but in 1983 he introduced most of the measures advocated by Turabi as the September Laws. Turabi urged that the *Shariah* should be applied to the South which he saw as a vacuum, without culture, which could be filled by Islam and he blamed international outcry at barbaric punishments upon distortion by the press. He himself fainted on the occasion that he witnessed an amputation. In March 1985 he quarrelled with Nimeiri whom he saw not only as too dependent upon the West and as lax in applying *Shariah* but also

as harbouring delusions that he could become a religious as well as a military leader and was imprisoned. He was freed after the fall of the regime the following month and with the legalisation of parties, formed the National Islamic Front. Opposing any relaxation of *Shariah* by the government of General Siwar al-Dhahab he was again briefly imprisoned after refusing to sign the Charter of the National Alliance of National Forces. He contested the general election of March 1986 but was defeated by a coalition of all the other parties against him. Nevertheless he became Attorney-General and then Minister of Justice in Saiyyid Sadiq's Cabinet and strongly influenced his brother-in-law against diluting or reversing *Shariah* in order to conciliate the South which had rebelled partly upon that issue. He was later Foreign Minister and Deputy Prime Minister. After the coup of General Bashir he was again briefly imprisoned but emerged to become what was generally believed to be the dominating figure behind the scenes. Despite previous close links with Saudi Arabia, he refused to sign the Mecca Declaration condemning the annexation of Kuwait by Saddam Hussain because he disapproved of the stationing of Western troops in the Holy land of the Arabian Peninsula. Turabi went instead to Baghdad to see if an Islamic solution could be found and later he led a delegation representing fundamentalist parties, many banned in their homelands, to Iran and around the Arab states most closely involved in the crisis. He formed the Popular Arab and Islamic Congress and a meeting on 25–8 April 1991 was attended by delegates from 55 countries and denounced the actions of the West in the Gulf. He attended the Tehran Anti-Peace Conference of October 1991 which condemned the Madrid Peace Conference. He called for global action against the tyrannical West and denounced the Egyptian and Algerian Governments for their crackdowns on Islamic fundamentalists. Turabi was by now an internationally important pan-Islamic figure with clandestine links in many countries particularly in the Horn of Africa. The Americans saw him as a global terrorist leader, akin to Umar Abd al-Rahman, the Tunisians linked him with Rashid Ghannouchi and the Algerians with the Front Islamique du Salut. He co-operated with Gulbadin Hikmatyar in Afghanistan and with Hamas on the West Bank, trying to mediate between it and other Palestinian groups. In May 1992 there was an attempt on his life by Sudanese exiles at Ottawa airport. In June 1992 he appeared to be advocating the severance of the Southern region so that Sudan could take its rightful place as a purely Islamic state in a united Muslim Umma. The abolition in October 1993 of the Revolutionary Command Council which had ruled since 1989 was seen as still further increasing his influence. In November he went to Kabul and tried to reconcile the warring leaders. In December 1993 he presided over a conference of the PAIC attended by 400 delegates, including some Christians, from 82 countries which aimed to settle disputes between warring factions within Muslim states. A small, bird-like man, always courteous, humorous and approachable, he was an extremely skilful politician, pragmatic in accepting compromise in periods of transition until he could influence a new regime from within: this association with despotic regimes tarnished his image.

TURKISH PETROLEUM COMPANY

The presence of oil in Iraq had been known since antiquity and the possibility of its commercial exploitation arose in the first decade of the twentieth century. In 1911 the Armenian financier Calouste Gulbenkian played an important part in reconciling conflicting interests and putting together a consortium with just under half its capital held by the Anglo-Persian Company, just under a quarter each by the Deutsche Bank and Shell and 5% by Gulbenkian himself. The shareholders bound themselves not to seek concessions elsewhere in the Ottoman Empire except as a group. This Turkish Petroleum Company was in June 1914 granted a concession for the vilayets of Baghdad and Mosul. The participation of Anglo-Persian in which it took a 51% stake in 1914, meant the direct involvement of the British Government. After the war the German share passed to the French but, citing the Open Door Principle, the Americans also demanded to participate. The TPC was finally reorganised in 1929 with 23.75% each in the hands of Anglo-Persian, Shell, the Compagnie Française des Pétroles and the Near Eastern Development Corporation which was a group that included Standard Oil. Gulbenkian retained his 5% and the TPC changed its name to that of the Iraq Petroleum Company. In the meanwhile in 1925, under strong British pressure, King Faysal had granted a concession that covered the entire country and in 1927 oil had been struck in abundance near Kirkuk.

TWA HIJACKING (1985)

On 15 June 1985 a TWA Boeing 727 airliner with more than a hundred Americans on board was hijacked by two Lebanese gunmen on a scheduled flight from Athens to Rome. The terrorists forced the pilot to fly to Beirut and then to Algiers and then back to Beirut where ten more gunmen joined it. In Beirut one of the Americans was murdered in cold blood, some were released and the rest hidden in groups throughout the city. Although there were indications that they were linked with Hizbullah, hijackers, negotiating through the Amal leader Nabih Berri demanded the release of 706 Shiah internees held by Israel. President Reagan cut short his weekend to preside over the National Security Council which declared that the US would not negotiate with terrorists. Special commandos were sent to the Mediterranean but could take no action without endangering the hostages, five of whom appeared at a press conference at the airport. After 18 days the hostages were released in Damascus through the help of President Assad whom Reagan had frequently accused of fomenting terrorism and the Israelis released some of the Shiah.

UBAYDAT, Ahmad (1938–)

Jordanian Prime Minister. He was born in a village north of Irbid and had his secondary education at Nablus before training as a lawyer at Baghdad University. In 1961 after a period as a teacher he transferred to the security service of which he became Director with the rank of General in 1974. Ubaydat was appointed Minister of the Interior in the Cabinet of Mudar Badran in April 1982 and in January 1984 succeeded him as Prime Minister. His government was soon involved in a fierce quarrel with Libya, breaking off relations. In January 1985 the Cabinet was shaken by the resignation of his Minister of Information, Laila, the widow of Abd al-Hamid Sharaf; she circulated a letter stating that Ubaydat was incapable of handling matters. The economic situation did not improve and there were terrorist attacks on Jordanian interests abroad. Relations with Syria became extremely tense and King Hussain considered that he needed a more skilful diplomat as Prime Minister. In April 1985 he therefore dismissed Ubaydat in favour of Zaid al-Rifai during whose previous administration relations with Damascus had been particularly cordial. In October 1986 Ubaydat published an open letter to President Mubarak protesting against the expenditure involved in a development plan for the West Bank. He was stripped of his membership of the Senate but in April 1990 was appointed to chair the committee set up to draft a new Charter for political life. Ubaydat was regarded as representative of the traditional East Bankers, a tough, hard man with a great knowledge of the country and very close to the King.

al-UBAYDI, Abd al-Ati Ibrahim (1939–)

Libyan "Prime Minister". The son of a landowner, he took a degree in Commerce at Tripoli University, followed by a higher degree in Science from Manchester. Returning home he became a Lecturer at the Libya University. When in January 1970 Colonel Qadafi formed a Cabinet, he chose Ubaydi as Minister of Labour and Social Affairs. He also acted as Foreign Minister with particular responsibility for establishing close contacts with Malta, then under the left-wing Prime Minister Dom Mintoff. At a meeting of Islamic Foreign Ministers in Kuala Lumpur in June 1974 he caused a storm by accusing the Philippines of genocide against their Muslim minority. Ubaydi was also responsible for the civil service. When in March 1977 the Sabhah Congress abolished ministries, establishing instead the General People's Committee, Ubaydi was elected as its Chairman, effectively Prime Minister.

Two years later when government itself was abolished and Qadafi divested himself of all duties save those of "Thinker and Symbol of the Revolution", Ubaydi succeeded him as Secretary-General of the General People's Congress. In January 1981 he was transferred to a new People's Bureau for External Liaison with the responsibility of co-ordinating the activities of all the Revolutionary People's Committees formed outside Libya. One of his first tasks was to visit African countries to persuade them that Libya would give them financial support in return for backing in Chad. Later he violently denounced the Fahd Plan as capitulation to Israel. It is unclear to what extent he personally was involved in the excesses of Libyan activities abroad – the attempts to bring about the overthrow of Presidents Mubarak and Nimeiri, the expensive meddling worldwide from Indonesia to Nicaragua and Surinam via Africa and Australia and the murder of "stray dogs" – Libyan refugees in Europe. In January 1984 he was replaced by Ali Abd al-Salam Turayki who was described as more hardline. In April 1992 as Ambassador to Brussels, Ubaydi represented Libya at the International Court against complaints of attempted destabilisation of Chad.

al-ULSHI, Jamil (c. 1880–?)

Syrian Prime Minister. He came from a middle-class Damascus family and after Military College in Istanbul became a Major in the Ottoman army. He then represented Faysal in Beirut and there were some suspicions that Ulshi betrayed him to the French. After the murder of Ala al-Din al-Durubi in whose Cabinet he had served, in August 1920 the French appointed Ulshi as Prime Minister but dismissed him after a few months. He then attached himself to his relative and close friend Taj al-Din al-Hassani who made him Minister of Finance and then of the Interior in his Cabinet from 1928–31. He was seen as the dominant figure in this government, a capable, cunning and unscrupulous politician who lined his own pockets very well. Shaykh Taj brought him back in his 1934 government. A British report of 1939 stated that he was no longer of any account but when in January 1943 the government of Husni al-Barazi collapsed in the middle of an economic crisis and quarrels with Shaykh Taj, now President, Ulshi became Prime Minister. He took over many of his predecessors's Ministers and was opposed by the National Bloc. In March he made way for a provisional government to supervise elections.

al-UMAR, Zahir (c. 1690–1775)

By origin probably a camel-driver, Zahir al-Umar was first heard of as a tax-farmer in the Safad district of Galilee in the late 1730s. He won over the people of his area by not exploiting them for short-term gain but by making them prosperous in the expectation of staying permanently in power. He therefore remitted taxes and gave out seed in bad years and made alliances with the bedouins to prevent raids upon his district. He provided security and encouraged trade. At the same time he satisfied the Ottoman by paying his dues regularly and bribing protectors at Court. They therefore acquiesced in his reducing the neighbouring shaykhs and taking their land and by about 1742 he was master of Galilee. This incensed Sulayman Pasha of Damascus who was worried at Zahir's increasing strength and his absorption of taxes formerly paid to Damascus. In 1742 the Pasha besieged Zahir in Safad for three months before having to compromise. Death prevented Sulayman from renewing the campaign the following year. In 1746 Zahir was granted the tax-farm for Acre and also seized Haifa, regularising his position with presents to the Ottoman Sultan and the Pasha of Sidon. Under his rule Acre became the most flourishing port in the Eastern Mediterranean. He opened trading relations with British and French merchants and Greeks emigrated from Cyprus to live under his rule. He was able to pay a regular army of North African mercenaries by establishing monopolies. He married frequently, often into bedouin tribes and while this brought him allies it also meant that if his sons became disaffected they had their own power bases. In 1760 Uthman al-Kurji became Pasha of Damascus and began an implacable personal campaign againt Zahir. In 1768 some of Zahir's sons revolted against him and Uthman hoped to profit from his embarrassment but his sons rallied to their father and defeated the Pasha. Zahir then formed an alliance with Ali, Bey of Egypt who had had personal clashes with Uthman years before. In June 1771 Zahir and an Egyptian army under Abu al-Dhahab captured Damascus. Probably for personal reasons Abu Dhahab withdrew and Uthman regained his capital. He then formed an alliance with the Druzes to crush Zahir but his own army was destroyed at Lake Hula, with many drowned in the Jordan and then the Druzes were defeated. In May 1772 Zahir was joined by Ali Bey who had lost power in Egypt and together they captured Jaffa. The French Consul now reported that Zahir was "acting as an independent sovereign" and he entered into alliance with the Russians who were then at war with Turkey. With the help of the Russian navy, Zahir besieged Beirut which was held for the Sultan by Jazzar Pasha. A relieving force of Turks was defeated by Zahir's son Ali at Zahle. In 1774 the Russians signed the Kucuk Kainardji Treaty with Constantinople and abandoned Zahir. He was able to make his peace with the Sultan keeping Acre. The following year, however, the Turks, Abu Dhahab Jazzar and the new Pasha of Damascus combined against Zahir who was betrayed by his officials then killed by one of his mercenaries as he attempted to escape from Acre. His state fell to pieces. It had survived so long merely due to his political skills and the weakness of the Pashas of Sidon and Damascus. Zahir maintained the most cordial relations with the Christians and it was the custom for the Franciscan Friars in his later years to present him with 1,000 crowns on each of his annual wedding days; usually his bride was 13 years old.

UMM KULTHUM (c. 1895–1975)

Egyptian singer. She was born Fatma Ibrahim al-Baltagi in a small village in Dakhaliyya Province but for nearly 50 years was one of the best known personalities in the Arab world. Egypt was seen as Nasser, the Pyramids and Umm Kulthum. She had a high-pitched, almost hypnotic voice which even in old age still attracted listeners throughout the Middle East, compelling them to switch on Radio Cairo for her concert on the first Tuesday of each month. They evoked an ecstatic reception, often bringing work to a stop during the transmission. Many of her songs, sung with a sincerity that was almost spiritual, had patriotic themes, welcoming the July Revolution and keeping up spirits during the War of Attrition but she was unmatched in love songs, settings of verses by classical and modern poets and religious themes. She also played an important part in building the Egyptian cinema industry into one of the largest in the world, although she would never allow herself to be kissed on the lips. Half a million people attended her funeral and more than a dozen years after her death, Cairo was still broadcasting her songs every first Tuesday.

UMM QASR DISPUTE

In the 1930s the Persians under Reza Shah resented the international agreements that had put their boundary line with Iraq along the eastern bank of the Shatt al-Arab instead of along the middle and occasionally they harassed shipping out of Basra which, anyway, was not suitable for large craft because of sand bars. In March 1938 Jamil al-Midfai asked British permission to build a deep water port on the Bay of Kuwait. London refused but suggested that Iraq should develop Umm Qasr on a creek off the Khor al-Zubayr. In November 1939 Nuri al-Said agreed but said that in order to assure access, Iraq should be given the Kuwaiti islands of Bubiyan and Warbah. The Foreign Office agreed but Shaykh Ahmad b. Jabir al-Sabah objected and was supported by the India Office. The position was made more difficult by the fact that the boundary between Iraq and Kuwait had not been delimited and it was uncertain on whose territory the best site was situated. In June 1940 the Iraqis asked for British financial help to develop Umm Qasr and although this was refused, in the following year the strategic situation altered with the need to increase troops in the area and fears that the pro-German Reza Shah might mine the Shatt. In July 1941, therefore, the British announced their determination themselves to build a port at Umm Qasr which would remain under their control after the war. Iraq, expecting to inherit it was pleased but Kuwait, fearing to lose trade, asked for an assurance that it would be destroyed when the wartime need had passed. In March 1942 the port was opened and in June the Iraqis published a schedule of customs charges. The Kuwaitis, backed by the British authorities in India and the Gulf objected that this prejudged the future ownership of Umm Qasr. Nuri refused to withdraw it but after the ousting of the Shah and British victories in North Africa Umm Qasr lost its military significance and in the spring of 1943 construction work ceased. There was some argument as to whether it was worth retaining in peacetime but by the end of 1944 London decided not to do so and the port was dismantled. Subsequently the Iraqis built an oil terminal on roughly the same site.

UMM SAID

Oil production began in 1949 at Dukhan on the west coast of the Qatari Peninsula and was pumped 49 miles across to a terminal on the east coast at Umm Said where, in 1956, the Qatar Petroleum Company established its headquarters. In the late 1960s, Shaykh Khalifah b. Hamad al-Thani who was effectively running the country, determined to make Umm Said a development area. In 1969 he entered into agreement with a consortium of six British banks to build a fertiliser plant which came into production in 1973, exporting to India and China. In 1974 a refinery was commissioned and in the same year the Qatar Petrochemical Company was established, jointly owned with a French company. Also in 1974 the Qatar Steel Company was set up with Japanese participation and Qatar claimed to be the third Arab country after Egypt and Algeria to have heavy industry. Since then the original plants have been increased in size and new ones, producing plastics, cement and flour for example, have been added. Much of the development of the industrial area comes from a power and desalination plant and from liquid gas.

UMMA PARTY (Sudan)

In 1945, worried by the pro-Egyptian activities of the Ashiqqa party and by the possibility that London might reach an agreement with Cairo prejudicial to the interests of the Sudan, Saiyyid Abd al-Rahman al-Mahdi organised his followers, the Ansar, into a more formal political structure. With his son Siddiq al-Mahdi as President and Abd Allah Khalil as Secretary-General and a membership of moderate intellectuals, tribesmen and peasants of the White Nile and Kordofan, it demanded independence for the Sudan through co-operation with Britain and opposed unity with Egypt. In the first national elections in 1953 it won only 22 out of 97 seats (none outside the Mahdist heartlands) but showed its power by mounting an enormous demonstration in Khartoum during the visit of the Egyptian President General Neguib. This latent threat that the Umma could start a civil war if union with Egypt were pressed through was an important factor in the decision of the Prime Minister Ismail al-Azhari to take independence for the Sudan. In July 1956, although conservative and pro-Western, the Umma joined forces with the radical and pro-Egyptian People's Democratic Party to bring down Azhari and Khalil became Prime Minister. In the elections of March 1958 it won 64 out of 173 seats and Khalil continued to lead a fractious coalition until the military take-over of General Abboud in November. Although its leaders had not opposed the coup, it was banned with all the other parties and its members continued their activities under the religious guise of Ansar. Later Ansar were prominent in opposing the military regime

and in the summer of 1961 led major riots in Khartoum. After the downfall of Abboud, in which it played an important part, the Umma resumed formal political activity and in the elections of May 1965 it emerged as the strongest single party with 75 out of 173 seats while its National Unionist Party allies gained another 52. The Umma party then provided Prime Ministers until the end of parliamentary government in 1969. At first Muhammad Ahmad Mahjoub formed a coalition but the Party began to split between a conservative wing following the Imam al-Hadi al-Mahdi supporting Mahjoub and a more radical reforming group under his nephew Sadiq al-Mahdi who had been too young to become Prime Minister in 1965. In 1966 Sadiq, now of age, formed an alliance with some NUP members, pushed through a vote of no-confidence in Mahjoub and became Prime Minister. The split continued and in May 1967 al-Hadi denounced his nephew's government as "a complete failure because of its weakness". In the same month the NUP members changed sides and Mahjoub resumed office. In April 1968 the Umma fought the elections as two separate parties, the Sadiq wing winning 36 out of 218 seats nationally while the al-Hadi wing had 30 with six more uncommitted. In November 1968 the split was formally healed by the marriage of Sadiq with a daughter of al-Hadi but six months later the Party was suppressed after the Nimeiri take-over. It continued its existence as Ansar and suffered severe casualties during the storming of Aba Island. The death of al-Hadi left Sadiq as undisputed leader and he took a prominent part in the National Front founded soon afterwards to oppose the regime but in 1977/8 in the National Reconciliation he apparently acquiesced in the suppression of the Umma by joining the Central Committee of the Sudan Socialist Union. Some 30 former members of the Umma were successful as SSU-approved candidates in the elections of February 1978 and some held ministerial office. Sadiq, however, opposed the Government's policy of close alliance with the Umma's old enemy Egypt even after Camp David and resigned. In 1980 the Ansar boycotted the elections for the Assembly. It formed part of the National Alliance for National Salvation, helped in the overthrow of Nimeiri and re-emerged as a political party. In March 1986 the Umma endorsed the Koka Dam Declaration which called for a non-sectarian Sudan. In the elections of the following month the Umma emerged as the largest single party with 100 seats and 38.2% of the national vote and Saiyyid Sadiq, forming a coalition with the Democratic Unionist Party and some smaller parties again became Prime Minister. During his three-year administration he several times changed his partners but always retained Umma ministers. After the take-over by General Bashir in June 1989 the Umma and all other parties were dissolved and some of its leaders imprisoned. In September 1991 one of its leaders, Abd al-Rahman Najd Allah was accused of plotting. The leaders in exile attacked Bashor for his support of Saddam Hussain during Operation Desert Storm and in June 1992 its representative in London deplored Sudanese Government attacks on Saudi Arabia.

UNEF

On 5 November 1956 the General Assembly of the UN called for a cease-fire in the Suez War, withdrawal to previous positions and the establishment of a United Nations Emergency Force to "secure and supervise the cessation of hostilities". The advance guard arrived on 15 November to replace British, French and Israeli troops. UNEF was under the command of the Canadian General Burns who had been in charge of UNTSO. It grew to nearly 6,000 men from Brazil, Canada, Colombia, Denmark, Finland, India, Indonesia, Norway, Sweden and Yugoslavia and was deployed in the Gaza Strip and Sinai as the Israelis refused to have it on their territory. Its task was to deter raids by patrolling the border and to assure the passage of ships into Eilat by a detachment at Sharm al-Shaykh. UNEF ran into financial difficulties as Russia and its satellites refused to pay their share and was reduced to about 3,600 men. In December 1963 the Secretary-General reported that the cost was $19 million a year. Its reports showed a minor ground incident every three or four days and an air violation at least once a day but there were no serious clashes. Its Commanders were General Burns until December 1959, followed by Generals Gyani (India) until January 1964, Chaves (Brazil) until January 1965, Sarmento (Brazil) until January 1966 and finally Rikhye (India). The more pugnacious Arabs such as the Syrians and the Iraqis started to taunt the Egyptians with sheltering behind it. In May 1967 Nasser asked General Rikhye to withdraw his men from the frontier. There was some confusion as to whether they were also required to leave Gaza and Sharm al-Shaykh but on 18 May Egypt informed the Secretary-General U Thant that it had "decided to terminate the presence of UNEF on its territory". U Thant decided that Egypt had the right to do this and ordered the recall of UNEF, a judgement for which he was later blamed. There are some indications that Nasser was prepared to change his attitude in order to win credit abroad but he was forestalled by an Israeli attack. During the June War Gaza and Sinai were occupied by the Israelis. In the attack on Gaza 14 Indian soldiers awaiting evacuation were killed.

UNEF (II)

After Israel and Egypt had accepted a UN call for a cease-fire in the October War the non-aligned members of the Security Council called for the establishment of an Emergency Force to police it. An American amendment, reluctantly accepted by the Russians, stipulated that no troops from the five Permanent Members should be included. The Chinese, objecting to the lack of condemnation of Israeli aggression, refused to participate in the debates. The Secretary-General, Kurt Waldheim reported that there would be a need for 7,000 men stationed in the area initially for six months at a cost of $30 million. An advance party of Finns, Swedes and Austrians under the command of the Chief of Staff of UNTSO, the Finn General Siilasvuo was joined by Irish and Canadian troops. They had to police the agreement signed at Kilometre 101 in November 1973. In April 1974 the Swedish General Bengt Liljestrand took command until he was succeeded by the Indonesian Rais Abdin in December 1976. The mandate of

UNEF was extended every six months until October 1975 when after the signature of the Second Sinai Agreement, it was extended annually. It had to supervise the separation area and the "oil strip" in Sinai and see that the military clauses of the agreement providing for buffer zones and areas of limited armaments were observed. In 1978 it consisted of 4,178 Finns, Ghanains, Indonesians, Swedes, Poles and Canadians with some Australian helicopters. In October 1978, after the signature of the Camp David Agreement, its mandate was extended for a final nine months. The Secretary-General stated that so far the cost of the force had been $443 million and estimated that it would need a further $59 million to take it up to its withdrawal on 31 May 1979. It ceased to have legal existence on 24 July 1979 when its supervisory functions were taken over by UNTSO.

UNIFICATION AND LIBERATION FRONT (Lebanon)

The Three Militia Agreement of December 1985, imposed by the Syrians on their Lebanese followers, made provisions for constitutional reform in the Lebanon. Elie Hobeika, however, who had signed on behalf of the Christian Lebanese Forces was disavowed and deposed by his co-religionists and the Maronites refused to abandon their traditional predominance and accept Syrian hegemony. In July 1987 Damascus sponsored a new grouping of its clients, Amal, the Progressive Socialist Party, the Lebanese Communist Party, members of the Baath and a few Christians and Nasserists to call for implementation of the Three Militia Agreement. Other demands were for the overthrow of the "sectarian regime" of President Amin Gemayel, for stress upon the "Arab identity" of Lebanon and for a special relationship with Syria. As all concerned were already known supporters of the Syrian line and co-operated with each other when it was in their interests to do so, the formation of the "Front" had little if any political impact.

UNIFICATION CRISIS (1976)

The agreement which brought into being the United Arab Emirates with Shaykh Zaid b. Sultan al-Nihayyan as its President, signed in 1971, stipulated that both these arrangements were valid for five years during which period a permanent Constitution should be devised. The five years showed a divergence between those led by Zaid who wanted a strong centralised government with authority over the army, the judiciary, the police, trade and immigration policies, and the budget, and those, led by Shaykh Rashid al-Maktum who argued that this would destroy the individuality of the constituent members and remove government from the grass roots. There were also disputes over the budget as the cost of federal institutions were paid for almost exclusively by Abu Dhabi, while Dubai, the second richest Emirate, paid nothing at all. There was also the question of whether oil policy should be regarded as a Federation matter or be dealt with by the individual states: the Oil Minister complained that he had only "nominal authority" outside Abu Dhabi. Rashid who had built up his defence forces to 2,000 men was unwilling to merge them as was Shaykh Saqr al-Qasimi of Ras al-Khaymah although Shaykh Sultan al-Qasimi of Sharjah put his under federal control; in May 1976, however, it was agreed to unite the forces under the operational command of a Jordanian officer with political control shared between Zaid's son Khalifah as Deputy Supreme Commander and Rashid's son Muhammad as Minister of Defence. There were also territorial disputes between members with particularly venomous exchanges between Dubai and Sharjah. There was an incredible waste of resources – there were already four international airports and proposals for two more. In July 1976 a lengthy document, in the drawing up of which an Egyptian legal expert had played a major role, was submitted to the Supreme Council of Rulers. This significantly strengthened the central power, making it obligatory, for example, for each member to contribute 75% of its revenue to state funds, removing the right of secession, abolishing the right of veto held only by Abu Dhabi and Dubai, members of the National Assembly were to be regarded as representative of the whole people and not of the government of individual Emirates, restricting the right to raise armed forces to the Federation. The Supreme Council rejected this new draft, resolving that the provisional constitution should continue for another five years. A fortnight later Zaid stated that this decision had "disappointed him a thousand times" and that he would not seek a second term as President as he was not receiving sufficient support in his efforts to make the Union a reality. The other Rulers concluded that without Zaid's leadership the structure would collapse and brought great pressure on him to remain in office. Dubai and Sharjah settled their quarrel. The Supreme Council accorded the President the sole right to levy troops, merged the intelligence services, put immigration, residence permits, public security, border control and information under his office and in response Zaid agreed to continue in office and to renew the interim constitution for another five years. The Cabinet was reshuffled with ministers chosen for individual merit rather than as part of the "share" of each Emirate. A second crisis arose in February 1978 when Zaid, attempting to make effective the unification of the armed forces, appointed his son Sultan as Commander-in-Chief. The decision was announced while he was on holiday outside the country and neither Rashid nor his son the Defence Minister had been consulted. There were rumours that Dubai would withdraw from the Union, setting itself up as a sort of Singapore, and that Britain, Saudi Arabia and Kuwait offered to mediate in the dispute which lasted over a year. Shaken by the Islamic Revolution in Iran, Zaid felt that Rashid should have a larger stake in the Federation and in April 1979 he invited him to become Prime Minister. A feature of this period was the support shown by citizens, particularly the young, for a stronger, more centralised Union.

UNIFIED ARAB COMMAND

One of the decisions of the Cairo Summit of 1964 was to create a Unified Arab Command in order to "consolidate Arab armed forces in the face of expansionist Zionism" which had just been shown in plans to divert the waters of the Jordan. An Egyptian General,

Ali Ali Amer, was put in overall command with the task of co-ordinating a united Arab response. Jordan was to receive financial help from Saudi Arabia and Egypt to re-equip and expand its armed forces. Commando raids should not give Israel a pretext for military action until the Arab armies were ready which, it was estimated, would be about the beginning of 1968. The Yemen War and the Kurdish Revolt (I) should be settled in order to free troops against the main enemy. The Command proved totally ineffective and its first real test, the destruction of Samu in November 1966 showed that it had no plan of action. As a crisis developed in the early summer of 1967 King Hussain sent his Chief of Staff to Cairo in an effort to concert plans but it appeared that the Command envisaged the Egyptian and Syrian armies fighting separately and no role for Jordan. The King himself then went to Cairo and agreed to put the Jordanian army under the command of the Deputy Chief of Staff of the UAC, the Egyptian General Abd al-Munim Riad with disastrous results in the June War. The UAC exercised no control over troops in the field and so was described as a "Paper Pyramid" – a head with no body: its principal use was in providing posts for Egyptian officers.

UNIFIED MILITARY COMMAND

Syria was greatly excited by Egypt's Czechoslovak Arms Deal and asked for a military alliance. Nasser was attracted by the idea as it would give him some control over the foreign and defence policy of Damascus without his becoming involved in its chaotic internal politics. An Agreement signed in Damascus on 20 October 1955 set up a Supreme Council of Foreign and War Ministers to control a joint Commander-in-Chief who was to be Field Marshal Abd al-Hakim Amer. There was to be a Council of the two Chiefs of Staff which was to plan training and co-operation, draw up a military budget, prepare statistics to facilitate joint planning etc. It was agreed that the two powers should consult in the event of international tension and that an attack on one would be regarded as an attack on both and all forces, including those on the Israeli frontiers would come under the C.-in-C. A week later Saudi Arabia adhered to the Alliance by the Jiddah Treaty which was subsequently joined by Yemen. When exactly a year later Britain, France and Israel launched the Suez War against Egypt the Unified Command was shown to exist only on paper.

UNIFIED POLITICAL COMMAND

The failure to implement the Tripartite Agreement reached in the Cairo Unity Talks of March/April 1963 led many Iraqi officers to consider a federal union with Egypt but without Syria. In May 1964 Presidents Nasser and Abd al-Salam Arif signed a preparatory unification agreement as "the first step towards full Arab unity". There would be a joint Presidential Council consisting of the two leaders, three ministers and three Cabinet members from each side to study the necessary steps to establish a union, co-ordinate political, military, economic and social planning and work for ideological unity of their popular organisations. Nasser had declared that only a socialist state could unite with Egypt and in July Iraq announced a programme of nationalisation. In October the two Presidents agreed to set up the Unified Political Command with themselves as the highest executive authority to bring about constitutional unity within two years. When Arif appointed Abd al-Rahman al-Bazzaz Prime Minister in September he ordered progress towards unity. A meeting of the Command in Cairo in February 1966 declared satisfaction at relations between the two and agreed to support the national struggle of Yemenis North and South, Palestinians, Cypriots, etc. and also the suppression of the Kurds. Apart from the adoption by Iraq of the Egyptian eagle on its flag and military insignia, that appears to have been the only achievement of the Unified Political Command. In Iraq only a minority of the Sunni Arabs, themselves a minority, approved of union and Nasser himself, after his experiences in Syria, was not really keen on adding to his own problems so the Command was never more than a fiction.

UNIIMOG
The Iran–Iraq War Security Council Resolution 598 which led to the cease-fire on 17 July 1988 established a Military Observer Group to monitor compliance with it. The vanguard arrived on 10 August and the force consisted of 403 men from 25 countries under the command of a Yugoslav Major-General, Slavko Jovic, who had a Swedish and a Bangladeshi Brigadier as his assistants in Iran and Iraq respectively. The force had difficulty in establishing crossing points between the two countries but there were few serious incidents, apart from the capture of several hundred Iranian soldiers shortly after its arrival. The Iranians claimed that the Iraqis had not evacuated some disputed areas and had set three oil wells on fire and would not allow them to be extinguished. In March 1990 the UN Secretary-General requested a renewal of UNIIMOG's mandate for another six months.

UNIKOM
One of the demands of the Resolution (Security Council) After Operation Desert Storm Number 687 of 3 April 1991 which laid down conditions for a cease-fire was the establishment of a demilitarised zone stretching 10 km into Iraq and 5 km into Kuwait from the 1963 border "to deter violations of the boundary and to observe hostile or potentially hostile actions". Resolution 689 of 9 April set up the United Nations Iraq–Kuwait Observer Mission for the purpose. Commanded by the Austrian General Gunther Greindl, a 15-member advance party arrived in Kuwait on 13 April. The force later increased to about 1,400, comprising 300 unarmed observers, protected by five battalions of infantry with mine clearers, logistics, an air unit, etc. from 34 nations with 15 permanent observation posts. UNIKOM replaced the 100,000 American troops who had been in Southern Iraq. They worked closely with UN officials engaged in the Kuwait–Iraq Frontier Delimitation. In August 1991 UNIKOM investigated a report of an Iraq incursion on Bubiyan Island which appeared to have been for purposes of smuggling and there were some 50 minor crossings of the frontier by armed Iraqis, but more seriously, in January 1993 Iraqi soldiers, without notifying UNIKOM, crossed

into the demilitarised zone to retrieve arms and dismantle buildings in an area newly assigned to Kuwait. On 19 January the UN Secretary-General Dr Butos-Ghali asked the Security Council to send 3 mechanised battalions and 20 helicopters which would have changed the observer force into a fighting force of 3,645 with less restrictive rules of engagement. On 3 February the Security Council approved the dispatch of a single Battalion of 750 Argentians. Despite condemnation by the Security Council, Iraqis crossed the frontier twice more but after an allied attack on missile sites near Baghdad, the Iraqis promised to refrain from further incursions.

UNION CONSTITUTIONELLE (Morocco)
In January 1983 the Prime Minister Maati Bouabid announced the formation of a new party, the Union Constitutionelle which would recruit mainly from the "post-Independence generation", seeking "more active political participation by the new élite". Its declared aims included "liberalism with a social conscience", support for constitutional monarchy, a multi-party system, private enterprise particularly for small businesses, women's rights, agrarian reform ("the land belongs to those who work it"), Arab unity, non-alignment, the Palestinians and liberation of the Presidios. These hardly differed from those of the Rassemblement National des Indépendents although Bouabid stressed pragmatism, stating that ideology and the pervasive state had caused most of the troubles of the Third World. An early meeting in Casablanca which attracted 10,000 was hailed by its leader as "the wedding night of democracy". The UC started to publish an Arabic daily and a French weekly. In June, contesting local elections, it was astonishingly successful with 2,731 seats representing 16% of the vote showing particular strength in Casablanca, Rabat and Tangier. In the parliamentary elections of September 1984 it emerged as the largest party with 55 seats, including the only Jew in an Arab legislature, with 25% of the votes and a further 27 indirectly elected. It was widely believed that such successes could only have been achieved with some help from the machinery of government. It contributed Ministers to the Cabinets of Karim Lamrani and Izz al-Din Laraki. In the communal elections of October 1992 it won 13% of the votes, making it the largest party after the RNI. The UC fought the parliamentary elections of June 1993 in alliance with the Mouvement Populaire and saw the number of its Deputies reduced to 27, considerably less than the main opposition parties. In the indirect elections, which many felt were conducted less honestly than the direct round, its numbers increased to 54 making it the largest of the Government parties.

UNION NATIONALE DES FORCES POPULAIRES (Morocco)
al-Ittihad al-Watani li-al-Quwwat al-Shaabiyyah. In September 1959 when the Istiqlal was the dominant party in Morocco, its younger and more left-wing leaders such as Mehdi Ben Barka, and Abd al-Rahim Bouabid, considering senior members such as Allal al-Fassi and Ahmad Balafrej excessively conservative and bourgeois, "spending too much time on talk and tea", after months

of disputes, formally broke away in January 1959 to create the Union Nationale des Forces Populaires. They were joined by Mahjoub Ben Sadiq who brought the alliance of the main labour movement, the Union Marocaine du Travail. Their other followers were mostly amongst the professional and student groups. Speaking in Marxist terms, they demanded more state intervention in the economy, nationalisation of key sectors such as banking, heavy industry and mining and more democracy at the expense of a theocratic monarchy to follow the election of a Constituent Assembly. They called for the removal of all vestiges of colonialism, particularly in the economic and military spheres, evacuation of foreign troops, reform of agriculture in the interests of the peasants, a unified Maghreb and help for nationalists in the Algerian War of Independence and Black Africa. After three months their newspaper was suspended and one of the leaders, Fqih Muhammad Basri arrested on the charge of fomenting a rising in the Riff. In February 1960 two of its leading members were arrested on charges of endangering public security and Ben Barka took refuge in France. In February 1960 18 UNFP leaders were arrested for plotting the murder of the future Hassan II. Nevertheless in the communal elections of May 1960, despite lack of time to organise, the party did well in urban areas, claiming 41 out of 45 seats in Casablanca and 31 out of 35 in Rabat. Later that year, after his dismissal as Prime Minister, Abd Allah Ibrahim joined the UNFP and edited its newspaper. The Party's second Congress in May 1962 called for the transformation of society by the total rejection of capitalism. In December 1962 the UNFP boycotted the referendum on the new Constitution. In May 1963 in the parliamentary elections UNFP won 28 seats (three of its Deputies were illiterate) out of 144 with 22% of the votes. In July the police stormed the party HQ and arrested 130 of its leaders, including 21 of its MPs, on charges of plotting to overthrow the King – the party itself alleged that 5,000 of its members were arrested. In November 104 were put on trial in Marrakesh and, after a patently unfair process, eleven, eight in absentia including Ben Barka, were sentenced to death amidst widespread international condemnation. None were executed and in April 1965 many were included in a general amnesty as the King tried to persuade the UNFP to enter a coalition under his Premiership but until the King suspended Parliament in June 1965 the UNFP and Istiqlal generally collaborated in opposition. In June 1966 a leading party member Umar Ben Jalloun, one of those condemned to death in 1963, was sentenced to six months for inciting student riots. In the October 1969 local elections the UNFP won 0.5% of the vote and 32 out of 9,000 seats: few doubted that the figures had been rigged by General Oufkir. The UNFP and the Istiqlal as the National Front, boycotted the referendum on the new Constitution in July 1970, the parliamentary elections the following month and a further Constitutional referendum in March 1972. In the winter of 1970/1 UNFP supporters were arrested charged with plotting subversion in conjunction with the Syrian Baath Party and in June 1971 193 were put on trial in Marrakesh. Five including Muhammad Basri, living in exile in Paris, were condemned to death

and over 130 received prison sentences but most were released early under amnesties. In the early 1970s relations between the Casablanca branch of the UNFP led by Ibrahim and the Rabat branch led by Bouabid deteriorated and in April 1973 the Rabat branch was outlawed after being linked with the March Plot for an armed rising with Libyan backing. In July 1976 about 300, mostly UNFP members, were brought to trial: two-thirds were acquitted and the remainder received light sentences. In September 1974 the Rabat branch had decided to go its own way as the Union Socialiste des Forces Populaires. After the start of the war in the Western Sahara the UNFP, alone of the parties, refused to support Morocco's claim and became marginalised. It officially boycotted the municipal elections of November 1976 but individual candidates took about 1% of the vote. In March 1977, again alone of the parties, its leader did not join the Cabinet that the King formed to ensure fair play in the June Assembly elections which it again boycotted. In March 1979, alone amongst the parties, it refused to participate in the National Defence Council. When in the same month one of its former Ministers, Maati Bouabid, became Prime Minister, the UNFP formally disowned him. The UNFP was the only one of the twelve parties to boycott the municipal elections of June 1983 and the parliamentary elections of September 1984 although its affiliated UMT won five of the indirectly elected seats. In February 1984 it had claimed that 120 of its members had been arrested in riots in the North over economic conditions. After more than a decade of sulking the UNFP agreed to collaborate with other opposition parties in preparations for the parliamentary elections of 1991 which were, however, in the event postponed. In May 1992 the UNFP refused to join the other opposition parties in the Democratic Bloc and boycotted the municipal elections in October.

UNION SOCIALISTE DES FORCES POPULAIRES (Morocco)

In April 1973 the Rabat branch of the Union Nationale des Forces Populaires, led by Abd al-Rahim Bouabid, was banned after its alleged involvement in the March Plot to stir up civil disturbances with the connivance of Colonel Qadafi. In the summer 157 accused were brought before a military tribunal in Kenitra and a further 81 in Casablanca and 16 were subsequently shot. In September 1974 Bouabid was permitted to revive the Rabat branch under the name of the Union Socialiste des Forces Populaires and at its inaugural Congress in January 1975 it called for general amnesty, curbs upon the Government's exceptional powers, ending restrictions on civil liberties, reversal of a 1973 order banning the student union, a lower voting age, municipal ownership of land, large-scale nationalisation and agrarian reform in a country where 70% were on the poverty line. It expressed strong support for Morocco's claims on the Western Sahara which it extended to include the Presidios of Ceuta and Melilla. It soon overtook the UNFP as spokesman for the moderate left, recruiting from the young urban middle class. In December 1975 one of its leaders, Umar Ben Jalloun, the editor of its newspaper was assassinated in Casablanca: the killers were never found. In the municipal elections of November 1976 it gained 6% of the votes, making it the third largest political party. In March 1977 Bouabid was one of the four party leaders who joined the Government to observe preparations for elections to the National Assembly which were held at the beginning of June. The USFP, campaigning on a platform of agricultural reform and expansion of industry, won 14.6% of the popular vote and made it the largest organised party after the Istiqlal although, with 16, it had fewer seats than the Mouvement Populaire. Bouabid, who failed to win his seat, resigned from the Government, the only party leader who complained that the elections had been unfair. The USFP went into opposition but in March 1979 agreed to nominate two members for the National Defence Council. An estimate in 1980 put its membership at 100,000 without counting its associated Trade Union, the Confédération Démocratique du Travail led by Ahmad Nubar al-Amawi. In June 1980 the USFP boycotted the referendum which extended the life of the National Assembly from four to six years. In May 1981 the Party boycotted the communal elections, claiming that they would not be fairly conducted. In June the CDT called a general strike which led to the Casablanca Riots in which the Party claimed that 637 people were killed. In August Party leaders criticised Hassan II for agreeing to a referendum on the Sahara which, they asserted, jeopardised Morocco's claims. Angered, the King put five, including Bouabid, out of the eight members of the Politburo on trial with 30 officials of the CDT and closed down their newspapers. Deputies who had been refusing to attend the Assembly which they considered illegal, were put under house arrest. Military reverses in the Sahara led to a renewed spirit of national unity, the members resumed their seats and Bouabid and his colleagues were released in February 1982, partly due to the intercession of President Mitterand with whose Socialists the USFP had established close links. Two prominent figures, Amawi and Mustafa Karchawi, the editor of its newpaper al-Muharrir, remained in detention until November 1983. During 1983 factional splits developed and the leftists, under Muhammad Ben Said, defected to form the Organisation de l'Action Démocratique et Populaire. The USFP considered fighting the June 1983 communal elections in concert with the "loyal opposition", the Rassemblement National des Indépendents but eventually went it alone to win only 6% of the votes and take 12 seats. In the parliamentary elections of September 1984, in which Muhammad al-Yazghi played a leading role as Bouabid was in poor health, the party improved to 17% of the votes with 34 seats directly elected with another four indirectly, putting it in fifth place. The OADP came bottom with 0.5% but one seat. In April 1985 the USFP left the Government because they disapproved of the economic policies proposed by the Prime Minister Karim Lamrani. Amawi took the lead in demanding compensation for the workers for the hardships these policies entailed and in April 1990 he called for a general strike in conjunction with the Istiqlal Union Géneral des Travailleurs Marocains. After the Government had promised discussions the strike was called off but when these did not materialise, the CDT and UGTM rescheduled the strike for December. This set off widespread

violence of which the Fez Massacre was the worst. In October 1991 there was another split as Abd al-Rahman Ben Ammar and Ahmad Benjalloun leaving to start the Parti de l'Avantgarde Démocratique Socialiste which was legalised in April 1992 as the sixteenth party. In January 1992 the USFP suffered a severe blow from the death of Bouabid as his successor, Abd al-Rahman Yusufi never enjoyed the same intimate relations with the King or the veneration of the rank and file. In April 1992 Amawi was jailed for slandering the Government. In May the USFP formed an alliance with Istiqlal and the Parti du Progrès et du Socialisme, issuing the Charter of the Democratic Bloc calling for more democracy and the end of corruption. In September, with the Istiqlal, it boycotted the referendum on a new Constitution. In the communal elections of October the USFP did well in the cities of Rabat and Casablanca, doubling its 1983 total of seats but nevertheless lost some strongholds: Yusufi blamed lack of militants and a failure to mobilise women voters. In February 1993 al-Yazghi, now Joint First Secretary suspended participation in the Commission preparing for the parliamentary elections as a protest against the imprisonment of Amawi. The campaign was fought on a joint Manifesto with Istiqlal, sufficiently vague not to offend the supporters of either party, after they had agreed that they would not oppose each other's candidates: Istiqlal was given a free run in 118 seats and the USFP in 104 but the PPS decided to go it alone. The elections of June 1993, generally agreed to have been fair, were seen as a triumph for the USFP which emerged as the largest party with directly elected 48 Deputies, an increase of 14. In July Amawi was pardoned. In the indirect elections the USFP won only a further 8 and Yusufi, resigned in protest at vote-rigging. The King tried to get the opposition into government, offering it 19 Ministries and the USFP appeared divided between the older men who hankered after a return to office and the younger radicals led by Amawi: the latter won and the party remained in opposition.

UNITED ARAB KINGDOM PLAN (1972)

In a speech on 15 March 1972 King Hussain set out a plan to replace the Hashemite Kingdom of Jordan by a United Arab Kingdom which would consist of two regions, Jordan and Palestine, each with its own capital but with Amman as federal capital. Each region would have its own Governor General, elected by Regional People's Councils. There would be regional Councils of Ministers but a central executive in Amman would remain responsible for "matters relating to the Kingdom as a sovereign international entity, ensuring the safety, stability and development of the Union". There would be a single army under the command of the King and a Supreme Court. Hussain emphasised that the plan would only operate after an Israeli withdrawal from the West Bank and confirmation by a referendum. The plan was immediately rejected by Israel, although Ben Gurion saw "merit" in it and, although many on the occupied West Bank supported it, by the Palestine Liberation Organisation. Although four former Prime Ministers were sent around the Arab world to stress that even semi-autonomy would be an advance for the Palestinian people the plan was almost unanimously criticised in the Arab states; President Sadat was so incensed that he broke off diplomatic relations with Jordan. The King, however, continued to insist that the offer was still open to the Palestinians until he finally disclaimed rule over the West Bank at the Rabat Summit of 1974. An adaptation of the concept of the two regions reappeared in the Reagan Peace Plan of 1982.

UNITED ARAB REPUBLIC

By 1957 Syrian politics were in a state of confusion. There had been a series of military coups, with one group wanting union with Iraq, another group, including the President Shukri al-Quwatli, on the Saudi payroll, the Baath wanting Arab unity with socialism but lacking muscle which they hoped that Nasser might provide, and the Syrian Social Nationalist Party wanting to annex Lebanon, driven underground but still active. There was also an extremely strong Syrian Communist Party whose leader Khalid Bakdash, allied to Khalid al-Azm, was one of the most important men in the country. The army was split with a pro-Communist Chief of Staff General Afif al-Bizri and the very powerful Chief of Intelligence Colonel Abd al-Hamid al-Sarraj who worked closely with the Baathist leader Akram al-Hawrani. So great was the threat of a communist take-over that there was a threat of a Turkish invasion, backed by the USA, to prevent them from controlling the country. In October 1957 the government of Sabri al-Assali requested the support of Egyptian troops in the north. The Baathist leaders Michel Aflaq and Salah al-Din Bitar who feared either a communist or an Iraqi take-over took the initiative in calling for union with Egypt despite the discouragement of the influential Egyptian Ambassador Mahmud Riad who argued that it would take five years to prepare. Syria had always considered itself as the "beating heart of Arabism" and in November 1957 and January 1958 Parliamentarians called for unity with Egypt. In January the army compelled the Government to go to Cairo with a formal request for union and the threat of imprisonment if they returned without it. Nasser, who had never visited the country, knew little of Syria except that it was difficult to govern, wanted to control its foreign policy without the burden of administering it with its fractious army and powerful tribes but, as the strident champion of Arab unity, found it difficult to refuse an obvious step towards it; he feared also that if he declined Syria might collapse into anarchy. Nasser, rejecting a draft Constitution brought by Bitar, set a deliberately high price, including the dissolution of all political parties except the Egyptian National Union. On 1 February 1958 the United Arab Republic was proclaimed and on 21 February a Constitution for "presidential democracy" was approved by a plebiscite in both countries: by 99.99% in Egypt and 99.98% in Syria where 39 people were reported to have voted against. It provided for a National Assembly of 300 Egyptians and 100 Syrians, appointed by the President with at least half the members chosen from the two dissolved Parliaments. There were also two Cabinets and two Regional Assemblies dealing with all matters except foreign affairs, defence, industrialisation, education and "national guidance" which were to be handled by a Central Government. Nasser was the only candidate for President and he appointed four Vice-Presidents Abd al-Hakim Amer, Abd al-Latif al-Baghdadi, Assali and Hawrani. The Central Cabinet consisted of one Syrian (Bitar in charge of Arab Affairs) and seven Egyptians including Mahmud Fawzi at Foreign Affairs and Amer, who was also Commander-in-Chief of the combined armies, at Defence. In October 1958 the Central Government was expanded to 14 Egyptians and 7 Syrians. Two Regional Executive Councils were appointed so that there were three Cabinets with 50 Ministers. The Councils were headed by little-known figures, Nur al-Din Tarraf for the South and Nur al-Din Kahalah for the North but all the key ministries were held by army officers. The two Chairmen were replaced during 1960 by Kamal al-Din Hussain and Sarraj. In July 1959 elections were held for committees of the National Union and in June 1960 a National Assembly as nominated by the President from their members: Anwar Sadat presided over its 600 members. The creation of the UAR evoked great enthusiasm in other Arab countries, the demand to join it contributed to the overthrow of the Monarchy in Iraq and led to the Muslims of Lebanon rising against the pro-Western Camille Chamoun. To the embarrassment of Nasser, the Imam Ahmad demanded admission for Yemen and a special status had to be found for an absolute Monarchy. The Syrian Communist Party was ruthlessly suppressed and the country, with Sarraj as Interior Minister, took on the atmosphere of a police state. Land was seized for distribution to peasants: the third tranche in January 1959 brought the total to over a million acres. The quick-witted Syrians regarded the slow Egyptian bureaucrats as arrogant and incompetent and considered that there were far too many of them: in the Syrian Ministry of Industry 7 of the top 13 officials were Egyptians. The Syrian élite was not consulted about decisions that affected them: as Bitar said Nasser would not "accept a necessary association of Arab progressive leaders in the management of the Arab cause". He had no intention of sharing power and he interfered enough in Syrian domestic matters to cause resentment but not enough to rule effectively. Egyptian officers were placed in key positions in Syria while Syrian officers were posted to remote desert garrisons in Egypt. Although the Syrian workers received new rights, the trade unions were curbed. In October 1959 Nasser gave Amer full powers over the Syrian Region to push through political, industrial and land reforms and entrench the National Union which had never taken root. Two months later the Baathists who had expected to be the ideological mentors of the Union and resented the fact that their party, its principal advocates, had been dissolved like the others, left the Government and went into clandestine opposition: there was by now little civilian support in Syria for the regime. Nasser on visits to the country in February 1958, February 1959 and February and September 1960 appeared to be received with diminishing enthusiasm but his "hero personality" was all that held the Union together as Arab nationalism proved no match for "Regionalism"; the two areas, separated by a hostile Israel, never coalesced into a single country. From the summer of 1960 there were rumours of plots. In February 1961 restrictions on foreign exchange and imports, long accepted in Egypt, were applied to Syria where they caused much resentment. The July Laws of 1961, promulgated without consultation with Syria, introduced a large measure of socialism repulsive to a nation of entrepreneurs and confiscated more land and there was a flight of capital; there was little opposition in Egypt. In August Cairo's political control over Syria was tightened with the Regional Councils abolished and all executive power, even over local councils, was concentrated in the central government. A new Cabinet included 7 Vice-Presidents (2 Syrian) and 36 Ministers (14 Syrian). The Syrians now saw the Egyptians not as partners but as overlords. There had been constant quarrels over jurisdiction, particularly over security, between Amer and Sarraj which in August Nasser resolved by transferring the latter to Cairo with the empty title of Vice-President for Internal Affairs. Sarraj, however, returned to Damascus to resume the struggle but Nasser ordered both men back to Cairo. On September 26 Sarraj resigned and Amer returned to Damascus where he found demonstrations of acute dissatisfaction. Early in the morning of 28 September the Syrian army, which had been seething with discontent, carried out a coup which declared the Union dissolved and Damascus Radio denounced Nasser's "odious tyranny". Hawrani, one of the architects of the Union, admitted that it had been based on sentimentality without working out the possible consequences. King Saud admitted that he had spent £12 million to wreck the Union. Nasser thinking at first that it was merely a local mutiny declared the secession illegal and prepared to crush it by force but was dissuaded. The new regine was immediately recognised by Jordan and Turkey and effectively by Nasser on 5 October. Even superficially friendly relations, however, were not restored until the Unity Talks of March 1963. The Egyptian people were largely indifferent to the Syrian secession although elsewhere it was seen as a set-back for Arab unity. Egypt continued to keep the UAR as its official title until it was dropped by Sadat in the summer of 1971.

UNITED ARAB STATES

At the end of 1957 the Imam Ahmad found himself under considerable pressure to liberalise his regime with unrest at home and propaganda attacks from *Sawt al-Arab* abroad. There had been a recent attack upon his life and the opposition *Ahrar* were receiving support from Cairo from where they were permitted to broadcast propaganda. The Imam's son Badr appeared to have fallen under the spell of the personality of Nasser whose backing could be of value in a possible succession struggle with his uncle Hassan. With great political skill and much cynicism Ahmad decided to disarm his opponents by a paper alliance with Nasser, exploiting his prestige as the champion of Arab nationalism and progress. He took advantage of the proclamation on 1 February 1958 of the United Arab Republic which invited the adhesion of other Arab states, to apply to join it and Nasser, though much embarrassed at finding himself linked with the most reactionary Arab country, was unable to refuse what was presented as a step towards Arab unity. The Pact of the United Arab States was signed on 8 March 1958. Each state was to preserve

its international personality and the Union was to be ruled by a Supreme Council of Heads of State who had to be unanimous so in fact Ahmad retained a veto in everything affecting Yemen. There was also to be a Federal Council of six members from each partner and there were to be subordinate bodies to co-ordinate defence, foreign, cultural and economic policies. The armed forces were to be unified under Field Marshal Abd al-Hakim Amer but this had no visible effect as the Yemen kept its own army. Customs duties and separate currencies were to remain. The permanent seat of the Union was to be Hudaydah. The Yemen was to pay 3% of the joint Budget. The *Ahrar* were no longer recognised as possible rulers of the Yemen and some such as Ahmad Muhammad Nu'man moved to Aden. Egyptian army officers took part in some operations against the British in the Aden Protectorate and Nasser switched his support from the pro-Egyptian South Arabian League to the pro-Yemeni Aden TUC of Abd Allah al-Asnaj. Medical and educational missions arrived in the Yemen but were kept on the tightest of reins by the Imam. The Union was little more than a fiction, perhaps taken seriously only by Badr who tried to use Egyptian officers to bolster his position while acting as Regent in the summer of 1959. On his return from medical treatment in Italy, Ahmad dismissed the Egyptians accusing them of being "tools of a foreign power" and relations with Nasser became icy. In June 1960 the Yemeni representatives were recalled from the Federal Council and never returned. In September 1961 when Syria defected from the Union, Ahmad declared that he too was leaving. In November Ahmad ridiculed Nasser in a poem which amused all literate Arabs with its wit and elegance and Cairo Radio riposted by dubbing him "The Enemy of God" and calling for his overthrow. In December Nasser formally dissolved the Union but it had served Ahmad's purpose by rendering the opposition practically powerless for over three years.

UNITED NATIONS WORLD CONFERENCE ON PALESTINE (1983)

The World Conference began on 29 August 1983 in Geneva which had been transformed into an armed camp guarded by 3,000 soldiers. It was attended by 137 nations although 20, mostly Western European, only sent observers while the US and Israel boycotted it. The Palestine Liberation Organisation, represented at first by Abu Lutf and then by Yassir Arafat attended as a full participant. The meeting declared the rights of the Palestinians to return to their homes and enjoy independence. The Israelis should return to their pre-June War boundaries. The annexation of Jerusalem and Jewish settlements on the West Bank were declared illegal. The plan put forward by the Fez Summit was endorsed as a guideline for a peace settlement. There should be an international peace conference of which the PLO should be a full member. The proceedings were endorsed on 13 December 1983 by the General Assembly by 124 votes to 4 with 15 abstentions in Resolution 38/58 which also called for 29 November to be observed as an International Day of Solidarity with the Palestine People.

UNITED POLITICAL ORGANISATION – NATIONAL FRONT (South Yemen)

Al-Tanzim al-siyassi al-muwahid – (al-Jibhah al-qawmiyyah). The National Liberation Front which had fought the Federation of South Arabia and the British in Aden and took power in November 1967 was a broad coalition of nationalists, socialists and extreme Marxists. The conservative, moderate first President Qahtan al-Shaabi was ousted in June 1969 by the Glorious Corrective Move led by Salim Rubai Ali, Muhammad Ali Haytham and Abd al-Fattah Ismail. Many Party members were purged and the left intensified its grip on the Party machinery. After the dismissal of Haytham in August 1971 a struggle developed between Ali as President and Ismail, the Secretary-General of the Party, for while Ali believed in local initiative, Ismail stood for a rigidly disciplined Vanguard Party which the masses had only to follow. At the Fifth Congress in March 1972 a Central Committee and a Politburo were created to exert more bureaucratic control. At the Sixth Congress of the National Front it was decided to unite with the technically illegal but previously tolerated Baath Party, the People's Vanguard and the Communist People's Democratic Union to form a new Vanguard Party. This was formally achieved at the Unification Congress of October 1975. As its name, the United Political Organisation – National Front, showed, the new organisation was dominated by the NF, although Cabinet posts were given to leaders of other groups. It was seen as a transitional party to prepare for a new type of Vanguard "guided by the principles of scientific socialism" and to "mobilise the creative energies of the people for the construction of a new society". Although he was made Assistant Secretary-General, the new grouping represented a setback for Ali as did the declaration that the socialist countries were "strategic allies" at a time when he was working for *rapprochement* with Saudi Arabia and the West. In October 1978, after the overthrow of Ali, the Yemeni Socialist Party was created and UPONF ceased to exist.

UNITY TALKS (1963)

The breakup of the United Arab Republic in September 1961 followed a military coup in Syria and was regretted by many who would have liked it to continue with more power in domestic matters retained in Damascus. Michel Aflaq, the founder of the Baath deplored the secession but his colleague Salah al-Din al-Bitar signed the document approving it. President Nasser refused to recognise the new regime. There was a strong body of officers who were pro-Nasser who followed an unsuccessful *putsch* in March 1962 with a take-over of power in March 1963. They appointed Bitar Prime Minister. The previous month the Baath had gained control of the government in Baghdad and it was natural that there should be talk of union. It was, however, clearly impractical to form a union of Syria and Iraq without the blessing of Nasser which was also necessary for the shaky Syrian Government to keep his supporters quiet. Unity talks began in Cairo within a week of the Syrian coup but Nasser soon made it plain that he had no confidence in the Baath and would not endorse any regime dominated by it. Syria was clearly so unstable that he wished to have no responsibilities there.

According to the record published by the Egyptians Nasser mocked and bullied Aflaq and Bitar making them appear ridiculous and ineffectual. However, no one could afford to be seen as opposing Arab unity so finally on 17 April Syria and Iraq accepted an agreement drafted by Nasser to establish a federal government to control foreign affairs, defence, economic planning, education and various other matters. Each country was to have a "political front" combining "all unionist, socialist and democratic forces" but it was not clear how these would operate. The problem of separate armies or a single one was not addressed. There was to be a referendum and the union was to come into being after 25 months. Few took the union seriously, by mid-May a propaganda war had broken out between Egypt and the Baathists and on 18 July an attempt by Nasserite officers in Damascus to seize power was put down with massive bloodshed. Finally on 23 July Nasser declared that he considered invalid an agreement signed with a "fascist regime .. built on fraud and treachery ... secessionist, inhuman and immoral".

UNKIAR-SKELESSI, Treaty of (1833)

In November 1831 Muhammad Ali Pasha invaded Syria and a year later his son Ibrahim Pasha crushed the Turkish army at Konia. The Ottoman Sultan Mahmud II appealed to the European Powers for help. Britain, preoccupied with internal matters after the passage of the first Reform Bill and with the affairs of Belgium, declined to become involved and France sympathised with Muhammad Ali so only Russia responded. An envoy was sent to Alexandria to persuade Muhammad Ali to halt Ibrahim's advance while a powerful fleet was sent to the Bosphorus in February 1833. The British, now alarmed at the extent of Russian influence brought pressure on the Sultan while France, equally worried, persuaded the Pasha to negotiate. The Kutayha Convention, concluded in April, halted a further Egyptian advance by conceding Muhammad Ali's main demands. Russia then demanded recompense for its services and the Treaty of Unkiar–Skelessi legitimised its role as the military protector of the Ottoman Empire. There should be reciprocal assistance in the event of war with another Power although a secret clause confined Turkey's role to closing the Dardanelles to non-Russian warships. The Treaty caused great apprehension in Britain and France and its annulment became a major objective of Lord Palmerston. He ultimately succeeded in the London Convention of July 1840.

UNOGIL

In the spring of 1958 Lebanon was in turmoil with many Muslims strongly attracted to the recently formed United Arab Republic while Christians feared the advance of Arab nationalism and socialism. At the same time President Camille Chamoun who in a corrupt election had secured a compliant Chamber of Deputies was seeking to amend the Constitution to secure a second term in office. In May Chamoun alleged that there was a rebellion fomented from the UAR and that there had been "massive infiltration" of men and arms as well as violent press and radio attacks and after getting no support from the Arab League he sent his Foreign Minister Dr Charles Malik to complain to the UN. On 11 June the Security Council resolved by 10 votes to 0 with Russia which disbelieved the Lebanese charges abstaining, to send a United Nations Observer Group to Lebanon to "ensure" that there was no illegal infiltration: it was not made clear whether "ensure" meant ascertain facts or take enforcement action but a strong measure would have been vetoed by the USSR. The Norwegian Major-General Odd Bull was put in command of a force that started with less than a hundred men but eventually rose to over 500. Stations and check points were set up and air observation was also used. On 3 July UNOGIL reported that there was no major infiltration. This statement was received with much scepticism by Chamoun and his supporters in the West. Before the matter could be debated Iraq underwent a Revolution, Chamoun requested American aid, and the US Marines arrived in Beirut. UNOGIL felt deceived and threatened to resign but was dissuaded by UN Secretary-General Dag Hammarskjöld. Shortly afterwards, at the request of King Hussain, British troops were sent to Jordan. After motions and counter-motions at the UN it was decided to leave matters in the hands of Hammarskjöld but in fact the Lebanese crisis was solved by the election as President of General Fuad Shihab. Shortly afterwards the Americans left Lebanon, the British left Jordan, Lebanon requested the withdrawal of her complaint against the UAR from the agenda, and, by 9 December, UNOGIL had come to an end.

UNRWA

The Lausanne Talks in the early summer of 1949 had shown that the dispute over the future of about 800,000 Arab refugees from Palestine was insoluble. The Americans were anxious that it should be treated as an economic rather than a political problem and despite Arab misgivings an Economic Survey was sent to the area. As a result of its report in December 1949 the General Assembly of the UN set up the UN Relief and Works Agency to aid and rehabilitate refugees with an initial budget of about $8 million. It provided housing and social services in the camps but attempts to resettle the refugees in other Arab countries failed because the demand that they should have the right to return to their original homes. The HQ was established in Vienna. The costs mounted with the years, reaching $30 million in the the 1960s, $100 million in the 1970s, $200 million in the 1980s and over $500 million in the early 1990s mostly provided by voluntary donations from governments. By this time UNRWA had a staff of about 17,000, mostly Palestinians although foreigners held the top posts. The number of refugees greatly increased after the June War and the Lebanese Civil War so in December 1991 UNRWA was providing essential services for over 2,500,000 of whom nearly 900,000 lived in 61 camps. Half the budget went on education: under the supervision of UNESCO over 600 schools, usually working in two shifts educated 365,000 pupils except when those on the West Bank and Gaza Strip were closed by the Israelis. There were also clinics and services for the distribution of food.

UNSCOM

One of the demands of the Resolution (Security Council) after Operation Desert Storm Number 687 of 3 April 1991 which laid down conditions for a cease-fire was for the full disclosure of all programmes to develop weapons of mass destruction and their subsequent elimination. This work was to be performed by a United Nations Special Commission comprising experts in nuclear, chemical, biological and ballistic weapons. As Iraq was estimated to have spent at least $10,000 million on this arsenal, it was a large task and after two years more than 55 teams, some of up to 50 members had visited military installations, supervising the destruction of prohibited material by local workers. The Iraqi Government was normally unco-operative until coerced and as early as August 1991 a second Resolution, Number 707, reinforced the demand for disclosure of all information demanded by UNSCOM. There was a belief that the Iraqis had hidden some 700 Scud missiles and in September President Bush threatened force to compel compliance. It was learned that Iraq could have had nuclear bombs by 1992/3 and UNSCOM demanded information about its suppliers which the Iraqis constantly promised to hand over. In October Resolution 715 ordered that most of Iraq's military and civilian installations should be put under permanent UN supervision. The Iraqi Super-Gun was destroyed and so, in May 1992 were two nuclear plants designed for electromagnetic isotope separation and another for solid fuel propellant for missiles. In eighteen months the destruction of 150 missiles was verified. In July 1992 there was a trial of wills as the Iraqis refused access to UNSCOM inspectors wishing to visit the Ministry of Agriculture. The UN officials sat in a car park for three weeks until the Iraqis gave way. In November 200 drums containing "uranium materials" were seized and later shipped out of the country. In January 1993, hoping that the change-over from Bush to Clinton would lead to a period of confusion, the Iraqis refused permission for the UNSCOM teams to land in their own aircraft. There was a period of tension as missile batteries both in the North and the South were attacked and finally, on 17 January, a Baghdad factory linked to the nuclear programme was hit by Tomahawk missiles. For some months the Iraqis hoped for a softening of attitude in Washington, promised again its list of suppliers, while in March 13,000 mustard gas shells were destroyed in addition to the 75 tons of nerve gas already found. In June 1993 the Iraqis refused to allow the installation of cameras to monitor a range where they could test the missiles with a range of up to 90 miles that they were permitted to develop: an alternative suggestion that machinery should be sealed was also rejected. The Iraqis tried to link compliance with the lifting of sanctions against them. After arguing for a month, during which time the Security Council, the Americans and the Russians all warned Baghdad of serious consequences, the UNSCOM chief, the Swedish diplomat Rolf Ekeus left the country. After threats that the sites would be destroyed by air attacks Ekeus returned and after several days of negotiations with Tariq Aziz it was agreed that the cameras would be installed but not immediately activated. The Dutch head of the chemical equipment team stated that his work was finished and the Iraqis claimed to have honoured 95% of their obligations. Ekeus warned of new methods of overflight surveillance on his first visit since July. Cameras were switched on at the end of September.

UNTSO

The United Nations Truce Supervision Organisation grew out of a Truce Commission for Palestine established by Security Council Resolution 48 of 23 April 1948 which consisted of the Consuls-General in Jerusalem of Belgium, France and the USA. They were asked to supply 63 military observers with auxiliary staff while the UN provided professional and administrative personnel and a security force. The Commission cooperated with the Mediator, Count Folke Bernadotte. There was little that could be done before the Rhodes Armistice but on 11 August 1949 Resolution 73 established UNTSO as a subsidiary organ of the UN. An American General W. E. Riley was appointed Chief of Staff, reporting to the Secretary-General and its strength grew to 300 officers and 300 other ranks. UNTSO chaired and worked through Mixed Armistice Commissions on each frontier and sent observers to any place where shooting had started to arrange a cease-fire and then investigate. The Chief of Staff could also issue orders for the discontinuation of work, such as irrigation, deemed likely to be provocative. Riley was replaced by the Danish General Vagn Bennike in July 1953. He was considered pro-Arab as was his successor, from September 1954, the Canadian General E. L. M. Burns who wrote a book about his experiences. The establishment of UNEF after the Suez War led to a sharing of functions on the Egyptian–Israeli armistice line and while Burns was particularly engaged there, the American Colonel Byron Leary acted as Chief of Staff. Burns was followed in March 1958 by the Swedish General von Horn, also criticised as pro-Arab and also the author of a book, who in June 1963 departed to head UNYOM. During the June War the HQ of his successor, the Norwegian General Odd Bull, was directly in the firing-line but he managed to act as an intermediary in securing a cease-fire. He established observer posts on the Syrian–Israeli cease-fire line and facilitated the exchange of prisoners. Before the war UNTSO had consisted of 140 observers and 261 other personnel but was increased by the recruitment of officers from Argentina, Austria, Burma, Chile and Finland. Annual Reports, submitted to the General Assembly showed that UNTSO had a particularly difficult time during the War of Attrition in 1970 and on the Lebanese frontier after 1975. Bull was succeeded in August 1970 by the Finn Ensio Siilvasvuo who remained in command until November 1973 when an Irish Colonel, Richard Bunworth took over on a temporary basis. The Swedish General Bengt Liljestrand was appointed in April 1974 and was replaced by the Ghanaian General Emmanuel Alexander Erskine in January 1976. This was a period of continual incidents on the Lebanese–Israeli frontier and in March 1978 Erskine and some of his staff were transferred to the new formation UNIFIL. It is unique amongst UN forces in being spread over 5 countries and providing personnel for new groups such as UNIFIL and UNDOF and the Chief of Staff acts as co-ordinator of all UN peace-keeping in his area. For the two years 1988 and 1989 the General Assembly voted $41,373,000 for the costs of UNTSO. Many officers, including the American Colonel killed were regarded as spies on behalf of their own governments.

UTHMAN, Ahmad (1930–)

Moroccan Prime Minister. He was born in Oudjdah and after a French education, accompanied the future Hassan II to Bordeaux University where they both took degrees in law. He then served on the private staff of Muhammad V. In 1957 he joined the Foreign Ministry, rising to become Head of the European Division and then of the American Division, attending meetings of the UN, OAU and Arab League. Uthman then held a series of posts – Secretary-General of the Defence Ministry, Ambassador to Bonn, Under-Secretary for Mines, President of the State Shipping Company and Ambassador to Washington, Ottawa and Mexico City and in 1964 he married the King's younger sister, Lalla Nazha. In October 1970 he joined the Cabinet of Ahmad Laraki as Minister of Administrative Affairs but in August 1971 he was moved to the key post of Director of the Royal Court. In August 1972 the Monarchy had appeared in danger after the attempt to shoot down the Royal Boeing and the mysterious death of General Oufkir, elections had to be postponed, and in November Uthman was appointed Prime Minister with instructions to form a widely based national coalition to show the country rallying around the Throne. He failed, however, to persuade the major parties, Istiqlal and the Union Nationale des Forces Populaires to join what became a basically non-political government. One of his first acts was to arrest the outgoing Minister of Agriculture for misappropriating funds and arrange trials for those involved in the attempt on the King which resulted in death sentences. He also had to face a hunger strike by political prisoners and a prolonged student strike which led to over 300 arrests and the dissolution of their union. In March 1973 Uthman took over the Defence Ministry which had been run by the King since the death of Oufkir. In the same month his government, attempting to placate the opposition by adopting measures that they had advocated, issued a series of Dahirs Moroccanising the economy with obligations laid upon foreign firms to have at least 50% Moroccan directors and to allocate at least 50% of their shares to Moroccan public agencies or to private investors who were given loans to encourage participation. Foreign-owned land, about 400,000 acres belonging to 2,000 farmers was taken over without compensation. These measures were accompanied by a Five-Year Development Plan. During the summer of 1973 there were lengthy political trials which showed that although the March Plot had failed, the Government had clearly been shaken. During the October War Moroccan troops saw action on the Golan Heights. Efforts at *rapprochement* with the opposition parties to bring them into the Government continued to be unsuccessful although there was less tension and in April 1974 when he reshuffled his government he could only bring several young technocrats into junior office. During 1974 Uthman was active on the international stage, negotiating the Madrid Tripartite Agreement which led to the Spanish withdrawal from the Western Sahara. Uthman was Prime Minister at the time of the Green March, during which he led a group across the frontier into the Spanish Sahara uniting the nation in a way which had not been seen since independence. In March 1976 he invited Moroccan Jews who had emigrated to Israel to return home. Profiting from the national unity, Uthman, or rather the King who was generally seen as ruling through him, reformed the Cabinet in March 1977 bringing in the leaders of all the main political parties to organise parliamentary elections which, held, in June, were generally seen to be amongst the fairest held in Africa. The majority of seats were won by independent loyalists whom the following year Uthman organised as the Rassemblement National des Indépendants. In October 1977 Uthman reorganised his Cabinet, retaining representatives of Istiqlal and the Mouvement Populaire and bringing in young technocrats. In a speech in November Uthman stressed the role of Morocco as an "open arena for the meeting of civilisations" – Western, Maghrebi, Arab, Islamic and African. He had been active in Africa during the year, being implicated in an embarrassing attempt to overthrow the government of Benin and sending troops, at the request of President Mobutu, to eject mercenaries from Zaire. Uthman was instrumental in providing administrative and diplomatic backing for the King and the generals running the Saharan War and helped to secure the neutrality of Russia during a visit in March 1978 in which he concluded a large trade deal. In March 1979, admitting that there had been corruption, inefficiency and waste the King replaced Uthman with Maati Bouabid who had close links with organised labour which had been showing dissatisfaction. Uthman himself said that he wished to devote more time to organising the RNI but accepted the chairmanship of a new National Defence Council which was to assist the Government in running the war.

UNYOM

After the overthrow of the Imamate by young officers with Egyptian backing in September 1962, Saudi Arabia intervened in the Yemen War to support the Royalists. By November the two countries themselves appeared to be on the brink of war and this caused great embarrassment in Washington which saw President Nasser as a bulwark against communism while the Kingdom was a major ally. After diplomatic activities by the veteran Ambassador Ellsworth Bunker, U Thant, Secretary-General of the UN announced on 30 April 1963 that an agreement had been reached between Egypt, Saudi Arabia and the Yemeni Republicans – the Royalists who controlled nearly half the country were ignored. Faysal would end military backing for the Imam while the Egyptians started to withdraw their forces. The UN Yemen Observation Mission was created to supervise the implementation of this agreement, establish a demilitarised zone for 20 km on either side of the Yemeni–Saudi border and station observers there. A force of 114 Yugoslav soldiers with Canadian air support was put under the command of the Swedish General Carl von Horn who had been Chief of Staff of UNTSO, and he arrived in Sanaa on 13 June. UNYOM had no executive powers, knew nothing of the area, was far too small to achieve anything and was chronically short of supplies. It was forbidden to contact the Royalists and refused co-operation by the Egyptians who made no effort to carry out their part of the agreement, refusing to allow monitoring of their troop movements at Hodeidah. After increasingly acrimonious correspondence with U Thant, von Horn resigned on 20 August saying that the policy of the UN was one of "calculated deceit" in refusing him the necessary resources. He then tried to withdraw his resignation but U Thant replaced him with the Indian General P. S. Gyani. At the end of the four months U Thant reported that it had been "virtually impossible for UNYOM to play a really helpful and constructive role", that the Saudis were still supplying the Royalists and the Egyptians not withdrawing. The Saudis who had refused to continue paying their share of the costs were persuaded by US pressure to change their minds and UNYOM received short-term extensions up to 4 September 1964 when it terminated having achieved nothing.

VENICE DECLARATION (1980)

In the summer of 1980 relations between the European Economic Community and Israel were cool as it had had to overcome considerable opposition to its wish to site its office in Tel Aviv and not in Jerusalem and it felt that the Israelis under Begin were dragging their feet over peace negotiations. In addition the British were selling sophisticated tanks to Jordan and the Foreign Secretary Lord Carrington had declared that he did not believe that the Palestine Liberation Organisation was a "terrorist organisation as such". A European Summit at Venice on 12–13 June issued a 11-point Declaration which, after reaffirming previous declarations opposing changes in the status of Jerusalem and stressing the inadmissibility of acquiring territory by force and its support for Resolution 242, broke new ground in calling for Palestinian self-determination and the need to associate the PLO with peace negotiations. The Nine stated that they were prepared to participate "within the framework of a comprehensive settlement in a system of concrete and binding international guarantees". They also commended the Euro-Arab Dialogue. The Americans were outraged that the Europeans should take an initiative in the Middle East, the PLO was angered that the Declaration did not name it as the sole representative of the Palestinian people while Israel bitterly denounced "a Munich-like capitulation to totalitarian blackmail" and an attempt to undermine Camp David. In these circumstances there was no possibility that the Declaration could have concrete results.

VILLAGE LEAGUES

The municipal elections of 1976 on the West Bank showed the strength of the support for the Palestine Liberation Organisation particularly in the towns. The Israelis hoped to mobilise against this radicalism the more conservative countryside and in 1978 Mustafa Dudin, a former Minister in the Jordanian Government, was encouraged to set up an "Association of the Hebron District Villages" which comprised 74 small communities. The Leagues were given by the occupation authorities financial support denied to the towns and were able to show substantial development. The replacement of the Military Government by a Civil Administration in November 1981 led to further encouragement of Village Leagues and new ones were established, most notable was one of 30 villages near Janin while a group of 20 near Nablus was seen as a counterweight to the strong nationalism of that town. The National Guidance Committee which had provided leadership for the people was outlawed in order to strengthen the influence of the collaborators. The Leagues had special access to the Israeli authorities, enjoyed considerable patronage in the issue of the numerous permits that an occupying force demands while some were even issued with weapons. There was an official attempt to separate those who thought "positively" from the nationalists who were punished ever more harshly. The leaders of the Leagues were attacked by the PLO as quislings and in March 1982 the Jordanian Government ordered them to renounce their membership within a month or face prosecution for treason. Although the leaders remained defiant, the rank and file membership faded away. It became increasingly obvious that the Begin government would never make real concessions and the Leagues lost all credibility.

VINCENNES INCIDENT (1988)

Using the pretext of the War of the Tankers the American Government sent a large naval force to the Gulf and was determined to use its presence to punish Iran for the humiliations of the seizure of its Embassy, the bungled attempt to rescue its diplomats and later the exposure of the fact that it had secretly been selling arms to the country and then illegally using the money to pay mercenaries against the regime in Nicaragua. The fleet threatened to fire upon any aircraft which approached nearer than five miles but took no action when an Iraqi plane attacked a warship killing 37 sailors. On 3 July 3 1988 an Iranian Airbus carrying 290 people on a regular scheduled flight from Tehran to Dubai was shot down by the cruiser *Vincennes*, a ship which had become notorious for its aggressive behaviour against small Iranian patrol boats. The *Vincennes* was engaging some small Iranian craft when, it was claimed, its supposedly infallible radar system misidentified a large civilian aircraft climbing as a small fighter plane diving to attack. The Iranians ruled out any retaliation against civilians. Later the Americans paid compensation to the families of the victims.

al-WADIAH DISPUTE
Al-Wadiah is a desert village 400 miles north-east of Aden, the possession of which is disputed between Saudi Arabia and South Yemen. King Faysal regarded the left-wing regime to his South with immense hostility and the sentiment was reciprocated by a government officially dedicated to spreading Revolution throughout the Peninsula. The Saudis subsidised and armed South Yemeni dissidents, encouraging them to raid across the border. In November 1969 the Aden Government said that it was expecting more incidents and later reported that the Saudis had occupied Wadiah, believing there to be oil in the vicinity. The Saudis said that without provocation the Yemenis had seized the frontier post. There followed a series of air clashes while Iraq and Jordan tried to mediate. On 5 December the Saudis claimed to have reoccupied it and later took journalists to see. They claimed to have killed 35 Adenis and to have been able to push on as far as Aden if not restrained by the moderation of the King. In 1973 after the signature of the Tripoli Agreement providing for the union of North and South Yemen, relations were particularly tense between Aden and Riyadh which wished to prevent the merger. In March the Saudis reported that two South Yemeni MiGs had attacked Wadiah. Aden denied any such incident and said that the Saudis were searching for a pretext for military intervention. In November 1977 after a brief *rapprochement*, relations between the two again deteriorated with both withdrawing their Ambassadors. In January 1978 newspapers reported further clashes at Wadiah and that four Saudi Lightning fighters had been shot down by an Adeni MiG. This was officially denied but in February there were reports of more fighting.

WAILING WALL INCIDENT (1929)
The Wailing Wall, the western wall of the temple built by King Herod and the only part of it remaining was regarded by Jews as the most hallowed site in Jerusalem. It and the property around it belonged to Muslims who for centuries put no restrictions in the way of Jews who wished to pray there. On the Day of Atonement in 1928 some Jews attempted to seize privileges there to which they were not entitled and were prevented by the police. In August 1929 on another religious occasion followers of the Revisionist Zionist Jabotinsky marched in procession to the Wall, demanded its ownership and swore to defend it. During the following week other incidents increased tension between the two communities and on Friday 23 August a large number of Arabs, armed with knives and staves attacked any Jew that they could find. Trouble spread to the neighbouring villages and to Hebron. The police, mainly Arabs, remained inactive and the British garrison which had been diminished had to be reinforced to restore order. During the disturbances about 130 Jews were killed by Arabs (half of them in Hebron), 6 Arabs were killed by Jews and 120 Arabs by the security forces; over 500 on the two sides were wounded. This was the first really serious clash between Arabs and Jews. The British set up a Commission under Sir Walter Shaw to report upon the causes of the incident.

WAR OF ALGERIAN INDEPENDENCE
Before the Second World War there was, apart from among some of the ulema and a few intellectuals and workers who had been in contact with French communists, less a general desire that the French should leave Algeria than a wish for better status under the existing regime. After the brutal repression of the Setif Uprising, there came a more widespread desire for independence and the conviction that it could only be obtained by force. Ait Ahmad and Ben Bella recruited and trained potential guerrilla fighters in the Organisation Spéciale in the west while Belkasim Krim led a gang of outlaws in Kabyle. In 1954, encouraged by the defeat of the French at the hands of the Vietnamese at Dien Bien Phu, the leading militants came together in the Comité Révolutionnaire d'Unité et d'Action which planned the All Saints' Day Uprising. Less than 2,000 men, perhaps a quarter of them armed, simultaneously attacked police posts, communications and isolated farmhouses throughout the country inflicting a few casualties and not a great deal of damage. Cairo Radio broadcast a call to arms in the name of the Front de Libération Nationale. The CRUA had divided the country into six *wilayas* but there was little communication between them and there was no direction of the war as the best-known leaders, the "externals", were in exile in Cairo and could only communicate spasmodically with the "internals" or arrange arms deliveries for them. For the next nine months there were occasional hit-and-run attacks with few successes outside the Aures where Ben Boulaid proved an effective leader. Much energy was spent in building a network of sympathisers and informants and in killing or terrorising those Muslims who refused their assistance. In January 1955 a new Governor-General Jacques Soustelle arrived with the intention of pacification through a mixture of strength and liberal measures to improve the standard of living of the peasantry by weakening the power of the grands colons. In April the FLN achieved its first

step towards international recognition with an invitation to the Bandung Conference while friendly Arab countries persuaded the UN to consider the Algerian question although France walked out of the debate. In August in a deliberate move to escalate the conflict Ben Tobal ordered a cold-blooded massacre of French civilians, including women and children at Philippeville: as he had intended reprisals by the colons antagonised hitherto neutral Muslims. The discovery of oil at Hassi Massaoud with its prospect of self-sufficiency for France increased the determination not to abandon Algeria. In February 1956 Soustelle was replaced by Robert Lacoste who also hoped that economic benefits would help to bring peace. In August the Soummam Valley Conference gave the FLN a more formal structure by concentrating the direction of the war in the hands of a 5-man Comité de Coordination et d'Exécution, asserting political control over the military and reducing the power of the "externals". In mid-October a ship bringing arms from Egypt to enable the FLN to open a new front in the Oran area was intercepted – a fact that reinforced the French willingness to participate in the Suez War which began a fortnight later. Before that, however, on 26 October an aircraft carrying Ben Bella and three others of the Neuf Historiques from Rabat to Tunis was forced to land at Algiers and the leading "externals" spent the rest of the war in captivity. This French action put paid to attempts by King Muhammad V and President Bourguiba to mediate a peaceful settlement and also destroyed the faith of many moderates that the French could be trusted to act in a legal fashion. These events intensified terrorist activity in Algiers where Yasif Saadi organised girls to place bombs in cafés and other civilian places while Ben Khedda and Ramdan Abane attempted to turn the Qasbah into a fortress impenetrable to the French, effectively challenging them to a pitched battle. In January 1957 Lacoste charged General Massu and his parachutists with bringing the capital back under control which after several months of extreme ruthlessness, they succeeded in doing. The Algiers Battle was a heavy defeat for the FLN but the routine torturing of suspects by the French then and thereafter aroused condemnation both abroad and at home where the war became increasingly unpopular. At around the same time the French began building the fortified Morice Line along the Tunisian frontier to prevent arms or the 10,000 men of the Armée de Libération Nationale training there from reaching the hard-pressed guerrillas of the interior. A series of large-scale battles took place early 1958 normally ending in heavy casualties for the Algerians. The French had by then some 400,000 troops in the country and had the assistance of perhaps 250,000 local Muslims – a number that far exceeded the number of the insurgents. Militarily the war was effectively won but senior officers and the colons feared that they would be betrayed in Paris where four governments had already collapsed since November 1954 and they took matters into their own hands. The Commander-in-Chief General Salan, without consulting the Government ordered the bombing of a suspected ALN stronghold at Sakiet Sidi Yusuf on Tunisian territory and this led to a political crisis and the collapse of a fifth government and a prolonged delay while there was a search for a new Prime Minister. Pierre Pfimlin was installed on 12 May but the locally-born Europeans, the *pieds noirs*, concluded that only one man could save the situation and on 13 May they seized the government buildings in Algiers in the name of General de Gaulle and set up Committees of Public Safety there and in the principal towns. They were immediately joined by Generals Massu and Salan. Massu's parachutists seized power in Corsica and prepared to capture key points in Paris. Pfimlin resigned and de Gaulle was invested as Prime Minister. Three days later he received in Algiers from crowds which included thousands of Muslims a hysterical reception of his opening words "*Je vous ai compris*" which was taken as an endorsement of "L'Algérie française". In fact he started almost immediately to find terms that would induce the FLN to agree to a cease-fire and in October he offered in the Constantine Plan a long-term policy of investment and development which would enable *pieds noirs* and Muslims to live together in prosperity. He offered also a *paix des braves* which would bring an end to the fighting without winners or losers. The FLN leadership which had recently constituted itself the Gouvernement Provisoire de la République Algérienne which won recognition from many Arab, communist and Third World states insisted that negotiation on independence should precede a cease-fire. In December 1958 de Gaulle, about to become President, replaced the hard-line Salan with General Challe and Lacoste with an unknown bureaucrat Paul Delouvrier. Early in 1959 Challe led a series of operations which snuffed out much of the remaining fighting strength of the *wilayas* while in Morocco and Tunisia the ALN increasingly well-trained and well-equipped under Colonel Boumédienne stood by, preparing to take power should Algeria achieve independence. The attitude of de Gaulle was mystifyingly ambiguous for after in May speaking of a "new Algeria bound forever to France" in September he formally offered self-determination which could lead to independence, although he thought that this would be disastrous; in November he offered a referendum after a cease-fire. Officers started to criticise the President and Massu who did so in the press was recalled. In January 1960 in "the week of the barricades" the *pieds noirs* rebelled but in one of the most dramatic speeches of his career de Gaulle refused to yield and the rebellion collapsed as the army denied them support. In June the first peace negotiations between the French Government and the GPRA took place in secret at Melun but broke down before matters of real substance could be discussed. In November de Gaulle spoke of "an Algerian Republic" and in the following month on a visit to the country he was cheered by the Muslims while *pieds noirs* bungled attempts to assassinate him and clashed with Muslim mobs. Later in the month the General Assembly by 63 votes to 8 with 27 abstentions recognised the right of the Algerian people to independence. Early in 1961 the French Government made secret contacts with the GPRA to discuss a resumption of negotiations and the possibility of this led *pied noir* extremists to form the Organisation Armée Secrète to resist by force the tranfer of power into Muslim hands. In April a group of Generals headed by Challe and Salan seized the vital centres of Algiers and called on the army to back their call for a French Algeria. Again de Gaulle stood firm and the *putsch* failed. International pressure upon France to make peace mounted by leading figures in Paris called upon conscripts to refuse to fight. Peace talks started at Evian in May but broke down over the future status of the *pieds noirs* and of the Sahara. The OAS started to attack the Muslim population, establishing a reign of terror in major cities and at the same time extended their activities to France even attempting the life of de Gaulle. Resumed peace talks ended on 18 March 1962 with agreement on a cease-fire. There followed some months of savage activity by the OAS against the Muslims in the hope of rekindling the war but these failed and the *pieds noirs* started to leave in large numbers. On 1 July a referendum was held in Algeria on the Evian Agreement with nearly 6,000,000 voting for independence and 16,000 against. By the end of August about 1,300,000 *pieds noirs* had moved to France leaving about 30,000 behind. The Muslims who had fought for the French were cynically abandoned by de Gaulle to the most atrocious tortures which extended to their families. According to French figures they lost during the War over 17,000 killed, 65,000 wounded and 1,000 missing – figures comparable to the numbers killed on the roads in the same period. They estimated that 141,000 FLN combatants had been killed by the security forces, 12,000 killed by the FLN in internal purges and some 70,000 other Muslims by the FLN: the Algerians themselves put their losses at a million.

WAR OF ATTRITION (1967–70)

The June War of 1967 left the Israelis on the east bank of the Suez Canal and despite the cease-fire there were clashes in August and September, culminating in a heavy Israeli bombardment of Port Suez after the sinking of their destroyer *Eilat* in October. The Russians had immediately started rearming the Egyptians and within six months had provided $150 million worth of military equipment, the aircraft virtually free. Resolution 242 and the subsequent Jarring Mission could not bring the two sides together and Nasser was anxious to prevent the *de facto* occupation of Arab territory solidifying into permanent frontiers as it had done after the Palestine War. He wished also to bring pressure on the Super-Powers to impose a peace settlement. He had also to restore national unity and satisfy growing clamour, particularly in the army, for revenge. In July 1968, after a visit to Moscow, he obtained a great increase in Russian aid including for the first time ground-to-ground missiles. Egyptian commandos ambushed Israeli forces across the Canal and practically the entire civilian population of Port Suez was evacuated after indiscriminate Israeli shelling. In October the Israelis penetrated 140 miles into Egypt to blow up a transformer station and two Nile bridges. The Israelis fortified their positions along the Canal as the Bar-Lev Line, named after their Chief of Staff. There were sporadic incidents and a major flare-up in March 1969 which extended almost the entire length of the Canal followed by further Egyptian commando raids. Eventually the Canal cities were destroyed and there were an estimated 750,000 refugees. There were also clashes

on the Jordanian front with Palestinian raids into Israel leading to reprisal attacks by aircraft. In April and June Israeli commandos destroyed targets 300 miles south of Cairo and more than 200 miles from their base in Sinai and there were fears that they might attack the Aswan High Dam. There were threats that they might launch a major offensive across the Canal. Alarmed by the escalation the Americans put forward the Rogers' Plan (I) which Nasser rejected saying that he could not conquer Israel but he could "wear them down by attrition". He showed his gratitude to the Russians by allowing them use of Alexandria naval base and by recognising East Germany and Vietnam. There were frequent air battles, Bar-Lev said that there had been 1,000 sorties over Egypt in 50 days, and in a single day the Israelis claimed to have destroyed 11 Egyptian aircraft while the Egyptians claimed 6 Israeli. On 9 September, after sinking two warships, the Israelis landed tanks to destroy a missile base on the Gulf of Suez. In November the Israelis claimed to have destroyed all missile and radar installations along the Canal and were now in almost complete control of the air over Egypt; this enabled them to bomb targets deep inside the country, including suburbs of Cairo. Defence Minister Moshe Dayan said that "the whole of Egypt is our battlefield". The Israelis did not attempt to conceal that their main objective was to humiliate Nasser and bring about his overthrow. The Israeli use of American aircraft caused strong anti-American feeling in Egypt. There were also aerial dogfights over Sinai. In January 1970 the Israelis had two spectacular successes, carrying off a 7-ton Russian-built radar system with its four Russian operators and fighting a major battle on the island of Shadwan in the Gulf of Suez. In February 88 civilian workers were killed when their factory was bombed and later 46 children were killed and 36 wounded when their school was destroyed. In January, Nasser, already ill, went to Moscow to beg that the Russians would support him as the Americans did their ally Israel; failing this the whole of Egyptian industry might be destroyed by deep penetration raids. Following this the Russians provided the most modern surface-to-air missiles, forming a "box" of 16 by 50 miles between the Canal and Cairo, operated by their own soldiers. These were defended by Russian aircraft, flown by about 80 Russian pilots who became involved in confrontations with Israeli flyers. There were estimates that there were up to 13,000 Russian military personnel in Egypt, some of whom were killed. In April and May Cairo claimed seven major crossings of the Canal, one by 600 troops. In retaliation the Israelis pounded Egyptian positions along the Canal from the air, destroying missile batteries but not those operated by the Russians which were held back some 20 miles. The situation was now so obviously explosive that on 25 June the Americans put forward Rogers' Plan (II). After some further clashes, it was accepted by Egypt but subsequently 5 Russian-flown MiGs were shot down by the Israelis. Eventually a cease-fire came into force on 7 August. Occasional incidents continued. Materially the War of Attrition had been extremely costly for Egypt but it probably fulfilled Nasser's objectives in launching it. He had also managed to postpone a definite choice between a peace settlement and an all-out war of liberation. The Israelis admitted that during the three years they had lost 1,000, killed, more than in the June War: Egyptian losses may have been as many as 10,000. The Egyptians lost 110 aircraft to 16 by Israel.

WAR OF THE CITIES

At the start of the Iran-Iraq War in September 1982 the Iraqis were equipped with Russian FROG-7 missiles with a range of about 70 miles and these were first used the following month causing casualties, mainly civilian, in Dizful. There was bombing on both sides, despite the outnumbering of the Iranian air force by three to one and an attack on Baghdad in June 1982 forced Saddam Hussein to lose much prestige by declaring that it was not a safe venue for the Non-Aligned Summit. The Iraqis had meanwhile acquired Russian SCUD-B missiles with a range of up to 170 miles and these were first fired against Dizful in October 1983 reportedly killing 64 civilians. In February 1984 the Iranians claimed that Iraqi bombing and missile attacks had killed 4,700 civilians and injured over 22,000. Russia had earlier resumed arms supplies to Iraq and those now included SS-12 missiles which, modified by Egyptian technicians, had a range of 500 miles, bringing every Iranian city except Mashhad within their range. There were tit-for-tat bombing and missile attacks on civilian targets throughout the first six months of 1984 until June when in response to a UN appeal, a moratorium was arranged which lasted until March 1985. Libya sent about 50 SCUD-B missiles to Iran which used them to attack Baghdad aiming, so it was believed, at the person of Hussain. Iraqi reprisals led to the evacuation of most foreign nationals from Tehran. Sixteen cities were hit in one day. There followed a pause for about six weeks until attacks on the two capitals were resumed at the end of May. Tehran was attacked for ten days in succession and the inhabitants camped out at night. On 15 June Hussain called for a 15-day moratorium after which attacks were spasmodic until mid-January 1986 when it was resumed for about a month during which the Iraqis claimed to have carried out 200 bombing raids against 35 cities in which the Iranians said that 4,000 civilians had been killed and over 12,000 injured. In early 1988 Iran said 1,143 had been killed and 4,000 wounded by SCUDS. In 1987 a Baghdad school was hit and 30 killed. In January 1987 29 Iranian cities were bombed in a fortnight and 1,786 killed. Iran was then 12 miles from Basra which was being shelled. Saddam threatened to wipe out whole cities. An attempt to stir up popular revolt against Khomeini's war deliberately exploited the evident terror. In August 1986 SCUDS hit Baghdad and in January 1987 Iranian aircraft bombed Basra – the first time for more than a year that Iranian aircraft had been in Iraqi airspace.

WAR OF THE TANKERS

Soon after Saddam Hussain started the Iran–Iraq War in September 1980 the Iranians destroyed oil facilities near Basra and were able to prevent Iraq from exporting its oil by sea although some could still go through pipelines to the Mediterranean. At the same time the main Iranian refinery at Abadan was destroyed and in December the Iraqis for the first time attacked the main Iranian terminal at Kharj Island. Iraq's export of 3 million barrels a day in early 1980 went down to less than one million while Iran, exporting 2 million barrels at a time of high prices, was able to continue to finance its war effort. By the summer of 1982 it was obvious that Iraq had no chance of winning the war on land so it determined to use its great superiority in the air to prevent or frighten ships, particularly tankers, from using Iranian ports. Therefore on 12 August, after sinking a Greek tanker, Baghdad announced a Maritime Exclusion Zone extending from the mouth of the Shatt al-Arab to south of Kharj and warned that any ship entering it would be liable to attack. Later they extended the war zone to include all other ports. In April 1983 Iraq again bombed Kharj and in May its attack on offshore Iranian oil wells set off a massive slick which threatened the maritime life of the Gulf. In the autumn of 1983 Iraq obtained from France Super-Etandard bombers equipped with deadly Exocet missiles which the previous year had inflicted great damage on the Royal Navy in the Falklands War. With these the Iraqis increased their effort to prevent export from Kharj and in March 1984 a British merchant vessel was sunk and the following month a Saudi tanker destroyed outside the MEZ. Altogether 51 ships were hit in 1984 and 42 in 1985. The Iraqi policy was to provoke an Iranian reaction and was gratified when Ayatollah Khomeini declared that if Iran could not send its oil through the Straits of Hormuz it would ensure that no one else should do so. The Iranians retaliated by attacking Saudi and Kuwaiti tankers and also occasionally stopped shipping to see if they carried contraband for Iraq. On 1 June 1984, the Iran–Iraq War, Security Council Resolution 552 condemned attacks on neutral shipping. The Iraqis, who had become dependent upon hand-outs from the Arab states managed by the end of 1985 to step up their oil exports with a second pipeline through Turkey and one across Saudi Arabia to the Red Sea. That summer they increased their attacks on Kharj and 120 were recorded in less than a year. The Iranians, who throughout the war showed much skill in improvisation, set up a make-shift terminal at Sirri to which small tankers could ferry oil to be loaded into the more vulnerable super-tankers. There appeared no shortage of seamen who for large bonuses were willing to risk their lives in these operations and the ship repair docks in Dubai enjoyed unprecedented prosperity. In August 1986 the Iraqis bombed Sirri, using in-flight refuelling, and damaged a UK-registered ship and killing 17 of its crew. The tanker war intensified during the winter with 98 ships hit in 1986 and 20 in the first four months of 1987. In May 1987 an American warship, the *Stark* was attacked, presumably in error, by an Iraqi jet and 37 sailors were killed. President Reagan declared that the Iranians were "the villains of the piece" and used the incident as a pretext to build up the American naval presence from seven ships to over seventy. The Iranians acquired Silkworm missiles from China and used fast patrol boats, operated by fanatics of the Revolutionary Guards, to attack shipping. The Kuwaitis who had suffered the worst, insurance premiums on ships bound there had doubled, called for international help to protect their tankers and when the Americans hesitated, appealed to the Russians. In July 1987 the USA agreed to give American flags to Kuwaiti tankers, thus qualifying them for naval protection. The Iranians then started to use mines, one of them damaging a reflagged Kuwaiti super-tanker which was preceding its US escort through dangerous waters. The ultra-modern American Navy was unable to deal with these supposedly obsolete weapons and had to call for minesweepers from its European allies. The American naval presence was unashamedly partisan, protecting shipping on the Arabian shore from attack while encouraging it on the Persian side. It also became increasing bellicose, shelling oil rigs, attacking Iranian patrol boats which had allegedly fired upon them or might have laid mines and finally in July 1988 an Iranian civilian aircraft with 290 passengers aboard was shot down by the cruiser *Vincennes*. The war ended a fortnight later. At the end Lloyds of London put the casualties in 546 attacks at 300 sailors killed and 300 wounded.

al-WAZZANI, Muhammad Hassan (1908–78)
Moroccan nationalist and party leader. He came from a very rich and influential family of descendants of the Prophet long-established in Fez and received a modern education, including the Hautes Écoles in Paris where he was Secretary-General of the North African students. He was one of the most violent opponents of the Berber Dhahir and was imprisoned. Wazzani then served as secretary to Shakib Arslan in Geneva from 1930 to 1933. Returning home he was one of the founders of the National Action Bloc and produced the left-wing *L'Action du Peuple* which was quickly banned with Wazzani being accused of republicanism and hostility to traditional religion. He was one of the draughtsmen of the Plan de Réformes Marocaines of 1934. He was by now with Allal al-Fassi regarded as the leader of the nationalist movement but the two men quarrelled in 1937 for Wazzani regarded his colleague as too Islamic and insufficiently modern in his outlook. He started to found his own party but in the same year was exiled into forced residence in the Sahara where he remained until 1946. After his release Wazzani founded the Parti Démocratique de l'Indépendance. He favoured negotiations with the French, feeling that Morocco should be reformed within the Protectorate as a prelude to independence. He remained in the Spanish zone or abroad much of the time until independence was achieved and even then was in no hurry to return. In 1956 he called for armed Moroccan intervention in the War of Algerian Independence. He continued active in politics, forming an alliance with the Berber Mouvement Populaire to oppose the Istiqlal Party in 1960. He served as a Minister in the Cabinet formed by Hassan II in June 1961 but by then the PDI had split and although he continued titular leader, he had little influence. He was amongst those wounded in the attempted coup at Skhirat in 1971.

WEST BANK
The cease-fire in the Palestine War of 1948 left the Arab Legion in occupation of about 2,200 square miles of what had previously been part of British Mandated territory with an original population of 400,000 swollen by another 250,000 refugees. In December 1948 the Jericho Conference of local notables asked Abd Allah to annex it to his Kingdon of Trans-Jordan (East Bank). His aggrandisement was attacked by other Arab states but welcomed by Israel, the USA and Britain which included it in the area guaranteed by the Anglo–Trans-Jordanian Treaty of 1946. In March 1949 military government was replaced by administrators who came under the appropriate Ministries in Amman some of which were soon headed by Palestinians. Unlike other Arab countries Jordan gave full citizenship to Palestinians who constituted half of the 40 Members of Parliament elected in April 1950. The Palestinian Deputies, although some were hostile to the King, called for complete unification of the two Banks. For the next seventeen years the West Bank provided about half of the country's population and an important part of its agriculture and industry. After the June War the West Bank and the Gaza Strip were occupied by the Israelis and although Resolution 242 called for their withdrawal the conditions under which this should take place could never be agreed. Despite condemnation by the UN, Israel insisted that its unilateral Jerusalem Annexation was not negotiable. Israeli occupation policy rested on three pillars: colonisation through strategically placed settlements, binding the territories to Israel by means of common roads, electricity, utilities, etc. and creating economic dependency by discouraging the growth of employment in the occupied areas while encouraging it in Israel proper, thus compelling over 30% of the workforce to take ill-paid jobs across the "Green Line" which marked the previous frontier. The Occupied Territories were not allowed to sell their produce directly overseas and it was bought by the Israelis at fixed prices and sold by them at considerable profit. Palestinians were subjected to numerous restrictions, having, for example different coloured identity documents and vehicle number plates and their press heavily censored with frequent closures of newspapers and imprisonment of journalists. Over 4,000 books were banned. Israeli military orders, eventually amounting to over 1,300, restricted every aspect of Palestinian life from picking wild thyme (an Israeli monopoly), to controlling the contents of school textbooks or holding a bank account. These were enforced by military courts presided over by officers with little legal training while the Palestinians had practically no redress for violations of their human rights. After 1967 about 1,200 were deported. In late 1967 and 1968 Yassir Arafat attempted to set up a Fatah network in the occupied areas but after this failed the Palestinian guerrillas regrouped in Jordan. Trade with Jordan continued, the traditional pro-Jordanian leadership still held much influence and Amman paid the salaries of local officials, but it soon became clear that the aspirations of the majority of the people were represented, particularly after Black September, not by King Hussain, whose plan for a United Arab Kingdom failed to attract much support, but by the Palestine Liberation Organisation. Neither, however, by calls for a boycott, could prevent a considerable turn-out in municipal elections in the spring of 1972. In 1973 a new, mainly professional class, leadership emerged and created the Palestine National Front to co-ordinate resistance groups. The Israeli Government began to expropriate more Arab land as *Lebensraum* for Jewish agricultural rather than strategic

settlements and to take water traditionally used by local farmers. A particularly unjust example led to the Land Day Riots of March 1976 but in September 1977 Agriculture Minister Ariel Sharon stated that there was a long-term plan to settle 2 million Jews in the Occupied Territories by the year 2000: this was an ideological pursuit of a Greater Israel. Land around Arab villages was declared unused and seized for Jewish expansion. Opposition intensified as the Israelis kept an increasingly ruthless grip despite UN condemnation of their policies of expelling people regarded as troublemakers and demolishing the houses of their relatives. In the Territories, always officially referred to as Judea and Samaria, the growth in discontent was shown by the sweeping victory of nationalist candidates in the municipal elections of April 1976: Mayors were the chosen spokesmen for the people. This represented a disavowal of Hussain's claims to speak for the Palestinians which he had maintained until obliged to abandon them officially at the Rabat Summit of 1974 although he still had hopes of reviving them with American backing. Attempts by the Government to rally the support of moderates by such means as Village Leagues proved unsuccessful and officials who collaborated with them were attacked by their own people. The Camp David agreement provided for eventual autonomy for the West Bank and although this was acceptable to conservative pro-Jordanian Mayors such as Elias Freij of Bethlehem and Rashad al-Shawwa of Gaza, it was opposed by more nationalist Mayors such as Bassam Shakaa of Nablus, Muhammad Milhem of Halhoul and Fahd Qawasmah of Hebron who formed the backbone of the National Guidance Committee. Israeli officials tried to restrict the activities of nationalist leaders by expelling some such as Milhem and Qawasmah, contrary to the Fourth Geneva Convention, while Israeli extremists tried to murder three other Mayors – on 2 June 1980 Shakaa had his legs blown off. Student demonstrations were followed by prolonged closure of schools and universities and police brutality: Bir Zeit University had at times to operate in private houses. The Begin government disregarded its pledges to introduce autonomy and restrict settlement and in March 1980 Resolution (Security Council) 465 unanimously condemned Israeli settlement policy although Zionist pressure forced President Carter to state that the American vote had been "an error". Fatah and the NGC radicals struggled for control of the Trade Unions and Universities, Fatah wanting united command exercised from outside while the NGC wanted democratic local initiative. In November 1981 the Military Government was replaced by a Civil Administration, headed by a Professor of Arabic Menaham Milson, but this was seen as a step towards spurious autonomy. Milson wanted to destroy the influence of the PLO by preventing it from bringing money from outside and by compromise and rejection of excessive force and collective punishment. He tried to create a different leadership by banning the NGC and giving a new emphasis to the Village Leagues but he was not provided with enough money for patronage and later resigned after the Sabra–Chatila Massacres. Arab terrorism increased and led to counter-terrorism by vigilantes and racist fanatics as in the Hebron Islamic

College Attack of July 1983 when the "Jewish Underground" killed two teachers and a student. Within the Arab community there was factionalism as supporters of Arafat clashed with those of Syria and Islamic fundamentalism grew after the Iranian Revolution. There were still attempts, such as that in the Reagan Plan to settle the problem of the West Bank by reviving its link with Jordan and for a time after the Amman Accord of 1985 it seemed possible that this might prove acceptable to Palestinian leaders. The *rapprochement* did not last long and then Hussain attempted to appeal to the West Bankers over the heads of the PLO by announcing a $1,300 million development scheme for the area. Neither the money, popular support nor Israeli acquiescence were forthcoming and the project never got off the ground although the King continued to subsidise educational establishments to compete with those dominated by the PLO. For twenty years of occupation the Palestinian people had prided themselves on the virtue of *Sumud* (steadfastness) but gradually on the West Bank and particularly in the Gaza Strip there grew a feeling of hopelessness that a spark could ignite and this was provided by a traffic accident in December 1987 which set off the *Intifadah*. This showed that the Israeli belief that promoting economic integration and a physical infrastructure would make annexation of the West Bank an irreversible fact was wrong. It showed also that Hussain had little influence over what was happening on the ground and at the Algiers Summit of June 1988 he accepted that the PLO was the "sole legitimate representative of the Palestinian people". The following month in his Separation Statement he cut the final links, dissolving the Parliament where West Bankers still held seats, stopping the payment of official salaries and pensions and ending the right of West Bankers to Jordanian citizenship. It was not clear whether this was merely a device to show that the PLO was in no position to fill the vacuum left by his withdrawal. The Iraqi annexation of Kuwait brought such overwhelming support for Saddam Hussain amongst the majority of West Bankers that the Gulf States ceased sending financial support. After the Temple Mount Massacre of October 1990 there were some attacks by Arabs on Jews and this led to the resurrection of the "Green Line" causing hardship to the Palestinians who crossed daily to work in Israel who were kept out for several days. After the start of Operation Desert Storm a curfew turned the Territories into a "collective prison" with not even the children allowed to leave their houses to play. Worship was restricted in Ramadan, farmers were compelled to leave their crops to rot and Arabs were denied admission to hospitals in case the beds were needed for Jewish casualties. Palestinians applauded enthusiastically when Iraqi Scud missiles landed in Israel. After the Iraqi defeat repression of the *Intifadah* continued with repeated condemnation of Israeli methods by the Security Council, the Red Cross, Amnesty International and Israeli Human Rights organisations such as Bet Salem. Plain clothes soldiers and police operated as murder squads and estimates varied from 5,000 to 18,000 for the number of Arab informants on the official payroll: some lived in separate fortified villages. The authorities stated that 14,000 Palestinians were held in prison; some spent 23 hours a day in underground cells, some had been detained since 1969. Bet Salem estimated that 5,000 a year were brutally interrogated and Amnesty pleaded for the end of the routine use of torture such as led to the death of Mustafa Akkawi. Schools were closed half of the academic year and one, Tulkarm, was reckoned to have had 100 days work in two years. The average annual income for West Bankers was $1,350 compared with $10,878 for Israelis. Under Likud Governments the number of Jewish settlements rose to over 100 with 100,000 residents, many of them from Russia, and there were estimates that the authorities had taken control of 65% of the land area since 1967. In November 1991 demonstrators with olive branches greeted the negotiators returning from the Madrid Peace Talks but later many opposed any negotiation which would not lead to complete Israeli withdrawal. The defeat of the Shamir government in June 1992 caused a new wave of hope and Rabin, the incoming Prime Minister, promised a freeze on settlements although as those under construction, 11,000 housing units, were allowed to continue, there was little apparent change with expectations that the number of settlers would rise to 170,000. Rabin also carved territory out of the West Bank to expand the area of "Greater Jerusalem" formally annexed to Israel. Early in 1993, after the deportation of alleged Islamic militants to Marj al-Zuhur the *Intifadah* flared up and in March the Territories were isolated from the outside world with workers banned indefinitely from crossing the "Green Line" to the jobs in Israel. This action, which incidentally stressed the separateness of the Palestinian entity, caused economic damage to Israeli businesses dependent on cheap labour and was gradually relaxed. In May 1993 as a good will gesture 30 deportees were allowed to return. The signature of the Israel–PLO Agreement in September opened a new chapter with the promise of the creation of the Jericho–Gaza Autonomous Areas. The World Bank estimated that $4,300 million was needed over ten years to give the Territories a modern infrastructure – for example the village of al-Ouja with 3,000 inhabitants had six telephones – but Palestinian sources put the need at $11,000 million. Large sums would be needed to resettle the refugees who had fled since 1967: nothing was to be done for those who had left before.

WEST BANK DEVELOPMENT SCHEME
At his accession the West Bank was part of the Hashemite state until it was lost when King Hussein took part in the June War. The Alexandria Summit of 1964 had already recognised the Palestine Liberation Organisation as the sole legitimate representative of the Palestinian people although the King did not fall into line until the Rabat Summit of 1974 after the failure of his 1972 proposal for a United Arab Kingdom. Jordan had continued to pay the salaries of some 20,000 officials, teachers, etc. on the West Bank, thus maintaining close links with the territory. It was also a major policy plank of the Americans, who refused to deal with the PLO, that the King should represent the Palestinians in any peace negotiations with Israel. The Palestinians appeared to acquiesce by agreeing on a confederal relationship in the short-lived Amman Accord of 1985/6. Hussain proposed to create 12,000

new jobs to stop people needing to work in Israel. The King then attempted to "buy" the West Bankers by offering them a better way of life through the inclusion of $1,290 million into their economy over five years – most of the money to come from outside. The largest allocation (43%) was to be given to building and construction. Education would take 22% in an attempt to increase the intelligent workforce. Agriculture would take 17%. There was opposition from the beginning. East Banker Ubaydat published an open letter to Mubarak protesting at the expense involved and the figure was later reduced to $1,015 million. The Saudis proposed a parellel programme for the East Bank which Jordan ended up paying for when Saudi funds never arrived. At its International Conference, on 8–10 November 1986, the PLO said that Hussain was collaborating with the US in an attempt to make the occupation materially rewarding. For strategic reasons Israel would not allow Jordan to deal with transport, telecommunications or energy. The West Bank programme failed and some of Hussain's closest advisers such as Zaid al-Rifai urged him to devote all his attention and resources to the East Bank. The outbreak of the *Intifadah* in December 1987 and its dominance by the Islamic fund of Hamas convinced Hussain that he really had very little influence on the Occupied Territories so in July 1988 in the Separation Statement he finally washed his hands of the West Bank influence.

WESTERN SAHARA WAR
After the signature of the Madrid Tripartite Agreement of 14 November 1975, Moroccan troops in alliance with Mauritania moved into the Spanish Sahara, an area of just over 100,000 square miles. They were attacked by guerrillas of Polisario and the first skirmish of the Western Sahara War took place at Smara on 28 November. The Moroccans continued their advance occupying the two main cities of al-Ayun and Villa Cisneros by early January 1976. The UN stated that about 45,000 Saharans fled to the Tindouf area of Algeria. From the first Algeria gave overt backing for Polisario, which declared itself the Saharan Arab Democratic Republic, and at the end of January Algerian and Moroccan regular troops clashed at Amgalla. There was a brief possibility that fighting might escalate into a full-scale war between Morocco, backed by the West, and Algeria supported by the Soviet Bloc but Boumédienne, despite his wish to do as much harm to Hassan II as possible, kept his troops thereafter within his own international boundaries. For Morocco the war was a matter of national pride rather than profit: the army was expanded by 50% during 1976 and a protracted campaign would have been impossible without support from the Arab oil states. It was also a means, skilfully exploited by the King, to preserve national unity, overcoming all other economic and political problems. In January 1976 the Sahrawis, with perhaps about 5,000 fighters, according to rumour including some Cubans and Vietnamese, began their tradition of wild exaggeration of Moroccan casualties, claiming 425 killed in a month. It declared all Morocco south of Agadir a war zone but the Sahrawis, many of whose leaders were Mauritanian dissidents, adopted the strategy of concentrating on their weaker enemy

and in June, in a brilliant operation organising supplies over a 2,000 km route, 200 guerrillas attacked Nouakchott, hoping to install a pro-Algerian regime. After Moroccan intervention, most of the party was captured and thenceforward Moroccan troops operated in Mauritania, taking increasing responsibility for its defence. After a year of fighting the Sahrawis claimed to have killed 6,500 Moroccan troops, taken 300 prisoners and destroyed 25 aircraft: actually the Moroccan force of 30,000 was losing about 100 a month but its air force was hampered by missiles supplied by Libya and the first year had cost $400 million – half of which was for arms. In May 1977, in a change of tactics, the Sahrawis launched a major attack on the Mauritian mining town of Zouerat in which for the first time foreign civilians were killed and some French citizens carried off. At other times they were able to seize Spanish and Portuguese sailors for hostages. Hassan II announced a Plan d'Urgence to win the allegiance of the Sahrawis by a $292 million crash programme of providing amenities in the towns, settling 65,000 nomads, developing fisheries and harbours, desalination schemes and building an Islamic University at Smara. In the course of time many Moroccans, lured by financial baits, moved into the new provinces, swamping the original inhabitants: in six years the population of al-Ayun grew from 28,000 to over 100,000. Arab leaders, including Crown Prince Fahd and President Mubarak made unsuccessful attempts at mediation. The West sold weapons to Morocco, and French aircraft occasionally helped them, but the Russians, primarily interested in establishing good trading links with Rabat, took no apparent interest in the conflict. During 1977 although the Mauritian army had been expanded from 2,200 to 12,000, the Moroccans had to take increasing responsibility for the country's defence: the armies held isolated settlements and strongpoints between which the Sahrawis moved at will. In December 1977 140 lorries of guerrillas raided into Mauritania to attack a railway, and the country appeared on the verge of collapse: in July 1978 the ould Daddah regime was overthrown but its successors continued the war, albeit in a half-hearted manner. In the same month the Sahrawis described a major attack on al-Ayun, killing 70 Moroccan soldiers but a visiting delegation of British MPs heard nothing of any battle: much of the fiercest fighting seems to have taken place only in the imagination of Polisario communiqué-writers. Their claim for 1978 was 6,794 Moroccan soldiers killed, 5,379 wounded, 322 taken prisoner with 10 aircraft, 801 vehicles and 36 locomotives destroyed. Economists calculated that the cost to Morocco during the year was $1,460 million, a sum roughly equal to its trade deficit, helping to cause 20% inflation. During 1978 the Sahrawis received weapons from Qadafi, then at the height of his anti-monarchist fervour, that often made them superior in fire-power to the Moroccan army and in January 1979 they shook their enemies by a raid on Tan-Tan, well within its old boundaries. In March the King set up a National Defence Council on which even the communists were represented. In August Mauritania sued for peace, renouncing any claim on its share of the Western Sahara which was promptly annexed by Morocco and sent representatives to Parliament in Rabat. The King suggested that Polisario could have Mauritania if it left him alone but they made a major attack which wiped out a Moroccan garrison at Lebouirate and almost succeeded in reaching Dakhla. The Moroccans admitted another defeat at Bir Enzaran, losing 100 killed to a force they estimated at 5,000: there were probably now 12,000 guerrillas under arms facing 60,000 Moroccans. There was heavy fighting near the Bu Craa mines and a town within Morocco was totally destroyed. In October there was a 36-hour conventional battle at Smara with both sides using armoured vehicles in which the Moroccans claimed to have killed 1,000, partly by air strikes. The King exploited these difficulties to frighten the West that the Libyan-supported Sahrawis might triumph and persuaded President Carter to authorise a long-delayed supply of arms although the Americans still refused to recognise Moroccan sovereignty over the Sahara. In November 1979 the Moroccan commander, Colonel Ahmad Dlimi, led what was described as the largest desert force since the days of Montgomery, with 6,000 men in 1,500 vehicles to drive the guerrillas from the territory. His success caused the King, comparing the advance to "windscreen wipers", to forecast that he would dictate peace terms during 1980 but during the year there were attacks on two towns well within Morocco. The Moroccans started to seal off the pacified and useful area by a series of *berms* (rock walls), the first was 3 metres high and 300 km long, protected by minefields and electronic devices said to be so sophisticated that they could spot a jackal at 30 km; this reversion to static defence was its first strategic use since the First World War. There were diplomatic moves for a *rapprochement* with Algeria which could bring pressure on the Sahrawis to accept a cease-fire leading to a referendum but Chadli refused to negotiate behind their backs. There was also an announcement of a railway which would link Marrakesh with al-Ayun and possibly Dakar. In October 1981, however, the Moroccans suffered their heaviest defeat so far when a garrison of 400 at Guelta Zammour was overwhelmed by 3,000 Sahrawis using Russian battle tanks and missiles which shot down Moroccan aircraft. Hassan, calling it "an event of the utmost gravity", said that the weaponry had been too sophisticated for guerrillas to have operated on their own. In January 1982 3,000 SADR regulars with tanks failed to breach the wall and another assault in July was repulsed. There was no further serious fighting for a year and then in July 1983, exasperated by the endless wrangling over a referendum and worried by rumours of a Moroccan–Algerian *rapprochement*, the Sahrawis, again using armour, attacked the wall, losing according to the Moroccans, 50 dead. At the end of 1983 25,000 Moroccan troops carried out a series of sweeps that enabled them, despite four major battles in April 1984, to build a fourth wall, 200 miles long, enclosing another 30,000 square miles including Hawza which had been described as the capital of the SADR. The guerrillas now found it easier to raid from Mauritania although in October they claimed that their frogmen had destroyed installations in al-Ayun. In the same month, just before a crucial OAU Summit, they committed a fifth of their army against the wall, leading to what the Moroccans described as the heaviest fighting since Guelta Zammour. The war was by now costing Morocco, already heavily indebted, over $2 million a day and the King described it as "a vampire". In January 1985 a fourth wall, ending 4 km from Tindouf was completed despite Sahrawi attacks and work immediately started on a fifth wall. Also in January in the course of a major battle in which the Sahrawis deployed three tank battalions a Moroccan aircraft was shot down with a missile fired from Algerian territory. In February Polisario shot down two civilian aircraft, one British and one German, and during the summer a German boat was sunk and Spanish sailors taken prisoner in dinghy-borne attacks. There was heavy fighting in July with the Sahrawis claiming to have carried out 179 attacks, killing 210 Moroccan soldiers and wounding 445. There were only minor skirmishes during 1986 but early in 1987 the Sahrawis claimed a major offensive with over a hundred armoured vehicles in 595 battles in which over 880 Moroccans were killed. The Moroccans admitted that a wall had been breached but claimed to have killed over 200 in sweeps into the "no-man's land" between the walls and international boundaries: this consisted of about 30,000 sq km of arid desert containing two villages. In April and May the Moroccans built a seventh wall, taking the total to over 1,800 miles. This final wall made access from Polisario's Algerian bases to the Atlantic possible only through Mauritania which complained that its neutrality was infringed. During 1987 the Sahrawis claimed to have 25,000 men under arms, the Moroccan estimate was 1,800 to 2,500 and others reckoned 8,000: estimates of the Moroccan army varied from 90,000 to over 150,000. Late in 1987 the UN started a new peace initiative which, in August 1988, resulted in both sides agreeing to a cease-fire which was quickly breached by Polisario making large-scale attacks: in September the Moroccans admitted losing 51 killed at Umm Dreiga while in November there was an armoured attack on the wall. Polisario declared a six-week cease-fire after the King's meeting with its leaders in Marrakesh and, announcing that it held 2,500 Moroccan prisoners of war, released 200 of them unconditionally. In October and November 1989 both sides reported the biggest battles since 1981 and Hassan said that he was ready to fight on for a hundred years. In April 1991 the UN set up MINURSO to monitor a cease-fire and a refer-endum but in August, before the peace-keepers were due to arrive, both sides attempted to assert control in the "no-man's land". When the cease-fire came into effect on 6 September 1991 Polisario claimed that in sixteen years of warfare they had killed or wounded 60,000 Moroccans: the Moroccans gave their own losses at "several hundred" and claimed to have killed 4,000 guerrillas. Minor incidents continued and in March 1992 the UN stated that of the 77 reported violations of the cease-fire, Morocco had been responsible for 75. There were no major battles in 1992 or 1993.

WOODHEAD REPORT (1938)

The Peel Report of 1937 concluded that the British Mandate for Palestine could not be fulfilled and that the country should be partitioned. There should be a small area still ruled by the British and an independent Jewish state while the rest of the territory should be annexed to Trans-Jordan. The following year the British Government sent Sir John Woodhead, an Indian Civil Servant and a lawyer and a Commission mostly of fellow members of the ICS to report on the practicality of partition. He put forward three plans of which he thought that the least objectionable was one to maintain Northern Palestine including Haifa and Nazareth and the Southern area of the Negev under the Mandate while a special enclave should be created around Jerusalem. A small coastal strip of about 400 square miles stretching north from Tel Aviv should be a Jewish state while the remainder including Janin, Hebron and Gaza should be an Arab state. However it was unlikely that the plan would be accepted by those concerned and it would be impossible to recommend boundaries which would afford reasonable prospects of self-supporting Arab and Jewish states. "Economic federalism" was recommended and fiscal autonomy might be withheld if the British Government were prepared to subsidise the two states. The Jewish state would be tiny and not have defensible boundaries. There would have to be compulsory transfers of Arabs from the Jewish areas which the Government had already refused to countenance as morally objectionable. In short, apart from the political difficulties, there would be enough administrative, financial and economic problems to render partition impractical.

al-YAFI, Abd Allah (1901–)

Lebanese Prime Minister. A Sunni from a middle-class family he went to the Jesuit University of Beirut and then took a doctorate in law from the Sorbonne. He practised law in Beirut and although he became a Deputy in 1932 and wrote some political newspaper articles was little known when he became Prime Minister in October 1938. The British Consulate reported that he was "moderately intelligent with strong nationalist sentiments". Like its predecessors, his Cabinet was mainly preoccupied with its internal intrigues with Ministers attending to the problems of their clientele rather than those of the country which were in the hands of the French and to a lesser extent those of President Emile Edde. In September 1939 the Constitution was suspended and executive power placed in the hands of a State Secretary. In 1944 Yafi was a member of the Lebanese delegation at the foundation of the Arab League and in 1945 of the UN. In 1950 as Minister of Agriculture he attempted some land reform and also to stamp out the cultivation of hashish – he later claimed that production was halved while he held office. In June 1951 after elections Bishara al-Khouri appointed Yafi Prime Minister but in February 1952 as opposition mounted the President felt he needed a stronger man with more support amongst the Sunnis and replaced him with Sami al-Sulh. Yafi thereupon joined the opposition and became an adherent of Camille Chamoun. In the crisis of September Yafi was appointed Prime Minister but failed to form a government. In August 1953 he was more successful and for just over a year was an active agent of Chamoun's desire to play a larger part in Arab politics. Yafi visited Cairo, Damascus and Baghdad. Development projects such as enlarging Tripoli harbour, improving electricity distribution, building a motorway and an irrigation scheme for the Litani area were inaugurated. In September 1954, feeling that more forceful leadership was needed to introduce reforms, Chamoun replaced Yafi with Saeb Salam as Prime Minister though he kept most of the rest of the Cabinet. In March 1956 Yafi was again Prime Minister, faced with the damage caused by a serious earthquake in the south and a dispute over royalties to be paid on the oil pipeline across Lebanon. There was a further problem as the Arab League, because of Algeria, called for a boycott of France with which Lebanon had such close cultural and economic ties. In November when he failed to persuade the President to break off diplomatic relations with Britain and France at the time of the Suez War, Yafi and Saeb Salam resigned and joined Chamoun's

opponents. An election rigged by Chamoun and Sami al-Sulh cost Yafi his seat in the Chamber and for a time he was out of mainstream politics. He advocated support for Nasser and Arab nationalism and welcomed the formation of the United Arab Republic. In May 1958 Yafi accused the President of seeking assistance from the Baghdad Pact countries and condemned his complaint to the Security Council against the UAR. In the 1960 election and again in 1964 Salam, who was emerging as his main rival for the leadership of the Beirut Sunnis, refused to support him and he failed to be elected. In April 1966, however, his old political ally President Charles Helou appointed him Prime Minister when Rashid Karami, who was the only Deputy in his own Cabinet, resigned to make way for a government of Parliamentarians. Yafi brought in Pierre Gemayel and Kamal Jumblatt but he held office only until December. There was a general feeling of insecurity, highlighted by the murder of the prominent newspaper editor Kamal Mrowa. There was also labour unrest, bloodshed in the Tripoli area and the Intra Bank Scandal. An attempt to call a National Conference to settle the nation's problems failed and the Government achieved little of note beyond banning cowboy and James Bond films. In February 1968 he began his final period of office as a caretaker Premier to prepare for elections, after which he offered to resign but received a vote of confidence. He strongly supported the Palestinians, applauded their victory at Karamah but found himself torn between the pressure of his constituents to take a militant line and his need to conform to the more cautious policies of President Helou. There was also a quarrel with Syria over transit dues. In October Yafi resigned but after great difficulty formed a Cabinet consisting only of Gemayel, Raymond Edde and Hussain al-Uwayni. There were demonstrations and riots and Yafi resigned in November but after one day decided to continue in office. On 28 December the Israelis raided Beirut airport, caught the Lebanese security totally unprepared and destroyed 13 aircraft on the ground. The popular outcry compelled the resignation of Yafi. In November 1974 he was one of the delegation led by President Sulayman Franjiyah and comprising nearly all the leading Lebanese politicians that went to lobby the UN on behalf of the Palestinians. In September 1975 he was a member of the National Dialogue Committee created in the hope of averting civil war and in October he was one of the "Security Committee" formed by the Prime Minister Karami after the attempted assassination of Pierre Gemayel. Yafi was generally regarded as an honest but not a forceful man. He wrote a book on the rights of women in Islam.

YAHYA, Tahir (1914–86)

Iraqi Prime Minister. His family came from Takrit but he was born in Baghdad, the son of a grain salesman. He trained as a teacher before entering the Military Academy and commanded armoured cars in the Palestine War. Although he had been retired from the army, suspected of political unreliability, Yahya was an early member of the Free Officers. After the July Revolution of 1958 he became Chief of Police but was dismissed and briefly imprisoned for involvement in the plot of Rashid Ali al-Gilani. He may also have had some connection with the Mosul Uprising and the attempt on the life of Abd al-Krim Qassim. He contacted Mulla Mustafa Barzani to gain Kurdish help for the overthrow of Qassim. In the early 1960s Yahya joined the Baath and in the February Revolution of 1963 he led a group of Party members to the principal barracks to prevent the garrison from coming to the rescue of Qassim. Yahya was then appointed Chief of Staff and conducted negotiations with the Syrian Baath, which came to power the following month, on military and political union. He also had further talks with Kurdish leaders. He became alienated by the irresponsible behaviour of the Baath National Guard and the attempt of the extremists to impose their will upon the Party so in the November Revolution of 1963 he joined with President Abd al-Salam Arif to smash it. Yahya was appointed Prime Minister, forming a Cabinet of which half were army officers and the majority were Nasserists. He pledged to make a reality of the Tripartite Agreement reached in the Cairo Unity Talks as "a nucleus for a general Arab union", a properly planned economy including the private sector, and agrarian reform. He ended martial law, banned paramilitary organisations, released political prisoners and welcomed back political refugees. Yahya declared himself for "democracy and socialism derived from Islam" but in general he had little time for ideology. In July 1964 he nationalised 30 large concerns including the banks but this was seen mainly as a step towards unity with Egypt. He failed in further efforts to reach a settlement with the Kurds and denounced Barzani as "a madman". His Cabinet was divided and unpopular and after reforming it in June 1964 he resigned in November. The President persuaded him to remain in office and he promised revival of parliamentary life within a year, isolation of the armed forces from politics, unity with Egypt and the restoration of national unity including Kurdistan. He then announced an ambitious Five-Year-Plan. After more than a year of negotiations in July 1965 he reached a new agreement in which the Iraq Petroleum Company relinquished some of its concessions. However Yahya was so well known to be financially dishonest that he was dubbed "The Thief of Baghdad" and the President, now anxious to be rid of a man who was appearing as a potential rival and wishing to make a gesture towards President Nasser by removing a man who had retained some Baathist links, hinted at a police investigation and the Prime Minister hastily resigned in September 1965. When in May 1967 the President Abd al-Rahman Arif decided to take over

as Prime Minister he appointed Yahya as one of four Deputy Premiers. Two months later, following Iraq's unimpressive participation in the June War, Arif found it impossible to combine the two posts and Yahya again became Prime Minister. He stated that the first task was to modernise the army, mobilise all patriotic forces in a single organisation based on socialism and recognise Kurdish national rights in a framework of Iraqi unity. He enforced the ban on oil exports to Britain and America and also added The Netherlands but later he restored relations with London but closed the American-run University. He made efforts to woo French and Russian oil interests to replace British and American and he established unusually friendly relations with Turkey and Iran. He made no progress with the Kurds. Again there was evidence of financial corruption and there was general dissatisfaction over economic conditions and his Cabinet, largely apolitical, was out of touch with public opinion. In April leading politicians including the former Prime Ministers Abd al-Rahman al-Bazzaz and Ahmad Hassan al-Bakr petitioned the President to dismiss the Government and hold free elections. Yahya resigned on 15 July 1968 and two days later the regime was overthrown in a palace coup. Yahya, charged with corruption, was imprisoned until November 1970 and then played no further part in politics.

YAMAMAH DEALS (1986 and 1988)

The AWACS Deal showed the Saudis the difficulties of obtaining sophisticated weaponry from the USA and in March 1985 they attempted to obtain Mirage fighters from France. This fell through and in February 1986 they signed an agreement with the British who agreed to provide 72 Tornado fighter-bombers, 30 Hawk fighter/training aircraft and 30 Orion surveillance aircraft, as well as missiles, training, technical support and spare parts. The value of the deal, estimated at over £5,000 million, the largest export contract ever won by Britain, was code-named *Yamamah* (Dove). It was to be paid for almost entirely in oil and the Saudis agreed to hand over 300,000 (some sources say 500,000) barrels a day (for two years?) which would be sold by Shell and British Petroleum who would pass the money to the Ministry of Defence for payment to British Aerospace. The first six Tornado aircraft were delivered in June 1986. At the time the agreement was concluded oil was selling for $28 a barrel but the price later dropped to $10 and although the amount of oil delivered was increased there was a shortfall in payments of $1,500 million which there was some difficulty in borrowing. Despite this a second *Yamamah* Deal was concluded in 1988 for an additional 48 Tornados, 60 Hawks and 88 Westland helicopters, some communications aircraft and six minesweepers. In addition, the British, in co-operation with a Dutch firm were to build two enormous bases. This was to be paid for by 400,000 barrels a day from 1990 to 1999. In addition the British undertook to invest $1,000 million in high technology industries in the Kingdom. In March 1989 British Aerospace stated that the two *Yamamah* deals could together amount to £150,000 million. The price of oil continued low and in 1988/9 the Saudis had to pay £2,000 million in cash. By the summer of 1990 over 40 of the Tornados of Yamamah-1 had been delivered but the Saudis decided not to buy 48 of those agreed in Yamamah-2 but instead to take more Hawks and helicopters. None of the deals was without controversy. In April 1989 the National Audit Office started investigating allegations that 30% of the deals estimated to be worth $150 billion over 20 years went in commissions. In March 1992 the investigation decided that there had been no corruption but refused to publish the report – not even the Commons Public Accounts Committee was allowed to see it and it was said that Prime Minister Thatcher had intervened to prevent publication. The Americans alleged that Westland paid bribes to land contracts and that Saudi Arabia paid a higher price to provide kick-backs. Khalid and Fahd b. Sultan were mentioned. In August 1992 allegations circulated that the Black Hawk helicopters would be furnished with US weapons which would thus be exported illegally. The *Yamamah* deals were not really contracts but in fact a list of possible purchases. Some of the spin-off projects were carried through. Michael Heseltine laid a foundation stone for one of the joint deals – the SR70 million pharmaceutical factory to be built by Glaxo in Jiddah – in January 1992. However, what appeared firm orders for defence equipment were cancelled or diverted to the US following Operation Desert Storm.

YAMANI, Ahmad Zaki (1930–)

Saudi Arabian Oil Minister. He came from a very distinguished Meccan family of juriconsults and scholars and after initial legal training at Cairo University, went on to take degrees in Comparative Law from New York University and Harvard Law School. His speciality was in multi-national corporations. He returned in 1956 to private practice in Jiddah but in 1957 was appointed Legal Adviser to the Oil Department of the Ministry of Finance, then run by Faysal whose *protégé* and close collaborator he became. Two years later he was appointed to the Cabinet as Minister of State without Portfolio before Faysal made him Oil Minister in March 1962. He founded Petromin and the College of Petroleum Technology in Dhahran. During the June War some of the Arab states called for the banning of oil exports to the supporters of Israel but Yamani considered this would only harm Saudi Arabia unless all producing states participated. He was therefore the main force behind the formation of OAPEC in September 1968. He always understood the interdependence of producers and customers and he took the opportunity to say that participation rather than nationalisation should be the future policy. When the oil companies resisted change, OPEC hardened its stance with Yamani acting as its spokesman. Yamani played a leading part in the negotiations of the Tehran Agreement of February 1973 which marked the beginning of the shift of power away from the companies to the producing states. Immediately afterwards Faysal sent Yamani to the US to warn that Saudi Arabia would not increase production to meet American needs unless it changed its attitude on the Palestine question. The outbreak of the October War was followed by the initiation of the Oil Weapon and a demand led by Yamani that the price of oil be doubled to $6 a barrel. Intending to profit by the ensuing crisis the Shah

announced that he would raise prices to over $20 which Yamani considered so high that it would damage the economies of the industrialised world and lead to a general slump which could cause communist take-overs in France or Italy: he persuaded the Shah to compromise on $12. This concern for viewing the world economy as a whole showed in a speech that he made to the General Assembly of the UN on the "North-South Divide" and in efforts to prevent rises in the price of oil. He also insisted that the "petro-dollars" be invested in the capitalist world. In June 1974 he signed an agreement which gave Saudi Arabia a 60% holding in ARAMCO. In March 1975 Yamani was standing beside Faysal when the King, who had treated him like a son, was murdered; and there was speculation that this event would mark the end of his influence. Later during the year he expected to lose his life during the OPEC Ministers Kidnapping when he spent four days in the hands of the terrorist "Carlos the Jackal". During the following years he was successful in keeping the oil price stable despite demands from the Shah and other leaders for rises which would have taken it to $100. Yamani's personal rivalry with his Iranian counterpart Jamshid Amouzegar further complicated the dispute. It was the fall of the Shah, however, that set off the second oil crisis when the price trebled. The 1979 rises caused so great a slump in Western economies that demand fell off and the prices started to fall. Yamani worked energetically to keep them steady by increasing or decreasing Saudi production which varied from 9 million barrels a day in 1980 to 3 million in 1985. This damaged the narrow interests of his country and the Budget for 1983/4 had cuts of up to 40% in some areas. Yamani managed to persuade his partners to accept quotas for production but many states quite openly cheated and the rise of non-OPEC producers had weakened the hold of the cartel. In 1986 the price fell to $9 and Saudi Arabia for the first time for decades found itself short of money. Many of the Princes felt that Yamani was somehow responsible for damaging their standard of living; they disliked also his Westernised habits and the way that his appetite for publicity made him appear to the world as more important than the King. Yamani was never as close to Fahd as he had been to his predecessors and in 1984 he was overruled in a deal in which aircraft were purchased from Boeing by increasing production. In the autumn of 1986 there arose the Al Yamamah Deal which Yamani also opposed to the great annoyance of middlemen who stood to lose enormous commissions. In the OPEC meeting of October it was obvious that he regarded the King's policy of increasing production while increasing prices as unrealistic and would bring the Organisation near collapse. After his return he was suddenly dismissed, learning the fact from watching television. There were reports that he was forbidden to leave the country but after some weeks he was able to go to Switzerland. Later he was a frequent commentator on oil matters and also took much interest in academic matters, lecturing at Universities. Yamani admitted that he was influenced by astrology in the timing of decisions. He was also very keen on yachting but was unable to move far without being surrounded by British bodyguards.

YANBU AND JUBAYL DEVELOPMENT SCHEMES

Yanbu was a small fishing village on the Red Sea which had some importance as the place where Egyptian pilgrims disembarked for Medina. Its pre-1939 population was about 3,000. Jubayl on the Gulf was even smaller. In September 1975 a Royal Decree established a Commission to develop these two sites as industrial cities. The importance attached to this Commission was shown by the appointment of Crown Prince Fahd as its Chairman. A 30-year master-plan was drawn up by American consultants. In addition to oil-linked industries it was determined to establish steel and light manufactures which would profit from cheap power. There were also to be training programmes, with 1,000 graduates a year in each city, to enable Saudis to replace expatriates. A new form of urban government was projected in self-contained, landscaped modern communities. Special attention was paid to health and environmental matters. It was anticipated that the population of Yanbu would exceed 130,000 and that of Jubayl 280,000 by 2010. Oil pipelines were built and a terminal for crude with a capacity of 1,600,000 barrels a day was in operation at Yanbu by July 1981. Refineries both for export and domestic consumption were also built. A naval base was built at Jubayl. These facilities proved invaluable during the War of the Tankers in the Gulf. In addition a 1,575 kilometre pipeline capable of carrying 1.65 million barrels a day of Iraqi crude to Yanbu was built at a cost of $2,700 million but was not opened until after the end of the war. Desalination plants were constructed – that at Jubayl supplying much of the needs of Riyadh. Yanbu was also important in a joint Saudi-Sudanese project to exploit minerals lying at the bottom of the Red Sea. Petromin and SABIC were responsible for the major projects but private enterprise was encouraged with tax exemptions and by 1990 120 industrial plants had been built at a cost of over $15,000 million. Altogether Yanbu and Jubayl represented one of the most ambitious schemes conceived by any developing country.

YASSIN, Abd al-Salam (c. 1927–)

Moroccan religious and political leader. His family claimed descent from the Idrisi Sharifs. After receiving a traditional Islamic education at the Yusufi University in Marrakesh, he became a teacher of Arabic and then an Inspector in the Ministry of Education. He was a pious Muslim but took little interest in politics until the early 1970s when he discovered the works of Hassan al-Banna and Saiyyid Qutb. In 1974 he addressed a 114-page letter to Hassan II warning him that his rule was tyrannical and a negation of Islam in its neglect of the poor, its tolerance of corruption and its failure to consult the people as the righteous Caliphs had done. He called for the abolition of political parties which contended for secular government. He supported the Western Sahara War on the grounds that there should be no boundaries between members of the Islamic Umma. Unwilling to make him a martyr, the King had him confined in a lunatic asylum. Upon his release in 1977, despite government obstruction he published an Islamic review which was banned in 1983 when he was forbidden to preach in mosques. After an attempt to publish another journal and riots in the North which were blamed on his followers he was imprisoned for two years. In jail he published a book on Leninism. Yassin was released early in 1986 but although kept under surveillance he attracted a considerable number of followers whom he organised as the Movement for Justice and Benevolence (al-Adl wa'l-Ihsan), promising the unemployed young, particularly those with education, that their lot would improve in an Islamic state. He abstained from direct criticism of the King and, opposing violence and advocating economic reform rather than calling for an Islamic state, he was seen as more moderate than the Islamic leaders in Algeria and Tunisia. In November 1986 24 of his followers, including 19 teachers, were sentenced to imprisonment for up to a year for belonging to an unauthorised organisation and possessing documents likely to cause a breach of the peace. In December 1989 he was put under house arrest in Sale and forbidden to receive visitors. In May 1990 the trial of six of his supporters for demonstrating outside his house sparked off a major riot. In February 1991 he recruited volunteers to fight but they were not organised before the fighting stopped. In April 1992 after some of his followers had occupied a University building near Casablanca after a clash with the police, Yassin was again arrested but released early in 1993 to facilitate dialogue with militants. Yassin was described as having twinkling eyes and a scraggy beard and an air of benevolence rather than fanaticism.

YASSIN, Ahmad (1935–)

Palestinian religious and political leader. He was born in Majdal near Ascalon from which his family was forced to flee in the Palestine War. They settled in the Shati refugee camp in the Gaza Strip where in 1951 he was crippled in a sporting accident. He was, however, able to marry and sire eleven children before becoming paralysed and confined to a wheelchair in 1980. He had joined the Muslim Brotherhood, which started to flourish in Gaza after the expulsion of the Egyptians and in 1983 he was arrested by the Israelis for organising a military wing which he called the Mujahidin of Palestine. He was also convicted of having arms in his house and was sentenced to 13 years' imprisonment. In 1985 he was released as part of a prisoner exchange between the Israelis and the Popular Front for the Liberation of Palestine – General Command. He taught Arabic and religion and acted as Imam while recruiting further members for the Muslim Brotherhood with his message of jihad and the need for mobility and change. He was dismissed from his post by the occupation authorities and earned his living by raising chicken and sheep. He opposed premature confrontation, feeling that the Palestinians were too weak and also needed to educate other Arab and Islamic countries so that they would be supported but by December 1987 he had gathered a group of militants which, after the outbreak of the Intifadah, he organised as Hamas. At first he worked with the Unified Leadership which was dominated by the Palestine Liberation Organisation but he came to see the secular leaders as too irreligious and too unenthusiastic. Hamas therefore escalated violence on its own and Yassin came to be seen as not merely the spiritual but the organisational leader of the Uprising. In May

1989 he was arrested, charged with ordering the abduction of two Israeli soldiers and the killing of three Palestinians. In October 1991 in plea-bargaining he admitted founding and directing a hostile organisation, homicide, incitement and possession of firearms and was sentenced to life imprisonment plus 15 years for ordering the killing of Palestinians. In December 1992 his supporters kidnapped an Israeli soldier whom they offered to exchange for the Shaykh. The authorities refused, the soldier was murdered and 400 alleged militants were deported to Marj al-Zuhur. In October 1993 Yassir Arafat made a special plea for the release of Shaykh Yassin.

YASSIN, Yusuf (c. 1890–1962)

Saudi Minister. He was born near Latakia and educated in Jerusalem where he became a teacher. According to some accounts in 1917 he joined Sharif Faysal and served him until the French entered Damascus. Faysal then found him a position with King Hussain who later sent him to Amman to work for his son Abd Allah. The two men did not get on and Yassin entered the service of Ibn Saud seeing him as the embodiment of Arab nationalism. According to other versions he was a journalist and agitator, who fled from Syria and was jailed by the British in Palestine. After the capture of Mecca, Ibn Saud appointed him editor of the official newspaper *Umm al-Qura*, and later he held an office variously described as Private Secretary to the King or Head of the Political Diwan of the Court. He was noticeably devoted to his master and had less difficulty in adapting to Wahhabi ways than many of the other Arabs who worked for Ibn Saud. He was frequently employed in dealing with foreign powers and Clayton found him an exasperating "vulture" in the negotiations for the Bahra and Hadda Agreements. He was regarded by foreign representatives as obstructionist, irritating, a hair-splitter, intolerant, fanatical and boorish; all, however, were impressed at the way in which he appeared able to read the King's mind and anticipate exactly how he would react. He made contact with the German Ambassador in Baghdad seeking arms and during the war he was extremely pro-Axis. He was a Saudi representative at the foundation of the Arab League and accompanied the King on his meetings with Churchill and Roosevelt and his state visit to King Farouq. He was believed to intrigue in Syrian politics for personal ends. In 1946 his position was formalised as Minister of State for Foreign Affairs and he increased his influence after the death of Fuad Hamza and appeared in complete charge of foreign affairs during the reign of King Saud. In 1955 evidence that he had bribed witnesses led to the collapse of the International Tribunal established to decide upon the ownership of Buraymi. It is probable that he was the instigator of the plot in which Saud paid a large sum to secure the assassination of Nasser. Although industrious and experienced, he was perhaps too disinclined to give the Ibn Saud unpalatable advice and too addicted to petty intrigue to be regarded as a statesman.

YATA, Ali (1920–)

Moroccan Communist leader. He was born near Oran of an Algerian father and a Moroccan mother and in 1943 went to France where he became a communist and also took French nationality. He returned to work as a teacher but when in 1945 it was considered that the leader of the Moroccan Communist Party should be a Moroccan, Yata was chosen as Secretary-General. He established cordial links with the nationalist Istiqlal Party. In June 1948 he was condemned to exile but went underground and was not caught until July 1950 when he was expelled to Algeria. Two weeks later he tried to return secretly and was sentenced to two years' imprisonment. After serving ten months he was again expelled to Algeria where he was again arrested in September 1952, accused of issuing subversive tracts. He spent much of the next few years in France and Eastern Europe, showing himself an orthodox communist with few original ideas and a supporter of Russia against China. After independence he made several attempts to return to Morocco but was not allowed to do so until 1958. The following year the MCP was banned and in 1960 Yata's attempt to form a left-wing front was also prohibited as anti-Islamic although he often claimed that Islam was "progressive and revolutionary" and always stressed that he was a practising Muslim. He stood as an Independent in Casablanca in the parliamentary elections of May 1963 but was defeated by the leader of the Jewish community. Although he had stated categorically that Morocco was not ready for revolution, in October he was briefly imprisoned as a danger to state security. In 1968 Yata attempted to reform the MCP as the Parti de la Libération et du Socialisme, demanding parliamentary democracy and support for popular struggles abroad but the movement was banned and in September 1969 he was arrested on his return from the Romanian Communist Party Congress and sentenced to ten months' jail. In July 1970 he supported the opposition National Front of the Istiqlal and the Union Nationale des Forces Populaires. After 1972 when Hassan II started to increase his contacts with the opposition, Yata showed himself a loyal supporter of the Monarchy. As the end of Spanish rule in the Western Sahara approached, Yata used his links with the communist bloc to put Morocco's case, visiting most of their capitals. In August 1974 he was allowed to establish the Parti du Progrès et du Socialisme. In June 1977 he was elected to Parliament and in March 1979 he was appointed to the National Defence Council. He took a strong line over the Sahara, in 1977 dismissing Polisario as a "gang of mercenaries paid by Algeria" and in 1982 publishing a book setting out Morocco's claims. He also supported the King's efforts to bring peace between the Arabs and Israel. A man of great political skill, Yata made the PPS respectable, operating within the law and co-operating with other opposition parties without advocating violence. He was also an intensely patriotic Moroccan, little interested in a worldwide class struggle: the collapse of communism in Europe appeared irrelevant to his efforts to improve the life of Moroccan workers. One of his twin sons was Director of Information on the national television service.

YEMEN WAR

On 26 September 1962 young officers with Egyptian support bombarded the palace of the Imam

Muhammad al-Badr. It was announced that he had been killed and a Republic was proclaimed under Colonel Abd Allah Sallal. Egyptian military aid – "to oppose any foreign intervention" in Nasser's words – arrived with such speed that it had clearly been held in readiness before the coup. The Royalists rallied under Badr's uncle Hassan who was proclaimed Imam: he called for the tribes to rally to him and established a government in Saudi Arabia. In addition to Saudi help, assistance was forthcoming from the Jordanians and Sharif Hussain al-Habili of Bayhan, with British connivance. In October the Royalists captured Marib in the East but failed to take Sada in the North. In November Egyptian aircraft bombed Saudi towns and the two countries appeared on the brink of open war. The following month Badr reappeared, gave a press conference and resumed the Imamate. The Americans recognised the Republican regime but the British refused to do so and their Legation was closed. In February 1963 after a visit by the Egyptian Commander-in-Chief Abd al-Hakim Amer and Anwar Sadat the Egyptians launched the Ramadan Offensive recapturing Marib and Harib and ending the fighting in the South. Skirmishes continued in the North and East in the mountains where the mobility and guerrilla skills of the tribesmen proved more than a match for the complete Egyptian monopoly of armour and aircraft. In April 1963 the UN tried to bring about a disengagement of Egyptian and Saudi forces by establishing UNYOM to supervise a cease-fire. The Royalists who had been ignored in this arrangement continued to fight and the Egyptians disregarded it, not ending their bombing of Saudi Arabia and starting to use poison gas and napalm. Two offensives by the Egyptians in the autumn and winter in the Jauf area, where they attempted to cut the Royalist supply route from Saudi Arabia failed and a Royalist counter-offensive in January and February 1964 achieved some successes, briefly cutting the Sanaa-Hodeidah road. At this time Egyptian forces numbered about 28,000 men and were doing most of the fighting as the Yemeni army was untrained and tribesmen were totally unreliable, usually taking subsidies from both sides. In April 1964 Nasser visited Sanaa and ordered further attacks which won some ground in the North, compelling the Imam to move his HQ nearer the Saudi frontier. In September 1964 UNYOM which had proved completely futile was withdrawn. Many Yemenis came to realise that their country merely provided a battlefield on which Nasser and King Faysal could contest the leadership of the Arab world so in October moderate Republicans and moderate Royalists attempted to make a peace between Yemenis at the Erkowit Conference. This provided for the withdrawal of Egyptian forces and of both Badr and Sallal but failed owing to the intransigence of the Egyptians and Sallal, who was regarded merely as their puppet. A cease-fire proclaimed on 8 November lasted only a few days and was followed by Royalist successes in one of which they claimed to have killed 1,000 Egyptians in a week-long battle. They recaptured Harib and Marib, leading to their control of a third of the country. The Republicans split with the moderates under Ahmad Muhammad Nu'man trying to make peace at the Khamir Conference in April 1965 but again their efforts

were frustrated by Sallal. Nasser, by now referring to "my Vietnam", realised that his superiority in conventional weapons would not bring victory over guerrillas in the mountains and facing other difficulties was anxious for peace but Faysal was unwilling to let him off the hook. Nasser had to humble himself and the result was the Jiddah Agreement of August 1965 which led to a cease-fire and a subsequent Conference at Haradh, which met in November. Some of the Egyptian troops, then numbering about 70,000, went home but in February 1966 the British Government issued their White Paper on Defence which stated their intention of leaving Aden by 1968. Nasser was convinced that if he could maintain his position in North Yemen he would be able to exercise much influence on the South after it attained independence. Declaring his willingness to stay for 20 years, he introduced the Strategy of the Long Breath which involved the concentration of his forces in the Sanaa–Taizz–Hodeidah triangle and the abandonment to the Royalists of the rest of the country. An attempt in August 1966 by Kuwait to mediate between Egypt and Saudi Arabia without any Yemenis being present failed because Nasser insisted on maintaining his military presence and he sent back to Sanaa Sallal who had been absent for most of a year to act as his Viceroy and detained a mission of Yemenis which came to ask him to make peace. Fighting was mostly confined to Egyptian bombing and gas raids, one of which on Kitaf killed 250 villagers, 95% of the population: the use of gas was confirmed by the Red Cross and by the British Prime Minister. During the winter of 1966/7 Royalist activities were diminished by internal feuding. After the Arab defeat in the June War, Nasser withdrew about 15,000 men but there was another Egyptian offensive in July. In August at the Khartoum Summit Nasser, now financially dependent upon Saudi Arabia, agreed to bring back all his troops. This was fiercely opposed by Sallal who feared for his own position but was completed by the end of November, by which time Sallal had been overthrown. The Royalists launched a major offensive and early in December succeeded in surrounding Sanaa. The Republicans, under General Hassan al-Amri conducted a vigorous defence in which they were supported firstly by the Russians and then by the National Liberation Front which had taken power in Aden. In February 1968 the siege was lifted when the Hodeidah road was reopened. Amri, without the help of the Egyptian forces, previously regarded as indispensable, succeeded in reconquering much of the country, helped by intensified Royalist feuding. In October and November Sanaa was again under threat. Many Royalist tribal supporters defected to the Republic and Badr withdrew to Saudi Arabia. In May 1969 President Abd al-Rahman al-Iryani said that not a shot had been fired since December. In September the Republicans recaptured Sada. The Royalists made a final effort and regained it in February 1970 but by then Faysal had decided that he could live with the moderate Republic of Iryani and indeed use it as an ally against the communist South. He therefore ceased aid to the Royalists and "ordered" them to stop fighting. Nearly all except members of the Ruling Family returned and were integrated in the new regime. It was estimated that during the war 200,000

Yemenis were killed – 4% of the population. Egyptian losses were never published but the morale of the army was fatally damaged and their financial reserves depleted.

YUNIS, Mahmud (1912–)

Egyptian engineer and administrator. He trained as an engineer, joined the army in 1937, taught at Staff College at the same time as Nasser and at the time of the July Revolution was a Colonel directing the Technical Section at Army HQ. Nasser put him in charge of technical and industrial affairs and according to Sadat he supervised a study of the feasibility of the Aswan High Dam. In July 1956, before he nationalised the Suez Canal, Nasser ordered Yunis to take over the Company's offices in Port Said when in a speech in Alexandria he said the words "Ferdinand de Lesseps" and to be responsible for its continued operation. When the British and French pilots walked out, he recruited replacements. His energy made nonsense of the key Western argument that the Egyptians were incapable of running an enterprise of world significance. After the Suez War he organised the rapid unblocking of the Canal with UN help. He improved services and also made it so profitable that tolls were not raised until 1964. In 1967 he was appointed Deputy Premier in charge of Electricity and Petroleum and had responsibilities for reconstruction added after the June War. In 1968 he left the Government and later settled in Beirut as a private consultant.

ZAID b. HUSSAIN, *Amir* (c. 1900–70)

The youngest son of the future King Hussain by a Turkish lady he received a modern education. T. E. Lawrence in 1916 described him as "a shy, white, beardless youth, calm and flippant, no zealot for the revolt" but later he was active in the field with his brother Faysal and commanded in operations around Medina. In June 1917 he defeated a force led by Saud b. Abd al-Aziz al-Rashid and in January 1918 with Jafar al-Askari, 60 regulars and 250 tribal irregulars he won a major battle against 1,000 Turks at Tafilah. After the War Zaid went with Faysal to Damascus, serving as his Deputy while the King was abroad and when they were expelled by the French, Zaid returned to the Hijaz. In 1922 after Faysal had become King of Iraq, Zaid went to Baghdad, was commissioned in the cavalry and acted briefly as Regent in 1924. In 1925 he went to Oxford where he studied agriculture and rowed in the Balliol boat. In 1928 he joined King Hussain, then in exile in Cyprus, staying until his father's death in 1931. He then served as Iraqi Minister in Ankara and Cairo and from 1946 to 1958 as Ambassador in London. After the July Revolution of 1958 he retired from public life, dividing his time between Amman, Paris and London. He was a kindly, generous, humorous man, always helpful to historical researchers: a Foreign Office report of 1934 stated that he was "generally regarded as the pick of the Hashemites".

ZAID IBN SHAKIR, *Sharif* (1932–)

Jordanian Field Marshal and Prime Minister. He was the son of Sharif Shakir who won a reputation as a commander of tribal levies during the Arab Revolt and later in the Khurmah Dispute before accompanying the Amir Abd Allah to Trans-Jordan where he became an influential adviser on tribal matters. Zaid was at Sandhurst with King Hussain to whom he became a trusted friend. In April 1957 as ADC to the King he convinced loyal troops during the Zerka Incident of his master's safety. During the June War he commanded an armoured brigade in the Hebron–Jerusalem sector but was given an impossible task by the Egyptian commander General Abd al-Munim Riad and his force suffered heavy casualties. In the June 1970 Brigadier Zaid was one of the strongest advocates of curtailing the licence enjoyed by the *fedayin* of the Palestine Liberation Organisation and was sacrificed in an attempt to gain their goodwill: his dismissal nearly caused a mutiny. When a showdown became inevitable he was recalled as Chief of Operations and drew up to the plans that led to their expulsion from Amman after the fighting of Black September. In 1972 he was appointed Chief of Staff and in January 1976 succeeded Field Marshal Habis al-Majali as Commander-in-Chief, a post that he held until his retirement in 1988. In April 1989 following the unrest that had brought down the government of Zaid al-Rifai, the Field Marshal was appointed Prime Minister with a brief to curb corruption, defuse discontent over unpopular economic measures and arrange a general election with all possible speed. After this had taken place in what was generally regarded as fair conditions, he handed over to Mudar Badran in December. He remained close to the King whom he served as Chief Adviser. In November 1991 after Tahir al-Masri had failed to keep his government together, Zaid was again appointed Prime Minister with instructions to reform the economy, work for Arab unity still damaged after the Iraqi invasion of Kuwait and reach accommodation with the Muslim Brothers, the strongest single group in Parliament which adamantly rejected Jordan's participation in the Madrid Peace Talks.

al-ZAYYAT, Muhammad Hassan (1915–93)

Egyptian diplomat. Born in Damietta, he took a degree at Cairo University where in 1950 he was appointed an Assistant Lecturer in Middle Eastern Studies. After a doctorate from Oxford he joined the Diplomatic Service and spent five years in Washington before being posted to Tehran as Chargé in 1955. In the early 1960s he represented Egypt at the Arab League and the UN and was briefly Ambassador to India. After the June War Zayyat was appointed Official Government Spokesman and became internationally known through his ability to present the Arab case in a form acceptable to the Western mind. He continued to do this after his selection as Permanent Representative to the UN in June 1969. Zayyat negotiated with Jarring and was the first to put forward the proposal that Egypt might recognise Israel in return for an agreement to hand back Sinai and limit the immigration of foreign Jews. In January 1972 he was appointed Minister of State for Information and in September, after Sadat had expelled Russian advisers, Foreign Minister. He immediately visited Europe, playing a large part in improving Egypt's relations. In October 1972 he declared that the credibility of the UN was severely damaged by its failure to agree collective action on the Middle East. Zayyat became known as an advocate of peace with Israel by any means short of total surrender. In October 1973 he gave up the Foreign Ministry but continued as a special adviser to the President on foreign affairs until his retirement in 1975. He then held Chairs as a Visiting Professor in Alexandria and California. In 1984 he was elected Deputy for Damietta, presiding over the National Assembly Commission of Immigration, Culture and Tourism.

ZBIRI, Taha (1924–)

Algerian military leader. Born in the Aures Mountains, he worked as a miner. He took part in the All Saints' Day Uprising and was in action several times before he was captured at the beginning of 1955. In November he escaped and continued fighting in the Aures, rising to command the first *wilaya* there. He was said to be the only senior officer never to have left the country during the war. Unlike some other *wilaya* commanders he supported Ben Bella against Ben Khedda in the power struggle that followed the Evian Agreement. In October 1963 Ben Bella profited from the absence of Boumédienne in Moscow to make Zbiri Chief of Staff, hoping to weaken the Defence Minister's hold on the army. Zbiri, however, became discontented with the too personal rule of Ben Bella and was the man who actually arrested him in June 1965. Later he considered that Boumédienne was no improvement upon his predecessor, refusing to consult anyone outside the Oudjdah Group and allowing the Industry Minister Abd al-Salam Belaid to follow technocratic rather than socialist policies. Boumédienne was also believed to be trying to get rid of those officers who had fought the War inside the country in favour of those who had been under his own command in Morocco and Tunisia. Zbiri therefore attempted a coup in December 1967 which failed when Boumédienne sent fighter aircraft against Zbiri's column of 22 tanks and a battalion of armoured cars. To save his men from slaughter Zbiri sent a message that he was abandoning them and set off by himself on foot. According to official figures 30 were killed during the incident. After some time underground Zbibi reached Tunisia which in May 1958 granted him asylum. He spent most of his exile in Europe and Morocco, returning home after the death of Boumédienne. Zbiri was a tough, humorous down-to-earth man, too honest to make a successful politician.

ZEMLA DEMONSTRATION (1970)

In December 1966 the UN passed Resolution 2072 calling for the decolonisation of Ifni and the Spanish Sahara and in 1969 Ifni reverted to Moroccan rule. The Spanish authorities determined to retain the Sahara by creating a "Hispano–Sahrawi Union" in which the Sahrawis would have second-class status unless they assimilated. This they wished to have endorsed by a Charter signed by the local notables who were summoned to meet on 17 June 1970. Islamic and nationalist dissidents called a for counter-demonstration at Zemla, on the outskirts of the capital Al-Ayun. Failing to prevent it, the Spanish authorities opened fire on the crowd of about 2,000, killing an unknown number of people. The leading nationalist, Muhammad Sid Ibrahim Bassiri, was arrested and never seen again. Morocco which earlier in the month had signed an agreement with Mauritania to collaborate for the liberation of the Sahara reaffirmed its claims to the area by

an official protest in Madrid. Spanish troops in the territory were reinforced but many Sahrawis came to feel that they could only achieve liberation by an armed struggle and several guerrilla groups were founded, the most important of which became known as Polisario.

ZERKA INCIDENT (1957)

During the spring of 1957 there was acute tension in Jordan as King Hussain struggled to maintain a pro-Western stance while his left-wing Prime Minister Sulayman al-Nabulsi wanted a close alliance with Egypt and diplomatic relations with Russia. The Chief of Staff, Major-General Ali Abu Nuwar, supposedly an intimate friend of the King, was secretly plotting to overthrow the Monarchy and on 8 April ordered an armoured car regiment to surround Amman; it was later rumoured that its commander had the King's abdication in his pocket. Hussain questioned Abu Nuwar who either lost his nerve or felt that the troops would refuse to act against the King and therefore ordered them back to barracks. On 10 April the King dismissed Nabulsi but found it difficult to find a new Prime Minister. On the evening of 13 April an artillery battalion commanded by a cousin of Abu Nuwar started to move out of Zerka camp in order to carry out a coup but their intentions were suspected by bedouin soldiers fiercely loyal to Hussain. Shooting broke out between the two groups and when the King heard of this he ordered Abu Nuwar to accompany him to Zerka. On the way they met bedouin soldiers rushing to Amman to protect the King: recognising him they declared their loyalty and asked his permission to kill Abu Nuwar. Hussain sent the General back to Amman and went on to Zerka which was still in a state of turmoil. He invited the soldiers to kill him if they thought him a traitor but they gave him enthusiastic support. The conspirators were later arrested and Abu Nuwar sent into exile. A coup which would have altered the future history of the Middle East was prevented by the personal courage and coolness of the King who was still only 21 years old.

ZEROUAL, Liamine (1941–)

Algerian President. Born Batna, he represented a generation of the Algeria military that had not served in the French army although he fought in the Algerian War of Independence. After training at military schools in France and Russia, he held a series of commands including both frontier areas and the Military Academy at Cherchel. He was a General and Commander of the Land Forces when he resigned in protest at the use of the army to put down the October Riots of 1988. Zeroual was sent as Ambassador to Romania but resigned in less than a year and went into retirement. In July 1993 he was recalled to succeed General Nezzar as Minister of Defence to cope with an Islamic Insurgency which amounted to civil war. He declared several times that the army would not get involved in partisan in-fighting and that its purpose was to help to "forge a national consensus". This set him apart from the hard-line Generals who wished to destroy the Front Islamique du Salut by force and later it was stated that he had held secret meetings with its imprisoned leaders. On 30 January 1994 the High Security Council nominated Zeroual as Head of State for a transition period of three years. He retained the Ministry of Defence. His appointment was welcomed by neighbouring states but condemned as illegitimate by FIS leaders in exile. His first public statement called for dialogue, declaring that a military solution was impossible. He was believed to be aiming for a coalition with old "trusties" from the Front de Libération Nationale in charge of Foreign Affairs, Defence and the Interior, economic portfolios held by technocrats, and those with a social dimension by the FIS. In April he got rid of hard liner Malik. He is a small man with a white quiff and bushy black eyebrows.

ZINJIBAR CONGRESS (1968)
From 2–8 March 1968 the National Liberation Front held its Fourth Congress, the first since becoming the ruling party of South Yemen. Attended by 167 delegates, the dispute between the left and right wings came out into the open. The President Qahtan al-Shaabi wished to build pragmatically upon what had been left by the British, not to antagonise neighbouring regimes and to avoid radical reforms and purges. The opposition led by two Ministers, Abd al-Fattah Ismail and Ali Salim al-Baydh, wanted a complete new beginning, "scientific socialism" based on village soviets with collectivisation of land, power to the workers, a Supreme People's Council, a People's Militia, nationalisation of banks, overseas trade, etc. They declared that the Revolution could not be regarded as complete until it had been exported to the neighbouring countries and Yemen unified; there should be support for left-wing movements such as the Vietcong throughout the world. The President was attacked for "pathetic phraseological socialism" and the left prevailed. On 20 March, in alliance with the army which felt threatened by the proposed militia, al-Shaabi arrested his opponents stating that they were planning a coup. Later, feeling that he had no need to fear them, he released them all but they succeeded in ousting him in the Glorious Corrective Move just over a year later.

ZUBARAH DISPUTE
About 1760 the Al Khalifah section of the Utub tribe left Kuwait and settled on the north-west coast of the Qatar Peninsula at Zubarah which was well-sited to be a base for pearl-fishing. The occupation of Basra by the Persians in the next decade attracted immigrant merchants to Zubarah, making it also a flourishing commercial centre. After several attempts by the Persians to destroy it, in 1783 the Al Khalifah made a counter-attack in which they wrested Bahrain from Persian occupation. The leading members of the family transferred themselves to their new conquest, leaving behind tribesmen of the Naim who were regarded as their subjects. Early in the next century Zubarah was occupied by the Saudis and then destroyed by Said b. Sultan Al Bu Said as part of his attempt to establish commercial domination over the Gulf. The Naim rebuilt it and in 1873 the Turks who had occupied the Hasa Province of Eastern Arabia claimed sovereignty over the Qatar Peninsula including Zubarah. Isa b. Ali al-Khalifah reasserted Bahrain's rights but was told by the British not to attempt to enforce them. In 1875

after the Naim had been attacked by tribal enemies, Isa was allowed to send them reinforcements but was later told to confine his activities to his own islands. In 1878 after the inhabitants had engaged in piracy, Zubarah was destroyed, with the consent of the British, by Jasim b. Muhammad al-Thani of Qatar. In 1888 there were reports that Jasim was planning to rebuild it as a base from which his son-in-law, a dissident member of the Al Khalifah, could attack Bahrain but he refrained after a warning from the British. In 1895 the Al Bin Ali, a dissident Bahraini tribe settled in the neighbourhood and prepared a fleet to invade the islands with the blessing of Jasim and the Turks. They disregarded British warnings and their ships were destroyed. In 1902 there were reports in a semi-official Constantinople newspaper that the Ottoman Government would establish administrative officials in Zubarah and in Udayd but after British protests at the highest level, they declared that there had been a mistaken initiative by a local official. The same thing happened in 1910. The Turks left Doha during the First World War and their claim to sovereignty passed to Qatar. In 1920 Abd Allah b. Jasim al-Thani asked British permission to develop the site but was instructed not to attempt to do so. In 1937 an oil company wished to prospect in the more or less deserted area. Hamad b. Isa al-Khalifah revived Bahrain's claim and started to arm the still loyal Naim. Abd Allah b. Jasim mounted a major attack and destroyed what was left of the settlement, building a fort which the British prevented Hamad from attacking. The Naim withdrew to Bahrain and Bahrain imposed an economic boycott on Qatar which caused considerable hardship there. The British tried to mediate, perhaps creating a neutral zone, but both sides refused to compromise. Sir Charles Belgrave said that the Al Khalifah were almost obsessed by what they saw as an assault upon their family dignity by the theft of their ancestral home and continued to pester the British for years but nothing was ever done. In 1949 Qatar withdrew its garrison and the Naim returned. The situation was thus restored to what it had been at the beginning of the century. The Al Khalifah regarded the sovereignty over Zubarah as the most important of political questions while the Qataris nursed similar grievances over Hawar.

al-ZUBAYDI, Muhammad Hamza
Became Prime Minister if Iraq in succession to Hammadi on 14 September 1991. In September 1993 he was dismissed, possibly because of his failure to prevent a coup attempt the month before. An official statement said that his dismissal was "to give momentum to Iraq's construction quest". Zubaydi is a Shi'i and Harvey Morris claims that he is a secret police thug. Zubaydi's name is on a list of war criminals compiled by INC.

ZURAYQ, Constantine (1909–)
Syrian scholar and diplomat. He was born in Damascus and educated at the American University of Beirut, Chicago and Princeton. Trained as a historian, he was Rector of Damascus University and Vice-President of AUB, and Syrian Minister to the US and the UN. He wrote several major historical works but his most

important publications were on contemporary themes. In 1939 his *Al-Wai al-Qawmi* – "National Consciousness" was one of the first attempts to define Arab nationalism and suggest how it might be achieved. Himself a Christian, he believed that Islam provided the essential means of uniting the Arabs. It had a powerful effect on Beirut students such as George Habash and Wadai Haddad. This was followed in 1948 by *Ma'na al-Nakba* – "The Meaning of the Disaster" in which he analysed the Arab defeat in Palestine. While many Arab leaders claimed that this was merely a setback, Zurayq argued that it was a disaster. He believed that there was total and comprehensive confrontation between the Arabs and the Zionists in the economic, social, political, military and technological spheres of life. Zionism was armed with modern Western science, advanced technology, a rational system of organisation, an expanding economy and a modern system of values and social practice. The Arabs on the other hand were basically traditional societies with tribal and parochial leadership, a lack of science and technology, a mainly religious value system, still dominated by colonial powers and ill at ease in the modern world. He maintained that Israel could not be defeated in a single battle but it would take a long struggle and the total transformation of Arab society. In order to achieve the transformation Zurayq maintained that it was necessary to adopt modern technology, train Arabs in empirical sciences, acquire a modern value system and separate Church and State. Then it would be possible to form a unified state with a progressive, dynamic mentality. His views caused intense debate amongst Arab intellectuals with some arguing for socialism and nationalism while others called for a return to the fundamentals of Islam.

al-ZUBAYRI, Muhammad Mahmud (c. 1917–65)

Yemeni statesman. He was a member of the *Qadi* class and, after a traditional education, entered government service about 1937. Disquietened by administrative injustices, he soon went to Cairo where he attended both religious and secular courses at Universities. He returned about 1941 and with Muhammad Ahmad Nu'man was one of the pioneers of the Ahrar which called for a reformed constitutional Imamate. He was close to the Crown Prince Ahmad whose son Badr he helped to tutor in the hope of forming a liberal ruler. In 1944 Ahmad saw in the Ahrar a threat to the dynasty, Zubayri and Nu'man fled to Aden from where they conducted a propaganda campaign. In 1948 when the Imam Yahya was murdered and Zubayri's patron Abd Allah b. Ahmad al-Wazir seized power he returned from Aden and was made Minister of Education but was away in Saudi Arabia seeking recognition for the new regime when it was overthrown. He thus escaped imprisonment, going first to Pakistan and then to Cairo where he was later joined by Nu'man. They established good relations with the Muslim Brothers and conducted a propaganda campaign for reform in the Yemen. Without specifically calling for the overthrow of the Imamate, their pamphlets demanded a constitution, civil liberties, education for all, freedom of movement and speech and the abolition of monopolies. Zubayri in Cairo met Crown Prince Badr with whom he still hoped to co-operate. When relations were bad between Ahmad and Nasser, Zubayri was given access to Cairo Radio which treated him as the leader of the Yemeni Liberation Movement. When the Imamate was overthrown he returned to Sanaa and was once again Minister of Education. He was later a Deputy Prime Minister and led the Republican delegation at the Erkowit Conference which in November 1964 was the first attempt to end the Yemen War. When this failed owing to the lack of co-operation from President Sallal and the Egyptians, Zubayri saw the Yemen as being subordinated to Nasser's interests. The following month with his old friends Nu'man and Abd al-Rahman al-Iryani he resigned, calling for a Council of Sovereignty to replace Sallal, the end of corruption and better security. He went to Jabal Barat near the Royalist-held area and amongst the tribes over which he had considerable influence, established God's Party (*Hizb Allah*) to act as a Third Force between the Imamate and military rule, calling for an Islamic Republic. On 1 April 1965 he was assassinated and it was generally believed that the Egyptians were responsible. The regime was severely shaken by the crime which led to the appointment of Nu'man as Prime Minister. Zubayri was a pious, level-headed intellectual, uncompromising on principle but moderate and liberal in his policies. He was also an extremely distinguished poet.